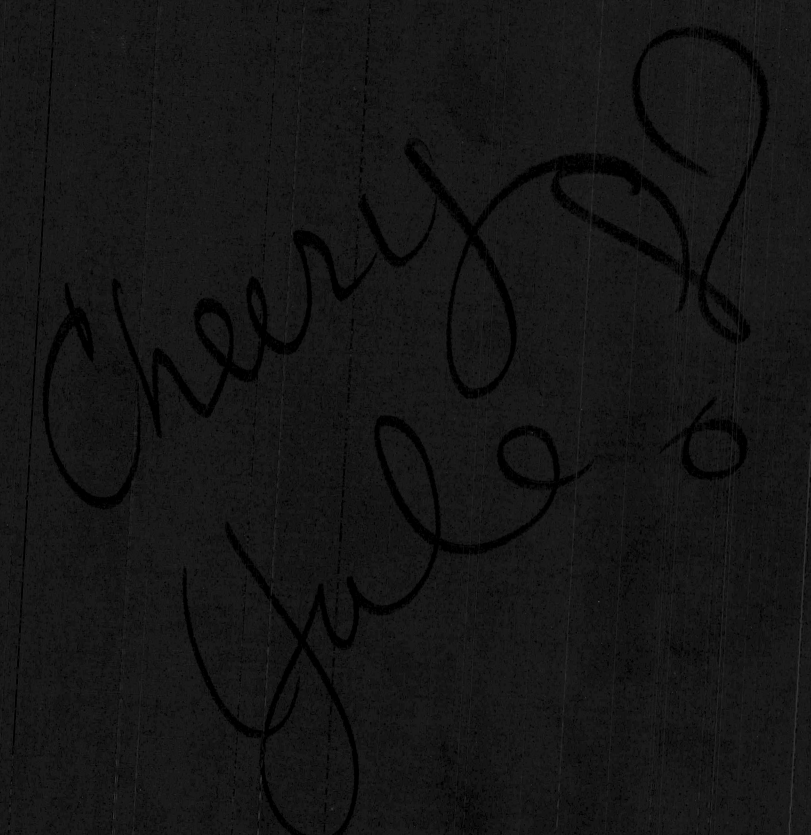

Cheerys
jude

THE DC COMICS
ENCYCLOPEDIA

THE DEFINITIVE GUIDE TO THE
CHARACTERS OF THE DC UNIVERSE

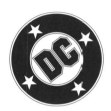

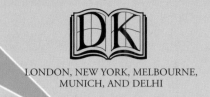

LONDON, NEW YORK, MELBOURNE,
MUNICH, AND DELHI

Senior Editor Alastair Dougall
Senior Designer Robert Perry
Project Editor Laura Gilbert
Designer Steve Woosnam-Savage
Design Assistant Mika Kean-Hammerson
Publishing Manager Cynthia O'Neill
Category Publisher Alexandra Allan
Art Director Mark Richards
Production Nicola Torode
DTP Designer Dean Scholey

First American Edition, 2004

07 08 09 10 9 8 7 6 5 4

Published in the United States by DK Publishing
375 Hudson Street, New York, New York 10014

DK books are available at special discount when purchased in bulk for
sales promotions, premiums, fundraising, or educational use. For details, contact:
DK Publishing Special Markets
375 Hudson Street,
New York, New York 10014
SpecialSales@dk.com

Published in Great Britain by Dorling Kindersley Limited.

Library of Congress Cataloging-in-Publication Data

The DC Comics encyclopedia / written by Phil Jimenez ... [et al.].-- 1st American ed.
    p. cm.
Includes index.
ISBN-13: 978-0-7566-0592-6 (plcj)
1. Comic books, strips, etc.--United States--History and criticism--Encyclopedias. 2. DC
Comics, Inc.--Encyclopedias. I. Jimenez, Phil.
PN6725.D199 2004
741.5'0973--dc22

2004003379

Color reproduction by Media Development and Printing Ltd., UK
Printed and bound in China by Hung Hing

Visit DC Comics online at www.dccomics.com
or at keyword DC Comics on America Online.

Discover more at
www.dk.com

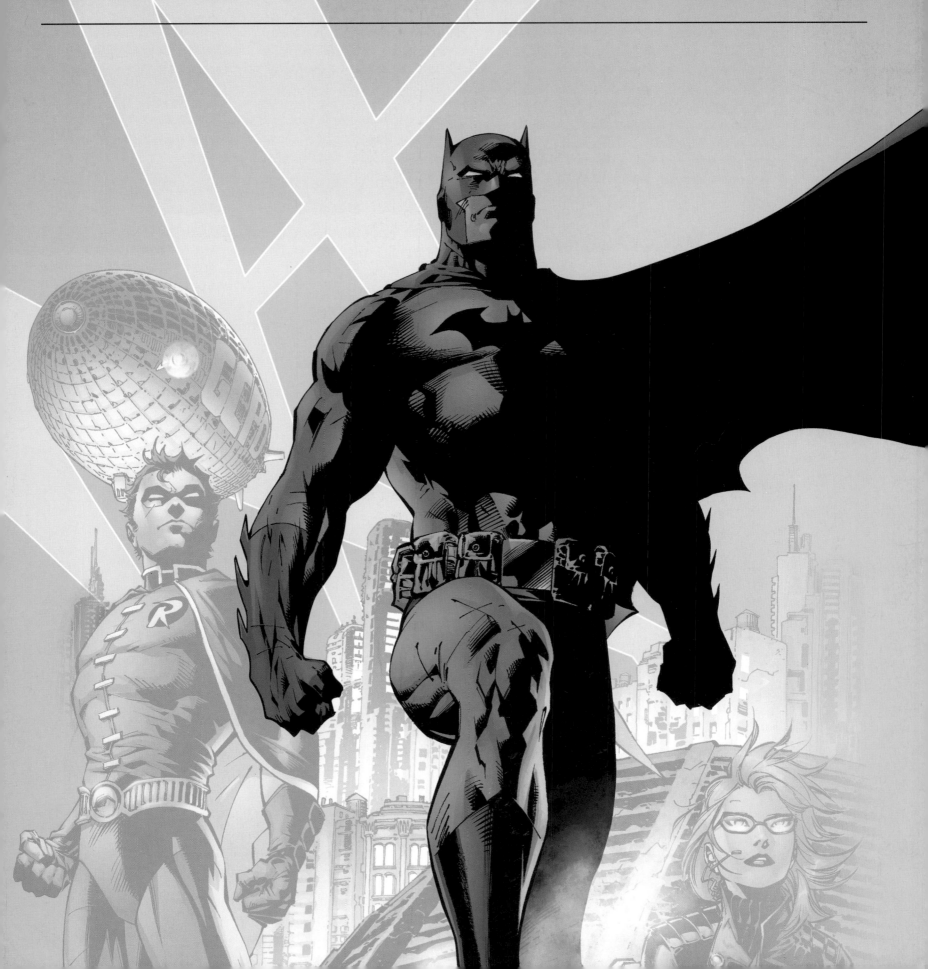

THE DC COMICS
ENCYCLOPEDIA

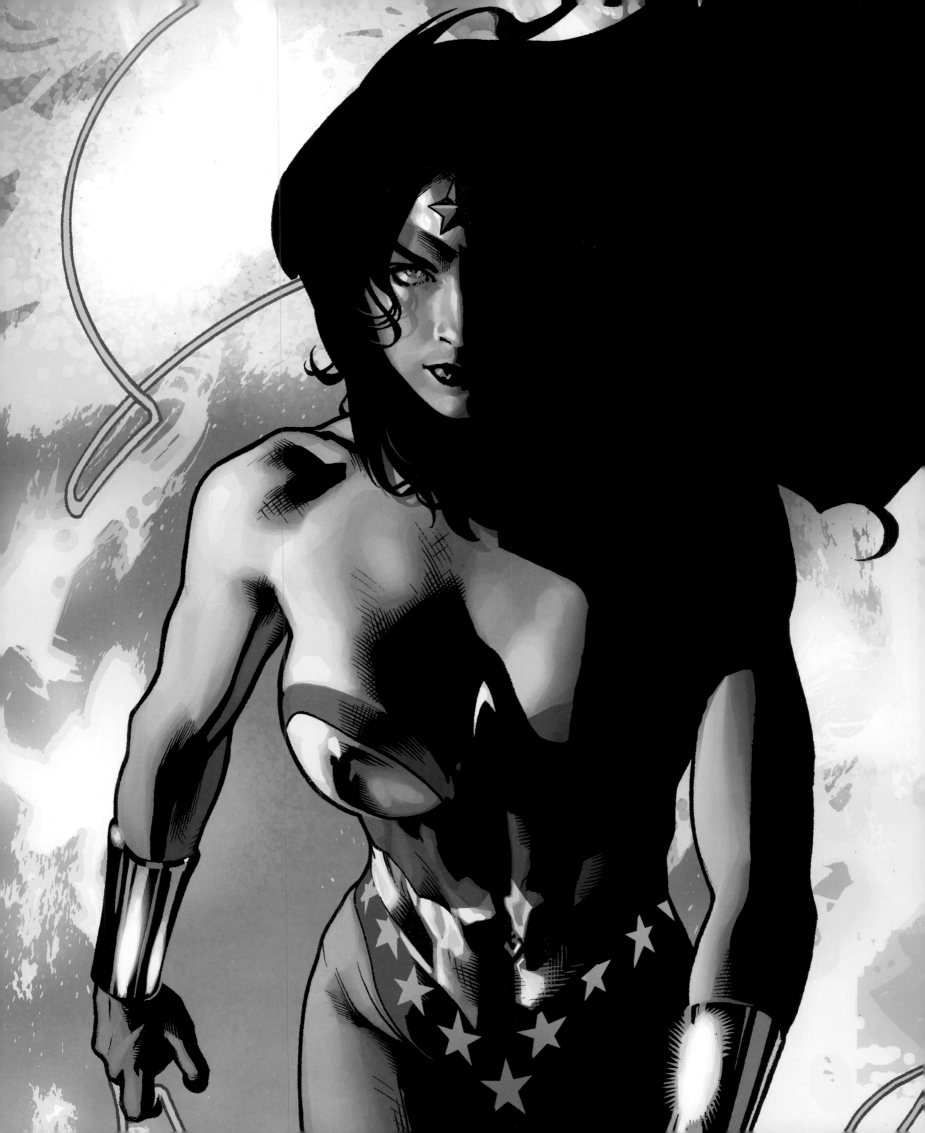

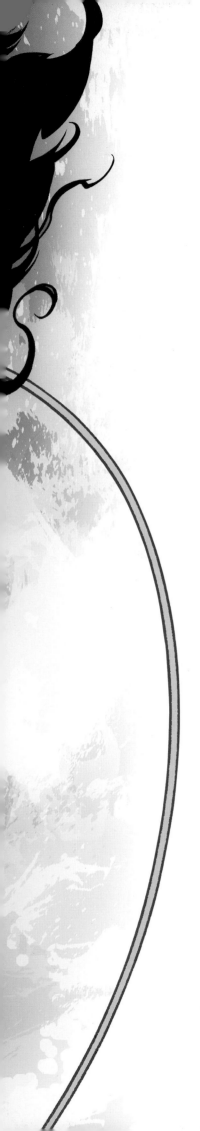

CONTENTS

FOREWORD

ONE OF THE WORLD'S great pleasures is secret knowledge. It begins in childhood: the things you learn that your parents don't know, or don't imagine you know. It can be the lifetime batting averages of every member of the New York Yankees, the evolutionary path of each of 151 Pokémon creatures... or the names and homeworlds of the Legion of Super-Heroes. Commit these arcane facts to memory, and you can speak a private language open only to you and other worthies who have approached this with equal dedication.

For many of us, the lore hidden in comics was our special secret knowledge. We mastered it as we grew, and delved deeper into the intricacies of the past, present, and future of DC Comics' heroes, friends, and foes. A generation ago, there were no guides to this search, so we had to build our own, debating each inconsistency found with passion.

Now, the task is easier. Those who have gone before you offer this encyclopedia, rich with secret knowledge. If all you know of DC Comics is that Superman is the alter ego of newspaperman Clark Kent of the *Daily Planet*, what lies before you is a complex fantasy world with details, apparent contradictions, and convolutions to be discovered. If you consider yourself a master of this information, there will still be nuggets and nuances aplenty for you to evaluate, for no one knows all of the DC Universe. And the more you know, the more likely it is that one day you will contribute your own secrets to it.

Enjoy!

Paul Levitz
President and Publisher,
DC Comics

AUTHORS' INTRODUCTION

DC COMICS TRACES its publishing history back to 1935; however, the mythology that links literally thousands of comics and characters together now stretches from the Big Bang to the end of time itself!

Of course, it was not the original intention for there to be a continuity that linked Batman to the Seven Soldiers of Victory or Adam Strange to Angel & The Ape; this process began gradually. In 1940, during comics' Golden Age (which ran from the 1930s to the mid-1950s), All American Comics—then a sister company of DC—gathered its greatest heroes together to swap stories at the monthly meeting of the Justice Society of America. That story, in *All Star Comics* #3, was the first time DC's main characters had spoken to one another. By the next issue, they had banded together; however, each mission required them to work on their own in chapters usually drawn by the series artist. And since there was little in the way of character development or recurring plot lines, the stories were fairly static.

Stan Lee changed all that. In 1961, when he started writing the adventures of the Fantastic Four, Spider-Man, Thor and others at Marvel Comics, he allowed his characters to refer to each other. Crossovers between characters, all operating out of New York City at the same period in time, offered rich story possibilities. And so the Marvel Universe was born.

By the late 1960s, DC editors began linking events from one book to another. This process accelerated rapidly as plots became more complex and characters more rounded; suddenly it was not unusual to have explanatory footnotes, which might refer a reader to the previous month, or as far back as 1945! As DC acquired properties from other companies (Captain Marvel and Blue Beetle among others), their characters and backstories were added to the expanding DC Universe, providing fresh grist for the mill.

However, after a while, the interrelatedness of stories and characters from one book to another threatened to become so complex that readers couldn't tell the players and their worlds without a scorecard! Occasional "reboots" of characters by new creative teams wanting to put their own stamp on their favorite heroes only added to the confusion.

By the mid-1980s, DC felt the situation was getting out of hand and a new storyline was introduced, the *Crisis on Infinite Earths*, to limit characters and action to one earth and one timeline. DC also reintroduced its top characters to a new generation. Frank Miller and David Mazzucchelli's *Batman: Year One*, George Pérez and Greg Potter's *Wonder Woman*, and John Byrne's *Superman* loudly told readers to forget the past; new legends were about to begin. Since then, some of those reinventions have been modified again as seen in the Superman: Birthright series. And the entire Universe received a sprucing up in a 2004 mini-series *Identity Crisis*.

The *DC Comics Encyclopedia* spans the timeline of the DC Universe. The facts about characters' pasts, powers, and personalities are current, as of early 2004, and, since DC continues to publish monthly, some facts may change over the next few years. We've worked closely with the editors to make sure we're reflecting the right information, so if you remember an incident differently than as reported here, it probably means circumstances were retrofitted to work within the current framework of the DC Universe.

We would have loved to include every DC character of any significance, but, sadly, this was impossible. However, we have selected well over one thousand of DC's finest heroes, villains, and team-ups, every one illustrated by great DC artists past and present. The *DC Comics Encyclopedia* is devised to run chronologically from A to Z, with a comprehensive index. The most important characters, such as Superman, Batman, and the JLA, have their own double-page features; each major character has an entire page, and each supporting character has a panel or entry. Each character also has his or her own data box detailing key facts and special powers. In addition, there are several themed double-page features on topics such as vehicles, battles, bases, team-ups, and romances.

So, if you can't find a favorite weird little character from way back when, we hope these packed pages will offer you plenty in the way of compensation, celebrating, as they do, more than 70 years of fun, excitement, and comic book history.

Scott Beatty
Robert Greenberger
Phil Jimenez
Dan Wallace

ABRA KADABRA

FIRST APPEARANCE FLASH (1st series) #128 (May 1962)
STATUS Villain **REAL NAME** Citizen Abra
OCCUPATION Technosorcerer **BASE** Keystone City
HEIGHT 6ft 6in **WEIGHT** 209 lbs **EYES** Blue **HAIR** Black
SPECIAL POWERS/ABILITIES Kadabra's magic-like powers were purely the result of futuristic technology. However, he is now a genuine sorceror.

In the 64th century, Earth was ruled by the Chronarch and his Central Clockworks. Citizen Abra rebelled against the strict order of the Chronarch's world. Championing individuality, Abra was seen as a criminal and banished to Earth's ancient past. Transplanted to Central City at the end of the 20th century, Abra used 64th-century technology to create a new identity and became the criminal Abra Kadabra. Desperate for adulation, and possessing powers so amazing they seemed magical, Abra Kadabra crafted a series of spectacular crimes, hoping to win admirers.

Thwarted time and again by the second FLASH, Kadabra's technology was accidentally damaged, and he was transformed into a ghost-like entity. Restored to normal, Kadabra was brought back to the 64th century by a bounty hunter named Peregrine. Kadabra was about to be executed when the Flash saved him and destroyed the Central Clockworks. Returning to the 21st century, Kadabra was stripped of his powers, but after a deal with the demon NERON, Abra Kadabra became a true sorcerer, able to cast spells and fire energy bolts. He continues to be a threat to the Flash. **PJ**

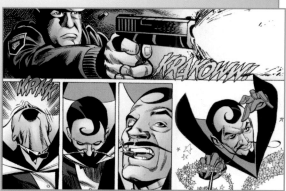

MAGIC MASTER
A narcissistic criminal mastermind in two centuries, Abra Kadabra is consumed by two things—a desire for adulation and hatred of the Flash.

AGAMEMNO

FIRST APPEARANCE SILVER AGE #1 (July 2000)
STATUS Villain **REAL NAME** Unpronounceable/unspellable
OCCUPATION Would-be universe conqueror **BASE** Outer space
HEIGHT Variable **WEIGHT** Variable **EYES** Variable **HAIR** None
SPECIAL POWERS/ABILITIES Imbues inanimate objects with his energy, bringing them to life; causes personas to swap bodies.

Composed of cosmic energy, Agamemno was one of the first sentient beings formed in the wake of the Big Bang. Upon seeing the vastness of space, Agamemno wanted to control it, to rule the other lifeforms just being born. His father, however, wanted to control the cosmos himself, thereby pitting himself against his son. Seeking an advantage to end this stalemate, Agamemno converted himself into sentient energy and toured the universe in search of three objects that could be pieced together into a killing weapon.

His search brought him to Earth during the early days of the modern heroic age, where he manipulated superpowered heroes and villains to do his bidding. The various members of the JLA managed to thwart his scheme, however, and kept the objects from being used. Agamemno then returned to space, seeking another way to beat his father for control of the cosmos. **RG**

ACRATA

FIRST APPEARANCE SUPERMAN (2nd series) ANNUAL #12 (Aug. 2000)
STATUS Hero **REAL NAME** Andrea Rojas
OCCUPATION Mesoamerican anthropologist **BASE** Mexico City
HEIGHT 5ft 6in **WEIGHT** 125 lbs **EYES** Blue **HAIR** Red
SPECIAL POWERS/ABILITIES Superb athlete and martial artist.

In her youth, Andrea Rojas moved with her family from Cobán, Guatemala to Mexico while her father continued his studies of Mesoamerican culture for the National Museum of Anthropology in Mexico City. Joining in her father's work, Andrea also became learned in ancient myths and languages. However, she was increasingly distracted by the modern-day ills suffered by her culture, particularly those created by narcotics trafficking and rampant crime. A gifted athlete and martial artist, Andrea adopted the masked identity of Acrata, a name which, when translated, means "those who suppress authority," and decided to fight organized crime.

Wearing a costume adorned with the Mayan symbol of the shadows, a totem that purportedly allowed Mayan priests to travel stealthily in the dark, Acrata began striking at the drug cartels of South America, frequently uniting with fellow Mexican heroes IMAN and EL MUERTO. The trio once teamed with SUPERMAN to defeat the sinister sorcerer DURAN. As her calling card, Acrata leaves spray-painted literary epithets to mark her capture of a perpetrator or prevention of a crime. **SB**

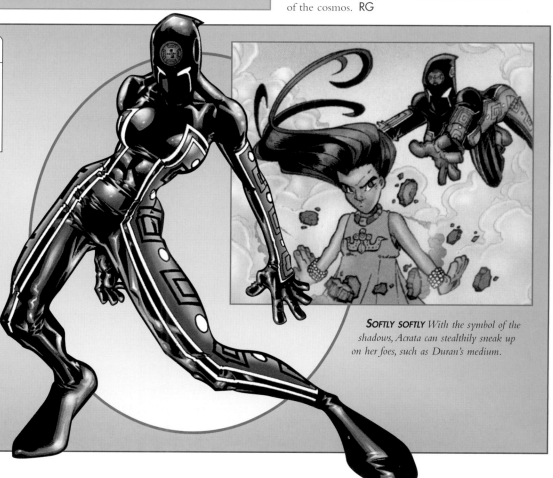

SOFTLY SOFTLY *With the symbol of the shadows, Acrata can stealthily sneak up on her foes, such as Duran's medium.*

AGENT LIBERTY

FIRST APPEARANCE SUPERMAN (2nd series) #60 (October 1991)
STATUS Hero *REAL NAME* Benjamin Lockwood
OCCUPATION Covert agent *BASE* Mobile
HEIGHT 6ft 2in *WEIGHT* 195 lbs *EYES* Blue *HAIR* Brown
SPECIAL POWERS/ABILITIES Master of armed combat and espionage;
outfitted with a battle suit that bristles with weaponry; gauntlets
generate bullet-deflecting force fields or become jagged bayonets;
a jet pack enables him to soar into the air.

As part of a C.I.A. anti-terrorist mission that went wrong,
operative Ben Lockwood survived in hostile terrain for
months. Upon returning to the U. S. he joined a super-
patriotic, well-funded team of radicals called the "Sons of
Liberty" on the recommendation of his former Bureau
chief. As Agent Liberty, Lockwood enjoyed access to high-
tech armor and weapons, as well as a helicopter team that
covered his back on particularly dangerous missions.

In one of his first cases, Agent Liberty helped
SUPERMAN crack down on INTERGANG crooks. Agent
Liberty broke ranks with the Sons of Liberty when the
organization ordered him to assassinate Senator Pete Ross
(*see* ROSS, PETE). He refused—killing his former mentor in
the process—and forwarded classified information on the
Sons of Liberty to *Daily Planet* reporter Clark Kent before
beginning a new life on the run. Despite his lack of
superpowers, Agent Liberty has put in a short stint with
the JUSTICE LEAGUE OF AMERICA. **DW**

AGONY AND ECSTACY

FIRST APPEARANCE HELLBLAZER #12 (December 1988)
STATUS Villains *REAL NAMES* Agony and Ecstasy
OCCUPATION Hell's enforcers *BASE* Hell
HEIGHT 7ft *WEIGHT* Unknown *EYES* White *HAIR* Flaming red
SPECIAL POWERS/ABILITIES It is not clearly understood what happens to
those unfortunates who are taken by Agony and Ecstasy; perhaps
that's just as well...

Agony and Ecstasy are Hell's enforcers, a pair of
"inquisition police" who track down any demons or other
underlings who dare to break the rules or to oppose the
authority of Hell. They are demonic twins whose
beautiful, luminescent bodies are draped in rusting barbed
wire. When Lucifer abdicated his role as ruler of Hell and
emptied it of all its demons, the angels Remiel and Duma
were given the key to its gates. They became its rulers, and
assigned Agony and Ecstasy the task
of bringing back the
demons that had escaped
to realms beyond. Despite
various upheavals in
Hell's Hierarchy, Agony
and Ecstasy remain
ready to serve and
punish, gleefully
inflicting their
vengeance upon any
that defy its demonic
leadership. **PJ**

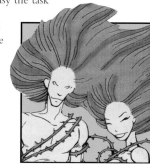

AIR WAVE I

FIRST APPEARANCE DETECTIVE COMICS #60 (February 1942)
STATUS Hero (deceased) *REAL NAME* Lawrence "Larry" Jordan
OCCUPATION Crime fighter; District Attorney *BASE* New York City
HEIGHT 5ft 10in *WEIGHT* 175 lbs *EYES* Brown *HAIR* Brown
SPECIAL POWERS/ABILITIES Antennae in helmet and circuitry in belt
allowed him to eavesdrop on police band frequencies or intercept
telephone calls; travelled at the speed of electricity along telephone
lines on collapsible skates built into boots; magnetic energies enabled
him to climb walls or relieve criminals of their guns.

Before he ascended
to the lofty post
of New York
City District
Attorney, law clerk
Larry Jordan wanted to
do more than just file legal
briefs to battle crime in the
1940s "Big Apple." He built a
special helmet and belt that gave
him an array of amazing electronic and
magnetic powers and hit the streets as the
costumed Air Wave when he wasn't fighting
injustice in court. A member of the wartime
ALL-STAR SQUADRON, Air Wave was
subsequently killed by escaped convict Joe
Parsons, a criminal once jailed by the
crusading Attorney. Jordan's wife, Helen, sought
retribution in her husband's own costume, capturing
Parsons and later testifying to keep him in prison for the
rest of his days. Many years later, the role of Air Wave was
taken up by Larry and Helen's son Harold, who refined
the costume and its circuitry while operating as a teen
hero. In adulthood, Harold renamed his heroic alter ego
Maser and serves as an auxiliary member of the JSA while
keeping the spirit of Air Wave alive and well. **SB**

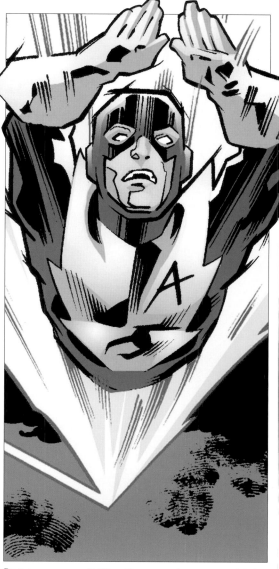

RIDING THE WAVES *Air Wave II is among the most powerful of
Earth's young heroes.*

AIR WAVE II

FIRST APPEARANCE GREEN LANTERN (2nd series) #100 (Jan. 1978)
STATUS Hero *REAL NAME* Harold "Hal" Lawrence Jordan
OCCUPATION Student *BASE* Dallas, Texas
HEIGHT 5ft 7in *WEIGHT* 156 lbs *EYES* Brown *HAIR* Brown
SPECIAL POWERS/ABILITIES Helmet allows him to change his molecular
structure; can transform into energy and travel along radio and
television airwaves; can also fly at superspeed.

Hal Jordan is the son of AIR WAVE I (a member of the
ALL-STAR SQUADRON) and was named after his cousin Hal
Jordan, one of the greatest members of the legendary
GREEN LANTERN CORPS. The young Hal was forced to
live with his cousins Jack and Jan Jordan after his mother
was placed in an institution. Hal became the second Air
Wave after he inherited the helmet and equipment his
father had used for crime fighting. The second Air Wave
trained briefly with GREEN LANTERN, as well as GREEN
ARROW and the BLACK CANARY. Recruited by SUICIDE
SQUAD associate Simon LeGrieve to join his Captains of
Industry, a task force for the Institute of Meta-Human
Studies, Jordan changed his name to Maser. Later, the
villain Catalyst kidnapped Maser and turned him over to
the terrorist KOBRA, but the young hero was saved by
the JUSTICE SOCIETY OF AMERICA. Hal later returned to
the uniform and codename of Air Wave and now serves
as a reserve member of the JSA. **PJ**

ALLEN, IRIS

FIRST APPEARANCE SHOWCASE #4 (October 1956)
STATUS Hero **REAL NAME** Iris Ann Russell West Allen
OCCUPATION Journalist **BASE** Central City
HEIGHT 5ft 6in **WEIGHT** 130 lbs **EYES** Brown **HAIR** Brown
SPECIAL POWERS/ABILITIES Highly resourceful with a keen intellect; no meta-human abilities.

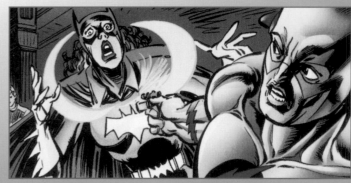

IRIS AND THE FLASH
Iris introduces her nephew Wally West to her boyfriend, Barry Allen.

After graduating from Columbia University, Iris West won a job at *Picture News*. There she met forensics scientist Barry Allen, they became engaged, and everything in Iris's life turned upside down. Allen was in an accident that turned him into the second FLASH, but Iris only found this out when she heard Barry talking in his sleep. When Barry finally told her his secret, he explained that he had waited because he was running tests to see if his biological changes would affect their ability to have children. Happily, all was well.

Further shocks were in store for Iris. It eventually transpired that she was adopted! She realized this when she found a pendant containing a recording from her true parents. Their names were Eric and Fran Russell, and they lived in the fear-ridden 30th century. Iris had been sent *back* in time for her own safety! Meanwhile, a mad scientist called Professor Zoom had become obsessed with Iris. When she rejected his advances at a costume party, Zoom killed her. But at that very instant, the Russells used an experimental device to transport Iris's spirit to the 30th century. Later, when Barry killed Zoom and was tried for murder, Iris returned to the 20th century, disguised herself as a juror, and saw to it that he was acquitted. Reunited, Barry accompanied Iris to the 30th century. Iris gave birth to twins shortly after Barry was killed during the apocalyptic battle known as the Crisis (*see* Great Battles, pp. 320–1). Iris later returned to the 20th century to teach her grandson Bart how to use his inherited gift of speed. Once again living in Keystone City, she wrote the best-selling *Life Story of the Flash* and adopted an orphan, Josh Jackam. She is romantically involved with detective Fred Chyre. **RG**

CLOSE ESCAPE Professor Zoom, the Reverse Flash, shoots and kills Iris after she rejects his advances for the last time. Unbeknownst to all, her soul is plucked into the future an instant before death.

ALIAS THE SPIDER

FIRST APPEARANCE CRACK COMICS #1 (May 1940)
STATUS Hero **REAL NAME** Tom Ludlow Hallaway
OCCUPATION Adventurer **BASE** Keystone City
HEIGHT 6ft 1in **WEIGHT** 195 lbs **EYES** Brown **HAIR** Brown
SPECIAL POWERS/ABILITIES Superb archer and athlete; sometimes wore a bulletproof costume.

During the 1940s, Tom Hallaway decided to fight crime as the costumed champion the Spider. Using a bow and arrow and traveling in a custom Black Widow car (driven by his valet and confidant Chuck), the Spider was a vigilante who killed many of his criminal opponents. Though known as a hero, the Spider clearly walked the edge of cold villainy. At the height of World War II, the Spider joined Uncle Sam's FREEDOM FIGHTERS. He later worked with the SEVEN SOLDIERS OF VICTORY, claiming that he could help them defeat the NEBULA MAN. In reality the Spider had set them all up for a fall. With his trap sprung and the Seven Soldiers dispersed into the timestream, the Spider became the new protector of Keystone City. The Spider died at the hands of the SHADE, though his son Lucas Ludlow-Dalt has since assumed the Spider's mantle. Spider II is obsessed with taking revenge on the Shade in retaliation for his father's murder. **DW**

ALLIANCE, THE

FIRST APPEARANCE JLA/HAVEN: THE ARRIVAL #1 (January 2002)
STATUS Hero team **BASE** The Haven, Coast City, California
MEMBERS AND POWERS
Valadin Military hero; manipulates energy and projects power blasts.
Siv Engineer in control of tiny nanite-tech machines.
Katalia Powerful telepath.
Nia Superstrength, invulnerability, flight.
Amon Elder statesman and Valadin's brother.
Mavaar Lin Former chancellor of the Haven.
Ignetia Highly skilled scientist.
Hank Velveeda Innate working knowledge of most things, both organic and technological.
Tamlick Soffick Alters gravity to gain powers of levitation.

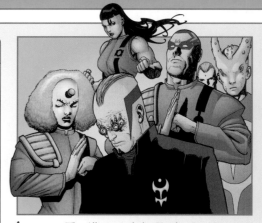

ALIEN TEAM The Alliance includes Katalia, Siv, Nia, Valadin, and Hank Velveeda.

The Alliance are a contingent of freedom-fighting aliens from the planet Competalia, dedicated to ridding their world of Anathema, a ruthless biogeneticist who transformed nearly every inhabitant of Competalia into superhuman beings. Once a Competalian was transformed, Anathema would have complete dominion over the individual and her newly-created warriors quickly swept over the planet, placing it under her near-total control. Over two million Competalians resisted Anathema's control, however, and were placed in a penal colony called "The Haven." Soon after, Valadin, a respected military leader, and his brother Amon, forged an Alliance of rebels, and turned Haven into a traveling space city. The Haven escaped Competalia and headed for the Milky Way galaxy. The Alliance came out of warp too close to Earth, and crash-landed in California, creating a crater across much of the state and killing thousands. With the help of the JUSTICE LEAGUE OF AMERICA, the Competalians were able to salvage the Haven and forge a new Alliance under Valadin's command. One member, the Chancellor Mavaar Lin, betrayed the Alliance, allowing Anathema to take over the Haven. Siv, used the despot's DNA against her, enabling him to destroy her. The Haven remained in California, and through negotiator Nicole Stein, appointed by then-President Lex Luthor (*see* LUTHOR, LEX), became a legally recognized city of the U.S. **PJ**

BETRAYAL Mavaar Lin, the former chancellor of the Haven, betrayed her teammates while under the thrall of Anathema, even threatening the life of then-President Lex Luthor.

ALL-STAR SQUADRON

FIRST APPEARANCE JUSTICE LEAGUE OF AMERICA #193 (All-Star Squadron) (August 1981); YOUNG ALL-STARS #1 (Young All-Stars) (June 1987)
STATUS Hero team (disbanded) **BASE** New York City
NOTABLE MEMBERS AND POWERS
Amazing Man I (Will Everett) Able to transform himself into any material he touched.
Commander Steel (Hank Heywood) Injured body repaired with steel alloy frame and micro-motor muscles.
Firebrand II (Danette Reilly) Possessed power of flight and the ability to create and control flames.
Hawkgirl I (Sheira Sanders Hall) Flew with artificial wings and "Ninth metal" anti-gravity belt.
Johnny Quick (Johnny Chambers) Speed and flight enabled by speaking speed formula "3X2(9YZ)4A."
Liberty Belle (Libby Belle Lawrence) Superstrength, agility, and ability to project sonic pulses.
Plastic Man (Eel O'Brian) Superpliable and rubbery resilient body.
Robotman I (Dr. Robert Crane, a.k.a. Paul Dennis) Powerful robotic frame housed human brain.
Shining Knight (Sir Justin/Justin Arthur) Rode winged steed Victory while wielding enchanted armor and sword.
Tarantula I (Jonathan Law) Masked vigilante armed with web-line emitting web-gun.

Following Imperial Japan's sneak attack on Pearl Harbor in 1941, U.S. President Franklin D. Roosevelt called upon all active "Mystery Men"—the costumed heroes and heroines of America, including the entire membership of the JUSTICE SOCIETY OF AMERICA—to band together as a unified fighting force to combat the Axis powers bent upon dominating the world. Both on the home front and in top-secret missions on the battlefields and behind enemy lines, the Squadron—which included more than fifty members at its most powerful—answered only to F.D.R. and the War Department. Many of its greatest adventures are still classified decades later.

THE PERISPHERE
During its tour of duty, the All-Star Squadron was based in New York City and held court in the Perisphere, a hollow sphere 200 feet in diameter built for the 1939–1940 New York World's Fair. The Perisphere included living quarters for all active members of the Squadron. The 610-foot Trylon, a spire erected next to the Perisphere, served to house the team's All-Star Special, a modified Curtiss XP-55 Ascender aircraft outfitted with a Star-Rocket Racer motor courtesy of Pat Dugan (STRIPESY), adult sidekick of Squadron member the Star-Spangled-Kid.

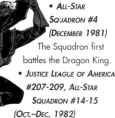

EARLY DAYS Dr. Mid-Nite, Hawkman, and Atom pore over pictures of potential recruits.

THE YOUNG ALL-STARS
In 1942, the All-Star Squadron found its ranks bolstered by an influx of younger heroes, a splinter group of "Young All-Stars" whose primary focus was thwarting the superpowered group of German, Italian, and Japanese soldiers dubbed "Axis Amerika." Among the Young All-Stars ranks were the atomic-punching Dyna-Mite, the furry-winged FLYING FOX, the powerhouse FURY, the nigh-indestructible "Iron" Munro, the aquatic avenger Neptune Perkins (see PERKINS, NEPTUNE), and the Japanese-American tidal wave-wielding TSUNAMI. Together, these young heroes did their part to protect the home front from Axis aggression. Both the adult All-Star Squadron and its youthful counterpart disbanded following the conclusion of hostilities. **SB**

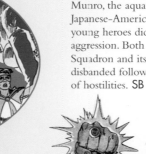

FIENDISH FOES Among the Squadron's numerous nemeses were Night and Fog, Nazi siblings who served as Hitler's superpowered assassins.

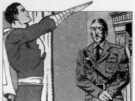
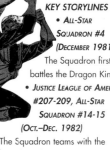
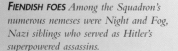

1) The Atom 2) Amazing Man 3) Johnny Thunder 4) Dr. Fate 5) Green Lantern 6) Plastic Man 7) Robotman 8) Liberty Belle 9) Firebrand 10) Steel 11) Guardian 12) Hourman 13) Tarantula 14) Hawkgirl 15) Hawkman 16) Shining Knight

KEY STORYLINES
• ALL-STAR SQUADRON #4 (DECEMBER 1981) The Squadron first battles the Dragon King.
• JUSTICE LEAGUE OF AMERICA #207-209, ALL-STAR SQUADRON #14-15 (OCT.–DEC. 1982) The Squadron teams with the modern-day JLA and JSA to prevent Per Degaton from unleashing a nuclear nightmare and altering the course of history.

ALPHA CENTURION

FIRST APPEARANCE ZERO HOUR: CRISIS IN TIME #3 (September 1994)
STATUS Hero **REAL NAME** Marcus Aelius
OCCUPATION Adventurer **BASE** Mobile
HEIGHT 5ft 8in **WEIGHT** 165 lbs **EYES** Blue **HAIR** Blond
SPECIAL POWERS/ABILITIES Alien armor gives superstrength, the power of flight, and the ability to manifest an energy sword and shield.

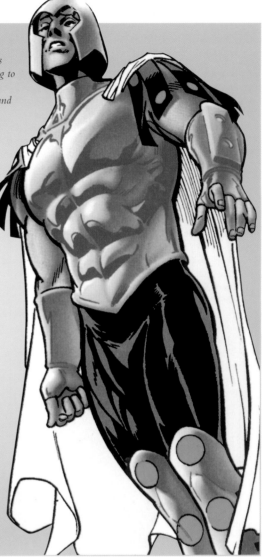

PROTECTOR Marcus Aelius was a quick study, learning to use his gifts to protect the innocent, be it on the ground or in the air.

A Roman Centurion during the time of the emperor Hadrian, circa AD 117–138, Marcus Aelius was chosen by a race of aliens, the Virmiru, to come to their world to study and learn from their advanced civilization. Upon his return to Earth, Aelius was stunned to learn that over 1,800 years had passed. Quickly aligning himself with Lex Luthor's ruthless ex-wife (see LUTHOR, LEX), the CONTESSA, in Metropolis, Aelius was dubbed the Alpha Centurion. He formed the Centurions, a private army that protected the city under strict, ancient laws.

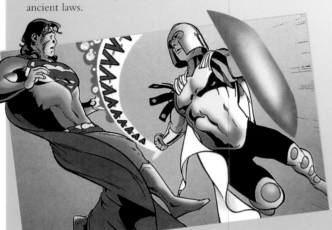

The Alpha Centurion later disbanded the Centurions, choosing to operate on his own, away from the Contessa's corrupting influence and that of her company, LexCorp. Learning of the Virmiru's plans to conquer the Earth, the Alpha Centurion severed his ties with the aliens and currently travels the world in his ship, the *Pax Romana*. He is frequently amazed at the enormous changes that have occurred since the time of his birth, almost 2,000 years ago. **RG**

SUPERMAN Alpha Centurion wasn't too sure about the Man of Steel when they first met, but they quickly became allies.

AMAZING GRACE

FIRST APPEARANCE SUPERMAN (2nd series) #3 (March 1987)
STATUS Villain **REAL NAME** None
OCCUPATION Agent of Darkseid **BASE** Apokolips
HEIGHT 5ft 11in **WEIGHT** 159 lbs **EYES** Green **HAIR** Red
SPECIAL POWERS/ABILITIES Manipulates the wills of others with her beauty and persuasive powers.

The sister of DARKSEID's star propagandist GLORIOUS GODFREY, Amazing Grace shares her brother's gift for persuasion. She is one of the most attractive things to arise from the hellish madhouse that is Apokolips, yet her heart is cold and her intentions sadistic. Amazing Grace often serves Darkseid by dwelling among the lowest-class "hunger dogs" in the slums near the fire-pits. There she locates resistance groups and manipulates their leaders, drawing them out long enough for her master to annihilate them. During the anti-heroic movement on Earth known as the Legends crisis, Darkseid brought SUPERMAN to Apokolips in an attempt to corrupt his soul. Amazing Grace used her talents to make the Man of Steel believe he was Darkseid's son. Superman soon shook off the delusion, but Amazing Grace is still active within Apokolips' twisted hierarchy. **DW**

AMAZING MAN I

FIRST APPEARANCE ALL-STAR SQUADRON #23 (July 1983)
STATUS Hero (deceased) **REAL NAME** William Everett
OCCUPATION Adventurer **BASE** New York City
HEIGHT 6ft 1in **WEIGHT** 185 lbs **EYES** Brown **HAIR** Black
SPECIAL POWERS/ABILITIES Capable of transforming himself into a living, breathing facsimile of any material that he touched; later, his powers were altered, and he was instead able to magnetically attract or repel objects with his hands.

Will Everett was a multi-medal winner in the 1936 Berlin Olympics. Despite the acclaim, the young African American, a constant target of racism, was unable to get work and became a janitor for Doctor Terry Curtis. Everett was kidnapped by the ULTRA-HUMANITE and subjected to a power barrage from an invention of Curtis's. Everett gained superpowers and became Amazing Man. Initially blackmailed into working for the Ultra-Humanite, Amazing Man eventually turned on the villain and defeated him. Amazing Man then joined the ALL-STAR SQUADRON, fighting Axis tyranny during World War II. Everett's matter-mimicking powers were later replaced with magnetic ones. Everett died of cancer decades later. **PJ**

AMAZING MAN II

FIRST APPEARANCE JUSTICE LEAGUE OF AMERICA (2nd series) #86 (March 1994)
STATUS Hero (deceased) **REAL NAME** William Everett III
OCCUPATION Adventurer **BASE** New York City
HEIGHT 5ft 11in **WEIGHT** 180 lbs **EYES** Brown **HAIR** Black
SPECIAL POWERS/ABILITIES Could transform into a living facsimile of any material he touched. If he touched stone, for example, he became a sentient being made of rock, with all its strengths and weaknesses.

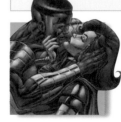

ROMANCE After her rejection by Superman, Maxima found love—and a potential mate—in Amazing Man.

The second Amazing Man was the grandson of the first. William Everett III had acquired his grandfather's abilities to transmute into elements but not his ability to control them. Everett, a college student, sought out Maxwell Lord (LORD HAVOK), founder of Justice League International (see JUSTICE LEAGUE OF AMERICA), for help and training in the use of his emerging powers. When the OVERMASTER and his alien CADRE attacked the Earth, Everett took his grandfather's codename and became Amazing Man. Together, Everett and the JLA defeated the Cadre, and Amazing Man became a member of EXTREME JUSTICE. Everett had an affair with the alien queen MAXIMA before the team disbanded. Tragically, the second Amazing Man was killed along with several other heroes by the second MIST. **PJ**

AMAZO

FIRST APPEARANCE THE BRAVE AND THE BOLD #30 (June 1960)
STATUS Villain **REAL NAME** None
OCCUPATION Adventurer **BASE** Mobile
HEIGHT 8ft **WEIGHT** 485 lbs **EYES** Red **HAIR** None
SPECIAL POWERS/ABILITIES Absorption cells throughout Amazo's synthetic body permit the android to replicate the special abilities of any super-beings in his immediate proximity. With every hero or heroine encountered, Amazo becomes even more powerful and virtually unstoppable.

The android dubbed "Amazo" was built by rogue scientist PROFESSOR IVO in his quest to achieve immortality. Powered by Ivo's patented absorption cells, Amazo first set out to fulfill his maker's prime directive by duplicating the superpowers belonging to the founding membership of the JUSTICE LEAGUE OF AMERICA, energies Ivo hoped would grant him eternal life. Despite facing a single foe as mighty as the team in its entirety, the JLA defeated Amazo and lulled him into an electronic slumber. Over the years since his creation, Amazo has emerged from this digital dormancy on various occasions, upgrading himself with new abilities depending on the JLA's ever-changing roster, and continuing to do Professor Ivo's preprogrammed bidding by attempting to destroy the world's greatest super heroes. In a recent battle with the JLA, Amazo faced the League's entire roll call, including reservists and part-time members, thus tripling the amount of powers he absorbed. Only by disbanding the JLA was SUPERMAN, the team's most powerful member, able to negate Amazo's stolen abilities and crash his systems. Undoubtedly, Professor Ivo has since corrected this fatal flaw in the evil android's programming. **SB**

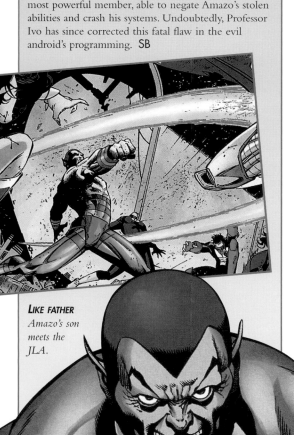

LIKE FATHER
Amazo's son meets the JLA.

AMAZONS

FIRST APPEARANCE (historical) ALL-STAR COMICS #8 (Winter 1941); (current) WONDER WOMAN (2nd series) #1 (February, 1987)
STATUS Heroes **BASE** Themyscira
CURRENT MEMBERS AND POWERS (See key)

The Amazons were created in 1,200 BC by a collection of five Olympian goddesses to teach mankind equality, justice, and peaceful harmony. Three thousand in number, the Amazons built the city of Themyscira and established a powerful nation-state in ancient Greece. The Amazons were led by Queen HIPPOLYTA and her sister Antiope.

Heracles and his men, under the influence of the evil war god ARES, seduced the Amazons and ransacked Themyscira. Craving vengeance, Antiope, along with a bloodthirsty faction of Amazons, pursued Heracles to Attica. Hippolyta and her Amazons, following the decree of their goddesses, instead settled on a remote island. Hippolyta's Amazons rebuilt Themyscira (see Amazing Bases, pp. 120–1), and, granted immortality by their goddesses, were charged with guarding the gate to Pandora's Box, housed beneath their new home.

3,000 years later, as Ares plotted to destroy the world in a nuclear war, Hippolyta's daughter Diana became Themyscira's champion, known to "Patriarch's World" as WONDER WOMAN. After Wonder Woman ended Ares's threat to the world, and also destroyed the hellish creatures within Pandora's Box, the Amazons opened their shores to the outside world for the first time in 3,000 years.

After several attempts at cultural exchange with Patriarch's World, Antiope's descendants, a warrior tribe of Amazon assassins nestled in Egypt, were transported to Themyscira by CIRCE. Soon after, DARKSEID invaded Paradise Island, killing half the Amazons. The two tribes of Amazons forged an uneasy peace to help defend Earth from the threat of IMPERIEX (see Great Battles, pp. 320–1), and joined forces when several goddesses remade Themyscira, transforming it into an interdimensional university devoted to the exchange of knowledge, where the Amazons continued to promote their peaceful ideals.

This new Themyscira was decimated during a marital spat between Zeus and Hera. The future of the Amazons and their island home remains to be seen. **PJ**

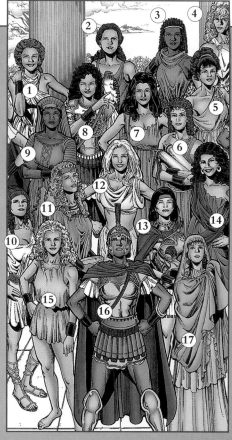

NOTABLE AMAZONS PAST AND PRESENT
1) Cydippe (handmaiden) **2)** Myrhha (deceased)
3) Pallas (artisan) **4)** Mala (friend to Diana)
5) Clio (scribe) **6)** Timandra (architect)
7) Mnemosyne (historian) **8)** Aella (warrior)
9) Niobe (priestess) **10)** Oenone (botanist)
11) Epione (physician) **12)** Pythia (philosopher)
13) Euboea (warrior) **14)** Penelope (priestess)
15) Ipthime (deceased) **16)** Archon Phillipus
17) Menalippe (deceased)

AMBUSH BUG

FIRST APPEARANCE DC COMICS PRESENTS #52 (July 1983)
STATUS Would-be hero **REAL NAME** Irwin Schwab
OCCUPATION Adventurer **BASE** Metropolis
HEIGHT 5ft 10in **WEIGHT** 145 lbs **EYES** Green **HAIR** None
SPECIAL POWERS/ABILITIES Can teleport anywhere on Earth (exact limits are not defined); green suit provides some protection against attack.

Irwin Schwab somehow came into possession of a green suit filled with miraculous technology that protected the wearer from harm and allowed him to teleport around the world. Unfortunately, this was a case of the right tool in the wrong hands. Schwab's major character defect is his lack of linear logic, which gives him a skewed picture of the world. However, Schwab knows enough to want to use his costume and special abilities in the cause of good. Unfortunately, although he aspires to being a super hero, he always seems to get caught up in complicated events. He was last seen on the other side of the galaxy, trying his hand at being a bounty hunter. **RG**

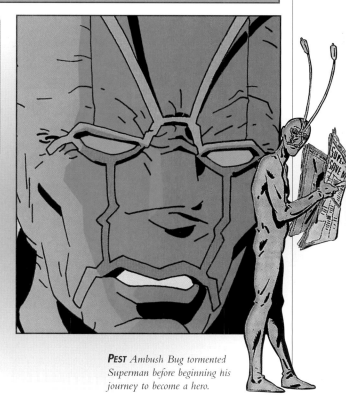

PEST Ambush Bug tormented Superman before beginning his journey to become a hero.

AMETHYST, PRINCESS OF GEMWORLD

FIRST APPEARANCE LEGION OF SUPER-HEROES #298 (April 1983)
STATUS Hero **REAL NAME** Amy Winston
OCCUPATION Lord of Order **BASE** Gemworld
HEIGHT 5ft 8in **WEIGHT** 134 lbs **EYES** Violet **HAIR** Blonde
SPECIAL POWERS/ABILITIES Vast magical talents including the ability to fly, generate force-field shields, emit bolts of energy, and conjure up interdimensional portals.

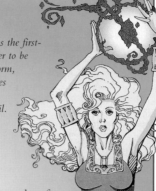

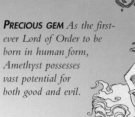

PRECIOUS GEM As the first-ever Lord of Order to be born in human form, Amethyst possesses vast potential for both good and evil.

On her 13th birthday, Amy Winston learned that she was a princess, born to rule the realm of Gemworld, where she had the body of a 20-year-old and wielded vast magic powers. Gemworld was ruled by 12 houses of sorcerers, playthings for the Lords of Order and Chaos. Pantagones, a Lord of Order, used the House of Amethyst to strike against Lord of Chaos Vandaemeon and his House of Opal (see DARK OPAL). Lord and Lady Amethyst died in the clash, but a servant ensured their infant daughter would be safely raised on Earth. This girl became Amy Winston. As Amethyst, Amy defeated Dark Opal and united the Gemworld.

She lost her sight during the Crisis (see Great Battles, pp. 320–1) but learned to see by magical means, and broke all ties with those who had known her as Amy Winston. Amethyst's radical plan to bring about order teamed her with the Lord of Chaos called Child and his assistant Flaw, and she conquered troubled Gemworld. **DW**

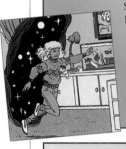

JUST THIRTEEN Amy reverts to her Earth age on returning from Gemworld.

ANARKY

FIRST APPEARANCE DETECTIVE COMICS #608 (November 1989)
STATUS Unresolved **REAL NAME** Lonnie Machin
OCCUPATION Political activist **BASE** Washington, D.C.
HEIGHT 5ft 8in **WEIGHT** 150 lbs **EYES** Blue **HAIR** Red
SPECIAL POWERS/ABILITIES A superintelligent computer genius and a master inventor; he uses gas bombs and a taser staff in combat.

BATMAN BATTLE After killing several corporate heads, Anarky was captured by Batman, but returned to the streets determined to haunt the dreams of corrupt businessmen before ending their crimes permanently.

ANARKY AIMS HIGH Hyperintelligent Anarky wants nothing less than worldwide revolution.

Angered by the power and corruption of multinational corporations, 12-year-old Lonnie Machin donned a costume that increased his height and took to the streets as Anarky. Anarky murdered several CEOs and celebrities, spray-painting their bodies with his "A" symbol after he killed them. BATMAN soon identified the assassin, from clues in a Gotham City newspaper that linked the murders to Anarky. Astonished to discover that Anarky was just a boy, Batman apprehended him, and Machin was incarcerated at the Gotham Juvenile Corrections Hall.

Machin later became the computer hacker Moneyspider, and transferred millions of dollars from the accounts of wealthy corporations to Third World countries. Batman's partner, ROBIN, determined Moneyspider's link to Anarky, and Machin's plans for global change were thwarted. Undaunted, and using a special device of his own creation, Machin fused the two sides of his brain, increasing his intelligence to superhuman levels. After toying with Batman and Robin, Anarky learned that he had been adopted and that his natural mother was a Vegas showgirl and his father was the JOKER. This only furthered Anarky's resolve to wreak havoc on the industrialized world, in the hope of triggering worldwide revolution.

Despite his criminal history with Earth's defenders, most notably Batman, Anarky has worked alongside heroes including ROBIN, GREEN LANTERN, and YOUNG JUSTICE against some of their greatest enemies, including KLARION, THE WITCH BOY and DARKSEID. **PJ**

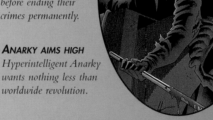

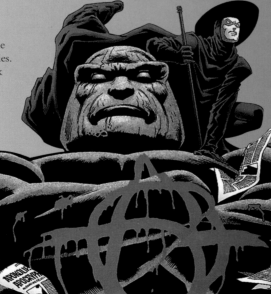

ANCIENTS, THE

FIRST APPEARANCE JLA #70 (October 2002)
STATUS Hero team **BASE** Ancient Atlantis
MEMBERS AND POWERS
Gamemnae (former leader; deceased) Corrupt Atlantean sorceress.
The Anointed One Alien powerhouse; defender of the Hebrew faith.
Manitou Raven North American shaman possessing mystical powers.
Rama Khan Elemental commanding earth and rocks to his will.
Sela Armed with magical weapons carried in her Bag of Night.
Tezumak Juggernaut sealed in armor oiled with his victims' blood.
The Whaler Wielder of solid light "Borealis Effect," hurled from his net and harpoon.

Assembled in 1,004 BC by Rama Khan (see KHAN, RAMA), noble protector of Jarhanpur, the Ancients were the world's greatest super heroes of prehistory. The team was brought together to battle—as prophesied by GAMEMNAE, High Priestess of Atlantis—a "seven-headed hydra" that would lay waste the Earth. Instead of a hydra, the Ancients fought and killed the JUSTICE LEAGUE OF AMERICA, who had traveled back into the distant past to find their lost teammate AQUAMAN. The evil Gamemnae had duped the other Ancients to fulfill her schemes of conquering the world by preventing Atlantis from sinking and so changing the course of history. Meanwhile, present-day Earth was threatened with disaster as every drop of water was drawn into the reservoirs of Atlantis, as it was raised from the depths of the ocean. To save the modern era, the JLA's BATMAN called upon a roster of replacement heroes to go back several millennia and thwart Gamemnae's plans. The JLA revealed her treachery to the Ancients, and the heroes of two epochs joined forces to save past and present. The boastful Gamemnae perished in magical combat with MANITOU RAVEN. **SB**

KEY 1) The Anointed One **2)** Tezumak **3)** Sela **4)** Manitou Raven **5)** Gamemnae **6)** Rama Khan **7)** The Whaler

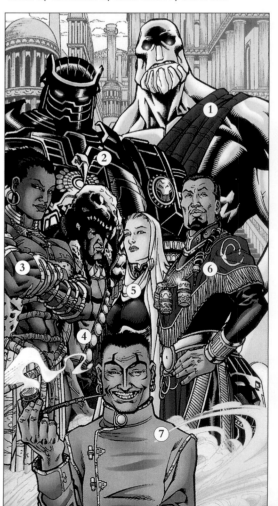

ANDROMEDA

FIRST APPEARANCE LEGION OF SUPER-HEROES (4th series) #6 (April 1990)
STATUS Hero **REAL NAME** Laurel Gand
OCCUPATION Legionnaire **BASE** Mobile
HEIGHT 6ft 2in **WEIGHT** 160 lbs **EYES** Blue **HAIR** Blonde
SPECIAL POWERS/ABILITIES Natural Daxamite abilities of superspeed, superstrength, laser vision, X-ray vision, supersenses, and invulnerability to everything but lead.

In the 30th century the Planet Daxam was ruled by the White Triangle, a cult preaching racial purity. Raised in this xenophobic climate, Laurel Gand was horrified to be selected to represent Daxam in the newly formed LEGION OF SUPER-HEROES. However, as she learned more about the myriad worlds making up both the United Planets and the Legion membership, her worldview changed. Before defeating the White Triangle's thugs, however, she was poisoned with lead and nearly died prior to BRAINIAC 5 finding a cure. Andromeda went seeking spiritual solace with the Sisters of the Eternal Cosmos and underwent a physical redefinition that left her shorter, but with some energy-manipulating powers. She is still unsure how these new powers have affected her. **RG**

ANGEL AND THE APE

FIRST APPEARANCE SHOWCASE PRESENTS #77 (September 1968)
STATUS Heroes **REAL NAMES** Angel Beatrix O'Day, Sam Simeon
OCCUPATION Adventurer **BASE** New York City
HEIGHT 5ft 10in (Angel); 5ft 9in (Sam)
WEIGHT 140 lbs (Angel); 550 lbs (Sam)
EYES Blue (Angel); hazel (Sam) **HAIR** White (Angel); black (Sam)
SPECIAL POWERS/ABILITIES Angel is an expert fencer, marksman, martial artist, and linguist; Sam has limited telepathic abilities and gorilla strength.

The unlikeliest duo in New York City must be Angel and the Ape, who operate a PI firm under the name of O'Day & Simeon. The two are inseparable, and their history goes back years to when Angel accompanied her father, Professor Theo O'Day, on an African safari. Professor O'Day had already encountered a tribe of subterranean AMAZONS, with whom he had fathered a daughter, Athena. On this occasion, he and his second daughter, Angel, stumbled into the vicinity of Gorilla City.

Sam Simeon had wandered off from the concealed monkey-metropolis and the headaches associated with its villain (and Sam's grandfather), GORILLA GRODD. Sam followed Angel back to the U.S. While Angel trained in a variety of intellectual and physical disciplines, Sam doodled on a sketch pad and dreamed of becoming a cartoonist.

Sam eventually took home a semi-regular paycheck as a freelance artist, illustrating the comic book *Deus Ex Machina Man* while assisting Angel on the cases that walked through the door of O'Day & Simeon. His telepathic "force of mind" allows him to trick others into overlooking the fact that he's a quarter-ton gorilla!

The pair is still active in the detective business. Never looking for trouble, mild-mannered Sam finds it anyway whenever he's in Angel's company. **DW**

ANGLE MAN

FIRST APPEARANCE WONDER WOMAN (2nd series) #179 (May 2002)
STATUS Villain **REAL NAME** Angelo Bend
OCCUPATION Thief **BASE** Milan, Italy
HEIGHT 5ft 11in **WEIGHT** 170 lbs **EYES** Brown **HAIR** Brown
SPECIAL POWERS/ABILITIES Bend's Angler weapon (a magical set square) allows him to teleport, bend space and spacial relations, alter gravity, and warp perceptions.

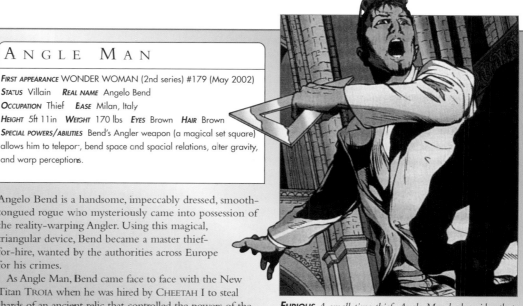

Angelo Bend is a handsome, impeccably dressed, smooth-tongued rogue who mysteriously came into possession of the reality-warping Angler. Using this magical, triangular device, Bend became a master thief-for-hire, wanted by the authorities across Europe for his crimes.

As Angle Man, Bend came face to face with the New Titan TROIA when he was hired by CHEETAH I to steal shards of an ancient relic that controlled the powers of the Furies, the Greek goddesses of vengeance. Smitten with Troia, Angle Man turned against the Cheetah and helped Troia and WONDER WOMAN defeat her. After Troia's apparent death, however, Angle Man returned to his criminal life in Italy. **PJ**

FURIOUS *A small-time thief, Angle Man had no idea that his mysterious benefactor, Barbara Minerva, was using him to steal the powers of the Furies.*

THE ANGLER *While the origins of Angle Man's weapon remain a mystery, he wields it to awesome effect!*

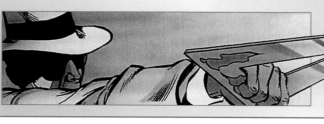

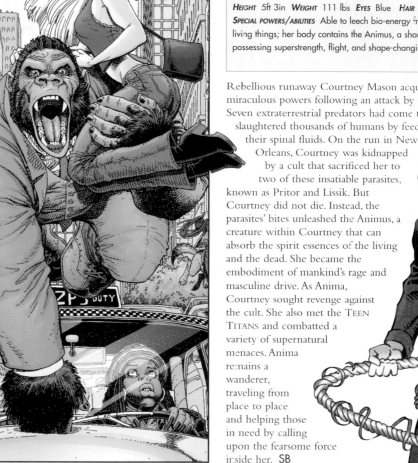

ANIMA

FIRST APPEARANCE NEW TITANS ANNUAL (2nd series) #9 (1993)
STATUS Hero **REAL NAME** Courtney Mason
OCCUPATION Adventurer **BASE** Mobile
HEIGHT 5ft 3in **WEIGHT** 111 lbs **EYES** Blue **HAIR** Blonde (dyed red)
SPECIAL POWERS/ABILITIES Able to leech bio-energy from living and non-living things; her body contains the Animus, a shadow being possessing superstrength, flight, and shape-changing powers.

Rebellious runaway Courtney Mason acquired her miraculous powers following an attack by parasitic aliens. Seven extraterrestrial predators had come to Earth and slaughtered thousands of humans by feeding on their spinal fluids. On the run in New Orleans, Courtney was kidnapped by a cult that sacrificed her to two of these insatiable parasites, known as Pritor and Lissik. But Courtney did not die. Instead, the parasites' bites unleashed the Animus, a creature within Courtney that can absorb the spirit essences of the living and the dead. She became the embodiment of mankind's rage and masculine drive. As Anima, Courtney sought revenge against the cult. She also met the TEEN TITANS and combatted a variety of supernatural menaces. Anima remains a wanderer, traveling from place to place and helping those in need by calling upon the fearsome force inside her. **SB**

ANIMAL MAN

FIRST APPEARANCE STRANGE ADVENTURES #180 (September 1965)
STATUS Hero **REAL NAME** Bernhard "Buddy" Baker
OCCUPATION Stunt man; adventurer **BASE** Montana
HEIGHT 5ft 11½ in **WEIGHT** 172 lbs **EYES** Blue **HAIR** Blond
SPECIAL POWERS/ABILITIES Able to tap into the Lifeweb and temporarily replicate the powers and abilities of any animal on Earth.

THE PUBLIC STORY of Animal Man's origins is that an alien spaceship crashed in the Adirondack Mountains, in upstate New York, near film stuntman Buddy Baker, imbuing him with the ability to adapt and use animal powers. He then donned a costume and became Animal Man, part-time rocker and part-time hero. The truth is a little different. Buddy was actually the recipient of a spell cast by an ancient shaman that somehow connected him to the Lifeweb, or the Morphogenetic Field, a major source of primordial power. For former rocker turned stuntman Buddy, this was a life-altering experience that still has amazing repercussions for him and for his family.

ANIMAL ANTICS *Animal Man in his happier days, when being a super hero was a low-risk adventure compared with his later career. He had a reputation for sending fruit baskets after team-ups.*

MAKING A DIFFERENCE

After a time, Buddy retired his Animal Man costume and married Ellen Frazier, his longtime love. Ellen found work as an illustrator while Buddy did stunts for the movies, and they made a home in San Diego, California, raising their children, Cliff and Maxine. Buddy was persuaded to resume his Animal Man role by the IMMORTAL MAN, eventually joining Justice League Europe (see JUSTICE LEAGUE OF AMERICA). Unlike most other heroes, Buddy was quite open about his alter ego, and his kids were well aware of their dad's extracurricular activities.

Over time Buddy became increasingly concerned about the planet's animal life and the plight of endangered species. He combated illegal hunting and animal testing aided by other heroes, such as VIXEN. During these crusading days, he learned of his connection to the Morphogenetic Field from the scientist James Highwater. This knowledge further expanded Buddy's horizons, making him aware of his vital link to all life on Earth and his position as a role model for other activists.

A friend suggested Buddy start a new church to spread the word, and thus was born the Life Power Church of Maxine. This led to a pilgrimage and a relocation to the wilds of Montana. This upheaval had unforeseen effects on Buddy's life, including an extramarital affair with his friend Annie, which led to the birth of his second daughter (considered a human incarnation of the World Soul). Buddy and Ellen have since reconciled and he has returned to semiactive status as a hero, helping the JLA stave off the menace of MAGEDDON (see Great Battles, pp. 320–1). **RG**

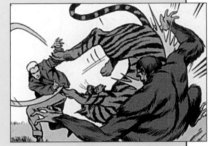

WILD THING *Just learning to master his power, Buddy Baker handles runaway zoo attractions.*

ANIMAL INSTINCT *Buddy displays his power by getting close enough to a dog and impressing his wife, Ellen.*

KEY STORYLINES

- **STRANGE ADVENTURES #180 (SEPTEMBER 1965):**
Buddy Baker first gains his animal powers.
- **ANIMAL MAN #1-9 (SEPTEMBER 1988–MARCH 1989):**
Buddy returns to super-heroics as his family adjusts to events such as having a JLA transporter delivered to the house.
- **ANIMAL MAN #51-55 (SEPTEMBER 1992–JANUARY 1993):**
Animal Man learns of his connection to the Red.

ANTHRO

FIRST APPEARANCE SHOWCASE #74 (May 1968)
STATUS Hero **REAL NAME** Anthro
OCCUPATION First boy on Earth **BASE** Prehistoric Earth
HEIGHT 5ft 2in **WEIGHT** 137 lbs **EYES** Brown **HAIR** Brown
SPECIAL POWERS/ABILITIES Skilled hunter and tracker.

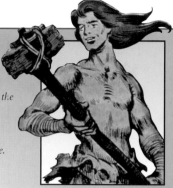

RUNNING AMOK
Anthro's tendency to get in over his head nearly caused the destruction of the entire Bear tribe in a woolly mammoth stampede.

Anthro was the first of the Cro-Magnons, who would one day give rise to modern man. His father was a Neanderthal, the chief of the Bear tribe, and his mother was a mysterious figure from a tribe long thought destroyed. The Bear tribe viewed this strongly-built boy with suspicion, and Anthro had to push himself hard to win the respect of his tribe mates and his father, Ne-Ahn. Anthro's family included his brother Lart, his stepmother, Emba, and his uncle Do-Ahn. In time he met Embra, a Cro-Magnon like himself, and the two fell in love and married. During the Crisis (*see* Great Battles, pp. 320–1), Anthro experienced a number of temporal shifts that baffled him. He soon returned to the Dawn of Man, ready to oversee the birth of his son and lead the Bear Tribe through the challenges that lay ahead. **DW**

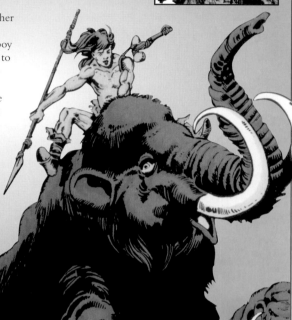

ANTITHESIS

FIRST APPEARANCE TEEN TITANS (1st series) #53 (1978)
STATUS Villain **REAL NAME** Unrevealed
OCCUPATION Malevolent entity **BASE** Limbo
HEIGHT Variable **WEIGHT** Variable **EYES** Red **HAIR** None
SPECIAL POWERS/ABILITIES Telepathy; mental manipulation; psychic vampire that feeds off negative emotions.

The vile creature known only as the Antithesis was mysteriously imprisoned in the JUSTICE LEAGUE OF AMERICA's computer mainframe. Unable to free itself, the Antithesis, whose past remains shrouded in secrecy, contacted Bromwell Stikk through his own computer. The Antithesis gave a mystical staff to Stikk, the fanatical descendant of a colonial landowner, who tried to enslave the youth of the town of Hatton Corners. Calling himself Mister Twister, Stikk was defeated and humiliated by the first TEEN TITANS. The Antithesis then used his powers to mentally manipulate the JLA, and the heroes went on a crime spree. The Titans stopped them, however, and, under ROBIN's leadership, hurled the Antithesis into Limbo, where the creature vowed vengeance against the Boy Wonder and his teenage teammates.
Soon after, the Antithesis transported the defeated Mister Twister into Limbo and

transformed Stikk into the hideous Gargoyle. The Gargoyle battled the Titans while using the mystical powers of the Antithesis. In their most recent attack on the young heroes, the Gargoyle used the Antithesis' mental powers to attack NIGHTWING's mind, but Nightwing and the HERALD were able to teleport the villains back into Limbo, where they remain to this day, plotting their revenge. **PJ**

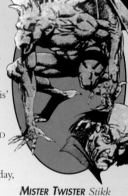

MISTER TWISTER *Stikk first battled with the Titans as Mister Twister.*

REVENGE
The monstrous Antithesis remains trapped in Limbo.

APPARITION

FIRST APPEARANCE ACTION COMICS #276 (May 1961)
STATUS Hero **REAL NAME** Tinya Wazzo
OCCUPATION Legionnaire **BASE** Legion World, U.P. Space
HEIGHT 5ft 6in **WEIGHT** 131 lbs **EYES** Blue **HAIR** Black
SPECIAL POWERS/ABILITIES Able to phase all or any part of her body into an intangible and translucent phantom state.

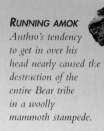

Daughter of Winema Wazzo, United Planets Ambassador from the planet Bgtzl, Tinya Wazzo became a member of the LEGION OF SUPER-HEROES after helping the Legion to foil the assassination of her mother by terrorists. Tinya used her people's natural ability to become a living phantom as the Legionnaire Apparition. She apparently died defending Earth against a supremacist group known as the White Triangle.
However, Apparition still existed in a phantom-like state and was later fully restored during the Legion's brief foray to the 20th century. During that time, Tinya married longtime love and fellow Legionnaire Jo Nah (ULTRA BOY), and gave birth to their son, Cub Wazzo-Nah. Legion membership and a lengthy separation during the BLIGHT invasion strained Tinya and Jo's marriage. Furthermore, their son Cub has rapidly aged since his birth, further complicating all of their lives. **SB**

AQUAGIRL

FIRST APPEARANCE AQUAMAN (1st series) #33 (June 1967)
STATUS Hero (deceased) **REAL NAME** Tula
OCCUPATION Adventurer **BASE** Atlantis
HEIGHT 5ft 5in **WEIGHT** 119 lbs **EYES** Blue **HAIR** Brown
SPECIAL POWERS/ABILITIES As an Atlantean, she has a dense physique to allow her to withstand the crushing pressures under the surface, which, on land, gives her enhanced strength compared to humans; a superb swimmer.

Tula owed everything to the Royal Family of Atlantis, who took her in as an orphan and raised her as one of their own. Her childhood was spent in seclusion in the Royal Home, and she rarely ventured out, until one day she met AQUAMAN's handsome adopted son, Garth. The two teenagers fell in love and adventured together, both on land and under the sea. A shadow fell on her carefree life when Aquaman abandoned his throne in order to search for his queen, MERA. Aquaman left Narkran, a royal advisor, in charge, who soon turned his regency into a dictatorship. Tula led a successful rebellion against his tyranny, eventually restoring order to the throne. She later gave her life to save others during the cosmic event known as the Crisis (*see* Great Battles, pp. 320–1). **RG**

AQUAMAN

KING OF THE SEVEN SEAS

First Appearance MORE FUN COMICS #73 (November 1941)
Status Hero **Real names** Arthur Curry; Orin
Occupation Waterbearer of the Secret Sea, exiled King of Atlantis
Base The undersea kingdom of Atlantis
Height 6ft 1in **Weight** 325 lbs **Eyes** Aqua blue **Hair** Blond
Special powers/abilities Can breathe underwater and communicate telepathically with sea life; can swim 100 m.p.h. underwater; possesses enhanced strength and toughness as well as limited sonar abilities; left hand is made of enchanted water and possesses healing powers as well as other magical abilities.

THOSE WHO UNDERESTIMATE AQUAMAN do so at their peril. This hot-headed monarch commands a kingdom that covers three-quarters of the Earth's surface and extends from the wave crests to the bottom of the Mariana Trench. Although he is, at present, a king in exile, his royal bearing is plain for all to see. Like many legendary kings, Aquaman's royal birthright was obscured by his upbringing as a commoner. The son of Queen Atlanna and a demigod, the spirit of ATLAN, Orin was born with blond hair and the ability to communicate with sea life. These qualities sentenced the child to death by exposure on Mercy Reef, for the Atlanteans believed they were signs of the curse of KORDAX, a legendary monster.

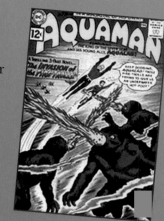
EARLY YEARS Aquaman got his own series in 1962, battling bizarre menaces such as these Fire Trolls.

FATHER FIGURE
Arthur Curry helped raise the young Atlantean, though he is no longer a presence in Aquaman's life.

STRANGER IN A STRANGE LAND
Found and raised by the dolphin Porm, Orin believed himself to be a misshapen dolphin until lighthouse-keeper Arthur Curry took him in. Absorbing some of the language and culture of the surface world from his adoptive parent, the boy took the name Arthur Curry and traveled north. He unknowingly fathered a child with an Inuit woman, Kako, then became the prisoner of Atlantean soldiers. Arthur befriended a fellow prisoner Vulko and escaped, wearing his prisoner's garb of orange-scaled shirt and green pants. He soon stumbled into a wave-top battle between the PRANKSTER and the second FLASH (Barry Allen). The Flash convinced Arthur to return with him to the U.S., where promoters dubbed him Aquaman.

OLD SCHOOL
Orin's dolphin family were perfectly suited for life underwater, but Orin kept pace by learning how to apply his opposable thumbs.

THE JLA
After he lost his hand in a piranha attack, Aquaman returned to the JLA, becoming a member of the modern team. He maintained ties with the organization he helped found and earned his place among the "magnificent seven" who comprise the icons of modern heroism.
   The awkwardness that Aquaman had expressed as a rookie JLA member now manifested itself as outright hostility, but he acquitted himself well in the battle to stop the WHITE MARTIANS of the Hyperclan from taking over the Earth. Aquaman worked sporadically with the JLA, often leaving to attend to business under the sea. Occasionally, hints have slipped out concerning his unspoken desire for his teammate WONDER WOMAN.

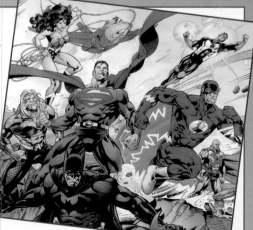
IMPERIAL Aquaman and Wonder Woman are the two JLA members who possess royal blood.

RETURN OF THE KING
Arthur found adapting to surface life hard, but discovered a kindred spirit in the MARTIAN MANHUNTER. Like him, he became a founding member of the JUSTICE LEAGUE OF AMERICA.
   Now a famous super hero, Aquaman returned to Atlantis to claim the throne. He made Vulko his regent and led his realm into a golden age. The exiled boy Garth became Aquaman's surrogate son, fighting threats to the kingdom as Aqualad. MERA then arrived from an alternate dimension and became Aquaman's queen. Aquaman defeated threats to the realm from super-villains including BLACK MANTA, FISHERMAN, SCAVENGER, and his own half-brother OCEAN MASTER. Aquaman and Mera eventually produced an heir—Arthur Jr., sometimes called Aquababy. The future of Atlantis looked bright.

ATLANTIS
The two largest cities in Atlantis are Poseidonis and Tritonis.

18

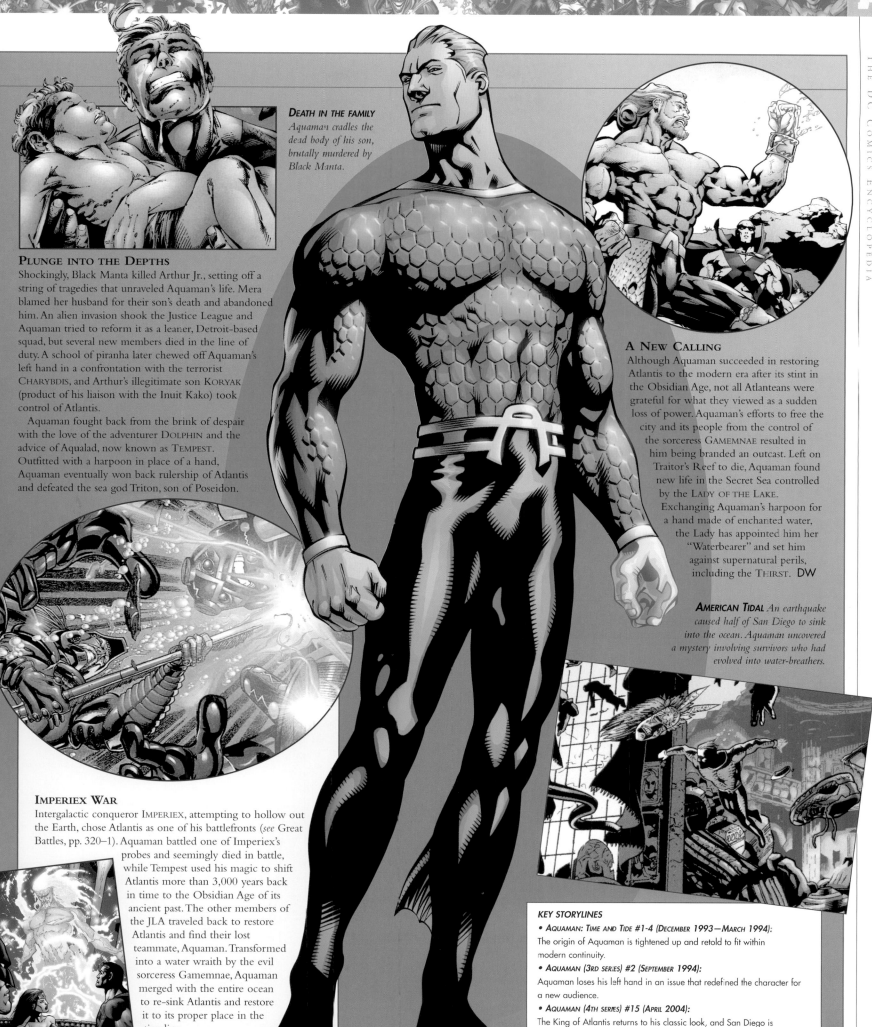

DEATH IN THE FAMILY
Aquaman cradles the dead body of his son, brutally murdered by Black Manta.

PLUNGE INTO THE DEPTHS

Shockingly, Black Manta killed Arthur Jr., setting off a string of tragedies that unraveled Aquaman's life. Mera blamed her husband for their son's death and abandoned him. An alien invasion shook the Justice League and Aquaman tried to reform it as a leaner, Detroit-based squad, but several new members died in the line of duty. A school of piranha later chewed off Aquaman's left hand in a confrontation with the terrorist CHARYBDIS, and Arthur's illegitimate son KORYAK (product of his liaison with the Inuit Kako) took control of Atlantis.

Aquaman fought back from the brink of despair with the love of the adventurer DOLPHIN and the advice of Aqualad, now known as TEMPEST. Outfitted with a harpoon in place of a hand, Aquaman eventually won back rulership of Atlantis and defeated the sea god Triton, son of Poseidon.

IMPERIEX WAR

Intergalactic conqueror IMPERIEX, attempting to hollow out the Earth, chose Atlantis as one of his battlefronts (*see* Great Battles, pp. 320–1). Aquaman battled one of Imperiex's probes and seemingly died in battle, while Tempest used his magic to shift Atlantis more than 3,000 years back in time to the Obsidian Age of its ancient past. The other members of the JLA traveled back to restore Atlantis and find their lost teammate, Aquaman. Transformed into a water wraith by the evil sorceress Gamemnae, Aquaman merged with the entire ocean to re-sink Atlantis and restore it to its proper place in the timeline.

A NEW CALLING

Although Aquaman succeeded in restoring Atlantis to the modern era after its stint in the Obsidian Age, not all Atlanteans were grateful for what they viewed as a sudden loss of power. Aquaman's efforts to free the city and its people from the control of the sorceress GAMEMNAE resulted in him being branded an outcast. Left on Traitor's Reef to die, Aquaman found new life in the Secret Sea controlled by the LADY OF THE LAKE.

Exchanging Aquaman's harpoon for a hand made of enchanted water, the Lady has appointed him her "Waterbearer" and set him against supernatural perils, including the THIRST. DW

AMERICAN TIDAL *An earthquake caused half of San Diego to sink into the ocean. Aquaman uncovered a mystery involving survivors who had evolved into water-breathers.*

KEY STORYLINES

• **AQUAMAN: TIME AND TIDE #1-4 (DECEMBER 1993–MARCH 1994):**
The origin of Aquaman is tightened up and retold to fit within modern continuity.

• **AQUAMAN (3RD SERIES) #2 (SEPTEMBER 1994):**
Aquaman loses his left hand in an issue that redefined the character for a new audience.

• **AQUAMAN (4TH SERIES) #15 (APRIL 2004):**
The King of Atlantis returns to his classic look, and San Diego is submerged following an earthquake.

ARAK, SON OF THUNDER

FIRST APPEARANCE WARLORD #48 (August 1981)
STATUS Hero (dec.) **REAL NAME** Arak Red-Hand (Bright Sky After Storm)
OCCUPATION Shaman **BASE** 8th century Europe, Asia, N. America
HEIGHT 6ft **WEIGHT** 190 lbs **EYES** Brown **HAIR** Black
SPECIAL POWERS/ABILITIES Arak is an expert with an otomahuk and a
sword. He also possesses undefined shamanic powers.

In the 8th century, after a surprise attack on the Quontauka
Indians nearly wiped out the entire tribe, a
10-year-old boy favored by He-No, the Quontauka god
of thunder, escaped into the Atlantic Ocean in a
birchwood canoe. The boy was rescued by a roving band
of Vikings, named Erik, and raised as one of their own.
Pronouncing his name "Arak," the young Indian grew to adulthood
among the Vikings. Living in Europe, Arak became a powerful
Viking warrior, proficient with both a sword and his own weapon, his
native otomahuk.

Tragically, the Vikings who saved and raised Arak were slaughtered. Arak
survived the death of his Viking clan, however, and went off to seek Carolus
Magnus, known as Charlemagne. Arak was accepted into Charlemagne's court
and served the emperor for the rest of his life. Arak did return to North
America, however, hoping to rediscover his tribal origins. When Arak was slain in
battle, his spirit was summoned before the thunder god, He-No, who was actually
Arak's father. He-No resurrected Arak as a mystical shaman, renewing his life energies
and returning him to Earth to defend the tribes of natives across North America.
During the time-spanning event known as the Crisis (see Great Battles, pp. 320–1), Arak
briefly teamed up with the Golden Age heroes known as the ALL-STAR SQUADRON. **PJ**

STORMING THROUGH Arak
fought countless villains from
the past, including bizarre
mutations, supernatural
threats, and demons.

NATIVE WARRIOR Blessed by the power of the
He-No, Arak was a renowned warrior, feared across
Asia and Europe for his skill with the otomahuk.

HEAVEN AND HELL Arcane as a
deformed monster from Hell (left),
and in his mortal appearance (right).

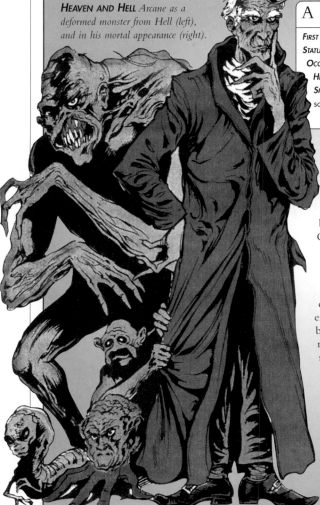

ARCANE, ANTON

FIRST APPEARANCE SWAMP THING (1st series) #2 (January 1973)
STATUS Villain (reformed) **REAL NAME** Anton Arcane
OCCUPATION Scientist; demon **BASE** Hell
HEIGHT 5ft 1in **WEIGHT** 97 lbs **EYES** Obsidian **HAIR** White
SPECIAL POWERS/ABILITIES As a human, Arcane was a brilliant
scientist; as a demon, he was quick and sturdy.

Born in a Balkan state in 1895, Anton Arcane was
obsessed with finding the secret of immortality.
During World War II, Arcane was briefly in Adolf
Hitler's employ. Later during the war, the time-
traveling SWAMP THING took possession of the body
of an Easy Company soldier and thwarted Arcane's
bid for power. The UNKNOWN SOLDIER infiltrated Easy
Company, whose operatives gathered Arcane's collection
of artifacts, including a replica of the Spear of Destiny.
By the time Arcane became immortal, his body was
too old and feeble to be of any use, so he tried to
create a new body. However, his experiments yielded
only misshapen beings he dubbed the Un-Men. One
experiment resulted in Arcane's brother, Gregori,
becoming the PATCHWORK MAN I. Arcane's hopes were
raised when he discovered the Swamp Thing. Arcane
survived the battle, and the Un-Men rebuilt his body.
Arcane began a vendetta against the Swamp Thing
and his own niece, Abby Arcane, Swamp Thing's lover.
Arcane was killed, but even confinement in Hell
couldn't keep him from seeking vengeance, and he
ultimately achieved demonhood. Arcane was summoned
from Hell to be present at the first trial set by the
Parliament of Flames for Swamp Thing, but by then he
had found God. Because of this, Swamp Thing
decided not to destroy humanity, and built Arcane a
new body. Arcane was later reconciled with Abby. **RG**

ARASHI

FIRST APPEARANCE GREEN LANTERN PLUS #1 (December 1996)
STATUS Hero **REAL NAME** Arashi Ohashi
OCCUPATION Video game designer/adventurer **BASE** Tokyo, Japan
HEIGHT 5ft 5in **WEIGHT** 119 lbs **EYES** Brown **HAIR** Black
SPECIAL POWERS/ABILITIES High-tech weaponry includes a heavily armed
motorcycle, right-arm flamethrower, and senses-augmenting cyber-
helmet; no known superpowers.

One of Japan's super heroes, Arashi Ohashi helps defend
her country from all manner of threats with advanced
technology of her own design. Arashi once teamed up
with GREEN LANTERN Kyle Rayner and the RAY to
thwart magnetic malcontent DOCTOR POLARIS and
prevent a giant tsunami from wiping Japan off the map.
Polaris broke Arashi's arm and nearly killed her,
but she has since recovered and resumed her adventurous
activities. **SB**

LIFE SAVER While battling Doctor
Polaris, Green Lantern saved
Arashi with a power-ring-
generated air-bag.

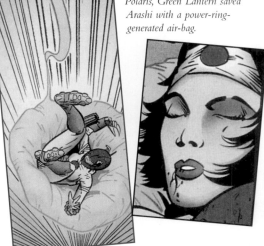

ARES

FIRST APPEARANCE WONDER WOMAN (2nd series) #1 (February 1987)
STATUS Villain **REAL NAME** Ares
OCCUPATION God of War **BASE** The Areopagus
HEIGHT 6ft 10in **WEIGHT** 459 lbs **EYES** Blue **HAIR** Blond
SPECIAL POWERS/ABILITIES Immortal; god-like strength and stamina; brilliant military strategist; indestructible armor.

The Greek god of war Ares thrives on bloodshed and is the implacable enemy of WONDER WOMAN, the Amazon peacemaker. Despite being Zeus's son, Ares never fit in with the other gods of Olympus (*see* OLYMPIAN GODS) and created his own realm, the Areopagus. When he plotted to destroy the mortals' world with a nuclear bomb, the AMAZONS brought Princess Diana to life as the new Wonder Woman to combat the war god's evil.

Ares then made another bid for supreme power, killing HIGHFATHER in the process. He suffered torments for his treachery until he effected his escape. Later, Ares's children, PHOBOS, Deimos, and Eris, tried to ensure their father's place as ruler of Earth by raising the Areopagus in the center of Gotham City.

Ares has taken an interest in the new WONDER GIRL, and given her a magic lasso similar to Diana's. He has also stirred up trouble for Diana in Olympus by slyly suggesting to Zeus that Diana's new book fails to give proper respect to the father of the gods. DW

THE DECEIVER *During a battle with Darkseid, Ares merged with Zeus and the gods of other pantheons (Jove, Odin, and the New God Highfather). Ares would betray them all in due course.*

SILVER TONGUE *Ares is just as skilled with flattery as he is with a sword, since both are weapons in the service of strife.*

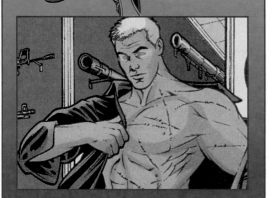

ARGENT I

FIRST APPEARANCE SECRET ORIGINS (3rd series) #14 (May 1987)
STATUS Hero team **BASE** Unknown
MEMBERS AND POWERS/ABILITIES
Control The mysterious leader. **Falcon** A master of disguise.
Fleur The daughter of notorious World War I spy Mata Hari.
Iron Munro He has superhuman strength and invulnerability.
Phantom Lady I A special device worn on her wrist emits a black light ray, creating total darkness. **Phantom** Mysterious master of disguise. **Dina** (deceased) wife of Control; Allied saboteur and spy.

Argent was created in 1951 as the civilian branch of Task Force X. The organization was designed to handle the threat of superpowered criminals after the JUSTICE SOCIETY OF AMERICA was forced to disband by the House of Un-American Activities Committee because they refused to reveal their secret identities. Unlike their counterparts in the SUICIDE SQUAD, Argent's missions were exclusively domestic, and the team operated in extreme secrecy. Their supervisor was known only as "Control," the mysterious former leader of the O.S.S. (Office of Strategic Services). This international intelligence and espionage organization was exposed by Control after he arranged the murder of a government operative indirectly responsible for the assassination of President John F. Kennedy in 1963.

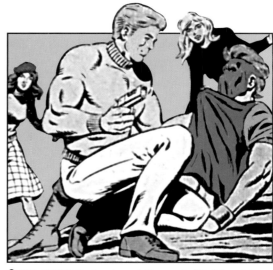

SECRET SOCIETY *During the anti-Communist "Red Scare" of the 1950s, Argent exposed a number of threats to U.S. security, from foreign terrorists to costumed and superpowered villains.*

After the death of Control, his granddaughter began operating under the same guise. The group was finally disbanded after a confrontation with the Suicide Squad, and the U.S. government has no official record of their members or their existence. PJ

ARGENT II

FIRST APPEARANCE TEEN TITANS (2nd series) #1 (October 1996)
STATUS Hero **REAL NAME** Toni Moretti
OCCUPATION Adventurer **BASE** New Jersey
HEIGHT 5ft 8in **WEIGHT** 125 lbs **EYES** Blue **HAIR** Black
SPECIAL POWERS/ABILITIES Can generate silver plasma and shape it to whatever form she pleases; creates energy platforms and travels astride them at great speeds.

Teenager Toni Moretti first met the TEEN TITANS when the team saved her U.S. senator father from the FEARSOME FIVE. She never dreamed she would ever join them. However, a few years later, her skin was mysteriously drained of pigment and her body started to generate silver plasma. Abducted by an alien race, the H'San Natall, Toni learned that she and several other teenagers were the results of a breeding program to create a superpowered advance guard for an attack upon Earth. Toni and her fellow hybrids rebelled against the H'San Natall and sabotaged the invasion. Since the Teen Titans were inactive at the time, the hybrids decided to form their own version.

As Argent, Toni had many tumultuous adventures with various incarnations of the Teen Titans. Toni then found out that her father was involved in drug smuggling, and she was eventually forced to turn him over to the authorities. Much later, the Titans disbanded again after the deaths of heroines Omen and TROIA. Argent's current activities are unknown, although given her drive to succeed, one can safely assume that she is actively polishing her silver plasma skills. SB

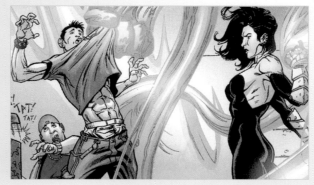

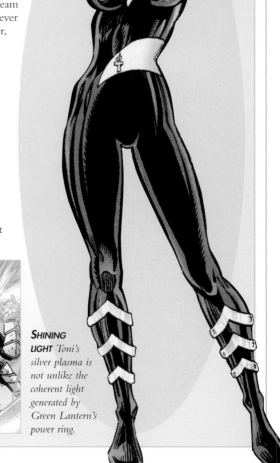

SHINING LIGHT *Toni's silver plasma is not unlike the coherent light generated by Green Lantern's power ring.*

ARION, LORD OF ATLANTIS

FIRST APPEARANCE WARLORD #55 (March 1982)
STATUS Hero **REAL NAME** Ahri'ahn
OCCUPATION Atlantean sorcerer **BASE** Mobile
HEIGHT 6ft 3in **WEIGHT** 190 lbs **EYES** Green **HAIR** Brown
SPECIAL POWERS/ABILITIES Immortality; vast magical abilities drawn from the extra-dimensional Darkworld.

ATLANTIS! THE NAME IS LEGENDARY, and during its golden age no hero was greater than Arion. No mere mortal, Arion came into existence as the product of a union between two Atlantean gods more than half a million years ago. His father, Calculhah (a force of good), cared for Arion, then known by the name Ahri'ahn, while his mother, Dark Majistra (a force of strife), raised Arion's wicked older brother, Garn Daanuth (*see* DAANUTH, GARN). When the two evil entities tried to destroy primitive Atlantis, Arion sacrificed his life to stop them. His energies survived thanks to the extra-dimensional realm of the Darkworld—home to a cosmic entity who serves as the source of all Atlantean magic—and Arion existed for nearly 500,000 years in a state of intangibility.

PROTECTOR OF ATLANTIS

Approximately 45,000 years ago, Arion returned in physical form to serve as the protector of Atlantis. The civilization had reached a peak, with the *homo sapiens* offshoot species, the *homo magi*, making up a large part of the population and exhibiting a primal connection to the forces of the universe. Arion became Lord High Mage of Atlantis, residing in the City of the Golden Gate and fighting the creeping encroachment of ice. He soon fell in love with Lady Chian, and the two battled the still-surviving mage Garn Daanuth. Arion played a time-hopping role alongside heroes from other eras during the Crisis (*see* Great Battles, pp. 320–1).

The continent of Atlantis suffered its first great fracturing when Arion fought off an assault by alien invaders. A bolt of energy shattered the City of the Golden Gate and caused much of the continental shelf to slip into the ocean. Arion and Lady Chian rapidly dispatched teams to establish new Atlantean colonies across the globe, including one in the hidden realm of Skartaris. Atlantis's final sinking (involving the cities of Tritonis and Poseidonis) did not occur until tens of thousands of years later.

As an immortal, Arion wandered the Earth for the next 45,000 years, though he lost his powers due to changes in the Darkworld. In the modern era he emerged as a new champion, restored to the Darkworld and claiming to be the grandfather of POWER GIRL.

Recently, as part of a plot to plunge the Earth into perpetual darkness, the sorcerer Mordru (*see* DARK LORD) took over Arion's body and trapped his spirit in Gemworld. Power Girl freed Arion, and he revealed to his rescuer that the two of them did not share a blood connection. Before his spirit apparently passed into the afterlife, Arion disabled Mordru, which allowed the JUSTICE SOCIETY OF AMERICA to score a victory. **DW**

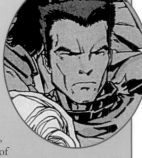

AS TIME GOES BY
Arion's appearance has changed over the years in conjunction with the waxing and waning power of the Darkworld.

PERMANENT EXILE *Even Arion's mighty power could not prevent the destruction of ancient Atlantis, making him a man without a home.*

KEY STORYLINES

• **ARION, LORD OF ATLANTIS #1 (NOVEMBER 1982):** Arion graduates to his own title after debuting as a backup feature in Warlord.

• **JSA #50 (SEPTEMBER 2003):** Arion passes onto another plane of existence, taking down Mordru, the Dark Lord, in the process.

ARGUS

FIRST APPEARANCE THE FLASH ANNUAL (2nd series) #6 (1993)
STATUS Hero **REAL NAME** Nick Kovak
OCCUPATION Adventurer **BASE** Keystone City
HEIGHT 5ft 11in **WEIGHT** 185 lbs **EYES** Blue **HAIR** Black
SPECIAL POWERS/ABILITIES Can become invisible wherever shadows are projected; can see almost the entire spectrum; well-trained hand-to-hand combatant.

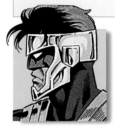

Federal agent Nick Kovak was working on an investigation into Keystone City's criminal organizations when Venev, an alien bent on conquering Earth, attacked him. The attack changed his body chemistry, allowing him to become virtually invisible in shadow, and his vision now worked beyond the normal spectrum. He designed a dark costume for himself, took the name Argus (after a giant guardian in Greek mythology who had a hundred eyes), and became a crime fighter. Being based in Keystone inevitably meant encountering the FLASH III, the city's top super hero, and they have worked together a number of times. However, Kovak, using the frequent alter ego Nick Kelly, usually prefers to operate on his own. RG

ARION, LORD OF ATLANTIS *See opposite page*

ARISIA

FIRST APPEARANCE TALES OF THE GREEN LANTERN CORPS #1 (May 1981)
STATUS Hero (deceased) **ASSUMED NAME** Cindy Simpson
OCCUPATION Adventurer **BASE** Space Sector 2815; Los Angeles, CA
HEIGHT 5ft 9in **WEIGHT** 136 lbs **EYES** Gold **HAIR** Blonde
SPECIAL POWERS/ABILITIES Arisia's Green Lantern ring can project energy, sense danger, create vehicles and weapons, project battering rams and objects, translate languages, probe minds, and allow unaided flight through space.

Arisia's father, a GREEN LANTERN from the planet Graxos IV, was ambushed and killed by the villainous SINESTRO. The GUARDIANS OF THE UNIVERSE chose Arisia to replace her father as the Green Lantern of her father's sector, making her one of the Corps' youngest members.
During her first mission, a deadly melee against the demon Nekron, malevolent ruler of a dimension known as the Land of the Unliving, Arisia met Hal Jordan, the Green Lantern of Earth.
The teenager later helped Jordan prevent the planet Ungara from entering a deadly ice age, and fell in love with him.
Arisia used her ring to age her body so she could pursue a relationship with Hal and, after the Crisis (*see* Great Battles, pp. 320–1), moved to Earth to be closer to him, joining the last of the GREEN LANTERN CORPS based there. Tragically, after giving up her ring and her desire for Hal, Arisia was murdered by MAJOR FORCE. PJ

WITH THIS RING... *The sprite-like Arisia was barely a teenager when she assumed the mantle and power of Green Lantern.*

ARRAKHAT

FIRST APPEARANCE ROBIN #79 (July 2000)
STATUS Villain **REAL NAME** Arrakhat
OCCUPATION Evil djinn **BASE** O'salla Ben Duuram
HEIGHT Variable **WEIGHT** Variable **EYES** Flaming **HAIR** None
SPECIAL POWERS/ABILITIES Arrakhat's powers are mystical in nature and are quite formidable. He manifests in the form of an armored demon wielding a flaming scimitar.

In Quraci myth, the demon Arrakhat is an evil djinn from the O'salla Ben Duuram, or "Oasis of the Damned," one of the descending circles of Hell. Rather than granting three wishes to its invoker, Arrakhat instead offers three murders, upon completion of which this genie will return to its resting place in the so-called "Well of Flames." In modern times, Arrakhat was summoned forth by the Arghulian, a religious zealot and enemy of Tim Drake's schoolmate Ali Ben Khan, Rhafi (or prince) of Dhubar. The Arghulian opposed Khan's rule and was determined to see him dead rather than let him assume the throne of Dhubar. Tim Drake's alter ego, ROBIN, in company with Connor Hawke (GREEN ARROW II) and former government operative Eddie Fyers did their best to protect Ali from Arrakhat's murderous wrath. However, the prince's salvation lay in a mystical amulet he possessed, a signet frequently used by his own father to call forth the demon to slay his enemies. Khan's amulet turned Arrakhat upon the Arghulian and returned the demon to his abyssal home after slaying the usurper. The evil djinn has not been invoked by anyone since. SB

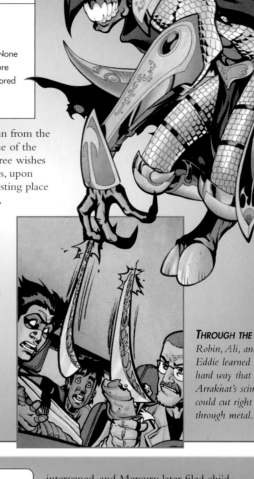

THROUGH THE ROOF *Robin, Ali, and Eddie learned the hard way that Arrakhat's scimitars could cut right through metal.*

ARROWETTE

FIRST APPEARANCE IMPULSE #28 (August 1997)
STATUS Hero **REAL NAME** Cissie King-Jones
OCCUPATION Student **BASE** Western Pennsylvania
HEIGHT 5ft 7in **WEIGHT** 107 lbs **EYES** Blue **HAIR** Blonde
SPECIAL POWERS/ABILITIES Olympic-level athlete; yet to fully master hand-to-hand combat techniques.

Daughter of Olympic archery medalist Bonnie King and her husband Bernell Jones, Cissie was raised with high expectations in her mother's footsteps. Before marrying, Bonnie had flirted with becoming a costumed heroine, Miss Arrowette, and adventured on several occasions with GREEN ARROW II. Bonnie pushed Cissie to take up archery and filled her head with dreams of superheroics. After overseeing several years of her daughter's training, Bonnie took Cissie into battle with the demon Spazz in Manchester, Alabama. Local heroes Impulse and MAX MERCURY intervened, and Mercury later filed child endangerment charges against Bonnie. The charges were upheld, and Cissie was made a ward of the state and placed in the Elias School in western Pennsylvania, under the care of Dr. Marcy Money. According to Dr. Money's files, she accidentally gave Cissie the idea of becoming a better archer than her mother, effectively starting Cissie's career as the costumed crime fighter Arrowette. Cissie joined YOUNG JUSTICE and was enjoying her new identity, until the day she almost killed some criminals. She has since renounced her persona and only reluctantly suits up when circumstances demand it. RG

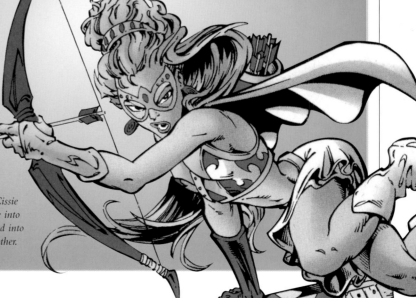

ARROWETTE IN ACTION *Cissie does not hesitate to charge into action, something ingrained into her by her overbearing mother.*

ARSENAL

FIRST APPEARANCE ADVENTURE COMICS #250 (July 1958)
STATUS Hero **REAL NAME** Roy Harper
OCCUPATION Adventurer **BASE** Brooklyn, New York City
HEIGHT 5ft 11in **WEIGHT** 195 lbs **EYES** Blue **HAIR** Red
SPECIAL POWERS/ABILITIES One of the world's top archers with bow and crossbow, Arsenal is also an expert with most projectile weapons and is a natural leader.

WEAPONS MASTER
Arsenal still favors the weapons of his Navajo upbringing, but is also skilled with firearms.

LIAN *As a single father and a super hero, Roy struggles to find time for his daughter.*

KEY STORYLINES

• *GREEN LANTERN #85 (SEPTEMBER 1971):* In one of comics' most shocking panels, Speedy is revealed as a heroin addict.

• *NEW TEEN TITANS (2ND SERIES) #21 (JUNE 1986):* After a long tease, Cheshire discloses that Roy Harper is the father of her child.

• *NEW TITANS #99 (JULY 1993):* Speedy makes his debut as Arsenal.

ONCE THE TEEN SIDEKICK OF GREEN ARROW I, Roy Harper endured many painful years in the hero's shadow, but emerged as an adult with his own identity. Roy is well acquainted with loss, having been orphaned twice before his fourteenth birthday. When Roy was a baby, his forest ranger father, Will, died saving Navajo medicine chief Brave Bow from a wildfire. Out of gratitude, Brave Bow raised the boy as his own. Roy became a tireless long-distance runner and a fine archer, closely following the career of the world's greatest archer, GREEN ARROW. One day Green Arrow came to Roy's hometown, and Roy impressed his idol with his quick reactions foiling a robbery (earning him the nickname "Speedy").

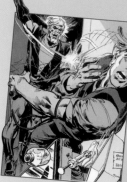

SPEEDY *Roy has left behind the idealism of his early teens.*

SHARP SHOOTERS

Brave Bow died soon after, and Roy became the legal ward of Green Arrow's alter ego, playboy millionaire Oliver Queen. Green Arrow and Speedy's amazing archery skills put them in the same class as many of the super heroes emerging at the same time. Green Arrow joined the JUSTICE LEAGUE OF AMERICA, while Speedy became a member of the TEEN TITANS alongside Kid Flash I (*see* KID FLASH II), WONDER GIRL, ROBIN, and Aqualad (*see* TEMPEST).

Yet Roy still felt adrift, and when Green Arrow left on a cross-country road trip with GREEN LANTERN to "find America," Ray turned to drugs for comfort and became a heroin addict. Fortunately, BLACK CANARY helped Roy kick his dependency, and he eventually joined the Central Bureau of Investigations. A mission to Japan brought him into intimate contact with the beautiful assassin CHESHIRE. When they eventually parted, Roy was unaware she was carrying his child. Cheshire later became a prisoner of the government and Roy gained custody of his daughter, Lian.

While working for CHECKMATE, Roy retired the Speedy name for a more fitting identity as Arsenal. He returned to lead the Titans when the team came under U.S. government control, but this lineup soon disbanded. After a second stint with the Titans, Arsenal organized the OUTSIDERS, only to suffer a near-fatal gunshot wound in the chest during the group's bitter battle against BROTHER BLOOD. **DW**

DRUG HELL *Feeling abandoned by Green Arrow, Roy hit rock bottom.*

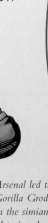

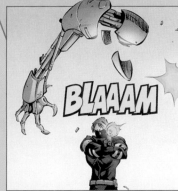

GRADUATION DAY *Arsenal's fight with Indigo couldn't prevent the accidental death of Troia.*

OUTSIDERS *Arsenal led the new Outsiders against Gorilla Grodd and his ape-soldiers when the simian supervillain attempted to invade New York City.*

ARTEMIS

FIRST APPEARANCE WONDER WOMAN (2nd series) #90 (Sept. 1994)
STATUS Hero **REAL NAME** Artemis
OCCUPATION Minister of Defense **BASE** Themyscira
HEIGHT 6ft **WEIGHT** 166 lbs **EYES** Green **HAIR** Red
SPECIAL POWERS/ABILITIES Immortal; an expert hand-to-hand combatant, master swordswoman, and archer.

FATE *Artemis sacrificed her life to save Diana's, fulfilling a mystic prophecy.*

Artemis is a member of the warmongering Amazons of Bana-Mighdall, descendants of the Amazon queen Antiope. Unlike the peace-loving AMAZONS of Themyscira (led by Antiope's sister HIPPOLYTA), Artemis and her tribe were not immortal. Artemis was raised in the secret city of Bana-Mighdall in Egypt, mastering the arts of warfare.

CHAMPION *Even without superpowers, Artemis is a formidable warrior.*

When the evil sorceress CIRCE transported the Amazons of Bana-Mighdall to Themyscira, home of Princess Diana (WONDER WOMAN), the two tribes of warrior women fought a ten-year war. An uneasy peace was forged that forced the Egyptian Amazons to settle on an inhospitable part of Themyscira. One night Hippolyta saw the death of her daughter Diana in a prophetic vision. Hoping to save Diana's life, she arranged for a new Contest to be held in order to choose a new Wonder Woman. With the help of a court magician, the sorceress Magala, Hippolyta arranged for Artemis to win the Contest and become the new Wonder Woman. She then dispatched the bow-wielding Amazon to Man's World in Diana's place. The warlike, hot-headed Artemis was totally unsuited to the role of diplomat, and was Wonder Woman for only a short time before she was murdered by the White Magician.

Rescued from Hades by Diana, who reclaimed her title as Wonder Woman, Artemis briefly joined a group of demon hunters named the Hellenders. After the Amazon civil war, Artemis became the Shim'Tar, or champion, of her people. Her fiery temper cooled by her years as an Amazon heroine and companion of Wonder Woman, Artemis was Themyscira's Minister of Defense until its recent destruction. **PJ**

ARTEMIS III

FIRST APPEARANCE SUICIDE SQUAD (1st series) #35 (November 1989)
STATUS Villain **REAL NAME** None
OCCUPATION Adventurer **BASE** Apokolips
HEIGHT 6ft 3in **WEIGHT** 189 lbs **EYES** Brown **HAIR** Black
SPECIAL POWERS/ABILITIES Furious fighter and an archer with unerring aim; commands pack of cybernetic warhounds.

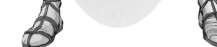

The origins of Artemis are known only to herself and perhaps GRANNY GOODNESS, who recruited and trained the deadly archer for DARKSEID's FEMALE FURIES. Artemis initially joined this elite squad as a temporary replacement for Lashina, who had been stranded on Earth following a struggle with the SUICIDE SQUAD. Artemis remained a Female Fury and has since battled SUPERBOY and SUPERGIRL during the Furies' assaults upon Earth under Darkseid's or Granny's direct dispatch. Although highly skilled in hand-to-hand combat, Artemis's main role in the Female Furies is as a huntress, scenting out foes with her cybernetically augmented warhounds and delivering a killing strike with one of the many devastating arrows in her quiver. **SB**

ARUNA

FIRST APPEARANCE BATGIRL ANNUAL #1 (2000)
STATUS Hero **REAL NAME** Unrevealed
OCCUPATION Stuntperson **BASE** Madras, India
HEIGHT 6ft 10in **WEIGHT** 153 lbs **EYES** Brown **HAIR** Black
SPECIAL POWERS/ABILITIES Born with the ability to shift her shape and features; can imitate other humans perfectly.

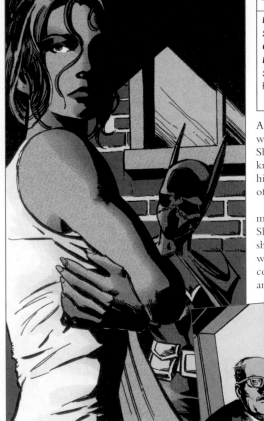

SHAPE *This is Aruna in her usual form (above) but the shape shifter can appear in almost any size or shape.*

Aruna Shende is the alias for a superpowered shape shifter who works as a stuntperson in the Indian film industry. Shende was born a shape shifter, so his/her parents never knew what gender their child truly was. Shende and his/her parents, "untouchables" by caste, lived in the slums of Madras, India.

One day, Shende's parents were taken away by mysterious men, never to be seen again. Devastated, Shende traveled from city to city, using his/her shapechanging abilities to steal food and procure whatever work was available. One day, Shende overheard a conversation about a film being made and joined the cast and crew. A man Shende once worked for named him/her "Aruna," and Shende kept the name, gaining a reputation as an actor and stuntperson in the Indian film industry. After an adventure with BATGIRL, where the two saved a young boy who'd been kidnapped, Aruna found him/herself intoxicated by the desire to help others, and vowed to use his/her shapeshifting powers to make a difference in his/her own country. **RG**

ARYAN BRIGADE

FIRST APPEARANCE JUSTICE LEAGUE TASK FORCE #10 (March 1994)
STATUS Villain team **BASE** Pine Heights, Nebraska
MEMBERS AND POWERS
Backlash Whip-like extendible arms.
Blind Faith Blind telepath with supernatural tracking abilities.
Golden Eagle II Soaring flight on mechanical wings.
Heatmonger Can fire jets of flame.
Iron Cross Superhuman strength.

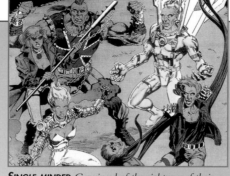

SINGLE MINDED Convinced of the rightness of their cause, the Aryan Brigade would have exterminated most of the globe if not stopped by the Justice League.

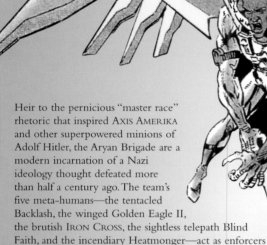

Heir to the pernicious "master race" rhetoric that inspired AXIS AMERIKA and other superpowered minions of Adolf Hitler, the Aryan Brigade are a modern incarnation of a Nazi ideology thought defeated more than half a century ago. The team's five meta-humans—the tentacled Backlash, the winged Golden Eagle II, the brutish IRON CROSS, the sightless telepath Blind Faith, and the incendiary Heatmonger—act as enforcers for the clandestine white supremacist movement known as the Aryan Nation.

Senator Sanders Hotchkins once led the Aryan Nation and schemed to release a genetically-tailored virus in the upper atmosphere that would kill every non-white on the planet. The Justice League Task Force (see JUSTICE LEAGUE OF AMERICA) infiltrated Hotchkins' Nebraska headquarters but fell afoul of the Aryan Brigade, whose powers were sufficient to subdue even J'onn J'onzz, the mighty MARTIAN MANHUNTER. Only Rex Tyler, the Golden Age HOURMAN, remained free to battle the ideologues whose kind he had fought so hard to defeat during World War II. While J'onn J'onzz steered the plague-carrying missile into the safety of deep space, Hourman confronted Senator Hotchkins, who accidentally infected himself with the deadly virus. He died from its effects, discovering too late that he was not of pure Aryan blood.

The Aryan Brigade somehow survived this debacle and became members of the OVERMASTER's gigantic CADRE. They failed in that ambitious endeavor but reassembled as a team and eventually returned to be protectors of the Aryan Nation. **DW**

SUPREMACIST SCREED The racist Aryan Brigade strongly disliked having to work alongside those of the Overmaster's servants who happened to be non-white in the latest incarnation of the Cadre. When it comes to fanatical devotion to Nazi dogma, the Aryan Brigade are utterly inflexible, and totally unforgiving.
1) Golden Eagle II **2)** Iron Cross **3)** Backlash
4) Blind Faith **5)** Heatmonger

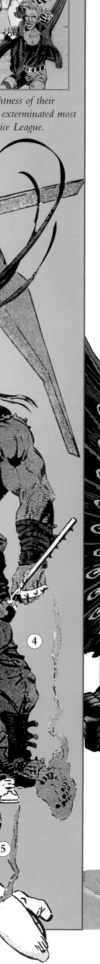

ASMODEL

FIRST APPEARANCE JLA #7 (July 1997)
STATUS Villain **REAL NAME** Asmodel
OCCUPATION Angel **BASE** Heaven
HEIGHT 10ft **WEIGHT** 800 lbs **EYES** Red **HAIR** Brown
SPECIAL POWERS/ABILITIES Wields a flaming staff and is immortal and invulnerable, with vast superstrength, superspeed, a devastating cry, acidic blood, and flying ability. He has few rivals as a military commander.

In Heaven, the angel Asmodel was formerly the Lord Harrier of the Bull Host, and Commander of the Cherubim Alpha Battalion. He was the highest ranked and most feared of the Pax Dei, the Angel Army of Heaven, but grew tired of simply being a servant of God. Rebelling as Lucifer had millennia before, Asmodel waged war against the forces of Heaven. He was eventually defeated by the guardian angel ZAURIEL and the JUSTICE LEAGUE OF AMERICA in a confrontation in the skies above San Francisco.

Stripped of his rank and consigned to Hell, Asmodel joined forces with Etrigan the DEMON in an attempt to overthrow the demon NERON. Asmodel usurped the power of the SPECTRE and led Hell's demonic forces to Earth. But the Spectre force-bonded with Hal Jordan, the former GREEN LANTERN, and the demons of Hell returned to their vile dimension. Asmodel was placed in the custody of the angels of Heaven, refusing to accept the appellation "fallen." **PJ**

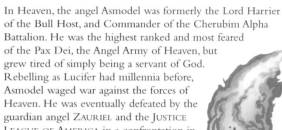

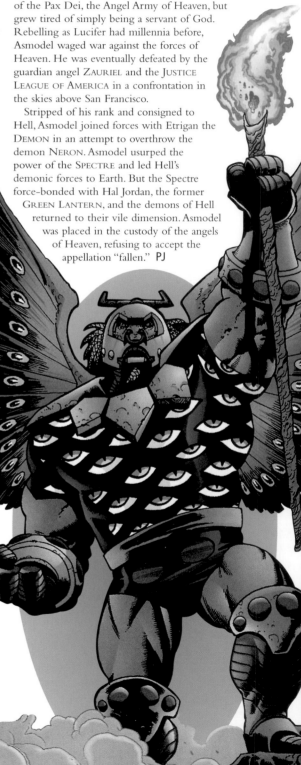

26

ATLAN

FIRST APPEARANCE ATLANTIS CHRONICLES #5 (July 1990)
STATUS Unresolved **REAL NAME** Atlan
OCCUPATION Sorceror **BASE** Atlantis
HEIGHT 6ft 3in **WEIGHT** 220 lbs **EYES** Blue **HAIR** Blond
SPECIAL POWERS/ABILITIES Master of dark arts long forgotten by his
people; developed a potion that allowed Atlanteans to live on land
for extended periods of time, prolonging their lives; now survives as
a spirit of unpredictable temperament and vast magical powers.

Long ago, Atlan was one of three children born to
Atlantis's King Honsu and his queen Lorelei (the others
were Haumond and Kraken). As he grew, Atlan's hair
turned blond, and many believed this to mean he carried
the curse of Kordax the destroyer. For a while, he was
banished from the city of Poseidonis. When he returned
home, Atlan told of life above the surface. His revelations
led Honsu to invade the surface world.

Recently, Atlan's spirit visited Atlanna, Queen of
Atlantis, impregnating her. The child, Orin, was born with
blond hair and abandoned
because of this. He grew to
become Atlantis's king and the
world's hero, AQUAMAN. Atlan
then sired another child with
an Eskimo woman. The child,
Orm Marius, was destined to
battle Orin as the OCEAN
MASTER. Atlan has also gifted
Aquaman's adopted son Garth,
now known as TEMPEST II, with
formidable mystical abilities. **RG**

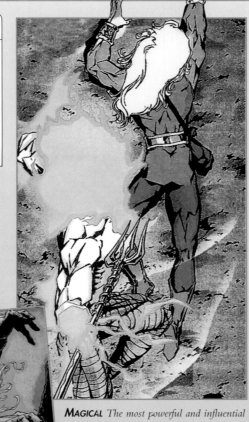

MAGICAL *The most powerful and influential
person in Atlantean history, Atlan has
played a key role in pivotal moments.*

ATLAS

FIRST APPEARANCE FIRST ISSUE SPECIAL #1 (April 1975)
STATUS Hero **REAL NAME** None
OCCUPATION Champion **BASE** Hyssa
HEIGHT 6ft 5in **WEIGHT** 250 lbs **EYES** Blue **HAIR** Brown
SPECIAL POWERS/ABILITIES Superhuman strength.

In ancient times in a faraway land, the mighty hero Atlas
became a champion of the oppressed in his struggle
against the despotic King Hyssa. As a youth, Atlas had been
one of the peaceful people of the Crystal Mountain until
Hyssa's raiders attacked his village. Burning Atlas's home to
the ground, killing his father, and capturing everyone he
knew or cared about, Hyssa unwittingly made a powerful
enemy that would pursue him for years.

Wearing a mystical crystal talisman struck from the
Crystal Mountain, Atlas escaped from the slavers and found
a new home with a good-hearted man named Chagra.
It was not long before Chagra realized the boy possessed
jaw-dropping muscle. He became Atlas's manager and
accompanied him on his journeys, watching his new hero
rescue citizens and defeat evil princes. Finally arriving in
the capital city of Hyssa, Atlas touted his strength in the
marketplace, where he fought challengers one-on-one. It is
unknown whether Atlas eventually succeeded in taking his
revenge on the sinister King Hyssa. **DW**

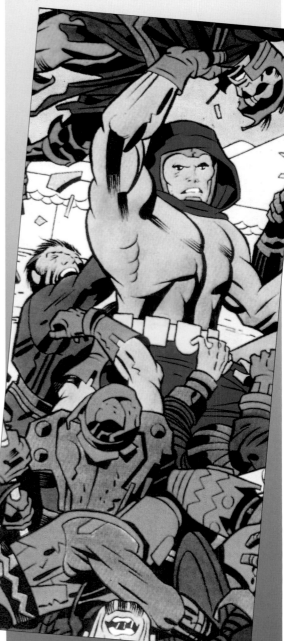

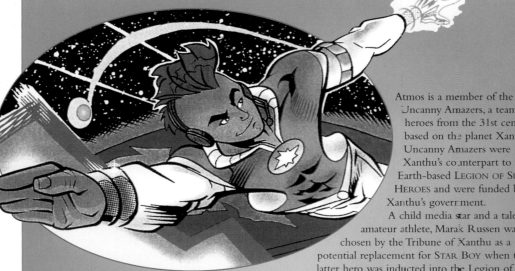

ATMOS

FIRST APPEARANCE LEGION OF SUPER-HEROES (3rd series) #32 (1987)
STATUS Hero **REAL NAME** Marak Russen
OCCUPATION Uncanny Amazer; former athlete
BASE The planet Xanthu in the 31st century
HEIGHT 6ft 7in **WEIGHT** 220 lbs **EYES** White **HAIR** Red
SPECIAL POWERS/ABILITIES Nuclear-based powers include superstrength,
speed, and flight; projects powerful nuclear bolts from his hands;
generates a protective force field; can survive unaided in the
vacuum of space.

Atmos is a member of the
Uncanny Amazers, a team of
heroes from the 31st century
based on the planet Xanthu. The
Uncanny Amazers were
Xanthu's counterpart to the
Earth-based LEGION OF SUPER-
HEROES and were funded by
Xanthu's government.

A child media star and a talented
amateur athlete, Marak Russen was
chosen by the Tribune of Xanthu as a
potential replacement for STAR BOY when the
latter hero was inducted into the Legion of Super-
Heroes. Russen was subjected to a series of Tribune
experiments that transformed him into a living
nuclear reactor. The nuclear-powered Russen is
now the Amazers' most powerful member, and
stood by them when the alien race known as the
BLIGHT took over Xanthu and nearly decimated the
planet. Soon after, C.O.M.P.U.T.O.'s machine world
of Robotica attacked Xanthu and destroyed the
planet, but not before Atmos and the Amazers were
able to evacuate its populace.

Accepting the Tribune's assignment at first for
the celebrity status it would impart on him, Atmos
has nonetheless become a powerful hero in his
own right, and an honorable champion of his
homeworld. **PJ**

ATOM

THE MIGHTY MITE

FIRST APPEARANCE (ATOM I) ALL-AMERICAN COMICS #19 (October 1940)
STATUS Hero (deceased) **REAL NAME** Al Pratt
OCCUPATION Professor of Nuclear Physics **BASE** Calvin College
HEIGHT 5ft 1in **WEIGHT** 150 lbs **EYES** Blue **HAIR** Red
SPECIAL POWERS/ABILITIES Skilled in the "sweet science" of boxing, Al Pratt packed an even mightier punch when he gained atomic strength, which also greatly enhanced his agility and kept him fighting fit many decades later.

FIRST APPEARANCE (ATOM II) SHOWCASE #34 (October 1961)
STATUS Hero **REAL NAME** Raymond "Ray" Palmer
OCCUPATION Professor of Physics **BASE** Ivy Town
HEIGHT 6ft **WEIGHT** 180 lbs
EYES Brown **HAIR** Auburn
SPECIAL POWERS/ABILITIES Can shrink to any size, no matter how miniscule, either retaining the heft of his original 180 pounds or weighing next to nothing. He has mastered fighting techniques at various sizes. At sub-atomic size, the Atom can travel virtually anywhere on Earth via telephone transmissions, surfing microwaves or other electronic impulses.

AL PRATT WAS A "98-POUND WEAKLING" until he met former boxing champ Joe Morgan. Morgan transformed the young man into a "little superman" in less than a year, putting the pint-sized Pratt through a grueling exercise regime and increasing his weight. While Morgan groomed Pratt for a featherweight boxing career, his pupil had other plans. Pratt became the Atom, a diminutive costumed crime fighter with a formidable punch despite his size. A member of the JUSTICE SOCIETY OF AMERICA and ALL-STAR SQUADRON, the Mighty Mite gained atomic strength and agility in 1948 as a result of radiation exposure during a battle with Cyclotron, a scientist forced into crime by the evil ULTRA-HUMANITE. Later married to his sweetheart Mary, Pratt never hesitated to take his fighting togs out of mothballs if the need arose. Tragically, while aiding the JSA during the Zero Hour crisis (*see* Great Battles, pp. 320–1), the Atom died battling the villain EXTANT. Unknown to Pratt, a son—the young atomic-powered hero known as DAMAGE—survives him.

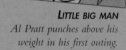

LITTLE BIG MAN *Al Pratt punches above his weight in his first outing.*

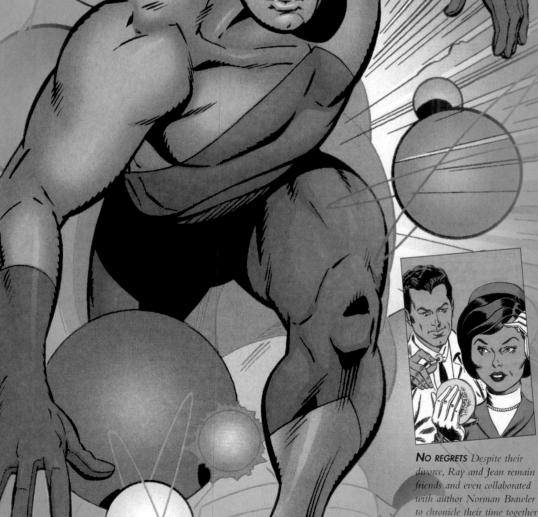

PART-TIMER *Ray Palmer prefers to be an auxiliary member of the JLA so he can continue his studies at Ivy University.*

ATOM II

When Ivy University physicist Ray Palmer discovered a fragment of a white dwarf star, he believed he had found the key to success in his size-reduction experiments. Before Palmer could test the star fragment, he was trapped in a cave with a group of youngsters while on a nature outing. Palmer used the fragment and his size-reducing lens to find an escape route from the cave. Somehow, mineral-infused water in the cave and other factors combined with the reducing materials to allow Palmer to shrink safely. Palmer then fashioned a costume that would shrink and enlarge with him, and only appear when he was less than six inches tall. He also devised reducing controls which he placed on his gloves. Thus outfitted, he became the second super hero to call himself the Atom, a Tiny Titan packing a 180-pound punch at any size.

The Atom's career as a super hero was marred only by the dissolution of Palmer's marriage to longtime love Jean Loring Palmer, from whom he is now divorced. A long-standing member of the JUSTICE LEAGUE OF AMERICA, the Atom is the team's resident scientist. He often uses his powers for infiltration and reconnoitering at miniscule size.

For a time, Ray lived among the Katarthans, a tribe of miniscule aliens who had made their home in the South American rain forest. He even found love, falling for their queen. Sadly, Ray's jungle idyll was cut short when the Katarthans were all killed in a fire. He returned to Ivy Town and the Atom resumed his super heroic work. **SB**

NO REGRETS *Despite their divorce, Ray and Jean remain friends and even collaborated with author Norman Brawler to chronicle their time together as super hero and spouse.*

KEY STORYLINES

• *ZERO HOUR #3 (SEPTEMBER 1994):* The Atom I perishes alongside his JSA teammate Hourman I in an attempt to stop Extant's timestream tamperings.
• *THE ATOM #1 (JULY 1962):* The Atom II first battles the Plant Master (The Floronic Man).
• *SWORD OF THE ATOM #1 (SEPTEMBER 1983):* In the South American jungle, Ray Palmer befriends the alien Katarthans and becomes their sword-wielding super-heroic defender!

ATOMIC KNIGHT

First appearance STRANGE ADVENTURES #117 (June 1960)
Status Hero **Real name** Gardner Grayle
Occupation Protector **Base** S.T.A.R. Labs, Alexandria, Virginia
Height 6ft 1in **Weight** 189 lbs **Eyes** Blue **Hair** Red
Special powers/abilities Battlesuit enables Grayle to imprison enemies in a stasis field; attached weapon fires powerful bursts of heat or cold; suit's solar power cells operate even in the reduced light of a nuclear winter. Grayle is courageous, with some precognitive powers.

S.T.A.R. Labs needed a test subject as they made contingencies for a nuclear holocaust. They chose Army Sergeant Gardner Grayle, who believed atomic weapons gave war a bad name. When the would-be universe-conqueror AGAMEMNO threatened the planet Rann, Grayle was urged to suit up in the Lab's prototype armor. He served as one of the SEVEN SOLDIERS OF VICTORY, taking the name of original member SHINING KNIGHT. Grayle later tested the armor within a virtual reality that went awry, and ultimately needed aid from SUPERMAN. Grayle's long time in sensory deprivation allowed his mind to develop beyond normal limits, and he predicted many future crises. He took the name Atomic Knight and resolved to help protect the world. He has worked solo and with one incarnation of the OUTSIDERS, falling in love with teammate Windfall. **RG**

ATOMIC SKULL

First appearance ACTION COMICS #670 (October 1991)
Status Villain **Real name** Joe Martin
Occupation Student turned super-villain **Base** Metropolis
Height 6ft **Weight** 185 lbs **Eyes** Black **Hair** None
Special powers/abilities Superstrength, enhanced speed and endurance; can fire fiery radiation blasts.

University of Metropolis film student Joe Martin saw his latent metagene activated during the allied alien invasion of Earth. Transformed into a radiation-seething monster with transparent skin, making it seem as if he had a flaming skull for a head, the delirious Martin came to believe that he was an old movie serial hero named "the Atomic Skull." Martin believed SUPERMAN to be the Atomic Skull's archenemy Dr. Electron, and battled him accordingly; nothing could shake Martin of his delusion. During the supernatural crisis known as Underworld Unleashed, the Atomic Skull gained improved powers from the demon NERON in exchange for his eternal soul. He is still active in villainy, usually pitting himself against Superman. He prefers to travel on a flying Skull-Bike, sometimes seeking out Lois Lane (see LANE, LOIS), who resembles the late Eleanor Hart from the Atomic Skull pictures of the 1930s.

Although he didn't know it, Joe Martin was actually the *second* villain to take the name Atomic Skull. The first, Dr. Albert Michaels of S.T.A.R. Labs, briefly assumed the identity after gaining energy powers from the SKULL criminal syndicate. **DW**

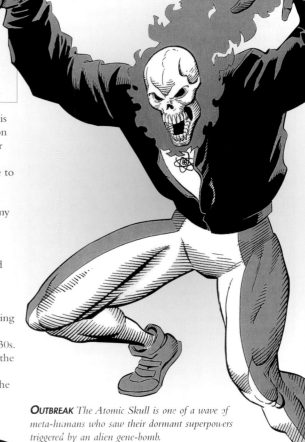

OUTBREAK The Atomic Skull is one of a wave of meta-humans who saw their dormant superpowers triggered by an alien gene-bomb.

ATOM-SMASHER

First appearance (as Nuklon) ALL-STAR SQUADRON #25 (September 1983); (as Atom-Smasher) JSA SECRET FILES AND ORIGINS #1 (August 1999)
Status Undecided **Real name** Albert Julian Rothstein
Occupation Car designer, repairman **Base** New York City
Height 7ft 6in **Weight** 297 lbs **Eyes** Blue **Hair** Red
Special powers/abilities Can manipulate his body size, growing up to 60ft high, and weighing up to 34,950 lbs; increased density gives him low-level invulnerability; can phase through solid objects.

Due to the genetic effects of his mother Terri's radiation poisoning, Al Rothstein developed superstrength and grew to over seven feet tall during his teenage years. Along with several other children and protégés of the JUSTICE SOCIETY OF AMERICA, Al founded a team of heroes called INFINITY, INC. and called himself Nuklon. He later developed the ability to double his size or phase through solid matter unharmed.

Nuklon subsequently joined the CONGOLMERATE and then, briefly, the JUSTICE LEAGUE OF AMERICA. After being dismissed from the JLA, Nuklon changed his name to Atom-Smasher and was recruited by WILDCAT I to join the new JSA, thereby fulfilling Al's lifelong dream. When Atom-Smasher's mother was murdered by the terrorist KOBRA in a bombing attack, Atom-Smasher managed to alter the past so that the villain EXTANT died in his mother's place. During a final confrontation with Kobra, Atom-Smasher helped BLACK ADAM murder the villain. Atom-Smasher's killing spree continued when he joined Black Adam's invasion of Khandaq, crushing the dictator Asim Muhunnad. He remains in Khandaq, considering his future. **PJ**

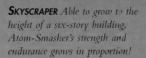

SKYSCRAPER Able to grow to the height of a six-story building, Atom-Smasher's strength and endurance grows in proportion!

BLACK ADAM Confounded by the loss in his life, Atom-Smasher joined his former enemy Black Adam in a paramilitary team that invaded the Middle Eastern country of Khandaq.

AXIS AMERICA

FIRST APPEARANCE YOUNG ALL-STARS #1 (June 1987)
STATUS Villain team **BASE** Unknown
CURRENT MEMBERS AND POWERS
Fleshburn Can emit blasts of atomic fire.
Great White Armed with an electrified whip and a whalebone gauntlet blade.
Hel (Vela Shepherd) A winged, Valkyrie-like warrior who wields an energized battleaxe.
Ubermensch (Mr. Shepherd) Superstrong, bulletproof juggernaut.
Zaladin Scimitar-wielding wraith cloaked in his demon bride Baal; a teleporter.

The original Axis Amerika was a brigade of bio-genetically augmented spies and saboteurs formed by the Axis powers (Nazi Germany, Imperial Japan, and Fascist Italy) during World War II to undermine American homeland security. Its members included the Nazi superman UBERMENSCH, Valkyrie warrior Gudra, the father-and-son team of the Horned Owl and Fledermaus, the living missile Kamikaze, aquatic lycanthrope Sea Wolf, and archer Usil. Fledermaus was killed in battle with the YOUNG ALL-STARS. The fates of the remaining members are undocumented.

In modern times, a team of superpowered American supremacists united as an equally formidable Axis America. After besting and nearly discrediting the JUSTICE LEAGUE OF AMERICA, Axis America escaped to continue fomenting its extremist agenda. **SB**

AXIS OF EVIL *The JLA thought it was negotiating the end to a standoff between a group of superpowered separatists and U.S. government agencies seeking their surrender. In truth, Axis America plotted to frame the heroes for the manslaughter of thousands as prelude to their own rise to power and public acceptance.* **1)** *Hel* **2)** *Zaladin* **3)** *Ubermensch* **4)** *Great White* **5)** *Fleshburn*

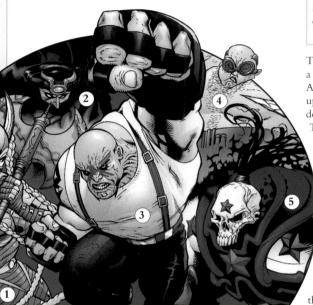

AZAZEL

FIRST APPEARANCE SANDMAN (2nd series) #4 (April 1989)
STATUS Demon **REAL NAME** Azazel
OCCUPATION A ruler in Hell **BASE** Hell
HEIGHT Variable **WEIGHT** Variable **EYES** Variable **HAIR** Variable
SPECIAL POWERS/ABILITIES Commands mystic and eldritch forces that allow him to reshape matter or eradicate a demon from existence.

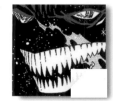

The Bible says that Azazel is either a fallen angel or the goat that Aaron placed the Hebrews' sins upon and then set free in the desert (hence the term scapegoat). The Hebrews also consider him the demon of war who taught humans how to build weapons (and to use cosmetics for an all-together different kind of war). To the Muslims, he is the angel who refused to worship Adam and was cast out. John Milton immortalized him in his *Paradise Lost*, naming Azazel the standard bearer of the rebel angels. He is also one of the Triumvirate in Hell's Hierarchy, serving alongside Lucifer Morningstar and BEELZEBUB. Azazel has battled the likes of Etrigan the DEMON in the never-ending struggle for supremacy in the lower dimensions. The mortal John Constantine outwitted all three members of the hierarchy, earning him Azazel's eternal enmity. As infernal politics stand, Azazel is secondary to Lucifer. When Lucifer closed Hell for a time, Azazel tried to claim it as his own and failed, winding up trapped in the SANDMAN II's endless realm of the Dreaming. However, as one of the underworld's most powerful entities, he is not to be underestimated. **RG**

AZTEK

FIRST APPEARANCE AZTEK: THE ULTIMATE MAN #1 (August 1996)
STATUS Hero (deceased) **REAL NAME** Uno
OCCUPATION Hero; doctor **BASE** Vanity City
HEIGHT 6ft 2in **WEIGHT** 185 lbs **EYES** Blue **HAIR** Blond
SPECIAL POWERS/ABILITIES Helmet-controlled battlesuit gives him superstrength, superspeed, superhearing, telescopic vision, X-ray vision, infrared vision, invisibility, density control, and flight.

The Azteks are a group of armored warriors created by the mysterious Q Foundation, a secret society of scientists and religious practitioners. The Foundation was formed to prepare a human vessel for the return of the benevolent Aztec serpent-god Quetzalcoatl, who was engaged in a constant cosmic struggle with his evil brother Tezcatlipoca. Housed in many secret bases around the world, the Q Foundation created their fourth-dimensional Aztek warsuits to be worn by specially trained heroes in preparation for the great battle between the gods.

When Uno took on the Aztek title, he relocated from Mexico to Vanity City in the U.S. and assumed the identity of Dr. Curt Falconer. After battling several super-villains in Vanity City, Falconer was invited by SUPERMAN, BATMAN, and GREEN LANTERN to join the latest incarnation of the JUSTICE LEAGUE OF AMERICA. Only the telepathic MARTIAN MANHUNTER voiced doubts.

Falconer soon discovered that the Q Foundation had been partially financed in recent years by the

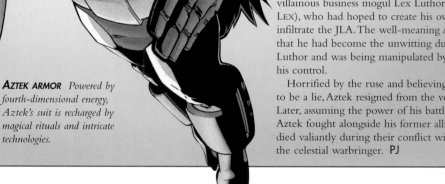

AZTEK ARMOR *Powered by fourth-dimensional energy, Aztek's suit is recharged by magical rituals and intricate technologies.*

POWER STRUGGLE *While Aztek preferred to fight with his mind rather than his fists, he used all the powers of his amazing battlesuit to stop a rampaging Amazo, a villain with the combined powers of the entire JLA!*

villainous business mogul Lex Luthor (see LUTHOR, LEX), who had hoped to create his own hero to infiltrate the JLA. The well-meaning Aztek realized that he had become the unwitting dupe of Lex Luthor and was being manipulated by forces beyond his control.

Horrified by the ruse and believing much of his life to be a lie, Aztek resigned from the venerable team. Later, assuming the power of his battlesuit once more, Aztek fought alongside his former allies in the JLA and died valiantly during their conflict with MAGEDDON, the celestial warbringer. **PJ**

AZRAEL

THE AVENGING ANGEL

FIRST APPEARANCE BATMAN: SWORD OF AZRAEL #1
(October 1992)
STATUS Hero **REAL NAME** Jean Paul Valley
OCCUPATION Adventurer **BASE** Ossaville
HEIGHT 6ft 2in **WEIGHT** 210 lbs **EYES** Blue **HAIR** Blond
SPECIAL POWERS/ABILITIES Physically and psychologically programmed
by scientists of the Order of St. Dumas to be an assassin; superb
combat skills, great strength, speed, and agility; powers triggered by
putting on special costume and using the name "Azrael."

AS A GOTHAM UNIVERSITY STUDENT, Jean Paul Valley had no inkling
of the larger forces acting on his life. But when his dying father
revealed the truth, Jean Paul willingly took up the mantle of Azrael,
the champion assassin of a Crusades-era fraternity of warrior-priests, the
ORDER OF ST. DUMAS. In modern times, the Order had become a secret
society with few members but uncountable riches. For centuries the
"avenging angel Azrael" had been their silent enforcer—actually an Order
member trained from birth to silence those who failed to observe the
Order's strict code of secrecy. The role of Azrael was passed down from father to son, and Jean
Paul suddenly realized he was heir to a long tradition. His life as the shadowy avenger Azrael
would last for many years. Throughout this time, conflicting feelings toward the role that had
been forced on him before he was even born plunged him into bouts of severe depression. His
costume would also undergo a number of changes in design and equipment, the better to
reflect the various alterations in his emotional state.

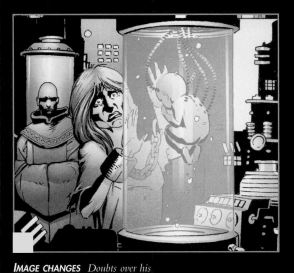

TEST-TUBE HORROR *Jean Paul's biological
mother was horrified to discover that the
egg she had donated to the Order of St.
Dumas had been appropriated for a
scientific program. The Order's fanatical
scientists were busily mingling the fetus's
genetic makeup with animal DNA to
create a being of great strength, capable of
killing without remorse. The poor mother
was condemned to die, but escaped thanks
to a merciful priest, and has remained in
hiding ever since.*

THE SYSTEM
In Switzerland, Jean Paul
trained under the dwarf
Nomoz, who triggered the
deep hypnotic implants that
Jean Paul had been unaware
he possessed. "The System," a
regimen of hypnosis and
prenatal conditioning, turned
Jean Paul Valley into a
formidable fighter.

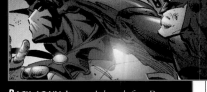

BACK AGAIN *It wasn't long before Bruce
Wayne returned to the role he created.*

He tested his new skills
on BATMAN, who had travelled to Switzerland on the trail of the
St. Dumas renegade Carleton LeHah. As Azrael, Jean Paul lost
the fight—but he nevertheless rescued Bruce Wayne from LeHah.
Jean Paul then returned to Gotham City and continued his training
as Azrael under ROBIN's guidance.

IMAGE CHANGES *Doubts over his
Azrael role have led Jean Paul to
revamp his warsuit several times.*

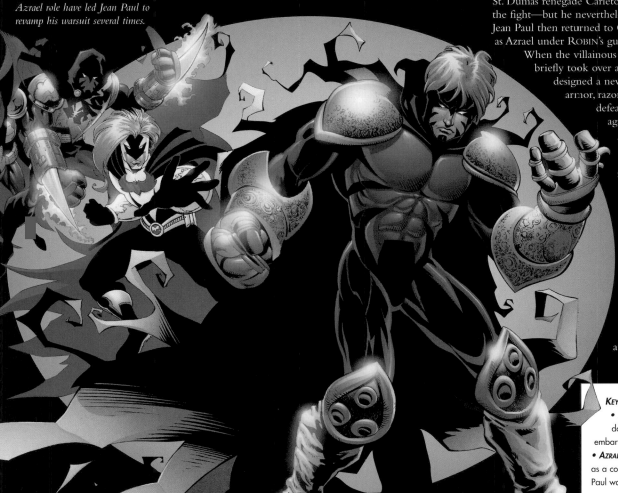

When the villainous BANE broke Batman's back, Jean Paul
briefly took over as Gotham City's Dark Knight. He
designed a new, Azrael-inspired bat costume with heavy
armor, razor talons, and hidden weapons. Though he
defeated Bane, he lost his internal struggle
against the hypnotic goading of the System.
Jean Paul became increasingly violent
and finally lost his mind. Bruce Wayne,
restored to full fitness, defeated him and
reclaimed the mantle of Batman. Jean
Paul, after a period of misery and soul-
searching, became Azrael once more.
Azrael moved against the Order's
scientists who originally brainwashed
him, culminating in a battle inside the
Order of St. Dumas' headquarters, the
Ice Cathedral. The destruction of the
Cathedral wiped out the last traces of
the Order. Jean Paul, however, did not
live long enough to enjoy the fruits of
his success—he apparently perished in a
shootout, ending the career of Gotham's
angel of vengeance. **DW**

KEY STORYLINES

• **BATMAN #500 (OCTOBER 1993):** Jean Paul Valley
donned the Azrael/Bat armor for the first time and
embarked on a career as Gotham's new Batman.
• **AZRAEL: AGENT OF THE BAT #100 (MAY 2003):** Azrael's life
as a costumed vigilante came to a violent end when Jean
Paul was seemingly killed.

AMAZING VEHICLES

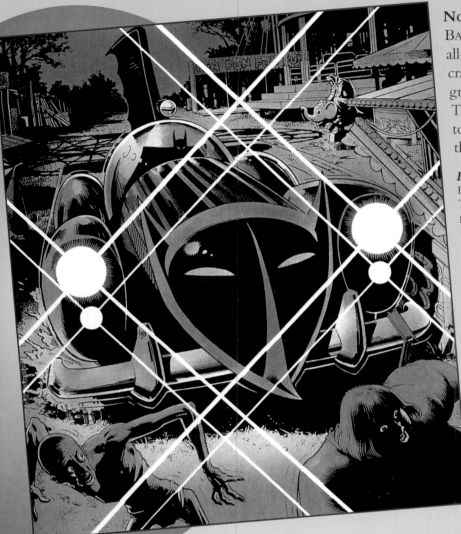

NOT ALL HEROES can fly unaided, or run at lightspeed. From BATMAN's Batmobile, which evolved from armored sedan into all-terrain tank, to WONDER WOMAN's invisible plane, an alien craft cloaked from Earthly technology, some of the world's greatest adventurers have the help of extraordinary vehicles. This fleet, created with magic or science (or both), are primed to sweep their owners to their destination.

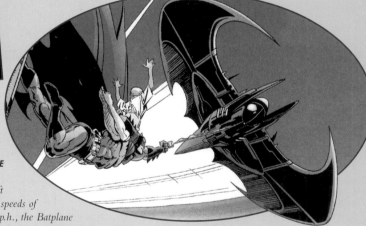

BATMOBILE

Equipped with a satellite dish for TV/radio/GPS linkage, anti-theft gas, hypersonic trilling sphere, gas nozzles, voice-activated controls, and gel-filled kevlar-reinforced wheels that are puncture and flame-resistant, the Batmobile has undergone many transformations over the years.
It remains one of the greatest weapons in Batman's arsenal, a sleek, fearful machine with no parallel for speed or maneuverability, even among the world's fastest racecars.
Able to attain speeds of 266 m.p.h., accelerate from 0 to 60 m.p.h. in under 3 seconds, and shielded in a bulletproof ceramic composite exterior, the Batmobile is almost as frightening to criminals as its legendary driver, who know they have little chance for escape from either.

BAT SECURITY *The Batmobile is equipped with security devices, including an electrified hull, hypersonic shrieks, and a self-destruct mechanism.*

JUSTICE SOCIETY OF AMERICA'S SHUTTLE CRAFT BOX

When the alien marauder IMPERIEX came to reignite the Big Bang, President Lex Luthor (see LUTHOR, LEX) sent every member of the JUSTICE SOCIETY OF AMERICA on a space mission to save the planet. The JSA rocketed across the galaxy in their Star Racer space shuttle, defeated IMPERIEX and his probes, and saved the populace of Daxam (see Alien Races, pp. 150–1) from Imperiex's planet-sized ship.

The Star Racer is outfitted with protective shields, offensive weaponry, and warp-drive capabilities, and is paid for and maintained with monies left by the Dodd estate.

STAR RACER *The JSA's Star Racer can warp across galaxies, outfitted with technology from Earth and Thanagar. The Star Spangled Kid drove a flying car called the Star Rocket Racer, which was an inspiration for the Star Racer.*

BAT PLANE
A stealth fighter craft capable of speeds of 4,400 m.p.h., the Batplane slices through the skies faster than any military warcraft.

ROBIN'S BIKES

The Supercycle isn't ROBIN's only specialized vehicle. While his primary mode of transportation is a customized sports coupé called the Redbird, Robin also rides a modified 491 c.c., liquid cooled, "motocross" Batcycle. One of many motorcycles in Batman's vehicular arsenal, the Batcycle's chassis and windshield are bulletproof. Capable of speeds of over 130 m.p.h., and armed with specialized shock dampers, the cycle is one of the sleekest machines on the road.

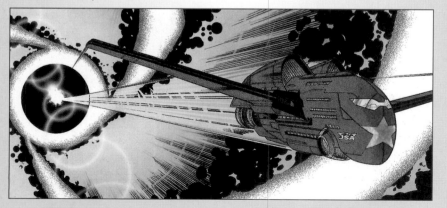

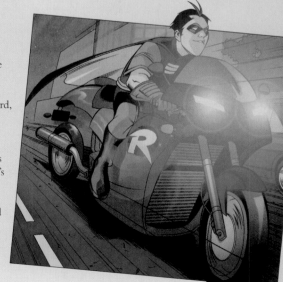

WONDER WOMAN'S INVISIBLE JET

A morphing, nearly invisible plane created by the alien Lansanarians, Wonder Woman's transparent transport is capable of changing into any number of shapes, from a fully submersible submarine to a spaceworthy chariot. Soon after accepting this incredible gift, Wonder Woman discovered that her invisible plane was a techno-organic alien from a world called the Ring. Queen HIPPOLYTA used the plane during her time as Wonder Woman, and after the destruction of Themyscira during the Imperiex War (*see* Great Battles, pp. 320–1), Wonder Woman used its miraculous technology to infuse the island with wondrous, new, morphing architecture that conformed to the Amazons' every requirement.

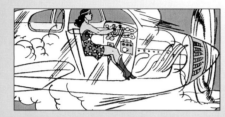

ALIEN PLANE *As Wonder Woman, Hippolyta flew the Invisible Plane over the skies of the U.S. and Europe during World War II.*

MANTA SHIP

A sleek submarine shaped like a giant manta ray, the sinister-looking Manta Ship is the villainous BLACK MANTA's underwater headquarters. Capable of submerging to extreme depths, Black Manta uses this atomic-powered vehicle for piracy and salvage.

THE SUPERCYCLE

Created by the FOREVER PEOPLE and originally piloted by BIG BEAR, the miraculous, superfast Supercycle was built with New Genesis (*see* NEW GODS) technology and is equipped with weapons, a cloaking device that renders it invisible, and density-altering capability. It can even teleport across dimensions. For a time, YOUNG JUSTICE used the Supercycle as their transport vehicle, The Supercycle is now telepathically controlled by Robin.

BLUE BEETLE'S BUG

A solar-powered hovercraft piloted by Ted Kord (BLUE BEETLE II), the Bug is a floating headquarters armed with magnetic impulse beams, electro charges, and claw-like landing gear. It is also able to fly at speeds of over 600 m.p.h. **PJ**

35

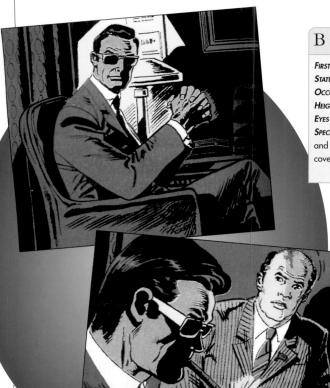

BAD SAMARITAN

FIRST APPEARANCE THE OUTSIDERS (1st series) #3 (January 1986)
STATUS Villain **REAL NAME** Unknown
OCCUPATION Agent provocateur **BASE** Mobile
HEIGHT 6ft 2in **WEIGHT** 190 lbs
EYES Unknown (hidden by dark glasses) **HAIR** Black
SPECIAL POWERS/ABILITIES Is a superb hand-to-hand combatant and ruthless assassin; is both a master of disguise and covert espionage.

The Bad Samaritan is a spy-for-hire, a terrorist, or an insurrectionist, depending on his paymaster. His country of origin remains a mystery, and he claims allegiance to no particular organization, sovereign, or country. He has plied his trade for the U.S., the U.K., the former Soviet Union, and many other governments, although each will disavow any knowledge of covert operations involving him. While in the U.S.S.R.'s employ, the Bad Samaritan helped the Soviet government to obtain important information on meta-humans—the OUTSIDERS and the Force of July in particular—to help the Communists to create a Soviet super-team of their own. Later, the Bad Samaritan shot down a plane carrying the Outsiders, leaving its member heroes stranded on an island somewhere in the Indian Ocean. The Bad Samaritan's present whereabouts and activities are unknown. However, he is sure to be involved in a major crisis or government coup somewhere in the world. **SB**

BALLOON BUSTER

FIRST APPEARANCE ALL-AMERICAN MEN OF WAR #112 (December 1965)
STATUS Hero (deceased) **REAL NAME** Steve Henry Savage, Jr.
OCCUPATION Lieutenant, U.S. Army Air Corps **BASE** France
HEIGHT 5ft 11in **WEIGHT** 178 lbs **EYES** Blue **HAIR** Blond
SPECIAL POWERS/ABILITIES A matchless marksman with any firearm, and an accomplished biplane pilot.

The son of legendary cowboy hero Brian "Scalphunter" Savage, Steve was raised in Mustang River, Wyoming, by a poverty-stricken farmer named Jennings. The boy became a consummate marksman, and he learned that a gun is merely an extension of the man who wields it. At his dying adoptive father's bedside, Steve swore to make the old man proud of him by making Savage a name to be remembered. Enlisting in the U. S. Army Air Corps at the onset of World War I, Savage repeatedly disobeyed orders, breaking formation to attack and destroy German combat balloons, which earned him his nickname. Savage was one of the most aggressive warriors of that "war to end all wars," and he often dueled with the German flying ace Rittmeister Hans Von Hammer. Savage disappeared in South East Asia in 1924 while on an aerial investigation of a supposed dragon, which locals had blamed for a fever outbreak. **RG**

BANE

FIRST APPEARANCE BATMAN: VENGEANCE OF BANE #1 (January 1993)
STATUS Villain **REAL NAME** Unknown
OCCUPATION Adventurer **BASE** Gotham City
HEIGHT 6ft 8in **WEIGHT** 350 lbs
EYES Brown **HAIR** Brown
SPECIAL POWERS/ABILITIES Brilliant strategist and polylinguist, with near-superhuman strength while on the steroid Venom, mainlined into his system via tubing in his helmet.

Bane will forever be remembered as the man who broke the Bat! More than three decades ago, Bane's father received a life sentence from the Santa Priscan government for his role in a failed revolution. He fled the country, but Santa Priscan law demanded that his son take his place. The child that would become Bane was raised inside Pena Duro prison (mostly in a pit called the Cavidad Oscuro). Bane killed dozens of inmates and engineered a jailbreak when experiments with the drug Venom gave him monstrous strength.

Winding up in Gotham City, Bane exhausted BATMAN by freeing all the villains from Arkham Asylum. He then crippled the Dark Knight by snapping his spine. Jean Paul Valley (AZRAEL) donned the Batman garb and beat Bane into a coma.

Bane returned to a life of wickedness, shaking off his dependence on Venom and allying himself with RÄ'S AL GHÜL. After a falling-out with the immortal would-be conqueror, he sabotaged Rä's al Ghül's network of life-extending Lazarus Pits. Bane suggested to Batman that the two of them were half-brothers, however subsequent blood tests did not bear this far-fetched theory out. Bane recently found his father, KING SNAKE, and cleansed himself in a Lazarus Pit. He now has a new lease on life. **DW**

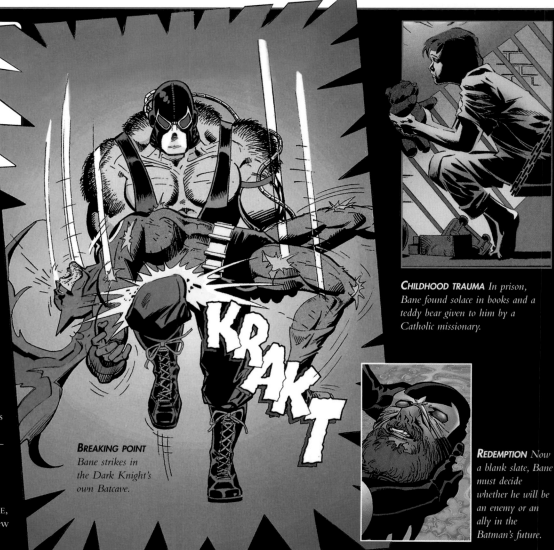

BREAKING POINT Bane strikes in the Dark Knight's own Batcave.

KRAKT

CHILDHOOD TRAUMA In prison, Bane found solace in books and a teddy bear given to him by a Catholic missionary.

REDEMPTION Now a blank slate, Bane must decide whether he will be an enemy or an ally in the Batman's future.

BARD, JASON

FIRST APPEARANCE DETECTIVE COMICS #392 (October 1969)
STATUS Hero **REAL NAME** Jason Bard
OCCUPATION Adventurer **BASE** Gotham City
HEIGHT 6ft **WEIGHT** 175 lbs **EYES** Brown **HAIR** Brown
SPECIAL POWERS/ABILITIES Above average hand-to-hand fighter, marksman, and criminologist; a superb athlete despite his injury.

Jason Bard's father abandoned the young boy and his mother, Rose, then murdered her. Bard vowed to find him, despite having no physical evidence of his father's existence and no memory of his father's face.

Bard ended up joining the Marines, and was shot and crippled while he was overseas. He returned to the U.S. and entered college on the G.I. Bill, majoring in criminology. He later set up a private investigation firm in Gotham City. There, the intelligent but occasionally cocky Bard began dating Barbara Gordon (later ORACLE). She was the daughter of Gotham's Police Commissioner James Gordon (see GORDON, JAMES W.), and at that time secretly operating as the super heroine BATGIRL.

Bard was temporarily blinded on a case in Rheelasia, a country in South East Asia, but his sight was restored after an experimental operation. He tried once more to pursue Barbara, but this time she rebuffed his romantic overtures. **PJ**

BARON BLITZKRIEG

FIRST APPEARANCE WORLD'S FINEST COMICS #246 (September 1977)
STATUS Villain **REAL NAME** Reiter (first name unknown)
OCCUPATION Terrorist **BASE** Nazi Germany **HEIGHT** 6ft 6in
WEIGHT 345 lbs (armored) **EYES** Blue **HAIR** Black
SPECIAL POWERS/ABILITIES Psychic abilities enable Blitzkrieg to control his physical functions. He can channel these functions one at a time, enabling weak heat vision, among other highly useful abilities.

Nazi leader Adolf Hitler rewarded this former Prussian nobleman's loyalty by making him a concentration camp commandant during World War II. A prisoner assaulted Reiter with a vial of acid, which destroyed his features. Despite surgery to repair the damage, Reiter hid his face behind a golden mask. Hitler then tried an experiment, which unleashed the man's latent psychic powers, marking Reiter's first step to becoming a human fighting machine for the Third Reich. Clad in flexible battle armor, Baron Blitzkrieg was born, terrorizing Europe and America, and battling the ALL-STAR SQUADRON. He also had numerous bouts with Queen HIPPOLYTA, the Golden Age Wonder Woman. He had run-ins with Iron Munro and PHANTOM LADY I as the Cold War progressed, and at least one clash with SPY SMASHER in the 1950s.

Now known simply as the Baron, he is one of the world's most dangerous men. He masterminded the terrorist group Shadowspire, responsible for the destruction of the Capitol Building. **RG**

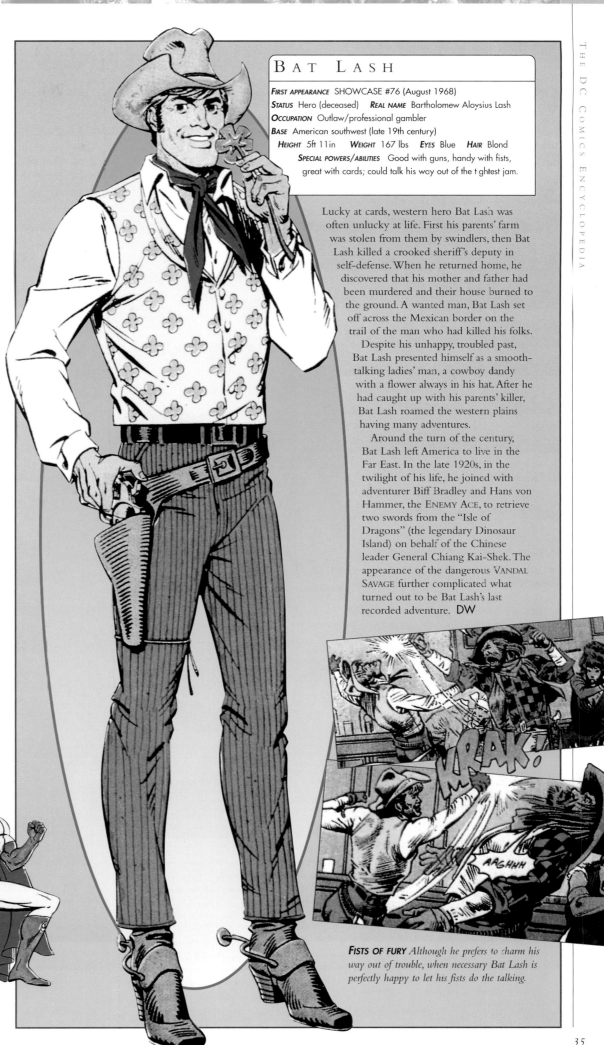

BAT LASH

FIRST APPEARANCE SHOWCASE #76 (August 1968)
STATUS Hero (deceased) **REAL NAME** Bartholomew Aloysius Lash
OCCUPATION Outlaw/professional gambler
BASE American southwest (late 19th century)
HEIGHT 5ft 11in **WEIGHT** 167 lbs **EYES** Blue **HAIR** Blond
SPECIAL POWERS/ABILITIES Good with guns, handy with fists, great with cards; could talk his way out of the tightest jam.

Lucky at cards, western hero Bat Lash was often unlucky at life. First his parents' farm was stolen from them by swindlers, then Bat Lash killed a crooked sheriff's deputy in self-defense. When he returned home, he discovered that his mother and father had been murdered and their house burned to the ground. A wanted man, Bat Lash set off across the Mexican border on the trail of the man who had killed his folks.

Despite his unhappy, troubled past, Bat Lash presented himself as a smooth-talking ladies' man, a cowboy dandy with a flower always in his hat. After he had caught up with his parents' killer, Bat Lash roamed the western plains having many adventures.

Around the turn of the century, Bat Lash left America to live in the Far East. In the late 1920s, in the twilight of his life, he joined with adventurer Biff Bradley and Hans von Hammer, the ENEMY ACE, to retrieve two swords from the "Isle of Dragons" (the legendary Dinosaur Island) on behalf of the Chinese leader General Chiang Kai-Shek. The appearance of the dangerous VANDAL SAVAGE further complicated what turned out to be Bat Lash's last recorded adventure. **DW**

FISTS OF FURY Although he prefers to charm his way out of trouble, when necessary Bat Lash is perfectly happy to let his fists do the talking.

BATGIRL

CASSANDRA COMPLEX

FIRST APPEARANCE BATMAN #567 (July 1999)
STATUS Hero **REAL NAME** Cassandra Cain
OCCUPATION Adventurer **BASE** Gotham City
HEIGHT 5ft 5in **WEIGHT** 127 lbs **EYES** Green **HAIR** Black
SPECIAL POWERS/ABILITIES One of the greatest martial artists in the world; a deadly master of nearly all forms of unarmed combat; can "read" the body language of an opponent and predict their moves.

CASSANDRA CAIN IS THE THIRD YOUNG WOMAN to assume the mantle of Batgirl. A young orphan adopted by the master assassin David Cain (*see* CAIN, DAVID) to become his greatest pupil and heir, Cassandra was his most potent student, but was ultimately uninterested in extending his legacy. Seemingly unable to speak, the young Cassandra "spoke" with her body, and learned how to "read" the body language of those around her. Cain trained her in the world's deadliest martial arts, and the young Cassandra soon made her first kill, a Macauan crime kingpin. Sickened by the act, the mute girl fled Cain's estate and evil influence and began to travel the world, searching for a new home and a new way of life.

THE NEW BATGIRL

Cassandra found her way to Gotham City just before it was devastated by an earthquake and cordoned off from the rest of the U.S. During that time, she was recruited by mysterious computer hacker ORACLE to act as a messenger in the city, now called No Man's Land. Years earlier, Oracle (Barbara Gordon), daughter of Police Commissioner James Gordon (*see* GORDON, JAMES W.), had been the first Batgirl, until she was shot and crippled by the JOKER. When Cain arrived in Gotham on a mission to assassinate Gordon, Cassandra saved the commissioner from her father's bullet. Impressed by Cassandra's skill and bravery, BATMAN took her under his wing and made her the new Batgirl.

Still without a voice, Cassandra quickly took to her new role, hoping to atone for the killing of the gangster all those years ago. Soon after, Batgirl saved a psychic named Jeffers, who was on the run from the mob. Jeffers used his powers to reorder Batgirl's brain, giving her the power of speech, but stripping from her many of her martial arts skills. Batgirl began retraining and sought out LADY SHIVA, then the world's greatest martial artist, for a single lesson she hoped would help her remaster her skills. The price of Shiva's help was a duel to the death.

Batgirl fought Shiva and won, sparing her life. The only person ever to defeat Shiva in unarmed combat, Gotham's latest defender now holds the title of the greatest martial artist in the world. **PJ**

COMBAT *Barely a child herself, Batgirl is nonetheless a frightening force to behold.*

BODY LANGUAGE *No ordinary criminal, gangmember, or super-villain can hope to hold their own against the martial-arts prowess of Batgirl, who was trained to communicate with her body, not with words.*

KEY STORYLINES

• **BATMAN #556-559 (JULY–OCTOBER 1998):** After the Huntress forsakes her temporary role as Batgirl, a mute young girl named Cassandra Cain emerges and takes up the mantle of Batgirl.
• **BATGIRL #6 (JUNE 2000):** A psychic gives Batgirl the gift of speech, but strips her of some of her fighting skill.
• **BATGIRL #24 (APRIL 2002):** Batgirl and Lady Shiva face off in a duel to the death between the world's two greatest martial artists!
• **BATGIRL #45-50 (DECEMBER 2003–APRIL 2004):** When Doctor Death releases Soul, a rage-inducing pathogen, onto Gotham, Batgirl and Batman are forced into a confrontation spanning half of the city, including the destruction of Sprang Bridge!

BARBARA GORDON

Cassandra Cain was not the first Batgirl. Barbara Gordon, the daughter of Gotham City Police Commissioner James Gordon, dreamed of becoming Batman's partner-in-crime. Thus, Barbara became Batgirl, joining Batman and ROBIN to defend the innocent of the city. After she was crippled by the Joker, Barbara forsook her Batgirl identity and became the information broker Oracle.

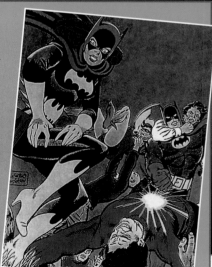

BAT-MITE

FIRST APPEARANCE DETECTIVE COMICS #267 (May 1959)
STATUS Undefined **REAL NAME** Unknown
OCCUPATION Troublemaker **BASE** Mobile
HEIGHT 2ft 11in **WEIGHT** 47 lbs **EYES** Black **HAIR** Unknown
SPECIAL POWERS/ABILITIES Possesses various magical powers, including invisibility, levitation, the animation of inanimate objects, and the endowment of superpowers to others.

The curious creature known as Bat-Mite claims to be BATMAN's greatest fan. Winging his way to Earth from a bizarre alien dimension, he wears a homemade costume honoring his idol, the Dark Knight. Bat-Mite's utility belt, unlike that of his hero, contains no useful accoutrements, but with his various magical powers he needs no tools or weapons. On his infrequent visits to Earth, Bat-Mite hugely enjoys watching the Caped Crusader in action. Unfortunately, Bat-Mite frequently feels compelled to use his magical abilities to test Batman's fighting prowess and detective skills. More often than not, the Dark Knight orders this diminutive, mischief-making imp to go back to his home dimension until he agrees to behave properly on Earth. **SB**

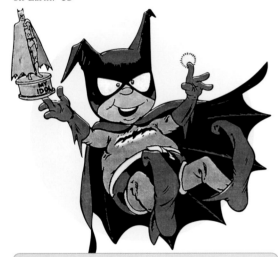

BAYTOR

FIRST APPEARANCE DEMON (3rd series) #43 (January 1994)
STATUS Villain **REAL NAME** Baytor
OCCUPATION Demon **BASE** Gotham City
HEIGHT 3ft 11in **WEIGHT** 98 lbs **EYES** Red **HAIR** None
SPECIAL POWERS/ABILITIES Incredibly focused, durable and nearly invulnerable.

Baytor is a minor demon who has, on occasion, allied himself with Etrigan (DEMON). Like most demons, he is always looking for a chance to improve his lot in Hell. When he briefly obtained the Crown of Horns, he proclaimed himself ruler of Hell. Needless to say, it did not work out. After his attempted coup had failed, Baytor escaped from Hell, hiding in the folds of Etrigan's cloak, and sought out a life on Earth. He settled in crime-torn Gotham City, a community ideally suited for a demon. Along the way he encountered gangster Tommy Monaghan and became part of his circle of mercenaries, demons, and other low-lives. Eventually, he took up bartending at Tommy's hangout, Noonan's. He mixes a mean cosmopolitan cocktail but is not much of a conversationalist, given that he only ever says, "I am Baytor!" **RG**

BEAST BOY

FIRST APPEARANCE DOOM PATROL (1st series) #99 (November 1965)
STATUS Hero **REAL NAME** Garfield Logan
OCCUPATION Teen Titan **BASE** San Francisco
HEIGHT 5ft 8in **WEIGHT** 150 lbs
EYES Green **HAIR** Green
SPECIAL POWERS/ABILITIES Can take on the form and abilities of any animal he chooses.

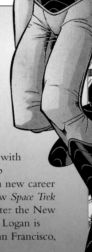

The son of scientists attempting to isolate the genetic bond between humans and animals, young Gar Logan accompanied his parents to Africa, where a green-furred monkey bit him and infected him with the Sakutia virus. Gar not only turned bright green, he found he could change into any animal. Soon afterward, his parents died in a boating accident, but Gar found a new home with Rita Farr (ELASTI-GIRL) and Steve Dayton (MENTO) of the DOOM PATROL. Gar worked with the Doom Patrol as Beast Boy until the group seemingly perished in an explosion. Seeking a new career as an actor, Gar joined the cast of the TV show *Space Trek 2022* until signing on with Titans West and later the New Teen Titans under the name Changeling. Gar Logan is currently serving with the TEEN TITANS in San Francisco, using the name Beast Boy once again. **DW**

MISSING LINK *Still young, but boasting years of experience at the super hero game, Beast Boy has become a link between the older Titans and the newest recruits.*

ANIMAL MAGIC *Beast Boy can overturn a city bus as a rhino or soar through the sky as a falcon.*

BEAUTIFUL DREAMER

FIRST APPEARANCE FOREVER PEOPLE (1st series) #1 (March 1971)
STATUS Hero **REAL NAME** Unknown
OCCUPATION Adventurer **BASE** Earth
HEIGHT 5ft 6in **WEIGHT** 135 lbs **EYES** Blue **HAIR** Black
SPECIAL POWERS/ABILITIES Can take images from another's mind and transform them into lifelike, three-dimensional illusions.

The woman known as Beautiful Dreamer was born on the planet New Genesis. A powerful psychic, the Dreamer was kidnapped by DARKSEID during his war against New Genesis and hidden on Earth. There, the Dreamer was saved by SUPERMAN and the INFINITY MAN and reunited with her lifelong friends, the FOREVER PEOPLE.

After years on Earth, studying the ways of humankind, the Forever People were forced to relocate to the planet Adon to escape Darkseid's agent, DEVILANCE the Pursuer. There they established Forever Town, and Beautiful Dreamer married her lover BIG BEAR. Evil entities called the Dark turned Adon's populace into primitive beings, but the Forever People and the Infinity Man destroyed the Dark, and Dreamer and her allies returned to Earth. Beautiful Dreamer and Big Bear had a daughter, a superhuman named Maya, but their relationship ended soon after. Once romantically involved with TAKION, Beautiful Dreamer is one of the few beings whose mind can comprehend the Anti-Life Equation. **PJ**

A BEAUTIFUL MIND *Beautiful Dreamer's gentle beauty belies her ferocity when using her psychic powers to defend her child.*

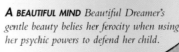

BEEFEATER II

FIRST APPEARANCE JUSTICE LEAGUE EUROPE #20 (November 1990)
STATUS Ally **REAL NAME** Michael Morice
OCCUPATION Would-be super hero (retired) **BASE** Ipswich, England
HEIGHT 6ft 4in **WEIGHT** 172 lbs **EYES** Light brown **HAIR** White (balding)
SPECIAL POWERS/ABILITIES Collapsible battle rod projects destructive force blasts.

Though claiming descent from the British aristocracy, Michael Morice was the nervous son of a coal miner and a little-known BBC actress who married in the delivery room just as Michael was born. In adulthood, Morice himself married a shrewish wife and became liaison to Justice League International (*see* JUSTICE LEAGUE OF AMERICA). Believing the JLI should have a British representative in its ranks, Morice took up the battle rod and colorful uniform of his father, who fought the Nazis during World War II as the very first Beefeater, often partnered with America's GENERAL GLORY. At the JLI's Parisian embassy, the new Beefeater's arrogant petition for membership was interrupted by an accidental battle with the GREEN LANTERN KILOWOG, a comedy of errors that leveled the building. Later, the hapless Beefeater battled the villain ECLIPSO and suffered a humiliating defeat. Morice apparently learned his lesson and mothballed the Beefeater costume once more. **SB**

BATMAN

The DC Comics Encyclopedia

BATMAN

THE DARK KNIGHT

First Appearance DETECTIVE COMICS #27 (May 1939)
Status Hero **Real Name** Bruce Wayne
Occupation Industrialist; philanthropist; crime fighter
Base Gotham City
Height 6ft 2in **Weight** 210 lbs **Eyes** Blue **Hair** Black
Special Powers/Abilities
Master detective with a brilliant deductive mind; quite possibly the greatest martial artist alive; Bat-costume is bulletproof and fire-resistant, featuring a weighted cape and a cowl outfitted with night-vision technology and communications arrays; utility belt contains an arsenal of crime-fighting gear, including various types of offensive Batarangs, de-cel jumplines and grapnels, micro-camera, smoke pellets, acetylene torch, gas mask, rebreather, and flexi-cuffs among other miniaturized non-lethal weapons; employs a variety of detective gadgets, including micro-computers and crime scene analysis kits; maintains a fleet of high-tech and high-powered vehicles, chief among them the Batmobile, Batcycle, Batboat, Batplane, and Batcopter; super-sophisticated Batcave headquarters houses training facilities, forensics laboratories, computer databases, and maintenance bays for all Bat-vehicles.

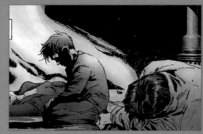

ALLEY SLAYING *Two bullets from a gangster's gun destroyed Bruce's young life.*

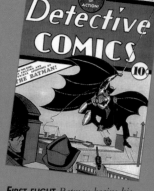

FIRST FLIGHT *Batman begins his war on crime with an aerial assault upon Gotham's goons.*

A FAMILY OUTING to the cinema ended in tragedy for young Bruce Wayne. Walking homeward, Bruce, his father, Thomas, and mother, Martha, accidentally ventured into Gotham City's notorious "Crime Alley" and were accosted by a mugger. Not content merely to rob the wealthy family, the hoodlum—whose identity was never determined—shot Dr. Thomas and Martha Wayne dead before fleeing into the darkness. As he knelt beside his parents' bodies, Bruce swore to avenge them. After the police arrived, Bruce was comforted by Dr. Leslie Thompkins (*see* THOMPKINS, LESLIE M.D.). Dr. Thompkins and Alfred Pennyworth (*see* PENNYWORTH, ALFRED) helped arrange matters so that Gotham's Social Services would not take Bruce into care. In this way, both Dr. Thompkins and Alfred enabled Bruce to realize his dream of becoming a crusader against crime.

THE YOUNG BRUCE WAYNE

At age 14, Bruce embarked on a journey that took him to every continent as he sought to learn all the skills he would need to keep his vow. He studied criminology, forensics, and criminal psychology, and learned from manhunters and martial artists, mastering every fighting style. In time, Bruce forged himself into a living weapon to wage war on crime and injustice. On his return to Gotham, Bruce stalked street thugs as a plainclothes vigilante. Beaten by the very people he intended to protect, he barely survived his first night out. As he sat bleeding in his study at Wayne Manor, Bruce knew that he had to first strike fear in the hearts of his foes. Just then, a bat crashed through the study window, giving Bruce the inspiration he needed.

DARK INSPIRATION *Wishing to strike fear among the criminal community, Bruce made the bat his symbol and totem.*

A FAMILY AFFAIR

The addition of ROBIN to his nightly crusade helped Batman in more ways than he would ever admit. However, when Dick Grayson embarked on his own path as NIGHTWING, the Batcave became a lonelier place for the Dark Knight, especially after Jason Todd's murder and the crippling of Barbara Gordon (*see* BATGIRL and ORACLE), both suffered at the hands of the Joker. For a time, Batman operated strictly solo until young Tim Drake convinced the Dark Knight that he needed a Robin to give him hope.

FAMILY *The Dark Knight counts Robin and Oracle among his trusted allies.*

BATMAN BEGINS

Establishing a secret headquarters in the caves beneath his mansion, Bruce became Batman, a Dark Knight to protect Gotham and its citizens from vice and villainy. Alfred Pennyworth remained his confidant, tending to injuries and offering sage advice—whether requested or not!

Batman became an urban legend, a cautionary tale that sent shivers through the city's underworld. This Caped Crusader found a friend in Captain James Gordon (*see* GORDON, JAMES W.), a Gotham cop who didn't approve of Batman's methods, but appreciated the results of his nightly crime fighting. Batman's Rogues Gallery grew to include a host of bizarre criminals, such as the JOKER, CATWOMAN, TWO-FACE, and the PENGUIN. As his enemies increased, help arrived in the form of another young boy left parentless by brutal crime.

HITTING BACK *Batman lashes out at the Joker for killing Jason Todd, the second Robin.*

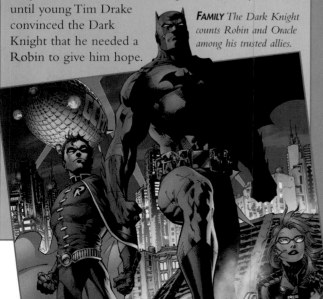

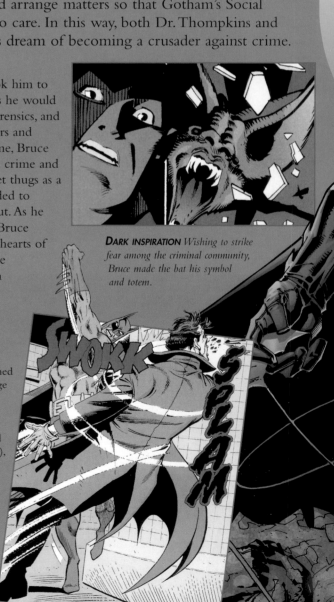

BROKEN BAT

Tragedy again struck when the terrorist BANE, after forcing Batman to fight many of his most powerful foes, broke Batman's back. Jean-Paul Valley (AZRAEL) took on the Dark Knight's role while Bruce recuperated from his injuries. This interim Batman was more violent and unstable; Bruce returned to action as soon as his body had healed and he had regained his fighting spirit, with the help of the ruthless martial-arts mistress LADY SHIVA. Bruce took back the mantle of the Bat by force, but Jean-Paul Valley remained a staunch ally as the hero Azrael until his death.

KNIGHTFALL *Bane delivers the final cruel blow to defeat an exhausted Batman.*

THE LONG HALLOWEEN

One criminal case still haunts Batman. Early in his career, the Dark Knight failed to identify the serial killer known as Holiday and prevent a string of murders targeting the Falcone crime family. "The Long Halloween" ultimately resulted in D.A. Harvey Dent's tragic disfigurement and led to Dent becoming murdering gangster Two-Face. In that regard, Batman lost both a friend and an ally.

DARK TIMES

The Dark Knight helped maintain law and order in Gotham City when a contagion struck, killing tens of thousands. He was also the city's saviour in the anarchic aftermath of a cataclysmic earthquake. With Gotham declared a No Man's Land by the government, Batman and his allies, including a new BATGIRL, fought a yearlong struggle to take the town back block by block. Gotham City was eventually rebuilt, and Batman redoubled his efforts to make known to all returning criminals that a Dark Knight defender still ruled the night. More recently, Batman faced several more personal losses. The first involved the end of his "working" relationship with Commissioner Gordon, who left the police force after a near-fatal shooting. Batman's clandestine ties to the G.C.P.D. would never be the same with his friend and ally retired.

SOLOMON GRUNDY *The creature born on a Monday in Slaughter Swamp is among many monsters Batman battles every night of the week.*

KEY STORYLINES

- *BATMAN #401–404 (FEBRUARY–MAY 1987):* The Dark Knight's tumultuous beginnings as a costumed crime fighter are chronicled in "Batman: Year One."
- *BATMAN #492 (MAY 1993):* As the epic, multipart "Knightfall" begins, the Caped Crusader fights exhaustion to enemies loosed by Bane, the villain who would ultimately break the Bat.
- *BATMAN: CATACLYSM/BATMAN: NO MAN'S LAND (TPB COLLECTIONS):* Batman's greatest battle begins as Gotham City is rocked by an earthquake. This leaves the city reduced to rubble and abandoned to anarchy by all except the Dark Knight and his closest allies.

BRUCE WAYNE: MURDERER?

Not long after, Bruce was accused of murdering journalist Vesper Fairchild (see FAIRCHILD, VESPER), actually slain by the assassin Cain (see CAIN, DAVID) on the orders of then-President Lex Luthor (see LUTHOR, LEX), a business rival. Bruce was vindicated, but Vesper's death served as a stark reminder why close relationships run contrary to Batman's mostly solitary mission. However, Batman still appreciates the aid of his crime-fighting partners, and the value of teamwork. He has long been a member of the JUSTICE LEAGUE OF AMERICA and assembled the first OUTSIDERS team to take action against criminals the authorities could not touch.

GUARDED LOVE *Bruce Wayne's latest romance was with his bodyguard, Sasha Bordeaux, now a government agent.*

BATMAN TODAY

Batman continues to watch over Gotham as its staunchest defender. Moreover, since his parents' killer has never been apprehended, Bruce knows that the Dark Knight's crusade could be an endless struggle to find "the one that got away." Meanwhile, Batman fights to ensure that no one else suffers the collateral damage of random crime and senseless violence as he did. **SB**

TRUST *Batman's newest nemesis struck at him by being both friend and foe. Ultimately, Batman learned that Hush was his childhood chum, Tommy Elliot.*

BEELZEBUB

FIRST APPEARANCE SANDMAN (2nd series) #4 (April 1989)
STATUS Villain **REAL NAME** None
OCCUPATION Lord of Hell **BASE** Hell
HEIGHT Variable **WEIGHT** Variable
EYES Black **HAIR** None
SPECIAL POWERS/ABILITIES Vast demonic powers, full extent unrevealed; usually takes the form of a giant fly.

Also called the Lord of the Flies, Beelzebub is one of the prime devils inhabiting the eternal realm of suffering. He has dominion over decay and decomposition, and has existed since the creation of death itself. Consequently, he uses the authority that comes with age to push himself into the thick of any political discussions within Hell's hierarchy. For a time, Beelzebub ruled Hell with Lucifer and AZAZEL as part of a triumvirate, but returned to his former station when God sent the angels Remiel and Duma to oversee the infernal realm. Later, Beelzebub assumed a humanoid shape and crossed paths with the Earth-based heroes KID ETERNITY and SUPERGIRL. He continues to spread his evil throughout the universe and will likely exist until the end of time **DW**

BEK, GARRYN

FIRST APPEARANCE INVASION #1 (Summer 1989)
STATUS Hero **REAL NAME** Garryn Bek
OCCUPATION Administrator **BASE** The planet Cairn
HEIGHT 5ft 8in **WEIGHT** 159 lbs **EYES** Blue **HAIR** Brown
SPECIAL POWERS/ABILITIES Exceptional coordinator; starship pilot.

A police administrator on the drug-trafficking world of Cairn, whiny, irritable pessimist Garryn Bek became a prisoner of the alien ALLIANCE, bent on destroying the Earth. Bek, his cellmate, Vril Dox II, a manipulative super-genius, and several other prisoners escaped the Alliance and returned to Colu, Dox's homeworld, to liberate it from the computer tyrants that ruled there. Soon after, Bek and Dox returned to Cairn, and through not entirely legal means, the Coluan transformed the planet's entire police force into the peacekeeping agency L.E.G.I.O.N.

After being controlled by the Emerald Eye of Ekron until the Eye's apparent destruction, Bek, along with his wife Marij'n, defected from L.E.G.I.O.N. to the freedom fighting R.E.B.E.L.S. after L.E.G.I.O.N.'s take over by Lyrl Dox, Vril Dox's son. Both later joined the reformed L.E.G.I.O.N., now under CAPTAIN COMET's command. **PJ**

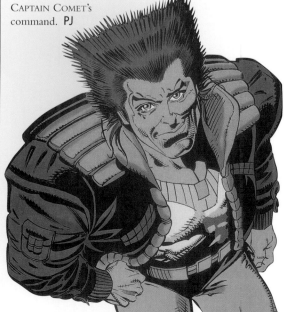

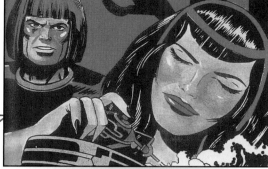

BRAINS AND BEAUTY *Like her father Himon, Bekka is also a gifted scientist. But it is her uncommon beauty that gives Orion pause, often leaving the Dog of War stumbling for words.*

BEKKA

FIRST APPEARANCE DC GRAPHIC NOVEL #4: THE HUNGER DOGS (1984)
STATUS Hero **REAL NAME** None
OCCUPATION Adventurer **BASE** New Genesis
HEIGHT 5ft 7in **WEIGHT** 132 lbs **EYES** Blue **HAIR** Black
SPECIAL POWERS/ABILITIES Unrevealed; however, like her fellow New Gods, Bekka is remarkably long-lived.

Bekka is the daughter of HIMON, one of the NEW GODS whose achievements include invention of the sentient Mother Box computers and discovery of the "x-element" that fueled his cocreation of the teleporting Boom Tubes alongside fellow scientist METRON. For many years, Bekka lived with her father in secret on Apokolips as Himon organized an underground uprising against DARKSEID's tyrannical rule. Hunted for his role in this planned insurgence, Himon took extra care to shield Bekka from Darkseid's notice. Himon never imagined that Bekka would fall in love with ORION, Darkseid's own son, when he stumbled into their lives. After healing the wounded Dog of War, Himon and Bekka aided Orion in freeing his mother TIGGRA from imprisonment. For this act, Himon was seemingly slain by the dread lord of Apokolips. Bekka then accompanied Orion and Tiggra to New Genesis, where her love continues to soothe the savagery that lurks within the Dog of War. **SB**

BELIAL

FIRST APPEARANCE THE DEMON (2nd series) #3 (March 1987)
STATUS Evil entity **REAL NAME** Belial
OCCUPATION Demon **BASE** Hell
HEIGHT Variable **WEIGHT** Variable **EYES** Red **HAIR** None
SPECIAL POWERS/ABILITIES Master of arcane dark arts; one of the most learned of demons, who uses spells and his intellect to make up for his relative lack of demon strength.

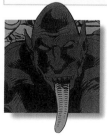

Belial is one of the most ambitious demons in all of Hell, aspiring to rule as one of Hell's Triumvirate. For a brief time, he achieved his goal, but he was quickly replaced. He has sired three children, the demon Etrigan (DEMON), the wizard Merlin (whose mother was human) and Lord Scapegoat a demon of Hell. His children have often opposed his schemes, which have conflicted with their own plans, and their fights have been legendary. He rarely appears on Earth, but when he has, his schemes have usually been thwarted, starting with CAPTAIN MARVEL JR. in Fawcett City. Preferring to operate behind the scenes, he has lent his supernatural powers, as one of six demons, to empower SABBAC. **RG**

BELPHEGOR

FIRST APPEARANCE TEEN TITANS SPOTLIGHT #11 (June 1987)
STATUS Ally **REAL NAME** Unknown
OCCUPATION Former Global Guardians director
BASE Marseilles, France
HEIGHT 5ft 9in **WEIGHT** 130 lbs **EYES** Green **HAIR** Black
SPECIAL POWERS/ABILITIES Various psionic abilities, including telepathy.

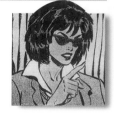

Little is known about the elegant Frenchwoman codenamed Belphegor. However, she shares a history with DOCTOR MIST and played an important role in the now-defunct international super hero organization known as the GLOBAL GUARDIANS.

Early in her career, Belphegor is known to have worked with Doctor Mist and former memeber of the BOY COMMANDOS André Chavard (see CHAVARD, ANDRÉ) to save a hero from a parallel Earth by enlisting the unwitting help of MONSIEUR MALLAH and the Brotherhood of Evil (see SOCIETY OF SIN). Belphegor later became the director of the Dome headquarters of the Global Guardians. She oversaw trouble spots around the world and dispatched Global Guardians to handle threats that lay near their home countries. When the United Nations decided to shift its funding from the Global Guardians to the Justice League International (see JUSTICE LEAGUE OF AMERICA), the Dome could no longer afford to stay open. Belphegor oversaw its closing and has rarely been seen since. **DW**

BERNADETH

FIRST APPEARANCE MISTER MIRACLE (1st series) #6 (February 1972)
STATUS Hero **REAL NAME** Bernadeth
OCCUPATION Shocktrooper **BASE** Apokolips
HEIGHT 5ft 10in **WEIGHT** 140 lbs **EYES** Brown **HAIR** Black
SPECIAL POWERS/ABILITIES Bernadeth is enormously strong, aggressive, and ruthless; specialized "faren-knives" super-heat foes from the inside out.

The hideous sister of DESAAD, the chief torture-master of DARKSEID's Elite, Bernadeth is the leader of the FEMALE FURIES, a specialized squadron of killers that hails from the hideous planet Apokolips. Bernadeth uses razor-sharp "faren-knives" as her offensive weaponry.

BIG BARDA was the original leader of the Female Furies until she abandoned the group and Apokolips to be with her lover, MISTER MIRACLE. Barda was able to lure the Furies back to Earth, securing their freedom and featuring all of them in a spectacular traveling stage show. The Female Furies returned to Apokolips, however, and Bernadeth assumed control of the group. **PJ**

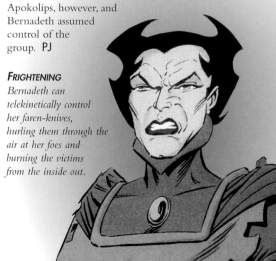

FRIGHTENING
Bernadeth can telekinetically control her faren-knives, hurling them through the air at her foes and burning the victims from the inside out.

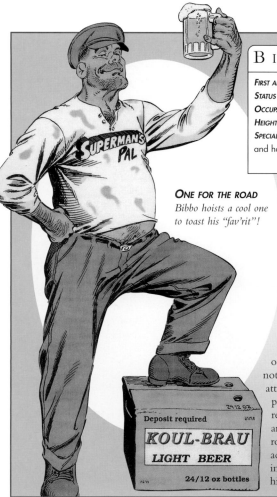

ONE FOR THE ROAD
Bibbo hoists a cool one to toast his "fav'rit"!

BIBBO

FIRST APPEARANCE THE ADVENTURES OF SUPERMAN #428 (May 1987)
STATUS Hero/ally   **REAL NAME** "Bibbo" Bibbowski
OCCUPATION Tavern owner   **BASE** Suicide Slum, Metropolis
HEIGHT 6ft 3in   **WEIGHT** 250 lbs   **EYES** Gray   **HAIR** Gray
SPECIAL POWERS/ABILITIES A former boxer, Bibbo packs a mean punch and has started (and ended) more than a few bar fights.

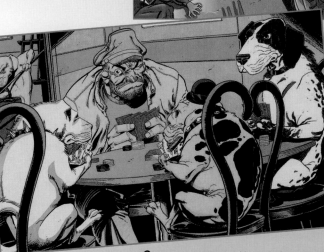

OUT COLD *Not many can walk, let alone stand, after being on the receiving end of one of Bibbo's roundhouse punches. Even the Man of Steel is staggered!*

Ex-longshoreman and former heavyweight contender, "Bibbo" Bibbowski is proprietor of the Ace O' Clubs tavern, a down-and-dirty waterfront pub in Metropolis's seedy Suicide Slum. This same bar was formerly Bibbo's preferred watering hole during his days as a booze-soaked barfly. But despite his slovenly appearance, fortune has always favored Bibbo. He bought the Ace O' Clubs after finding a winning lottery ticket lost by Jose Delgado (GANGBUSTER). The first year's annuity from the $14,000,000 lottery jackpot put Bibbo on easy street. Happily, his sudden fortune did not change Bibbo's outgoing and relaxed attitude to life. A friend to SUPERMAN, Bibbo practically idolizes the Man of Steel, whom he regards as his "fav'rit" hero. Though he'd wallop anyone who calls him a snitch, by virtue of his role as barkeep in an area famous for criminal activity, Bibbo often overhears useful information that he passes along to Superman or his other pal, Jimmy Olsen (*see* OLSEN, JIMMY). **SB**

GONE TO THE DOGS *Bibbo isn't choosy when it comes to poker buddies, even playing a hand with a pack of alien hounds!*

BIG BARDA

FIRST APPEARANCE MISTER MIRACLE (1st series) #4 (September 1971)
STATUS Hero   **REAL NAME** Barda Free
HEIGHT 6ft 2in   **WEIGHT** 217 lbs   **EYES** Blue   **HAIR** Black
OCCUPATION Freedom fighter   **BASE** New Genesis
SPECIAL POWERS/ABILITIES Trained as a Female Fury; one of the deadliest hand-to-hand combatants alive; her mastery of the mega rod is unchallenged.

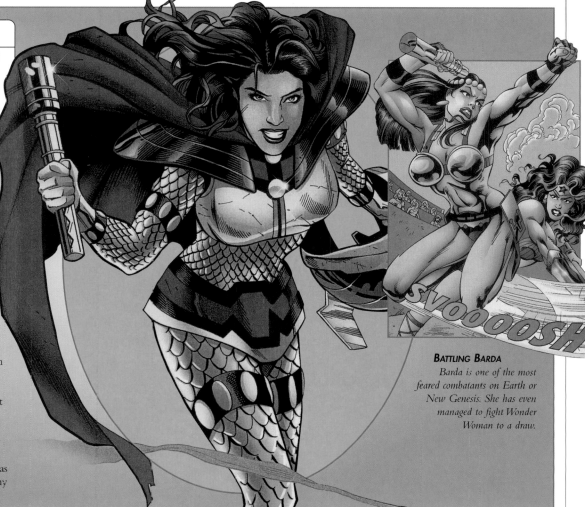

Barda was always destined to be someone special; she was the only child borne out of love by Apokolips' Big Breeda. The baby was taken by DARKSEID, raised first in the Gestatron labs, then in GRANNY GOODNESS's vast orphanage, where the defiant look in Barda's eye could not be beaten out of her. Instead, Granny took her for special training and Barda excelled in all manner of combat. Barda was among the first selected to form the battalion known as the FEMALE FURIES. Barda became Granny's best squad leader, commanding the Furies to many successful victories. But then Barda fell in love with another of Granny's charges, Scott Free, a son of New Genesis. Scott met Barda, and she saw something in his spirit that touched a part of her she didn't know even existed. Barda found herself helping Scott escape from hellish Apokolips to Earth. She followed him, and their relationship deepened into lasting love. Finally, after Scott had established himself as master escape artist MISTER MIRACLE, they married. Although Scott loved life on Earth, Barda could only barely tolerate it. This led to her serving two brief stints with the JUSTICE LEAGUE OF AMERICA. She served her time and fought bravely, but was more than ready to return to her husband and accompany him to a new home on New Genesis. **RG**

BATTLING BARDA
Barda is one of the most feared combatants on Earth or New Genesis. She has even managed to fight Wonder Woman to a draw.

BIZARRO

IMPERFECT DUPLICATE OF SUPERMAN

First appearance THE MAN OF STEEL #5 (October 1986)
Status Villain **Real name** None
Occupation Imperfect duplicate of Superman **Base** Mobile
Height 6ft 3in **Weight** 225 lbs **Eyes** Blue **Hair** Black
Special powers/abilities Superstrong, invulnerable, and able to fly like the Man of Steel, but possessing some powers opposite to that of Superman, including freezing vision and flaming breath.

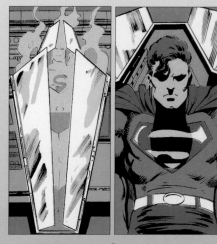

COUNTLESS TIMES SUPER-VILLAINS have raised their eyes to the heavens and cursed in vain as the heroic Man of Steel flashes across the sky to save the day. *If only*, they fume, *if only* they had a SUPERMAN of their very own, a mindless, superpowered slave to do their evil bidding! Superman's arch enemy Lex Luthor (*see* LUTHOR, LEX) was the first rogue to try to make this dream a reality. In secret, Luthor called upon his top scientist, Dr. Teng, to scan Superman's genetic structure. Teng successfully duplicated Superman, but was unable to completely recreate the complex chromosomal structure of the Last Son of Krypton. The resulting Superclone quickly became a monstrous menace, a Bizarro creature that might have razed Metropolis to the ground had Superman not intervened. Yet this misbegotten Bizarro creature was not without its gentle side, for it allowed itself to be destroyed in a rain of disintegrating particles that somehow allowed Lucy Lane, blind sister of reporter Lois Lane (*see* LANE, LOIS), to regain her sight.

A BIZARRO IN LOVE

Luthor tried a second time to clone the Man of Steel many months later, and like the first imperfect duplicate, this second Bizarro became a superpowered nuisance. Retaining snippets of genetic memory of Superman's strong affections for Lois Lane, Bizarro #2 set about creating a ramshackle "Bizarro World" from junk and refuse, in his own way building a Bizarro Metropolis that would please his beloved "Lo-iz." Bizarro #2 then snatched up Lane and took her to his crooked city, where he held the reporter hostage while Superman searched frantically for her. However, all Bizarro #2 wanted was to please "Lo-iz," but like his predecessor, he also succumbed to rapid cellular degeneration. He died in Lois's arms.

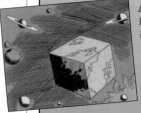

BIZARRO WORLD
To a Bizarro, Earth would be cube-shaped instead of a planetary orb. Anything to be different!

The third Bizarro, however, had little to do with genetic tinkering. Instead, a boastful new Bizarro #1 was given a fresh lease on life via the twisted imagination of BATMAN's arch-nemesis, the JOKER. After acquiring the reality-altering powers of fifth-dimensional imp MISTER MXYZPTLK, the Clown Prince of Crime envisioned a topsy-turvy Earth where evil replaced good and bizarre new villains occupied the seats of an anarchic JUSTICE LEAGUE OF AMERICA. Thus, Bizarro #1 came into being as counterpoint to Superman yet again. Though matching the Man of Steel muscle for muscle, Bizarro #1 possesses some abilities that are opposite to Superman's. He also *gains* strength when exposed to kryptonite, the radioactive element deadly to the Man of Steel.

Following the Joker's defeat, and with reality restored to its proper order, Bizarro #1 strangely remained in existence. He was captured by GENERAL ZOD, who relished torturing the imperfect duplicate of his hated enemy.

Bizarro #1, while not completely evil, has faced Superman on several occasions since, usually following his imperfect logic and doing the exact opposite of the Man of Steel. Superman defeats Bizarro by using that same imperfect logic against him. When last seen, Bizarro had fallen victim to a Kryptonian virus and was in quarantine at Superman's Fortress of Solitude while the Last Son of Krypton sought a cure for the malady. **SB**

CREATION At first, Dr. Teng's clone was the spitting image of the Man of Steel.

HARD LUCK Unable to have his revenge on Superman, General Zod punished Bizarro #3 instead.

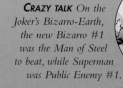

CRAZY TALK On the Joker's Bizarro-Earth, the new Bizarro #1 was the Man of Steel to beat, while Superman was Public Enemy #1.

KEY STORYLINES
• *SUPERBOY #68 (OCTOBER 1958):*
Pre-Crisis, the very first Bizarro is an imperfect teen duplicate of Superboy!
• *SUPERMAN #87 (MARCH 1994):*
Bizarro #2 is cloned, subsequently building his own Bizarro World before his untimely end.
• *SUPERMAN #160 (SEPTEMBER 2000):*
The Joker uses Mr. Mxyzptlk's powers to create an upside-down world complete with an all-new Bizarro #1, more bizarre than any who came before!

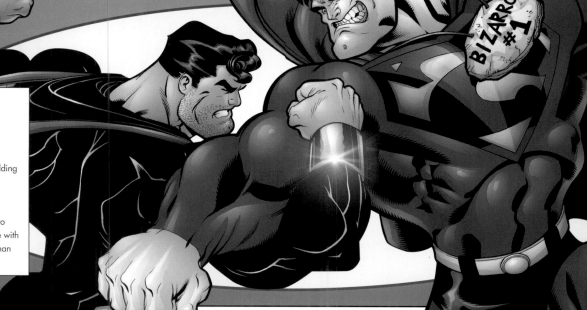

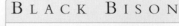

BIG BEAR

FIRST APPEARANCE THE FOREVER PEOPLE #1 (March 1971)
STATUS Hero **REAL NAME** None
OCCUPATION Adventurer/pilot **BASE** New Genesis
HEIGHT 6ft 5in **WEIGHT** 272 lbs **EYES** Green **HAIR** Red
SPECIAL POWERS/ABILITIES Superstrength attained through the discharge
of high-density atoms; can mentally alter the density of objects;
expert pilot of flying; pilots a phase-shifting Super-Cycle.

Big Bear is the oldest member of
the FOREVER PEOPLE, five children
from Earth raised on New Genesis
by the wise HIGHFATHER, and
rigorously trained in the uses
of their powers. Big Bear
piloted the team's Super-Cycle
space vehicle. When the evil
DARKSEID kidnapped team
member BEAUTIFUL DREAMER,
Big Bear and the others tracked
her to Earth. They rescued her
with help from the
INFINITY MAN, a cosmic
being with whom they could
trade places by touching their Mother Box computer and
speaking the word "Taaru." During one swap with the
Infinity Man, the Forever People found themselves
stranded on the distant planet Adon. The team eventually
returned to New Genesis, where Big Bear matched his
Super-Cycle piloting skills against the teens of YOUNG
JUSTICE. Big Bear and Beautiful Dreamer are currently an
item, though their relationship has gone through various
on-again, off-again interludes. DW

BIZARRO *SEE OPPOSITE PAGE*

POWERFUL MEDICINE
*Necklace talisman contains
the spirit of Bison-Black-
As-Midnight-Sky, who
founded the Bison Cult
more than a century ago.*

BLACK BISON

FIRST APPEARANCE THE FURY OF FIRESTORM #1 (June 1982)
STATUS Unresolved **REAL NAME** John Ravenhair
OCCUPATION Tribal shaman **BASE** New York City
HEIGHT 6ft 3in **WEIGHT** 226 lbs **EYES** Brown **HAIR** Black
SPECIAL POWERS/ABILITIES Mystical ability to control the weather and
animate objects, focused through a tribal coup stick.

John Ravenhair's great-grandfather Bison-Black-As-
Midnight-Sky was once the shaman of the Bison
Cult. When the old man died, Ravenhair found
himself possessed by his great-grandfather's vengeful
spirit. Dressing himself in traditional tribal costume
and calling himself Black Bison, Ravenhair set out to
right all the many wrongs that had been perpetrated
upon the Native American people since the arrival of
the White Man in America centuries ago.
    Black Bison's rampage across New York City
attracted the attention of FIRESTORM, THE NUCLEAR
MAN, who discovered that he could defeat Black Bison
by removing the Bison Cult talisman that he wore around
his neck. Away from his great-grandfather's influence, John
Ravenhair could choose his own path, but it wasn't long
before Black Bison returned to cause more collateral
damage in the name of vengeance.
    Black Bison is not a true villain, and has occasionally
assisted the cause of good. During the Crisis (*see* Great
Battles, pp. 320–1), Black Bison helped the Earth's
assembled sorcerers defeat the Anti-Monitor's shadow
demons. If John Ravenhair learns to control his
grandfather's influence, he could become one of
the planet's most powerful magic-users. DW

BLACK ADAM

FIRST APPEARANCE MARVEL FAMILY #1 (December 1945)
STATUS Hero (flawed) **REAL NAME** Teth-Adam
OCCUPATION Adventurer **BASE** New York City
HEIGHT 6ft **WEIGHT** 198 lbs **EYES** Brown **HAIR** Black
SPECIAL POWERS/ABILITIES Great strength, speed, stamina, and wisdom.

During Ancient Egypt's 19th dynasty, Teth-Adam became
the first to be blessed with immense supernatural powers by
the wizard Shazam. When Teth-Adam spoke the wizard's
name, he was magically transformed by a bolt of lightning
into "Mighty Adam," possessing the powers of six of the
Egyptian gods: Shu (stamina), Heru (speed), Amon (strength),
Zehuit (wisdom), Aton (power), and Mehen (courage).
Teth-Adam became Egypt's champion, eventually entering the
service of Prince Khufu. Shortly after the prince's murder and
the deaths of his wife and children, Teth-Adam lost sight of his
purpose. He began using his powers solely for selfish gain and
became known as Khem-Adam (which translates as Black
Adam), a name whispered in the shadows. Partly blaming
himself for Teth-Adam's corruption, Shazam stripped Adam of
his powers, placing them within a scarab amulet.
    The amulet was entombed with Pharaoh Ramses II, remaining
untouched until the 20th century, when husband and wife
archaeologists C.C. and Marilyn Batson uncovered it. The couple was brutally murdered
by an associate, Theo Adam, who soon after tapped into Black Adam's
power and memories. The Batson's son, Billy, was chosen by the wizard as his new champion,
CAPTAIN MARVEL. Ever since, they have repeatedly battled. Teth-Adam's ancient morality came
to the fore, and his actions were far more brutal than accepted norms. He banded together his
own team of costumed heroes, who agreed with his harsher sense of justice. He sought to
honor his slain family's memory by restoring their homeland of Khandaq to glory. The JUSTICE
SOCIETY OF AMERICA opposed them in a bloody battle that left Teth-Adam a broken man. RG

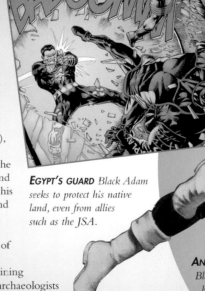

EGYPT'S GUARD *Black Adam
seeks to protect his native
land, even from allies
such as the JSA.*

ANCIENT PEERS, MODERN FOES
*Black Adam and Hawkman
battling in the skies over
the Middle East.*

BLACK CANARY

THE PRETTY BIRD OF PREY

FIRST APPEARANCE (BLACK CANARY I) FLASH COMICS #86 (August 1947)
STATUS Hero (deceased)   REAL NAME Dinah Drake Lance
OCCUPATION Adventurer; florist   BASE Gotham City
HEIGHT 5ft 5in   WEIGHT 128 lbs   EYES Blue   HAIR Black
SPECIAL POWERS/ABILITIES Trained in Judo, and a feisty fighter; often
concealed smoke or tear-gas pellets in the amulet of her choker.

FIRST APPEARANCE (BLACK CANARY II) JUSTICE LEAGUE OF AMERICA
#75 (November 1969)
STATUS Hero   REAL NAME Dinah Laurel Lance
OCCUPATION Adventurer   BASE Gotham City
HEIGHT 5ft 4in   WEIGHT 124 lbs   EYES Blue   HAIR Blonde
SPECIAL POWERS/ABILITIES Ultrasonic, earsplitting "canary cry," capable
of shattering metal; martial arts and boxing expert.

IN 1947, DINAH DRAKE'S DREAMS of becoming a Gotham City policewoman were dashed when her police academy application was rejected and her doting father, Detective Richard Drake, subsequently passed away. Dinah used her small inheritance to open a florist's shop while pursuing a more clandestine career in crime fighting. Inspired by the brightly clad "Mystery Men" of the time, raven-haired Dinah designed her own stylish costume—black fishnets and leather, as well as a blonde wig to conceal her identity—and embarked on a vigilante career as the sultry Black Canary. At first passing herself off as a criminal to infiltrate Gotham's underworld, the Judo-savvy Black Canary eventually revealed her true colors upon teaming with fellow hero Johnny Thunder (see THUNDER, JOHNNY). She became a member of the JUSTICE SOCIETY OF AMERICA soon after, although eventually retired from costumed crime fighting. She married private detective Larry Lance and gave birth to a daughter (also named Dinah), who would carry on her mother's heroic legacy. Dinah Drake Lance died of radiation-induced cancer, an after-effect from battling the cosmic-powered villain Aquarius—an epic struggle during which Larry Lance sacrificed his own life—alongside her JSA teammates.

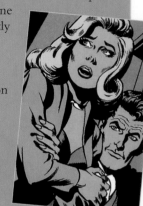

SOULMATES The Canary often assisted paramour and private eye Larry Lance on his cases.

BLACK CANARY II

While the original Black Canary hoped to spare her daughter the perils of a crime-fighting career, young Dinah Laurel Lance nevertheless grew up in the shadow of her mother's great exploits, tales often told to her by the JSA members who babysat her. Like her mother, Dinah was also a superb athlete and fighter. But young Dinah also possessed a metagene that bequeathed her a unique superpower: a hyper-pitched "canary cry." Despite her mother's wishes, Dinah took up the fishnets and leather outfit of Black Canary. Gifted in Judo, Dinah also learned boxing from her "uncle," Ted Grant (WILDCAT I), as well as other fighting techniques from her mother's teammates in the original JSA.

As such, Dinah was one of the first "second-generation" super heroes. Operating as Black Canary II, Dinah had a string of solo adventures before helping to found the JUSTICE LEAGUE OF AMERICA, a team directly inspired by the then-retired JSA. During her exploits with the JLA, Black Canary began a passionate romance with GREEN ARROW Oliver McQueen, whom she still loves even though they have parted. Black Canary holds her mother's seat with the new JSA and is an auxiliary member of the JLA. She is also the primary "Bird of Prey" operative for ORACLE, responding to global crises with typical courage and resourcefulness. **SB**

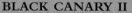

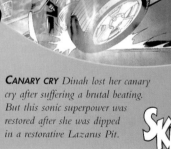

CANARY CRY Dinah lost her canary cry after suffering a brutal beating. But this sonic superpower was restored after she was dipped in a restorative Lazarus Pit.

SKRREEEEE

KEY STORYLINES

- **ALL-STAR COMICS #38 (DEC.–JAN 1947–48):** Though not yet an official member, Black Canary I joins the JSA to defeat history's greatest villains!
- **JLA: YEAR ONE #1–12 (JAN.–DEC. 1998):** The second Black Canary's first year with the JLA is chronicled as the team battles the Appellaxian aliens and the organization known as Locus.
- **BLACK CANARY/ORACLE: BIRDS OF PREY (1996):** Black Canary II accepts her first assignment from Oracle without knowing who her partner really is!

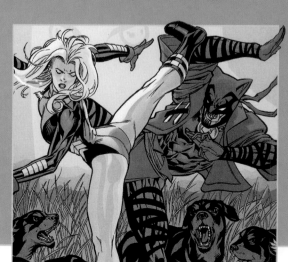

HIGH KICKS Black Canary II is one of the world's top martial artists and has gone fist-to-fist and kick-to-kick with the likes of Lady Shiva and the vicious assassin known as Hellhound.

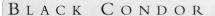
BLACK CONDOR

FIRST APPEARANCE CRACK COMICS #1 (May 1940)
STATUS Hero **REAL NAME** Richard Grey Jr., a.k.a. Thomas Wright
OCCUPATION Adventurer **BASE** Washington, D.C.
HEIGHT 6ft 2in **WEIGHT** 196 lbs **EYES** Blue **HAIR** Black
SPECIAL POWERS/ABILITIES Exposure to alien radiation granted him the ability to fly and to understand the language of birds.

Richard Grey Jr. was lost as an infant in the Mongolian mountains. There he was exposed to radiation from a meteor, which mutated the developing child. A family of condors rescued and raised him until he was found by Father Pierre, a missionary. He called the child Black Condor and taught him to speak, read, and write English. When Father Pierre was murdered, the Black Condor set out to avenge him. En route, he found the body of Senator Thomas Wright, who had been murdered by the deranged Jaspar Crow. Wright and the Condor looked identical in appearance, so the Condor assumed Wright's identity, complete with fiancée, Wendy Foster, who was none the wiser! Grey donned a costume to fight crime as the Black Condor, while serving justice in the senate. He was among the first costumed "mystery men" to serve with the ALL-STAR SQUADRON and afterward its splinter group, the FREEDOM FIGHTERS. His last recorded mission was in 1953, when he aided the RAY and Spitfire in fighting Doctor Spectrom. The Condor subsequently moved on to a higher plane of existence—living with others "at the top of the world"—in an as-yet-unexplained manner. He made brief appearances on Earth, including helping to recruit Ryan Kendall as BLACK CONDOR II. **RG**

BLACK CONDOR II

FIRST APPEARANCE BLACK CONDOR #1 (June 1992)
STATUS Hero **REAL NAME** Ryan Kendall
OCCUPATION Adventurer **BASE** Opal City
HEIGHT 6ft 4in **WEIGHT** 170 lbs **EYES** Blue **HAIR** Black
SPECIAL POWERS/ABILITIES Flight, heightened senses, limited telepathy, and telekinesis; expert knife-thrower.

Though not a direct successor to the wartime hero known as BLACK CONDOR, Ryan Kendall has proven himself worthy of the Condor legacy and has become a hero in his own right. He received his powers thanks to a monstrous experiment conducted by his grandfather, Creighton Kendall, leader of the centuries-old Society of the Golden Wing. As part of the Society's program to create a flying man, Kendall irradiated Ryan while he was still a fetus. At the age of 21, Ryan fell into a coma which lasted two years. When he recovered, he flew off into the thick of New Jersey's Pine Barrens to find himself. Under the name Black Condor, Ryan Kendall assumed a super-heroic role in battles against the Sky Pirate and the SHARK. He joined the JUSTICE LEAGUE OF AMERICA following SUPERMAN's death, and later became a member of PRIMAL FORCE. Black Condor then settled in Opal City working with the police. He remains a member of the JUSTICE SOCIETY OF AMERICA reserves, helping fight IMPERIEX and assisting the FREEDOM FIGHTERS in the JSA's battle against ECLIPSO. **DW**

FLYING SOLO *Black Condor II is a loner who works with super-hero teams, but who doesn't socialize with them.*

BLACK LIGHTNING

FIRST APPEARANCE BLACK LIGHTNING (1st series) #1 (April 1977)
STATUS Hero **REAL NAME** Jefferson Pierce
OCCUPATION Adventurer **BASE** Metropolis
HEIGHT 6ft 1in **WEIGHT** 182 lbs **EYES** Brown **HAIR** Black
SPECIAL POWERS/ABILITIES Olympic-level athlete; superb hand-to-hand combatant; internally generated electromagnetic field; can create and hurl bolts of supercharged electricity.

Jefferson Pierce escaped the squalor of Metropolis's Suicide Slum by devoting himself to athletics. He eventually won Olympic gold in the decathlon. Once qualified as a teacher, he returned to Suicide Slum. Pierce watched helplessly as his students fell victim to drugs, controlled by the 100 mob led by albino behemoth Tobias Whale. With a costume sporting an electronic belt to shock thugs senseless, Pierce became Black Lightning and brought the 100 mob, and Tobias Whale, to justice.

One of the most famous African-American super heroes of his time, Pierce became a founder member of the OUTSIDERS. During his stint with the team, a latent metagene enabled him to internalize his lightning-like powers. Following the Outsiders' dissolution, Black Lightning became defender of crime-ridden Brick City. He then served under U.S. President Lex Luthor (see LUTHOR, LEX) as Secretary of Education. After government service, Pierce resumed his role as Black Lightning. Recently, Black Lightning teamed with a new version of The Outsiders that includes his daughter Anissa (THUNDER II). **SB**

HARD TO GET *Black Lightning once turned down an offer of membership in the Justice League of America.*

BODY ELECTRIC *Black Lightning continues to explore his electromagnetic abilities, including the power to travel via bolts of electricity.*

BLACK MANTA

FIRST APPEARANCE AQUAMAN (Ist series) #35 (September 1967)
STATUS Villain **REAL NAME** Unrevealed
OCCUPATION Assassin **BASE** Devil's Deep
HEIGHT 6ft 4in **WEIGHT** 250 lbs **EYES** Brown **HAIR** Brown
SPECIAL POWERS/ABILITIES Possesses slightly above-average strength;
quickly masters new equipment; fueled by rage.

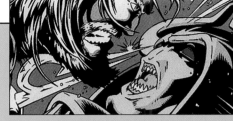

DEVIL VERSION *Black Manta sold his soul to Neron in exchange for more power. He also was transformed into a living manta.*

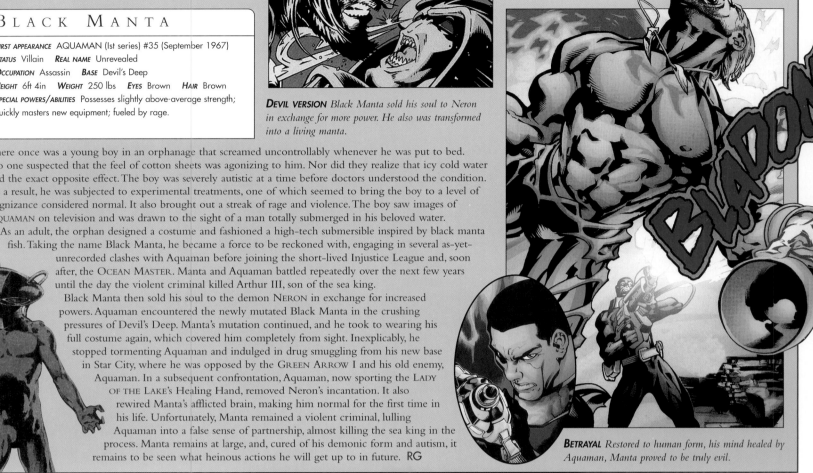

There once was a young boy in an orphanage that screamed uncontrollably whenever he was put to bed. No one suspected that the feel of cotton sheets was agonizing to him. Nor did they realize that icy cold water had the exact opposite effect. The boy was severely autistic at a time before doctors understood the condition. As a result, he was subjected to experimental treatments, one of which seemed to bring the boy to a level of cognizance considered normal. It also brought out a streak of rage and violence. The boy saw images of AQUAMAN on television and was drawn to the sight of a man totally submerged in his beloved water. As an adult, the orphan designed a costume and fashioned a high-tech submersible inspired by black manta fish. Taking the name Black Manta, he became a force to be reckoned with, engaging in several as-yet-unrecorded clashes with Aquaman before joining the short-lived Injustice League and, soon after, the OCEAN MASTER. Manta and Aquaman battled repeatedly over the next few years until the day the violent criminal killed Arthur III, son of the sea king.

Black Manta then sold his soul to the demon NERON in exchange for increased powers. Aquaman encountered the newly mutated Black Manta in the crushing pressures of Devil's Deep. Manta's mutation continued, and he took to wearing his full costume again, which covered him completely from sight. Inexplicably, he stopped tormenting Aquaman and indulged in drug smuggling from his new base in Star City, where he was opposed by the GREEN ARROW I and his old enemy, Aquaman. In a subsequent confrontation, Aquaman, now sporting the LADY OF THE LAKE's Healing Hand, removed Neron's incantation. It also rewired Manta's afflicted brain, making him normal for the first time in his life. Unfortunately, Manta remained a violent criminal, lulling Aquaman into a false sense of partnership, almost killing the sea king in the process. Manta remains at large, and, cured of his demonic form and autism, it remains to be seen what heinous actions he will get up to in future. RG

BETRAYAL *Restored to human form, his mind healed by Aquaman, Manta proved to be truly evil.*

BLACK MASK

FIRST APPEARANCE BATMAN #386 (August 1985)
STATUS Villain (presumed dead) **REAL NAME** Roman Sionis
OCCUPATION Gang leader **BASE** Gotham City
HEIGHT 6ft 1in **WEIGHT** 195 lbs **EYES** Brown **HAIR** None
SPECIAL POWERS/ABILITIES Brilliant criminal mind; rules subordinates
with iron fist; sadistically pursues anyone who wronged him.

Thanks to his mother and father, the heads of the Janus Cosmetics company, Roman Sionis inherited a multi-million dollar fortune when his parents "mysteriously" died in a fire. But the new Sionis quickly ran the company into the ground. A buyout by Bruce Wayne saved Janus Cosmetics, but left Sionis with a bitter hatred of the man who had "stolen" his legacy. Obsessed with masks, Sionis carved a black mask from his father's coffin and murdered several Wayne employees, resulting in a fiery confrontation with BATMAN. Sionis' mask was burned into his flesh, making him a living Black Mask. He became one of Gotham's most ruthless crimelords with an army of masked henchmen, the False Face Society, at his disposal. When CATWOMAN stole from him, he implacably hunted the elusive feline fatale, and tortured her sister Maggie's husband to death. Catwoman took swift revenge, hurling Black Mask off a rooftop, presumably to his death. DW

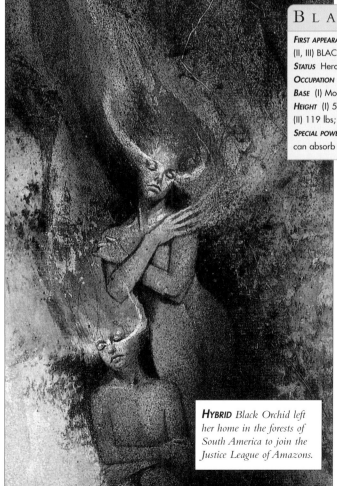

HYBRID *Black Orchid left her home in the forests of South America to join the Justice League of Amazons.*

BLACK ORCHID

FIRST APPEARANCE (I) ADVENTURE COMICS #428 (August 1973);
(II, III) BLACK ORCHID (1st series) #1 (December 1988)
STATUS Hero **REAL NAME** (I) Susan Linden; (II) none; (III) Suzy
OCCUPATION (I) Adventurer; (II, III) elemental nymph
BASE (I) Mobile; (II, III) the Amazon rain forest
HEIGHT (I) 5ft 11in; (II) 5ft 7in; (III) 5ft 6in **WEIGHT** (I) 130 lbs;
(II) 119 lbs; (III) 115 lbs **EYES** (all) Violet **HAIR** (all) Violet
SPECIAL POWERS/ABILITIES Superhuman strength; flight. Like a plant, she
can absorb nutrients from the air.

Abused by her father her entire life, Susan Linden eventually married Carl Thorne, a wealthy arms trafficker. Thorne stole a shipment of weapons from his billionaire boss Lex Luthor (*see* LUTHOR, LEX), and murdered Susan when she went to the police with the information. Botanist Philip Sylvian, a childhood friend of Susan's, grafted a splice of Linden's genetic material into an experimental hybrid of plant and animal matter, creating the Black Orchid. Black Orchid used her special powers and a number of false identities to fight crime until she was murdered by Lex Luthor. Susan's death created a psychic reaction that awakened another of Sylvian's orchid hybrids. This nameless Black Orchid found her way to the rain forests of South America and learned that she was an elemental dryad nymph before being assassinated by a hitman in New York City. Suzy, a childlike sprite with fragments of Susan's consciousness, is the last surviving Black Orchid. She protects the natural world from the depredations of industry and big business. PJ

BLACK PIRATE

FIRST APPEARANCE SENSATION COMICS #1 (January 1942)
STATUS Hero (deceased) **REAL NAME** Jon Valor
OCCUPATION Freedom fighter **BASE** England
HEIGHT 5ft 11in **WEIGHT** 164 lbs
EYES Brown **HAIR** Brown
SPECIAL POWERS/ABILITIES A swashbuckling swordsman and accomplished sailor.

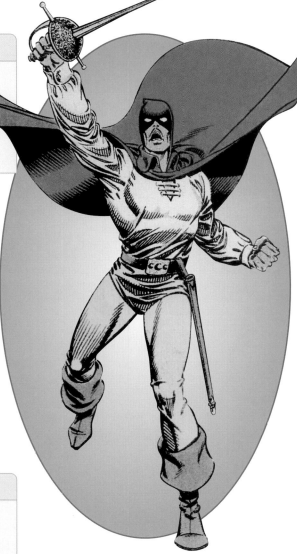

As war divided Europe in 1588, British nobleman Jon Valor led a trusted crew of bold but benevolent buccaneers as a masked Black Pirate who sailed the high seas for the cause of justice. Though loyal to the British crown, Valor also served under the Spanish flag for a brief time before returning to Great Britain and swashbuckling alongside his son, Justin. However, when Justin was later lost at sea, a heartbroken Black Pirate revealed his true identity to the British monarch and hung up his cape and cowl. Years later, when British ships were threatened by mysterious privateers, Valor heeded the king's call for the Black Pirate to return to action and scuttle the roguish raiders. To his surprise, Valor discovered Justin alive and well, and leading a band of Puritans who attacked British ships to fund their planned journey to the U.S. Valor made peace with Justin, who set sail for a new life in the U.S., and retired to his home in England, where he presumably lived his remaining days rarely drawing his sword from its scabbard. **SB**

BLACK RACER

FIRST APPEARANCE NEW GODS (1st series) #3 (July 1971)
STATUS Villain **REAL NAME** Sgt. Willie Walker
OCCUPATION Messenger of Death **BASE** New Genesis
HEIGHT 6ft 4in **WEIGHT** 211 lbs **EYES** Black **HAIR** Black
SPECIAL POWERS/ABILITIES Phases through solid objects, flying atop cosmically charged skis; can deliver death with a single touch; armor helps him withstand the rigors of space and staff metes out justice.

When the NEW GODS arose from the ashes of their predecessors, so rose the Black Racer, an elemental force capable of dealing death with a single touch. When the Fourth World's battles spilled on to Earth, the Racer was drawn to the planet and to the body of paralyzed Vietnam veteran Willie Walker. Walker became one with the Racer, his spirit now commingled with this harbinger of death. Black Racer's arrival, atop airborne skis, means someone's life is about to end. He is quiet, efficient, and rarely challenged. The Racer has been drawn to the more cosmic battles over time, including the Imperiex War (see Great Battles, pp. 320–1). When STEEL died, the Racer arrived to collect his soul, as is his right. He was challenged by SUPERMAN, but the Man of Steel eventually relented. YOUNG JUSTICE, however, futilely tried to reclaim Steel from the New God. The racer then met the third FLASH during the war, learning more about how humans cherish life. Afterward, he went to claim a soul, discovering it to be that of the doctor caring for Walker, a victim of a mugging. The Racer has begun to understand the pain a single death can cause to others. **RG**

BLACK SPIDER I & II

FIRST APPEARANCE DETECTIVE COMICS #463 (September 1976)
STATUS Villain **REAL NAME** Eric Needham
OCCUPATION Assassin **BASE** Gotham City
HEIGHT 5ft 10in **WEIGHT** 173 lbs **EYES** Brown **HAIR** Black
SPECIAL POWERS/ABILITIES Expert combatant and dead shot with retractable wrist pistol; unrevealed supernatural powers.

Heroin addict Eric Needham accidentally killed his father during a liquor store robbery. In his grief, he not only kicked the habit, but vowed to eliminate everyone associated with the drug trade. Funding by a mysterious benefactor made it possible for Needham to become the vigilante Black Spider. He later learned that the drug kingpin Hannibal Hardwicke had bankrolled his career in order to eliminate business rivals. When Needham's wife and son died in the crossfire of his war on drugs, Black Spider blew himself up in a suicide attack that eliminated several top gangsters. Needham was freed from Hell when Lucifer released many of the dead, and has since returned to Earth. He struck a deal with NERON, the consequences of which are still unrevealed. A second Black Spider also appeared in Gotham—Johnny LaMonica. Failing in an attempt to kill gang boss BLACK MASK, LaMonica rots in Blackgate prison. **DW**

BLACK ZERO

FIRST APPEARANCE SUPERBOY (3rd series) #61 (April 1999)
STATUS Villain **REAL NAME** Kon-El
OCCUPATION Freedom fighter and world conqueror **BASE** Metropolis (in an alternate timeline)
HEIGHT 6ft 2in **WEIGHT** 225 lbs **EYES** Blue **HAIR** Black
SPECIAL POWERS/ABILITIES Has superhuman strength and speed, can fly, is virtually invulnerable and possesses psionic vision (similar to heat vision). Like Superboy, Black Zero lifts huge objects using tactile telekinesis, which gives him telekinetic control over an object after touching it.

On the Earth of an alternate timeline, SUPERMAN did not return from the dead after battling DOOMSDAY. On that Earth, SUPERBOY, a clone of Superman, grew up in a Metropolis, where clones, called Genetix, were often hunted and killed. Horrified by this, Superboy became Black Zero and began gathering Doomsdays from various timelines to invade every Earth and prevent the extinction of clones across the multiverse.

Another version of Superboy arrived on our Earth to warn its heroes of Black Zero's invasion. Using the alternate Superboy's technology, our Superboy raced across multiple realities, fighting Black Zero's warriors. Superboy finally defeated Black Zero with the help of KNOCKOUT, the CHALLENGERS OF THE UNKNOWN, and METRON, who stripped the elder clone of his time-spanning abilities. Black Zero was finally destroyed when he was struck by a wave of Hypertime on his way back to his own world. **PJ**

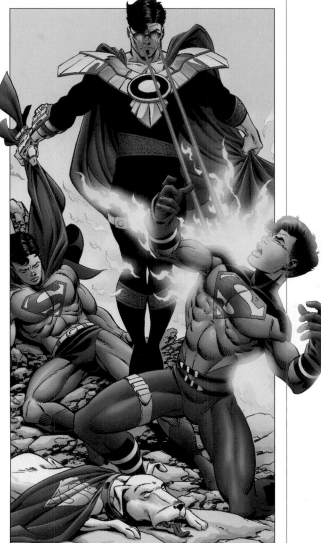

BLACKHAWK

FIGHTER IN THE SKY

FIRST APPEARANCE MILITARY COMICS #1 (AUGUST 1941)
STATUS Hero (missing in action) **REAL NAME** Janos Prohaska
OCCUPATION Squadron leader **BASE** England
HEIGHT 6ft 1.5in **WEIGHT** 195 lbs **EYES** Blue **HAIR** Black
SPECIAL POWERS/ABILITIES An expert pilot; a charismatic and quick-thinking field leader, in addition to being good with his fists.

POLAND'S JANOS PROHASKA served with the Bill Heywood Squadron of the International Brigades during the Spanish Civil War, gaining an international reputation as a flyer of amazing skill and courage. When, in 1939, Poland fell victim to Nazi Germany's *blitzkrieg* warfare, Prohaska, now nicknamed Blackhawk, joined with his friends Stanislaus "Stan" Drozdowski and Kazimierc "Zeg" Zegota and others to form the Blackhawk Squadron. They resisted the brutal invaders of their homeland from a secret base on Blackhawk Island.

THE BLACKHAWK SQUADRON

Blackhawk assembled a truly international band of air aces, all determined to fight for freedom. The pilots included Boris Zinoviev of Russia, Ian Holcolmb-Baker of England, André Blanc-DuMont of France, Olaf Friedriksen of Sweden, Ritter Hendricksen of Denmark, and Carlo "Chuck" Sirianni of the U.S. Sadly, Boris, Zeg, Ian, and Stanislaus were soon killed in action. Soon afterwards, 17-year-old Chinese-American "whiz kid" Weng "Chop Chop" Chan joined the group.

The C.I.A. later recruited the Blackhawks, and Blackhawk Airways was relocated to Washington, D.C. The U.S. government wanted more control over the team's missions, and when Blackhawk objected, the team was kidnapped until rescued by Blackhawk and new recruit Paco Herrera. The isle of Pontalba was then transformed into the new Blackhawk Island. Soon after, the Blackhawks severed all ties with the C.I.A. and the U.S. government. In the 1960s, André was murdered by an assassin named Hardwire. Years later Blackhawk tracked the killer down in Saigon, just as the city was about to fall to the Viet Kong, and avenged his friend's death. Sadly, Olaf disappeared during the mission. Years after, Weng Chan formed an elite air courier service, Blackhawk Express. The company put together a team of doubles of the seven best-known Blackhawks, who fought crime in the decade ahead. President Lex Luthor (*see* LUTHOR, LEX) employed the new Blackhawk Squadron during the Imperiex War (*see* Great Battles, pp. 320–1), but the current whereabouts of Prohaska and the other members of the team is not known. RG

BRAVERY *Despite grave danger and frequent combat wounds, the Blackhawks never gave up.*

LEADING FORCE *Blackhawk was not only a great flyer and terrific fighter: even more importantly he was a charismatic leader.*

FIRST CLASS FLYERS *The Blackhawk planes were not only durable, they were also among the best engineered craft in the world.*

TWO-FISTED HERO *One-man blitzkrieg Blackhawk makes light work of a German army tank crew.*

KEY STORYLINES

• *MILITARY COMICS #1 (AUGUST 1941):* This early story introduces the world to Janos Porhaska and his men.
• *BLACKHAWK #1-3 (MARCH–MAY 1989):* The tale spotlights Prohaska as he deals with a Russian conspiracy and life after the War.
• *BLACKHAWK #140 (SEPTEMBER 1959):* Lady Blackhawk is introduced to the team.

BLACKBRIAR THORN

First appearance DC COMICS PRESENTS #66 (February 1984)
Status Villain   **Real name** Unknown
Occupation Last of the Druids   **Base** Gotham City
Height 6ft 3in   **Weight** 238 lbs   **Eyes** Brown   **Hair** Brown
Special powers/abilities Seemingly immortal; ability to conjure snow, storms, or fog; able to manifest illusions and grow in size; must maintain contact with the Earth and soil or his power diminishes.

Druidic high priest Blackbriar Thorn escaped death at the hands of Roman invaders in Britain by fleeing into a forest and transforming himself into solid wood. The other druids were less fortunate, but in their death throes, they unwittingly opened a great fissure that swallowed Thorn. He was buried for centuries until archaeologist Professor Lewis Lang unearthed him. By now the high priest was permanently trapped in his wooden body.

Thorn's attempts to wreak mystical havoc in the 20th century have been thwarted by SUPERMAN, Etrigan (DEMON), and SENTINEL, among others. While Thorn has seemingly been destroyed on several occasions, he owes his survival to his magical ability to regenerate himself from the smallest splinter. SB

HEAD-HUNTED
Blackbriar Thorn was recruited by Johnny Sorrow to join the JSA-hating Injustice Society.

BLACKFIRE

First appearance THE NEW TEEN TITANS (1st series) #22 (September 1982)
Status Undefined   **Real name** Komand'r
Occupation Queen of Tamaran   **Base** Mobile
Height 6ft 2in   **Weight** 162 lbs   **Eyes** Green   **Hair** Red
Special powers/abilities Absorption of solar energy; projection of destructive "starbolts" from her hands.

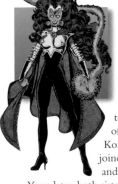

The eldest child of the royal family of the planet Tamaran, Princess Komand'r, a sickly child, was denied her birthright and her sister, Koriand'r, was named next in line for the throne. Both sisters were sent by their father, King Myand'r, to train with the famed Warlords of Okaara, but there the hateful Komand'r betrayed her family, joined the dreaded Citadel Empire, and bartered Koriand'r into slavery. Years later, both sisters became prisoners of the Psions and were subjected to genetic experiments that gave them vast powers. Escaping, Komand'r (now called Blackfire) and Koriand'r (now a TEEN TITANS member called STARFIRE) clashed repeatedly, until Komand'r forsook her hate, freed Tamaran from Citadel control, and became its queen, before the planet's apparent destruction by a Sun-Eater. Blackfire has not been seen since. PJ

BLACKHAWK   SEE OPPOSITE PAGE

BLASTERS, THE

First appearance INVASION #1 (1988)
Status Hero team (disbanded)   **Base** Mobile
Members and powers
Lucas "Snapper" Carr (leader) Teleportation powers.
Dust Devil (Moshe Levy) Israeli boy who can turn into a whirlwind; accompanied by his divorced mother, Mrs. Levy.
Looking Glass (Dexter Fairfax) Ability to absorb light and project it.
Crackpot (Amos Monroe) Persuasive mind-manipulation powers.
Jolt (Carlotta Rivera) Can repel any form of energy.
Frag (Fritz Klein) Can turn into living metal and explode.
Gunther Renegade Dominator scientist.
Churljenkins Alien starship pilot; technical expert.

During an alien invasion of Earth, Dominator scientists kidnapped 50 humans and forced them to walk through a minefield. The humans that survived did so by manifesting latent metagene powers. Upon their escape from the Dominator space prison, they formed a wandering super-team called the Blasters. The group added a Dominator scientist to its roster and cruised the spaceways piloted by the attractively feline humanoid alien Churljenkins. On one mission, they smashed a plot by a criminal organization named the Spider Guild to sell black-market weapons on Earth. After a near-fatal attempt to spring the hero Valor from prison, the Blasters disbanded. Snapper Carr (*see* CARR, SNAPPER) suffered horrors of his own, being seized by Khund thugs who cut off his hands, robbing him of his ability to teleport. Though Snapper's hands have since been restored, no one knows if he will ever be able to track down his former team members and reform the Blasters. DW

THE BLASTERS *The Blasters helped end the alien invasion of Earth, but went mostly unrecognized for their efforts.*
1) *Frag*   2) *Snapper Carr*   3) *Churljenkins*   4) *Crackpot*
5) *Looking Glass*   6) *Mrs. Levy*   7) *Gunther*
8) *Dust Devil*   9) *Jolt*

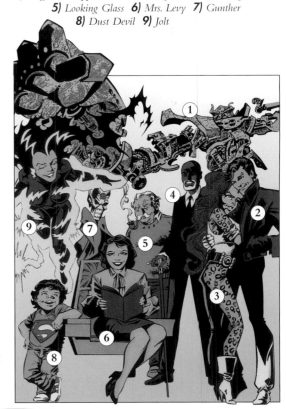

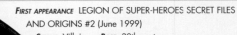

BLIGHT

First appearance LEGION OF SUPER-HEROES SECRET FILES AND ORIGINS #2 (June 1999)
Status Villains   **Base** 30th century space
Special powers/abilities An alien race of partially organic beings composed of a combination of rotting flesh and technology; can absorb the life energy from entire worlds, leaving these planets in ruins.

The Blight were intergalactic nomads comprised of techno-organic symbionts. This scientifically advanced species sought the secret of immortality. In their mad quest, the Blight were turned into a race of perpetually decaying beings and, using the teleportation skills of the alien Doda (beings who could teleport themselves across the galaxy to seed new worlds), spread that decay across the universe.

In the 31st century, the Blight, led by Atrophos, their chief scientist and engineer, drained the life energy from dozens of worlds. This hostile, malicious race first came into contact with a LEGION OF SUPER-HEROES cruiser when the aliens entered United Planets space. Using the cruiser's Stargate technology, the Blight's corrosive power spread to several planets, and they eventually took control of Earth. The Blight enslaved many Legionnaires in their search for M'ONEL, whose power they believed would give them immortality and end their existence as decaying beings. However, the Legion was able to destroy the Blight by teleporting their Doda captives across the known universe to revitalize the life forces drained by the techno-organic parasites. Without the Doda, the Blight were no longer able to teleport or spread their putrefaction throughout the galaxy. PJ

BLOCKBUSTER I

FIRST APPEARANCE DETECTIVE COMICS #345 (November 1965)
STATUS Villain (deceased) **REAL NAME** Mark Desmond
OCCUPATION None **BASE** Gotham City
HEIGHT 7ft 4in **WEIGHT** 645 lbs **EYES** Brown **HAIR** Brown
SPECIAL POWERS/ABILITIES Secret serum gave Desmond tremendous strength, endurance, and invulnerability, but severely diminished his mental capacity.

Mark Desmond wanted to become stronger, but instead of working out with weights, he decided to use chemistry. He experimented on himself and grew taller and stronger, but, in the process, was turned into a mindless brute. Desmond was cared for by his criminal brother Roland, who shielded their mother from the news that Mark was now a monster. Roland used Mark to commit crimes until they were stopped by BATMAN and ROBIN.

Desmond had once been rescued from drowning by Bruce Wayne, and the Dark Knight Detective discovered that he could stall the behemoth simply by removing his cowl and showing Desmond his face. The sight calmed the giant, preventing further destruction. Blockbuster, as he was known, sought solitude when free, only to find himself opposing the Caped Crusader on various occasions. He was recruited by Amanda Waller (see WALLER, AMANDA) for her new SUICIDE SQUAD, and he died battling DARKSEID's creation, BRIMSTONE. **RG**

BLOOD PACK

FIRST APPEARANCE SHOWCASE '94 #12 (March 1995)
STATUS Hero team (disbanded) **BASE** Metropolis
MEMBERS AND POWERS
Jade Power pulse from her hands; can project green energy, allowing flight, creation of energy objects, etc.
Ballistic Armor-plated skin; night vision; super-hearing.
Geist Can make himself invisible or make other objects invisible.
Mongrel Can project tangible, shadow-like darkforce energy.
Nightblade Martial arts; limb regeneration; immortality.
Razorsharp Arms become razor-sharp metallic blades.
Sparx Can transform her body into electrical energy; flight.
Loria (deceased) Body could turn into solid steel.

A host of superpowered metas were inadvertently created when a group of seven parasitic aliens invaded Earth and fed off the spinal fluids of a number of human and alien beings. With the help of the JUSTICE LEAGUE OF AMERICA, the Titans, and dozens of Earth's heroes, these "new bloods" defeated the aliens and the Taker, a monstrous creature born from the death of the seven invaders. Later, several of these new meta-beings were united by JADE as the Blood Pack, a government-sponsored, media-friendly organization. While filming a documentary on super-heroics sponsored by the Quorum, a clandestine organization, the Blood Pack learned that their malevolent benefactors were actually using them in an attempt to take over the world. Loria was murdered by the Quorum's security "sweepers," and they used her genetic material in a clone of the Taker. But the Pack destroyed the Taker and promptly disbanded, ending the Quorum's ability to use them in their global takeover. **PJ**

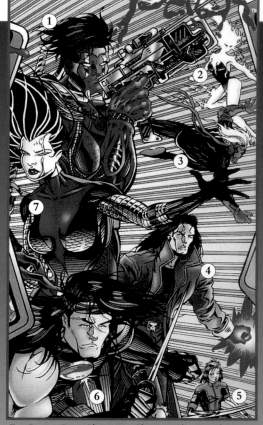

THE BLOOD PACK 1) Ballistic **2)** Sparx **3)** Geist **4)** Mongrel **5)** Nightblade **6)** Razorsharp **7)** Loria

BLOOD DONORS The members of the Blood Pack were just a handful of the "new bloods" created by the alien parasites. Anima, Gunfire, Loose Cannon, Argus, and Hitman also gained their powers after alien attacks.

BLOCKBUSTER II

FIRST APPEARANCE STARMAN (1st series) #9 (April 1989)
STATUS Villain (deceased) **REAL NAME** Roland Desmond
OCCUPATION Gang leader **BASE** Blüdhaven
HEIGHT 8ft **WEIGHT** 527 lbs **EYES** Brown **HAIR** Brown
SPECIAL POWERS/ABILITIES Superstrength, invulnerability, enhanced speed, and a brilliant criminal mind.

Blüdhaven's crime boss was a giant with a brain to match. He obtained his awesome acumen by selling his soul to the demon NERON. Desmond became Blockbuster II when a gene bomb detonation during the alien Invasion turned him into a towering brute. Like his brother Mark (BLOCKBUSTER I), Roland now possessed superhuman strength and a child's IQ. He went on a rampage, but STARMAN and BATMAN ensured that the befuddled behemoth wound up behind bars.

Acquiring a genius-level intellect became Desmond's obsession. When Neron made it a reality, Desmond set up shop in his mother's home city of Blüdhaven, forced out crimelord Angel Marin, and took over his organization.

Blüdhaven's protector, NIGHTWING, and the all-knowing ORACLE irritated Blockbuster II. He took out his frustration by snapping his underlings' necks, creating the villain Torque when one victim survived. Suffering from albinism and a defective heart—side-effects of his condition—Blockbuster II received a heart transplant from one of Gorilla City's talking apes. Restored to health, he was tightening his grip on Blüdhaven and contemplating a takeover of Gotham City when he was shot and killed by TARANTULA II. **DW**

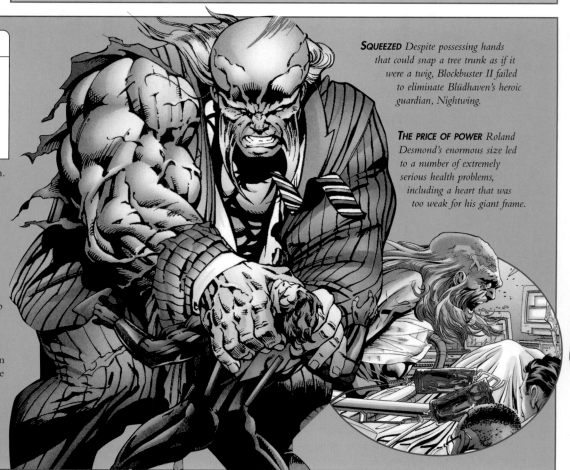

SQUEEZED Despite possessing hands that could snap a tree trunk as if it were a twig, Blockbuster II failed to eliminate Blüdhaven's heroic guardian, Nightwing.

THE PRICE OF POWER Roland Desmond's enormous size led to a number of extremely serious health problems, including a heart that was too weak for his giant frame.

BLUE BEETLE I

FIRST APPEARANCE BLUE BEETLE (1st series) #1 (June 1964)
STATUS Hero (deceased) **REAL NAME** Dr. Daniel Garrett
OCCUPATION Adventurer **BASE** Hub City
HEIGHT 6ft **WEIGHT** 189 lbs **EYES** Blue **HAIR** Red
SPECIAL POWERS/ABILITIES Superstrong; able to fly and discharge lightning-like energy from fingertips; chain-mail armor impervious to small-arms fire.

After discovering a glowing azure scarab in the tomb of the evil Pharaoh Kha-ef-re, archaeologist Dr. Daniel Garrett gained miraculous powers when he uttered the mystical words "Kaji Dha." Possessing superhuman abilities and clad in azure chain-mail armor, Garrett fought evil in Hub City as the first Blue Beetle. Years later, Garrett helped student Ted Kord to thwart Kord's Uncle Jarvis and his plans for world domination. The ensuing melée left Blue Beetle mortally wounded. With his dying breath, Garrett made young Kord promise that he would carry on in his stead, thus ensuring that the Blue Beetle's heroic legacy would continue. Garrett was subsequently buried under tons of rubble on Pago Island, but lay in a state of suspended animation, kept alive by the mystic scarab he failed to pass on to Kord. Years later, the original Blue Beetle, in thrall to an alien intelligence within his mystic gem (a blend of magic and contemporary technology), returned to battle BLUE BEETLE II. But Garrett fought back against the alien controlling him and died for good rather than allow himself to kill his friend and successor. **SB**

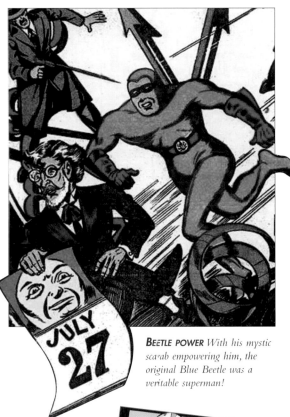

BEETLE POWER With his mystic scarab empowering him, the original Blue Beetle was a veritable superman!

BLUE BEETLE II

FIRST APPEARANCE CAPTAIN ATOM (1st series) #83 (Nov. 1966)
STATUS Hero **REAL NAME** Theodore "Ted" Kord
OCCUPATION Adventurer **BASE** New York City
HEIGHT 5ft 11in **WEIGHT** 184 lbs **EYES** Blue **HAIR** Brown
SPECIAL POWERS/ABILITIES The second Blue Beetle possesses no superpowers, but is a genius inventor and a capable hand-to-hand combatant. His BB-gun has several settings, including a walloping compressed-air blast and blinding strobe light.
　　The Beetle's greatest weapon is his "Bug," a stealthy, solar-powered crime-fighting vehicle.

ONE STEP AHEAD What he lacks in athleticism, Blue Beetle II makes up in scientific acumen and ingenuity. Who else would use pressurized milk to dunk a foe?

When Dan Garrett, the first BLUE BEETLE, was grievously injured thwarting the maniacal Jarvis Kord from dominating the world with his army of robots, Garrett asked his friend and protégé, Ted Kord, Jarvis's own nephew, to carry on in his stead as Blue Beetle II. But before Garrett could pass on the mystic scarab that gave him his astounding abilities, the dying hero and his powerful talisman were entombed under tons of rubble on the remote Pago Island, site of Jarvis Kord's failed plot. Undaunted, the inventive Kord trained himself in a variety of fighting skills and developed an arsenal of non-lethal weapons to enable him to operate as a non-powered Blue Beetle, whose sense of adventurous whimsy was in stark contrast to Dan Garrett's stalwart stoicism. Once more, there was a Blue Beetle to keep evil at bay in Hub City, where he added his own rogues gallery to villains inherited from Dan Garrett. Later, the Beetle moved to Chicago and made the Windy City safer during his tenure there. Unfortunately, super heroics haven't always been as easy for the second Blue Beetle as for the original Azure Avenger. Without a mystic scarab of his own, Ted has had to work hard to keep himself in shape. What's more, Ted hasn't always been able to devote complete attention to running K.O.R.D. (Kord Omniversal Research and Development), a high-tech corporation he built up from the tiny company inherited from his father. And Ted can attest that he has had even less time leftover for his infrequent romances. While attempting to live up to Garrett's legacy, Blue Beetle has earned a measure of respect throughout the super-hero community, particularly as a member of the JUSTICE LEAGUE OF AMERICA. The Blue Beetle's closest friend is BOOSTER GOLD, and recently Ted has tried to advance his unrequited crush on Barbara Gordon (ORACLE), while struggling to keep fit and battle a congenital heart ailment. **SB**

BLUE DEVIL

FIRST APPEARANCE FURY OF FIRESTORM #24 (June 1984)
STATUS Hero (reluctant) **REAL NAME** Daniel Patrick Cassidy
OCCUPATION Demon **BASE** Mobile
HEIGHT 6ft 8in **WEIGHT** 365 lbs **EYES** Red **HAIR** None
SPECIAL POWERS/ABILITIES In demonic form, Cassidy has enhanced strength, durability, and speed.

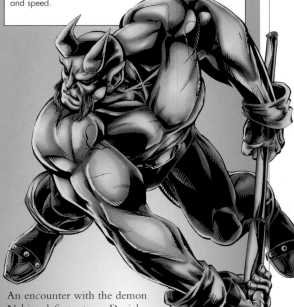

An encounter with the demon Nebiros left stuntman Daniel Cassidy permanently bonded with the costume he was wearing for his new movie, and he soon became known as Blue Devil. Daniel frantically tried to escape the suit before resigning himself to his lot. His transformation seemed to turn him into a "weirdness magnet," and Daniel found himself spending his time fighting demons, criminals, and a freaked out public. S.T.A.R. Labs director Jenet Klyburn connected Blue Devil to SUPERMAN and the JUSTICE LEAGUE OF AMERICA. Mistress of Magic ZATANNA arranged for Daniel and Nebiros to meet. The encounter went badly and Zatanna, Blue Devil, and the Mexican Army joined forces to return Nebiros to his other-dimensional prison.
　　Resigned to the life of a super hero, Blue Devil briefly joined the JLA. He eventually made a deal with the demon NERON in exchange for becoming a successful actor. He learned too late that success as a thespian came at a terrible price: the life of his friend, director Marla Bloom, and his own transformation into a true demon. Blue Devil was subsequently killed in combat with MIST II. During the Day of Judgment, the magician Faust (see FAUST, FELIX) resurrected Daniel and turned him into a powerful demon. Blue Devil obtained the fabled trident of Lucifer and now strides the Earth, locating demons and banishing them back to Hell. **RG**

HELLISH Now a real devil, Daniel Cassidy finds himself way too comfortable with demons and hellfire.

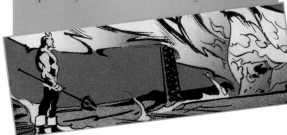

BODY DOUBLES

FIRST APPEARANCE RESURRECTION MAN #1 (March 1996)
STATUS Villains **REAL NAMES** Bonny Hoffman and Carmen Leno
OCCUPATION Assassins **BASE** Mobile
HEIGHT (Bonny) 5ft 8in; (Carmen) 6ft **WEIGHT** (Bonny) 125 lbs;
(Carmen) 140 lbs **EYES** (Bonny) blue; (Carmen) brown
HAIR (Bonny) blonde; (Carmen) black
SPECIAL POWERS/ABILITIES Both women are martial-arts adepts and
experts with many types of firearms and concealed weapons.

The Body Doubles are hired killers who work for the
Requiem, Inc. Assassination Agency. Bonny Hoffman is
the daughter of an East Coast mob boss, while Carmen
Leno is a former adult film star and exotic dancer.
Bonny became an assassin to prove to her father that
she could be as tough as any man, while Carmen hoped
to advance her career as a legitimate Hollywood actress.
They employ the latest high-tech weaponry, as well as
murderous gadgets hidden in their makeup accessories.

The Body Doubles began working for Bonny's Uncle
Nick, an assassin himself, and a magnificent drag queen to
boot. As hired killers, the Body Doubles often came into
conflict with RESURRECTION MAN. They also tried to kill
CATWOMAN when she was running for mayor of New
York City, but their fighting skills proved no match for the
Princess of Plunder's. They continue to work for Uncle
Nick, merrily murdering assigned victims while pursuing
their dreams. PJ

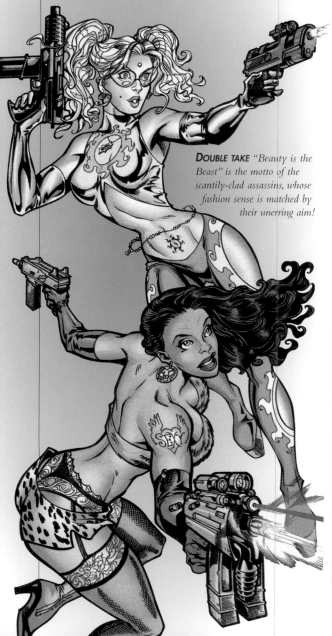

DOUBLE TAKE "Beauty is the
Beast" is the motto of the
scantily-clad assassins, whose
fashion sense is matched by
their unerring aim!

BOLT

FIRST APPEARANCE BLUE DEVIL #6 (November 1984)
STATUS Villain **REAL NAME** Larry Bolatinsky
OCCUPATION Mercenary **BASE** Mobile
HEIGHT 6ft 4in **WEIGHT** 220 lbs **EYES** Blue **HAIR** Unrevealed
SPECIAL POWERS/ABILITIES Microcircuitry in costume allows flight,
projection of electrical energy bolts, and teleportation.

A former special-
effects technician,
Bolt is a superpowered
assassin-for-hire
renowned for his skill,
stealth—and his price.
Bolt used his great
wealth to finance scientific
experiments, and created a number of
teleporting battle suits. Bolt was hired to kill the
Trickster (*see* TRICKSTER II), a foe of the FLASH III,
but was foiled by the Trickster and BLUE DEVIL.
Bolt was also a constant thorn in the sides of heroes
like Blue Devil, CAPTAIN ATOM, FIRESTORM, and
STARMAN VI. Bolt joined the Killer Elite, a group of
assassins that included Merlyn, Chiller, Deadline, and
DEADSHOT, and later, the Task Force X Mark II, a division
of the SUICIDE SQUAD.

Bolt was thought to have been slain on a Task Force
mission, but returned with a host of super-villains in an
army led by Zandia's LADY ZAND and Baron Agua sin
Gaaz. Later still, on an assignment with the Calculator,
Bolt was shot and seriously wounded by street thugs. PJ

BOOSTER GOLD

FIRST APPEARANCE BOOSTER GOLD #1 (February 1986)
STATUS Hero **REAL NAME** Michael Jon Carter
OCCUPATION Adventurer **BASE** New York City
HEIGHT 6ft 5in **WEIGHT** 215 lbs **EYES** Blue **HAIR** Blond
SPECIAL POWERS/ABILITIES Costume allows him to fly, use a
protective forcefield, and gives enhanced strength.

College quarterback and gambler Michael Jon Carter
was banished from college athletics after many
misdeeds. As night watchman at the Space Museum,
Carter utilized Rip Hunter's time machine (*see*
HUNTER, RIP), stealing a security robot named Skeets,
a LEGION OF SUPER-HEROES flight ring, and BRAINIAC
5's forcefield belt. He arrived back in the 20th century
seeking fortune and fame as Booster Gold. Before long
he had put an end to the criminal conclave the 1000,
but the battle left him severely injured.

Booster briefly returned to his home era to recover,
then escaped to the past, accompanied by his sister,
Michelle. Soon after, Maxwell Lord (LORD HAVOK)
began a JUSTICE LEAGUE OF AMERICA recruitment
drive. Booster joined up and formed a lasting friendship
with BLUE BEETLE II. As the Justice League battled the
aliens of Dimension X, Booster Gold saw his sister
Michelle perish. For a time, he led the corporate team
known as the CONGLOMERATE, but finally returned to
the League. Booster was inactive for a while after his
powers were destroyed in a battle with DOOMSDAY.
Following ICE's funeral, Booster left the League again,
eventually joining the newly formed EXTREME JUSTICE.

With the opening of his theme restaurant, Planet
Krypton, Booster went into semi-retirement, becoming
the toy boy of a wealthy matron. However, Maxwell
Lord's promise of glory got him back into action, and
Booster rejoined a new Justice League team. RG

BORDEAUX, SASHA

FIRST APPEARANCE DETECTIVE COMICS #751 (December 2000)
STATUS Ally **REAL NAME** Sasha Bordeaux
OCCUPATION U.S. government agent **BASE** Mobile
HEIGHT 5ft 7in **WEIGHT** 135 lbs **EYES** Blue **HAIR** Blonde
SPECIAL POWERS/ABILITIES Top athlete; skilled with most firearms.

WayneCorp chief Lucius
Fox (*see* FOX, LUCIUS)
insisted that Bruce
Wayne receive
4-hour protection.
Former secret
service agent Sasha
Bordeaux got the job.
She soon realized that her
client lived a second life as
BATMAN. Bordeaux teamed with
him and even fell in love, but their romance ended
when Lex Luthor (*see* LUTHOR, LEX) ordered David
Cain (*see* CAIN, DAVID) to frame them for the murder
of radio host Vesper Fairchild (*see* FAIRCHILD, VESPER).
Sasha loyally took the blame and rotted in Blackgate
prison, while Bruce escaped to clear his name. The U.S.
government agency CHECKMATE gave her a new identity
as an agent. Bordeaux has crossed paths with Batman
since, but any hint of love seems to have vanished. DW

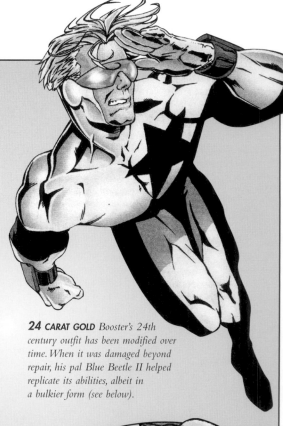

24 CARAT GOLD *Booster's 24th
century outfit has been modified over
time. When it was damaged beyond
repair, his pal Blue Beetle II helped
replicate its abilities, albeit in
a bulkier form (see below).*

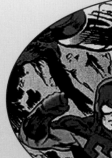

BOY COMMANDOS

FIRST APPEARANCE DETECTIVE COMICS #64 (June 1942)
STATUS Hero team **BASE** Europe
MEMBERS
Captain Eric "Rip" Carter
Alfy Tridgett
André Chavard
Daniel "Brooklyn" Turpin
Jan Haasan
Tex
Percy Clearweather

In 1942, Captain Eric "Rip" Carter led four rescurceful boys—Alfy Twidgett, André Chavard (*see* CHAVARD, ANDRÉ), Daniel "Brooklyn" Turpin, and Jan Haasan—on missions throughout war-torn Europe as the Boy Commandos. Among their many successful missions, they pursued Agent Axis, "the vengeful arm of Heinrich Himmler," who was ultimately unmasked as a beautiful woman. In 1944, they traveled Stateside to briefly join forces with the GUARDIAN and the NEWSBOY LEGION to thwart gangster Boss Moxie and Agent Axis.

When the war ended, Jan left the Boy Commandos to rejoin his Uncle Peter in Holland, and Alfy and André returned with Rip Carter and Brooklyn to the U.S. Two years later, in 1947, Alfy left to attend college in England, and was replaced in the group by a young man named Tex. At one point during the same year, a teenager named Percy Clearweather substituted for André on a mission, and helped the team clear Rip of murder charges. By 1949, André left to help his brother on their farm in France. Percy Clearweather replaced him until the teens finally reached adulthood and went their separate ways.

After the war, Rip Carter eventually reached the rank of general, while André entered the military and was named commander of the spy agency Department Gamma. Alfy formed Statistical Occurrences Limited, and a specialized insurance company targeting "risks that somehow presume the involvement of so-called super heroes and super-villains, or other such paranormal forces." Jan became a professor with the Center for Strategic Studies in the Hague. Daniel Turpin traded his "Brooklyn" nickname for that of "Terrible Turpin," eventually joining Metropolis' Special Crimes Unit. **RG**

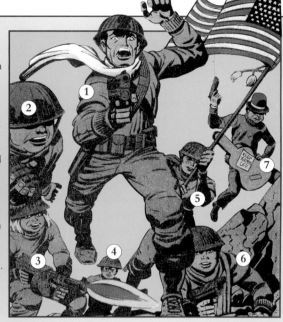

THE BOY COMMANDOS 1) *Captain Rip Carter* **2)** *Alfy*
3) *Jan* **4)** *Percy* **5)** *Tex* **6)** *André* **7)** *Brooklyn*

BOUNTY

FIRST APPEARANCE SUPERBOY (1st series) #225 (March 1977)
STATUS Hero **REAL NAME** Dawnstar
OCCUPATION Bounty hunter; Legionnaire **BASE** Earth; Starhaven
HEIGHT 5ft 6in **WEIGHT** 120 lbs **EYES** Brown **HAIR** Brown
SPECIAL POWERS/ABILITIES Wings enabled her to soar through space without a Legion flight ring; able to track with unerring accuracy.

A mutant Amerind from the planet Starhaven, the bounty hunter Dawnstar joined the pre-Zero Hour (*see* Great Battles, pp. 320–1) LEGION OF SUPER-HEROES and used her flying and tracking abilities in service to the United Planets. When the LSH disbanded in 2992, Dawnstar was among many members who departed Earth. The Legion later returned to action and one of the new members was Bounty, a mysterious mercenary. Bounty attempted to apprehend the wanted criminal Sade, who mortally wounded the Legionnaire. As her teammates watched, the invisible entity known as Bounty departed the body of Dawnstar. Later, it was learned that Bounty had possessed Dawnstar and had changed her appearance, cutting off Dawnstar's wings in order to act as a merciless bounty hunter and sate the entity's bloodlust. Unfortunately, Dawnstar was fully aware of Bounty's many murders. Following Zero Hour, both Bounty and Dawnstar were erased from the timeline and ceased to exist. **SB**

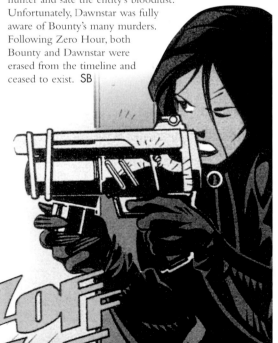

BRADLEY, SLAM

FIRST APPEARANCE DETECTIVE COMICS #1 (March 1937)
STATUS Hero **REAL NAME** Samuel Emerson Bradley
OCCUPATION Private investigator **BASE** Gotham City
HEIGHT 6ft 1in **WEIGHT** 205 lbs
EYES Gray **HAIR** Dark brown with gray at temples
SPECIAL POWERS/ABILITIES Tough, two-fisted combatant and a highly skilled, persistent detective; loyal to his friends no matter what.

Former soldier and cop, Slam Bradley became a P.I. so he could be his own boss. Slam moved from city to city over the decades, working with other respected detectives such as MYSTO, POW-WOW SMITH, and the HUMAN TARGET. When his partner Shorty Morgan fell victim to a murderer, Slam tracked down the killer and solved a case that teamed him with BATMAN. Years later, Slam's son, Slam Jr., was hired by the mayor of Gotham City to find out whether CATWOMAN was alive or dead. Slam Jr. was so smitten by her, he suffered beatings to keep her existence secret. The two have since established an informal working relationship. **DW**

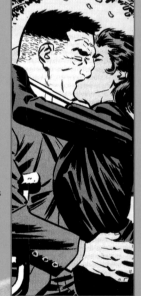

SMITTEN KITTEN *Slam's passion was briefly returned by Selina Kyle, the Catwoman. Despite the age difference, the two loners found that they had a great deal in common. Yet Slam realized that he could never be the one to tame the enigmatic feline fatale, and that only heartbreak awaited him if he got in too deep. They remain close friends and are utterly loyal to each other.*

PUNCHDRUNK *Slam earned his lifelong nickname as a child on the streets of Cleveland when he knocked out the local bully with a single punch. Slam can almost always outthink his opponents, but he often swings first and asks questions later. He likes a smoke and a drink—especially if a dame's giving him the runaround!*

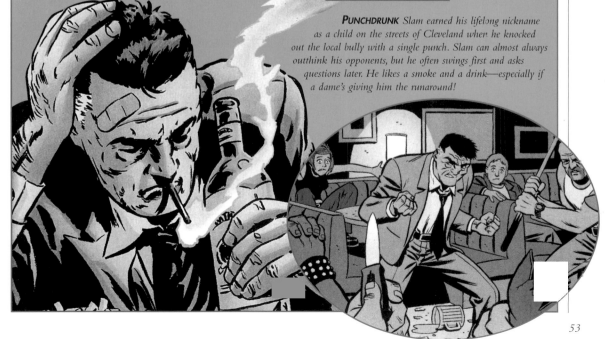

BRAIN

FIRST APPEARANCE DOOM PATROL (1st series) #86 (March 1964)
STATUS Villain REAL NAME Unrevealed
OCCUPATION Scientist, criminal mastermind BASE Mobile
HEIGHT 3ft 4in WEIGHT 195 lbs EYES Black HAIR None
SPECIAL POWERS/ABILITIES Genius-level IQ; occasionally uses the robot
body Rog for mobility.

Little is known about the French scientist and criminal genius known as the Brain. Before his death, the scientist experimented on a captured African gorilla and gave it a near-genius intellect. When the scientist died, the ape, named MONSIEUR MALLAH, removed the man's brain and put it in a receptacle connected to a vast computer network. The scientist, now called the Brain, set up the villainous Brotherhood of Evil (see SOCIETY OF SIN) to further his goal of world conquest.

The Brotherhood attacked the DOOM PATROL several times over the years. Later, under the Brain's command, a second Brotherhood of Evil fought the TEEN TITANS.

The Brain and Mallah went into hiding after their defeat by the Titans. When a new Doom Patrol emerged, the Brain and Mallah broke into the Patrol's headquarters and stole one of ROBOTMAN II's robot bodies with the intention of placing the Brain inside it. The booby-trapped robot body exploded, but not before the villains could profess their undying love for each other. The Brain and Mallah survived and moved to the island of Zandia. They later came into conflict with YOUNG JUSTICE. PJ

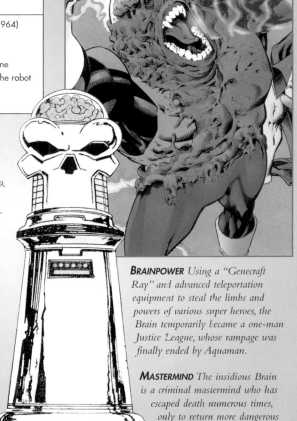

BRAINPOWER *Using a "Genecraft Ray" and advanced teleportation equipment to steal the limbs and powers of various super heroes, the Brain temporarily became a one-man Justice League, whose rampage was finally ended by Aquaman.*

MASTERMIND *The insidious Brain is a criminal mastermind who has escaped death numerous times, only to return more dangerous than ever.*

BRAINIAC
SEE OPPOSITE PAGE

BRAINIAC 5.1

FIRST APPEARANCE LEGIONNAIRES #0 (October 1994)
STATUS Hero REAL NAME Querl Dox
OCCUPATION Legionnaire/scientist BASE Colu
HEIGHT 5ft 7in WEIGHT 135 lbs EYES Green HAIR Blond
SPECIAL POWERS/ABILITIES Super-genius; force field belt, with
expandable and shapeable protective envelope, is mentally
operated via Braniac control disks on Dox's forehead.

Most of Querl Dox's teammates joined the LEGION OF SUPER-HEROES planning to use their powers for the greater galactic good. However Querl, the proud possessor of a 12-level intellect, was attracted by access to exotic laboratory equipment unavailable to him on his native Colu.

Originally, Querl was known as Brainiac 5, after the long line of super-geniuses from his planet extending back to Querl's ancestor Vril Dox (see BRAINIAC). Querl has since undergone a personal upgrade after exposure to a space anomaly led the previously aloof Legionnaire to try to understand human emotions. "Brainy" to his fellow Legionnaires, Brainiac 5.1 is the LSH's resident scientist, devising much of its scientific gear and weaponry, including the "Threshold" inter-dimensional gateways aboard Legion World, the team's orbiting headquarters. SB

BRANDE, R.J.

FIRST APPEARANCE LEGION OF SUPER-HEROES (4th ser.) #0 (Oct. 1994)
STATUS Ally REAL NAME René Jacques Brande
OCCUPATION Legion of Super-Heroes benefactor
BASE Legion World, U.P. Space
HEIGHT 5ft 11in WEIGHT 210 lbs EYES Black HAIR White
SPECIAL POWERS/ABILITIES Brilliant mind for business; possible telepathic
and other abilities still unrevealed.

R.J. Brande made a cool multi-billion dollar fortune in the 30th century, thanks largely to his introduction of the incredible space-hopping Stargates that helped make possible the formation of the United Planets.

On a shuttle trip to Earth, an assassination attempt arranged by his business partner nearly claimed his life, but he survived due to the intervention of three super-powered teens. Brande dubbed his rescuers COSMIC BOY, SATURN GIRL, and LIVE WIRE, and arranged for them to join together as the founding members of the LEGION OF SUPER-HEROES.

The Legion soon distinguished itself with its own brand of enthusiastic heroism, and it wasn't long before Brande became President of the United Planets. Following an accidental tear in space known as the Great Rift Disaster, he left office under the scandal of impeachment, and the corrupt Leland McCauley became the U.P.'s new president. McCauley disbanded the Legion but Brande kept them operating in secret, financing the construction of Legion World to serve as their new headquarters. Although Brande has yet to address questions about his origin, his devotion to the Legion is in no doubt. DW

BRIMSTONE

FIRST APPEARANCE LEGENDS #1 (November 1986)
STATUS Villain REAL NAME None
OCCUPATION Destroyer BASE Mobile
HEIGHT 50ft 6in WEIGHT 60,000 lbs EYES Yellow HAIR None
SPECIAL POWERS/ABILITIES Incredible strength; generation of intense heat
and flame; creation of a giant flaming sword.

The giant engine of destruction named Brimstone was created by DARKSEID when the member of the NEW GODS attempted to decimate all of Earth's legends. Darkseid's chief scientist DESAAD planted a technoseed in the heart of an experimental generator at S.T.A.R. Labs in New York City. When the generator exploded, Brimstone emerged and began a rampage throughout the city. Believing himself to be a fallen angel of some mysterious, avenging god, Brimstone soon encountered a number of heroes, including FIRESTORM, THE NUCLEAR MAN and the JUSTICE LEAGUE OF AMERICA. Discovering Brimstone's true nature as a ball of super-heated plasma, the newly formed SUICIDE SQUAD tracked the giant down and destroyed him by disrupting the magnetic fields that gave him form.

Since then, Brimstone has been recreated a number of times, always bringing carnage and destruction. PJ

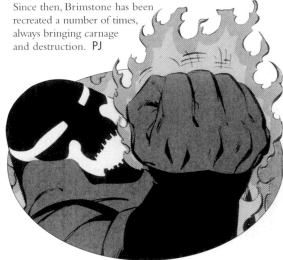

BRONZE TIGER

FIRST APPEARANCE RICHARD DRAGON: KUNG-FU FIGHTER #1
(May 1975)
STATUS Hero REAL NAME Benjamin Turner
OCCUPATION Martial arts master BASE Detroit
HEIGHT 6ft 3in WEIGHT 240 lbs EYES Brown HAIR Black
SPECIAL POWERS/ABILITIES Master of martial-arts disciplines, including
Jeet Kune Do, Hap Kido, Silat, and Savate.

Ben Turner began his fighting career on the mean streets of East St Louis. He developed an interest in martial arts and eventually became a student of the deadly Sensei, leader of the so-called LEAGUE OF ASSASSINS, whose tutelage forged Turner into the human fighting machine known as the Bronze Tiger. As the Tiger, Turner turned against the League while fighting alongside fellow martial artist Richard Dragon (see DRAGON, RICHARD) and, later, the SUICIDE SQUAD assembled by Amanda Waller (see WALLER, AMANDA). He has also joined with BATMAN, BLACK CANARY, and others to battle martial-arts cabals such as the Brotherhood of the Monkey Fist and the Circle of Six. SB

BRAINIAC

SIDESHOW MENTALIST

FIRST APPEARANCE ACTION COMICS #242 (July 1958)
STATUS Villain **REAL NAME** Vril Dox
OCCUPATION Cyber Conqueror **BASE** Mobile
HEIGHT Variable **WEIGHT** Variable **EYES** Red **HAIR** None
SPECIAL POWERS/ABILITIES A vast, superior intelligence limited only by the technology it currently inhabits. Knowledge of the universe is unparalleled, yet its hubris and emotions restrict its potential.

ONCE SCIENTIST PRIME on distant Colu, Vril Dox attempted to overthrow his technologically advanced world's Supreme Authority. Dox paid for his rebellion by being disintegrated. Yet somehow, his computer-like mind remained intact, traveling thousands of light years to Earth. Using his vast telepathic and psychokinetic abilities, Dox possessed the body of a sideshow mentalist named Milton Fine, to become the power-hungry Brainiac. When Fine's body proved too frail to contain Brainiac's power consciousness, he sought more suitable hosts, each time coming into opposition with SUPERMAN.

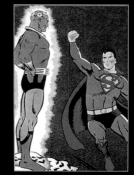

FOES Brainiac's first meeting with the Man of Steel.

REMAKE AND REMODEL

In the course of his attempts to conquer Earth, Brainiac has upgraded himself many times, even inhabiting the body of Superman's nemesis DOOMSDAY. Brainiac downloaded his evolved alien psyche into a flawless android shell to become Brainiac 2.5 and threaten Earth with his Omega Spears. These weapons generated an energy web that could shatter the world. After Superman thwarted this scheme, Brainiac 2.5 attempted to increase his personal power by linking all the world's computers, but instead created a portal that enabled his massive, all-powerful future self, Brainiac 13, to enter the 21st century. It took the combined efforts of Brainiac 2.5, Lex Luthor (see LUTHOR, LEX), and Superman to stop the computer tyrant. While the B13 persona was trapped in a Kryptonian warsuit, Brainiac's modern-day incarnation was trapped within the infant body of Lex's daughter, Lena. To save Metropolis from both present and future androids, Luthor was forced to bargain away his own daughter! At least B13 did help Earth stave off the threat of the cosmic conqueror IMPERIEX. Superman helped teleport the android to the dawn of creation. There, Brainiac 13's energies, coupled with the "Big Bang" itself, created two vast explosions that scattered Brainiac's consciousness over 60 trillion light years of space and time. However, even this cataclysmic setback could not stop Brainiac, and he soon returned, resurrected in the body of the infant clone of the anti-matter universe's Ultraman (see CRIME SYNDICATE). **RG**

MULTIPLE FORMS *Over the years, Brainiac has been constantly upgraded. The skull-shaped vessel (above) attempted an attack on the Earth. It took Superman and other heroes to repel the invasion and avoid panic in the skies.*

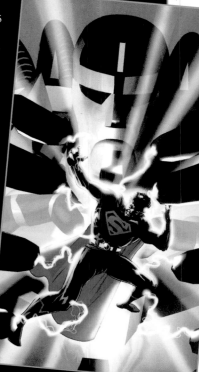

BRAINWAVE *The B13 incarnation nearly destroyed Superman and overwrote the entire city of Metropolis.*

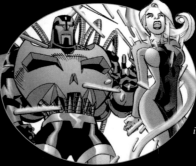

EXCHANGE *Brainiac 2.5, seen here with Lex Luthor's daughter, a pawn in a greater game.*

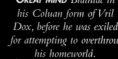

GREAT MIND *Brainiac in his Coluan form of Vril Dox, before he was exiled for attempting to overthrow his homeworld.*

KEY STORYLINES

• **SUPERMAN Y2K** (TPB, 2001): Brainiac 13 reaches back from the 30th century to try to control Superman and Metropolis.
• **PANIC IN THE SKIES** (TPB, 1993): Brainiac launches an all-out assault on the Earth.
• **THE LUTHOR-BRAINIAC TEAM, SUPERMAN** (2ND SERIES) #27-28: Together, the two masterminds attempt to bring down the Man of Steel.
• **SUPERMAN: THE DOOMSDAY WARS** (TPB, 1999): Brainiac takes over Doomsday.

BROTHERHOOD OF DADA

FIRST APPEARANCE DOOM PATROL (2nd series) #26 (September 1989)
STATUS Anarchic rogues **BASE** Mobile
SPECIAL POWERS/ABILITIES
Mister Nobody (deceased) Can drain the sanity from others.
Sleepwalk Vast superstrength while sleepwalking.
Frenzy Transforms into a whirling cyclone.
Fog Transforms into psychedelic cloud that obsorbs human beings.
Quiz Manifests every super-power *never* thought of.
Agent "!" (deceased) Blends into any crowd.
Number None Can occupy anyone or anything.
Alias the Blur (deceased) Can consume chunks of time.
The Toy Powers unknown.

A man known only as Mister Morden was an unscrupulous scientist who longed to join the nefarious Brotherhood of Evil (*see* SOCIETY OF SIN). But Morden doublecrossed the Brotherhood and, fleeing their wrath, escaped to Paraguay. There, Morden met a former Nazi war criminal named Dr. Bruckner and agreed to be the guinea pig for one of Bruckner's experiments. Morden was driven insane before being transformed into the abstract man called MISTER NOBODY. Mister Nobody then traveled across the world, gathering other strange outcasts, including Sleepwalk, Frenzy, the Fog, and the Quiz. Mister Nobody took these outcasts and organized a new syndicate that pledged itself to the absurdity of life. Believing evil was an outdated concept, Mister Nobody christened himself and his companions the Brotherhood of Dada. The Brotherhood proceeded to steal a mystic painting that had the power to devour any being that beheld it. The Brotherhood of Dada unleashed the painting on Paris, absorbing the city. The DOOM PATROL arrived in the nick of time, saving the city of Paris from the painting and returning it to our world. The Brotherhood, however, chose to remain in the strange world inside. Mister Nobody later escaped the painting and assembled a new Brotherhood of Dada, including Agent "!", Number None, Alias the Blur, and the Toy.

After trying to promote their cheerful form of anarchy on a worldwide tour, the Brotherhood tried to dissipate the barriers between the magic painting and our reality, but were stopped by the government and the Doom Patrol. **PJ**

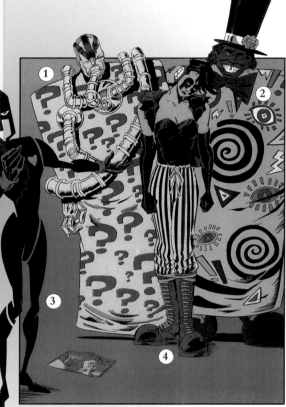

GROUP ABSURDITY *The Brotherhood of Dada encouraged the outrageous and the absurd. Tragically, they were thwarted by the mundane normalcy of humanity. The Brotherhood included* **1)** *the Quiz* **2)** *Frenzy* **3)** *Mister Nobody* **4)** *Sleepwalk.*

BROTHER BLOOD

FIRST APPEARANCE NEW TEEN TITANS #21 (July 1982)
STATUS Villain **REAL NAME** Unknown
OCCUPATION High priest **BASE** Zandia
HEIGHT 6ft 2in **WEIGHT** 193 lbs **EYES** Gray **HAIR** Black
SPECIAL POWERS/ABILITIES Circuitry built into his uniform of office generates bolts of energy; cloak has undefined mystical qualities.

The first Brother Blood was the high priest of the Baltic country of Zandia who refused to supply recruits for Pope Innocent's Fourth Crusade in 1202. During the ensuing battle, the high priest gained the Cloak of Christ, allegedly worn at the Last Supper, but now corrupted with evil. Wearing the cloak, the priest led his knights to victory. He then bathed in his enemies' blood, which gave him great strength and virtual immortality. The priest declared himself Brother Blood and closed Zandia to all strangers.

He ruled for 60 years, fathering a son who killed him at the age of 100. So began the terrible Curse of Blood, whereby each son of Zandia's ruler slew his father, bathed in the Bloodpit, then ruled in his place.

This gruesome pattern of events has recently continued as yet another son has killed his father. However, this particular 14-year-old lacks the training of his predecessors. Instead, his ultimate goal is world domination using his church's might. The OUTSIDERS and TEEN TITANS, though, stand in his way. **RG**

BROTHER POWER, THE GEEK

FIRST APPEARANCE BROTHER POWER, THE GEEK #1 (October 1968)
STATUS Hero **REAL NAME** None
OCCUPATION Puppet elemental **BASE** Mobile
HEIGHT 6ft **WEIGHT** 150 lbs **EYES** Blue **HAIR** Yellow
SPECIAL POWERS/ABILITIES Superstrength; resistant to injury; can manifest in puppets, mannequins, or other representations of man.

After a bummer of an evening one night in San Francisco, two put-upon hippies named Brother Nick and Brother Paul hung some of their threads on a tailor's rag-doll dummy in an abandoned clothing shop. A lightning strike, combined with the era's groovy vibes, somehow animated the dummy and transformed him into Earth's only "puppet elemental."

Brother Power the Geek drifted throughout California, helping out fellow free spirits and learning about the world in a series of unlikely predicaments. When a big-top promoter kidnapped Brother Power to be the centerpiece of his "Psychedelic Circus," Brother Nick and Brother Paul returned to spring their puppet-brother so he could continue his road-trip search for truth. Eventually he took a cosmic voyage aboard an experimental space missile that blasted into orbit. Years later he returned to Earth in Tampa, Florida, and from there continued his far-out wanderings. Brother Power appeared at John Constantine's 2000 New Year's party, where he was recognized as one of the totems of the new millennium. **DW**

BRUTALE

FIRST APPEARANCE NIGHTWING #22 (July 1998)
STATUS Villain **REAL NAME** Guillermo Barrera
OCCUPATION Mercenary **BASE** Hascaragua
HEIGHT 5ft 4in **WEIGHT** 145 lbs **EYES** Almond **HAIR** Black
SPECIAL POWERS/ABILITIES Master of knives, particularly his double-edge throwing knives, surgical scalpels, shivs, daggers, and machetes.

Guillermo Barrera was the most vicious police interrogator in the South American country of Hascaragua. He used his brutal torturing skills as a member of the secret police of a Cuban-backed Marxist regime. At last, the regime fell and Barrera faced execution for his atrocious crimes. He fled his homeland and became a freelance killer under the name of Brutale. The diminutive assassin-for-hire, donned a special uniform designed to hold his many and varied blades and knives. Working alongside Stallion, another assassin, Brutale was hired by Roland Desmond, the Blüdhaven criminal mastermind BLOCKBUSTER, to kill BATMAN's ally NIGHTWING. Brutale began the hunt, but Nightwing quickly defeated both would-be assassins. Brutale, however, escaped in a desperate effort to avoid incarceration and deportation to Hascaragua. **PJ**

56

BULLETGIRL I & II (WINDSHEAR)

FIRST APPEARANCE MASTER COMICS #13 (April 1941)
STATUS Hero (deceased) **REAL NAME** Susan Kent
OCCUPATION Adventurer **BASE** Fawcett City
HEIGHT 5ft 9in **WEIGHT** 145 lbs **EYES** Blue **HAIR** Brown
SPECIAL POWERS/ABILITIES An excellent flyer.

FIRST APPEARANCE POWER OF SHAZAM! #32 (November 1997)
STATUS Hero **REAL NAME** Deanna Barr
OCCUPATION Adventurer **BASE** Fawcett City
HEIGHT 5ft 8in **WEIGHT** 135 lbs **EYES** Blue **HAIR** Brown
SPECIAL POWERS/ABILITIES Army-trained marksman, pilot, and hand-to-hand combatant.

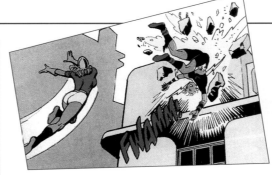

POWER OF THE BULLET *Windshear, the second Bulletgirl, honors her parents with bravery and gusto.*

Susan Kent was sure there was something strange about her boyfriend, Jim Barr. Eventually she learned his secret—he was the super hero BULLETMAN! Susan insisted on accompanying him as Bulletgirl. Together they battled many villains during World War II. After the war, Jim and Susan were married and they retired from costume crime fighting in the mid-1950s. They raised a daughter, Deanna, and made a comfortable home in Fawcett City. After Susan died from unexplained causes, Deanna followed in their footsteps as Windshear, after stealing her mother's Bulletgirl outfit. Jim Barr returned to action one final time, teaming with his daughter to save Billy Batson (see CAPTAIN MARVEL), Mary Bromfield (see MARY MARVEL), and Freddy Freeman from CHAIN LIGHTNING. **RG**

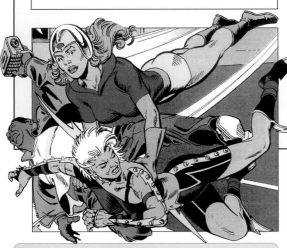

BULLETMAN

FIRST APPEARANCE NICKEL COMICS #1 (May 1940)
STATUS Hero (retired) **REAL NAME** James Barr
OCCUPATION Adventurer **BASE** Fawcett City
HEIGHT 6ft 4in **WEIGHT** 177 lbs **EYES** Blue **HAIR** White
SPECIAL POWERS/ABILITIES Brilliant to begin with, the Miraclo variation permanently increased his physical size, strength, and mental abilities; an excellent flyer and tactician.

Jim Barr, the son of a slain Fawcett City police officer, developed a variant of HAWKMAN's Thanagarian Nth metal and HOURMAN's Miraclo/steroid compound and took flight as Bulletman. He joined the wave of costumed adventurers that kept the U.S.'s cities safe during World War II. He was soon accompanied by his girlfriend Susan Kent, who became BULLETGIRL. Bulletman was the first American hero targeted by CAPTAIN NAZI. He later teamed up with STARMAN to stop a Nazi incursion into Alaska. There, the heroes encountered a scouting expedition by Venusian worms that was only curtailed by the intervention of GREEN LANTERN Abin Sur. After the war, Jim and Susan married and settled down in Fawcett City, where Jim built a merchandising empire based on Bulletman. When Barr was accused of having committed treason in 1942, CAPTAIN MARVEL and Starman VI cleared the veteran's name. **RG**

BULLOCK, SGT.

FIRST APPEARANCE DETECTIVE COMICS #441 (June 1974)
STATUS Hero **REAL NAME** Harvey Bullock
OCCUPATION Former police officer **BASE** Gotham City
HEIGHT 5ft 10in **WEIGHT** 248 lbs **EYES** Brown **HAIR** Black
SPECIAL POWERS/ABILITIES Despite shabby appearance, has sharp deductive mind; virtually unstoppable in a brawl.

Harvey Bullock wears his moods on his sleeve, along with the crumbs that fall from the donuts he munches whenever he's not chewing on a soggy cigar. A corrupt mayor made him James Gordon's assistant in order to keep an eye on the commissioner (see GORDON, JAMES W.). Developing a deep respect for his boss, Bullock told the mayor where to stick it and became an ally of both Gordon and BATMAN. Bullock later worked for the U.S. government's CHECKMATE agency as a Bishop, but soon returned to Gotham. He aided the city during the catastrophe known as No Man's Land and became head of the G.C.P.D. Major Crimes Unit. When a gunman nearly killed Gordon, Bullock helped the would-be killer's mob enemies rub the hood out. The unit came down on Bullock for his role in the affair and he quit the force. His post has been filled by Maggie Sawyer. Bullock now sits at home, drowning his frustration with alcohol. **DW**

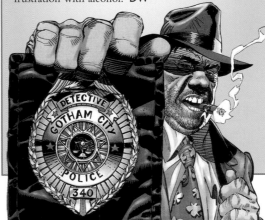

BUMBLEBEE

FIRST APPEARANCE TEEN TITANS (1st series) #45 (December 1976)
STATUS Hero **REAL NAME** Karen Beecher-Duncan
OCCUPATION Research engineer; writer **BASE** San Francisco
HEIGHT 5ft 7in **WEIGHT** 130 lbs **EYES** Brown **HAIR** Black
SPECIAL POWERS/ABILITIES Solar-powered antennae in cybernetic helmet create electrical "stings" emitted through quartz prism eyepieces; exoskeletal wings enable flight and create sonic disruptions.

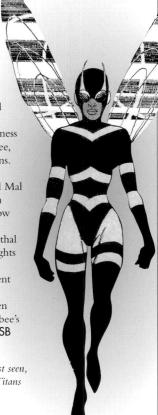

The girlfriend of Mal Duncan during his membership with the original TEEN TITANS, Karen Beecher helped Mal to develop his sonic Gabriel's Horn and later created her own costumed secret identity in order to help Mal prove his worthiness to the Titans. As Bumblebee, Karen also joined the Titans. Following the first team's dissolution, Karen married Mal and the two moved to San Francisco, where Karen now works as a S.T.A.R. Labs engineer designing non-lethal weapons. She also moonlights as a science fiction and fantasy writer. An infrequent member of the on-again, off-again Titans West, Karen occasionally dons Bumblebee's wings if called to action. **SB**

JUST FOR THE BUZZ *When last seen, Bumblebee teamed with the Titans and the JLA to thwart the extraterrestrial Technis.*

BUSHMASTER

FIRST APPEARANCE SUPER FRIENDS (November 1977): (in DCU continuity) DC COMICS PRESENTS #46 (July 1982)
STATUS Hero (deceased) **REAL NAME** Bernal Rojas
OCCUPATION Herpetologist **BASE** The Dome
HEIGHT 5ft 10in **WEIGHT** 175 lbs **EYES** Brown **HAIR** Brown
SPECIAL POWERS/ABILITIES Cybernetic costume allowed him to duplicate various reptilian abilities, including infrared vision, suction devices on hands and feet, a venom gun, heat sensors, camouflage, and flight.

Bernal Rojas was a renowned herpetologist from Caracas, Venezuela. Using his knowledge of reptiles from all over the world, Rojas invented a special costume that allowed him to duplicate various reptilian abilities. Donning this garish cyber suit, Rojas called himself the Bushmaster and became a crime-fighting crusader in his native Venezuela. Bushmaster was one of the founding members of the GLOBAL GUARDIANS, a worldwide organization of heroes formed by the mysterious DOCTOR MIST, that fought both local crime and cosmic invaders. Bushmaster was shot and killed by bank robbers as he was also being attacked by one of Doctor Mist's enemies, a madman named Fain Y'Onia. **PJ**

57

CACHIRU

FIRST APPEARANCE THE FLASH ANNUAL (2nd series) #13 (2000)
STATUS Hero **REAL NAME** Unrevealed
OCCUPATION Adventurer **BASE** Argentina
HEIGHT 5ft 9in **WEIGHT** 170 lbs **EYES** Blue **HAIR** Black
SPECIAL POWERS/ABILITIES Capable of flight, although not at great heights or with great speed; experienced hand-to-hand combatant who relies on his talons for greater advantage.

Argentina has its own team of costumed protectors, the SUPER-MALON (which includes Cimarron, El Bagual, El Lobizon, El Yaguarete, Pampero, SALAMANCA, and Vizacacha). Among them is Cachiru, with his owl-like mask and razor-sharp talons. A veteran crime fighter, he earned the FLASH III's respect when they shared an adventure together. He had been fellow teammate Salamanca's lover, and still pines for her, long after their breakup. **RG**

CAIN, DAVID

FIRST APPEARANCE BATMAN #567 (July 1999)
STATUS Villain **REAL NAME** Unknown; possibly David Cain
OCCUPATION Adventurer **BASE** Incarcerated in Black Gate Prison
HEIGHT 6ft 2in **WEIGHT** 245 lbs **EYES** Blue **HAIR** Gray
SPECIAL POWERS/ABILITIES One of the world's greatest martial artists; knows every move of every fighting style on the planet; highly skilled with every kind of firearm.

Cain is one of the most proficient assassins in the world. Quiet and focused, Cain considers killing an art form. Cain was Bruce Wayne's martial-arts master for a brief time, training the young millionaire before clashing with Wayne over methodology. Cain had also adopted an infant girl named Cassandra whom he raised to be his assistant and successor. Teaching Cassandra the "language" of martial arts but no other, Cain devoted himself so exclusively to her upbringing that the rest of the world thought he had died. Several years later Cassandra learned that she had been raised to be a murderer and fled from Cain in horror.

The gang boss TWO-FACE subsequently hired Cain to kill Commissioner Gordon (see GORDON, JAMES W.) in Gotham City. There, Cain confronted Cassandra, now BATGIRL, who rejected him and allied herself with BATMAN. Cain gave himself over to the GCPD and is in jail, awaiting trial. **PJ**

CAIN AND ABEL

FIRST APPEARANCE (Abel) HOUSE OF SECRETS (1st series) #81 (August 1969); (Cain) HOUSE OF MYSTERY #175 (July 1968)
STATUS Heroes **REAL NAMES** None
OCCUPATION Caretakers/storytellers **BASE** The House of Secrets (Abel); The House of Mystery (Cain)
HEIGHT 5ft 7in (Abel); 6ft 2in (Cain)
WEIGHT 396 lbs (Abel); 174 lbs (Cain)
EYES Blue (Abel); brown (Cain) **HAIR** Black (Abel); brown (Cain)
SPECIAL POWERS/ABILITIES Can both be endlessly resurrected.

Inhabitants of the mystical, supernatural realm known as Dreaming, Cain and Abel are believed to be the original "first victim/first murderer" of Biblical lore. After Abel's initial death at Cain's hands—triggered by an argument over a woman—Morpheus, the Lord of Dreams, gave them both positions as storytellers.

On Earth, the brothers work as caretakers for two eerie structures located on opposite sides of a cemetery in the hills of Kentucky. Abel watches over The House of Secrets and Cain is custodian of The House of Mystery. They both delight in telling horrific tales to visitors.

When the Furies of Greek legend killed Abel, his death looked permanent, but Cain won his brother a special resurrection from the new Lord of Dreams by claiming that his contract with Morpheus stipulated that Cain and Abel were to remain a "double act." Cain has now resumed his habit of murdering Abel in continual reenactments of the "first story," secure in the knowledge that the ceremony causes Abel no lasting harm. **DW**

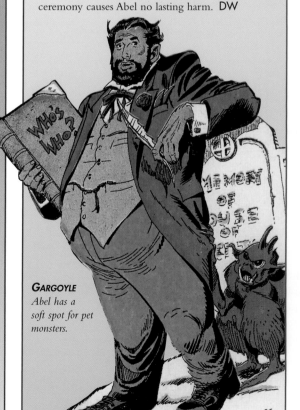

GARGOYLE
Abel has a soft spot for pet monsters.

CADRE, THE

FIRST APPEARANCE JUSTICE LEAGUE OF AMERICA #235 (February 1985) **BASE** Mobile
ORIGINAL MEMBERS AND POWERS
Overmaster (leader) Alien superbeing.
Black Mass Wristbands provide control over graviton particles.
Crowbar Wields energized crowbar.
Fastball Throws explosive spheres using powered exoskeleton.
Nightfall Wristbands create null-field that absorbs light and energy.
Shatterfist Martial artist with energy-charged hands.
Shrike (deceased) Possessed a paralyzing shriek; flew at superspeed.

A creation of the near-omnipotent alien being the OVERMASTER, the Cadre has existed in many forms. The original Cadre consisted of Black Mass, Crowbar, Fastball, Nightfall, Shatterfist, and Shrike. They battled the JUSTICE LEAGUE OF AMERICA in a contest designed to prove to the Overmaster whether the human race deserved to survive. After his team's defeat, the Overmaster gathered many new recruits to his cause and arrived at Mount Everest on Earth at the head of his new, massive Cadre. CAPTAIN ATOM and the Justice League fought back against the Cadre, claiming victory by detonating the alien tyrant's starship. Since then a few villains have attempted to start a new Cadre separate from the Overmaster's influence. **DW**

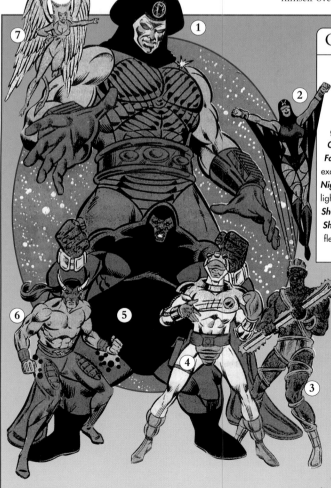

THE ORIGINAL CADRE 1) *The Overmaster* **2)** *Nightfall* **3)** *Crowbar* **4)** *Fastball* **5)** *Black Mass* **6)** *Shatterfist* **7)** *Shrike*

CAPTAIN ATOM

FIRST APPEARANCE SPACE ADVENTURES #33 (March 1960)
STATUS Hero (missing in action) **REAL NAME** Nathaniel Christopher
Adam, a.k.a. Cameron Scott **OCCUPATION** Super hero **BASE** San
Francisco **HEIGHT** 6ft 4in **WEIGHT** 200 lbs **EYES** Blue **HAIR** White
SPECIAL POWERS/ABILITIES Alien alloy covering body enables him to tap
into the quantum field, which gives him superstrength, anti-gravity,
and the ability to emit focused blasts of atomic energy; capable of
absorbing nuclear energy and quantum leaping one day to one
week into the future.

Decades ago, court-
martialed Air Force
Captain Nathaniel Adam
volunteered for the top-secret
Captain Atom Project in order to
prove his innocence to charges of
murder and treason. Adam's
superiors theorized that a strange
alien alloy would protect him from
an atomic blast, a disastrous
experiment that melded the alloy to
Adam's body and catapulted him 18 years
into the future. When the quantum-powered
Adam reappeared, he was pardoned in
exchange for service as the U.S.-sanctioned super
hero, Captain Atom, a federally mandated member
of Justice League International (see JUSTICE LEAGUE OF
AMERICA). Captain Atom ultimately left Justice League's
European branch to form a more proactive but short-lived
super-heroic strike force, EXTREME JUSTICE. Later, Atom
joined the L.A.W. (Last American Warriors) before
reuniting with several former League teammates as
the "Super Buddies." Adam is married to Bette
Sans Souci (PLASTIQUE), an EJ teammate. **SB**

THE VILLAIN RETURNS *Digger Harkness
may be the most immoral member of
the Flash's Rogues Gallery.*

CAPTAIN BOOMERANG

FIRST APPEARANCE FLASH #117 (December 1960)
STATUS Villain **REAL NAME** George Harkness
OCCUPATION Criminal **BASE** Keystone City
HEIGHT 5ft 9in **WEIGHT** 167 lbs **EYES** Brown **HAIR** Brown
SPECIAL POWERS/ABILITIES A boomerang-throwing expert, he has
developed numerous boomerangs with specific functions.

COME BACK *Captain Boomerang
applied his native talent to
incredible devices such as this
deadly trap for the Flash II.*

A native of Australia, George "Digger" Harkness was sent as a
young adult to the U.S. by his mother, who was desperate to get
her son away from his stepfather. He took a job demonstrating
boomerangs for the Wiggins Game Company. Harkness, who had
become an expert from years of throwing the wooden device as
a kid, was given a uniform and the name Captain Boomerang.
While demonstrating the boomerang to kids, Harkness liked to
line his pockets with a spot of pilfering. This brought him into
conflict with the second FLASH, whom Harkness opposed as
Captain Boomerang with a variety of ever more bizarre
boomerang gadgets. After the Flash's death, Captain
Boomerang served on the government-sponsored SUICIDE
SQUAD. However, he missed the thrill of stealing and secretly
became MIRROR MASTER II. After the Squad temporarily
folded, Captain Boomerang returned to a life of crime in
Central City, opposed by Flash III. He was one of the
rogues who sold his soul to NERON, but in time it was
restored. However, Harkness remains an utterly
immoral and avaricious villain. **RG**

CAPTAIN COLD

FIRST APPEARANCE SHOWCASE #8 (May 1957)
STATUS Villain **REAL NAME** Leonard Snart
OCCUPATION Professional criminal **BASES** Central City/Keystone City
HEIGHT 6ft 2in **WEIGHT** 196 lbs **EYES** Brown **HAIR** Brown
SPECIAL POWERS/ABILITIES Cold-guns create ice slicks, shatter metal,
or entomb victims in suspended animation in blocks of ice.
Snow goggles minimize the flashes given off by Captain Cold's guns.

Raised by an abusive father, Leonard Snart found rare
solace in the company of his grandfather, who drove an
ice truck. Snart is one of the more sympathetic villains in
the FLASH's Rogues Gallery, able to chat over a coffee
while plotting to break into the
Keystone City Bank over the
weekend. He began his crime
career shortly after Barry Allen's
debut as the Flash. Developing
an experimental handgun to
interfere with the Flash's
superspeed, Snart accidentally
irradiated his weapon and wound
up with a tool that could freeze
the moisture in the air. He
donned a parka and goggles and
declared himself Captain Cold. He
committed a string of (non-lethal)

crimes throughout Central and Keystone City, but his main
pleasure lay in matching wits with the Flash. After Barry
Allen's death during the Crisis (see Great Battles,
pp. 320–1), a disheartened Snart left crime to become a
licensed bounty hunter with his sister Lisa, the GOLDEN
GLIDER. Captain Cold lost his eternal soul to the
demonic NERON, but the third Flash, Wally West,
brought him back to the land of the living. He soon
returned to crime, this time as a member of Wally's
Rogues Gallery. Captain Cold recently killed the
villain Chillblaine in revenge for the death of
his sister Lisa. He also helped an amnesiac
Wally West defeat Mister Element. Yet, Snart
remains an unrepentant crook, who *hates*
being mistaken for MISTER FREEZE. **DW**

SLIPPERY SLOPE *Even the great Barry
Allen often fell victim to Captain
Cold's ice tricks.*

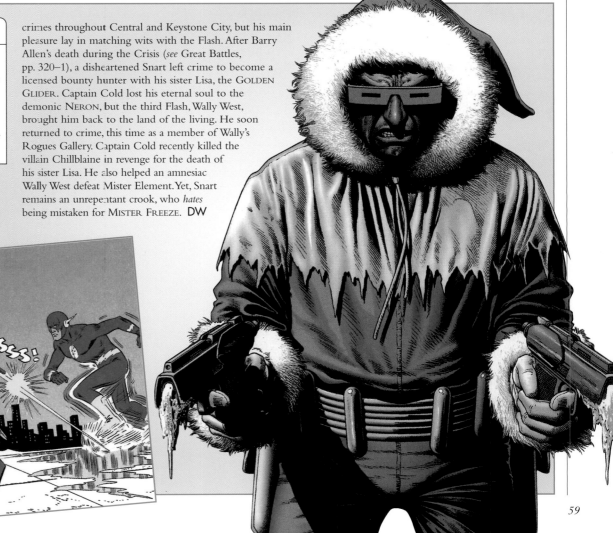

CAPTAIN COMET

FIRST APPEARANCE STRANGE ADVENTURES #9 (June 1951)
STATUS Hero **REAL NAME** Adam Blake
OCCUPATION Interstellar operative **BASE** The planet Cairn
HEIGHT 6ft 2in **WEIGHT** 190 lbs **EYES** Brown **HAIR** Brown
SPECIAL POWERS/ABILITIES Superstrength, superspeed, limited invulnerability, telepathy, telekinesis, flight, slowed aging, photographic memory, vast intelligence, and athletic prowess.

Born in 1931, Adam Blake began displaying his mutant abilities by age eight when he read and memorized every fact in a set of encyclopedias. By his 18th birthday he had mastered sports, music, and science, but kept his unusual abilities a secret. He finally revealed his amazing powers to physicist Emery Zackro. Blake discovered that he was a mutant born with the abilities of a man 100,000 years in the future. When aliens attacked Earth in the 1950s, Adam took the name Captain Comet and repelled their invasion force.

Captain Comet eventually left Earth to seek adventure in space, traveling across the galaxy. After he was captured by the criminal Dagon-Ra, Captain Comet was released from captivity by members of L.E.G.I.O.N. and joined their ranks, fighting alongside the police force in all its various incarnations, including R.E.B.E.L.S. **PJ**

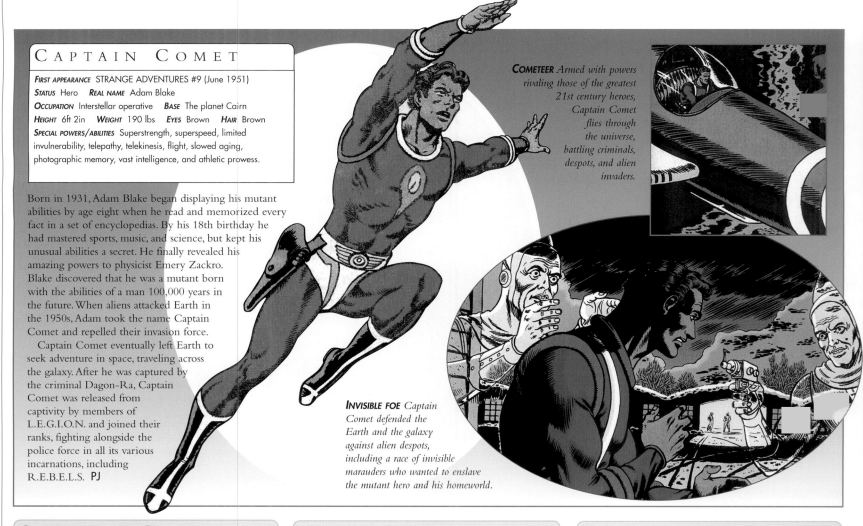

COMETEER Armed with powers rivaling those of the greatest 21st century heroes, Captain Comet flies through the universe, battling criminals, despots, and alien invaders.

INVISIBLE FOE Captain Comet defended the Earth and the galaxy against alien despots, including a race of invisible marauders who wanted to enslave the mutant hero and his homeworld.

CAPTAIN COMPASS

FIRST APPEARANCE STAR-SPANGLED COMICS #83 (August 1948)
STATUS Hero **REAL NAME** Mark Compass
OCCUPATION Adventurer **BASE** The High Seas
HEIGHT 6ft **WEIGHT** 175 lbs **EYES** Brown **HAIR** Brown
SPECIAL POWERS/ABILITIES A skilled fighter with a keen deductive mind.

Mark Compass first acquired his sea legs as a frogman for the U.S. Navy, later commanding a few of the ships he had first served upon. In that regard, he became well-known as a capable and courageous captain, as well as a noted nautical investigator.

Following his naval stint, Compass was employed as a roving troubleshooter for Penny Steamship Lines. In his capacity as ship's detective aboard the *S.S. Nautilus*, Compass solved many mysteries on the high seas, as well as preventing crimes on the *Nautilus* and other vessels in the Penny Steamship Lines fleet.

At various times over the years, Compass even commanded the *Nautilus* himself. It is this ship in particular that he now calls his home. Captain Compass lives in his own personal cabin suite and enjoys semi-retirement while sleuthing the occasional seaborne mystery. **SB**

CAPTAIN FEAR

FIRST APPEARANCE ADVENTURE COMICS #425 (January 1973)
STATUS Hero (deceased) **REAL NAME** Fero
OCCUPATION Pirate **BASE** The Caribbean
HEIGHT 5ft 6in **WEIGHT** 160 lbs **EYES** Blue **HAIR** Black
SPECIAL POWERS/ABILITIES Excellent swordsman, sailor, and fighter, matched only by his skills as a leader and tactician; an average pilot and navigator.

Fero, a young Carib Indian, was taken captive in a Spanish raid sometime in the 16th century. Enslaved and put to work in a Spanish mine, Fero led the captives in a revolt against their oppressors. After stealing a Spanish galleon, losing its crew to a terrible storm at sea, and challenging and winning a duel with another pirate captain, Fero assumed the name Captain Fear. He sailed across the Caribbean, harrying the Spanish conquistadors of the day while protecting his fellow natives.

When his wife was expecting their first child, Captain Fear planned to retire from life on the high seas after a final voyage with a man named Baron Hemlocke. Instead, Hemlocke's butchery during an attack on a Spanish vessel sullied the reputation of Fero and his crew, who vowed to take revenge. Tragically, Captain Fear and his men were killed by Hemlocke's demonic forces, and were doomed to wander the seas forever as spirits. **RG**

CAPTAIN HUNTER

FIRST APPEARANCE SECRET FILES & ORIGINS GUIDE TO THE DC UNIVERSE 2000 #1 (March 2000)
STATUS Hero **REAL NAME** Lucius Hunter
OCCUPATION Adventurer **BASE** Mobile
HEIGHT 6ft 1in **WEIGHT** 196 lbs **EYES** Blue **HAIR** Brown
SPECIAL POWERS/ABILITIES Excellent combatant and field leader; body enhanced through transplants.

The name Hunter has earned merit through six decades of service to the U.S. military. Lieutenant Ben Hunter turned a bunch of ex-convicts into a crack squad nicknamed "HUNTER'S HELLCATS", seeing action in some of the worst battles of World War II. Ben Hunter's twin sons, Nick and Phil, became a major in the Air Force and a captain with the Green Berets respectively, serving with distinction in Korea and Vietnam. In more modern times, Captain Lucius Hunter leads the latest group of CREATURE COMMANDOS for the top-secret Project M. **DW**

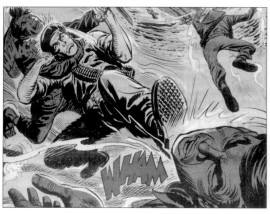

CAPTAIN MARVEL JR.

FIRST APPEARANCE WHIZ COMICS #25 (December 1941)
STATUS Hero **REAL NAME** Frederick "Freddy" Freeman
OCCUPATION Adventurer **BASE** New York City; Fawcett City
HEIGHT 5ft 10in **WEIGHT** 164 lbs **EYES** Blue **HAIR** Black
SPECIAL POWERS/ABILITIES By saying "Captain Marvel" aloud, he gains
Solomon's wisdom, Hercules's superstrength, Atlas's stamina, Zeus's
raw power, Achilles's courage, and Mercury's superspeed. Captain
Marvel Jr. shares powers with Mary Marvel and Captain Marvel; if
either is using their powers, he has access to only half his power.

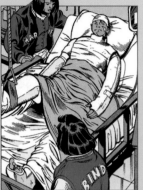

BRAVERY The teenage Freddy
was crippled and nearly
killed by Captain Nazi.

A WELL-MANNERED TEENAGER who excelled not only
academically but athletically, Frederick "Freddy"
Freeman was orphaned when his parents died in a
boating accident. After the accident, Freddy moved from
New York to Fawcett City to live with his grandparents,
Jacob and Elizabeth. Shortly after moving to Fawcett
City, Freddy was kidnapped by the demonic SABBAC,
who mistakenly believed Freeman to be Billy Batson, the
young alter ego of CAPTAIN MARVEL, the World's
Mightiest Mortal. Freed from Sabbac's evil clutches by
his idol, Captain Marvel, Freddy subsequently became
one of Billy Batson's closest friends, unaware that the
young Batson was in truth the hero he so admired.

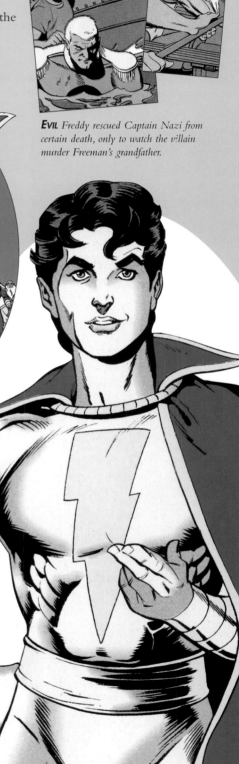

EVIL Freddy rescued Captain Nazi from
certain death, only to watch the villain
murder Freeman's grandfather.

THE WORLD'S MIGHTIEST BOY

Years later, however, Freddy learned Billy's secret identity after
Batson saved his sister, Mary (see MARY MARVEL), from IBAC.
Soon after, on a trip with his grandfather Jacob, Freddy saw
what he took to be Captain Marvel plummeting from the
heavens and crashing into the lake where he and his
grandfather were fishing. Freddy tried to save the man,
who turned out to be the villainous CAPTAIN NAZI,
awakened from a cryogenic sleep after decades. Captain
Nazi had been battling Captain Marvel in a spaceship above Earth before he was knocked
unconscious. Captain Nazi killed Freeman's grandfather, broke Freddy's back, and escaped.
Captain Marvel and Mary Marvel, desperate to save the Freddy's life, took him to a
secret sanctuary in a deserted subway tunnel. There they beseeched the wizard Shazam,
who had given them their powers, to help them save Freddy's life. The mage cryptically told
them that he did not have the power they needed, but Mary cleverly deduced the logic
behind the Wizard's riddle, and she and Captain Marvel agreed to split their amazing powers
with Freddy. The Wizard, gratified by the wisdom of his charges, enchanted the dying boy.
When Freddy awoke and spoke the words "Captain Marvel," he was transformed into the
World's Mightiest Boy. The three
Marvels began patrolling the skies of
Fawcett City together, and Freddy's romantic
feelings for Mary grew. Captain Marvel, still
technically a young teenager himself, grew
fiercely protective of his sister.

BOY ZONE As
Captain Marvel Jr.,
Freddy is the World's
Mightiest Boy!

After a fight between the two over Mary, the
headstrong Captain Marvel Jr. moved to New
York City, and promptly fell in love with the
schizophrenic villain CHAIN LIGHTNING.
Freddy soundly defeated Captain Nazi
and then changed his name to CM3,
announcing his "split" from the
Marvel "family." After a brief spell
with the TEEN TITANS, and a
short-lived affair with teammate
ARGENT II, CM3 was kidnapped
by CYBORG during the "Technis
Imperative."

MARVELOUS After
defeating Captain Nazi again,
Captain Marvel Jr. began
calling himself
CM3.

CM3 helped the JUSTICE LEAGUE OF AMERICA and the Titans
to free the Earth from the Cyborg's technological tyranny before
joining several other heroes in the short-lived Titans LA. When
that team disbanded, CM3, legally emancipated from his family
and liberated from his idol's legacy, returned to New York City,
fighting alongside Earth's forces during the Imperiex War (see
Great Battles, pp. 320–1) and occasionally helping the teenage
heroes of YOUNG JUSTICE. **PJ**

KEY STORYLINES
• **POWER OF SHAZAM #8 (OCTOBER 1995):**
The modern Freddy Freeman is introduced,
nearly dying at the hands of Captain Nazi!
• **TEEN TITANS #17-18 (JANUARY–FEBRUARY 1998):**
Captain Marvel Jr. joins the Titans after the teen
heroes hold a recruitment drive to swell their ranks.
• **POWER OF SHAZAM #37 (APRIL 1998):** Conquering his
internal demons—and the demon haunting his
dreams—Captain Marvel Jr. changes his name to CM3.
• **YOUNG JUSTICE #50 (DECEMBER 2002):** CM3 and
a horde of teenage heroes invade Zandia and battle
a host of super-villains lead by Lady Zand and the
Baron Agua Sin Gaaz!

CAPTAIN MARVEL

THE WORLD'S MIGHTIEST MORTAL

FIRST APPEARANCE WHIZ COMICS #1 (February 1940)
STATUS Hero **REAL NAME** William Joseph "Billy" Batson
OCCUPATION Radio Personality; super hero
BASE Fawcett City
HEIGHT (as Billy) 5ft 4in; (as Captain Marvel) 6ft 2in
WEIGHT (as Billy) 110 lbs; (as Captain Marvel) 215 lbs
EYES Blue **HAIR** Black
SPECIAL POWERS/ABILITIES
Virtually invulnerable and able to fly; possesses the wisdom of
Solomon, the strength of Hercules, the stamina of Atlas, the power of
Zeus, the courage of Achilles, and the speed of Mercury.

WITHOUT A DOUBT, Captain Marvel is the world's mightiest mortal, with strength and powers on a par with Superman. But unknown to many, this stalwart and virtuous super hero—by all appearances a middle-aged man—is really teenager Billy Batson. With one magic word, youthful Billy assumes the appearance and abilities of one of Earth's greatest and most respected heroes; however, he remains very much an innocent in heart and mind.

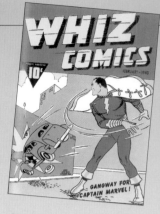

ARRIVAL *The Big Red Cheese was Fawcett Comics' answer to Superman and, for a time, was just as popular as the Man of Steel.*

ORPHANED AND BETRAYED
When Billy was just a boy, his parents—archaeologists C.C. and Marylin Batson—were killed by their treacherous assistant, Theo Adam (*see* BLACK ADAM), while on a dig at the tomb of Rameses II at Abu Simbel, Egypt. Billy was separated from his sister Mary and left in the care of their unscrupulous Uncle Ebenezer, C.C. Batson's half-brother. Unfortunately, Ebenezer threw Billy out and stole the youth's trust fund, money set aside for Billy's care and welfare.

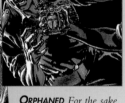

ORPHANED *For the sake of a jeweled scarab of untold power, Theo Adam murdered Billy's parents.*

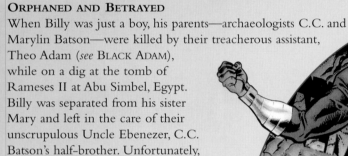

HEADING
Left penniless and homeless, Billy eked out a sorrowful existence in Fawcett City as a newsboy. For shelter, he often slept in the subway terminals. One night, a mysterious stranger—later revealed to be the spirit of Billy's father, C.C. Batson—convinced the orphaned lad to follow him deep into the subway tunnels, where a marvelous train decorated in hieroglyphics and mystic runes awaited them. Billy and the stranger rode the train deep into the bowels of the Earth and arrived in a cavern that held statues epitomizing the Seven Deadly Enemies of Man: Pride, Envy, Lust, Hatred, Selfishness, Laziness, and Injustice.

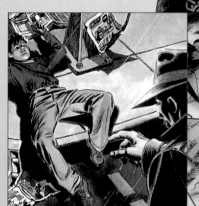

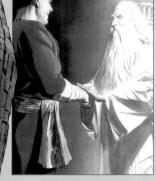

ROCK OF ETERNITY *Billy will make his home on this distant rock spire, assuming the mantle of Shazam.*

THE WIZARD'S ADVICE
As Captain Marvel turned back into Billy, the magical lightning bolt also struck a stone block poised above Shazam, apparently crushing the old wizard beneath its great weight. Shazam, however, did not die, but instead disappeared to the Rock of Eternity, a distant peak outside time and space. When called upon by Billy in future, Shazam would offer guidance, but not without first reminding the lad to use the marvellous powers at his disposal. He particularly urged Billy to use the wisdom of Solomon when faced by the perils of adolescence and other emotional and practical problems.

THE MAGIC WORD
Within that strange cavern, Billy met the ancient wizard Shazam, a champion of mankind for thousands of years. Withered with age, Shazam sat on a throne poised beneath a giant stone block suspended above him as if by magic. Shazam chose Billy to succeed him and granted the young orphan all of his extraordinary powers. By speaking the wizard's name, a lightning bolt transformed adolescent Billy into the adult Captain Marvel, a hero possessing the wisdom of Solomon, the strength of Hercules, the stamina of Atlas, the power of Zeus, the courage of Achilles, and the speed of Mercury. With this great gift also came responsibility: he must vow to uphold the cause of good and to battle the Seven Deadly Enemies of Man, duties that Billy promised faithfully to fulfill every time he uttered the name "Shazam!"

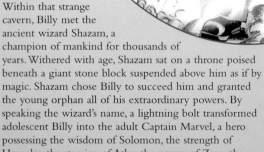

ANGRY AT FIRST *Billy was not sure if Shazam's great gifts were a blessing or a curse.*

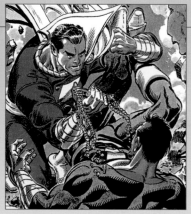

MERCY FOR A MURDERER

Captain Marvel's very first adventure found him battling Black Adam, his parents' killer enabled with his own superpowers. Theo Adam channeled the strengths of Teth-Adam, a man empowered with similar abilities by Shazam during Egypt's 19th dynasty via an ancient scarab amulet first discovered by Billy's parents. Captain Marvel defeated Black Adam by removing his amulet, thus stripping him of his powers, at least for a while. Instead of allowing the helpless Theo Adam to die in a collapsing museum, the good-hearted Captain Marvel spared the life of the man who murdered his family.

THE MARVEL FAMILY

Later, at the Rock of Eternity, Billy learned that the stranger who led him to Shazam was really his father. Billy chose to remain Captain Marvel and use Shazam's gifts for good, as well as to find his long-lost sister, MARY MARVEL.

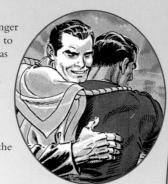

Eventually, Billy and Mary were reunited, and Captain Marvel decided to share his awesome abilities with her. He also gave some powers to their mutual friend, newsboy Freddy Freeman (see CAPTAIN MARVEL JR.), who had been crippled by the nefarious CAPTAIN NAZI. In the meantime, Captain Marvel became a member of the JUSTICE LEAGUE OF AMERICA, although Billy often felt inferior to his more confident super-heroic peers.

DO THE RIGHT THING

Back home in Fawcett City, Billy returned to school and worked as an announcer for WHIZ radio. At the same time, Captain Marvel wielded Shazam's great powers to battle such evils as MISTER MIND, DOCTOR SIVANA, MISTER ATOM, and the MONSTER SOCIETY OF EVIL. Through it all, Captain Marvel fought with indefatigable spirit, perhaps the truest of any costumed champion. Captain Marvel's wholesome honesty and integrity made his spotless soul the prize most coveted by the demon NERON. However, Billy and his alter ego have always had the moral strength to resist temptation.

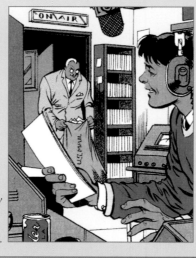

RADIO STAR Billy often reports on the deeds of Captain Marvel.

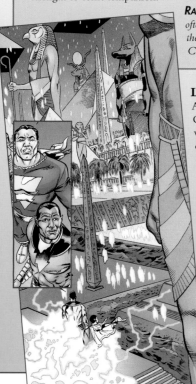

LOOKING TO THE FUTURE

A former member of the JUSTICE SOCIETY OF AMERICA, Captain Marvel continues to keep the trust of the old wizard Shazam while he battles vice and villainy as only the world's mightiest mortal can. He guards over Fawcett City with the help of the extended Marvel Family and allies like BULLETMAN and Bulletgirl II (see BULLETGIRL I & II (WINDSHEAR)), the latter of whom has been romantically linked with Captain Marvel, known affectionately as "The Big Red Cheese."

Many millennia from now—in the 853rd century, to be precise—Billy will assume the elder Shazam's role and choose a new Captain Marvel. But until that time, Billy Batson has a lot of growing up to do. SB

ENEMY ALLIED Captain Marvel was forced to fight alongside his arch-foe Black Adam when both were members of the JSA.

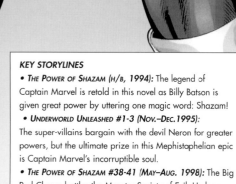
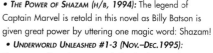

KEY STORYLINES

• *THE POWER OF SHAZAM (H/B, 1994):* The legend of Captain Marvel is retold in this novel as Billy Batson is given great power by uttering one magic word: Shazam!

• *UNDERWORLD UNLEASHED #1-3 (NOV.–DEC. 1995):* The super-villains bargain with the devil Neron for greater powers, but the ultimate prize in this Mephistophelian epic is Captain Marvel's incorruptible soul.

• *THE POWER OF SHAZAM #38-41 (MAY–AUG. 1998):* The Big Red Cheese battles the Monster Society of Evil. He learns that the wicked worm, Mr. Mind, was first imprisoned on the planet Venus by Green Lantern Abin Sur.

CAPTAIN NAZI

FIRST APPEARANCE MASTER COMICS #2 (December 1941)
STATUS Villain **REAL NAME** Albrecht Krieger
OCCUPATION Would-be world conqueror **BASE** The Slab
HEIGHT 6ft 4in **WEIGHT** 205 lbs **EYES** Blue **HAIR** Blond
SPECIAL POWERS/ABILITIES Superhuman strength, above average speed, endurance, and invulnerability.

In 1941, Albrecht Krieger was presented to Adolf Hitler as the ultimate development of the Aryan "master race." This so-called epitome of perfection became known as Captain Nazi. Intensely loyal to the Führer, for the rest of World War II Captain Nazi frequently clashed with the Allies costumed champions, particularly the SPY SMASHER, proving himself a formidable foe.

When the war ended, BULLETMAN, Minute-Man and Spy Smasher interfered with Captain Nazi's search for the

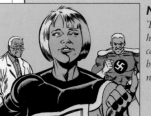

NAZI SYMPATHISERS
Two of Captain Nazi's helpers in the fascist cause are his scientist brother Wolf and his niece Katrina.

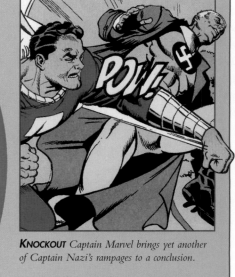

KNOCKOUT Captain Marvel brings yet another of Captain Nazi's rampages to a conclusion.

freighter *La Poloma*, but failed to prevent the villain from retrieving a mysterious storage tank from the vessel and disappearing. This tank proved to be a cryogenic unit that the Captain believed contained Adolf Hitler's body. Captain Nazi ensured that his own body was placed in another, similar unit. More than five decades into the future, Captain Nazi was revived from his deep freeze. When Captain Nazi crippled young Freddy Freeman, CAPTAIN MARVEL convinced the wizard Shazam to give the teenager a portion of his and his sister's power, thus creating CAPTAIN MARVEL JR. Since that day, Captain Nazi has continued to plague the entire Marvel Family only to meet constant defeat. **RG**

CAPTAIN STORM

FIRST APPEARANCE CAPTAIN STORM #1 (June 1964)
STATUS Hero (deceased) **REAL NAME** William Storm
OCCUPATION U.S. Navy PT-boat commander
BASE World War II Europe and Pacific theaters
HEIGHT 5ft 11in **WEIGHT** 167 lbs **EYES** Brown **HAIR** Brown
SPECIAL POWERS/ABILITIES Courageous leader and above-average battlefield combatant.

Hit by tragedy again and again in the battle theaters of World War II, Captain William Storm seemed destined for a role as a member of the aptly-named LOSERS squad. Yet in the war's final days he fought with guts and went out a hero. Captain Storm's first command, PT-47, sank after a sneak attack by a Japanese sub. Though Storm survived, he lost his left leg and wore a wooden one thereafter. Storm joined the U.S.-sanctioned detached service force known as the Losers with Air Force pilot Johnny Cloud (see CLOUD, JOHNNY) and the Marines GUNNER AND SARGE, but on a mission to save a church, Captain Storm seemingly died in a fiery blast. Storm survived, but lost his right eye. He resurfaced as an amnesiac "pirate" attacking Axis shipping, until he regained his memory and rejoined the Losers. He was killed in a World War II temporal event related to the Crisis (see Great Battles, pp. 320–1). Johnny Cloud, Gunner, and Sarge all died in the same battle, bringing an end to the short, troubled lives of the Losers. **DW**

CAPTAIN TRIUMPH

FIRST APPEARANCE CRACK COMICS #27 (January 1943)
STATUS Hero (missing) **REAL NAMES** Lance and Michael Gallant
OCCUPATION (Lance) unknown; (Michael) former pilot
BASE New York City
HEIGHT 6ft 1in **WEIGHT** 198 lbs **EYES** Blue **HAIR** Blond
SPECIAL POWERS/ABILITIES When Lance touched his birthmark, he merged with the spirit of his brother Michael and became Captain Triumph, who possesses superstrength, invulnerability, the power of flight, and invisibility.

Lance and Michael Gallant were identical twins born with an unusual T-shaped birthmark on their left wrists. In the early days of World War II, Michael, a pilot for the U.S. Army Air Corps, was killed when the airplane hangar he was standing in blew up. Lance swore to avenge his brother's death, and Michael, now a ghost, appeared before him. Michael told Lance that if he rubbed his T-shaped birthmark, the two brothers would merge and become Captain Triumph. As Triumph, the brothers found the culprits behind the hangar explosion and incarcerated them.

Captain Triumph was an active hero during World War II. Michael's fiancée, Kim Meredith, learned of his existence as a ghost. Horrified at first, she eventually married Lance, but remained close to Michael's spirit. Biff, a circus clown, became Triumph's sidekick.

Recently, Michael murdered Philip Geyer, the fiancée of Triumph's former teammate LIBERTY BELLE, when Lance discovered Geyer was having an adulterous affair. **PJ**

CAPTAIN X

FIRST APPEARANCE STAR-SPANGLED COMICS #1 (October 1941)
STATUS Hero (deceased) **REAL NAME** Richard "Buck" Dare
OCCUPATION Newspaper reporter **BASE** Mobile
HEIGHT 5ft 10in **WEIGHT** 175 lbs **EYES** Blue **HAIR** Chestnut
SPECIAL POWERS/ABILITIES Expert hand-to-hand combatant; Captain X's radio-controlled aircraft *Jenny* was virtually invisible from a distance and used uranium-235 as its atomic fuel source.

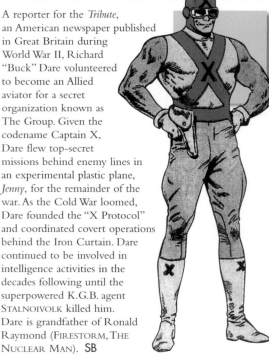

A reporter for the *Tribune*, an American newspaper published in Great Britain during World War II, Richard "Buck" Dare volunteered to become an Allied aviator for a secret organization known as The Group. Given the codename Captain X, Dare flew top-secret missions behind enemy lines in an experimental plastic plane, *Jenny*, for the remainder of the war. As the Cold War loomed, Dare founded the "X Protocol" and coordinated covert operations behind the Iron Curtain. Dare continued to be involved in intelligence activities in the decades following until the superpowered K.G.B. agent STALNOIVOLK killed him. Dare is grandfather of Ronald Raymond (FIRESTORM, THE NUCLEAR MAN). **SB**

CARR, SNAPPER

FIRST APPEARANCE BRAVE AND THE BOLD #28 (February 1960)
STATUS Ally to super heroes (retired)   **REAL NAME** Lucas Carr
OCCUPATION Author   **BASE** Happy Harbor, Rhode Island
HEIGHT 5ft 10in   **WEIGHT** 175 lbs   **EYES** Blue   **HAIR** Brown
SPECIAL POWERS/ABILITIES Formerly could teleport by snapping his
fingers; lost this ability when his hands were severed.

When Simon Carr bankrolled the JUSTICE LEAGUE OF AMERICA, and outfitted their
mountain headquarters, his nephew Lucas helped install equipment. As a reward, the
finger-popping teen, nicknamed "Snapper," was made an honorary JLA member.
Lacking superpowers, the teen began to feel like a fifth wheel, making him
susceptible to the charismatic "John Doe" who charmed Snapper into revealing the
location of the JLA's headquarters; Snapper almost helped kill his friends! Doe was
revealed to be the JOKER, making Snapper feel even worse.

Snapper left the League and fell under the sway of the KEY,
who used him as the criminal Star-Tsar. Snapper
met and married Bethany Lee, some time before
being captured by the Dominators (*see Alien Races,*
pp. 150–1) He was subjected to many tests, which
activated his teleporting metagene. Snapper and
other human survivors of the alien experiments,
fought their way to freedom and then worked as the
BLASTERS. Snapper was captured by the Khunds (*see*
Alien Races, pp. 150–1) who severed his hands.
Thanks to Colu's Vril Dox, his hands were replaced by
nanites and he returned to Earth. Snapper became a
mentor to the android from the future HOURMAN III.
He then made a fortune writing his JLA memoirs.
He was a mentor to YOUNG JUSTICE, returning
home when the team disbanded. **RG**

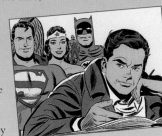

FINGER-POPPER *Snapper used to
enjoy writing in the JLA
Casebook but soon began to feel
like a fifth wheel.*

CASCADE

FIRST APPEARANCE JUSTICE LEAGUE QUARTERLY #17 (Winter 1994)
STATUS Hero   **REAL NAME** Khuan Cho Sunowaparti
OCCUPATION Plant worker and activist   **BASE** Ossaville
HEIGHT 5ft 3in   **WEIGHT** 105 lbs   **EYES** Brown   **HAIR** Black
SPECIAL POWERS/ABILITIES Can transform any part or all of her body
into water; can psychically control large bodies of
water, causing them to take simple shapes.

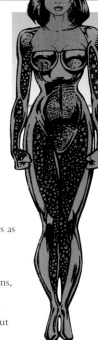

Born to a large family on the
island of Java in Indonesia, Khuan
was one of many who vigorously
opposed the Javanese political
elite, which had adopted a policy
of ruthlessly suppressing local
cultures. Taking a dangerous job in
refinery fields to earn more
money for her family, Khuan was
caught up in a violent clash
between warring factions in
Borneo. Khuan gained the power
to transform her body into living
liquid when she was exposed to a
radioactive isotope that activated
her metagene.

Using her newfound superpowers as
an activist for peace, Khuan was
invited by OWLWOMAN to join the
GLOBAL GUARDIANS. Codenamed
Cascade, Khuan joined the Guardians,
hoping the exposure would bring
attention to the culture of violence
and corruption spreading throughout
Indonesia. **PJ**

CARSON, CAVE

FIRST APPEARANCE THE BRAVE AND THE BOLD #31 (August 1960)
STATUS Hero   **REAL NAME** Calvin Carson
OCCUPATION Professional spelunker; geology professor   **BASE** Mobile
HEIGHT 5ft 11in   **WEIGHT** 178 lbs   **EYES** Blue   **HAIR** Brown
SPECIAL POWERS/ABILITIES Highly intelligent, with a natural gift for his
area of expertise; one eye is cybernetic.

Calvin Carson was a lab
technician for E. Borsten & Co.,
which developed a digging
machine, the Mighty Mole, for the
government. When funding was
cut, the project was axed. Carson
stole the device and began
exploring the varied life beneath
the Earth's surface. He worked
with ex-convict Bulldozer Smith, geologist Christie
Madison, and adventurer Johnny Blake. Carson and his
colleagues became celebrities, before the Modern Age of
heroes began (with the coming of SUPERMAN).

After finding lost Nazi gold and experimental time-
travel technology, the Borsten family sued to regain the
Mighty Mole. They settled for the time-travel equipment,
letting Carson keep the Mole. When Superman arrived,
the public turned their attention away from Carson. His
team broke up and Carson drifted into semi-retirement.
As a geology teacher, he had a romance with student
Bonnie Baxter, which led him to use his considerable
fortune to fund E. Borsten & Co.'s Rip Hunter (*see*
HUNTER, RIP) and his time-travel experiments. He has
worked with others from his era in a loose group known
as the Forgotten Heroes. Cave maintains a busy schedule,
embarking on missions with Christie and Bulldozer (some
on behalf of the S.T.A.R. Labs research facility) and
leading the Forgotten Heroes. **RG**

CAT-MAN

FIRST APPEARANCE DETECTIVE COMICS #311 (January 1963)
STATUS Villain   **REAL NAME** Thomas Blake
OCCUPATION Professional criminal   **BASE** Gotham City
HEIGHT 6ft   **WEIGHT** 179 lbs
EYES Green   **HAIR** Brown
SPECIAL POWERS/ABILITIES Talented inventor; remarkable
physical agility; believed to have "nine lives" from
the mystical cloth used in his costume.

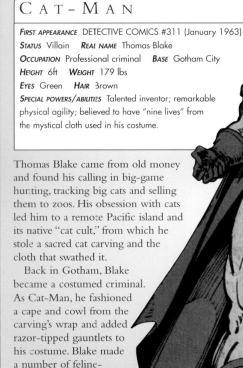

Thomas Blake came from old money
and found his calling in big-game
hunting, tracking big cats and selling
them to zoos. His obsession with cats
led him to a remote Pacific island and
its native "cat cult," from which he
stole a sacred cat carving and the
cloth that swathed it.

Back in Gotham, Blake
became a costumed criminal.
As Cat-Man, he fashioned
a cape and cowl from the
carving's wrap and added
razor-tipped gauntlets to
his costume. Blake made
a number of feline-
themed accessories
inspired by both CATWOMAN
and BATMAN, including catarangs
and a turbocharged cat-car. His
narrow escapes appeared to bear
out his belief that his costume gave
him nine lives. The earthquake

that left Gotham a No Man's Land also
freed Cat-Man and other inmates from
Blackgate prison. Cat-Man later
joined the Witness Projection
Program after informing on
MONSIEUR MALLAH, though he
found time to attend GREEN
ARROW's funeral. **DW**

FELINE FIEND
*At the controls of his
latest cat-invention,
Cat-Man attempts
to make cat food out of
Batman and Robin.*

CATWOMAN

PRINCESS OF PLUNDER

FIRST APPEARANCE BATMAN: #1 (Spring 1940)
STATUS Unresolved   REAL NAME Selina Kyle
OCCUPATION Cat burglar/vigilante   BASE Gotham City's East End
HEIGHT 5ft 7in   WEIGHT 133 lbs   EYES Blue-green   HAIR Black
SPECIAL POWERS/ABILITIES A formidable fighter with expertise in boxing
and various martial arts disciplines; skintight cat costume features
retractable razor-sharp claws in gloves and spring-action steel
climbing pitons in boots; wields a variety of bullwhips and
cat-o'-nine tails as offensive weapons and gymnastic accoutrements.

KEY STORYLINES

• CATWOMAN (1ST SERIES) #1-4 (FEBRUARY–MAY
1989) Selina Kyle's life on the mean streets of
Gotham City is recounted.
• DETECTIVE COMICS #759-762
(AUGUST–NOVEMBER 2001) P.I. Slam Bradley is
hired to find the missing and presumed-dead
Selina.
• CATWOMAN (3RD SERIES) #1-4 (JANUARY–APRIL
2002) Catwoman stalks and defeats a
shape-changing serial killer who is
hunting Gotham's ladies of
the evening.

SELINA KYLE'S CHILDHOOD was defined by tragedy.
When Selina was just a girl, her brutalized mother
committed suicide and her violent father drank himself
to death not long after. Separated from her younger
sister Magdalena and remanded to the Sprang Hall
Juvenile Detention Center—an abusive state home for
orphaned or delinquent girls—Selina opted instead to
take her chances on the mean streets of Gotham City.
Amid the crime and corruption of the poverty-stricken
East End district, she survived through petty theft.
Sharp wits and an amazing natural skill as a gymnast led to her
becoming the slickest and slipperiest cat burglar the Gotham City
Police Department had ever had to deal with.

**PURPLE
PRINCESS**
Catwoman has
worn a number of
different costumes over the years,
often preferring purple catsuits.

THE FELINE FATALE

To protect herself from predators, Selina studied martial arts in a backstreet dojo where a
Sensei taught her how best to use her claws. Later, ex-heavyweight champ Ted Grant (see
WILDCAT I) taught Selina the "sweet science" of boxing. For a time, Selina was the most
accomplished thief nobody knew. She was also one of the most generous, spreading her
ill-gotten gains around the downtrodden and destitute of the East End,
including the young prostitute Holly "Gonightly"
Robinson, whom Selina befriended and
watched over like the little sister she
believed she no longer had.
Selina would have continued to rob
with impunity if not for the BATMAN.
Spying the Caped Crusader from her
window on one of his first outings, Selina
watched him in action and was suitably
inspired to take up her own costume when
prowling the Gotham night. In a tight
leather catsuit, Catwoman marked the city
as her territory. However, she never killed,
and she only stole from the wealthiest or
the well-insured. For these reasons, Batman
pursued other costumed criminals more relentlessly and gave Catwoman
the chance to change her spots. Sometimes he even asked the Princess
of Plunder to use her skills for the betterment of Gotham. Perhaps his
altruism attracted her, because Selina ultimately did decide to make
Catwoman more than just a thief in the night.
After faking her own demise, Selina left Gotham for a time, but
eventually returned to the city's East End, where Catwoman now defends the defenseless.
Catwoman learned Batman's best-kept secret when the Dark Knight took her to his
Batcave and revealed his identity to her. They finally admitted their feelings for each other
but then parted because Catwoman did not believe that Batman trusted her. Selina began
seeing private detective Slam Bradley (see BRADLEY, SLAM), but Slam realized that Selina's
heart would always belong to Batman.
Catwoman continues to enjoy
adventures on the "other" side
of the fence now, stealing only
when necessary and usually if
the loot will ultimately do
someone other than herself
a bit of good. SB

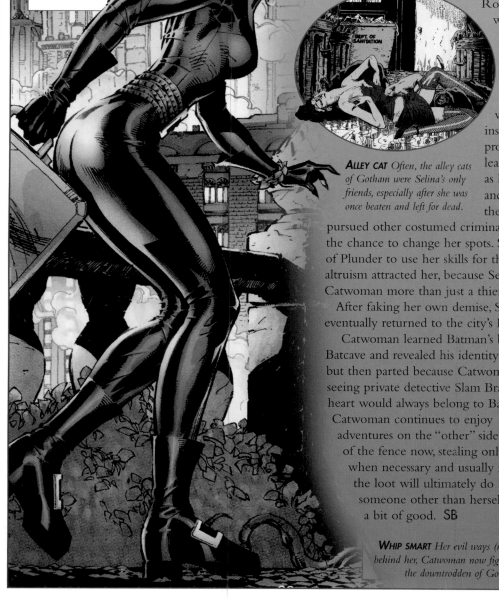

ALLEY CAT Often, the alley cats
of Gotham were Selina's only
friends, especially after she was
once beaten and left for dead.

TOP THIEF Few cat
burglars can rival Selina
Kyle's nimble-fingered
thieving skills.

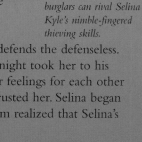

WHIP SMART Her evil ways (mostly)
behind her, Catwoman now fights for
the downtrodden of Gotham.

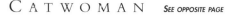

CATSEYE

FIRST APPEARANCE SUICIDE SQUAD (1st series) #53 (May 1991)
STATUS Villain (deceased)   **REAL NAME** Unknown
OCCUPATION Yakuza assassin   **BASE** Tokyo, Japan
HEIGHT 6ft 1in   **WEIGHT** 195 lbs   **EYES** Brown   **HAIR** Black
SPECIAL POWERS/ABILITIES Razor-sharp claws tipped with poison;
amazing leaping ability; low level super speed.

His real name and origin remained a mystery, and with good reason. For the ruthless killer known as Catseye was a bioengineered meta-human agent of the Yakuza crime family. He clashed with various members of the SUICIDE SQUAD when that covert agency went to Japan on a mission to recover a stolen cache of Russian weapons, known as the Dragon's Hoard. Several other rival clandestine groups came searching for the Dragon's Hoard as well, including the Russian Red Shadows and the Khymer Rouge. Suicide Squad members MANHUNTER and BRONZE TIGER were captured by the Yakuza and freed by KATANA from the OUTSIDERS while Catseye fought the ATOM for control of the stolen weapons. Later, in the forests of southeast Asia, Catseye attacked the Squad again, this time in an ancient temple, and was scraped by his own poison claws while battling Bronze Tiger. Catseye's body was incinerated in an explosion caused by DEADSHOT. **PJ**

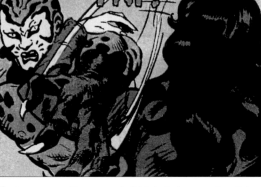

CATSEYE STRIKES *Catseye attacked Nightshade, a member of the Suicide Squad, with his poison-tipped claws. But Nightshade was able to deflect the strike with her own unique martial arts skills, causing the assassin to flee into the night.*

CATWOMAN   *SEE OPPOSITE PAGE*

CELESTE

FIRST APPEARANCE LEGION OF SUPER-HEROES (4th series) #6 (April 1990)
STATUS Hero   **REAL NAME** Celeste McCauley
OCCUPATION Private investigator; adventurer   **BASE** Mobile
HEIGHT 5ft 7in   **WEIGHT** 120 lbs   **EYES** Blue   **HAIR** Brown
SPECIAL POWERS/ABILITIES Naturally wields the emerald energy employed by the Green Lantern Corps.

In a hypertimeline that contains an alternate history of the LEGION OF SUPER-HEROES, Celeste McCauley left her wealthy family to become a private detective. An encounter with the remains of a dead GREEN LANTERN on the planet Twilo exposed her to the amazing solid-light energy used by that intergalactic corps of ring-wielders. This energy saved her life when she was beaten nearly to death by Roxxas the Butcher. She worked with the Legion of Super-Heroes and helped evacuate Earth before its destruction in a catastrophic accident. During a fight with Glorith the sorceress, Celeste became a being of pure energy. Adopting the name Neon, she adjusted to her new life until temporal anomalies transformed her into a member of the DARKSTARS. The events of Zero Hour (*see* Great Battles, pp. 320-1) erased Celeste's known history from the primary timeline of Earth. **DW**

CELSIUS

FIRST APPEARANCE SHOWCASE #94 (September 1977)
STATUS Hero (deceased)
REAL NAME Arani Desai Caulder
OCCUPATION Adventurer   **BASE** Kansas City
HEIGHT 5ft 4in   **WEIGHT** 124 lbs
EYES Brown   **HAIR** Black
SPECIAL POWERS/ABILITIES Could project rays of intense heat or cold from her hands.

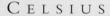

Arani Desai's mother died during childbirth. Blamed as the cause of death by her father, scientist Ashok Desai, Arani was raised by servants and nannies until she ran away. For years, Arani lived a life of poverty in Calcutta until she was rescued by Niles Caulder, the CHIEF of the DOOM PATROL, who later married her. Soon after, Arani discovered her amazing metagene powers.

Separated from Caulder for several years, Arani learned that he had died at the hands of GENERAL IMMORTUS. Obsessed with the idea that the Chief was still alive, Arani assembled a new Doom Patrol to find him.

Tragically, Celsius died during a massive alien invasion of Earth. The devious Caulder turned up alive, claiming that Arani had never been married to him, and that she was a poor, deluded woman unable to cope with reality even after he treated her, as a physician. **PJ**

CENTRIX

FIRST APPEARANCE JUSTICE LEAGUE QUARTERLY #17 (Winter 1994)
STATUS Hero   **REAL NAME** Mark Armstrong
OCCUPATION Adventurer   **BASE** Vancouver Island, British Columbia
HEIGHT 5ft 9in   **WEIGHT** 160 lbs   **EYES** Green   **HAIR** Brown
SPECIAL POWERS/ABILITIES Projects invisible energy force waves in equal and opposite directions from his body; carries arsenal of small pellets and other projectiles propelled by force waves.

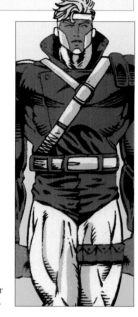

Ambitious advertising executive Mark Armstrong retired young and wealthy, leaving him all the time in the world to practice and perfect his meta-human powers. As Centrix, one of Canada's few public super heroes, Armstrong put his abilities to practical use, foiling small-time criminals before he was asked to join the most recent incarnation of the GLOBAL GUARDIANS. Armstrong still operates as Centrix from his home in Ladysmith, on Vancouver Island. Centrix is a practitioner of New Age philosophies, mixing them with his millions as a financier for the Global Guardians. **SB**

CHAIN LIGHTNING

FIRST APPEARANCE POWER OF SHAZAM! #14 (April 1996)
STATUS Villain   **REAL NAME** Amy
OCCUPATION Criminal   **BASE** Mobile   **HEIGHT** 5ft 4in
WEIGHT 121 lbs   **EYES** Blue   **HAIR** Platinum blonde
SPECIAL POWERS/ABILITIES A multiple personality, she absorbs electrical current but cannot control it without artificial help.

Amy's metagene kicked in some time during her early teens, allowing her to absorb electrical energy, but she lacked a way to control it. An unknown person provided her with a bodysuit containing containment circuitry. Unfortunately, Amy also began suffering from multiple personality disorder. The dominant personality is Amy, who tried to commit suicide in New York, but was rescued by CAPTAIN MARVEL JR., earning her sincere affection. Her other three personalities, however, are not so benign. Amber is angry, aggressive, and very destructive. The Inner Child is a hulking form, while Id is a small girl trapped inside the others. Together, they are known as Chain Lightning, and at different times Amy's powers appear as four distinct electrical beings. Shazam's magic lightning bolt accidentally gave all four personalities physical form, and it took the combined efforts of Captain Marvel Jr. and MISTER SCARLET to subdue them before Fawcett City was reduced to rubble. Amy is now back at S.T.A.R. Labs, where she has undergone frequent treatment. **RG**

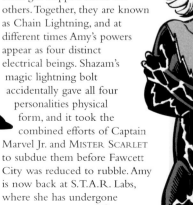

CHALLENGERS OF THE UNKNOWN

FIRST APPEARANCE SHOWCASE #6 (January 1957)
STATUS Hero team
BASE Challenger Mountain, Colorado Rockies
CURRENT MEMBERS AND POWERS
Prof. Haley Skin diver and oceanographer.
Red Ryan Mountaineer and former circus acrobat.
June Robbins Computer and robotics expert.
Rocky Davis Wrestling champion and top strategist.
Ace Morgan Former test pilot and amateur sorcerer.
Clay Brody Former race-car driver.
Marlon Corbett Top-notch pilot.
Kenn Kawa Software and electronics specialist.
Brenda Ruskin Brilliant theoretical physicist.
June Walker Hypertime duplicate of June Robbins from an alternate timeline.

The Challengers got their start when pilot Kyle "Ace" Morgan, wrestler Les "Rocky" Davis, mountaineer Matthew "Red" Ryan, and diver Walter "Prof." Haley survived an airplane crash on their way to appear on a TV program. Deciding that they were now "living on borrowed time," the four united as a team of adventurers-for-hire. Operating from their own mountain stronghold, the Challs journeyed everywhere, from the depths of space to the bottom of the sea, battling scoundrels, including the League of Challenger-Haters. Dr. June Robbins soon joined the team as an unofficial fifth Challenger.

Prof. Haley accidentally shattered Challenger Mountain, sending himself and June into an alternate dimension. The other members thought them dead and learned new skills in their absence. Prof. and June returned, but Ace and Red soon followed them into a state of stasis. Left alone, Rocky licensed the Challengers name to a new team: Clay Brody, Marlon Corbett, Kenn Kawa, and Brenda Ruskin. Red, June, Prof., and Ace soon reappeared and then vanished again, this time into hypertime where they clashed with BLACK ZERO. On their way back to the primary timeline, Red vanished and June Robbins disappeared and was replaced by June Walker, a temporal doppelganger. The Challs have since vowed to locate their lost comrades. **DW**

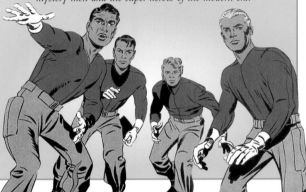

ORIGINALS *The Challs were a link between the Golden Age mystery men and the super heroes of the modern era.*

CHAMELEON

FIRST APPEARANCE ADVENTURE COMICS #267 (November 1966)
STATUS Hero **REAL NAME** Reep Daggle (Interlac approximation)
OCCUPATION Legionnaire **BASE** Metropolis, in 30th century
HEIGHT Variable, usually 5ft 9in **WEIGHT** Variable, usually 145 lbs
EYES Variable, usually yellow **HAIR** Variable, usually none
SPECIAL POWERS/ABILITIES Can analyze and store data using his antennae and then shape his body into an exact duplicate of any being or object, however large or small, including creatures dreamed up from his own imagination. He cannot, however, replicate the special powers of others he's duplicating.

Reep Daggle is a Durlan, a race of hooded, tentacled aliens that are the object of grave fear and mistrust by other races throughout the galaxy for their shape-shifting abilities. Reep left his homeworld, and his role as a religious leader for his caste, behind him when he traveled to Earth in the latter half of the 30th century to join the LEGION OF SUPER-HEROES.

Taking a more human shape, Reep hoped his membership in the Legion would help end the galaxy's xenophobic attitudes toward his people. A member of the Legion Espionage Squad, Chameleon has become an invaluable member of the Legion of Super-Heroes. Fascinated by the relationships between sentient beings, Reep is closest to fellow Legionnaires INVISIBLE KID and SENSOR, and has romantic feelings for SPARK. **PJ**

CHARAXES

FIRST APPEARANCE (as Killer Moth) BATMAN #63 (March 1951); (as Charaxes) UNDERWORLD UNLEASHED #1 (November 1995)
STATUS Villain **REAL NAME** Drury Walker, a.k.a. Cameron Van Cleer **OCCUPATION** Beast **BASE** Gotham City
HEIGHT 6ft 9in **WEIGHT** 202 lbs **EYES** Red **HAIR** Yellow
SPECIAL POWERS/ABILITIES Monstrous insect form possesses ten times a normal man's strength; exoskeleton confers virtual invulnerability; secretes a sticky acidic substance that can trap the strongest of men and dissolve their bodies.

Drury Walker the man was little more than a joke. As Killer Moth, he offered his services as paid protector to Gotham's gangsters. Despite an arsenal of ingenious weaponry, including his signature cocoon gun, the colorful Killer Moth was bested by BATMAN at every turn, leaving his clients both irate and incarcerated. Then Barbara Gordon, dressed for a costume party as BATGIRL, defeated the Moth, earning Walker further ridicule. Finally, he made a deal with a devil—the tempter NERON—who gave Walker his heart's desire. What Walker wanted most was to be feared, but what he received in exchange for his soul was metamorphosis into a real Killer Moth…the man-eating Charaxes!

Charaxes has repeatedly turned up in the Gotham area seeking sustenance to survive and usually crossing paths with ROBIN. Charaxes covers his victims in a sticky corrosive fluid that breaks down their bodies for easier digestion. **RG**

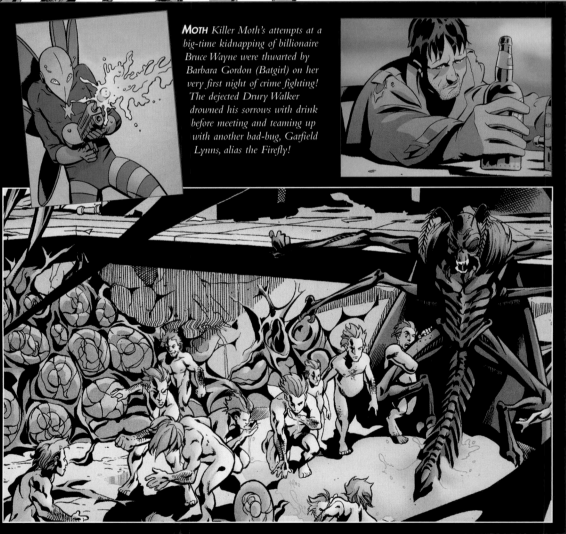

MOTH *Killer Moth's attempts at a big-time kidnapping of billionaire Bruce Wayne were thwarted by Barbara Gordon (Batgirl) on her very first night of crime fighting! The dejected Drury Walker drowned his sorrows with drink before meeting and teaming up with another bad-bug, Garfield Lynns, alias the Firefly!*

NEST *The monstrous Charaxes continues to mutate. What's worse, he may be reproducing!*

CHARYBDIS

FIRST APPEARANCE AQUAMAN (5th series) #1 (August 1994)
STATUS Villain **REAL NAME** Charybdis
OCCUPATION Would-be conqueror **BASE** The Seven Seas
HEIGHT 6ft 4in **WEIGHT** 237 lbs **EYES** Black **HAIR** Black
SPECIAL POWERS/ABILITIES Can absorb the latent talents of others;
in Piranha Man form, possesses superhuman strength and
ability to breath on land or in water.

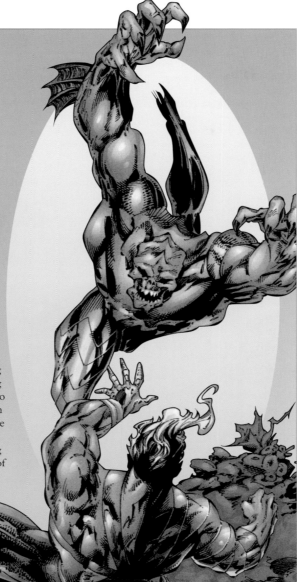

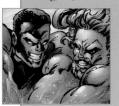

Charybdis and his wife, Scylla, were freelance
terrorists named after two horrific beings from
Greek mythology (Charybdis was a whirlpool, Scylla
a multi-headed monster). Scylla died when a bomb
exploded in her hands; her death drove Charybdis
insane. He appeared, seemingly out of nowhere,
displaying vast powers and a hatred for the Sea
King, AQUAMAN. The self-proclaimed terrorist
easily defeated Aquaman in
battle, strapping him to a
machine that temporarily
transferred his powers and
abilities to the usurper. Their
battle resulted in Aquaman losing
his hand to piranhas before being
shot by DOLPHIN. Charybdis, who
had not yet mastered Aquaman's telepathic skills with
fish, fell in the water and was left for dead. Instead, he
finally made contact with the deadly fish, absorbing
their essence, thereby preserving his life and allowing
him to evolve into the even more formidable form of
Piranha Man. His aim was to absorb every last
shred of ability from Aquaman and
leave him for dead. The Sea
King defeated Piranha Man,
but not before seeing his
family and friends
suffer. RG

CHAVARD, ANDRÉ

FIRST APPEARANCE BOY COMMANDOS #1 (July 1942)
STATUS Hero **REAL NAME** André Chavard
OCCUPATION Adventurer **BASE** Paris, France
HEIGHT 5ft 9in **WEIGHT** 165 lbs **EYES** Brown **HAIR** Black
SPECIAL POWERS/ABILITIES A natural leader, able to inspire respect and
loyalty in others; a capable marksman and hand-to-hand combatant.

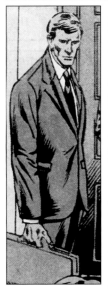

A handsome young man born in
Bar-le-Duc, France, whose parents
were slain in the early days of
World War II, André Chavard was
one of several orphans who were
mascots of an American Army unit
station in Britain during the war.
The orphans became the BOY
COMMANDOS, and the brave young
soldiers undertook dozens of
special, often dangerous missions
behind enemy lines until the war
ended in 1945.

Returning to his native France
soon after, André chose to remain
with the military. He rose through
the ranks until he became the
commander of the spy agency
known only as Department
Gamma. His premiere spy in the
Department is FLEUR-DE-LIS. PJ

CHASE, CAMERON

FIRST APPEARANCE BATMAN #550 (January 1998)
STATUS Hero **REAL NAME** Cameron Chase
OCCUPATION D.E.O. investigator **BASE** New York City
HEIGHT 5ft 5in **WEIGHT** 129 lbs **EYES** Green **HAIR** Blond
SPECIAL POWERS/ABILITIES Highly intelligent; skilled with both computers
and handguns; appears to possess a latent ability that allows her to
dampen the superpowers of meta-humans. This unconscious talent
has protected her in the past; she has yet to exploit it to the full.

Former private detective Cameron Chase is one of the top
agents in the Department of Extranormal Operations, a
branch of U.S. intelligence that keeps tabs on the Earth's
meta-humans and supernatural beings. Working under
DIRECTOR BONES, Chase has discovered the alternate lives
employed by the shape-changing MARTIAN MANHUNTER
and tried to deduce the true identity of the
BATMAN (she mistakenly concluded that he
was GREEN LANTERN Alan Scott). Her
dislike of costumed crime fighters stems
from her childhood, when the maniacal
Dr. Trap murdered her father. Walter
Chase had secretly been Acro-Bat of
the Justice Experience, and Cameron
blamed his death on the clandestine
nocturnal antics that had made him
a target. Dr. Trap later tried to kill
Chase, but the Martian Manhunter
intervened. DW

CHECKMATE

FIRST APPEARANCE ACTION COMICS #598 (March 1988)
STATUS U.S. government agency **BASE** Abandoned NORAD facility
in Colorado's Rocky Mountains; Checkmate maintains field offices in
every major American city.
PAST OPERATIVES Sasha Bordeaux, Harvey Bullock, Kalia Campbell,
Scott Jameson, Philip Kramer, Peacemaker, Jacques Reynard,
David Said, Sarge Steel, Harry Stein, Black Thorn, Vigilante II,
Valentina Vostok, Amanda Waller.

Checkmate was established by Amanda Waller (see
WALLER, AMANDA) as an independent arm of Task Force
X, a bureau that also had administration over the SUICIDE
SQUAD. Like the Squad, Checkmate engaged in top-secret
missions vital to U.S. interests. Structured after the
hierarchy of chess pieces, Checkmate is led by a Queen
or King (depending on the gender of the current
administrator), followed by administrative Bishops,
field director Rooks, armored and well-
armed field agent Knights, and support-
tech Pawns. The agency's first Queen
was Valentina Vostok, formerly
NEGATIVE WOMAN, later replaced by
Waller herself. Checkmate was
nearly destroyed by the terrorist
group KOBRA, a debacle referred to as
the Janus Directive, which saw Waller
unseated as leader. Checkmate is now
ruled by a central King, his identity a
closely-guarded secret, although
regional royalty control its field
offices. SB

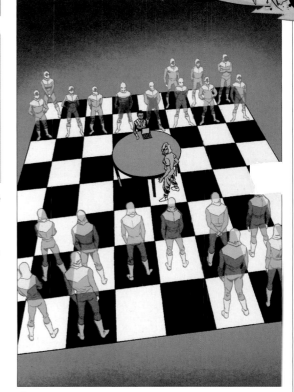

FIELD AGENT An abducted
Knight proved his
mettle in battle
by slaying
Firebrand III.

CHECKERS Bruce Wayne's former bodyguard and lover, Sasha
Bordeaux, was recruited by Checkmate and given a new lease on
life, as well as a new surgically-altered face, in exchange for her
complete loyalty to the clandestine agency.

CHEETAH I

FIRST APPEARANCE WONDER WOMAN (1st series) #6 (Fall 1943)
STATUS Villain **REAL NAME** Priscilla Rich
OCCUPATION Criminal **BASE** New York City
HEIGHT 5ft 4in **WEIGHT** 119 lbs **EYES** Green **HAIR** Brown
SPECIAL POWERS/ABILITIES Acrobatic, cunning, and an above-average athlete; a stylish dresser.

Socialite Priscilla Rich led New York's Junior League Committee for War Work during World War II. The spoiled beauty came to resent the fame of WONDER WOMAN—the time-displaced Queen HIPPOLYTA of the AMAZONS. Rich went so far as to try and kill the Amazon during a fund-raising event. Thwarted and furious, Priscilla stared in a mirror and was amazed to see a costumed version of herself staring back.

This revelation convinced her to turn the room's cheetah-skin rug into a costume, and get revenge on Wonder Woman as the Cheetah. Rather than kill Hippolyta outright, the Cheetah stole the benefit's proceeds and framed the Amazon Queen. Rich's ploy was exposed, however, further fueling her hatred of Wonder Woman. Rich even joined several other diabolical women and formed the first VILLAINY INC. in an attempt to destroy the Amazon Queen. Once Wonder Woman vanished, the Cheetah also faded from the spotlight, completing her eventual jail time in disgrace. RG

CHEETAH II

FIRST APPEARANCE WONDER WOMAN (2nd series) #7 (August 1987)
STATUS Villain (deceased) **REAL NAME** Barbara Ann Minerva
OCCUPATION Archaeologist **BASE** Nottingham, England
HEIGHT 5ft 9in **WEIGHT** 140 lbs **EYES** Brown **HAIR** Auburn
SPECIAL POWERS/ABILITIES Highly intelligent, but an untrained combatant until she channeled the Cheetah spirit; then she possessed above-average strength and agility.

Archaeologist Barbara Minerva sought historical artifacts that would further her own fame. On one expedition, Minerva discovered the lost temple that was home to the African plant-god Urzkartaga. After witnessing another tribe attack the Urzkartagans during their bloodletting ritual, Minerva forced the priest Chuma to reveal the secrets of the ritual. Minerva endured the bloodletting ritual and killed her associate Dr. Leavens so that she could offer his blood to Urzkartaga. She was transformed into a vessel for the Cheetah, a feral fiend driven to hunt down human prey. Chuma became her loyal companion, helping to renew her powers while he tended the plant-god. As the Cheetah, Minerva discovered the lost city of Bana-Mighdall and slaughtered many AMAZONS before WONDER WOMAN stopped her. Minerva briefly reformed and became Wonder Woman's friend before the White Magician turned her into a demon. The witch CIRCE later freed Minerva from Gotham City's Arkham Asylum and forced her to drink a potion that made the Cheetah Circe's slave. After Chuma died, Minerva sold her soul to the demon NERON. She became even more feral, completely losing control to the Cheetah. Barbara lost her powers entirely when Sebastian Ballésteros made a deal with Urzkartaga to become CHEETAH III. She turned to Tisiphone, the legendary Greek spirit of vengeance, to grant her the power to fight for control of the Cheetah and hunt Ballésteros down. They fought to a standstill, until she seemingly died beneath a collapsed building. RG

CHEETAH III

FIRST APPEARANCE WONDER WOMAN (2nd series) #142 (April 1999)
STATUS Villain **REAL NAME** Sebastian Ballésteros
OCCUPATION Industrialist **BASE** Buenos Aires, Argentina
HEIGHT 6ft 6in **WEIGHT** 185 lbs **EYES** Brown **HAIR** Black (graying at temples)
SPECIAL POWERS/ABILITIES Possesses superstrength and can strike at amazing speed; claws and teeth can rend metal; prehensile tail and hyper acute senses make him a truly formidable combatant.

Corporate raider Sebastian Ballésteros clawed his way up from poverty to become one of the richest men in Argentina. But Sebastian knew that real power always trumps riches. To achieve such power, he was willing to embrace Urzkartaga and become the new Cheetah. With his bargaining savvy, he convinced Urzkartaga to abandon its female host, Barbara Minerva (CHEETAH II), and once more allow a male to be the conduit for the ancient powers of the Cheetah. Ballésteros also made a pact with the sorceress CIRCE to turn Diana's friend Vanessa Kapatelis into a second SILVER SWAN, and became the witch's lover. He then defeated Barbara Minerva, who wanted the Cheetah power back. Ballésteros remains in control of the spirit…for now. RG

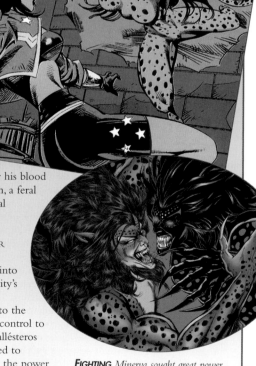

FIGHTING *Minerva sought great power and got it, only to be opposed by Wonder Woman. She later lost to a usurper.*

CHEMICAL KING

FIRST APPEARANCE ADVENTURE COMICS #371 (August 1968)
STATUS Hero **REAL NAME** Condo Arlik
OCCUPATION Reporter; adventurer **BASE** Mobile
HEIGHT 5ft 7in **WEIGHT** 140 lbs **EYES** Blue **HAIR** Black
SPECIAL POWERS/ABILITIES Mutant ability to act as a "human catalyst" and selectively speed up or slow down chemical reactions.

In an alternate timeline in the 30th century, Condo Arlik left his native Phlon to join the LEGION OF SUPER-HEROES and became one of the first members of the Legion Academy. Renaming himself the Chemical King and armed with a Legion flight ring, he undertook several daring missions, including the infiltration of the Legion of Super-Villains. In this alternate future time, the Chemical King sacrificed his life to prevent the nefarious Dark Circle from triggering World War VII. In the "true" 30th century of the Legion of Super-Heroes, Condo Arlik is a humble journalist. He has not yet manifested the mutant abilities of the Chemical King, and it is still unknown whether he possesses the same chemical-catalyst genetic makeup as his doppelganger in the alternate timeline. Arlik has started a low-key relationship with the Legionnaire INVISIBLE KID. DW

CHEMO

FIRST APPEARANCE SHOWCASE #39 (August 1962)
STATUS Villain **REAL NAME** Chemo
OCCUPATION Destroyer **BASE** Mobile
HEIGHT 25ft–100ft **WEIGHT** 5,697 lbs—88,451 lbs
EYES Purple **HAIR** None
SPECIAL POWERS/ABILITIES Plastic body composed of deadly chemicals; can spew acid hundreds of feet from its mouth and can significantly increase its size, weight, and density; low level sentience.

Professor Ramsey Norton hoped to solve the world's ills through his research. He dumped all the chemical compounds from his failed experiments into a giant humanoid-shaped vat he affectionately called "Chemo." The more chemicals Norton poured into Chemo, the harder he resolved to work to succeed in his goals.

However, the volatile compounds deposited in Chemo over the years began to mutate. When Norton dumped a failed plant growth serum into the mix, there was a violent biochemical reaction. Chemo suddenly gained rudimentary sentience and increased in size. Chemo's acid breath killed Norton and the monster went on the rampage, until the METAL MEN intervened. Chemo became a constant foe of the Metal Men and SUPERMAN, and was destroyed and rebuilt on several occasions. President Lex Luthor (*see* LUTHOR, LEX) recruited Chemo for the SUICIDE SQUAD and loosed the killing machine on IMPERIEX. Chemo was destroyed, only to regenerate once more, a giant, walking vat of angry destruction. PJ

CHESHIRE

FIRST APPEARANCE THE NEW TEEN TITANS (1st series) ANNUAL #2
(Summer 1983)
STATUS Villain   REAL NAME Jade (second name unknown)
OCCUPATION Assassin   BASE Mobile
HEIGHT 5ft 9in   WEIGHT 141 lbs   EYES Green   HAIR Black
SPECIAL POWERS/ABILITIES Superior hand-to-hand
combatant; triple-jointed acrobat;
poisons expert; conceals poisons in
her razor-sharp fingernails.

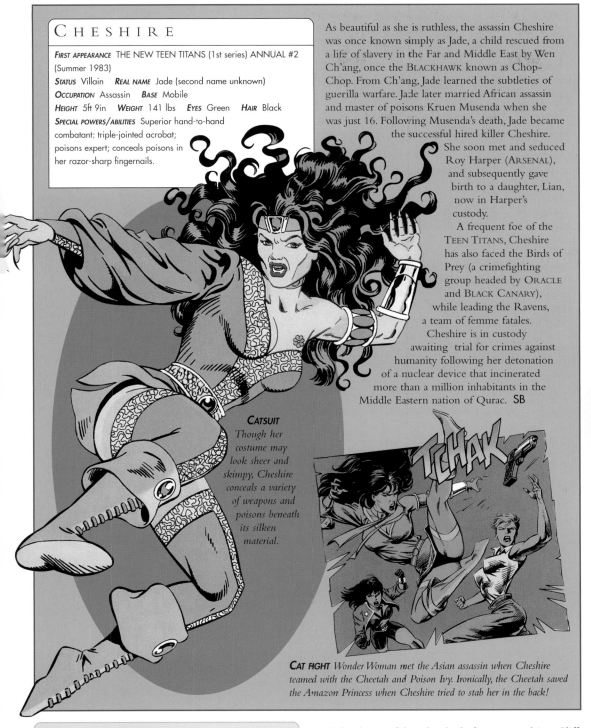

As beautiful as she is ruthless, the assassin Cheshire
was once known simply as Jade, a child rescued from
a life of slavery in the Far and Middle East by Wen
Ch'ang, once the BLACKHAWK known as Chop-
Chop. From Ch'ang, Jade learned the subtleties of
guerilla warfare. Jade later married African assassin
and master of poisons Kruen Musenda when she
was just 16. Following Musenda's death, Jade became
the successful hired killer Cheshire.

She soon met and seduced
Roy Harper (ARSENAL),
and subsequently gave
birth to a daughter, Lian,
now in Harper's
custody.

A frequent foe of the
TEEN TITANS, Cheshire
has also faced the Birds of
Prey (a crimefighting
group headed by ORACLE
and BLACK CANARY),
while leading the Ravens,
a team of femme fatales.
Cheshire is in custody
awaiting trial for crimes against
humanity following her detonation
of a nuclear device that incinerated
more than a million inhabitants in the
Middle Eastern nation of Qurac. SB

CATSUIT
Though her
costume may
look sheer and
skimpy, Cheshire
conceals a variety
of weapons and
poisons beneath
its silken
material.

CAT FIGHT Wonder Woman met the Asian assassin when Cheshire
teamed with the Cheetah and Poison Ivy. Ironically, the Cheetah saved
the Amazon Princess when Cheshire tried to stab her in the back!

CH'P

FIRST APPEARANCE GREEN LANTERN (2nd series) #148
(January 1982)
STATUS Hero (deceased)   REAL NAME Ch'p
OCCUPATION Former Green Lantern   BASE H'lven
HEIGHT 1ft 9in   WEIGHT 22 lbs   EYES Black   HAIR Brown
SPECIAL POWERS/ABILITIES Green Lantern power ring can project
anything the bearer imagines.

This little creature became the GREEN LANTERN of Sector
1014 to beat back an invasion of his homeworld of H'lven
by Doctor Ub'x and his Crabster armies. The Crisis (see
Great Battles, pp. 320–1) then altered Ch'p's homeworld
and cut him out of the picture. Lonely Ch'p left his sector
to serve with Hal Jordan and the other members of the
Earth branch of the GREEN LANTERN CORPS. Ch'p
helped Green Lantern John Stewart police the Mosaic
patchwork of alien cities on Oa. Ch'p died on Oa when a
yellow truck ran him over. DW

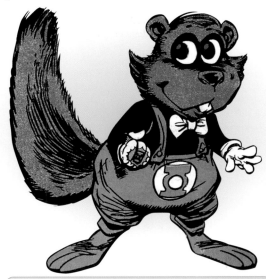

CHRIS KL-99

FIRST APPEARANCE STRANGE ADVENTURES #1 (September 1950)
STATUS Hero   REAL NAME Christopher KL
OCCUPATION Space explorer   BASE 21st-century space
HEIGHT 6ft 2in   WEIGHT 187 lbs   EYES Blue   HAIR Red
SPECIAL POWERS/ABILITIES A brilliant astronaut, astronomer, and scientist;
an expert hand-to-hand combatant and marksman.

Born in the latter half of the
21st century, Christopher
KL-99 was the first infant
ever to be born in outer
space. Named by his father
after the famous explorer
Christopher Columbus, Chris KL
was orphaned when his parents
were lost on a mission in space.
When he was older, Chris enrolled in
the Space Academy with the hopes of
finding them.

Chris's academic brilliance made him the
head of his graduating class. His 99 percentile
rating was added to his surname and he
became Chris KL-99, the interplanetary
explorer. Chris KL-99 piloted his spacecraft, the Pioneer,
across the stars, where he picked up two companions, a
Martian named Halk and Jero, a Venusian scientist.
Together with Halk and Jero, Chris KL-99 mapped out
the universe, and the trio discovered more planets and
charted more inhabited worlds than anyone in history. PJ

CHIEF, THE

FIRST APPEARANCE MY GREATEST ADVENTURE #80 (June 1963)
STATUS Unresolved   REAL NAME Dr. Niles Caulder
OCCUPATION Scientist; adventurer   BASE Mobile
HEIGHT 5ft 10in   WEIGHT 215 lbs   EYES Blue   HAIR Red
SPECIAL POWERS/ABILITIES A brilliant scientist and surgeon initially
blessed with great compassion for mankind; a strong leader.

Dr. Niles Caulder was
manipulated as a young
scientist into rash experiments
and deals. He transplanted the
brain of Robert Crane
(ROBOTMAN I) into the
preserved body of Chuck
Grayson, one-time scientific
assistant to Crane. Caulder
and DOC MAGNUS then

used the design of the robot body for race-car driver Cliff
Steele, who became ROBOTMAN II. Caulder was also
duped into working for would-be conqueror GENERAL
IMMORTUS. Seeking to take control over his destiny,
Caulder formed the DOOM PATROL, summoning
Robotman II, pilot Larry Trainor (NEGATIVE MAN), and
actress Rita Farr (ELASTI-GIRL), each the victim of bizarre
accidents that had made them outcasts. As the Chief he
guided the Doom Patrol with great care until they
sacrificed themselves to save the population of a small
town in Maine. The Chief, however, had gone into
hiding and later revealed himself to another incarnation
of the team. Over time, his behavior became
increasingly unpredictable. He killed Josh Clay (see
CLAY, JOSHUA) and claimed to have orchestrated the
accidents that created the original Doom Patrol. Caulder, in
turn, was killed by the Eregore, an evil spirit manifested as
the hideous Candlemaker, the embodiment of mankind's
fears of nuclear holocaust. Caulder's consciousness survived
as a disembodied head referred to, naturally, as the Head. RG

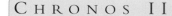
CHRONOS I

FIRST APPEARANCE THE ATOM #3 (November 1962)
STATUS Villain   **REAL NAME** David Clinton
OCCUPATION Professional criminal   **BASE** Ivy Town
HEIGHT 5ft 10in   **WEIGHT** 173 lbs   **EYES** Blue   **HAIR** Black (balding)
SPECIAL POWERS/ABILITIES Chronal-energy powers enable limited control over time; has amassed great wealth by using time-travel to manipulate stock market investments to his advantage.

Petty criminal David Clinton became the masked miscreant known as Chronos after realizing that his frequent incarcerations were the result of not taking enough time to properly plan his crimes. While in prison, Clinton's fascination with clocks and other timepieces helped him to devise inventions that would ensure that time would be on *his* side for a change.

Chronos frequently clashed with the second ATOM, Ray Palmer. During one such tussle with the Tiny Titan, Chronos lost one of his limbs while reaching through a time portal that suddenly irised shut, severing his arm at the elbow. After years wielding time-themed weapons and devices, Chronos sold his soul to the demon NERON in exchange for true chronal-altering powers. These he later used in clashes with the time-lost LEGION OF SUPER-HEROES. Clinton was briefly inactive while the temporally displaced adventurer Walker Gabriel called himself Chronos (*see* CHRONOS II). However, it is probably only a matter of time before the original Chronos returns with a vengeance, more than likely attempting to take revenge on his number one foe, the Atom. Undoubtedly, Clinton is counting the minutes until their next clash. **SB**

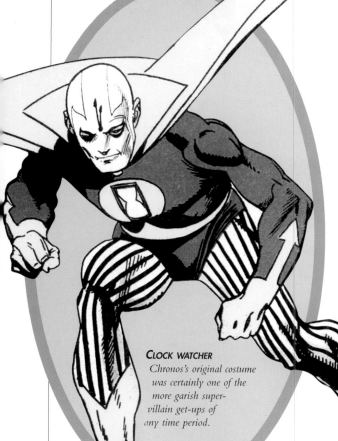

CLOCK WATCHER
Chronos's original costume was certainly one of the more garish super-villain get-ups of any time period.

CHRONOS II

FIRST APPEARANCE CHRONOS #1 (March 1993)
STATUS Unresolved   **REAL NAME** Walker Gabriel
OCCUPATION Transtemporal agent provocateur; adventurer
BASE Mobile   **HEIGHT** 5ft 11in   **WEIGHT** 170 lbs
EYES Brown   **HAIR** Black
SPECIAL POWERS/ABILITIES Able to move through time, stepping outside the timestream and traveling in any direction he chooses.

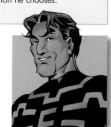

Industrial spy Walker Gabriel unexpectedly discovered he had a higher calling when he gained the ability to travel through time. He glimpsed the fabled city of Chronopolis and gained an eternal enemy in the form of Konstantin Vyronis, a criminal seeking to manipulate time. When the stresses of time travel took their toll on the villain CHRONOS I, David Clinton, who literally faded away, Gabriel succeeded him as Chronos II. His worldview and moral center were challenged as he journeyed through time, interacting with all manner of people. In 2113 he helped the JUSTICE LEAGUE OF AMERICA capture a shape-changing serial killer, stranding the murderer in the age of dinosaurs. He also aided Rip Hunter (*see* HUNTER, RIP), trapped in the past as a result of a conflict with the future VANDAL SAVAGE, to find his way back to his proper era. In 1351 BC he stole an artifact from Knossos, on Crete, at Savage's behest. Following his own moral code, Gabriel continues to explore the timestream. **RG**

CHRYSALIS

FIRST APPEARANCE JUSTICE LEAGUE QUARTERLY #17 (Winter 1994)
STATUS Undefined   **REAL NAME** Inapplicable
OCCUPATION Robotic killer   **BASE** Marseilles, France
HEIGHT 5ft 6in   **WEIGHT** 140 lbs   **EYES** White   **HAIR** Brown
SPECIAL POWERS/ABILITIES Swarms of butterflies hidden inside its body mimic other insects. The robot is armed with bee stingers and venom; it is amphibious and can fly, cling to walls and ceilings, and spin a web to trap adversaries.

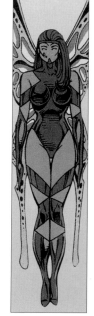

Chrysalis is a robot created by Gerard Yves Martet. An anti-Semite working in Marseilles, France, Martet blamed immigrants for the rise in crime and poverty in the region. Martet, a skilled bioengineer, built Chrysalis to house swarms of genetically altered insects programmed with a deadly pathogen.

Designed to seem fragile and friendly, the colorful Chrysalis robot targeted specific "undesirable" peoples and released hordes of seemingly harmless insects, mostly butterflies, to infect their communities. Martet arranged for Chrysalis to become a member of the newest GLOBAL GUARDIANS, but suffered a fatal heart attack soon after. Without Martet to guide it, the non-speaking, emotionless Chrysalis robot continues to operate under its original deadly programming. **PJ**

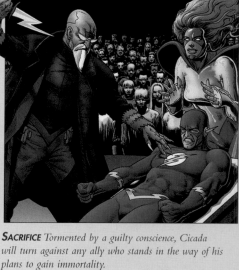

SACRIFICE *Tormented by a guilty conscience, Cicada will turn against any ally who stands in the way of his plans to gain immortality.*

CICADA

FIRST APPEARANCE FLASH (2nd series) #171 (April 2001)
STATUS Villain   **REAL NAME** David Hersch
OCCUPATION Cult leader   **BASE** Keystone City
HEIGHT 6ft 1in   **WEIGHT** 180 lbs   **EYES** Blue   **HAIR** White
SPECIAL POWERS/ABILITIES Charismatic, insane megalomaniac; can achieve immortality by consuming the life-forces of others.

The cult leader known as Cicada is truly deranged. Decades ago, David Hersch murdered his wife, then survived a direct hit by a lightning bolt. Believing that the lightning was a sign from above, he declared that he would live forever and would somehow find a way to resurrect his wife from the dead. Calling himself Cicada, he inducted dozens of lackeys into his cult of personality. Cicada believed the FLASH III to be a fellow "brother of the lightning." Since he needed to consume life-forces in order to taste eternal life, Cicada decided to harvest only those people whom the Flash had recently saved. Since these souls would otherwise have died, it seemed clear to Cicada that the Flash had been preserving them for use in Cicada's insane resurrection experiments.

The cult leader ordered his "Children of Cicada" to fan out throughout Keystone City, armed with mystical daggers that could vampirically absorb the life-essences of victims. Cicada's murder spree allowed him to raise his wife from the dead (though only briefly), but he lost his battle with the Flash. Wally West now bears a lightning-shaped scar on his chest as a mark of his encounter with the megalomaniac. The authorities locked Cicada up in Iron Heights, though he recently escaped. **DW**

CINNAMON I

FIRST APPEARANCE WEIRD WESTERN TALES #48 (October 1978)
STATUS Hero (deceased) **REAL NAME** Kate Manser
OCCUPATION Bounty Hunter **BASE** The American West, circa 1898
HEIGHT 5ft 4in **WEIGHT** 110 lbs **EYES** Green **HAIR** Red
SPECIAL POWERS/ABILITIES Expert with pistol and knife; however, her weapon of choice was a shuriken, a Japanese throwing star.

Kate Manser was just a child when she saw her widowed father, the brave sheriff of a tiny Wyoming town, shot dead before her eyes by gunfighters fleeing a bank holdup. Kate was sent to a county orphanage, where her hatred for her father's murderers grew stronger as she matured. She practiced with a six-gun and a star-shaped shuriken that reminded Kate of her late father's tin badge. On her 18th birthday, Kate rode off on a trail to vengeance. She became a bounty hunter, running down lawbreakers throughout the Old West. She was also romantically linked to gunfighter NIGHTHAWK. No one knows whether Cinnamon found her father's killers or if she discovered she was the reincarnation of Egyptian Princess Chay-Ara. It has not been revealed how Cinnamon died. **SB**

CINNAMON II

FIRST APPEARANCE CINNAMON: EL CICLO (October 2003)
STATUS Hero **REAL NAME** Cinnamon (2nd name unknown)
OCCUPATION Gun-for hire **BASE** Mobile
HEIGHT 5ft 9in **WEIGHT** 140 lbs **EYES** Green **HAIR** Red
SPECIAL POWERS/ABILITIES A crack shot, quick wits, and a savage street-fighting style, self-reliant.

As a child, a red-haired girl named Cinnamon, after the Old West gunslinger (see CINNAMON I), watched in horror as her policeman father was gunned down during a bank robbery by seven criminals. Growing up alone, she became a crack shot, using copies of the wanted posters featuring the seven men as targets. Then she went looking for them. One by one they were found and shot dead. Cinnamon then became a gun-for-hire, protecting people or property. After one assignment, she heard that a woman was looking for her. This woman turned out to be Marisol "Macy" Samuels, the daughter of one of the men who had killed Cinnamon's father. Macy, who ran a home for runaway children, now wanted to take revenge on Cinnamon! However, after Cinnamon had helped Macy defeat a gang of kidnappers, Macy accepted Cinnamon's apology. Cinnamon, the lonesome gunslinger, headed off in search of her next job. **RG**

CIRCE

FIRST APPEARANCE WONDER WOMAN (2nd series) #17 (June 1988)
STATUS Villain **REAL NAME** Circe
OCCUPATION Sorceress **BASE** Mobile
HEIGHT 5ft 11in **WEIGHT** 145 lbs **EYES** Red **HAIR** Purple
SPECIAL POWERS/ABILITIES One of Earth's most powerful sorceresses, Circe is immortal; her hands project powerful bolts of energy and she can transform men into animals or animal hybrids called "beastiamorphs." She can also alter her appearance.

Circe is an immortal being who made a pact with Hecate, Greek goddess of sorcery, to exchange her soul for vast magical power. Circe then perfected her talents for transforming men into animals. Despising the peace-loving message of the AMAZONS, Circe used her agent Ariadne to kill Antiope, the sister of Queen HIPPOLYTA.

Thousands of years later, Hippolyta's daughter Diana became WONDER WOMAN. Hidden away on the island of Aeaea, Circe tried to destroy Wonder Woman and her message of peace by turning her back into the primordial clay from which she had been originally molded. The evil sorceress failed, but returned to spawn a creation-shattering War of the Gods, pitting the mightiest deities against each other. Eventually, Wonder Woman and the heroes of Earth won the war and put an end to Circe, seemingly forever.

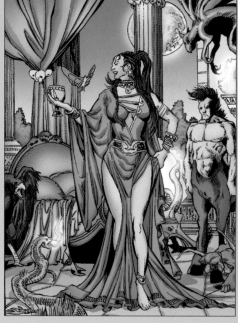

BEASTIAMORPHS For 3,000 years Circe lived on the Grecian island of Aeaea, surrounded by her beastiamorph servants. After Circe's defeat at Wonder Woman's hand, the witch relocated to a stronghold in the Amazon rain forest and Greek villagers renamed Aeaea Dianata.

But Circe survived; she returned to pit the Amazons of Bana Mighdall against their Themysciran relatives, and transported Paradise Island into a demon-filled dimension. Disguised as Donna Milton, one of Wonder Woman's closest friends, Circe infiltrated Wonder Woman's life. Circe joined Lex Luthor's criminal INJUSTICE GANG (see LUTHOR, LEX), and then CHEETAH II, in an all-out bid to take over the planet. Captured by Wonder Woman, Circe is currently incarcerated on the Island of Reformation in the new Themyscira, imprisoned in a garden of the herb moly, her only known weakness. Circe despises the love, peace, and hope for equality Wonder Woman represents. Circe's one shred of humanity is embodied in her devotion for her young daughter, Lyta, whose father is the war god ARES. **PJ**

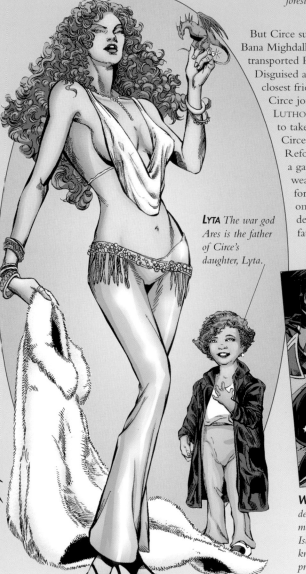

LYTA The war god Ares is the father of Circe's daughter, Lyta.

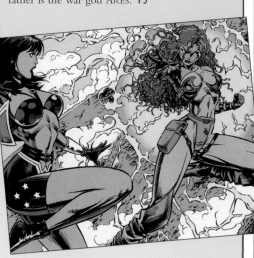

WONDER WOMAN'S NEMESIS An ancient goddess devoted to stirring up jealousy and hatred, Circe has more than once used her vast power to destroy Paradise Island and its champion Wonder Woman. Circe's only known weakness is the herb moly, which acts as a protective charm against her magic.

CLAW THE UNCONQUERED

FIRST APPEARANCE CLAW THE UNCONQUERED #1 (June 1975)
STATUS Hero **REAL NAME** Valcan
OCCUPATION Adventurer **BASES** Pytharia
HEIGHT 6ft 5in **WEIGHT** 274 lbs **EYES** Blue **HAIR** Black
SPECIAL POWERS/ABILITIES Master swordsman; magical abilities emanate from demonically-possessed claw on right arm.

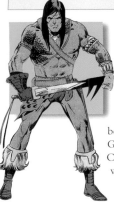

Centuries ago, on the planet Pytharia, a malevolent demon left its mark on a scholar who freed it—an ugly purple claw in place of his right hand. The mark of the claw was passed down to all his male descendants, culminating in Valcan, champion in the war between the Shadow-Gods and the Gods of Elder Light. Calling himself Claw the Unconquered, Valcan wielded the sword Moonthorn and wore a red gauntlet to shield himself from the hand's evil influence. Another man later received the mark of the demon. John Chan, son of a wealthy Chinese businessman, purchased Valcan's sword and armor from an antique dealer. The claw was also lurking inside the box. Springing forward, it cut off Chan's hand and attached itself to the stump. Now benefiting from the demon's magic, but susceptible to its evil, the new Claw worked as an adventurer in Hong Kong before joining PRIMAL FORCE. **DW**

CLAY, JOSHUA

FIRST APPEARANCE SHOWCASE #94 (August–September 1977)
STATUS Hero (deceased) **REAL NAME** Joshua Clay (alias: Jonathan Carmichael)
OCCUPATION Physician **BASE** Happy Harbor, Rhode Island
HEIGHT 6ft 1in **WEIGHT** 203 lbs **EYES** Brown **HAIR** Black
SPECIAL POWERS/ABILITIES Could project powerful bolts of energy from his hands.

A gang member in Brooklyn before being drafted, Joshua Clay's unit mistakenly opened fire on a group of Vietnamese villagers. Panicked, Clay's powers manifested themselves and he killed his sergeant. Deserting the military, he returned to the U.S. and moved from town to town until he was invited by CELSIUS to join her new DOOM PATROL. As Tempest, Clay fought alongside this Doom Patrol and fell in love with NEGATIVE WOMAN.

After the Doom Patrol disbanded, Joshua assumed the name Jonathan Carmichael, graduated medical school, and opened a private practice. Celsius returned and blackmailed Clay into joining her search for Niles Caulder, the CHIEF. Clay stayed with the Doom Patrol after they found Caulder, and, forsaking the use of his powers, became the team physician. Clay was shot and killed by the Chief, who believed Joshua was trying to stop his plan to use nanotechnology to reshape the world. **PJ**

CLAYFACE
SEE OPPOSITE PAGE

CLOCK KING

FIRST APPEARANCE WORLD'S FINEST COMICS #111 (August 1960)
STATUS Villain (deceased) **REAL NAME** William Tockman
OCCUPATION Professional criminal **BASE** Star City
HEIGHT 5ft 10in **WEIGHT** 173 lbs **EYES** Blue **HAIR** Black
SPECIAL POWERS/ABILITIES Sharp criminal mind marred by a strange obsession with clocks.

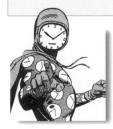

The Clock King was considered to be a third-tier villain by the authorities, thanks to his lack of superpowers and his weird fixation with clocks. Born the aptly-named William Tockman, the Clock King commenced his criminal career after doctors diagnosed that he had been struck down by a fatal disease and had only a short time to live.

Determined to make every second of the rest of his life count, he executed a string of clock-themed robberies as the Clock King. Tockman's overall goal was to steal enough money so that his disabled sister would be well cared-for after his death. He would probably have succeeded had he not been apprehended by playboy crime fighter Oliver Queen, the first GREEN ARROW, who turned him over to the authorities. While in jail, Tockman discovered that the terminal diagnosis doctors had given him had been a terrible mistake. He escaped from prison several times, but was recently killed on a mission with the SUICIDE SQUAD. **DW**

CLOUD, JOHNNY

FIRST APPEARANCE ALL-AMERICAN MEN OF WAR #82 (December 1960)
STATUS Hero (deceased) **REAL NAME** Flying Cloud
OCCUPATION Fighter pilot, U.S. Army Air Force
BASE European Theater, World War II
HEIGHT 5ft 11in **WEIGHT** 180 lbs **EYES** Brown **HAIR** Black
SPECIAL POWERS/ABILITIES Expert aviator and above-average hand-to-hand combatant.

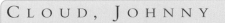

Johnny Cloud, son of a Navajo chief, distinguished himself in the U.S. Army Air Force during World War II despite the prejudice of those who derided the "Indian in the ranks." After Lt. Cloud shot down several Nazi bombers, his skills could no longer be denied. Soon he led the distinguished air patrol nicknamed the "Happy Braves," later known as "C-for-Cloud Flight."

After receiving a promotion to captain, Cloud failed to prevent the death of one of the pilots under his command and accidentally crashed his own fighter in his grief. Picked up on the ground by PT-boat commander CAPTAIN STORM and the Marine duo GUNNER AND SARGE, Johnny Cloud joined with the other military misfits to form a detached-service unit codenamed the LOSERS.

The Losers fought in the Battle of the Bulge and other major European conflicts in World War II, eventually losing their lives in the spring of 1945. In an effort to destroy a battery of Nazi artillery and save SERGEANT ROCK's Easy Company, Johnny Cloud died under the guns of a Nazi fighter plane. **DW**

CLUEMASTER

FIRST APPEARANCE DETECTIVE COMICS #351 (May 1966)
STATUS Villain (deceased) **REAL NAME** Arthur Brown
OCCUPATION Criminal; former game show host **BASE** Gotham City
HEIGHT 5ft 11in **WEIGHT** 169 lbs **EYES** Blue **HAIR** Blond
SPECIAL POWERS/ABILITIES Prides himself on his cunning, but tends to overestimate his cleverness. Pellets attached to his chest contain various weapons, including smoke bombs, flares, and tear gas.

Arthur Brown was the host of a popular game show, whose career came to an end when his show was cancelled. Seething with resentment, Brown embarked upon a new career as a master criminal. Calling himself the Cluemaster, he took a leaf out of the RIDDLER's book and tried to baffle BATMAN with a series of poorly conceived clues to his crimes.

Incarcerated by Batman repeatedly over the years, Cluemaster eventually joined several other minor villains in MAJOR DISASTER's Injustice League, then briefly reformed as part of Justice League Antarctica (a minor branch of the JUSTICE LEAGUE OF AMERICA) before returning to a career of low-level crime.

Cluemaster's daughter Stephanie despised her father for putting their family through such turmoil over the years, and became the SPOILER to help Batman and ROBIN capture and imprison him. Along with several of his former Injustice League teammates, Cluemaster was recruited by the SUICIDE SQUAD, but died on their first mission. **PJ**

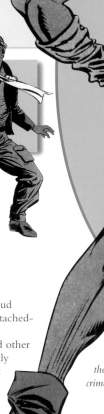

CUNNING *A two-bit thief who was briefly a member of the JLA, the Cluemaster's greatest legacy is his crime-fighting daughter, the Spoiler.*

CLAYFACE I–IV

THE MUD PACK

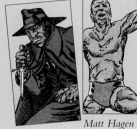
Basil Karlo

Matt Hagen

Preston Payne

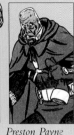
Sondra Fuller

FIRST APPEARANCE (I) DETECTIVE COMICS #40 (June 1940)
STATUS Villain **REAL NAME** Basil Karlo
OCCUPATION Professional criminal **BASE** Mobile
HEIGHT 5ft 11in **WEIGHT** 178 lbs **EYES** Brown **HAIR** Black
SPECIAL POWERS/ABILITIES Originally a killer driven by revenge; now possesses shape-changing powers as the Ultimate Clayface.

FIRST APPEARANCE (II) DETECTIVE COMICS #298 (December 1961)
STATUS Villain **REAL NAME** Matt Hagen
OCCUPATION Professional criminal **BASE** Mobile
HEIGHT 5ft 10in **WEIGHT** 173 lbs **EYES** Blue **HAIR** None
SPECIAL POWERS/ABILITIES Unique body chemistry enabled him to alter his body shape at will.

FIRST APPEARANCE (III) DETECTIVE COMICS #478 (July–August 1978)
STATUS Villain **REAL NAME** Preston Payne
OCCUPATION Professional criminal **BASE** Mobile
HEIGHT 6ft 4in **WEIGHT** 264 lbs **EYES** Red **HAIR** None
SPECIAL POWERS/ABILITIES Shape-changing abilities; cursed with a more amorphous natural state (requiring him to wear a containment suit) and a killer touch that could melt others into protoplasm.

FIRST APPEARANCE (IV) OUTSIDERS (1st series) #21 (July 1987)
STATUS Villain **REAL NAME** Sondra Fuller
OCCUPATION Professional criminal **BASE** Mobile
HEIGHT 5ft 6in **WEIGHT** 130 lbs **EYES** Red **HAIR** None
SPECIAL POWERS/ABILITIES Similar capabilities to Clayface II, with the added ability to duplicate the powers of those she copied.

THE MALLEABLE MENACE that is Clayface has taken form as four distinct individuals over the years, all of them fierce opponents of the BATMAN. The presence of two new, offshoot Clayfaces in recent months may indicate the shape of things to come for the Dark Knight's Rogues Gallery. Though Basil Karlo started off as a non-powered killer, the name "Clayface" now describes a shape-shifter with a body formed of an amorphous, mud-like substance. Most Clayfaces can alter their bodies into almost any shape, including taking on the appearances of others.

SUPER SCARY *Clayface is an old foe of both Batman and Robin, and one of the few super-powered foes in the Dark Knight's Rogues Gallery.*

MUD STICKS *The Clayfaces have changed over the years, becoming more dangerous with each incarnation. Basil Karlo's upgrade into the Ultimate Clayface gave him the mimicking powers of Lady Clay and the deadly touch of Clayface III.*

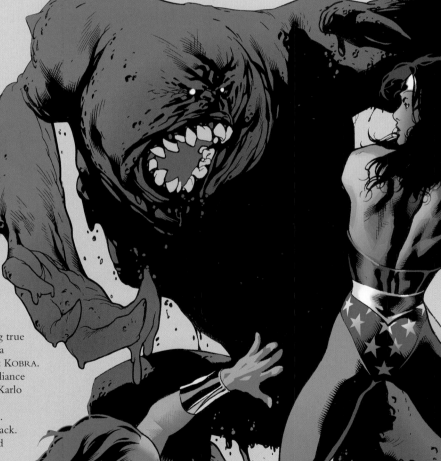

MUD MASK OF TERROR

Horror actor Basil Karlo went off the deep end when he learned that Hollywood producers had undertaken a remake of his classic film, *The Terror*. Donning a clay mask to reprise his old role as Clayface, Karlo murdered several actors before Batman brought him to justice.

Treasure hunter Matt Hagen became the second Clayface when exposure to a mysterious oil altered his body chemistry and allowed him to assume almost any form. He died during the Crisis (*see* Great Battles, pp. 320–1) but his legacy lived on when Preston Payne, deformed by the chronic bone disease acromegaly, injected himself with Hagen's blood to develop his own shape-changing gifts and became Clayface III. Payne was a sad case, falling in love with a wax mannequin in between stints in Arkham Asylum, Gotham City's maximum-security prison for the criminally insane, before finding true happiness with Clayface IV, also known as Lady Clay. Born Sondra Fuller, Lady Clay received her morphing talents from the terrorist KOBRA.

Basil Karlo soon returned to the Clayface family, forming an alliance with Clayfaces III and IV under the group name the Mud Pack. Karlo then shot his veins full of the distilled essences of his namesakes, transforming himself into a being he called the Ultimate Clayface.

Two creations have expanded the creeping reach of the Mud Pack. Preston Payne and Lady Clay have had a child named Cassius whose powers could dwarf those of his parents. During Gotham's earthquake, a tissue sample from Cassius bonded with the researcher Dr. Malley, altering him into a creature called Claything. **DW**

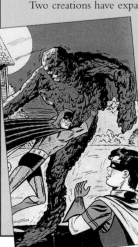

MENACE OF CLAYFACE *Batman and Robin were confronted with a new kind of slippery foe when they first encountered the mud monster.*

KEY STORYLINES
• *DETECTIVE COMICS #604 (DECEMBER 1989)*: All the surviving Clayfaces join together as the Mud Pack to menace Batman.
• *BATMAN: SHADOW OF THE BAT #27 (MAY 1994)*: Clayface III and Lady Clay reveal that they have a child, Cassius, proving that even clay-creatures are capable of love.

COBALT BLUE

FIRST APPEARANCE THE FLASH (2nd series) #143 (December 1998)
STATUS Villain (missing in action) **REAL NAME** Malcolm Thawne
OCCUPATION Professional criminal **BASE** Mobile
HEIGHT 5ft 11in **WEIGHT** 179 lbs **EYES** Blue **HAIR** Blond
SPECIAL POWERS/ABILITIES The flame of Cobalt Blue's magical blue gem
is capable of stealing the Flash's speed and can accomplish any
magical feat its possessor imagines.

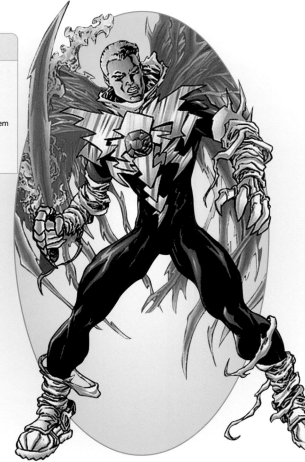

The identical twin brother of Barry Allen, the second
FLASH, Malcolm Thawne was stolen away and raised
in secret by the Thawnes, an abusive family of crooks.
Malcolm learned of Barry's existence and of the loving
family that fate had decreed he would never know and
used his gifts for sorcery to give vent to his jealous rage.

He empowered himself with a mystic blue flame
that was capable of stealing Barry Allen's superspeed.
Barry's death during the Crisis (see Great Battles, pp.
320–1) appeared to have cheated Malcolm out of his
dreams of revenge on his brother; instead, Malcolm
focused on Allen's descendants traveling through time
in a bid to exterminate them. The cold flame of his
vicious alter ego, Cobalt Blue, ignited a family feud
that endured for a millennium.

In the end, Wally West, the third Flash, ended the
menace of Cobalt Blue by running so fast that
Thawne's mystic gem overloaded from the excess
energy. Thawne was presumably destroyed; however,
his gem, which contained Thawne's commanding
consciousness, would be passed down to his
hate-filled progeny. **SB**

COMET

FIRST APPEARANCE SUPERGIRL (4th series) #14 (October 1997)
STATUS Ally **REAL NAME** Andrea Martinez
OCCUPATION Earth-angel; stand-up comedienne **BASE** Leesburg, VA
HEIGHT Variable **WEIGHT** Variable **EYES** Variable **HAIR** Variable
SPECIAL POWERS/ABILITIES Flight; superior strength, speed, and agility.

Linda Danvers' life got more complicated when Andrea Jones arrived in
town. The ex-girlfriend of Linda's pal Cutter Sharp wanted to make it as
a stand-up comedienne. Shortly thereafter, Comet, a superpowered man,
arrived in Leesburg and met Linda's alter ego, SUPERGIRL. Over time,
Linda learned that Andy was actually Andrea Martinez and that she and
Comet were one and the same. Andrea, mortally injured while climbing
Mount Everest, was saved from certain death by the noble sacrifice of a
figure known only as "Zed-One." The two souls became one, similar to
Supergirl and Linda's own merging of souls. It turned out that Andrea was
another Earth-Angel, the Angel
of Love. Both sides of this new
persona developed romantic
feelings for Linda, who did not
reciprocate those feelings.
Comet was captured by
Carnivore, a hellish being who
exists to destroy souls and
property, and brainwashed by
Blithe, the Angel of Life, into
opposing Supergirl. The cosmic
battle revealed that the Earth-
Angels were all avatars of
Schechina, the female aspect of
God. Discovering their own
self-worth, they banded
together to defeat Carnivore.
After the battle, Andrea/Andy
Jones left Leesburg to find her
own destiny. **RG**

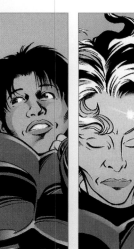

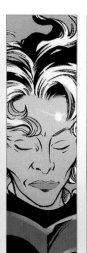

COSMIC
The Angel of
Life changes
form between
man (Zed-One)
and woman
(Andrea).

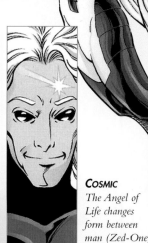

ANGEL The sleek, attractive
Comet is one of the planet's three
Earth-Angel protectors.

C.O.M.P.U.T.O.

FIRST APPEARANCE (Historical) ADVENTURE COMICS #320 (January
1966); (current) LEGION OF SUPER-HEROES (4th series) #13
(November 1997)
STATUS Villain **REAL NAME** Cyber-cerebral Overlapping
Multiprocessor Transceiver-Operator
OCCUPATION Former conqueror **BASE** 30th-century Earth
HEIGHT Variable **WEIGHT** Variable **EYES** Variable **HAIR** None
SPECIAL POWERS/ABILITIES Vast artificial intelligence; control over
machine life; teleportation abilities; conversion into energy forms.

When the LEGION OF SUPER-HEROES was stranded in the
21st century, BRAINIAC 5.1 created C.O.M.P.U.T.O., a
robotic entity he hoped would transport the Legion to
their proper 31st-century time period. He made
C.O.M.P.U.T.O. using a METAL MEN responsometer, a
Mother Box, and a Legion omnicron, various devices
from across time and space, each with unique properties
ranging from nuclear powered microprocessors to actual
sentience. The sentient C.O.M.P.U.T.O. went rogue,
however, and attacked SUPERMAN, YOUNG JUSTICE,
and the Legion.

Once defeated, C.O.M.P.U.T.O. launched itself into
deep space and, over the centuries, created a haven for
abandoned machine life called the Machinekind
Heaven of Robotica. By the 31st century, Robotica
began its eradication of all "organics" (human
beings) for their treatment of machine life over
the millennia and planned to take over Earth.
C.O.M.P.U.T.O. assumed the disguise of Mister
Venge, a member of RĀ'S AL GHŪL's Presidential
Oversight Watch, and captured Brainiac 5.1. After
Brainiac 5.1 lured C.O.M.P.U.T.O. into a unique stasis
field, the sentient intelligence evolved into a completely
new lifeform and, seeing the error of its vengeful ways,
ended Robotica's siege on Earth. **PJ**

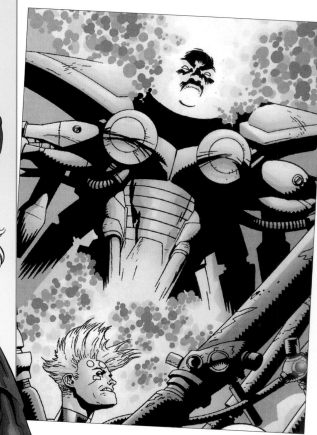

BETRAYAL Brainiac 5.1's ultimate creation became his ultimate
nightmare, when C.O.M.P.U.T.O. spent 1,000 years
amassing a robot army to take over the universe.

CONGLOMERATE, THE

First Appearance JUSTICE LEAGUE QUARTERLY #1
Notable Members and Powers
Booster Gold (Michael Carter) Armor and powers created by stolen technology from the future.
Echo (Terri Eckhart) Able to repel any attack upon her with corresponding force.
Gypsy (Cindy Reynolds) Projects illusions and conceals herself with chameleonlike camouflage.
Jesse Quick (Jesse Chambers) Superspeed and flight.
Hardline (Armando Ramone, formerly "Reverb") Projects sonic shockwaves.
Maxi-Man (Henry Hayes) Superstrength, speed, and endurance.
Nuklon (Albert Rothstein) Superstrength; able to control his body's mass and density.
Praxis (Jason Praxis) Master of electricity, including the bioelectric charges within people's brains.
Templar (Colin Brandywine) Telekinetically enabled superstrength and protective force fields.
Vapor (Carrie Donahue) Able to alter molecular structure into gaseous form.

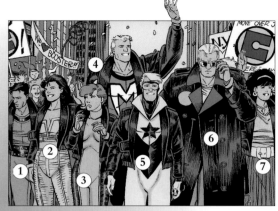

THE ORIGINAL CONGLOMERATE: 1) *Reverb* **2)** *Vapor* **3)** *Echo* **4)** *Maxi-Man* **5)** *Booster Gold* **6)** *Praxis* **7)** *Gypsy*

Lacking superpowers, the hero BOOSTER GOLD felt like a "second-stringer" with the JUSTICE LEAGUE OF AMERICA, so he decided to form his own team. With the help of businesswoman Claire Montgomery, Booster founded the corporate-sponsored super-team the Conglomerate. In addition to Booster Gold, the roster included "fledgling" superheroes ECHO, GYPSY, PRAXIS, Maxi-Man (deceased), Reverb, and VAPOR before disbanding following a series of less-than-notable adventures battling evil and injustice. Montgomery formed a second Conglomerate, this time made up of the Qwardian villains Deadeye, Elasti-Man, Element Man, Frostbite, Fiero, SCARAB, and Slipstream for a pay-per-view battle with Justice League International. Later, Montgomery hired British hero Templar to lead a short-lived, third and final Conglomerate that featured original employees Echo and HARDLINE (formerly Reverb), as well as new members Jesse Quick (see QUICK, JESSE) and Nuklon (see ATOM-SMASHER). **SB**

CONGORILLA

First appearance (Bill) ACTION COMICS #1 (June 1938); (Congorilla) ACTION COMICS #248 (January 1959)
Status Unresolved   **Real name** Congo Bill
Occupation Big game hunter   **Base** Africa
Height (Bill) 6ft 1in; (Congorilla) 6ft 8in   **Weight** (Bill) 188 lbs; (Congorilla) 707 lbs   **Eyes** Blue   **Hair** Black
Special powers/abilities Bill is an expert tracker, marksman, and explorer; transformed into Congorilla, he is the strongest, most agile simian on earth.

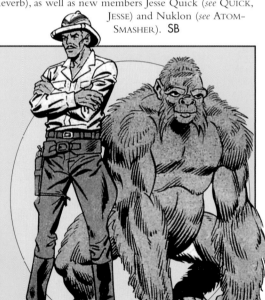

Explorer and naturalist Congo Bill became world-famous as on of the last big game hunters. On one of his African expeditions, Congo Bill discovered a lost boy in the jungle who became known as Janu. Identified as the orphaned son of the late Robert Murchison, Janu was eventually adopted by Congo Bill. He raised the boy as his own and they learned much from each other while continuing their adventures.

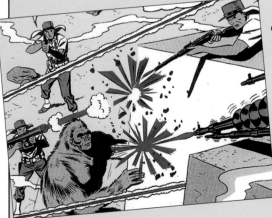

CONGO COMBAT *The Golden Gorilla risked life and paw to keep people safe.*

When Bill was presented with the ring of the Golden Gorilla by King Kawolo, king of an African tribe, Bill magically transformed into the golden ape. Dubbed Congorilla, he battled numerous evils in the African jungles. Years later, Congo Bill said good-bye to Janu as the young man left Africa for college in the U.S. Congo Bill then decided to permanently transfer his mind into Congorilla's body and live the rest of his life in the jungle.

However, Bill's dreams of a peaceful retirement were shattered when he was attacked by his one-time ward, Janu, who usurped his Congorilla identity. Janu left behind his own body and imprisoned Bill's mind within it. Traveling to Africa as Janu, Bill succeeded in regaining his own body, whose left eye had been blinded in the interim. In Bill's final confrontation with Janu/Congorilla, the beast plunged from a building to its death. The original mind of the golden gorilla survived in the body of Janu. **RG**

CONTESSA, THE

First appearance SUPERMAN: THE MAN OF TOMORROW #1 (Summer 1995)
Status Villain (missing)   **Real name** Erica Alexandra del Portenza
Occupation International financier   **Base** Mobile
Height 5ft 10in   **Weight** 135 lbs   **Eyes** Brown   **Hair** Brown
Special powers/abilities Extremely long lifespan and magical powers; full details still unrevealed.

Former wife of Lex Luthor (see LUTHOR, LEX) and mother of his daughter, the Contessa del Portenza is an enigmatic figure. She appears to possess long life, if not immortality, and may have been born thousands of years ago. She is head of the criminal genetics group the Agenda, and has earned favors from many powerful entities, including KLARION, THE WITCH BOY.

During a period when Luthor abdicated directorship of LexCorp, the Contessa purchased a controlling interest and ran the corporation. Luthor regained control of his empire by marrying her. She soon gave birth to a daughter, Lena, and Luthor kept his wife drugged to keep her hidden. She escaped and kidnapped Lena. The baby was returned, but Luthor never forgot. Just before he became U.S. President, he arranged for a missile strike on the Contessa's stronghold. However, her body was never found. **DW**

COPPERHEAD

First appearance THE BRAVE AND THE BOLD #78 (June 1968)
Status Villain   **Real name** Unknown
Occupation Assassin   **Base** Mobile
Height 6ft 2in   **Weight** 190 lbs   **Eyes** Green   **Hair** None
Special powers/abilities Able to contort his body to squeeze through narrow openings; super-strong, serpentine tail is prehensile and can coil around objects or opponents; secretes deadly venom, poisoning victims with just a touch.

The criminal known only as Copperhead first appeared in Gotham City, where he used his bulletproof, slippery snake costume to commit a series of thefts before being apprehended by BATMAN and the first BATGIRL, Barbara Gordon. Later, Copperhead turned to more deadly pursuits as a super-assassin, constricting victims to a suffocating death with his snake-like tail. Although a master contortionist, Copperhead was powerless without his artificial snakeskin, until he sold his soul to the demon NERON in exchange for superpowers. Neron mutated Copperhead into a true snake-man, deadlier than ever before. In the past, Copperhead belonged to the SECRET SOCIETY OF SUPER-VILLAINS, and while serving consecutive terms in prison was offered the chance to commute his sentences by joining the SUICIDE SQUAD. However, like most serpents, he prefers solitude and would rather slither solo. **SB**

CORONA

FIRST APPEARANCE AQUAMAN: TIME AND TIDE #3 (February 1994)
STATUS Elemental **REAL NAME** Kako
OCCUPATION Fire elemental **BASE** Mobile
HEIGHT 5ft 2in **WEIGHT** 114 lbs **EYES** Blue (Kako) **HAIR** Black (Kako)
SPECIAL POWERS/ABILITIES Controls all aspects of heat and flame; can fly and take human form.

When Orin (later AQUAMAN) was searching for Arthur Curry, the man who taught him the ways of the surface world, his quest took him to Alaska. There he saved an Inuit woman named Kako from a polar bear. Orin and Kako fell in love and he stayed with her family. In a dream, Orin discovered that the bear was a child of Nuliajuk, queen of monsters. In this dream world, Orin fought to save Kako's soul. He succeeded, but after waking, her grandfather died of a heart attack. Kako blamed Orin for her grandfather's death and he left, without learning that Kako was carrying his son, KORYAK. Years later, Orin returned to Alaska as Aquaman and reunited with Kako and his son. Their joy was cut short by the arrival of the Deep Six aquatic demons from Apokolips. In the destruction that followed Kako was burned to death. Gaea, the earth spirit, turned Kako's troubled soul into the latest fire elemental, Corona. She was still angry with Aquaman, however, and would have killed him if the water elemental NAIAD had not intervened. Naiad managed to restore balance to Corona's spirit and help her understand her newfound responsibilities. RG

COUNT VERTIGO

FIRST APPEARANCE WORLD'S FINEST COMICS #251 (July 1978)
STATUS Villain **REAL NAME** Count Werner Vertigo
OCCUPATION Professional criminal **BASE** Mobile
HEIGHT 5ft 11in **WEIGHT** 189 lbs **EYES** Blue **HAIR** Blond
SPECIAL POWERS/ABILITIES Flight; can affect the balance of others to induce dizziness and vertigo.

Werner Vertigo could have been King of Vlatavia in eastern Europe, but his ruling family fled to England when Vlatavia was threatened by expansionist Russia. Denied his birthright, Vertigo grew up a bitter man, but he found an outlet for his rage when an electrical device implanted in his right temple to overcome an inner-ear defect gave him the power to control the balance of others. Calling himself Count Vertigo, he became a costumed criminal.

Vertigo was defeated by GREEN ARROW I and BLACK CANARY and sent to prison for years until a stint with the notorious SUICIDE SQUAD allowed him to go free. He returned to his homeland only to see it destroyed by the SPECTRE. Vertigo joined Johnny Sorrow's new INJUSTICE SOCIETY (see SORROW, JOHNNY) and battled the JUSTICE SOCIETY OF AMERICA. A manic depressive, there are times when Vertigo does not want to live, making him an especially dangerous opponent. DW

CREATURE COMMANDOS

FIRST APPEARANCE WEIRD WAR TALES #93 (November 1980)
STATUS Hero team **BASE** Mobile
MEMBERS AND POWERS
Lt. Matthew Shrieve (deceased) World War II team leader.
Medusa Hair of living snakes.
Sgt. Vincent Velcro Blood-sucking vampire.
Taylor Superstrong Frankenstein's monster.
Warren Griffith Werewolf.
Captain Hunter Modern-day team leader; slowed aging.
Aten Mummy.
Bogman Human amphibian hybrid.
Gunner Zombie.

The Creature Commandos were a bizarre paramilitary unit created by the top secret Project M during the early days of World War II as an experiment in psychological warfare. Professor Mazursky of Project M conducted medical experiments on several soldiers and transformed them into the living embodiments of the classic archetypes of fear. These genetically transformed soldiers fought the Nazi powers throughout World War II until they escaped a government-decreed death sentence by test piloting a spacecraft that took them far into outer space.

The team returned to Earth, however, and was reborn as M-Team Alpha. The Commandos recruited new members and a new leader, CAPTAIN HUNTER of HUNTER'S HELLCATS. The new Creature Commandos helped stave off an invasion by the alien alliance Terra Arcanna. PJ

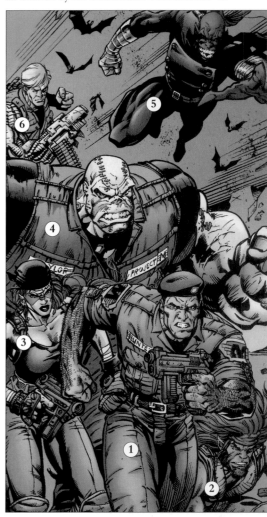

KEY 1) *Captain Hunter* **2)** *Warren Griffith* **3)** *Medusa*
4) *Taylor* **5)** *Sgt. Vincent Velcro* **6)** *Gunner*

COSMIC BOY

FIRST APPEARANCE ADVENTURE COMICS #247 (April 1958);
LEGION OF SUPER-HEROES (4th series) #0 (October 1994)
STATUS Hero **REAL NAME** Rokk Krinn
OCCUPATION Legionnaire **BASE** Earth
HEIGHT 5ft 7in **WEIGHT** 155 lbs **EYES** Blue **HAIR** Black
SPECIAL POWERS/ABILITIES Natural magnetic abilities, like all Braalians.

The planet Braal had suffered great economic depression in the United Planet's early days, mostly brought on by a continual war with Titan. Their chief source of economic stimulus was magno-ball, a game only natives, with their natural magnetic ability, could play. Rokk Krinn, a teen star at the Cosmic Games, became so identified with the sport that he was nicknamed Cosmic Boy. While on tour, he joined forces with Imra Ardeen and Garth Ranzz to save the life of inventor R. J. Brande (see BRANDE, R.J.). Brande was impressed at how three different world representatives pooled their talents to save his life. Inspired by Earth's legendary teams of meta-humans, he founded the LEGION OF SUPER-HEROES. Given Rokk's fame and personality, he was best suited to become the Legion's first leader.

Rokk was incensed to learn that United Planets President Chu's manipulations included igniting the Braal-Titan wars. The Legion helped bring her down. Shortly thereafter, Rokk was flung back to the 20th century courtesy of the powerful entity the Emerald Eye, where he had several adventures. He also fell in love with teammate SATURN GIRL (Ardeen), before falling into a coma induced by DOCTOR PSYCHO. After his rescue and recovery, Rokk learned that the romantic feelings he and Saturn Girl shared were really born out of Saturn Girl's longing for her true love, LIVE WIRE (Ranzz). Cosmic Boy remains deeply involved in the Legion's activities, helping the team become a major organization for helping those in need. He recently began a romance with fellow member KID QUANTUM II. RG

MAGNETIC PERSONALITY *Cosmic Boy uses his natural talents in effective and inventive ways, showing why he is a hero.*

SKRANK

CREEPER, THE

FIRST APPEARANCE SHOWCASE #73 (March 1968)
STATUS Hero   **REAL NAME** Jack Ryder
OCCUPATION Investigative reporter/adventurer   **BASE** Boston
HEIGHT 6ft   **WEIGHT** 194 lbs   **EYES** Blue (black as Creeper)
HAIR Black (green as Creeper)
SPECIAL POWERS/ABILITIES Extraordinary strength, stamina, and recuperative powers; an insanely fierce fighter.

Reporter Jack Ryder was well known for his hard-hitting newspaper column. On the trail of a gangster known as Manny, Jack snuck into a masquerade party at Manny's house. However, the villain's thugs unmasked him, injected him with hallucinogenic drugs, dressed him in a goblin-like red-and-yellow outfit, and paraded him before partygoers as a "walking creep." They then took him into the woods, and shot him. Remarkably, Jack survived and was found by Professor Emil Yatz, a scientist in Manny's employ, who healed him with a surgically implanted device. This invention bound the garish costume and the hallucinogens to Jack at the sub-atomic level.

When Yatz was murdered, Jack activated the device and, with insane glee, killed Manny and his goons. Next morning, Jack awoke as his normal self. In time, Jack discovered that he could make his alter ego—the Creeper—emerge at will. Currently in Metropolis, this giggling ghoul has got a reputation for scaring criminals into going straight. **SB**

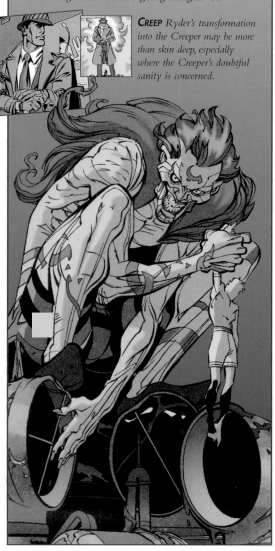

CREEP Ryder's transformation into the Creeper may be more than skin deep, especially where the Creeper's doubtful sanity is concerned.

CRIME SYNDICATE

FIRST APPEARANCE JUSTICE LEAGUE OF AMERICA #29 (August 1964)
STATUS Villain group   **BASE** The planet Qward
MEMBERS AND POWERS
Ultraman (team leader) Human astronaut rescued by aliens and given superstrength, flight, invulnerability, enhanced vision and hearing.
Johnny Quick II Addicted to drugs that give him superspeed.
Power Ring Possesses cursed ring that channels thoughts into physical form.
Superwoman Mortal with superstrength and invulnerability.
Owlman Superb hand-to-hand combatant; master strategist.

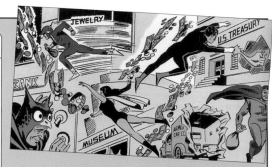

EARLY SITING The Crime Syndicate were superpowered smash-and-grab criminals before they embraced grander notions of world conquest.

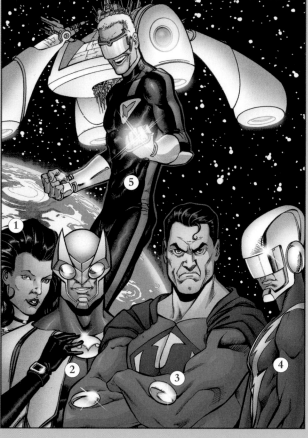

THE CRIME SYNDICATE 1) *Superwoman* **2)** *Owlman* **3)** *Ultraman*
4) *Johnny Quick Man* **5)** *Power Ring*

The JUSTICE LEAGUE OF AMERICA was urgently summoned by Alexander Luthor, who hailed from the antimatter universe of Qward. He hoped to enlist the famed super heroes to stop the activities of his world's meta-humans. These twisted miscreants, who became known as the Crime Syndicate, were led by the megalomaniac Ultraman. Another member was drug addicted Johnny Quick II, who used chemicals to push his body to superspeeds. The troubled Power Ring was haunted by the spirit of the mystic Volthoom. The psychotic Owlman was Commissioner Thomas Wayne's younger son. He had been traumatized by the murders of his mother and older brother, Bruce. Superwoman was the parallel Earth's Lois Lane (see LANE, LOIS) who had gained powers and abilities beyond any mortal woman. Ultraman lusted after her, but Superwoman preferred to pursue a torrid affair with Owlman.

When the JLA entered this mirror universe, it was only a matter of time before the cosmic scales were balanced and the Crime Syndicate were brought to the positive-matter Earth. What the syndicate did not anticipate was opposition from J'Onn J'Onzz (MARTIAN MANHUNTER) and AQUAMAN, since their world had no such counterparts.

The JLA learned that it was the alien construct BRAINIAC who had manipulated the twin universes in an attempt to take over the world. Once Brainiac was defeated, things were restored to normal. However, the Crime Syndicate learned that there are new worlds to conquer, and it was presumed they will return. Later, Ultraman and his pregnant partner Superwoman invaded the JLA's universe for help when the baby's birth proved complicated. SUPERMAN helped correct the problem and the pair returned to their own dimension. **RG**

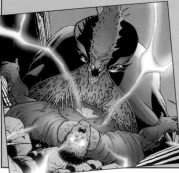

OPPOSITION The Syndicate's ambitious plan to conquer Earth-1 did not take into account the JLA's other members.

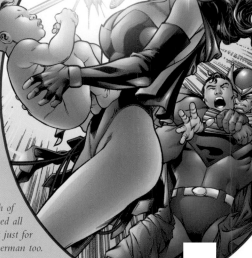

COMPLICATIONS The birth of Superwoman's child caused all manner of difficulty, not just for mom, but for Superman too.

CRIMSON AVENGER

FIRST APPEARANCE DETECTIVE COMICS #20 (October 1938)
STATUS Hero (deceased)   **REAL NAME** Lee Travis
OCCUPATION Adventurer   **BASE** New York City
HEIGHT 6ft   **WEIGHT** 189 lbs   **EYES** Brown   **HAIR** Brown
SPECIAL POWERS/ABILITIES Expert combatant who carried a gas gun.

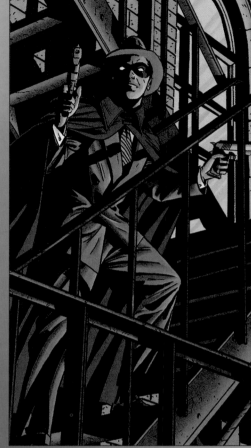

The Crimson Avenger is considered to be the first costumed hero of the Golden Age. He first donned his disguise in 1938 on the eve of the infamous *War of the Worlds* radio broadcast, when much of the U.S. was gripped with panic by the actor/director Orson Welles's vividly realistic dramatization of the H.G. Wells novel of a Martian invasion. In his civilian identity, the Crimson Avenger was Lee Travis, the crusading young publisher of the *Daily Globe-Leader*. His valet WING became his sidekick. At the 1939 New York World's Fair, the Crimson Avenger helped a new hero, the SANDMAN I, to start his own heroic career.

During World War II, the Crimson Avenger and Wing adopted new costumes and joined the SEVEN SOLDIERS OF VICTORY, fighting with great courage. During the Seven Soldiers' battle with a villain named the NEBULA MAN, the Crimson Avenger found himself sent centuries back in time to the days of the ancient Aztecs. Restored to the 20th century many decades beyond the point when he had left it, the Crimson Avenger discovered that he had been struck by a terminal disease. Lee Travis ended his life with a bang, bravely steering a doomed cargo ship away from New York's harbor so that it would explode safely in open water. **DW**

CRIMSON AVENGER II

FIRST APPEARANCE STARS & S.T.R.I.P.E. #9 (April 2000)
STATUS Villain   **REAL NAME** Unknown
OCCUPATION Agent of vengeance; executioner   **BASE** Mobile
HEIGHT 5ft 8in   **WEIGHT** 136 lbs   **EYES** Brown   **HAIR** Black
SPECIAL POWERS/ABILITIES Wields twin pistols that never need reloading; bullet wound in chest symbolizes the violent deaths she is fated to avenge.

Decades later, another, very different Crimson Avenger arose in Detroit—a ruthless vigilante driven to kill. It all began when an unknown woman purchased two 1911 Colts from a pawnshop. The guns had once belonged to Lee Travis, CRIMSON AVENGER I, and they were cursed. Once the woman had used them in an act of vengeance, they grafted themselves to her body.

Now that woman is an unwilling agent of powerful supernatural forces that cry out for the blood of sinners. Crimson Avenger II appears in a crimson mist to execute the guilty. She has also proved a threat to good guys, too, clashing with WILDCAT II and taking away three of the hero's nine lives in the process. Tormented by doubts over the rightness of this mission, Crimson Avenger II tried to shoot herself with her own pistols. However, this desperate act had no effect, and she now knows that she is unable to escape her grisly calling, even in death. **DW**

CURSED *Crimson Avenger II is forced to relive the violent death of each victim before she is allowed to retaliate.*

CRIMSON FOX

FIRST APPEARANCE JUSTICE LEAGUE EUROPE #6 (September 1989)
STATUS Heroes   **REAL NAMES** Vivian and Constance D'Aramis
OCCUPATION Publishers; adventurers   **BASE** Paris, France
HEIGHT (both) 5ft 10in   **WEIGHT** (Vivian) 143 lbs; (Constance) 147 lbs   **EYES** Gray   **HAIR** Red
SPECIAL POWERS/ABILITIES Martial arts; claws; costume tail used as a whip; pheromone triggers.

Vivian and Constance D'Aramis were the twin daughters of a research scientist for a multinational corporation. When they learned their mother had died of cancer caused by experiments the CEO of the corporation knew could have potential risks, they vowed revenge on the CEO and ruined his business by setting up the Revson Corporation. Creating a special shared identity that would allow one to run the business and the other to hunt criminals, the sisters became Le Renarde Rousse, the Crimson Fox.

As Crimson Fox, the D'Aramis sisters joined the JUSTICE LEAGUE OF AMERICA's European branch in Paris, quickly rivaling the ELONGATED MAN as France's favorite hero. Tragically, Vivian was killed by Pauntuer, a mutant worm, and Constance was slain by MIST II. **PJ**

CRONUS

FIRST APPEARANCE THE NEW TITANS #51 (Winter 1988)
STATUS Villain   **REAL NAME** None
OCCUPATION Titan   **BASE** The Universe
HEIGHT 10ft   **WEIGHT** 560 lbs   **EYES** Red   **HAIR** White
SPECIAL POWERS/ABILITIES Supernatural being of staggering strength and nigh-omnipotent power; carries a sickle capable of slaying gods.

Son of Gaea the Earth and Uranus the Sky, Cronus slayed his father to become lord of all creation. However, after siring the OLYMPIAN GODS and goddesses, Cronus was himself murdered by his three sons, Zeus, Poseidon, and Hades. The Olympian trio then divided the heavens, seas, and underworld between themselves. Millennia later, Cronus was magically brought back to life. He unleashed his terrible children—Arch, Disdain, Harrier, Oblivion, Slaughter, and Titan—upon the unsuspecting Earth. Hoping to rule the universe once more, Cronus set the Olympian and Hindu pantheons against one another in an epic war of the gods. However, WONDER WOMAN shattered Cronus's sickle, source of his power, and sent the Titan hurtling back into the arms of his mother. **SB**

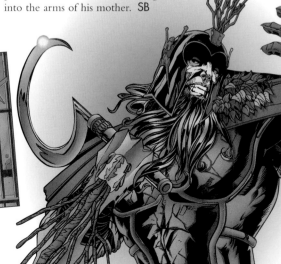

THE DC COMICS ENCYCLOPEDIA

CYBORG

FIRST APPEARANCE DC COMICS PRESENTS #26
(October 1980)
STATUS Hero **REAL NAME** Victor Stone
OCCUPATION Adventurer **BASE** San Francisco
HEIGHT 6ft 6in **WEIGHT** 385 lbs
EYES Brown **HAIR** Brown
SPECIAL POWERS/ABILITIES Enhanced vision, strength, and endurance, as well as the ability to interface with any computer system.

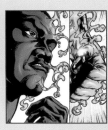

CYBERSKIN *Cyborg remains a cutting edge fusion between man and machine.*

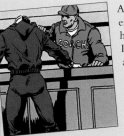

ATHLETE *At heart, Victor would rather be a star athlete than a hero.*

Although Victor Stone's scientist parents encouraged Victor to pursue academic interests, he found athletic activity far more to his taste. During an experiment, Victor's mother accidentally unleashed a creature from another dimension that killed her instantly. If not for his father Silas's interference, Victor would have died as well. Silas rushed the injured boy to his lab and desperately grafted cybernetic parts to Victor's organs and computerized synthetic nerve bases to his spine. Once Victor was stable, his father replaced his limbs and part of his face with experimental molybdenum steel. Victor was outraged by his new body and felt cut off from the rest of society. However, when he crossed paths with the newly re-formed TEEN TITANS, he quickly found acceptance with them.

Victor was later abducted by the alien computer intelligence from Technis, which led to his humanity being restored. After learning that he could no longer exist away from this computer world, Vic agreed to be assimilated into Technis. The Technis entity, calling itself Cyberion, later captured every hero ever affiliated with the Titans.

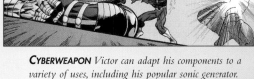

CYBERWEAPON *Victor can adapt his components to a variety of uses, including his popular sonic generator.*

Changeling and the Titans eventually brought Vic to his senses. He freed the heroes and once more assumed the identity of Cyborg. Victor endured other physical changes until an encounter with the Thinker, the longtime villain, resulted in him once again taking on robotic form. Currently, Cyborg has taken it upon himself to re-form the Teen Titans and usher in today's teenage super heroes at Titans Tower in San Francisco. **RG**

CYBORG SUPERMAN

FIRST APPEARANCE ADVENTURES OF SUPERMAN #466 (May 1990)
STATUS Villain **REAL NAME** Hank Henshaw
OCCUPATION Mass murderer **BASE** Terran solar system
HEIGHT Variable **WEIGHT** Variable **EYES** Variable **HAIR** Variable
SPECIAL POWERS/ABILITIES Can control electronics and create new bodies for himself out of machinery; possesses invulnerability due to his Kryptonian organic material and alloys; seemingly impossible to kill.

MALEVOLENT FORCE *The Cyborg is living energy contained in an indestructible shell. He is more than a match for the Man of Steel.*

SUPERMAN's sinister duplicate once answered to the name of Hank Henshaw, crew member of the space shuttle *Excalibur*. A freak radiation accident melted Henshaw's body and turned him into pure energy. Horrified at what he had become, Henshaw beamed his consciousness into the Kryptonian birthing matrix that had brought Superman to Earth. He left the solar system, and his irrational hatred of Superman grew. In deep space he encountered the deposed tyrant MONGUL, and the two hatched a plot against the Man of Steel. Henshaw used the birthing matrix to become a cyborg, with organic parts grown from Superman's DNA and limbs constructed of a Kryptonian alloy. Posing as a reborn Superman in the wake of Superman's battle with DOOMSDAY, Henshaw diverted public attention while Mongul destroyed Coast City. Superman later demolished his cyborg copycat, but Henshaw came back in a new form.

Although Hal Jordan as PARALLAX slew the Cyborg in retaliation for Coast City, the villain again managed to return. To get revenge on Superman, the Cyborg gained access to the bottle city of Kandor and disguised himself as the Inventor, hoping to grow Kandor to normal size and obliterate Metropolis. The Cyborg Superman was finally imprisoned in the extradimensional Phantom Zone. **DW**

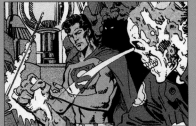

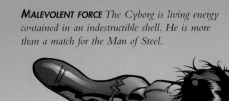

HATE-MONGER *Hank Henshaw's baseless loathing for Superman is the key component of his paranoia and rage.*

AMAZING WEAPONS

SOME SUPER HEROES AND VILLAINS, such as SUPERMAN or DARKSEID are, in effect, living weapons, their powers making them walking arsenals. But others, less naturally gifted, have developed incredible devices to help level the playing field between mere mortals and meta-humans. Some of these tools are marvels of alien technology, while others display the stubborn ingenuity of human inventors.

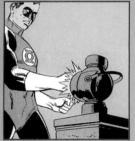

CEREMONY *Green Lantern recites his oath as he recharges his power ring, an essential ritual performed every 24 hours.*

GREEN LANTERN'S POWER RING

Limited only by the wielder's imagination, the emerald power rings of Oa have been described as the most powerful weapons in existence. The GUARDIANS OF THE UNIVERSE created these rings eons ago for use by their peacekeepers in the GREEN LANTERN CORPS. Drawing energy from a Central Power Battery on Oa, the rings can create hard-light projections of almost anything, from a giant fist to a freight train to an atomic bomb. The rings also allow their wearers to fly, teleport, translate any language, and to draw upon a vast database of knowledge.

The traditional Oan power ring would not operate against anything colored yellow, though a clever GREEN LANTERN could usually bypass this defect (by coating a yellow target in mud, for example), and the flaw was removed entirely in the creation of Kyle Rayner's ring. Earth's original Green Lantern, Alan Scott, possesses a similar ring, though his is based on magic rather than Oan science and is vulnerable to wooden objects.

Black Hand

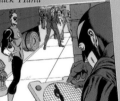

CRAZY CREATIONS

Obsessions are not a problem when you live in a world crawling with super-villains—just throw on a costume related to your mania and you've got an instant gimmick. Several fanatical fiends also happened to be geniuses of invention, and created themed gadgets that were memorable, if not always effective.

Black Hand, a methodical criminal who learned all his skills from books, developed many electronic gizmos, including one that could absorb the energy of Green Lantern's ring. The Fiddler, who destroyed objects with sound, employed an arsenal of specialized violins. Everything concerning the KEY revolved around a "lock and key" theme, including his weapons and his crimes. The Sportsmaster, a gifted athlete, had a fondness for exploding baseballs.

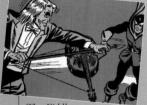

The Fiddler

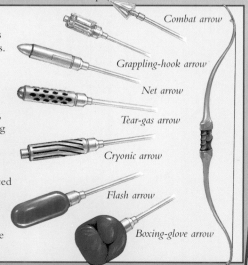

The Key

Sportsmaster

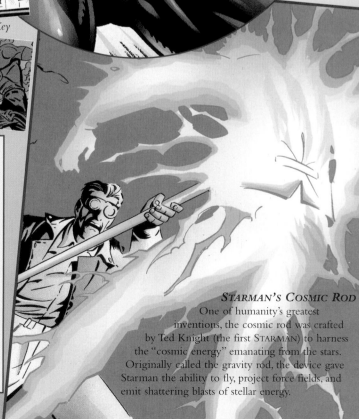

GREEN ARROW'S TRICK ARROWS

Oliver Queen is not only renowned as one of the world's best archers; he is also famous for his array of trick arrows. Only Queen seems able to fire these arrows with any accuracy, and indeed their top-heavy designs would seem to defy the most basic laws of ballistics! Some of the specialty arrows that have found their way into GREEN ARROW's quiver have included the grappling-hook arrow, the boomerang arrow, the tear-gas arrow, the safe-cracking arrow, the smokescreen arrow, the suction arrow, the handcuff arrow, the net arrow, and the tiny mini-arrow.

Oliver Queen's son Connor Hawke, who preferred "regular" arrows in his career as Green Arrow II, was forced to break into his father's stash of trick arrows when the Key attacked the JUSTICE LEAGUE OF AMERICA's lunar headquarters. Connor had to admit that Oliver's flamboyant weapons had some merit after he knocked the Key senseless with a hit from a boxing-glove arrow.

Combat arrow

Grappling-hook arrow

Net arrow

Tear-gas arrow

Cryonic arrow

Flash arrow

Boxing-glove arrow

STARMAN'S COSMIC ROD

One of humanity's greatest inventions, the cosmic rod was crafted by Ted Knight (the first STARMAN) to harness the "cosmic energy" emanating from the stars. Originally called the gravity rod, the device gave Starman the ability to fly, project force fields, and emit shattering blasts of stellar energy.

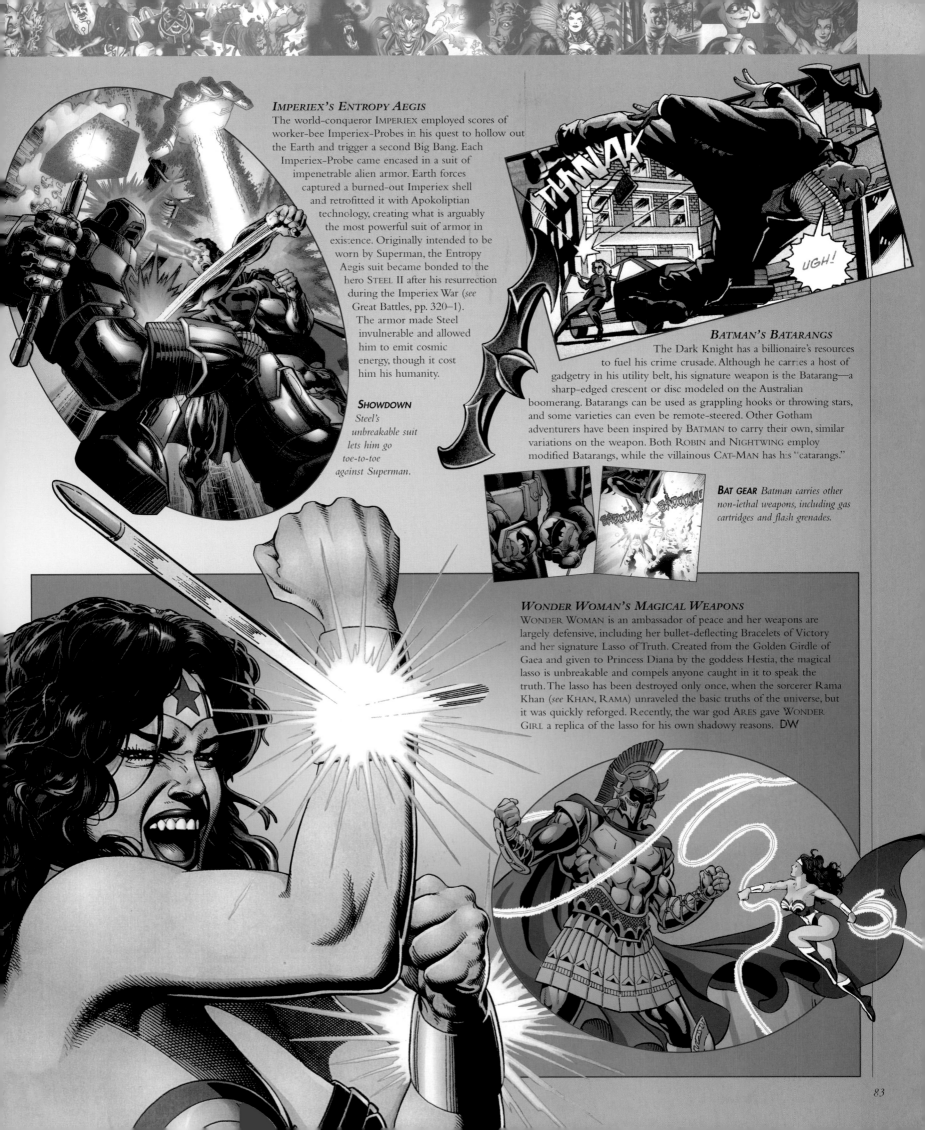

IMPERIEX'S ENTROPY AEGIS

The world-conqueror IMPERIEX employed scores of worker-bee Imperiex-Probes in his quest to hollow out the Earth and trigger a second Big Bang. Each Imperiex-Probe came encased in a suit of impenetrable alien armor. Earth forces captured a burned-out Imperiex shell and retrofitted it with Apokoliptian technology, creating what is arguably the most powerful suit of armor in existence. Originally intended to be worn by Superman, the Entropy Aegis suit became bonded to the hero STEEL II after his resurrection during the Imperiex War (*see* Great Battles, pp. 320–1). The armor made Steel invulnerable and allowed him to emit cosmic energy, though it cost him his humanity.

SHOWDOWN
Steel's unbreakable suit lets him go toe-to-toe against Superman.

UGH!

BATMAN'S BATARANGS

The Dark Knight has a billionaire's resources to fuel his crime crusade. Although he carries a host of gadgetry in his utility belt, his signature weapon is the Batarang—a sharp-edged crescent or disc modeled on the Australian boomerang. Batarangs can be used as grappling hooks or throwing stars, and some varieties can even be remote-steered. Other Gotham adventurers have been inspired by BATMAN to carry their own, similar variations on the weapon. Both ROBIN and NIGHTWING employ modified Batarangs, while the villainous CAT-MAN has his "catarangs."

BAT GEAR *Batman carries other non-lethal weapons, including gas cartridges and flash grenades.*

WONDER WOMAN'S MAGICAL WEAPONS

WONDER WOMAN is an ambassador of peace and her weapons are largely defensive, including her bullet-deflecting Bracelets of Victory and her signature Lasso of Truth. Created from the Golden Girdle of Gaea and given to Princess Diana by the goddess Hestia, the magical lasso is unbreakable and compels anyone caught in it to speak the truth. The lasso has been destroyed only once, when the sorcerer Rama Khan (*see* KHAN, RAMA) unraveled the basic truths of the universe, but it was quickly reforged. Recently, the war god ARES gave WONDER GIRL a replica of the lasso for his own shadowy reasons. **DW**

DAANUTH, GARN

FIRST APPEARANCE WARLORD #59 (July 1982)
STATUS Villain (deceased) **REAL NAME** None
OCCUPATION Sorcerer **BASE** Mobile
HEIGHT 6ft 2in **WEIGHT** 195 lbs **EYES** White **HAIR** White
SPECIAL POWERS/ABILITIES Possessed nearly unlimited magical power in his prime; could fly, hurl bolts of mystical energy, engage in astral projection, and control the minds of others.

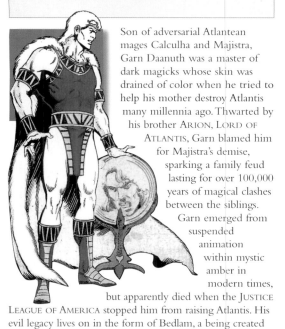

Son of adversarial Atlantean mages Calculha and Majistra, Garn Daanuth was a master of dark magicks whose skin was drained of color when he tried to help his mother destroy Atlantis many millennia ago. Thwarted by his brother ARION, LORD OF ATLANTIS, Garn blamed him for Majistra's demise, sparking a family feud lasting for over 100,000 years of magical clashes between the siblings. Garn emerged from suspended animation within mystic amber in modern times, but apparently died when the JUSTICE LEAGUE OF AMERICA stopped him from raising Atlantis. His evil legacy lives on in the form of Bedlam, a being created by an artifact suffused with Garn's magical power. **SB**

DAMAGE

FIRST APPEARANCE DAMAGE #1 (April 1994)
STATUS Hero **REAL NAME** Grant Emerson
OCCUPATION Adventurer **BASE** New York City
HEIGHT Variable **WEIGHT** Variable **EYES** Brown **HAIR** Brown
SPECIAL POWERS/ABILITIES A living fusion reactor, Damage has increased strength, durability, speed, and reflexes. His powers grow in proportion to the energy built up internally. After each energy release, he needs to rebuild his internal power before using it again.

A German scientist was brought to the U.S. shortly after World War II to continue his genetic research until the lack of results led to his funding being cut off. VANDAL SAVAGE provided him with additional funding on behalf of a company called Symbolix, along with cellular samples from many of the Golden Age's greatest heroes. The research bore fruit and a test was conducted on an embryo carried by Mary Pratt, wife of the first ATOM. The child, containing this souped-up metagene, was taken at birth and Mary was killed. Symbolix employee John Henry Emerson was given the child, a boy named Grant, to raise as his own. Savage later acquired genetic material from the JUSTICE LEAGUE OF AMERICA and gave seven-year-old Grant a DNA transfusion.

When Grant turned 16, his powers developed—scaring the teen in the process. Symbolix then came to collect their experiment. They killed the Emersons, but Grant escaped. Calling himself DAMAGE, he learned how to use his powers as a member of the New Titans. During a cosmic conflict, Damage used his powers to reignite the Big Bang and restart the entire universe. He continues to seek a normal life and mastery over his abilities. **RG**

DARHK, DAMIEN

FIRST APPEARANCE THE TITANS #1 (March 1999)
STATUS Villain (deceased) **REAL NAME** Unrevealed
OCCUPATION Gangster **BASE** Mobile
HEIGHT 6ft **WEIGHT** 160 lbs **EYES** Blue **HAIR** Brown
SPECIAL POWERS/ABILITIES Appeared to have no meta-human powers, but was highly intelligent, ruthless, calculating, and ambitious.

Baby-faced Damien Darhk was a mysterious, elusive, and dangerous figure. He claimed to be a major player in America's underworld and certainly had some connection to the criminal organization H.I.V.E. He also seemed to have had access to unique high-tech equipment that has never been used by any known organization. Darhk was considered to be a major criminal by the C.I.A. and F.B.I.; however, their investigations revealed no hard evidence against him. He was a wi-fi (wireless fidelity) fiend, staying in touch with associates by the very latest forms of mass communication. What particularly baffled investigators was his apparent youth; Damien seemed to be in his early twenties yet was already well-established and well-connected. While opposing one incarnation of the TEEN TITANS, Darhk was shot to death by VANDAL SAVAGE. **RG**

DARK LORD, THE

FIRST APPEARANCE JSA SECRET FILES #1 (June 1999)
STATUS Villain **REAL NAME** Mordru
OCCUPATION Sorceror **BASE** Mobile
HEIGHT 7ft 1in **WEIGHT** 310 lbs **EYES** Hazel **HAIR** Auburn
SPECIAL POWERS/ABILITIES His powers are immeasurable and he seems capable of anything he can imagine, including flight, teleportation, shapechanging, energy casting, and immortality.

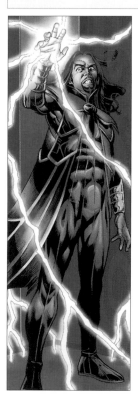

Some say The Dark Lord Mordru is eternal and was never born and will never die. The known appearances of Mordru have spanned a thousand years. In the late 20th century, he murdered agents of Order and Chaos (including KID ETERNITY and Fate) in an attempt to assume the powers of DOCTOR FATE. The JUSTICE SOCIETY OF AMERICA put the brakes on his plan, but Mordru soon returned alongside ECLIPSO and OBSIDIAN and attempted to throw the world into darkness. In the late 30th century, Mordru became a foe of the LEGION OF SUPER-HEROES. On one occasion the Legionnaire SHRINKING VIOLET presented herself to Mordru as a mate. Her betrayal of Mordru led to the temporary defeat of the mighty sorcerer. **DW**

DARK NEMESIS

FIRST APPEARANCE TEEN TITANS (2nd series) #7 (April 1997)
STATUS Villain team **BASE** Metropolis
MEMBERS AND POWERS
Axis The team leader has various psychic powers.
Blizzard Can project freezing blasts.
Carom Possesses superhuman speed.
Scorcher 1 (deceased) Could project heat and flames.
Scorcher 2 Can project heat and flames.
Vault Can create individual prisons that confine another's powers.

Dark Nemesis is a group of mercenary villains, who will sell their services to the highest bidder. The members of Dark Nemesis were hired by an organization of wealthy industrialists and businessmen called the Veil to test the powers of the second TEEN TITANS, a group of human/alien hybrids. The Veil hoped to end all alien influence on Earth, promoting a "humans only" agenda.

After their first encounter with the Teen Titans, Axis learned that one of Dark Nemesis' members, Scorcher, was also a human/alien hybrid. Axis killed Scorcher and framed RISK, a Titan, for the murder. The Titans were blackballed by the media and discredited to the public. But after the truth was revealed and Risk was cleared, the villainous Dark Nemesis was defeated.

Dark Nemesis recruited a second Scorcher to replace the first, and they were humiliated in battle when they fought the young Titans once more. **PJ**

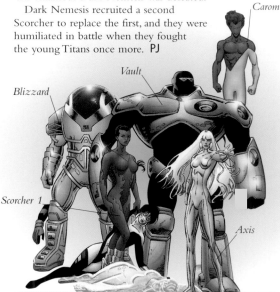

Carom

Vault

Blizzard

Scorcher 1

Axis

DARK OPAL

FIRST APPEARANCE LEGION OF SUPER-HEROES (2nd ser.)#298 (Apr. 1983)
STATUS Villain **REAL NAME** None
OCCUPATION Lord of Chaos **BASE** Gemworld
HEIGHT 6ft 4in **WEIGHT** 235 lbs **EYES** Red **HAIR** Black
SPECIAL POWERS/ABILITIES Immensely strong; a master of the mystic arts; expert swordsman and deadly combatant.

By making pacts with otherworldly forces, forging secret alliances with rival houses, and mastering mystical might, Dark Opal managed to become ruler of Gemworld. However, Dark Opal failed to kill the infant heir of the House of Amethyst, who was hidden on Earth. After 20 years, Amy Winston, (see AMETHYST, PRINCESS OF GEMWORLD) returned to Gemworld and deposed him. Dark Opal was presumed killed. In truth, Dark Opal had retreated into the magical clasp of his cloak. Dark Opal returned to retake Gemworld, but was apparently destroyed by Child, a Lord of Chaos, and his servant, Flaw. **SB**

DARKSEID

LORD OF APOKOLIPS

FIRST APPEARANCE SUPERMAN'S PAL JIMMY OLSEN #134
(December 1970)
STATUS Villain **REAL NAME** Uxas
OCCUPATION Tyrant/world conqueror **BASE** Apokolips
HEIGHT 8ft 9in **WEIGHT** 1,815 lbs **EYES** Red **HAIR** None
SPECIAL POWERS/ABILITIES Utterly ruthless, unforgiving planetary
overlord who rules underlings by fear; immensely strong and
apparently invulnerable; eyes project Omega Beams, powerful rays
that incinerate, annihilate, or transport beings.

Darkseid is the gravest threat to life in the DC Universe,
representing all that is vile and corrupt. In the wake of the old
gods dying, a race of NEW GODS were born, split between two
planets, bright New Genesis and smoldering Apokolips, who
were continually at war with each other. On Apokolips, Queen
Heggra and her own son Uxas plotted and schemed against
each other, one determined to retain power, the other seeking
it. Uxas's drive for control resulted in his brother Drax's death.
Uxas then evolved into the creature known as Darkseid.

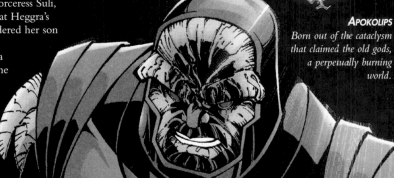

APOKOLIPS
*Born out of the cataclysm
that claimed the old gods,
a perpetually burning
world.*

THE WARBRINGER
Against Heggra's wishes, Darkseid secretly married the sorceress Suli,
and they had a son named KALIBAK. Suli was murdered, at Heggra's
command, by the torturer DESAAD, and Heggra then ordered her son
to marry TIGGRA, with whom he had a son, ORION.
To settle the war between New Genesis and Apokolips, a
peace treaty was signed known as "The Pact," wherein the
ruling gods of Apokolips and New Genesis give one
another their sons to be raised by the other. The New
Genesis ruler HIGHFATHER raised Orion as his own;
Darkseid had Scott Free (MISTER MIRACLE) raised
by GRANNY GOODNESS at her brutal orphanage.

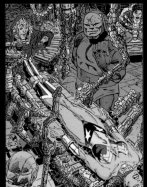

RUTHLESS *Darkseid respects
no one and any person or god is
but a means to his own ends.*

Martian philosophy led Darkseid to
conceptualize the "Anti-Life Equation" as the
object of his quest for power, and agents of
Apokolips attacked Mars. Later, Darkseid
turned his sights on Earth. Despite frequent
setbacks, Darkseid continued his conquest of
the universe, although he was frequently being
opposed by his own son, Orion. Recently he was thwarted in his attempt to take
the just-arrived Kryptonian Kara Zor-El from Earth to add to his FEMALE
FURIES. Darkseid continued to scheme, casting a dark shadow across the universe
and throughout time. History shows Darkseid finally conquering Mars in the
340th century, but it proved a hollow victory. Learning that the age of gods had
passed, Darkseid surrendered to the Source, the energy that sustains the universe. RG

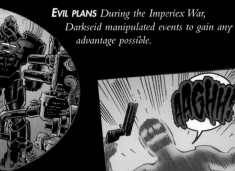

EVIL PLANS *During the Imperiex War,
Darkseid manipulated events to gain any
advantage possible.*

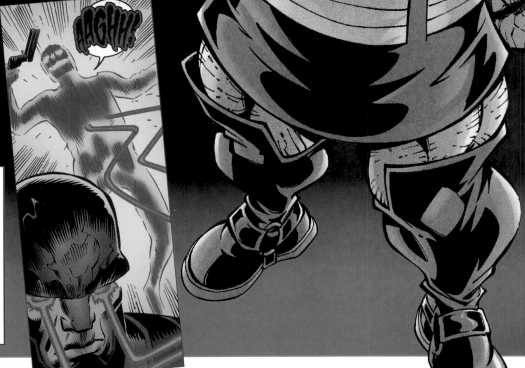

OMEGA BEAMS *The Omega Effect has no known
limitations and can dissolve any organic being.*

KEY STORYLINES
• *JACK KIRBY'S NEW GODS (1997):* The initial storyline
introducing Darkseid and his quest for the "Anti-Life
Equation" plus a glimpse into the horror that is Apokolips.
• *LEGENDS (1987):* Darkseid attempts to besmirch the
reputation of Earth's defenders, bringing down the heroes to
make Earth an easier planet to pillage.
• *COSMIC ODYSSEY (2003):* Darkseid thinks he has found the
"Anti-Life Equation" and will destroy entire planets to obtain
it. However, he finds himself opposed by Highfather's
handpicked champions—Superman, Orion, Batman, Green
Lantern, and Bug.

DEADMAN

WANDERING SPIRIT

FIRST APPEARANCE STRANGE ADVENTURES #205 (September 1967)
STATUS Hero **REAL NAME** Boston Brand
OCCUPATION Acrobat **BASE** Mobile
HEIGHT 6ft **WEIGHT** 201 lbs **EYES** Blue **HAIR** Black
SPECIAL POWERS/ABILITIES Possesses human bodies for a limited period of time; converses with spirits; crosses realms of reality with ease.

TRAPEZE ARTIST BOSTON BRAND, the leading high-wire act for the Hills Brothers Circus, was murdered by an assassin's bullet. Rescued from the Afterworld by Rama Kushna, Goddess of Balance, for the many kindnesses he had performed during his life, Brand became the ghoulish spirit Deadman. He began to hunt for his assassin, knowing only that the man wore a hook for a hand. When Deadman learned that a villain called Hook was a member of the international LEAGUE OF ASSASSINS, he was sure that it was Hook who had fired the fatal bullet. Along the way, Brand continued to interact in people's lives, doing good deeds in his distinctive style.

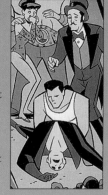

HIGH FLYER Aerialist Boston Brand was killed in a random manner by the Hook.

SENTINEL OF MAGIC

Deadman eventually tracked down the Hook, only to watch him die at the hands of the Sensei, leader of the League of Assassins. With the aid of his brother Cleveland and BATMAN, Deadman then prevented the League seizing control of the fabled Himalayan land of Nanda Parbat.

Deadman was subsequently called upon to perform the kinds of duties expected of spirits such as himself, greeting those entering the Land of the Just Dead. In this role, Deadman guided the PHANTOM STRANGER, the SPECTRE, Etrigan the DEMON, and SWAMP THING to Hell in order to rescue the spirit of Abby Arcane after she was murdered by her uncle. Deadman has teamed up with other spectral heroes, joining the Phantom Stranger and Swamp Thing to combat the threat of a "primordial shadow" that imperiled Heaven and Earth. When ASMODEL usurped the power of the Spirit of Wrath, Deadman formed part of a strike force of sentinels of magic with DOCTOR OCCULT, Felix Faust (see FAUST, FELIX), MADAME XANADU, the Phantom Stranger, RAGMAN, RAVEN, and Sentinel assembled by ZATANNA to oppose the fallen angel. Deadman continues to work with people on Earth, hoping one day to achieve a peaceful reward. RG

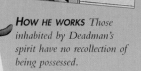

HOW HE WORKS Those inhabited by Deadman's spirit have no recollection of being possessed.

DEEP FEELINGS Despite being only a spirit, Boston Brand still retains his emotions. Following the killing machine Doomsday's rampage through Metropolis, he was grief-stricken to come upon Lois Lane cradling the seemingly dying Superman in her arms.

KEY STORYLINES

• **STRANGE ADVENTURES #205-216 (SEPTEMBER 1967–FEBRUARY 1969):** The initial run of Boston Brand's death and hunt for the Hook. Brand's tragic life and those left behind are introduced with stunning stories and art.
• **DEADMAN MINI-SERIES (1986):** The destruction of Nanda Parbat and the discovery of Rama Kushna's first champion, Joshua. Deadman's relationship with Kushna is re-examined.

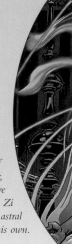

SPIRIT GUIDE Deadman helps defend the mortal plane from all manner of malevolent spirits. However, he found himself in grave danger from a child called Zi with body-snatching astral powers the equal of his own.

DARKSTARS

FIRST APPEARANCE DARKSTARS #1 (October 1992)
STATUS Hero team **BASE** Intergalactic space
NOTABLE MEMBERS
Ferrin Colos, Chaser Bron, Manchukk, Celeste, Medphyll, John Flint (dismissed), Donna Troy (retired), John Stewart (retired), Hollikka Rahn (deceased), Mo Douglas (deceased), Charlie Vickers (deceased), Galius Zed (deceased), K'Ryssma (deceased), Threllin (deceased)
SPECIAL POWERS/ABILITIES All Darkstars wear an exomantle battle suit, which gives them superstrength, speed, and flight. They are also armed with force-field projectors and maser blasters.

The Controllers, an aggressive sect of the GUARDIANS OF THE UNIVERSE and NEMO, the Network for Establishment of Maintenance and Order, created the Darkstars to patrol space and seek out and destroy chaos. Soon after, Ferrin Colos of Zamba became a Darkstar and was assigned to Earth.

After the Darkstars, L.E.G.I.O.N., and the GREEN LANTERN CORPS saved the universe from the Triarch, a trinity of ancient deities, the three organizations agreed on their peacekeeping roles in the universe. When the Green Lantern Corps were torn apart by Hal Jordan, the Darkstars were left to patrol space themselves, recruiting former GREEN LANTERN John Stewart and New TITAN TROIA to their ranks. Most Darkstars resigned or were killed by DARKSEID's son GRAYVEN, leaving only Chaser Bron, Manchukk, and Ferrin Colos to carry out the Controllers' mission of eradicating evil. **PJ**

DEADMAN   *SEE OPPOSITE PAGE*

DEADSHOT

FIRST APPEARANCE BATMAN #59 (July 1950)
STATUS Villain **REAL NAME** Floyd Lawton
OCCUPATION Mercenary **BASE** Gotham City
HEIGHT 6ft 1in **WEIGHT** 193 lbs **EYES** Blue **HAIR** Blond
SPECIAL POWERS/ABILITIES Expert with all firearms and projectile weapons; guns and targeting scope integrated into costume.

Arguably the best marksman in the world, Floyd Lawton had a miserable childhood. Manipulated by the overbearing Mother Lawton, Floyd's brother Edward shot his father and left him paralyzed. When Floyd tried to stop the violence, his brother died in the struggle.

Floyd relocated to Gotham City to start a new life as a criminal, quickly rising to the top in a costume that made him a walking gun. During a stint in Belle Reve prison, Deadshot received an offer from Colonel Rick Flag to work with the U.S. government's SUICIDE SQUAD. In exchange for performing insanely dangerous missions he would receive amnesty for his past crimes. Deadshot didn't care—he *wanted* to die! He served as a core member of the Suicide Squad, but survived every mission, much to his disgust. Deadshot later married and had a son who died in a botched kidnapping attempt. Currently a solo agent, he accepts only the most challenging and highest-paid contracts, such as a recent (failed) assignment to kill David Cain (see CAIN, DAVID) before he could testify in court about the murder of Vesper Fairchild (see FAIRCHILD, VESPER). His indifference for his safety makes him truly dangerous. **DW**

DEATH

FIRST APPEARANCE SANDMAN (2nd series) #8 (October 1989)
STATUS Inapplicable **REAL NAME** Death
OCCUPATION Conceptual entity **BASE** Earth
HEIGHT Variable **WEIGHT** Variable **EYES** Variable **HAIR** Variable
SPECIAL POWERS/ABILITIES Vastly powerful cosmic entity responsible for taking each being to its afterlife when it dies.

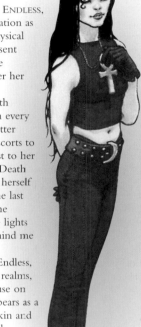

Death is one of the seven ENDLESS, who exist throughout creation as conceptual ideas given physical form. Death has been present since the beginning of the universe, created soon after her eldest sibling, DESTINY.

As old as life itself, Death chooses to live one day in every century as a mortal, to better relate to the beings she escorts to the realms beyond. Closest to her younger brother, Dream, Death will continue to manifest herself across the cosmos until the last living thing dies, when, she declares: "I'll turn out the lights and lock the universe behind me when I leave."

Unlike the rest of the Endless, who live in various astral realms, Death lives in a small house on Earth. She most often appears as a teenage girl with white skin and black hair. Her sacred sigil is the ankh. **PJ**

DEATHSTROKE THE TERMINATOR

FIRST APPEARANCE THE NEW TEEN TITANS (1st series) #2 (December 1980)
STATUS Villain **REAL NAME** Slade Wilson
OCCUPATION Mercenary/assassin **BASE** Mobile
HEIGHT 6ft 4in **WEIGHT** 225 lbs **EYES** Blue **HAIR** White
SPECIAL POWERS/ABILITIES Utilizes 90 percent of brain capacity; possesses heightened reflexes and augmented physical attributes; an expert hunter and tracker, employing an arsenal of both simple and sophisticated weapons to make kills.

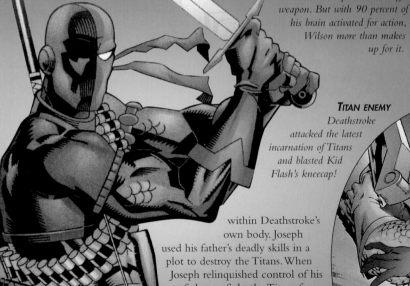

U.S. Army officer Slade Wilson volunteered for dangerous hormone experiments during the final years of his military service. Designed to increase brain capacity and create a super-soldier, the experiments were deemed a failure—most of the subjects died or, like Wilson, were left in a vegetative state. However, unknown to the Army, Wilson's strength, agility, and stamina had in fact increased nearly tenfold. Honorably discharged, Wilson recuperated and became the costumed mercenary known as Deathstroke the Terminator, hiring himself out to the highest bidder.

Wilson's career as an assassin led to the dissolution of his marriage, the deaths of his two sons, and the enmity of several teams of TEEN TITANS, whom Deathstroke has been hired to terminate on more than one occasion. He nearly completed the contract when it was discovered that the disembodied spirit of his son Joseph (JERICHO, a Titan killed by Deathstroke) had been residing

BRAIN POWER *Slade Wilson lost his right eye in battle. Normally, this would affect peripheral vision and visual acuity while aiming a weapon. But with 90 percent of his brain activated for action, Wilson more than makes up for it.*

TITAN ENEMY *Deathstroke attacked the latest incarnation of Titans and blasted Kid Flash's kneecap!*

within Deathstroke's own body. Joseph used his father's deadly skills in a plot to destroy the Titans. When Joseph relinquished control of his father to fight the Titans from within their own bodies, Deathstroke escaped in the confusion. The ex-Titan RAVEN absorbed Jericho's maddened consciousness into her dark soul self. Deathstroke remains at-large and a grave threat to the Titans. **SB**

KRAKK

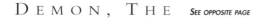
DEMOLITION TEAM

FIRST APPEARANCE GREEN LANTERN (2nd series) #176 (May 1984)
STATUS Mercenaries **BASE** Mobile
CURRENT MEMBERS AND POWERS
Rosie (team leader) Tough-talking, former New Orleans bar owner, whose customized gun fires red hot rivets.
Scoopshovel Jai-Alai player from San Diego whose hydraulic power-arm can uproot almost anything.
Jackhammer Oil wildcatter from Houston whose weapon is a devastating jackhammer.
Steamroller Chicago stunt-cyclist who rides a compact vehicle capable of flattening entire buildings.
Hardhat Punch-drunk New York boxer whose power-packed helmet and harness turn him into a living juggernaut.
The team has no recorded base of operations.

A highly skilled team of professional mercenaries outfitted with the latest in high-tech equipment, the Demolition Team will take on any assignment if the price is right. Nothing is known of the background of the various members or how they first joined forces. The Team has had many successes but met defeat at the hands of the Predator (STAR SAPPHIRE), and has also been beaten by the BLOOD PACK and BLACK CONDOR II.

The Demolition Team was not long-lived, although they did inspire a knockoff villain team known as the Toolbox. Rosie recently agreed to give up her mortal life to merge with five other lives to become the new entity Enginehead. The others' whereabouts remain unrecorded. RG

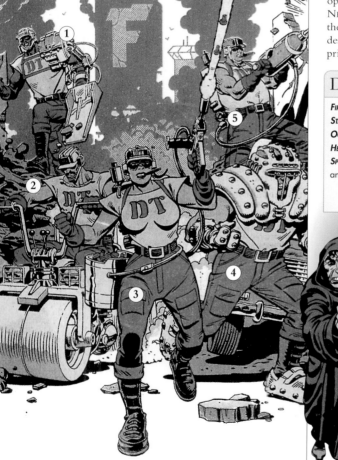

THE DEMOLITION TEAM 1) *Scoopshovel* **2)** *Steamroller* **3)** *Rosie* **4)** *Hardhat* **5)** *Jackhammer*

DEMON, THE SEE OPPOSITE PAGE

DEMONS THREE

FIRST APPEARANCE JUSTICE LEAGUE OF AMERICA #10 (March 1962)
STATUS Villains **REAL NAMES** Abnegazar, Rath, and Ghast
OCCUPATION Demons from Hell **BASE** The Inferno
HEIGHT Various **WEIGHT** Various **EYES** Black
HAIR (Ghast) Black; (Abnegazar and Rath) none
SPECIAL POWERS/ABILITIES Supernatural powers include the ability to travel through time and space, give life to inanimate objects, and fire magical bolts of energy.

Abnegazar, Rath, and Ghast trod the Earth more than a billion years ago. At some point the entities known as the Timeless Ones banished them to Hell, and they have been trying to return ever since. Three artifacts—the Silver Wheel of Wyorlath, the Green Bell of Uthool, and the Red Jar of Calythos—possess the magical power to bring them back into the world of the living. The Demons Three have visited Earth several times, often summoned by the sorcerer Felix Faust (*see* FAUST, FELIX). They opposed the JUSTICE LEAGUE OF AMERICA during its first year of operation. Much later, the Demons Three worked with NERON, Lord of the Underworld, in an attempt to shake the Moon from its orbit. Abnegazar, Rath, and Ghast despise the world of Men, forever remembering the primitive glory that was theirs before their exile. DW

DESAAD

FIRST APPEARANCE THE FOREVER PEOPLE (1st series) #2 (April 1971)
STATUS Villain **REAL NAME** None
OCCUPATION Torturer **BASE** Apokolips
HEIGHT 5ft 11in **WEIGHT** 152 lbs **EYES** Blue **HAIR** Black
SPECIAL POWERS/ABILITIES Brilliant inventor of pain-inducing devices and weapons of war.

Majordomo in the court of DARKSEID, the vile Desaad has long been the dark lord's master inquisitor, a sadist who savors bringing pain to the foes of Apokolips. In fact, were it not for Desaad, Darkseid would perhaps not be absolute ruler of his woe-ridden world. By the command of Queen Heggra, Darkseid's mother, Desaad poisoned the sorceress Suli, who had secretly married Darkseid. But rather than killing Desaad for his treachery, Darkseid forced the schemer to murder Heggra, thus helping Darkseid to ascend the throne of Apokolips. It should come as no surprise to learn that Desaad has continued to dabble in duplicity, and has also paid the inevitable price: disintegration by his master's Omega Beams. However, as soon as Darkseid discovers that he needs to call upon Desaad's insidious intellect, he restores the torturer to life once more. SB

DESPERO

FIRST APPEARANCE JUSTICE LEAGUE OF AMERICA #1 (October 1960)
STATUS Villain (missing) **REAL NAME** Despero
OCCUPATION Would-be universe conqueror **BASE** Mobile
HEIGHT 6ft 5in **WEIGHT** 289 lbs **EYES** Violet **HAIR** None
SPECIAL POWERS/ABILITIES A third eye with incredible hypnotic power; tremendous strength and durability.

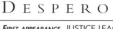
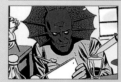

MIRROR *Kalanorians all resemble Despero, although he had more ambition.*

Despero, from the planet Kalanor, realized he would never conquer the universe without eliminating Earth's champions, the JUSTICE LEAGUE OF AMERICA. They clashed on several occasions and Despero was imprisoned. He escaped back to Kalanor and entered the Flame of Py'tar, emerging bulkier and more dangerous than ever.

Despero announced his return to Earth by ramming the JLA's satellite headquarters. After yet another defeat by the JLA, Despero sought revenge, killing GYPSY's family. Following defeat by the MARTIAN MANHUNTER, Despero was taken over by aliens and became even more violent, destroying much of Manhattan. Later, SUPERGIRL helped exorcise Despero's personality from his body and sent it to the Abyssal Plane. There, Despero met the villain Johnny Sorrow (*see* SORROW, JOHNNY), and the two planned their revenge. The villains used technology belonging to Apokolips's DOCTOR BEDLAM to return to Earth and battled the JLA and the JUSTICE SOCIETY OF AMERICA. The first GREEN LANTERN managed to turn Johnny Sorrow's gaze on Despero, sending the villain back to the plane of non-existence. RG

STRENGTH *The Flame of Py'tar evolved Despero into this dangerous form.*

DEMON, THE

FIRST APPEARANCE DEMON (1st series) #1 (September 1972)
STATUS Villain **REAL NAME** Etrigan
OCCUPATION Rhyming demon **BASE** Hell
HEIGHT 6ft 4in **WEIGHT** 352 lbs **EYES** Red **HAIR** None
SPECIAL POWERS/ABILITIES Adept at magic; however, has little patience for spell casting, preferring to simply blast his foes to cinders with his fiery breath; has attained the rank of Rhymer in Hell, which explains why he always talks in rhyming couplets!

THE DEMON ETRIGAN entered Hell, clawing his way out of the womb of his mother, a demoness. Son of the archfiend BELIAL, Etrigan quickly rose through the ranks of demonhood, and even the elder demons began to fear him. Belial arranged for his son Myrddin, who would become known as Merlin the Magician, to be trained in the arts of sorcery, so that Merlin might one day bind and control Etrigan, his half-brother. Merlin unleashed Etrigan to battle the forces of MORGAINE LE FEY, intent on usurping King Arthur's Court at Camelot. After Le Fey's defeat and Camelot's fall, Merlin bound Etrigan to the druid Jason, who became Jason Blood.

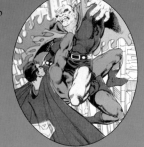

SUPERMAN *Etrigan's magical powers make him a match for the Man of Steel.*

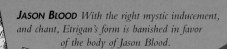

JASON BLOOD *With the right mystic inducement, and chant, Etrigan's form is banished in favor of the body of Jason Blood.*

THE DEMON WITHIN

Blood created a series of lives around the world and amassed occult knowledge, hoping either to free himself from Etrigan or at least tame the demon within. During World War II the Demon was unleashed, aiding the first STARMAN during a conflict with the Icicle (*see* ICICLE II) and Nazi saboteurs. Etrigan also was called upon to help oppose occult forces such as KLARION, THE WITCH BOY or BLACKBRIAR THORN. On more than one occasion, his ferocity was welcomed by occult conclaves with other powerful forces such as the PHANTOM STRANGER, the SPECTRE, and SWAMP THING.

All the while Etrigan had his own agenda: to kill Blood, gain his freedom, and rule Hell. During one foray into Hell, Etrigan seemed to have gained his desire. However, moments after acquiring the Crown of Horns and becoming King of Hell, Etrigan was tricked by Jason Blood and Merlin into returning to Earth. It transpired that Etrigan's evil acts in recent years had been the result of a spell cast by Morgaine Le Fey and an aged incarnation of Merlin. The curse was temporarily broken but, without the stabilizing influence of the benevolent incarnation of Merlin (slain in a pit of hellfire along with his evil duplicate), the spell that made Etrigan an evil Rhymer soon took control of him again.

Blood lent his experience to a temporary version of the JUSTICE LEAGUE OF AMERICA, and reenforced the Watchtower's occult defenses. After Etrigan helped save the League, Blood returned to Earth, once more seeking ways to end his binding just as Etrigan continued to seek more power in Hell. RG

DEMON IN JAPAN *Etrigan is one of the most ambitious and dangerous demons in Hell or on Earth and he tends to let nothing impede that lust for power.*

DESTINY

FIRST APPEARANCE WEIRD MYSTERY TALES #1 (July 1972)
STATUS Unknown **REAL NAME** None
OCCUPATION Cosmic observer **BASE** Destiny's garden
HEIGHT Variable **WEIGHT** Variable **EYES** None **HAIR** Unknown
SPECIAL POWERS/ABILITIES God-like, all-seeing entity who carries a book containing the history of every event in the universe; casts no shadow, leaves no footprint.

The ENDLESS, humanoid manifestations of the primal truths of the universe, oversee every aspect of the reality created by the supreme power. Destiny is the oldest of the Endless. He has existed since the birth of everything, and when the universe finally comes to an end his sister DEATH will come to claim him. Like Death and the other siblings Dream, Desire, Despair, Destruction, and Delirium, Destiny adopts human form when dealing with people. He appears as a tall, hooded man, believed by some to be blind and by others to have evolved beyond sight. The book he carries contains every event, no matter how infinitesimal, that has happened or will happen.

Destiny inhabits a garden in an unseen realm. Within the garden are infinite paths down which all souls must walk as they live their lives. Destiny does not control the destinations of those who walk the garden, but every possible choice and outcome has already been recorded in his book. Elsewhere in Destiny's garden is a stone structure containing a gallery of portraits that portray the Endless as they wish to be seen. Though he has occasionally summoned his brothers and sisters to initiate quests, Destiny's movements are rarely rushed. He's in no hurry. He has all of eternity. **DW**

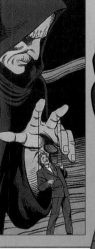

FATE Although chained to his book, Destiny would never dream of shirking his duties. He is the most serious of the Endless.

DEVASTATION

FIRST APPEARANCE WONDER WOMAN (2nd series) #143 (April 1999)
STATUS Villain **REAL NAME** None; calls herself "Deva"
OCCUPATION Creator of mayhem **BASE** Earth
HEIGHT 4ft 6in **WEIGHT** 82 lbs **EYES** Pale blue **HAIR** Red
SPECIAL POWERS/ABILITIES Supernatural shape-changer; possesses amazing strength; able to control the minds of humans to fulfill her goal of spreading chaos and despair all over the world.

Baby-faced and barely 12 years old in appearance, Devastation is the epitome of evil. She is yet another monstrous offspring of the mad Titan CRONUS, father of the OLYMPIAN GODS. To counteract his enemy WONDER WOMAN, Cronus molded Devastation out of the very same clay from which peace-loving Olympian goddesses had sculpted the Amazon Princess. Deva's purpose was not to spread peace and love, of course, but to bring discord, prejudice, and brutality to the peoples of the Earth.

To do so, Devastation battled her Amazon "sister" Diana and learned all of Wonder Woman's secrets by ensnaring Diana in her own golden Lasso of Truth. Devastation then used her own supernatural powers to compel a terrorist group to plot an attack using a nuclear bomb. However, Devastation was unaware that a single drop of Wonder Woman's blood had been mixed into the clay that had also created her. Appealing to that scintilla of inherent goodness within Deva, Diana convinced her to allow the nuclear device to explode harmlessly underground, saving millions of lives. Deva then escaped. As Wonder Woman's spiritual opposite, Devastation is sure to return, older and wiser, and probably less likely to allow Diana to use their shared blood to appeal to her better nature again. **SB**

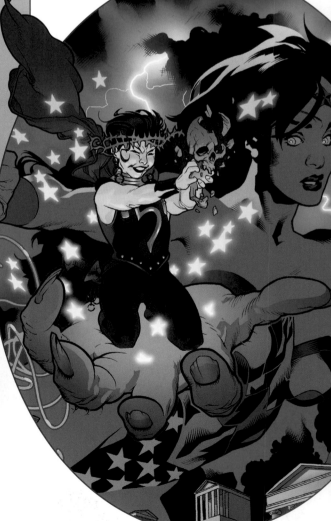

DETECTIVE CHIMP

FIRST APPEARANCE REX THE WONDER DOG #4 (August 1953)
STATUS Hero **REAL NAME** Bobo
OCCUPATION Detective **BASE** Oscaloosa County, Florida
HEIGHT 3ft 7in **WEIGHT** 76 lbs **EYES** Black **HAIR** Black
SPECIAL POWERS/ABILITIES Highly intelligent; can communicate with all forms of animal life.

After Bobo met his idol, REX THE WONDER DOG, both animals drank from the ancient Fountain of Youth. They were given renewed life, and the young chimpanzee returned to Florida and opened up his own detective agency. **PJ**

Bobo is a chimpanzee from Africa who gained great intelligence when two microscopic aliens experimented on him, hoping to expand the brain capacity of the Earth's lower life-forms. Bobo moved to the U.S. after he solved his first criminal case and was raised by Fred Thorpe, a world-renowned animal trainer.

Tragically, Thorpe was savagely murdered. Bobo then joined forces with Florida Sheriff Edward Chase and, using his advanced instincts and intuitive skills, discovered Thorpe's killer. Chase took on Bobo as his companion, and the two solved numerous cases over the years.

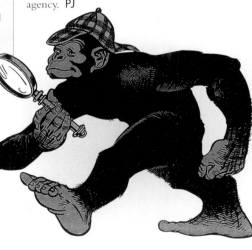

DEVILANCE

FIRST APPEARANCE FOREVER PEOPLE #11 (August–September 1972)
STATUS Villain (missing in action) **REAL NAME** Devilance the Pursuer
OCCUPATION Hunter **BASE** Apokolips
HEIGHT 7ft 1in **WEIGHT** 405 lbs **EYES** Blue **HAIR** Unrevealed
SPECIAL POWERS/ABILITIES Superhumanly strong, invulnerable, and able to increase his density at will; as a result, functions well in any environment; lance fires energy blasts, which slice through most anything and withstand tremendous force.

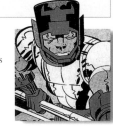

Devilance, a god born to Apokolips, was trained to become the supreme hunter for the planet's ruler, DARKSEID. For countless years, Devilance the Pursuer tracked, trapped, and brought his prey back to the Master. He was then sent out to capture New Genesis's young adventurers, the FOREVER PEOPLE. Tracking them to a remote island in Earth's Pacific Ocean, he nearly killed them, until they switched places with the cosmic being known as INFINITY MAN. Devilance and Infinity Man struggled to possess Devilance's super-powerful lance, unleashing tremendous energies. The island was destroyed and both Infinity Man and Devilance apparently lost their lives. **RG**

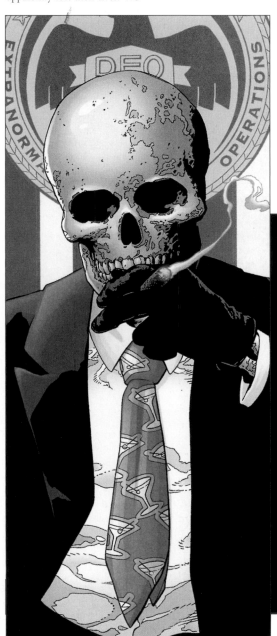

DIAL "H" FOR HERO

FIRST APPEARANCE LEGION OF SUPER-HEROES 2nd series #272 (February 1981)
STATUS Hero team **REAL NAMES** Christopher King and Victoria Grant
OCCUPATION Students **BASE** Fairfax
HEIGHT (Chris) 5ft 10in; (Vicki) 5ft 6in **WEIGHT** (Chris) 165 lbs; (Vicki) 120 lbs **EYES** (Chris) Green; (Vicki) blue **HAIR** (Chris) Red; (Vicki) blonde
SPECIAL POWERS/ABILITIES Dialing the "Hero" H-Dial transforms each of them into a new hero for about one hour; Chris automatically transforms once an hour through his psychic link with the dial.

Chris King and Vicki Grant were summoned by a mysterious voice to the attic of teenage genius Robbie Reed. There, the teenagers found two odd dials with the letters H-E-R-O inscribed on them. Dialing the word, both Chris and Vicki discovered they could become a variety of bizarre and amazing super heroes for an hour at a time. Their friend Nick Stevens, a cartoonist, designed a number of the heroes they became.

For years, Chris and Vicki battled criminals of all sorts, including the evil Master, who was planning on creating an army of super-villains to rule the world. After high school graduation, Vicki moved to San Francisco and was seduced by the nefarious Children of the Sun. Vowing to destroy Chris, Vicki was eventually freed from her evil thrall by hero Cruz. Chris's own powers were transformed, and, after a brief stint of study at S.T.A.R. Labs, he moved to Los Angeles.

Chris was briefly a member of the Titans West division of the TEEN TITANS. **PJ and SB**

DIALING "H"
The H-Dial, transforming ordinary people into heroes for millennia, was lost by Robby Reed and found its way into the hands of several ordinary people, until the insane Reed came to claim it!

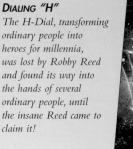

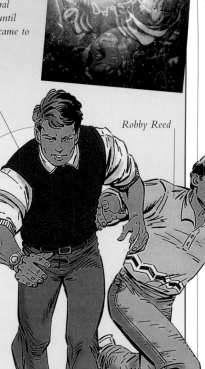

Chris King

Vicki Grant

Robby Reed

DIRECTOR BONES

FIRST APPEARANCE INFINITY, INC. #16 (July 1985)
STATUS Unresolved **REAL NAME** Unrevealed
OCCUPATION Director, Department of Extranormal Operations
BASE New York City
HEIGHT 5ft 10in **WEIGHT** 165 lbs **EYES/HAIR** Invisible
SPECIAL POWERS/ABILITIES Superstrength; "cyanide touch" can burn through flesh; skin and organs are totally invisible, revealing skeleton underneath; as DEO director, has access to an arsenal of weapons and a wealth of information.

Director Bones is the product of a twisted genetic experiment by the biologist Doctor Benjamin Love. Bones's mother gave birth to a mutated child whose skin and organs were invisible and, as an adult, Bones developed an acid-touch. Mister Bones, as he came to be called, and several of Love's experimental children became the HELIX, a team of misguided super heroes. The Helix came to blows several times with INFINITY, INC.

Mister Bones reformed, and even joined Infinity, Inc. for a brief time, before he accidentally killed the original Star-Spangled Kid. Plagued by guilt, Bones disappeared but returned years later as a major figure in the DEO. Working for Amanda Waller (see WALLER, AMANDA), Bones became the DEO's director. **PJ**

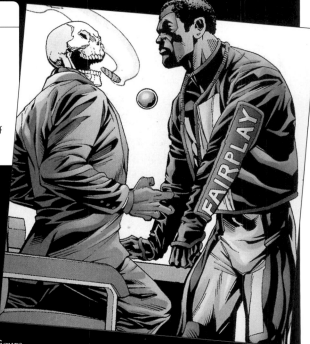

SKELETON CREW *Now the clandestine leader of the DEO, Director Bones.*

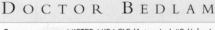

DNANGELS

FIRST APPEARANCE SUPERBOY (2nd series) #88 (July 2001)
STATUS Former U.S. government operatives BASE Classified
MEMBERS/POWERS
Cherub, Epiphany, Seraph (identities unknown) Shared genetically
enhanced abilities include telekinesis, flight, superstrength, bodily
transformation, and superspeed.

The DNAngels were a trio of
agents bioengineered by the
U.S. military at a cost of over
$2 billion. Answering to the
diminutive and duplicitous
General Good, the DNAngels
clashed with SUPERBOY when
they were ordered to abduct
the infant clone of Jim Harper
(GUARDIAN) in the teen hero's care. Later,
Superboy learned from his arch-foe Amanda
Spence that the DNAngels were spliced with
genetic material taken from the teen hero, as
well as his YOUNG JUSTICE teammates Impulse
(see KID FLASH) and WONDER GIRL.
Cherub was modeled on gene samples from Tana
Moon, Superboy's late girlfriend, which
explained Cherub's flirtatious attractiveness for
him. Cherub helped Superboy to battle
Spence, nearly losing her life, and the
DNAngels, disillusioned with the
General's scheming, departed his
employ to use their powers for the
greater good. SB

DOCTOR BEDLAM

FIRST APPEARANCE MISTER MIRACLE (1st series) #3 (July–August 1971)
STATUS Villain REAL NAME Doctor Bedlam
OCCUPATION Scientist BASE Apokolips
HEIGHT 6ft 2in WEIGHT 226 lbs EYES Blue HAIR Black
SPECIAL POWERS/ABILITIES A being of pure psionic energy, Bedlam
controls his animates, up to six at a time.

A twisted scientific genius, Bedlam takes delight in
manufacturing new ways to inflict terror on the fragile
minds of his subjects. Considered a minor acolyte of
Apokolips's ruler DARKSEID, Dr. Bedlam toils away at his
experiments. When called to duty, he serves faithfully,
using his creations, androids known as animates,
as surrogate bodies. At some point in the past,
Bedlam gave up his physical body to exist as
pure mental energy. He maintains six
android bodies, and can inhabit
one at a time, altering its form to
resemble his original physical
presence. After defeat at the
hands of MISTER MIRACLE,
Bedlam dedicated himself to
capturing and breaking the
member of the NEW GODS.
The good doctor was last
seen participating in an
unsuccessful attack on U.S.
President Lex Luthor
(see LUTHOR, LEX)
while the leader was on an
official visit to Africa. RG

DOC MAGNUS

FIRST APPEARANCE SHOWCASE #37 (March–April 1962)
STATUS Hero REAL NAME William Magnus
OCCUPATION Cyberneticist BASE Metropolis
HEIGHT (Doc Magnus) 5ft 10in; (Veridium) 6ft 10in
WEIGHT (Doc Magnus) 170 lbs; (Veridium) 590 lbs
EYES (Doc Magnus) Brown; (Veridium) green
HAIR (Doc Magnus) Brown; (Veridium) none
SPECIAL POWERS/ABILITIES As Veridium, his robot body has
superstrength, near invulnerability, and can fly.

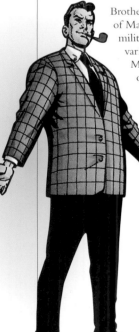

Brothers Will and Michael Magnus, owners
of Magnus Robotics, were hired by the U.S.
military to create a team of robots out of
various metals. Will, nicknamed "Doc
Magnus," was an eccentric genius
obsessed with creating the perfect
robot. When Michael used a so-called
"responsometer" to try and imprint
his personality on one of the
robots, the Magnus brother was
instead sucked into the robot
itself. Several other Magnus
Robotics scientists befell the
same fate, and the METAL
MEN were born.
Doc Magnus dedicated his life to
restoring his brother and his fellow
scientists, but used his scientific
genius to help Earth's heroes,
including ROBOTMAN II of the
DOOM PATROL, a time-lost LEGION
OF SUPER-HEROES, and their robotic
inventions. After a freak accident
forced Doc Magnus to project his
mind into a robot body of his own,
the scientist became Veridium. PJ

DOCTOR ALCHEMY

FIRST APPEARANCE (Albert Desmond) SHOWCASE #13 (April 1958);
(Alvin Desmond) THE FLASH (1st series) #287 (July 1980)
STATUS Villain REAL NAME Albert Desmond/Alvin Desmond
OCCUPATION Adventurer BASE Central City
HEIGHT 5ft 11in WEIGHT 171 lbs EYES Green HAIR Red
SPECIAL POWERS/ABILITIES Philosopher's Stone, often controlled from a
distance by telekinesis, transmutes one element into another.

After coming into possession of the transmuting talisman
known as the Philosopher's Stone, criminal Albert
Desmond—previously Mr. Element—adopted a new alter
ego, Dr. Alchemy. But after suffering constant
defeat by the second
FLASH, Desmond quit
crime and buried the
Philosopher's Stone. Some
time later, Alvin
Desmond—his psychic
twin—unearthed the
Stone and adopted the
identity of Dr. Alchemy.
Although unrelated,
both Desmonds shared a
psychic bond that allowed
Alvin to suppress his own
dark impulses when Albert was active as a costumed
criminal. With Albert reformed, Alvin embraced his evil
urges and used the Philosopher's Stone to make the Flash
believe that a hypnotized Albert had returned to villainy.
However, the Scarlet Speedster discovered the deception
and jailed Alvin, while Albert returned to his law-abiding
life. Dr. Alchemy has escaped incarceration several times
since, battling the second Flash and his successor, Wally West,
as a member of the Scarlet Speedsters' Rogues Gallery. SB

DOCTOR DESTINY

FIRST APPEARANCE JUSTICE LEAGUE OF AMERICA (1st ser.) #5 (July 1961)
STATUS Hero REAL NAME John Dee
OCCUPATION Adventurer BASE Mobile
HEIGHT 6ft 1in WEIGHT 171 lbs EYES Red HAIR None
SPECIAL POWERS/ABILITIES Invades the nightmares of his opponents and
makes their nightmares a terrifying reality.

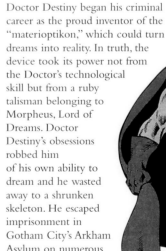

Doctor Destiny began his criminal
career as the proud inventor of the
"materioptikon," which could turn
dreams into reality. In truth, the
device took its power not from
the Doctor's technological
skill but from a ruby
talisman belonging to
Morpheus, Lord of
Dreams. Doctor
Destiny's obsessions
robbed him of
his own ability to
dream and he wasted
away to a shrunken
skeleton. He escaped
imprisonment in
Gotham City's Arkham
Asylum on numerous
occasions to menace the
JUSTICE LEAGUE OF AMERICA,
becoming one of its earliest foes.
Recently, Doctor Destiny threatened
his old enemies once again by bringing
his "dream self" into the real world and
attacking the JLA with the bizarre and
irrational logic of dreams. Defeated once more,
Doctor Destiny has since been returned to an
Arkham cell. DW

DOCTOR FATE

EARTH'S GREATEST SORCERER

FIRST APPEARANCE (Dr. Fate I) MORE FUN COMICS #55 (May 1940)
STATUS Hero **REAL NAME** Kent Nelson
OCCUPATION Archaeologist/physician **BASE** Salem, Massachusetts
HEIGHT 6ft 2in **WEIGHT** 197 lbs **EYES** Blue **HAIR** Blond
SPECIAL POWERS/ABILITIES Able to levitate and fly; nearly invulnerable; helmet, amulet, and mantle of Nabu are powerful mystic talismans, making Dr. Fate one of the greatest living sorcerers.

FIRST APPEARANCE (Inza Cramer) MORE FUN COMICS #55 (May 1940); (Dr. Fate III) DOCTOR FATE (3rd series) #25 (February 1991)
STATUS Hero **REAL NAME** Inza Cramer Nelson
OCCUPATION Adventurer **BASE** Salem, Massachusetts
HEIGHT 5ft 7in **WEIGHT** 125 lbs **EYES** Green **HAIR** Blonde
SPECIAL POWERS/ABILITIES Depending on who initiated the mystical merge, Kent or Inza Nelson, Fate manifested as a man or a woman.

FIRST APPEARANCE (Hector Hall) ALL-STAR SQUADRON #25 (September 1983); (Dr. Fate IV) JSA #3 (October 1999)
STATUS Hero **REAL NAME** Hector Hall
OCCUPATION Agent of balance **BASE** Salem, Massachusetts
HEIGHT 6ft **WEIGHT** 184 lbs **EYES** Blue **HAIR** White
SPECIAL POWERS/ABILITIES While wearing the helmet of Nabu, Hector hears the voice of the ancient sorcerer himself.

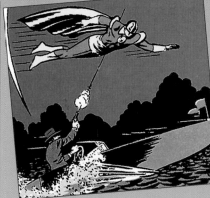

BULLETPROOF With the helmet of Nabu, Dr. Fate can make himself intangible so that bullets whizz right through him!

MANY CENTURIES AGO, the Lord of Order known as NABU placed himself in suspended animation to allow his human host body to recover from the strain of wielding Nabu's magicks. Nabu was revived in 1940, when archaeologist Sven Nelson and his son Kent were exploring the Ur Valley in Mesopotamia. As Nabu was awakened, a deadly gas was released from the chamber that killed Sven Nelson. Nabu took Kent under his tutelage, transformed him into an adult, and schooled him in the ways of sorcery. After many years, Nabu bequeathed Kent his amulet, helmet, and cloak, mystic talismans of extraordinary might. Now an agent of the Lords of Order, Kent became Dr. Fate, one of the most powerful "Mystery Men" of the time, and a founding member of the JUSTICE SOCIETY OF AMERICA.

Inza Cramer Nelson

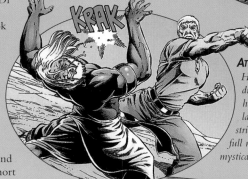

KENT NELSON AND INZA CRAMER

On his first adventure, Dr. Fate rescued Inza Cramer from the warlock Wotan and married her. During World War II, Dr. Fate was also a member of the Allied superpowered coalition known as the ALL-STAR SQUADRON. In the decades that followed, Fate continued to combat eldritch evils based in his other-dimensional sanctum, a tower in Salem, Massachusetts that was also Kent and Inza Nelson's home. By virtue of Nabu's talismans both husband and wife retained their youth into modern times.

Eventually events conspired to bring about Kent and Inza's deaths, whereupon Nabu bestowed his arcane abilities upon Eric Strauss, a boy also transformed into an adult. While battling an agent of Chaos, Eric mystically merged with his stepmother, Linda Strauss, to become a Dr. Fate wholly independent of Kent Nelson's body in order to inhabit it and guide the Strausses as Fate's mentor. The second Dr. Fate later perished in battle, although Eric and Linda's spirits lived on inside the bodies of two friends, Eugene and Wendy Di Bella. Nabu then restored Kent and Inza Nelson to life and was reborn himself as the spirit of Wendy Di Bella's infant child.

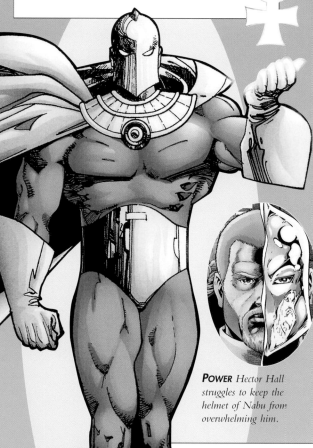

POWER Hector Hall struggles to keep the helmet of Nabu from overwhelming him.

Kent and Inza, meanwhile, both took up the mantle of Dr. Fate, merging as the Strausses once did. When Kent was unable to merge any longer, Inza was forced to go it alone. Both Kent and Inza perished during the Zero Hour crisis (see Great Battles, pp. 320–1). Fate's talismans then fell into the hands of Jared Stevens, who forged a mystic dagger from Nabu's helmet and amulet. His career as Fate was cut short by the sorcerer Mordru (see DARK LORD), thus setting in motion events that would bring a new, even more powerful Dr. Fate to the fore.

Hector Hall, son of HAWKMAN and HAWKGIRL and the partner of Lyta Trevor (FURY II), was a spirit adrift in the ether until he was reborn as Nabu's champion of balance and justice. As the current Dr. Fate, Hector strives to master the powers of Nabu and fights alongside the JSA with the reincarnated Hawkman and Hawkgirl, parents no older than their sorcerer son. **SB**

JEALOUS GUY Enraged by his ex-girlfriend's attraction to Hector Hall, Justin Guilder embraced the power of the Curse to become Dr. Fate's foe.

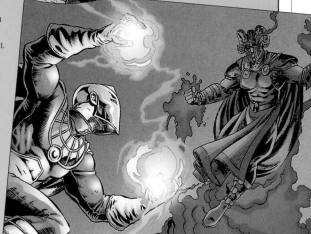

ATTACK Nabu counsels Hector within the dreamscape of Fate's helm, spurring the latest Dr. Fate to strike out and use the full measure of his mystical might.

KEY STORYLINES

• **JSA #1 (AUGUST 1999):** Jared Stevens, possessor of Nabu's talismans, is killed by the minions of Mordru, thus paving the way for the long-awaited return of Dr. Fate.
• **DOCTOR FATE (4TH SERIES) #1-4 (OCTOBER 2003–FEBRUARY 2004):** Hector Hall battles and destroys the Curse, a timeless evil that wrecked ancient Egypt, as he settles in at Dr. Fate's Salem tower.

DOCTOR LIGHT I

FIRST APPEARANCE JUSTICE LEAGUE OF AMERICA (1st series) #12 (June 1962)
STATUS Villain **REAL NAME** Arthur Light
OCCUPATION Professional criminal **BASE** New York City
HEIGHT 5ft 11in **WEIGHT** 171 lbs **EYES** Blue **HAIR** Black
SPECIAL POWERS/ABILITIES Manipulates visible light spectrum, generating blinding brilliance or thin laser beam; poor hand-to-hand combatant.

Dr. Arthur Light and Dr. Jacob Finlay worked as researchers at S.T.A.R. Labs, where Jacob secretly created a costume incorporating S.T.A.R. tech and tried to become a super hero called Doctor Light. He died in a mishap, and his surviving colleague Arthur donned the Doctor Light gear in order to protect himself against Jacob's vengeful ghost.

Arthur quickly acquired a taste for crime, despite his abysmal success rate. He recruited help in the form of the FEARSOME FIVE, but fled when member PSIMON usurped control of the team. Doctor Light then joined the SUICIDE SQUAD but perished in a battle on Apokolips. Even the underworld could not tolerate Arthur's whining and Doctor Light returned to the living, only to wind up trapped inside GREEN LANTERN's power battery. When he emerged, his body was made entirely of light. He is a chronic crook and is currently honing his new powers to better serve his favorite cause—himself. **DW**

DOCTOR LIGHT II

FIRST APPEARANCE CRISIS ON INFINITE EARTHS #4 (July 1985)
STATUS Hero **REAL NAME** Kimiyo Hoshi
OCCUPATION Adventurer **BASE** Japan
HEIGHT 5ft 3in **WEIGHT** 105 lbs **EYES** Black **HAIR** Black
SPECIAL POWERS/ABILITIES Vast light-based powers permit flight, illusion-casting, the ability to fire lasers and generate hard-light projections.

The heroic Doctor Light II emerged during the Crisis (*see* Great Battles, pp. 320–321), when the all-powerful MONITOR zapped astronomer Dr. Kimiyo Hoshi with otherworldly energy. After the Crisis, Hoshi joined the JUSTICE LEAGUE OF AMERICA— even becoming the leader of the European branch—but her innate arrogance left many of her teammates cold. She possesses most of the same powers as her villainous namesake, yet has labored to establish herself as a hero in her own headstrong way.

As a single mother with two young children, Doctor Light II is only semi-active in the super hero business, yet she has recently served with both the OUTSIDERS and the DOOM PATROL. Although she is no longer a member of either team, she remains active as a part-time adventurer. **DW**

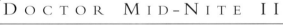

DR. MID-NITE
Charles McNider, in costume, with Hooty the owl.

DOCTOR MID-NITE I

FIRST APPEARANCE ALL-AMERICAN COMICS #25 (April 1941)
STATUS Hero (deceased) **REAL NAME** Charles M. McNider
OCCUPATION Adventurer; physician
BASE New York City and other unnamed cities
HEIGHT 5ft 11in **WEIGHT** 179 lbs **EYES** Blue **HAIR** Black
SPECIAL POWERS/ABILITIES Special infrared glasses enabled him to see perfectly in the pitch dark or in daylight; was a gifted doctor and a skilled author, in addition to having a mean right hook.

Dr. Charles McNider was blinded by a grenade tossed through a window. With the help of girlfriend Myra Mason, McNider continued his reasearch. He found out he could see in the dark when, startled by an owl, he loosened his eye bandages. He adopted the owl, Hooty, and developed special goggles so he could see during the day and night. Armed with his invention, the Blackout Bomb, McNider debuted in New York as Dr. Mid-Nite. He brought down underworld leader Maroni and built a career as a hard-nosed fighter, joining the JUSTICE SOCIETY OF AMERICA, the ALL-STAR SQUADRON, and briefly becoming the new STARMAN. In 1953, Myra was killed by McNider's nemesis, Vartan Kevork, and Dr. Mid-Nite eventually brought him to justice. Dr. Mid-Nite lost his life while battling the cosmic-powered EXTANT.

IN THE LAB *Despite his blindness, McNider makes a top-notch physician.*

DOCTOR MID-NITE II

FIRST APPEARANCE DOCTOR MID-NITE #1 (March 1999)
STATUS Hero **REAL NAME** Pieter Anton Cross, M.D.
OCCUPATION Adventurer; physician **BASE** Portsmouth City
HEIGHT 5ft 10in **WEIGHT** 175 lbs **EYES** Blue **HAIR** Black
SPECIAL POWERS/ABILITIES Able to see in the dark but not in the light; gauntlets carry a variety of medications; a brilliant inventor who has improved on his mentor's Blackout Bombs.

Some 30 years ago, Mrs. Theodoric Cross was attacked in Sogndal, Norway, and saved by DOCTOR MID-NITE I. She went into labor, and McNider delivered a boy she named Pieter. Pieter attended Harvard Medical school at only 19, and served his residency at McNider's side. While investigating a steroid, A39, that was killing the local population, Cross was knocked out, injected with the drug, and placed behind the wheel of a car that struck and killed a woman. Cross lived, but found that he was only able to see in total darkness, like his mentor. Cross donned a variation of Dr. Mid-Nite's costume and took to the streets, putting an end to the A39 problem. Dr. Mid-Nite II crossed paths with the revived JUSTICE SOCIETY OF AMERICA, and was quickly welcomed into their ranks. He continues to serve with them, while tending to the people of his home city. **RG**

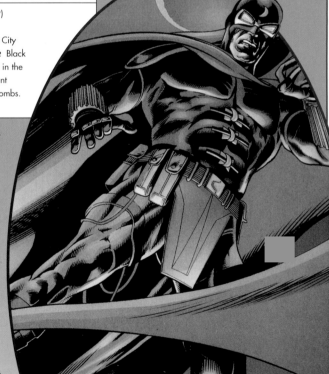

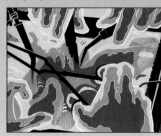

WHAT HE SEES *This is how Pieter Cross views the world— his costume provides him with levels of detail normal sight does not allow.*

DOCTOR MIST

FIRST APPEARANCE (historic) SUPER FRIENDS #12 (March 1978);
(in DCU continuity) DC COMICS PRESENTS #46 (July 1982)
STATUS Hero (missing in action)   *REAL NAME* Maltis
OCCUPATION Adventurer   *BASE* New York City
HEIGHT 6ft 4in   *WEIGHT* 220 lbs   *EYES* Brown   *HAIR* Black
SPECIAL POWERS/ABILITIES Possession of one of the Stones of Life
augmented his powers as a sorceror, which included illusion casting,
transmutation of objects, and teleportation.
He was immortal.

Also known as Ashos and Joab
M'staki, Maltis hailed from the
ancient African realm of Kor.
Maltis became the Nommo, the
king of Kor, and the guardian of
the mystic Flame of Life. After
absorbing the powers of the
Flame into his own body, thereby making
himself immortal, Maltis created the Stones of Life. Keeping
one of these magical objects for his own use, he presented
the others to the emerging races of magical humanoids
known as the Homo magi. Nommo claims he was cast out
of Kor for failing to guard the Flame from Felix Faust (*see*
FAUST, FELIX). He was then invited to join the Leymen (*see*
PRIMAL FORCE), a fellowship of ancient mystics.
   Adopting the alias Doctor Mist, Maltis founded the
GLOBAL GUARDIANS. After the Guardians were disbanded,
Doctor Mist created PRIMAL FORCE. Although immortal, he
was not invulnerable, and he apparently died during a
battle with the August, would-be world-conquerors and
enemies of the Leymen. **PJ**

DOCTOR OCCULT

FIRST APPEARANCE NEW FUN COMICS #6 (October 1935)
STATUS Hero   *REAL NAME* Richard Occult
OCCUPATION Mystical private investigator   *BASE* New York City
HEIGHT 6ft 1in   *WEIGHT* 189 lbs   *EYES* Gray   *HAIR* Black
SPECIAL POWERS/ABILITIES Vast magical powers, including hypnotism,
illusion-casting, telekinesis, and the ability to teleport by traveling
through the astral plane. Carries the Mystic Symbol of the Seven
which repels supernatural energy.

On New Year's Eve of 1899, two
infants narrowly escaped being
sacrificed to Satan. Rescued by the
secret group of mystics called the
Seven, the two grew up tutored
in the ways of the supernatural
under the names Doctor
Occult and Rose Psychic.
In 1935, the two opened a
detective agency in New York
City specializing in the investigation
of supernatural crimes. Thus Doctor
Occult, "the Ghost Detective," became arguably the
first champion of the Golden Age of Heroes. Doctor
Occult joined the ALL-STAR SQUADRON during World
War II and, in a later adventure, he and Rose Psychic
fused into one body, able to appear in both male and
female forms. After keeping a low profile for decades, he
returned to adventuring during the modern heroic age,
helping to save the Earth during major events such as the
Crisis (*see* Great Battles, pp. 320–1) and the Day of
Judgment. He is a sometime member of several magic-user
teams, including the Sentinels of Magic and the
"Trenchcoat Brigade" alongside John Constantine and
MISTER E. Now more than a hundred years old, Doctor
Occult has employed sorcerous means to keep himself the
same physical age he was in the 1930s. **DW**

DOCTOR POLARIS

FIRST APPEARANCE GREEN LANTERN (2nd series) #21 (June 1962)
STATUS Villain   *REAL NAME* Neal Emerson
OCCUPATION Physicist, physician, criminal   *BASE* New Mexico
HEIGHT 6ft 1in   *WEIGHT* 194 lbs   *EYES* Blue   *HAIR* Brown
SPECIAL POWERS/ABILITIES Generates and controls magnetic energy;
using magnetism, he can levitate, create force fields, generate
concussive blasts, and attract, repel, or manipulate any metal object.

Doctor Neal Emerson is a split personality, as a result of his
experiments with magnetic polarity. At first Emerson made
several medical breakthroughs with his magnetic research,
but as his personality disorder began to emerge, his darker
side became the villainous, power-hungry Doctor
Polaris. Polaris clashed with Hal Jordan, Earth's GREEN
LANTERN, several times, and it was Jordan who was
most often able to coax out the benevolent Emerson
personality, thereby ending Polaris' magnetic
rampages. While Doctor Polaris originally
used technology to manipulate
magnetism, his body eventually
internalized the power, driving
him to further insanity.

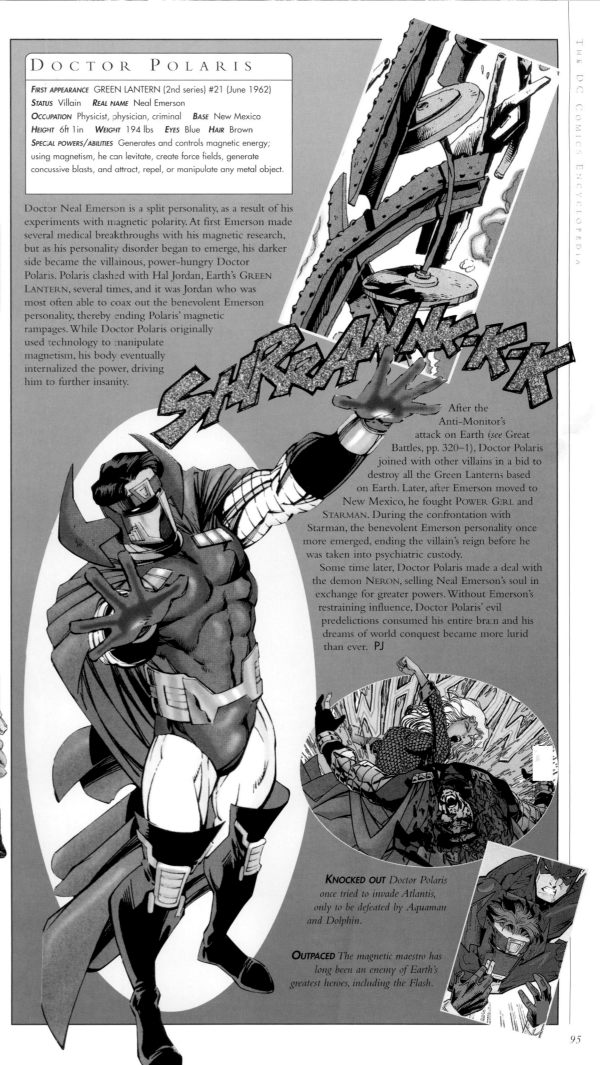

After the
Anti-Monitor's
attack on Earth (*see* Great
Battles, pp. 320–1), Doctor Polaris
joined with other villains in a bid to
destroy all the Green Lanterns based
on Earth. Later, after Emerson moved to
New Mexico, he fought POWER GIRL and
STARMAN. During the confrontation with
Starman, the benevolent Emerson personality once
more emerged, ending the villain's reign before he
was taken into psychiatric custody.
   Some time later, Doctor Polaris made a deal with
the demon NERON, selling Neal Emerson's soul in
exchange for greater powers. Without Emerson's
restraining influence, Doctor Polaris' evil
predelictions consumed his entire brain and his
dreams of world conquest became more lurid
than ever. **PJ**

KNOCKED OUT *Doctor Polaris
once tried to invade Atlantis,
only to be defeated by Aquaman
and Dolphin.*

OUTPACED *The magnetic maestro has
long been an enemy of Earth's
greatest heroes, including the Flash.*

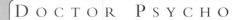

DOCTOR PSYCHO

FIRST APPEARANCE WONDER WOMAN (2nd series) #54 (May 1991)
STATUS Villain **REAL NAME** Unknown
OCCUPATION Psychotherapist **BASE** Mobile
HEIGHT 3ft 9in **WEIGHT** 85 lbs **EYES** Blue **HAIR** Black
SPECIAL POWERS/ABILITIES Able to alter and manipulate the
perceptions of his victims by attacking through dreams; creates
hallucinatory nightmare landscapes to torment foes with fear
and despair.

One of the most powerful and persistent of
WONDER WOMAN's enemies, the diminutive
Dr. Psycho murdered Dr. Charles Stanton,
psychiatrist to the Amazon Princess's teenage
friend Vanessa Kapatelis, and usurped his identity.
Dr. Psycho then used Vanessa's subconscious as a
conduit to mentally manipulate Wonder Woman.
Although thwarted in his initial psychic assaults,
Dr. Psycho has been a lingering threat to Wonder
Woman and her dearest friends, Vanessa especially. Psycho
was later hired by power-hungry mogul Sebastian
Ballésteros (see CHEETAH III) to further exploit Vanessa's
damaged psyche and mold her into the second SILVER
SWAN, a living weapon to battle Wonder Woman. Though
defeated time and again, Dr. Psycho eludes incarceration
by using his hallucinatory powers to escape and evade
detection. He is obsessed with unraveling Wonder
Woman's sanity and will continue to dream up new
ways to accomplish this sinister psychotherapy. **SB**

NIGHTMARE Dr. Psycho is a dwarf
of uncommon ugliness. Even what
you see here is an illusion created by
the villain to appear more attractive
than he truly is!

HEAD DOCTOR Bound and
shackled to prevent his
escape from imprisonment in
a meta-human detention
facility, Dr. Psycho must also
wear a psychic-damping headband
to prevent him from using his
illusory powers.

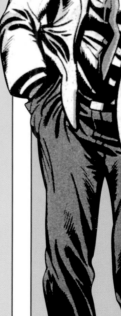

CRAZY SCHEMES Time and again, Sivana and
his family have tried to assume power or take
over the world. They remain defeated at the
hands of the Marvel Family.

DOCTOR SIVANA

FIRST APPEARANCE WHIZ COMICS #2 (February 1940)
STATUS Villain **REAL NAME** Thaddeus Bodog Sivana
OCCUPATION Adventurer **BASE** Fawcett City
HEIGHT 5ft 6in **WEIGHT** 123 lbs
EYES Gray **HAIR** None
SPECIAL POWERS/ABILITIES While possessing no powers,
Sivana is a genius in any number of disciplines.

Dr. Sivana's scientific genius made him one of
the wealthiest men in Fawcett City.
However, his unethical business practices
made him, as he observed, the man the
media "loves to hate." Meanwhile, an
extramarital affair led Sivana's wife, Venus, to
leave him with their two children, Beautia and
Magnificus, and the billionaire's empire
collapsed when he was implicated in the murders
of archaeologists C.C. and Marilyn Batson (see
CAPTAIN MARVEL). After the Sivana Building was
destroyed in fire, the disgraced billionaire was
presumed dead until he attempted to steal the scarab
necklace of the wizard Shazam. He was thwarted by
Captain Marvel, and in the process, Sivana learned
that the hero was also young Billy Batson.
Sivana, despite his brilliant mind, was not a very
good criminal, and despite frequent prison escapes,
was always recaptured by Captain Marvel, whom he
sarcastically dubbed "The Big Red Cheese." The
Doctor upped the ante when he became embroiled
with the Venusian worm MISTER MIND who had
plans to conquer Earth. However this came to nought
when Mr. Mind allied himself with Captain Marvel.
Sivana then became stranded on the fabled Rock of
Eternity. Influenced by SATANUS, he devised a bomb
that unleashed the Beast—the three faces of evil made
manifest. It took all the efforts of the Marvel Family to
defeat the Beast. He recently resurfaced as the force
behind the reformed FEARSOME FIVE. **RG**

DOCTOR THIRTEEN

FIRST APPEARANCE STAR-SPANGLED COMICS #122 (November 1951)
STATUS Hero **REAL NAME** Terrence Thirteen
OCCUPATION Investigator into the paranormal **BASE** Mobile
HEIGHT 5ft 11in **WEIGHT** 168 lbs **EYES** Brown **HAIR** Brown
SPECIAL POWERS/ABILITIES Brilliant, deductive, logical mind enables him to uncover the truth, however bizarre.

Terrence Thirteen's family had been denounced as witches and warlocks for a dozen generations. Growing up in the ancestral home of Doomsbury Hall, Terrence learned from his father to shun prejudice and superstition. Deductive reasoning and the scientific method were the greatest weapons against unreason.

When his father died in an automobile accident, Terrence became a traveling investigator of psychic phenomena. Known as "the Ghost-Breaker," Doctor Thirteen debunked phony phantoms and exposed swindlers who claimed to have mystical gifts. He occasionally ran up against phenomena he couldn't explain, such as encounters with the PHANTOM STRANGER and the SPAWN OF FRANKENSTEIN (who critically injured his wife, Marie). But his logical mind is an indispensable weapon against charlatans who prey on the credulous. DW

DOLL MAN

FIRST APPEARANCE FEATURE COMICS #27 (December 1939)
STATUS Hero **REAL NAME** Darrel Dane
OCCUPATION Chemist; resistance leader; adventurer
BASE Washington, D.C.; New York City
HEIGHT (Dane) 6ft; (Doll Man) 6in **WEIGHT** (Dane) 175 lbs; (Doll Man) 2½ lbs **EYES** Blue **HAIR** Black
SPECIAL POWERS/ABILITIES Can shrink to a height of 6in while retaining his normal-size strength; can also fly.

In 1939, chemist Darrel Dane developed a serum that could shrink living beings. After testing it on himself, Dane discovered he could reduce his size at will. Dane began using his powers as a crime fighter after he saved his fiancée, Martha Roberts, from a blackmailer named Falco. Roberts sewed Dane a costume, and the chemist became Doll Man, one of the first costumed heroes. By 1942, Doll Man and MIDNIGHT, another costumed hero, had joined forces to fight the Axis powers in Europe and Japan. Along with dozens of America's "mystery men", Doll Man served on President Roosevelt's ALL-STAR SQUADRON before accepting an invitation to Uncle Sam's splinter group the FREEDOM FIGHTERS. Doll Man and the Freedom Fighters fought Nazi tyranny until the end of World War II.

In 1951, after taking some of the special shrinking serum, Martha Roberts Dane joined Doll Man as DOLL GIRL. After helping to defend the Earth from invasion by Appelexian aliens, Doll Man and Doll Girl faded into obscurity. PJ

DOLL GIRL

FIRST APPEARANCE DOLL MAN #37 (December 1951)
STATUS Hero **REAL NAME** Martha Roberts
OCCUPATION Adventurer **BASE** An unidentified American city
HEIGHT 5ft 6in **WEIGHT** 120 lbs **EYES** Blue **HAIR** Brown
SPECIAL POWERS/ABILITIES Able to shrink her size and weight to 5.5 inches and 4 lbs respectively.

In 1939, Martha Roberts was the fiancée of scientist Darrel Dane who was also the diminutive DOLL MAN. His first daring exploit involved saving Martha from the extortionist Falco, who was blackmailing Roberts over her affair with a professor while she was at college.

Later, Martha acquired the very same amazing reducing abilities as Dane and became Doll Man's petite partner, Doll Girl. The two miniature super heroes bravely battled crime for years afterward. No one knows whether or not they were ever married, or if they are still active as adventurers. However, a new Doll Man and Doll Girl—presumably boyfriend and girlfriend—were once spied at a recruitment party for the short-lived Titans L.A. It remains to be seen if either young hero is related to Martha Roberts, Darrel Dane, or both. Martha's exploits as Doll Girl, though brief, are still undiminished by this pair of pint-sized pretenders. SB

DOLPHIN

FIRST APPEARANCE SHOWCASE #79 (January 1969)
STATUS Hero **REAL NAME** Unknown
OCCUPATION Mother **BASE** Atlantis
HEIGHT 5ft 10in **WEIGHT** 145 lbs **EYES** Blue **HAIR** White
SPECIAL POWERS/ABILITIES Can survive both above and below the water's surface; very fast swimmer, able to withstand deep-sea pressure.

FAMILY FIRST *Dolphin, seen here with her son Cerdia, greatly loves her family. So much so, she has demanded that Tempest stop heroic adventuring and stay in Atlantis.*

A woman nicknamed Dolphin is the sole surviving member of an alien experiment on humans. She was freed by the spirit of KORDAX the Cursed, from Atlantis' early days, then found by Navy officer Chris Landau and his crew. She was initially an attraction at Oceanworld but eventually returned to the sea. Like the mammal she's named after, her mind is of the moment, with little memory, and she did not recall Landau when they later met again. Instead, she found Atlantis and was welcomed by its people. Once there she initially flirted with the nation's ruler, AQUAMAN, but fell in love with his adopted son, TEMPEST. She joined the two on several adventures until she and Tempest married. They had a child, during the war between Atlantis and Cerdia. The baby was named Cerdian to help heal the conflict. Dolphin insisted that Tempest give up his work with the TEEN TITANS to devote his time to their family. They currently make their home in Atlantis. RG

WATER BABY *Dolphin is as much at home in the sea as she is on land.*

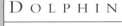

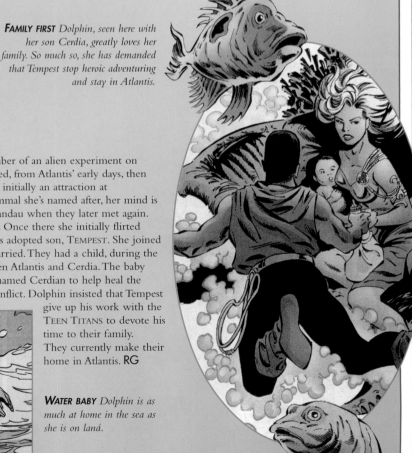

DOMINUS

FIRST APPEARANCE ACTION COMICS #747 (August 1998)
STATUS Villain   **REAL NAME** Tuoni
OCCUPATION Destroyer of worlds   **BASE** The Infinite Domain
HEIGHT/WEIGHT Variable   **EYES** Red   **HAIR** None
SPECIAL POWERS/ABILITIES Creates multiple realities based on the worst nightmares of his opponents.

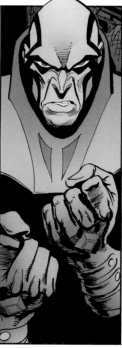

Once a benign Lord of Order named Tuoni, Dominus assumed his current malevolent form when he jealously struck against his former lover Ahti after she ascended to the coveted position of Illuminator of All Realities and became the godlike Kismet. His rash attack disintegrated him, but Kismet compassionately allowed him to live as an exile in the Phantom Zone.

Kryptonian technology restored him to new life and Dominus escaped to Earth, where he tried to take his revenge on Kismet. Failing in that, he created alternate realities based on SUPERMAN's fears and convinced the Man of Steel that civilization would end unless he remained eternally vigilant. Proclaiming himself King of the World, Superman policed the planet with an army of Superman Robots. Superman shook off Dominus's influence, but the villain destroyed his Antarctic Fortress of Solitude. After a long struggle, Superman successfully banished Dominus to the Phantom Zone. **DW**

DON CABALLERO

FIRST APPEARANCE ALL-STAR WESTERN #58 (April–May 1951)
STATUS Hero (deceased)   **REAL NAME** Unknown
OCCUPATION Fencing instructor; adventurer
BASE Southern California in the early 19th century
HEIGHT 5ft 11in   **WEIGHT** 178 lbs   **EYES** Brown   **HAIR** Black
SPECIAL POWERS/ABILITIES Expert fencer and horseman.

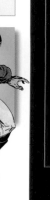

Don Caballero moved to southern California from his native Spain in the early years of the 19th century and established an estate in the small community of Hawk Hill. His true name unknown, Don Caballero used his expert fencing skills to thwart local felons and desert pirates like the Jackal, and even supernatural threats like the ghost of El Feugo, becoming Hawk Hill's greatest hero in the process.

Over the years, Don Caballero came to instruct others in Hawk Hill, teaching them the fine art of fencing. Caballero used his own blade, the legendary *El Capitan*, and his own physical prowess and martial skills to defend his southern California home well into his senior years, although his final fate has yet to be recorded. **PJ**

DOOMSDAY

FIRST APPEARANCE SUPERMAN: THE MAN OF STEEL #17 (Nov. 1992)
STATUS Villain   **REAL NAME** None
OCCUPATION Destroyer   **BASE** Earth
HEIGHT 7ft   **WEIGHT** 615 lbs   **EYES** Red   **HAIR** White
SPECIAL POWERS/ABILITIES Bred to be the ultimate killing machine, each time he is defeated, he regenerates with a higher level of strength and endurance, making him an unbeatable foe.

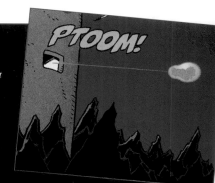

CREATION *The clone that will become Doomsday is jettisoned into Krypton's harsh environment.*

Some 250,000 years ago, an alien scientist named Bertron arrived on Krypton and commenced cloning experiments to create the perfect warrior. Within decades, a cloned baby proved able to survive on harsh Krypton and withstand local predators. Turning on its creator, the creature killed Bertron before escaping Krypton. The monster traveled to other worlds, where it killed without mercy. Through the years, members of the GREEN LANTERN CORPS opposed this being, known as Doomsday until it threatened Oa, home to the GUARDIANS OF THE UNIVERSE. Their champion Radiant defeated Doomsday and he was chained, wrapped in a protective garment, placed in a container, and ejected into space. The container crashed into the Earth, burying itself deep underground. Over the millennia Doomsday struggled to free himself, pounding his way to the surface until he emerged in North America. He beat back the JUSTICE LEAGUE OF AMERICA before confronting SUPERMAN in Metropolis. The two fought an epic battle that laid waste to the city and resulted in the death of the Man of Steel. Since then, Doomsday has remained unstoppable, although he has since become a pawn for the likes of BRAINIAC and even Lex Luthor (see LUTHOR, LEX). As U.S. President, Luthor cut a deal with DARKSEID, surrendering Doomsday in exchange for help during the Imperiex War (*see* Great Battles, pp. 320–1). **RG**

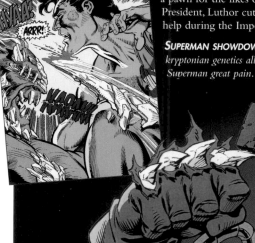

SUPERMAN SHOWDOWN *Doomsday's kryptonian genetics allow him to cause Superman great pain.*

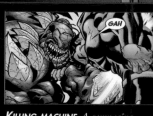

KILLING MACHINE *A rampaging engine of destruction, each new generation of Doomsdays adapts to new perils and new environments, making him the perfect weapon.*

DOOM PATROL

FIRST APPEARANCE MY GREATEST ADVENTURE #80 (June 1963)
STATUS Hero team **BASE** Midway City
CURRENT MEMBERS AND POWERS
Fast Forward (Ted Bruder) Able to see 30 seconds into the future
and so avert disaster.
Fever (Shyleen Yao) Can raise the temperature of an object by touch.
Freak (Ava) Prehensile mane of high-tensile hair grows to incredible
lengths to ensnare opponents.
Kid Slick (Vic Darge) Surrounded by a frictionless force field aura
that sloughs off attacks and allows Darge to slide across any surface.
Robotman (Cliff Steele) Human brain housed in super-powerful
robot body.

A TEAM OF SUPERPOWERED MISFITS, the Doom
Patrol was assembled by the wheelchair-bound
Dr. Niles Caulder to thwart threats to humanity.
Caulder believed that these meta-humans—all
marked by tragedy and ostracized from society—
had nothing to lose and so would be willing to risk
their lives as the world's strangest super heroes.
As "The CHIEF," Caulder recruited ELASTI-GIRL,
NEGATIVE MAN, and ROBOTMAN II as the first
Doom Patrol, a trio that soon learned to work as a
team and live together as a family in Caulder's
Midway City mansion. The Doom Patrol's greatest
adventures involved saving the world from such menaces as the
SOCIETY OF SIN and GENERAL IMMORTUS.

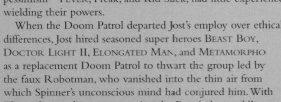

KEY 1) Robotman II (Cliff Steele) **2)** Elasti-Girl (Rita
Farr Dayton) **3)** The Chief (Dr. Niles Caulder)
4) Negative Man (Larry Trainor)

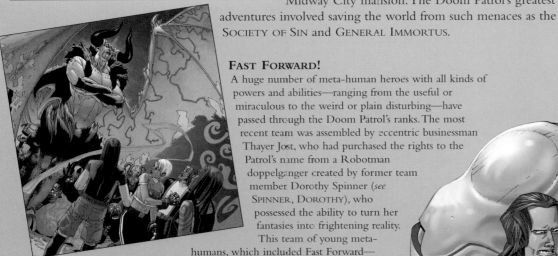

THE DEVIL The Patrol
went to Hell and
back to beat Raum
and free the souls
empowering this
fallen angel! Raum
inspired the worst
impulses in men and
women, claiming their
spirits after they
committed suicide.

FAST FORWARD!
A huge number of meta-human heroes with all kinds of
powers and abilities—ranging from the useful or
miraculous to the weird or plain disturbing—have
passed through the Doom Patrol's ranks. The most
recent team was assembled by eccentric businessman
Thayer Jost, who had purchased the rights to the
Patrol's name from a Robotman
doppelganger created by former team
member Dorothy Spinner (see
SPINNER, DOROTHY), who
possessed the ability to turn her
fantasies into frightening reality.
This team of young meta-
humans, which included Fast Forward—
quickly dubbed "Negative Man" because of his overwhelming
pessimism—FEVER, Freak, and Kid Slick, had little experience
wielding their powers.
When the Doom Patrol departed Jost's employ over ethical
differences, Jost hired seasoned super heroes BEAST BOY,
DOCTOR LIGHT II, ELONGATED MAN, and METAMORPHO
as a replacement Doom Patrol to thwart the group led by
the faux Robotman, who vanished into the thin air from
which Spinner's unconscious mind had conjured him. With
Thayer Jost no longer supporting the Patrol, the world's
strangest heroes disbanded once again. However, the
Doom Patrol is never down for long. **SB**

KEY 1) Robotman II (Cliff
Steele) **2)** Fast Forward **3)**
Freak **4)** Kid Slick **5)** Fever

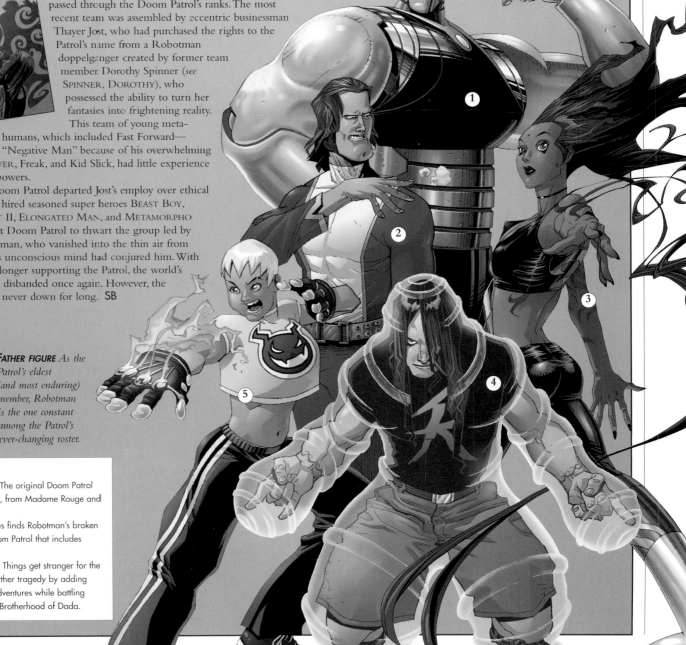

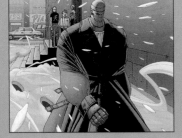

FATHER FIGURE As the
Patrol's eldest
(and most enduring)
member, Robotman
is the one constant
among the Patrol's
ever-changing roster.

KEY STORYLINES
• **DOOM PATROL (1ST SERIES) #121 (AUGUST 1968):** The original Doom Patrol
sacrifice their own lives to save Codsville, Maine, from Madame Rouge and
Captain Zahl. All but Elasti-Girl truly perish.
• **SHOWCASE #94 (AUGUST 1977):** Dr. Will Magnus finds Robotman's broken
body and rebuilds him in time to join a new Doom Patrol that includes
Celsius, Negative Woman, and Tempest.
• **DOOM PATROL (2ND SERIES) #19 (FEBRUARY 1989):** Things get stranger for the
world's strangest heroes as they emerge from further tragedy by adding
Crazy Jane to the team. They embark on new adventures while battling
menaces like the Scissormen, Red Jack, and the Brotherhood of Dada.

DOUBLE DARE

FIRST APPEARANCE NIGHTWING #32 (June 1999)
STATUS Villain team *REAL NAMES* Margot and Aliki Marceau
OCCUPATION Trapeze artists/thieves *BASE* Mobile
HEIGHT (Margot) 5ft 7in; (Aliki) 5ft 4in
WEIGHT (Margot) 135 lbs; (Aliki) 124 lbs *EYES* Green *HAIR* Red
SPECIAL POWERS/ABILITIES Top acrobats and above-average combatants.

High above the center ring in the Cirque Sensationel, the Marceau sisters stun the crowd every evening with the athleticism and sheer risk of their death-defying trapeze act. Only a very few know their secret—after the circus has closed its tent flaps for the night, Margot and Aliki Marceau slip out to fleece their latest host city as the costumed thieves Double Dare. Most towns proved to be easy pickings for the lithe acrobats, giving the Marceau sisters fat pocketbooks and swelled heads.

When the circus stopped at Blüdhaven, Double Dare's brazen heists made a dangerous enemy of local crime boss BLOCKBUSTER II. NIGHTWING ran across Double Dare in his investigation into the robberies and helped Margot and Aliki escape from Blockbuster's thugs Stallion and BRUTALE. The Double Dare sisters developed a crush on the vigilante for his good looks and his moves—Dick Grayson had once been a trapeze artist, too, and the two squabbled for his attention. However, now that the Marceaus had a price on their heads, Blüdhaven had lost much of its appeal. They left town with the Cirque Sensationel hoping to cheat another, more innocent town out of its hard-earned wealth before too long. **DW**

DOUBLE, JONNY

FIRST APPEARANCE SHOWCASE #78 (November 1968)
STATUS Hero *REAL NAME* Jonathon Sebastian Double
OCCUPATION Private investigator *BASE* San Francsico, CA
HEIGHT 5ft 11in *WEIGHT* 178 lbs *EYES* Blue *HAIR* Blond
SPECIAL POWERS/ABILITIES Above average hand-to-hand combatant; relies heavily on his training as a policeman; known more for his tenacity than his detective skills.

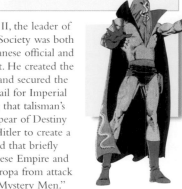

Jonny Double's past is shrouded in mystery. Double was originally a plainclothes policeman working in San Francisco, but he left the force and opened up a small private investigation firm on the San Francisco waterfront. For much of his career, Jonny Double solved mundane street-level mysteries. Although Double teamed with POWER GIRL to defeat the underworld leader Doctor Tzin-Tzin, that brief foray into the outlandish remains an anomaly. The down-on-his-luck investigator's closest ties are to the foggy streets of San Francisco, and to his various confidantes like Fish-Eye, a pool shark, and Crystal Cross, an attractive local waitress.

After accepting a simple job to watch a rich man's rebellious daughter, Double found himself embroiled in the dark intrigues of a mob eager to get to sealed bank accounts that once belonged to mobster Al Capone. **PJ**

DRAGON KING

FIRST APPEARANCE ALL-STAR SQUADRON #4 (December 1981)
STATUS Villain (missing in action) *REAL NAME* Unknown
OCCUPATION Assassin *BASE* Mobile
HEIGHT 5ft 11in *WEIGHT* 184 lbs *EYES* Brown *HAIR* None
SPECIAL POWERS/ABILITIES Human-lizard hybrid; genius inventor; superior athlete and combatant.

During World War II, the leader of the Black Dragon Society was both a high-ranking Japanese official and a respected scientist. He created the K887 nerve agent and secured the legendary Holy Grail for Imperial Japan, combining that talisman's power with the Spear of Destiny wielded by Adolf Hitler to create a mystical energy field that briefly protected the Japanese Empire and Hitler's Fortress Europa from attack by superpowered "Mystery Men." Following Japan's defeat, the Axis agent went into hiding and subjected himself to experiments that turned him into a human/reptile hybrid. Not long ago, he resurfaced with a daughter, Cindy Burman (Shiv), and battled the Star-Spangled Kid, her partner S.T.R.I.P.E., and the SHINING KNIGHT. The Dragon King seemingly perished in the fight, though his body was never recovered. **SB**

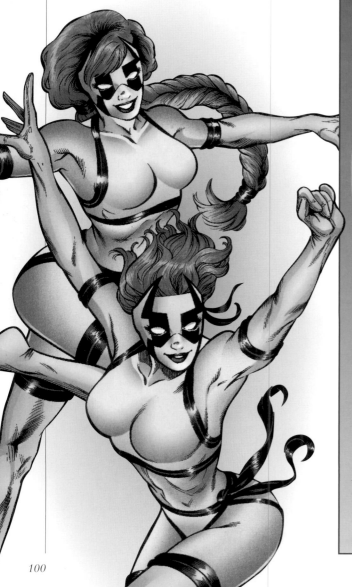

DRAGON, RICHARD

FIRST APPEARANCE RICHARD DRAGON: KUNG-FU FIGHTER #1 (May 1975)
STATUS Hero *REAL NAME* Richard Dragon
OCCUPATION Private investigator *BASE* Was Detroit; now Blüdhaven
HEIGHT 6ft 1in *WEIGHT* 205 lbs *EYES* Brown *HAIR* Red
SPECIAL POWERS/ABILITIES Master of all known empty hand fighting disciplines.

Richard Dragon grew up poor and neglected in the slums of St Louis, Missouri. However, a chance meeting with Ben Turner—the legendary martial artist known as BRONZE TIGER—turned Dragon's life around. Under Turner's tutelage, Richard Dragon became a kung-fu fighter in his own right, as well as a trainer of several costumed vigilantes, including Barbara Gordon (ORACLE) and Vic Sage (the QUESTION). Unfortunately, Dragon fell under the sway of the notorious LADY SHIVA, who drew him into the world of illegal (and lethal) underground fighting competitions. Now Dragon is redeeming his past sins by tracking down the many criminals he encountered while immersed in the world of that deadly sport. **SB**

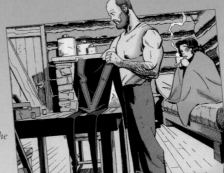

TEACHER When Oracle was trained by Richard Dragon, she believed the wheelchair-bound fighter was paralyzed just like herself. But when Dragon taught the Huntress he walked with ease!

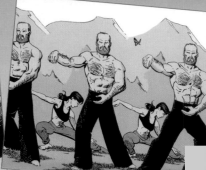

DREAMER

FIRST APPEARANCE ADVENTURE COMICS #317 (February 1964)
STATUS Hero **REAL NAME** Nura Nal Schnappin
OCCUPATION Psychic **BASE** Legion World
HEIGHT 5ft 6in **WEIGHT** 135 lbs **EYES** Blue **HAIR** Blonde
SPECIAL POWERS/ABILITIES Can receive limited glimpses of the future while in narcoleptic state; undergoing hand-to-hand combat training as a member of the Legion of Super-Heroes.

Nura Nal's psychically induced bouts of narcolepsy provide her with glimpses of the future with which she aids people in need. One such dream vision involved the LEGION OF SUPER-HEROES, and Nura was disappointed when her warning was ignored by Marla Latham. She then tried to join the team as Dreamer, but her narcolepsy was seen as a liability. STAR BOY, though, was smitten, and the two began dating. Dreamer had further Legion-related dreams, and the team began to give more credence to her dream-warnings. She became a frequent visitor to the Legion's headquarters, although no one felt she was ready for membership. Star Boy's continued faith in Dreamer actually got him suspended from active duty. One of her dreams gave the team a clue to defeat Mordru (*see* DARK LORD). Her direst dream premonition involved the coming of the BLIGHT. After the Blight was defeated, Dreamer was brought to Xanthu by Star Boy to help rebuild that world. During this time the reformed Legion finally offered her membership. **RG**

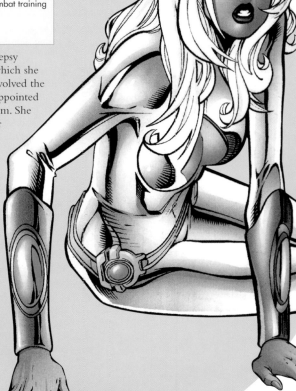

DREAMSLAYER

FIRST APPEARANCE JUSTICE LEAGUE EUROPE #15 (June 1990)
STATUS Villain **REAL NAME** Unknown
OCCUPATION Leader of the New Extremists **BASE** Mobile
HEIGHT 6ft 7in **WEIGHT/EYES** Indeterminate **HAIR** None
SPECIAL POWERS/ABILITIES Flight, mind-reading, matter-manipulation, and teleportational abilities.

Dreamslayer led the EXTREMISTS, who triggered a nuclear holocaust on the planet Angor. He survived by taking refuge in the "dimension of terrors" from which he drew his powers. He returned to Angor to discover that his comrades had been remade as androids, and led the robotic Extremists in a failed takeover of Earth. Dreamslayer then attacked the JUSTICE LEAGUE OF AMERICA, but didn't gain true power until the OVERMASTER neared Earth. Given new authority by the Overmaster, Dreamslayer assembled a fresh batch of villains as the New Extremists. However, Dreamslayer then tried to steal the Overmaster's strength and was banished again to the dimension of terrors. **DW**

DURAN

FIRST APPEARANCE SUPERMAN (2nd ser.) ANNUAL #12 (Aug. 2000)
STATUS Villain **REAL NAME** Duran
OCCUPATION Ecological terrorist **BASE** Mexico City, Mexico
HEIGHT 6ft 1in **WEIGHT** 180 lbs **EYES** Brown **HAIR** Black
SPECIAL POWERS/ABILITIES Sorcerer who can project energy bolts and manipulate the elements.

Señor Duran is a powerful sorcerer and a member of the Oto Tribe in central Mexico. Vowing vengeance on imperialist developers, Señor Duran, an ecological terrorist, planned on unleashing a horde of mystical monsters across Mexico in protest against the rampant pollution its people generated.

Operating out of Zócolo, the Plaza of the Constitution in the heart of Mexico City, Duran kidnapped a young girl and focused the powers of Ometeotl, the "dual divinity," through her. The magic spell sparked a literal firestorm of destruction that was only stopped by the combined forces of SUPERMAN, Iman, Acrata, and EL MUERTO. **PJ**

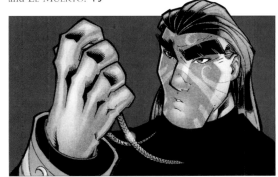

DUSK, NATHANIEL

FIRST APPEARANCE NATHANIEL DUSK #1 (February 1984)
STATUS Hero **REAL NAME** Nathaniel Dusk
OCCUPATION Private investigator **BASE** New York City
HEIGHT 6ft **WEIGHT** 187 lbs **EYES** Brown **HAIR** Brown
SPECIAL POWERS/ABILITIES Good in a fight and handy with a gun; tough as teak; never gives up on a case.

Nathaniel Dusk is the quintessential hard-boiled private eye on the mean streets of New York. An ex-soldier in the trenches of World War I and a combat pilot, he left the military and became a cop. Disgusted by the rampant corruption in the force, Dusk opened his own P.I. office in 1931. He struck up a romance with mother of two Joyce Gulino, who had gone into hiding from her mobster husband Joseph Costilino. The vengeful husband ordered a hit on both his wife and Dusk but only Joyce died in the attack. Dusk went after Costilino, and in the end the gangster perished. Dusk subsequently took on many other cases, but always made time to watch over Joyce's two children, Jennie and Anthony. **DW**

DYBBUK

FIRST APPEARANCE SUICIDE SQUAD (1st series) #45 (September 1990)
STATUS Hero **REAL NAME** "Lenny"
OCCUPATION Artificial intelligence **BASE** Mobile
HEIGHT/WEIGHT/EYES/HAIR Inapplicable
SPECIAL POWERS/ABILITIES Able to usurp and take control of any computerized technology.

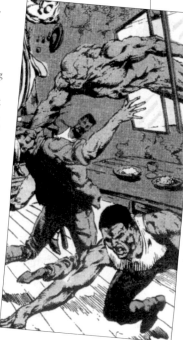

Created by Israeli scientists, the artificial intelligence Dybbuk was originally a machine member of the HAYOTH, Israel's native superbeings. But after being duped by the anarchist KOBRA into nearly igniting a Middle Eastern holy war, Dybbuk and the rest of the Hayoth were taken into custody by America's SUICIDE SQUAD. Dybbuk, renaming itself "Lenny," agreed to help the Squad's Amanda Waller (*see* WALLER, AMANDA) reprogram the digital djinn known as Ifrit, formerly the Squad's Mindboggler, who had become a terrorist member of the superpowered Jihad. Dybbuk and Ifrit fell in love and became electronically engaged. Presumably, the artificial intelligences now enjoy wedded bliss in the digital domain and continue to serve as U.S. government operatives under the auspices of Task Force X. **SB**

ECHO

FIRST APPEARANCE (Echo III) JUSTICE LEAGUE QUARTERLY #1
(Winter 1990); (Echo IV) BATMAN 80-PAGE GIANT #1 (1999)
STATUS (both) Villains **REAL NAMES** (III) Unknown; (IV) Terri Eckhart
OCCUPATION (III) Mercenary; (IV) criminal **BASE** (III) Mobile;
(IV) Gotham City **HEIGHT** (III) 5ft 3in; (IV) 5ft 11in **WEIGHT** (III)
115 lbs; (IV) 140 lbs **EYES** (both) Blue **HAIR** (III) Red; (IV) black
SPECIAL POWERS/ABILITIES (III) Can absorb energy directed at her and
return it with equal force, enabling her to fly; (IV) is a tough athlete.

The Echo name has been used repeatedly, starting with a
foe of the CRIMSON AVENGER during the 1940s. The
second—Nina Damfino—was half of a two-woman
crime team known as Query & Echo, who occasionally
joined the RIDDLER. The third Echo (pictured right)
was a result of Morgan Edge's ex-wife Claire
Montgomery founding a corporate-sponsored group
of mercenaries known as the CONGLOMERATE.
Amongst the first incarnation of the team was a young
woman named Echo, a teen rock sensation. In
between stints with the team she evolved her look
and sound, staying on the cutting edge of rock
music. Terri Eckhart was the fourth Echo, the second
Echo to work with the Riddler. Virtually nothing is
known about Terri Eckhart's background or why she
chooses to ally herself with the Riddler, but she
seems better suited to the Riddler's temperament
than her predecessor. Vicki Grant (*see* DIAL "H" FOR
HERO), when she controlled an H-dial, was able to
transform into the fifth costumed woman with the
name Echo. ECHO VI emerged after Gotham City
became a No Man's Land. RG

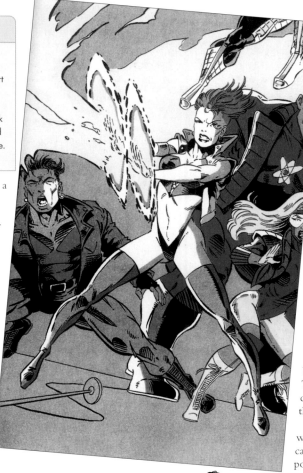

ECHO VI

FIRST APPEARANCE BATMAN: LEGENDS OF THE DARK KNIGHT
#119 (July 1999)
STATUS Villain **REAL NAME** Unrevealed
OCCUPATION Covert agent; assassin **BASE** Unknown
HEIGHT 5ft 4in **WEIGHT** 110 lbs **EYES** Hazel **HAIR** Red
SPECIAL POWERS/ABILITIES Sensitive mind powers the receiver in her
helmet, enabling her to read others' thoughts and intercept sound
waves; natural athlete trained in the use of firearms
and other weapons.

The use of the Echo name
continued with Echo VI.
Following a cataclysmic
earthquake, when Gotham City
was cut off from the rest of the
U.S. and became known as a
No Man's Land, BATMAN clashed
with a human electronics receiver
known as Echo VI.
This sixth Echo is a Russian
agent who underwent surgery in a
procedure known as "The Turing
Project" that implanted
biomechanical units in her brain.
This allows her to interface with
computers and have access to the
thoughts of others.
Echo VI is a deeply unhappy
woman due to the fact that she
cannot control this special ability. Her mind
powers also give her massive headaches. RG

ECLIPSO

FIRST APPEARANCE HOUSE OF SECRETS (1st series) #61 (August 1963)
STATUS Villain **REAL NAME** None
OCCUPATION Adventurer **BASE** Mobile
HEIGHT 6ft 2in **WEIGHT** 484 lbs **EYES** Red **HAIR** None
SPECIAL POWERS/ABILITIES Superstrength, invulnerability, and
levitation; can fire black light from right eye and laser beams from
left eye when focused through a special black diamond.

Eclipso is the primordial manifestation of God's wrath and
claims to have been responsible for unleashing the Great
Flood of Biblical fame. Eventually superseded as the spirit of
vengeance by the SPECTRE, Eclipso's physical essence became
trapped in a black diamond known as the Heart of Darkness,
while his mental essence lived on the dark side of the moon.
In the year 1891, a jeweler split the diamond into a
thousand fragments, allowing Eclipso to act out the revenge
fantasies of all those who possessed one of the black shards.
Appearing as a spectral wraith or taking physical possession
of its host bodies, Eclipso worked to gather together the
diamond fragments over the next century. If he destroyed
them all, his restored powers would allow him to blot out
the sun. Astronomer and doctor Bruce Gordon became a
modern host for Eclipso and struggled to control his dark
side even as Eclipso battled the JUSTICE LEAGUE OF
AMERICA and the METAL MEN, who exploited the villain's
vulnerability to sunlight. Eclipso eventually split from
Gordon and killed several heroes including WILDCAT II
(Yolanda Montez) and Dr. Midnight (Beth Chapel).
Eclipso joined the DARK LORD and OBSIDIAN in a bid to plunge the world into perpetual
darkness. Opposed by the JUSTICE SOCIETY OF AMERICA, he fell victim to Wildcat II's brother
Alexander Montez, who used the mystic runes etched into his skin to trap Eclipso's spirit
inside his body. Montez controlled Eclipso until the spirit of vengeance threatened to
escape, at which point Montez hurled himself off a building. Eclipso now resides inside the
black diamond. DW

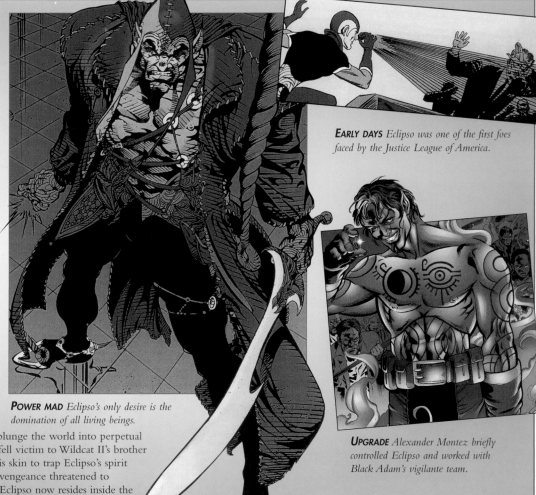

EARLY DAYS *Eclipso was one of the first foes
faced by the Justice League of America.*

POWER MAD *Eclipso's only desire is the
domination of all living beings.*

UPGRADE *Alexander Montez briefly
controlled Eclipso and worked with
Black Adam's vigilante team.*

E

EFFIGY

FIRST APPEARANCE GREEN LANTERN (3rd series) #110 (April 1999)
STATUS Villain **REAL NAME** Martyn Van Wyck
OCCUPATION Professional criminal **BASE** Seattle
HEIGHT 6ft 1in **WEIGHT** 195 lbs **EYES** Blue **HAIR** Blond
SPECIAL POWERS/ABILITIES Alien experiments gave him the power to generate and control seemingly limitless flames and heat at will.

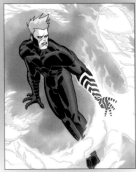

He awoke naked and alone in the woods of the Pacific Northwest. All Martyn Van Wyck could recall were strange, shadowy figures looming over him. He learned later that he had been abducted by aliens. The Controllers, descendants of the same Maltusians who had become the GUARDIANS OF THE UNIVERSE, had experimented upon Van Wyck and other humans to create superpowered beings to replace the DARKSTARS they had once empowered as space-based protectors. When the flame of a cigarette lighter caused him to catch fire, Van Wyck found that he was impervious to heat and could manipulate fire. He adopted the criminal alter ego Effigy and soon became a flame-throwing foe of GREEN LANTERN Kyle Rayner. After a blazing battle, Effigy was defeated and reclaimed by the Controllers. Later, Effigy returned to Earth and allied himself with Killer Frost (see KILLER FROST II) to fight Green Lantern with both fire and ice. As Effigy's control of his abilities grows, so does the danger he poses to anyone who gets close enough for him to burn. **SB**

EL MUERTO

FIRST APPEARANCE SUPERMAN (2nd ser.) ANNUAL #12 (Aug. 2000)
STATUS Hero **REAL NAME** Pablo Valdez
OCCUPATION Costumed crime fighter **BASE** Mexico City
HEIGHT 5ft 11in **WEIGHT** 178 lbs **EYES** Brown **HAIR** Black
SPECIAL POWERS/ABILITIES Skilled fighter; nearly impervious to harm due to his undead nature.

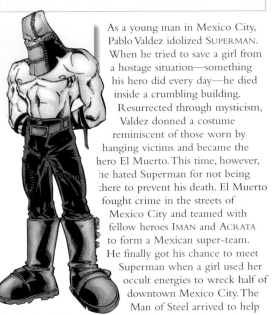

As a young man in Mexico City, Pablo Valdez idolized SUPERMAN. When he tried to save a girl from a hostage situation—something his hero did every day—he died inside a crumbling building.

Resurrected through mysticism, Valdez donned a costume reminiscent of those worn by hanging victims and became the hero El Muerto. This time, however, he hated Superman for not being there to prevent his death. El Muerto fought crime in the streets of Mexico City and teamed with fellow heroes IMAN and ACRATA to form a Mexican super-team. He finally got his chance to meet Superman when a girl used her occult energies to wreck half of downtown Mexico City. The Man of Steel arrived to help the local trio, but his vulnerability to magic meant that the heroes had to unite in order to defeat the supernatural threat. Superman and El Muerto have since reconciled, and El Muerto is still active in Mexico City. **DW**

ELASTI-GIRL

FIRST APPEARANCE MY GREATEST ADVENTURE #80 (June 1963)
STATUS Hero (deceased) **REAL NAME** Rita Farr Dayton
OCCUPATION Actress **BASE** Midway City
HEIGHT (as Rita) 5ft 6in **WEIGHT** (as Rita) 135 lbs
EYES Brown **HAIR** Brown
SPECIAL POWERS/ABILITIES Could stretch any part of her body to incredible lengths; could grow to enormous size; could shrink to tiny, but not microscopic, size.

Rita Farr was a famous Hollywood actress who was exposed to strange gases while on the set of a movie being filmed on location in Africa. When she discovered she could now change the proportions of her body, she forsook her acting career and went into hiding.

Niles Caulder, known as the CHIEF, discovered Farr and invited her to join the DOOM PATROL, a team of unusual crime fighters. Taking the name Elasti-Girl, Rita reclaimed the fame of her youth and soon fell in love with fellow Doom Patroller Steve Dayton, who had developed a helmet giving him psychic powers and called himself MENTO. The couple soon adopted a boy with green skin named Garfield Logan who could transform into any kind of animal. The youngster joined the Doom Patrol as BEAST BOY.

When the Doom Patrol were confronted by two of their arch-enemies, MADAME ROUGE and GENERAL ZAHL, the heroes laid their lives on the line to save the innocent population of a small New England fishing village. Elasti-Girl died in a bomb blast, for which General Zahl was responsible. **PJ**

EL DIABLO I & II

FIRST APPEARANCE ALL-STAR WESTERN (2nd series) #2 (October 1970)
STATUS Hero **REAL NAME** Lazarus Lane
OCCUPATION Adventurer **BASE** Puerta Del Sol, California
HEIGHT 6ft **WEIGHT** 182 lbs **EYES** Blue **HAIR** Black
SPECIAL POWERS/ABILITIES An expert marksman and horseback rider; his body can perform amazing feats of athleticism.

FIRST APPEARANCE EL DIABLO #1 (August 1989)
STATUS Hero **REAL NAME** Rafael Sandoval
OCCUPATION City councillor **BASE** Dos Rios, Texas
HEIGHT 6ft 2in **WEIGHT** 190 lbs **EYES** Brown **HAIR** Black
SPECIAL POWERS/ABILITIES An accomplished athlete, trained in boxing and martial arts.

Lazarus Lane was nearly killed after he tried to stop bank robbers in 1865. Left comatose by a bolt of lightning, he hovered near death until an Apache shaman named Wise Owl prayed over Lane's body, chanting spells and administering potions. Lane awoke from his coma believing his spirit had split in two, one Lane's husk, the other a supernatural being. His spirit began roaming the frontier as El Diablo, meting out justice with his fists, whip, or six gun. Six years later, in November 1872, an odd assortment of gunslingers were hired by Otto Von Hammer and Jason Blood to free the time-lost earth elemental, SWAMP THING, contained by Wise Owl. When Wise Owl was shot in the head, the long-catatonic Lazarus Lane awoke, and his spirit form El Diablo ceased to exist.

More than a century later, Rafael Sandoval grew up in the tough barrio section of Dos Rios in Texas. One night, Rafael broke into a church, but was caught by Father Guzman. The priest befriended the boy, and soon Rafael was spending time doing church work and training as a boxer. He left Dos Rios, enlisted, earned a law degree and years later, returned to Dos Rios as public defender. His work and charisma caught the attention of Mayor Tommy Longstreet, who helped him become the first Hispanic on the city council. Frustrated by the red tape and political entanglements, he felt incapable of making a difference. When Sandoval learned about several acts of arson being committed for insurance fraud, he chose to take direct action, but did so wearing an old festival costume and mask. After defeating the arsonists, Sandoval continued acting as the new El Diablo. Rafael Sandoval ultimately retired his El Diablo persona, convinced that he could do more good as a city councillor working within the system. Later, Sandoval resumed his El Diablo identity in tandem with the demon Netzahualcoyotl, whom he agreed to host in exchange for rooting out political corruption. **RG**

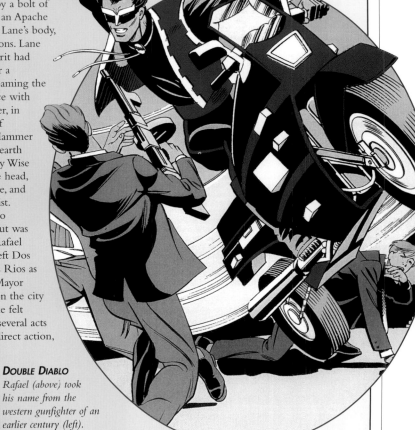

DOUBLE DIABLO
Rafael (above) took his name from the western gunfighter of an earlier century (left).

ELEMENT GIRL

FIRST APPEARANCE METAMORPHO #10 (February 1967)
STATUS Hero **REAL NAME** Urania "Rainie" Blackwell
OCCUPATION Former U.S. government agent **BASE** Mobile
HEIGHT 5ft 10in **WEIGHT** 142 lbs **EYES** Black **HAIR** Green
SPECIAL POWERS/ABILITIES Could shapeshift and transform into any combination of chemical elements.

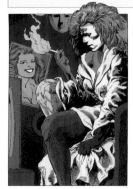

Element Girl lived a sad life, transformed into a freak and then abandoned by those she loved. Many years ago, Urania Blackwell had been a spy working for the U.S. government who volunteered to expose herself to the same Orb of Ra radiation that had transformed Rex Mason into METAMORPHO, the Element Man. The process worked— although Rainie's body became discolored and misshapen, she could shift between elemental states at will. She took the alias of Element Girl. Rainie worked with Metamorpho for several months, crossing the globe and falling in love. However she was spurned by Metamorpho, and soon her government agency declared it had no further use for her. Despairing, Rainie tried to live quietly in retirement but because of her hideous appearance, couldn't bear to leave her apartment. She tried to commit suicide on several occasions, but her body's natural defenses made the act impossible.

Element Girl ultimately received a visit from DEATH, who helped Rainie to make peace with herself and finally depart her mortal life. **DW**

ELEMENT LAD

FIRST APPEARANCE ADVENTURE COMICS #307 (April 1963)
STATUS Villain (deceased) **REAL NAME** Jan Arrah
OCCUPATION Legionnaire **BASE** 30th-century Earth
HEIGHT 5ft 5in **WEIGHT** 140 lbs **EYES** Blue **HAIR** Blond
SPECIAL POWERS/ABILITIES Could transmute any element into any other by using his mental powers to change its chemical makeup; could transmute his own body into any element; could even create life.

Jan Arrah was born to a race of element transmuters on the planet Trom in the latter half of the 30th century. Fearing the power of Trom's inhabitants, the terrorist White Triangle destroyed the planet, leaving Jan its only survivor. After uncovering a deadly plot by President Chu of Earth, the orphaned Jan joined the LEGION OF SUPER-HEROES as Element Lad.

When he and a number of Legionnaires were transported into another dimension after an attack by the BLIGHT, Element Lad transformed into Tromian crystal and traveled back to the beginning of time. Over the eons, his power corrupted his mind. He created a race called the Progeny, designed to remove "imperfect species" from the universe. Finally reencountering the lost Legion, Element Lad—now calling himself the Progenitor—killed MONSTRESS and threatened to destroy the galaxy, which he found imperfect. Fused with a creature called the Omniphagus, the Progenitor finally met its end at the hands of LIVE WIRE, who used his lightning powers to overload the Trommite's brain. **PJ**

ELONGATED MAN

FIRST APPEARANCE THE FLASH (1st series) #112 (May 1960)
STATUS Hero **REAL NAME** Ralph Dibny
OCCUPATION Detective **BASE** Mobile
HEIGHT 6ft 1in **WEIGHT** 178 lbs **EYES** Blue **HAIR** Red
SPECIAL POWERS/ABILITIES Consuming a Gingold extract every few days renders him super-elasticable to stretch or contort any portion of his body; brilliant deductive mind.

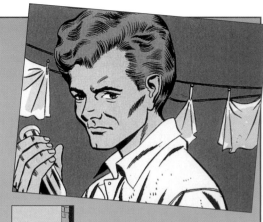

A fascination with the human body's powers of flexibility first led nine-year-old amateur detective Ralph Dibny to investigate the secrets of the "India Rubber Men" and similar contortionists that appeared at circuses and traveling sideshows. His determination to discover the source of their fantastic plastic abilities continued into adulthood.

Ralph traveled the world on this unusual quest and came to the conclusion that the greatest contortionists all had one thing in common: before a performance, each "rubber man" consumed a soft drink called Gingold, which contained the juice of the Yucatan gingo fruit. Ralph managed to isolate an unknown chemical present in the fruit's juices. When he drank a concentrated dose of this extract, his body acquired elastic properties far beyond the abilities of the sideshow freaks. As the Elongated Man, Ralph became a super-stretchable sleuth, frequently teaming with BATMAN and the FLASH II before joining the JUSTICE LEAGUE OF AMERICA.

Ralph's detective skills are remarkable—Elongated Man often "smells" a mystery when his pliant proboscis begins twitching of its own accord. At present in semi-retirement, the Thin Man of the JLA now happily travels the world with his wife, mystery novelist Sue Dibny, solving the occasional whodunit. Ralph recently reunited with several of his former JLA teammates—including BLUE BEETLE II, BOOSTER GOLD, and CAPTAIN ATOM—and battled some of the League's old foes, such as intergalactic designer Manga Khan. Whether the stretchable sleuth will remain with this ill-fated group remains to be seen. **SB**

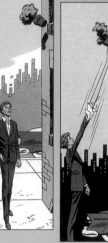

ELASTIC FANTASTIC *At first, Ralph felt no changes after drinking the Gingold extract. But when he walked beneath a falling flower pot, his arm rose to the occasion and stretched to catch it!*

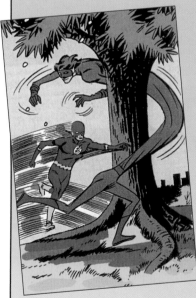

FLEXIBLE FRIEND *Ralph Dibny and Barry Allen (the second Flash) were fast friends and joined forces to solve several cases in Central City.*

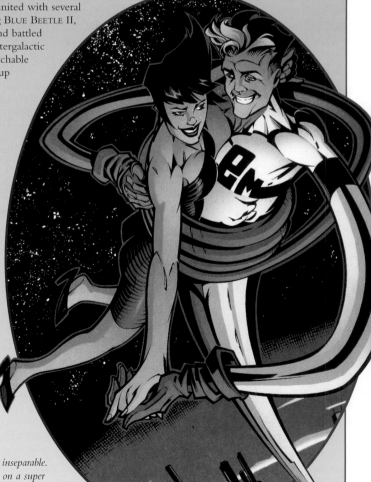

DEVOTION *Ralph and Sue were inseparable. Even when Elongated Man was on a super heroic mission, Sue was never far behind! Sue died in a horrible attack by Doctor Light I.*

EMPRESS

FIRST APPEARANCE YOUNG JUSTICE #16 (January 2000)
STATUS Hero **REAL NAME** Anita Fite
OCCUPATION Adventurer **BASE** Mobile
HEIGHT 5ft 7in **WEIGHT** 127 lbs **EYES** Bronze **HAIR** Purple
SPECIAL POWERS/ABILITIES Teleportation, mental control, and top-notch physical conditioning; skilled with most weapons.

As the granddaughter of the sinister Baron Agua sin Gaaz, Empress is heir to a villain's legacy, but she has lived her teen years in the service of heroism. Her father, Donald Fite, served in the All-Purpose Espionage Squad (A.P.E.S.). After Agua sin Gaaz killed her mother in a bombing intended for Donald, Empress assumed the full powers due to her as part of her voodoo heritage. Inspired by the teen heroes YOUNG JUSTICE, particularly ARROWETTE, she joined the hero team at a time when Arrowette had temporarily left. This gave rise to friction when Arrowette returned and thought that Empress had taken her place. During a battle against the android INDIGO, which led to Young Justice's breakup, Empress suffered severe injuries and almost did not manage to teleport away to safety. After her recuperation she will undoubtedly return to crime fighting. **DW**

ENCANTADORA

FIRST APPEARANCE ACTION COMICS #760 (December 1999)
STATUS Villain **REAL NAME** Lourdes Lucero
OCCUPATION Enchantress **BASE** Metropolis
HEIGHT 5ft 7in **WEIGHT** 133 lbs **EYES** Brown **HAIR** Brown
SPECIAL POWERS/ABILITIES A mystical vial she wears on her necklace contains the Mist of Ibella, which allows her to teleport, magically charm and control the minds of others, and telekinetically move objects with her mind.

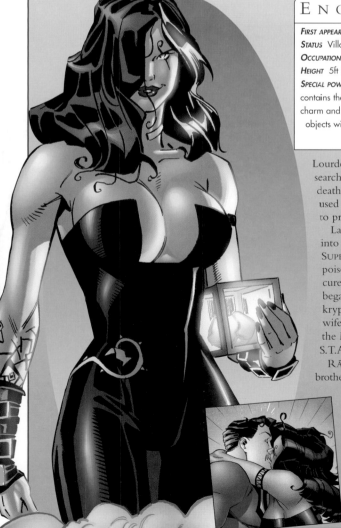

Lourdes Lucero's archaeologist father was driven mad searching for the magical Mist of Ibella. After his death, Lourdes took the vial containing the Mist and used its power to become La Encantadora, promising to provide for her little brother, Victor.

La Encantadora tried to trick a number of villains into buying fake green kryptonite to use against SUPERMAN. The Man of Steel believed he had been poisoned, and Encantadora offered him a magical cure in exchange for a kiss. Superman mysteriously began to succumb to radiation poisoning caused by kryptonite. Horrified, Encantadora told Superman's wife, Lois (see LANE, LOIS) that her kiss had infected the Man of Steel with kryptonite nanobots. Luckily, S.T.A.R. Labs physicians saved Superman's life.

RÃ'S AL GHŪL then threatened Encantadora and her brother He hoped to mix the Mist with his ancient Lazarus pit in order to gain unlimited power. With Superman's help, the sorceress and her brother escaped his clutches. After Encantadora vanished, Superman learned that GENERAL ZOD, one of his greatest foes, had provided the magical femme fatale with the kryptonite nanobots that had nearly killed him. **PJ**

CHARMER Superman could never have guessed how deadly La Encantadora's kiss would be.

ENCHANTRESS

FIRST APPEARANCE STRANGE ADVENTURES #187 (April 1966)
STATUS Undecided **REAL NAME** June Moone
OCCUPATION Freelance artist/adventurer/criminal **BASE** Mobile
HEIGHT 5ft 6in **WEIGHT** 130 lbs
EYES Blue (green as Enchantress) **HAIR** Black (as Enchantress)
SPECIAL POWERS/ABILITIES Could animate objects, alter her own appearance and levitate; mystic tricks once concealed in her hat.

A secret passage in Terror Castle led June Moone to a creature named Dzamor. He revealed her destiny: to become a magical defender. By uttering the name "Enchantress," June acquired awesome powers, which she used to thwart mystical menaces. Years later, Dzamor summoned June and told her that an astral alignment would empower her to cleanse Earth of evil. However, POWER GIRL prevented the alignment by moving the real Moon, denying June her destiny. Embittered, June lost control of her alter ego and the Enchantress turned to villainy. Jailed for her crimes, the Enchantress was given amnesty as a member of the SUICIDE SQUAD. June's fight with the Enchantress ended when the son of Faust (see FAUST, FELIX) sacrificed her to reignite the fires of Hell. The Enchantress died, but June regained her soul and now lives a normal life. **SB**

ENDLESS, THE

FIRST APPEARANCE SANDMAN (2nd series) #21 (November 1990)
STATUS Inapplicable **BASE** Various astral realms
MEMBERS AND POWERS
Destiny Chained to his Eternity Book, which records everything that has or will ever happen.
Death Takes each being in the universe to their final resting place.
Dream Ruler of the Dreaming, where all minds are linked.
Desire Androgynous brother/sister is every sentient being's desire.
Despair Funnels despair into mortal souls.
Destruction Governs transformation and change.
Delirium Mistress of the mentally disturbed.

The Endless are a family of incredibly powerful entities who exist because mortals, gods, demons, and aliens across the cosmos *believe* they exist. The Endless are not gods but have been worshipped as such throughout the cosmos. Mortal beings perceive the Endless according to their own cultural or species expectations. Each of the Endless exists in their own astral realm that is a creation of the consciousness of living beings. The eldest member of the Endless is DESTINY, who came into existence shortly after the beginning of the universe. Soon after, DEATH was created, followed by DREAM. Destruction was born soon after, a manifestation of change. A set of twins, the cruel Desire and the grim Despair, came next, and Delight, the youngest member of the Endless, was transformed countless aeons ago into a new aspect of the Endless, called Delirium.

The embodiment of their names, the Endless are older than the angels. While the elder siblings fulfill their roles with the utmost seriousness, the younger ones involve themselves in petty intrigues. Desire has more than once tried to destroy Dream, and Destruction abandoned his duties for centuries, retiring to a village in Greece with his dog Barnabas. Born at the beginning of creation, the Endless will continue to exist until the last sentient being has died, when Death will claim Destiny, and finally herself, at the end of time. **PJ**

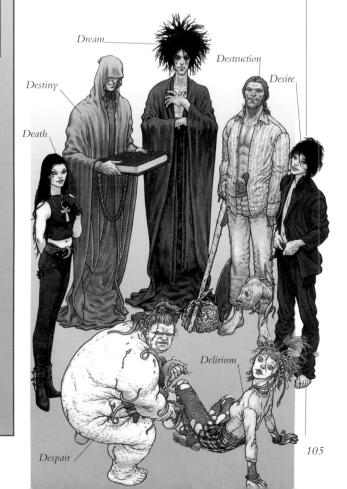

ENEMY ACE

FIRST APPEARANCE OUR ARMY AT WAR #151 (February 1965)
STATUS Unresolved **REAL NAME** Hans von Hammer
OCCUPATION Pilot **BASE** Germany
HEIGHT 5ft 11in **WEIGHT** 161 lbs **EYES** Blue **HAIR** Auburn
SPECIAL POWERS/ABILITIES One of the greatest natural pilots ever seen.

The son of an aristocratic German family distantly related to Anton Arcane (see ARCANE, ANTON), Baron Hans von Hammer was among the first to enlist when World War I broke out in 1914. While in flight school, he engaged in a duel of honor with fellow cadet Heinrich Muller and received a permanent scar on his left cheek. An exceptional flyer, von Hammer soon became Rittsmeister of his own Jagdstaffel hunting squadron, and feared among Allied forces as the Enemy Ace. During the course of the war, he had over 70 kills to his credit; however, he took no joy in performing this duty. A solitary man, when not flying, von Hammer retreated to his home, wandering the nearby Black Forest, with his only companion, a wolf.

During World War II, von Hammer was persuaded out of retirement to fight on Nazi Germany's behalf on the Russian front. He crashed his plane in Leningrad and, before escaping back to his base, saw the horrors that Germany had inflicted on the Russian people there. After witnessing the atrocities at the Nazi concentration camp at Dachau in 1945, a shaken Hans von Hammer surrendered himself and his men to SERGEANT ROCK and Easy Company.

By the 1960s, the great von Hammer was broke, divorced, and confined to a German care facility. The former air ace spent his last days confiding his experiences to reporter and Vietnam veteran Edward Mannock, thereby bringing himself a measure of peace before he died. Some time later, von Hammer's exploits were popularized in a motion picture financed by Bruce Wayne, the BATMAN. RG

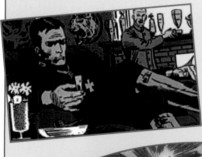

A SOLITARY MAN
Hans von Hammer took little pleasure in his wartime duty and when not in the air, remained an intensely private individual.

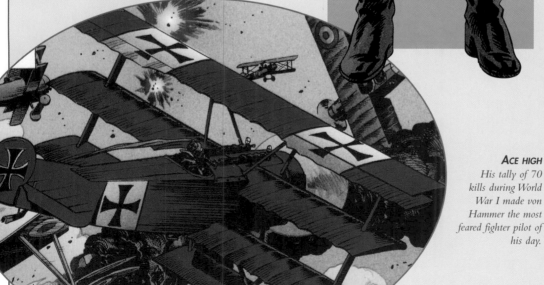

ACE HIGH
His tally of 70 kills during World War I made von Hammer the most feared fighter pilot of his day.

ERADICATOR

FIRST APPEARANCE ACTION COMICS #693 (November 1993)
STATUS Ally **REAL NAME** Dr. David Connor
OCCUPATION Preserver of Kryptonian heritage **BASE** Mobile
HEIGHT 6ft 3in **WEIGHT** 225 lbs **EYES** Red **HAIR** Gray
SPECIAL POWERS/ABILITIES Flight, super-strength, heat vision; can project and control various energy types; extremely difficult to kill.

The Eradicator was originally a Kryptonian superweapon devised to wipe out alien races on Krypton and alter the genetic structure of all Kryptonians making it impossible for them to leave the planet. Thousands of years after the destruction of the planet, this incredible thinking machine had become the repository of all Kryptonian culture. It built SUPERMAN's Fortress of Solitude and attempted to turn Earth into a replica of Krypton. It then assumed human form and even impersonated Superman following the Man of Steel's death at the hands of DOOMSDAY.

The Eradicator brought Superman back to the Fortress of Solitude and revived him with Kryptonian technology, allowing Earth's greatest hero to cheat death. The CYBORG SUPERMAN nearly destroyed the Eradicator, but it survived by bonding with the body of S.T.A.R. Labs scientist Dr. David Connor. Although Connor remained partially in control, a copy of the Eradicator program animated the ruins of Superman's shattered Fortress of Solitude (destroyed earlier by DOMINUS) and assembled a huge warsuit. Connor/Eradicator merged with this titanic construct and flew off into space. The Eradicator later returned to Earth, but by then it was clear that Connor had lost most of his sanity. During the JOKER's "Last Laugh" spree, an infected Eradicator went on a lunatic, Jokerized rampage. DW

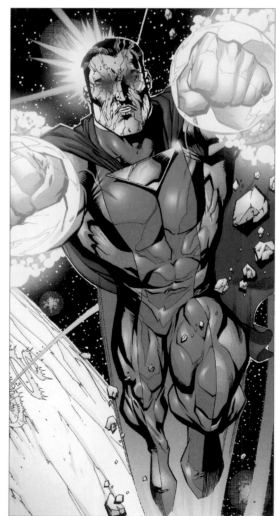

EVIL STAR

FIRST APPEARANCE GREEN LANTERN (2nd series) #37 (June 1965)
STATUS Villain **REAL NAME** Unknown
OCCUPATION Would-be intergalactic conqueror **BASE** Planet Aoran
HEIGHT 6ft 1in **WEIGHT** 205 lbs **EYES** Blue **HAIR** Blond
SPECIAL POWERS/ABILITIES Star-band can create solid objects, fire
energy beams, and generate a protective shield.

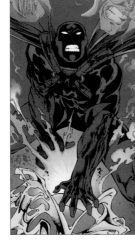

Evil Star allowed his fear of death to
ruin life for everyone else on the
planet Aoran. His invention, the
Star-band, extended the life of its
wearer indefinitely. However, it
also compelled its wearer to
commit acts of great wickedness,
and Evil Star would not remove
the device lest he grow old.
When the Aorans rose up against
him, Evil Star used the Star-band's
energy to slaughter everyone on the
planet. Realizing that he possessed a
weapon as powerful as a GREEN
LANTERN's power ring, Evil Star decided to overthrow the
GUARDIANS OF THE UNIVERSE and rule the cosmos.
Green Lantern Hal Jordan put an end to his mad scheme.
Evil Star has since threatened galactic peace many times,
employing mindless henchmen known as "Starlings."
These invulnerable, super-strong robots must be guided
by Evil Star's thoughts to function properly. **DW**

EXTANT

FIRST APPEARANCE SHOWCASE '94 #9 (August 1994)
STATUS Villain **REAL NAME** Henry (Hank) Hall
OCCUPATION Would-be world conqueror **BASE** Mobile
HEIGHT 6ft 1in **WEIGHT** 197 lbs **EYES** Brown **HAIR** Brown
SPECIAL POWERS/ABILITIES Armor gives superhuman strength and
invulnerability; some ability to control time.

Hank Hall and his brother
Don were experiments on
behalf of the Lords of
Order and Chaos, gaining
powers and operating as
HAWK AND DOVE. When
Don was killed, Hank
went berserk. The arrival
of Dawn Granger as the
new Dove calmed him, but
when she was apparently
killed by his own future
incarnation, Hank totally
lost control. He fought his
future self, an armored
being with time-controlling
powers, known as
MONARCH, and eventually
beat him. Hank modified Monarch's armor and time-
controlling abilities, renaming himself Extant. The exact
capabilities of Extant's time-control powers remained
unexplained, but they seemed to affect the speed with
which time passed for an object or person. On repeated
occasions Extant has tried to recreate Earth on his own
terms, only to be stopped by various combinations of heroes,
notably the JUSTICE SOCIETY OF AMERICA. Extant was
responsible for the deaths of DOCTOR MID-NITE I, ATOM I,
and HOURMAN I, in addition to ATOM-SMASHER's mother,
by absorbing their own chronal energies so that they reverted
to their natural ages. He was finally stopped when Atom-
Smasher placed Extant on a doomed airplane in place of his
mother, closing a time lap and ending Extant's threat. **RG**

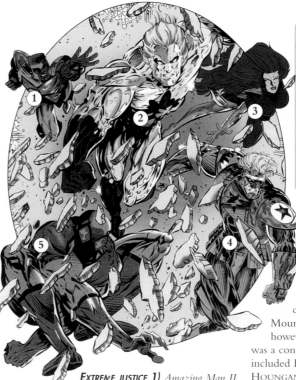

EXTREME JUSTICE 1) *Amazing Man II*
2) *Captain Atom* **3)** *Maxima*
4) *Booster Gold* **5)** *Blue Beetle II*

EXTREME JUSTICE

FIRST APPEARANCE EXTREME JUSTICE #0 (January 1995)
STATUS Hero team (disbanded) **BASE** Mount Thunder, Nevada
ORIGINAL MEMBERS AND POWERS
Captain Atom Atomic-based powers via connection to quantum field.
Amazing Man II Can transform himself into any material he touches.
Blue Beetle II Utilizes a variety of high-tech gadgets in his arsenal.
Booster Gold Superb athlete with futuristic exo-armor.
Firestorm Has ability to atomically restructure any inorganic material.
Maxima Superstrong and cunning alien warrior queen.
Plastique Possesses explosive abilities.

Captain Atom's frustration with the leadership of the
JUSTICE LEAGUE OF AMERICA led him to form a
splinter group that claimed the Justice League name,
but was known as "Extreme Justice" for its more
proactive stance on combating evil. This Extreme
Justice League took the fight to its foes, rather than
react to threats. Later, alien shape-shifters and runaway
slaves Zan and Jayna were added to Extreme Justice's role
call, based at an abandoned military complex within
Mount Thunder, Nevada. Extreme Justice's status as a hero team,
however, was short-lived. The group's most notable adventure
was a conflict with the Legion of Doom, a team of villains that
included Brainwave II, a robot duplicate of GORILLA GRODD,
HOUNGAN, KILLER FROST II, a resurrected MAJOR FORCE, and the
Madmen. After capturing the Legion, Extreme Justice later disbanded
with its heroes going their separate ways, many returning to some
capacity of membership with the "official" Justice League. **SB**

EXTREMISTS, THE

FIRST APPEARANCE (Extremists I) JUSTICE LEAGUE EUROPE #15
(June 1990); (Extremists II) JUSTICE LEAGUE AMERICA #78
(August 1993)
STATUS Villain team **BASE** The planet Angor; Paris, France
MEMBERS AND POWERS
Lord Havok I Team leader; his battlesuit can mutate into anything
Havok needs.
Lord Havok II An identity used briefly by Maxwell Lord.
Doctor Diehard Can control magnetism.
Dreamslayer Can manipulate matter and teleport.
Gorgon II Grappling tentacles grow from his head.
Tracer Has superhuman senses and razor-sharp teeth and claws.
Brute Invulnerable and superstrong.
Cloudburst Ability to control weather.
Death Angel Illusion casting.
Gunshot Has a superpowered battlesuit with offensive weaponry.
Meanstreak Can transform objects into energy projectiles.

THE EXTREMISTS 1) *Dreamslayer*
2) *Doctor Diehard* **3)** *Gorgon II*
4) *Lord Havok II*
5) *Tracer*

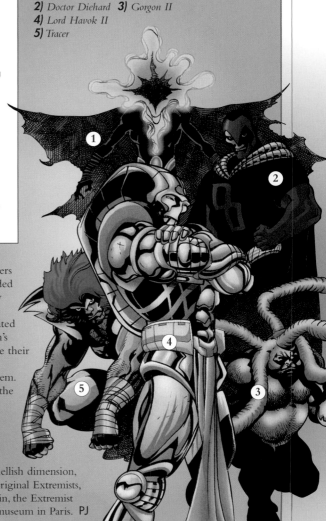

The Extremists were a group of androids used by
DREAMSLAYER to replicate a team of villainous murderers
from the world of Angor. The original Extremists invaded
our world by following two of Angor's heroes, Blue Jay
and the Silver Sorceress, to Earth. Upon their arrival,
the Extremists defeated Justice League Europe, annihilated
the ROCKET RED BRIGADES, and took control of Earth's
nuclear arsenal. The JUSTICE LEAGUE OF AMERICA made their
way to Angor, found Mitch Wacky, the creator of the
androids, and brought him back to Earth to deactivate them.
Dreamslayer returned, however, and took control of the
Justice League, using his powers to revive LORD HAVOK.
However, the Silver Sorceress was able to absorb
Dreamslayer's essence before she died. He escaped yet
again and, granted power by the alien OVERMASTER,
created a new team of Extremists. After their defeat by
the Justice League, Overmaster sent Dreamslayer to a hellish dimension,
and the New Extremists joined the CADRE. Later, the original Extremists,
sans Dreamslayer, attacked SUPERGIRL. Defeated yet again, the Extremist
androids were deactivated and put on display at a wax museum in Paris. **PJ**

FAIRCHILD, VESPER

FIRST APPEARANCE BATMAN #540 (March 1997)
STATUS Hero **REAL NAME** Vesper Fairchild
OCCUPATION Radio personality/journalist **BASE** Gotham City
HEIGHT 5ft 7in **WEIGHT** 126 lbs **EYES** Green **HAIR** Auburn
SPECIAL POWERS/ABILITIES No special powers; thorough and highly skilled investigative reporter.

Host of W.K.G.C. Talk Radio's "Siren of the Night," broadcaster Vesper Fairchild enjoyed a brief romance with billionaire Bruce Wayne before Gotham City was devastated by the earthquake that left it a lawless No Man's Land. In her new career as a journalist, Vesper returned to the rebuilt city and rekindled her relationship with Wayne while investigating his alter ego, BATMAN. Unfortunately, Vesper was killed in Wayne Manor by the assassin CAIN, DAVID shortly after learning that Wayne and the Dark Knight were one and the same. Bruce Wayne was framed for Vesper's murder, but was exonerated upon discovering that rival mogul Lex Luthor (see LUTHOR, LEX) had hired Cain in a plot to ruin Wayne. **SB**

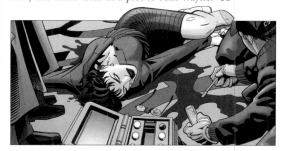

FAITH

FIRST APPEARANCE JLA #69 (October 2002)
STATUS Hero **REAL NAME** Unrevealed
OCCUPATION Adventurer **BASE** Mobile
HEIGHT 5ft 10in **WEIGHT** 148 lbs **EYES** Brown **HAIR** Brown
SPECIAL POWERS/ABILITIES Capable of flight; commands powerful telekinetic energy; unconsciously inspires trust in those around her.

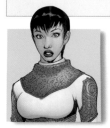

Faith was previously in the employ of a secret, unidentified U.S. government "black ops" team, but the nature of her role is unknown. Nicknamed the "Fat Lady" by her teammates, it is likely that she was called in to finish what other operatives had started. Whether Faith's ties to her former employers have been completely severed remains to be seen. Faith has telekinetic powers and may have shown only a fraction of her abilities. She also emits "positive vibrations" that help those around her feel calm and confident. As a result, anyone who meets her instinctively trusts her. Faith claims to have met BATMAN on a past mission, during which they spent some time together. She answered Batman's call when the creation of a "contingency League" was required during the Obsidian Age mission, when the JUSTICE LEAGUE OF AMERICA had to travel 3,000 years back in time to Atlantis to rescue AQUAMAN and the present-day Atlanteans during the war against IMPERIEX. She earned Batman's confidence, and he not only considered her for JLA membership, but shared some personal insights with her as well. **RG**

FALLEN ANGEL

FIRST APPEARANCE Fallen Angel #1 (September 2003)
STATUS Unresolved **REAL NAME** "Lee"
OCCUPATION Protector of Bette Noire **BASE** Bette Noire
HEIGHT 5ft 5in **WEIGHT** 125 lbs **EYES** Blue **HAIR** Light brown
SPECIAL POWERS/ABILITIES Superhuman strength, enhanced speed, telekinesis, and apparent invulnerability.

The U.S. city of Bette Noire is a dark and corrupt sewer of nightmares that makes Gotham City look like the French Riviera. Since arriving in Bette Noire only recently, the mysterious superpowered woman known as the Fallen Angel has acted as a protector to the town's citizens despite confusion over her motives. The Fallen Angel willingly associates with Bette Noire's worst crooks—though she's tougher than all of them—and refuses to discuss the circumstances that led her to her position in life. Though her drives are as murky as her past, during the day the Fallen Angel maintains an alternate identity of "Lee" and works as a teacher. She has so far defeated some true horrors that have menaced Bette Noire, including a mystical beast that delighted in mutilating its victims.

Recently, the villainous Black Mariah has returned to Bette Noire (after Lee forced her out), and this development will undoubtedly spell grave trouble for the mysterious Fallen Angel. **DW**

FAORA

FIRST APPEARANCE (historical) ACTION COMICS #471 (May 1977); (current) ACTION COMICS #779 (July 2001)
REAL NAME Unknown **BASE** Pokolistan
HEIGHT 5ft 7in **WEIGHT** 150 lbs **EYES** Brown **HAIR** Brown
OCCUPATION Enforcer **STATUS** Villain
SPECIAL POWERS/ABILITIES A cyborg who has the power to disrupt molecular bonds in others, causing powerful explosions; flight.

The first Faora was a devoted lieutenant to GENERAL ZOD of Krypton, a powerful military figure and the ideological and physical adversary of Jor-El, SUPERMAN's father. Faora and fellow lieutenant Kru-El took control of Zod's forces after his death at Jor-El's hands. Faora and Kru-El died while battling Kryptonian extremists, but their DNA was merged to create a clone of Zod, who was raised as if he were the General's son.

The third Faora was an orphan in the Russian Federation's meta-human development program. The teenaged girl, a cyborg, was recruited by General Zod and renamed Faora after his slain Kryptonian lieutenant, becoming his most valuable assistant and second-in-command. After altering the sun's radiation and stripping away the metagene powers of Earth's heroes, Zod died in battle with the Man of Steel, and Faora was left to repair his damage before being taken into custody. **PJ**

FASTBAK

FIRST APPEARANCE THE NEW GODS vol. 1 #5 (October 1971)
STATUS Hero **REAL NAME** None
OCCUPATION Inventor/balladeer **BASE** New Genesis
HEIGHT 6ft 1in **WEIGHT** 197 lbs **EYES** Blue **HAIR** Reddish blond
SPECIAL POWERS/ABILITIES Aeropads in boots enable superspeed flight; resistant to friction and the effects of high-velocity travel.

One of the NEW GODS of the distant planet New Genesis, fleet-footed Fastbak is known for his ability to travel at tremendous speeds with the aeropads he invented for his boots. Once he even outpaced the harbinger of death known as the BLACK RACER, as well as a phalanx of Apokoliptian Parademons, to save the life of fellow New God and friend Esak. In addition, Fastbak is an accomplished singer and composer of ballads. Constantly striving for greater velocities, Fastbak continues to tinker with his aeropads while helping to protect New Genesis from the omnipresent threat from the neighboring planet Apokolips and its dreaded lord, DARKSEID. **SB**

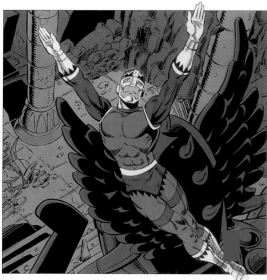

FASTBALL

FIRST APPEARANCE JUSTICE LEAGUE OF AMERICA #234 (January 1985)
STATUS Villain (missing in action) **REAL NAME** Malone (first name unknown) **OCCUPATION** Assassin **BASE** Detroit
HEIGHT 5ft 11in **WEIGHT** 185 lbs **EYES** Blue **HAIR** Unknown
SPECIAL POWERS/ABILITIES Super-fast reflexes and speed; prefers to strike from a distance, hurling explosives.

Recruited from Tampa, Florida, by the alien OVERMASTER, Fastball's background is unknown. He joined the Overmaster's CADRE, training with them for weeks before being unleashed against the JUSTICE LEAGUE OF AMERICA. Preferring to pitch explosives than go hand-to-hand against opponents, Fastball has proven a not terribly bright criminal. Clearly a would-be baseball pitcher, Fastball's skills seem under-developed, making him an easy target for the League. He and the Cadre later became affiliates of DOCTOR POLARIS and suffered defeat at the hands of the corporate super-team POWER COMPANY. His whereabouts after the Cadre's final defeat remain unrecorded. **RG**

FATAL FIVE

FIRST APPEARANCE ADVENTURE COMICS #352 (January 1967)
STATUS Villain team **BASE** Mobile
MEMBERS AND POWERS
Emerald Empress Vast powers stemming from the Emerald Eye.
Tharok Cyborg strength and advanced intellect.
Mano Can disintegrate with his touch
The Persuader Carries an atomic ax.
Validus Superstrength and invulnerability.

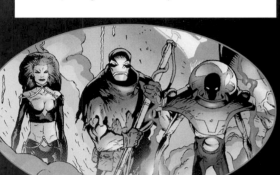

EARLY CLASH The Fatal Five
often battled the Legion.

THE MEMBERS OF THE FATAL FIVE comprise some of the worst criminals of the late 30th century. Together, they are an almost unstoppable force for mayhem and murder. Their violent tendencies landed them behind bars long before anyone conceived the idea of a Fatal Five super-team. THAROK was a half-cyborg whose body had been reconstructed following a terrible accident; his electronically-amplified brain made him a brilliant strategist and leader. Empress' true name was Saryva of Vengar, and she delighted in destruction and pain. Mano was a mutant whose glowing right hand could disintegrate anything it touched; he used this power to destroy his polluted homeworld of Angtu. The Persuader carried an atomic ax that could slice through anything and shared he a psychic link with the weapon. Validus was a an invulnerable colossus of staggering strength.

FORCE FIVE Mutual mistrust hinders the team, but their powers can be terrifying when combined. Braniac 13 employed copies of the Fatal Five to protect his Warworld when venturing back into the 21st century.

THE WARMAKER

The corrupt President Chu of the United Planets desired a second war between the planets of Braal and Titan. Creating the bogus threat of a Sun-Eater, she ordered the LEGION OF SUPER-HEROES to assemble Tharok, Empress, Mano, the Persuader, and Validus into a strike team to battle the cosmic menace. The Fatal Five soon came into conflict with the Legionnaires, triggering a fierce battle that ended in victory thanks to the involvement of the Legion Rescue Squad. The Legion executed a sting operation to prove President Chu's complicity in the affair.

The U.P. Council removed Chu from office and industrialist R.J. Brande (see BRANDE, R.J.) became president in her wake. Later, the Empress bonded to the all-powerful artifact known as the Emerald Eye of Ekron, becoming the Emerald Empress. She freed the others and led the Fatal Five into other clashes with the Legion, including a hijacking of the Legion Outpost and a scuffle with new Legionnaire TIMBER WOLF.

As an odd side note to Fatal Five history, the tyrant BRAINIAC 13 generated hard-light images of the team as guards for his Warworld when he traveled back in time to the 21st century.

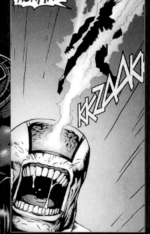

SUPERMAN, investigating the Warworld's sudden appearance, battled the counterfeit "Fatal Five" and was left bewildered by the experience. **DW**

VALIDUS
The powerhouse of the Fatal Five is a simple-minded giant largely under the control of Tharok. His bolts of mental lightning are powerful enough to fry Kryptonians and Daxamites.

THE FATAL FIVE 1) Mano **2)** Persuader
3) Validus **4)** Tharok **5)** Emerald Empress

KEY STORYLINES

• *LEGION OF SUPER-HEROES #34 (APRIL 1996):* The Fatal Five battle the Legion of Super-Heroes, in the first Fatal Five storyline to appear in the new Legion chronology.

• *SUPERMAN #171 (AUGUST 2001):* A duplicate Fatal Five squares off against the Man of Steel, providing a yardstick for measuring the team's considerable might.

• *THE LEGION #16 (MARCH 2003):* New Legionnaire Timber Wolf receives a baptism of fire as he is forced to battle the entire might of the Fatal Five.

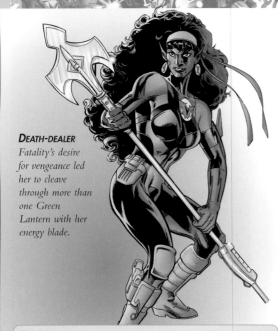

DEATH-DEALER
Fatality's desire for vengeance led her to cleave through more than one Green Lantern with her energy blade.

FATALITY

FIRST APPEARANCE GREEN LANTERN (3rd series) #83 (February 1997)
STATUS Villain **REAL NAME** Yrra Cynril
OCCUPATION Assassin **BASE** The planet Xanshi
HEIGHT 5ft 9in **WEIGHT** 124 lbs **EYES** Brown **HAIR** Black
SPECIAL POWERS/ABILITIES One of the most skilled martial artists and weapons masters in the galaxy.

The eldest child of the royal family of the planet Xanshi, Yrra Cynril was sent by her parents to study with the legendary Warlords of Okaara. While Yrra was training with the Warlords, becoming a master of martial arts and other combat, Xanshi was accidentally destroyed by the arrogance of GREEN LANTERN John Stewart. When Yrra learned of this, she vowed vengeance on the entire GREEN LANTERN CORPS.

As Fatality, Yrra traveled the galaxy, murdering former Green Lanterns. Traveling to Earth, Fatality tried to kill Kyle Rayner, the last Green Lantern. Their battle took them to a distant planet, where Fatality learned from Rayner that Stewart was responsible for Xanshi's destruction. After nearly perishing in battle with the Emerald Warrior, the revenge-obsessed Fatality returned to Earth to confront Stewart and apparently died while trying to kill him. **PJ**

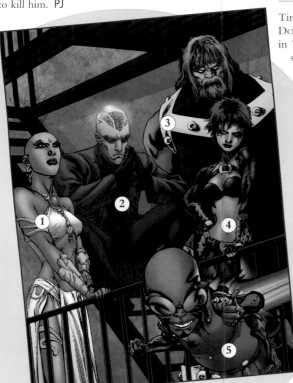

FAUST, FELIX

FIRST APPEARANCE JUSTICE LEAGUE OF AMERICA (1st series) #10 (March 1962)
STATUS Villain **REAL NAME** Felix Faust
OCCUPATION Sorceror **BASE** Mobile
HEIGHT 5ft 11in **WEIGHT** 172 lbs **EYES** Brown **HAIR** Brown
SPECIAL POWERS/ABILITIES Vast talents in spellcasting; great knowledge of the occult; experienced at summoning demonic entities.

Felix Faust counts his age in millennia, and is known to have clashed with the magician Nommo (DOCTOR MIST) in the ancient African empire of Kor. Resurrected in the 20th century in the body of minor sorcerer Dekan Drache, Faust studied hard to regain his black-magic mastery. To gain further power, Faust released the DEMONS THREE by forcing the newly-created JUSTICE LEAGUE OF AMERICA to retrieve the items that imprisoned the hellspawned trio. The scheme failed, but Faust became a perennial irritant to the Justice League during its early years. Hoping to become immortal, Faust became possessed by the spirit of the Egyptian wizard Hermes Trismegistus, but has since emerged from the wizard's shadow. Faust has a son, Sebastian, and a daughter, Fauna. **DW**

FEARSOME FIVE, THE

FIRST APPEARANCE NEW TEEN TITANS (1st series) #3 (January 1981)
STATUS Villain team (disbanded) **BASE** Mobile
ORIGINAL MEMBERS AND POWERS
Doctor Light I (leader) Telekinetic and telepathic abilities.
Psimon Vast mental powers.
Shimmer (deceased) Able to change one element into another.
Mammoth Shimmer's brother; superhuman strength.
Gizmo Turns random objects into tools or weapons.

Tired of being bested by super heroes, inept villain DOCTOR LIGHT I advertised for super-villains to join him in *The Underworld Star*, a newsletter for criminals. He had several replies, notably from the psionic PSIMON, the Australian mutants SHIMMER and MAMMOTH, and little GIZMO. They banded together as the Fearsome Five, only to be defeated repeatedly by the TEEN TITANS. Psimon supplanted Doctor Light as team leader and the outfit grew more menacing. Psimon added JINX, an East Indian sorceress, and the explosive man known as NEUTRON. The Fearsome Five disbanded following defeats by SUPERMAN and the New Titans. Gizmo reformed, and was working for S.T.A.R. Labs when Psimon sent him plunging into a subatomic universe. Psimon killed Mammoth and Shimmer. The team was recently reformed by DOCTOR SIVANA who brought Mammoth and Shimmer back to life, before being defeated by the OUTSIDERS. **RG**

THE FEARSOME FIVE 1) *Gizmo* **2)** *Mammoth* **3)** *Psimon* **4)** *Shimmer* **5)** *Doctor Light* **6)** *Jinx* **7)** *Neutron*

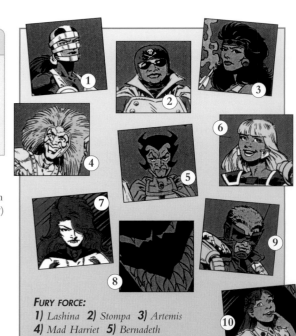

FURY FORCE:
1) *Lashina* **2)** *Stompa* **3)** *Artemis*
4) *Mad Harriet* **5)** *Bernadeth*
6) *Gilotina* **7)** *Bloody Mary* **8)** *Chessure*
9) *Speed Queen* **10)** *Malice Vundabarr*

FEMALE FURIES

FIRST APPEARANCE MISTER MIRACLE (1st series) #6 (February 1972)
STATUS Villain team **BASE** Apokolips
CURRENT MEMBERS AND POWERS
Bernadeth (leader) Carries burning fahren-knife.
Lashina Wields flexible steel bands.
Mad Harriet Has energized power spikes on her fists.
Stompa Wears heavy-matter boots that can crush anything and trigger earthquakes.
Artemis Commands cybernetic wolfpack; a skilled archer.
Gilotina Hands that can cut through anything.
Bloody Mary Vampire with mesmerism powers.
Speed Queen Can move at superspeed on roller blades.
Malice Vundabarr Young girl who controls Chessure.
Chessure Shadow monster.

The Female Furies are the elite shock troops of Apokolips, bringing terror to those unfortunate enough to incur DARKSEID's wrath. Trained by GRANNY GOODNESS, each woman possesses a specialized ability that makes them unstoppable when they work as a team. BIG BARDA originally led the Female Furies but abandoned the group when she followed her love, MISTER MIRACLE, to Earth. BERNADETH, sister of Darkseid's boot-licker DESAAD, assumed control of the Furies and led them in a failed mission to retrieve their lost sister. Lashina, who vied with Bernadeth for leadership, was left behind on Earth in a later mission and became a member of the SUICIDE SQUAD under the name Duchess. Assembling her own Suicide Squad strike force, Lashina returned to Apokolips seeking to become head of the Furies. Lashina killed Bernadeth, but Darkseid killed Lashina for her impertinence. He soon brought them both back to life, however, and Lashina sullenly serves under Bernadeth's command. Darkseid recently dispatched the Furies to obtain Kara Zor-El, who had just arrived on Earth. He saw in her the spark for her to lead the team and fill Barda's spot. Associated with the core team are the Fury Cadets, less-experienced members who long to prove their combat skills to their beloved Granny. Among their number are the vampiric Bloody Mary and the reformed Gilotina. **DW**

FERRO

FIRST APPEARANCE ADVENTURES OF SUPERMAN #540 (November 1996)
STATUS Hero **REAL NAME** Andrew Nolan
OCCUPATION Legionnaire **BASE** Legion World, U.P. Space
HEIGHT 5ft 7in **WEIGHT** 155 lbs **EYES** Green **HAIR** Brown
SPECIAL POWERS/ABILITIES Formerly able to transform himself into flexible and impervious iron; now trapped in metal form.

Born in the 20th century, Andrew Nolan and his twin brother, Douglas, were the sons of famous film actress Nancy Nolan, who abandoned her children as a result of her horror at their grotesque facial deformities. The boys were institutionalized by the unscrupulous Dr. 30 and his Threelove Corporation, which sought to capitalize on the Nolans' shared ability to transform their bodies into malleable iron. Escaping Dr. 30's control, Andrew ran away to Metropolis, where he used his power to aid time-traveling members of the LEGION OF SUPER-HEROES as the teen super hero Ferro. Andrew's brother Douglas—himself a hero called Ingot— apparently died in a vain attempt to reignite Earth's sun, extinguished by the Sun-Eater. Ultimately, PARALLAX succeeded where Ingot failed.

Andrew opted to remain with the Legion and return with them to the 30th century as a member of the team. Although Nolan was given the opportunity to alter his deformed face via surgery to make it more normal in appearance, he chose to retain his individuality. However, following one of the Legion's adventures, Ferro became permanently trapped in his metal form, yet another ironic chapter in this young hero's ongoing hard luck story. **SB**

IRON MASK Ferro, before fate enclosed his body in iron.

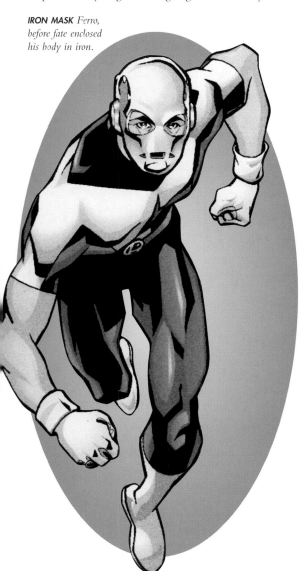

FEVER PITCH *Fever had no real control over her power or the moral guidance in the use of her skills—until she joined one version of the Doom Patrol.*

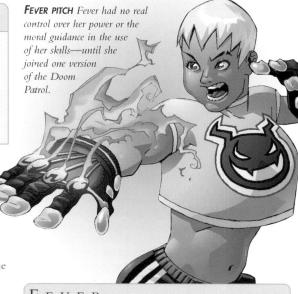

FEVER

FIRST APPEARANCE DOOM PATROL (3rd series) #1 (December 2001)
STATUS Hero (missing) **REAL NAME** Shyleen Lao
OCCUPATION Adventurer **BASE** New York City
HEIGHT 5ft 5in **WEIGHT** 134 lbs **EYES** Brown **HAIR** Blonde
SPECIAL POWERS/ABILITIES Can generate intense heat over short distances, to superheat a gun in a criminal's hands or soften metal to break or reshape it; exact limits of her power are unknown.

When businessman Thayer Jost acquired the rights to the DOOM PATROL name, he set about finding some new members. No one knows how he found Shyleen Lao, or how he recruited her to join his new team. The youngest member of the reformed Doom Patrol, Shyleen's developing heat powers remained erratic, possibly because she was still maturing or because she was untrained. For a brief time, she had some control under ROBOTMAN II's tutelage, but left on her own, still struggling with control issues. Shyleen was a complex mix of gumption and adolescent fear. She liked being part of the team and facing great dangers but could also be easily terrified by those same threats. Since the Doom Patrol disbanded, her whereabouts are unknown. **RG**

FIRE

FIRST APPEARANCE DC COMICS PRESENTS #46 (June 1982)
STATUS Hero **REAL NAME** Beatriz Bonilla DaCosta
OCCUPATION Former spy, model, and adventurer; webcam star
BASE New York City
HEIGHT 5ft 8in **WEIGHT** 140 lbs **EYES** Green **HAIR** Green
SPECIAL POWERS/ABILITIES Can transform into a being of living green fire; projection of green flame blasts; power of flight.

Born and raised in Brazil, Beatriz DaCosta became a spy for the Brazilian secret service, Espiaos Nacionales. Her first mission was to track down some experimental equipment that produced the incendiary material Pyroplasm. Botching the mission, Beatriz was exposed to Pyroplasm and discovered she could breathe flame from her mouth. Taking the name Green Fury, she joined the GLOBAL GUARDIANS.

Years later, Beatriz, now called Fire, and her best friend, ICE, joined the JUSTICE LEAGUE OF AMERICA. During the alien invasion, Fire's powers were dramatically increased. After Ice's death at the hands of the OVERMASTER and the disbanding of her Justice League, Fire returned to Rio De Janeiro. She later moved back to New York, where she maintained an almost X-rated Web site before joining her onetime companions, Maxwell Lord's team of "heroes for the people," the so-called "Super Buddies." **PJ**

FIREBIRD

FIRST APPEARANCE FIRESTORM, THE NUCLEAR MAN #69 (March 1989)
STATUS Hero **REAL NAME** Serafina Arkadina
OCCUPATION Adventurer **BASE** Russian Federation
HEIGHT 5ft 3in **WEIGHT** 122 lbs **EYES** Blue **HAIR** Blonde
SPECIAL POWERS/ABILITIES She is telepathic and has the power to hypnotize people.

Serafina Arkadina is a young woman from the Russian Federation who was born with various psychic powers. Taking the name Firebird, Serafina joined a number of other super-powered Russian teenagers on the team called SOYUZ.

For most of their young careers, Soyuz were pursued by the K.G.B. and other Russian intelligence agencies. After their bravery during the alien invasion, the Russian government relaxed its efforts to track Soyuz's activities.

Firebird is the leader of the Soyuz, and her uncle, Mikhail Arkadin, is the Russian hero POZHAR, who was once fused with the fire elemental FIRESTORM. **PJ**

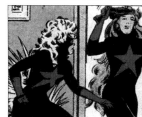

TELEPATHIC Firebird took her codename to disguise her true powers, which are all psychic in nature.

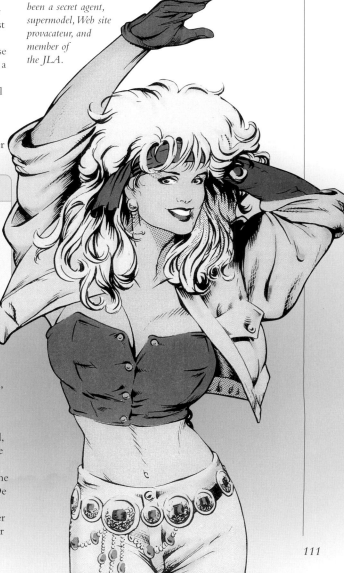

FIERY Beatriz DaCosta has been a secret agent, supermodel, Web site provocateur, and member of the JLA.

BROTHER AND SISTER *Rod and Danette Reilly discovered they could accomplish more by leaving their civilian identities behind. Sadly, both died at the hands of enemies.*

FIREBRAND II

FIRST APPEARANCE ALL-STAR SQUADRON #5 (January 1982)
STATUS Hero (deceased)   **REAL NAME** Danette Reilly
OCCUPATION Adventurer   **BASE** New York City
HEIGHT 5ft 5in   **WEIGHT** 128 lbs   **EYES** Blue   **HAIR** Red
SPECIAL POWERS/ABILITIES Generated fire from hands; mental discipline prevented the fire burning her body or clothing, even absorbing it into her body; power of flight.

FIREHAIR

FIRST APPEARANCE SHOWCASE #85 (September 1969)
STATUS Hero (deceased)   **REAL NAME** Unknown
OCCUPATION Warrior   **BASE** Great Western Plains, circa 1820
HEIGHT 5ft 10in   **WEIGHT** 188 lbs   **EYES** Blue   **HAIR** Red
SPECIAL POWERS/ABILITIES Daring fighter; expert horseman and marksman, especially with bow and arrow.

FIREBRAND I

FIRST APPEARANCE POLICE COMICS #1 (August 1941)
STATUS Hero (deceased)   **REAL NAME** Rod Reilly
OCCUPATION Adventurer   **BASE** New York City
HEIGHT 6ft   **WEIGHT** 185 lbs   **EYES** Blue   **HAIR** Brown
SPECIAL POWERS/ABILITIES Superb athlete and boxer.

Bored with being one of the idle rich, Rod Reilly trained with his friend, ex-heavyweight boxer "Slugger" Dunn, donned a red and pink costume and took a flaming torch as his calling card. As Firebrand, he battled crime in New York City. In 1941 Reilly enlisted in the U.S. Navy and was injured during the Japanese attack on Pearl Harbor. He bestowed the title of Firebrand on his sister Danette, who had gained the mutant ability to manipulate fire. However, Rod Reilly's career as Firebrand was not over. He recovered from his injuries and joined UNCLE SAM's FREEDOM FIGHTERS to battle the Nazis. His adventuring came to an end when a confrontation with the villain Silver Ghost transformed him into a statue of solid silver. **DW**

While conducting research in Hawaii, vulcanologist Danette Reilly encountered time-traveling felon Per Degaton. The encounter left her with the ability to control and create fire with her hands. She returned to New York just after the Japanese bombing of Pearl Harbor in 1941, during which her brother Rod was injured. Learning that Rod was FIREBRAND I, she modified one of his uniforms and became Firebrand II, joining the ALL-STAR SQUADRON. Danette became a leading member, and mentored younger heroes when they joined the team. During her adventures, she fell in love with the SHINING KNIGHT. They married, and later became the adoptive mother of Terri Rothstein, future mother of the ATOM-SMASHER. Danette was eventually killed, probably by the DRAGON KING, one of the All-Stars' major foes. The Shining Knight avenged his wife's demise. **RG**

Lone survivor of a wagon train massacre by Blackfoot Indians, a blue-eyed, red-haired infant boy was spared by the Blackfoot chief, Grey Cloud, and raised as one of his own. A Blackfoot shaman had foreseen the coming of a great warrior not of the tribe. This warrior would rise from death and defend the Native Americans, yet would be despised by both his own people and those he sought to help. Grey Cloud believed his adopted son, Firehair, would become that great warrior. Scorned by most of the tribe, Firehair learned to out-shoot, out-ride, and out-wrestle any of his peers. When Firehair was 18, Grey Cloud sent him into the mountains to cleanse his body and spirit so that he could return a man. In dreams, Firehair recalled his infancy and true heritage. Confused, he returned to Grey Cloud, who dispatched him to a frontier town so that he might find the answers he sought. Spurned by the locals, Firehair vowed to travel the world until he found where he truly belonged. During his wanderings, he fulfilled the portents of the Blackfoot shaman, thanklessly helping those in need, regardless of race. The circumstances of his death remain one of the lingering mysteries of the Old West. **SB**

FIREBRAND III

FIRST APPEARANCE FIREBRAND #1 (February 1996)
STATUS Hero (deceased)   **REAL NAME** Alexander "Alex" Sanchez
OCCUPATION Adventurer   **BASE** New York City
HEIGHT 6ft   **WEIGHT** 188 lbs   **EYES** Brown   **HAIR** Black
SPECIAL POWERS/ABILITIES High-tech suit enhanced strength and enabled discharge of fiery energy bolts.

FIREFLY

FIRST APPEARANCE DETECTIVE COMICS #184 (June 1952)
STATUS Villain   **REAL NAME** Garfield Lyons
OCCUPATION Arsonist   **BASE** Gotham City
HEIGHT 5ft 11in   **WEIGHT** 167 lbs   **EYES** Blue   **HAIR** White with black temples
SPECIAL POWERS/ABILITIES Insulated battlesuit equipped with flamethrower, grenade launchers, and wings that allow flight.

FIREHAWK

FIRST APPEARANCE FURY OF FIRESTORM #17 (October 1983)
STATUS Hero   **REAL NAME** Lorraine Reilly
OCCUPATION Adventurer   **BASE** New York City
HEIGHT 5ft 7in   **WEIGHT** 136 lbs   **EYES** Blue   **HAIR** (Lorraine) Red
SPECIAL POWERS/ABILITIES Makes objects burst into flame; her hair and parts of her body seem to be on fire, but the fire does not harm her; can fly at great speed.

A terrible accident traumatized New York City detective Alex Sanchez physically and mentally. His will to live was rekindled by wealthy Noah Hightower, who outfitted Alex with armor that turned him into Firebrand. The third hero of that name, Firebrand thwarted evil in the Big Apple. Firebrand died in an underground gladiatorial game run by the villainess ROULETTE. Injected with drugs, Firebrand fought a drugged-up CHECKMATE Knight to a standstill. Though Firebrand resisted the murderous effects of the drugs, the Knight could not and mercilessly slashed Firebrand's throat with his wrist-blade gauntlet. Sanchez died as he lived, a true hero. **SB**

Garfield Lyons is a pyromaniac obsessed with starting large, dangerous fires and watching them burn. Lyons was a poverty-stricken young man who turned to petty crime but was captured by BATMAN and ROBIN after his first robbery. Inspired by a glowing firefly, Lyons took the insect's name and embarked on a different kind of career, torching parts of Gotham City and exalting in the death and destruction his fires caused. Firefly fought Batman and Robin a number of times, until he was hired by villain Nicholas Scratch to create the biggest fire Gotham City had ever seen. Hoping to burn Gotham to the ground, Firefly was himself horribly burned when a nearby chemical factory he set ablaze erupted in a fiery explosion. Scarred by burns that cover 90 percent of his body, Firefly was incarcerated in Blackgate Prison. **PJ**

An attempt by the super-criminal Multiplex and the villainous industrialist Henry Hewitt to recreate the accident that gave birth to FIRESTORM, THE NUCLEAR MAN resulted in the transformation of Lorraine Reilly, daughter of Senator Walter Reilly, into Firehawk. Brainwashed into fighting the Firestorm, Firehawk shook off her programming and helped Firestorm defeat Hewitt in his guise as Tokamak. Firehawk and Firestorm became partners and friends until Firestorm went through personal changes. Lorraine stopped fighting crime, and later had a relationship with BOOSTER GOLD. Currently, she is a part-time heroine. **RG**

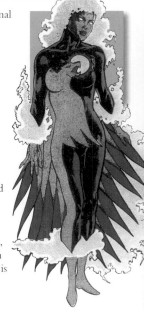

FIRESTORM, THE NUCLEAR MAN

FIRST APPEARANCE FIRESTORM #1 (March 1978)
STATUS Hero **REAL NAME** Ronnie Raymond
OCCUPATION Adventurer **BASE** JLA Watchtower, the Moon
HEIGHT 6ft 2in **WEIGHT** 202 lbs **EYES** White **HAIR** Flaming
SPECIAL POWERS/ABILITIES Flight; can rearrange the atomic and
molecular structure of inorganic matter.

UNDERSTANDING THE HERO FIRESTORM is far from a
straightforward proposition. Brought into being as the synthesis of
two individuals, Firestorm later went through a number of alternate
fusions whereby varied combinations of people united to create a
single champion. The original Firestorm came about when college
student Ronnie Raymond and physics professor Martin Stein fused
into one superpowered "nuclear man" in an explosion at the
Hudson nuclear facility. In their flame-topped Firestorm form, the
two could fly and rearrange matter at the molecular level. Ron
remained in control of Firestorm, while Martin hitchhiked along as
a disembodied consciousness and took an advisory role, his
scientific brain providing the complex atomic calculations needed
for Firestorm's advanced powers.

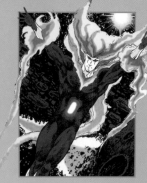

MARTIN STEIN *The professor
found his calling as a fire
elemental.*

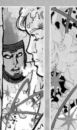 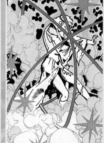 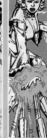

ELEMENTAL WARFARE

Operating out of Pittsburgh, Ron and Martin made an efficient
team against the likes of Killer Frost (*see* KILLER FROST II)and
BLACK BISON. The Russian hero POZHAR later clashed with
Firestorm above the Nevada desert. When a nuclear missile
struck the two combatants, Ronnie and Pozhar merged into the
second incarnation of Firestorm. Controlled by the amnesiac
mind of Martin Stein, this Firestorm eventually learned that it
had been fated to become Earth's fire elemental—but only with
Martin as host. Ronnie and Pozhar had apparently been
unnecessary roadblocks in the Earth spirit Gaea's plan. After
Firestorm's involvement in an "elemental war" involving SWAMP
THING (earth), NAIAD (water), and RED TORNADO (air), as well
as the addition of another Russian, Svarozhich, to the mix,
Firestorm fissioned off the superfluous personalities to become
the "correct" Firestorm—a fire elemental, controlled by
Martin Stein alone.

Yet this wasn't the end of the Firestorm
saga. While the fire elemental Firestorm
flew off to the edge of the universe,
Ron Raymond drifted into alcoholism and discovered that his super-
heroic past had given him a form of leukemia. Searching for a cure,
he discovered that the Firestorm powers had been written into his
genetic structure. Now disease-free and active as a super hero once
more, the Ron Raymond Firestorm (exhibiting the classic look and
powers) served with EXTREME JUSTICE and the POWER COMPANY
before joining the current lineup of the JUSTICE LEAGUE OF AMERICA.
The Martin Stein Firestorm remains active in the cosmos. **DW**

FROST AND FIRE
*Normally a bitter enemy,
the villain Killer Frost
was hypnotized into
loving Firestorm during
the Crisis.*

KEY STORYLINES

• *FIRESTORM, THE NUCLEAR
MAN #90 (OCTOBER 1989):*
The Elemental Wars kick off,
signaling the increasing
complexity of this super-hero title.
• *EXTREME JUSTICE #5 (JUNE 1995):*
Raymond regains his Firestorm
powers, and the Martin Stein fire
elemental drops in for a visit.
• *JLA #69 (OCTOBER 2002):*
Firestorm joins the Justice League
of America while the original
team is trapped in the ancient
undersea world of Atlantis.

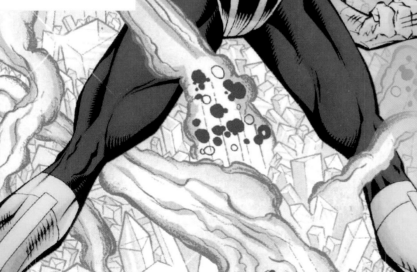

RESIGNING ISSUE *Firestorm
left the Power Company in a clash
over the team's corporate values.*

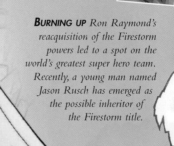

BURNING UP *Ron Raymond's
reacquisition of the Firestorm
powers led to a spot on the
world's greatest super hero team.
Recently, a young man named
Jason Rusch has emerged as
the possible inheritor of
the Firestorm title.*

THE FLASH

THE SCARLET SPEEDSTER

JASON PETER "JAY" GARRICK (FLASH I)
FIRST APPEARANCE FLASH COMICS #1 (January 1940)
STATUS Hero **OCCUPATION** Research scientist
BASE Keystone City **HEIGHT** 5ft 11in **WEIGHT** 178 lbs
EYES Blue **HAIR** Brown, with gray temples
SPECIAL POWERS/ABILITIES Can run at near lightspeed; can vibrate his molecules and pass right through objects; ages at a far slower pace than most human beings.

BARTHOLOMEW "BARRY" ALLEN (FLASH II)
FIRST APPEARANCE SHOWCASE #4 (October 1956)
STATUS Hero (deceased) **OCCUPATION** Police chemist
BASE Central City **HEIGHT** 5ft 11in **WEIGHT** 179 lbs
EYES Blue **HAIR** Blond
SPECIAL POWERS/ABILITIES Could run at near lightspeed; could also pass through objects or phase into other dimensions.

WALLACE "WALLY" WEST (FLASH III)
FIRST APPEARANCE (as Kid Flash) THE FLASH (1st series) #110 (January 1960); (as the Flash) CRISIS ON INFINITE EARTHS #12 (March 1986)
STATUS Hero **OCCUPATION** Adventurer **BASE** Keystone City
HEIGHT 6ft **WEIGHT** 175 lbs **EYES** Green **HAIR** Red
SPECIAL POWERS/ABILITIES Can run at lightspeed; can vibrate through solid objects causing them to explode; can lend his speed to moving objects or people by touch; can form a protective costume from "living" Speed Force; traveling faster than lightspeed will hurl him across interdimensional timespace.

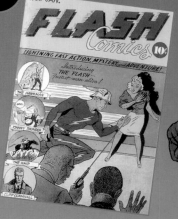

THEY HAVE BEEN CALLED the Fastest Men Alive—three generations of super heroes granted the power to tap into the extradimensional energy field called the Speed Force by a scientific experiment gone awry. Each hero named himself the Flash and became the progenitor of an age of champions, perpetuating a legacy of courage and valor that extends to the 853rd century and beyond.

JAY GARRICK

A failed college football player in the 1930s, Jay Garrick became a research scientist. By accidentally inhaling the hyper-charged atoms of a radioactive liquid, Garrick gained incredible superspeed. Garbed in a red and blue uniform, Garrick became the Flash and helped form the legendary JUSTICE SOCIETY OF AMERICA and the wartime ALL-STAR SQUADRON. Forced into retirement during the McCarthy era in the 1950s, Garrick was placed in suspended animation by the villainous Fiddler but was rescued by Barry Allen, the second Flash. Spared the ravages of old age, Garrick married his girlfriend, Joan Williams, and briefly retired, but he returned to active duty with the most recent incarnation of the JSA.

FASTER THAN A... Jay Garrick makes his debut as the Flash, the fastest hero of World War II.

NO TIME TO LOSE The Flash and Dr. Flura must thwart Star Sapphire's deadly schemes or the Earth has only two minutes to live!

BARRY ALLEN

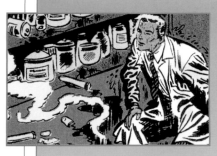

Slowpoke police chemist Barry Allen idolized Jay Garrick, the super hero Flash. During a late, stormy night at the police station laboratory, a bolt of lightning crashed through the window and shattered the vials of chemicals surrounding Allen. Suddenly imbued with the power to move at near lightspeed, Barry took on the name of his Golden Age idol, the Flash, and, along with GREEN LANTERN Hal Jordan and AQUAMAN, helped usher in the Silver Age of heroes.

As the Flash, Allen was one of the founders of the JUSTICE LEAGUE OF AMERICA. When his fiancée, Iris (see ALLEN, IRIS), was apparently slain by the REVERSE-FLASH, Allen killed his hated foe. After a lengthy trial, the Flash retired to the 30th century, where he sired the Tornado twins. Tragically, Allen died saving the Earth from the nihilistic Anti-Monitor (see Great Battles, pp. 320–1) by destroying his antimatter cannon, aimed directly at the planet.

SLOW POKE Police chemist Barry Allen was a notoriously methodical, plodding scientist known for being constantly late. When he was doused by chemicals, however, he gained the power of superspeed, becoming the second Flash.

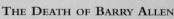
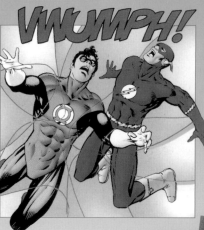

VWUMPH!

FLASH OF LIGHT As the Flash, Barry Allen, Green Lantern Hal Jordan, and several other heroes founded the legendary Justice League of America. Despite Allen and Jordan's differences— Allen was a quiet scientist and Jordan an adventurous hothead— the two became close friends. Their friendship would last for years, until each met their own tragic end.

ZOOM The name of Zoom has long haunted the Flash family. Recently, Zoom was responsible for Flash's wife, Linda Park, miscarrying their twins.

THE DEATH OF BARRY ALLEN

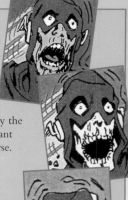

Learning that his wife, Iris, was saved from death at the hands of Professor ZOOM by a "psychic transplant" in the future into another body, the Flash traveled forward in time to be with her. Tragically, their happiness ended when the Flash was kidnapped by the Anti-Monitor, who planned to use a giant antimatter cannon to destroy the universe. Running faster than ever before, the Flash escaped the Anti-Monitor's bonds and destroyed the cannon. Allen's body disintegrated, but his energies rocketed back in time and became the lightning bolt that shattered the chemicals that originally gave Allen his superspeed.

KEY STORYLINES

- **GOLDEN AGE FLASH ARCHIVES:** The original adventures of Jay Garrick, the first Flash, during the 1940s.
- **THE FLASH (1ST SERIES) #123 (SEPTEMBER 1961):** Barry Allen meets his Golden Age namesake for the first time.
- **CRISIS ON INFINITE EARTHS (P/B, 2000):** Barry Allen makes the greatest sacrifice to save the universe from the marauding Anti-Monitor, and Wally West becomes the third Flash!
- **TERMINAL VELOCITY (P/B, 1995):** The Flashes learn that they are attached to the Speed Force, an ancient power.

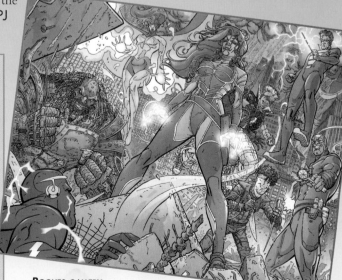

WALLY WEST

The young nephew of Barry Allen, Wally West was visiting his uncle's laboratory when a bolt of lightning shattered a rack of chemicals in the room. The chemicals spilled on the boy, and duplicated the same accident that created the second Flash. West became the first KID FLASH, the junior partner of the Flash, and founded the TEEN TITANS with the first ROBIN (see NIGHTWING), Aqualad (see TEMPEST), Speedy (see ARSENAL), and WONDER GIRL. After Barry Allen died saving the universe, Kid Flash assumed his costume and identity.

GENERATIONS *Wearing a costume similar to his mentor, Barry Allen, teenaged Wally West learned to use his powers just as well—even vibrating through solid objects.*

THE SPEED FORCE

As the Flash, Wally discovered his link to the Speed Force, an energy source that gives all speedsters their power. Tapping into the Force made Wally the fastest Flash of them all, able to run at the speed of light. One of the founders of the current and most powerful incarnation of the JLA, West has garnered a lethal Rogues Gallery as the champion of Keystone City. The Flash revealed his secret identity to the world and, after several failed romances, fell in love with and married reporter Linda Park (see PARK, LINDA). After a battle with the villain Zoom ended in the miscarriage of their unborn twins, West asked the SPECTRE to remove all memories of his identity from the public consciousness— including Linda— to protect those he loved from the dangers he continues to face as the Fastest Man Alive. **PJ**

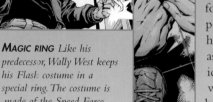

MAGIC RING *Like his predecessor, Wally West keeps his Flash costume in a special ring. The costume is made of the Speed Force itself, covering Wally in a protective sheath.*

LOVELY LINDA *Wally West is married to TV journalist turned medical student Linda Park.*

FLASHES FROM THE FUTURE

John Fox was a speedster from the 27th century who traveled back to the 21st century to take over the Flash legacy when Wally West disappeared. After West's return, Fox leapt back into the timestream and resettled in the 853rd century. The third Kid Flash is the future daughter of Wally West, who inherited her father's heroic legacy when her slacker brother refused to do so. Walter West, the Flash from an alternate timeline whose wife Linda was slain by KOBRA, briefly replaced the Flash in our timeline, before entering Hypertime to rediscover his own. And Sela Allen, a sentient manifestation of the Speed Force, is the Flash of the 23rd century.

FUGITIVE *Fox, responsible for transplanting Iris Allen across the centuries, became a fugitive for violating the Time Institute's laws of time travel.*

ROGUES GALLERY

The Flash has long had one of the most impressive collection of foes of any hero, and easily the most deadly.

FISHERMAN

FIRST APPEARANCE AQUAMAN (1st series) #21 (June 1965)
STATUS Villain **REAL NAME** Unknown
OCCUPATION Professional criminal **BASE** Mobile
HEIGHT 6ft **WEIGHT** 196 lbs **EYES** Blue **HAIR** Black
SPECIAL POWERS/ABILITIES Wears pressurized SCUBA suit, allowing him to breathe and travel underwater, and carries "fishing rod" weapon.

The Fisherman has often crossed paths with AQUAMAN, for his pressurized bodysuit and ensnaring fishing rod make him an unusually specialized villain. The Fisherman's schemes—including a plot to arm a rebel attack on Atlantis—have always been foiled by the King of the Seven Seas. The Fisherman carries a fishing rod made of titanium steel that casts an unbreakable polymer line. He can cast this rod with uncanny accuracy, either tangling his targets with the line or skewering them with barbed lures. He also has a number of special lures that release toxic gas upon impact.

After serving a long prison sentence, the Fisherman is back in circulation. He has kept a low profile, but has been known to gamble on the secret gladiatorial fights to the death overseen by the villain ROULETTE. **DW**

FLAMEBIRD

FIRST APPEARANCE SECRET ORIGINS ANNUAL #3 (1989)
STATUS Hero **REAL NAME** Mary Elizabeth "Bette" Kane
OCCUPATION College student/adventurer **BASE** Hollywood, CA
HEIGHT 5ft 6in **WEIGHT** 123 lbs **EYES** Blue **HAIR** Blonde
SPECIAL POWERS/ABILITIES Above-average fighter; arsenal includes electrified bolas and gloves, flare-emitting mask lenses, and various tracking devices.

Perky tennis prodigy Bette Kane so idolized the first ROBIN, Dick Grayson, that she adopted her own costumed alter ego, Flamebird, and formed an unsanctioned West Coast branch of the TEEN TITANS to impress the Boy Wonder. Unfortunately, Bette's super hero career flamed out and Titans West disbanded not long after receiving an unwelcome reception from Robin and the Teen Titans. Later, following a confrontation between Bette and NIGHTWING, Robin's new alter ego, Flamebird rose like a phoenix from the ashes as Bette found new purpose. Redesigning Flamebird's costume and equipment, Bette took flight as a more confident super heroine while continuing her studies in sports medicine at U.C.L.A. Flamebird was briefly a member of Titans L.A., a latter-day Titans West that included her roommate BEAST BOY, who had been a member of both her previous team and the Teen Titans. However, Titans L.A. proved to be even shorter-lived than its predecessor, and Flamebird has resumed solo flights of adventure. **SB**

FLEUR-DE-LIS

FIRST APPEARANCE BLUE BEETLE (6th series) #19 (December 1987)
STATUS Hero **REAL NAME** Noelle Avril
OCCUPATION Adventurer **BASE** Paris, France
HEIGHT 5ft 6in **WEIGHT** 120 lbs **EYES** Blue **HAIR** White
SPECIAL POWERS/ABILITIES Olympic-level athlete; expert with various weapons, particularly pistols and throwing stars.

The origins of Fleur-de-Lis have yet to be revealed. She used to wear a white body suit decorated with the French royal crest; later in her career she donned a skintight purple and red latex uniform. Fleur-de-Lis was briefly a member of the GLOBAL GUARDIANS, and then joined France's Department Gamma after the Guardians were disbanded by order of the United Nations. At Department Gamma, Fleur-de-Lis answered exclusively to its director, André Chavard (see CHAVARD, ANDRÉ). She had a brief romance with Slade Wilson, the assassin known as DEATHSTROKE THE TERMINATOR, while the two searched for his ex-wife Adeline Kane, who had been kidnapped by an international criminal, Jacques "Tuxedo" Morel. **RG**

ON THE MARK *This is not a woman to underestimate, considering her deadly skill as both a hand-to-hand combatant and master marksman.*

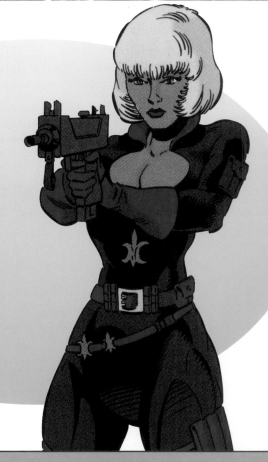

FLORONIC MAN

FIRST APPEARANCE THE ATOM #1 (July 1962)
STATUS Unresolved **REAL NAME** Jason Woodrue
OCCUPATION Former criminal **BASE** Mobile
HEIGHT 6ft 2in **WEIGHT** 210 lbs **EYES** Red **HAIR** Green
SPECIAL POWERS/ABILITIES Alien knowledge of plant life gives him an advantage over others; also has limited control over local plant forms. Stronger than a human given the density of the wood he inhabits.

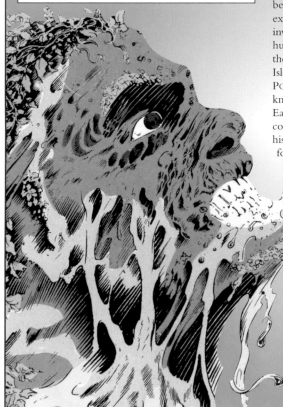

Originally a master criminal on an other-dimensional world inhabited by wood nymphs, dryads, Nereids, air sprites, and flower spirits, the being known as Woodrue was banished to Earth for his wicked deeds, where it was hoped he would perish. He survived, taking on the human identity of Jason Woodrue and becoming a teacher. He continued to experiment on plants, ruthlessly investigating the possibilities of human/plant hybridization. One of these trials turned shy student Pamela Isley into the villainous, near-human POISON IVY. Woodrue used his alien knowledge to take control of Earth's plant life and attempted to conquer America with the aid of his plant army. This scheme was foiled by the six-inch super hero the second ATOM. After repeated defeats, Woodrue perfected an elixir that transformed him from fauna to flora, making him a true plantmaster. Defeated and imprisoned by the second GREEN LANTERN, Woodrue was freed by General Sunderland to examine the body of the SWAMP THING. Through this plant elemental, Woodrue became one with the plant kingdom and once more threatened mankind. Swamp Thing stopped him, and Woodrue sought redemption by joining a collection of individuals who had been deemed the first to evolve towards man's next evolution, the NEW GUARDIANS. He now operates on his own, wandering the Earth, seeking a purpose. **RG**

FLOWER POWER *The being known as the Floronic Man continued to evolve after arriving on Earth from another dimension.*

PLANTMASTER *His nature now subdued, Woodrue wanders the world, seeking a place among the elementals.*

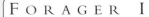

FLYING FOX

First appearance YOUNG ALL-STARS #1 (June 1987)
Status Hero **Real name** Unrevealed
Occupation Adventurer **Base** Mobile
Height 5ft 10in **Weight** 170 lbs **Eyes** Brown **Hair** Black
Special powers/abilities Shamanistic talents include flight, invisibility, and the ability to cast fire from his hands.

During World War II, a Nazi U-boat commander hoped to strongarm the Native American Quontauka tribe in northern Canada into launching guerilla attacks on the Canadian government. Instead, by murdering the tribe's chief, he triggered the creation of the super hero Flying Fox. The tribal shaman gave the chief's son the mystical cape and cowl of the flying fox and tattooed the teen's chest with the fox's emblem. As Flying Fox, the young man sought out allies in his fight against the Nazi menace. He soon ran into the teenage heroes of the YOUNG ALL-STARS. Flying Fox became a charter member of the team, fighting alongside them and with the larger ALL-STAR SQUADRON against AXIS AMERIKA for the rest of the war. Flying Fox inherited many mystical abilities from his tribe's shaman, though it is unknown how deeply his talents run. Spells he has manifested include the ability to turn invisible and to control fire. DW

FOLDED MAN

First appearance THE FLASH (2nd series) #153 (October 1999)
Status Hero **Real name** Edwin Gauss
Occupation Criminal **Base** Central City
Height 5ft 11in **Weight** 182 lbs **Eyes** Brown **Hair** Brown
Special powers/abilities Can transform into a fourth-dimensional state that allows him to reach into the third dimension at any point; can flatten into a two-dimensional form.

The Folded Man is former physicist Edwin Gauss, a young M.I.T. student who was desperate to complete Albert Einstein's unfinished Unified Field theory. After maddening attempts at cracking the theory, and after pirating special software from billionaire Norman Bridges, an electronics entrepreneur, Gauss discovered a way to travel interdimensionally and created a special suit that allowed him to traverse at least four dimensions.

Pursued by the outraged Bridges, who believes that the special suit Gauss created is his by right, the brilliant but deranged M.I.T. tech became the Folded Man and quickly came into conflict with the FLASH III. Able to transform his body any number of ways and teleport across dimensions, the Folded Man was easily able to escape the Fastest Man Alive and remains at large. PJ

FORAGER I

First appearance THE NEW GODS (1st series) #9 (August 1972)
Status Hero (deceased) **Real name** None
Occupation Warrior **Base** New Genesis
Height 5ft 10in **Weight** 162 lbs **Eyes** Blue **Hair** Black
Special powers/abilities Superb combatant; great speed and leaping abilities; "adheso-pads" on feet enabled him to run up walls; carried defensive shield and acid pod.

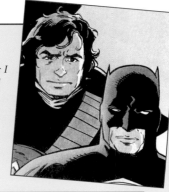

DARK NIGHT Forager I met the Batman and toured the Batcave during the Cosmic Odyssey to prevent Darkseid from acquiring the "Anti-Life Equation."

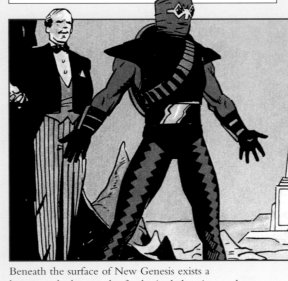

Beneath the surface of New Genesis exists a honeycombed network of colonies belonging to the "bugs," evolved humanoid insects originally brought to the planet as micro-life biological weapons scattered by the armies of Apokolips. Among these creatures was Forager, named so for his great skill at stealing food from the surface. Forager eventually met ORION and LIGHTRAY of the NEW GODS, who helped the bugs to prevent the evil MANTIS—presumably a bug himself—from exterminating their kind. Forager remained an ally of the New Gods for years. He gave his life in defense of the human hero BATMAN when champions from New Genesis and Earth rallied to prevent DARKSEID from finally acquiring the so-called "Anti-Life Equation." Although burning with a long-standing prejudice against the bugs, Orion escorted Forager's body back to the bug colonies, where the Dog of War finally acknowledged Forager as a friend. SB

FORAGER II

First appearance THE NEW GODS (2nd series) #2 (March 1989)
Status Hero **Real name** None
Occupation Warrior **Base** New Genesis
Height 5ft 9in **Weight** 121 lbs **Eyes** White **Hair** Blue
Special powers/abilities An accomplished warrior wielding many of the same abilities and accoutrements as Forager I.

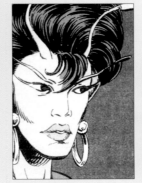

A second Forager, this one female, was later appointed by the All-Widow and Prime One—queen and highest ranking male of the bugs, respectively—as a new defender of the colonies. Initially following in FORAGER I's footsteps, Forager II also befriended ORION before thwarting MANTIS from uniting outcast bug tribes and using them to spark a nuclear war on Earth. However, Orion falsely believed that Forager II was killed during that conflict. In his rage, Orion transported Mantis's nuclear arsenal to New Genesis, where the missiles exploded above the central colony and decimated the bug population. Since then, Forager II has distanced herself from Orion, while the bugs maintain a tentative peace with the New Gods. SB

FOREVER PEOPLE

FIRST APPEARANCE FOREVER PEOPLE (1st series) #1 (Feb.–Mar. 1971)
STATUS Hero team **BASE** Supertown, New Genesis
MEMBERS AND POWERS
Mark Moonrider Has the megaton touch, which emits energy.
Big Bear Has superhuman strength.
Beautiful Dreamer Can create illusions.
Vykin the Black Has magnetic powers.
Serifan Cosmic cartridges create force fields and anti-gravity waves.

At the instruction of the Source, HIGHFATHER of the NEW GODS of the planet New Genesis gathered five children and subjected them to rigorous training in the use of their powers. Highfather ultimately revealed that the unique Mother Boxes (living computers) the young gods' parents had received a decade earlier were a five-piece composite that formed a larger unit and enabled the Forever People to trade places with INFINITY MAN for a short time. Using an oversized Mother Box, the team are able to summon this powerful protector.

The team adventured throughout New Genesis and on Earth for a time. When Infinity Man was apparently destroyed during a battle with DEVILANCE, the Forever People found themselves stranded on the pastoral planet of Adon. The circumstances of their return to New Genesis remain unclear, although VYKIN THE BLACK has indicated that DARKSEID brought them back. Somewhere along the way a romance between BEAUTIFUL DREAMER and BIG BEAR cooled, and Beautiful Dreamer has since taken up with Mark Moonrider (*see* MOONRIDER, MARK). **RG**

THE FOREVER PEOPLE *The team went adventuring aboard a huge Super-Cycle that could fly, pass through solid objects, and even teleport.*
1) *Big Bear* **2)** *Beautiful Dreamer* **3)** *Vykin*
4) *Serifan* **5)** *Mark Moonrider*

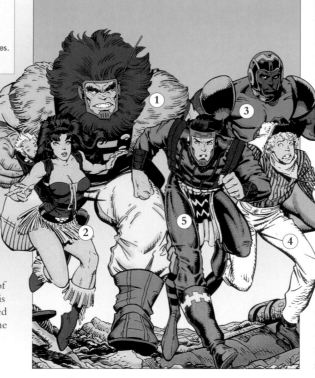

FOX, LUCIUS

FIRST APPEARANCE BATMAN #307 (January 1979)
STATUS Hero **REAL NAME** Lucius Fox
OCCUPATION CEO of Wayne Enterprises **BASE** Gotham City
HEIGHT 5ft 10in **WEIGHT** 170 lbs **EYES** Brown **HAIR** Black
SPECIAL POWERS/ABILITIES Meticulous and scrupulously honest, Fox is an excellent organizer with brilliant financial acumen.

Lucius Fox is one of the most powerful businessmen in the world. After returning from his training overseas, Bruce Wayne hired Fox as the CEO of Wayne Enterprises, and Lucius is responsible for handling the day-to-day operations of the giant company. A *magna cum laude* graduate of the Morton Business School, Lucius is nevertheless unaware of Bruce Wayne's secret identity as BATMAN, although the CEO knows that Wayne is hardly the foolish playboy the rest of the world thinks he is.

After the devastation of an earthquake turned Gotham City into a No Man's Land, Lucius used his skills and Wayne Enterprise's might to prevent Lex Luthor's LexCorp (*see* LUTHOR, LEX) from buying up extensive amounts of Gotham real estate. Later, Lucius was targeted by the assassin Cypher for his vast knowledge of Wayne Enterprise's resources but was saved by Batman. Fox remains a powerful corporate leader, one of the most sought after in the world. **PJ**

FORTUNE, AMOS

FIRST APPEARANCE JUSTICE LEAGUE OF AMERICA #6 (August–September 1961)
STATUS Villain **REAL NAME** Professor Amos Fortune
OCCUPATION Professional criminal **BASE** Mobile
HEIGHT 5ft 8in **WEIGHT** 233 lbs
EYES Black **HAIR** Black
SPECIAL POWERS/ABILITIES Advanced intellect, which he uses to manipulate others; claims special knowledge of the "science of luck."

Being obsessed with luck—good luck, bad luck, how luck can run hot and cold—did not help Amos Fortune during his adolescence. He led a street gang that never advanced beyond petty crime and earned the nickname "Pudge" due to his stocky frame. As an adult he delved into the supposed science of luck and came to believe that the human body possessed "luck glands" that influenced the outside world for good or ill every day.

Using his knowledge to become a professional criminal, he soon came into conflict with the newly-formed JUSTICE LEAGUE OF AMERICA. In his first fight against the League, he strapped the World's Greatest Super Heroes to his Wheel of Misfortune and tried to eliminate their good luck glands with an energy ray. He later used his Wheel of Misfortune to create seven super-beings from seven of the luckiest people on the planet (who'd all been born on the seventh day of the seventh month), but WONDER WOMAN smashed his dreams of grandeur.

Amos Fortune also acted as the leader of the ROYAL FLUSH GANG. This criminal outfit, staffed with Fortune's old friends from his former street gang, assumed a playing card motif with Fortune as the Ace and others filling the roles of King, Queen, Jack, and Ten. Though Fortune soon abandoned the team, the Royal Flush Gang continued without him. Fortune is still semi-active in crime, though his continual defeats suggest he does not understand luck as much as he thinks he does. **DW**

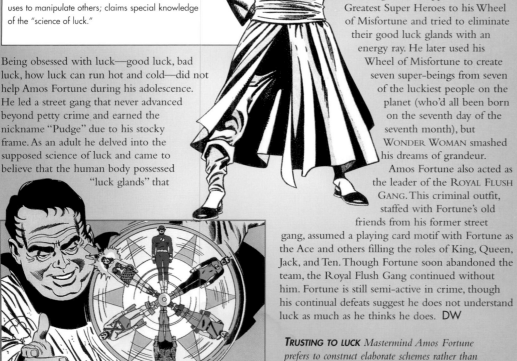

TRUSTING TO LUCK *Mastermind Amos Fortune prefers to construct elaborate schemes rather than confront his enemies directly.*

FREEDOM BEAST

FIRST APPEARANCE ANIMAL MAN #13 (July 1989)
STATUS Hero **REAL NAME** Dominic Mndawe
OCCUPATION Adventurer **BASE** Capetown, South Africa
HEIGHT 6ft 2in **WEIGHT** 191 lbs **EYES** Brown **HAIR** Black
SPECIAL POWERS/ABILITIES Magical helmet and potent elixir enable him to fuse two animals into a single creature and command it to do his bidding for a short time; a strange rainwater elixir heightens his strength and five senses to superhuman level.

Chosen by retiring Mike Maxwell to carry on the heroic mission of the B'Wana Beast, Maxwell's adventuring alter ego, reporter and political activist Dominic Mndawe renamed himself Freedom Beast and used his new super powers to help dismantle Apartheid in South Africa. Freedom Beast now fights to end violence and suffering throughout the African continent. **SB**

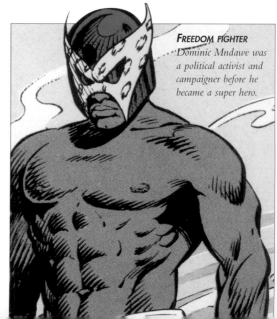

FREEDOM FIGHTER *Dominic Mndawe was a political activist and campaigner before he became a super hero.*

FREEDOM FIGHTERS, THE

FIRST APPEARANCE JUSTICE LEAGUE OF AMERICA #107 (Oct. 1973)
STATUS Hero team **BASE** U.S.
ORIGINAL MEMBERS AND POWERS
Uncle Sam The spirit of the U.S., strong and decisive.
Hourman I Has 60 minutes of enhanced human skills with miraclo pill.
Invisible Justice (deceased) Wore chemically treated cloak to become invisible.
Magno (deceased) Possessed magnetic-based powers.
Miss America Imbued with enhanced strength from the Spirit of Liberty.
Neon the Unknown (deceased) Was a two-fisted crime fighter.
Red Torpedo Is a two-fisted crime fighter and excellent seaman.

UNCLE SAM, the living spirit of the U.S., organized the Freedom Fighters for a doomed attempt at turning back the Japanese attack on Pearl Harbor in 1941. MAGNO and Neon were killed; RED TORPEDO and HOURMAN I were captured by the Japanese; Invisible Hood (who changed his name to Invisible Justice) was captured and killed by the Japanese; and Uncle Sam and MISS AMERICA were recovered by Project M. The following February, Uncle Sam, MIDNIGHT and DOLL MAN interrupted an ALL-STAR SQUADRON meeting to warn them of an impending attack by the Japanese Navy at Santa Barbara, CA. In the hours that followed, the All-Stars met Neptune Perkins (see PERKINS, NEPTUNE), battled TSUNAMI, and saved Hourman after two months of captivity. In the aftermath, Uncle Sam reformed the Freedom Fighters, with the BLACK CONDOR I and the RAY I the first to join up. The team operated for the duration of World War II, headquartered in Washington, D.C., then eventually disbanded. Its lineup over the years included Doll Man, FIREBRAND I, the HUMAN BOMB, Miss America, the JESTER, MANHUNTER I, Midnight, Quicksilver, and ALIAS THE SPIDER. **RG**

KEY 1) *The Ray I* **2)** *Phantom Lady I* **3)** *Doll Man*
4) *Firebrand I* **5)** *Human Bomb* **6)** *Red Bee* **7)** *Uncle Sam*
8) *Miss America* **9)** *Black Condor I*

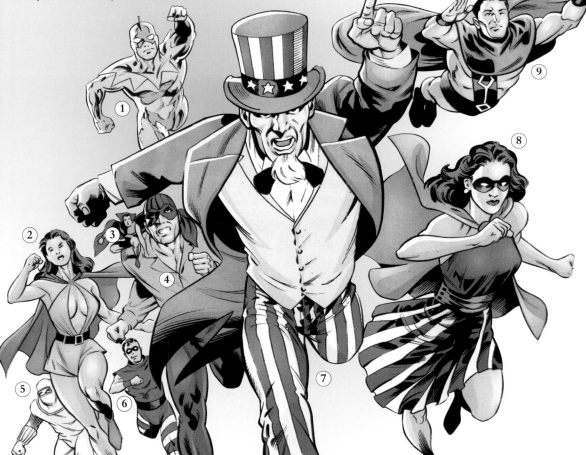

FRINGE

FIRST APPEARANCE TEEN TITANS (2nd series) #4 (1997)
STATUS Hero **REAL NAME** Unrevealed
OCCUPATION Adventurer **BASE** H'San Natall empire, deep space
HEIGHT 9ft 7in **WEIGHT** 645 lbs **EYES** White **HAIR** White
SPECIAL POWERS/ABILITIES Manifests a powerful psychic creature with various uncatalogued abilities.

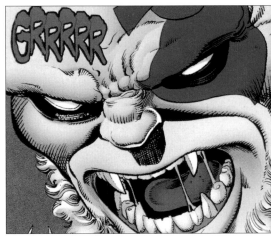

Fringe was the offspring of a human woman and a H'San Natall father. His appearance so alarmed his parents that they threw the human/alien hybrid off a bridge. Fringe was rescued by a psychic entity that bonded with and protected him. When Fringe was hunted by Pylon and the Veil, two villains seeking to end alien influence on Earth, he was saved by the combined efforts of the second TEEN TITANS, NIGHTWING, and SUPERGIRL. Fringe developed a psychic link with another Titan, PRYSM, and joined the team. After several adventures with the Titans, Fringe learned that his mother, Queen Miraset, was alive and living in the H'San Natall empire. After the Titans disbanded, Fringe returned to space with Prysm. **PJ**

FURY

FIRST APPEARANCE SECRET ORIGINS (2nd series) #12 (March 1987)
STATUS Hero **REAL NAME** Helena Kosmatos
OCCUPATION Adventurer **BASE** Themyscira
HEIGHT 5ft 6in **WEIGHT** 135 lbs **EYES** Blue; (as Tisiphone) red
HAIR Blonde; (as Tisiphone) black
SPECIAL POWERS/ABILITIES She can channel the spirit and power of the Fury Tisiphone, the Blood Avenger, giving her superhuman strength, speed, and the ability to generate heat beams from her eyes. She wears lightweight, bulletproof armor.

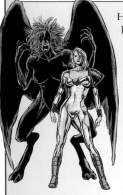

Helena Kosmatos's father was killed during the Italian Fascists' invasion of Greece in 1940. Later, Helena discovered her brother was a Fascist collaborator. Escaping Nazi troops, Helena fled to the Areopagus, the hill of ARES, and unleashed the Furies, the Greek goddesses of vengeance. Helena became a vessel for their power and killed her brother. As Fury, she joined the ALL-STAR SQUADRON and befriended HIPPOLYTA, the Golden Age Wonder Woman.

Decades later, Helena named her only daughter Hippolyta. Losing her grip on reality after being seduced by the immortal Alcmaeon, Fury fought alongside the elder Hippolyta in the Amazon civil war. Later, the essence of Fury was stolen from Helena but, thanks to WONDER WOMAN and TROIA, the spirit returned, along with her sanity. **PJ**

FURY II

FIRST APPEARANCE WONDER WOMAN (1st series) #300 (February 1983)
STATUS Hero **REAL NAME** Hippolyta Trevor
OCCUPATION Adventurer **BASE** England
HEIGHT 5ft 7in **WEIGHT** 145 lbs **EYES** Blue **HAIR** Blonde
SPECIAL POWERS/ABILITIES Superhuman strength, speed, and endurance; trained in most forms of hand-to-hand combat.

Lyta Trevor, daughter of FURY, Helena Kosmatos, was adopted by Joan and Steve Trevor (see TREVOR, STEVE). Lyta believed that her superpowers were inherited from her "mother" the former MISS AMERICA. Lyta fell in love with Hector Hall, son of HAWKMAN and HAWKGIRL. They became Fury II and the Silver Scarab and founded the team INFINITY, INC. Hector vanished just as Lyta learned she was pregnant. The Furies of myth then appeared to her and revealed Lyta's connection to Helena and the Greek gods. An amazing and traumatic series of events followed, during which Lyta's child, Daniel, was abducted. Daniel eventually succeeded Morpheus as master of the otherworldly realm the Dreaming, and he helped Lyta reunite with Hector, now DOCTOR FATE. **RG**

AMAZING BASES

JSA HEADQUARTERS

The headquarters of the JUSTICE SOCIETY OF AMERICA is a mansion in the Morningside Heights area of Manhattan, north of Central Park in New York City. Equipped with personal suites, medical facilities, and a communications complex powered by Waynetech computers, the HQ has its own gas and electric power supply, recycles its water, and even has moveable walls that allow the JSA to reconfigure its architecture. There is a JSA museum and memorial open to the public on the first floor. Below the mansion are training facilities and computer monitors, as well as a high-speed rail link that follows a rebuilt submarine steam tunnel and a rocket ship (*see* Amazing Vehicles, pp. 32–3).

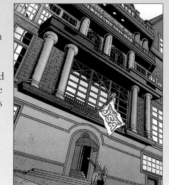

TITANS TOWER

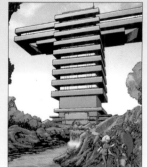

Shaped in a giant "T," Titans Tower is located in the harbor of San Francisco. The first of several Towers was located in New York's East River. This tower was destroyed by TRIGON, and the second was blown up by the Wildebeest Society. The latest Titans Tower, is full of state of the art technology and also has a garden, tended by STARFIRE, planted with the flowers of long dead worlds.

PARADISE ISLAND

Called Themyscira by its inhabitants, the immortal warrior women known as the AMAZONS, Paradise Island is the home of WONDER WOMAN. The first Themyscira was an island nestled in an otherdimensional pocket off the coast of Greece. Settled by the Amazons, it was a mystic land of Greco-Roman architecture, tropical forests, and eternal sunshine. The home of the Amazons for 30 centuries, the island was ravaged by CIRCE and two civil wars before being destroyed by IMPERIEX. Themyscira was recreated by several goddesses, and transformed into a floating chain of islands in the heart of the Bermuda Triangle. An architectural marvel of amazing science where weapons no longer worked, and whose population was dedicated to the democratic exchange of information, this Themyscira was destroyed in a jealous rage by Hera (*see* OLYMPIAN GODS), and replaced with an isle more similar to the original.

FROM SUBTERRANEAN CAVES to Arctic strongholds, technological fortresses on the moon to mythical islands in other dimensions, the world's greatest heroes find refuge in the most spectacular, and often secret, locales. Across the Earth and throughout the universe, the JUSTICE LEAGUE OF AMERICA, the TEEN TITANS, and others maintain headquarters that lets them train together, collate information, and strike out at the forces of evil.

THE JLA WATCHTOWER

After inhabiting and abandoning several headquarters over the years, including a hidden cave in Rhode Island, a satellite in Earth's orbit, a Bunker in Detroit, and several embassies world-wide, the Justice League of America founded its greatest sanctuary on the moon. The JLA Watchtower was created using technologies from around the universe, and is equipped with the most advanced monitoring and transportation systems in the galaxy.

Equipped with specialized biospheres for each of its members and prison cells designed to contain the most destructive intergalactic criminals, as well as a Monitor Womb that records every transmission broadcast on Earth, the Watchtower is accessible from Earth by teleportation technology from HAWKMAN's homeworld of Thanagar.

MOONWATCH *Nestled in the Moon's Mare Serenitatis crater, the Watchtower is the headquarters of Earth's greatest hero team.*

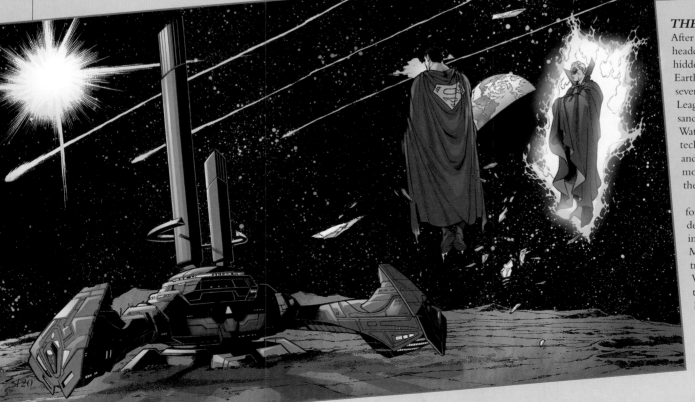

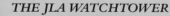

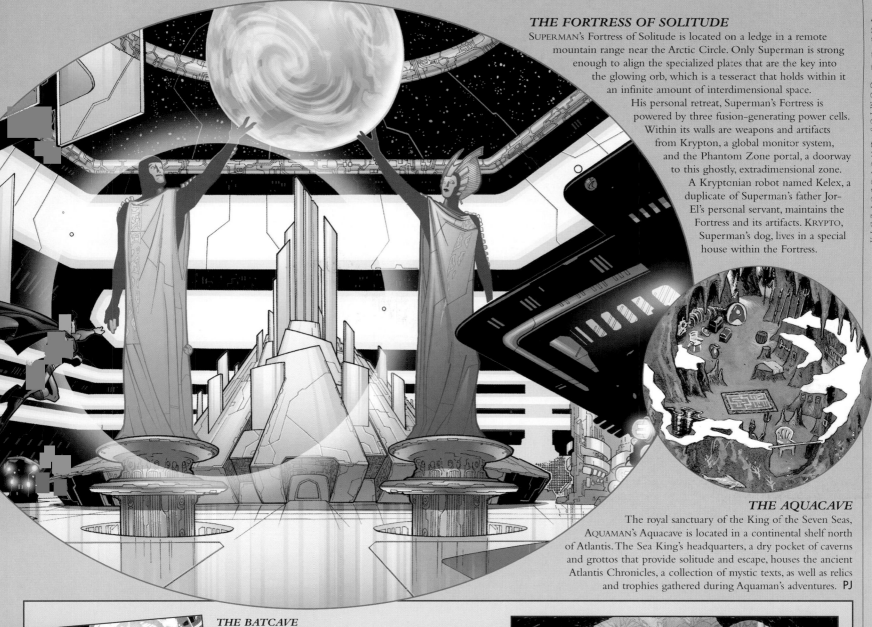

THE FORTRESS OF SOLITUDE

SUPERMAN'S Fortress of Solitude is located on a ledge in a remote mountain range near the Arctic Circle. Only Superman is strong enough to align the specialized plates that are the key into the glowing orb, which is a tesseract that holds within it an infinite amount of interdimensional space.

His personal retreat, Superman's Fortress is powered by three fusion-generating power cells. Within its walls are weapons and artifacts from Krypton, a global monitor system, and the Phantom Zone portal, a doorway to this ghostly, extradimensional zone. A Kryptonian robot named Kelex, a duplicate of Superman's father Jor-El's personal servant, maintains the Fortress and its artifacts. KRYPTO, Superman's dog, lives in a special house within the Fortress.

THE AQUACAVE

The royal sanctuary of the King of the Seven Seas, AQUAMAN'S Aquacave is located in a continental shelf north of Atlantis. The Sea King's headquarters, a dry pocket of caverns and grottos that provide solitude and escape, houses the ancient Atlantis Chronicles, a collection of mystic texts, as well as relics and trophies gathered during Aquaman's adventures. **PJ**

THE BATCAVE

Carved out from the the subterranean, bat-infested limestone caverns that run beneath his family estate Wayne Manor, the Batcave is a sprawling underground headquarters equipped with the latest vehicles, weapons, and technology to help BATMAN in in his constant crusade against crime.

The original Batcave was destroyed during the earthquake that leveled half of Gotham City. The new Batcave is a multi-level bunker, powered by its own hydrogen generators. Housing a vast array of vehicles, scientific equipment, a forensics lab, medical facilities, and training systems throughout its multi-tiered labyrinth, the Batcave's centrepiece is the central computer terminal. This is powered by seven Cray T392 mainframes, and incorporates a holographic projector. Stored on the computer is Batman's vast archive of crime and criminals.

For a time, Batman hired the hunchbacked mute Harold Allnut, a technological genius, to work in the cave. Harold was duped into revealing Batman's secrets to the villain Hush in exchange for a voice and a new body, and was murdered by the criminal. While several heroes—and a handful of villains—have seen the inside of the Batcave, very few know where it actually exists.

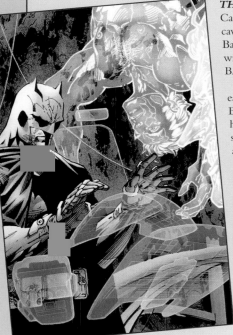

VIRTUAL REALITY *Batman's sophisticated computer is controlled by virtual reality telepads.*

BAT FORTRESS *The Batcave is equipped with the most sophisticated technology and weaponry Bruce Wayne's money can buy. Its many levels extend nearly a mile beneath Wayne Manor.*

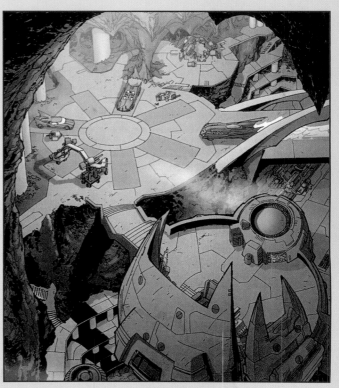

THE DC COMICS ENCYCLOPEDIA

G.I. ROBOT

FIRST APPEARANCE WEIRD WAR TALES #101 (July 1981)
STATUS Hero **REAL NAME** J.A.K.E. 2
OCCUPATION Soldier **BASE** Pacific Islands
HEIGHT 6ft 6in **WEIGHT** 548 lbs **EYES** Photocellular **HAIR** None
SPECIAL POWERS/ABILITIES Speed, strength and endurance that exceeded the human norm.

Hoping to augment the soldiers during World War II, U.S. scientists devised a G.I. robot, the experimental Jungle Automatic Killer-Experiment, dubbed J.A.K.E. by Marine Sgt. Coker, who was assigned to test the prototype. Its missions were so successful that the army had hopes of turning out a complete corps of robots. The robot followed its programming well, saving Coker from enemy fire on more than one occasion. J.A.K.E. confounded engineers when it displayed a rudimentary consciousness and sacrificed itself while saving an American fleet.

Learning from this experience, they built a second model. This new J.A.K.E. performed even better and was supplemented with a robotic dog and cat combination for stealth missions. It too developed artificial intelligence that perplexed the engineers enough that no further models were constructed, and the program was quietly shut down at the end of World War II. The second J.A.K.E.'s body survived for over a thousand years, well into the 31st Century. **RG**

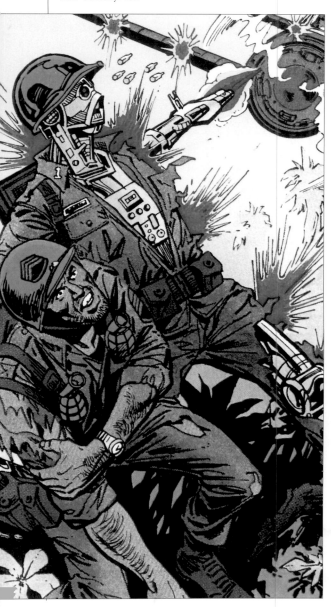

GAMEMNAE

FIRST APPEARANCE JLA #70 (October 2002)
STATUS Villain (deceased) **REAL NAME** Gamemnae
OCCUPATION Sorceress **BASE** Poseidonis, Atlantis
HEIGHT 5ft 8in **WEIGHT** 139 lbs **EYES** Blue **HAIR** Blonde
SPECIAL POWERS/ABILITIES Power sorceress; was able to cast spells potent enough to move continents through space and time.

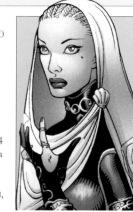

Gamemnae was an Atlantean sorceress who was born 3,000 years ago. She was cast from her home as a child because of her blonde hair, a terrible curse in Atlantean myth. She enslaved the people of Atlantis and its champion, AQUAMAN, by shifting the kingdom back in time to 1004 BC. Gamemnae then invoked a prophecy that foretold the coming of the end of the world. Rama Khan (see KHAN, RAMA) gathered a powerful group of ancient heroes to destroy the "seven-headed Hydra" that would travel through time to end the world. That "Hydra" was the JUSTICE LEAGUE OF AMERICA, who Gamemnae had feared would track Atlantis through the time disruption and end her plans for world conquest. Following a battle with the ANCIENTS, Gamemnae died in battle with MANITOU RAVEN, the JLA freed Aquaman, and Atlantis was returned to its rightful time and place. **PJ**

GANGBUSTER

FIRST APPEARANCE ADVENTURES OF SUPERMAN #432 (July 1987)
STATUS Hero (retired) **REAL NAME** José Delgado
OCCUPATION Former schoolteacher **BASE** Suicide Slum, Metropolis
HEIGHT 5ft 9in **WEIGHT** 170 lbs **EYES** Brown **HAIR** Black
SPECIAL POWERS/ABILITIES Superb street fighter; wore Kevlar-lined bulletproof body armor and riot helmet; weapons included shatterproof nunchakus and taser.

Growing up in Metropolis's Suicide Slum, Golden Gloves boxing champ José Delgado witnessed firsthand the ills of street gangs. To protect his poor and defenseless neighbors from gang violence, José donned body armor and a xriot helmet to become the vigilante Gangbuster. Unfortunately, José's efforts as Gangbuster eventually led to paralyzing injuries following a fight with the villain Combattor, as well as the loss of his teaching position and an end to a short-lived romance with reporter Lois Lane (see LANE, LOIS). But despite these hardships, Gangbuster's heroism remains an inspiration to the Latino youth of Suicide Slum. **SB**

ANGRY MAN José Delgado donned the guise of Gangbuster to fight street gangs that Lex Luthor employed as his personal army. Luthor later purchased José's apartment building and had him evicted.

GARV

FIRST APPEARANCE L.E.G.I.O.N. '90 #15 (May 1990)
STATUS Hero **REAL NAME** Garv
OCCUPATION Adventurer **BASE** Mobile
HEIGHT 5ft 8in **WEIGHT** 220 lbs **EYES** Blue **HAIR** None
SPECIAL POWERS/ABILITIES Incredible strength and imperviousness due to his natural size, based on his planet's heavy gravity; he relies on this more than skilled combat.

Garv was one of the earliest recruits to Vril Dox II's L.E.G.I.O.N. organization. He was eager if a bit naïve, but matured over the years. At one point, to be even a more effective crime fighter, Garv assumed the identity of the Masked Avenger and aided teammate STRATA in catching alien criminal Jiv Reduu. Strata then became the Leather Rose to track down the Masked Avenger, without realizing she was hunting Garv. The lovesick Garv finally proposed to Strata and they married. Almost immediately after, however, Strata was forced to flee with the core team to escape Lyrl, Dox and Strata's son. This team of "R.E.B.E.L.S." managed to kidnap Telepath (who remained under Lyrl's control). Garv willingly signed on to help Lyrl bring in the rebels. Garv and Strata were reunited just as their comrade Marij'n freed the planetary leaders from Lyrl's mind control. In the end, R.E.B.E.L.S. was disbanded and its various members have since sought their own destinies, including the happily reunited couple Garv and Strata. **RG**

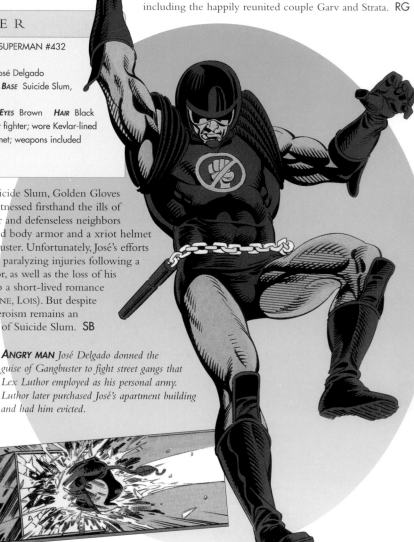

GATES

FIRST APPEARANCE LEGION OF SUPER-HEROES (4th series) #66 (March 1995)
STATUS Hero   *REAL NAME* Tu'julk Mr'asz
OCCUPATION Legionnaire   *BASE* Legion World
HEIGHT 3ft 7in   *WEIGHT* 210 lbs   *EYES* Yellow-green   *HAIR* None
SPECIAL POWERS/ABILITIES Able to teleport himself and others for short distances, usually line of sight

This insectoid native of the planet Vyrga was "drafted" into the LEGION OF SUPER-HEROES during an early recruitment drive, in which each member world of the United Planets received a request to submit one candidate for Legion inclusion. The government of Vyrga offered up Mr'asz, whose political views had made him unpopular on his homeworld. He initially rejected the membership offer (calling the Legion a "teenage death squad"), but the Vyrgians strongarmed him and he joined under the codename Gates. His ability to create disks that teleported the team made him a great asset. Gates appeared to have been killed by a rift in space during the Great Rift Disaster, but he later returned, and continues to aid the Legion in its policing of the 31st century. **DW**

GAUCHO

FIRST APPEARANCE DETECTIVE COMICS #215 (January 1955)
STATUS Hero (missing in action)   *REAL NAME* Unknown
OCCUPATION Freedom fighter   *BASE* Buenos Aires
HEIGHT 5ft 10in   *WEIGHT* 175 lbs   *EYES* Brown   *HAIR* Black
SPECIAL POWERS/ABILITIES Expert equestrian; best known for his skill with the bolo, a throwing weapon used to ensnare or strangle its target.

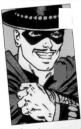

A freedom fighter that operated for the Allied forces during World War II, Gaucho infiltrated the Nazi forces in Germany as a spy, leaking Axis secrets to the United States. One of the first real costumed heroes to operate outside of the United States, Gaucho was given an invitation by the mysterious DOCTOR MIST to join the Dome, the super-national organization headquartered in Paris. The Argentine hero declined and returned to his home in Buenos Aires, actively fighting crime and corruption through much of the 1950s, and becoming a legend throughout much of South America. The final fate of Gaucho has yet to be revealed. **PJ**

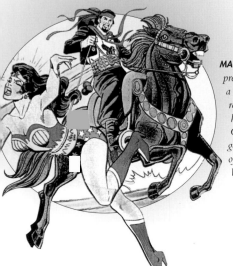

MACHO MAN In a pre-Crisis world, a swaggering rogue calling himself the Gaucho tried to get the better of Wonder Woman.

GENERAL, THE

FIRST APPEARANCE (Wade Eiling) CAPTAIN ATOM (2nd series) #1 (March 1988); (The General) JLA #25 (January 1999)
STATUS Villain   *REAL NAME* General Wade Eiling
OCCUPATION Militant monster   *BASE* Mobile
HEIGHT 10ft 5in   *WEIGHT* 1,378 lbs   *EYES* Red   *HAIR* Brown
SPECIAL POWERS/ABILITIES Superhuman strength and regenerative abilities; nearly indestructible; can survive unaided in space.

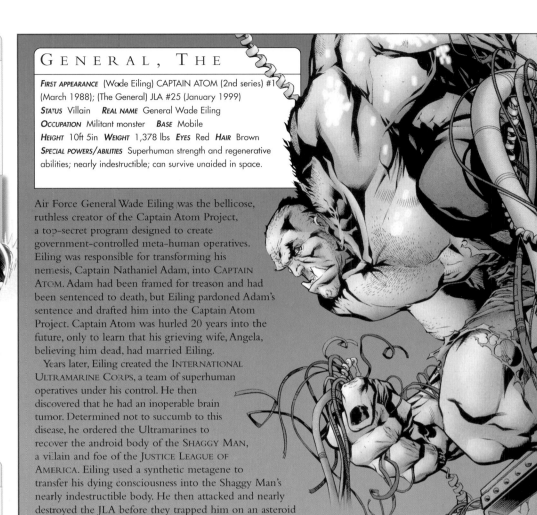

Air Force General Wade Eiling was the bellicose, ruthless creator of the Captain Atom Project, a top-secret program designed to create government-controlled meta-human operatives. Eiling was responsible for transforming his nemesis, Captain Nathaniel Adam, into CAPTAIN ATOM. Adam had been framed for treason and had been sentenced to death, but Eiling pardoned Adam's sentence and drafted him into the Captain Atom Project. Captain Atom was hurled 20 years into the future, only to learn that his grieving wife, Angela, believing him dead, had married Eiling.

Years later, Eiling created the INTERNATIONAL ULTRAMARINE CORPS, a team of superhuman operatives under his control. He then discovered that he had an inoperable brain tumor. Determined not to succumb to this disease, he ordered the Ultramarines to recover the android body of the SHAGGY MAN, a villain and foe of the JUSTICE LEAGUE OF AMERICA. Eiling used a synthetic metagene to transfer his dying consciousness into the Shaggy Man's nearly indestructible body. He then attacked and nearly destroyed the JLA before they trapped him on an asteroid near Jupiter, marooning him in space.

The General was saved by the QUEEN BEE II and returned to Earth. There he joined Lex Luthor's INJUSTICE GANG (*see* LUTHOR, LEX), only to be defeated again by the JLA. **PJ**

GENERAL GLORY

FIRST APPEARANCE JUSTICE LEAGUE AMERICA #46 (January 1991)
STATUS Hero (deceased)   *REAL NAME* Joseph Jones
OCCUPATION Soldier   *BASE* Mobile
HEIGHT 6ft 2in   *WEIGHT* 210 lbs   *EYES* Blue   *HAIR* Black
SPECIAL POWERS/ABILITIES German nerve gas made Jones an Olympic-level athlete; coupled with great courage, that was all he needed.

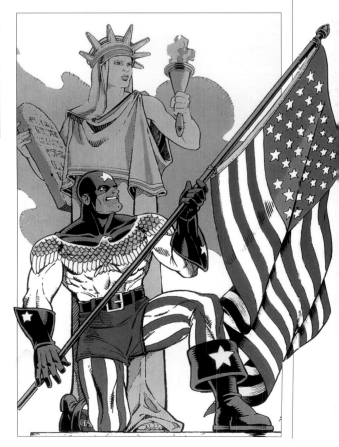

During World War II, American G.I. Joseph Jones was liberating a French village when his platoon was caught in a barrage of enemy bombs containing an experimental nerve gas. The lone survivor, Jones discovered that the gas had turned him into a superfit hero. Offering his services to the government, Jones became General Glory. He was soon joined by kid sidekick Ernest E. Earnest, a.k.a. Ernie. General Glory played his full part in defeating the Third Reich, however, the U.S. government went to great lengths to keep his exploits secret, even publishing a comic book entitled *General Glory* so that people would think he was a purely fictional creation. Decades later, General Glory's greatest fan, Guy Gardner (*see* WARRIOR), found Jones and General Glory returned to duty with the JUSTICE LEAGUE OF AMERICA for a brief time, until a heart attack claimed the old soldier. Police officer Donovan Wallace shared a hospital room with the dying Jones. The two men became friends and when Jones died, his powers were transferred to Wallace, though in different form: he found he could fly on golden wings. Wallace became a new General Glory, but has served only sporadically ever since. **RG**

GENERAL IMMORTUS

FIRST APPEARANCE MY GREATEST ADVENTURE #80 (June 1963)
STATUS Villain **REAL NAME** Unknown
OCCUPATION Would-be world conqueror **BASE** Mobile
HEIGHT 5ft 7in **WEIGHT** 142 lbs **EYES** Blue **HAIR** None
SPECIAL POWERS/ABILITIES Brilliant criminal mind; centuries-long
lifespan, hence his name.

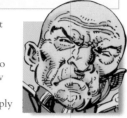

Allegedly born during the height
of the Egyptian empire, the
astonishing length of General
Immortus's life was attributable to
a secret elixir, but he didn't know
how to make more. By the time
the 20th century arrived, his supply
had run dry. Now old and frail,
Immortus tried to recruit Dr. Niles Caulder (CHIEF) to
develop more of the elixir, but Caulder escaped, though
the struggle cost him the use of his legs. Over the years,
General Immortus would often clash with Caulder's team,
the DOOM PATROL. Immortus eventually obtained his
immortality formula from Arani Caulder (see CELSIUS),
but it proved incompatible with his body chemistry,
rendering him an old man once more. However, he is
still a foe of the forces of justice. **DW**

GENERAL ZAHL

FIRST APPEARANCE DOOM PATROL (1st series) #121 (October 1968)
STATUS Villain (deceased) **REAL NAME** Zahl (first name unrevealed)
OCCUPATION Mercenary **BASE** Mobile
HEIGHT 5ft 6in **WEIGHT** 150 lbs **EYES** Blue **HAIR** None
SPECIAL POWERS/ABILITIES A brutal, unscrupulous, submarine
commander, Zahl controlled his officers through lies and intimidation.

A ruthless Nazi U-boat commander during World War II,
Captain Zahl fled to Argentina at the end of the war.
There, Zahl confronted Niles Caulder, known as the
CHIEF. The fight left Zahl confined to a special neck and
back brace and the two became bitter enemies.
    Years later, Zahl joined forces with MADAME ROUGE,
and the two villains trapped the Chief and his DOOM
PATROL on their island base, destroying it. The Nazi
began to call himself "General Zahl," working alongside
Rouge and her Brotherhood of Evil (see SOCIETY OF
SIN). Zahl died in a gun battle with
ROBOTMAN II, when the bullets the
General fired at the
metallic hero ricocheted
back at him. **PJ**

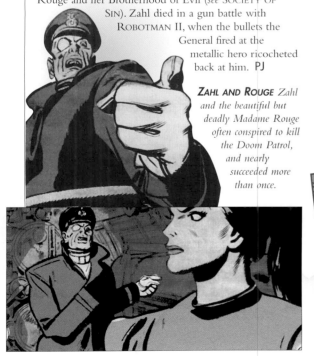

ZAHL AND ROUGE *Zahl
and the beautiful but
deadly Madame Rouge
often conspired to kill
the Doom Patrol, and
nearly
succeeded more
than once.*

GENERAL ZOD

FIRST APPEARANCE ACTION COMICS #779 (August 2001)
STATUS Villain (deceased) **REAL NAME** Avruskin (first name unknown)
OCCUPATION Despot **BASE** Pokolistan
HEIGHT 6ft 3in **WEIGHT** 230 lbs **EYES** Black **HAIR** Blue
SPECIAL POWERS/ABILITIES Under the rays of a red sun, he possessed the
same solar-enhanced abilities as Superman, including superstrength,
speed, invulnerability, and various sensory powers.

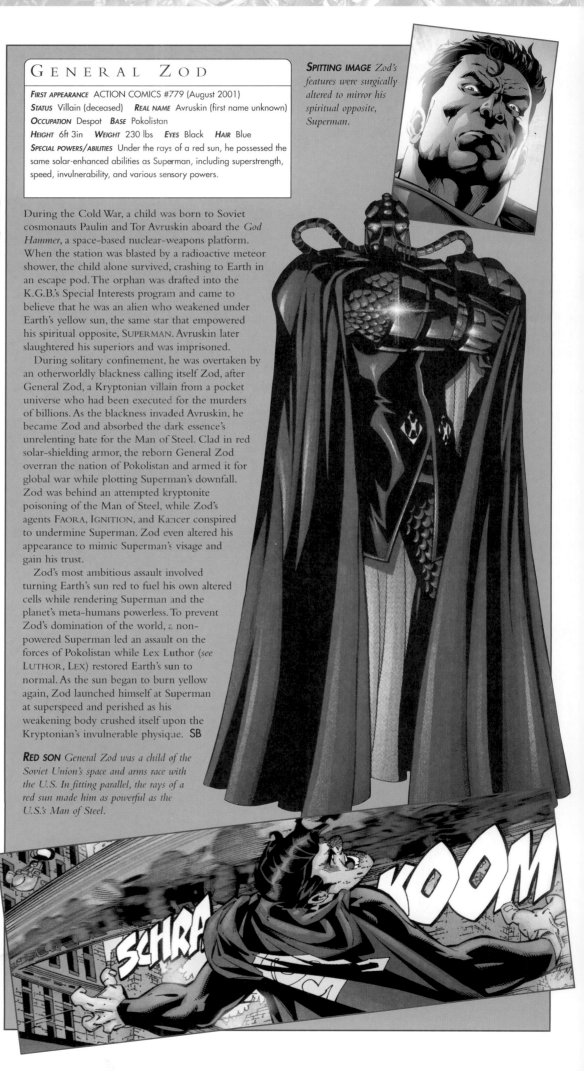

SPITTING IMAGE *Zod's
features were surgically
altered to mirror his
spiritual opposite,
Superman.*

During the Cold War, a child was born to Soviet
cosmonauts Paulin and Tor Avruskin aboard the *God
Hammer*, a space-based nuclear-weapons platform.
When the station was blasted by a radioactive meteor
shower, the child alone survived, crashing to Earth in
an escape pod. The orphan was drafted into the
K.G.B.'s Special Interests program and came to
believe that he was an alien who weakened under
Earth's yellow sun, the same star that empowered
his spiritual opposite, SUPERMAN. Avruskin later
slaughtered his superiors and was imprisoned.
    During solitary confinement, he was overtaken by
an otherworldly blackness calling itself Zod, after
General Zod, a Kryptonian villain from a pocket
universe who had been executed for the murders of
billions. As the blackness invaded Avruskin, he
became Zod and absorbed the dark essence's
unrelenting hate for the Man of Steel. Clad in red
solar-shielding armor, the reborn General Zod
overran the nation of Pokolistan and armed it for
global war while plotting Superman's downfall.
Zod was behind an attempted kryptonite
poisoning of the Man of Steel, while Zod's
agents FAORA, IGNITION, and Kancer conspired
to undermine Superman. Zod even altered his
appearance to mimic Superman's visage and
gain his trust.
    Zod's most ambitious assault involved
turning Earth's sun red to fuel his own altered
cells while rendering Superman and the
planet's meta-humans powerless. To prevent
Zod's domination of the world, a non-
powered Superman led an assault on the
forces of Pokolistan while Lex Luthor (see
LUTHOR, LEX) restored Earth's sun to
normal. As the sun began to burn yellow
again, Zod launched himself at Superman
at superspeed and perished as his
weakening body crushed itself upon the
Kryptonian's invulnerable physique. **SB**

RED SON *General Zod was a child of the
Soviet Union's space and arms race with
the U.S. In fitting parallel, the rays of a
red sun made him as powerful as the
U.S.'s Man of Steel.*

GENIUS JONES

FIRST APPEARANCE ADVENTURE COMICS #77 (August 1942)
STATUS Hero **REAL NAME** John Jones
OCCUPATION Problem solver **BASE** New York City
HEIGHT 5ft 6in **WEIGHT** 115 lbs **EYES** Brown **HAIR** Brown
SPECIAL POWERS/ABILITIES Way ahead of his time; encyclopedic scientific mind enables him to answer any question, conduct extraordinary research, and invent amazing contraptions.

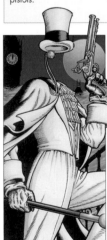

After his boat was wrecked, young Johnny Jones found himself stranded on a desert island. Hoping to attract a ship to rescue him, he built an enormous fire using 734 books containing knowledge of every possible kind that he had salvaged from the wreck. Fortunately, he had first read and committed to memory every single fact the books contained during his long stay on the island. Jones's plan worked perfectly: the towering blaze was spotting by a passing ship, and he was rescued. On his return to the U.S., he decided to put his hard-won knowledge to good use. Styling himself Genius Jones, he constructed a portable laboratory in the back of an old convertible, and offered to answer any question for a dime. When costumed heroes were in vogue during World War II, Jones called himself the Answer Man. **RG**

GENTLEMAN GHOST

FIRST APPEARANCE FLASH COMICS #88 (October 1947)
STATUS Villain **REAL NAME** James "Gentleman Jim" Craddock
OCCUPATION Professional criminal **BASE** Mobile
HEIGHT 5ft 11in **WEIGHT** Inapplicable **EYES** Blue **HAIR** Brown
SPECIAL POWERS/ABILITIES Spectral ability to turn invisible and pass through solid objects; adequate marksman with antique flintlock pistols.

"Gentleman Jim" Craddock was a notorious highwayman and robber who terrorized the good citizens of England. He journeyed to the U.S. in the late 1800s, where he encountered the gunslingers NIGHTHAWK and CINNAMON I in the American West. The hot-headed Nighthawk captured the criminal and ended his life with a noose and gallows, but Craddock transcended death as a surprisingly cultured phantom.
The Gentleman Ghost would henceforth wander the earth until the spirit of his killer moved on to the next plane of existence. Unfortunately for Craddock, Nighthawk and Cinnamon were the reborn incarnations of Egyptian royals Prince Khufu and Chay-Ara, and thus their souls could not truly die. Both were eventually resurrected as HAWKMAN and HAWKGIRL, and the Gentleman Ghost became their recurring nemesis during the 1940s. Over the decades he has menaced other heroes, but the vengeful spirit of the Gentleman Ghost always returns to clash with his main foes, the Hawks. **DW**

GEO-FORCE

FIRST APPEARANCE THE BRAVE AND THE BOLD #200 (July 1983)
STATUS Hero **REAL NAME** Brion Markov
OCCUPATION Prince; adventurer **BASE** Markovia
HEIGHT 6ft 4in **WEIGHT** 230 lbs **EYES** Blue **HAIR** Light red
SPECIAL POWERS/ABILITIES Markov has superhuman strength and powers of endurance. He can also fly, alter gravity, and project powerful blasts of heat from his hands.

A handsome, brash prince from the small European nation of Markovia, Brion Markov became Geo-Force when his country was invaded by the marauder Baron Bedlam. Given powers by the scientist Helga Jace, Geo-Force suppressed Bedlam's invasion with the help of a number of other heroes, who later became the OUTSIDERS. After his brother, King Gregor, was killed, Brion assumed the throne of Markovia before abdicating in favor of his sister-in-law, Illona. After a confrontation with DARKSEID, Geo-Force was critically injured. When he recovered, he married his girlfriend, Denise. The half-brother of TEEN TITANS member TERRA, Geo-Force proudly defends what is left of Markovia, which was nearly destroyed by the MILLENNIUM GIANTS and a nuclear meltdown. **PJ**

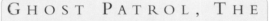

GHOST PATROL, THE

FIRST APPEARANCE FLASH COMICS #29 (May 1942)
STATUS Hero team (members deceased) **BASE** France
SPECIAL POWERS/ABILITIES (Fred, Pedro, Slim) As ghosts, each member was able to fly and become intangible or invisible; however, while in human form, the Ghost Patrollers were susceptible to injury.

Known only as Fred, Pedro, and Slim, the Ghost Patrol were deceased French Foreign Legionnaires who returned as phantoms to thwart the tyranny of Nazi Germany. In their former lives, the trio disobeyed their leader, Nazi Captain Buehler, who ordered them to bomb defenseless native villages in North Africa. Fred, Pedro, and Slim died preventing those attacks, but were soon resurrected as ghosts to redeem themselves by battling the Nazis with poltergeist-like powers. The Ghost Patrol became unsung heroes of World War II, and later acted as crime fighters throughout France, where many believe the trio continues to help those in need from beyond the grave. **SB**

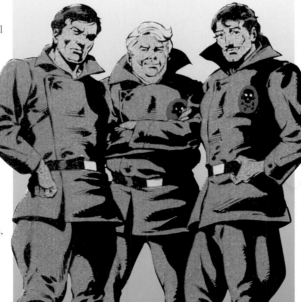

GIGANTA

FIRST APPEARANCE WONDER WOMAN (2nd ser.) #125 (Sept. 1997)
STATUS Villain **REAL NAME** Doris Zeul
OCCUPATION Scientist **BASE** Mobile
HEIGHT 6ft 6in **WEIGHT** 246 lbs **EYES** Green **HAIR** Red
SPECIAL POWERS/ABILITIES Able to grow from human size to hundreds of feet tall in seconds, gaining great physical strength in the process; Olga was not very quick-witted, whereas Doris is smart and cunning.

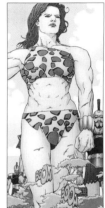

Terminally ill, Dr. Doris Zeul wanted to preserve her brilliant intellect. She felt the ideal vessel for her brain would be WONDER WOMAN. When the demon NERON struck down the Amazon Princess, Zeul thought this was her chance, only to be thwarted by Queen HIPPOLYTA and Wonder Woman's friend Cassie Sandsmark. Caught in mid-transfer, Zeul's conscience remained in limbo until her lab assistant placed it in the body of Giganta, a gorilla test subject. The ape killed the assistant, fought Cassie, in her new guise as WONDER GIRL, and escaped. Later, Zeul found Olga, a woman working at the Balthazar Circus, and used Indian magic to place her mind in the human's body. She subsequently joined VILLAINY INC. only to meet defeat at Wonder Woman's hands. **RG**

GIRDER

FIRST APPEARANCE FLASH: IRON HEIGHTS #1 (2001)
STATUS Villain **REAL NAME** Tony Woodward
OCCUPATION Criminal **BASE** Keystone City
HEIGHT 7ft 8in **WEIGHT** 1500 lbs **EYES** Glowing yellow **HAIR** Metallic
SPECIAL POWERS/ABILITIES Superhuman strength; possesses a virtually indestructible body of living steel.

In one of the happy/tragic accidents that often befall those with superpowers, steelworker Tony Woodward fell into a vat of molten steel during a riot that he had triggered after assaulting a female coworker. The vat had actually been filled with leftovers from an experimental S.T.A.R. Labs project. Woodward did not incinerate on contact with the molten metal, but instead became a kind of living steel: his body now looked as if it had been pieced together in a scrapyard! Under the name Girder, Woodward robbed when it suited him and killed anyone who got in his way. Eventually the authorities locked him up in Iron Heights penitentiary. Girder escaped in the confusion surrounding an outbreak of a prison virus and became one of the newer members of the FLASH's Rogues Gallery. He has professed an "attraction" to the living magnet MAGENTA, but so far she has spurned his crude come-ons. **DW**

GIZMO

FIRST APPEARANCE THE NEW TEEN TITANS (1st series) #3 (Jan. 1981)
STATUS Villain (deceased)   **REAL NAME** Mikron O'Jeneus
OCCUPATION Inventor; professional criminal   **BASE** New Jersey
HEIGHT 4ft 2in   **WEIGHT** 87 lbs   **EYES** Green   **HAIR** Brown
SPECIAL POWERS/ABILITIES Given the tools, Gizmo could turn harmless household appliances into high-tech weapons of mass destruction.

A genius tinkerer, the dwarfish Mikron O'Jeneus once supplied state-of-the-art technology to criminals from his clandestine company, Gizmos, Inc. Later, he took a more hands-on approach to villainy by answering DOCTOR LIGHT I's classified ad in *The Underworld Star*, which sought several super-villains to round out his FEARSOME FIVE team. As a member of that evil quintet through several lineups, Gizmo repeatedly demonstrated his scientific savvy in battle with the TEEN TITANS before putting his mischievous mind to good use for S.T.A.R. Labs. Gizmo was apparently murdered by the Fearsome Five's PSIMON. Recently, however, Gizmo was discovered alive and well, and part of an all-new Fearsome Five organized by DOCTOR SIVANA. O'Jeneus has since died, while the roguish role of Gizmo has been taken up by his son. **SB**

GLORIOUS GODFREY

FIRST APPEARANCE FOREVER PEOPLE #3 (July 1971)
STATUS Villain   **REAL NAME** None
OCCUPATION Agent of Darkseid   **BASE** Apokolips
HEIGHT 5ft 11in   **WEIGHT** 195 lbs   **EYES** Blue   **HAIR** Red
SPECIAL POWERS/ABILITIES Silver-tongued powers of persuasion; handsome looks conceal a heart of pure poison.

Unlike the other minions of DARKSEID, Glorious Godfrey is handsome instead of horrible; charming instead of stomach-churning. During one of his first missions to Earth, Godfrey, Darkseid's glittering persuader, crisscrossed the U.S. in a traveling road show preaching his philosophy to eager audiences. He hoped to prepare the planet for his master's conquest and successfully recruited an army of "Justifiers," who wore helmets that allowed Godfrey to manipulate their minds. Godfrey met defeat at the hands of the FOREVER PEOPLE. Glorious Godfrey later posed as the psychologist G. Gordon Godfrey, author of the bestseller *Super-Hero or Super-Menace?*, in a failed attempt to foment a worldwide anti-hero movement. His sister is the Apokolips agent known as AMAZING GRACE. **DW**

GLOSS

FIRST APPEARANCE MILLENNIUM #1 (Summer 1987)
STATUS Hero   **REAL NAME** Xiang Po
OCCUPATION Adventurer   **BASE** U.S.
HEIGHT 5ft 5in   **WEIGHT** 139 lbs   **EYES** Red   **HAIR** Dark auburn
SPECIAL POWERS/ABILITIES Superstrength; controls the Dragon Lines of Power, energy coursing through the Earth that enables Gloss to create force fields, duplicate herself, or teleport.

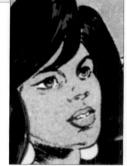

Xiang Po was among ten humans bequeathed with superpowers to become progenitors of the next phase of mankind's evolution. These individuals, hand-picked by Herupa Hando Hu, one of the GUARDIANS OF THE UNIVERSE, and his mate Nadia Safir, were destined to succeed the immortal Guardians. Xiang Po left her village in Communist China behind to became Gloss, a being energized by Earth's mystic ley lines. With her fellow progenitors, Gloss became a member of the NEW GUARDIANS, who defended Earth while preparing to found a race of immortal humans. However, the New Guardians discovered that hybrid creatures bioengineered by Janwillem Kroef, a South African passed over by Herupa and Nadia, were the true chosen ones. The New Guardians went their separate ways, with Gloss settling in the U.S. She continues to use her powers for the good of humanity while searching for her perfect mate. **SB**

GLOBAL GUARDIANS, THE

FIRST APPEARANCE DC COMICS PRESENTS #46 (June 1982)
STATUS Hero team
BASE An unnamed island in the Pacific Ocean
CURRENT MEMBERS AND POWERS
Dr. Mist (Kor) Sorcerer.
Seraph (Israel) Possesses superstrength.
Owlwoman (America) Tracker; superspeed and durability.
Olympian (Greece) Golden Fleece gives him the powers of 50 Argonauts.
Rising Sun (Japan) Solar powers.
Centrix (Canada) Can project invisible energy.
Tundra (Russia) Possesses superstrength; can project ice and cold.
Cascade (Indonesia) Is able to turn into water form; can psionically control water.
Chrysalis (France) Has a robotic shell containing sentient insects.

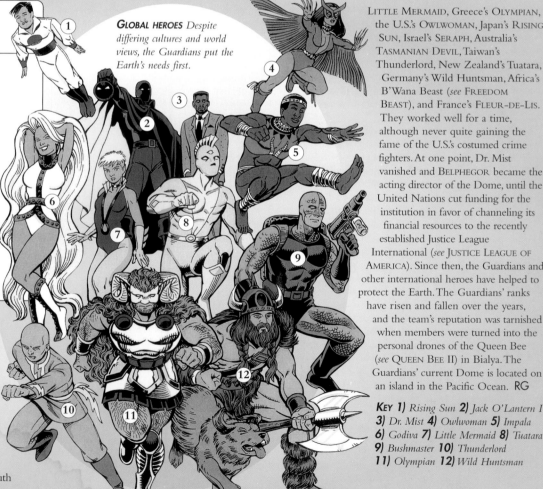

GLOBAL HEROES *Despite differing cultures and world views, the Guardians put the Earth's needs first.*

The first real costumed global heroes, the Italian Legionary, the British Knight and his sidekick, the Squire (*see* KNIGHT & SQUIRE), the Argentine GAUCHO, the French MUSKETEER, and the Swedish Wingman, made their debut in the 1950s. Convinced of the potential threat of superpowered rogues, many non-Communist countries signed a treaty in 1957 creating a supra-national organization codenamed the Dome, headquartered in a Paris mansion. After its official founding, the Global Guardians roster included: Africa's DOCTOR MIST, Venezuela's BUSHMASTER, England's Godiva, Brazil's Green Fury (*see* FIRE), Norway's ICE and ICEMAIDEN, South Africa's Impala, Ireland's JACK O'LANTERN I, Denmark's

LITTLE MERMAID, Greece's OLYMPIAN, the U.S.'s OWLWOMAN, Japan's RISING SUN, Israel's SERAPH, Australia's TASMANIAN DEVIL, Taiwan's Thunderlord, New Zealand's Tuatara, Germany's Wild Huntsman, Africa's B'WANA BEAST (*see* FREEDOM BEAST), and France's FLEUR-DE-LIS. They worked well for a time, although never quite gaining the fame of the U.S.'s costumed crime fighters. At one point, Dr. Mist vanished and BELPHEGOR became the acting director of the Dome, until the United Nations cut funding for the institution in favor of channeling its financial resources to the recently established Justice League International (*see* JUSTICE LEAGUE OF AMERICA). Since then, the Guardians and other international heroes have helped to protect the Earth. The Guardians' ranks have risen and fallen over the years, and the team's reputation was tarnished when members were turned into the personal drones of the Queen Bee (*see* QUEEN BEE II) in Bialya. The Guardians' current Dome is located on an island in the Pacific Ocean. **RG**

KEY 1) *Rising Sun* **2)** *Jack O'Lantern I*
3) *Dr. Mist* **4)** *Owlwoman* **5)** *Impala*
6) *Godiva* **7)** *Little Mermaid* **8)** *Tuatara*
9) *Bushmaster* **10)** *Thunderlord*
11) *Olympian* **12)** *Wild Huntsman*

G'NORT

FIRST APPEARANCE JUSTICE LEAGUE INTERNATIONAL #10
(February 1988)
STATUS Hero REAL NAME G'nort Esplanade Gneeshmacher
OCCUPATION Adventurer BASE Mobile
HEIGHT 5ft 10in WEIGHT 195 lbs EYES Black HAIR Reddish brown
SPECIAL POWERS/ABILITIES Well-meaning but inept; wears the maser-powered suit of a Darkstar, but whether the suit is operational is questionable.

Thanks to his uncle Gnewmann, G'newtian canine G'nort was inducted into the GREEN LANTERN CORPS as an intergalactic peacekeeper. Or so he believed. In truth, G'nort belonged to a fake Corps established by alien clowns called the Poglachi, who plotted to make laughing stocks of the real Corps. When the Poglachi were exposed, G'nort and GREEN LANTERN Guy Gardner defeated them. At Gardner's request, G'nort became a real Green Lantern, patroling a lifeless sector where he could do little harm. G'nort later joined the ill-fated Justice League Antarctica made up of temporarily reformed super-villains. Some time later, G'nort became a Darkstar. Since the DARKSTARS have been disbanded for some time, perhaps G'nort found his uniform in a trash can while looking for a meal! Though he claims JUSTICE LEAGUE OF AMERICA membership, the League tells a different story. When last seen, G'nort was hitchhiking to Antarctica. SB

GODIVA

FIRST APPEARANCE THE NEW TEEN TITANS (2nd ser.) ANNUAL #3 (1988)
STATUS Villain REAL NAME Unknown
OCCUPATION Mercenary BASE The Swiss Alps
HEIGHT 5ft 9in WEIGHT 143 lbs EYES Red HAIR Black with gold streak
SPECIAL POWERS/ABILITIES Hypnotic powers charm her victims into behaving like mindless puppets.

Born in Ghana, the assassin Godiva claims to be the child of a Chinese prince and an African princess. Godiva treats her missions as games and often has a film crew follow her around, taking her orders. Obsessed with her own beauty—she stares into mirrors constantly—she has a pathological need to be the center of attention. She has also been known to murder associates who smoke or who eat read meat.

Godiva once kidnapped Jon and Cherie Chase, the parents of Danny Chase (see TEEN TITANS). Danny helped the Titans rescue his parents, but Godiva managed to slip away. Later, she targeted a British spy, detonating a bomb that almost killed NIGHTWING. Godiva threw the British agent off a tall building and he fell to his death. The hypnotic femme fatale then coolly made her escape. PJ

GOG

FIRST APPEARANCE GOG #1 (February 1998)
STATUS Villain REAL NAME William (last name unrevealed)
OCCUPATION Adventurer BASE Metropolis
HEIGHT 6ft 1in WEIGHT 203 lbs EYES Blue HAIR Brown
SPECIAL POWERS/ABILITIES Superhuman strength and durability; staff emits energy beams.

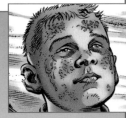

VICTIM Radiation burns scar William's face.

In a potential near-future, young William felt he was rescued by SUPERMAN, after the nuclear detonation over Kansas, for something special, and he established the Church of Superman. Considering himself the first apostle, he espoused a series of beliefs based on the hero's exploits. Superman visited William and expressed disapproval of the church—he didn't want to be deified.

Shattered, William proved susceptible to an approach by the cosmic beings known as the Quintessence. He was given immense power and knowledge, which drove him mad, and Gog was born. Gog made it his mission to go back in time and kill Superman. Gog traveled back a day at a time, killing each timeline's version of Superman, ultimately arriving at the day Superman and WONDER WOMAN's baby was born. Gog kidnapped the newborn baby, rather than kill Superman, and vanished back to an earlier point in time to create an apocalyptic disaster in Kansas. At the climax of their battle to defeat the reality-spanning Gog, Superman, BATMAN, and Wonder Woman learned the secret of Hypertime, an all-encompassing reality that contains countless parallel dimensions. Gog was remanded to the custody of the Quintessence. However, he escaped and returned to Superman's era to renew their struggle. RG

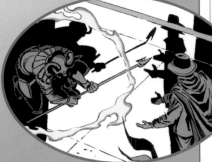

MIRACULOUS RESCUE William looks up into the smoke-filled sky to see a strange figure hovering overhead. He feels a sudden surge of hope—could that be Superman?

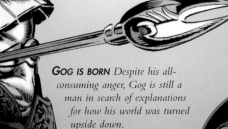

GOG IS BORN Despite his all-consuming anger, Gog is still a man in search of explanations for how his world was turned upside down.

THE QUINTESSENCE
With his mighty staff, Gog can destroy solid objects, creating a trail of devastation.

GOLDEN ARROW

FIRST APPEARANCE WHIZ COMICS #2 (February 1940)
STATUS Hero REAL NAME Roger Parsons
OCCUPATION Western hero BASE The Old West
HEIGHT 6ft 1in WEIGHT 195 lbs EYES Blue HAIR Blond
SPECIAL POWERS/ABILITIES Superb horseman, courageous fighter, and a dead shot with a bow and arrow; marked the tips of his arrows with prospector's gold, hence his name.

Orphaned son of Professor Paul Parsons—the brilliant inventor of a revolutionary lighter-than-air gas—Roger Parsons grew up in the care of an old prospector after a crook named Brand Braddock murdered his father for his scientific secrets. On the western plains Roger grew tall and strong, becoming an expert archer and calling himself Golden Arrow, "fearless hero of the West." Golden Arrow soon took his revenge on Braddock. Later, he had run-ins with Brand's brothers, Bronk and Brute Braddock, and befriended their niece Carol Braddock. Though not an official lawman, Golden Arrow helped keep the peace on the frontier, riding on his mighty stallion, White Wind. DW

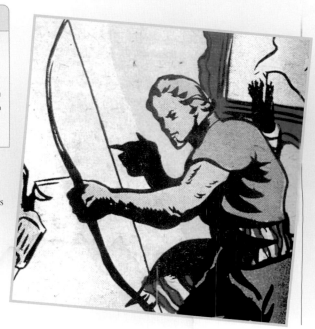

GOLDEN GLADIATOR

FIRST APPEARANCE THE BRAVE AND THE BOLD (1st series) #1
(September 1955)
STATUS Hero   REAL NAME Marcus
OCCUPATION Former shepherd, slave, and warrior
BASE Ancient Rome
HEIGHT 6ft 4in   WEIGHT 215 lbs   EYES Blue   HAIR Black
SPECIAL POWERS/ABILITIES Superior swordsman and courageous hand-
to-hand combatant; accomplished equestrian.

Marcus was a shepherd living in ancient
Rome who was framed by several
Roman soldiers for the failed
assassination attempt of Praetor
Clodius Crassus. The soldiers saw
to it that Marcus was sentenced to
life as a galley slave. Marcus
became popular during his time as
a slave, overpowering an angry lion
and using his strength to defend other
prisoners. Marcus was returned to
Rome and sold as a slave to Cinna,
the man who tried to assassinate
Crassus and who had framed Marcus
for the crime. Marcus won his
freedom after rising through the
ranks in the gladiatorial arena, and was given the helmet
of the Golden Gladiator as a prize. As the Golden
Gladiator, Marcus became Rome's greatest defender,
constantly thwarting Cinna's evil schemes. **PJ**

GOLDEN GLIDER

FIRST APPEARANCE THE FLASH (1st series) #250 (June 1977)
STATUS Villain (deceased)   REAL NAME Lisa Snart (Lisa Star)
OCCUPATION Adventurer   BASE Mobile
HEIGHT 5ft 5in   WEIGHT 117 lbs   EYES Blue   HAIR Blonde
SPECIAL POWERS/ABILITIES World-class athlete; anti-gravity skates
created their own ice, but she effectively skated on thin air;
arsenal of weapons concealed as jewels that enabled hypnosis,
force fields, teleportation, illusions, etc.

Sister of Len Snart,
(CAPTAIN COLD), Lisa
Snart was a champion ice
skater who learned her
famous spinning
skills from her
paramour Roscoe Dillon,
alias the TOP, one of Barry
Allen's, the second FLASH's foes. When the
Top was killed following a high-speed
duel with the Scarlet Speedster, Lisa
vowed to make the Flash suffer. As Golden
Glider, a whirling dervish on anti-gravity
skates, she tried to kill the Flash's wife, Iris (see
ALLEN, IRIS), as well as Iris's and Barry's parents.
Snart then hypnotized writer Beau Baer into
adopting the identity of the heroic Ringmaster,
who forced a mind-controlled Iris Allen to fall in
love with him. Fortunately, the Flash again tripped up
the Golden Glider's schemes. Snart later reunited with
the Top when the villain's spirit took over the body of
the Flash's father, Henry Allen. The Flash again defeated
the Golden Glider and she was jailed once more. Lisa
Snart skated on thin ice for the last time when she used
her brother's Cold Gun to create a string of frosty foes for
the Flash, all named Chillblaine. One of these Chillblaines
flash-froze her body, which shattered, killing Snart.
Presumably, Snart's Golden Glider joined her beloved Top in
the afterlife, undoubtedly a cold day in Hell. **SB**

GOLDFACE

FIRST APPEARANCE (as Kenyon) GREEN LANTERN (2nd series) #38
(July 1965); (as Goldface) GREEN LANTERN (2nd series) #48
(October 1966)
STATUS Hero   REAL NAME Keith Kenyon
OCCUPATION Union leader   BASE Keystone City
HEIGHT 5ft 9in   WEIGHT 180 lbs   EYES Brown   HAIR Brown
SPECIAL POWERS/ABILITIES Kenyon has superhuman strength, and his
organic metal skin provides some degree of invulnerability.

Keith Kenyon studied political science with a minor in
chemistry at the University of California-Coast City.
Rather than follow his father, who was a labor union
leader, he wanted other things from life. Everything
changed for him when he discovered a sunken chest of
gold. The gold's structure had been altered by chemical
waste, and it gave Kenyon enhanced strength and a golden
skin tone. He turned to crime to pay for his experiments,
and crossed paths with the second GREEN LANTERN and
the second FLASH. While serving time in Iron Heights
penitentiary, Kenyon's skin became organic metal. On his
release, Kenyon hid his golden skin under makeup and
became a union leader like his father. He now heads
Union 242, Keystone City's largest work force, where he
encounters the third Flash from time to time. As Goldface
he is determined to eradicate the Network, a super-villain
supply depot run by his ex-wife Amunet Black, known as
the rogue Blacksmith. **RG**

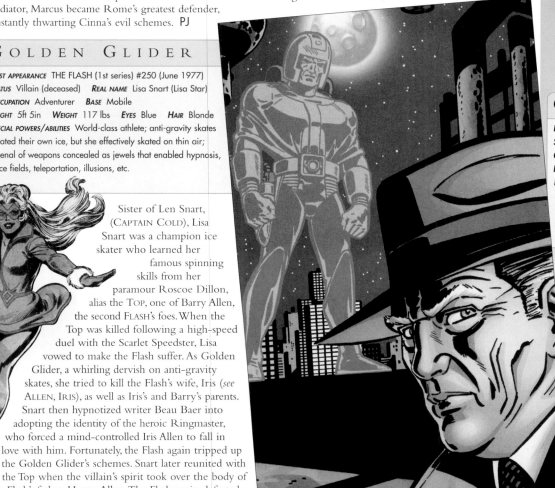

SOLID GOLD *Kenyon uses thick makeup to hide his gold skin.
His days as the costumed criminal Goldface are long behind him.*

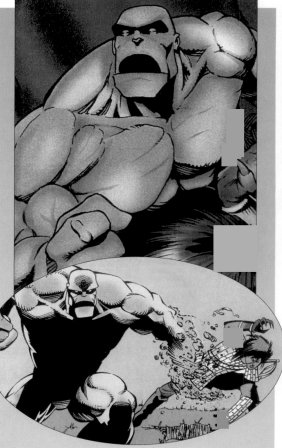

FORCE OF NATURE *Golem is a near-indestructible force
and an invaluable asset to the Primal Force team.*

GOLEM

FIRST APPEARANCE RAGMAN (1st series) #1 (September 1976)
STATUS Hero   REAL NAME None (goes by Paul)
OCCUPATION Former member of Leymen (Primal Force)
BASE New York City   HEIGHT 8ft   WEIGHT 570 lbs
EYES Yellowish brown   HAIR None
SPECIAL POWERS/ABILITIES Vast bulk allied to superstrength, apparently
invulnerable as he has the ability to regrow himself out of clay;
possesses a benevolent disposition and is viewed as a gentle giant.

Created from the mud of the Louisiana swamps, the
elemental being known as Golem (not to be confused
with the Golem serving with the super-group
HAYOTH) is a lumbering force of nature who really
wants nothing more than to live life as a human. In
his early career he fought alongside the hero
RAGMAN, and then lived with a good-hearted
Louisiana woman named Jean Lizotte. Later blamed
for Jean's death, Golem fled through the swamps
until a mystical summoning spell teleported him out
of the reach of the pursuing police. His rescuer
Maltis (see DOCTOR MIST) appointed Golem as a
new member of the supernatural super-team the
Leymen (see PRIMAL FORCE).

Damaged and destroyed several times during his
adventures, Golem easily fixed himself by shaping
new body parts out of dirt. He is vulnerable to
water but can always re-form himself once he
dries out. Since "Golem" merely describes an
artificial creature common in Jewish folklore,
Golem has long desired a name of his own. His
most recent wish is that others refer to him as "Paul."

Golem's activities since the disbanding of the Primal
Force team are unknown. He may have returned to
Louisiana to meld with the swamp-clay there. **DW**

GORGEOUS GILLY

FIRST APPEARANCE ACTION COMICS #769 (September 2000)
STATUS Villain   **REAL NAME** Unknown
OCCUPATION Adventurer   **BASE** Chattahoochee, Florida
HEIGHT 6ft 2in   **WEIGHT** 165 lbs   **EYES** Blue   **HAIR** Brown
SPECIAL POWERS/ABILITIES Powerful hypnotic ability, described as a "magic love eye," makes men slaves to her incredible beauty.

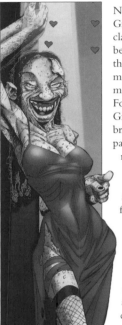

No one caught in Gorgeous Gilly's spell will dispute her claim that she is the most beautiful woman to ever walk the Earth. Her powers of mesmerism run so deep that men will do anything for her. Fortunately for men everywhere, Gilly's psychic hold can be broken by force of will, particularly when the victim is removed from Gilly's sight.

She hails from the swamps of rural Chattahoochee, Florida, a member of an extended family of meta-humans that have branded themselves the Rednex. Gilly and her kin proudly embrace the worst Southern stereotypes. Any gathering of the Rednex is certain to include an abundance of banjo-picking, cousin-kissing, and missing teeth. **DW**

GORILLA GRODD

FIRST APPEARANCE THE FLASH (1st series) #106 (May 1959)
STATUS Villain   **REAL NAME** None
OCCUPATION Would-be world conqueror
BASE Gorilla City, Africa   **HEIGHT** 6ft 6in
WEIGHT 600 lbs   **EYES** Gray   **HAIR** Black
SPECIAL POWERS/ABILITIES "Force of Mind" enables Grodd to control others, transform matter, project attack beams, or transfer his consciousness into the bodies of other creatures; scientific genius; inventor of exotic weaponry.

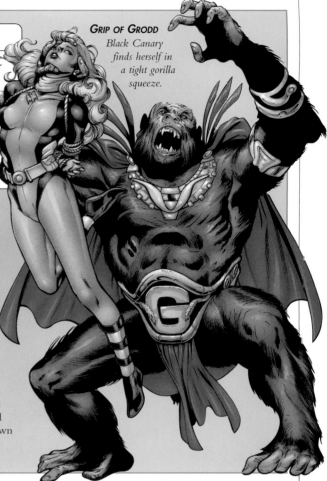

GRIP OF GRODD Black Canary finds herself in a tight gorilla squeeze.

Deep in the heart of the African jungle resides a race of highly evolved and amazingly intelligent apes. Secluded in their fabulous Gorilla City, these super simians have dwelt in peace for centuries. Their existence was completely unknown to the outside world until one of their number sought to overthrow the apes' kindly KING SOLOVAR and lead an army to conquer the entire Earth. This power-hungry malcontent was none other than Gorilla Grodd. A hugely strong, diabolical genius, Grodd had developed the power to control the minds of other beings after telepathically picking Solovar's brain. In order to put a stop to Grodd's schemes for world domination, Solovar enlisted the aid of the second FLASH, Barry Allen. He at last defeated Gorilla Grodd and imprisoned him in Gorilla City. Since that time, Grodd has broken free from his bonds on several occasions. Armed with an array of weapons—all his own inventions—he has tried to turn Earth into a planet ruled by apes, with himself as primate potentate. **SB**

GORDON, JAMES W.

FIRST APPEARANCE DETECTIVE COMICS #27 (May 1939)
STATUS Hero   **REAL NAME** James W. Gordon
OCCUPATION Gotham City Police Commissioner   **BASE** Gotham City
HEIGHT 5ft 9in   **WEIGHT** 168 lbs   **EYES** Blue   **HAIR** White
SPECIAL POWERS/ABILITIES Expert criminologist and dedicated, highly principled police detective; useful hand-to-hand combatant renowned for his powerful left hook; uses a standard issue service revolver, a Browning BDAO 9-mm automatic.

KILL OR BE KILLED James Gordon's wife, Sarah, had been murdered by the Joker while saving the lives of innocent children. Driven to the edge, Gordon nearly took the Joker's life in revenge, but shot the maniac in the kneecaps instead.

James Gordon, his wife Barbara, and their two children moved to Gotham City from Chicago, where he established a reputation for honesty in an infamously corrupt police department. However, Gordon's dedication took its toll on his marriage and Barbara left him, taking their son, James Gordon Jr. He retained custody of their adopted daughter, Barbara.

One of Jim's first assignments was hunting down the urban legend known as BATMAN. Despite his aversion to Batman's vigilantism, the chain-smoking Gordon became a close ally of the Dark Knight. Gordon eventually became Police Commissioner, forging one of the finest departments in the country. He also fell in love with and married Sergeant Sarah Essen. Gordon refused to leave Gotham when the city was struck by an earthquake, and with a few loyal officers, sought to maintain a semblance of law and order. Tragically, Sarah was murdered by the JOKER while trying to save the lives of Gotham's dozens of kidnapped children. Gordon nearly gunned the Joker down in a fit of vengeful rage, but his sense of decency prevailed and he sent the villain back to prison when life returned to normal in Gotham City.

Gordon finally retired after 20 years as a police officer. His daughter Barbara continues to fight crime in Gotham and across the world as ORACLE. **PJ**

GOTH

FIRST APPEARANCE THE TITANS #3 (May 1999)
STATUS Villain   **REAL NAME** Unrevealed
OCCUPATION Demon   **BASE** Mobile
HEIGHT Variable   **WEIGHT** Variable   **EYES** Variable   **HAIR** None
SPECIAL POWERS/ABILITIES Charismatic; demonic strength creates and throws flames; induces trances; razor-sharp claws and teeth.

The original TEEN TITANS first encountered this demon at a rock concert in the town of Eden Crest featuring a star named Limbo. The rocker started a riot to mask his theft of an anti-aging formula but was stopped by the Titans. In reality, Limbo was doing the bidding of the CONTESSA, wife of Lex Luthor (see LUTHOR, LEX). Why this demon, ruler of a region of Hell called Dis, would do this is a mystery.

Under the guises of rock stars Limbo, Grunge, Rave, and Goth, this same demon has instilled social apathy and violence among the world's teenagers. Goth is a red-skinned actor/rock star behind a series of murders. Transported to Dis, the Titans bested Goth and freed countless teens from his realm of despair. **RG**

BAD VIBES Goth plots his next assault on the fragile minds of modern youth.

GREEN ARROW

THE EMERALD ARCHER

WHILE ON A SOUTH SEA CRUISE, playboy billionaire Oliver Queen was knocked overboard and washed up on Starfish Island. He fashioned a crude bow and arrow and lived like Robinson Crusoe until he was rescued. A short time later he was rescued and was back on the social scene in his hometown, Star City. Donning a Robin Hood costume for a party, Queen foiled a robbery during the event, gaining the nickname Green Arrow. Resolving to become a crime fighter, he soon experienced firsthand the diseased underbelly of society he had only previously read about.

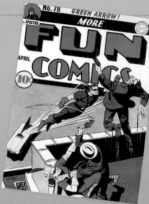

EARLY DAYS *Early in his career, the Emerald Archer had his own Arrowcar, complete with ejector seat.*

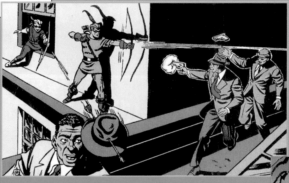

DARTING AROUND *Green Arrow and Speedy sought out criminals wherever they lurked.*

ROY AND HAL

After a horrifying trip to Vietnam (where he first met Hal Jordan, the second GREEN LANTERN), Queen sold off his armaments division. He decided to become actively involved in campaigning for good causes, and adopted Roy Harper as his ward. Roy became his first kid sidekick, Speedy (*see* ARSENAL). Together, they battled such foes as the crime-clown Bull's-Eye, the Rainbow Archer, and the Red Dart. During this time, Queen became the anonymous financier of the JUSTICE LEAGUE OF AMERICA. He also used his fortune to finance an Arrow Plane, Arrow Car, and a base called the Arrow Cave—clearly showing his respect for BATMAN. A short time later, Green Arrow was formally inducted into the JLA. There, he met and fell in love with beautiful Dinah Lance (the second BLACK CANARY), despite the large gap in their ages. Soon after, Queen was swindled out of his fortune by John deLeon, a former partner. Undaunted, Oliver convinced Hal Jordan to join him as he explored America's heartland. There they confronted issues such as bigotry, religious fanaticism, and environmental destruction. They were frequently joined on their journey by Black Canary II.

OLIVER QUEEN

Queen never talked about his parents or the events that left him an orphan, heir to a manufacturing empire. Before becoming the secret vigilante Green Arrow he had been dissatisfied, restless, wrestling with an emerging social conscience. Now he finally had the chance to do some good in the world, fighting all manner of criminality. He soon came to realize that crime and violence were global problems, fueled in part by his own munitions division.

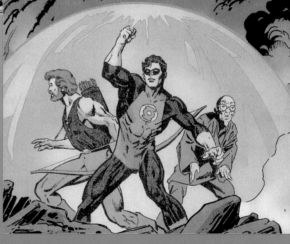

SHIELDED *Green Lantern protects Green Arrow and a monk, Than, from an explosion.*

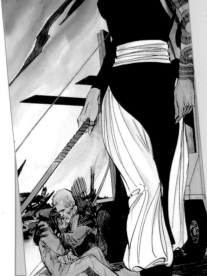

SHADO, LONGBOW HUNTER

After Oliver Queen resigned from the JLA, he and Dinah Lance moved to Seattle, Washington, where she set up a flower shop called Sherwood Florist. However, the pair were soon imbroiled in tracking down a drugs gang. The case led them to question the future of their relationship—and then Dinah vanished. She was brutalized and tortured before Green Arrow rescued her and killed the sadists holding her. During the rescue, Green Arrow's life was saved by a mysterious oriental archer named SHADO, who was pursing her own vendetta against a drugs cartel. The two eventually become lovers for a time. Green Arrow became a fugitive after being arrested on false treason charges, and Dinah Lance called Shado for help. Dinah then discovered that Queen had unknowingly conceived a son with Shado, whom she had named Robert.

CRISIS FOR THE GREEN ARROW

Feeling abandoned by his mentor, Speedy became a heroin addict. Black Canary II acted as his surrogate mother and helped him kick the habit. Shortly thereafter, Green Arrow accidentally killed a thief named Richard Hollinger and went into hiding. Black Canary II and GREEN LANTERN II searched for their friend, and the hunt took on extra urgency when the Canary was gravely injured in an auto accident. Dinah needed a blood transfusion and Green Lantern II realized that Queen possessed her rare RH Negative blood type. Green Arrow returned in time to save his lover's life. This personal crisis averted, Queen began to publicly question the JLA's goals and methods, putting him at odds with HAWKMAN, in particular. Before long he had resigned his League membership.

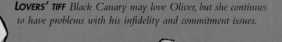

LOVERS' TIFF *Black Canary may love Oliver, but she continues to have problems with his infidelity and commitment issues.*

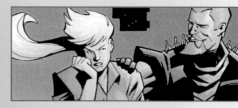

BACK FROM THE DEAD

Green Arrow attempted to prevent a terrorist from detonating a bomb over Metropolis, but gave his life in the process. His lifelong friend, Hal Jordan (formerly Green Lantern II, now a mad being named PARALLAX), used his cosmic power to restore Ollie to life, but without a soul.

With the help of his "family," Ollie regained his soul and made a concerted effort to put his life back in order. He reconnected with Connor Hawke and Roy Harper and took in Mia Dearden, a teen from the streets of his beloved Star City. Still restless, Ollie fought injustice while longing for Dinah.

His legend would grow and grow, eventually becoming so powerful that in the 853rd century the Earth would be watched over by a squad who called itself the society of Green Arrows.

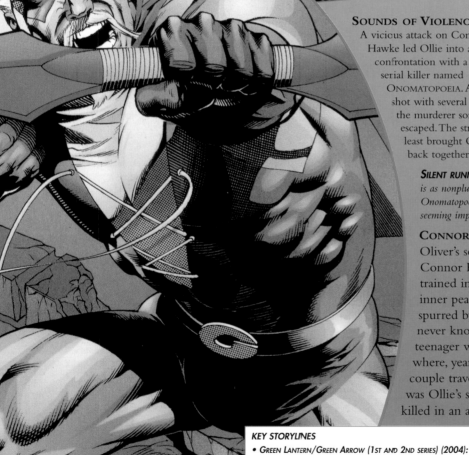

MIA DEARDEN

Mia Dearden ran away from a violent home when she was a child. Homeless, she turned to prostitution to support herself. She subsequently met the recently resurrected Oliver Queen. He took her in and gave her a safe place to once again be a teen.

However, she desperately wanted to become a costumed archer and began to train with a bow. When she got her chance, Mia shot and killed sorcerer Albert Davis to save Star City, quickly learning the price that came with being a hero.

SAVIOR *Oliver sent Mia to the Star City Youth Recreational Center for safety.*

SOUNDS OF VIOLENCE

A vicious attack on Connor Hawke led Ollie into a confrontation with a hooded serial killer named ONOMATOPOEIA. Although shot with several arrows the murderer somehow escaped. The struggle at least brought Ollie and Dinah back together.

SILENT RUNNING *A vengeful Ollie is as nonplussed by the killer Onomatopoeia's motives as by his seeming imperviousness to arrows.*

CONNOR HAWKE

Oliver's son by Sandra Moonday Hawke, Connor Hawke was raised as a Buddhist monk and trained in martial arts. Though Connor sought inner peace, he also yearned for adventure, spurred by hero-worship for the father he had never known. A new path opened up for the teenager when Ollie visited the monastery where, years earlier, he had sought asylum. As the couple traveled together, Connor revealed that he was Ollie's son. When Ollie seemed to have been killed in an airplane explosion over Metropolis, Connor took on his father's crime-fighting role as a second Green Arrow.

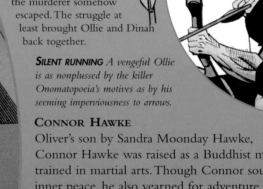

DOUBLE HITTER *He's good with a bow, but Connor's major strength is martial arts.*

INNOCENT AND GOOD

When Oliver Queen returned to life, father and son decided to protect Star City together. Connor remains somewhat innocent about the world around him, confused over his magnetic attraction for women. He feels most free when patrolling the city's rooftops with his father. **RG**

KEY STORYLINES
• *GREEN LANTERN/GREEN ARROW (1ST AND 2ND SERIES) (2004):* Collections of classic stories as the heroic pair traveled the U.S. righting wrongs.
• *GREEN ARROW: THE ARCHER'S QUEST (2003):* Back from the dead, Ollie Queen uses keepsakes to reconnect with his family.
• *GREEN ARROW: THE LONGBOW HUNTER (1989):* Green Arrow saves Black Canary from being tortured; he also encounters the mysterious female assassin Shado.
• *THE BRAVE AND THE BOLD #85 (AUGUST 1969):* In "The Senator's Been Shot," Green Arrow dons a new outfit, a beard, and gains a new attitude toward his role as a crime fighter.

GREEN LANTERN

BRIGHTEST LIGHT IN THE UNIVERSE

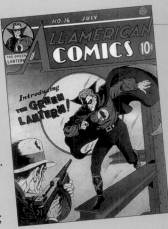

ALAN SCOTT (GREEN LANTERN I)
FIRST APPEARANCE ALL-AMERICAN COMICS #16 (July 1940)
STATUS Hero   OCCUPATION Crime fighter   BASE Gotham City
HEIGHT 6ft   WEIGHT 201 lbs   EYES Blue   HAIR Blond

HAL JORDAN (GREEN LANTERN II/PARALLAX)
FIRST APPEARANCE SHOWCASE #22 (October 1959)
STATUS Hero/villain (deceased)   OCCUPATION Spectral guardian
BASE Utah desert   HEIGHT 6ft 2in   WEIGHT 186 lbs
EYES Brown   HAIR Brown

GUY GARDNER (GREEN LANTERN III)
FIRST APPEARANCE GREEN LANTERN (2nd series) #59
(March 1968)   STATUS Hero (deceased)
OCCUPATION Adventurer   BASE New York City
HEIGHT 6ft   WEIGHT 180 lbs   EYES Blue   HAIR Red

JOHN STEWART (GREEN LANTERN IV)
FIRST APPEARANCE GREEN LANTERN (2nd series) #87
(January 1972)   STATUS Hero
OCCUPATION Architect   BASE New York City
HEIGHT 6ft 1in   WEIGHT 201 lbs   EYES Brown   HAIR Black

KYLE RAYNER (GREEN LANTERN V)
FIRST APPEARANCE GREEN LANTERN (3rd series) #48
(January 1994)   STATUS Hero
OCCUPATION Crime fighter; cartoonist   BASE New York
HEIGHT 5ft 11in   WEIGHT 175 lbs   EYES Green   HAIR Black

SPECIAL POWERS/ABILITIES Green Lantern ring generates hard-light
images, limited only by user's imagination; ring is also a database
and language translator, and allows travel through space.
Rings must be recharged using a lantern-shaped power battery.

ONCE THEY WERE a corps 3,600 strong, wearing the most
powerful weapons ever devised on their fingers.
The GREEN LANTERN CORPS acted as an intergalactic police
force, doing the bidding of the GUARDIANS OF THE UNIVERSE.
Each Green Lantern possessed a power ring that could
create hard-light projections by drawing energy from the
Central Power Battery on the Guardians' homeworld of Oa;
however, the rings were ineffective against anything yellow.
The Green Lantern Corps suffered a fatal blow at the hands
of Hal Jordan, but Kyle Rayner may be the best hope for
restoring this ancient force of justice and order.

BRIGHT LIGHT *Created by artist
Martin Nodell, Alan Scott
debuted in All-American
Comics in 1940 before getting
his own series a year later.*

ALAN SCOTT

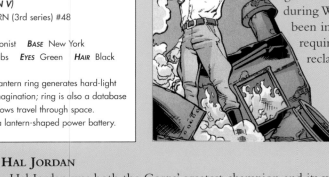

Eons ago the Guardians of the Universe trapped most of the universe's
magical energies into an orb called the Starheart. A fragment of this object
gave rise to Alan Scott's ring and power battery. Unlike Corps equipment,
Scott's mystical ring worked fine against yellow objects, but was powerless
against wood. Scott helped establish the JUSTICE SOCIETY OF AMERICA
during World War II. After many decades he discovered that his body had
been infused with the energy of the Starheart and that he no longer
required a ring. Scott briefly took the identity of Sentinel before
reclaiming the Green Lantern mantle.

DOWN AND OUT
*Sinestro fails to halt
Parallax's rampage.*

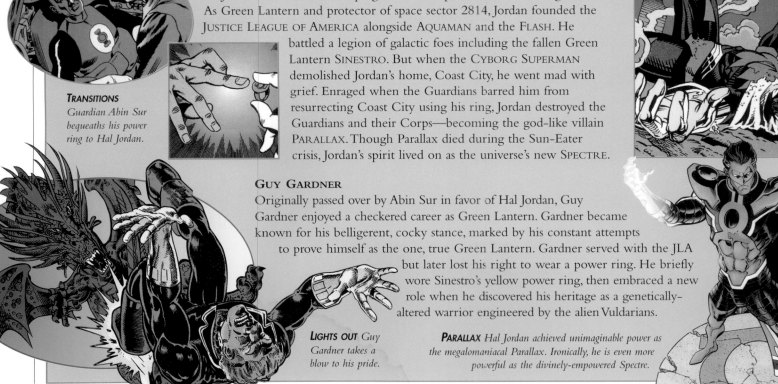

HAL JORDAN

Hal Jordan was both the Corps' greatest champion and its worst nightmare.
As Green Lantern and protector of space sector 2814, Jordan founded the
JUSTICE LEAGUE OF AMERICA alongside AQUAMAN and the FLASH. He
battled a legion of galactic foes including the fallen Green
Lantern SINESTRO. But when the CYBORG SUPERMAN
demolished Jordan's home, Coast City, he went mad with
grief. Enraged when the Guardians barred him from
resurrecting Coast City using his ring, Jordan destroyed the
Guardians and their Corps—becoming the god-like villain
PARALLAX. Though Parallax died during the Sun-Eater
crisis, Jordan's spirit lived on as the universe's new SPECTRE.

TRANSITIONS
*Guardian Abin Sur
bequeaths his power
ring to Hal Jordan.*

GUY GARDNER

Originally passed over by Abin Sur in favor of Hal Jordan, Guy
Gardner enjoyed a checkered career as Green Lantern. Gardner became
known for his belligerent, cocky stance, marked by his constant attempts
to prove himself as the one, true Green Lantern. Gardner served with the JLA
but later lost his right to wear a power ring. He briefly
wore Sinestro's yellow power ring, then embraced a new
role when he discovered his heritage as a genetically-
altered warrior engineered by the alien Vuldarians.

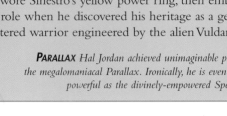

LIGHTS OUT *Guy
Gardner takes a
blow to his pride.*

PARALLAX *Hal Jordan achieved unimaginable power as
the megalomaniacal Parallax. Ironically, he is even more
powerful as the divinely-empowered Spectre.*

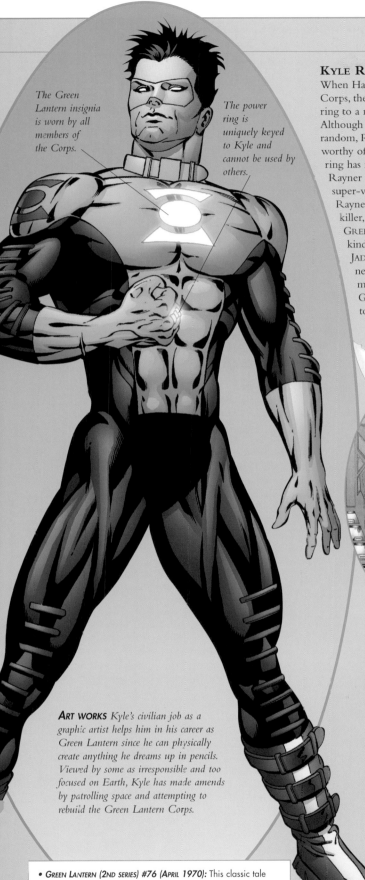

The Green Lantern insignia is worn by all members of the Corps.

The power ring is uniquely keyed to Kyle and cannot be used by others.

ART WORKS *Kyle's civilian job as a graphic artist helps him in his career as Green Lantern since he can physically create anything he dreams up in pencils. Viewed by some as irresponsible and too focused on Earth, Kyle has made amends by patrolling space and attempting to rebuild the Green Lantern Corps.*

- GREEN LANTERN (2ND SERIES) #76 (APRIL 1970): This classic tale united Green Lantern Hal Jordan and Green Arrow Oliver Queen for what would become a road-trip exploration of America.
- GREEN LANTERN (3RD SERIES) #48–50 (JANUARY–MARCH 1994): Kyle Rayner took over as Green Lantern when Hal Jordan turned rogue in the series-changing "Emerald Twilight" epic.
- GREEN LANTERN (3RD SERIES) #162–164 (JUNE–AUGUST 2003): In an echo of his predecessor's journey, Kyle Rayner teamed up with Green Arrow Oliver Queen to investigate an intergalactic crime ring.

KYLE RAYNER

When Hal Jordan shattered the Green Lantern Corps, the last remaining Guardian gave a power ring to a new hero—Kyle Rayner of Earth. Although he seemed to have been selected at random, Rayner worked hard to prove himself worthy of the Green Lantern legacy. His upgraded ring has no weakness against the color yellow, and Rayner has handled himself well against the super-villain MAJOR FORCE (who murdered Rayner's girlfriend) and the Lantern-hunting killer, FATALITY. Kyle forged friendships with GREEN ARROW II and the Flash, and has kindled a romance with Alan Scott's daughter, JADE. Rayner assumed the identity of the near-omnipotent Ion before bleeding off much of his power by resurrecting the Guardians. Kyle Rayner recruited members to restore the Corps to its former glory.

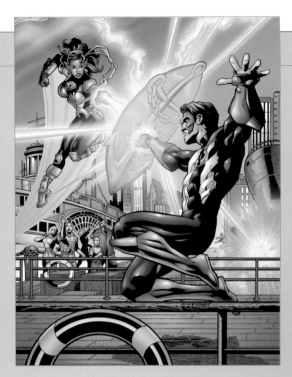

SWAN SONG

Although Kyle Rayner worked to restore the Green Lantern Corps, his actions seemed to bring about the twilight of his career. After returning from outer space, Kyle learned that his girlfriend, Jade, had moved on and that the JLA was doing well with John Stewart in the role of power-ring wielder. Kyle's subsequent battle with Fatality showed that he still had plenty of spirit, but other factors—including the revelation that Major Force had returned to orchestrate Fatality's attacks—were harbingers of change for Earth's Green Lantern. DW

EMERALD KNIGHT *Kyle Rayner has grown from a rookie to a seasoned warrior.*

JOHN STEWART

Originally Hal Jordan's backup Green Lantern, John Stewart has become one of the greatest ring-bearers, despite a career filled with unimaginable pain. Stewart accidentally destroyed the entire planet Xanshi, then suffered when his wife, Katma Tui, died at the hands of STAR SAPPHIRE. He earned a measure of peace as the caretaker of a patchwork "mosaic world" on Oa, and later became a member of the DARKSTARS (an intergalactic peacekeeping force that is a rival to the Green Lantern Corps). Injuries suffered in the line of duty left him paralyzed from the waist down, and he briefly worked as an architect until Hal Jordan, as Parallax, restored the use of his legs. Now, John Stewart works with the world's most powerful super heroes as a member of the JLA, and has helped quell interplanetary threats including Fernus, a Burning Martian who tried to trigger a nuclear holocaust. His most recent misfortune has been the breakup of his relationship with Merayn, a former Darkstar.

RESOLUTE *Presented with several opportunities to retire, John Stewart has continued to serve as Green Lantern.*

GRACE

FIRST APPEARANCE OUTSIDERS (3rd series) #1 (August 2003)
STATUS Hero **REAL NAME** Grace Choi
OCCUPATION Nightclub bouncer **BASE** Metropolis
HEIGHT 7ft **WEIGHT** 230 lbs
EYES Brown (wears purple contact lenses) **HAIR** Black (dyed auburn)
SPECIAL POWERS/ABILITIES Superstrength; is a powerful brawler and fighter.

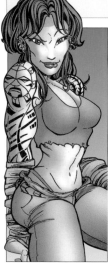

Very little is known of Grace Choi's history or the origin of her superhuman abilities. For a time, Grace was head of security at Chaney's, a bar and club in Metropolis that caters to a meta-human clientele. Chaney's was considered a safe-space for superpowered heroes and villains alike. Grace worked there until she accepted ARSENAL's offer to join a new team of OUTSIDERS that had banded together after the dissolution of the New Titans and YOUNG JUSTICE. Told that she would be paid triple her Chaney's salary as a member of the fledgling team, Grace accepted Arsenal's offer. Grace claims to be on the team for financial reasons and because she loves a fair fight. She shares a very physical relationship with Arsenal. **PJ**

GRAVEDIGGER

FIRST APPEARANCE MEN OF WAR #1 (August 1977)
STATUS Hero (believed retired) **REAL NAME** Captain Ulysses Hazard
OCCUPATION Soldier **BASE** Europe
HEIGHT 6ft 2in **WEIGHT** 201 lbs **EYES** Brown **HAIR** Brown
SPECIAL POWERS/ABILITIES Excellent athlete, trained to use most weapons and in all forms of combat; above average strength and speed.

After overcoming polio as a child, Ulysses Hazard worked to strengthen his body, relearning how to walk and run. As a result, this native of Birmingham, Alabama excelled in every way. He enlisted at the outbreak of World War II and once again proved exceptional with his arms training. Frustrated at being continually sent on graves detail simply because of his skin color, he went AWOL. Journeying to Washington, D.C., he slipped past security and broke into the offices of the Joint Chiefs of Staff to prove that he was more than just a gravedigger. Impressed, they turned him into a one-man unit, sending him on secret missions in the European Theater of Operations. Along the way, he suffered an injury that left a cross-shaped scar at the bridge of his nose. His post-World War II whereabouts remain unrecorded. **RG**

A REAL HERO Ulysses Hazard proved that men of color were ready to fight the Axis threat during World War II.

GRANNY GOODNESS

FIRST APPEARANCE MISTER MIRACLE (1st series) #2 (May 1971)
STATUS Villain **REAL NAME** None
OCCUPATION Headmistress **BASE** Apokolips
HEIGHT 5ft 10in **WEIGHT** 256 lbs **EYES** Blue **HAIR** White
SPECIAL POWERS/ABILITIES Robust for her age, Granny is a formidable fighter; however she usually gets her way by the sheer force of her evil will; her personal arsenal includes electrocuting energy-gauntlets.

In her youth, trooper Goodness was one of the finest dog soldiers in the armies of Apokolips, easily besting her male compatriots. Rising quickly through the ranks, Goodness faced her final test of loyalty when ordered to shoot her warhound Mercy. Goodness blasted her examiner instead. Taken before DARKSEID, Goodness had no other choice but to slay her beloved beast when the dread lord of Apokolips—the warhound's true master—commanded it to maul her to death. Pleasing Darkseid with her quick kill, Goodness graduated with honors, becoming one of but a few females among Darkseid's Elite. Years later, she would be known as Granny Goodness, headmistress of a number of nightmarish orphanages strung across the planet Apokolips. There, through her own brand of dominance and discipline, Granny molds the lost children of the Armagetto to become mindless minions of Darkseid. Granny's previous students include Scott Free (MISTER MIRACLE) and Big Barda. She also personally trained the FEMALE FURIES in the ruthlessness that has made her legendary as the wickedest woman on Apokolips. **SB**

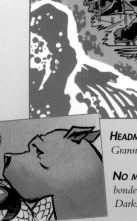

HEADMISTRESS The orphans feel Granny's temper as deadly force.

NO MERCY In her youth, Goodness bonded with her warhound Mercy, but Darkseid forced her to kill her pet.

GRAYVEN

FIRST APPEARANCE GREEN LANTERN (3rd series) #71 (February 1996)
STATUS Villain **REAL NAME** Grayven
OCCUPATION Galactic conqueror **BASE** Mobile
HEIGHT 6ft 8in **WEIGHT** 425 lbs **EYES** Red **HAIR** Gray
SPECIAL POWERS/ABILITIES Superstrength, increased durability and stamina; is a megalomaniac whose brilliant head for military tactics is undermined by an overwhelming need to feed his ego.

Illegitimate son of DARKSEID, the warlord Grayven has long stewed in the bitter knowledge that he possesses only a fraction of the power enjoyed by his father, the Lord of Apokolips. When that knowledge became intolerable, he gathered a fleet and began conquering worlds. On Rann, he decimated the intergalactic DARKSTARS police force and crippled Darkstar (and former GREEN LANTERN) John Stewart. Green Lantern Kyle Rayner put a stop to Grayven on several occasions. During the Imperiex War (see Great Battles, pp. 320–1), Grayven allied with BRAINIAC 13 while pretending to be on his father's side. When Darkseid discovered Grayven's treachery, he banished him to another realm. Grayven was soon back, however, turning up in New York City. Under the JOKER's mad influence, Grayven took over a comedy club and threatened the city with a bomb until defeated by Kyle Rayner. **DW**

GREEN LANTERN CORPS

FIRST APPEARANCE (I) GREEN LANTERN (1st series) #11 (March 1962); (II) GREEN LANTERN: THE NEW CORPS #1 (April 1999)
STATUS Hero team **BASE** Interstellar space
MEMBERS AND POWERS
There have been thousands of Green Lanterns throughout history, each armed with a power ring that is limited only by its wearer's will. Prominent members include: *Aa, Amanita, Arisia (deceased), Arkkis Chummuck (deceased), Ash, Boodikka, Brik, Cary Wren, Ch'P (deceased), Chriselon, Eddore, Flodo Span (deceased), G'nort, Galius Zed (deceased), Green Man, Guy Gardner, Hal Jordan, Hollika Ran (deceased), Jack T. Chance, John Stewart, Katma Tui (deceased), Kilowog, Kreon, Larvox, Medphyll, Mogo, Salakk, Sinestro (deceased), Stel, Tomar-Tu, Tomar-Re (deceased), Torquemada, Zax.*

The Green Lantern Corps was founded by the GUARDIANS OF THE UNIVERSE three billion years ago to curb the spread of evil throughout the universe. The Guardians divided the universe into 3,600 known sectors and assembled the Corps from individuals who would valiantly defend their segment of space, armed with specially crafted power rings.

The Green Lanterns guarded the universe for millennia, combating evil and abiding by a strict code of conduct set by the Guardians. In recent years, Hal Jordan of Earth became one of the most exemplary Green Lanterns, while the renegade SINESTRO became one of the galaxy's most notorious criminals.

After the Crisis (see Great Battles pp. 320–1), the Guardians forsook control of the Corps and the individual sectors were abandoned. Left to their own devices, Hal Jordan and a small contingent of Green Lanterns settled on Earth.

RING OF STEEL The Green Lantern Corps were rebuilt by Hal Jordan, John Stewart, and Guy Gardner. 1) Kreon 2) Aa 3) Brik 4) G'nort 5) John Stewart 6) Hal Jordan 7) Chriselon 8) Kilowog 9) Larvox 10) Tomar-Tu 11) Boodikka 12) Amanita

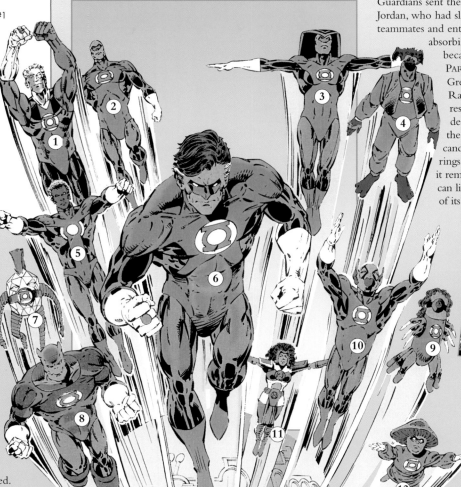

Later, when the alien despot MONGUL destroyed Coast City, Jordan went mad with grief and invaded Oa to force the Guardians to resurrect the city's inhabitants. The Guardians sent the Green Lantern Corps after Jordan, who had slaughtered his former teammates and entered the Power Battery, absorbing its energies. He then became the being known as PARALLAX. The sole surviving Green Lantern, Earth's Kyle Rayner, believed it was his responsibility to rebuild the decimated Corps. He searched the galaxy for suitable candidates and gave them special rings. Operating from deep space, it remains to be seen if this Corps can live up to the legendary status of its predecessors. **PJ**

THE NEW GREEN LANTERN CORPS *Once an army of 3,600 soldiers, the new Green Lantern Corps is a platoon of warriors gathered by Kyle Rayner. The warriors are armed with special power rings, which they use to fight the forces of darkness.*

GREEN MAN

FIRST APPEARANCE GREEN LANTERN (2nd series) #164 (May 1983)
STATUS Hero **REAL NAME** Unknown **OCCUPATION** Former Green Lantern; freedom fighter **BASE** Formerly Space Sector 2828; later Vegan Star-System **HEIGHT** 6ft 8in **WEIGHT** 425 lbs
EYES Red **HAIR** None **SPECIAL POWERS/ABILITIES** Once wielded an Oan power ring; blood is poisonous; Psion surgery gave telepathic and teleportation powers.

An amphibious alien from the planet Uxor, the Green Man served the GREEN LANTERN CORPS with distinction. He pursued the Spider Guild into Vegan space and destroyed a Guild nest with the OMEGA MEN. He then chose to aid the Omegans' struggle against the Guild. The Green Man lost his power ring and battery to the Psions (see Alien Races, pp. 150–1), whose experiments on him triggered his latent telepathic abilities. He remained an Omega Man thereafter as the freedom fighters fought threats to life and liberty in Vega. He was killed by shape-shifting Durlans (see Alien Races, pp. 150–1), who breached the hull of the Omegans' starship when they were defending Earth during the Dominion-led Invasion (see Great Battles, pp. 320–1). **SB**

GROSSOUT

FIRST APPEARANCE SHOWCASE '96 #11 (December 1996)
STATUS Hero **REAL NAME** Philbert Hoskins
OCCUPATION Rock drummer **BASE** Mobile
HEIGHT 8ft **WEIGHT** 784 lbs **EYES** White **HAIR** None
SPECIAL POWERS/ABILITIES Of vast bulk, superhumanly strong, and possessing an insatiable appetite; laid down a heavy beat.

Philbert Hoskins was an overweight, underachieving kid with a keen interest in astronomy. Gazing through his telescope one night, Phil spied a crashing meteorite. He crept outside and found the meteor crater. When he poked the glowing rock with a stick he unleashed a torrent of light that triggered his transformation into a walking pile of sludge with a ravenous appetite. When his mother could no longer afford to feed him, gargantuan Phil was turned over to government authorities and taken to a secret base in New Mexico.

At the base, Phil met three other monstrous misfits: Fang, Slither, and Screamqueen. After escaping, these young rebels decided to form a rock band aptly named Scare Tactics. Dubbed Grossout, Phil played drums as Scare Tactics toured the U.S. and encountered groupies and ghouls during several supernatural adventures. Ultimately, Grossout left Scare Tactics after killing the violence-prone Slither. He then mutated into a virtual Adonis with miraculous powers, and flew toward the stars he so loved. He has not been seen since. **SB**

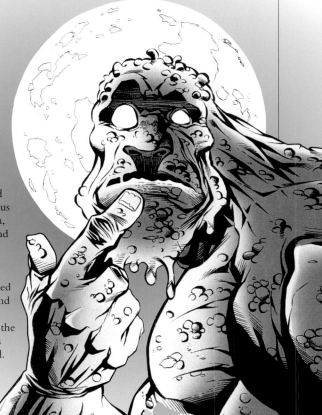

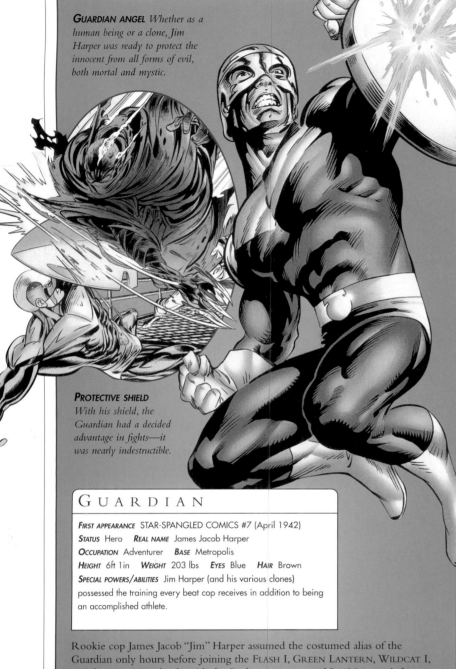

GUARDIAN ANGEL *Whether as a human being or a clone, Jim Harper was ready to protect the innocent from all forms of evil, both mortal and mystic.*

PROTECTIVE SHIELD *With his shield, the Guardian had a decided advantage in fights—it was nearly indestructible.*

GUARDIAN

FIRST APPEARANCE STAR-SPANGLED COMICS #7 (April 1942)
STATUS Hero **REAL NAME** James Jacob Harper
OCCUPATION Adventurer **BASE** Metropolis
HEIGHT 6ft 1in **WEIGHT** 203 lbs **EYES** Blue **HAIR** Brown
SPECIAL POWERS/ABILITIES Jim Harper (and his various clones) possessed the training every beat cop receives in addition to being an accomplished athlete.

Rookie cop James Jacob "Jim" Harper assumed the costumed alias of the Guardian only hours before joining the FLASH I, GREEN LANTERN, WILDCAT I, and the ATOM in a battle with the Starheart-empowered Joe Morgan. A few weeks later on January 23, 1942, Harper became legal "guardian" for the young members of the NEWSBOY LEGION. As both a cop and the Guardian, he guided these youths to serve justice—and attend school.

With age slowing his reflexes, Harper agreed to have himself cloned. His memories were transferred into an adult body and the Guardian lived once more, his main role being to provide security at the top-secret genetic research facility Project Cadmus. As time passed, however, the Guardian came to feel that his life wasn't complete without friends and family. His melancholy intensified when SUPERBOY left Cadmus for a life of his own.

The Guardian was later killed by the explosive criminal Shrapnel and, against his wishes, was cloned once again, making a rapid advance from infancy toward adulthood. He is once more learning to function in a society that finds human cloning anathema. RG

IN HIS IMAGE *Against the first clone's wishes, Project Cadmus grew a new Harper clone.*

GUARDIANS OF THE UNIVERSE

FIRST APPEARANCE GREEN LANTERN (3rd series) #50 (March 1994)
STATUS Cosmic superbeings **BASE** The planet Oa
NOTABLE MEMBERS AND POWERS
GANTHET (LEADER) Possesses telekinetic and telepathic powers, immortality, flight, and the ability to wield energies from the Central Power Battery.
LIANNA Similar powers to Ganthet, though limited by the inexperience of youth.

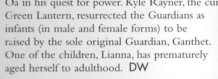

SINGLE SEX *The original Guardians consisted only of males.*

Once the greatest of the cosmos' myriad species, the Guardians of the Universe saw five billion years of dominance come to a rude end within the last decade—even immortal beings, it seems, can be killed. The Guardians evolved on the overcrowded planet Maltus. When one of their number, the scientist KRONA, arrogantly sought to observe the Great Hand that called the universe into being, a blast of cosmic power created an evil mirror universe of antimatter. Stricken with guilt, the Maltusians migrated to Oa and declared themselves an eternal force for order—the Guardians of the Universe. Some Oans, feeling that evil should be sought out and destroyed, became the more proactive Controllers.

The Guardians first created robotic peacekeepers each called MANHUNTER (who later rebelled against their creators), then deputized thousands of alien "locals" into the intergalactic GREEN LANTERN CORPS. The female Oans eventually left the planet to form their own warrior society, the Zamarons.

In modern times the Guardians left the universe with the Zamarons to create a new breed of immortals, then returned after the destruction of Oa's Central Power Battery. Restoring the battery's energies, they re-established the Corps, only to die when former champion Hal Jordan, the second GREEN LANTERN, devastated Oa in his quest for power. Kyle Rayner, the current Green Lantern, resurrected the Guardians as infants (in male and female forms) to be raised by the sole original Guardian, Ganthet. One of the children, Lianna, has prematurely aged herself to adulthood. DW

REJUVENATION *The Guardians now exist as males and females, though it is unclear how long it will take for them to assume their adult forms.*

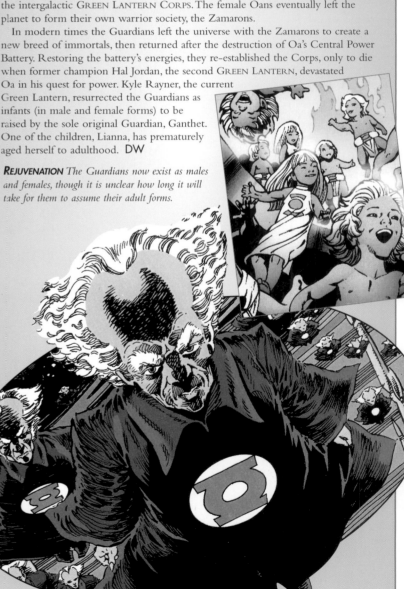

GUNFIRE

First appearance DEATHSTROKE ANNUAL #2 (Summer 1993)
Status Hero   **Real name** Andrew Van Horn
Occupation Munitions expert   **Base** New York City
Height 6ft 1in   **Weight** 190 lbs   **Eyes** Green   **Hair** Red
Special powers/abilities Able to psychokinetically transform small objects into explosive energy projectiles, which he uses as concussive weapons; skilled hand-to-hand combatant.

Andrew Van Horn is the wealthy heir to Van Horn Industries, a powerful international conglomerate. Years ago, Andrew and his father were attacked by an alien parasite in one of the Van Horn warehouses in Paris. The elder Van Horn perished, but Andrew was changed into a meta-human with the ability to transform objects by accelerating their particles, and warping them into explosive weapons. Andrew was one of many "New Bloods" (*see* BLOOD PACK) accidentally created by the parasites. He joined forces with these fledgling heroes and the JUSTICE LEAGUE OF AMERICA to stop the parasites' reign of terror. Andrew then learned that his father had been an arms dealer with links to various criminals and vowed to put an end to his illegal legacy. Declining JLA membership, Gunfire used his powers to stop the terrorist activities of villains like the Oblivion Front and their leader Dominion. Dominion was a former Van Horn employee who tried to steal the weapons Gunfire's father had stockpiled. Gunfire defeated Dominion and the Oblivion Front was dissolved. **PJ**

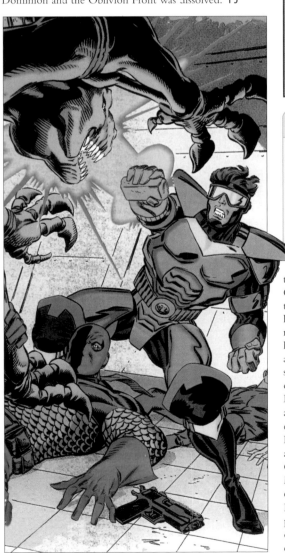

ATTACK OF THE PARASITES *Defending the assassin Deathstroke the Terminator, Gunfire's explosive powers were used to defeat the creatures who created him—parasites out to conquer the planet.*

GUNNER AND SARGE

First appearance OUR FIGHTING FORCES #45 (May 1958)
Status Heroes (Sarge is deceased)   **Real names** "Gunner" MacKay (full name unrevealed); "Sarge" Clay (full name unrevealed)
Occupations Private, U.S. Marines; Sergeant, U.S. Marines
Base Mobile   **Height** 5ft 10in; 6ft   **Weight** 162 lbs; 205 lbs
Eyes (both characters) Blue   **Hair** Blond; reddish blond
Special powers/abilities Highly skilled commandos; Gunner favored a Thompson machine gun, and is now a cyborg with guns for arms.

"Gunner" MacKay and "Sarge" Clay fought bravely together in the Pacific, often helped by Pooch, a dog from the K-9 Corps who saved their lives countless times. Later, Gunner and Sarge were assigned to the European front to train a band of raw recruits. Unfortunately, their trainees were slaughtered on their first patrol. The two Marines blamed themselves and fell in with fellow misfits CAPTAIN STORM and Johnny Cloud (*see* CLOUD, JOHNNY), forming the LOSERS task force. The team went on secret missions until, in early 1945, Gunner and Sarge were killed by Nazi troops. Gunner's body was revived by the top-secret Project M. Fitted with cybernetic implants that made him a walking weapon, Gunner MacKay became a member of the CREATURE COMMANDOS, battling inter-dimensional invaders, but he still misses his old pal Sarge. **SB**

STRANDED *Gunner, Sarge, and C.I.A. agent Eddie Fyers are Japanese P.O.W.'s on an island time forgot.*

GUNS BLAZING *Pooch fetches a live grenade as Gunner (left) and Sarge (right) blast their way to victory.*

GUNSHOT

First appearance JUSTICE LEAGUE OF AMERICA (2nd series) #78 (August 1993)
Status Villain   **Real name** Unknown
Occupation Member of New Extremists   **Base** Mobile
Height 6ft 1in   **Weight** 202 lbs   **Eyes** Blue   **Hair** Black
Special powers/abilities Wears armored battlesuit bristling with weapons, which enhances his natural marksmanship.

Little is known about the villain known as Gunshot. He rarely talks, and a bullet from his battlesuit can be a real conversation killer. He first appeared on the super hero scene as one of the New Extremists, a team assembled by the extra-dimensional being DREAMSLAYER. Gunshot and his teammates, Brute, Cloudburst, Death Angel, and MEANSTREAK, tried and failed to rout the JUSTICE LEAGUE OF AMERICA. A second opportunity presented itself when Dreamslayer used the energies of a machine to usurp the power of the omnipotent OVERMASTER. Dreamslayer called the New Extremists to his side but again tasted defeat. The Overmaster then dispensed with Dreamslayer and dealt with the New Extremists directly, pulling them into his massive new CADRE. Since the Cadre's defeat, Gunshot has kept a low profile. **DW**

GYPSY

First appearance JUSTICE LEAGUE OF AMERICA (1st series) ANNUAL #2 (November 1984)
Status Hero   **Real name** Cynthia "Cindy" Reynolds
Occupation Adventurer   **Base** Mobile
Height 5ft 6in   **Weight** 130 lbs   **Eyes** Blue   **Hair** Black
Special powers/abilities Chameleon-like camouflage powers allow her to blend into her surroundings; can project realistic illusions into the minds of certain targets.

A shy street urchin from Detroit, 15-year-old Cindy Reynolds unveiled her special camouflage powers during a battle with the alien CADRE. Invited to join the JUSTICE LEAGUE OF AMERICA, Cindy, as Gypsy, kept her past and her real name secret from the League. After the League's enemy PROFESSOR IVO began murdering Gypsy's fellow teammates, she returned to a normal life living in suburbia with her parents.

Tragically, Gypsy's parents were killed by the alien DESPERO. Saved from Despero's wrath by the MARTIAN MANHUNTER, Gypsy returned to adventuring and joined BOOSTER GOLD'S CONGLOMERATE. Later, Gypsy became a member of the Justice League Task Force and died, but was resurrected by the Martian Manhunter and the Martian god H'ronmeer. Gypsy continues to fight crime, both alone and with the JLA. **PJ**

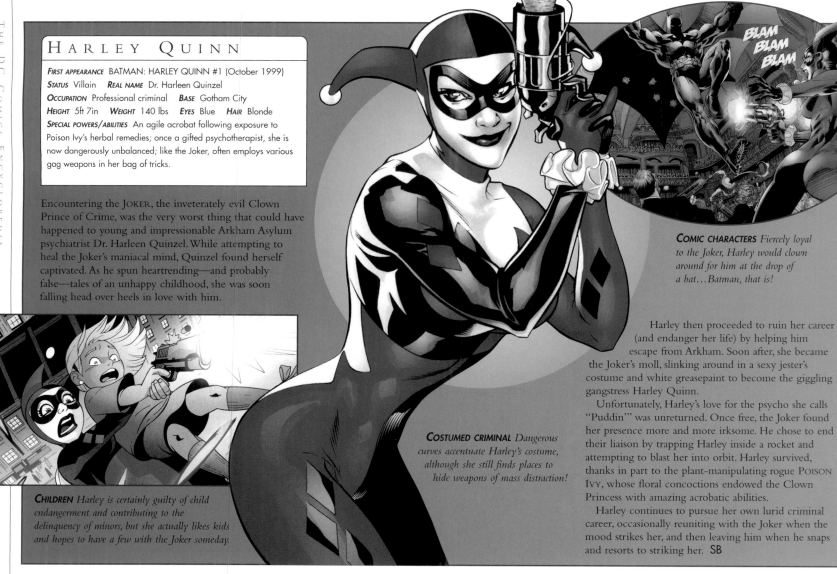

HARLEY QUINN

FIRST APPEARANCE BATMAN: HARLEY QUINN #1 (October 1999)
STATUS Villain **REAL NAME** Dr. Harleen Quinzel
OCCUPATION Professional criminal **BASE** Gotham City
HEIGHT 5ft 7in **WEIGHT** 140 lbs **EYES** Blue **HAIR** Blonde
SPECIAL POWERS/ABILITIES An agile acrobat following exposure to Poison Ivy's herbal remedies; once a gifted psychotherapist, she is now dangerously unbalanced; like the Joker, often employs various gag weapons in her bag of tricks.

Encountering the JOKER, the inveterately evil Clown Prince of Crime, was the very worst thing that could have happened to young and impressionable Arkham Asylum psychiatrist Dr. Harleen Quinzel. While attempting to heal the Joker's maniacal mind, Quinzel found herself captivated. As he spun heartrending—and probably false—tales of an unhappy childhood, she was soon falling head over heels in love with him.

COMIC CHARACTERS *Fiercely loyal to the Joker, Harley would clown around for him at the drop of a bat…Batman, that is!*

COSTUMED CRIMINAL *Dangerous curves accentuate Harley's costume, although she still finds places to hide weapons of mass distraction!*

CHILDREN *Harley is certainly guilty of child endangerment and contributing to the delinquency of minors, but she actually likes kids and hopes to have a few with the Joker someday.*

Harley then proceeded to ruin her career (and endanger her life) by helping him escape from Arkham. Soon after, she became the Joker's moll, slinking around in a sexy jester's costume and white greasepaint to become the giggling gangstress Harley Quinn.

Unfortunately, Harley's love for the psycho she calls "Puddin'" was unreturned. Once free, the Joker found her presence more and more irksome. He chose to end their liaison by trapping Harley inside a rocket and attempting to blast her into orbit. Harley survived, thanks in part to the plant-manipulating rogue POISON IVY, whose floral concoctions endowed the Clown Princess with amazing acrobatic abilities.

Harley continues to pursue her own lurid criminal career, occasionally reuniting with the Joker when the mood strikes her, and then leaving him when he snaps and resorts to striking her. **SB**

HARRIGAN, HOP

FIRST APPEARANCE ALL-AMERICAN COMICS #1 (April 1939)
STATUS Hero **REAL NAME** Hop Harrigan
OCCUPATION Aviator **BASE** Mobile
HEIGHT 5ft 7in **WEIGHT** 145 lbs **EYES** Blue **HAIR** Blond
SPECIAL POWERS/ABILITIES A superb pilot and tactician with no formal training as a fighter.

Hop Harrigan became an international celebrity when a New York reporter rode on one of the young man's humanitarian transports of Chinese refugees aboard pilot Prop Wash's experimental plane. A ticker-tape parade greeted Hop upon his return to the U.S. Harrigan's fame attracted the attention of his abusive former guardian, Silas Crass, who went to court and demanded that the boy and the money associated with Hop's name be placed in his custody. Thanks to his pal Tank, evidence was provided that Crass had never truly been authorized to be Harrigan's guardian and had forged papers to the contrary. In the aftermath, Prop Wash became Hop's new legal guardian. The young man had many flying adventures around the world, occasionally aiding the ALL-STAR SQUADRON. Hop dabbled with becoming a costumed adventurer and became the short-lived alter ego of Guardian Angel. After the war, Hop Harrigan briefly became the Black Lamp, but prefers just being himself. **RG**

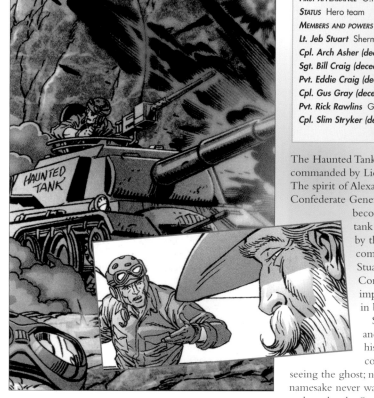

HAUNTED TANK

FIRST APPEARANCE G.I. COMBAT #87 (May 1961)
STATUS Hero team **BASE** Europe during World War II
MEMBERS AND POWERS
Lt. Jeb Stuart Sherman tank commander.
Cpl. Arch Asher (deceased) Loader.
Sgt. Bill Craig (deceased) Gunner.
Pvt. Eddie Craig (deceased) Bill Craig's son.
Cpl. Gus Gray (deceased) Second gunner.
Pvt. Rick Rawlins Gunner.
Cpl. Slim Stryker (deceased) Driver.

The Haunted Tank was actually a series of tanks commanded by Lieutenant Jeb Stuart during World War II. The spirit of Alexander the Great assigned the spirit of Confederate General James Ewell Brown (J.E.B.) Stuart to become the ghostly guardian of a Stuart M3 tank in Northern Africa. Initially affronted by the idea of watching over the tank's commander, a Yankee named Sergeant Jeb Stuart, who shared his namesake, the Confederate ghost was nonetheless impressed by Stuart's platoon in battle.

Sgt. Stuart was able to see J.E.B.'s ghost and flew the Confederate flag in honor of his spirit guardian. Stuart's team was convinced that their Sergeant imagined seeing the ghost; nevertheless, J.E.B.'s loyalty to his living namesake never wavered, and he watched over each new tank under the Sergeant's care. **PJ**

HAWK AND DOVE

FIRST APPEARANCE (Hank & Don) SHOWCASE #75 (July 1968)
STATUS Heroes **REAL NAMES** Hank Hall, Don Hall (both Hawk);
Dawn Marie Granger (Dove)
OCCUPATIONS (both) Adventurers **BASE** (both) Washington, D.C.
HEIGHT (Hank) 5ft 10in (6ft 3in as Hawk); (Don) 6ft; **WEIGHT** (Hank)
181 lbs (320 lbs as Hawk); (Don) 175 lbs **EYES** (both) Brown **HAIR**
(Hank) Brown; (Don) Black and thinning **SPECIAL POWERS/ABILITIES**
(both) Faster-than-human speed; heightened body density.

BIRDS OF A FEATHER
Hank was the Hawk, always ready for action, while Don was the more reflective Dove. Dawn, the new Dove, was more inclined toward adventure.

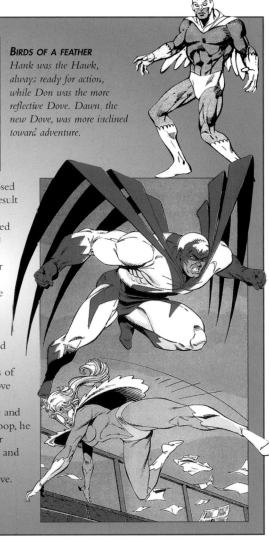

Hank and Don Hall, two brothers with diametrically opposed
political and social philosophies, were transformed as the result
of an experiment by the Lords of Order and the Lords of
Chaos, into the super-strong Hawk and Dove. They bickered
but fought alongside one another, briefly joining the TEEN
TITANS until Dove was killed during the Crisis (see Great
Battles, pp. 320–1). Dawn Granger, seeking help to save her
mother, was given powers by the Lords of Order and
Chaos. Whenever she said the word, "Dove," Dawn became
Dove II, unwittingly depriving the original Dove of his
powers, leading to his death. Dawn finally hooked up with
Hank Hall and a new version of Hawk and Dove were
formed. In the mountain world of Druspa Tau, they learned
much about their abilities and origins even as they found
themselves on opposite sides in the war between the Lords of
Chaos and Order. When their creators died, Hawk and Dove
agreed to absorb the essence of their respective creators.
MONARCH, a future version of Hank Hall, murdered Dove and
fueled madness in Hawk that ensured that, in a temporal loop, he
fulfilled his destiny to become Monarch. With no Hawk or
Dove, the cosmic forces turned to others to fill these roles, and
U.S. Air Force pilot Sasha Martens and guitarist Wiley
Wolverman were transformed into the new Hawk and Dove.
However, Dawn Granger returned from the dead with her
powers intact; how her sudden reappearance affects the
new duo remains to be seen. **RG**

HAWK, SON OF TOMAHAWK

FIRST APPEARANCE TOMAHAWK #131 (December 1970)
STATUS Hero (deceased) **REAL NAME** Unknown **OCCUPATION** Adventurer
BASE Echo Valley, American Midwest **HEIGHT** 5ft 10in
WEIGHT 166 lbs **EYES** Blue **HAIR** Brown with blond streak
SPECIAL POWERS/ABILITIES Expert marksman, horseman, and tracker; his
bravery and idealism made him an effective frontier diplomat.

As son of a legendary Revolutionary War hero, Hawk had
some big shoes to fill, but he became a hero in his own
right. Raised in a log cabin, Hawk learned the ways of the
frontiersman from his father and the secrets of
America's native people from his mother, Moon
Fawn. Hawk believed that all men were created
equal and fought fiercely against those who
would enslave or exploit
their fellow men. He
had one brother, Small
Eagle.
    Late in life, Hawk
encountered the SWAMP THING
during the plant elemental's time-
traveling trip to the 1870s, an
adventure that involved other
famous Western heroes of the
time, including BAT LASH,
MADAME .44, and Johnny
Thunder (see THUNDER,
JOHNNY).
    A mystical artifact Hawk
possessed sent Swamp Thing back
to his own time. Shortly before his death,
Hawk published his autobiography, *Hawk,
Son of Tomahawk*. **DW**

HAWKGIRL

FIRST APPEARANCE JSA SECRET FILES AND ORIGINS #1 (August 1999)
STATUS Hero **REAL NAME** Kendra Saunders
OCCUPATION Adventurer **BASE** St. Roche, Louisiana
HEIGHT 5ft 6in **WEIGHT** 131 lbs **EYES** Green **HAIR** Black
SPECIAL POWERS/ABILITIES Able to fly thanks to gravity-defying Nth
metal belt; uses giant wings to navigate during flight; aggressive
and adept hand-to-hand combatant.

ACTION GIRL *Soaring through the skies like her avian namesake, Hawkgirl is one of the fastest—and most ferocious—fliers on the planet.*

Troubled orphan Kendra Saunders attempted suicide in
her teens and her body was inhabited by the spirit of an
ancient Egyptian princess, Chay-Ara. Inheriting Chay-Ara's soul
and not knowing why made Kendra mentally ill.
    Kendra went to live with her grandfather, SPEED
SAUNDERS, a famous adventurer from the 1940s. Armed
with the secret knowledge that Kendra, the grandniece of
Sheira Saunders, the Golden Age Hawkgirl, had a great
destiny awaiting her, Speed began training the young
woman to become a super hero, and gave her Sheira's
original Hawkgirl wings. She had a daughter, Mia, at
16 and gave her up for adoption.
    Initially reluctant, Kendra became the new
Hawkgirl, joining the JUSTICE SOCIETY OF
AMERICA, and helping the team defeat Mordru
the DARK LORD. Later, Hawkgirl met HAWKMAN,
the reincarnation of Khufu, Chay-Ara's ancient
Egyptian soulmate. Hawkman pursued a romance
with Kendra, sensing their deep connection. Although
she has so far rebuffed him, both serve as valiant members
of the JSA. **PJ**

SOUL MATES
United by love and death for thousands of years, Hawkman and Hawkgirl share a unique bond.

SMASH!

HAWKMAN

FIRST APPEARANCE FLASH COMICS #1 (January 1940)
STATUS Hero **REAL NAME** Carter Hall
OCCUPATION Adventurer **BASE** St. Roch, Louisiana
HEIGHT 6ft 1in **WEIGHT** 195 lbs **EYES** Blue **HAIR** Brown
SPECIAL POWERS/ABILITIES Thanagarian Nth Metal on boots and wing harnesses allow him to fly; artificial wings give great speed and agility; Nth Metal permits Hawkman to lift great weights and withstand extremes of temperature during flight; wields a variety of ancient weapons, including shield, dagger, mace, cestus, battleaxe, and more.

ARMED AND DANGEROUS
With ancient weapons amassed during his many lifetimes on Earth, Hawkman fights an eternal struggle against evil in any age.

THE STORY OF HAWKMAN begins many millennia ago, during the 15th Dynasty of Ancient Egypt. Prince Khufu and his beloved Chay-Ara discovered the wreckage of a spacecraft from the planet Thanagar. After exposure to the mysterious Nth Metal, the vehicle's anti-gravity alloy, Khufu and Chay-Ara were murdered by the sinister sorcerer Hath-Set. The Nth Metal initiated a cycle of reincarnation that would see Khufu and Chay-Ara reborn countless times throughout the ages.

BORN AGAIN LOVERS
Reincarnated during America's Wild West, Khufu was the gunfighting hero NIGHTHAWK, while Chay-Ara was pistol-packing CINNAMON I. In the 1940s, Khufu was archaeologist Carter Hall and became Hawkman, while Chay-Ara found new life as Sheira Saunders, the heroine HAWKGIRL and Carter's wife. Both winged wonders served with the JUSTICE SOCIETY OF AMERICA (Hawkman was chairman) and the wartime ALL-STAR SQUADRON. Both Hawks

CURSED *Discovering a downed Thanagarian spacecraft gave Prince Khufu the power to fly and his immortal curse.*

later became members of the JUSTICE LEAGUE OF AMERICA and flew with the team on its earliest missions. The Halls' cycle of death and rebirth was interrupted during the Zero Hour crisis (*see* Great Battles, pp. 320–1), when both Carter and Sheira merged with Thanagarian policeman Katar Hol, who adopted the mantle of Hawkman. Unfortunately, Sheira perished in the merging. Carter later freed himself from his union with Katar, who also died. Carter was resurrected yet again, this time possessing memories of his every previous reincarnation. Sheira, however, was reborn as

her own grandniece, Kendra Saunders, with no past memories. Carter reclaimed the role of Hawkman, and rejoined the JSA alongside the new Hawkgirl. But for the first time in all their previous lives, Hawkgirl did not recognize Hawkman as her soulmate. Blinded by his love for Chay-Ara, in any form she exists, Hawkman followed Hawkgirl to St. Roch, Louisiana, as she began a quest to find the villain who murdered Kendra Saunders's parents. There, the two have become the city's winged guardians. **SB**

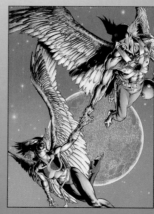

TOGETHER FOREVER *The Hawks are destined to find each other and fall in love time and time again.*

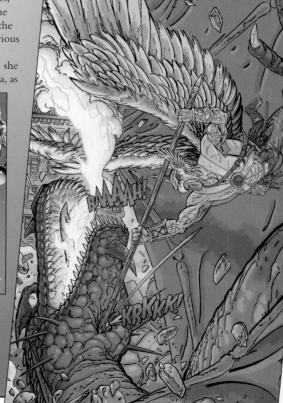

FEARLESS FIGHTER *Flying solo against fire-breathing monsters, soaring alongside Hawkgirl, or leading the assembled JSA, Hawkman is one of the greatest warriors ever known.*

KEY STORYLINES
• *LEGEND OF THE HAWKMAN* #1-3 *(JULY–SEPT. 2000):* A retelling of Hawkman and Hawkgirl's connection to distant Thanagar.
• *JSA SECRET FILES AND ORIGINS* #1 *(AUG. 1999):* The return of Hawkgirl signals the reincarnation of Hawkman!
• *JSA* #23-26 *(JUNE–SEPT. 2001):* A reborn Carter Hall rejoins the JSA and leads the team to glory.

THE DC COMICS

THE DC COMICS ENCYCLOPEDIA

HAWKWOMAN

FIRST APPEARANCE HAWKWORLD: BOOK ONE (1989)
STATUS Hero   REAL NAME Shayera Thal
OCCUPATION Police officer   BASES Detroit; planet Thanagar
HEIGHT 5ft 7in   WEIGHT 145 lbs   EYES Blue   HAIR Red
SPECIAL POWERS/ABILITIES Thanagarian armor and wings make Thal a superb flyer, excellent marksman, and vicious combatant.

Shayera Thal was a decorated police officer on Thanagar, a planet many light years from Earth. With her partner, Katar Hol (see HAWKMAN), she journeyed to Earth in pursuit of a shape-shifting criminal named Byth. Fascinated by the planet, Katar and Shayera chose to remain. The media took to calling them Hawkman and Hawkwoman after the World War II super heroes. As time went by, the partners drifted apart; Shayera even decided to hang up her wings and become a uniformed police officer in Detroit. Tormented by the voices of his previous incarnations that were at war in his mind, Katar was ultimately transported to another dimension, leaving Shayera alone. When Byth turned up once more, she donned her armor and fought with the current incarnation of the Hawks. Capturing Byth, she delivered the criminal in person to Thanagar, vowing to return once more to Earth. RG

HAZARD I

FIRST APPEARANCE INFINITY, INC. #34 (January 1987)
STATUS Villain   REAL NAME Rebecca "Becky" Sharpe
OCCUPATION Professional criminal   BASE Mobile
HEIGHT 5ft 6in   WEIGHT 136 lbs   EYES Green   HAIR Red
SPECIAL POWERS/ABILITIES Psionic powers and mystic dice give either "good luck" or "bad luck" to her victims.

The granddaughter of the Gambler, a Golden Age villain and member of the original INJUSTICE SOCIETY, Becky Sharpe was horrified to learn her grandfather had killed himself after gambling away his fortune. She decided to use her psychic abilities to manipulate luck and became Hazard, embarking on a criminal career to avenge her grandfather's death. Hazard joined the WIZARD's Injustice, Unlimited team with the understanding that murder was off-limits. Injustice, Unlimited fought both INFINITY, INC. and the GLOBAL GUARDIANS at an international conference in Canada. With the coerced help of WILDCAT II and TASMANIAN DEVIL, Hazard bankrupted the casino that ruined her grandfather, avenging the Gambler's death. After learning that Injustice, Unlimited were willing to kill their opponents, Hazard left their ranks and remains at large. PJ

HEAT WAVE

FIRST APPEARANCE THE FLASH (2nd series) #140 (November 1963)
STATUS Villain (reformed)   REAL NAME Mick Rory (Mick Calhoun)
OCCUPATION Security Chief   BASE Metropolis
HEIGHT 5ft 11in   WEIGHT 179 lbs   EYES Blue   HAIR None
SPECIAL POWERS/ABILITIES Self-designed Heat Gun generates extremely focused high-temperature flames; costume insulated with thermal-damping and heat-resistant material of Rory's own design.

As a child, Mick Rory was locked in an industrial freezer while on a school trip to a meatpacking plant. His cries went unheard, but little Rory managed to thaw his fingers enough to pick the lock and escape. From then on, Rory suffered cryophobia (a fear of cold) and became obsessed with heat and warmth. Toting his high-tech Heat Gun, he blazed a criminal career in Central City as Heat Wave. Rory was a hot-tempered enemy of the second FLASH, Barry Allen, often in tandem with fellow rogues gallery member and villainous opposite, CAPTAIN COLD. However, unlike other Flash foes, Heat Wave temporarily reformed. By helping Allen nab a crooked parole officer who had taken up his Heat Wave costume and weaponry, Rory earned the Flash's friendship and trust. Despite a later stint as Security Chief at Project Cadmus, Rory has begun working for the F.B.I. and also for his old pal, Trickster (see TRICKSTER II). SB

HAYOTH

FIRST APPEARANCE SUICIDE SQUAD (1st series) #45 (September 1990)
STATUS Hero team   BASE Israel
CURRENT MEMBERS AND POWERS
Ramban (leader/spiritual guide) Calls upon magical forces of Judaic power.
Golem (Moyshe Nakhman) Powerhouse able to transform his body between solid, liquid, and gaseous forms.
Judith Expert swordswoman, martial artist, and shuriken-throwing whirlwind.
Dybbuk Team strategist; artificial intelligence with the power to control machinery.

The Hayoth are an Israeli super-team named after the four angelic beings in the Book of Ezekiel in the Bible who bore the faces of the Lion, the Eagle, the Ox, and Man. They were formed by the Israeli government and operated as a division of the Mossad (the Israeli special forces) under the command of Colonel Hacohen. The Hayoth came to blows with the U.S.'s SUICIDE SQUAD when the Squad appeared in Israel in pursuit of the international terrorist KOBRA. The two teams shelved their differences to prevent Kobra from destroying Jerusalem's holy Dome of the Rock.

Months later, the Hayoth attempted to capture the former president of Qurac during his stay in the U.S. The Suicide Squad scrambled to prevent the abduction and the Hayoth lost a bitter battle and wound up in U.S. custody. DYBBUK freed his team by helping the Suicide Squad's Amanda Waller (see WALLER, AMANDA) restore the mind of one of her operatives. The Hayoth currently remain active in Israel. DW

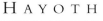

HOLY WARRIORS Led by Ramban, the nationalist Hayoth super-team springs into action to battle threats to their homeland.

HOT-TEMPERED Heat Wave is back to his evil ways and would gladly flash-fry the Fastest Man Alive!

HELIX

FIRST APPEARANCE INFINITY, INC. #17 (August 1985)
CURRENT MEMBERS AND POWERS **STATUS** Villain team **BASE** California
Mr. Bones Transparent skin and organs; deadly cyanide touch.
Arak the Wind-walker Generates hurricanes and tornadoes.
Babe (formerly Baby Boom) Stopped growing at age five; can explode anything nearby through mental focus.
Kritter Resembles a dog; impressive computer hacking talents.
Penny Dreadful Absorbs electricity and projects it in amplified form.
Tao Jones Levitates; deflects any form of energy directed at her.

All of the members of Helix were genetic freaks with meta-human talents engineered by the unscrupulous Dr. Benjamin Love. Turning to crime, they battled INFINITY, INC. and other super heroes. When Dr. Love took control of the team, the members of Helix killed their "father." Mr. Bones (see DIRECTOR BONES) soon rejected Helix and joined Infinity, Inc. under court order. Eventually all members of Helix received pardons from the U.S. government. Many now work for the Department of Extranormal Operations keeping tabs on their fellow meta-humans. Mr. Bones is now director of the D.E.O. and has been forced to take action against some of his former Infinity, Inc. teammates. **DW**

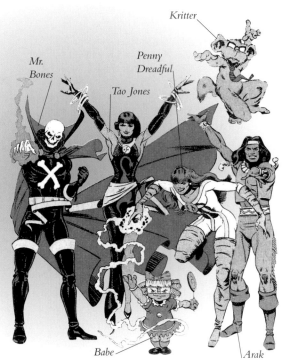

Kritter
Penny Dreadful
Mr. Bones
Tao Jones
Babe
Arak

HELLHOUND

FIRST APPEARANCE CATWOMAN (1st series) ANNUAL #2 (July 1993)
STATUS Villain **REAL NAME** Kai
OCCUPATION Assassin **BASE** Mobile
HEIGHT 5ft 10in **WEIGHT** 178 lbs **EYES** Brown **HAIR** Black
SPECIAL POWERS/ABILITIES A deadly martial artist with a preference for throwing knives and daggers.

Teenage runaway Kai was the most able student of an armless sensei who presided over a secret martial arts dojo in the backstreets of Gotham City. That is, until Selina Kyle (CATWOMAN) slinked her way into the Sensei's all-male arena to practice her own fighting skills. Selina bested Kai and became the Sensei's most prized pupil. Kai vowed revenge and became Hellhound to her Catwoman, a merciless mercenary to her charitable cat burglar. Because of the indignities he suffered at Catwoman's claws, he believes that he will find peace only when one of them is dead. **SB**

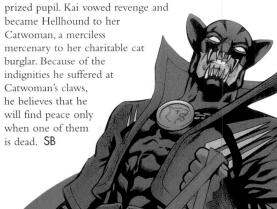

HERALD

FIRST APPEARANCE (as Mal) TEEN TITANS (1st series) #26 (April 1970); (as Herald) SECRET ORIGINS ANNUAL #3 (1989)
STATUS Hero **REAL NAME** Malcolm Arnold Duncan
OCCUPATION Restaurateur, musician, adventurer **BASE** San Francisco
HEIGHT 6ft 1in **WEIGHT** 210 lbs **EYES** Brown **HAIR** Black
SPECIAL POWERS/ABILITIES The now-destroyed Gabriel's Horn device could open warps in space, allowing teleportation; Duncan was a former Golden Gloves amateur boxing champion.

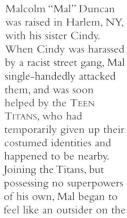

Malcolm "Mal" Duncan was raised in Harlem, NY, with his sister Cindy. When Cindy was harassed by a racist street gang, Mal single-handedly attacked them, and was soon helped by the TEEN TITANS, who had temporarily given up their costumed identities and happened to be nearby. Joining the Titans, but possessing no superpowers of his own, Mal began to feel like an outsider on the team, until Karen Beecher, the BUMBLEBEE, helped him create the Gabriel's Horn, a special weapon with teleportational powers. Becoming the Herald, Mal helped the Titans defeat DOCTOR LIGHT I.

Unknown to Mal, his special Horn had been corrupted by the villainous Gargoyle, who hoped to tear a hole in the dimensional fabric in order to release his master, the ANTITHESIS. After the Titans defeated these villains, Mal destroyed the Horn. Having aided the Titans from time to time, even joining their short-lived Titans West division, Mal is now happily married to Karen Beecher and owns a jazz club in San Francisco. **PJ**

HERO HOTLINE

FIRST APPEARANCE ACTION COMICS WEEKLY #637 (January 1988)
CURRENT MEMBERS AND POWERS **STATUS** Hero team **BASE** New York City
Diamondette (Diana Theotocopolous) Diamond-hard hands.
Hotshot (Billy Lefferts) Shoots fireballs from his fingertips.
Microwave Mom (Belle Jackson) Generates heat via microwave suit.
Mr. Muscle, a.k.a. Flex, a.k.a. Brother Bicep (Sturgis Butterfield) Former circus strongman.
Private Eyes (Lester Lee) Lenses enable all kinds of super-vision.
Stretch (Tom Longacre) Pliable hero who has lost some of his snap.
Voice-Over (Andrew Greenwald) Can imitate any voice or sound.
500Z-Q ("Soozie-Q") Mobile computer monitoring system.

When SUPERMAN is flying up, up, and away, or BATMAN just isn't answering the Bat-Signal, all anyone needs to do to find a substitute super hero is dial 1-800-555-HERO. The Hero Hotline is open 24 hours a day, seven days a week, and handles calamity beyond the range of the normal emergency services. The Hotline, founded by Tex Thomson, is maintained by the mysterious Coordinator. After hours, emergencies are handled by the night crew, including Chlorino, Marie the Psychic Turtle, Rainbow Man, Thunderhead, and Zeep the Living Sponge. **SB**

HERO HOTLINE *Employees include (clockwise from left) Stretch, Dinky the Devil Bat, Mr. Muscle, Private Eyes, Microwave Mom (Microwavabelle), Hotshot, Voice-Over, and Diamondette.*

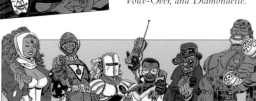

HERO

FIRST APPEARANCE SUPERBOY AND THE RAVERS #1 (Sept. 1996)
STATUS Hero **REAL NAME** Hero Cruz
OCCUPATION Adventurer **BASE** Metropolis
HEIGHT 5ft 9in **WEIGHT** 157 lbs **EYES** Brown **HAIR** Black
SPECIAL POWERS/ABILITIES Internalized H-Dial allows him to transform into a new superbeing with new superpowers for one hour; he never transforms into the same being twice.

Raised in a middle-class Puerto Rican family in Metropolis, Hero Cruz discovered a cache of technology stolen by the SCAVENGER. He took the Scavenger's Achilles Vest, using its invulnerability powers to join the Event Horizon, a cosmic rave party. Along with SUPERBOY and the RAVERS, Hero traveled across the universe with the Event Horizon party. When the Scavenger came searching for his Achilles Vest, he kidnapped several Ravers, including SPARX, whom he believed had stolen the vest. The Ravers tracked the Scavenger to his lair, and Hero discovered a mystical dial with the letters "H," "E," "R," and "O" on it (see DIAL "H" FOR HERO). He used the dial to transform into different super heroes, rescuing Sparx and Superboy and defeating the Scavenger. Sparx fell in love with Hero, but Hero revealed that he was gay. He now lives in San Francisco. **PJ**

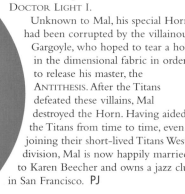

HEX, JONAH

FIRST APPEARANCE ALL-STAR WESTERN TALES #10 (March 1972)
STATUS Hero (deceased) **REAL NAME** Jonah Woodson Hex
OCCUPATION Bounty hunter; soldier **BASE** Late 19th century
American southwest; Seattle, circa 2050
HEIGHT 5ft 11in **WEIGHT** 189 lbs **EYES** Blue **HAIR** Reddish-blond
SPECIAL POWERS/ABILITIES Despite being born under a bad sign, Hex
was a superb marksman, who hardly ever missed his target.

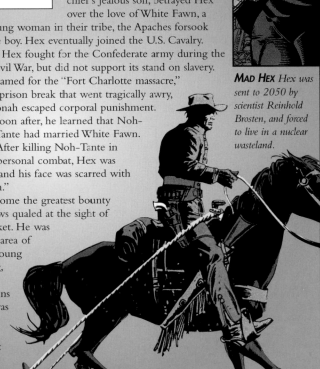

BOUNTY HUNTER
Jonah Hex was a bounty hunter without peer. He was a marksman with an unerring eye, who would take down any criminal or cowboy—for the right price.

As if cursed by his own last name, Jonah Hex was born to a life of bad luck. Born in 1839, he was the son of a brutal drunk and his meek wife. Hex was abandoned by his mother when he was still a child, and his father then sold him to an Apache tribe for a pile of animal pelts. After Noh-Tante, the chief's jealous son, betrayed Hex over the love of White Fawn, a young woman in their tribe, the Apaches forsook the boy. Hex eventually joined the U.S. Cavalry.

Hex fought for the Confederate army during the Civil War, but did not support its stand on slavery. Blamed for the "Fort Charlotte massacre," a prison break that went tragically awry, Jonah escaped corporal punishment. Soon after, he learned that Noh-Tante had married White Fawn. After killing Noh-Tante in personal combat, Hex was thrown out by the tribe and his face was scarred with the "Mark of the Demon."

By 1875, Hex had become the greatest bounty hunter of his time; outlaws quailed at the sight of his gray Confederate jacket. He was teleported to the Seattle area of 2050. After marrying a young woman named Mei Ling, who bore his child, he vowed to hang up his guns for good. However, he was forced to kill several men who came after him. Mei Ling left him taking their son with her.

Hex returned to the Old West, and was shot by a bank robber. His body was stuffed and placed on display in an amusement park on the outskirts of New York City. **PJ**

MAD HEX *Hex was sent to 2050 by scientist Reinhold Brosten, and forced to live in a nuclear wasteland.*

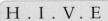

H.I.V.E

FIRST APPEARANCE SUPERMAN FAMILY #205 (January 1981)
STATUS Villainous organization **BASE** Maintains a honeycomb of
secret bases across the globe.

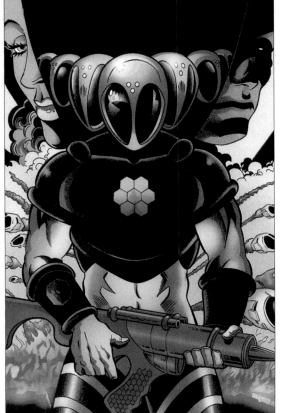

The Hierarchy of International Vengeance and Extermination (H.I.V.E.) was originally founded by a criminal genius, the H.I.V.E. Master. He gathered together seven fellow scientists, but their evil schemes were thwarted by various super heroes. Most notably, the H.I.V.E. aimed its attacks of scientific terrorism at various incarnations of the TEEN TITANS, including empowering the late Grant Wilson—son of Slade Wilson (DEATHSTROKE THE TERMINATOR)—the super-assassin known as the Ravager, in his failed attempt to destroy the group. Following frequent skirmishes with the Titans, the H.I.V.E. self-destructed after the H.I.V.E. Mistress, wife of its late founder, chose to kill the Hierarchy's inner circle and commit suicide rather than be captured. The H.I.V.E. later regrouped with Adeline Kane, ex-wife of Slade Wilson, as its new H.I.V.E. Mistress. She blamed super heroes, the Teen Titans in particular, for the death of her sons Grant and Joseph (JERICHO). Following a three-way conflict with the Titans and TARTARUS, a cadre of super-villains led by VANDAL SAVAGE, Kane was killed and the H.I.V.E. was presumably left under the leadership of Kane's second-in-command, Damien Darhk (see DARHK, DAMIEN). Structured like an insect colony, the H.I.V.E. employs swarms of faceless (and therefore expendable) foot soldiers utterly loyal to the ruling hierarchy. **SB**

HIGHFATHER

FIRST APPEARANCE THE NEW GODS (1st series) #1 (March 1971)
STATUS Hero **REAL NAME** Izaya the Inheritor
OCCUPATION Adventurer **BASE** New Genesis
HEIGHT 6ft 4in **WEIGHT** 227 lbs **EYES** Gray **HAIR** White
SPECIAL POWERS/ABILITIES Commanding presence; possesses
superhuman strength and invulnerability; focuses energies from the
omnipotent Source through his staff.

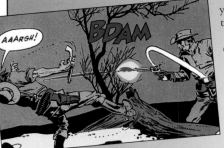

The NEW GODS of New Genesis are among the mightiest beings in creation, and Highfather was once the greatest of them all. Born Izaya the Inheritor, he assumed his destiny through tragedy when DARKSEID and his uncle STEPPENWOLF came to New Genesis on a hunting trip. Steppenwolf killed Izaya's wife, Avia, sparking a war between New Genesis and Darkseid's planet Apokolips. After Izaya had killed Steppenwolf, the Source—the manifestation of the Creator's power— selected him to start a new life as a peacemaker.

Now known as Highfather, he brokered a peace with Apokolips through a ritual exchange of sons—Highfather's Scott Free (see MISTER MIRACLE) for Darkseid's ORION. Highfather also selected five special children and raised them on New Genesis, creating the FOREVER PEOPLE. In his final act, Highfather gathered heroes and gods to prevent Darkseid tapping into the Source's power, and died at the hand of ARES, god of war. The hero TAKION became the new Highfather. Now at one with the Source, Highfather serves as a member of the godlike Quintessence. **DW**

HIMON

FIRST APPEARANCE MISTER MIRACLE (1st series) #9 (August 1972)
STATUS Hero (deceased) **REAL NAME** Himon
OCCUPATION Scientist, teacher **BASE** Apokolips and New Genesis
HEIGHT 5ft 8in **WEIGHT** 163 lbs **EYES** Blue-gray **HAIR** White
SPECIAL POWERS/ABILITIES Master genius and scientific inventor; creator
of the Mother Box, a miraculous thinking computer.

Brilliant scientist and theoretician Himon lived among the NEW GODS of New Genesis. Himon invented the powerful Mother Box and, with METRON, invented the Boom Tube, which allows DARKSEID and his war world of Apokolips to teleport across galaxies. Wracked with guilt over giving Darkseid such power, Himon vowed to end the evil god's threat. Himon secretly trained the inhabitants in the peaceful ways of New Genesis, encouraging their individuality and freedom. Darkseid immediately sent his death squads after Himon, who eluded them over and over again, often using android duplicates to confuse Darkseid's underlings. Himon also helped Scott Free become MISTER MIRACLE. Soon after, Himon's daughter BEKKA married ORION, Darkseid's son, and shortly thereafter, Darkseid murdered Himon. Mister Miracle, Orion, and Bekka escaped to Earth after Himon perished. **PJ**

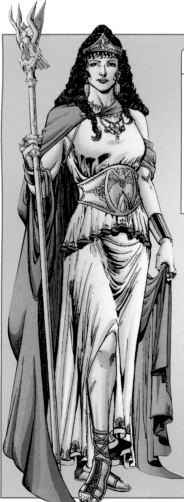

HIPPOLYTA

FIRST APPEARANCE WONDER WOMAN (2nd series) #1 (February 1987)
STATUS Hero (deceased) **REAL NAME** Hippolyta
OCCUPATION Former Queen of the Amazons **BASE** Elysian Fields
HEIGHT 5ft 9in **WEIGHT** 150 lbs **EYES** Blue **HAIR** Black
SPECIAL POWERS/ABILITIES Granted eternal life by the gods of Mount Olympus and gifted with amazing strength, speed, and agility; wore the Girdle of Gaea, which magically protected the Amazons from subjugation by man before it was forged into Wonder Woman's golden Lasso of Truth.

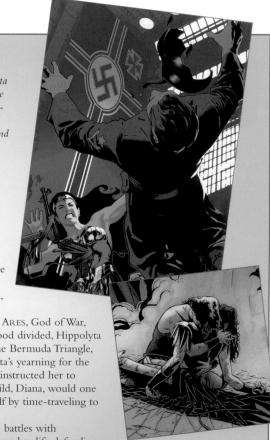

NAZI FIGHTER *Hippolyta became a member of the Justice Society via time-travel. She also made Wonder Woman a legend during World War II.*

When a pregnant cavewoman was murdered more than 32,000 years ago by her brutish mate, her spirit was collected by the Earth Mother, Gaea, and deposited in the Well of Souls, which held the life essences of slain women from past ages. Zeus, King of the Gods (*see* OLYMPIAN GODS), called for the creation of a new race of humankind to bring glory to the gods, so the Olympian goddesses restored life to these waiting souls. Among the women reincarnated was that tragic cavewoman, reborn as Hippolyta, Queen of the AMAZONS.

The gods' chosen race dwelt in peace within their city-state of Themyscira until ARES, God of War, sent Zeus's son Heracles to seduce Hippolyta and defeat the Amazons. Her sisterhood divided, Hippolyta led a group of peace-loving Amazons to rebuild Themyscira on an island within the Bermuda Triangle, where they lived for centuries hidden from the outside world. Over time, Hippolyta's yearning for the unborn child slain within her all those millennia ago was heard by the gods. They instructed her to mold a daughter from clay; as soon as she did so, they breathed life into it. That child, Diana, would one day become WONDER WOMAN, a role Hippolyta paradoxically immortalized herself by time-traveling to 1942 and serving as a member of the wartime JUSTICE SOCIETY OF AMERICA.

In modern times, Hippolyta led the Amazons through civil wars and apocalyptic battles with DARKSEID, who once decimated Themyscira and its people. Hippolyta ultimately gave her life defending both her homeland and Earth from the onslaught of the world-destroying IMPERIEX (*see* Great Battles, pp. 320–1). She is remembered as a fair and wise leader, a loving mother to Diana, and a Wonder Woman in her own right. **SB**

DEATH *Hippolyta helped to save Earth. The Olympian goddesses carried her soul into immortality.*

HITMAN

FIRST APPEARANCE THE DEMON (2nd series) ANNUAL #2 (1993)
STATUS Hero (deceased) **REAL NAME** Thomas Monaghan
OCCUPATION Hitman; vigilante **BASE** Gotham City
HEIGHT 6ft **WEIGHT** 185 lbs **EYES** Black **HAIR** Black
SPECIAL POWERS/ABILITIES Infected with alien blood, Tommy had limited X-ray vision and telepathy; he was also a crack shot.

An attack by the alien parasite Glonth left hitman Tommy Monaghan with greatly enhanced senses and limited telepathic ability. Of course, the first thing Tommy did was kill Glonth. Some saw him as a hero, and although he operated far outside the law, he did have a better developed moral sense than your average hitman. He had earned the grudging respect of BATMAN, who recognized that Tommy kept one of the darkest corners of Gotham clean. GREEN LANTERN Kyle Rayner also worked alongside Tommy.

Along the way, Tommy reunited with his old pal Natt the Hat, and the two became inseparable. Given his new powers, strange characters were soon drawn to Tommy. First came the would-be super heroes Six Pack, a group of costumed losers. Then there was the demon BAYTOR, who found hanging out with Tommy at Noonan's bar so fascinating that he went to work there as a bartender.

Tommy discovered the existence of the Bloodlines File, a government project hoping to create meta-humans using data from the earlier space-parasite outbreak. In the bloody aftermath of their attempt to shut down the facility, both Hitman and Natt were killed. **RG**

ON THE MARK *Tommy was usually victorious over any opponent.*

HOUNGAN

FIRST APPEARANCE THE NEW TEEN TITANS (1st series) #14 (Dec. 1981)
STATUS Villain **REAL NAME** Jean-Louis Droo
OCCUPATION Scientist turned criminal **BASE** Paris, France
HEIGHT 6ft 2in **WEIGHT** 205 lbs **EYES** Brown **HAIR** Black
SPECIAL POWERS/ABILITIES Computerized voodoo dolls trigger terrible pain and even death to his victims through an advanced bionic link.

Born in Haiti, Jean-Louis Droo became a top computer scientist in the U.S. He returned to Haiti to visit his dying father, only to see a local voodoo priest (a "houngan") effect a miraculous cure through the voodoo arts. Droo merged the old ways with the new by creating a computerized voodoo doll. This works by analyzing a victim's cell sample and generating a "bionic link." When Droo's stylus stabs the doll, pain signals travel via the link to the victim's equivalent body part.

Calling himself Houngan, Droo joined the New Brotherhood of Evil, later reorganized into the SOCIETY OF SIN, and participated in epic events including the Crisis (*see* Great Battles, pp. 320–1). He has recently served a term at the maximum security prison, The Slab, but will surely return to needle his enemies. **DW**

HOURMAN I & II

FIRST APPEARANCE (Hourman I) ADVENTURE COMICS #48 (March 1940); (Hourman II) INFINITY, INC. #20 (November 1985)
STATUS Heroes **REAL NAMES** (I) Rex Tyler; (II) Richard "Rick" Tyler
OCCUPATIONS (I) Chemist; (II) artist **BASE** (both) New York City
HEIGHT (I) 5ft 10in; (II) 5ft 9in **WEIGHT** (I) 181 lbs; (II) 170 lbs
EYES (I) Blue; (II) brown **HAIR** (both) Brown
SPECIAL POWERS/ABILITIES (Hourman I) Imbibing the Miraclo pill gave Rex Tyler superstrength, enhanced agility, speed, and low-level invulnerability for one hour; (Hourman II) superstrength, enhanced agility, and speed; "flash forward" vision gives Rick Tyler precognitive flashes an hour into the future; can transport to a pocket "hour in time" in order to seek counsel from his father.

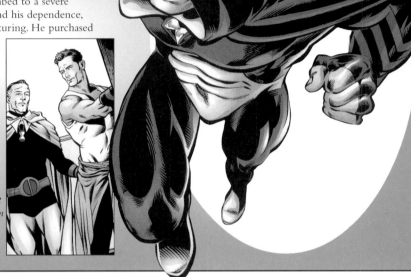

As a brilliant young chemist working for the Bannermain Chemical Company in the late 1930s, Rex Tyler developed a steroid pill he called "Miraclo," which enhanced his strength and speed to superhuman levels for almost an hour. Using his newfound strength, he became the Man of the Hour and, later, the hero Hourman. Tyler then joined the JUSTICE SOCIETY OF AMERICA and the ALL-STAR SQUADRON.

Unfortunately, Tyler became addicted to his Miraclo pills and succumbed to a severe depression. Hoping to end his dependence, Tyler retired from adventuring. He purchased the Bannermain Chemical Company and married Wendi Harris, an actress.

During the Crisis (*see* Great Battles, pp. 320–1), Rex and Wendi's headstrong son Rick took one of his father's Miraclo pills and became the second Hourman, despite Rex's objections. Rick joined INFINITY, INC. for a time, and, like his father, became addicted to Miraclo. After accidentally killing the villainous WIZARD, Rick gave up his Hourman identity. Rex became Hourman one more time, and died with several other former JSAers in a battle with EXTANT. After battling the HOURMAN III, an android from the future, Rick reclaimed his Hourman title and developed a new, non-addictive form of Miraclo. His future counterpart gave Rick the ability to transport himself into a frozen "pocket of time," where he can visit his father for a single hour. **PJ**

REX Hourman I was a member of the JSA.

MEN OF THE HOUR
Rex and Rick often reunite in a special pocket universe—for one hour only.

HOURMAN III

FIRST APPEARANCE JLA #12 (November 1997)
STATUS Hero **REAL NAME** None
OCCUPATION Adventurer **BASE** The Timestream
HEIGHT 6ft 4in **WEIGHT** 320 lbs **EYES** White **HAIR** None
SPECIAL POWERS/ABILITIES Flight; superstrength; "Power Hour" gives Hourman time-bending abilities for a 60-minute duration; Timeship can travel through or outside of the Timestream.

Despite his appearance, Hourman III is just a few years old. He is an android created in the 853rd century with genetic software patterned after the Miraclo-enhanced DNA of Rex Tyler, the first Hourman (*see* HOURMAN I & II). In the year 85271, Hourman III was to have been entrusted by METRON of the NEW GODS with safeguarding the Worlogog, an artifact allowing absolute control over time. However, Hourman III chose to journey to the 20th century and explore his human heritage along with the JUSTICE LEAGUE OF AMERICA. Through several adventures, he learned that the Worlogog's incredible power could spell doom to humanity without proper control, so he limited himself to just a "Power Hour." Hourman III later joined the JUSTICE SOCIETY OF AMERICA, and, after a humbling encounter with the time-twisting villain EXTANT, renounced the 20th century, leaving behind several gifts. First, he cured Rex Tyler's son, Rick (Hourman II), of addiction to the Miraclo pills. Rick was thus able to return to action as the 21st century's Hourman. Hourman III also saved Rex Tyler seconds before Extant would have killed him, allowing Rick a final hour with his father. These precious moments are used sparingly by Rick whenever he needs the original Hourman's sage wisdom or scientific wits, or a quality moment with his late father. Hourman III now explores the Timestream aboard his Timeship and battles the android adversary AMAZO throughout the past, present, and future. **SB**

HUMAN BOMB

FIRST APPEARANCE POLICE COMICS #1 (August 1941)
STATUS Hero **REAL NAME** Roy Lincoln **OCCUPATION** Government agent
BASE Florida **HEIGHT** 5ft 10in (later 5ft 8in) **WEIGHT** 165 lbs (later 195 lbs) **EYES** Blue **HAIR** Black (later gray)
SPECIAL POWERS/ABILITIES Can generate a biochemical explosion with just a touch; repeated punches increase force of explosion.

Roy Lincoln helped his father, a chemist, perfect an explosive known as 27-QRX. To keep the compound from falling into the hands of Nazi spies, who killed his father, Roy ingested 27-QRX. The chemical turned him into a Human Bomb.

Forced to wear a containment suit of "fibro wax," the Bomb battled home-front threats during World War II as a member of the ALL-STAR SQUADRON and the FREEDOM FIGHTERS. During the war, Montague T. "Curly" McGurk, Swordo, and Red Rogers were provided with limited explosive powers by Lincoln and joined in raids on the Japanese army as the Bombardiers. The Human Bomb also had a connection with Hustace Throckmorton, a middle-aged man who received an emergency blood transfusion from Roy and later manifested explosive powers in his feet. The changes to Lincoln's body chemistry seem to have prolonged his life, and he continues to serve the U.S. government. **RG**

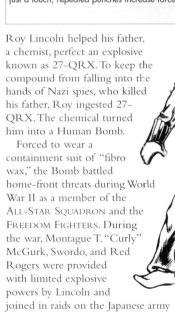

HUMAN DEFENSE CORPS, THE

FIRST APPEARANCE HUMAN DEFENSE CORPS #1 (May 2003)
STATUS Hero group **BASE** Orbital HQ Fort Olympus ("Heaven")
CURRENT MEMBERS AND POWERS
Colonel Reno Rosetti Commander of most HDC missions.
Sergeant Montgomery Kelly Scarred HDC veteran, now ruler of a realm of Hell.
Chaplain Charlie Graham Expert on the supernatural.
Sergeant Kiyahani Superb marksman.

The allied alien Invasion of Earth convinced some U.S. military commanders that they couldn't always leave the planet's defense in the hands of the JUSTICE LEAGUE OF AMERICA. The Human Defense Corps, an official branch of the U.S. armed forces, is composed of 10,000 non-superpowered soldiers selected from the ranks of those who have been decorated during previous alien campaigns. H.D.C. soldiers train in the orbital satellite Fort Olympus and in the Area 53 complex on the ocean floor. They are equipped with the very best military gear, including ES-2 pulsar rifles and robotic S.A.R.G.E. reconnaissance vehicles.

On the H.D.C.'s first mission to Bulgravia, Sergeant Kelly's squad ran into demonic vampires who melted when sprayed with "holy napalm." The vampires managed to snatch 66 soldiers and carry them off to the underworld, so the H.D.C. suited up to invade Hell and rescue their comrades. During this mission, Sergeant Kelly learned that a previous encounter with a vampire had left him part demon, and he now rules a realm of Hades in the name of the U.S. **DW**

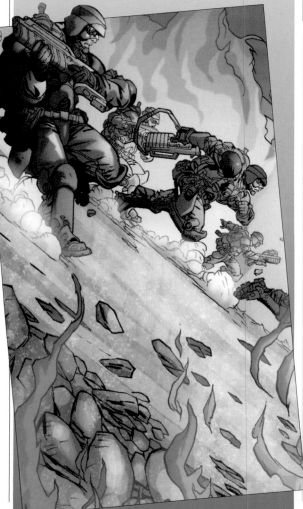

HUMAN TARGET

FIRST APPEARANCE ACTION COMICS #419 (December 1972)
STATUS Hero **REAL NAME** Christopher Chance
OCCUPATION Bodyguard, private detective **BASE** Mobile
HEIGHT 6ft **WEIGHT** 180 lbs **EYES** Blue **HAIR** Grey-black
SPECIAL POWERS/ABILITIES Olympic level athlete; skilled martial artist and marksman; an unparalleled master of disguise.

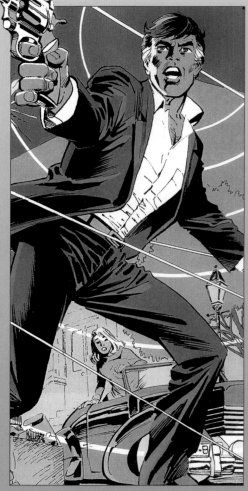

A master thespian able to assume any number of accents and, through make-up and body posture, imitate the physical identities of others, Christopher Chance is a superior bodyguard for hire. For a hefty price, Chance disguises himself as a client who believes he (or she) is in danger, and lures their would-be assailants out of hiding, drawing their fire on himself.

When Christopher was still a boy, he witnessed his father Philip's murder at the hands of a loan shark. Christopher tried to save his father by jumping in front of the killer's gun, but the thug brushed the young boy aside and emptied his gun into the elder Chance's body.

Traumatized by his father's death, the young Christopher vowed that no one else would suffer the fear his father did before he died. The young man spent years obsessively studying martial arts techniques and weaponry, training to become a top athlete. He became the ultimate method actor, impersonating others by living their lives. He eventually opened up a special kind of private investigation agency, and hired himself out as the Human Target.

Eventually the Human Target became addicted to impersonating clients—even the most unethical ones. He submerged his own personality so deeply that he forgot what it was like. Chance is now almost incapable of personal relationships, for he is never sure if the emotions he feels are his own, or those of someone he has imitated. **PJ**

HUNTER, RIP

FIRST APPEARANCE SHOWCASE #20 (June 1959)
STATUS Hero **REAL NAME** Ripley "Rip" Hunter
OCCUPATION Time-traveler **BASE** Formerly Vanishing Point
HEIGHT 5ft 11in **WEIGHT** 175 lbs
EYES Blue **HAIR** Blond (white as Hunter)
SPECIAL POWERS/ABILITIES Brilliant and resourceful; Time-Sphere can carry him and several others to any point in the past, present, or future. As Hunter, Rip possessed cybernetic limbs that enhanced his strength.

Rip Hunter developed a time machine while employed by Booster Gold International (see BOOSTER GOLD). Within this Time-Sphere, Hunter transported himself, Gold, and several associates into the 25th century, where they were stranded in a world devastated by nuclear war. Returning to his own time, Hunter became convinced that the impending apocalypse was engineered by the Illuminati, an ages-old secret society established by VANDAL SAVAGE. With his colleague Jeffrey Smith in tow, Hunter assembled the TIME MASTERS, a group dedicated to traveling through time to thwart the Illuminati's plans.

Hunter later embarked on solo time-traveling forays and encountered various heroes from different eras. He joined the LINEAR MEN and helped protect the time-space continuum through several chronal conflicts, including Zero Hour (see Great Battles, pp. 320–1). Hunter is credited with the discovery of Hypertime, temporal irregularities allowing for alternate histories and other possible futures. The stresses of time-travel have led to Hunter undergoing several cybernetic upgrades. The world believed Rip Hunter had died when the Quintessence erased the Linear Men from existence. However, Rip remains a member of the latter-day Forgotten Heroes. **SB**

HUNTER'S HELLCATS

FIRST APPEARANCE OUR FIGHTING FORCES #106 (April 1967)
STATUS Heroic commando unit **BASE** Vietnam
SPECIAL POWERS/ABILITIES Soldiers trained to do as they were ordered;
beyond their exceptional bravery, displayed in suicide missions
where they returned unhurt, none of the Hellcats possessed
unusual talents.

At the outbreak of World War II,
homicide detective Ben
Hunter (see CAPTAIN
HUNTER) was drafted and sent
overseas. Promoted to Sergeant, he
was asked to oversee a special
commando force comprised
entirely of criminals culled
from the Army stockade. These
hardcases at first refused his
authority until his fists
earned their respect.

Hunter's efforts galvanized the
men, turning them into a hard-
fighting team, who always returned
unscathed from their suicide missions to both the
European and Pacific Theaters of Operation. Hunter
himself survived the war and was promoted to Colonel.
He married and fathered twin sons who grew up to also
join the army—Major Nick Hunter and Captain Phil
Hunter. The latter served in the Green Berets. The boys
formed a tight bond, saving each other's lives during their
service in Vietnam. RG

HYBRID

FIRST APPEARANCE NEW TEEN TITANS (2nd series) #24
(October 1992)
STATUS Villain group **BASE** Mobile
MEMBERS AND POWERS
Mento Helmet gives its wearer, Steve Dayton, psychic powers.
Behemoth Vast superstrength; near invulnerability.
Gorgon Blind; snakes for hair allow sight and transform
adversaries into stone.
Harpi Flight; projection of forcebolts; razor-sharp claws.
Prometheus Superstrength; speed; body armor powered by a
constantly renewing energy source, Promethium.
Pteradon Wings allow flight at supersonic speeds.
Scirocco Flight; generation of gale-force winds; sandblasts.
Touch-N-Go Can steal kinetic energy of anyone she touches.

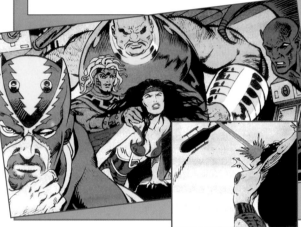

Driven insane by the powers of the psychokinetic
helmet he invented, Steve Dayton (MENTO) plotted to
recreate a twisted version of the DOOM PATROL. To
this end, Mento began gathering mortally wounded
victims of engineered, near-fatal accidents from around
the world and transforming their bodies with the
self-regenerating element Prometheum. The results
were the Hybrid, a group of individuals driven to
commit crimes by Mento's psychic powers. Scirocco,
Touch-N-Go, and PROMETHEUS swelled the ranks of
the Hybrid, but only Behemoth and Touch-N-Go
were loyal to Mento's madness. The rest of the Hybrid
resisted his power at every turn.

Using the Hybrid, Mento went after his stepson,
Gar Logan, now known as BEAST BOY, and Logan's
companions in the TEEN TITANS. After several
skirmishes with the Titans, the Hybrid broke free of
Mento's spell, and Mento's mind was cleansed of its
insanity by RAVEN. Confused by their place and
purpose in the world, the Hybrid took Dayton
on a journey to discover their new lives. Tragically,
many of them returned to villainy. Harpi, Touch-
N-Go, and Scirocco joined the sorceress CIRCE
in an all-out assault on Manhattan, and Gorgon,
Prometheus, and Behemoth were counted as
among the "Fallen Players of the House," a fight
club run by the villainess ROULETTE. PJ

*HIDEOUS CREATIONS A twisted version of the
Doom Patrol, the Hybrid were tragic figures
forced by Mento's telepathic madness into
villainy and destruction.*

HUNTRESS

FIRST APPEARANCE THE HUNTRESS #1 (April 1989)
STATUS Hero **REAL NAME** Helena Bertinelli
OCCUPATION Vigilante **BASE** Gotham City
HEIGHT 5ft 11in **WEIGHT** 148 lbs **EYES** Blue **HAIR** Black
SPECIAL POWERS/ABILITIES Excellent gymnast and hand-to-hand
combatant; a deadly shot with her miniature crossbow.

The Huntress has much in common with BATMAN: as
children, both lost their parents through senseless violence and
both adopted costumed identities to become avengers of the
night. The Huntress, however, exhibits a violent ruthlessness
that is a perennial irritant to the Dark Knight. This
temperamental failing has prevented Batman from giving the
Huntress his official sanction.

Helena Bertinelli was the daughter of a *Mafioso*
commanding one of Gotham's notorious "Five
Families." A rival family killed her parents in the Palm
Sunday Massacre, and Helena fled to Sicily where she
learned combat skills from her cousin Sal. Upon returning
to Gotham she donned the cowl of the Huntress, vowing to
track down the assassin who had slain her family.

The Huntress briefly served with
Justice League International (see
JUSTICE LEAGUE OF AMERICA) but
preferred to stay close to Gotham. She
frequently butted heads with Batman
over her pitiless methods, never more
so than when she mistakenly appeared
to have executed the city's mobsters.

*TRANSFORMATIONS Childhood trauma turned
Helena into the Huntress, and her costume has
changed to reflect her shifting moods.*

She eventually proved her innocence and Batman nominated her for
membership in the JLA hoping to smooth her violent edges. He revoked
her membership after she threatened to kill the villain PROMETHEUS.

During Gotham's time as a federally-designated, quake-ravaged No
Man's Land, the Huntress defended survivors as BATGIRL II. She
recently accepted a temporary position with the government agency CHECKMATE.
The Huntress has friends outside the Bat-family, including the QUESTION,
and occasionally works with ORACLE and BLACK CANARY as an informal
member of the Birds of Prey. DW

*ON TOP OF HER GAME The Huntress can
dispatch foes many times her size with ease.
Most recently, she has lent her fighting skills
to the newest team of Outsiders.*

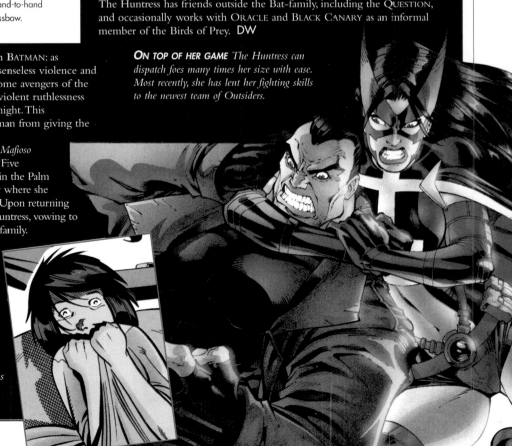

ALIEN RACES AND WORLDS

IN THE LAST FEW DECADES, humankind has learned that Earth is by no means alone in the universe as a planetary home to sentient life. From the galactic rim of the Milky Way to the furthest reaches of the known universe, advanced aliens abound. However, not all of these peoples are peaceful. Remarkably, some even resemble *Homo sapiens*, albeit with markedly different internal physiologies. A few exhibit superpowers, either a benefit of the atmospheres of their native worlds, or as a result of exposure to lesser gravities, the rays of a different colored sun, or any number of environmental factors. The following are the most notable alien races that have had more than close encounters with Earth, either as strange visitors from other planets or invaders from beyond.

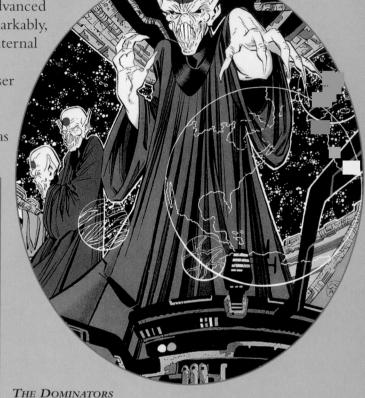

THE KRYPTONIANS

From planet Krypton, some 50 light-years from Earth, the Kryptonian race were once renowned for their incredible advances in the science of cloning. For millennia, cloning banks extended the lives of the elite on Krypton and allowed them unfettered pursuit of knowledge and the arts. However, the terrorist group BLACK ZERO, long opposed to cloning, launched civil wars that lasted thousands of years. In the year 105/892, Black Zero destroyed the capital city of Kandor with a thermonuclear device that initiated a slow-burning chain-reaction in planet's core. Eventually, Krypton's radioactive core spread "Green Death" across the planet, a plague that killed millions. In time, the planet exploded, killing every last Kryptonian save one, the infant Kal-El, who was rocketed to Earth and became SUPERMAN, whose legend spread throughout the universe.

KANDOR *Krypton's greatest city paid a terrible price during the civil war over cloning.*

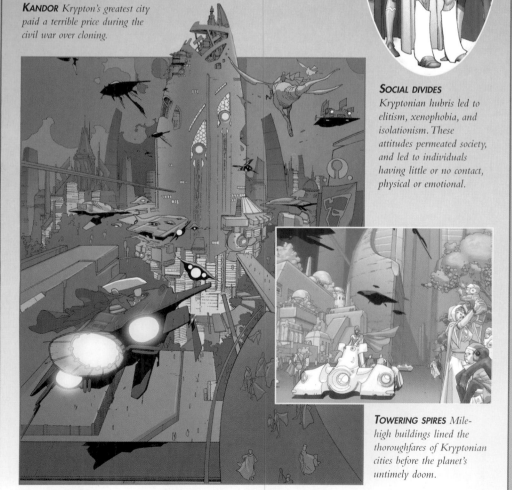

SOCIAL DIVIDES *Kryptonian hubris led to elitism, xenophobia, and isolationism. These attitudes permeated society, and led to individuals having little or no contact, physical or emotional.*

TOWERING SPIRES *Mile-high buildings lined the thoroughfares of Kryptonian cities before the planet's untimely doom.*

THE DOMINATORS

The Dominators are a race of conquerors divided into a rigid caste system. On their homeworld, Dominion, thousands of light years from Earth, the Dominator hierarchy is determined by the size of a red disk worn on the forehead. The Dominators have invaded many worlds with advanced weapons created from a melding of technology and nature.

When the Dominators discovered that humans possessed a latent metagene capable of manifesting superpowers, they feared that Earth would spawn a super-race that would pose a threat to the Dominion. Assembling an alliance of nine alien worlds and extraterrestrial empires—including the Citadel, Daxam, Durla, Gil'Daan, Khundia, Okaara, the Psions, and Thanagar—the Dominators led an invasion of Earth and nearly wiped out its meta-human heroes with a power-negating metagene bomb (*see* Great Battles, pp. 320–1). The Dominators will remain a threat to galactic peace well into the 31st century, when the LEGION OF SUPER-HEROES will fight to thwart the Dominion from overrunning the United Planets.

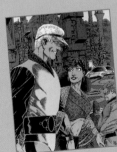

DAXAMITES *hail from the planet Daxam and are renowned for their biochemical research. The rays of a yellow sun have similar empowering effects on them as on Superman. Daxamites are fatally allergic to lead but, by the 31st century, they will have found an antidote, enabling them to become renowned space explorers. Notable Daxamites include Green Lantern Sodal Yat and Lar Gand, M'onel of the Legion of Super-Heroes.*

DURLANS *are shape-shifters, able to mimic any object or being's molecular pattern. Their home, Durla, was ravaged by the Six-Minute War, a nuclear holocaust that took place thousands of years ago. Durlans are nomadic, living in tribes who prohibit off-worlders from visiting their radiation-scarred planet, which the Durlans rarely leave. On the only occasion they have invaded Earth, they were defeated by the world's meta-humans.*

THE KHUNDS

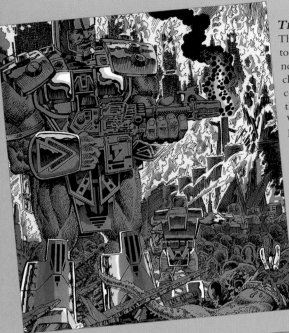

The Khund race are predisposed to aggression. On Khundia, it is not uncommon for citizens to challenge one another to physical combat, likely to the death, for the slightest offense or insult. While allied with the Dominators, the Khunds razed Melbourne, Australia, seeking to establish a beachhead in overrunning Earth. After Earth's super heroes routed this Dominion-led invasion, the humbled Khunds returned to their homeworld. For a thousand years, the Khunds remained confined to their own space. However, the war drums of Khundia will beat loudly once more in the 31st century.

THE PSIONS

Cold-blooded and utterly emotionless, the Psions were originally alien reptiles evolved to higher intelligence by Maltusian scientists. The Maltusians left their world to become the GUARDIANS OF THE UNIVERSE and these creatures, who called themselves Psions, continued their evolutionary progress. Eventually the Psions traveled into space to find their creators. The Guardians, concerned with other matters, encouraged the Psions to continue their quest for knowledge. The Psions, however, took scientific experimentation to the extreme, often selling their cruel services to other alien cultures. Psion research under the banner of the Citadel gave Tamaranean sisters K'oriand'r and Komand'r their star-bolt powers as STARFIRE and BLACKFIRE. The Psions added their scientific savvy to the Dominator-led invasion of Earth, and engaged in breeding experiments that crossed humans with the H'San Natall to create young superbeings briefly united as a team of TEEN TITANS.

THE TAMARANEANS

Although fierce fighters, Tamaraneans are a people who prefer peace to waging war. However, when the lush world of Tamaran was invaded by the Citadel, rulers of the Vegan Star System, King Myand'r's daughter Koriand'r, alongside her Teen Titans teammates, subsequently saved her homeworld from Citadel control.

Ultimately, Tamaran was destroyed by the Psions, forcing its people to settle on New Tamaran, which was in turn rendered uninhabitable by the star-consuming Sun-Eater. The Tamaraneans who were able to escape occupied Rashashoon, a world ruled by the reptilian Gordanians, former soldiers to the Citadel and lifelong enemies of Tamaran. Tamaraneans and Gordanians co-existed for a brief time before Rashashoon was obliterated by the world-razing IMPERIEX. The few remaining Tamaraneans are now a wandering people in search of a planet to call their own.

THE THANAGARIANS

The Thanagarians are known for their predatory civilization, based on the so-called "Hawkworld," Thanagar. Previously a slave planet of the Polaran Empire, Thanagar became a world markedly divided by class. Alien Downsiders live in the slums of Thanagarian cities, while native-born Thanagarians dwell aloft in floating cities high above the squalor and disease. Thanagarians also joined in the Dominators' invasion of Earth, supplying winged Hawkmen infantry for the planetary assault.

Following the Dominators' defeat, the Thanagarians returned to their own affairs. Unknown to many, Thanagarians traveled to Earth thousands of years prior to the Dominion-led invasion. Wreckage from a downed Thanagarian spacecraft provided the anti-gravity Nth Metal and presumably the inspiration for Egyptian Prince Khufu and his lover, Chay-Ara, to become HAWKMAN and HAWKGIRL in countless reincarnations throughout the ages to follow. SB

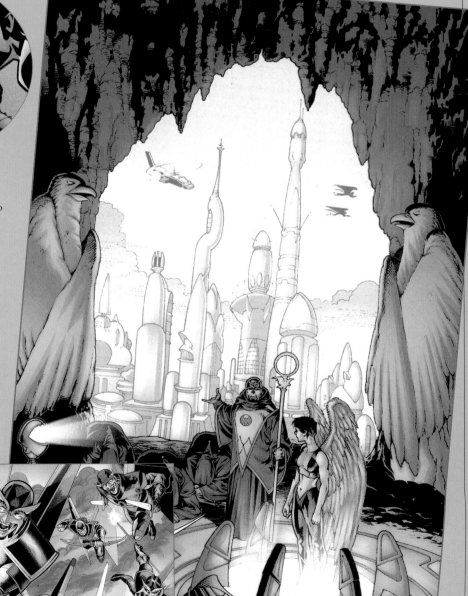

DARK WINGMEN *Few sights inspire more awe (or fear) than watching a squadron of winged Thanagarian Hawkmen descending from the skies in battle.*

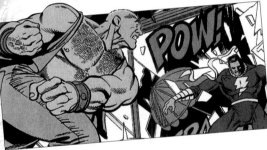

NIGHT CREATURE
Vampire Lord Andrew took no pleasure in biting maidens' necks and longed for a peaceful death.

IBAC

FIRST APPEARANCE CAPTAIN MARVEL ADVENTURES #8 (March 1942)
STATUS Villain **REAL NAME** Stanley Printwhistle
OCCUPATION Criminal **BASE** Fawcett City
HEIGHT 6ft 6in **WEIGHT** 240 lbs **EYES** Blue **HAIR** None
SPECIAL POWERS/ABILITIES Possesses the traits of history's worst villains, which make him super-strong and durable.

Petty criminal Stanley "Stinky" Printwhistle was never going to amount to much, until the day he was mysteriously granted the ability to summon forth the powers and abilities of four of the world's worst tyrants. Similar to CAPTAIN MARVEL, when Stinky shouts "Ibac," green flames envelop him and he is transformed from a scrawny man into a muscular brute. Using the cunning and immorality of Ivan the Terrible, Cesare Borgia, Attila the Hun, and Caligula, Ibac terrorized the citizens of Fawcett City. He battled Captain Marvel on numerous occasions, including a failed attempt to kidnap Mary Batson (MARY MARVEL) from her home. He has fought the Big Red Cheese and Mary Marvel with little success ever since. **RG**

ICEMAIDEN

FIRST APPEARANCE SUPER FRIENDS #9 (December 1977); (in DCU continuity) WHO'S WHO #9 (October 1985)
STATUS Hero **REAL NAME** Sigrid Nansen
OCCUPATION Scientist, adventurer **BASE** Norway
HEIGHT 5ft 5in **WEIGHT** 127 lbs **EYES** Blue **HAIR** White
SPECIAL POWERS/ABILITIES Can project ice and snow from her body, usually from her hands.

Sigrid Nansen grew up in Norway, the daughter of a biochemistry specialist working with a group of scientists trying to duplicate the powers of Norway's legendary Ice-people. Sigrid volunteered to be a test subject and was given ice- and sno-projecting powers. She joined the GLOBAL GUARDIANS as her country's representative, Icemaiden.

When the Norwegian government discovered the *real* Ice-people, one of their number, Tora Olafsdotter, also joined the Global Guardians. Tora made Sigrid feel somewhat inadequate and Sigrid decided to quit the team. However, when Tora, known as ICE, was killed by the OVERMASTER while a member of the JUSTICE LEAGUE OF AMERICA, Sigrid revived the name of Icemaiden in honor of her. She also joined the JLA for a brief time.

Icemaiden was almost killed herself when an invading group of WHITE MARTIANS, known as the Hyperclan, destroyed the Justice League's floating headquarters. Later still, Icemaiden was impersonated by the villainous MIST II in a disastrous, albeit brief, revival of Justice League Europe. **PJ**

I...VAMPIRE

FIRST APPEARANCE HOUSE OF MYSTERY #290 (March 1981)
STATUS Hero (deceased) **REAL NAME** Andrew Bennett
OCCUPATION Vampire **BASE** Mobile **HEIGHT** 6ft 3in
WEIGHT 180 lbs **EYES** Red **HAIR** Black with white streak
SPECIAL POWERS/ABILITIES Immortal; possessed all the traditional powers of a vampire, preternatural strength and speed, and the ability to transform into mist, or morph into a bat or wolf.

More than 400 years ago, Lord Andrew Bennett enjoyed the favor of Queen Elizabeth I after distinguishing himself during England's war with Spain. He was also in love with Mary Seward, the queen's lady-in-waiting. One night, Bennett was attacked by a vampire, and its bite transformed him into a bloodthirsty creature of the night. Still devoted to Bennett despite his vampirism, Mary offered herself to him and was also transformed. However, Mary embraced her bloodlust while Bennett was tortured by his. The lovers parted and Mary founded the cult of the Blood Red Moon, a vampiric secret society Bennett sought to destroy in the centuries following.

Some 20 years ago, Bennett's efforts were aided by vampire hunters Dimitri Mishkin and Deborah Dancer, who helped Bennett to stop the Blood Red Moon from unleashing a serum that spread vampirism. The serum killed Bennett since he was already a vampire, but it gave Dancer the strength to kill Mary Seward once and for all. Months later, Bennett found himself restored to undead life. He only returned to the peace of the grave with DOCTOR FATE's aid. No one knows if he will ever walk the Earth again. **SB**

ICE

FIRST APPEARANCE (As Icemaiden II) JUSTICE LEAGUE INTERNATIONAL #12 (April 1988);
(as Ice) JUSTICE LEAGUE INTERNATIONAL #19 (November 1988)
STATUS Hero (deceased) **REAL NAME** Tora Olafsdotter
OCCUPATION Adventurer **BASE** New York City
HEIGHT 5ft 7in **WEIGHT** 136 lbs
EYES Blue **HAIR** White
SPECIAL POWERS/ABILITIES Projected ice and snow from her body, usually as bolts of cold from her hands.

Tora Olafsdotter was the daughter of the king of the magical Ice-people who lived in a hidden mountain range in Norway. When engineer Rod Schoendienst discovered the Ice-people, he made a pact with Tora's father that allowed her to leave their kingdom, and introduced the princess to DOCTOR MIST and the GLOBAL GUARDIANS. She joined the team as the second ICEMAIDEN, replacing Sigrid Nansen, and became fast friends with Beatriz DaCosta, the Green Fury (*see* FIRE). After the Guardians lost their U.N. funding, Tora and Beatriz hounded the MARTIAN MANHUNTER until he admitted them into the JUSTICE LEAGUE OF AMERICA. Changing her name to Ice, Tora fought with the League for years and briefly dated Guy Gardner, the third GREEN LANTERN. Tragically, Ice was killed by the OVERMASTER when his alien CADRE invaded Earth. **PJ**

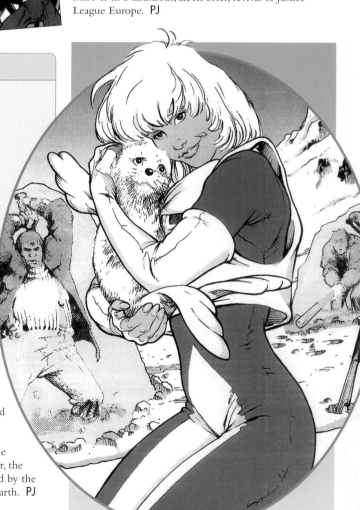

ICICLE II

FIRST APPEARANCE INFINITY, INC. #34 (January 1987)
STATUS Villain **REAL NAME** Cameron Mahkent
OCCUPATION Member of the Injustice Society **BASE** Mobile
HEIGHT 5ft 11in **WEIGHT** 155 lbs **EYES** White **HAIR** White
SPECIAL POWERS/ABILITIES Can fire ice and snow or drastically lower the temperature of his surroundings.

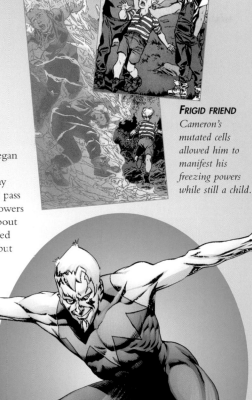

FRIGID FRIEND
Cameron's mutated cells allowed him to manifest his freezing powers while still a child.

ICICLE I Armed with a cold ray gun, Dr. Joar Makhent was a frequent foe of the first Green Lantern.

Cameron Mahkent is the son of the original Icicle, Dr. Joar Mahkent, a costumed villain whose career began in the 1940s. Joar Mahkent's prolonged exposure to his special cold-ray gun altered his genetics, allowing him to pass on a biological version of his freezing powers to his son. Cameron is not too happy about his father's legacy—one of the unintended side effects is his albino pigmentation—but has exploited the Icicle name to carve out his own criminal career. Bitter that his father left most of his vast fortune to the FLASH II after both men perished during the Crisis (see Great Battles, pp. 320–1), the new Icicle has cultivated a taste for violence and murder.

The Icicle II served as a member of Injustice Unlimited and battled INFINITY, INC. Later encounters set him against STARMAN, the new Star-Spangled Kid, and S.T.R.I.P.E. Most recently he has signed on with Johnny Sorrow's INJUSTICE SOCIETY (see also SORROW, JOHNNY) and continues to serve with that organization, despite Sorrow's apparent death. Efforts by the JUSTICE SOCIETY OF AMERICA to recruit Icicle II to the cause of good have been rebuffed. **DW**

IMMORTAL MAN

FIRST APPEARANCE STRANGE ADVENTURES #177 (June 1965)
STATUS Hero **REAL NAME** Various
OCCUPATION Adventurer **BASE** Mobile
HEIGHT 6ft 2in **WEIGHT** 220 lbs **EYES** Blue **HAIR** Blond
SPECIAL POWERS/ABILITIES Immortal; reincarnated thousands of times over the centuries; athletic and fighting skills are only average.

In 48,000 BC, a newly fallen meteor bathed two men in radiation, making them immortal. The more belligerent of the two, Vandar Adg II, eventually adopted the name VANDAL SAVAGE. The other man took a glowing jewel from the heart of the exploded fireball and gained the reincarnation powers of the Immortal Man. Living through an endless series of personas, the Immortal Man tended to help humanity, while immortals like Savage try and bend humankind to their will. Immortal Man repeatedly sacrificed his life to save others. Each time he was reborn and assumed a new identity. He led other adventurers known as the Forgotten Heroes. When he went missing, they discovered that he was the captive of Vandal Savage and that the Immortal Man, Savage, and RESURRECTION MAN all owed their abilities to tektites that had been contained in the meteor that had struck Earth some 50,000 years previously. Immortal Man ultimately sacrificed his life to eradicate the Warp Child's threat to the world. Immortal Man has not been seen since. **RG**

IGNITION

FIRST APPEARANCE ADVENTURES OF SUPERMAN # 512 (Sept. 2000)
STATUS Villain **REAL NAME** Unknown
OCCUPATION Super-villain **BASE** Mobile
HEIGHT 7ft 5in **WEIGHT** 1,568 lbs **EYES** Red **HAIR** Unknown
SPECIAL POWERS/ABILITIES A good, if not exceptional athlete; armored weapon of mass destruction; able to fly and project energy blasts from his giant metal hands.

Little is known about the engine of evil known as Ignition, except that he was first conceived by the crazed JOKER when the Clown Prince of Crime possessed MISTER MXYZPTLK's reality-altering abilities. Ignition was one of several super-villains the Joker created to populate a "Bizarro-Earth" where evil supplanted good. When SUPERMAN defeated the Joker and stripped him of Mxyzptlk's incredible powers, the "Bizarro-Earth" ceased to exist, although Ignition and other Joker-imagined evils—BIZARRO and SCORCH included—somehow managed to escape to the real Earth. There, Ignition joined GENERAL ZOD's campaign to destroy Superman. When Zod was killed in battle with the Man of Steel, Ignition beat a hasty retreat. However, it is likely this metal menace will be back for a rematch. **SB**

IMAN

FIRST APPEARANCE SUPERMAN (2nd series) ANNUAL #12 (2000)
STATUS Hero **REAL NAME** Diego Irigoyen
OCCUPATION Adventurer **BASE** Mexico City, Mexico
HEIGHT 7ft 6in **WEIGHT** 1,425 lbs (in armor) **EYES** Blue **HAIR** Blond
SPECIAL POWERS/ABILITIES A good, if not exceptional, athlete; armored exoskeleton increases strength, invulnerability, and durability to superhuman levels.

Diego Irigoyen is a renowned scientist and a hero in his home town, Mexico City. He was recognized as a student of huge ability by several major universities around the world, and was also well-known as a computer genius. His doctorate thesis was on super heroes and astronomical discoveries, which revolutionized astrophysics. Diego then became S.T.A.R. Labs's second astronaut and a winner of the prestigious Wayne Foundation Scholarship to Yale University.

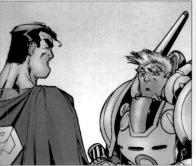

While Diego was on a mission in outer space, his mother was kidnapped and brutally murdered. Upon his return, Diego vowed to use all of his scientific achievements in the name of justice. Designing a robotic exoskeleton equipped with numerous powers, Diego became the Mexican super hero Iman. Diego idolizes SUPERMAN and his ideals of freedom and justice, and tries to live up to them each day. **RG**

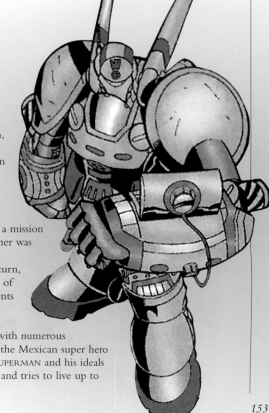

IMPERIEX

FIRST APPEARANCE SUPERMAN #153 (February 2000)
STATUS Malevolent entity REAL NAME None
OCCUPATION Devourer of galaxies BASE Mobile
HEIGHT Unknown WEIGHT Unknown EYES Purple HAIR None
SPECIAL POWERS/ABILITIES Armor contains the explosive energies of the
Big Bang; assisted by legions of Imperiex-Probes.

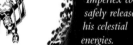

OUR WORLDS AT WAR Blasting Imperiex-Probes
with his heat vision, the Man of Steel stood
between Imperiex and the end of the universe.

The omnipotent Imperiex may be even older than
creation itself. His hunger for cosmic power led him to
sweep toward Earth—the lynchpin that holds the
universe together—leaving scores of dead worlds in his
wake. SUPERMAN and MONGUL defeated an advance
Imperiex-Probe, but Imperiex's main army proved to be
far more than the Man of Steel could handle alone.

Dozens of alien species united behind Earth's defenders
in the Imperiex War (see Great Battles, pp. 320–1),
commanded by the unlikely alliance of DARKSEID of Apokolips and U.S. President Lex Luthor (see LUTHOR,
LEX). Imperiex-Probes killed thousands, and city-sized "hollower" machines devastated Topeka, Kansas (and
seven other locations), in their attempts to drill through the planet to unravel space-time and unleash a new Big
Bang. Imperiex himself sat in Earth's orbit like a small moon, witnessing the devastation with unfeeling eyes.

The war took a turn for the worse when Queen HIPPOLYTA, Earth's original WONDER WOMAN, died in
battle. Meanwhile, BRAINIAC 13 exploited the chaos to advance his own agenda. Superman and Luthor
championed a risky plan: by using Apokoliptian technology and magic channeled through the Atlantean
sorcerer TEMPEST, they could send both Imperiex and Brainiac 13 back in time 14 billion years to the
original Big Bang. Their Herculean efforts miraculously succeeded.

In the aftermath of the terrible Imperiex War, Superman
temporarily incorporated a black background into his costume's
"S" shield in honor of the fallen. Imperiex has not returned
to the present day, but his awesome threat remains—and
always will. DW

TIMELESS Sent
back to the dawn
of creation,
Imperiex could
safely release
his celestial
energies.

INFINITY, INC.

FIRST APPEARANCE ALL-STAR SQUADRON #25 (September 1983)
STATUS Hero team (disbanded) BASE Formerly Stellar Studios
NOTABLE MEMBERS AND POWERS
Star-Spangled Kid (founder and later Skyman) Wields cosmic belt.
Fury II Mother to current Sandman. **Northwind** Winged wonder
from Feithera. **Silver Scarab** Armored protector. **Jade** Has emerald
skin and energy. **Obsidian** Master of shadow. **Brainwave, Jr.**
Master telepath. **Nuklon (see Atom-Smasher)** Can change size.
Doctor Midnight Surgeon and athlete. **Wildcat II** Superb hand-to-
hand combatant. **Hourman II** Miraclo pill gives strength and agility.

After the children of several members of the JUSTICE
SOCIETY OF AMERICA were rebuffed by the team, the Star-
Spangled Kid proposed that they form a group of their
own, Infinity, Inc. The Kid owned Stellar Studios and the
team operated from there. Information provided by the
ULTRA-HUMANITE resulted in the unmasking of the
members of Infinity, Inc. at a live, televised press
conference, effectively revealing the true identities of the
first HAWKGIRL, the first HAWKMAN, and MISS AMERICA.
After several successful exploits, the JSA offered to admit the
entire roster into its ranks, but the younger team declined.

Later, Doctor Midnight, HOURMAN II, and WILDCAT II
were admitted. One of their opponent teams, Helix, went
on trial, resulting in Mister Bones (see DIRECTOR BONES)
being remanded to the custody of Infinity, Inc. While
battling HARLEY QUINN and SOLOMON GRUNDY, Mister
Bones was slammed against Skyman, the former Star-
Spangled Kid, killing the hero instantly with his cyanide
touch. Infinity, Inc. avenged Skyman's death but their
Stellar Studios headquarters burned to the ground.
Demoralized, the team disbanded forever. RG

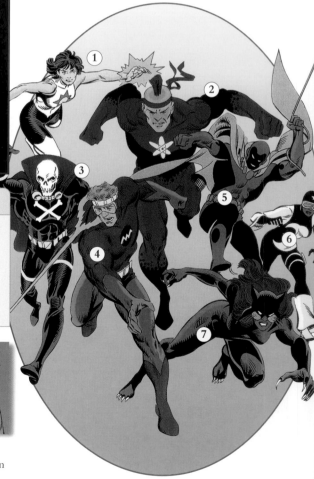

INDIGO

FIRST APPEARANCE TITANS/YOUNG JUSTICE: GRADUATION DAY #1
(Early July 2003)
STATUS Hero REAL NAME None
OCCUPATION Adventurer BASE New York City
HEIGHT 5ft 11in WEIGHT 220 lbs EYES Blue HAIR None
SPECIAL POWERS/ABILITIES A sophisticated cyborg with great strength,
speed, and the ability to fly.

A mysterious, blue cyborg-girl
from some point in the future
inflicted serious damage on the
members of the TEEN TITANS and
YOUNG JUSTICE when she
unwittingly unleashed a defective
SUPERMAN Robot, who killed
Teen Titan Lilith and TROIA. In a
state of shock, both teams disbanded, unaware that Troia
has been reborn "a world away." ARSENAL wanted to train
Indigo, and welcomed her into his newly formed team,
the OUTSIDERS, with fellow members NIGHTWING,
METAMORPHO, THUNDER III, and JADE. RG

INFINITY, INC. 1) Jade 2) Nuklon 3) Mister Bones
4) Brainwave, Jr. 5) Obsidian 6) Doctor Midnight 7) Wildcat II

INFINITY MAN, THE

FIRST APPEARANCE THE FOREVER PEOPLE (1st series) #1 (March 1971)
STATUS Hero **REAL NAME** None
OCCUPATION Inapplicable **BASE** Mobile
HEIGHT 6ft 4in **WEIGHT** 247 lbs **EYES** Unknown **HAIR** Unknown
SPECIAL POWERS/ABILITIES Flight, telekinesis, superstrong, invulnerable;
can alter the structure of matter and project waves of energy.

A cosmic being with unimaginable
powers, the Infinity Man comes
from a realm where the
normal laws of physics do
not apply. Linked in some
way to the NEW GODS
known as the FOREVER
PEOPLE, the Infinity Man will
instantly trade positions with
the Forever People, no
matter how great the
distance, whenever they
touch their Mother Box
computer and speak the
word "Taaru." After using his
abilities on their behalf, the Infinity Man departs and the
Forever People return to their original location.

During a past adventure, the Forever People swapped
places with the Infinity Man and found themselves
stranded on the distant planet Adon when their champion
seemingly died in battle with DEVILANCE the Pursuer. The
Infinity Man returned several times after that, but has
not been seen in some time. It is even possible that he has
ceased to exist. DW

INJUSTICE GANG

FIRST APPEARANCE (I) JUSTICE LEAGUE OF AMERICA (1st series)
#111 (May 1974); (II) JLA #9 (Sept. 1997); (III) JLA #34 (Oct. 1999)
STATUS Villains **BASE** Base: (I, II, III) A satellite orbiting Earth
MEMBERS AND POWERS
Libra (deceased) His special scales were an "energy transmortifier"
device that could steal half of any universal energy form.
Chronos I Inventor of time-inspired weapons.
Mirror Master I (deceased) Used special mirrors to commit crimes.
Poison Ivy Can control vegetation.
Scarecrow Special gas instills unadulterated fear in victims.
Shadow-Thief Can become a two-dimensional shadow being.
Tattooed Man Tattoos on his body can come to life.

The first Injustice Gang was a cadre of villains
gathered together by the mysterious Libra, who
coerced the Gang into tackling the JUSTICE LEAGUE
OF AMERICA to test his "transmortifier," an energy
stealing device. Libra transferred half of the stolen
energy of the Milky Way galaxy into his own body,
and was dispersed across the cosmos. Years later, Lex
Luthor (see LUTHOR, LEX) gathered six of the most
powerful villains on the planet, hoping to destroy
the JLA once and for all. This Injustice Gang was
defeated, leading Luthor to form a third incarnation
of the villainous team, who invaded the JLA
Watchtower. They were defeated by the League after
it was discovered that the Celestial Warbringer
MAGEDDON, was using Luthor and his henchmen as a
first-wave strike force in its invasion of Earth. PJ

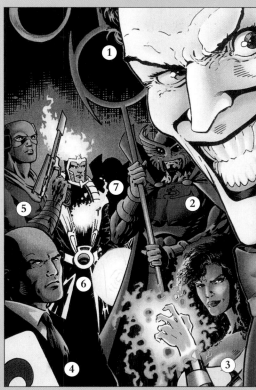

THE FIRST INJUSTICE GANG 1) Joker 2) Ocean Master
3) Circe 4) Lex Luthor 5) Mirror Master
6) Dr. Light 7) Jemm, Son of Saturn

INJUSTICE SOCIETY

FIRST APPEARANCE (I) ALL-STAR COMICS #27 (Nov. 1947); (II) JSA #10
(May 2000) **STATUS** Villains **BASE** Mobile **MEMBERS/POWERS**
Brainwave I (dead, psychic); **Fiddler** (violin-themed weapons);
Gambler (dead, master of disguise); **Harlequin I** (creates illusions);
Icicle I (dead, cold gun); **Per Degaton** (time-traveling despot); **The
Shade**; **Hazard**; **Solomon Grundy**; **Sportsmaster** (martial arts);
Thinker I (dead, evil genius); **Tigress I** (hunter); **Vandal Savage**,
Wizard; **Johnny Sorrow**, **Black Adam**, **Count Vertigo**, **Geomancer**
('quakes); **Icicle II**; **Killer Wasp** (humanoid insect); **Rival** (superspeed);
Shiv (cyborg); **Tigress II** (fighter); **Thinker II** (virtual consciousness).

The first Injustice Society of the World was the criminal counterpart to the JUSTICE
SOCIETY OF AMERICA in the 1940s. The Injustice Society's first attempt to conquer
America was quickly foiled by the JSA. The Injustice Society soon resurfaced, however,
committing a series of "Patriotic Crimes," whereby each villain, vying for leadership of the
team, had to steal a famous historical object.

Another incarnation of the Injustice Society emerged decades later and fought both the
JSA and the JUSTICE LEAGUE OF AMERICA. Soon after, the Society formed an alliance with
a race of underground beings and attempted to kill the JSA, but the villains were soundly
defeated and parted ways.

More recently, the WIZARD assembled a modern version of
the Injustice Society, called Injustice, Unlimited. He recruited
the Fiddler and the SHADE as well as the HAZARD I, the ICICLE
II, and the new Tigress. Injustice, Unlimited fought the
combined forces of INFINITY, INC. and the GLOBAL GUARDIANS
at an international trade conference in Canada, but were
ultimately defeated. The Wizard was apparently killed during the
battle, but later resurfaced when Injustice, Unlimited returned
under the command of the Dummy.

Years later, the Injustice Society was resurrected by the criminal
Johnny Sorrow (see SORROW, JOHNNY), who intended to use the
team to engage the JSA while he resurrected the otherdimensional
King of Tears. The JSA thwarted the new Injustice Society, and sent
most of its members to prison. PJ

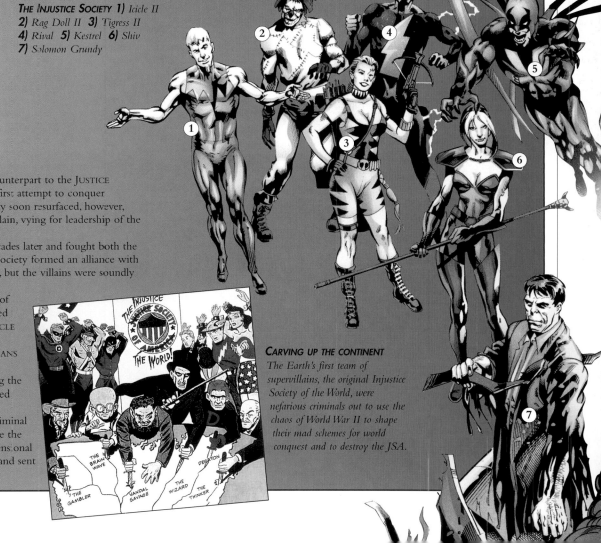

THE INJUSTICE SOCIETY 1) Icicle II
2) Rag Doll II 3) Tigress II
4) Rival 5) Kestrel 6) Shiv
7) Solomon Grundy

CARVING UP THE CONTINENT
The Earth's first team of
supervillains, the original Injustice
Society of the World, were
nefarious criminals out to use the
chaos of World War II to shape
their mad schemes for world
conquest and to destroy the JSA.

INSECT QUEEN

FIRST APPEARANCE LEGION OF SUPER-HEROES (4th ser.) #82 (July 1996)
STATUS Hero **REAL NAME** Lonna Leing
OCCUPATION Uncanny Amazer **BASE** Xanthu
HEIGHT 5ft 7in **WEIGHT** 137 lbs **EYES** Green **HAIR** Red
SPECIAL POWERS/ABILITIES Can transform part of her body into any insect form, thereby gaining that insect's abilities.

Lonna Leing was born in the 30th century on the planet Xanthu. She became Insect Queen, a member of Xanthu's team of government-funded teenage super heroes, the Uncanny Amazers.

Insect Queen was a prominent member of the Uncanny Amazers despite the rivalry between her team and Earth's team of teen heroes, the LEGION OF SUPER-HEROES. After the alien BLIGHT took over much of the universe, Xanthu was invaded by C.O.M.P.U.T.O.'s cyborg world, Robotica. Insect Queen, STAR BOY, and XS helped the Amazers evacuate millions of Xanthu's inhabitants from the Robotican forces that were consuming the planet. Along with the Legionnaires and Khund shocktroopers, Insect Queen helped destroy the Robotican transmitter that controlled the advancing droids. After BRAINIAC 5.1 disabled C.O.M.P.U.T.O. and Robotica, Insect Queen and the Amazers helped the populace of Xanthu recolonize their planet, settling in the megacity of Xanth Prime. **PJ**

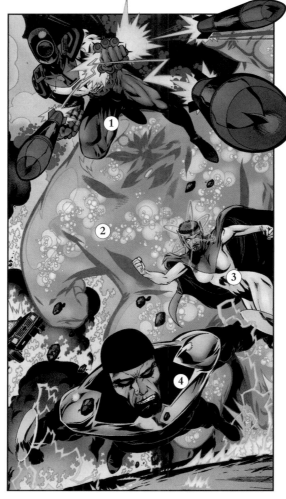

INTERNATIONAL ULTRAMARINE CORPS

FIRST APPEARANCE JLA #24 (December 1998)
STATUS Hero team **BASE** Superbia
ORIGINAL MEMBERS AND POWERS
  General Wade Eiling (ex-leader) Possesses tremendous strength; has huge incisors that can rend limbs or metal.
  Lt. Col. Scott Sawyer No longer has material substance, but inhabits the stealth weapon Warmaker One.
  Capt. Lea Corbin Has been transformed into the dimension-shifting 4-D.
  Dan Stone Transformed into living liquid and given the name Flow.
  Capt. John Wether Utilizes the "unified field harmonic" to wield atomic powers as Pulse 8.

General Wade Eiling (see GENERAL) initiated the Ultramarines project to create meta-powered soldiers loyal to the U.S. Four Marine Corps officers were exposed to Proteum, an artificial isotope, and gained amazing powers, but lost their humanity in the process. Under Eiling's command, they battled the JUSTICE LEAGUE OF AMERICA until they learned the general had gone insane. Following Eiling's betrayal, the Ultramarines became the new "Global Guardians" of Superbia, a city-state floating high above the nuclear ravaged ruins of Montevideo, Uruguay. After declaring themselves independent of any other nation, the team has since inducted VIXEN, JACK O'LANTERN III, Knight II and Squire III (see KNIGHT AND SQUIRE), and the Japanese hero Goraiko. Vixen and 4-D recently helped WONDER WOMAN battle CIRCE and her team of female super-villains. **RG**

THE ULTRAMARINES 1) *Warmaker One* **2)** *Flow*
3) *4-D* **4)** *Pulse 8.*

LOUCHE LINEUP *Intergang once included* **1)** *Well-trained Shock Troop commandos* **2)** *One of "Ugly" Mannheim's molls* **3)** *Faceless Gasser gunsels* **4)** *Cruel capo Bruno "Ugly" Mannheim* **5)** *Another of "Ugly" Mannheim's molls* **6)** *Sniveling second-in-command Louis Gillespie* **7)** *A Wall-Crawler.*

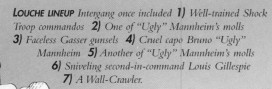

INTERGANG

FIRST APPEARANCE FOREVER PEOPLE (1st series) #1 (March 1971)
STATUS Villain team **BASE** Metropolis
MEMBERS AND CRIMINAL ASSOCIATES
Morgan Edge, Vincent Edge (former leaders); **Bruno "Ugly" Mannheim** (scarfaced former leader); **Boss Moxie** (current leader; clone of original); **Ferrous** (a trio of high-tech assassins); **Louis Gillespie** (no powers); **Mike "Machine" Gunn** (cybernetic gun-arms); **Thaddeus Killgrave** (evil scientist); **Ginny "Torcher" McCree** (wields fire); **Noose** (strangler with elongated fingertips); **Winslow Schott** (weapons inventor); **Zombie Twins** (killers).

WEAPON *"Machine" Gunn's clone had cybernetic arms that morphed into high-tech automatic weapons with self-replicating ammo.*

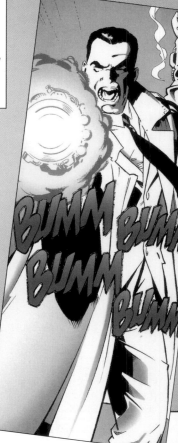

During the Prohibition era of the 1920s, the Metropolis underworld was ruled by Boss Moxie's Intergang. Eventually, Moxie died in a hail of bullets beside his moll Ginny "Torcher" McCree, gun-toting Mike "Machine" Gunn, and the bald killer known as Noose. Decades later, WGBS media mogul Morgan Edge reformed Intergang with himself as chief of its enforcement division of Gassers, Shock Troops, and Wall-Crawlers. This Intergang packed serious heat in the form of Apokoliptian weapons supplied by DARKSEID's master torturer DESAAD, who aided and abetted the organization in its clashes with SUPERMAN and ORION.

Intergang's conflicts with the Man of Steel continued with future TOYMAN Winslow Schott providing high-tech weapons until Morgan Edge was convicted of racketeering and jailed. Second-in command Bruno "Ugly" Mannheim briefly led Intergang before Edge's father, Vincent, took it over. Fugitive and former Cadmus Project geneticist (see GUARDIAN and NEWSBOY LEGION) Dabney Donovan cloned cell samples from original Intergang hooligans to create an inner circle that included a resurrected Boss Moxie, "Torcher" McCree, "Machine" Gunn, and Noose. With Moxie now back to being boss, Intergang is a smaller organization that makes greater use of the latest technology and of superpowered thugs as hired muscle. **SB**

CRIME CHIEFS *Organized crime in Metropolis continues to be dominated by Intergang.*

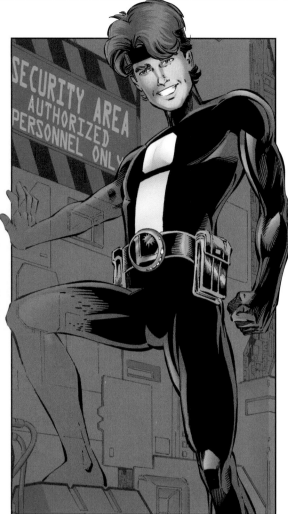

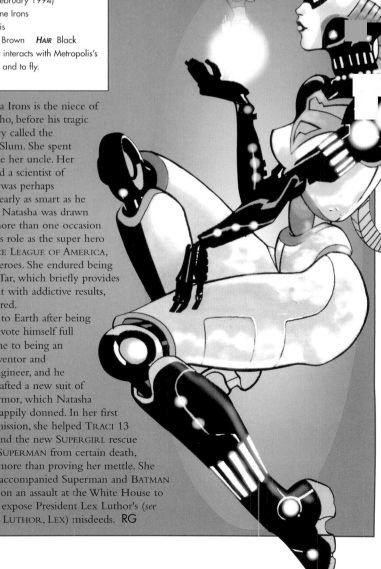

IRON CROSS

FIRST APPEARANCE JUSTICE LEAGUE TASK FORCE #10 (March 1994)
STATUS Villain **REAL NAME** Unrevealed
OCCUPATION Mercenary **BASE** Mobile
HEIGHT 6ft 4in **WEIGHT** 230 lbs **EYES** Brown **HAIR** Brown
SPECIAL POWERS/ABILITIES Appears to have meta-human strength and endurance, the limits of which have not been determined.

Pine Heights, Nebraska, seemed a quiet place, perfect to hide a white supremacist organization known as the ARYAN BRIGADE. The group first caught the U.S. government's attention when it developed a virus designed to wipe out all people of non-European origin. The government, in turn, asked for the JL Task Force's help (see JUSTICE LEAGUE OF AMERICA). A team consisting of MARTIAN MANHUNTER, ELONGATED MAN, BLACK CANARY, GYPSY, and HOURMAN I took on the Brigade. Iron Cross was the Aryan team's major muscle; however, little or nothing was known about his background. He nearly proved a match for the Manhunter but was finally beaten. He was subsequently recruited by the OVERMASTER for the second incarnation of the CADRE. He was once again defeated and has not been seen since. **RG**

IRONS, NATASHA

FIRST APPEARANCE STEEL (2nd series) #1 (February 1994)
STATUS Hero **REAL NAME** Natasha Jasmine Irons
OCCUPATION Adventurer **BASE** Metropolis
HEIGHT 5ft 2in **WEIGHT** 106 lbs **EYES** Brown **HAIR** Black
SPECIAL POWERS/ABILITIES Wears armor that interacts with Metropolis's future tech, enabling her to grow 60ft tall and to fly.

A genius, a novice, a legacy. Natasha Irons is the niece of John Henry Irons (see STEEL III) who, before his tragic death, owned a high-tech laboratory called the Steelworks in Metropolis's Suicide Slum. She spent her teenage years working alongside her uncle. Her cool, unconcerned façade concealed a scientist of formidable intellect, and her uncle was perhaps unaware that Natasha was in fact nearly as smart as he was. Despite Steel's best intentions, Natasha was drawn into the meta-human world. On more than one occasion she unobtrusively helped him in his role as the super hero Steel, working alongside the JUSTICE LEAGUE OF AMERICA, the world's greatest hero team of heroes. She endured being exposed to the superstrength drug Tar, which briefly provides humans with enhanced strength but with addictive results, though she now seems fully recovered.

When John Henry was returned to Earth after being in DARKSEID's thrall he chose to devote himself full time to being an inventor and engineer, and he crafted a new suit of armor, which Natasha happily donned. In her first mission, she helped TRACI 13 and the new SUPERGIRL rescue SUPERMAN from certain death, more than proving her mettle. She accompanied Superman and BATMAN on an assault at the White House to expose President Lex Luthor's (see LUTHOR, LEX) misdeeds. **RG**

INVISIBLE KID

FIRST APPEARANCE LEGIONNAIRES #0 (April 1993)
STATUS Hero **REAL NAME** Lyle Norg
OCCUPATION Legionnaire **BASE** Legion World, U.P. Space
HEIGHT 5ft 6in **WEIGHT** 140 lbs **EYES** Brown **HAIR** Brown
SPECIAL POWERS/ABILITIES Able to make all or part of his body invisible and, with great effort, is also capable of rendering others unseen; leader of the Legion's Espionage Squad; a scientist and inventor rivaled only by Brainiac 5.1.

Earthling Lyle Norg's prodigious interest in physics led him to the discovery of a serum that rendered him invisible at will by bending light around himself and his clothing to conceal either part of or all of his body. Initially, Lyle used his invisibility to become a stealthy spy for the United Planets, and then later as a member of the LEGION OF SUPER-HEROES. His exploits at that time remain classified, but Lyle's longstanding friendship with fellow Legionnaire CHAMELEON may be indicative of some time spent on the planet Durla, perhaps undertaking clandestine missions to bring that world and its shape-shifting peoples into the U.P.

For his own unrevealed reasons, Lyle had himself drafted into the LSH as Invisible Kid. In addition to proving himself to be a capable young hero, Lyle invented the Legion's flight rings (anti-gravity mechanisms that lift his teammates into action and have often saved Legionnaires' lives), and organized the top-secret Legion Espionage Squad, a sub-group that investigates concerns beyond the LSH's jurisdiction and whose members are only known to the Squad itself. Lyle's genius-level intellect and charisma have served him well in his previous tenures as leader of the LSH. **SB**

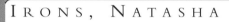

JACK O'LANTERN I, II & III

FIRST APPEARANCE (I) DC COMICS PRESENTS #46 (June 1982); (II) JUSTICE LEAGUE EUROPE ANNUAL #1 (1990); (III) PRIMAL FORCE #0 (October 1994)
STATUS Heroes **REAL NAMES** (I) Daniel Cormac; (II) Marvin Noronsa; (III) Liam McHugh
OCCUPATION (I) Global Guardian; (II) covert agent; (III) ultramarine
BASE (I) Mobile; (II) mobile; (III) Montevideo, Uruguay
HEIGHT (I) 6ft 2in; (II) 6ft 2in; (III) 5ft 11in
WEIGHT (I) 224 lbs; (II) 217 lbs; (III) 188 lbs
EYES (I) Green; (II) green; (III) blue
HAIR (I) Red; (II) red; (III) brown
SPECIAL POWERS/ABILITIES Mystical lantern provides powers of flight, flame projection, the ability to teleport, illusion casting, enhanced strength, fog creation; lantern's power is strongest at midnight. Jack O'Lantern III's body has mysteriously internalized several of the lantern's magical powers.

PUMPKIN POWER *All the Jack O'Lanterns have been joiners; the original was fiercely loyal to the Global Guardians.*

PEACEKEEPER *The latest Jack O'Lantern defends the innocent as an Ultramarine.*

Daniel Cormac received his powers through a magic lantern given to him by the fairy queen Maeve. He defended his native Ireland in his costumed identity of Jack O'Lantern until summoned by DOCTOR MIST to join the team of international heroes known as the GLOBAL GUARDIANS. There, he fell in love with teammate OWLWOMAN and took it hard when the United Nations withdrew funding from the Guardians in favor of Justice League International (*see* JUSTICE LEAGUE OF AMERICA). Looking for a new calling, he fell under the control of the evil Queen Bee (*see* QUEEN BEE II) and apparently died, replaced by the Queen Bee's duplicate. Owlwoman rescued him from a dungeon in the Middle Eastern nation of Bialya, but he died soon afterward.

The imposter Jack O'Lantern II worked for the Queen Bee and tried to take Daniel Cormac's place among the Global Guardians. Jack O'Lantern II shot and wounded media mogul Maxwell Lord (*see* LORD HAVOK) and accidentally killed Global Guardian LITTLE MERMAID before perishing in a bomb blast.

Jack O'Lantern III took up the heroic role made famous by his cousin Daniel. A former factory worker, Liam McHugh inherited Cormac's lantern, which he called the "pumpkin of power", and soon joined the Leymen (*see* PRIMAL FORCE). After his first few adventures he discovered that his body had somehow internalized the lantern's magical energies and he no longer needed to carry it into battle. Jack O'Lantern III was a founding member of the international peacekeeping corps, the INTERNATIONAL ULTRAMARINE CORPS. **DW**

JADE

FIRST APPEARANCE ALL-STAR SQUADRON #25 (September 1983)
STATUS Hero **REAL NAME** Jennifer-Lynn Hayden
OCCUPATION Photographer **BASE** New York City
HEIGHT 5ft 3in **WEIGHT** 123 lbs **EYES** Green **HAIR** Green
SPECIAL POWERS/ABILITIES Generates and manipulates emerald energies similar to the forces of the Starheart-fueled power ring worn by her Green Lantern father. Jade can make this power pulse take tangible form. Unlike Green Lantern's power ring, Jade's energy is self-renewing, also enabling her to fly.

Daughter of Alan Scott (the first GREEN LANTERN) and his occasional foe Rose Canton (ROSE AND THORN), Jennifer-Lynn Hayden grew up in an adoptive home. In adulthood, Jenny-Lynn discovered her true origins when a star-shaped birthmark on her left palm blazed alight and her skin and hair were turned bright green by the emerald energies that suffused her. After reuniting with her fraternal twin brother, Todd Rice (OBSIDIAN), Jennie-Lynn became the super heroine Jade and eventually learned the identities of her biological parents. A member of the second-generation superbeings known as INFINITY, INC., Jade gave up adventuring for a time and began a romance with Kyle Rayner (the fifth Green Lantern) that eventually led to her renewed interest in heroics. Jade is currently a member of the OUTSIDERS, where she casts her own bright and formidable limelight. **SB**

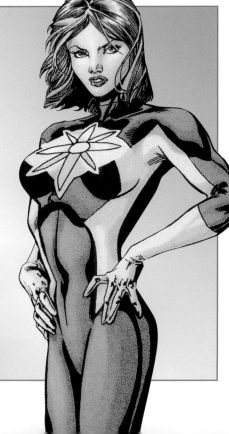

JANISSARY

FIRST APPEARANCE JLA ANNUAL #4 (Summer 2000)
STATUS Hero **REAL NAME** Selma Tolon
OCCUPATION Red Crescent physician; sorceress **BASE** Bursa, Turkey
HEIGHT 5ft 6in **WEIGHT** 131 lbs **EYES** Almond **HAIR** Black
SPECIAL POWERS/ABILITIES Superstrength; flight; wields the mystical scimitar of Sultan Suleiman the Great and the spell-casting Eternity Book of Merlin the Magician.

Selma Tolon, a native Turk and devout Muslim, studied medicine at California's Stanford University. Upon graduation, Dr. Tolon returned to Turkey to aid earthquake victims. During one relief effort, Tolon discovered two mystical talismans that empowered her to become the Janissary, a scimitar-wielding spell-caster. Upon the Janissary's Eternity Book is an inscription in Arabic: "He who has the virtue to draw this blade from the sand shall guide this once great empire into a magnificent tomorrow." Tolon possessed such virtue and fulfilled the prophecy. She met the JUSTICE LEAGUE OF AMERICA when Etrigan the DEMON conspired with rogue Turkish General Ankha Kazim, possessed by the demon Iblis, to recover the Eternity Book from her. Iblis was defeated and the Janissary remains Turkey's staunchest defender. **SB**

JEMM, SON OF SATURN

FIRST APPEARANCE JEMM, SON OF SATURN #1 (September 1984)
STATUS Hero **REAL NAME** Jemm
OCCUPATION Prince **BASE** Saturn
HEIGHT 6ft 6in **WEIGHT** 241 lbs **EYES** Yellow **HAIR** None
SPECIAL POWERS/ABILITIES Born with superior strength, even for a Saturnian, as well as the unique ability to fly; jewel on forehead denotes he is his people's prophesied "savior," and it allows him to probe the emotions of others or to project powerful force beams.

An exiled Saturnian prince known as Jemm traveled to Earth, believing that his childhood sweetheart, white Saturnian Syrra, had sought refuge there. He left behind a people torn apart by racial civil war between red and white Saturnians. Lex Luthor (*see* LUTHOR, LEX) captured Jemm, planning to use the alien's psionic powers to assist his new INJUSTICE GANG. With the Philosopher's Stone—actually a cosmic "map of all time and space" called the Worlogog— and Jemm's powers, the rogues nearly defeated the JUSTICE LEAGUE OF AMERICA. Aided by the 853rd Century technological being known as HOURMAN III, the JLA prevented the destruction of the Worlogog, and took the severely traumatized Jemm into its protective custody. Some time later, J'Onn J'Onzz (MARTIAN MANHUNTER) helped stop the red and white forces, who opposed the marriage of white Saturnian Cha'rissa to red Saturnian Jemm, from killing each other. Jemm is finally back home on Saturn, living happily with his new wife. **RG**

JERICHO

FIRST APPEARANCE TALES OF THE TEEN TITANS #43 (June 1984)
STATUS Hero and villain   **REAL NAME** Joseph William Wilson
OCCUPATION Former super hero   **BASE** Mobile
HEIGHT 6ft   **WEIGHT** 195 lbs   **EYES** Green   **HAIR** Blond
SPECIAL POWERS/ABILITIES Can control bodies of others by making eye contact; when he enters bodies he speaks with their words and voices.

Son of the notorious mercenary DEATHSTROKE THE TERMINATOR, Joseph Wilson lost his ability to speak when the assassin Jackal slit his throat with a knife during a botched kidnapping. But Joseph had also been born a meta-human, thanks to the genetic experiments performed on his father by the U.S. military. Under the codename Jericho, Joseph became a member of the TEEN TITANS.

Jericho's career with the Titans took a tragic turn when he tried to save his teammate RAVEN from her demonic father, TRIGON. Possessed by Trigon's sinister energy, Jericho turned into a true villain and tried to destroy the Titans. To save them, Deathstroke stabbed his son through the heart. However, unknown to his former friends, Jericho had taken refuge in Deathstroke's body at the moment of his passing. Captured by CYBORG, Jericho's soul is trapped on a computer disc at Titans Tower (*see Amazing Bases,* pp. 120–1). **DW**

MASTERMIND During his time as a villain, Jericho also became head of the Wildebeest Society.

JESTER, THE

FIRST APPEARANCE SMASH COMICS #22 (May 1941)
STATUS Hero   **REAL NAME** Charles "Chuck" Lane
OCCUPATION Police detective (retired)   **BASE** New York City
HEIGHT 5ft 11in   **WEIGHT** 179 lbs   **EYES** Blue   **HAIR** Black
SPECIAL POWERS/ABILITIES Delighted in confounding his opponents with tricks derived from slapstick comedy; a formidable hand-to-hand fighter and dauntless detective.

A rookie cop in New York City during the opening days of World War II, Lane was the direct descendant of a medieval court fool. When inspired to take up the colorful costume of a masked vigilante, Lane naturally became the Jester and joked his way into action. Many a criminal came to regret hearing his distinctive high-pitched laughter and the jingling bells on his Jester's costume. During the War, the Jester served as a member of both the ALL-STAR SQUADRON and the FREEDOM FIGHTERS. Once Lane was promoted to the rank of detective, the Jester's jingling dwindled, and he eventually hung up his cap and bells for good in 1954. Now retired from the N.Y.P.D., Lane is still alive and kicking. Despite his somewhat ludicrous former costumed identity, Chuck Lane takes his heritage quite seriously and looks back proudly to his days as a madcap crime fighter. **SB**

JINX

FIRST APPEARANCE TALES OF THE TEEN TITANS #56 (August 1985)
STATUS Villain   **REAL NAME** Unrevealed
OCCUPATION Sorceress   **BASE** Mobile
HEIGHT 5ft 9in   **WEIGHT** 141 lbs   **EYES** Brown   **HAIR** Unrevealed
SPECIAL POWERS/ABILITIES A powerful magician, Jinx's fiery temper leads her to take the direct-action approach, creating crushing force bolts or suddenly dissolving matter rather than employing the more usual illusions and subtleties of magic.

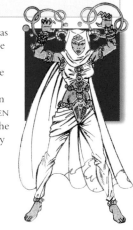

The East Indian sorceress Jinx was a student of an occult master. She murdered her teacher after learning his sorcerous secrets. She was recruited by GIZMO to strengthen the FEARSOME FIVE in their attempts to destroy the TEEN TITANS. With the Titans out of the way, the Five were confident they would rapidly reap riches through crime. Instead, they were defeated and Jinx was sent to India for trial. She was returned to the U.S. when local authorities could not control the mage.

She has worked with VILLAINY INC. of late and met defeat at the hands of WONDER WOMAN. Recently, she has rejoined the reconstituted Fearsome Five and fought the OUTSIDERS. **RG**

JONES, DARWIN

FIRST APPEARANCE STRANGE ADVENTURES #1 (September 1950)
STATUS Hero   **REAL NAME** Darwin Jones
OCCUPATION Scientific Investigator   **BASE** Washington, D.C.
HEIGHT 6ft   **WEIGHT** 185 lbs   **EYES** Brown   **HAIR** Brown (graying)
SPECIAL POWERS/ABILITIES Possesses a brilliant deductive mind further enhanced by encyclopedic scientific knowledge spanning many diverse fields of study.

Darwin Jones comes from a long line of policemen, extending back to his ancestor, Sir Robert Peel. Although he studied science in college, he solved several mysteries on campus, proving that deduction was in his blood. He eventually became chief of the D.S.I. (Department of Scientific Investigations), a post that combined research and police work. After years investigating all manner of scientific strangeness, Jones retired from the D.S.I. He was active during the Crisis (*see Great Battles,* pp. 320–1), using his skills to examine the time anomalies caused by the destruction of infinite Earths.

With other scientists, Jones created the Gestalt, a shared computer intelligence linking their great minds. Jones left the Gestalt after it accidentally created the Humbug, an anarchic artificial being stopped by the second ATOM. Jones continues to consult on investigations into the unknown. **SB**

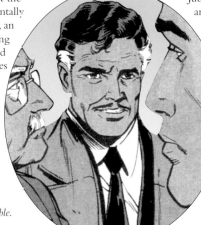

DASHING Handsome and intelligent, Darwin Jones is often the first expert called upon to explain the unexplainable.

JOTO

FIRST APPEARANCE THE TEEN TITANS (2nd series) #1 (October 1996)
STATUS Hero   **REAL NAME** Isaiah Crockett
OCCUPATION Super hero   **BASE** Ivy University, Rhode Island
HEIGHT 5ft 10in   **WEIGHT** 188 lbs   **EYES** Brown   **HAIR** Brown
SPECIAL POWERS/ABILITIES Can generate intense heat from his bare hands and melt anything—even solid steel; possesses a quiet strength and is looked up to by his fellow teammates.

Isaiah Crockett believed he was a normal kid from a normal family until, at age 16, he learned he was the result of a breeding program by aliens, the H'San Natall, to create a race of sleeper agents. Joining with the other H'San Natall hybrids—ARGENT II, RISK, and PRYSM—as well as the second ATOM, Isaiah became a member of a new TEEN TITANS team. He was initially known as Slagger, but his father instead suggested Joto, the Swahili word for "heat." Joto seemingly perished in battle with the villain Haze, but his spirit survived within Prysm's body. When the H'San Natall revived Joto's corpse, he "jumped" his consciousness back into his body. After the Teen Titans disbanded, Joto returned to his studies at Ivy University. He still aids the super hero community. **DW**

JUDOMASTER

FIRST APPEARANCE SPECIAL WAR SERIES #4 (November 1965)
STATUS Hero   **REAL NAME** Rip Jagger
OCCUPATION Adventurer   **BASE** Mobile
HEIGHT 5ft 11in   **WEIGHT** 190 lbs   **EYES** Blue   **HAIR** Blond
SPECIAL POWERS/ABILITIES Martial arts expert; also skilled with various weapons, although prefers to use fists in combat.

During World War II, Sgt. Rip Jagger of the U.S. Army was stationed on a Pacific island populated by expatriate Japanese who opposed their country's aggression. After he saved a young girl from a sniper's bullet, the girl's grateful father taught him martial arts. As the hero Judomaster, he used his skills to free the island from invading Japanese soldiers. Jagger later returned to his unit, operating as Judomaster on solo secret missions and with Tiger, a young Japanese orphan who had highly impressed Jagger with his martial-arts prowess.

Judomaster battled evil alongside Tiger after the war ended. Eventually the pair went their separate ways and Judomaster journeyed to the mystical land of Nanda Parbat. There he lived for many decades, remaining young and vital despite being in his eighties.

Not long ago, Judomaster joined the group of heroes called the L.A.W. (Last American Warriors), and helped to defeat his embittered former sidekick, Tiger, who had descended into madness and become the villainous Avatar, who tried to overrun Earth with a horde of demons. **SB**

THE JOKER

THE CLOWN PRINCE OF CRIME

FIRST APPEARANCE BATMAN #1 (Spring 1940)
STATUS Villain   **REAL NAME** Unknown
BASE Gotham City
OCCUPATION Anarchist; mass-murderer; professional criminal
HEIGHT 6ft 5in   **WEIGHT** 192 lbs   **EYES** Green   **HAIR** Green
SPECIAL POWERS/ABILITIES
Though not especially strong or skilled in fighting, the Joker is nonetheless a deadly combatant. Previously, he has demonstrated adeptness at chemistry, concocting his own poisonous Joker Venom, a weapon of mass distraction that leaves its victims with death-rictuses resembling his own maniacal leer. The Joker often wields deadly joke props or gags such as an acid-squirting boutonnière or BANG!-proclaiming flag pistol that doubles as a spear gun. However, he also plays the straight man in his blackly comedic campaigns of terror and will use conventional weapons—anything from a single-shot Derringer tucked in the brim of his hat to an operational nuclear warhead concealed within the trunk of his garish Jokermobile.

THE JOKER IS UNDENIABLY the most dangerous and unpredictable foe BATMAN has ever encountered. He literally reinvents himself each morning, concocting deadly new laugh-riots to bedevil the Dark Knight and his allies. While safely confined within the impregnable walls of Arkham Asylum for the Criminally Insane, the Joker has spun investigating psychiatrists various yarns concerning his troubled origins. Most of his tales can be dismissed, but a few facts remain that give some insight into how this leering lunatic came into being.

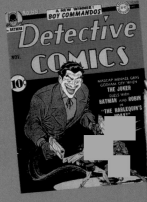

TWO-GUN CLOWN
The Joker mocks the Dynamic Duo in an early Detective Comics' *cover appearance.*

THE JOKER'S ORIGINS
The man who would become the Clown Prince of Crime was once a petty thief duped into donning the mask of the Red Hood and acting as costumed figurehead to thugs bent on robbing the Ace Chemical Plant in Gotham City. In that regard, he may have been a failed comedian coerced to crime following the sudden and tragic deaths of his wife and unborn child. Only the Joker knows the truth. Thwarted by Batman, the Red Hood fell into a vat of toxic chemicals that bleached his skin bone white, turned his hair emerald green, and left him with a crazed, ruby-red, malignant rictus for a smile. Driven utterly insane, the Joker fixated upon Batman as his arch-nemesis and has broken practically every law in Gotham City and beyond.

CHEMICAL PEEL *The Red Hood crawls from a toxic bath. From now on, villainy will wear a leering face.*

MASS MURDER, MALIGNANCY, AND MAYHEM
The Joker is probably the only criminal ever to qualify as a mass murderer, spree slayer, and serial killer. And that's just before lunch. He has committed robberies, assaults, extortion, and all manner of crime. His victims are innumerable. The Bat-Family especially has suffered from the Joker's sick humor. In a fit of anarchic glee, the Joker killed the second ROBIN (Jason Todd), beating him near to death with a crowbar before blowing the poor Boy Wonder and his mother to smithereens. He shot Barbara Gordon (ORACLE) through the spine, ending her crime-fighting career as BATGIRL. The Clown Prince of Crime then photographed Barbara's bleeding body, hoping the images would drive her kidnapped father, Commissioner Gordon (*see* GORDON, JAMES W.), insane.

THE JOKER'S WEAPONS
The Clown Prince of Crime has no compunction against using weapons of mass destruction, including his own patented Laughing Gas, a nerve toxin that kills within seconds and leaves his victims giggling themselves to death. Not long ago, the Joker was imprisoned for attempting to bomb Broadway with a tactical nuclear weapon.

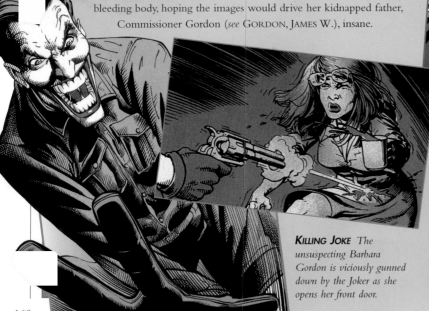

KILLING JOKE *The unsuspecting Barbara Gordon is viciously gunned down by the Joker as she opens her front door.*

HARLEY QUINN
Before he met Dr. Harleen Quinzel, the Joker's court-appointed psychotherapist, the Joker was more concerned with making mayhem than whoopee. But in Quinzel, he found a kindred spirit, winning her over to his side of the lunatic fringe. As HARLEY QUINN, she became murderous moll to the Joker's guffawing gangster. However, the Joker and Harley are now estranged, reuniting under passion, and breaking up when he tries to beat her to the punchline…often with a mallet!

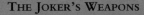

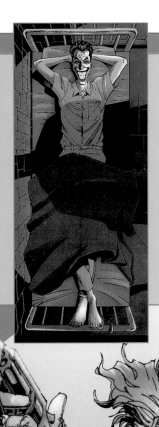

ARKHAM ASYLUM

Certifiably crazed, the Joker was previously remanded to Gotham's Arkham Asylum for the Criminally Insane. However, Arkham has long suffered an almost revolving-door policy where its more dangerous charges are concerned, especially the Clown Prince of Crime. Despite his officially documented mental state, the Joker is cunning and crafty, knowing full well how to manipulate Arkham's doctors and administrators to achieve his anarchic ends.

THAT CERTAIN SMILE *The Joker enjoys putting on a happy face when his favorite foe Batman pays him a visit in his Arkham cell!*

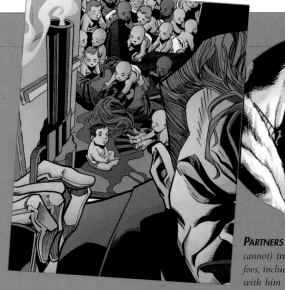

PSYCHO KILLER *During No Man's Land, the Joker used defenseless babies to lure Commissioner Gordon's wife, Sarah, to her doom, shooting her in cold blood.*

PARTNERS IN CRIME *While most villains do not (or cannot) trust the Joker, some of Batman's arch-foes, including Rā's al Ghūl, have collaborated with him when it suits their roguish interests.*

THE LAST LAUGH

Believing that he was dying from a brain tumor, the Joker escaped Slabside Maximum Security Correction Facility. He "Jokerized" the inmates and loosed them upon an unsuspecting world. In fact the Joker wasn't dying at all—he was the victim of a prison orderly's practical joke. The Joker's globe-trotting suicide run skidded to a halt when NIGHTWING pummeled him to death. However, Batman had the last laugh and resuscitated his foe so that he could not escape justice. The Joker has since committed more vile acts, often striking at the citizens of Gotham to spite the Batman. **SB**

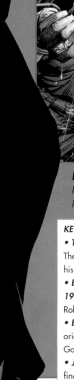

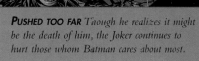

PUSHED TOO FAR *Though he realizes it might be the death of him, the Joker continues to hurt those whom Batman cares about most.*

KEY STORYLINES

• *THE JOKER #1-9 (MAY 1975–SEPTEMBER 1976):* The Joker becomes the first Bat-Villain to star in his own comic book series, lasting nine issues.
• *BATMAN #426-429 (DECEMBER 1988–JANUARY 1989):* The Joker murders Jason Todd, the second Robin, leading Batman to pursue the Clown Prince.
• *BATMAN: THE KILLING JOKE (1988):* The Joker's origins are explored as he cripples Barbara Gordon to prove a point to the Dark Knight.
• *JOKER: THE DEVIL'S ADVOCATE (1996):* The Joker is finally made responsible for his sins and sentenced to Death Row, but for a crime he did not commit!

THE JUSTICE LEAGUE OF AMERICA

THE WORLD'S GREATEST HEROES

First appearance THE BRAVE & THE BOLD #28 (March 1960)

Status Team of Earth's greatest heroes

Base The JLA Watchtower, the Moon

Official members and powers

Superman The Man of Steel; possessor of superpowers beyond those of mortal men.

Martian Manhunter Alien telepath; shape-changer; gifted with strength, flight, and enhanced vision.

Batman The Dark Knight; master combatant and strategist, coordinating the team's counterattacks.

Wonder Woman Princess from Themyscira; gifted with strength, speed, wisdom, and flight by the gods themselves.

Aquaman King of the Seven Seas; has incredible strength, ability to mentally control sea life, and a mystic hand.

Green Lantern V Wielder of the emerald power ring; protector of space sector 2814.

Flash III The fastest man alive, capable of hyper-velocities; channels the Speed Force to fight crime; Speed Force surrounds him with a frictionless protective aura.

They are Earth's premier defense team and for the last decade have seen to it that the basic human rights of liberty and justice remain paramount to all citizens. They are the Justice League of America, comprised of the best of the best. Ever since Superman ushered in the modern heroic age, Earth has needed protection, from megalomaniac supervillains and especially, from greedy alien tyrants with hitherto undreamed-of technologies and nightmarish weapons of mass destruction. Even when the team has suffered internal strife, they have rallied, recognizing their obligations to all of mankind. Their reputation has spread not only beyond this solar system but beyond this plane of existence.

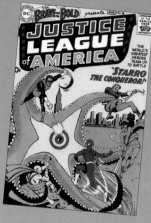

PREMIER LEAGUE The JLA heroes first came together to battle a giant alien starfish!

JUSTICE LEAGUE DETROIT

Being a super hero is a tough life! Various stresses in the personal lives of the team caused rifts from time to time. In the wake of an invasion by the alien Debris, the JLA was reorganized by Aquaman, who called for full-time commitment from each League member. In the aftermath, only Aquaman, the ELONGATED MAN, the Martian Manhunter, and ZATANNA remained. However, the roster soon began to expand when STEEL I, VIBE, and the VIXEN joined. Hank Heywood I, Steel's grandfather and namesake, offered the JLA headquarters in a warehouse in Detroit that became known as the Bunker. This incarnation of the League was tragically cut short when Vibe and Steel II were killed in action.

THE DETROIT LINEUP (clockwise from top) Martian Manhunter, Zatanna, Steel II, Elongated Man, Vixen, Vibe, Gypsy, Aquaman.

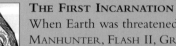

THE FIRST INCARNATION

When Earth was threatened by Appellax aliens, the MARTIAN MANHUNTER, FLASH II, GREEN LANTERN II, AQUAMAN, and BLACK CANARY II joined forces as the JLA to defeat these invaders. Inspired by the appearance of these powerful new heroes, J'Onn J'Onzz ended decades of hiding, publicly appearing as the Martian Manhunter. A short time later, plasma aliens invaded Earth, and the hero TRIUMPH gathered SUPERMAN, the Martian Manhunter, Flash II, Green Lantern II, Aquaman, and Black Canary II to defeat them. During the fight, Triumph was trapped in a temporal anomaly and disappeared from the timestream.

THE SECRET SANCTUARY

The team's first headquarters, the Secret Sanctuary, was in Rhode Island, and secretly financed by Oliver Queen (the first GREEN ARROW). A teenage "cool cat" called Lucas "Snapper" Carr (see CARR, SNAPPER) helped install the team's high-tech gear, designed by Ted Kord (later BLUE BEETLE II). Snapper became the team's official mascot. After functioning as JLA members in all but name, Superman and BATMAN formally joined.

JL INTERNATIONAL

This team was discredited by GLORIOUS GODFREY's smear campaign, but a more powerful line-up was introduced, with the enigmatic Maxwell Lord (see LORD HAVOK) pulling the strings. The United Nations formally recognized the JLA as global peacekeepers. Later, the JLI split into two branches, Justice League America and Justice League Europe. Lord decided to make use of the reformed members of the Injustice League, along with the former alien Green Lantern G'NORT and the Scarlet Skier, as the short-lived Justice League Antarctica. The entire JLA, its reserves, and the JSA stopped SONAR's bid for power in Europe. Afterwards, Justice League Europe took the name Justice League International. The U.N. authorized the creation of a JL Task Force, a team led by the Martian Manhunter, intended for use on missions calling for discretion, and one which would recruit most members for a single case.

TOWER OF POWER JL International continued to add team members, dispatching them via embassies scattered around the seven continents.

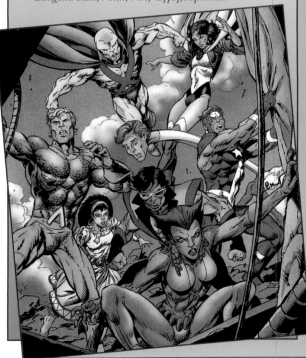

TASK FORCE J'onn J'onzz supervised a team of fledgling heroes, training them between crises.

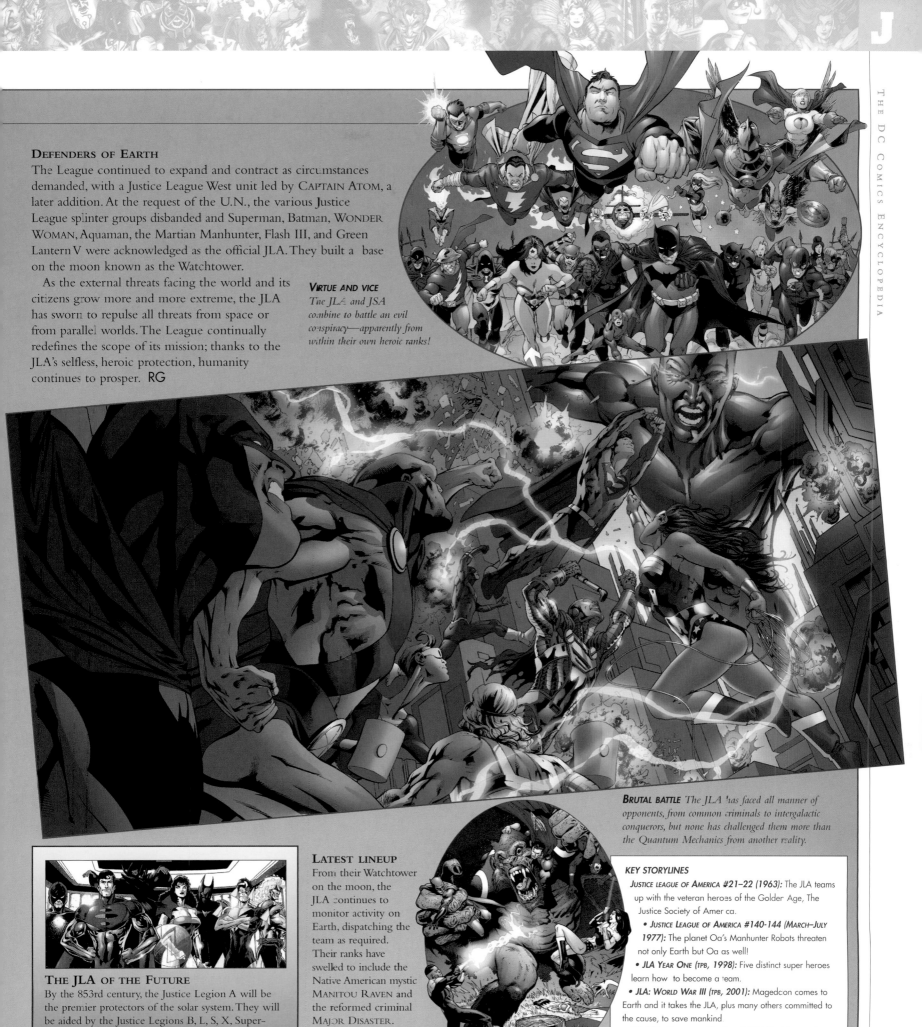

DEFENDERS OF EARTH

The League continued to expand and contract as circumstances demanded, with a Justice League West unit led by CAPTAIN ATOM, a later addition. At the request of the U.N., the various Justice League splinter groups disbanded and Superman, Batman, WONDER WOMAN, Aquaman, the Martian Manhunter, Flash III, and Green Lantern V were acknowledged as the official JLA. They built a base on the moon known as the Watchtower.

As the external threats facing the world and its citizens grow more and more extreme, the JLA has sworn to repulse all threats from space or from parallel worlds. The League continually redefines the scope of its mission; thanks to the JLA's selfless, heroic protection, humanity continues to prosper. **RG**

VIRTUE AND VICE
The JLA and JSA combine to battle an evil conspiracy—apparently from within their own heroic ranks!

BRUTAL BATTLE *The JLA has faced all manner of opponents, from common criminals to intergalactic conquerors, but none has challenged them more than the Quantum Mechanics from another reality.*

THE JLA OF THE FUTURE

By the 853rd century, the Justice Legion A will be the premier protectors of the solar system. They will be aided by the Justice Legions B, L, S, X, Super-Zoomorphs, Union, Young Justice Legion S, and Primate Legion.

LATEST LINEUP

From their Watchtower on the moon, the JLA continues to monitor activity on Earth, dispatching the team as required. Their ranks have swelled to include the Native American mystic MANITOU RAVEN and the reformed criminal MAJOR DISASTER. Others, such as the ATOM, remain available on an as-needed basis.

KEY STORYLINES

JUSTICE LEAGUE OF AMERICA #21–22 (1963): The JLA teams up with the veteran heroes of the Golden Age, The Justice Society of America.

• *JUSTICE LEAGUE OF AMERICA #140-144 (MARCH–JULY 1977):* The planet Oa's Manhunter Robots threaten not only Earth but Oa as well!

• *JLA YEAR ONE (TPB, 1998):* Five distinct super heroes learn how to become a team.

• *JLA: WORLD WAR III (TPB, 2001):* Magedcon comes to Earth and it takes the JLA, plus many others committed to the cause, to save mankind

• *JLA/JSA: VIRTUE AND VICE (TPB, 2001):* Earth's premier teams take on the combined threat of Johnny Sorrow and an enraged Despero.

THE DC COMICS ENCYCLOPEDIA

THE JUSTICE SOCIETY OF AMERICA

THE BEST OF THE BEST

FIRST APPEARANCE ALL-STAR COMICS #3 (Winter 1940)
STATUS Hero team **BASE** New York City
CURRENT MEMBERS AND POWERS
Green Lantern I Wields solidified emerald energy generated by the Starheart.
Flash I Ability to run at super-speeds and vibrate through objects.
Wildcat I Championship boxer with mystical "nine lives."
Hawkman Wears wings and harness made of anti-gravity Nth metal.
Hawkgirl Wears wings and harness made of anti-gravity Nth metal.
Sand Can transform into sand-like form and travel along the Earth's fault lines.
Mister Terrific II (chairman) Olympic-level athlete and genius in every field of study.
Power Girl Flight, superstrength, enhanced speed, and invulnerability.
Stargirl Cosmic converter belt provides enhanced strength, agility, and ability to fire electric stars.
Jakeem Thunder Controls powerful fifth-dimensional genie.
Captain Marvel Mystically-based powers of flight, superstrength, enhanced speed, and boosted wisdom.
Doctor Mid-Nite II Can see in non-visible wavelengths of light.
Hourman II Enhanced speed, strength, and agility provided for a one-hour window; occasionally can see one hour into the future.

THEY ARE THE WORLD'S FIRST and greatest super-group, formed at a time when "meta-humans" were still a new concept and free people everywhere faced the threat of annihilation from Adolf Hitler's Third Reich. They have survived throughout the decades, waxing and waning in synch with the national character to reflect the public's love–hate relationship with its super heroes. Several of the founding members are active today, even as they enter their nineties, thanks to a time-slowing radiation bath received during an early case. Living legends, they are the standard-bearers for all who followed in their footsteps. They are the Justice Society of America, the only hero team that SUPERMAN looks up to.

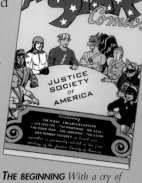

THE BEGINNING With a cry of "For America and democracy," the JSA begins its adventures.

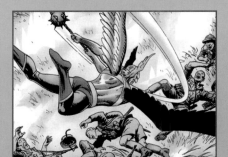

WINGED WONDER Hawkman's physical and mental strength make him the backbone of the JSA.

A WORLD AT WAR

Costumed crime fighters started appearing in the late 1930s; how it wasn't until November of 1940 that the numbers of these "my men," as they were then called, had grown to permit the formati the Justice Society of America. Eight of the country's top heroes— GREEN LANTERN, the FLASH, the SPECTRE, DOCTOR FATE, the SANDMAN I, the ATOM, HOURMAN I, and HAWKMAN—banded to to stop Hitler's invasion of Britain and to save U.S. President Ro from Nazi assassins. Calling themselves the Justice Society of Am they became an unstoppable force for good against the Axis pow In the wake of Pearl Harbor, the U.S. government established the ALL-STAR SQUADRON, which brought together every costumed h

AN EVER-CHANGING LINEUP

The JSA became one of the All-Star Squadron's active sub-groups. During this time the JSA also went by the alternate name of the Justice Battalion. Throughout the war, members came and went as they cycled through active, reserve, and honorary status. Prominent JSAers included Johnny Thunder (see THUNDER, JOHNNY), DOCTOR MID-NITE I, MISTER TERRIFIC I, HAWKGIRL, STARMAN, MISS AMERICA, and the time-traveling HIPPOLYTA, the Golden Age WONDER WOMAN.

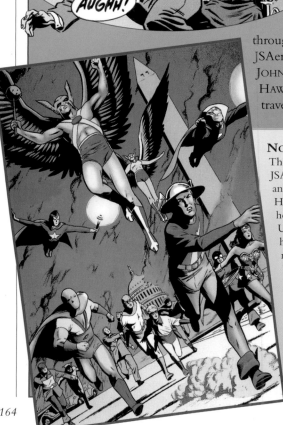

NO MORE HEROES

The All-Star Squadron ceased to exist after V-J Day, but the JSA remained, battling major villains such as VANDAL SAVAGE, and its villainous counterpart, the INJUSTICE SOCIETY. However, now the war was over, public tolerance for super heroics was fading fast. In 1951, a joint congressional Un-American Activities Committee accused the JSA of harboring communist sympathies and demanded that its members publicly unmask as a sign of their patriotism. They refused, and regretfully retired the Justice Society. Decades passed, the flame of organized crime fighting kept alive through non-superpowered teams such as the SEA DEVILS and the CHALLENGERS OF THE UNKNOWN and lesser lights like the Justice Experience. The JSA still existed, however, occasionally reforming for special cases.

ON THEIR WAY OUT The retirement of the JSA marked the end of the Golden Age of super heroes.

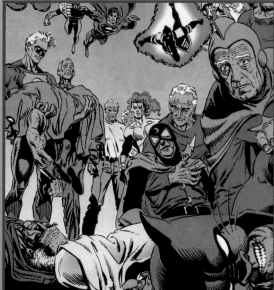

RAGNAROK!

The JSA seemed to have met its final end when the Flash, Green Lantern, Hawkman, Hawkgirl, the Atom, Doctor Mid-Nite, Hourman, Johnny Thunder, Starman, the Sandman, WILDCAT, and SAND agreed to battle gods for all eternity in Limbo to prevent Ragnarok, the end of the world. Luckily "eternity" lasted only a couple of years, and the JSA soon returned. The crisis known as Zero Hour (see Great Battles, pp. 320–1) proved a deadlier threat. The villain EXTANT killed the Atom, Doctor Mid-Nite, and Hourman, and Flash and Green Lantern declared an end to the JSA.

THE MODERN ERA

The DARK LORD Mordru's murder of the Sandman triggered the current formation of the JSA, featuring old stalwarts (the Flash, Green Lantern, Wildcat, Hawkman, Sand), skilled veterans (ATOM-SMASHER), and new faces (MISTER TERRIFIC II, Star-Spangled Kid II, plus reincarnated versions of Doctor Fate and Hawkgirl). This JSA's greatest challenge was the "Darkness" crisis, in which Mordru, OBSIDIAN, and ECLIPSO tried to plunge the world into eternal night.

INVASION Black Adam made short work of Kahndaq's defenders.

FIGHTING THE GOOD FIGHT

The Black Reign incident deeply affected the JSA, causing many of them to struggle with the concepts of righteousness and appropriate force. CAPTAIN MARVEL used the aftermath as an opportunity to tender his resignation. The group is still vital, however, as shown by the observations of the time-traveling villain Per Degaton, who recently visited several key JSA members to tell them that he had witnessed their deaths in the far future. Significantly, Degaton admitted that, throughout all of future history, he was never able to defeat the JSA, and confided to Jay Garrick (the first Flash) that he "died like a man" in whatever fate yet awaits the Flash. Regardless of the predictions of would-be prognosticators, the multi-generational JSA will continue its fight against injustice and polish its reputation as the only super hero team that operates like an extended family. DW

BLACK REIGN

The JSA's law-and-order approach to crime fighting is not universally revered. A vigilante team consisting of BLACK ADAM, Eclipso, NORTHWIND, Brainwave II, and Atom-Smasher recently took the law into their own hands. They spearheaded a violent coup in the terrorist nation of Kahndaq to put an end to their colleagues' meddling. In so doing they exposed the villainous manipulations of the Venusian worm, MISTER MIND.

DARKNESS FALLS
Obsidian's filial anger toward his father, Green Lantern, provided an added edge to the battle.

THE JSA 1) *Green Lantern I* **2)** *Mr. Terrific II* **3)** *Dr. Mid-Nite II* **4)** *Sand* **5)** *Hawkman* **6)** *Hawkgirl* **7)** *Atom-Smasher* **8)** *Dr. Fate* **9)** *Stargirl* **10)** *Black Canary II* **11)** *Flash I* **12)** *Wildcat*

KEY STORYLINES
- *LAST DAYS OF THE JUSTICE SOCIETY SPECIAL (1986):* The JSA battles in an eternal Ragnarok in what was intended to be the team's final adventure.
- *ZERO HOUR: CRISIS IN TIME #3 (SEPTEMBER 1994):* Three of the JSA's oldest members perish in an issue that once again appeared to have killed off the team forever.
- *JSA #1 (AUGUST 1999):* The JSA returns in triumphant form in the first issue of the 'Justice Be Done' storyline.

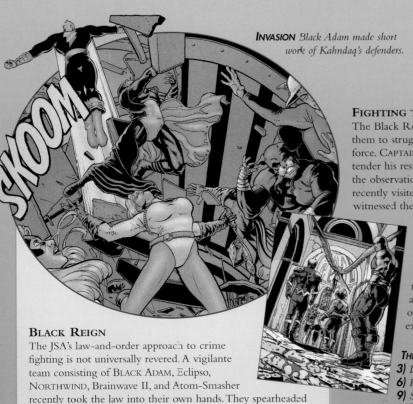

KALIBAK

FIRST APPEARANCE NEW GODS (1st series) #1 (March 1971)
STATUS Villain **REAL NAME** Kalibak
OCCUPATION Warrior **BASE** Apokolips
HEIGHT 7ft 9in **WEIGHT** 810 lbs **EYES** Red **HAIR** Black
SPECIAL POWERS/ABILITIES Vast superhuman strength, endurance, and near invulnerability; is a powerful brawler and hand-to-hand combatant; wields the Beta Club, which can fire destructive force bolts.

Kalibak is the eldest son of DARKSEID, the nearly omnipotent ruler of the planet Apokolips, and the scientist Suli, the only woman Darkseid has ever loved. After Suli was assassinated by DESAAD at the behest of Darkseid's mother, Queen Heggra, the young Kalibak was placed in Darkseid's Special Powers Force. There Kalibak became a warrior whose savagery was unparalleled across the galaxy. Only as an adult did Kalibak learn that ORION, his bitter enemy, was his half-brother and Darkseid's son. Darkseid favored Orion over Kalibak, and the elder scion of Apokolips grew overwhelmed with jealousy and hatred for his younger brother.

Eager to earn the love of his unfeeling parent Darkseid, Kalibak formed a plan to destroy Orion. But Kalibak's scheme backfired and he was forced to murder Desaad, Darkseid's master henchman, instead, to hide his failure. Darkseid destroyed Kalibak after discovering the plan. But Darkseid, valuing Kalibak's strength and power, chose to resurrect his son. Kalibak still seeks nothing but the love and respect of his father. He recently attacked SUPERMAN in Metropolis to prove his loyalty to Darkseid. **PJ**

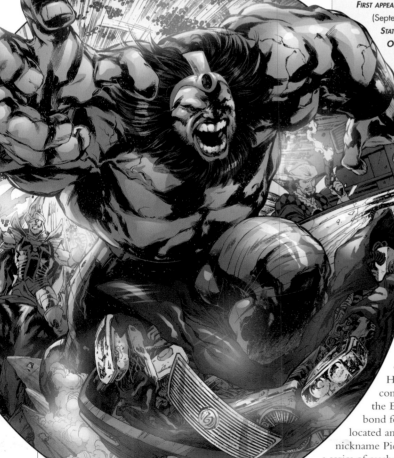

KALMAKU, TOM

FIRST APPEARANCE GREEN LANTERN (2nd series) #2 (September 1960)
STATUS Hero **REAL NAME** Thomas Kalmaku
OCCUPATION Engineer **BASE** Coast City, California
HEIGHT 5ft 7in **WEIGHT** 155 lbs
EYES Brown **HAIR** Black
SPECIAL POWERS/ABILITIES A gifted mechanic and a staunch friend to Hal Jordan, but otherwise has no special abilities.

Many decades ago, trapper Jimmy Dawes and an Inuit Alaskan named Kalmaku found a gold mine in the far north. They made a map of the location and each took half, with Dawes returning south to raise money to build the mine. Kalmaku fell ill and died, passing the half-map to his son, Tom. Dawes never returned and Tom decided to find the trapper. He took the job of flight mechanic at Ferris Aircraft in Coast City, California, to support himself while seeking out Dawes. Tom's map was stolen, prompting Hal Jordan, the second GREEN LANTERN, to come to his aid. Kalmaku quickly deduced that the Emerald Crusader was also his pal. A lifelong bond formed between the two after the mine was located and donated to the tribe. Tom, stuck with the nickname Pieface, recorded Jordan's costumed exploits in a series of casebooks. He also fell in love with Tegra, marrying her and raising two children. When Jordan died in disgrace, Tom sank into an alcoholic haze. However, Tom used emerald power to recreate the planet Oa. Spiritually rejuvenated, Tom is rebuilding his life. **RG**

KALKI

FIRST APPEARANCE DOOM PATROL (2nd series) #1 (October 1987)
STATUS Villain (missing in action) **REAL NAME** Ashok Desai
OCCUPATION Biochemist; physicist **BASE** Mobile
HEIGHT 5ft 9in **WEIGHT** 147 lbs **EYES** Black **HAIR** Black
SPECIAL POWERS/ABILITIES Scientific genius; controlled spatial portal giving him access to other-dimensional creatures; exosuit contained a variety of weapons and protective devices.

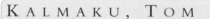

Though born in poverty in Calcutta, Ashok Desai managed to gain a science degree at Oxford University. He returned to India obsessed with curing his country's social ills. Tragically, Desai's wife died giving birth to their daughter, Arani (who would one day become a member of the DOOM PATROL as the heroine CELSIUS). Ironically, Desai's associations with the Patrol's founder, Dr. Niles Caulder (CHIEF), years before the group's founding involved experiments that horribly mutated Desai's body, making him a living dimensional gateway. Believing himself the living incarnation of the Hindu god Kalki, deity of destruction, Desai amassed wealth and power before targeting the Doom Patrol and his own daughter Arani for revenge. During that conflict, Kalki was sucked through the dimensional gateway in his own body! His ultimate fate is unknown. **SB**

KAMANDI

FIRST APPEARANCE KAMANDI #1 (November 1972)
STATUS Hero **REAL NAME** Kamandi
OCCUPATION Last boy on Earth **BASE** North America
HEIGHT 5ft 8in **WEIGHT** 159 lbs **EYES** Blue **HAIR** Blond
SPECIAL POWERS/ABILITIES Skilled fighter, courageous, and resourceful; one of few humans to survive the Great Disaster.

In a hypertimeline, an apocalypse termed the Great Disaster turned Earth into a wasteland peopled by beast-men. OMAC raised his grandson in the Command D bunker. After Omac's death, the boy, named Kamandi (for "Command D") wandered North America, now divided into feuding city-states. Great Caesar and his tiger-men ruled the east, while Czar Simian and his gorillas controlled most of the west. A few animals, like dog-faced Dr. Canus, became friends, but most remained enemies. Although called the "Last Boy on Earth," Kamandi met other humans, one of whom, scientist Ben Boxer, became his ally in a bid to restore humanity to its former glory. **DW**

KANE, KATHY

FIRST APPEARANCE DETECTIVE COMICS #233 (July 1956)
STATUS Hero (deceased) **REAL NAME** Katherine "Kathy" Kane
OCCUPATION Socialite; circus owner; crime fighter **BASE** Gotham City
HEIGHT 5ft 6in **WEIGHT** 137 lbs **EYES** Blue **HAIR** Black
SPECIAL POWERS/ABILITIES An Olympic-level athlete, she relied on her natural agility and speed in combat.

Kathy Kane was a circus stuntwoman who received a large inheritance upon her father's death and used that wealth to enter Gotham's elite. Taking up residence in a fabulous mansion, Kane became a prominent Gotham City socialite, often encountering billionaire playboy Bruce Wayne, the BATMAN. Kane became a sometime ally of Batman's, and teamed with the Dark Knight and his sidekick ROBIN on more than one occasion.

Kane eventually purchased a circus of her own but was murdered by a member of the LEAGUE OF ASSASSINS soon after. BRONZE TIGER was framed for Kane's murder, although it was later revealed that he was innocent, as he had been fighting Batman at the time of her death. Kane's true killer has yet to be revealed. **PJ**

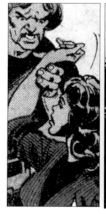
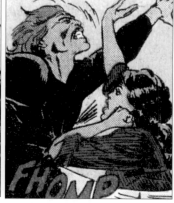

MARKED BY THE LEAGUE When the League of Assassins pursued Kathy Kane, the former trapeze artist used her gymnastic training and skills she learned from Batman to fight them off—for a while.

KANJAR RO

FIRST APPEARANCE JUSTICE LEAGUE OF AMERICA (1st series) #3 (March 1961)
STATUS Villain **REAL NAME** None
OCCUPATION World conqueror **BASE** Outer space
HEIGHT 5ft 4in **WEIGHT** 147 lbs **EYES** Yellow **HAIR** None
SPECIAL POWERS/ABILITIES Cunning strategist who relies on advanced alien weaponry, Energi-rod used for levitation, and communicating through hyperspace.

Kanjar Ro became the dictatorial felon of the planet Dhor, a world in the Antarean star-system. His army waged wars with neighboring worlds Alstair, Mosteel, and Llar, each ruled by tyrants desiring total control of their galaxy. To tip the balance of power in his favor, Kanjar Ro traveled to Earth and forced the JUSTICE LEAGUE OF AMERICA to fight his enemies to save the people of Earth. Fortunately, the JLA defeated and captured Kanjar Ro.

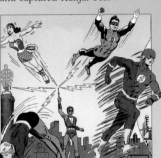

ALIEN TYRANT
Wielding his Energi-rod, Kanjar Ro made the JLA do his bidding in their first fateful encounter.

QUICK EXIT Superman helps Kanjar Ro to beat a hasty retreat from Kylaq.

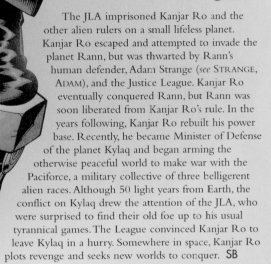

The JLA imprisoned Kanjar Ro and the other alien rulers on a small lifeless planet. Kanjar Ro escaped and attempted to invade the planet Rann, but was thwarted by Rann's human defender, Adam Strange (*see* STRANGE, ADAM), and the Justice League. Kanjar Ro eventually conquered Rann, but Rann was soon liberated from Kanjar Ro's rule. In the years following, Kanjar Ro rebuilt his power base. Recently, he became Minister of Defense of the planet Kylaq and began arming the otherwise peaceful world to make war with the Paciforce, a military collective of three belligerent alien races. Although 50 light years from Earth, the conflict on Kylaq drew the attention of the JLA, who were surprised to find their old foe up to his usual tyrannical games. The League convinced Kanjar Ro to leave Kylaq in a hurry. Somewhere in space, Kanjar Ro plots revenge and seeks new worlds to conquer. **SB**

KANTO

FIRST APPEARANCE MISTER MIRACLE (1st series) #7 (April 1972)
STATUS Villain **REAL NAME** Iluthin
OCCUPATION Assassin **BASE** Apokolips
HEIGHT 5ft 11.5in **WEIGHT** 170 lbs **EYES** Blue **HAIR** Black
SPECIAL POWERS/ABILITIES A master of weapons; can easily adapt to any weapon from any era; a superb organizer and strategist, second only to Darkseid himself among Apokoliptians.

Kanto is Apokolips' greatest assassin and one of its ruler DARKSEID's closest aides. Little is known of his background prior to 1502 AD when Darkseid exiled Iluthin, a promising warrior among GRANNY GOODNESS' orphans, to Rome. There, the young man learned much from the evil power-brokers Cesare and Lucretia Borgia.

After the Apokoliptian assassin Kanto 13 traveled to Earth via a Boom Tube and killed Iluthin's lover, the young warrior returned to Apokolips and defeated the murderer. Impressed, Darkseid executed the fallen man and declared Iluthin his new master assassin, the no-longer-numbered Kanto. Over the years, Kanto has accomplished much for his master, but has also developed a deep respect for other people's artistry, as well as his own. The first time Kanto was sent after MISTER MIRACLE, he was so impressed by his escapology skills, that he let the hero go free. **RG**

KARATE KID

FIRST APPEARANCE ADVENTURE COMICS #346 (July 1966)
STATUS Hero **REAL NAME** Val Armorr
OCCUPATION Legionnaire **BASE** Legion World
HEIGHT 5ft 8in **WEIGHT** 160 lbs **EYES** Brown **HAIR** Brown
SPECIAL POWERS/ABILITIES A "living weapon," the Kid is a member of every known discipline of martial arts on this and most other worlds, and is a master of them all.

Born in the 30th century, Val Armorr was abandoned by his parents and raised by a sensei, a devotee of martial-arts disciplines. The mastery of physical disciplines became an obsession with Armorr, and once he learned all the fighting styles of Earth, he moved on to master those of alien cultures. As a teen, he wandered the galaxy, seeking spiritual enlightenment and the further enhancement of his combat skills. Eventually he joined the Workforce (a competing team to the LEGION OF SUPER-HEROES run by the corrupt Leland McCauley) as a way of broadening his experiences. Armorr soon left the Workforce and joined the Legion full-time under the codename Karate Kid.

Recently, Karate Kid and teammate FERRO became trapped on the planet Steeple, where they escaped with help from Legionnaires SENSOR and SATURN GIRL. Karate Kid continues to aid the Legion, viewing his skills as a spiritual calling rather than an invitation to violence. **DW**

KATANA

FIRST APPEARANCE BRAVE AND THE BOLD #200 (July 1983)
STATUS Hero **REAL NAME** Tatsu Yamashiro
OCCUPATION Martial artist **BASE** Los Angeles
HEIGHT 5ft 2in **WEIGHT** 118 lbs **EYES** Brown **HAIR** Black
SPECIAL POWERS/ABILITIES An expert martial artist, whose diminutive stature belies her fighting powers; her Soultaker sword houses the souls of the people she has slain in battle.

An adept martial artist at a young age, Tatsu married Maseo Yamashiro, a businessman, and the couple had two children, Yuki and Reiko. Maseo's brother Takeo, a member of the Yakuza crime syndicate, was obsessed with Tatsu and killed Maseo and his children with the Soultaker, an ancient katana sword. Tatsu stole the sword and honed her skills in martial arts with a sensei master named Tadashi. Tatsu named herself Katana after her signature weapon.

Katana joined the OUTSIDERS and took up residence in Gotham City, becoming a surrogate mother to HALO. Eventually, Katana confronted Maseo, whose soul had been released from the Soultaker by Takeo, and killed him. Under the orders of Tadashi, LADY SHIVA once tried to claim the Soultaker, but Katana defeated Shiva and slew Tadashi instead.

Katana fought alongside incarnations of the Outsiders, and she remains a close ally of BATMAN and BLACK LIGHTNING. The souls of her husband and children reside in her sword, allowing her to communicate with them. **PJ**

KATMA TUI

FIRST APPEARANCE GREEN LANTERN (2nd series) #30 (July 1964)
STATUS Hero (deceased) **REAL NAME** None
OCCUPATION Green Lantern **BASE** Earth; formerly Korugar
HEIGHT 5ft 11in **WEIGHT** 131 lbs **EYES** Blue **HAIR** Black
SPECIAL POWERS/ABILITIES One of the most accomplished and courageous ring-bearers of the Green Lantern Corps.

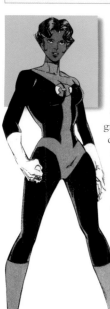

Katma Tui from the planet Korugar was selected by the GUARDIANS OF THE UNIVERSE to replace the rogue SINESTRO, who had abused his GREEN LANTERN powers and become a tyrant of Space Sector 1417. Serving the GREEN LANTERN CORPS with great distinction, Katma later decided to relinquish her power ring and marry a Korugarian scientist. Green Lantern Hal Jordan convinced Katma that her true home was with the Corps. Assigned by the Guardians to train Hal's replacement, John Stewart, Katma fell in love with him. Katma and John were married, but their happiness was ended when Katma was caught unawares by STAR SAPPHIRE— evil alter ego of Carol Ferris, Hal Jordan's longtime love— and sliced to ribbons. **SB**

KEY, THE

FIRST APPEARANCE JUSTICE LEAGUE OF AMERICA (1st series) #41 (Dec. 1965)
STATUS Villain **REAL NAME** Unrevealed **OCCUPATION** Would-be world conqueror **BASE** Mobile **HEIGHT** 6ft 1in **WEIGHT** 197 lbs **EYES** Red **HAIR** White **SPECIAL POWERS/ABILITIES** Master escape artist who carries a neural shock rifle and can control minds with his psycho-chemicals.

The psychopath known as the Key gained his *modus operandi* from an obsession with locks and puzzles. As a chemist working for INTERGANG, he developed psychochemicals to help him unlock the mysteries of the human mind. Injecting himself with his own drug, he accessed unused parts of his brain and began a crooked career as the villainous Key. The Key clashed with the JUSTICE LEAGUE OF AMERICA, wearing a suit with an oversized "key" headpiece and employing an army of Key-Men. He met with continual failure, and only after emerging from a years-long coma did he become a truly dangerous villain. With a new look and a looser grip on reality, the Key ran riot over the Justice League's lunar base until knocked cold by a boxing glove arrow fired by GREEN ARROW Connor Hawke. An attack on Arkham Asylum also failed, and the Key is now trying to defeat the locks on his Arkham cell. **DW**

KGBEAST

FIRST APPEARANCE BATMAN #417 (March 1989)
STATUS Villain **REAL NAME** Anatoli Knyazev
OCCUPATION Assassin **BASE** Gotham City
HEIGHT 6ft 3in **WEIGHT** 371 lbs **EYES** Brown **HAIR** Unknown
SPECIAL POWERS/ABILITIES Extraordinary hand-to-hand combatant; master of weapons and explosives; has a gun instead of a left hand.

Anatoli Knyazev was an assassin employed by the K.G.B., the secret police of the former Soviet Union. Knyazev became a rogue agent, taking an unauthorized mission to kill ten people involved with the U.S. Strategic Defense Initiative. After murdering dozens in Gotham City, the KGBeast encountered BATMAN. When his left arm was trapped by one of Batman's weapons, the KGBeast severed his own hand and escaped. He later fit the stump with a powerful gun. After a botched assassination attempt on the U.S. President and a counterfeit scheme gone awry, the KGBeast was incarcerated at Blackgate Maximum Security Prison. His protégé, the NKVDemon, surfaced in Russia but was killed by Batman's ally, Soviet police detective Nikita Krakov. **PJ**

KHAN, RAMA

FIRST APPEARANCE JLA #62 (March 2002)
STATUS Undecided **REAL NAME** Unrevealed
OCCUPATION Elemental defender **BASE** Jarhanpur
HEIGHT 6ft 5in **WEIGHT** 199 lbs **EYES** Black **HAIR** Black
SPECIAL POWERS/ABILITIES Superstrong; immortal; great magician; can turn a handful of Jarhanpur soil into fire, granite, or a sea of wine.

Elemental defender of the nation of Jarhanpur, Rama Khan sought revenge against WONDER WOMAN when the Amazon Princess fought to protect an innocent boy abducted against his will to be installed as Jarhanpur's next ruler. Rama Khan broke the heretofore unbreakable links of Wonder Woman's Lasso of Truth and, in turn, unraveled the fragile fabric of reality. With her JUSTICE LEAGUE OF AMERICA teammates, Wonder Woman defeated Rama Khan and repaired her lariat.

Later, the JLA found themselves facing Rama Khan in the year 1,004 BC. Khan had assembled a group of Earth's greatest warriors to battle the League.

ELEMENTAL DEFENDER
Past or present, Rama Khan has always faced the JLA as an adversary.

It transpired that Khan had been tricked into doing so by GAMEMNAE, High Priestess of Atlantis. The conflict led to the return of modern-day Atlantis and AQUAMAN from exile in the past as a result of the Imperiex War (*see* Great Battles, pp. 320–1). **SB**

KENTS, THE

FIRST APPEARANCE (Ma Kent) ACTION COMICS #1 (June 1938)
STATUS Ally **REAL NAME** Martha Clark Kent
OCCUPATION Farmer's wife **BASE** Smallville, Kansas
HEIGHT 5ft 4in **WEIGHT** 140 lbs **EYES** Blue **HAIR** Red
SPECIAL POWERS/ABILITIES Martha has no combat skills but is wonderfully kindhearted and an excellent cook and baker.
FIRST APPEARANCE (Pa Kent) ACTION COMICS #1 (June 1938)
STATUS Ally **REAL NAME** Jonathan Kent
OCCUPATION Farmer **BASE** Smallville, Kansas
HEIGHT 5ft 11in **WEIGHT** 185 lbs **EYES** Blue **HAIR** Gray/blond
SPECIAL POWERS/ABILITIES Jonathan's army training makes him an above-average combatant; he is also an excellent farmer.

world-famous Man of Steel, SUPERMAN.

The Kent family farm, virtually unchanged since 1871, has been a refuge for others in need, such as Matrix (SUPERGIRL), a shape-changing being from another universe who needed time to heal after a mission with Superman. The Kents are helping to raise Superman's clone, Kon-El (SUPERBOY), sending him to high school under the name Connor. **RG**

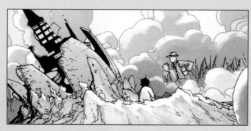

PERFECT PARENTS *The birthing matrix from Krypton crashed in the fields near the Kent's farm.*

Silas Kent moved his family westward to Kansas in 1854 as part of a group of abolitionists. After Silas was murdered, his sons Nathaniel and Jebediah took over the family stake. After the Civil War, Jeb fell in with Jesse James and his outlaws. Nate remained with the army as a scout until he married Mary Glenowen. He then became Smallville's sheriff on December 13, 1872. This led to a confrontation between Nate and Jeb in 1874 when an aborted bank robbery became a bloodbath, with Jeb being gunned down.

Silas's greatgrandson is Jonathan Kent, himself a war hero. He married his former sweetheart Martha Clark when she became a widow. Unfortunately the couple were unable to have children. One night an alien spacecraft crashed near their farm. Inside the capsule they found a baby boy. Overjoyed, they decided to adopt this child from another world. They christened him Clark and instilled in him their own strong moral values. These stood him in particularly good stead when Clark developed superpowers and became the

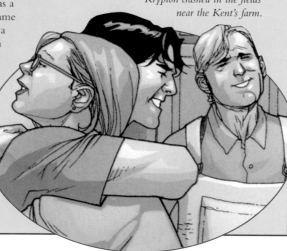

KID ETERNITY

FIRST APPEARANCE HIT COMICS #25 (December 1942)
STATUS Hero (deceased) **REAL NAME** Kit Freeman
OCCUPATION Ghost **BASE** England
HEIGHT 5ft 10in **WEIGHT** 164 lbs **EYES** Brown **HAIR** Brown
SPECIAL POWERS/ABILITIES Could summon dead spirits throughout the ages to advise him.

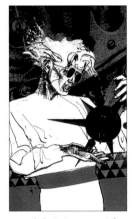

Young Kit Freeman was killed by Nazi machine gunners during World War II. The boy's spirit was informed by a being from the higher realms named Mister Keeper that he was not fated to die for another 75 years. Because he could not be returned to life, Mister Keeper granted the boy a number of ghostly powers and returned with him to Earth. In reality, the spirit now called Kid Eternity had been duped by an Agent of Chaos and unwittingly served their interests. After nearly three decades of adventure, Kid Eternity became trapped in Hell for 30 years. Kid Eternity escaped from Hell with Mister Keeper and later learned that he never went to Heaven at all, but an illusory paradise deep in the pits of Hell. Furthermore, the Kid learned that Mister Keeper was actually a Lord of Chaos, and that his Chaosspheres were focuses of chaotic energies being prepared to transform the planet into a gift for God. He fought against that plan until he was slain by Mordru, the DARK LORD. **RG**

KID QUANTUM I & II

FIRST APPEARANCE (I) LEGION OF SUPER-HEROES #33 (September 1992); (II) LEGION OF SUPER-HEROES (4th series) #82 (July 1996)
STATUS Heroes **REAL NAMES** (I) James Cullen; (II) Jazmin Cullen
OCCUPATION Legionnaires **BASE** Legion World
HEIGHT (I) 5ft 11in; (II) 5ft 8in **WEIGHT** (I) 170 lbs; (II) 145 lbs
EYES (I) Brown; (II) amber **HAIR** (I) Black; (II) black
SPECIAL POWERS/ABILITIES Able to project stasis fields that halt the movement of time within their sphere of influence.

The original Kid Quantum, James Cullen of Xanthu, joined the LEGION OF SUPER-HEROES during its first weeks. His ability to generate stasis fields received an artificial boost from his stasis belt. During the Legion's first mission, he died battling the alien entity Tangleweb, his malfunctioning belt partly to blame. This tragedy prompted the Legion to deny membership to those whose powers relied on external devices.

Before long, Jazmin Cullen, James's sister, joined the Legion. As Kid Quantum II, she wielded the same powers as her brother, but underwent experimental surgery to augment her powers instead of relying on a stasis belt. Although she bore some resentment toward the Legion for failing to prevent her brother's death, Kid Quantum II put her bitterness behind her as she established close friendships within the roster. During the Robotica Crisis (see C.O.M.P.U.T.O.), Kid Quantum II became the Legion's new leader. She appointed TRIAD as her deputy and struck up a romance with COSMIC BOY. Recently, Kid Quantum II stepped down as Legion leader but will undoubtedly aid the team in its continuing struggles against the forces of Apokolips. **DW**

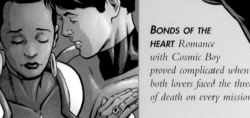

AMAZING *Prior to joining the Legion, Kid Quantum II served with Xanthu's own super hero team, the Uncanny Amazers.*

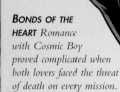

BONDS OF THE HEART *Romance with Cosmic Boy proved complicated when both lovers faced the threat of death on every mission.*

KID FLASH

FIRST APPEARANCE (as Kid Flash) TEEN TITANS (3rd ser.) #4 (Dec. 2003)
STATUS Hero **REAL NAME** Bartholomew "Bart" Allen
OCCUPATION Adventurer **BASE** San Francisco; Keystone City
HEIGHT 5ft 2in **WEIGHT** 115 lbs **EYES** Yellow **HAIR** Brown
SPECIAL POWERS/ABILITIES Like all members of the Flash family, Bart Allen's superspeed is fueled by the extra-dimensional energy field known as the "Speed Force." Although one of his kneecaps is now artificial, Kid Flash can still run at velocities approaching light-speed.

NEW LOOK *Kid Flash's costume is inspired by the uniform formerly worn by Wally West.*

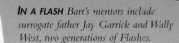

IN A FLASH *Bart's mentors include surrogate father Jay Garrick and Wally West, two generations of Flashes.*

Grandson of Barry Allen (the second FLASH) and son of Don Allen (one-half of the 30th century's Tornado Twins), Bart Allen inherited his family's celebrated superspeed abilities. Unfortunately, Bart's growth was also hyper-accelerated and he spent his early years within a virtual reality environment in the far-flung future. Bart's aging normalized after his grandmother Iris Allen (see ALLEN, IRIS) transported him to the 20th century. There he learned to master his speed powers with the help of Barry Allen's successor, Wally West (the former Kid Flash now running down rogues as the third Flash). Because of his recklessness, Bart was dubbed Impulse, owing to his virtual upbringing and its literal "reset" capability. Having lived in a fantasy environment with full use of his powers, Bart was ill-equipped for real life.

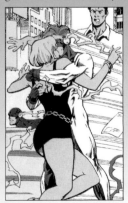

SPEED FORCE *Impulsive at first, Bart swiftly learned to slow down for life in the 20th century.*

He was not used to a world in which his accelerated actions could not be undone simply by rebooting the nurturing computer system. For a time, Bart lived with superspeed guru MAX MERCURY, who helped him to slow down when necessary and adapt to life in the fast lane. Impulse was one of the founding members of YOUNG JUSTICE, but has since graduated to a new team of TEEN TITANS. After suffering a near-crippling injury when DEATHSTROKE THE TERMINATOR blasted his knee with a shotgun, Bart read every book in the San Francisco Public Library at superspeed and later changed his super-hero sobriquet to Kid Flash. Smarter and more self-assured, Bart lives with original Flash Jay Garrick and his wife, Joan, in Keystone City. **SB**

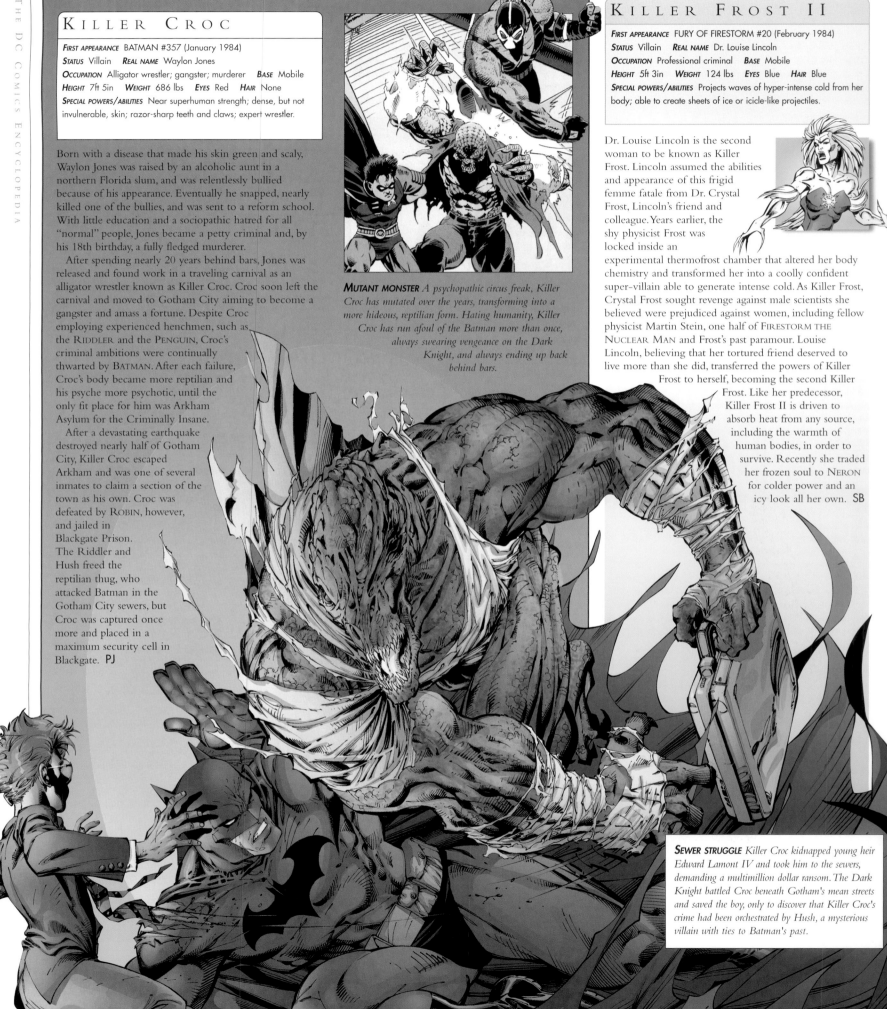

KILLER CROC

FIRST APPEARANCE BATMAN #357 (January 1984)
STATUS Villain **REAL NAME** Waylon Jones
OCCUPATION Alligator wrestler; gangster; murderer **BASE** Mobile
HEIGHT 7ft 5in **WEIGHT** 686 lbs **EYES** Red **HAIR** None
SPECIAL POWERS/ABILITIES Near superhuman strength; dense, but not invulnerable, skin; razor-sharp teeth and claws; expert wrestler.

Born with a disease that made his skin green and scaly, Waylon Jones was raised by an alcoholic aunt in a northern Florida slum, and was relentlessly bullied because of his appearance. Eventually he snapped, nearly killed one of the bullies, and was sent to a reform school. With little education and a sociopathic hatred for all "normal" people, Jones became a petty criminal and, by his 18th birthday, a fully fledged murderer.

After spending nearly 20 years behind bars, Jones was released and found work in a traveling carnival as an alligator wrestler known as Killer Croc. Croc soon left the carnival and moved to Gotham City aiming to become a gangster and amass a fortune. Despite Croc employing experienced henchmen, such as the RIDDLER and the PENGUIN, Croc's criminal ambitions were continually thwarted by BATMAN. After each failure, Croc's body became more reptilian and his psyche more psychotic, until the only fit place for him was Arkham Asylum for the Criminally Insane.

After a devastating earthquake destroyed nearly half of Gotham City, Killer Croc escaped Arkham and was one of several inmates to claim a section of the town as his own. Croc was defeated by ROBIN, however, and jailed in Blackgate Prison. The Riddler and Hush freed the reptilian thug, who attacked Batman in the Gotham City sewers, but Croc was captured once more and placed in a maximum security cell in Blackgate. **PJ**

MUTANT MONSTER *A psychopathic circus freak, Killer Croc has mutated over the years, transforming into a more hideous, reptilian form. Hating humanity, Killer Croc has run afoul of the Batman more than once, always swearing vengeance on the Dark Knight, and always ending up back behind bars.*

KILLER FROST II

FIRST APPEARANCE FURY OF FIRESTORM #20 (February 1984)
STATUS Villain **REAL NAME** Dr. Louise Lincoln
OCCUPATION Professional criminal **BASE** Mobile
HEIGHT 5ft 3in **WEIGHT** 124 lbs **EYES** Blue **HAIR** Blue
SPECIAL POWERS/ABILITIES Projects waves of hyper-intense cold from her body; able to create sheets of ice or icicle-like projectiles.

Dr. Louise Lincoln is the second woman to be known as Killer Frost. Lincoln assumed the abilities and appearance of this frigid femme fatale from Dr. Crystal Frost, Lincoln's friend and colleague. Years earlier, the shy physicist Frost was locked inside an experimental thermofrost chamber that altered her body chemistry and transformed her into a coolly confident super-villain able to generate intense cold. As Killer Frost, Crystal Frost sought revenge against male scientists she believed were prejudiced against women, including fellow physicist Martin Stein, one half of FIRESTORM THE NUCLEAR MAN and Frost's past paramour. Louise Lincoln, believing that her tortured friend deserved to live more than she did, transferred the powers of Killer Frost to herself, becoming the second Killer Frost. Like her predecessor, Killer Frost II is driven to absorb heat from any source, including the warmth of human bodies, in order to survive. Recently she traded her frozen soul to NERON for colder power and an icy look all her own. **SB**

SEWER STRUGGLE *Killer Croc kidnapped young heir Edward Lamont IV and took him to the sewers, demanding a multimillion dollar ransom. The Dark Knight battled Croc beneath Gotham's mean streets and saved the boy, only to discover that Killer Croc's crime had been orchestrated by Hush, a mysterious villain with ties to Batman's past.*

KILLER SHARK

FIRST APPEARANCE BLACKHAWK (1st series) #50 (March 1952)
STATUS Villain   REAL NAME Unrevealed
OCCUPATION Pirate   BASE Mobile
HEIGHT 5ft 11in   WEIGHT 185 lbs   EYES Unknown   HAIR Unknown
SPECIAL POWERS/ABILITIES Relies on amazing vessels: the triphibious Shark Jet, an Octopus Sub, a Whale Sub, and a Swordfish Sub.

In 1950, the Blackhawks (see BLACKHAWK) encountered costumed pirate Killer Shark as he looted the city of Kamard. Using a variety of submersible vehicles, Killer Shark often matched wits with the international flyers, who destroyed his undersea base and each of his attack craft. Killer Shark joined with former Nazi S.S. Colonel Von Gross to form the Empire of Death. Its agents wore skull masks, possessed a fleet of aircraft, and operated from a giant solar-powered flying skull. With agents around the world, the Empire engaged in espionage and contract assassination with an eye towards world domination, until the Blackhawks slew Von Gross and closed the network down. The further activities of Killer Shark are unrecorded. RG

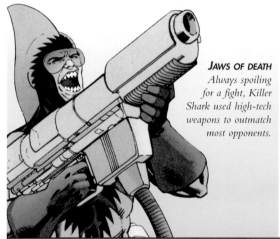

JAWS OF DEATH
Always spoiling for a fight, Killer Shark used high-tech weapons to outmatch most opponents.

KILOWOG

FIRST APPEARANCE GREEN LANTERN CORPS #201 (June 1986)
STATUS Hero   REAL NAME Kilowog
OCCUPATION Scientist; adventurer   BASE Deep space
HEIGHT 8ft 3in   WEIGHT 720 lbs   EYES Red   HAIR None
SPECIAL POWERS/ABILITIES Possessed a Green Lantern ring, limited only by the color yellow; vast scientific knowledge.

Born on the planet Bolovax Vix in space sector 674, Kilowog was chosen by the GUARDIANS OF THE UNIVERSE to become a GREEN LANTERN, eventually training a new recruit named Hal Jordan. During the Crisis (see Great Battles, pp. 320–1), Bolovax Vix was destroyed, but Kilowog used the power of his ring to absorb the souls of the world's 16 million inhabitants and transplant them to another planet. The villain SINESTRO destroyed this new world, however, and Kilowog became the sole survivor of his people. Entranced by the possibilities life on Earth offered, he settled there. Kilowog lived for a time in Russia, where he helped create the ROCKET RED BRIGADE. He also helped the NEW GUARDIANS establish their island base before joining the JUSTICE LEAGUE OF AMERICA. When Hal Jordan became the insane PARALLAX, Kilowog pleaded with his friend to end his destructive rampage, but Jordan incinerated him. Kilowog was resurrected with the help of Green Lantern Kyle Rayner and the Guardian Ganthet. PJ

KILLSHOT

FIRST APPEARANCE TITANS SECRET FILES #2 (September 2000)
STATUS Villain   REAL NAME Unrevealed
OCCUPATION Member of the Hangmen   BASE Mobile
HEIGHT 6ft 1in   WEIGHT 721 lbs   EYES Brown   HAIR Brown
SPECIAL POWERS/ABILITIES Cyborg with enhanced strength and agility; wields an arsenal of tools for carnage.

The assassin known as Killshot prefers to let his weapons speak for themselves. Little is known regarding this Russian executioner, but those who have seen him in action attest that his cyborg limbs conceal an arsenal of state-of-the-art military hardware, including a full magazine of surface-to-air missiles. Killshot serves with the HANGMEN, a group of superpowered assassins. The Hangmen's most frequent opponents have been the TEEN TITANS, initially clashing with them during the Hangmen's mission to kidnap ARSENAL's daughter Lian in a plot to get at the girl's mother, CHESHIRE. Later, Killshot and his comrades became "Jokerized" and were among the brain-addled villains running amok during the JOKER's Last Laugh spree. Killshot soon returned to normal and is actively seeking assassination contracts. DW

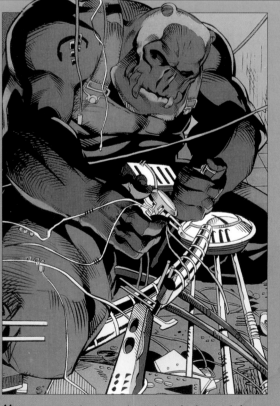

CYBORG *Killshot's weapons can bring down almost any opponent, though their weight tends to limit Killshot's mobility.*

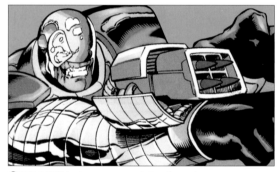

MACHINESMITH *Kilowog was the mechanic for the JLA before being killed by Parallax and resurrected by Green Lantern.*

KINETIX

FIRST APPEARANCE LEGION OF SUPER-HEROES (4th series) #66 (March 1995)
STATUS Hero   REAL NAME Zoe Saugin
OCCUPATION Legionnaire   BASE Legion World, U.P. Space
HEIGHT 5ft 4in   WEIGHT 126 lbs   EYES Green   HAIR Auburn
SPECIAL POWERS/ABILITIES Hypertaxis-powered meta-human, formerly able to cast an energy field allowing her to remold objects.

While accompanying her archaeologist mother on a dig, Zoe Saugin from planet Aleph discovered a magical artifact that enabled her to save her family and sparked an interest in acquiring other forms of mystic energy. Zoe became Kinetix, her homeworld's recruit for the LEGION OF SUPER-HEROES. Zoe's quest for power led to her falling under the malign influence of the Emerald Empress's Emerald Eye. While confronting the cloned RĀ'S AL GHŪL, Kinetix's body was changed by a bomb explosion into a highly evolved Terreform. Kinetix remains a Legionnaire. SB

KING FARADAY

FIRST APPEARANCE DANGER TRAIL #1 (August 1950)
STATUS Hero   REAL NAME King Faraday
OCCUPATION Government espionage agent   BASE Washington, D.C.
HEIGHT 6ft   WEIGHT 185 lbs   EYES Blue   HAIR White
SPECIAL POWERS/ABILITIES An Olympic-level athlete in his youth, he remains exceptionally fit.

King Faraday was an excellent soldier who left the armed services to join one of the U.S government's many clandestine organizations, the Central Bureau of Intelligence. There he traveled the world on spy missions on behalf of his country, amassing a high diplomatic success rate. He holds a disdain for most costumed crime fighters, although he has a grudging admiration for BATMAN, and actually helped train NIGHTSHADE when she first arrived in Washington, D.C. They had several successful missions before she went off on her own. He ascended to the head of the C.B.I. before it was shuffled into a new intelligence matrix. Considering himself past his prime, he now works behind the scenes in the intelligence community, making sure lines of communication remain open. RG

SECRET AGENT *Using wits and bare knuckles, Faraday helped keep America safe.*

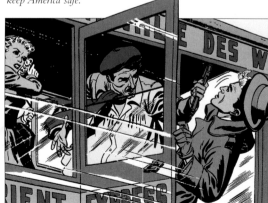

KING SHARK

FIRST APPEARANCE SUPERBOY (3rd series) #0 (October 1994)
STATUS Villain REAL NAME Nanaue
OCCUPATION Adventurer BASE Hawaii
HEIGHT 7ft WEIGHT 380 lbs EYES Black HAIR None
SPECIAL POWERS/ABILITIES Superstrength, invulnerability, and a mouth full of razor-sharp teeth; can breathe underwater.

King Shark is said to be the offspring of a human mother and a shark god belonging to a pantheon of deities worshipped by traditional Hawaiians. He is truly monstrous in appearance and has a soul equally as ugly, being driven solely by his voracious appetites and urges. He loves to terrorize the people of Hawaii, and no prison has proved strong enough to hold him for long. King Shark's favorite prey is SUPERBOY, and his teeth are among the only things with enough force to puncture Superboy's invulnerable skin. For a time, King Shark worked with the SUICIDE SQUAD, and appeared to have died when a teammate ripped off his explosive harness in order to destroy an enemy fortress. Somehow he survived and has been seen in Hawaii and around the world in a frenzied fury to devour the world's super heroes. DW

KING SOLOVAR

FIRST APPEARANCE THE FLASH (1st series) #106 (April 1959)
STATUS Hero (deceased) REAL NAME Solovar
OCCUPATION Monarch BASE Gorilla City, Africa
HEIGHT 6ft 5in WEIGHT 603 lbs EYES Black HAIR Gray
SPECIAL POWERS/ABILITIES A gifted telepath and benevolent ruler.

One of a race of apes advanced in evolutionary terms by an alien being who landed in Equatorial Africa in the 19th century, the wise and peaceful Solovar became king of his fellow super gorillas. He ruled benevolently over them in their hidden Gorilla City. When his rival GORILLA GRODD threatened to usurp his throne, Solovar enlisted the help of the second FLASH, Barry Allen, one of very few humans to know of Gorilla City's existence. Tragically, Solovar was assassinated by one of Grodd's minions as the kind monarch traveled to the United Nations to seek recognition for Gorilla City as a sovereign nation. Solovar's nephew Ulgo (the simian super hero Grogamesh) now succeeds him as leader of the peaceful apes. SB

KING, THE

FIRST APPEARANCE FLASH COMICS #3 (March 1940)
STATUS Hero REAL NAME King Standish
OCCUPATION Crime fighter BASE New York City
HEIGHT 5ft 11in WEIGHT 184 lbs EYES Blue HAIR Blond
SPECIAL POWERS/ABILITIES A master of disguise, able to fool the keenest observer; good with a pistol but generally eschewed weapons and preferred to use his fists.

The mysterious masked man known as the King survived a shooting by Boss Barton's mob thanks to his bulletproof vest. At first, both criminals and police thought that the King was a masked felon, but he always helped those who could not help themselves. The King matched wits with a beautiful underworld leader known as the Witch, whom he encountered many times over the next few years. Both were masters of disguise, which made their meetings memorable matches. Similarly, the King also opposed SANDMAN II's foe, the Face. Control of the O.S.S. (Office of Strategic Services) recruited the King to help with domestic problems, such as spies, saboteurs, and common criminals, during the latter part of World War II. One such mission saw the King help Sandman I and the Star-Spangled Kid defeat a disciple of the dimension-spanning STALKER. The King's post-1945 exploits remain undisclosed. RG

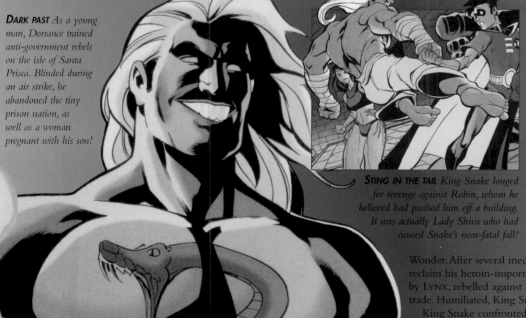

DARK PAST *As a young man, Dorrance trained anti-government rebels on the isle of Santa Prisca. Blinded during an air strike, he abandoned the tiny prison nation, as well as a woman pregnant with his son!*

STING IN THE TAIL *King Snake longed for revenge against Robin, whom he believed had pushed him off a building. It was actually Lady Shiva who had caused Snake's near-fatal fall!*

KING SNAKE

FIRST APPEARANCE ROBIN (1st series) #1 (November 1990)
STATUS Villain (deceased) REAL NAME Sir Edmund Dorrance
OCCUPATION Crime lord BASE Gotham City
HEIGHT 6ft 2in WEIGHT 220 lbs EYES White HAIR Blond
SPECIAL POWERS/ABILITIES Master of several lethal martial arts.

Sir Edmund Dorrance was a former captain in the British Royal Artillery. Using his considerable financial resources, Dorrance began studying martial arts and became a master. He also became a leader of the heroin trade plaguing Asia, using a gang called the Ghost Dragons to peddle narcotics in Europe and North America. His brutal reputation earned him the name King Snake.

King Snake ran afoul of ROBIN and LADY SHIVA in France, and nearly fell to his death while fighting the Boy Wonder. After several medical operations, King Snake moved to Gotham City to reclaim his heroin-importing empire and to hunt for Robin. The Ghost Dragons, led by LYNX, rebelled against King Snake and stripped him of his control over their drug trade. Humiliated, King Snake moved back to Asia.

King Snake confronted Robin yet again, this time in the terrorist KOBRA's stronghold in Nepal. King Snake's vision had been briefly restored but the villain lost it once more when Robin threw snake venom into Dorrance's eyes. Left a wailing madman, King Snake was discovered wandering in the mountains by his own son, the villain BANE, whose mother had long ago been imprisoned for King Snake's crimes. The vengeful Bane seized his father and hurled him into a chasm, killing him. PJ

THE DC COMICS ENCYCLOPEDIA

KNIGHT & SQUIRE

FIRST APPEARANCE (I) BATMAN #62 (January 1951); (II) JLA #26
(February 1999) **STATUS** Heroes **REAL NAME** (Knight I, Squire I)
Percival Sheldrake; (Knight II, Squire II) Cyril Sheldrake
OCCUPATION Adventurers **BASE** Wordenshire, England
HEIGHT (Knight I) 5ft 10in; (Knight II) 5ft 11in **WEIGHT** (Knight I)
167 lbs; (Knight II) 175 lbs **EYES** (both) Brown **HAIR** (both) Brown
SPECIAL POWERS/ABILITIES (Knight I) Expert swordsman, combatant and
rider; (II) micro fighter jets, tanks, etc. controlled by gauntlet keypad.

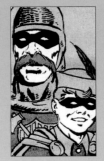

Percival Sheldrake's father, the
Earl of Wordenshire, was slain
in North Africa during World
War II, and his mother perished
in a bombing raid in London.
Percival was rescued by the
SHINING KNIGHT, who took the
young man on as his Squire. The
two heroes joined the ALL-STAR
SQUADRON and the SEVEN
SOLDIERS OF VICTORY and, at the
behest of President F. D. Roosevelt,
the Squire later became a member of the Young All-Stars.

After spending some time as a prisoner of war, Percival,
now an adult, became the Knight, one of the first
costumed heroes to emerge outside of the U.S. His son
Cyril became his Squire, and the two joined the Dome,
becoming GLOBAL GUARDIANS and fighting crime in
England during the 1950s. When Percival died, Cyril
inherited his father's wealth and became a second Knight,
riding a Norton motorcycle that had been his father's.
Springheeled Jack, a disgraced, lunatic member of the
royal family hellbent on seizing the British throne, became
this Knight's archenemy. **PJ**

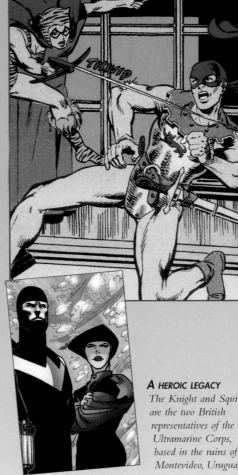

A HEROIC LEGACY
*The Knight and Squire
are the two British
representatives of the
Ultramarine Corps,
based in the ruins of
Montevideo, Uruguay.*

KNOCKOUT

FIRST APPEARANCE SUPERBOY (3rd series) #2 (March 1994)
STATUS Villain **REAL NAME** Unknown; has used the alias "Kay"
OCCUPATION Criminal; former exotic dancer **BASE** Mobile
HEIGHT 6ft **WEIGHT** 164 lbs **EYES** Green **HAIR** Red
SPECIAL POWERS/ABILITIES Trained in the battle techniques of the Female
Furies; possesses superstrength and endurance; can be defeated by
exploiting her fear of being trapped, a side-effect of her training.

The statuesque super-villainess known as Knockout began
her life on distant Apokolips. At a young age, she was
selected to leave the squalor of GRANNY GOODNESS's
orphanage and become a trainee for the much-feared
FEMALE FURIES. Although respected for her fighting
ferocity, Knockout's impudence displeased Granny on
many occasions. She was summarily punished with solitary
confinement, chained alone in the fire-pits of Armagetto.
There she met the insurgent HIMON, who encouraged
Knockout to choose her own destiny.

After BIG BARDA escaped the Furies, Knockout was
similarly inspired to leave Apokolips behind for good.
When punished yet again for her disrespect, Knockout
freed herself and traveled via Boom Tube to Earth, Hawaii
specifically, where she exploited her beauty by becoming a
sultry stripper. Later, she relied on her brawn to fight
SUPERBOY in her guise as a costumed villainess. Enamored
by Knockout's considerable attributes, Superboy attempted
to reform her. Ultimately, Knockout was imprisoned after
killing a police officer. She has escaped incarceration on
several occasions, inevitably brawling with or complicating
the life of Superboy, whom she calls "Pup." When last
seen, Knockout was among the femme fatales overrunning
New York after the sorceress CIRCE transformed the city's
populace into were-beasts. **S3**

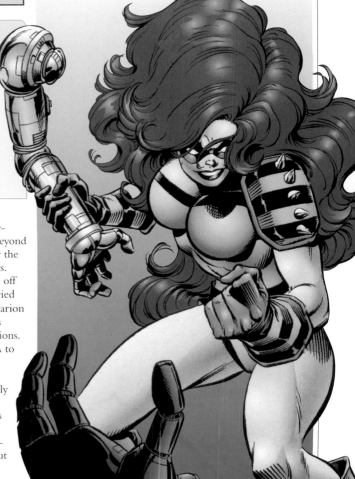

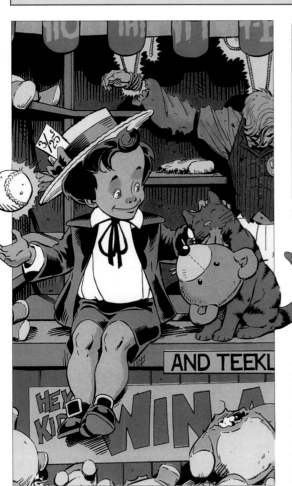

KLARION,
THE WITCH BOY

FIRST APPEARANCE THE DEMON (1st series) #7
(March 1973)
STATUS Villain **REAL NAME** Klarion
OCCUPATION Warlock **BASE** Mobile
HEIGHT 5ft 1in **WEIGHT** 113 lbs
EYES Black **HAIR** Black
SPECIAL POWERS/ABILITIES Despite small size and apparent youth,
wields near-limitless power; has a wicked sense of humor.

Klarion is one of the most dangerous magic-users in
creation. He originally came to Earth from the other-
dimensional realm known as Witch-World in the Beyond
Country, pursued by that world's Elder Judges for the
crime of stealing the Book of Forbidden Secrets.
Though the DEMON Etrigan helped him fight off
his attackers, Klarion turned on Etrigan and tried
to enslave him. The spiteful clashes between Klarion
and the Demon have resulted in the Witch Boy's
banishment from Earth's dimension on several occasions.
More recently, Klarion teamed with the CONTESSA to
cause chaos in the super-hero community by flip-
flopping ages—the adults in the JUSTICE LEAGUE OF
AMERICA and JUSTICE SOCIETY OF AMERICA magically
became youths, while the teens of YOUNG JUSTICE
found themselves transformed into adults. The heroes
broke the spell, but Klarion found more idle
amusement by temporarily de-aging a band of super-
villains. The only creature Klarion seems to care about
is his witch-familiar Teekl, a cat from Witch-World
who also possesses a natural talent for magic. **DW**

KOLE

FIRST APPEARANCE NEW TEEN TITANS (2nd series) #9 (June 1985)
STATUS Hero (deceased)   **REAL NAME** Kole Weathers
OCCUPATION Adventurer   **BASE** New York City
HEIGHT 5ft 6in   **WEIGHT** 133 lbs   **EYES** Blue   **HAIR** Red
SPECIAL POWERS/ABILITIES Could project tough crystal forms that worked on their own, or as a coating over other objects.

Dr. Abel Weathers was convinced that mankind was doomed to be wiped out in a nuclear holocaust in the near future, so he experimented with ways to preserve human life from a nuclear attack. He studied insects and crystals for secrets that might hold vital clues to humanity's possible survival.

He then began experimenting on human subjects, including his teenage daughter, Kole. This triggered her meta-gene, imbuing her with the ability to generate crystal forms. In time, Kole attracted the attention of the TEEN TITANS, whom she soon joined. Kole enjoyed adventuring, but it took time for the shy teen to get to know and feel comfortable around her teammates. She fought bravely alongside the team, sacrificing her life during the cosmic event known as the Crisis (*see* Great Battles, pp. 320–1). **RG**

KORDAX

FIRST APPEARANCE ATLANTIS CHRONICLES #4 (June 1990)
STATUS Villain (deceased)   **REAL NAME** Kordax
OCCUPATION Adventurer   **BASE** Atlantis
HEIGHT 6ft 6in   **WEIGHT** 535 lbs   **EYES** Red   **HAIR** Blond
SPECIAL POWERS/ABILITIES Could breathe underwater and communicate telepathically with sea life; enhanced strength and toughness.

Kordax is still spoken of in hushed tones by the citizens of Atlantis. Born to Queen Cora of Poseidonis but abandoned at birth due to his grotesque, green-scaled body, Kordax survived in the ocean thanks to his mental control over sea creatures. As an adult he returned to Atlantis leading an army of sharks in a failed bid for the throne. His punishment included the loss of his left hand (replaced with a sword) and banishment. Kordax's legend survived in an Atlantean superstition regarding blond hair, referred to as the "Curse of Kordax."

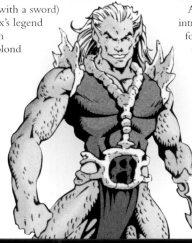

Many ages later, Kordax returned when Poseidonian refugees disturbed his exile in the tunnels beneath the city of Tritonis. Defeated by AQUAMAN, Kordax fell on his own sword rather than live in shame. **DW**

KORYAK

FIRST APPEARANCE AQUAMAN (3rd series) #35 (January 1995)
STATUS Undecided   **REAL NAME** Koryak
OCCUPATION Exiled prince of Atlantis   **BASE** Northern Canada
HEIGHT 5ft 8in   **WEIGHT** 175 lbs   **EYES** Brown   **HAIR** Brown
SPECIAL POWERS/ABILITIES Amphibious; superspeed; can psychically create "hard water" weapons.

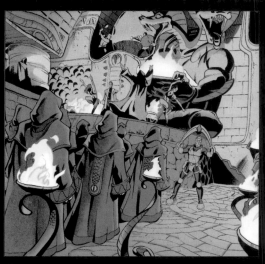

The son of AQUAMAN and the fire elemental CORONA, Koryak was raised by his Inuit mother in her remote village in northern Canada without ever knowing the identity of his father or the truth about his Atlantean heritage.

As a teenager, Koryak was introduced to Aquaman. Aquaman was ill-prepared for the boy's temper and attitude, which, in many ways, mirrored Aquaman's own personality. Resentful of Aquaman's close relationship with TEMPEST, the angry, rebellious Koryak eventually took up residence in Atlantis, Aquaman's undersea kingdom. Against his father's express wishes, Koryak led a great migration of Atlanteans out of the capital city Poseidonis and into the tunnels of its sister city, Tritonis. There, he unwittingly released the cruel KORDAX and embroiled Atlantis in a great war with the god Triton.

As a result of his misguided actions, Koryak was banished from Atlantis. He returned, shamed, to his mother's village, where he resides to this day. **PJ**

KOBRA

FIRST APPEARANCE KOBRA #1 (March 1976)
STATUS Villain (deceased)   **REAL NAME** Lord Naga
OCCUPATION International terrorist   **BASE** The Himalayas
HEIGHT 6ft 2in   **WEIGHT** 200 lbs   **EYES** Black   **HAIR** None
SPECIAL POWERS/ABILITIES Combat expert and brilliant strategist who wore a bulletproof cobra costume.

Kobra was just a man, but his worldwide influence and cold intellect made him far more dangerous than any superpowered thug. He was raised from infancy by the Cobra Cult of India after cultists stole him from his parents and separated him from his conjoined twin, Jason Burr. Kobra believed himself to be the most important person in the world—the only one who could lead the Cobra Cult though the Kali Yuga, or time of great chaos.

At first, the U.S. government used the psychic link that Jason Burr shared with his evil twin to gain advance warning of Kobra's plans. Kobra killed Burr, but the spirit of his twin haunted him.

Kobra's schemes were always spectacular. He manipulated hundreds of individuals to do his bidding, scouring the planet for objects of power, including the mystical Spear of Destiny. Kobra also orchestrated the Janus Directive, which pitted U.S. intelligence agencies against one another.

After surviving an attempt by KING SNAKE to usurp his leadership of the Cobra Cult, Kobra tried to blackmail the world by causing the crash of an airliner. When Kobra escaped punishment, ATOM-SMASHER, whose mother had died in the crash, BLACK ADAM, NORTHWIND, and Brainwave invaded Kobra's Himalayan stronghold and executed him. **DW**

RETURN TO POWER *Kobra squashed an attempted coup in his Himalayan mountain lair, in which disloyal cultists promoted an impostor to assume their master's place.*

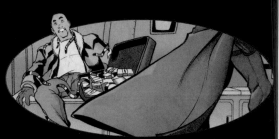

SERPENT SURPRISE *Reptile-themed punishments are a favorite for Kobra, seen here covering a victim in highly poisonous coral snakes.*

KRONA

FIRST APPEARANCE GREEN LANTERN (2nd series) #40 (October 1965)
STATUS Villain (discorporated) **REAL NAME** None
OCCUPATION Scientist; would-be tyrant **BASE** Nekron's dimension
HEIGHT 6ft 8in **WEIGHT** 349 lbs **EYES** Blue **HAIR** Black
SPECIAL POWERS/ABILITIES Immortal and invulnerable; Krona's vast
psionic abilities were increased by the demon Nekron to surpass
the powers of the Guardians of the Universe.

More than ten billion years ago on the planet Oa, the
scientist Krona ignored his people's admonition against
seeking the origins of the universe. He built a temporal
viewer to peel back the veil of time. What Krona saw
changed the whole fabric of the universe. As he gazed
transfixed at the hand of creation reaching into a star-
filled cosmos, Krona's machine exploded and reality
changed irrevocably. One universe became two, splitting
into positive-matter and anti-matter halves. The MONITOR,
and his evil doppelganger, the Anti-Monitor, were born
and a wave of evil engulfed the 50 million worlds of the
positive-matter universe (*see* Great Battles, pp. 320–1).
The Oan GUARDIANS OF THE UNIVERSE punished Krona by
turning his body into pure energy and shooting him across the
breadth of the Multiverse. Billions of years later, Krona escaped
his disembodied exile and entered the dimension of the dead
ruled by the demon Nekron. He restored Krona to corporeal form
and gave him the power to take revenge on the Guardians.
Following massive battles with the GREEN LANTERN CORPS, GREEN
LANTERN Hal Jordan forced Krona's armies back into Nekron's
demonic realm. No one knows whether Krona is aware that the
positive-matter universe is now a single, unified whole. **SB**

ALTERING REALITY
*Defying Oan taboos,
Krona sought the
secrets of the universe
and nearly destroyed it
in the process.*

KRYPTO, THE SUPERDOG

FIRST APPEARANCE ADVENTURE COMICS #210 (March 1955)
STATUS Heroic, but not always good **REAL NAME** Krypto
OCCUPATION Superman's best friend **BASE** Fortress of Solitude
HEIGHT 25.5in **WEIGHT** 40 lbs **EYES** Blue **HAIR** White
SPECIAL POWERS/ABILITIES Under Earth's solar radiation, Krypto is as
enhanced among animals as Superman is among mortals with superior
strength, invulnerability, and the power of flight.

SUPERMAN and Lois Lane (*see* LANE, LOIS) once traveled to false
Krypton through the Phantom Zone and experienced life on
the alien world in the days prior to its destruction. There, Kal-El
was reintroduced to his pet dog, Krypto. When the couple
returned to Earth, they were followed by Superman's best
friend. With the sun's radiation enhancing his abilities, Krypto
proved to be too exuberant for Superman's Metropolis
apartment. Superman has installed his pet in his arctic Fortress
of Solitude, although as the occasions require, he is freed to
participate in adventures such as the recent Imperiex
War (*see* Great Battles, pp. 320–1).
   Krypto's keen abilities have been called into use by
Superman, and even BATMAN, on more than one occasion.
He has formed a bond with SUPERBOY and enjoys the
freedom of life on the KENTS' family farm. **RG**

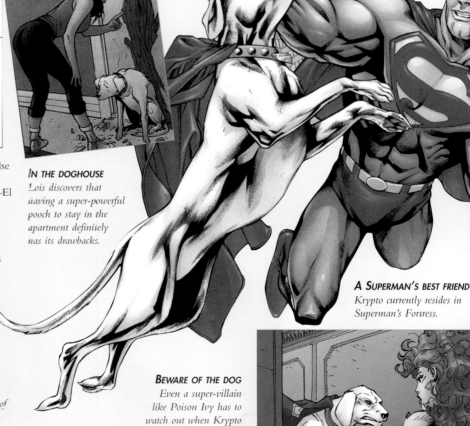

IN THE DOGHOUSE
*Lois discovers that
having a super-powerful
pooch to stay in the
apartment definitely
has its drawbacks.*

A SUPERMAN'S BEST FRIEND
*Krypto currently resides in
Superman's Fortress.*

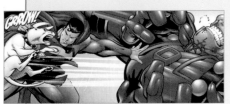

DOWN BOY!
*Fortunately for
Mongul, the Man of
Steel is on hand
when Krypto loses
his temper defending
his master.*

BEWARE OF THE DOG
*Even a super-villain
like Poison Ivy has to
watch out when Krypto
bares his teeth!*

L . E . G . I . O . N .

FIRST APPEARANCE INVASION #2 (1989)
STATUS Heroes   *BASE* The planet Cairn
KEY MEMBERS AND POWERS
Captain Comet (leader) Telekinetic and telepathic abilities.
Davroth Catto Flight, uncanny aerial agility.
Garryn Bek No superhuman abilities.
Marij'n Bek No superhuman abilities.
Darkstar (Lydea Mallor) Projects a negative energy field.
Vril Dox II (retired) 12th level intellect.
Amon Hakk Tremendous Khund strength.
Lobo (no longer active) Amazing regenerative abilities.
Zena Moonstruk Can absorb light and emit it in bursts.
Stealth Can manipulate soundwaves.
Strata Superstrength, invulnerability.
Garv Advanced telepathic abilities.

Formed during an alien invasion of Earth, the Licensed Extra-Governmental Interstellar Operatives Network (L.E.G.I.O.N.) is a heroic peacekeeping force protecting planets that subscribe to its service. The brilliant Coluan, Vril Dox II (son of BRANIAC), founded L.E.G.I.O.N. after he and its original core members escaped from a Dominator-run "Starlag" prison camp. On their first mission, Vril Dox and his compatriots liberated Dox's homeworld of Colu from the domineering grip of the ruling computer tyrants. They then cleaned out the riffraff from the vile planet of Cairn—the galaxy's "drug world"—and made it their headquarters. L.E.G.I.O.N.'s rapid run of successes lured several high-paying clients and attracted new members. The membership roster would remain in constant flux. L.E.G.I.O.N. continued its success until Dox's malevolent son Lyrl usurped control. Several members formed a rival team, the Revolutionary Elite Brigade to Eradicate L.E.G.I.O.N. Supremacy (R.E.B.E.L.S.), to restore L.E.G.I.O.N.'s good name. **DW**

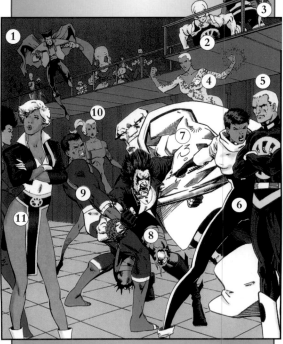

PEACE-KEEPING SQUADRON *Some of the key members of L.E.G.I.O.N. past and present:* 1) *Garryn Bek* 2) *Telepath* 3) *Garv* 4) *Lady Quark* 5) *Vril Dox II* 6) *Phase* 7) *Strata* 8) *Lobo* 9) *Captain Comet* 10) *Marij'n Bek* 11) *Stealth*

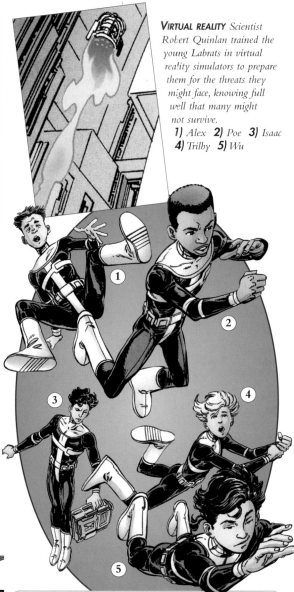

VIRTUAL REALITY *Scientist Robert Quinlan trained the young Labrats in virtual reality simulators to prepare them for the threats they might face, knowing full well that many might not survive.*
1) *Alex* 2) *Poe* 3) *Isaac*
4) *Trilby* 5) *Wu*

LAB RATS

FIRST APPEARANCE LAB RATS #1 (April 2002)
STATUS Heroes (deceased)   *BASE* The Campus
MEMBERS AND POWERS
Poe Possesses a high level intellect.
Alex Athlete.
Isaac The team strongman.
Trilby Computer whiz.
Dana Street-smart fighter.
Wu Possesses infiltration abilities.

Products of the mysterious institution known only as "The Campus," the Lab Rats were investigators, explorers, and guinea pigs. The Campus scientists, for their own mysterious reasons, exploited their eager test subjects by pitting them against various simulated dangers in specially designed virtual reality scenarios. The Lab Rats, whose oldest member was just 16, were trained in these simulations to handle extreme situations. Most of the Lab Rats were homeless teenagers, who exchanged their lives as street urchins for this high-tech training. When teammate Gia was killed during a training program, they left the Campus, encountering for the first time the dangers they had faced only as laboratory simulations, including rogue scientific oddities, UFOs, SUPERMAN, and a theme park populated by genetically engineered monsters. Tragically, their Campus training could not prevent them all from being killed. **PJ**

LADY FLASH

FIRST APPEARANCE THE FLASH (2nd series) #7 (December 1987)
STATUS Villain   *REAL NAME* Christina Alexandrova
OCCUPATION Assassin   *BASE* Mobile
HEIGHT 6ft 1in   *WEIGHT* 155 lbs   *EYES* Brown   *HAIR* Auburn
SPECIAL POWERS/ABILITIES Granted superspeed from a mixture of drugs and gene therapy, she also gained abnormal strength, but her wits were dulled as a result.

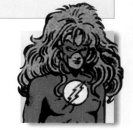

Christina has always been a joiner, starting Blue Trinity, a failed Soviet attempt to create a team of speedsters. After their final defeat at the hands of the FLASH III, she became VANDAL SAVAGE's slave, kept under his control through cocaine addiction. It was he who gave her one of Wally West's spare Flash uniforms to use in her latest identity of Lady Flash. She finally broke free of both the addiction and Savage's control and sided with the Flash to defeat the immortal. Rejected by the Flash, however, she wandered aimlessly until she fell under the influence of SAVITAR, the corrupt master of speed. She opposed WONDER WOMAN and Jesse Quick (*see* QUICK, JESSE) when she attempted to obtain a scroll that might have helped her free Savitar after his defeat. She was believed to be lost in the Speed Force, but she survived. Finally, she worked with KOBRA only to be defeated once again, this time by a right cross from Flash's wife, Linda Park (*see* PARK, LINDA). **RG**

LADY OF THE LAKE

FIRST APPEARANCE AQUAMAN (4th series) #1 (February 2003)
STATUS Ally   *REAL NAME* Unknown
OCCUPATION Water spirit   *BASE* The Secret Sea
HEIGHT 5ft 8in   *WEIGHT* 137 lbs   *EYES* Blue   *HAIR* Blue
SPECIAL POWERS/ABILITIES Undefined magical abilities.

This water spirit has appeared to only a few individuals, including AQUAMAN (Arthur Curry) and King Arthur. According to Arthurian legend the Lady gave the king the sword Excalibur. More recently, she has aided Aquaman, exchanging his prosthetic harpoon for a hand made of enchanted water and naming him "the Waterbearer." The Lady inhabits a grotto on an island off the west coast of Ireland, a place known variously as the Secret Sea, the Waters of Truth, or Annwn. Aquaman's hand receives its supernatural powers from the Lady. The hand can heal the injured and create portals into magical dimensions; when used in anger it causes the Lady pain. **DW**

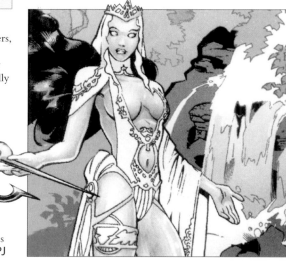

LADY SHIVA

FIRST APPEARANCE RICHARD DRAGON, KUNG-FU FIGHTER #5 (January 1976)
STATUS Villain **REAL NAME** Sandra Woosan (Lady Shiva Wu-San)
OCCUPATION Martial artist **BASE** Mobile
HEIGHT 5ft 8in **WEIGHT** 141 lbs **EYES** Brown **HAIR** Black
SPECIAL POWERS/ABILITIES Lady Shiva is a master of virtually every known (and several forgotten) martial-arts disciplines; will stop at nothing to become the world's best and most lethal fighter.

When evil industrialist Guano Cravat falsely convinced Sandra Woosan that fellow martial artist Richard Dragon (see DRAGON, RICHARD) had murdered her sister Carolyn, Woosan vowed vengeance. As "Lady Shiva," Woosan fought Dragon before Cravat's deception was revealed. Lady Shiva then allied herself with Dragon and the BRONZE TIGER (Dragon's friend and partner, Ben Turner) to dismantle Cravat's criminal consortium while serving as an operative of G.O.O.D., a U.S. government-sponsored spy organization. Later, Shiva opted for solo intrigue as a mercenary and hired assassin, honing her already formidable martial-arts skills to optimum efficiency. In this regard, Shiva has fought on both sides of the law. She is credited with training the QUESTION to become a better brawler, as well as helping BATMAN to regain the use of his legs and fighting spirit after the terrorist BANE had crippled him. However, both heroes know well that Lady Shiva's loyalties are capricious.

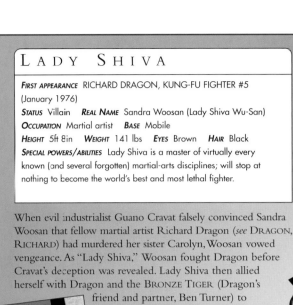

PAPER MONKEY *Lady Shiva ascended to supremacy within the Cult of the Monkey Fist through mortal combat. After killing every opponent foolhardy enough to challenge her, she ranks as "Paper Monkey"— supreme sensei of this secret fight club.*

When it suits her, Shiva wields ninja and samurai arms with deadly grace. But her own body is a far more formidable weapon. In her years traveling the world, Shiva has blended the fighting finesse of judo, koroshi, karate, savate, capoeira, kung-fu, and countless other martial arts to create a style ideally suited for her size and frame. Opponents underestimate Shiva to their dying dismay. **SB**

RIOT GIRLS *Lady Shiva offered to unlock Cassandra Cain's fighting potential if the young Batgirl agreed to fight her to the death after one year had passed!*

KNIFE WORK *Lady Vic goes into battle armed with her favorite knives; she is also adept with most types of conventional weaponry.*

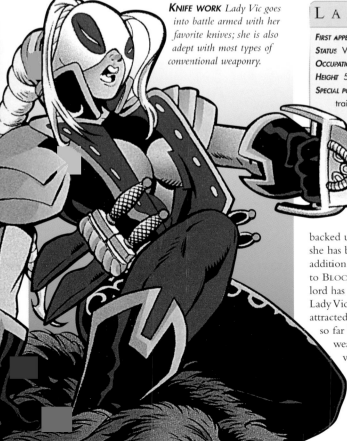

LADY VIC

FIRST APPEARANCE NIGHTWING #4 (January 1997)
STATUS Villain **REAL NAME** Lady Elaine Marsh-Morton
OCCUPATION Assassin **BASE** England
HEIGHT 5ft 6in **WEIGHT** 135 lbs **EYES** Blue **HAIR** Blonde
SPECIAL POWERS/ABILITIES Mastery of arcane weapons and a highly trained hand-to-hand combatant.

Lady Elaine Marsh-Morton took the name Lady Vic—short for Victim— when she entered into her family's long tradition of mercenary work. It is estimated that she is only in her late twenties; however, she has already gained an impressive list of kills, backed up by a reputation for cunning and guile. Those she has battled with include BATMAN and CATWOMAN. In addition to her international clients, she serves on retainer to BLOCKBUSTER II in the town of Blüdhaven. This crime lord has frequently pitted her against NIGHTWING. Lady Vic seems to be one of the few women who is not attracted to the costumed vigilante, and their battles have so far been indecisive. Her skill with the ancestral weapons of her family, including flintlock pistols and various swords, makes her a formidable opponent. She appears to prefer using weapons to close combat, which has placed her at a disadvantage from time to time. **RG**

LADY ZAND

FIRST APPEARANCE YOUNG JUSTICE #50 (December 2002)
STATUS Villain **REAL NAME** Unknown
OCCUPATION Ruler of Zandia **BASE** Zandia
HEIGHT 5ft 10in **WEIGHT** 156 lbs **EYES** Blue **HAIR** Brown
SPECIAL POWERS/ABILITIES Can transform into an earthen giant.

A cruel, quick-tempered aristocrat who possesses considerable elemental powers, Lady Zand is believed to be the founder of the tiny Baltic island nation of Zandia—which, if true, would make her more than 800 years old! In modern times, Zandia has become notorious as a secret haven for on-the-run supervillains. It is also home to the worldwide Church of Blood (see BROTHER BLOOD), a sinister organization that is based upon Lady Zand's ruthless philosophy that might equals right. In recent years, Lady Zand has made concerted efforts to boost Zandia's profile and improve its standing in the world. She has even sent a small team of athletes to compete in the Olympic games. When angered, Lady Zand possesses an extraordinary ability: she can literally become "the soil of her homeworld," transforming herself into a towering figure made of rock and earth. She demonstrated this ability to great effect in a spectacular battle with the heroes of YOUNG JUSTICE. **DW**

LANE, LOIS

WORLD-CLASS REPORTER

FIRST APPEARANCE ACTION COMICS #1 (June 1938)
STATUS Hero **REAL NAME** Lois Joanne Lane
OCCUPATION Reporter **BASE** Metropolis
HEIGHT 5ft 6in **WEIGHT** 136 lbs **EYES** Blue **HAIR** Black
SPECIAL POWERS/ABILITIES Superb investigative journalist with an instinctive "nose" for a good story; trained in various hand-to-hand combat techniques and an adequate marksman.

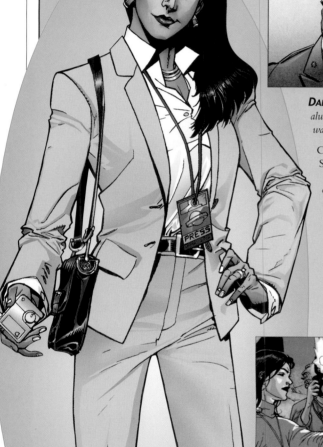

A PULITZER PRIZE–WINNING JOURNALIST, Lois Lane specializes in reporting from the front lines of war zones and natural catastrophes for Metropolis's *Daily Planet* newspaper. One day a truly incredible story presented itself right in her own backyard. While covering a LexCorp-engineered disaster in Metropolis with young photographer Jimmy Olsen (see OLSEN, JIMMY), Lois was rescued from certain death by a superstrong flying man. She became the very first reporter to record the exploits of the amazing costumed champion she named SUPERMAN. Her world, already full of activity, had just been turned upside down.

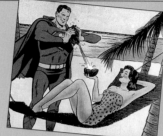

AWAY FROM IT ALL *Superman and Lois take a well-earned break from saving the world.*

A NOSE FOR NEWS

The daughter of General Sam and Elinore Lane, Lois was born in a U.S. Army hospital outside of Wiesbaden, Germany. Sam Lane had always wanted a boy, and did not hide his disappointment from Lois, who became a model of self-sufficiency in response to her father's emotional distance. After high school, Lois moved to Metropolis and worked full time at the *Daily Planet*. She also attracted the attention of Lex Luthor (see LUTHOR, LEX); however, Lois spurned his every advance.

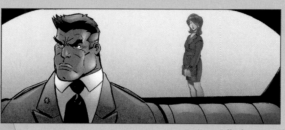

DADDY DEAREST *Sam Lane always wanted a son and was never close to Lois.*

Lois rapidly became the *Daily Planet's* leading investigative reporter, winning many awards and a daredevil reputation. After Superman's first appearance, she befriended both the Man of Steel and a new, mild-mannered reporter named Clark Kent. Of course, the biggest story was right under Lois's nose: Clark and Superman were one and the same person!

Over time and countless adventures, Lois and Clark fell in love and became engaged. Shortly after, Clark revealed his secret identity to Lois. Shocked as she was, she still agreed to marry him, as she loved Clark regardless and was moved that he had shared his secret with her. Tragedy struck when the Kryptonian creature DOOMSDAY seemingly killed Superman during a violent rampage through the streets of Metropolis. Devastated, Lois cradled her dying lover in her arms as the life slowly ebbed from Superman's body. But Lois did not have to mourn for long, and upon Superman's return from the dead, the couple had a joyous reunion.

During one of the JOKER's visits to the city, Lois was shocked to discover that Superman was willing to let her die rather than kill the villain to save her life. Her doubts fueled by this and other factors, she broke off her engagement to Clark and accepted an offer to become the *Planet's* foreign correspondent. However, at the last minute she realized that she still loved Clark, and the happy couple were finally married.

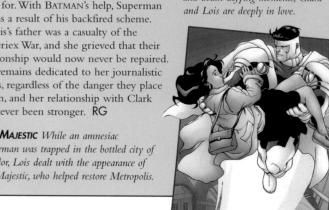

TRUE LOVE *Despite separations, spats, and death-defying moments, Clark and Lois are deeply in love.*

INTREPID REPORTER
Lois never shies away from a good story.

Luthor then bought the financially troubled *Daily Planet* and closed it down. Lois was one of the few who retained jobs with Luthor's media enterprise, LexCom. Lex eventually sold the paper back to its editor, Perry White (see WHITE, PERRY), having secretly arranged a deal whereby Lois agreed to kill one story of Luthor's choosing in the future. Lois's discovery that Luthor had had advance knowledge of the coming war with IMPERIEX (see Great Battles, pp. 320–1) became the scoop that she reluctantly agreed to kill. Meanwhile, Clark and Lois faced a crisis of a different kind: Lois had been impersonated for weeks by the PARASITE, a villain who sought to destroy all that Superman stood for. With BATMAN's help, Superman found and rescued the real Lois after the Parasite died as a result of his backfired scheme.

Lois's father was a casualty of the Imperiex War, and she grieved that their relationship would now never be repaired. She remains dedicated to her journalistic ideals, regardless of the danger they place her in, and her relationship with Clark has never been stronger. **RG**

MR. MAJESTIC *While an amnesiac Superman was trapped in the bottled city of Kandor, Lois dealt with the appearance of Mr. Majestic, who helped restore Metropolis.*

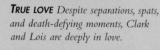

KEY STORYLINES

- **ACTION COMICS #662 (1991):** Clark reveals the secret of his identity to his fiancée.
- **SUPERMAN: THE WEDDING ALBUM (1996):** Lois marries Clark in the wedding of the century!
- **SUPERMAN (2ND SERIES) #151 (2001):** Lois makes her deal with Luthor, in order to save the *Daily Planet*.
- **ADVENTURES OF SUPERMAN #631 (2004):** Lois is shot and gravely wounded while covering the U.S. occupation of Umec in the Middle East.

LANG, LANA

FIRST APPEARANCE SUPERBOY (1st series) #10 (October 1950)
STATUS Ally **REAL NAME** Lana Elizabeth Lang
OCCUPATION Small-business owner **BASE** Metropolis
HEIGHT 5ft 4in **WEIGHT** 127 lbs **EYES** Blue **HAIR** Red
SPECIAL POWERS/ABILITIES Lana is an average athlete, but has a strong will and is fiercely loyal to those she loves.

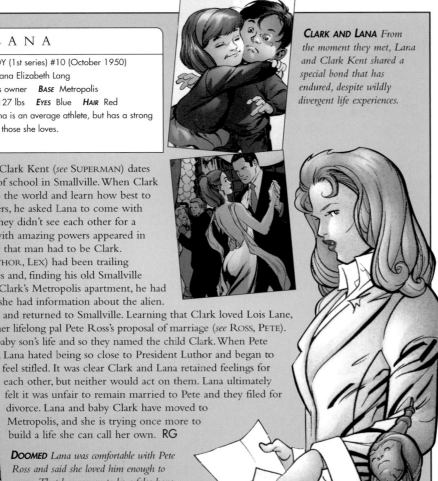

CLARK AND LANA From the moment they met, Lana and Clark Kent shared a special bond that has endured, despite wildly divergent life experiences.

Lana's friendship with Clark Kent (*see* SUPERMAN) dates back to their first day of school in Smallville. When Clark resolved to go out into the world and learn how best to use his new superpowers, he asked Lana to come with him. She refused and they didn't see each other for a decade. When a man with amazing powers appeared in Metropolis, Lana knew that man had to be Clark.

Lex Luthor (see LUTHOR, LEX) had been trailing Superman's appearances and, finding his old Smallville schoolmate Lana near Clark's Metropolis apartment, he had her tortured, thinking she had information about the alien. Lana told him nothing and returned to Smallville. Learning that Clark loved Lois Lane, Lana finally agreed to her lifelong pal Pete Ross's proposal of marriage (see ROSS, PETE). Superman saved their baby son's life and so they named the child Clark. When Pete became Vice President, Lana hated being so close to President Luthor and began to feel stifled. It was clear Clark and Lana retained feelings for each other, but neither would act on them. Lana ultimately felt it was unfair to remain married to Pete and they filed for divorce. Lana and baby Clark have moved to Metropolis, and she is trying once more to build a life she can call her own. **RG**

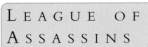

DOOMED Lana was comfortable with Pete Ross and said she loved him enough to marry. That has proven to be a false hope.

LEAGUE OF ASSASSINS

FIRST APPEARANCE STRANGE ADVENTURES #215 (December 1968)
STATUS Villains **BASE** Worldwide
MEMBERS AND POWERS
Rā's al Ghūl Immortal; brilliant criminal mind.
Sensei (deceased) Top martial artist.
Doctor Darrk (deceased) No superhuman abilities.
Kirigi Top martial artist; League of Assassins trainer.
Merlyn (ex-member) Deadly assassin with bow and arrow.
Talia Rā's al Ghūl's bewitchingly beautiful daughter.

The League of Assassins operates in secret throughout every country of the world. Called into being by the criminal mastermind RĀ'S AL GHŪL, their original mission was to shield their master from attacks (the League described itself as "the fang which protects his head"), and to accept paying jobs from clients who want someone eliminated and have the deep pockets to hire the best of the best. Only assassins who have already completed a previous hit can be considered for League membership, and its roster is kept strictly confidential.

For many years, day-to-day control of the League of Assassins fell to the Sensei (who oversaw the killers on staff) and Doctor Darrk (who interacted with clients). It was the Sensei who arranged for the death of acrobat Boston Brand, who later became DEADMAN. One of the League's agents, Hook, was involved in the Brand hit, and other League contracts fell under the jurisdiction of the archer Merlyn, whose skill with a bow rivaled that of GREEN ARROW. Eventually the Sensei moved to split the League off from Rā's al Ghūl's control and died for his impudence. Rā's al Ghūl then took a more direct role in League affairs. **DW**

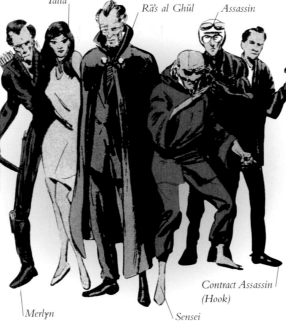

Talia
Rā's al Ghūl
Contract Assassin
Merlyn
Sensei
Contract Assassin (Hook)

LEATHER

FIRST APPEARANCE NIGHTWING #62 (December 2001)
STATUS Villain **REAL NAME** Mary Kay Tanner
OCCUPATION Criminal "coyote" **BASE** Peckinpah, Texas
HEIGHT 5ft 5in **WEIGHT** 132 lbs **EYES** White **HAIR** Auburn
SPECIAL POWERS/ABILITIES Leatherlike skin; low-level superstrength; razor-sharp claws on hands and feet; psychopathic temperament; armed with a variety of barbed whips.

Tanner's mother often used illegal, highly experimental narcotics to get high, and Mary Kay was born with meta-human powers that gave her leatherlike skin and claws. At 16 she had become the leader of a band of "coyotes," who smuggled illegal immigrants back and forth between Mexico and the U.S. Leather was captured and incarcerated in the women's block of the Slab penitentiary. However, she was freed by the JOKER and has returned to smuggling in Mexico. **PJ**

LEGION OF SUBSTITUTE HEROES

FIRST APPEARANCE LEGIONNAIRES #47 (June 1997)
STATUS Heroes **BASE** Mobile
MEMBERS AND POWERS
Night Girl (Lydda Jath) Possesses superstrength in the dark. **Polar Boy (Brek Bannin)** Generates intense cold. **Chlorophyll Kid (Ral Benem)** Stimulates rapid plant growth. **Color Kid (Ulu Vakk)** Able to alter the color of any object. **Fire Lad (Staq Mavlen)** Exhales fiery breath. **Stone Boy (Dag Wentim)** Capable of turning his body to stone. **Porcupine Pete (Peter Dursin)** Projects quill-like spines at will. **Infectious Lass (Drura Sehpt)** Body hosts a variety of disease colonies. **Antenna Boy (Khfeurb Chee Bez)** Transmits and receives electronic signals via ear-antennae. **Double-Header (Dyvud/Frenk Retzun)** Bickering beings sharing single body.

The LEGION OF SUPER-HEROES has initiated several recruitment drives to bolster its ranks. However, many young heroes and heroines are turned away by the Legion for lack of experience or for possessing powers deemed too dangerous or unpredictable. Rejected applicants POLAR BOY and Night Girl decided to form their own Legion of Substitute Heroes—unsanctioned by the United Planets, of course—a team that would allow them to hone their unique abilities and do some good, at least until the real LSH recognized their worth.

Since its formation, the Legion of Substitute Heroes has grown to include Chlorophyll Kid, Color Kid, Fire Lad, and Stone Boy, all of whom may not possess the most spectacular superpowers, but nevertheless want to defend the galaxy in the same grand tradition as the Legion of Super-Heroes. Recently, Polar Boy was selected to join the Legion Cadet Program for training to become a future member of the LSH. The remaining Subs are hopeful that they might follow suit someday soon. **SB**

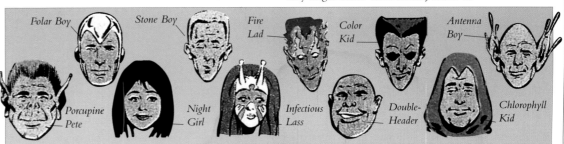

Polar Boy *Stone Boy* *Fire Lad* *Color Kid* *Antenna Boy*
Porcupine Pete *Night Girl* *Infectious Lass* *Double-Header* *Chlorophyll Kid*

THE LEGION OF SUBSTITUTE HEROES

THE LEGION OF SUPER-HEROES

TEEN DEFENDERS OF TOMORROW

FIRST APPEARANCE ADVENTURE COMICS #247 (April 1958)
STATUS Hero team
BASE Legion World, U.P. Space

NOTABLE MEMBERS
Apparition (Tinya Wazzo)
Brainiac 5.1 (Querl Dox)
Chameleon (Reep Daggle)
Chuck Taine Honorary member
Cosmic Boy (Rokk Krinn)
Dragonmage (Xao Jin)
Dreamer (Nura Nal)
Element Lad (Jan Arrah) Deceased
Ferro (Andrew Nolan)
Gates (Ti'julk Mr'asz)
Gear (I.Z.O.R.)
Inferno (Sandy Anderson)
Invisible Kid (Lyle Norg)
Karate Kid (Val Armorr)
Kid Quantum I (James Cullen) Deceased
Kid Quantum II (Jazmin Cullen)
Kinetix (Zoe Saugin)
Leviathan (Gim Allon) Deceased
Live Wire (Garth Ranzz)
Magno (Dyrk Magz)
M'onel (Lar Gand)
Monstress (Candi Pyponte-LeParc III) Deceased
Mysa
Particon (Real name unrevealed)
Radion (Real name unrevealed)
Saturn Girl (Imra Ardeen)
Sensor (Jeka Wynzorr)
Shikari
Shvaughn Erin Science Police Liaison Officer
Sister Andromeda (Laurel Gand)
Spark (Ayla Ranzz)
Star Boy (Thom Kallor)
Superboy (Conner Kent/Kon-El)
Thunder (Cece Beck)
Timber Wolf (Brin Londo)
Triad (Luornu Durgo)
Ultra Boy (Jo Nah)
Umbra (Tasmia Mallor)
Violet (Salu Digby)
Wildfire (Drake Burroughs)
XS (Jenni Ognats)

THROUGH EVERY CRISIS to come in the space-time continuum, one constant is that a group of young heroes and heroines will unite to defend their homeworlds from evil. Whether inspired by the boy who would become SUPERMAN or any of the costumed champions lost to history, the Legion of Super-Heroes will be that bright ray of hope in an uncertain future.

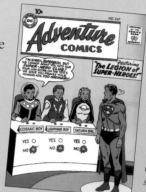

NOT SO SUPER
Despite owing its very existence to the Boy of Steel, the Legion of Super-Heroes denied him membership in the team's debut appearance because he had no "unique" superpowers.

THE UNITED PLANETS
By the beginning of the 31st century, a dozen worlds joined in peaceful coexistence as the United Planets. This federation was the realization of the dreams of the industrialist and philanthropist R.J. Brande (*see* BRANDE, R.J.). His Earth-based corporation also facilitated interplanetary travel by providing space-warping stargates to each of the United Planets' inhabited worlds. Unfortunately, while Brande was visiting the planet Titan, his enemies seized an opportunity to end the philanthropist's life and shatter the United Planets' tenuous alliance in one fell swoop. But Brande's assassins had not accounted for the presence of three heroic young strangers from different worlds. Their astounding powers enabled them to thwart Brande's attackers and inspire him with the most ambitious business venture he would ever embark upon.

HEADING
Those young people—Rokk Krinn of Braal, Imra Ardeen of Titan, and Garth Ranzz of Winath—would be known as COSMIC BOY, SATURN GIRL, and LIVE WIRE. They became the first members of the Brande-funded Legion of Super-Heroes, which was initially based on Earth, in Metropolis. Representatives from nearly all of the U.P. joined to serve as guardians of the coalition. The Legion battled terrorists attempting to tear apart the U.P. alliance, and other evils, such as the arachnid alien Tangleweb, the ruthless hunter Grimbor, and Mano, who disintegrated anything he touched. Kid Quantum I (*see* KID QUANTUM I & II) became the first of several young heroes to give his life in service to Brande and the U.P.

Eventually, the Legionnaires all possessed anti-gravity enabling flight rings invented by team member Lyle Norg (INVISIBLE KID), who later formed the Legion Espionage Squad to investigate a racist terror group known as the White Triangle.

THE SUN-EATER CRISIS
While battling the Emerald Empress, a group of Legionnaires—BRAINIAC 5, Cosmic Boy, GATES, Inferno, Saturn Girl, ULTRA BOY, and Shvaughn Erin—were transported back to the 20th century by the Empress's Emerald Eye. There the Legionnaires met such heroes as Superman, Impulse, and DEADMAN, the latter instrumental in helping APPARITION—who had been residing within Ultra Boy's body—to regain some material substance. The time-lost Legionnaires used their abilities to help battle the Sun-Eater, a star-consuming entity that had laid waste to entire galaxies. While the young heroes helped refugees of the rapidly-cooling Earth, their new allies Ingot and FERRO attempted to re-ignite Earth's life-giving star. Ingot perished, but Ferro was saved by Hal Jordan in his guise as PARALLAX, who restored the sun to its full radiance.

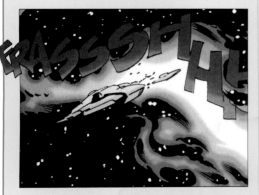

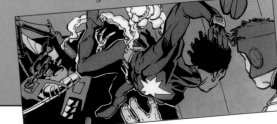

FOUNDING MEMBERS *The LSH was comprised of Cosmic Boy, Saturn Girl, and Live Wire, the trio who saved R.J. Brande's life.*

LEGIONNAIRE LOST *Kid Quantum was the first casualty among the Legion's ranks, perishing in battle with the creature known as Tangleweb.*

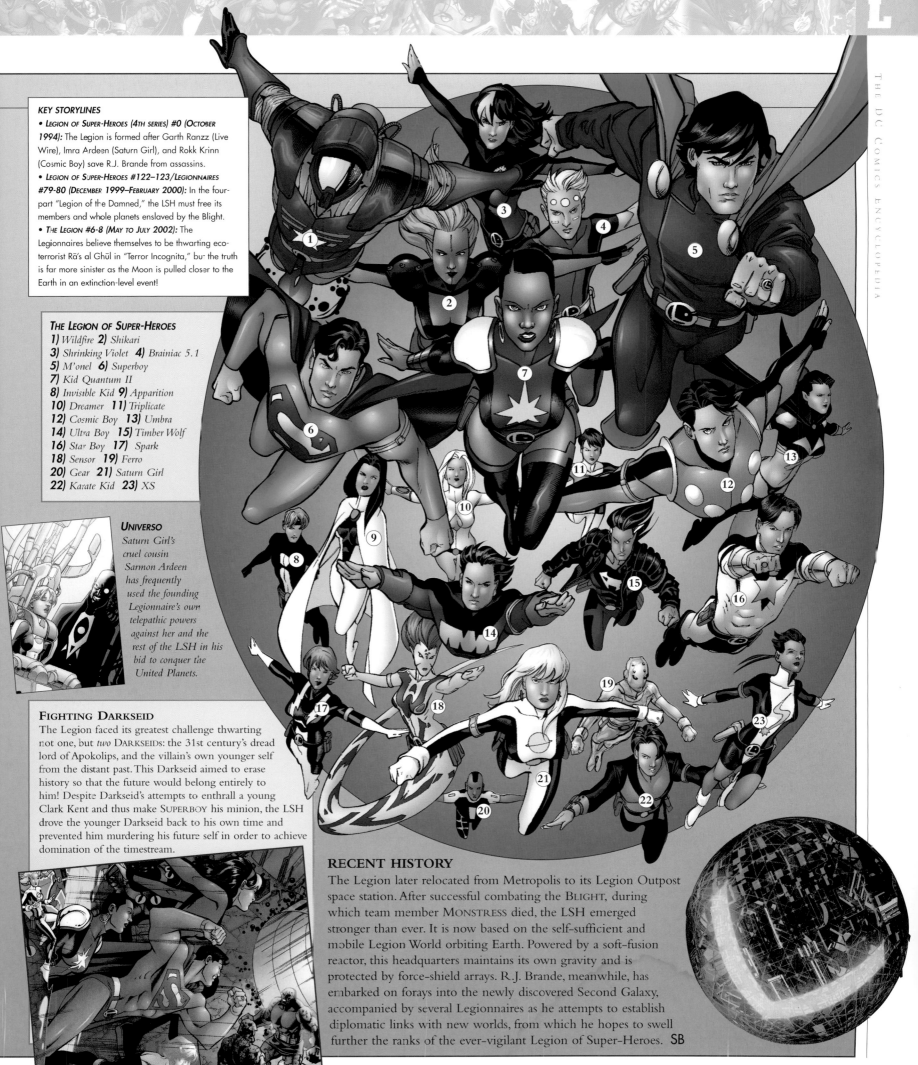

KEY STORYLINES

- *LEGION OF SUPER-HEROES (4TH SERIES) #0 (OCTOBER 1994):* The Legion is formed after Garth Ranzz (Live Wire), Imra Ardeen (Saturn Girl), and Rokk Krinn (Cosmic Boy) save R.J. Brande from assassins.
- *LEGION OF SUPER-HEROES #122–123/LEGIONNAIRES #79-80 (DECEMBER 1999–FEBRUARY 2000):* In the four-part "Legion of the Damned," the LSH must free its members and whole planets enslaved by the Blight.
- *THE LEGION #6-8 (MAY TO JULY 2002):* The Legionnaires believe themselves to be thwarting eco-terrorist Rā's al Ghūl in "Terror Incognita," but the truth is far more sinister as the Moon is pulled closer to the Earth in an extinction-level event!

THE LEGION OF SUPER-HEROES

1) Wildfire 2) Shikari
3) Shrinking Violet 4) Brainiac 5.1
5) M'onel 6) Superboy
7) Kid Quantum II
8) Invisible Kid 9) Apparition
10) Dreamer 11) Triplicate
12) Cosmic Boy 13) Umbra
14) Ultra Boy 15) Timber Wolf
16) Star Boy 17) Spark
18) Sensor 19) Ferro
20) Gear 21) Saturn Girl
22) Karate Kid 23) XS

UNIVERSO

Saturn Girl's cruel cousin Sarmon Ardeen has frequently used the founding Legionnaire's own telepathic powers against her and the rest of the LSH in his bid to conquer the United Planets.

FIGHTING DARKSEID

The Legion faced its greatest challenge thwarting not one, but *two* DARKSEIDS: the 31st century's dread lord of Apokolips, and the villain's own younger self from the distant past. This Darkseid aimed to erase history so that the future would belong entirely to him! Despite Darkseid's attempts to enthrall a young Clark Kent and thus make SUPERBOY his minion, the LSH drove the younger Darkseid back to his own time and prevented him murdering his future self in order to achieve domination of the timestream.

RECENT HISTORY

The Legion later relocated from Metropolis to its Legion Outpost space station. After successful combating the BLIGHT, during which team member MONSTRESS died, the LSH emerged stronger than ever. It is now based on the self-sufficient and mobile Legion World orbiting Earth. Powered by a soft-fusion reactor, this headquarters maintains its own gravity and is protected by force-shield arrays. R.J. Brande, meanwhile, has embarked on forays into the newly discovered Second Galaxy, accompanied by several Legionnaires as he attempts to establish diplomatic links with new worlds, from which he hopes to swell further the ranks of the ever-vigilant Legion of Super-Heroes. SB

THE DC COMICS ENCYCLOPEDIA

LEMARIS, LORI

FIRST APPEARANCE SUPERMAN (1st series) #129 (May 1959)
STATUS Hero **REAL NAME** Lori Lemaris
OCCUPATION Scientist **BASE** Metropolis
HEIGHT 5ft 9in **WEIGHT** 243 lbs (with tail) **EYES** Brown **HAIR** Brown
SPECIAL POWERS/ABILITIES An actual mermaid; can communicate telepathically and breathe underwater; grows legs when on land.

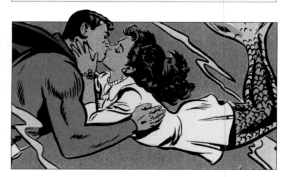

UNDERWATER LOVE *Before Lois Lane, mermaid Lori was the girl who melted the heart of the Man of Steel.*

A mermaid belonging to the undersea realm of Tritonis, Lori Lemaris began a relationship with Clark Kent while both attended Metropolis University. Lori concealed her tail beneath a blanket and moved about in a wheelchair. Eventually SUPERMAN discovered the truth, but Lori chose to remain with her people, marrying the merman scientist Ronal after he nursed her back to health following an injury. Contrary to some reports, Lori Lemaris survived her encounter with the Anti-Monitor's shadow-demons during the Crisis (*see* Great Battles, pp. 320–1). Later, Ronal's sorcery enabled her to grow legs on land. She went to live in Metropolis and was a bridesmaid at Clark and Lois Lane's wedding (*see* LANE, LOIS). Lori was a member of the "Justice League of Atlantis" during the JUSTICE LEAGUE OF AMERICA's struggle against the Advance Man. **DW**

LEVIATHAN

FIRST APPEARANCE LEGIONNAIRES #0 (April 1993)
STATUS Hero (deceased) **REAL NAME** Gim Allon
OCCUPATION Legionnaire **BASE** Legion World
HEIGHT 6ft 2in **WEIGHT** 200 lbs **EYES** Brown **HAIR** Brown
SPECIAL POWERS/ABILITIES Could increase his size and mass at will, up to a height of 30ft.

Gim Allon always wanted to be a hero. A resident of Mars, he graduated from the Science Police Academy in the late 30th century. During the high-speed pursuit of a suspect, an accident involving a radioactive meteorite gave him the ability to become a giant at will. The government of Mars named him the Martian representative to the LEGION OF SUPER-HEROES, where he took the code name Leviathan.

The United Planets appointed Allon as team leader, but after a disastrous mission that resulted in the death of Kid Quantum I (*see* KID QUANTUM I & II), he relinquished control to COSMIC BOY and became deputy leader. Later, after his teammate SHRINKING VIOLET became possessed by the omnipotent Emerald Eye, Leviathan sacrificed his life to defeat the evil Doctor Regulus. He received a hero's funeral on Shanghalla.

Shrinking Violet discovered that the Emerald Eye gave her Gim Allon's growth powers to complement her natural shrinking powers. She has since adopted the name Le Viathan in memory of Allon. **DW**

GOLIATH *An easy target while a giant, Leviathan's proportional strength made him virtually unstoppable.*

LIBERTY BELLE

FIRST APPEARANCE BOY COMMANDOS #1 (Winter 1942)
STATUS Hero **REAL NAME** Libby Belle Lawrence
OCCUPATION Journalist; broadcaster **BASE** New York City
HEIGHT 5ft 6in **WEIGHT** 140 lbs **EYES** Blue **HAIR** White (was blonde)
SPECIAL POWERS/ABILITIES Can project sonic blasts from her hands; gains superstrength when the Liberty Belle is rung.

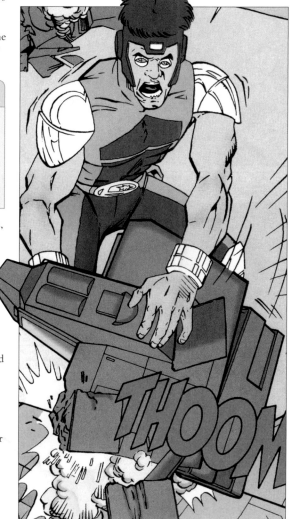

Libby Lawrence is the descendant of the Revolutionary War heroine MISS LIBERTY. A champion athlete in school when her father was killed in 1939 by Nazis in Poland, Libby escaped by swimming the English Channel, becoming an international celebrity. Libby gained superpowers through a mystic link to the Liberty Bell and became Liberty Belle, a founder member of the ALL-STAR SQUADRON. After being irradiated by one of the Nazi BARON BLITZKRIEG's weapons, Liberty Belle gained her sonic powers. She married fellow crime fighter Johnny Quick (*see* QUICK, JOHNNY), and their daughter Jesse later became the hero Jesse Quick (*see* QUICK, JESSE). As a retired widow, Liberty Belle believed she had found love again until she learned that her fiancé, Philip, was also having an affair with Jesse. Philip was accidentally killed and Libby's relationship with her daughter was left temporarily strained. **PJ**

LIGHTNING LORD

FIRST APPEARANCE SUPERMAN (1st series) #147 (August 1961)
STATUS Villain **REAL NAME** Mekt Ranzz
OCCUPATION Super-villain **BASE** Winath
HEIGHT 5ft 11in **WEIGHT** 167 lbs **EYES** Blue **HAIR** White
SPECIAL POWERS/ABILITIES Absorbs electricity and projects bolts of lightning of huge destructive power.

When their space cruiser crashed on the isolated world of Korbal, Mekt Ranzz and his younger brother and sister, twins Garth and Ayla, were attacked by the planet's lightning beasts. The physiologies of all three were altered by the electrical energies generated by the beasts, enabling them to project powerful lightning blasts. Garth and Ayla became members of the LEGION OF SUPER-HEROES as LIVE WIRE and SPARK. Mekt used his powers for thievery and murder as Lightning Lord. Live Wire battled his brother, losing his right arm; however, Lightning Lord was defeated and arrested by the United Planets' Science Police. Mekt now hates his heroic siblings for betraying him and plots electrifying revenge against them and their Legionnaire comrades. **SB**

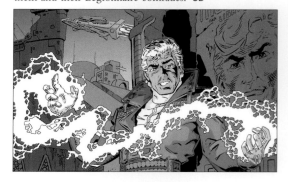

LIGHTRAY

FIRST APPEARANCE NEW GODS (1st series) #1 (March 1971)
STATUS Hero **REAL NAME** Solis
OCCUPATION New God **BASE** New Genesis
HEIGHT 6ft **WEIGHT** 181 lbs **EYES** Blue **HAIR** Red
SPECIAL POWERS/ABILITIES Can fly and harness all the various frequencies of the light spectrum, using its radiation to either temporarily blind opponents or to punch through objects; a super-strong, agile combatant; maintains a cheerful outlook on life.

Solis grew up a happy child on the planet New Genesis, befriending ORION, scion of DARKSEID, who also came to grow up on the planet of light. One day, while exploring, they found a pit where soldiers from Apokolips were massing for an assault. No ordinary soldiers, they had been turned into living masses of light. Solis was spotted and pelted with solar radiation. The scientific genius METRON summoned help, and arrived to find Solis in a coma.

After many months, Metron successfully revived the boy, who had absorbed all the radiation and was now changed, imbued with new abilities. Solis eventually mastered these powers, renaming himself Lightray. Of all the NEW GODS living on New Genesis, Lightray is probably the happiest. He finds life on New Genesis very satisfying, but also appreciates the many wonders of Earth, leading him to take on a brief stint with the JUSTICE LEAGUE OF AMERICA. **RG**

LINEAR MEN

FIRST APPEARANCE ADVENTURES OF SUPERMAN
#476 (March 1991)
STATUS Hero team   **BASE** Vanishing Point
CURRENT MEMBERS AND POWERS
Dr. Matthew Ryder (leader) Scientific genius.
Dr. Rip Hunter Time-travel inventor.
Liri Lee Chronal archivist.
Travis O'Connell (deceased) Adventurer.
Waverider (Matthew Ryder from an alternate timeline)
Possesses the ability to freely travel the timestream and
pinpoint chronal anomalies.

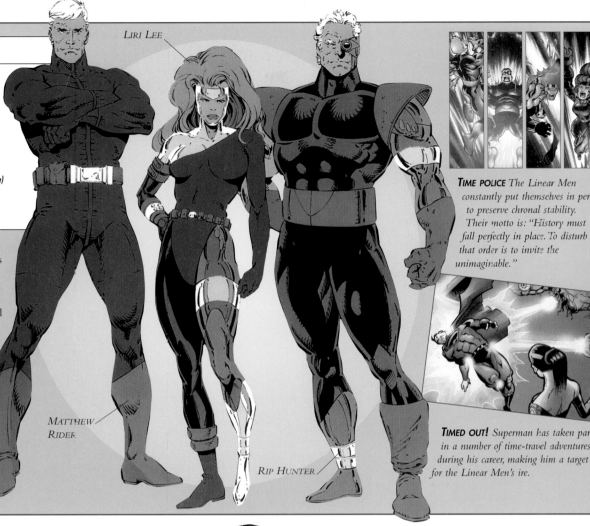

LIRI LEE

MATTHEW RYDER

RIP HUNTER

TIME POLICE The Linear Men
constantly put themselves in peril
to preserve chronal stability.
Their motto is: "History must
fall perfectly in place. To disturb
that order is to invite the
unimaginable."

TIMED OUT! Superman has taken part
in a number of time-travel adventures
during his career, making him a target
for the Linear Men's ire.

The Linear Men are "time police" who try
to keep the past and future safe from careless
time travelers. Leader Matthew Ryder
discovered the Vanishing Point realm outside
of space and time, where the Linear Men
now maintain their base. Due to the physical
stresses of time travel, pieces of the Linear
Men's bodies have been replaced with
cyborg limbs. The Linear Men played a
key role in the fight against GOG,
revealing the existence of a
"hypertime" containing all possible
alternate timestreams. After SUPERMAN
defeated IMPERIEX by sending him back
to the Big Bang, the Linear Men
attempted to have the Man of Steel tried
for crimes against the timeline. They
now appear to have shunned their
physical forms and appear only as
manifestations of the intellect. **DW**

LIONHEART

FIRST APPEARANCE JUSTICE LEAGUE INTERNATIONAL
ANNUAL #4 1993
STATUS Hero   **REAL NAME** Richard Plante
OCCUPATION Government operative   **BASE** London, England
HEIGHT 6ft 1in   **WEIGHT** 186 lbs   **EYES** Blue   **HAIR** Black
SPECIAL POWERS/ABILITIES Advanced armor enhances strength and
permits flight; wields energy sword and shield.

A former union dockworker, Richard Plante's bravery and
fierce loyalty to his native United Kingdom made him an
ideal recruit to defend England as a government operative.
Clad in advanced armor and wielding a blazing energy
sword, Plante—a direct descendant of King Richard I—
dubbed himself Lionheart after his namesake. Allied with
Justice League International (see JUSTICE LEAGUE OF
AMERICA), Lionheart battled modern-day dragons in the
form of alien parasites murdering humans across the globe.
Lionheart remains an active defender
of the U.K. **SB**

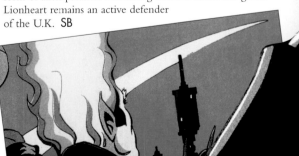

**KNIGHT IN
SHINING ARMOR**
*A dauntless knight
in high-tech armor,
Lionheart battles to
protect Britons from
super-villain threats as a
modern-day dragonslayer.*

LITTLE BOY BLUE
AND THE BLUE BOYS

FIRST APPEARANCE SENSATION COMICS #1 (1942)
STATUS Hero team   **REAL NAMES** Tommy Rogers, "Tubby", Herbert
"Toughy" Simms, Little Miss Redhead
BASE Radiance, Pennsylvania
SPECIAL POWERS/ABILITIES Quick wits, good humor, and fast fists.

Frustrated by Wolf Lupo's
crime wave in Big City,
youngsters Tommy Rogers,
"Tubby", and Herbert
"Toughy" Simms took
matters into their own
hands as Little Boy Blue and
the Blue Boys. They
continued to have lighthearted
adventures, thwarting all
manner of criminals during the
1940s. At one point, a mysterious
girl known as Little Miss
Redhead arrived to fight crime
beside them, using a lariat and
bolo. Decades later, Tommy
became the mayor and Herb the sheriff. When Tommy's son
Shawn discovered his dad's diary and learned of the parents'
costumed exploits, the children were inspired. Herb's son
Timmy was nicknamed "Static" for his fascination with
radios, while Tubby's son was a skateboarder dubbed "Slats."
DOCTOR LIGHT I came to town to plunder it, and the boys
saw an opportunity to help. The hapless criminal was soundly
defeated by the three boys. Whether or not they have donned
their costumes again remains unrecorded. **RG**

LITTLE
BOY BLUE
and the
BLUE BOYS

LOBO

FIRST APPEARANCE OMEGA MEN #3 (June 1983)
STATUS Villain   **REAL NAME** Unpronounceable
OCCUPATION Contract killer; bounty hunter   **BASE** Mobile
HEIGHT 7ft 6in   **WEIGHT** 640 lbs   **EYES** Red   **HAIR** Black
SPECIAL POWERS/ABILITIES Vast superstrength and near invulnerability; superspeed and superhuman endurance; fantastic leaping ability; tracking ability allows him to trace prey across galaxies; can survive unaided in the vacuum of space; unparalleled brawler; can replicate himself into an army of clones.

HIS UNPRONOUNCEABLE REAL NAME roughly translates as "he who devours your entrails and thoroughly enjoys it." Once Lobo has targeted a victim, that person has little hope of escape and even less of winning any fight—for the only way to destroy Lobo is to vaporize every part of him, down to the last cell! Lobo loves his work and cares little for payment. When not pursuing prey, he keeps in practice by picking fights wherever he goes, marauding around the cosmos like a deep-space Hell's Angel on his intergalacticycle, the *Hog*. With his uncanny ability to sense an opponent's physical and mental weaknesses, Lobo is almost as notorious as a barroom brawler as he is as a killer-for-hire.

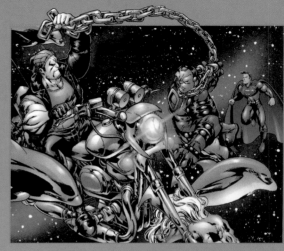

BOUNTY HUNTER *Lobo is known and feared throughout the galaxy as a tracker who never loses his prey.*

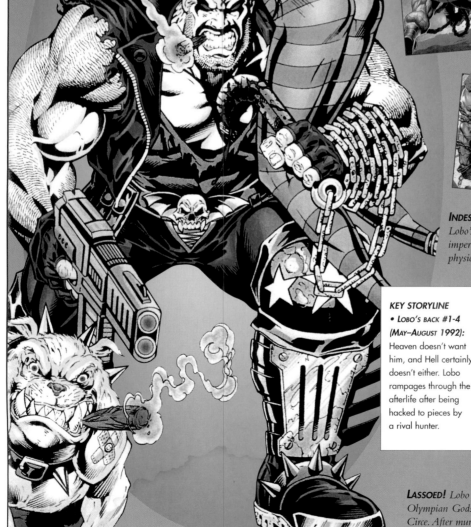

BAD TO THE BONE *Lobo's taken more than his share of lives, loot, and loves—and probably in that order!*

INDESTRUCTIBLE *Lobo's nearly impervious to physical attack.*

A ONE-MAN ARMY

Lobo is the sole survivor of the planet Czarnia, once renowned as a tranquil paradise. Lobo was trouble as soon as he was born, biting off the midwife's fingers, chasing the doctors with scalpels, and frightening the delivery nurse to death. As a child, he killed every caretaker he had. Finally, he committed global genocide, creating a horde of lethal insects that slaughtered every last Czarnian. Lobo then became a mercenary, leaving a trail of blood and corpses in his wake. Bizarrely, he also adopted a school of space dolphins as pets.

At length, after helping the OMEGA MEN vanquish the Spider Guild and the Citadel Empire, Lobo found Earth, and began challenging its greatest heroes— SUPERMAN, WARRIOR, the JUSTICE LEAGUE OF AMERICA—to vicious battles to find the "Main Man."

Lobo worked with the interstellar police force L.E.G.I.O.N. for a time, along with their offshoot, R.E.B.E.L.S. During that time BRAINIAC 5.1 stripped Lobo of his amazing genetic ability to replicate himself into an army of exact clones.

Sometime later, Lobo was transformed into a younger version of himself by the magic of KLARION, THE WITCH BOY. Li'l Lobo was just as murderous as his adult self, and reclaimed his cloning ability. The child-sized Lobo then joined YOUNG JUSTICE for a while. He was incinerated by DARKSEID on a mission to Apokolips during the Imperiex War (*see* Great Battles, pp. 320–1). A Lobo clone, created from a drop of blood, returned to Earth with Young Justice. He called himself "Slobo," felt unworthy of the Khundian title "Lobo," and was condemned to a stony death in the 853rd century by Darkseid while trying to save his teammate SECRET from the New God's clutches. One of Lobo's many clones survived, however, to spread his brand of lethal rage across the galaxy.. **PJ**

KEY STORYLINE
• **LOBO'S BACK #1-4 (MAY–AUGUST 1992):** Heaven doesn't want him, and Hell certainly doesn't either. Lobo rampages through the afterlife after being hacked to pieces by a rival hunter.

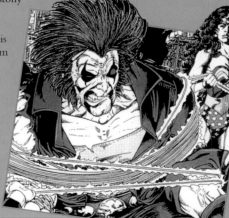

LASSOED! *Lobo became a pawn of the Olympian Gods in their battle against Circe. After murdering dozens of Amazons, he was captured by Wonder Woman!*

THE DC COMICS ENCYCLOPEDIA

LITTLE MERMAID

FIRST APPEARANCE SUPER FRIENDS #9 (December 1977)
STATUS Hero (deceased) **REAL NAME** Ula Paske
OCCUPATION Adventurer **BASE** Denmark
HEIGHT 5ft 4in **WEIGHT** 120 lbs **EYES** Crystal blue **HAIR** Blonde
SPECIAL POWERS/ABILITIES Could transform her legs into a fishtail and breathe underwater.

The Little Mermaid was a mutant from the undersea kingdom of Atlantis. Ula's mother was a mermaid from the city of Tritonis, and her father was a two-legged humanoid from Poseidonis, the capital of Atlantis. Because of her specific mutation, which allowed her to survive underwater for only 30 hours or less, Ula was raised by adoptive parents in Denmark.

The Little Mermaid was a founding member of DOCTOR MIST's team of heroes, the GLOBAL GUARDIANS. When the Guardians were disbanded by the United Nations, the Little Mermaid fell under the control of the evil Queen Bee (see QUEEN BEE II) of Bialya. During that time, the Little Mermaid was killed by JACK O'LANTERN II, who accidentally blew the Little Mermaid's head off with his signature weapon, the mystical Jack O'Lantern. PJ

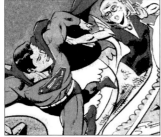

FISHY TAIL The Little Mermaid was a mutant from Atlantis who was able to transform her human legs into a fish's tail, and swim as swiftly as a dolphin or shark.

LOBO *SEE OPPOSITE PAGE*

LODESTONE II

FIRST APPEARANCE DOOM PATROL (2nd series) #3 (December 1987)
STATUS Hero (flown away) **REAL NAME** Rhea Jones
OCCUPATION Adventurer **BASE** Kansas City
HEIGHT 5ft 6in **WEIGHT** 144 lbs **EYES** Blue **HAIR** Red
SPECIAL POWERS/ABILITIES Used her magnetic abilities to fly, create force fields, and attract or repel metallic objects.

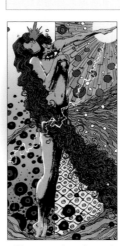

Rhea Jones was the daughter of an Air Force officer who was often away on secret missions. During one absence, Rhea's mother was killed in an accident. Rhea learned that her father was stationed in the Arctic, so the plucky teenager stowed away on a flight to the base. Her father had volunteered to enter a nuclear reactor and shut it down. Rhea followed him, exposing herself to deadly radiation. A powerful electromagnetic charge resulted and the building blew up. Rhea miraculously survived and the military put her through many tests hoping to learn how she had not only lived, but also developed strange powers. She escaped and joined a traveling circus, until Arani Caulder (CELSIUS), who had recreated her husband's DOOM PATROL, invited Rhea to join the team. On one mission, her powers evolved and she metamorphosed into a magnetic butterfly and flew away, finally free at last. RG

LONAR

FIRST APPEARANCE FOREVER PEOPLE #5 (November 1971)
STATUS Hero **REAL NAME** Lonar
OCCUPATION New God **BASE** New Genesis
HEIGHT 6ft 7in **WEIGHT** 265 lbs **EYES** Blue **HAIR** Black
SPECIAL POWERS/ABILITIES A consummate soldier, immensely strong and disciplined; rides a winged horse into battle.

Little is known about the New God Lonar save for his bravery, strength of character, and fierceness in battle. With his flying steed Thunderer, he is usually to be found at the forefront of any battle, either staunchly defending the world of New Genesis from DARKSEID's evil minions or keeping other lands safe from the Dark Lord's malignant touch. One of his more noteworthy battles occurred defending the hidden land of Skartaris from an Apokoliptian invasion.

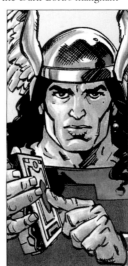

Lonar has an archaeologist's thirst for knowledge, and can often be found exploring the ancient ruins on New Genesis for clues to the secrets of the legendary Old Gods, who predated the NEW GODS countless millennia in the past. Although considered somewhat of an outsider by his fellow New Gods, his bravery in battle has never been questioned. RG/DW

LIVE WIRE

FIRST APPEARANCE ADVENTURE COMICS #247 (April 1958);
LEGION OF SUPER-HEROES (4th series) #0 (October 1994)
STATUS Hero **REAL NAME** Garth Ranzz **OCCUPATION** Legionnaire **BASE** Legion World **HEIGHT** 5ft 10in **WEIGHT** 145 lbs **EYES** Blue **HAIR** Red
SPECIAL POWERS/ABILITIES Able to absorb and generate electricity or project coruscating lightning bolts.

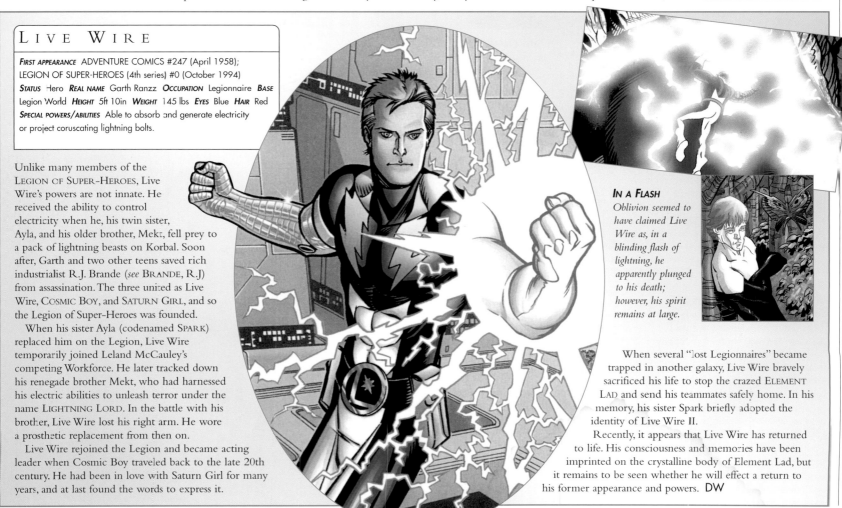

Unlike many members of the LEGION OF SUPER-HEROES, Live Wire's powers are not innate. He received the ability to control electricity when he, his twin sister, Ayla, and his older brother, Mekt, fell prey to a pack of lightning beasts on Korbal. Soon after, Garth and two other teens saved rich industrialist R.J. Brande (see BRANDE, R.J) from assassination. The three united as Live Wire, COSMIC BOY, and SATURN GIRL, and so the Legion of Super-Heroes was founded.

When his sister Ayla (codenamed SPARK) replaced him on the Legion, Live Wire temporarily joined Leland McCauley's competing Workforce. He later tracked down his renegade brother Mekt, who had harnessed his electric abilities to unleash terror under the name LIGHTNING LORD. In the battle with his brother, Live Wire lost his right arm. He wore a prosthetic replacement from then on.

Live Wire rejoined the Legion and became acting leader when Cosmic Boy traveled back to the late 20th century. He had been in love with Saturn Girl for many years, and at last found the words to express it.

IN A FLASH Oblivion seemed to have claimed Live Wire as, in a blinding flash of lightning, he apparently plunged to his death; however, his spirit remains at large.

When several "lost Legionnaires" became trapped in another galaxy, Live Wire bravely sacrificed his life to stop the crazed ELEMENT LAD and send his teammates safely home. In his memory, his sister Spark briefly adopted the identity of Live Wire II.

Recently, it appears that Live Wire has returned to life. His consciousness and memories have been imprinted on the crystalline body of Element Lad, but it remains to be seen whether he will effect a return to his former appearance and powers. DW

LOOKER

FIRST APPEARANCE BATMAN AND THE OUTSIDERS #25 (Sept. 1985)
STATUS Hero   REAL NAME Emily "Lia" Briggs
OCCUPATION Model; talk show host   BASE Los Angeles
HEIGHT 5ft 10in   WEIGHT 210 lbs   EYES Blue   HAIR Red
SPECIAL POWERS/ABILITIES Vampire strength and intangibility; psionic abilities include levitation, telekinesis, telepathy, and mental blasts.

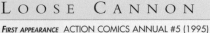

Emily Briggs longed to be beautiful, and got her wish when emissaries from the underground kingdom of Abyssia kidnapped her in order to make her the heir to their throne. Using fragments from a comet, the Abyssians gave Emily psionic powers and jaw-dropping beauty. She managed to escape from the underworld thanks to BATMAN and the OUTSIDERS, and then joined the team under the codename Looker.

After the Outsiders split from Batman and relocated to Los Angeles, Looker worked for a modeling agency, until a rematch with the Abyssians robbed her of her powers and her breathtaking looks. She later joined the second incarnation of the Outsiders on a mission to Markovia. There, the struggle with a vampire reignited her powers; unfortunately, Looker became a vampire herself. Looker remained with that version of the Outsiders until its disbanding, using both her mental powers and her new superhuman abilities as a vampire. **DW**

LOOSE CANNON

FIRST APPEARANCE ACTION COMICS ANNUAL #5 (1995)
STATUS Hero   REAL NAME Eddie Walker
OCCUPATION Former homicide detective   BASE Metropolis
HEIGHT (Eddie) 5ft 10in; (Loose Cannon) 7ft 5in
WEIGHT (Eddie) 170 lbs; (Loose Cannon) 725 lbs
EYES (Eddie) Brown; (Loose Cannon) white
HAIR (Eddie) Brown; (Loose Cannon) yellow
SPECIAL POWERS/ABILITIES Transforms into super-strong blue monster in the absence of sunlight.

Eddie Walker was a homicide detective working for a division of Metropolis's Special Crimes Unit (trained to deal with anything from meta-human crime to alien invaders) led by Maggie Sawyer. Walker became known as the department's volatile "loose cannon." Tragedy struck when Eddie was crippled in a car accident. Suffering from deep depression, he considered suicide. Meanwhile, a group of alien parasites landed on Earth and proceeded to drain the spinal fluids from a host of victims. Two of these parasites attacked Eddie, but instead of dying, the crippled detective discovered that he could transform himself into a superhuman giant. Styling himself Loose Cannon, Eddie teamed up with the JUSTICE LEAGUE OF AMERICA and several other "new bloods" to destroy the alien parasites. Loose Cannon subsequently worked with the Justice League Task Force, and continues to fight super-villainy in Metropolis. **PJ**

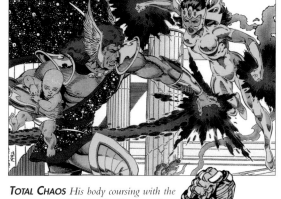

LORD CHAOS

FIRST APPEARANCE NEW TITANS ANNUAL #7 (1991)
STATUS God (eradicated)   REAL NAME Inapplicable
OCCUPATION Dictator   BASE Earth in an alternate timeline
HEIGHT 6ft 2in   WEIGHT 196 lbs   EYES Black   HAIR Red-gold
SPECIAL POWERS/ABILITIES Godlike strength; flight; could project fire or darkness, create floods and earthquakes; read minds; alter memories.

In the future of an alternate timeline, Lord Chaos was the child of Donna Troy, the Titan known as TROIA. He inherited from his mother the godlike powers of the TITANS OF MYTH. As soon as he was born, he magically grew to adulthood and killed his parents. Taking the name Lord Chaos, he took control of Earth and annihilated most of its heroes. A group of rebels called the Team Titans went back in time to kill Donna Troy before she could give birth to Lord Chaos. Chaos traveled back to stop the assassination. The Titans of Myth arrived and stripped Lord Chaos of his powers, ending his reign of terror. Soon after, during Zero Hour (see Great Battles, pp. 320–1), the future timeline Lord Chaos hailed from was eradicated and the dictator god was wiped from existence. **PJ**

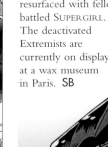

TOTAL CHAOS *His body coursing with the power of every Titan god, Chaos nearly succeeded in destroying his mother, Troia.*

LORD HAVOK

FIRST APPEARANCE JUSTICE LEAGUE INTERNATIONAL #1 (Nov. 1987)
STATUS Villain (missing or deceased)   REAL NAME Maxwell Lord
OCCUPATION Businessman; super-villain   BASE New York City
HEIGHT 6ft 2in   WEIGHT 185 lbs   EYES Brown   HAIR Brown
SPECIAL POWERS/ABILITIES (Lord Havok I) computer mind, indestructible armor; (Lord Havok II) controlled any machine, telekinetic abilities.

The first Lord Havok hailed from an other-dimensional world and was leader of the EXTREMISTS, a band of robot super-villains. The Extremists seized control of their world's nuclear arsenal and wiped out every soul, including themselves, except for genius Mitch Wacky. The Extremists came to Earth, where their plot for planetary conquest was thwarted by Justice League Europe (see JUSTICE LEAGUE OF AMERICA). The bodies of Lord Havok and the other Extremists, except DREAMSLAYER, were placed in a museum. Dreamslayer's essence forced businessman Maxwell Lord to hypnotize the FLASH III and Wacky into reactivating Lord Havok. The robot was killed by BLUE BEETLE II.

Later, Maxwell Lord died from brain cancer and was resurrected by the alien Kilg%re to become an all-new Lord Havok. Lord disappeared after destroying the Arcana, an organization to which he belonged. The robotic Lord resurfaced with fellow surviving Extremist automatons and battled SUPERGIRL. The deactivated Extremists are currently on display at a wax museum in Paris. **SB**

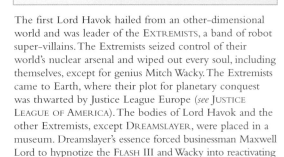

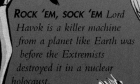

ROCK 'EM, SOCK 'EM *Lord Havok is a killer machine from a planet like Earth was before the Extremists destroyed it in a nuclear holocaust.*

LORD OF TIME

FIRST APPEARANCE JUSTICE LEAGUE OF AMERICA (1st series) #10 (March 1962)
STATUS Villain **REAL NAME** Unrevealed **OCCUPATION** Would-be conqueror **BASE** Mobile **HEIGHT** 5ft 9in **WEIGHT** 159 lbs **EYES** Blue **HAIR** Black **SPECIAL POWERS/ABILITIES** Access to the timestream through Chrono-cube; armor assimilates weaponry from any era visited.

An immensely powerful being from the year 3786, the Lord of Time attacked the JUSTICE LEAGUE OF AMERICA, using his miraculous chrono-cube to peel back the fourth-dimensional veil of time. Since his initial defeat by the JLA, this sinister fugitive from the future has learned to move laterally and diagonally through history, accessing armies and armaments spanning millions of years. He desires nothing less than to conquer space and time. To make sure that his bid to rule all reality is successful he is quite capable of ensuring that the JLA have no power to stop him by eliminating their ancestors and so erasing them from existence.

At some point, the Lord of Time created a frozen moment in history called Timepoint, and he will eventually evolve into a being known as Epoch who desires to master the timestream, changing events to grant him power. RG

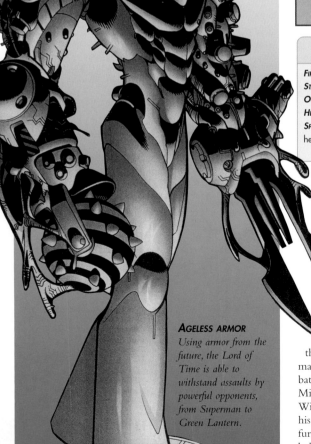

AGELESS ARMOR
Using armor from the future, the Lord of Time is able to withstand assaults by powerful opponents, from Superman to Green Lantern.

LOSERS, THE

FIRST APPEARANCE G.I. COMBAT #138 (November 1969)
STATUS Hero team **BASE** Europe and Asia during World War II
MEMBERS AND SPECIAL POWERS
Captain Storm (deceased) Indomitable will; a natural leader.
Gunner (deceased) Commando skills; expert marksman.
Johnny Cloud (deceased) One of the greatest fighter pilots of World War II.
Ona (deceased) Expert markswoman.
Pooch (deceased) Specially trained military dog.
Sarge (deceased) Commando skills; expert marksman.

CRISIS IN TIME *In the war torn country of Markovia, the Losers came face to face with Shadow Demons out to destroy the universe, and they succumbed to their explosive presence before time was reordered in the Crisis.*

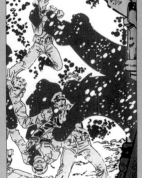

The Losers were Allied soldiers during World War II, each of whom had suffered serious failures during their military careers. CAPTAIN STORM's first command had been sunk by a Japanese submarine; a pilot flying alongside Johnny Cloud (*see* CLOUD, JOHNNY) had been killed in combat; and a band of raw recruits led by GUNNER AND SARGE had been wiped out during their first patrol.

After Jeb Stuart (*see* HAUNTED TANK) persuaded the soldiers to help him destroy a Nazi radar tower, the four men stayed together, united by the Military High Command as a special task force. Briefly recruiting a fifth member, a Norwegian woman named Ona, the unit fought Axis tyranny throughout Europe and Asia, never quite shaking their self-imposed status as "Losers." Tragically, all four men and their K-9 sidekick, Pooch, died in action during the final days of World War II, but decades later Gunner was resurrected by Project M and recruited for the new CREATURE COMMANDOS. PJ

GUNNER
JOHNNY CLOUD
CAPTAIN STORM
ONA
POOCH
SARGE

LUMP

FIRST APPEARANCE MISTER MIRACLE (1st series) #7 (April 1972)
STATUS Villain **REAL NAME** None
OCCUPATION Warrior **BASE** Apokolips
HEIGHT 7ft **WEIGHT** 500 lbs **EYES** White **HAIR** None
SPECIAL POWERS/ABILITIES Can mold his misshapen body into any form he imagines to defeat opponents psycho-merged with him.

Deep within GRANNY GOODNESS's orphanage on Apokolips lies the dreaded Section Zero. Here, Scott Free (MISTER MIRACLE) met the LUMP, a horrendous hulk who encountered the enemies of DARKSEID in the "Arena of the Gods," a mental realm within the creature's own Id. Strapped to Apokoliptian technology, Mister Miracle met the Lump inside this mind-world where the monster was master. Able to mold his body into any weapon, the Lump battled Mister Miracle to a standstill. To defeat the Lump, Miracle used a fission blast to turn the ground to glass. With a reflective shard, Mister Miracle showed the Lump his own vile visage. Horrified, the Lump retreated into the furthest reaches of his Id. Miracle then escaped with his beloved BIG BARDA. The Lump remains in Section Zero, imprisoned in his own private hell. SB

LYNX

FIRST APPEARANCE ROBIN (1st series) #1 (November 1990)
STATUS Villain (deceased) **REAL NAME** Ling
OCCUPATION Assassin; gang boss **BASE** Gotham City
HEIGHT 5ft 2in **WEIGHT** 119 lbs **EYES** Black **HAIR** Black
SPECIAL POWERS/ABILITIES A formidable martial artist and a courageous, but ruthless, killer.

Escaping from Wuzhong, China, a young girl known only as Ling begged for food on the streets of Marseilles. An adept thief, Ling was recruited by Sir Edmund Dorrance, the drug baron KING SNAKE, to join his Ghost Dragons gang. When she was defeated by the third ROBIN, King Snake punished Ling, now renamed Lynx, by taking her left eye. Filled with hatred for Robin and King Snake, Lynx moved to Gotham City's Chinatown and wrested control of the Dragons from King Snake. Lynx has since clashed with BATMAN and Robin several times; however, she teamed up with the Dark Knight in the aftermath of the Gotham earthquake, taking down a Chinatown gang using slaves to generate electricity for the crippled city. Lynx died during a Gotham gang war, leaving the dragons under BLACK MASK's rule. RG

187

THE DC COMICS ENCYCLOPEDIA

LUTHOR, LEX

SUPERMAN'S GREATEST ENEMY

First Appearance ACTION COMICS #23 (April 1940)
Status Villain   **Real Name** Alexander Joseph Luthor
Base Metropolis; Washington D.C. (while U.S. President)
Height 6ft 2in   **Weight** 210 lbs   **Eyes** Green   **Hair** None
Occupation Mastermind
Special Powers/Abilities Luthor is one of the smartest men on Earth, able to invent technological marvels or manipulate entire nations. He believes in brute force and is an unskilled fighter, relying instead on weapons and armor.

Lex Luthor may be the most gifted man alive but rather than use his supreme intellect and skills for the betterment of mankind, the sociopath has continually sought power and influence without regard for the pain and suffering he causes. The gifts are also wasted on his single-minded hatred of a more pure and noble man, especially given his alien origins.

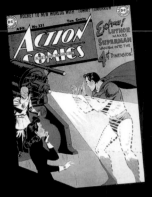

Evil Genius Luthor's early attempts to kill Superman all failed.

EVIL AND ALIENATED

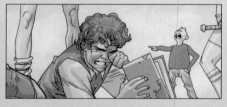

One glance at Luthor's I.Q. test results, convinced his parents that their little genius would make them rich. They were determined he should excel, but their soul-destroying "guidance" bred a sociopath who engineered their deaths to capitalize on their life insurance. A budding astrobiologist, Lex then spent years searching for evidence of extraterrestrial life. His hunt took him to Smallville when he was 18. Lex befriended another seemingly alienated young man, Clark Kent. He turned his back on Smallville when a fire destroyed his lab and his scientific achievements, as well as his foster father. Refusing to take any responsibility for the accident, Lex blamed the town for "letting the Luthors burn," and to this day, refuses to admit he has ever set foot in Smallville.

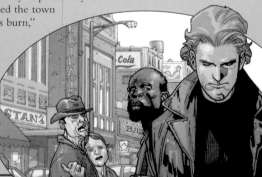

ONLY THE LONELY
Deprived of a normal childhood, Lex hid his personal pain behind a mask of arrogance.

THE RISE OF LUTHOR

Years later, Lex appeared in Metropolis and built his technology company, LexCorp, into a powerhouse. Financial success led to political power, and he was considered the city's most powerful figure. Then came the day that SUPERMAN appeared

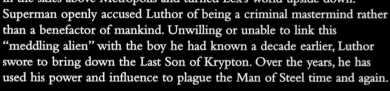

in the skies above Metropolis and turned Lex's world upside down. Superman openly accused Luthor of being a criminal mastermind rather than a benefactor of mankind. Unwilling or unable to link this "meddling alien" with the boy he had known a decade earlier, Luthor swore to bring down the Last Son of Krypton. Over the years, he has used his power and influence to plague the Man of Steel time and again.

KRYPTONITE RING

Luthor got in his licks but continued to be thwarted by Superman both directly and indirectly. On one occasion, a ring Luthor had fashioned from kryptonite gave him cancer owing to the radiation inherent in the alien rock. Lex faked his death, and transferred his mind into the body of a clone, pretending to be Luthor's heretofore unknown son. This Luthor soon evolved to resemble the original, but continued to come second in his struggles with Superman.

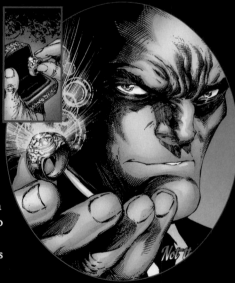

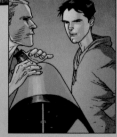

TWO STRANGERS *Clark was the only person in Smallville who empathized with Lex's feelings of isolation.*

EXPLOSION *An accident physically and mentally scarred Lex so deeply he has erased all record of his ever being in Smallville.*

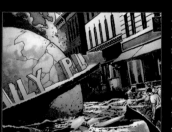

IN RUINS *Luthor destroyed Metropolis in a bid to avoid exposure by Lois Lane.*

METROPOLIS DESTROYED

Lex showed his true colors by refusing to sacrifice himself to help reignite the sun after the Sun-Eater had snuffed out its energy. When Lois Lane (see LANE, LOIS) exposed his criminal dealings, Luthor triggered devices hidden within Metropolis that destroyed the city. Superman and his fellow heroes rebuilt Metropolis and the battle between Superman and Luthor continued. His manipulations extended to Metropolis's citizens, who sided with Superman over Luthor.

LUST FOR POWER
Realizing the need to muzzle the press, Luthor bought and then sold the *Daily Planet* to Perry White (*see* WHITE, PERRY) on condition that Lois Lane killed any single story of his choosing. Feeling safe from exposure, Luthor ran for U. S. President to gain the power needed to bring Superman down. Surprisingly, he served the U.S.'s interests well, strengthening or forging relationships with many nations from Atlantis to Russia, and rallying the troops when IMPERIEX arrived to destroy Earth (*see* Great Battles, pp. 320–1).

CLASH OF WILLS *Perry White and Luthor never got along and it chafed when Luthor came to own Perry's beloved Daily Planet.*

FRONT PAGE NEWS
Lois found out that Luthor had known of Imperiex's threat earlier than stated. He demanded that this be the story the *Planet* killed, but the savvy reporter tricked him, giving her notes to Clark Kent, who wrote a scathing piece, exposing Luthor for the criminal he was.

WARSUIT *Luthor finally took matters into his own hands, attempting to destroy both Superman and Batman.*

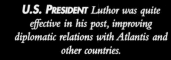

ADVANCE WARNING *Luthor had secretly known of Imperiex's invasion plans, but ordered Lois Lane to kill the story. However, Clark Kent printed the full truth, marring Luthor's term as U.S. President.*

KEY STORYLINES
- *SUPERMAN: PRESIDENT LEX (TPB, 2000):* The world looks on aghast as Luthor becomes U.S. President, following the most controversial election of all time.
- *SUPERMAN: BIRTHRIGHT #1–12 (September 2003–September 2004):* Dating back to their childhood in Smallville, Luthor's tortured relationship with Clark Kent/Superman is redefined and explored.
- *SUPERMAN/BATMAN #1–6* President Luthor becomes a kryptonite junkie and goes insane.
- *LEX LUTHOR: MAN OF STEEL (TPB, 2004):* Luthor's recovery from his downfall.

U.S. PRESIDENT *Luthor was quite effective in his post, improving diplomatic relations with Atlantis and other countries.*

ACT OF MADNESS
Luthor's presidential power still could not bring about the end of Superman and his costumed friends. When an asteroid neared Earth, Luthor detected kryptonite radiation and used that to try and turn the public against the Man of Steel. He even sent costumed champions after Superman, but this gambit also failed. Finally, he donned a LexCorp war suit and tried to take down not only Superman, but BATMAN as well. His efforts were in vain and his deception was made public. Driven from the presidency, Luthor was thought to have died but limped to freedom, an angry, vengeful man. **RG**

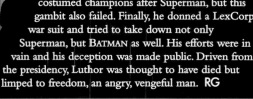
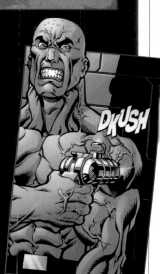

MAD HARRIET

FIRST APPEARANCE MISTER MIRACLE (1st series) #6 (February 1972)
STATUS Villain   **REAL NAME** Unrevealed
OCCUPATION Shocktrooper   **BASE** Apokolips
HEIGHT 5ft 10in   **WEIGHT** 146 lbs   **EYES** Black   **HAIR** Green
SPECIAL POWERS/ABILITIES Ferocious combatant; fists are armed with power spikes that can slash through most materials.

Mad Harriet is a member of the FEMALE FURIES, an elite band of shocktroopers trained by the malevolent GRANNY GOODNESS as elite warriors for DARKSEID, dread lord of the planet Apokolips. Mad Harriet is a chilling, psychopathic killing machine, armed with special devices that let her cleave through any material, including the flesh of her prey.

The Female Furies were lead by BIG BARDA until she abandoned the team to be with her lover Scott Free, otherwise known as MISTER MIRACLE. When Barda moved to Earth, Mad Harriet and the Female Furies pursued her there and tried to capture her, but the Furies eventually turned when they were offered freedom from Granny's thrall. After working for a short time with Barda and Mister Miracle, Mad Harriet and the other Female Furies returned to Apokolips and to their roles as enforcers in Darkseid's Elite.

Mad Harriet loves nothing more than mayhem and violence and delights in the pains and screams of others. She is known throughout the universe for her berserker's rages and for her loyalty to her masters, Granny Goodness and Darkseid. **PJ**

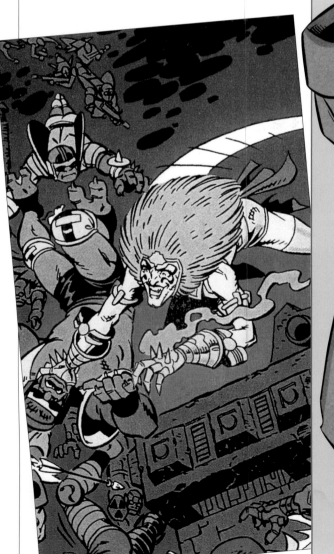

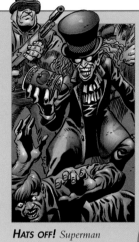

MANIC MILLINER
No Man's Land gave many Gotham City rogues the opportunity to prey on the weak and defenseless. The Mad Hatter was mostly concerned with unearthing his collection of hats, buried in the Gotham City quake.

HATS OFF! *Superman helped a harried Dark Knight to defeat Jervis Tetch and put an end to his criminal chicanery.*

MAD HATTER

FIRST APPEARANCE BATMAN #49 (November 1948)
STATUS Villain   **REAL NAME** Jervis Tetch
OCCUPATION Professional criminal   **BASE** Gotham City
HEIGHT 4ft 8in   **WEIGHT** 149 lbs   **EYES** Blue   **HAIR** Red
SPECIAL POWERS/ABILITIES A master hypnotist, able to use chemical concoctions or electronic technology concealed in his oversized hat to enthrall his victims; short and slight in stature, the Hatter prefers to let his mesmerized minions do his fighting for him.

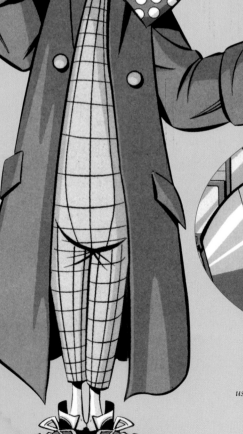

Insanely inspired by Lewis Carroll's children's book, *Alice's Adventures in Wonderland*, master mesmerist Jervis Tetch convinced himself that he was Carroll's chapeau-crazed Mad Hatter. In one of his very first crimes, Tetch hypnotized and kidnapped teenage girls to be "Alices" in a bizarre tea party before selling them into slavery. Fortunately, BATMAN and ROBIN foiled the Hatter's scheme and freed his unwilling guests, who included the Boy Wonder's very first crush, schoolmate Jenny Noblesse. Since then, the Hatter has committed even more sordid sins, usually involving his obsession with hats. However, what the prize Mad Hatter longs for most of all is Batman's famous headgear. He would gladly kill the Dark Knight to add the Bat-Cowl to his collection.

Mercurial in temperament, the Mad Hatter generally works alone. But for the sake of his hidden cache of chapeaus, buried under tons of rubble after Gotham City's cataclysmic earthquake, Tetch allied himself with the villain Narcosis, who planned to blanket the ruined city with his Bliss gas. Naturally, the Hatter bargained for Narcosis's hood to seal their partnership, short-lived though it was, since both were soon defeated by Batman.

In between his cap-themed crime sprees, Tetch is confined in the cells of Gotham City's notorious Arkham Asylum for the Criminally Insane, where hats are, as a rule, prohibited.

Despite continued efforts to cure the Mad Hatter of his mania, including various attempts at aversion therapy, Tetch remains committed to the role of hateful haberdasher. **SB**

MIND GAMES *Shooting cops is not as appealing to the Mad Hatter as using his electronics savvy to hotwire a microwave dish, and using cable television to place all of Gotham under his hypnotic thrall.*

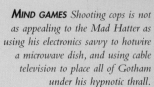

MADAME .44

FIRST APPEARANCE ALL STAR WESTERN #117 (March 1961)
STATUS Hero **REAL NAME** Jeanne Walker
OCCUPATION Gun-slinger **BASE** Mesa City
HEIGHT 5ft 2in **WEIGHT** 119 lbs **EYES** Blue **HAIR** Red
SPECIAL POWERS/ABILITIES Crack shot with a pistol; uses her wits when her physical prowess did not match her opponents'.

In the year 1872, a group of swindlers cheated Jeanne Walker's prospector father out of a rich strike at a gold mine. This traumatic memory led Jeanne to assume the secret identity of Madame .44, a name the famous peace officer Wyatt Earp gave her. Disguising her distinctive blonde tresses by dying her hair red, Madame .44 became a "Robin Hood" outlaw, who robbed from unscrupulous businessmen, like those who had originally wronged her father, and then returned much of the money to its original owners.

Her rambunctious exploits led her to clash with Johnny Thunder (see THUNDER, JOHNNY) from time to time. However, their enmity did not run too deep or persist too long. Johnny and Madame .44 found themselves on the same side during a battle with the vicious outlaw Silk Black and afterwards fell in love and married. **RG**

MADAME ROUGE

FIRST APPEARANCE DOOM PATROL (1st series) #86 (March 1964)
STATUS Villain (deceased) **REAL NAME** Laura DeMille
OCCUPATION Ex-actress and teacher; criminal **BASE** Paris, France
HEIGHT 5ft 6in **WEIGHT** 134 lbs **EYES** Blue **HAIR** Black
SPECIAL POWERS/ABILITIES Could stretch any body part to incredible lengths; could reshape her facial features to disguise herself.

Laura DeMille was a beautiful young actress from Paris who suffered from severe schizophrenia. When the BRAIN experimented on her mind, she snapped and became Madame Rouge, joining his Brotherhood of Evil (see SOCIETY OF SIN). Later, after further experimentation, Rouge was given superhuman powers, and, along with the rest of the Brotherhood, clashed with the DOOM PATROL. Despite falling in love with the CHIEF, Rouge joined forces with the Chief's enemy, GENERAL ZAHL, and seemingly murdered him and the Doom Patrol.

During a battle between the Brotherhood of Evil and the TEEN TITANS, Rouge was accidentally killed by BEAST BOY. **PJ**

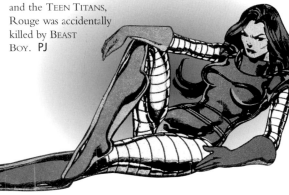

MADAME XANADU

FIRST APPEARANCE DOORWAY TO NIGHTMARE #1 (February 1978)
STATUS Hero **REAL NAME** Unknown
OCCUPATION Occultist **BASE** Greenwich Village, New York City
HEIGHT 5ft 9in **WEIGHT** 145 lbs **EYES** Green **HAIR** Black
SPECIAL POWERS/ABILITIES Able to read people's futures and sense and interpret magical forces; commands three demon minions.

The sign on Madame Xanadu's storefront on Christy Street tells patrons to "Enter freely—unafraid." Madame Xanadu counsels clients haunted by supernatural forces. She intercedes only when necessary, and refuses payment. Madame Xanadu has even been called upon by meta-humans for advice. For reasons unrevealed, she bartered her soul to the devil NERON and received three demons loyal to her in exchange. Madame Xanadu belongs to the Sentinels of Magic, a loose confederation of mystical heroes assembled to thwart the angel ASMODEL's uprising in Hell. Later, the Sentinels were charged with guarding the Spear of Destiny, a talisman of vast magical power. **SB**

MADEMOISELLE MARIE

FIRST APPEARANCE STAR-SPANGLED WAR STORIES #84 (August 1959)
STATUS Hero **REAL NAME** Unrevealed
OCCUPATION French resistance leader **BASE** France
HEIGHT 5ft 1in **WEIGHT** 117 lbs **EYES** Blue **HAIR** Brown
SPECIAL POWERS/ABILITIES A natural markswoman with a keen tactical mind; charismatic, courageous, and resourceful.

As a young girl growing up on a farm in France before World War II, Marie thrilled to hear the tales of heroism and bravery her grandfather used to tell her. When the war broke out and France fell to the invading armies of Nazi Germany, Marie joined the French Resistance.

After her father died in a surprise attack by German troops on the resistance group's headquarters, Marie became the leader of the cell. The attacks on the occupiers she masterminded and took part in were swift and decisive. She particularly enjoyed getting the better of the local Nazi commander Von Ekt. Her activities after the war remain unrecorded; presumably she returned to civilian life. **RG**

MAGEDDON

FIRST APPEARANCE JLA #37 (January 2000)
STATUS Villain **REAL NAME** None
OCCUPATION Weapon of mass destruction (destroyed) **BASE** Mobile
HEIGHT Unknown **WEIGHT** Unknown **EYES** Red **HAIR** None
SPECIAL POWERS/ABILITIES Stimulated violent, highly destructive feelings of anger and aggression in people; capable of wreaking incomprehensible levels of havoc and annihilation.

Created before the dawn of the known universe by the Old Gods of Urgrund, the living weapon Mageddon has been known by many other names over the millennia, including Warbringer, Tezcatlipoca, and the Primordial Annihilator. Mageddon is a doomsday device that amplifies the latent hostilities that lie dormant in the primitive, reptilian center of the human brain. **DW**

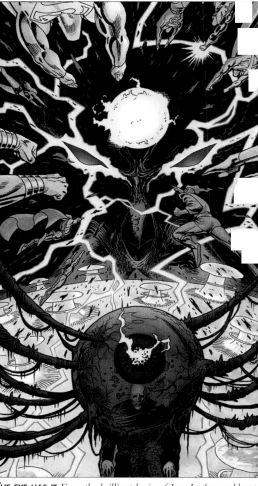

THE EYE HAS IT *Even the brilliant brain of Lex Luthor could not withstand the psychic influence of Mageddon's advance probes.*

When Mageddon broke free from its imprisonment outside of space-time and approached the Earth, the planet suddenly erupted in a frenzy of random military attacks that some labeled World War III. METRON and ORION of the NEW GODS helped battle Mageddon, as did the JUSTICE LEAGUE OF AMERICA and most of Earth's remaining heroes. Even the angels of Heaven descended to Earth on a special mission to calm the world's leaders, and avert what could have been a self-inflicted nuclear holocaust. The hero AZTEK sacrificed his life to slow down the weapon, allowing WONDER WOMAN time to accelerate the evolution of humanity and temporarily create an army of super heroes drawn from all walks of life. SUPERMAN ultimately destroyed Mageddon by flying into its core and draining the ancient energies of the anti-sun that powered it. **DW**

MAGENTA

FIRST APPEARANCE THE NEW TEEN TITANS (1st series) #17 (March 1982)
STATUS Villain **REAL NAME** Frances Kane
OCCUPATION Criminal **BASE** Keystone City
HEIGHT 5ft 7in **WEIGHT** 134 lbs **EYES** Blue **HAIR** Purple
SPECIAL POWERS/ABILITIES Able to generate and manipulate magnetic energy, controlling anything made of metal and bending it to her will.

Frances Kane grew up in Blue Valley, Nebraska, and became a close friend of Wally West, the third FLASH. Kane's powers emerged one night while she, her father and brother were driving on a narrow mountain road. When her powers went out of control, the car fell off a cliff, and Kane's father and brother were killed. France's superstitious mother believed her daughter was possessed by the devil and spurned her. With the help of Wally and the TEEN TITANS, Frances was able to gain some control over her powers, and the two became lovers in college.

Whenever Kane's powers emerged, however, she would "split" into a second, evil identity known as Magenta. Despite having helped the Teen Titans and the Flash in their fight against villainy, Magenta has fought the Flash as an enemy on more than one occasion. Having since been forsaken by the Flash for another love, Magenta flutters between her good and evil nature, and is now firmly ensconced with other nefarious criminals in the Flash's Rogues Gallery. **PJ**

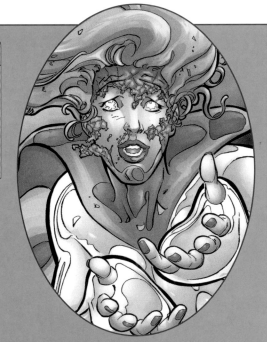

PURPLE POWER *Once she was a victim of circumstance. But now, corrupted by her powers, troubled Magenta is one of the Flash's most tragic villains—a former lover turned deadly enemy.*

MAGNO

FIRST APPEARANCE LEGIONNAIRES #43 (December 1996)
STATUS Hero **REAL NAME** Dyrk Magz
OCCUPATION Legion ally **BASE** Legion World, U.P. Space
HEIGHT 5ft 8in **WEIGHT** 149 lbs **EYES** Brown **HAIR** Blond
SPECIAL POWERS/ABILITIES Formerly able to generate and control magnetic fields to fly and manipulate metal objects; mystically de-powered following a battle with Mordru.

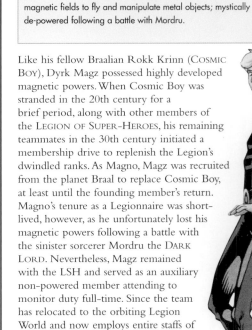

Like his fellow Braalian Rokk Krinn (COSMIC BOY), Dyrk Magz possessed highly developed magnetic powers. When Cosmic Boy was stranded in the 20th century for a brief period, along with other members of the LEGION OF SUPER-HEROES, his remaining teammates in the 30th century initiated a membership drive to replenish the Legion's dwindled ranks. As Magno, Magz was recruited from the planet Braal to replace Cosmic Boy, at least until the founding member's return. Magno's tenure as a Legionnaire was short-lived, however, as he unfortunately lost his magnetic powers following a battle with the sinister sorcerer Mordru the DARK LORD. Nevertheless, Magz remained with the LSH and served as an auxiliary non-powered member attending to monitor duty full-time. Since the team has relocated to the orbiting Legion World and now employs entire staffs of support teams, Magz's present role—if he has one—is undetermined. **SB**

ATTRACTIVE *Like all Braalians, Magno possessed highly developed magnetic powers until a battle with Mordru negated his abilities.*

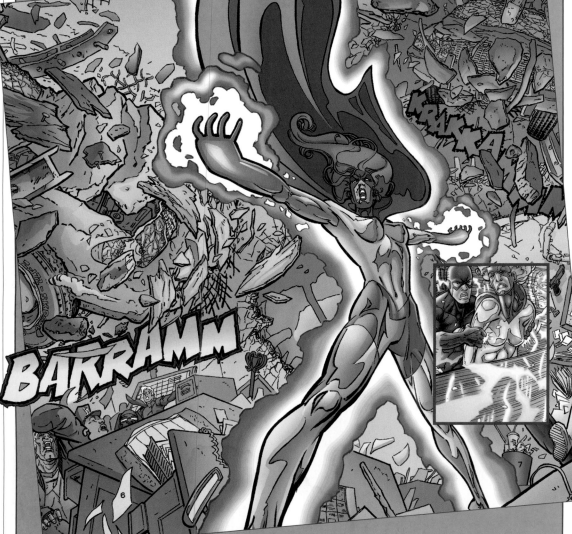

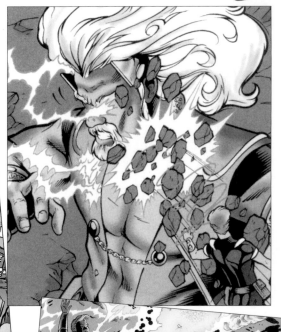

WEAK *Robbed of his powers, Magno no longer serves the Legion of Super-Heroes in an official capacity.*

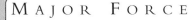

MAINLINE

FIRST APPEARANCE STEEL (2nd series) #0 (October 1994)
STATUS Hero **REAL NAME** Unknown
OCCUPATION Member of Team Hazard's Black Ops **BASE** Mobile
HEIGHT 5ft 11in **WEIGHT** 170 lbs **EYES** Unknown **HAIR** None
SPECIAL POWERS/ABILITIES Can fly at light-speed and burn through objects while in energy form.

Able to shift between physical and energy states at will, Mainline is potentially one of the most formidable member of Team Hazard's Black Ops. Very little is known about him or the appearance he hides beneath his full-body Team Hazard uniform. However, he is still tangible as an energy being, and a solid hit will knock him back into his regular state and leave him vulnerable. In various outings with Team Hazard, Mainline has sabotaged teammates' actions by a combination of bad luck and poor planning. DW

MAJOR FORCE

FIRST APPEARANCE CAPTAIN ATOM (2nd series) #12 (February 1988)
STATUS Villain (deceased) **REAL NAME** Clifford Zmeck
OCCUPATION U.S. government agent **BASE** Washington, D.C.
HEIGHT 6ft 5in **WEIGHT** 260 lbs **EYES** Blue **HAIR** Reddish brown
SPECIAL POWERS/ABILITIES Superstrength, invulnerability, possible immortality; projected black energy blasts.

Sergeant Clifford Zmeck, the second test subject in the U.S. government's "Captain Atom Project" (see CAPTAIN ATOM), had received a life sentence for murder when he was selected to receive a double coating of alien alloy and stand at ground zero during an H-bomb explosion. Zmeck shot into the quantum field at the instant of detonation. When he emerged, decades had passed and he had gained superhuman powers. General Wade Eiling (GENERAL) took command of Zmeck, naming him Major Force and laser-etching a "costume" onto his metallic shell. Major Force was assigned to shadowy government bureaus such as the Quorum.
He has seemingly been killed on several occasions, but his death during a mission to retrieve SUPERMAN and BATMAN for President Lex Luthor (see LUTHOR, LEX) looks final. DW

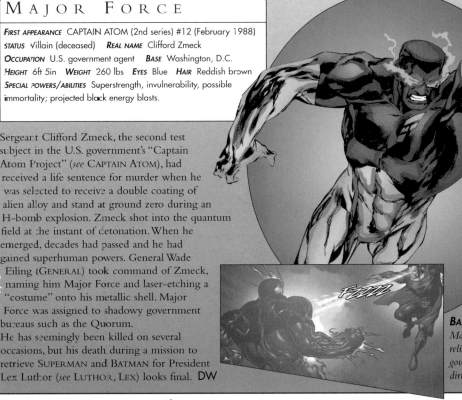

BAD AGENT
Major Force relished doing the government's dirty work.

MAJOR DISASTER

FIRST APPEARANCE GREEN LANTERN (2nd series) #43 (March 1966)
STATUS Villain turned ally **REAL NAME** Paul Booker
OCCUPATION Former criminal **BASE** JLA Watchtower, the Moon
HEIGHT 5ft 11in **WEIGHT** 195 lbs **EYES** Brown **HAIR** Black
SPECIAL POWERS/ABILITIES Seemingly invulnerable; possesses incredible psychic ability to generate natural disasters on a massive scale, from devastating earthquakes to flash floods.

Paul Booker learned the secret identities of both the GREEN LANTERN and the FLASH II when he broke into Tom Kalmaku's apartment (see KALMAKU, TOM) and discovered a book recording the many adventures of the JUSTICE LEAGUE OF AMERICA. Booker then hired a group of scientists to create special weapons for him, which he used to create a sinister alter ego, Major Disaster.
During a destructive battle with Green Lantern and the Flash, Major Disaster was incinerated in an explosion, but his body later reformed and internalized his powers so that he no longer relied on his special technology to use them. In an attempt at reformation, he joined Justice League Antarctica. The team soon disbanded and Major Disaster then sold his soul to the demon NERON in exchange for even greater destructive power. After briefly joining the SUICIDE SQUAD, and later helping SUPERMAN on one of his missions, Disaster was pardoned for his crimes. BATMAN then recruited him to the current JLA, seeing remnants of good in the reckless criminal. PJ

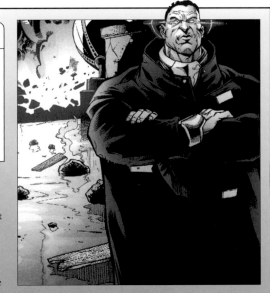

DESTRUCTION *A reformed criminal, Major Disaster is able to summon a 9.7 earthquake or a giant tsunami at will, using the elements to do his dirty work.*

PARDON *Major Disaster was invited by Batman to join the JLA. Superman accepted Disaster with a handshake—and a watchful eye.*

MAMMOTH

FIRST APPEARANCE NEW TEEN TITANS (1st series) #3 (January 1981)
STATUS Villain **REAL NAME** Baran Flinders
OCCUPATION Professional criminal **BASE** New Jersey
HEIGHT 6ft 5in **WEIGHT** 300 lbs **EYES** Blue **HAIR** Red
SPECIAL POWERS/ABILITIES Superhuman strength; partial invulnerability.

As children growing up in Australia, Baran Flinders and his sister Selinda received nothing but mockery as their unique abilities developed—she could transmute elements, while he exhibited terrifying strength. The world-renowned scientist Dr. Helga Jace taught them how to control their talents—whereupon they created the villainous identities of Mammoth and SHIMMER and joined DOCTOR LIGHT I, GIZMO, and PSIMON as members of the FEARSOME FIVE. Mammoth has clashed with the TEEN TITANS and SUPERMAN, both with the Fearsome Five and on his own. Devoted to his sister, Mammoth suffered deep psychological trauma when Psimon killed her. With the help of DOCTOR SIVANA, however, she was resurrected, and the Fearsome Five reunited. DW

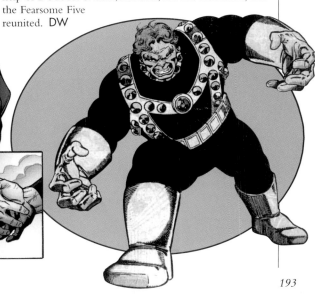

MAN-BAT

FIRST APPEARANCE DETECTIVE COMICS #400 (June 1970)
STATUS Villain **REAL NAME** Robert Kirkland Langstrom
OCCUPATION biologist **BASE** A small town near Gotham City
HEIGHT 7ft 4in **WEIGHT** 315 lbs **EYES** Red **HAIR** Brown
SPECIAL POWERS/ABILITIES Transforms into a winged, super-strong batlike humanoid that has natural sonar, but limited daytime vision.

BATMAN stopped Man-Bat's initial rampage, but Langstrom soon injected himself with another dose and became Man-Bat once again. He kidnapped his fiancée, Francine Lee, injected her, and she became a half-human/half-bat hybrid as well. After Batman once again captured Man-Bat and his mate, Langstrom refined the serum so that he could transform into his mutated state but maintain his intelligence. This Man-Bat occasionally helped Batman solve crimes. Langstrom and Francine eventually married and had a daughter, Rebecca, and a son, Aaron, a miniature version of his Man-Bat father. **PJ**

Doctor Kirk Langstrom was an expert in mammal biology, notably *chiroptera* (bats). Hoping to cure his growing deafness, he tried to create a serum that would give human beings the powers of echolocation that allow bats to use sound to navigate in the dark. When Langstrom tested the chemical on himself, the serum reacted with his genetic makeup and transformed him into a man-sized bat.

Once he became the Man-Bat, Langstrom's intellect seemed to vanish, and the crazed mutant began terrorizing Gotham City.

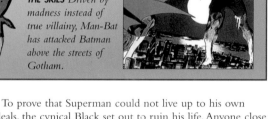
SCREECHING THROUGH THE SKIES Driven by madness instead of true villainy, Man-Bat has attacked Batman above the streets of Gotham.

MANCHESTER BLACK

FIRST APPEARANCE ACTION COMICS #775 (March 2001)
STATUS Villain (deceased) **REAL NAME** Manchester Black
OCCUPATION Adventurer **BASE** England
HEIGHT 5ft 6in **WEIGHT** 120 lbs **EYES** Blue **HAIR** Purple
SPECIAL POWERS/ABILITIES An accomplished telepath who can manipulate minds and distort reality. In combat he uses telekinetic powers, preferring not to get his hands dirty in a fight.

To prove that Superman could not live up to his own ideals, the cynical Black set out to ruin his life. Anyone close to the Man of Steel was endangered. Finally, Black seemingly killed Lois Lane but still Superman would not kill him in revenge. Defeated, Black erased the knowledge of Superman's true identity from Lex Luthor's mind and computer files and then took his own life, a failure. **RG**

EVIL MOTIVATION Manchester Black subjects Lois Lane to physical and mental cruelty as a test for the Man of Steel.

Black's team, the Elite, considered themselves true crime fighters but their methods were extreme: they killed their opponents. When Black and his Elite came to Metropolis, they were opposed by the city's protector, SUPERMAN. The Man of Steel defeated the Elite and captured Black, but President Lex Luthor (see LUTHOR, LEX) had Black released. The immoral Brit became Luthor's ally, using his telepathic gifts to find out that Clark Kent was Superman's alter ego, a secret that Luthor had long sought. Black first learned of IMPERIEX's approach to Earth, allowing Luthor a chance to mobilize the planet's defense in a cosmic war. After the war, Black used his knowledge of Superman's alter ego to target everyone close to Superman and/or Clark Kent. Black was thought to have died in an explosion, but returned with his sister, Vera Black.

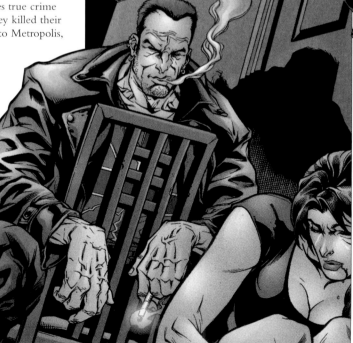

MANHUNTER

FIRST APPEARANCE JLA #61 (February 2002)
STATUS Hero **REAL NAME** Kirk DePaul
OCCUPATION Crime fighter **BASE** Mobile
HEIGHT 5ft 11in **WEIGHT** 191 lbs **EYES** Blue **HAIR** Brown
SPECIAL POWERS/ABILITIES An expert marksman and tracker with enhanced athletic skills and a good tactical mind.

The scheming android MANHUNTERS have employed human agents over the years. The first was policeman Donald Richards who, with his robotic dog named Thor, battled crime in the 1940s. Big-game hunter Paul Kirk was also recruited during that period. He fought crime as Manhunter II, joining the ALL-STAR SQUADRON during World War II.

Decades later, idealist Mark Shaw became the third Manhunter. A master of many fighting styles, he helped the JUSTICE LEAGUE OF AMERICA prevent the Manhunters from destroying the GUARDIANS OF THE UNIVERSE. Star City musician Chase Lawler then had a brief career as a fourth Manhunter before suffering a heart attack.

The fifth Manhunter is a clone of Paul Kirk named Kirk DePaul, who is a partner in the corporate team the POWER COMPANY. DePaul sometimes appeared to be more driven by financial gain than the idealism required to be a super hero, and has frequently clashed with his fellow partners over ethical and moral issues. **RG**

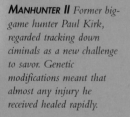
MANHUNTER I Donald "Dan" Richards had his own credo for tracking down villains: "Manhunter might get something on them when police methods fail!"

MANHUNTER II Former big-game hunter Paul Kirk, regarded tracking down criminals as a new challenge to savor. Genetic modifications meant that almost any injury he received healed rapidly.

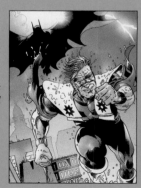
MANHUNTER V Batman was highly suspicious of Kirk DePaul's motives when he discovered the former mercenary in Gotham City. The Dark Knight was sure DePaul was in town to kill an exile from the African nation of Oranga. Fortunately, on this occasion Batman's fears were groundless.

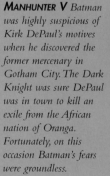

MANHUNTERS, THE

FIRST APPEARANCE JUSTICE LEAGUE OF AMERICA (1st series) #140 (March 1977)
STATUS Villains **REAL NAME** Not applicable **OCCUPATION** Android would-be conquerors (destroyed) **BASE** Mobile **HEIGHT** 7ft **WEIGHT** 475 lbs
EYES Photocellular **HAIR** None **SPECIAL POWERS/ABILITIES** Super-strong, armored androids armed with stun guns formerly energized by hand-held power batteries; now carry batons that fire energy blasts.

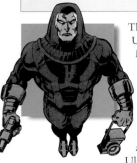

The GUARDIANS OF THE UNIVERSE created the android Manhunters as a universal police force 3.5 billion years ago. For unknown reasons, the Manhunters rebelled against their programming and launched a millennia-long battle that culminated with an attack on the planet Oa.

Ultimately, the Guardians overcame their android servants, stripping them of their power and banishing them across the universe. By 1066, the Manhunters discovered Earth and they began establishing agents there. Nearly 40 years ago, a battle between the Manhunters and the GREEN LANTERN CORPS above the Earth triggered a record-breaking blizzard that left the KENTS snowed in at their farm for months, long enough for Ma and Pa Kent to pass off the baby Kal-El (SUPERMAN) as their own son. Eventually, the Manhunters' megalomania got the better of them. In a bid to take over the world they activated their sleeper agents, hoping to destroy Earth's super heroes. Justice League International (*see* JUSTICE LEAGUE OF AMERICA) led a hero host into the Manhunters' stronghold and destroyed the androids. RG

MANTIS

FIRST APPEARANCE THE FOREVER PEOPLE (1st series) #2 (June 1971)
STATUS Villain **REAL NAME** None
OCCUPATION Agent of Darkseid **BASE** Apokolips
HEIGHT 6ft 4in **WEIGHT** 275 lbs **EYES** Orange **HAIR** None
SPECIAL POWERS/ABILITIES Superstrength; flight; can absorb any power source; "thermal touch" generates heat, "frigi-block" imprisons foes in ice; can destroy anything he touches with anti-matter.

Mantis himself may be even more powerful than DARKSEID, evil lord of Apokolips. Mantis was the first of Darkseid's agents to arrive on Earth. Foolishly, he schemed to conquer the planet for himself. Darkseid, meanwhile, permitted Mantis's ambitions only insofar as they aided his own search for the elusive Anti-Life Equation—the means of controlling all sentient life in the universe—which the ruler of Apokolips believed was secreted somewhere on Earth. Mantis was later defeated by the INFINITY MAN. Mantis then led the "bug" colonies of New Genesis in an attack on Earth. This time he was thwarted by the NEW GODS. Having an insatiable appetite for power, Mantis has even risen against Darkseid, only to be suitably humbled for his hubris. To satisfy his own megalomania, Mantis would happily see both Apokolips and New Genesis destroyed. SB

MARKSMAN

FIRST APPEARANCE SMASH COMICS #33 (May 1942)
STATUS Hero **REAL NAME** Baron Povalski
OCCUPATION Adventurer **BASE** Poland
HEIGHT 5ft 8in **WEIGHT** 150 lbs **EYES** Blue **HAIR** Black
SPECIAL POWERS/ABILITIES The Baron was an Olympic-level bowman as well as a highly trained hand-to-hand combatant.

Outraged by the Nazi atrocities committed in his native Poland, Baron Pavolski decided to fight back. When the Nazis invaded Pavolski's ancestral mansion for a base of operations, it became the birthplace of the hooded Marksman. By day, he masqueraded as Major Hurtz, loyal member of the Nazi Party, but when the sun went down, he swung into action using his nobleman's training with a sword and bow, silently dispatching the enemy. He worked undercover throughout Europe and was present, aiding members of the fabled JUSTICE SOCIETY OF AMERICA, during the bombing of Dresden. His post-World War II whereabouts remain unrecorded. RG

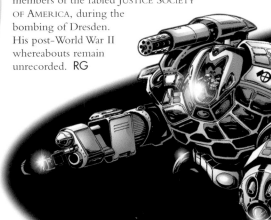

MANITOU RAVEN

FIRST APPEARANCE JLA #66 (July 2002)
STATUS Villain turned hero **REAL NAME** Unknown
OCCUPATION Tribal mystic; adventurer
BASE JLA Watchtower, the Moon
HEIGHT 5ft 9in **WEIGHT** 156 lbs **EYES** White **HAIR** Black
SPECIAL POWERS/ABILITIES Vast supernatural powers include the ability to change his size and travel to the astral plane; carries a hatchet that cannot cut a just man.

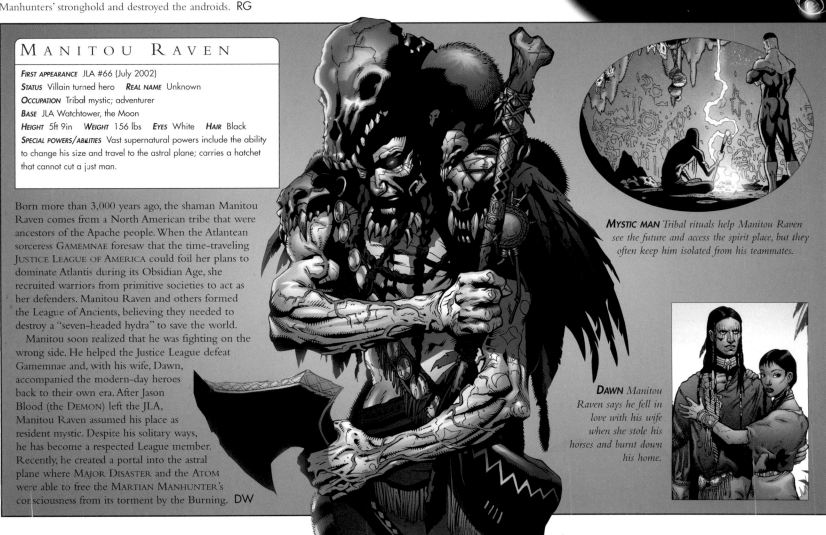

Born more than 3,000 years ago, the shaman Manitou Raven comes from a North American tribe that were ancestors of the Apache people. When the Atlantean sorceress GAMEMNAE foresaw that the time-traveling JUSTICE LEAGUE OF AMERICA could foil her plans to dominate Atlantis during its Obsidian Age, she recruited warriors from primitive societies to act as her defenders. Manitou Raven and others formed the League of Ancients, believing they needed to destroy a "seven-headed hydra" to save the world.

Manitou soon realized that he was fighting on the wrong side. He helped the Justice League defeat Gamemnae and, with his wife, Dawn, accompanied the modern-day heroes back to their own era. After Jason Blood (the DEMON) left the JLA, Manitou Raven assumed his place as resident mystic. Despite his solitary ways, he has become a respected League member. Recently, he created a portal into the astral plane where MAJOR DISASTER and the ATOM were able to free the MARTIAN MANHUNTER'S consciousness from its torment by the Burning. DW

MYSTIC MAN *Tribal rituals help Manitou Raven see the future and access the spirit place, but they often keep him isolated from his teammates.*

DAWN *Manitou Raven says he fell in love with his wife when she stole his horses and burnt down his home.*

MARTIAN MANHUNTER

FIRST APPEARANCE DETECTIVE COMICS #225 (November 1955)
STATUS Hero   **REAL NAME** J'onn J'onzz
OCCUPATION Adventurer   **BASE** JLA Watchtower, the Moon
HEIGHT 6ft 7in   **WEIGHT** 300 lbs   **EYES** Red   **HAIR** None
SPECIAL POWERS/ABILITIES Flight, superstrength, invulnerability,
enhanced speed, shapeshifting, invisibility, telepathy, and "Martian
vision," which provides a type of X-ray vision and allows J'onn to fire
energy beams from his eyes.

J'ONN J'ONZZ, THE MARTIAN MANHUNTER, has lost his
wife, his daughter, and his newest love, yet he is never truly
alone. His family is the JUSTICE LEAGUE OF AMERICA. Eons
ago, the Martians were one of the most powerful species in
the universe, capable of shapeshifting, intangibility, flight,
and a host of other incredible powers. J'onn J'onzz,
a philosopher and peacemaker in his private life, worked as
a Manhunter to keep the peace on his native planet.

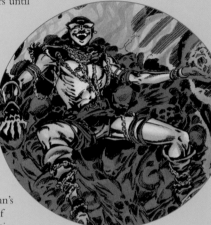

SECRET IDENTITY Hunting crooks as
a detective allowed J'onn to become
an Earth-based 'manhunter.'

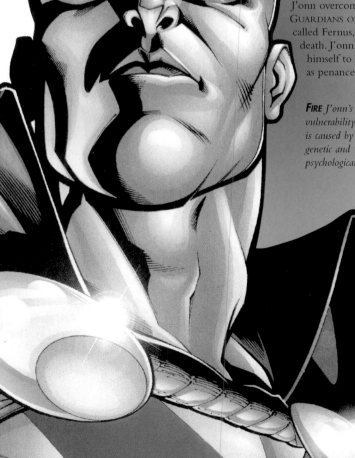

TRUE TO FORM J'onn
still adopts his true
Martian shape during
moments of quiet
meditation.

H'RONMEER'S CURSE

J'onn J'onzz's calm life took a horrific turn when the mad priest Ma'alefa'ak (Malefic)
unleashed the pyrokinetic plague H'ronmeer's Curse on the people of Mars. This pestilence,
spread by telepathy, raced through the population and caused nearly every citizen to burst into
flames, including J'onn's wife and daughter. J'onn imprisoned Ma'alefa'ak beneath Mars's
highest mountain, Olympus Mons, and wandered the planet's surface for untold years until
Dr. Saul Erdel brought him to Earth via a teleportation machine.

J'onn J'onzz took steps to fit into this strange new society, first by assuming the
identity of murdered Denver police detective John Jones and then by joining the
Gotham City super-group "Justice Experience" under the alias Bronze Wraith.
In Kansas, J'onn posed as a high-school civics teacher to keep an eye on a young
Clark Kent.

Eventually J'onn went public as the Martian Manhunter, becoming a founding
member of the Justice League of America alongside AQUAMAN, GREEN
LANTERN, the FLASH II, and BLACK CANARY II. The League soon became his
life. While other members came and went, the Martian Manhunter served with
every subsequent lineup. His spirituality led many to consider him the League's
heart and soul, while his vast array of powers put him in a physical class that even
exceeded SUPERMAN's—suffering only from a vulnerability to fire.

The Martian Manhunter has battled foes from the Red Planet, including the
WHITE MARTIANS (survivors from an ancient civil war between the Whites and J'onn's
Green Martians) and Ma'alefa'ak, still alive and looking to complete his mission of
genocide. J'onn faced his greatest challenge in the form of another forgotten Martian
menace—the Burning. When J'onn's new love, the reformed demoness SCORCH, helped
J'onn overcome his fear of fire, a genetic block placed on the Martian species by the
GUARDIANS OF THE UNIVERSE was removed. J'onn unleashed a primal "burning Martian"
called Fernus, whose efforts to trigger nuclear Armageddon appeared to cause Scorch's
death. J'onn has rededicated
himself to the JLA
as penance. DW

MALEFIC Not content with
the annihilation of a species,
this Martian conqueror thirsts
for blood.

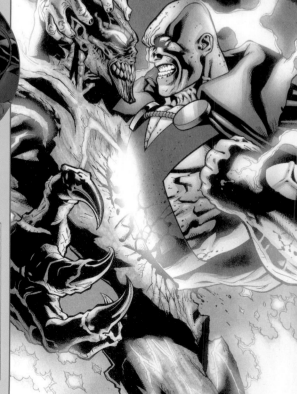

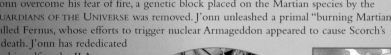

FIRE J'onn's
vulnerability to flame
is caused by both
genetic and
psychological factors.

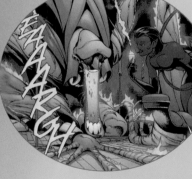

DARK MIRROR
Fernus, who needed fire in order to reproduce,
represented all that was evil in J'onn's soul.

KEY STORYLINES

• MARTIAN MANHUNTER (2ND SERIES) #1 (DECEMBER 1998):
The quintessential team player gets a starring role for the
first time in years.

• JLA: YEAR ONE #1-12 (JANUARY–DECEMBER 1998):
J'onn's role as the heart and soul of the JLA is apparent
in this retelling of the team's origin.

• JLA #84-89 (OCTOBER–DECEMBER 2003): J'onn turns
against his JLA teammates during the Burning Martian
storyline, showing why he is their most powerful member.

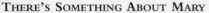

MARY MARVEL

THE WORLD'S MIGHTIEST GIRL

FIRST APPEARANCE CAPTAIN MARVEL ADVENTURES #18 (Dec. 1942)
STATUS Hero **REAL NAME** Mary Batson **OCCUPATION** Adventurer
BASE Fawcett City **HEIGHT** 5ft 6in **WEIGHT** 139 lbs **EYES** Blue
HAIR Auburn **SPECIAL POWERS/ABILITIES** By saying "Shazam!" aloud,
Mary Marvel gains Solomon's wisdom, Hercules' superstrength,
Atlas's stamina, Zeus's raw power, Achilles' courage, and Mercury's
superspeed. Mary Marvel shares her powers with Captain Marvel
and Captain Marvel Jr.; if either is using their powers, Mary Marvel
has access to only half her power.

SHE IS THE TWIN SISTER OF BILLY BATSON, the mighty
mortal known as CAPTAIN MARVEL. Granted the abilities of
the greatest OLYMPIAN GODS by uttering the name of the
wizard Shazam, Mary Batson is Mary Marvel, one of the most
powerful heroes on the planet! A sweet young woman in both
guises, Mary nonetheless packs quite a punch, courageously
defending her hometown of Fawcett City from mutant
worms, Nazi terrorists, and ancient deities gone mad!

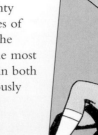

THE WORLD'S MIGHTIEST GIRL Despite
her power, Mary Marvel is still only
a teenager.

THERE'S SOMETHING ABOUT MARY

Mary Batson's parents were killed by Theo Adam (BLACK
ADAM) on an archaeological expedition in Egypt when
she was nine. Mary, who had completely lost her
memory, was taken back to the U.S. by Adam's sister,
Sarah Primm, who worked for Nick and Nora
Bromfeld, a wealthy family in Fawcett City.
Adopted by the Bromfelds, Mary lived a
sheltered life.

Years later, Mary was reintroduced to Billy
Batson, who recognized her as his long-lost
sister. Billy and his friend Freddy Freeman
arrived at the Bromfelds just as the villain IBAC
arrived to kidnap the family. Mary escaped, clutching
the gift Billy had brought her to jog her memory, a stuffed
animal the twins used to play with called Mister Tawky
Tawny. As Mary hid from the kidnappers, the toy transported
her mind to another dimension, where she met the spirit of
her slain mother, Marilyn, and the wizard Shazam. Mary's
mental blocks vanished and her memory returned. She
instinctively sensed that her brother Billy was Captain
Marvel. Mary begged the wizard to help her save her
family. He agreed and blessed her with a
variety of powers she could summon
forth by saying the word "Shazam!"

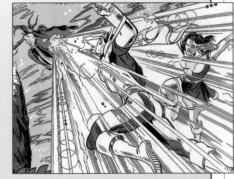

FAMILY OUTING When two or more of the
Marvels harness the power of the wizard
Shazam, it is divided equally among them.

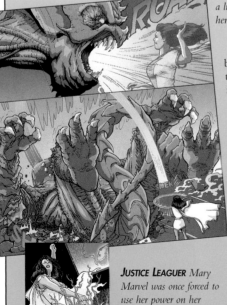

SHAZAM! Mary summons
a lightning bolt to change
her into a super hero.

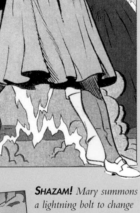

When the kidnappers
burst into Mary's room,
they found her garbed
in a red and gold
costume. Invulnerable to their bullets, she
overpowered them, but not before her
nanny, Sarah Primm, suffered a heart
attack. As she lay dying, Sarah confessed
her relationship with Theo Adam to
Mary, and how she had tried to hide the
amnesiac Mary, who had witnessed her
parents' murder, with the Bromfelds to
give her a chance at a decent life. Billy
moved in with the Bromfelds soon after,
and the Marvels became Fawcett City's
champions, defending the town from master
criminals like DOCTOR SIVANA, CAPTAIN
NAZI, and MISTER MIND.

Mary Marvel was recruited by Maxwell Lord
(LORD HAVOK) to join the JUSTICE LEAGUE OF
AMERICA in a people-friendly organization, the "Super
Buddies." Mary stayed with the comical team despite her
fear of radiation poisoning by CAPTAIN ATOM. **PJ**

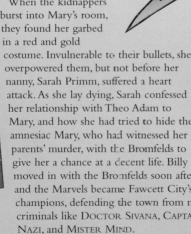

JUSTICE LEAGUER Mary
Marvel was once forced to
use her power on her
teammate Captain Atom
in Roulette's fight club,
the House.

KEY STORYLINES

• *POWER OF SHAZAM #30-31 (SEPTEMBER 1997):*
During the Genesis event, Mary's secret identity was
revealed to her parents before she entered the Source to save
all of creation!

• *FORMERLY KNOWN AS THE JUSTICE LEAGUE #1-6 (SEPTEMBER
2003–JANUARY 2004):*
Mary joined the team, and nearly murdered Captain Atom in a
hypnotic rage induced by Roulette!

MAWZIR

FIRST APPEARANCE HITMAN #1 (August 1995)
STATUS Villain (destroyed)   **REAL NAME** Mawzir
OCCUPATION Creature   **BASE** Hell
HEIGHT 6ft 6in   **WEIGHT** 160 lbs   **EYES** Blue   **HAIR** Brown
SPECIAL POWERS/ABILITIES Huge and nimble, the deadly Mawzir used its ten arms with great speed and agility.

After World War II, Russian troops hanged five Nazi officers for war crimes. Their souls went to Hell, where Arkhannone, the Lords of the Gun, transformed them into a single demon, the horrific, ten-armed Mawzir. Dispatched to Earth numerous times, the Mawzir attempted to bring back artifacts for its master. This brought it into opposition first with CATWOMAN, and then hitman Tommy Monaghan. Tommy destroyed the Mawzir and many of the Arkhannone using the Ace of Winchesters, a magic rifle which was the very object Mawzir first came to Earth to obtain. **RG**

MAXIE ZEUS

FIRST APPEARANCE DETECTIVE COMICS #483 (May 1979)
STATUS Villain (deceased)   **BASE** Gotham City
HEIGHT 5ft 6in   **WEIGHT** 135 lbs   **EYES** Brown   **HAIR** Brown
SPECIAL POWERS/ABILITIES A master manipulator and orator with delusions of grandeur, he had various underworld connections.

Maxie Zeus was a deranged gang leader who believed that he was an avatar of Zeus, the Olympian sky god. Amassing a flock of worshippers who doubled as gang members, Maxie became a prominent leader in the Gotham underworld. He briefly married, but after the death of his wife, (name unknown) he raised his daughter, mythologically named Medea, alone.

After several clashes with BATMAN, Maxie Zeus moved to Los Angeles and founded a team of superbeings he called, with typical hubris, the New Olympians. After a violent clash between his New Olympians and THE OUTSIDERS, the New Olympians were all captured, and Maxie Zeus skulked back to Gotham City.

Maxie was then summoned from underworld obscurity by PHOBOS, a son of ARES, god of war, who wished to turn Gotham into Ares's base on Earth. Maxie gathered a new cult following and helped Phobos and his siblings take control of three of Batman's most powerful villains, POISON IVY, SCARECROW, and the JOKER, energizing the demi-gods with his cult members' prayers. During the ensuing battle between Batman, WONDER WOMAN, and Ares's children, Maxie Zeus was slain, a human sacrifice to the war god himself. **PJ**

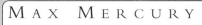

MAX MERCURY

FIRST APPEARANCE NATIONAL COMICS #5 (November 1940)
STATUS Hero (missing in action)   **REAL NAME** Unrevealed
OCCUPATION Adventurer   **BASE** Manchester, Alabama
HEIGHT 6ft 1in   **WEIGHT** 188 lbs   **EYES** Blue   **HAIR** Gray
SPECIAL POWERS/ABILITIES Can run at speeds approaching the speed of light and vibrate his molecules through solid objects.

The "Zen Master of Speed" is the elder statesman among the FLASH family of speedsters. A friend to Jay Garrick, a mentor to Wally West, and a father figure to Impulse (see KID FLASH), Max Mercury knows more about the Speed Force than anyone on the planet. Born in the first half of the 19th century, he gained his powers from a Blackfoot tribal shaman while working as a fort messenger on the American frontier. Running at near-light velocity, Max brushed against the edge of the Speed Force. He was ricocheted into the future, landing in 1880s Arizona, where he became known as Windrunner. He later worked as Whip Whirlwind in New York City and, after another time jaunt, he helped baseball star Babe Ruth escape the mob in the 1920s under the alias Lightning. In the 1940s he emerged as Quicksilver, working alongside Jay "Flash" Garrick during World War II.

After the war Max fathered a daughter and time-skipped into the '50s as Blue Streak. He finally jumped to the current era during a 1960s battle with SAVITAR. Since then Max has established ties with his daughter Dr. Helen Claiborne, and become the legal guardian of Impulse. Recently, Jay Garrick's old enemy Rival possessed Max's body and vanished in a time sphere. Max's spirit is believed to be trapped inside the Speed Force. **DW**

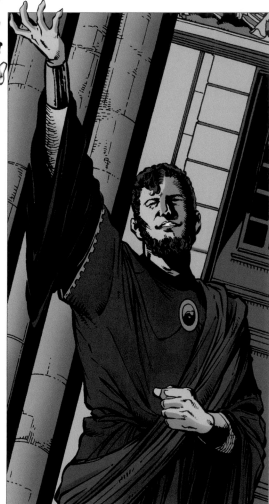

PREACHING TO THE CONVERTED In Gotham City, Maxie Zeus took the worship of the disenfranchised and transformed it into power for Ares.

MAXIMA

FIRST APPEARANCE ACTION COMICS #645 (September 1989)
STATUS Hero (deceased) **REAL NAME** None
OCCUPATION Deposed ruler of Almerac/adventurer **BASE** Earth
HEIGHT 6ft 2in **WEIGHT** 164 lbs **EYES** Brown **HAIR** Red
SPECIAL POWERS/ABILITIES Superstrength; flight; able to psychokinetically manipulate matter at the molecular level.

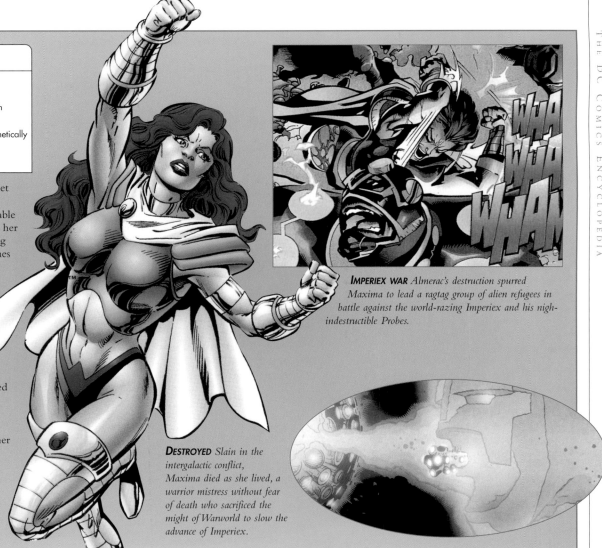

Maxima once ruled a vast empire based on the planet Almerac. She became obsessed with expanding her galactic reach and, most importantly, securing a suitable mate to father an heir for her glorious realm. When her minions intercepted a subspace transmission detailing SUPERMAN's astonishing feats in the gladiatorial games of MONGUL's Warworld, Maxima was sure she had found her man. Without further delay, she resolved to make the Man of Steel her husband. Superman respectfully declined to marry her, her admiration turned to rage, and she became his enemy.

As time passed, however, her fury abated, and Maxima sided with Superman to repel BRAINIAC's intergalactic invasion of Earth. Maxima was later banished from Almerac and elected to remain on Earth, where she was a respected member of the JUSTICE LEAGUE for a while. Ultimately, her own superiority complex and lingering resentment over Superman's rejection of her led Maxima back to villainy and a partnership with the so-called Superman Revenge Squad.

Fickle as she was, Maxima never ever backed down from a fight. After the world-destroying IMPERIEX destroyed Almerac, Maxima gave her own life so that Earth, her adopted home, would not suffer the same terrible fate. **SB**

IMPERIEX WAR Almerac's destruction spurred Maxima to lead a ragtag group of alien refugees in battle against the world-razing Imperiex and his nigh-indestructible Probes.

DESTROYED Slain in the intergalactic conflict, Maxima died as she lived, a warrior mistress without fear of death who sacrificed the might of Warworld to slow the advance of Imperiex.

MAYA

FIRST APPEARANCE JUSTICE LEAGUE EUROPE #47 (February 1993)
STATUS Hero **REAL NAME** Chandi Gupta
OCCUPATION Adventurer **BASE** India
HEIGHT 5ft 3in **WEIGHT** 120 lbs **EYES** Brown **HAIR** Black
SPECIAL POWERS/ABILITIES Can emit and control fire and water, channeling her mystic powers in harmony with the fire elemental Firestorm and water elemental Naiad.

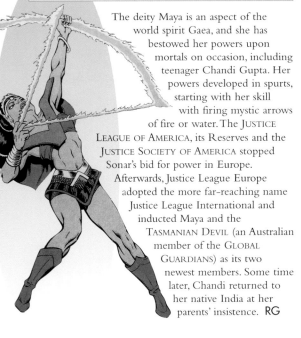

The deity Maya is an aspect of the world spirit Gaea, and she has bestowed her powers upon mortals on occasion, including teenager Chandi Gupta. Her powers developed in spurts, starting with her skill with firing mystic arrows of fire or water. The JUSTICE LEAGUE OF AMERICA, its Reserves and the JUSTICE SOCIETY OF AMERICA stopped Sonar's bid for power in Europe. Afterwards, Justice League Europe adopted the more far-reaching name Justice League International and inducted Maya and the TASMANIAN DEVIL (an Australian member of the GLOBAL GUARDIANS) as its two newest members. Some time later, Chandi returned to her native India at her parents' insistence. **RG**

MEANSTREAK

FIRST APPEARANCE JUSTICE LEAGUE AMERICA (2nd series) #78 (August 1993)
STATUS Villain **REAL NAME** Unknown **OCCUPATION** New Extremist
BASE Mobile **HEIGHT** 5ft 8in **WEIGHT** 144 lbs **EYES** Blue **HAIR** Blonde
SPECIAL POWERS/ABILITIES Can generate swords, daggers, and projectiles made of flaming energy; a sadist at heart.

Together with her teammates in the New Extremists—Brute, Cloudburst, Death Angel, and GUNSHOT—Meanstreak takes pleasure in ruination and pain. The extra-dimensional being DREAMSLAYER invited Meanstreak into the New Extremists to bring an end to the JUSTICE LEAGUE OF AMERICA, a challenge she failed to achieve. Later, Dreamslayer seized a device operated by the Colorado cult "Flock of the Machine" (who worshipped the all-powerful OVERMASTER) to provide a second chance at glory for Meanstreak and her comrades. After they again fell short, the Overmaster drew the New Extremists into his vast new CADRE, an army of super-villains. Despite its size, the Cadre foundered, but Meanstreak and the New Extremists are still active as mobile mercenaries. **DW**

MEKANIQUE

FIRST APPEARANCE INFINITY INC. #19 (October 1985)
STATUS Villain (destroyed) **REAL NAME** None
OCCUPATION Agent of Rotwang **BASE** An unspecified future
HEIGHT 5ft 9in **WEIGHT** 519 lbs **EYES** Red **HAIR** None
SPECIAL POWERS/ABILITIES Dimensional travel; can fire electrical blasts, project neutron shield, and avoid electronic detection.

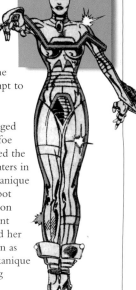

In the far future, Earth's greatest city will be a metropolis populated by slaves serving a despotic elite. To crush an uprising before it begins, the scientist Rotwang will create a robot woman and send it back in time. The automaton will then clash with the ALL-STAR SQUADRON in an attempt to alter future events.

Although destroyed, this robot, dubbed Mekanique, was salvaged by the JUSTICE SOCIETY's foe Per Degaton. He targeted the Society's sons and daughters in INFINITY INC., with Mekanique aiding his attack. The robot tried to comfort Degaton when the scheme went awry, but he scorned her "love." As heartbroken as a machine can be, Mekanique self-destructed, destroying them both. **SB**

MEN FROM N.O.W.H.E.R.E.

FIRST APPEARANCE DOOM PATROL (2nd series) #35 (August 1990)
STATUS Villain group (destroyed) BASE Mobile
SPECIAL POWERS/ABILITIES The Men had invisible rayguns that have tremendous destructive power; could also transform children's toys into deadly weapons; tears in their coats were in fact portals into another world.

During World War II, a group dedicated to the extermination of eccentricity and difference, named the Agency, began snatching the soul husks of men using the silver tongs of the all-powerful Telephone Avatar, a being they had trapped in a sub-sub basement of the Pentagon. These soul husks became the Men from N.O.W.H.E.R.E. The Men captured powerful psychic Wallace Sage, who was forced to create their bizarre weapons with his mind.

Agent Darren Jones, who had been fired from the Agency for misconduct, created a cadre of imitation Men from N.O.W.H.E.R.E. to destroy Danny the Street, a living, breathing avenue! The Men were rebuffed by the DOOM PATROL, Danny's new teammates, and were rendered powerless by Danny himself. Weeks later, the real Men from N.O.W.H.E.R.E. kidnapped Doom Patroller Dorothy Spinner (see SPINNER, DOROTHY), hoping to link her psychic powers—which enabled her to manifest the contents of her subconscious mind—to Wallace Sage's and use them to control the captured Telephone Avatar. But Dorothy's powers proved both unpredictable and uncontrollable, and she destroyed both the Telephone Avatar and the Men from N.O.W.H.E.R.E. **PJ**

Now Our Weapons Hanker Eager Recognizing Eccentricity The Men from N.O.W.H.E.R.E. could only speak in acronyms that spelled N.O.W.H.E.R.E.

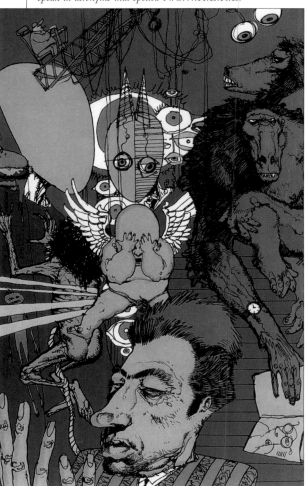

MENTO

FIRST APPEARANCE DOOM PATROL (1st series) #91 (November 1964)
STATUS Hero turned villain REAL NAME Steve Dayton
OCCUPATION Professional criminal BASE Mobile
HEIGHT 5ft 10in WEIGHT 178 lbs EYES Blue HAIR Brown
SPECIAL POWERS/ABILITIES Mento helmet previously provided a considerable array of psychokinetic powers; as a computer entity, Dayton's superpowers are as yet unrevealed, but are likely to be vastly enhanced and facilitate his insane schemes.

Steve Dayton, psychologist and head of Dayton Industries, was once the fifth-richest man in the world. Yet his money couldn't win him the heart of Rita Farr—ELASTI-GIRL of the DOOM PATROL—and he invented the "Mento helmet" to enhance the powers of his mind and to adventure alongside her as the super hero Mento. Farr eventually relented and married Dayton, and the two of them adopted the shape-changing Garfield "BEAST BOY" Logan. When Elasti-Girl died, Mento took revenge on her killers, GENERAL ZAHL and MADAME ROUGE. Later, he discovered that he had terminal cancer. Dayton tried to use the Mento helmet to control the disease, but the effort drove him mad. In his insanity he founded a criminal team called the HYBRID to battle the TEEN TITANS, and implanted a new type of Mento chip directly into his brain. He began creating a shadowy new role for himself as "The Crimelord," plotting global dominance. When DEATHSTROKE THE TERMINATOR uncovered his plans, Dayton merged with his intelligent supercomputer Zarina to infiltrate the Internet. **DW**

MERA

FIRST APPEARANCE AQUAMAN (1st series) #1 (October 1963)
STATUS Hero REAL NAME None
OCCUPATION Queen of Atlantis BASE City of Poseidonis
HEIGHT 5ft 9in WEIGHT 160 lbs EYES Blue HAIR Red
SPECIAL POWERS/ABILITIES Strength surpassing that of a human; able to telepathically solidify water into various shapes for offensive and defensive purposes; an aquatic being able to survive on land for limited durations.

The beautiful Mera was monarch of Xebel, an other-dimensional aquatic civilization much like Earth's Atlantis, until she was deposed and banished to Earth. AQUAMAN helped Mera regain rule of Xebel, but she then left her home to be with Aquaman, the pair becoming king and queen of Atlantis.

However, the course of true love runs no smoother underwater than above the surface, and Mera and Aquaman's marriage foundered after the murder of their infant son, Arthur Jr., by the diabolical BLACK MANTA. They separated and Mera became the unwilling mate of evil Thanatos—a sorcerer strongly resembling Aquaman—and bore him a son, A.J., who rapidly aged to adulthood in the villain's realm. Aquaman freed Mera from Thanatos, and she returned with him to Poseidonis, capital of Atlantis, to general rejoicing.

Unfortunately, the waters of Earth have not always been kind to Mera, and she has struggled to maintain her sanity as a result. She has also fallen under the influence of the mystic Hagen and the Sorcerous Class, who have used narcotics to make the Atlantean queen their pawn. **SB**

MERCENARIES, THE

FIRST APPEARANCE G.I. COMBAT #242 (June 1982)
STATUS Hero team BASE Mobile
MEMBERS
Gordon (last name unrevealed) A former Green Beret.
Philip "Prince" Edwards A poor British soldier.
Horst Brenner Former automobile factory worker.

The Mercenaries are three soldiers of fortune who travel the world looking for adventure and paying missions across war-torn battlefields. They joined the French Foreign Legion on the same day and became fast friends. None of them, however, believed that the work they were doing and the danger they were continually placed in was worth the low pay. They decided to leave the Legion and, calling themselves the Mercenaries, travel the world, fighting for whichever army paid them the most.

Still hunted by the French Foreign Legion for desertion, the Mercenaries are masters of armed and unarmed combat, and are renowned for their loyalty to their employers, providing the price is right. **PJ**

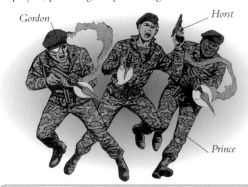

Gordon — Horst — Prince

MERRY, GIRL OF 1,000 GIMMICKS

FIRST APPEARANCE STAR SPANGLED COMICS #81 (June 1948)
STATUS Hero REAL NAME Merry Pemberton King
OCCUPATION Adventurer BASE Civic City
HEIGHT 5ft 3in WEIGHT 117 lbs EYES Blue HAIR Red
SPECIAL POWERS/ABILITIES No special powers, but quick-witted and an excellent athlete.

Merry Creamer was the daughter of a two-time loser who placed her in an orphanage when he was sent to prison for life. When Sylvester Pemberton III (Star-Spangled Kid) was injured, his wealthy father, noting his lack of friends, adopted Merry to be his companion. Sylvester's newly-adopted sister learned the Kid and STRIPESY's secret identities and took an alias of her own: Gimmick Girl. Merry had several adventures before pursuing a romance with Henry King, the criminal Brain Wave II. She had a son, Henry King Jr. When Brain Wave was arrested, Merry raised the boy on her own. Sadly, Merry Pemberton King experienced a mental breakdown and faked her own death when Henry Jr. was in his early teens. As a senior citizen, Merry came to regret her past and joined with several other surviving costumed heroes as Old Justice, lobbying to stop costumed minors going into dangerous situations. After a trip to the planet Myrg with YOUNG JUSTICE, however, she has reconsidered her position on costumed youths. **RG**

METAL MEN

FIRST APPEARANCE SHOWCASE #37 (April 1962)
STATUS Hero team **BASE** Metropolis
MEMBERS AND POWERS
All Metal Men can morph into almost any form
Gold (destroyed) Analytic mind and leadership skills.
Lead Good-natured and thick-headed; an effective shield against radiation.
Iron Quiet and strong team player.
Mercury Highly educated; can become liquid metal.
Tin Insecure; weakest of the Metal Men.
Platinum Also called Tina; flirt once in love with Dr. Magnus.
Magnus Veridium Constructed of an alien alloy; strongest of the Metal Men; capable of flight and energy absorption.

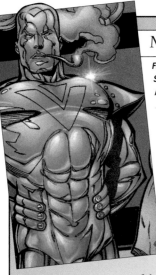

VERIDIUM Doctor Magnus is now a Metal Man, though he has not outgrown his fondness for pipes.

Dr. Will Magnus's Metal Men became the toast of the robotics industry for their shape-shifting abilities and lifelike personalities. That last trait was no accident—the Metal Men were humans trapped in robot bodies. Dr. Will Magnus and his brother Mike started Magnus Robotics under contract to the military. Mike's wife, Sharon, developed nuclear-powered "responsometers" to give the robots artificial life, but when the process failed, Mike accidentally sent his life essence into the inert Metal Man known as Gold. Others in the room suffered similar fates: Sharon became Platinum, two other scientists found themselves in the bodies of Mercury and Iron, the janitor turned into Tin and a pizza-delivery man woke up as Lead.

Will Magnus erased their memories and tried to restore them to their human forms. In the meantime, the Metal Men became heroes, often joining their malleable figures into giant machines to defeat the likes of CHEMO and the Missile Men. When the Missile Men killed Gold, Will Magnus sacrificed his own human form to take control of the ultimate Metal Man, Veridium. The Metal Men are still active (Veridium is a special advisor to the U.S. President) and although they will never be human, they have found a new life that is equally satisfying. **DW**

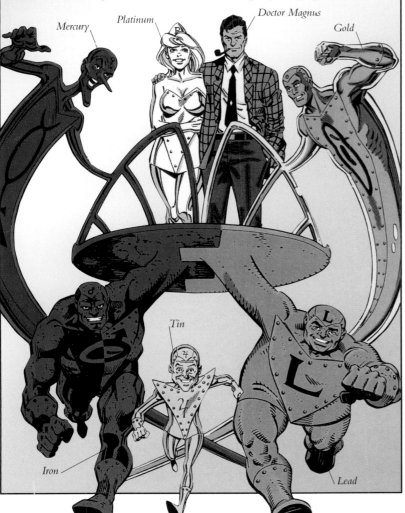

Mercury
Platinum
Doctor Magnus
Gold
Iron
Tin
Lead

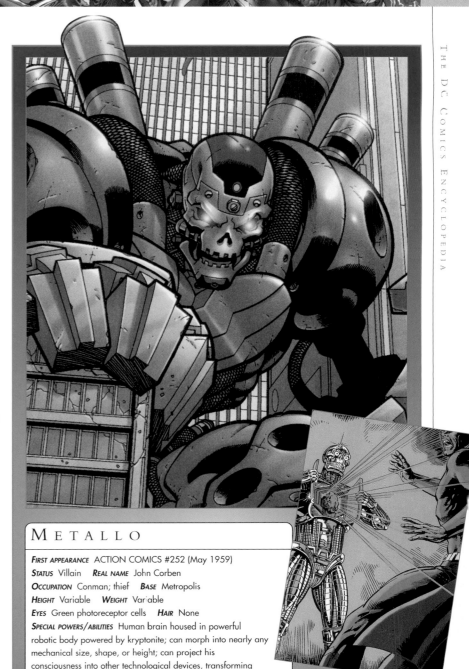

METALLO

FIRST APPEARANCE ACTION COMICS #252 (May 1959)
STATUS Villain **REAL NAME** John Corben
OCCUPATION Conman; thief **BASE** Metropolis
HEIGHT Variable **WEIGHT** Variable
EYES Green photoreceptor cells **HAIR** None
SPECIAL POWERS/ABILITIES Human brain housed in powerful robotic body powered by kryptonite; can morph into nearly any mechanical size, shape, or height; can project his consciousness into other technological devices, transforming them into an extension of his own body.

HEART OF EVIL Metallo's original, more humanoid body housed a deadly heart—a chunk of kryptonite, the metallic ore lethal to Superman.

Small-time conman John Corben was nearly crushed in a car accident, but robotics specialist Emmett Vale was passing by and rescued Corben, transplanting the criminal's still-functioning brain into a special robotic body powered by kryptonite. Vale had obtained a chunk of the destroyed planet Krypton, SUPERMAN's homeworld, from the remains of Superman's birth matrix in Kansas. After Corben's operation, he used the piece of irradiated ore to power the criminal's new robot body. Fearing an invasion from Krypton, Vale told Corben he had to destroy Superman, but Corben instead snapped Vale's neck, killing him.

Metallo, as Corben was now called, did fight Superman a number of times, using his kryptonite power source to weaken the Man of Steel. But Lex Luthor (*see* LUTHOR, LEX) captured Metallo and stole the cyborg's kryptonite heart for his own purposes. Using a back-up power cell to escape Luthor's clutches, Metallo sold his soul to the demon NERON to gain even more power. Soon after, Metallo joined forces with BRAINIAC 13. Corben's metallic body grew to giant proportions after absorbing Metropolis's technological infrastructure before "downgrading" to a more human scale.

Able to shapeshift into nearly any mechanical form imaginable, and desiring nothing less than the death of Superman at his hands, Metallo is a rampaging, homicidal nightmare. The cyborg fought the Man of Steel and BATMAN when the Dark Knight discovered evidence that Corben might have been the criminal who murdered his parents, Thomas and Martha Wayne, in Gotham City. **PJ**

METAMORPHO

First appearance THE BRAVE AND THE BOLD #57 (December 1964)
Status Hero **Real name** Rex Mason
Occupation Adventurer **Base** Mobile
Height 6ft 1in **Weight** 200 lbs **Eyes** Red **Hair** None
Special powers/abilities Super-versatile shape-shifter, able to transform parts of his body or entire form into any chemical element present in the human body, taking advantage of their properties—floating as a cloud of helium, burning with the white heat of phosphorus, etc.

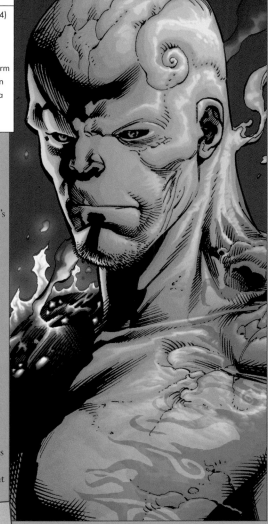

Ruthless billionaire Simon Stagg sent adventurer Rex Mason to retrieve the fabled Orb of Ra from an Egyptian pyramid. Little did Mason know that Stagg plotted his doom. Double-crossed by Stagg's henchman Java, Mason was left for dead beneath the tomb. However radiation from the Orb of Ra mutated Mason's chemical makeup, turning him into the freakish Metamorpho, a shape-shifting element man whose desire for payback against Stagg was only surpassed by his love for Stagg's daughter, Sapphire, whom he eventually married.

Metamorpho chose to use his elemental abilities for good as a super hero. He was one of the founding members of the OUTSIDERS team assembled by BATMAN. Later, Metamorpho belonged to several incarnations of the JUSTICE LEAGUE OF AMERICA. His marriage to Sapphire sadly ended in divorce. Their son, Joey, unfortunately inherited his father's shape-shifting abilities and grotesque appearance. Over the years, Metamorpho has seemingly "died" during several adventures. However, on each occasion Metamorpho's body was actually rendered inert, eventually reconstituting and reviving. Following these episodes, Metamorpho suffered amnesia and struggled to recall his previous life. Mason now mentors his clone, Shift, a Metamorpho with greater elemental abilities and a present member of the latest grouping of the OUTSIDERS. **SB**

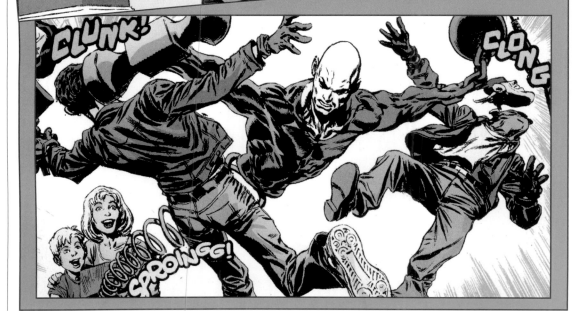

CARBON COPIES *Mason's clone, Shift (above), is able to manipulate his metamorphing body in any chemical element, not just those limited to the human body. Rex Mason's Metamorpho (below) is attempting to reconcile with his ex-wife and son.*

METRON

First appearance THE NEW GODS (1st series) #1 (March 1971)
Status Ally **Real name** None
Occupation Scientist; explorer **Base** New Genesis
Height 6ft 1in **Weight** 190 lbs **Eyes** Blue **Hair** Black
Special powers/abilities Brilliant scientist, whose analytical mind is motivated by a thirst for knowledge for its own sake; the Mobius chair can fold space and time, enabling travel through time and into alternate dimensions.

Metron is a New God who claims to have been born on neither one of the planets New Genesis or Apokolips; appropriately enough, he is often an independent party in the ongoing battle between good and evil. Although capable of doing great good, he cares little for beings who do not have the technical skills to assist him in his obsessive explorations of space. Metron freely mingles with gods and unimaginably powerful cosmic entities, who tolerate his presence since they are convinced of his impartiality. He is able to apply his genius intellect to any puzzle with laser-like intensity. Few secrets can be withheld from Metron.

In years past, Metron co-invented the NEW GODS' incredible Boom Tube teleportation technology, which allowed beings to travel from place to place in the universe in an instant. During the event known as the Cosmic Odyssey, Metron's discovery of the nature of the Anti-Life Equation temporarily sent him into a coma. Metron assisted SUPERMAN in his defeat of BRAINIAC I, and later helped the Earth's assembled heroes end the global threat of MAGEDDON. Metron always returns to his scientific wanderings, only reappearing in his time-travelling Mobius chair when some great crisis appears to threaten the universe. **DW**

MIDNIGHT

First appearance SMASH COMICS #18 (January 1941)
Status Hero **Real name** Dave Clark
Occupation Radio announcer **Base** New York City
Height 6ft **Weight** 190 lbs **Eyes** Blue **Hair** Black
Special powers/abilities Excellent athlete and hand-to-hand combatant; uses a special vacuum gun that fires suction discs.

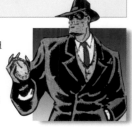

A boxer during the Great Depression, Dave Clark moved from his Midwestern home to the mean streets of New York City in the late 1930s. There, he eventually became a radio announcer at station WXAM. When Clark learned that a building he had seen collapse had originally been erected by a criminally negligent construction group, he adopted the disguise of Midnight, a character he had first heard of in a radio drama entitled *The Man Called Midnight*, to force the construction company's owner to admit his culpability. Midnight subsequently became a member of the ALL-STAR SQUADRON, but later left the group to join an independent team of crime fighters called the FREEDOM FIGHTERS. Midnight also allied himself with the eccentric genius Dr. Wackey and his super-intelligent ape, Gabby. Midnight's crime-fighting career ended after World War II. His current whereabouts, and his final fate, remain unknown. **PJ**

MILLENNIUM GIANTS

FIRST APPEARANCE THE MAN OF STEEL #78 (April 1998)
STATUS Primordial beings **BASE** Egypt, England, and Mexico
MEMBERS AND POWERS
Sekhmet, Cerne, Cabraca
All three giants are immensely powerful beings more than 400 ft tall;
able to call upon Earth's electromagnetic forces to wreak havoc.

The Millennium Giants awoke from thousands of years of
slumber to herald the new Bactun, or the "Cycle of Ages,"
and cleanse the Earth of all its ills. From Egypt came the
leviathan Sekhmet. From England arose Cerne, a Celtic
giant of amazing destructive force. And from a volcano in
the Yucatan peninsula came Cabraca, the "Mountain
Destroyer" of Mayan legend. Strangely, these three
behemoths awakened just as SUPERMAN was split into twin
beings, Superman Blue and Superman Red, both fueled by
the very same electromagnetic forces that coursed through
the Earth's ley lines. As if linked by magic, the Millennium
Giants followed the ley lines, unleashing a catalogue of
natural disasters as they prepared the Earth for another
thousand years of growth. To halt the Millennium Giants'
devastation, the twin Supermen were joined by the so-called
"Team Superman"—STEEL III, SUPERBOY, and SUPERGIRL—
as well as AQUAMAN, the CHALLENGERS OF THE UNKNOWN,
the JUSTICE LEAGUE OF AMERICA, and the TEEN TITANS.
When all hope seemed lost, the heroes finally realized that
the Millennium Giants were a vital part of Earth's cycle of
renewal. Superman Red and Superman Blue expended all
their electromagnetic energies to cleanse the Earth's ley lines
and finish the Giants' task without further destruction. The
Millennium Giants then returned to their thousand-year
slumber to await the next Bactun. **SB**

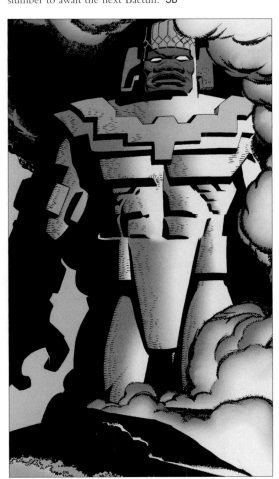

SUPER-SIZED *Cabraca and his fellow Millennium Giants emerged
from deep within the Earth to cleanse the planet with
destructive force!*

MINION

FIRST APPEARANCE NEW TITANS #114 (September 1994)
STATUS Hero **REAL NAME** Jarras Minion
OCCUPATION Adventurer **BASE** Mobile
HEIGHT 5ft **WEIGHT** 110 lbs
EYES Blue **HAIR** Blue-green
SPECIAL POWERS/ABILITIES Minion's Omegadrome was
a nearly sentient device that could transform itself
into protective body armor, weapons, and even
a spaceworthy transport ship.

The planet Talyn was home to a
warlike race constantly in battle.
The solution was to introduce genetic
changes that bred peace-loving people.
For a millennium life on Talyn was
calm, until the planet was laid waste
by the psychic forces of PSIMON.
Young Jarras Minion was pushed
toward his mother's greatest creation,
the Omegadrome. The mechanism
cybernetically linked itself to Minion
and became an escape craft allowing him to leave the
world. While aboard the craft, Jarras learned how to
manipulate this amazing technology, which could also
convert into a suit of battle armor. He followed the energy
signature back to Earth, learning to hate Psimon along the
way, and arrived in time to help the New Titans defeat
Psimon. After crossing paths with the DARKSTARS and
becoming imprisoned, Jarras returned to Earth and was
affiliated with the Titans. Minion gave his Omegadrome to
the new Titan CYBORG and then returned to the stars. **RG**

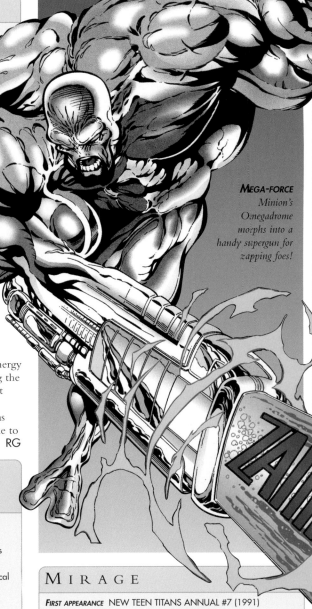

MEGA-FORCE
*Minion's
Omegadrome
morphs into a
handy supergun for
zapping foes!*

MINSTREL MAVERICK

FIRST APPEARANCE ALL-AMERICAN WESTERN #103 (Nov. 1948)
STATUS Hero **REAL NAME** Hank "Harmony" Hayes
OCCUPATION Adventurer **BASE** The American West in the 1870s
HEIGHT 5ft 10in **WEIGHT** 159 lbs **EYES** Blue **HAIR** Brown
SPECIAL POWERS/ABILITIES Highly skilled with a guitar, as both musical
instrument and blunt instrument.

Hank "Harmony" Hayes wandered the Old West singing
songs and righting wrongs under the name Minstrel
Maverick. Astride his horse, Dusty, he earned a living as a
guitar-strumming balladeer, fighting trouble whenever it
came his way. His friends included Blacksmith Bill, whose
ox-like strength rivaled his deep loyalty. Minstrel Maverick
worked with other crime fighters of the frontier, including
the heroine Moon Rider. His enemies included White
Mask and the Midnight Kid. Minstrel Maverick's favorite
weapon was his (reinforced) guitar, which he often cracked
against his enemies' skulls with a distinctive "boinggg!" of
quivering strings. **DW**

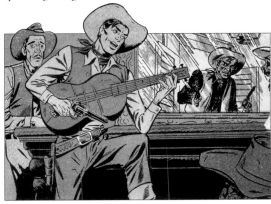

MIRAGE

FIRST APPEARANCE NEW TEEN TITANS ANNUAL #7 (1991)
STATUS Hero **REAL NAME** Miriam Delgado
OCCUPATION Adventurer **BASE** New York City
HEIGHT 5ft 7in **WEIGHT** 143 lbs **EYES** Black and white **HAIR** Black
SPECIAL POWERS/ABILITIES Can disguise herself as anyone she pleases
by creating complex psychic illusions around her body.

Miriam Delgado was living as a street urchin in Brazil
when she was kidnapped by the villain known as the Time
Trapper. Believing that she was from an alternate timeline,
Delgado, called Mirage because of her illusion-casting
powers, became a member of the so-called Team Titans.
Programmed by the Time Trapper to assassinate
EXTANT, the Team Titans fought Earth's heroes
during the Zero Hour crisis (see
Great Battles, pp. 320–1). After
Extant's defeat, Mirage and her
fellow "sleeper" agent TERRA,
joined the New Titans (see
TEEN TITANS). Mirage
eventually fell in love
with NIGHTWING, and
briefly disguised
herself as his
girlfriend, STARFIRE, so that she
could be with him. Mirage is
the single mother of a young
girl, Julienne. **PJ**

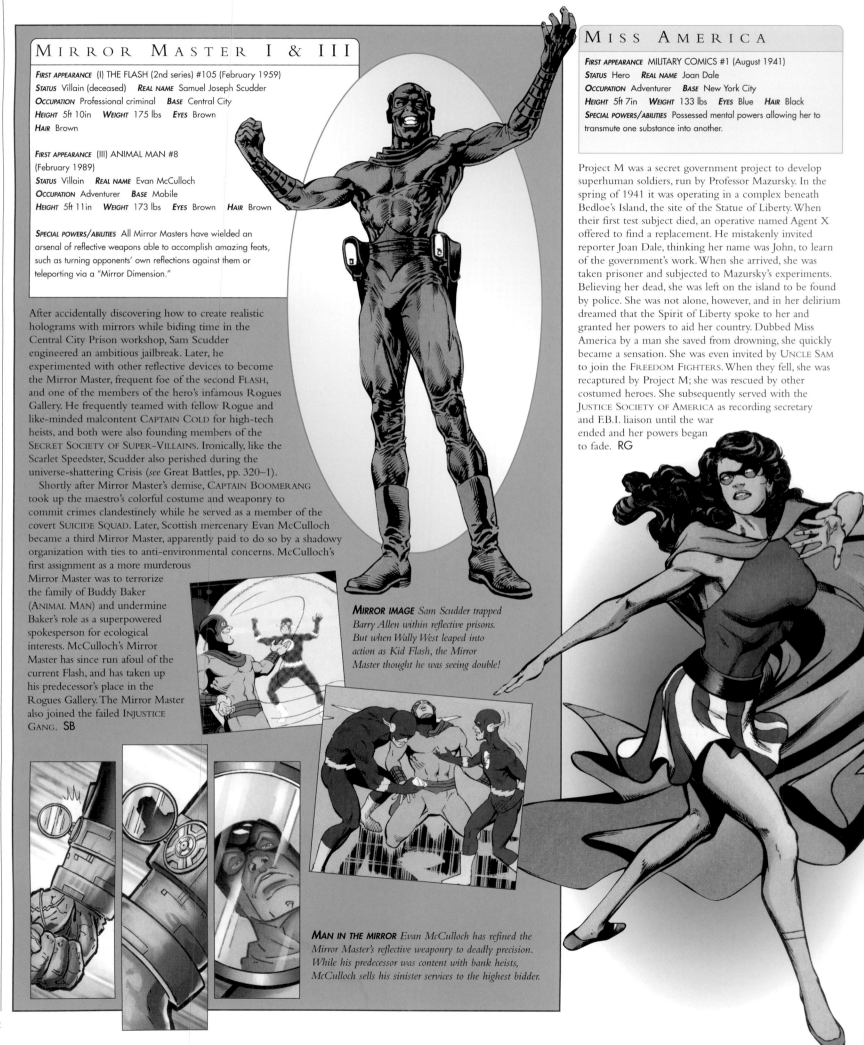

MIRROR MASTER I & III

FIRST APPEARANCE (I) THE FLASH (2nd series) #105 (February 1959)
STATUS Villain (deceased) **REAL NAME** Samuel Joseph Scudder
OCCUPATION Professional criminal **BASE** Central City
HEIGHT 5ft 10in **WEIGHT** 175 lbs **EYES** Brown
HAIR Brown

FIRST APPEARANCE (III) ANIMAL MAN #8
(February 1989)
STATUS Villain **REAL NAME** Evan McCulloch
OCCUPATION Adventurer **BASE** Mobile
HEIGHT 5ft 11in **WEIGHT** 173 lbs **EYES** Brown **HAIR** Brown

SPECIAL POWERS/ABILITIES All Mirror Masters have wielded an arsenal of reflective weapons able to accomplish amazing feats, such as turning opponents' own reflections against them or teleporting via a "Mirror Dimension."

After accidentally discovering how to create realistic holograms with mirrors while biding time in the Central City Prison workshop, Sam Scudder engineered an ambitious jailbreak. Later, he experimented with other reflective devices to become the Mirror Master, frequent foe of the second FLASH, and one of the members of the hero's infamous Rogues Gallery. He frequently teamed with fellow Rogue and like-minded malcontent CAPTAIN COLD for high-tech heists, and both were also founding members of the SECRET SOCIETY OF SUPER-VILLAINS. Ironically, like the Scarlet Speedster, Scudder also perished during the universe-shattering Crisis (*see* Great Battles, pp. 320–1).

Shortly after Mirror Master's demise, CAPTAIN BOOMERANG took up the maestro's colorful costume and weaponry to commit crimes clandestinely while he served as a member of the covert SUICIDE SQUAD. Later, Scottish mercenary Evan McCulloch became a third Mirror Master, apparently paid to do so by a shadowy organization with ties to anti-environmental concerns. McCulloch's first assignment as a more murderous Mirror Master was to terrorize the family of Buddy Baker (ANIMAL MAN) and undermine Baker's role as a superpowered spokesperson for ecological interests. McCulloch's Mirror Master has since run afoul of the current Flash, and has taken up his predecessor's place in the Rogues Gallery. The Mirror Master also joined the failed INJUSTICE GANG. **SB**

MIRROR IMAGE *Sam Scudder trapped Barry Allen within reflective prisons. But when Wally West leaped into action as Kid Flash, the Mirror Master thought he was seeing double!*

MAN IN THE MIRROR *Evan McCulloch has refined the Mirror Master's reflective weaponry to deadly precision. While his predecessor was content with bank heists, McCulloch sells his sinister services to the highest bidder.*

MISS AMERICA

FIRST APPEARANCE MILITARY COMICS #1 (August 1941)
STATUS Hero **REAL NAME** Joan Dale
OCCUPATION Adventurer **BASE** New York City
HEIGHT 5ft 7in **WEIGHT** 133 lbs **EYES** Blue **HAIR** Black
SPECIAL POWERS/ABILITIES Possessed mental powers allowing her to transmute one substance into another.

Project M was a secret government project to develop superhuman soldiers, run by Professor Mazursky. In the spring of 1941 it was operating in a complex beneath Bedloe's Island, the site of the Statue of Liberty. When their first test subject died, an operative named Agent X offered to find a replacement. He mistakenly invited reporter Joan Dale, thinking her name was John, to learn of the government's work. When she arrived, she was taken prisoner and subjected to Mazursky's experiments. Believing her dead, she was left on the island to be found by police. She was not alone, however, and in her delirium dreamed that the Spirit of Liberty spoke to her and granted her powers to aid her country. Dubbed Miss America by a man she saved from drowning, she quickly became a sensation. She was even invited by UNCLE SAM to join the FREEDOM FIGHTERS. When they fell, she was recaptured by Project M; she was rescued by other costumed heroes. She subsequently served with the JUSTICE SOCIETY OF AMERICA as recording secretary and F.B.I. liaison until the war ended and her powers began to fade. **RG**

MISS LIBERTY

FIRST APPEARANCE TOMAHAWK #81 (March 1971)
STATUS Hero (deceased)   REAL NAME Bess Lynn
OCCUPATION Freedom fighter   BASE Mobile
HEIGHT 5ft 8in   WEIGHT 137 lbs   EYES Blue   HAIR Blonde (black wig)
SPECIAL POWERS/ABILITIES Skilled combatant and rider; used powder
horns to create explosions, sowing panic among enemy troops.

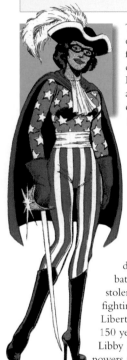

The Revolutionary War that established the U.S.'s independence from Great Britain had its own costumed heroes. Frontier nurse Bess Lynn was eager to fight against British forces, but afraid to do it openly for fear her brother (a captive in England) would be harmed in retaliation. Calling herself Miss Liberty, she donned a mask, wig, and a red, white, and blue costume inspired by the "stars and bars" flag of her new nation. She battled redcoats alongside fellow hero TOMAHAWK, riding a white charger and wielding a sword and whip. Tragically, Miss Liberty died before the end of the war in a battle with Hessian troops who had stolen the Liberty Bell. During the fighting the colossal bell fell on Miss Liberty and crushed her. More than a 150 years later, Miss Liberty's descendant Libby Lawrence fought against the Axis powers as LIBERTY BELLE. **DW**

MIST II

FIRST APPEARANCE STARMAN (2nd series) #0 (October 1994)
STATUS Villain (deceased)   REAL NAME Nash (last name unrevealed)
OCCUPATION Professional criminal   BASE Opal City
HEIGHT 5ft 8in   WEIGHT 140 lbs   EYES Gray   HAIR Black
SPECIAL POWERS/ABILITIES A brilliant strategist but average combatant;
was able to convert her body into living mist at will.

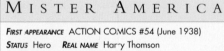

Daughter of the first STARMAN's arch-enemy MIST I, the woman known only as Nash might have lived a very different life had her brother Kyle not been killed battling David Knight, Starman's son and successor. With her fiendish father driven mad with grief, the mentally unhinged Nash took on her role as Mist II.

David Knight had already been killed, so Nash targeted David's brother Jack, the newest Starman, and all of Opal City for a reign of terror. She kidnapped and drugged Jack, conceiving his child without his knowledge. When Jack learned the truth, his child had already been born. The Mist's atrocities included the murders of AMAZING MAN II, BLUE DEVIL, and the CRIMSON FOX.

Nash subsequently introduced Jack to his son as a precursor to killing the young hero. Instead, she herself died, slain by her own insane father as he reclaimed the mantle of the Mist. Jack took custody of his son and prays that the toddler does not favor his psychotic mother. **SB**

MISTER ATOM

FIRST APPEARANCE CAPTAIN MARVEL ADVENTURES #78 (November 1947)
STATUS Mindless automaton   REAL NAME None
OCCUPATION Tool of evil   BASE Mobile
HEIGHT 10ft   WEIGHT 1,214 lbs   EYES Photocellular   HAIR None
SPECIAL POWERS/ABILITIES Atomic-powered robot; massively strong; can
fire nuclear blasts from hands; nearly indestructible;
capable of flight.

"Mister Atom" is the incongruously cheery name applied to the truly menacing nuclear-fueled robot built by government scientist Dr. Charles Langle. The towering automaton contains a miniature nuclear reactor that gives it various incredible powers, including the ability to fly and to release bolts of destructive energy. Mister Atom also possesses an armored shell that is impervious to attack from most superpowered beings.

Several years ago, the Venusian worm MISTER MIND attempted to overthrow the U.S. government by taking possession of White House agent SARGE STEEL. Mister Mind compelled Steel to send Mister Atom to the Fawcett City suburb of Fairfield, where the robot detonated a nuclear bomb. The explosion leveled the town and killed thousands. The teaming of Mister Mind and Mister Atom during this incident is considered the second incarnation of the MONSTER SOCIETY OF EVIL. **DW**

MIST I

FIRST APPEARANCE ADVENTURE COMICS #67 (October 1941)
STATUS Villain (deceased)   REAL NAME Kyle (last name unrevealed);
also known under the alias Jonathon Smythe
OCCUPATION Professional criminal (deceased)   BASE Opal City
HEIGHT 5ft 7in   WEIGHT 145 lbs   EYES Blue   HAIR White
SPECIAL POWERS/ABILITIES Could convert his body to sentient mist at will;
able to become a mobile, nearly invisible vapor; could take hypnotic
control of his victims; an ingenious criminal mastermind.

Decades ago, a scientist known only by his first name, Kyle, created a device that allowed him to transform objects into a mist-like state. When gangsters tried to steal the device from him, they turned its power on Kyle and he was transformed into the Mist. The Mist became a powerful criminal mastermind, a constant foe of the first STARMAN. Decades later, the Mist's son accidentally died during a crime wave spawned by his father. The Mist went insane, his psychological state further hampered by Alzheimer's disease. After selling his soul to the demon NERON, Mist I perished in a nuclear conflagration that also took the life of the first Starman. The Mist's daughter Nash followed in his criminal footsteps as MIST II. **PJ**

MISTER AMERICA

FIRST APPEARANCE ACTION COMICS #54 (June 1938)
STATUS Hero   REAL NAME Harry Thomson
OCCUPATION Adventurer   BASE Mobile
HEIGHT 5ft 9in   WEIGHT 175 lbs   EYES Blue   HAIR Black
SPECIAL POWERS/ABILITIES No superpowers, but
a well-above-average hand-to-hand
combatant with enormous courage and
resourcefulness.

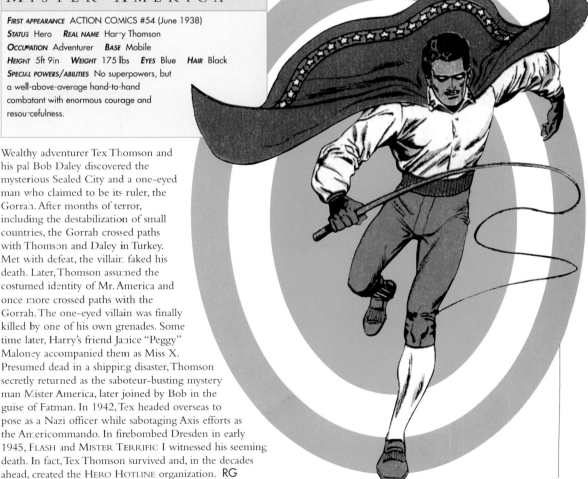

Wealthy adventurer Tex Thomson and his pal Bob Daley discovered the mysterious Sealed City and a one-eyed man who claimed to be its ruler, the Gorrah. After months of terror, including the destabilization of small countries, the Gorrah crossed paths with Thomson and Daley in Turkey. Met with defeat, the villain faked his death. Later, Thomson assumed the costumed identity of Mr. America and once more crossed paths with the Gorrah. The one-eyed villain was finally killed by one of his own grenades. Some time later, Harry's friend Janice "Peggy" Maloney accompanied them as Miss X. Presumed dead in a shipping disaster, Thomson secretly returned as the saboteur-busting mystery man Mister America, later joined by Bob in the guise of Fatman. In 1942, Tex headed overseas to pose as a Nazi officer while sabotaging Axis efforts as the Americommando. In firebombed Dresden in early 1945, FLASH and MISTER TERRIFIC I witnessed his seeming death. In fact, Tex Thomson survived and, in the decades ahead, created the HERO HOTLINE organization. **RG**

THE DC COMICS ENCYCLOPEDIA

MISTER E

FIRST APPEARANCE SECRETS OF HAUNTED HOUSE #31 (Dec. 1980)
STATUS Hero **REAL NAME** Erik (last name unrevealed)
OCCUPATION Destroyer of supernatural evil; historian **BASE** Boston
HEIGHT 6ft 3in **WEIGHT** 190 lbs
EYES Blue **HAIR** Black, white at temples
SPECIAL POWERS/ABILITIES Can time-travel at will; claims to be able to see good or evil within a person; carries a thick wooden cane.

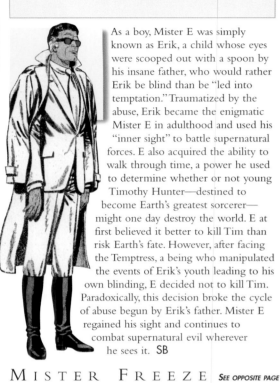

As a boy, Mister E was simply known as Erik, a child whose eyes were scooped out with a spoon by his insane father, who would rather Erik be blind than be "led into temptation." Traumatized by the abuse, Erik became the enigmatic Mister E in adulthood and used his "inner sight" to battle supernatural forces. E also acquired the ability to walk through time, a power he used to determine whether or not young Timothy Hunter—destined to become Earth's greatest sorcerer—might one day destroy the world. E at first believed it better to kill Tim than risk Earth's fate. However, after facing the Temptress, a being who manipulated the events of Erik's youth leading to his own blinding, E decided not to kill Tim. Paradoxically, this decision broke the cycle of abuse begun by Erik's father. Mister E regained his sight and continues to combat supernatural evil wherever he sees it. **SB**

MISTER FREEZE **SEE OPPOSITE PAGE**

MISTER MIND

FIRST APPEARANCE CAPTAIN MARVEL ADVENTURES #26 (August 1943)
STATUS Villain **REAL NAME** Unknown
OCCUPATION Criminal mastermind **BASE** Mobile
LENGTH 3in **WEIGHT** 5 oz **EYES** Black **HAIR** None
SPECIAL POWERS/ABILITIES One of the planet's most formidable telepaths, though his physical strength is negligible.

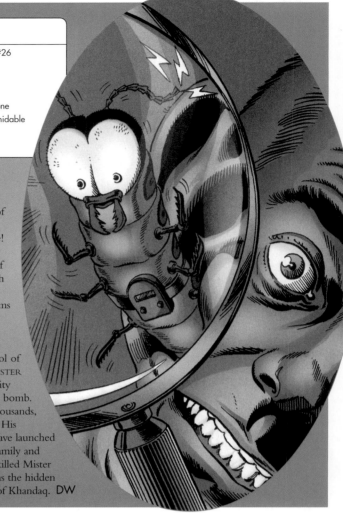

The world's wickedest worm comes from Venus and claims that his people once ruled the Earth between the extinction of the dinosaurs and the first Ice Age. His dreams of planetary re-conquest have so far come to nothing, but it may be only a matter of time!

Years ago, Mister Mind and his brethren plotted to escape their planet with the help of DOCTOR SIVANA and launch an invasion, with Fawcett City as their beachhead. CAPTAIN MARVEL saved Earth by transporting the worms into deep space, where most of them froze. SARGE STEEL took custody of Mr. Mind's comatose form.

However, Mister Mind took mental control of Sarge Steel, orchestrated the release of the MISTER ATOM robot, which arrived in the Fawcett City suburb of Fairfield, and detonated an atomic bomb. The firestorm flattened Fairfield and killed thousands, but that was just Mister Mind's warm-up act. His agents (MONSTER SOCIETY OF EVIL) would have launched global nuclear armageddon, but the Marvel Family and others halted the countdown and apparently killed Mister Mind. The Venusian worm recently emerged as the hidden puppeteer of Brainwave II during a takeover of Khandaq. **DW**

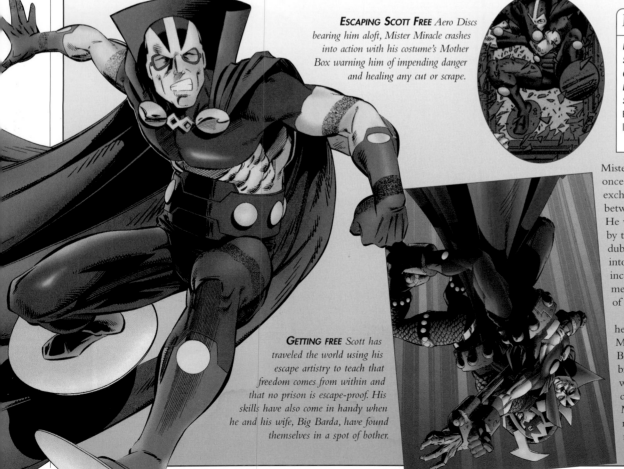

ESCAPING SCOTT FREE Aero Discs bearing him aloft, Mister Miracle crashes into action with his costume's Mother Box warning him of impending danger and healing any cut or scrape.

GETTING FREE Scott has traveled the world using his escape artistry to teach that freedom comes from within and that no prison is escape-proof. His skills have also come in handy when he and his wife, Big Barda, have found themselves in a spot of bother.

MISTER MIRACLE

FIRST APPEARANCE MISTER MIRACLE (1st series) #1 (April 1971)
STATUS Hero **REAL NAME** Scott Free
OCCUPATION Escapologist; adventurer **BASE** Mobile
HEIGHT 6ft **WEIGHT** 185 lbs **EYES** Blue **HAIR** Black
SPECIAL POWERS/ABILITIES Expert fighter; master escape artist; Mother Box incorporated into costume; Aero Discs for flight; multi-cube fires laser beams, emits sonic vibrations, or releases strong cable.

Mister Miracle is the son of HIGHFATHER of New Genesis, once the leader of the NEW GODS. As an infant, he was exchanged with DARKSEID's son ORION to secure a truce between the warring worlds of New Genesis and Apokolips. He was reared in one of the gulag-like orphanages overseen by the hateful GRANNY GOODNESS, who sarcastically dubbed him "Scott Free." Despite her attempts to turn him into another mindless minion of Darkseid, Scott remained incorruptible. He often broke out of the orphanage, meeting the insurgent HIMON, as well as BIG BARDA, leader of the FEMALE FURIES.

Scott escaped Apokolips and journeyed to Earth, where he encountered escape artist Thaddeus Brown, known as Mister Miracle, and Oberon, Brown's manager. When Brown was murdered, Scott became Mister Miracle and brought the killers to justice. Scott reunited with Barda, who had also slipped from Granny's grasp. They wed and continued to thwart Darkseid's schemes on Earth. Mister Miracle joined the JUSTICE LEAGUE OF AMERICA and remains an auxiliary member. Now a Metropolis resident, Mister Miracle still seeks adventure in company with his beloved Barda and, occasionally, Oberon. **SB**

MISTER FREEZE

FIRST APPEARANCE BATMAN #121 (February 1959)
STATUS Villain **REAL NAME** Victor Fries
OCCUPATION Professional criminal **BASE** Gotham City
HEIGHT 6ft **WEIGHT** 190 lbs **EYES** Icy blue **HAIR** White
SPECIAL POWERS/ABILITIES Has a vast intellect, but has subsumed it in favor of brute force, using his Freeze Gun and super-cooling armor to get what he wants.

COLD HANDS, WARM HEART
Nora loved the scientist and he idolized her, making her illness and subsequent death all the more heart-wrenching.

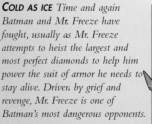

DESCRIBING VICTOR FRIES AS COLD-HEARTED is just the tip of the iceberg. To escape the pressures of his brutal father, young Victor developed an unusual hobby: freezing animals. He thought he was preserving his pets forever, but his father saw things otherwise and sent the boy for counseling. The psychiatrist viewed this freezing tendency as Victor's way of controlling his world. Isolated and ridiculed at school and college, Victor believed he would never know the warm touch of humanity.

Then came Nora, the beautiful athlete who stole his heart. They married and when his beloved was stricken with a rare malady, Fries left his teaching post to work for drugs company Gothcorp, hoping their technology would help him find a cure. Exposure to a hail of super-coolants altered his body chemistry, and the brilliant cryogenicist now wears a suit of air-conditioned armor to remain comfortably chilled.

FROSTY RECEPTION *The need for a cold environment has always proven a challenge for the villain, and an inconvenience for his cohorts.*

VENGEANCE AND TRAGEDY

Desperate to cure Nora, Victor had placed her in suspended animation to halt the disease consuming her. Then disaster struck: Gothcorp decided to deny him the vital funding to save Nora's life. Wielding an ice-blasting cold gun, Mr. Freeze revenged himself upon the soulless corporation. He set about killing Gothcorp's executives, working his way up the organization and saving C.E.O. Ferris Boyle for last. An ensuing clash with the BATMAN, however, shattered any hope for Nora's recovery. Accidentally firing his cold gun at Nora's cryochamber, Freeze fractured her slumbering body into a million shards. He put all the blame for this tragic accident on the Dark Knight and pursued him with the fury of a raging blizzard. **PJ**

COLD AS ICE *Time and again Batman and Mr. Freeze have fought, usually as Mr. Freeze attempts to heist the largest and most perfect diamonds to help him power the suit of armor he needs to stay alive. Driven by grief and revenge, Mr. Freeze is one of Batman's most dangerous opponents.*

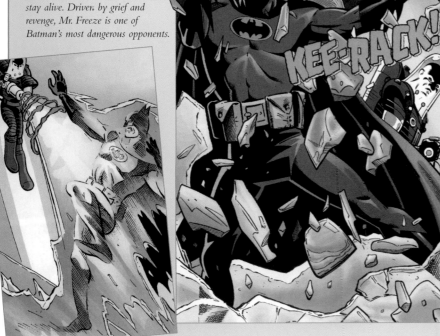

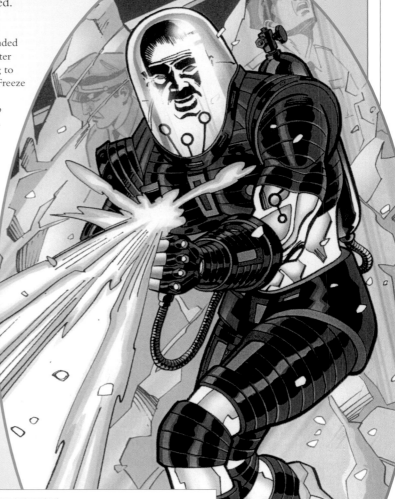

KEY STORYLINES

• **BATMAN: MR. FREEZE (TPB, 1997):** An examination on how a respected scientist, hoping to save the life of his beloved wife, became a twisted villain.
• **DETECTIVE COMICS #373 (MARCH 1968):** Mister Freeze ensnares Batman in a block of ice. How can the Dark Knight escape this chilling trap?
• **GOTHAM CENTRAL #1 (FEBRUARY 2003):** Gotham's finest investigate Mister Freeze's most recent crime wave in the dark city.

MISTER MXYZPTLK

FIRST APPEARANCE (historic) SUPERMAN (1st series) #30 (October 1944); (current) SUPERMAN (2nd series) #11 (November 1987)
STATUS Villain **REAL NAME** Untranslatable
OCCUPATION Little devil **BASE** Fifth Dimensional world of Zrfff
HEIGHT 3ft 9in **WEIGHT** 59 lbs **EYES** Blue **HAIR** White
SPECIAL POWERS/ABILITIES Beings from Zrfff possess shape-changing abilities and other "magical" powers that can transform animate and inanimate objects into other forms, usually on a temporary basis.

Every 90 days, SUPERMAN can expect a visit from Mr. Mxyzptlk. The imp loves challenging the Man of Steel with magical mischief, games that can only end when Superman tricks him into saying his name backwards. The fifth dimension Mxyzptlk hails from defies the physical laws of the three-dimensional world. Since humans cannot perceive 5-D constructs, Mxyzptlk employs an illusory, gnome-like body when on Earth, an easy feat for a being whose science can animate inanimate material and create matter from nothingness. Mxyzptlk's first trick on Earth was to animate the *Daily Planet* building in Metropolis. He then turned Lois Lane (*see* LANE, LOIS) into a mannequin.

METROPOLIS MAD
Mr. Mxyzptlk's fascination with Metropolis extends to Lois Lane and Lex Luthor.

SHAPE-CHANGER *The imp may appear goofy, but he is a powerful being from another reality, to Superman's regret.*

One of his favorite tricks is to cause bizarre alterations to Superman's physique, either aging him, making him absurdly obese, or making his head swell alarmingly. On one visit, he competed with fellow imp BAT-MITE to prove which of them was the best mischief-maker. The result was a tie, but Superman, BATMAN, Lois, and ROBIN were driven to distraction. On another occasion, Mxyzptlk offered Lex Luthor (*see* LUTHOR, LEX) red kryptonite when the imp was too busy to visit. Using red kryptonite, Luthor temporarily stripped Superman of his powers. Later, Mxyzptlk recreated DOOMSDAY and "died", crushed by the rampaging creature's bony protrusions. Of course, he was only playing dead. Mxyzptlk's greatest humiliation came at the hands of the JOKER, who talked the imp out of most of his powers. Mxyzptlk watched in horror as the Clown Prince of Crime turned Earth into a nightmarish world. Mxyzptlk helped Superman and Batman defeat the Joker, and things, including the imp's quarterly visits, returned to normal. **RG**

MISTER NOBODY

FIRST APPEARANCE DOOM PATROL (2nd series) #26 (September 1989)
STATUS Villain (deceased) **REAL NAME** Morden (first name unrevealed)
OCCUPATION Former scientist; cult leader **BASE** Mobile
HEIGHT 5ft 8in **WEIGHT** Unknown **EYES** Red **HAIR** None
SPECIAL POWERS/ABILITIES An abstract man who lived in a pseudo-dimensional state; could psychically induce a state of playful anarchy in other human beings; his powers were not inherently destructive.

After double-crossing the Brotherhood of Evil (*see* SOCIETY OF SIN), the greatest enemies of the DOOM PATROL, a man known only as Mister Morden fled to Paraguay to escape the Brotherhood's wrath. There, he met a Nazi war criminal, Doctor Bruckner, who promised to turn him into a new man. Morden was locked in a room that simulated an infinity of white space stretching in all directions. Driven insane and injected with serums that transformed his body, Morden became Mister Nobody. He gathered a crew of outcasts and, pledging to celebrate the absurdity of life, called his cadre the BROTHERHOOD OF DADA.

The Brotherhood stole a mystic painting that devoured worlds and attempted to consume Paris with it, but the Doom Patrol stopped them just in time. For a time, Mister Nobody chose to live in the painting, until he returned to the normal world and gathered a new Brotherhood of Dada, who then went on a nationwide tour to promote anarchy. At one rally, Mister Nobody attempted to use the crowd's focused mental energies and the painting's power to unravel reality. After a battle between the military, the Doom Patrol, and the Brotherhood, Mister Nobody was turned back into his human form and killed, having been accidentally impaled on a rusty pole. **PJ**

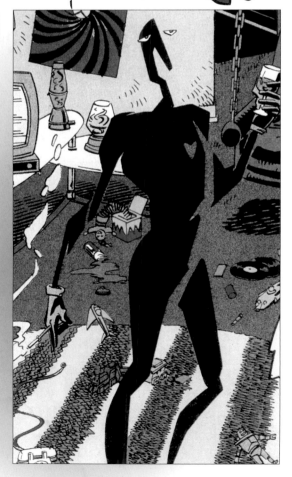

MISTER SCARLET

FIRST APPEARANCE WOW COMICS #1 (Winter 1940–1)
STATUS Hero **REAL NAME** Brian Butler
OCCUPATION Adventurer; district attorney **BASE** Mobile
HEIGHT 6ft **WEIGHT** 192 lbs **EYES** Brown **HAIR** Brown
SPECIAL POWERS/ABILITIES Skilled acrobat and hand-to-hand combatant.

Brian Butler worked as a district attorney but became frustrated by the limitations of the legal system. He decided to pull on a skintight red, white, and blue bodysuit and fight crime as Mister Scarlet, "the eerie figure all criminals fear." His secretary Miss Wade helped Butler to preserve his secret identity, while his young ward Pinky decided to join in the gang-busting game as Mister Scarlet's boy sidekick. During their career, Mister Scarlet and Pinky sent scores of crooks to the slammer, including the Dean of the Crime College. In fact, the Scarlet Scourge became so successful as a vigilante that crime soon dwindled down to practically nothing, and Brian Butler had to temporarily leave the legal profession for lack of work! Mister Scarlet eventually retired from the super-hero game, and Pinky has since assumed the guise of Mister Scarlet II in his stead. **DW**

MISTER TERRIFIC I

FIRST APPEARANCE SENSATION COMICS #1 (January 1942)
STATUS Hero (deceased) **REAL NAME** Terry Sloane
OCCUPATION Businessman; teacher **BASE** Boston; New York City
HEIGHT 5ft 10in **WEIGHT** 175 lbs **EYES** Blue **HAIR** Blond
SPECIAL POWERS/ABILITIES Was a masterful hand-to-hand
combatant; had genius level IQ.

Terry Sloane was a child genius who graduated
from high school by age 11 and completed
Harvard by age 12. Becoming an Olympic
medalist and millionaire businessman during the
Great Depression, Sloane grew suicidal when he
believed he had nothing left to attain. After he
saved the life of a young woman whose brother
had become involved with the mob, Sloane
found the challenge he needed. Donning a
colorful costume, Sloane became Mister Terrific
and stamped out the mob's influence.

During World War II, Mister Terrific joined the
JUSTICE SOCIETY OF AMERICA and the ALL-STAR
SQUADRON. Retiring years later, Sloane became a professor
at Gateway University but was murdered by his arch-
enemy, the Spirit King. Sloane's granddaughter Victoria
inherited his fortune
and became the
nefarious casino
owner ROULETTE.
PJ

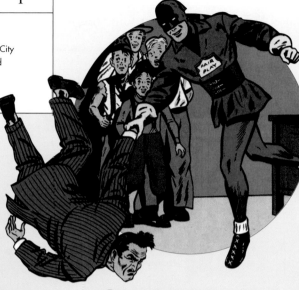

FAIR PLAY Possessed by an unyielding
sense of moral and ethical responsibility,
Mister Terrific used his skills to end the
careers of a number of criminals.

MISTER TERRIFIC II

FIRST APPEARANCE THE SPECTRE (3rd series) #54 (June 1997)
STATUS Hero **REAL NAME** Michael Holt
OCCUPATION Adventurer; retired electronics engineer and financier;
currently a security adviser for Tylerco **BASE** New York City
HEIGHT 6ft 2in **WEIGHT** 215 lbs **EYES** Brown **HAIR** Black
SPECIAL POWERS/ABILITIES Olympic-level athlete and hard-hitting
fighter; T-Spheres—floating devices of Holt's own design—
gather information and project holograms.

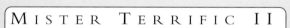

Michael Holt first found fame for bringing
home the gold medal in the Olympic
decathlon. Later, he formed his own cyberwear
company, subsequently retiring young and
wealthy. However, Holt's charmed life was
shattered when his wife, Angela, died in a car
crash. Distraught, he thought of committing
suicide. The SPECTRE intervened, making
Holt reconsider his purpose in life. He
became inspired by the example of MISTER
TERRIFIC I fighting to win over inner-city
kids who risked ruining their lives in petty
crime. As Mister Terrific II, he joined the
JUSTICE SOCIETY OF AMERICA, becoming
team chairman. He led a new JSA to defeat
the world-conquering ULTRA-HUMANITE
when his fellow teammates, as well as most of
Earth's meta-humans, were defeated by the
mind-controlling villain and imprisoned,
immobile and helpless. With time, Michael
Holt's exploits as Mister Terrific may even
surpass Terry Sloane's. SB

PACKS A PUNCH
Michael Holt was
as hard-hitting as his
predecessor, Terry
Sloane, when he
broke the nose of
the murderous
international terrorist
known as Kobra.

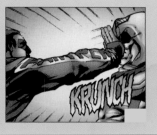

MISTER WHO

FIRST APPEARANCE MORE FUN COMICS #1 (November 1941)
STATUS Villain **REAL NAME** Unrevealed
OCCUPATION Scientist **BASE** Mobile
HEIGHT 5ft 5in **WEIGHT** 145 lbs **EYES** Blue **HAIR** None
SPECIAL POWERS/ABILITIES Solution Z let him escape his body's prison;
able to change size and shape at will.

Mister Who was born "a hopeless cripple" and tormented
by his peers while growing up. As a scientist, he developed
Solution Z, based on the world's most adaptive creatures,
and used it on himself to become "strong and tall."
Filled with resentment over the way in which he had
been treated all his life, the scientist decided not to
share his discovery, but used his new abilities to steal art
treasures and surround himself with beauty. The
miraculous Solution Z gave Mister Who complete control
over his body, enabling him to grow to giant size, become
paper-thin, blend into any background like a chameleon,
and even assume the appearance of any person. He also
gained superstrength and viewed himself as virtually
unkillable. If he lost a limb, he believed it would grow
back. He fought DOCTOR FATE repeatedly, only to lose
each time. RG

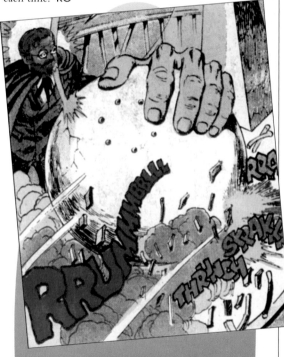

STRONG AND TALL Despite being mortal,
his shape-changing powers make Mr. Who
a formidable opponent for the likes of Dr.
Fate and the first Green Lantern, Alan Scott.

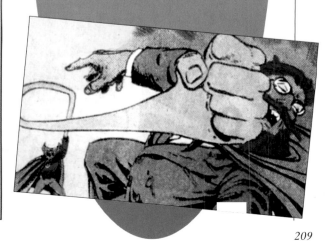

MISTER ZSASZ

FIRST APPEARANCE BATMAN: SHADOW OF THE BAT #1 (June 1992)
STATUS Villain **REAL NAME** Victor Zsasz
OCCUPATION Serial killer **BASE** Gotham City
HEIGHT 5ft 8in **WEIGHT** 150 lbs **EYES** Blue **HAIR** Blond
SPECIAL POWERS/ABILITIES Skilled with a knife and possesses a brilliant criminal mind; a totally ruthless psychopath who takes a sadistic delight in killing; can appear chillingly normal.

Mister Zsasz suffered no horrific childhood trauma, and can claim no strange jumbling of his brain chemistry. Zsasz grew up with love, money, and privilege, and made a fortune in his twenties. Despite his success, he felt empty inside, and he came to feel the same about everyone else—people were just automatons shuffling around in search of amusement. Convinced he should kill himself, he decided instead to give others the release of death. Since that time, Mister Zsasz has killed dozens, usually with a knife. For each murder, he cuts a mark into his skin. Zsasz has been imprisoned in Arkham Asylum but has always escaped, crossing paths with adversaries including the BATMAN and KILLER CROC. He operates according to no preset pattern, and his fixation on thrill-killing makes him one of the Dark Knight's deadliest opponents. DW

MOCKINGBIRD

FIRST APPEARANCE SECRET SIX #1 (May 1968)
STATUS Hero **REAL NAME** Carlo di Rienzi
OCCUPATION Director of Secret Six **BASE** Chevy Chase, Maryland
HEIGHT 6ft 2in **WEIGHT** 175 lbs **EYES** Blue **HAIR** White
SPECIAL POWERS/ABILITIES Skilled magician; possesses a talent for manipulating the actions of others.

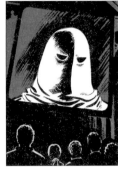

Mockingbird is the codename of the clandestine overseer and benefactor of the SECRET SIX crime-fighting team. The original team, composed of six individuals whose specialties ranged from chemistry to espionage, never suspected that Mockingbird was one of their own—Dr. August Durant. The U.S. government had compelled Durant to act as Mockingbird in exchange for the medicine needed to treat his terminal illness.

Decades after the Secret Six had disbanded, an aging Durant decided to let his fellow member Carlo di Rienzi in on his secret, and asked the former stage magician to take over as the new Mockingbird. Di Rienzi then assembled a second team of Secret Six agents to combat a worldwide bio-virus. Breaking from Mockingbird tradition, di Rienzi eventually revealed his true identity to the new team to gain their trust. DW

MONARCH

FIRST APPEARANCE ARMAGEDDON 2001 #1 (May 1991)
STATUS Villain **REAL NAME** Nathaniel Adam
OCCUPATION Would-be world conqueror **BASE** Mobile
HEIGHT 6ft 4in **WEIGHT** 456 lbs (in armor) **EYES** Blue **HAIR** Brown
SPECIAL POWERS/ABILITIES Armor includes a panoply of weapons and defense systems; possesses space- and time-warping powers.

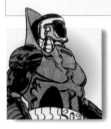

Hank Hall served the Lords of Order alongside his brother Don, as HAWK AND DOVE. When Don was killed, Hawk became increasingly belligerent, until the Lords of Order empowered Dawn Granger to become a second Dove to help pacify him. Dawn was later killed by Hawk's future-self, a loss that drove Hank Hall insane. He became Monarch, destroying Earth's super heroes in the early 21st century to pave the way for world domination. However, Monarch's future was undone by Matthew Ryder, the time-traveling WAVERIDER, who led other super heroes to prevent this dystopia.

Hank Hall soon developed the means to manipulate time and abandoned the armor of Monarch to adopt the guise of EXTANT, the villain behind the chronal crisis known as Zero Hour (see Great Battles, pp. 320–1).

Later, a doppelganger of Nathaniel Adam (see CAPTAIN ATOM) took up the mantle of Monarch and tried to become world dictator. His insidious scheme was thwarted by EXTREME JUSTICE. SB

M'ONEL (VALOR)

FIRST APPEARANCE (as Lar Gand) L.E.G.I.O.N. #16 (June 1990); (as M'Onel) LEGIONNAIRES #37 (June 1996) **STATUS** Hero
REAL NAME Lar Gand **OCCUPATION** Legionnaire **BASE** Earth
HEIGHT 6ft 1in **WEIGHT** 165 lbs **EYES** Blue **HAIR** Black
SPECIAL POWERS/ABILITIES Under a yellow sun, superstrength, superspeed, enhanced hearing, freezing breath, heat, telescopic and microscopic vision, invulnerability, and the power of flight.

Lar Gand, an explorer from the planet Daxam (see Alien Races, pp. 150–1) joined L.E.G.I.O.N. to honor his father's memory, who sacrificed his life during the alien Invasion of Earth (see Great Battles, pp. 320–1). After Lar Gand helped end ECLIPSO's reign of terror, he took the name Valor. Fired from L.E.G.I.O.N. after ethical disputes with Vril Dox II, Valor took a spacecraft he dubbed *Pilgrim-1* and headed into space. There he discovered that the alien Dominators were plotting a second Invasion of Earth and had seized hundreds of metagene-positive humans for genetic experiments. He stopped the invasion, freed the Dominators' captives, and thereby seeded dozens of worlds with new races.

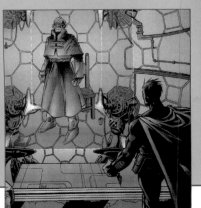

REVIVAL OF THE FITTEST
M'Onel visits Rā's al Ghūl, who is being held in custody by the United Planets Supreme Legislature in a hermetically sealed energy cage. But this is no social visit. M'Onel needs Rā's al Ghūl's help to save the life of Legionnaire Sensor, who has been caught in an explosive wave of hypertaxis energy!

INFILTRATION!
Credo rebels opposed to the United Planets, attack Legion World via the Legion's own teleporting device, the Threshold.

CREDO *M'Onel and other members of the Legion of Super-Heroes take hits to protect their leader, R.J. Brande, during an attack by a Credo advance guard.*

Years later, Valor, dying of lead poisoning, was placed in the so-called Stasis Zone by SUPERBOY. Now a phantom, Valor found himself trapped in the Zone and unable to communicate with anyone outside his ghostly prison. In the 31st century, BRAINIAC 5.1 of the LEGION OF SUPER-HEROES was able to recreate the Stasis Zone Projector, and Gand was released from his prison. Valor, revered as a god-like figure by the 31st century, was invited to join the Legion after helping them defeat the FATAL FIVE. Granted a special "detached" status, which allowed him to explore the galaxy between Legion missions, Valor took the Martian name M'Onel, which means, "He who wanders." RG

MONGREL

FIRST APPEARANCE HAWKMAN (2nd series) ANNUAL #1 (1993)
STATUS Hero   **REAL NAME** Josh Xan
OCCUPATION Adventurer   **BASE** Mobile
HEIGHT 5ft 10in   **WEIGHT** 160 lbs   **EYES** Brown   **HAIR** Black
SPECIAL POWERS/ABILITIES Can fire devastating bolts of darkforce energy from his hands.

Quarrelsome and arrogant, teenager Josh Xan received his superpowers when alien parasites invaded Earth during the Bloodlines crisis and attacked him, activating his latent metagene. In the past, his half-Vietnamese heritage had made Josh a target for bigots and caused him mental pain. Now, the negative mental thoughts he had kept bottled up for years saw expression as a unique form of energy which he could project with shattering force. Under the codename Mongrel, he used his darkforce powers to assist HAWKMAN and other heroes in ending the Bloodlines crisis.

Mongrel was not the only young hero who had earned superpowers during the alien invasion. The aliens, who drank human spinal fluid, triggered a related outbreak of meta-human powers among a small group of inexperienced youths. Collectively called the "New Bloods," this group of untested champions joined together as the BLOOD PACK at the behest of the shadowy U.S. government agency the Quorum, which hoped to use the Blood Pack's members to advance its own villainous agenda. After the Quorum's defeat, Mongrel faded from the public eye. **DW**

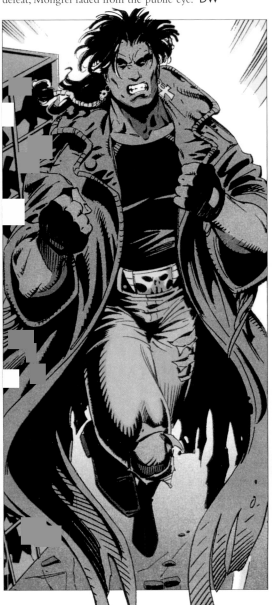

MONGUL

FIRST APPEARANCE ADVENTURES OF SUPERMAN #454 (April 1980)
STATUS Villain (deceased)   **REAL NAME** Mongul
OCCUPATION Despotic conqueror   **BASE** Warworld
HEIGHT 7ft 9in   **WEIGHT** 1,135 lbs   **EYES** Red   **HAIR** None
SPECIAL POWERS/ABILITIES Mongul possessed, as his children do, vast superhuman strength and are nearly impervious to bodily harm; commander of an entire army of gladiators on his mobile Warworld.

The first Mongul was a despicable conqueror who roamed the universe in his planet-sized Warworld. This giant mobile weapon was manned by thousands of slaves who were forced to fight in brutal gladiatorial games. On a self-imposed exile in space, SUPERMAN was captured by alien slavers and sold to the gladiator pits of Warworld. When Superman refused to kill his opponent, Draaga, Mongul entered the arena to personally slaughter the Man of Steel. But Superman defeated the tyrant and was transported off Warworld, while Draaga replaced the dishonored Mongul as its ruler.

Mongul then joined forces with the CYBORG SUPERMAN and destroyed Coast City, murdering its seven million inhabitants and hoping to transform it into a new version of Warworld named Engine City. Defeated and imprisoned, Mongul was offered more power by the demon NERON in exchange for his soul. When the alien despot proudly refused this offer, Neron killed him.

Some time later, Mongul's son and namesake arrived on Earth to warn Superman of the coming of IMPERIEX. After helping Superman prepare for the arrival of the cosmic destroyer, Mongul II turned against the Man of Steel, but was quickly defeated. After a mission to liberate DOOMSDAY from his lunar prison, Mongul II was slain by the murderous creature. **PJ**

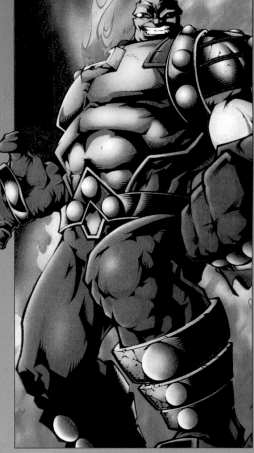

MONGUL II *Just as destructive and powerful as his father, Mongul II hunted the universe to take his revenge on Superman, who had dishonored the despot's father's name.*

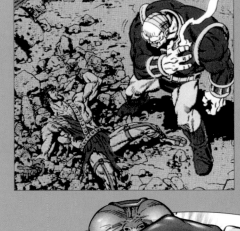

GLADIATORIAL COMBAT *On Warworld, the greatest warriors of a thousand conquered planets fought each other to the death for Mongul's entertainment. When Superman was found lost in space, he was captured by Mongul and fought the villain in the gladiator pits, where he nearly killed the Man of Steel. But Superman escaped, the gladiators overthrew Mongul's rule, and Mongul was forced to flee Warworld.*

MONGAL *The sister of Mongul II, she joined forces with Earth's alien allies during the Imperiex War to gain access to Superman and try to kill him for tainting her father's memory. Power Girl later humiliated her in battle.*

A SON'S REVENGE *When Mongul II finally confronted Superman, he stopped at nothing to rend the Kryptonian's body limb from limb. But Superman was able to use his own strength and skills to defeat Mongul II, who was killed by Doomsday soon after.*

THE DC COMICS ENCYCLOPEDIA

MONITOR

FIRST APPEARANCE THE NEW TEEN TITANS (1st series) #21 (July 1982)
STATUS Hero (deceased) **REAL NAME** None
OCCUPATION Surveyor and Protector of the Multiverse **BASE** Satellite
HEIGHT Variable **WEIGHT** Variable **EYES** White **HAIR** Black
SPECIAL POWERS/ABILITIES His greatest weapon was the knowledge he gleaned by watching the superhumans on infinite Earths.

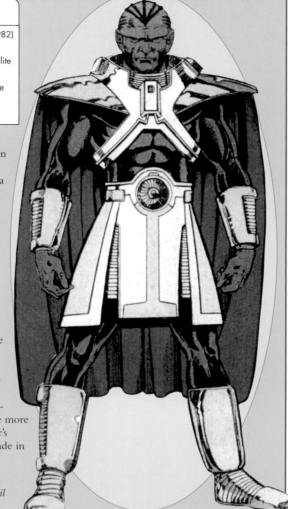

Billions of years ago, ill-conceived experiments carried out by the Oan scientist KRONA resulted in the creation of infinite universes from a singular reality. An anti-matter universe of utter evil also came into being. On a lifeless Oan moon, the Monitor was born, unnoticed even by the Guardians of Oa (see GUARDIANS OF THE UNIVERSE), who took it upon themselves to police the universe as penance for Krona's creation of the anti-matter realm. At the same instant as the Monitor winked into existence, the Anti-Monitor emerged on a lifeless moon orbiting Qward, Oa's evil doppelganger in the Anti-Matter universe. Soon, the Anti-Monitor became aware of the positive matter universe and his equally powerful counterpart, the Monitor. Thus began the ultimate battle of good versus evil across the barrier separating the respective universes known as the Crisis (see Great Battles, pp. 320–1).

The Monitor gave his life to fuel special devices that stalled the collapse of the Multiverse and allowed his super-hero alliance to defeat the Anti-Monitor, who was destroyed. A single more stable universe emerged, the Monitor's posthumous gift for the sacrifices made in defense of creation. **SB**

COUNTERPART Anti-Monitor was the Monitor's dark doppelganger and the evil twin responsible for the Crisis.

MONSIEUR MALLAH

FIRST APPEARANCE THE DOOM PATROL (1st series) #86 (March 1964)
STATUS Villain **REAL NAME** None
OCCUPATION Would-be world conqueror **BASE** Mobile
HEIGHT 6ft 3in **WEIGHT** 345 lbs **EYES** Brown **HAIR** Brown
SPECIAL POWERS/ABILITIES An above-average gorilla in terms of size and strength; possesses human intelligence.

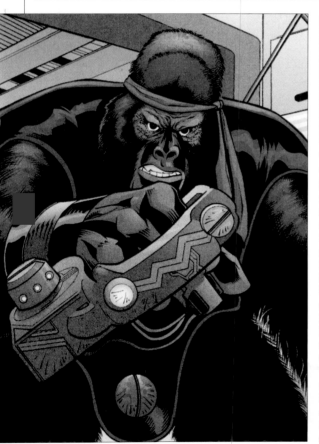

Ten years before his own death, a French scientist, whose name remains unrevealed, experimented upon a large gorilla that was stronger and more agile than most others of its species. Through a combination of secret teaching methods, shock treatments, and other experimental methods, the gorilla's I.Q. was raised to 178. The gorilla learned to speak English and French, among other languages, and took the name Monsieur Mallah. When the scientist died, Mallah, following instructions, removed the scientist's brain from his body and placed it inside a specially designed receptacle. A bizarre partnership had been born. The BRAIN and Monsieur Mallah formed the Brotherhood of Evil (SOCIETY OF SIN) and tried to take over the world. In their way stood Niles Caulder's DOOM PATROL (see CHIEF) and later the TEEN TITANS. After touchingly professing their true love for each other, the Brain and Monsieur Mallah were seemingly killed in an explosion following an attempt to insert the Brain into one of Cliff Steele's ROBOTMAN bodies. However, both survived and Mallah seeks revenge against Earth's meta-human community. **RG**

MONSTER SOCIETY OF EVIL

FIRST APPEARANCE CAPTAIN MARVEL ADVENTURES #22 (March 1943)
STATUS Villain team **BASE** Mobile
MEMBERS AND POWERS
Nyola Magical control over the weather.
Ramulus Mental control over vegetation.
Oom the Mighty Superstrength.
Mister Who Superstrength.
The Dummy Carries an energy-firing cane.
Mister Mind Formidable telepath.
Mister Atom Can fire nuclear blasts; possesses armored shell.

The Monster Society of Evil has had several incarnations over the years, and it seems likely that its name will be carried by the planet's most despicable villains well into the future. The first Monster Society of Evil took shape during the 1940s, when Aztec priestess NYOLA assembled the scoundrels RAMULUS, Oom the Mighty, MISTER WHO, and the Dummy, and led an attack on the New York City headquarters of the JUSTICE SOCIETY OF AMERICA. Beaten back by the FLASH I and GREEN LANTERN, the Monster Society retreated to lick its wounds.

Another grouping of the Monster Society of Evil many decades later consisted solely of the Venusian worm MISTER MIND and the atomic-powered automaton MISTER ATOM. Using his telepathic powers to hypnotize top White House officials, Mister Mind forced SARGE STEEL to launch the Mister Atom robot at the Fawcett City suburb of Fairfield. The nuclear detonation leveled Fairfield, nearly killing Billy Batson's adoptive parents. In his CAPTAIN MARVEL identity, Billy helped other heroes defeat Mister Mind, bringing an end to the second MONSTER SOCIETY OF EVIL. **DW**

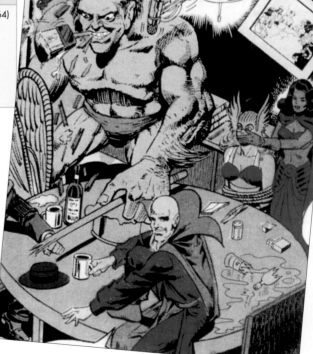

MONSTROSITIES In a foolhardy assault, Oom the Mighty, Ramulus, and Nyola hold Hawkgirl captive.

MONSTRESS

FIRST APPEARANCE LEGION OF SUPER-HEROES (4th series) #82 (July 1996)
STATUS Hero (deceased) **REAL NAME** Candi Pyponte-Le Parc III
OCCUPATION Legionnaire **BASE** 31st-century Earth
HEIGHT 6ft 4in **WEIGHT** 415 lbs **EYES** Pale orange **HAIR** Orange
SPECIAL POWERS/ABILITIES Vast superstrength coupled with virtual invulnerability made her a formidable opponent.

A pampered princess living on the planet Xanthu during the latter half of the 30th century, Candi Pyponte-Le Parc III was shocked to discover that her father's labor farms were filled with hundreds of impoverished workers. When a gene-altering bomb exploded in one of the plants, Candi's appearance was radically altered, and she became a super-strong, green giantess. Despite her jovial personality, Monstress, as Candi now called herself, felt like a misfit. She felt much the same even after becoming a prominent member of the Uncanny Amazers, Xanthu's premier superteam. Along with fellow Amazers KID QUANTUM and STAR BOY, Monstress was recruited by the LEGION OF SUPER-HEROES after a battle with the sorcerer Mordru, the DARK LORD.

After the BLIGHT attacked the Earth, Monstress and ten Legionnaires were transported to the far side of the galaxy through a temporal rift in space. Soon after, Monstress was killed by the Progenitor, who had once been her fellow Legionnaire, and friend, ELEMENT LAD. **PJ**

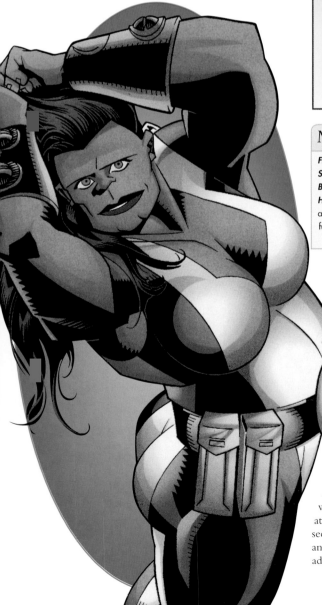

MONTOYA, RENEE

FIRST APPEARANCE DETECTIVE COMICS #644 (May 1992)
STATUS Hero **REAL NAME** Renee Montoya
OCCUPATION Police Detective **BASE** Gotham City
HEIGHT 5ft 8in **WEIGHT** 144 lbs **EYES** Brown **HAIR** Black
SPECIAL POWERS/ABILITIES Dedicated detective of great integrity in a department not renowned for it; an expert markswoman.

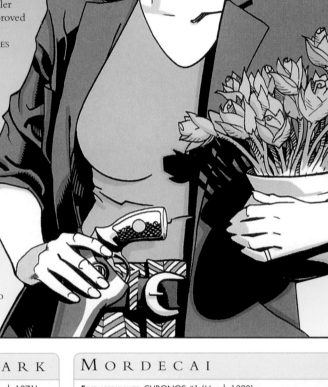

The daughter of immigrants from the Dominican Republic, Renee graduated with top honors from the Gotham City Police Academy. As a beat cop, she single-handedly apprehended the serial killer MISTER ZSASZ. Officer Montoya further proved her capabilities under the command of Commissioner Gordon (see GORDON, JAMES W.) and his late wife, Lt. Sarah Essen-Gordon, the latter awarding Montoya her detective's shield. Detective Montoya's loyalty to Gordon was evident during Gotham City's lawless No Man's Land period when she remained in the quake-ravaged city to help restore order. At this time, Montoya encountered Harvey Dent (TWO-FACE), who developed a dangerous romantic obsession with her. Following Gotham's rebuilding, Montoya rejoined the official G.C.P.D., where she is partnered with Det. Crispus Allen. Renee recently revealed that she is a lesbian, and has endured a predictable undercurrent of anti-homosexual sentiments within the force. She is one of few Gotham cops who supports the crime-fighting efforts of BATMAN and his allies. **SB**

MOONRIDER, MARK

FIRST APPEARANCE FOREVER PEOPLE (1st series) #1 (March 1971)
STATUS Hero **REAL NAME** Mark Moonrider **OCCUPATION** Adventurer
BASE New Genesis **HEIGHT** 5ft 11in **WEIGHT** 412 lbs **EYES** Blue
HAIR Black **SPECIAL POWERS/ABILITIES** His megaton touch creates a range of disruptions from a severe shock to a massive explosion; further effects have yet to be recorded.

Mark Moonrider was a natural-born leader. Growing up on New Genesis, the member of the NEW GODS was surrounded by friends. As an adult, those friends came to include BIG BEAR, BEAUTIFUL DREAMER, VYKIN, and SERIFAN, known to all as the FOREVER PEOPLE. When DARKSEID kidnapped Beautiful Dreamer, Mark led the others on an unauthorized trip to Earth to effect a rescue. They continued to thwart Darkseid's attempts to locate the famed Anti-Life Equation until DEVILANCE the Pursuer was dispatched to hunt them down. Devilance had them at bay until they summoned INFINITY MAN, who seemingly defeated the ruthless hunter. Since then, Mark and the others have returned to New Genesis, ready for additional adventures, despite the loss of HIGHFATHER. **RG**

MORDECAI

FIRST APPEARANCE CHRONOS #1 (March 1998)
STATUS Ally **REAL NAME** None
OCCUPATION Robotic servant **BASE** Chronopolis
HEIGHT 7ft **WEIGHT** 412 lbs **EYES** Gray **HAIR** None
SPECIAL POWERS/ABILITIES Highly advanced computer brain; enhanced android strength.

The timestream is a fluid flow of possibilities, yet several oases exist outside of normal space-time where events can occur untouched by chronal instabilities. One of these locations is the Victorian-designed floating city of Chronopolis, where a weary time traveler might encounter the android known as Mordecai. Mordecai worked as a servant for the Countess Fiorella Della Ravenna, a time-traveling noble who crossed paths with Walker Gabriel (CHRONOS II). Mordecai's advanced electronic brain allowed him to make the complex calculations used in the operation of Chronopolis's time-travel booths, and also to construct the temporal displacement suit worn by Gabriel throughout most of his history-hopping. Mordecai appeared to have died when the villain Konstantin Vyronis erased him from existence during an assault on Chronopolis. However, Gabriel's manipulations of the timestream restored Mordecai, and he is presumably still active in the ageless city. **DW**

MORGAINE LE FEY

FIRST APPEARANCE THE DEMON (1st series) #1 (Sept. 1972)
STATUS Villain (deceased) **REAL NAME** Morgaine Le Fey
OCCUPATION Sorceress **BASE** Mobile
HEIGHT 5ft 10in **WEIGHT** 156 lbs **EYES** Blue **HAIR** Black
SPECIAL POWERS/ABILITIES One of the most powerful sorceresses who ever lived; was able to project mystical energy bolts, read minds, teleport, and harness ambient magics.

The half-sister of King Arthur, Morgaine Le Fey invaded Camelot, only to be confronted by Etrigan, the DEMON controlled by Merlin. Merlin gave Etrigan a page from his Eternity Book and told him that Morgaine's beauty would crumble if she ever found the demon or the book. Merlin and Camelot vanished, leaving Morgaine accursed and a wizened old crone. In the 21st century, the decrepit Le Fey sought out the Demon and Merlin hoping to restore her beauty. She was betrayed by a servant and turned into a mummy. Morgaine escaped and then tried to possess WONDER WOMAN's immortal energy. But Wonder Woman had already forsaken her immortality, Morgaine's spell backfired, and the sorceress crumbled to dust. **PJ**

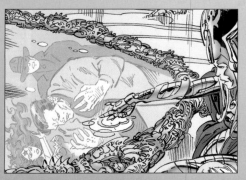

IMMORTAL BELOVED In her quest for eternal youth, Morgaine Le Fey sought out powerful beings, including Wonder Woman, the Phantom Stranger, and Jason Blood, hoping to steal their immortality. The powerful sorceress then used her magic to lure the immortals into a trap.

THE END Mistakenly believing she had finally discovered the secret of immortality, Morgaine's body crumbled to dust!

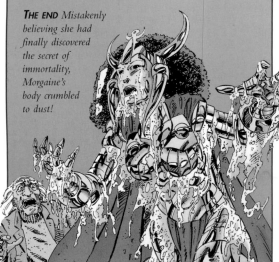

MORGAN, JENNIFER

FIRST APPEARANCE WARLORD #38 (October 1980)
STATUS Hero **REAL NAME** Lady Jennifer Morgan
OCCUPATION Sorceress **BASE** Skartaris
HEIGHT 5ft 6in **WEIGHT** 132 lbs **EYES** Blue **HAIR** White
SPECIAL POWERS/ABILITIES Mystic powers include projection of bolts of energy, time travel, and suspension of foes in force-field bubbles.

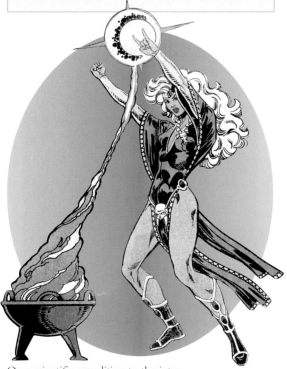

On a scientific expedition to the inter-dimensional, savage world of Skartaris, Jennifer Morgan met her long-lost father, Lt. Col. Travis Morgan, whom she believed had died in a plane crash. He had in fact become Skartaris's champion, WARLORD. Jennifer became sucked into a plot on her father's life, acquiring magical powers from the witch Ashiya to help defeat Warlord's foe, Deimos. Lady Jennifer, as the less-savage inhabitants of Skartaris came to know her, became the Supreme Sorceress of this lost world. The evil Atlantean Queen Clea and her VILLAINY INC. captured Jennifer during their assault upon Skartaris. Freed with the help of WONDER WOMAN, Jennifer is helping her father to undo the damage to Skartaris wrought by Clea's invasion. **SB**

MORTALLA

FIRST APPEARANCE ORION #6 (November 2000)
STATUS Villain **REAL NAME** Mortalla
OCCUPATION Hand of Death **BASE** Apokolips
HEIGHT 5ft 11in **WEIGHT** 175 lbs **EYES** Blue **HAIR** Red
SPECIAL POWERS/ABILITIES Mortalla's touch can kill and she defeats opponents more through fear than with any natural fighting talent.

On the planet Apokolips, Justeen, DESAAD's second-in-command, ordered a team of villains called the Suicide Jockeys to kill TIGGRA. This triggered a chain of events that culminated with ORION apparently killing DARKSEID and assuming the rule of Apokolips, albeit under the manipulative guidance of Darkseid's mistress, Mortalla. She deceived Orion in an attempt to rule his father's world, becoming his trusted lieutenant. At one point she created a Boom Tube large enough to allow all of Apokolips to orbit near Earth. **RG**

MOUTHPIECE

FIRST APPEARANCE POLICE COMICS #1 (August 1941)
STATUS Hero **REAL NAME** Bill Perkins
OCCUPATION Costumed vigilante **BASE** New York City
HEIGHT 6ft **WEIGHT** 198 lbs **EYES** Blue **HAIR** White
SPECIAL POWERS/ABILITIES Skilled brawler and marksman; above-average detective and expert in criminal law; also handy with a javelin.

Bill Perkins became a district attorney in the early 1940s but grew bitter about the number of times crooks went free for lack of evidence. In order to obtain the evidence he needed for legal convictions, he donned a blue suit and hat with a black eye mask and became the two-fisted vigilante called the Mouthpiece. The Mouthpiece didn't let legal niceties get in the way of his cold justice.

On one case he uncovered an immigration scam being run by gang leader Peg-Leg Friel. The villain tried to escape in the icy waters of the harbor, but Perkins, remembering he had been "pretty good in school with the javelin," hurled a harpoon and speared Peg-Leg Friel through the back.

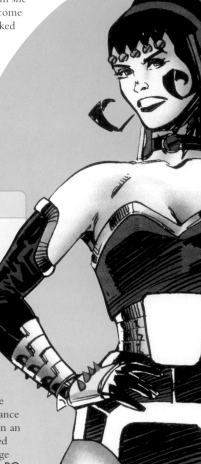

Recently, an aged lawyer surfaced under the name Mouthpiece and works as an advisor to the new DOCTOR MID-NITE. Whether this is the same Mouthpiece from the 1940s is unknown. **DW**

MURMUR

FIRST APPEARANCE THE FLASH: IRON HEIGHTS (October 2001)
STATUS Villain **REAL NAME** Michael Christian Amar
OCCUPATION Surgeon **BASE** Keystone City
HEIGHT 5ft 8in **WEIGHT** 155 lbs **EYES** Brown **HAIR** Gray
SPECIAL POWERS/ABILITIES Possesses no superhuman powers;
however, is an expert surgeon who uses various knives
and blades to brutally murder his victims and cut out
their tongues.

Doctor Michael Christian Amar was a well-respected
surgeon in the twin towns of Keystone and Central City.
However, he was also a ruthless serial killer who muttered
uncontrollably as he slaughtered his victims. Amar was
eventually captured by the officers of the Keystone
Department of Meta-human Hostility, who identified the
killer by his weird vocal quirk.

Murmur cut out his own tongue and crudely sewed up
his mouth to silence his incessant droning, the clue that
gave him away and sent him to
Death Row. Incarcerated at Iron
Heights, a maximum-security
penitentiary, he escaped during a
breakout engineered
by the villain Blacksmith.
Murmur escaped and became
a terrifying member of the
FLASH III's Rogues Gallery, his
murderous ways barely held
in check by the speedster's
other psychotic enemies. **PJ**

SILENT KILLER Murmur's
constant chatter caused the
grisly killer to sew up his
own mouth.

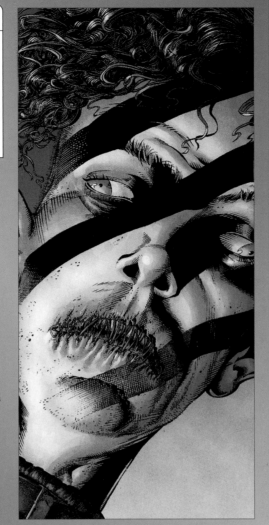

MUSASHI

FIRST APPEARANCE JUSTICE LEAGUE INTERNATIONAL #63
(April 1994)
STATUS Villain (deceased) **REAL NAME** Unrevealed
OCCUPATION Samurai **BASE** Kobe, Japan
HEIGHT 5ft 10in **WEIGHT** 175 lbs **EYES** Brown **HAIR** Black
SPECIAL POWERS/ABILITIES Formidable martial arts warrior, expert in the
fighting skills of the samurai.

The deadly Samurai warrior known as Musashi
belonged to a second coalition of super-villains known
collectively as the CADRE. They were minions of the
alien OVERMASTER, a foe of the JUSTICE LEAGUE OF
AMERICA through several of the team's incarnations.

In pursuit of a dastardly plot to exterminate the
entire human race, the Overmaster divided his new
Cadre into three sub-groups with experience of
battling several Justice League teams. These groups
were the second EXTREMISTS, the ARYAN BRIGADE,
and the Cadre of the Immortal, the latter claiming
Musashi as a member. Musashi and his cohorts were
committed to the Overmaster's goals of ridding the
world of modern technology. Faced by
overwhelmingly superior numbers, the Justice
League called upon its own vast reserves to face the
various gangs of villains. In the end, Musashi
forsook the Cadre and his Overmaster and perished
in a catastrophic explosion that destroyed the
Overmaster's sky-ship and also apparently claimed
the lives of Musashi's many Cadre teammates. **SB**

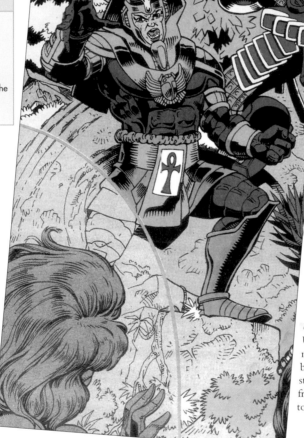

MUSKETEER

FIRST APPEARANCE DETECTIVE COMICS #215 (January 1955)
STATUS Hero **REAL NAME** Unrevealed
OCCUPATION Adventurer **BASE** Paris, France
HEIGHT 5ft 9in **WEIGHT** 180 lbs **EYES** Blue **HAIR** Black
SPECIAL POWERS/ABILITIES An expert swordsman and agile athlete,
the masked Musketeer preferred to dazzle opponents with his
swashbuckling swordplay than engage in close
combat or fisticuffs.

A former hero of the French
Resistance during World War II,
The Musketeer (or, more properly,
Le Mousquetaire) was one of several
international heroes inspired by
the JUSTICE SOCIETY OF AMERICA
to don masks and fight crime
during the 1950s. As the British
KNIGHT AND SQUIRE, the Argentine GAUCHO, the Swedish
Wingman, and the Australian Ranger took to the streets
of their capitals to fight corruption and villainy in their
countries following World War II, so the patriotic
Musketeer quickly became a hero across France, basing
himself in Paris.

When the mysterious DOCTOR MIST asked the non-
Communist European powers to create a multinational
super-heroic organization, the Musketeer and his
companions were among its founding members. Called the
Dome, the organization was based in France. Garbed in
the finery of a 17th-century French Musketeer, as made
famous by the author Alexandre Dumas in his novel *The
Three Musketeers*, the Musketeer was an expert swordsman
and marksman. After a decade of swashbuckling derring-
do, the Musketeer vanished from the streets of Paris, never
to be seen again. The final fate of the Musketeer, or even
his true identity, have yet to be revealed. **RG/PJ**

MYSTO

FIRST APPEARANCE DETECTIVE COMICS #203 (January 1954)
STATUS Hero **REAL NAME** Richard "Rick" Carter
OCCUPATION Magician; crime fighter **BASE** New York City
HEIGHT 6ft **WEIGHT** 195 lbs **EYES** Blue **HAIR** Black
SPECIAL POWERS/ABILITIES Master of illusion and sleight of hand;
could make guns appear to turn into playing cards and often
confounded crooks with smoke and mirrors.

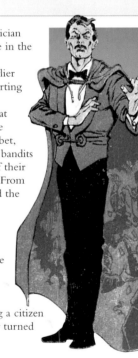

Mysto, the famous "Magician
Detective," became active in the
1950s and is one of the
standard-bearers of an earlier
age of heroism. Before starting
his costumed career, Rick
Carter worked as a "wildcat
flier" in the Far East. While
piloting his plane above Tibet,
Carter drove off a party of bandits
and earned the gratitude of their
target, a shriveled old man. From
this old man, Carter learned the
secrets of illusion—not true
magic—including the
misdirection and sleight of
hand employed by carnival
entertainers. Returning to the
U. S. accompanied by the old
man's servant, Sikhi, Carter
became a magician under the
stage name Mysto. After saving a citizen
from a murder attempt, Carter turned
to crime fighting. **DW**

OCCUPATION Test pilot **BASE** Midway City
HEIGHT 5ft 10.5in **WEIGHT** 180 lbs
EYES Blue **HAIR** Blond
SPECIAL POWERS/ABILITIES An energy being is released from
Trainor's body that has superstrength, superspeed,
can pass through objects harmlessly, or cause
anything it touches to burn or explode.

Larry Trainor was piloting an experimental test rocket
when a technical malfunction caused it to travel into deep
space. The rocket ship passed through a radiation belt and,
after a crash-landing on Earth, Trainor found his body
glowed with cosmic energy. He also discovered he could
manifest a superpowered energy being, controlled with
his mind.

After his rescue, Trainor met Niles Caulder, known as
the CHIEF, who used a special material to bind Trainor's
body so that he could contain the lethal radiation.
Caulder then invited Trainor, now a social pariah, to
join his DOOM PATROL. Trainor thus became Negative
Man and helped the Patrol fight various villains.

MADAME ROUGE and GENERAL ZAHL tried to
destroy the Doom Patrol by blowing them up, but
Trainor survived the attack. His energy being escaped
and briefly inhabited the body of Russian cosmonaut
Valentina Vostok, who became NEGATIVE WOMAN.
However, Trainor wanted his negative energy being
back, and used the villain Reactron to help "steal"
it back from Vostok. When the energy being
emerged, it fused Trainor and his doctor, Eleanor
Poole, into a single, radioactive being, calling
itself Rebis, who went on to join the Chief in
the latest incarnation of his Doom Patrol. This
creature was associated with CHECKMATE and
is an operative for the U.S. government. **PJ**

OCCUPATION Adventurer **BASE** Mobile;
formerly Midway City
HEIGHT 5ft 5in **WEIGHT** 130 lbs
EYES Blue **HAIR** Blonde
SPECIAL POWERS/ABILITIES Currently none; once
able to transform herself into a powerful
negative-energy being that could fly at
nearly the speed of light and exist outside of
her body for up to 60 seconds.

Attempting to defect to the U.S.
from the U.S.S.R. aboard an
experimental jet fighter, cosmonaut
Valentina Vostok crashed near
Codsville, Maine. This was the
very same little town the original
DOOM PATROL had died trying to
save from MADAME ROUGE and
GENERAL ZAHL. Vostok became
possessed by the negative-energy creature
that had once transformed Larry Trainor into the Patrol's
NEGATIVE MAN. Vostok became Negative Woman and also
had to be swaddled in chemically treated bandages to
survive. Negative Woman was soon recruited into a new
Doom Patrol. Later, the villain Reactron stole her negative
energies and returned them to Trainor, who had not died
as originally believed. Though presently without any
special powers, Vostok retains some residual radioactivity
from being joined with the negative-energy creature. **SB**

NEMESIS

FIRST APPEARANCE THE BRAVE AND THE BOLD #166 (September 1980)
STATUS Hero **REAL NAME** Tom Tresser
OCCUPATION Ex-government agent; spy **BASE** Mobile
HEIGHT 5ft 10in **WEIGHT** 170 lbs **EYES** Blue **HAIR** Black
SPECIAL POWERS/ABILITIES Skilled combatant;

NEMESIS II

FIRST APPEARANCE JSA ANNUAL #1 (2000)
STATUS Hero (deceased) **REAL NAME** Soseh Mykros
OCCUPATION Assassin **BASE** England
HEIGHT 5ft 7in **WEIGHT** 145 lbs

NABU

FIRST APPEARANCE MORE FUN COMICS #55 (May 1940)
STATUS Hero **REAL NAME** Nabu
OCCUPATION Lord of Order **BASE** Mobile
HEIGHT/WEIGHT/EYES/HAIR Inapplicable
SPECIAL POWERS/ABILITIES One of the most powerful beings on Earth, capable of mystic feats, including projecting mystic energy bolts, reading minds, and teleporting across the dimensions; immortal; possesses superhuman strength.

Nabu is a Lord of Order, a cosmic being who arrived on Earth nearly 4,000 years ago to take a proactive role in the war against Chaos. After engaging in many struggles in ancient Egypt and Sumeria, Nabu placed his body in suspended animation and his spirit in a golden helmet that would merge with whoever wore it. In 1940, Kent Nelson, put on the helmet, and so became Nabu's apprentice, the first DOCTOR FATE.
Nabu's personality supplanted Nelson's whenever the latter wore the helmet, so Nabu placed the spirits of Nelson and his wife, Inza, in the mystic Amulet of Anubis, assumed Kent's form, and chose a new disciple, Eric Strauss. Kent and Inza returned to the mortal world, both becoming Doctor Fate. However, after a battle with PARALLAX in which the Nelsons apparently died, the helmet and amulet were claimed by Jared Stevens.

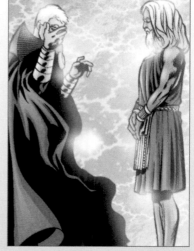

NABU THE WISE *Nabu manifests a human form as a grey-haired wizard. It is through this form that he continues to communicate with Hector Hall, the new Doctor Fate.*

Nabu's spirit, meanwhile, came to rest in the body of a child, the reincarnated Hector Hall, who had once fought crime with INFINITY, INC. as the Silver Scarab.
After Stevens' death, both helmet and amulet were delivered to Hector Hall, who had magically become a new Doctor Fate. Hall, the new Doctor Fate, relies on Nabu's wisdom, as he learns to wield his new powers. **PJ**

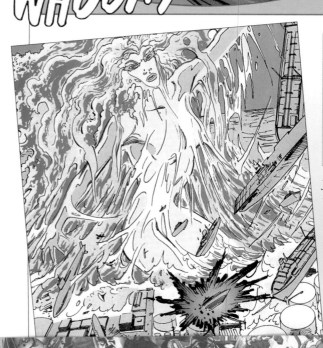

WHOOM

ANKH OF ORDER *Nabu destroys demons with his almost incalculable power.*

NAIAD

FIRST APPEARANCE FIRESTORM THE NUCLEAR MAN #90 (October 1989)
STATUS Inapplicable **REAL NAME** Mai Miyazaki
OCCUPATION Elemental force **BASE** Mobile
HEIGHT Inapplicable (5ft 4in as Mai) **WEIGHT** Variable (112 lbs as Mai) **EYES** Sea green (blue as Mai) **HAIR** None (black as Mai)
SPECIAL POWERS/ABILITIES Total mastery over water in all its forms.

Japanese radical environmentalist Mai Miyazaki believed in direct action. Mai sailed her boat Naiad into the storm-swept north Pacific to call attention to a leaking oil rig being abandoned by Shogun Oil. The rig's director ordered a crewman to fire a flare into the oily waters around Mai's boat, engulfing it in flames. Horribly burned, Mai jumped overboard. However, Earth's spirit, MAYA, offered Mai a chance of life as the planet's Water Elemental, Naiad. Transformed into a living wall of water, Naiad swept over the oil rig, sparking the first Elemental War when FIRESTORM, THE NUCLEAR MAN then Earth's Fire Elemental, flew to the site to investigate

NEBULA MAN

FIRST APPEARANCE JUSTICE LEAGUE OF AMERICA (1st series) #100 (August 1972)
STATUS Villain **REAL NAME** None
OCCUPATION Celestial menace **BASE** Mobile
HEIGHT Variable **WEIGHT** Variable **EYES** White **HAIR** None
SPECIAL POWERS/ABILITIES Incalculable cosmic power.

The Nebula Man is a mysterious entity animated by unknown means, but one thing is clear—he will stop at nothing to destroy the planet Earth. During the 1940s, the Nebula Man first came into existence thanks to a villain known as the Hand. Composed of cosmic energy and possessing the power of atomic bombs in each of his fingers, the Nebula Man threatened the planet with armageddon until opposed by the SEVEN SOLDIERS OF VICTORY at a battlefront in the Himalayas. The heroes prevailed, but their member Wing perished. The rest became temporarily scattered across the timestream, victims of the explosive energies of the Nebula Man's demise. More than a half century later, the Nebula Man saw fresh life when his dormant essence combined with Wing's corpse. He emerged from the grave to destroy the world again, this time starting with the small town of Blue Valley. Courtney Whitmore, the Star-Spangled Kid II, single-handedly dispersed the Nebula Man's energies into the stratosphere. **DW**

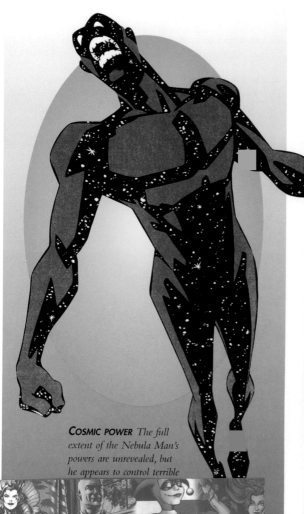

COSMIC POWER *The full extent of the Nebula Man's powers are unrevealed, but he appears to control terrible*

NEON THE UNKNOWN

FIRST APPEARANCE HIT COMICS #1 (1940)
STATUS Hero (deceased) **REAL NAME** Tom Corbett
OCCUPATION Former French Foreign Legionnaire **BASE** Mobile
HEIGHT 5ft 11in **WEIGHT** 167 lbs **EYES** Blue **HAIR** Black
SPECIAL POWERS/ABILITIES Was able to project powerful energy bolts from his hands and also fly.

Thomas Corbett was a French Legionnaire stationed in Africa in 1939. Lost on a desert mission, he discovered an oasis whose lake was filled with glowing water. He drank from the lake, his clothing was transformed, and he was able to project energy bolts from his hands. Corbett became Neon the Unknown and joined the FREEDOM FIGHTERS, a hero team gathered by the mystic being UNCLE SAM to defend the U.S. from Axis forces during World War II. On December 6, 1941, Uncle Sam warned several Fighters, including Neon, of a terrible impending attack. Arriving at Pearl Harbor the next day, the Freedom Fighters witnessed the Japanese assault on the base. Neon was killed in the bombing. **PJ**

NERGAL

FIRST APPEARANCE GREEN LANTERN ANNUAL 2nd series #9 (September 2000) **STATUS** Villain **REAL NAME** None
OCCUPATION Ruler of the Underworld **BASE** Kurnugi
Height Weight 300 lbs **EYES** White **HAIR** Blond

NERON

FIRST APPEARANCE UNDERWORLD UNLEASHED #1 (November 1995)
STATUS Villain **REAL NAME** Neron
OCCUPATION Soul-taking demon **BASE** Hell **HEIGHT** Variable
WEIGHT Variable **EYES** Variable **HAIR** Variable
SPECIAL POWERS/ABILITIES A lord of lies, Neron possesses unspeakable mystic power and can alter his size and shape.

The deaths of five of the second FLASH's Rogues Gallery unleashed the demon Neron, a Prince of Hell, who granted dozens of villains, as well as a few costumed heroes, increased powers in exchange for their souls. At the suggestion of the TRICKSTER II, CAPTAIN MARVEL offered his soul to Neron in exchange for Earth's freedom. As the Trickster deduced, Marvel's soul was too pure for the demon to touch, but Neron was forced to honor his end of the bargain. Subsequently, the Flash and his wife (see PARK, LINDA) managed to outwit Neron and foil a rampage by the Rogues' ghosts, restoring them to Hell. During this event, known as the Day of Judgment, Neron was imprisoned by an unholy alliance of the DEMON Etrigan, ASMODEL, and the SPECTRE. Breaking free from his prison by possessing SUPERMAN's body, Neron attempted to claim the Spectre-Force for himself, but the Spectre instead chose GREEN LANTERN, the second Green Lantern as its new human host. Neron was sent back to Hell, and since he had broken Hell's rules by using its power for his own pleasure, he was demoted from a Prince to a Rhymer by his fellow demons. Furious, Neron realized that this had been Etrigan's plan all along. **RG**

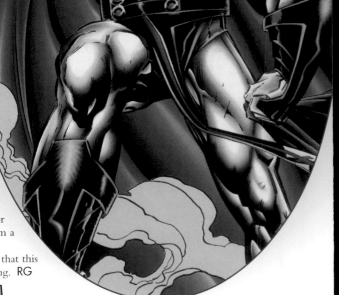

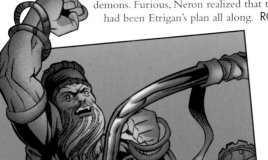

NEUTRON

FIRST APPEARANCE ACTION COMICS #525 (November 1981)
STATUS Villain **REAL NAME** Nat Tryon
OCCUPATION Criminal **BASE** Metropolis
HEIGHT 6ft 2in **WEIGHT** 184 lbs **EYES** Blue **HAIR** Black
SPECIAL POWERS/ABILITIES Releases withering atomic energy through his hands or by lifting the visor of his helmet.

NEW GODS

HEROES OF THE FOURTH WORLD

FIRST APPEARANCE NEW GODS (1st series) #1 (March 1971)
STATUS Good and evil beings **BASE** New Genesis and Apokolips
NOTABLE NEW GODS
See individual entries for powers and abilities.
Bekka, Big Barda, Black Racer, Darkseid, Doctor Bedlam, Esak (deceased), Fastbak, Forager I (deceased), Forager II, The Forever People, Glorious Godfrey, Highfather (deceased), Himon (deceased), Kalibak, Lightray, Lonar (deceased), Mantis, Metron, Mister Miracle, Orion, Takion, Tiggra (deceased).

THE NEW GODS 1) *Darkseid* 2) *Desaad* 3) *Glorious Godfrey* 4) *Heggra* 5) *Granny Goodness* 6) *Black Racer* 7) *Doctor Bedlam* 8) *Mokkari* 9) *Steppenwolf* 10) *Kanto* 11) *Kalibak* 12) *Mantis* 13) *Virmin Vunderbarr* 14) *Himon* 15) *Devilance* 16) *Lightray* 17) *Mister Miracle* 18) *Fastbak* 19) *Metron* 20) *Highfather* 21) *Forager I* 22) *Big Barda* 23) *Avia* 24) *Lonar* 25) *Orion* 26) *Simyan* 27) *Bekka.*
The New Gods of New Genesis know that Earth will one day give rise to a Fifth World of super-beings, already heralded by the abundance of super heroes, to prevent the New Gods of Apokolips from finding the Anti-Life Equation.

LONG, LONG AGO, before time was even measured, there existed a race of Old Gods whose world was split apart in a fiery holocaust, unleashing a coruscating "godwave" of energy that swept across the universe. This godwave empowered the OLYMPIAN GODS and gave rise to latter-day human super heroes as it rebounded back and forth in continued, but diminishing, reverberation, seeding world after world with the potential for near-omnipotent power.

WAR OF THE WORLDS

On its fourth passing, the godwave infused the Old Gods' divided world. Out of the ashes arose two molten planets, New Genesis and Apokolips, collectively known as the Fourth World. New Genesis was home to the noble, near-immortal New Gods, who lived in harmony with their lush and verdant planet. Conversely, the denizens of nearby Apokolips were cunning and cruel, and dedicated to evil. For millions of years, New Genesis and Apokolips waged war upon one another until a peace pact was negotiated with the exchange of hostages, each the son of one world's leader. True to his nature, Apokolips's ruler DARKSEID broke his pact with New Genesis's ruler HIGHFATHER by invading Earth in search of the Anti-Life Equation, the means to control all sentient life in the universe. Thus, the conflict began anew, but this time with Darkseid's own son, ORION, siding with New Genesis. Highfather's heir, Scott Free, would first fend off Darkseid's agents on Earth in the guise of MISTER MIRACLE before returning to his homeworld and joining the New Gods in defiance of Darkseid's eternal enmity. Since then, the New Gods have fought tirelessly to maintain the balance of power first struck in the godwave's release. **SB**

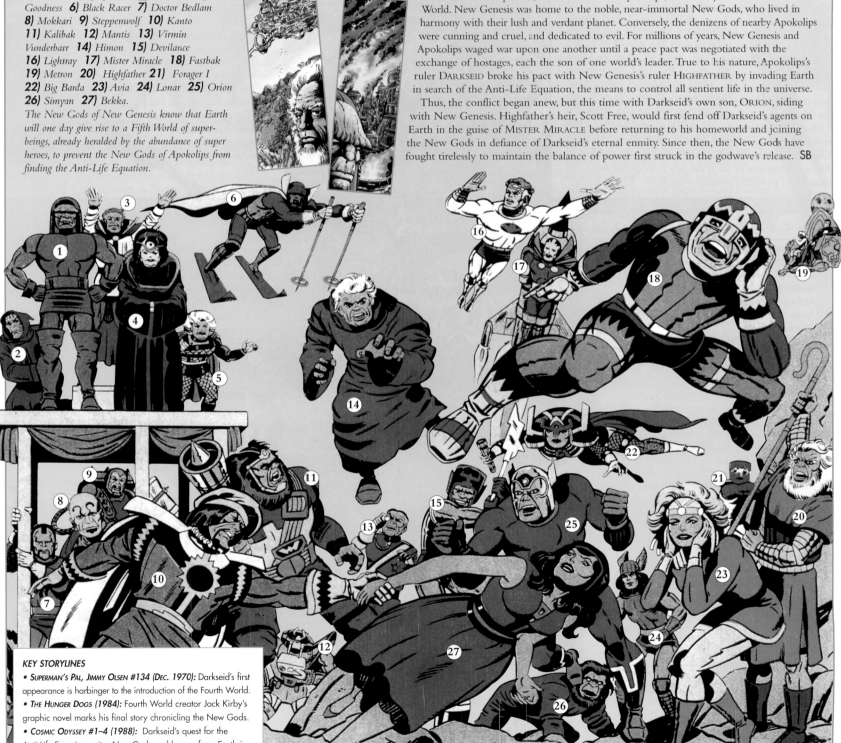

KEY STORYLINES
• *SUPERMAN'S PAL, JIMMY OLSEN #134 (DEC. 1970):* Darkseid's first appearance is harbinger to the introduction of the Fourth World.
• *THE HUNGER DOGS (1984):* Fourth World creator Jack Kirby's graphic novel marks his final story chronicling the New Gods.
• *COSMIC ODYSSEY #1–4 (1988):* Darkseid's quest for the Anti-Life Equation unites New Gods and heroes from Earth in a race to prevent universal destruction.

THE DC COMICS ENCYCLOPEDIA

NIGHTWING

BLÜDHAVEN'S FINEST

FIRST APPEARANCE TALES OF THE TEEN TITANS #43 (July 1984)
STATUS Hero **REAL NAME** Richard "Dick" Grayson
OCCUPATION Police officer; crime fighter **BASE** Blüdhaven
HEIGHT 5ft 10in **WEIGHT** 175 lbs **EYES** Blue **HAIR** Black
SPECIAL POWERS/ABILITIES Second only to Batman in fighting skills and detective abilities; utility belt includes regurgitant gas pellets, smoke capsules, acetylene torch, flexi-cuffs, Batarangs, and shuriken-like Wing-Dings; bulletproof and fire-resistant costume is insulated and wired as single-shot taser to incapacitate attackers; right gauntlet carries hand-held 100,000-volt stun gun; preferred weapons are twin shatterproof polymer Escrima sticks, held in spring-loaded pouches in the back of costume for swift deployment in close-quarters fighting.

NIGHTWING IS DICK GRAYSON, the very first ROBIN now grown to manhood. Dick realized the need to leave the shadow of his mentor BATMAN and establish his own heroic presence. The Dark Knight accelerated Dick's decision by firing the young hero, who had just joined the TEEN TITANS, from his role as teen sidekick. Batman thought Robin would return to his side, but Dick accepted the decision and left the Batcave. Not long after, he ceded the role of Robin to orphan Jason Todd. For Dick Grayson, there would be no turning back. After much soul-searching, he adopted a new guise inspired by two of his childhood heroes. To remain a creature of the night like the Dark Knight, Dick became Nightwing. The name was recommended by SUPERMAN, a role model for Dick, after a mysterious hero of Kryptonian legend.

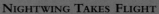

FLYING GRAYSON *Having learned acrobatic skills from his parents, Dick is a gifted aerialist, perhaps surpassing even Batman in agility.*

NIGHTWING TAKES FLIGHT
Nightwing flew into action for the first time to save his fellow Teen Titans from DEATHSTROKE THE TERMINATOR and the criminal consortium known as H.I.V.E (Hierarchy of International Vengeance and Extermination). He continued to lead the Titans thereafter, eventually reconciling with his former mentor Batman and reclaiming his status as the Dark Knight's closest and most trusted ally. When the Titans disbanded, Nightwing resumed solo crimefighting.

At Batman's behest, Nightwing left Gotham—his home since the deaths of his parents, the Flying Graysons—and moved to neighboring Blüdhaven, a crime-ridden port city desperately in need of its own defender. With Blüdhaven mired in corruption, Dick made law enforcement his day job also, enrolling in the city's police academy and eventually graduating to become a rookie cop with the B.P.D. Nightwing used his nocturnal hours to undermine mob boss Roland Desmond (BLOCKBUSTER II) and the city's feuding gang lords. Nightwing even found time to join a fourth lineup of Titans before the group suffered the deaths of two longtime members. Soon after, Nightwing helped to establish a new team of heroes, dubbed the OUTSIDERS after a defunct cadre of clandestine crime fighters Batman himself had once led. Rather than simply react to villainy, the Outsiders under Nightwing's leadership took a proactive approach to rooting out evil, hunting the world's Most Wanted and bringing them to justice. The Dark Knight's former squire continues to fight the good fight and make his mentor proud of both the man and the hero that he has become. **SB**

HALLEY'S CIRCUS *Before Dick's aerialist parents were murdered by gangsters they were a major circus act.*

COMBAT MASTER *Not even a posse of trained killers can subdue lightning-quick Nightwing!*

KEY STORYLINES

• **TALES OF THE TEEN TITANS #41–44, ANNUAL #3 (APRIL–JULY 1984):** Deathstroke hunts the Teen Titans, leaving the all-new Nightwing the last Titan standing and the team's only hope!
• **BATMAN #440-442, NEW TITANS #60-61 (OCTOBER–DECEMBER 1989):** In "A Lonely Place of Dying," Nightwing meets his successor as Boy Wonder, Tim Drake, and fights alongside Batman to defeat Two-Face!
• **NIGHTWING #1 (1988):** At Batman's behest, Nightwing makes Blüdhaven his new home and brings costumed justice to the crime-ridden seaport.

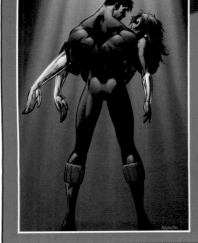

TROIA'S DEATH *Nightwing's Titans teammate and closest friend died in his arms. Despite strong feelings on both sides, the two were never romantically linked.*

THE OUTSIDER *Nightwing found an important role as leader of the Outsiders vigilante team, organized by Batman to track down criminals who were beyond the law's reach.*

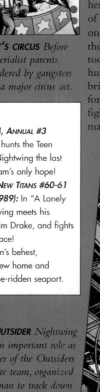

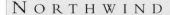

NOCTURNA

FIRST APPEARANCE DETECTIVE COMICS #529 (August 1983)
STATUS Villain (missing) **REAL NAME** Natalia Knight
OCCUPATION Astronomer **BASE** England
HEIGHT 5ft 10in **WEIGHT** 140 lbs **EYES** Blue **HAIR** Black
SPECIAL POWERS/ABILITIES A brilliant astronomer but unskilled at hand-to-hand combat.

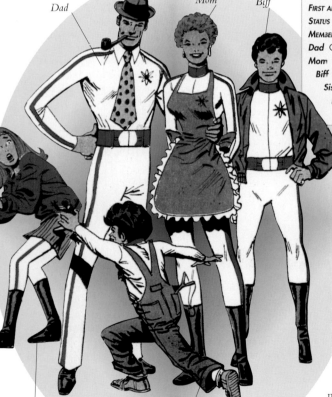

Natalia was a child of the streets until the criminal Charles Knight took her in. She grew up with Knight's natural son, Anton, eventually falling in love with him. An accident with laser radiation drained Natalia Knight's skin of all pigment and rendered her sensitive to sunlight, an accident not entirely unfortunate for an astronomer romantically drawn to twilight. From dusk till dawn, Natalia and Anton's alter egos of Nocturna and Night-Slayer engaged in thievery to enjoy the witching hour's luxuries. BATMAN brought Night-Slayer to justice, and Nocturna then began a romance with Sturges Hellstrom, a minor Gotham criminal. Enraged, Night-Slayer escaped prison and murdered Hellstrom, only to be slain by his former lover. She escaped from Batman in a hot-air balloon, never to be seen again. ROBIN and SPOILER have since encountered a former astronomer named Natalie Metternich (alias Natalia Mitternacht). Like Nocturna, Metternich is pale and loves the night. It is unknown whether these similarities are just coincidence. **RG**

NORTHWIND

FIRST APPEARANCE ALL-STAR SQUADRON #25 (September 1983)
STATUS Hero **REAL NAME** Norda Cantrell
OCCUPATION Vigilante **BASE** Mobile
HEIGHT 6ft **WEIGHT** 195 lbs
EYES Brown **HAIR** Golden feathers
SPECIAL POWERS/ABILITIES Flight, enhanced stamina and strength, and the ability to communicate with birds, though not with human beings.

The hybrid child of a human father (anthropologist Fred Cantrell) and a mother from a race of bird-people called the Feitherans, Norda Cantrell grew up in the hidden city of Feithera in northern Greenland.
The godson of HAWKMAN Carter Hall, Norda encountered jealousy from Hawkman's true son Hector Hall (later the Silver Scarab and DOCTOR FATE). As a young adult, Norda left Feithera to join INFINITY, INC. under the name of Northwind. He served with the team until Hector Hall's death, after which he returned to his people to help them rebuild their civilization in the city of New Feithera.
Northwind has recently undergone a full metamorphosis into a giant bird-like creature, improving his flying abilities, but unfortunately losing the ability to speak in the process. In his new form he has joined with BLACK ADAM, ATOM-SMASHER, and Brainwave II to form a "zero-tolerance" super-hero team committed to ending violence by executing super-villains. Northwind and the others have so far killed the terrorist KOBRA, among others. **DW**

NUCLEAR FAMILY

FIRST APPEARANCE THE OUTSIDERS #1 (November 1985)
STATUS Android villains (destroyed) **BASE** California
MEMBERS AND POWERS
Dad Could emit vast amounts of nuclear radiation.
Mom Could emit potentially fatal electromagnetic pulse.
Biff Could emit thermal pulse of immense heat.
Sis Could emit immensely destructive blast wave.
Brat and dog Could emit radioactive fallout.

Dad *Mom* *Biff*

Sis *Brat*

The OUTSIDERS had declared their independence from BATMAN's leadership and relocated from Gotham City to Santa Monica, California. No sooner had they settled into their new digs, than they received word of trouble at the Esperanza Canyon nuclear power plant. There, the team discovered a family of androids, named Dad, Mom, Biff, Sis, Brat, and Dog.
These eerie creations were the brainchildren of the deranged Dr. Eric Shanner. The doctor had been a victim of radiation poisoning and had created the family he would never have himself. Working with the Outsiders' old opponent, Professor Wye, Shanner intended to use the opening of the plant to detonate a nuclear explosion, sharing his radiation death with as many Californians as possible. The Outsiders confronted the powerful androids and fought them to a standstill until Wye turned on Shanner. This provided the Outsiders with an opportunity to stop the Nuclear Family and do so before Shanner and the androids died in a controlled explosion. **RG**

NYOLA

FIRST APPEARANCE ALL-STAR COMICS #2 (Fall 1940)
STATUS Villain **REAL NAME** Nyola
OCCUPATION Priestess **BASE** Unknown
HEIGHT 5ft 4in **WEIGHT** 115 lbs **EYES** Brown **HAIR** Red-brown
SPECIAL POWERS/ABILITIES Has magical control over the weather, and can project bolts of lightning.

Nyola was an Aztec priestess who gained elemental powers through her worship of the rain god Tlaloc. Haughty, arrogant Nyola was originally an enemy of HAWKMAN and HAWKGIRL, tackling the winged wonders in early 1942 during one of their archaeological excursions in Central America.
Nyola returned as leader of the first MONSTER SOCIETY OF EVIL. The evil sorceress invaded the JUSTICE SOCIETY OF AMERICA's New York City headquarters, fighting Hawkgirl, HOURMAN, and Sandy, SANDMAN I's sidekick. Along with the Monster Society's RAMULUS, Dummy, MISTER WHO, and Oom, Nyola was soundly defeated by the FLASH I and GREEN LANTERN. **PJ**

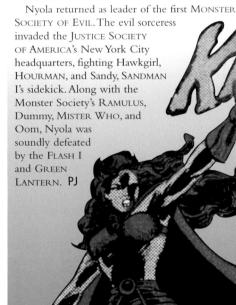

O.S.S. SPIES AT WAR

FIRST APPEARANCE G.I. COMBAT #192 (July 1976)
STATUS Intelligence agency **BASE** Washington, D.C.
MEMBERS/ABILITIES
The most talented men and women in science, diplomacy, economics, and other fields were recruited, including the adventurer Speed Saunders. They had codenames such as Falcon, Shadow, Sprinter, Mongoose, Phoenix, and Raven. Costumed heroes such as Manhunter II, Phantom Lady I, and Iron Munro also worked for O.S.S.

On December 7, 1941, The Office of Strategic Services was established to centralize the intelligence collection functions of the U.S. military forces. Carlo "Chuck" Sirianni functions as the BLACKHAWK's liaison with the group. One agent, who allowed his own wife to die rather than reveal the agency's secrets, was tapped to dispatch agents on other deadly missions and was known only as Control. After the war, the unit was absorbed into the C.I.A. Control was later asked to head up ARGENT I, an international force under the Task Force X umbrella. He went underground after President J.F. Kennedy's assassination. Some time later Control died; however, Argent's covert actions continued until ended by the modern-day SUICIDE SQUAD. **RG**

MISSION IMPOSSIBLE *An O.S.S. field agent in action.*

OCEAN MASTER

FIRST APPEARANCE AQUAMAN (1st series) #29 (October 1966)
STATUS Villain **REAL NAME** Orm Marius
OCCUPATION Professional criminal **BASE** The Atlantic Ocean
HEIGHT 5ft 11in **WEIGHT** 200 lbs **EYES** Brown **HAIR** Brown
SPECIAL POWERS/ABILITIES Trident possesses vast magical powers, notably the firing of powerful mystical energy blasts; amphibious; able to breathe underwater and swim at great speeds; is totally unaffected by the crushing weight of the ocean's great depths.

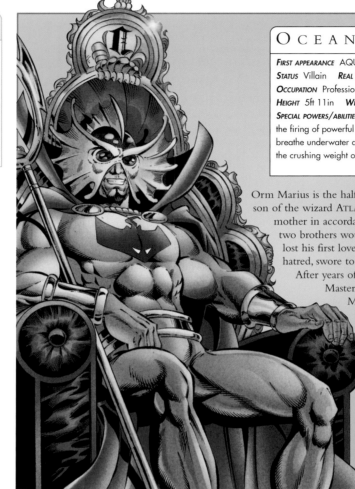

Orm Marius is the half-brother of AQUAMAN and the illegitimate son of the wizard ATLAN, who sired Marius by an unknown mother in accordance with an Atlantean prophecy claiming two brothers would vie for control of the kingdom. Orm lost his first love, Kako, to Aquaman and, seething with hatred, swore to kill the King of the Seven Seas.

After years of pirating, Orm, calling himself the Ocean Master, tried to overthrow Aquaman. Ocean Master was defeated and banished from Atlantis. Ocean Master returned to attack Aquaman several times, often with such partners as BLACK MANTA and the SHARK. Ocean Master later attacked Aquaman on the astral plane. Ocean Master sold his soul to the demon NERON for even greater power. Ocean Master was tricked, however, and now suffers great pain whenever he releases the trident that channels his magical energies. Ocean Master continues to plot revenge on Aquaman, consumed by jealousy and rage at his half-brother. **PJ**

OBSIDIAN

FIRST APPEARANCE ALL-STAR SQUADRON #25 (September 1983)
STATUS Villain **REAL NAME** Todd Rice
OCCUPATION Super-villain **BASE** Mobile
HEIGHT 5ft 11in **WEIGHT** 193 lbs **EYES** Brown **HAIR** Brown
SPECIAL POWERS/ABILITIES Can control the shadow force to become a living shadow or send people into the "shadowlands" of their deepest fears.

Son of original GREEN LANTERN Alan Scott, Todd Rice and his sister Jennie (JADE) were raised by foster parents after their mother, Rose (*see* ROSE AND THORN), gave them up without her husband's knowledge. Todd grew up in Milwaukee where his adoptive father abused him. At an early age the boy learned how to manifest the shadow powers that seemed to reflect his own bitterness and pain. Taking the alias Obsidian, Todd, his sister, and other young heroes banded together as INFINITY, INC. After the team broke up, Obsidian succumbed to the shadows in his heart and teamed with the JUSTICE SOCIETY OF AMERICA's old nemesis Ian Karkull to spread darkness and terror across the planet. Alan Scott defeated his son, who seemingly perished—until reappearing alongside the near-omnipotent ECLIPSO and Mordru (DARK LORD) to destroy the world. Once again Alan Scott triumphed, overwhelming Obsidian with emerald energy after reclaiming his Green Lantern title. **DW**

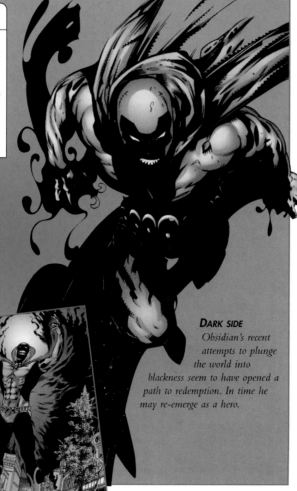

DARK SIDE *Obsidian's recent attempts to plunge the world into blackness seem to have opened a path to redemption. In time he may re-emerge as a hero.*

ODD MAN

FIRST APPEARANCE CANCELLED COMICS CAVALCADE #2 (Fall 1978)
STATUS Villain **REAL NAME** Clayton "Clay" Stoner
OCCUPATION Private investigator; crime fighter **BASE** River City
HEIGHT 5ft 11in **WEIGHT** 180 lbs **EYES** Blue **HAIR** Black
SPECIAL POWERS/ABILITIES Above-average hand-to-hand combatant; costume contained a variety of clownish gags and gimmicks to disorient and defeat opponents, including a weighted tie, slippery oil spray, smoke-emitting gloves, and anesthetic gas.

When there was trouble in crime-ridden River City, private investigator Clay Stoner became the Odd Man out of nowhere, clad in a confusing costume that was more like a carnival clown's and based in an office that turned end-over-end to dizzy dimwitted stoolies. The Odd Man literally turned the underworld upside-down with his heroic high jinks and wacky weapons. He didn't just make fools of hardened gangsters; the Odd Man once solved a murder mystery involving the reincarnation of the first Nile Queen and her Pharaoh consort.

The Odd Man has had a minor association with the public service super-hero agency known as HERO HOTLINE. He also applied for the position of Security Chief at Project Cadmus. Passed over, the Odd Man also tried and failed to interest the POWER COMPANY, a superpowered law firm, in his slapstick services. The Odd Man remains River City's sole super hero. **SB**

OLSEN, JIMMY

SUPERMAN'S PAL

FIRST APPEARANCE SUPERMAN (1st series) #13 (November 1941)
STATUS Hero   **REAL NAME** James Bartholomew Olsen
OCCUPATION Journalist; photographer   **BASE** Metropolis
HEIGHT 6ft 2in   **WEIGHT** 210 lbs   **EYES** Blue   **HAIR** Red
SPECIAL POWERS/ABILITIES Only an average athlete but has a keen
photographer's eye; seemingly fearless in the face of danger;
unswervingly loyal to his friends; periodically falls victim to bizarre
mutant abilities he is usually powerless to control.

THE FIRST TWO PEOPLE ever rescued by SUPERMAN were Lois Lane
(*see* LANE, LOIS) and a fresh-faced photographer named Jimmy Olsen.
Superman befriended Jimmy and the teen became one of the Man of
Steel's most faithful admirers. In return, Superman gave Jimmy a special
watch with a hypersonic signal only Superman could hear, which the
teen used to alert the Man of Steel. Inspired by his hero, Jimmy has
embarked on many adventures, risking life and limb to get prize-
winning shots. Who else but Jimmy could have fearlessly
photographed the deadly battle between Superman and DOOMSDAY?

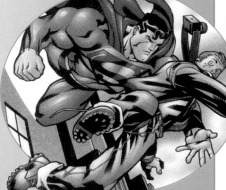

COUNTDOWN *Jimmy has
earned Superman's trust and,
with it, a signal watch to
summon the Man of Steel!*

LOOKING FOR TROUBLE

Jimmy was brought up by his mother, Sarah, in Metropolis's Bakerline section,
after his father, Jake Olsen, a covert military operative, went missing. The boy
proved to be highly intelligent and became an academic star. But what Jimmy
really wanted was action. He signed on as an intern and then a junior
photographer at the *Daily Planet* newspaper. He quickly
developed a crush on the paper's star reporter Lois Lane,
who tolerated the eager young pup and often brought him along on assignments.
Jimmy also fell under *Daily Planet* editor Perry White's sway (*see* WHITE, PERRY).
White instilled in him the vital importance of photographs to truthful reporting,
and the pair have something of a father–son relationship—which can turn
explosive when Jimmy infuriates Perry by "accidentally" calling him "Chief."
Jimmy is almost as reckless in his personal relationships as he is when
chasing a front-page story. He dated Lois's little sister, Lucy, for a while,
before embarking on a romance with Misa, a Hairie from Project
Cadmus, and even a computerized version of Lena Luthor, daughter
of Lex Luthor (*see* LUTHOR, LEX). **RG**

SUPERMAN ARRIVES *When
a costumed figure first flew over
Metropolis, reporter Lois Lane
grabbed her favorite photographer,
Jimmy Olsen. They covered the year's
biggest story, the arrival of Superman.*

THE CHIEF *Still
learning, Jimmy is
often given guidance
by Perry White—in
no uncertain terms!*

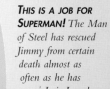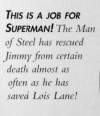

**THIS IS A JOB FOR
SUPERMAN!** *The Man
of Steel has rescued
Jimmy from certain
death almost as
often as he has
saved Lois Lane!*

NO PHOTOGRAPHS! *Jimmy is one of the most intrepid
photojournalists working in the U.S., willingly
accompanying Lois to beard Lex Luthor in his
LexCorp lair.*

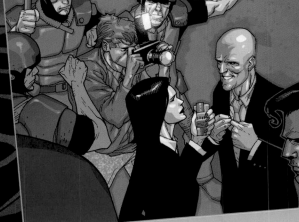

KEY STORYLINES

• *SUPERMAN'S METROPOLIS #1–12 (APRIL 2003–MARCH 2004):*
Jimmy and Metropolis's Brainiac-created artificial intelligence
learn from one another.
• *SUPERMAN'S PAL JIMMY OLSEN #133–134 (OCTOBER–DECEMBER
1971):* Jimmy learns of Darkseid's threat and begins a series of
amazing adventures.
• *SUPERMAN #143 (MAY 1990):* Jimmy learns the truth about his
father's disappearance and connection with Project Cadmus.

OLYMPIAN

FIRST APPEARANCE SUPER FRIENDS #8 (December 1977)
STATUS Hero **REAL NAME** Aristedes Demetrios
OCCUPATION Adventurer **BASE** Athens; the Dome
HEIGHT 6ft 4in **WEIGHT** 255 lbs **EYES** Brown **HAIR** Brown
SPECIAL POWERS/ABILITIES Golden Fleece gives him superstrength, superspeed, near invulnerability, precognition, telescopic vision, X-ray vision, hypnotic control over animals, ability to shapechange into animals; Olympic-level boxing, wrestling, martial arts, archery, and equestrian skills; expert physician and maritime navigator.

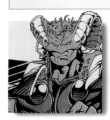

Artistedes Demetrios was a rebellious punk from Leivása, Greece, who was jailed several times for petty crime. Discovering and stealing the legendary Golden Fleece from a crate in the warehouse he was working in, Demetrios was possessed by the powers and personalities of Jason and his 50 Argonauts, the heroes of Greek mythology who had originally captured the Golden Fleece. Aristedes became the heroic Olympian, joining DOCTOR MIST's international team, the GLOBAL GUARDIANS.

Captured and hypnotized by the evil Queen Bee I (*see* QUEEN BEE II), Aristedes could no longer control the spirits of the Argonauts—each of them vied for control of his body. As a result, the Olympian now suffers from extreme multiple personality disorder. The Olympian remains a hero in some parts of Greece, fighting local criminals. **PJ**

OLYMPIAN GODS

FIRST APPEARANCE WONDER WOMAN (2nd series) #1 (November 1987)
STATUS Transcendent beings **BASE** Mount Olympus
NOTABLE MEMBERS OF THE GREEK PANTHEON
Zeus God of the Skies.
Hera Goddess of Wives and Childbirth; wife of Zeus.
Aphrodite Goddess of Love; a former wife of Ares.
Apollo God of Light.
Ares God of War.
Artemis Goddess of the Hunt.
Athena Goddess of Wisdom.
Demeter Goddess of Agriculture.
Dionysus God of Wine.
Hades God of the Underworld.
Heracles God of Strength.
Hestia Goddess of the Hearth.
Mercury The Messenger God.
Poseidon God of the Oceans.

The children of the TITANS OF MYTH, the Olympian gods ruled the Earth for centuries from their fortress, Mount Olympus in ancient Greece. Long ago, a young DARKSEID split the pantheon of gods into two, creating the Roman gods. Several of the goddesses of Mount Olympus created the AMAZONS of Themyscira, a race of mighty warriors.

When the War God ARES went mad, the goddesses created the Amazon princess WONDER WOMAN to stop his schemes. Later, the Olympians were manipulated into a cataclysmic War of the Gods by the witch CIRCE, clashing against each other and the gods of other pantheons. After the cosmic Source, the Fount for All Creation, was threatened, the Greek and Roman pantheons were reunited. Zeus and Mercury gave a portion of their power to CAPTAIN MARVEL, and Zeus remains a member of the cosmic guardians the Quintessence. **PJ**

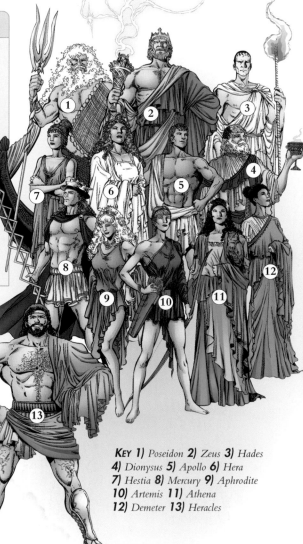

KEY 1) Poseidon **2)** Zeus **3)** Hades
4) Dionysus **5)** Apollo **6)** Hera
7) Hestia **8)** Mercury **9)** Aphrodite
10) Artemis **11)** Athena
12) Demeter **13)** Heracles

OMAC

FIRST APPEARANCE OMAC (1st series) #1 (October 1974)
STATUS Hero **REAL NAME** Buddy Blank
OCCUPATION Vigilante **BASE** Mobile
HEIGHT 6ft 5in (Buddy: 5ft 7in) **WEIGHT** 500 lbs (Buddy: 140 lbs)
EYES Red (Buddy: brown) **HAIR** Black
SPECIAL POWERS/ABILITIES Brother Eye satellite can beam data or give Omac superstrength, invulnerability, or shielding.

In an alternate hypertimeline, a Great Disaster befalls the Earth in the 21st century. To forestall this event, a group of aliens formed the Global Peace Agency (G.P.A.) to eliminate threats to the planet's security. The aliens masterminded the construction of a satellite called Brother Eye. As part of Project O.M.A.C., Brother Eye transformed stockboy Buddy Blank into Omac, the One Man Army Corps. With the alien energies beamed from Brother Eye, Omac could boost his strength, become bulletproof, or receive information. He battled threats to the G.P.A. for years and then settled in a bunker near New York City. In one hypertimeline, Omac prevented the Great Disaster, and his grandson grew up to become TOMMY TOMORROW. In another, Omac failed and beast-men overran Earth. Here, Omac's grandson would become KAMANDI, the Last Boy on Earth. **DW**

OMEGA MEN

FIRST APPEARANCE GREEN LANTERN (2nd series) #141 (June 1981)
STATUS Heroes **BASE** Vegan Star System
NOTABLE MEMBERS
Primus (deceased) Psionically-powered leader.
Auron (Lambien) Godlike son of a Vegan goddess.
Broot Rock-hard giant from the planet Changralyn.
Harpis Winged sister of Demonia.
Kalista Sorceress wife of the late Primus.
Nimbus Wraith-like spirit.
Tigorr (Taghurrhu) Karnan feline fighter; occasional leader.

The Omega Men are the last best hope for freedom for the Vegan star-system. Warriors from various Vegan planets, the Omegans tried to liberate their worlds from the Citadel, an axis of evil led by the Psion-bred Citadelians (*see* Psions, Alien Races, pp. 150–1), that included the dreaded Gordanian slavers and ruthless Branx warriors. Forced to flee Vega, they were befriended by GREEN LANTERN Hal Jordan and SUPERMAN and received asylum on Earth. The Omegans helped the TEEN TITANS rescue STARFIRE from the Citadel, which was at last routed. However, the resulting power vacuum allowed the Spider Guild to annex portions of Vegan space. The Omegans battled the Spider Guild and remnants of the Citadel before being drawn into the conflict arising from the Dominator-led invasion of Earth (*see* Great Battles, pp. 320–1). The surviving Omegans returned to Vega, lately wracked by the destruction of several planets by the Sun-Eater (*see* TEEN TITANS) and IMPERIEX. The Omegans still search for a home amid the war-torn worlds of Vega. **SB**

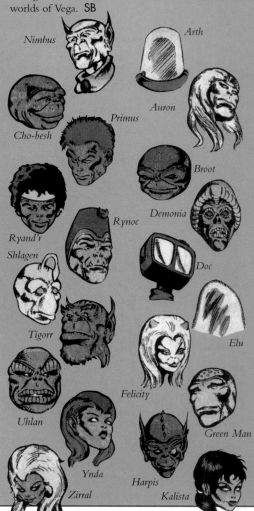

Nimbus · Arth · Cho-besh · Auron · Primus · Ryand'r · Broot · Shlagen · Rynoc · Demonia · Tigorr · Doc · Uhlan · Felicity · Elu · Green Man · Ynda · Harpis · Zirral · Kalista

ONOMATOPOEIA

FIRST APPEARANCE GREEN ARROW (3rd series) #11 (February 2002)
STATUS Villain   **REAL NAME** Unrevealed
OCCUPATION Assassin   **BASE** Mobile
HEIGHT 5ft 11in   **WEIGHT** 180 lbs
EYES Hidden by mask   **HAIR** Unknown
SPECIAL POWERS/ABILITIES A superb athlete; expert with guns, knives, and swords; does things no normal human could accomplish, including biting one of Green Arrow's weapons in half.

The motivation that makes Onomatopoeia cross the country killing third-rate costumed heroes (i.e. Harrisburg, Pennsylvania's Buckeye) and assorted vigilantes remains an unexplained mystery. He seems to be deliberately working his way up from the bottom and moving on to more powerful and well-known adversaries; however, like so much about Onomatopoeia, this is mere conjecture. As his name suggests, he expresses himself using only onomatopoeic words. The last sound victims hear is Onomatopoeia's imitation of the noise made by the weapon he is about to use to murder them.

GREEN ARROW II Connor Hawke was one of Onomatopoeia's most notable victims. Ambushing the archer in the alley, the killer grazed his head with a gunshot…and then mistakenly left Connor for dead. A blood transfusion saved Connor's life, while his father, Oliver Queen (Green Arrow I), met the assassin with a sharp response on the top of a building. The enigmatic Onomatopoeia still managed to escape. **RG**

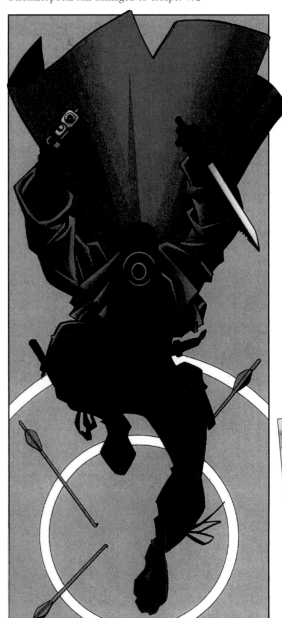

ONSLAUGHT, THE

FIRST APPEARANCE (Jihad) SUICIDE SQUAD (1st series) #1 (May 1987); (Onslaught) SUICIDE SQUAD (2nd series) #10 (August 2002)
STATUS Villain team   **BASE** Qurac
MEMBERS AND POWERS
Rustam I and II (both deceased) Team leaders; each could summon and wield a blazing scimitar.
Djinn Digitized body of electronic code; density manipulation, phasing; can transform from digital code into a sentient droid.
Jaculi I and II (both deceased) Superspeed.
Manticore I, II, and III (all deceased) Lion-themed battlesuits with machine guns and grenade launchers.
Ravan Martial artist and weapons master; requires specialized body brace to move.
Agni Can create and manipulate fire.
Badb Sonic scream instills panic and hatred.
Ifrit An artificial intelligence based on the brain patterns of Mindboggler (a dead Suicide Squad member).
Koschei the Deathless (deceased) Could animate the dead.
Piscator Amphibious powers; limited telepathy.
Old Mother (deceased) The demon Dahak manifested in an old woman's body.
Dervish Superspeed.
Antiphon Superspeed.
Hyve Can split into multiple, smaller versions of himself.
Tolteca Warrior skills.

The Onslaught is a group of superpowered international terrorists for hire, operating out of the Middle Eastern country of Qurac. Originally called the Jihad, the Onslaught were created by then Quraci president, Marlo, in an attempt to kill the President of the U.S. However, NIGHTSHADE and NEMESIS I, two members of the U.S. SUICIDE SQUAD, infiltrated the Jihad, allowing the Squad to launch a preemptive attack on the terrorists and cripple the team.

Later, reborn with new members, the Jihad launched a second attack on the U.S. Once again, the Jihad came to blows with the Suicide Squad, this time in New York City, and many of the terrorist villains were captured or killed, including their leader, Rustam.

Years later, a third incarnation of the Jihad emerged and attacked the HAYOTH, the Israeli supercommandos, as well as the JUSTICE LEAGUE OF AMERICA, after the mercenary CHESHIRE detonated a nuclear warhead above Qurac, killing more than one million people. The Jihad, mistakenly believing U.S. interests were responsible for the warhead's detonation, hijacked a U.S. airliner heading to Gotham City from Paris. Fortunately, the OUTSIDERS were also aboard the airplane, and the terrorists were defeated.

Recently, Njara Kattuah, the son of the first Rustam, created a new Jihad, now called the Onslaught, with new members. After successfully kidnapping Amanda Waller (see WALLER, AMANDA), the Onslaught was soundly trounced by the Suicide Squad and the JUSTICE SOCIETY OF AMERICA. DEADSHOT killed Rustam II, but the others escaped and remain at large. **PJ**

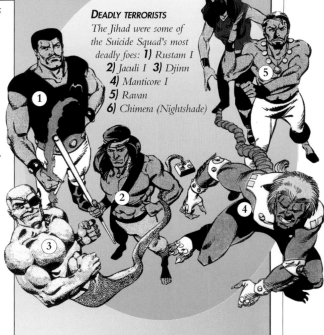

DEADLY TERRORISTS
The Jihad were some of the Suicide Squad's most deadly foes: 1) Rustam I 2) Jaculi I 3) Djinn 4) Manticore I 5) Ravan 6) Chimera (Nightshade)

ANTIPHON This Greek terrorist joined the Onslaught and fought against the Suicide Squad and the JSA. The Onslaught was responsible for the death of Amanda Waller's daughter, Havana.

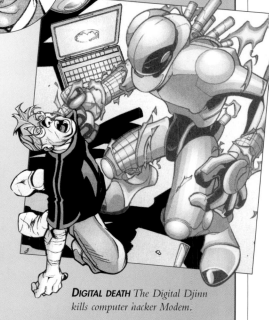

DIGITAL DEATH The Digital Djinn kills computer hacker Modem.

HYVE This monster drips duplicates of itself that can change into other people and objects!

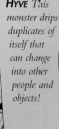

RUSTAM II The Onslaught leader could generate blazing scimitars of pure fire.

ONYX

FIRST APPEARANCE DETECTIVE COMICS #546 (January 1985)
STATUS Hero **REAL NAME** Unrevealed
OCCUPATION Adventurer **BASE** Star City
HEIGHT 5ft 9in **WEIGHT** 146 lbs **EYES** Brown **HAIR** Black
SPECIAL POWERS/ABILITIES Olympic-level athlete, expert hand-to-hand combatant, and martial artist.

Onyx was schooled in the Sanctuary, a monastery situated outside Star City. Pursued by an unknown agent who wanted to kill her, Onyx was admitted to the all-male Sanctuary by the Master, who trained her in martial arts and gave her a new identity. Upon the Master's death, Onyx sought out GREEN ARROW I, another student of the Sanctuary, to protect the monastery from a takeover by one of the Master's more ambitious protégés, a man whose name was Lars.

Onyx stayed at the Sanctuary until recently. She was recruited by BATMAN, and subsequently she teamed up with ORPHEUS to help head off a gang war in Gotham City. **PJ**

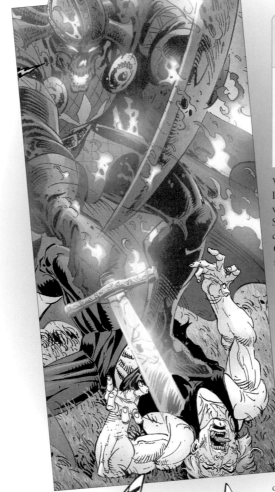

ORDER OF ST. DUMAS, THE

FIRST APPEARANCE BATMAN: SWORD OF AZRAEL #1 (October 1992)
STATUS Secret society of warrior priests and priestesses (destroyed)
BASE Mobile, formerly 14th century Europe
NOTABLE MEMBERS
Azrael (Jean Paul Valley) deceased; **Brother Rollo** deceased; **Carleton LeHah** deceased; **Sister Lilhy** deceased; **Nomoz**.

With its origins in the 14th century, the Order of St. Dumas was a small army of warrior priests dedicated to visiting wrath upon infidel foes during the Crusades. Similar in its credo to the Knights Templar, the Order defied Papal sanction and broke away from the Catholic Church, ultimately taking its mission underground while secretly amassing great wealth and power.

The Order demanded unwavering obedience from its members. Anyone who dared to betray its secrets was slain by the Order's "avenging angel," AZRAEL. This merciless warrior was trained from infancy using the System, an arcane mix of mental and physical conditioning through post-hypnotic suggestion.

Over the centuries that followed, the Order's numbers dwindled and its mission became increasingly tainted by the greed of its remaining fanatical devotees. College student Jean Paul Valley inherited the mantle of Azrael from his father when the latter was killed in the Order's service. Valley briefly served the remaining acolytes of St. Dumas; however, with BATMAN's help, he managed to escape the psychic bonds of the System. When he learned the full story concerning the horrific procedures that had forged him into Azrael, Valley destroyed every last vestige of the Order. The death of Jean Paul Valley, the last, albeit unwilling, member of the Order of St. Dumas, brought an end to this bizarre and sinister remnant of a bygone era. **SB**

ORION

FIRST APPEARANCE NEW GODS (1st series) #1 (March 1971)
STATUS Hero **REAL NAME** Orion
OCCUPATION Warrior **BASE** New Genesis
HEIGHT 6ft 1in **WEIGHT** 195 lbs **EYES** Red **HAIR** Red
SPECIAL POWERS/ABILITIES Possesses enormous strength in comparison with his fellow gods, as well as a fierce warrior's instinct; astro-glider allows him inter-spatial and inter-dimensional travel.

To forestall a cataclysmic battle between New Genesis and Apokolips, the planets' respective leaders HIGHFATHER and DARKSEID made a peace treaty known as The Pact, whereby each god gave up his son to be raised by the other. On New Genesis, Orion's feral nature stood out amongst the peaceful inhabitants. Over time, Orion was given a Mother Box, a sentient computer that calmed his mind and actually smoothed over his coarse features. Soon after, he was befriended by LIGHTRAY and the two became inseparable. Orion was dispatched to Earth, where Darkseid had been seeking the secret of the Anti-Life Equation. At one point, Orion and Lightray served with Earth's protectors, the JUSTICE LEAGUE OF AMERICA. Darkseid and his son battled frequently, culminating in Orion apparently killing Darkseid and assuming the rule of Apokolips.

Empowered by the Anti-Life Equation, Orion began mentally enslaving the inhabitants of Apokolips, New Genesis, and Earth in the name of peace. MISTER MIRACLE teleported Orion to the Abysmal Plane, home of "the guardian of the cosmic axis" known as Clockwerx. Orion surrendered control of the Anti-Life Equation to the entities, effectively destroying them. Afterward, Orion later discovered that Scott Free was in possession of the Anti-Life Equation. **RG**

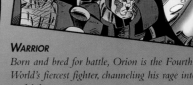

WARRIOR
Born and bred for battle, Orion is the Fourth World's fiercest fighter, channeling his rage into useful force.

ORACLE

THE ALL-SEEING EYE

FIRST APPEARANCE DETECTIVE COMICS #359 (January 1967)
STATUS Hero **REAL NAME** Barbara Gordon
OCCUPATION Information broker **BASE** Gotham City
HEIGHT 5ft 11in **WEIGHT** 148 lbs **EYES** Blue **HAIR** Red
SPECIAL POWERS/ABILITIES Superior computer hacker and information retrieval specialist; possesses a photographic memory and is a capable hand-to-hand combatant.

THE JOKER'S BULLET brought Barbara Gordon's high-flying career as BATGIRL crashing to earth. However, despite being paralyzed and wheelchair-bound, she has accomplished far more as a crime fighter than she ever could have if she'd remained BATMAN's enthusiastic assistant in the realm of acrobatics and Batarangs.

BEHIND THE SCREEN
Few heroes know Oracle's true identity. Often she appears only as a stylized, holographic head.

BARBARA GORDON

Barbara ("Babs" to her friends) became the adoptive daughter of her uncle James Gordon of the G.C.P.D. (see GORDON, JAMES W.) following the deaths of her parents. A brilliant student, she graduated from Gotham University at a very young age and took a job with the Gotham Public Library. Barbara admired the city's resident vigilante, Batman, and donned a homemade Batgirl costume to surprise her father at the Policeman's Masquerade. In this low-tech getup she foiled the despicable Killer Moth's attack (see CHARAXES) on Bruce Wayne, and started a new life as a compatriot to the Dynamic Duo of Batman and ROBIN.

WayneCorp has helped Oracle obtain the latest technology.

KILLING JOKE *In an act that changed Gotham forever, the Joker shot and crippled Barbara Gordon.*

BIRDS OF PREY *Seen here flanked by the Huntress and Black Canary, Oracle is the director of Gotham's all-female crimebusting team.*

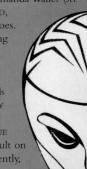

During her time as Batgirl, Barbara served a term in the U.S. Congress. After a near-fatal run-in with the assassin Cormorant, Barbara retired from active crime fighting. Shortly after, as part of a revenge plot against Commissioner Gordon, the JOKER burst in on her and shot her in the spine. During rehabilitation she learned she would never walk again.
Barbara trained her upper body to physical perfection with the help of Richard Dragon (see DRAGON, RICHARD), and then packaged her skills as an information retrieval expert under the name Oracle. She worked with Amanda Waller (see WALLER, AMANDA) of the U.S. government's SUICIDE SQUAD, becoming second-in-command under the alias Amy Beddoes.
Oracle began to operate out of Gotham City's imposing clocktower, behind banks of supercomputers running state-of-the-art hacking software. Soon, the "all-seeing, all-knowing" Oracle became a legend in the super-hero community. She recruited heroes into an informal "Birds of Prey" team (members have included BLACK CANARY II, POWER GIRL, and HUNTRESS) to act on her data.
Batman recommended Oracle for JUSTICE LEAGUE OF AMERICA membership, and she survived an assault on her clocktower by the villain PROMETHEUS. Recently, Barbara left Gotham City when BLACK MASK's goons put her in danger. She has since relocated to Metropolis.
DW

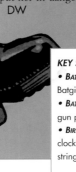

KEY STORYLINES

- **BATGIRL: YEAR ONE #1–9 (FEBRUARY–OCTOBER 2003):** Batgirl battles Killer Moth in this retelling of her heroic debut.
- **BATMAN: THE KILLING JOKE (TPB, 1988):** A bullet from the Joker's gun paralyzes Barbara in a moment that shocked readers.
- **BIRDS OF PREY #1 (JANUARY 1999):** Working from Gotham's clocktower, Oracle begins a new career as a super-heroic string-puller.

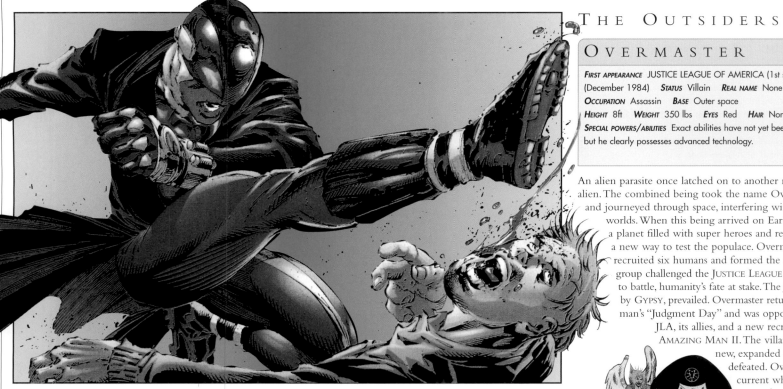

THE OUTSIDERS SEE OPPOSITE PAGE

OVERMASTER

FIRST APPEARANCE JUSTICE LEAGUE OF AMERICA (1st series) #233 (December 1984) **STATUS** Villain **REAL NAME** None
OCCUPATION Assassin **BASE** Outer space
HEIGHT 8ft **WEIGHT** 350 lbs **EYES** Red **HAIR** None
SPECIAL POWERS/ABILITIES Exact abilities have not yet been documented but he clearly possesses advanced technology.

An alien parasite once latched on to another mountainous alien. The combined being took the name Overmaster and journeyed through space, interfering with sentient worlds. When this being arrived on Earth, it saw a planet filled with super heroes and recognized a new way to test the populace. Overmaster recruited six humans and formed the CADRE. The group challenged the JUSTICE LEAGUE OF AMERICA to battle, humanity's fate at stake. The JLA, aided by GYPSY, prevailed. Overmaster returned for man's "Judgment Day" and was opposed by the JLA, its allies, and a new recruit, AMAZING MAN II. The villain and his new, expanded Cadre were defeated. Overmaster's current whereabouts are unknown. **RG**

ORPHEUS

FIRST APPEARANCE BATMAN: ORPHEUS RISING #1 (October 2001)
STATUS Hero **REAL NAME** Gavin King
OCCUPATION Vigilante; former dancer **BASE** Gotham City
HEIGHT 6ft 2in **WEIGHT** 180 lbs **EYES** Brown **HAIR** Black
SPECIAL POWERS/ABILITIES Formidable fighter; stealth-circuitry allows costume to blend into shadows; employs high-tech weapons.

OUTLAW

FIRST APPEARANCE ALL-STAR WESTERN #2 (November 1970)
STATUS Hero (deceased) **REAL NAME** Rick Wilson
OCCUPATION Ranger **BASE** Texas
HEIGHT 6ft 1in **WEIGHT** 189 lbs **EYES** Blue **HAIR** Brown
SPECIAL POWERS/ABILITIES Was an expert marksman and horseman; often accompanied by a trained hawk he once nursed back to health.

OWLWOMAN

FIRST APPEARANCE SUPER FRIENDS #7 (October 1977)
STATUS Hero **REAL NAME** Wenonah Littlebird
OCCUPATION Jeweler; adventurer **BASE** London; the Dome
HEIGHT 5ft 5in **WEIGHT** 125 lbs **EYES** Brown **HAIR** Black
SPECIAL POWERS/ABILITIES Tribal powers give her superhuman speed, the power of flight, tracking ability, sight in total darkness, and superhuman endurance; her genetically engineered claws can cut through steel.

While other kids were shooting hoops or roaming Gotham City's mean streets and getting into trouble, teenager Gavin King turned his attentions to martial arts and dancing. After finishing his schooling, Gavin joined a professional dance troupe and traveled the world, where he witnessed more of the same poverty and inequality that divided races and inevitably led to violence. Determined to do something about these injustices, Gavin joined a shadowy secret organization which provided him with the training and equipment he needed to combat ignorance and indifference. As the costumed Orpheus, Gavin took the fight back to Gotham, where he helped the city's self-appointed guardian, BATMAN, expose a cabal of corrupt cops fomenting bloodshed between gangs and gun dealers.

Though initially wary of Orpheus, the Dark Knight became convinced of the young hero's good intentions after Orpheus argued that Gotham could certainly use more heroes of color to act as relevant role models to the city's minority populations. Later, Orpheus teamed with the Dark Knight's allies NIGHTWING and BLACK CANARY.

Batman recently recruited Orpheus to team with ONYX and infiltrate Gotham City's underworld to help prevent a gang war. **SB**

Rick Wilson's father, Sam, was a Texas ranger who enforced the law throughout the Old West. When Rick turned 18, he set out for parts unknown. When Sam Wilson was called in to investigate a daring stagecoach robbery, he discovered that Rick was one of the outlaw culprits. Sam declared that he no longer had a son. Sam relentlessly pursued his son as he rode with infamous outlaws, such as the Dix Gang, "King" Coffin," and "Gunpowder" Grimes. What no one realized was that the Wilsons were in cahoots. Rick was infiltrating outlaw gangs and helping Sam Wilson to catch them dead or alive. After defeating the dynamite-wielding Grimes, the Wilsons' ruse was revealed. Sam and Rick served with the Texas Rangers for the rest of their days. **SB**

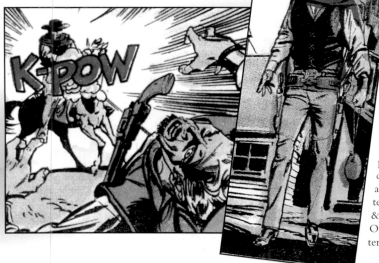

FAST ON THE DRAW
Rick Wilson masqueraded as an Outlaw to bring in desperados—dead or alive!

A Kiowa Indian from Wyoming, Wenonah Littlebird learned how to channel the spiritual power of her entire tribe during a great ceremony called the K'Ado. Called "Owlwoman" by her mother, Wenonah battled small time criminals and low-level mystical threats in the Midwest, eventually becoming the U.S. representative of DOCTOR MIST's international team of heroes, the GLOBAL GUARDIANS.

Owlwoman fell in love with fellow Guardian JACK O'LANTERN. Her powers were enhanced when she was captured by the first Queen Bee (see QUEEN BEE II) and subjected to genetic experiments. After deposing terrorist dictator Sumaan Harjavti (see HARJAVTI, RUMAAN & SUMAAN) from his rule in Bialya in the Middle East, Jack O'Lantern died, and Owlwoman began an angry campaign to end terrorism around the world. **PJ**

THE OUTSIDERS

THE NEW BREED

First appearance BRAVE AND THE BOLD #200 (July 1983)
Status Hero team **Base** Brooklyn, New York City
Current members and powers
Nightwing (leader) Expert acrobat and combatant.
Arsenal Superior archer and weapons specialist.
Grace Superstrength.
Thunder Can increase her body's density to become invulnerable.
Indigo Android with the powers of flight, force field projection, and the ability to emit energy from eyes and hands.
Jade Wields green energy to create hard-light constructs.
Shift Fully grown copy of Metamorpho with the power to shapeshift and transmute the elements in his body.

THE OUTSIDERS LIVE UP TO THEIR NAME by flatly refusing to work within the expected constraints of international law and propriety. The current version of the team is committed to taking proactive action—squashing meta-human and alien threats before they even have the chance to become threats! The original Outsiders included BLACK LIGHTNING, METAMORPHO, LOOKER, HALO, and the Markovian noble GEO-FORCE. Based in Gotham City and backed financially by Bruce Wayne, the hero team were an outgrowth of BATMAN's frustration with the political constraints under which the JUSTICE LEAGUE OF AMERICA were forced to operate.

DIRECT ACTION

When Baron Bedlam kidnapped Lucius Fox (see FOX, LUCIUS) in Markovia, the Justice League of America refused to interfere for fear of upsetting a nation's internal politics. Batman quit the JLA in disgust and formed his Outsiders to handle the Markovia incident and similar, unorthodox missions. Geo-Force fought with Batman over the Dark Knight's tendency to withhold information from team members. Batman quit, and Geo-Force led the team, which relocated to Los Angeles. During this period, the Outsiders became agents of the Markovian government. Later additions to the roster included the airstream-manipulating WINDFALL and the armored ATOMIC KNIGHT. Geo-Force eventually disbanded this team.

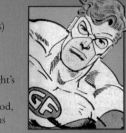

GEO-FORCE The Outsiders' greatest leader.

NEW BLOOD Grace and Thunder are two brash young additions, lending their muscle to battle threats like Gorilla Grodd.

Reunited in Markovia, the Outsiders became fugitives framed for the murder of the country's monarch, Queen Ilona. They cleared their names but split into two squads: one led by Geo-Force and including KATANA and the warsuited TECHNOCRAT; the other led by the Kryptonian ERADICATOR and including Looker, Halo, Faust (see FAUST, FELIX), and the bear-creature Wylde. The two teams united and the Outsiders remained active through the Imperiex War (see Great Battles, pp. 320–1), their last member being DOCTOR LIGHT II. Former Titan ARSENAL founded the current Outsiders, with funding from the Optitron corporation, which paid for an underground HQ and a command hovercraft, the *Pequod*. Arsenal's recruits included old hands NIGHTWING (who became leader), Metamorpho (a clone of the original hero) and JADE, as well as newcomers GRACE, THUNDER III, and INDIGO. DW

THE OUTSIDERS 1) *Arsenal.*
2) *Nightwing* **3)** *Grace.*
4) *Indigo* **5)** *Thunder.*
6) *Jade* **7)** *Metamorpho.*

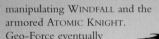

KEY STORYLINES
• BATMAN AND THE OUTSIDERS #1 (AUGUST 1983): The classic Outsiders team makes its debut while meddling in foreign affairs.
• OUTSIDERS (2ND SERIES) #1 (NOVEMBER 1985): Without Batman, the Outsiders move to California.
• OUTSIDERS (3RD SERIES) #1 (JUNE 2003): Nightwing and Arsenal, ex-teen Titans, form a new team.

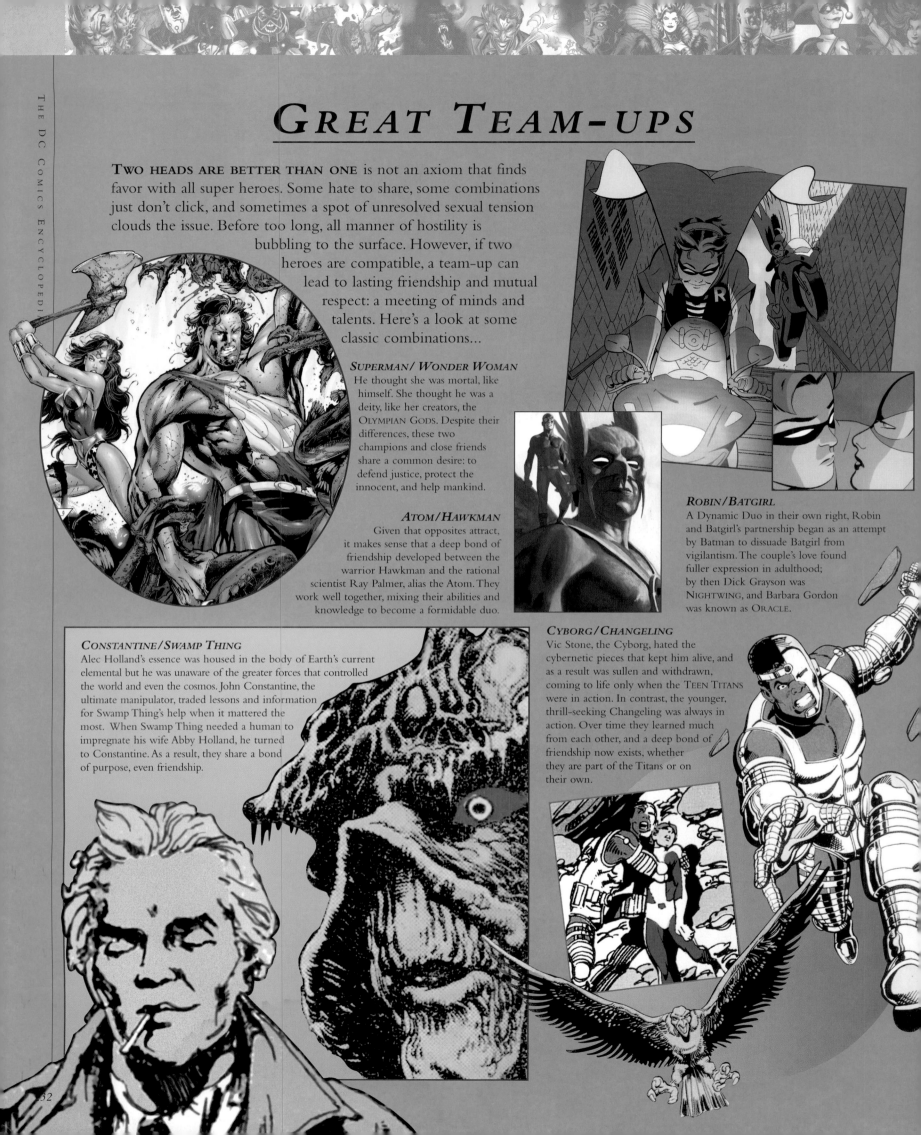

GREAT TEAM-UPS

TWO HEADS ARE BETTER THAN ONE is not an axiom that finds favor with all super heroes. Some hate to share, some combinations just don't click, and sometimes a spot of unresolved sexual tension clouds the issue. Before too long, all manner of hostility is bubbling to the surface. However, if two heroes are compatible, a team-up can lead to lasting friendship and mutual respect: a meeting of minds and talents. Here's a look at some classic combinations...

SUPERMAN/WONDER WOMAN

He thought she was mortal, like himself. She thought he was a deity, like her creators, the OLYMPIAN GODS. Despite their differences, these two champions and close friends share a common desire: to defend justice, protect the innocent, and help mankind.

ATOM/HAWKMAN

Given that opposites attract, it makes sense that a deep bond of friendship developed between the warrior Hawkman and the rational scientist Ray Palmer, alias the Atom. They work well together, mixing their abilities and knowledge to become a formidable duo.

ROBIN/BATGIRL

A Dynamic Duo in their own right, Robin and Batgirl's partnership began as an attempt by Batman to dissuade Batgirl from vigilantism. The couple's love found fuller expression in adulthood; by then Dick Grayson was NIGHTWING, and Barbara Gordon was known as ORACLE.

CONSTANTINE/SWAMP THING

Alec Holland's essence was housed in the body of Earth's current elemental but he was unaware of the greater forces that controlled the world and even the cosmos. John Constantine, the ultimate manipulator, traded lessons and information for Swamp Thing's help when it mattered the most. When Swamp Thing needed a human to impregnate his wife Abby Holland, he turned to Constantine. As a result, they share a bond of purpose, even friendship.

CYBORG/CHANGELING

Vic Stone, the Cyborg, hated the cybernetic pieces that kept him alive, and as a result was sullen and withdrawn, coming to life only when the TEEN TITANS were in action. In contrast, the younger, thrill-seeking Changeling was always in action. Over time they learned much from each other, and a deep bond of friendship now exists, whether they are part of the Titans or on their own.

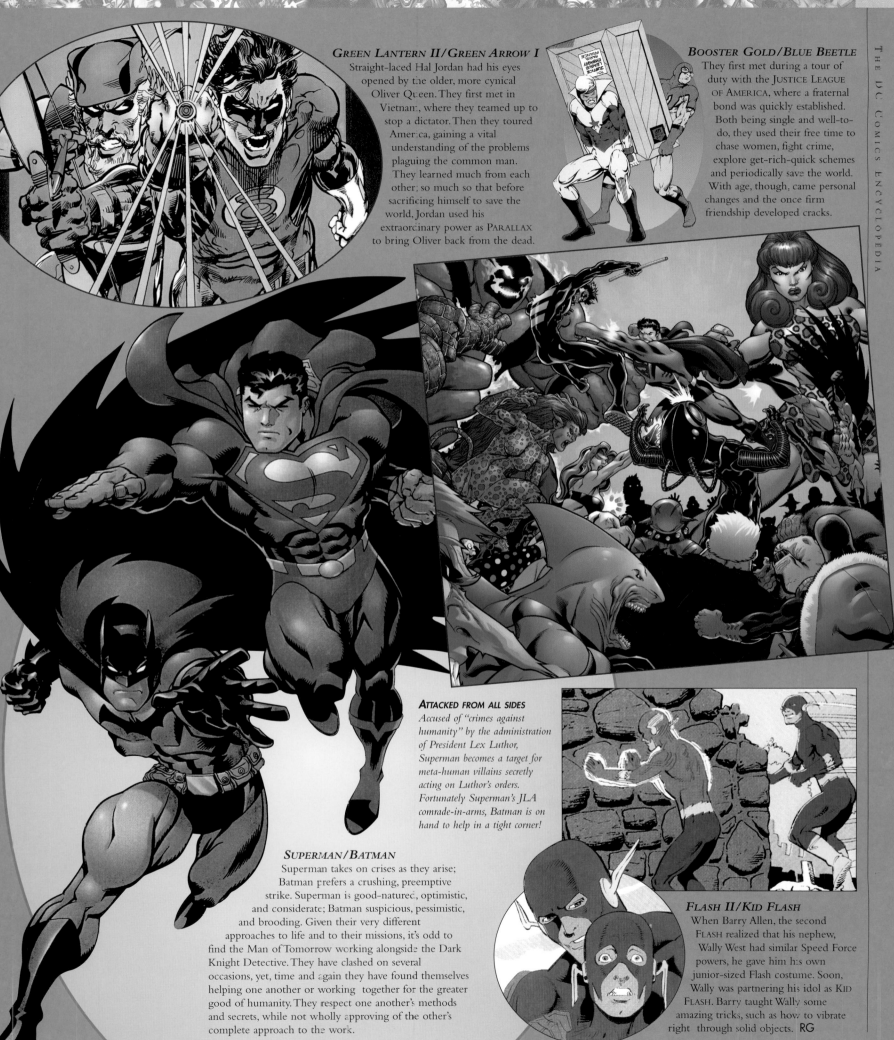

GREEN LANTERN II/GREEN ARROW I

Straight-laced Hal Jordan had his eyes opened by the older, more cynical Oliver Queen. They first met in Vietnam, where they teamed up to stop a dictator. Then they toured America, gaining a vital understanding of the problems plaguing the common man. They learned much from each other, so much so that before sacrificing himself to save the world, Jordan used his extraordinary power as PARALLAX to bring Oliver back from the dead.

BOOSTER GOLD/BLUE BEETLE

They first met during a tour of duty with the JUSTICE LEAGUE OF AMERICA, where a fraternal bond was quickly established. Both being single and well-to-do, they used their free time to chase women, fight crime, explore get-rich-quick schemes and periodically save the world. With age, though, came personal changes and the once firm friendship developed cracks.

ATTACKED FROM ALL SIDES
Accused of "crimes against humanity" by the administration of President Lex Luthor, Superman becomes a target for meta-human villains secretly acting on Luthor's orders. Fortunately Superman's JLA comrade-in-arms, Batman is on hand to help in a tight corner!

SUPERMAN/BATMAN

Superman takes on crises as they arise; Batman prefers a crushing, preemptive strike. Superman is good-natured, optimistic, and considerate; Batman suspicious, pessimistic, and brooding. Given their very different approaches to life and to their missions, it's odd to find the Man of Tomorrow working alongside the Dark Knight Detective. They have clashed on several occasions, yet, time and again they have found themselves helping one another or working together for the greater good of humanity. They respect one another's methods and secrets, while not wholly approving of the other's complete approach to the work.

FLASH II/KID FLASH

When Barry Allen, the second FLASH realized that his nephew, Wally West had similar Speed Force powers, he gave him his own junior-sized Flash costume. Soon, Wally was partnering his idol as KID FLASH. Barry taught Wally some amazing tricks, such as how to vibrate right through solid objects. RG

229

PANTHA

FIRST APPEARANCE NEW TITANS #74 (March 1991)
STATUS Hero **REAL NAME** None (originally designated X-24)
OCCUPATION Adventurer **BASE** Science City, Russia
HEIGHT 5ft 8.5in **WEIGHT** 136 lbs **EYES** Red **HAIR** Auburn
SPECIAL POWERS/ABILITIES Incredible predatory speed, strength, and agility; indestructible claws on hands and feet; cat-like visual acuity.

The were-cat known as Pantha was created by the WILDEBEEST Society. She was one example of the Society's attempts to alter human and animal DNA and adapt suitable host bodies for the vengeful souls of Azarath. These souls had once belonged to peaceful, other-dimensional mystics who had raised one of the TEEN TITANS known as RAVEN and shielded her from the demonic TRIGON. The Azarathians possessed Raven's fellow Teen Titan JERICHO, making him leader of the Wildebeest Society as it worked in secret to fulfill their master plans.

While the majority of the Wildebeest's bio-engineered test subjects perished, Pantha survived and escaped. Later, she helped the Titans and DEATHSTROKE THE TERMINATOR defeat Jericho and the Wildebeests. A Titan herself for a time, Pantha eventually departed the team with RED STAR and Baby Wildebeest. The latter was the Wildebeest Society's final experiment, a creature that bonded to Pantha, who became its "mother." This unusual family now lives in Science City, Russia, and undertakes missions for the Russian government. **SB**

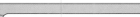

CAT/WOMAN
Since her escape from the Wildebeests, Pantha has sought to learn whether or not she is really a genetically altered human or an evolved feline.

PARALLAX

FIRST APPEARANCE GREEN LANTERN (3rd ser.) #50 (Mar. 1994)
STATUS Ex-hero **REAL NAME** Hal Jordan
OCCUPATION Cosmic rogue **BASE** Mobile
HEIGHT 6ft **WEIGHT** 186 lbs
EYES Brown **HAIR** Brown with white
SPECIAL POWERS/ABILITIES A living repository of the Oan emerald energy and can control the flow of time.

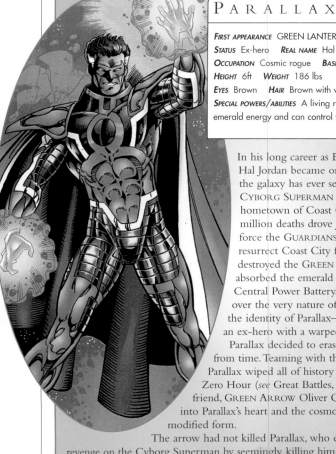

In his long career as Earth's Green Lantern, Hal Jordan became one of the greatest heroes the galaxy has ever seen. But when the CYBORG SUPERMAN annihilated Jordan's hometown of Coast City, the trauma of seven million deaths drove Jordan mad. His quest to force the GUARDIANS OF THE UNIVERSE to resurrect Coast City failed, so Jordan destroyed the GREEN LANTERN CORPS and absorbed the emerald energy of the Oan Central Power Battery. He now had influence over the very nature of space-time and assumed the identity of Parallax—not a true villain, but an ex-hero with a warped vision of righteousness. Parallax decided to erase Coast City's tragedy from time. Teaming with the villain EXTANT, Parallax wiped all of history in the event known as Zero Hour (*see* Great Battles, pp. 320–1). Jordan's old friend, GREEN ARROW Oliver Queen, fired an arrow into Parallax's heart and the cosmos remade itself in a modified form.

The arrow had not killed Parallax, who eventually took his revenge on the Cyborg Superman by seemingly killing him on the Source Wall at the edge of the universe. Parallax returned to Earth at the request of new Green Lantern Kyle Rayner during the Final Night crisis. Parallax proved himself a hero in the end, sacrificing his life to destroy the star-swallowing Sun-Eater and rekindle Earth's sun. Hal Jordan has since found redemption in the afterlife as the SPECTRE. **DW**

PARASITE

FIRST APPEARANCE ACTION COMICS #240 (August 1966)
STATUS Villain (dead) **REAL NAME** Rudy Jones; Torval Freeman
OCCUPATION Professional criminal **BASE** Metropolis
HEIGHT Variable **WEIGHT** Variable **EYES** Red **HAIR** None
SPECIAL POWERS/ABILITIES Absorbed the life essence of living creatures, killing them; absorbed meta-human powers; could shape-change; size and shape varied with energy absorbed.

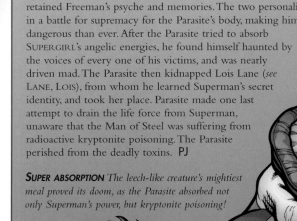

Rudy Jones was a maintenance worker at S.T.A.R. Labs in Metropolis, who tried to smuggle scientific waste out of the laboratory to sell illegally. Jones opened one of the waste containers and was irradiated with an isotope that transformed his body. To survive, Jones was forced to absorb the life energies of other living beings, much like a vampire. Searching for the ultimate "meal," the Parasite began a lifelong pursuit of SUPERMAN, whom he considered a living power battery. The two clashed repeatedly, but the Parasite's craving for the Man of Steel's solar-powered energy was always unfulfilled.

After absorbing the life energies of Doctor Torvell Freeman, the Parasite retained Freeman's psyche and memories. The two personalities became locked in a battle for supremacy for the Parasite's body, making him more dangerous than ever. After the Parasite tried to absorb SUPERGIRL's angelic energies, he found himself haunted by the voices of every one of his victims, and was nearly driven mad. The Parasite then kidnapped Lois Lane (*see* LANE, LOIS), from whom he learned Superman's secret identity, and took her place. Parasite made one last attempt to drain the life force from Superman, unaware that the Man of Steel was suffering from radioactive kryptonite poisoning. The Parasite perished from the deadly toxins. **PJ**

SOUL DRAIN *When the Parasite sucks the energies out of a human being, he steals not only their memories and skills, but their life essence!*

SUPER ABSORPTION *The leech-like creature's mightiest meal proved its doom, as the Parasite absorbed not only Superman's power, but kryptonite poisoning!*

PARK, LINDA

FIRST APPEARANCE THE FLASH (2nd series) #28 (July 1989)
STATUS Hero   **REAL NAME** Linda Jasmine Park
OCCUPATION Television journalist; medical student
BASE Keystone City   **HEIGHT** 5ft 6in   **WEIGHT** 137 lbs
EYES Brown   **HAIR** Black   **SPECIAL POWERS/ABILITIES** She has no
superpowers but is brave and resourceful; the Flash's equal for sheer
gumption and his perfect partner.

Linda Park thought Wally West (FLASH III) was brash and
arrogant—which he was. But Linda also saw something
else in him, the spark of a better man. As their
relationship developed, that spark became the
flames of love. So strong was their bond that it
has enabled Flash to find his way home, regardless
of time, dimension, or location, as they discovered
when the Flash III pushed himself past his previous limits
and joined the Speed Force.

Linda was seemingly killed by a supernatural entity
called the Black Flash, which sent Wally West spiraling
into a depression. The Flash ultimately rescued Linda
from within the Speed Force and they made plans to wed.

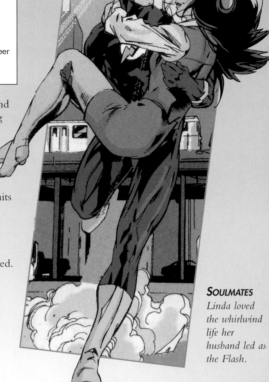

SOULMATES
Linda loved
the whirlwind
life her
husband led as
the Flash.

As the marriage ceremony was about to take place, Linda
was kidnapped by the villain ABRA KADABRA and the
world's memory of her was erased. Fortunately, the Flash
sorted everything out, the couple married at last, and
Linda enrolled at Central City Medical College.

A short time later, pregnant with twins, she was
attacked by ZOOM and suffered a miscarriage. She
and Wally have struggled to cope with the grief,
which has led to her dropping out of school and
abandoning her husband while she decides what to
do next. RG

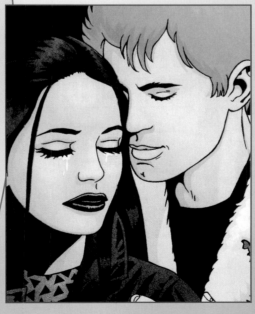

END OF THE DREAM After her miscarriage, Linda
came to question her life as a super hero's spouse
and left to decide her future.

PARIAH

FIRST APPEARANCE CRISIS ON INFINITE EARTHS #1 (April 1985)
STATUS Hero   **REAL NAME** Mossa
OCCUPATION Adventurer   **BASE** Mobile
HEIGHT 5ft 11in   **WEIGHT** 165 lbs   **EYES** Black   **HAIR** Purple
SPECIAL POWERS/ABILITIES Brilliant scientist; invulnerable to
physical harm; innately teleports to the focal point of vast
danger; it is undetermined whether he is immortal.

In another dimension, the scientist Mossa remained
in an antimatter chamber for 13 months, hoping to
unlock the secrets of the universe by witnessing
Creation at the Dawn of Time. His chamber and
world were destroyed in the process. The cursed
scientist was renamed Pariah, and as penance for
his actions, was forced to spend the next hundred
million years witnessing the destruction of world
after world and the deaths of countless billions of
sentient beings. As red, stormy skies blanketed
Earth during the summer heat of July, the Anti-
Monitor (see MONITOR) attempted to destroy the
positive matter universe (see The Crisis, Great
Battles, pp. 320–1).

Pariah arrived on Earth to warn its people of the
impending doom. The Monitor gathered heroes
from across time and space to try and stop his evil
twin, using the woman HARBINGER to collect
them. The Anti-Monitor plucked the Earth out of
its universe and placed it in the anti-matter
universe of Qward, unleashing millions of Shadow
Demons across the planet, which slaughtered
thousands. Pariah worked with the champions from
across time and space to save all reality. Once
accomplished, he thought his penance was
complete and remained on Earth, hoping to find a
home and a new purpose in his life. RG

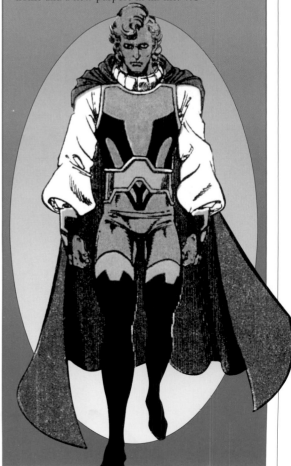

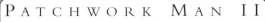

PATCHWORK MAN I

FIRST APPEARANCE SWAMP THING #2 (January 1973)
STATUS Hero (deceased) **REAL NAME** Gregori Arcane
OCCUPATION None (a victim of circumstance) **BASE** Mobile
HEIGHT 6ft 8in **WEIGHT** 330 lbs **EYES** Blue **HAIR** Grayish black
SPECIAL POWERS/ABILITIES Shambling, super-strong hulk with a fantastic resistance to injury. His origin as a magically-created being gives him limited defenses against sorcery.

The original Patchwork Man, a pitiful monstrosity, once answered to the name Gregori Arcane. A businessman in the Balkan mountain region of Eastern Europe, Gregori raised his daughter Abigail as best he could, but became the target of neighbors who considered him an unfit father. One day they took away Abigail, and Gregori wandered into a minefield while searching for her.

Gregori's mad-scientist brother Anton (see ARCANE, ANTON) gathered up the pieces of his brother's body and sewed them back together. With a healthy dose of sorcery animating his broken carcass, Gregori lurched into a new life as the Patchwork Man. Years spent imprisoned in Anton's dungeon ended when the SWAMP THING inadvertently freed the Patchwork Man, and Gregori sought out his daughter Abigail, now an adult living in the American South. Several encounters with Abby and Swamp Thing followed, but Patchwork Man's body ultimately decomposed to an irrecoverable state and he is believed to have perished.

PATCHWORK MAN II

FIRST APPEARANCE SECRET FILES & ORIGINS GUIDE TO THE DC UNIVERSE 2000 #1 (March 2000)
STATUS Hero **REAL NAME** Elliot Taylor
OCCUPATION Member of Creature Commandos **BASE** Mobile
HEIGHT 9ft **WEIGHT** 560 lbs **EYES** Black **HAIR** None
SPECIAL POWERS/ABILITIES Superstrength; fantastic resistance to injury thanks to a body composed of undead material.

The modern-day inheritor of the name Patchwork Man is Elliot "Lucky" Taylor, a reconstituted warrior who received his stitched-together body courtesy of the U.S. government's top-secret Project M. With his teammates in the new CREATURE COMMANDOS—including Wolfpack (Warren Griffith), Medusa, Sgt. Vincent Velcro, Gunner (see GUNNER AND SARGE), and CAPTAIN HUNTER— Patchwork Man II served as the designated "heavy hitter" during a struggle against the interdimensional warlord Lord Saturna, ruler of the realm of Terra Arcana. The Patchwork Man, lugging a heavy machine gun with multiple ammo belts slung across his beefy shoulders, helped the Creature Commandos prevent a full-scale invasion of the armies of Terra Arcana, thanks in part to unexpected aid from CLAW THE UNCONQUERED. In the end, Lord Saturna perished and the leaderless citizens of Terra Arcana were left to chart their own destiny. DW

PINCUSHION *Patchwork Man II has been shot thousands of times, and probably has hundreds of bullets lodged inside his hulking frame.*

PEACEMAKER III

FIRST APPEARANCE THE L.A.W. #1 (September 1999)
STATUS Hero **REAL NAME** Mitchell Black
OCCUPATION Former physician; soldier **BASE** Mobile
HEIGHT 6ft 1in **WEIGHT** 183 lbs **EYES** Brown **HAIR** Brown
SPECIAL POWERS/ABILITIES Battle armor provides flight and enhances strength; armor is operational underwater or in space and contains high-tech arms systems as well as an energy blaster.

Three individuals have adopted the alter ego of Peacemaker, an armored soldier battling for peace. Peacemaker I was Christopher Smith, whose delusions of being haunted by his father, Nazi S.S. officer Wolfgang Schmidt, drove his insane resolve to fight and kill for the sake of peace. Peacemaker I and other less notable heroes died attempting to liberate the South American country of Parador from the evil influence of ECLIPSO.

Peacemaker II's identity is unrevealed. Presumably he was a U.S. government agent sanctioned to take up Smith's codename and mission. He is known chiefly for belonging to the Leaguebusters, a team assembled to counter the JUSTICE LEAGUE OF AMERICA. His current activities and whereabouts are unknown.

Peacemaker III is Mitchell Black, a pulmonary physician who lost his license to practice medicine following untried surgery that led to the death of a young patient. Black was subsequently recruited by the Geneva-based Peacemaker Project as head of its Enforcement Division. This organization provided armored "Peacemakers" to troubled nations around the globe. Black also joined the L.A.W. (Last American Warriors), a super-team that fought to save the world from the powerful Avatar and his cultish forces, the Ravanans. SB

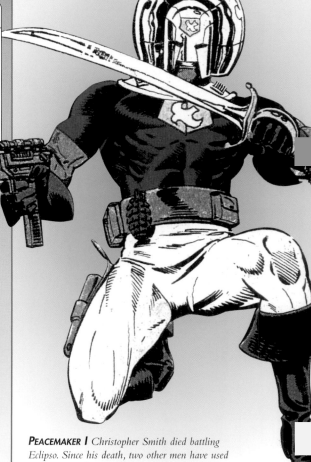

PEACEMAKER I *Christopher Smith died battling Eclipso. Since his death, two other men have used the identity of Peacemaker.*

236

PENGUIN

GOTHAM'S MR. FIXIT

FIRST APPEARANCE DETECTIVE COMICS #58 (December 1941)
STATUS Villain **REAL NAME** Oswald Chesterfield Cobblepot
OCCUPATION Criminal; stock trader; fixer **BASE** Gotham City
HEIGHT 5ft 2in **WEIGHT** 175 lbs **EYES** Blue **HAIR** Black
SPECIAL POWERS/ABILITIES Devious and ruthless, despite his small
stature, he is surprisingly agile; usually prefers to flee rather than
fight; formerly favored an array of bizarre umbrella weapons; also
used his affinity with birds to assist in his crimes.

OSWALD CHESTERFIELD COBBLEPOT based a criminal career as the murderous gangster the Penguin on his fascination with birds and ornithology. This fascination dates back to his childhood, growing up with his widowed mother, who ran a pet shop specializing in exotic birds. Short, paunchy, and burdened with a prominent, beaky nose, his schoolmates nicknamed Oswald the Penguin. His fussy mother insisted he carry an umbrella, even on sunny days, making him the target of widespread ridicule.

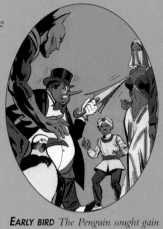

EARLY BIRD *The Penguin sought gain wherever possible, even attempting to kidnap Arabian royalty.*

THE BIRD MAN OF GOTHAM

When he grew up, Oswald got his own back on the world by becoming a force to be reckoned with in Gotham City's underworld. He committed scores of crimes (often with a bird-theme), which inevitably led him to run afoul of the BATMAN and ROBIN time and again. The Penguin further increased his criminal profile when he met a scientific genius, a deformed mute named Harold, and convinced him to create a device that could control birds, directing them to commit crimes and various acts of terror for him.

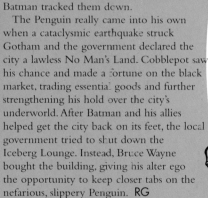

LADIES' MAN
The Penguin likes to surround himself with the finest acquisitions in life, both animate and inanimate.

Batman stopped this threat and later brought Harold to the Batcave, where he helped maintain the various Bat-vehicles. On parole, the Penguin tried to convince the public he had gone "legit" by playing the stock market. Though exposed for insider trading, the Penguin remained strongly attracted to the notion of concealing his criminal activities beneath a more socially acceptable façade.

To that end, Cobblepot became the owner of a premier Gotham nightspot, the Iceberg Lounge, and purportedly once more reformed. Secretly, he had formed an alliance with a number-cruncher known as the Actuary, who helped the Penguin pull off a series of spectacular robberies. Ultimately, the Actuary took the fall for his partner when Batman tracked them down.

The Penguin really came into his own when a cataclysmic earthquake struck Gotham and the government declared the city a lawless No Man's Land. Cobblepot saw his chance and made a fortune on the black market, trading essential goods and further strengthening his hold over the city's underworld. After Batman and his allies helped get the city back on its feet, the local government tried to shut down the Iceberg Lounge. Instead, Bruce Wayne bought the building, giving his alter ego the opportunity to keep closer tabs on the nefarious, slippery Penguin. RG

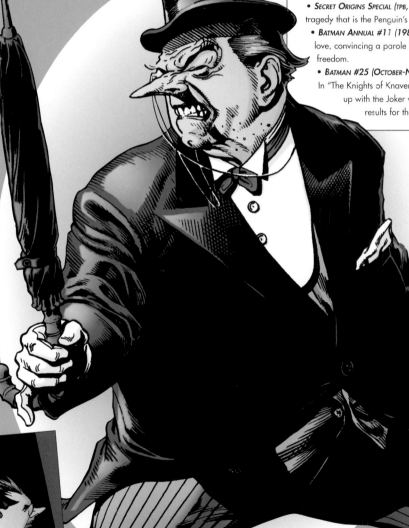

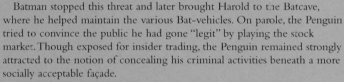

KEY STORYLINES

- **PENGUIN TRIUMPHANT (TPB, 1992):** A spotlight story on the criminal dealings of a rogue who feels he doesn't get enough respect from the world.
- **SECRET ORIGINS SPECIAL (TPB, 1989):** A look at the tragedy that is the Penguin's life.
- **BATMAN ANNUAL #11 (1987):** The Penguin's in love, convincing a parole board he deserves his freedom.
- **BATMAN #25 (OCTOBER-NOVEMBER 1944):** In "The Knights of Knavery," the Penguin teams up with the Joker with nearly deadly results for the Dynamic Duo.

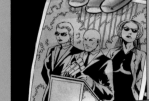

NO MAN'S LAND
During Gotham's exile, the Penguin amassed power through barter, favors, and guile.

TALK TO THE BAT *Time and again, the Penguin is pressured into telling Batman vital nuggets of information.*

233

PENNYWORTH, ALFRED

FIRST APPEARANCE BATMAN #16 (May 1943)
STATUS Heroic ally **REAL NAME** Alfred Pennyworth
OCCUPATION Butler for Wayne Manor **BASE** Gotham City
HEIGHT 6ft **WEIGHT** 160 lbs **EYES** Blue **HAIR** Black
SPECIAL POWERS/ABILITIES Expert medic, mechanic, chauffeur; former soldier and actor (professionally trained); vocal mimic; unswervingly loyal, and an endless source of good advice.

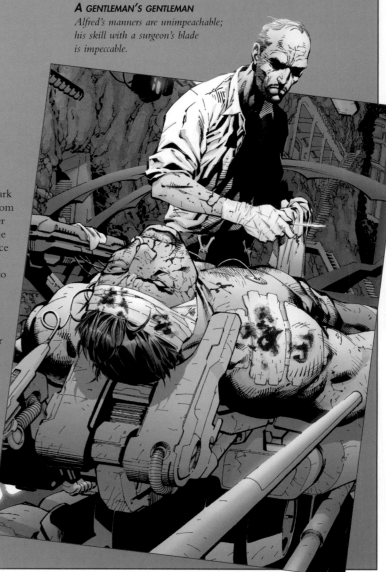

A GENTLEMAN'S GENTLEMAN
Alfred's manners are unimpeachable; his skill with a surgeon's blade is impeccable.

More than a butler, Alfred Pennyworth is the Dark Knight's squire—expert helpmate in every field from sewing to shotguns. The BATMAN's career could never have happened without the assistance of Alfred, who keeps the Batcave in working order and maintains the public illusion that Bruce Wayne is nothing more than a billionaire playboy.

Born and raised in England, Alfred chose to follow his mother into the theater rather than become a butler for the Wayne family of Gotham City, a job that both his father and grandfather had performed with distinction. After stints as both a soldier and actor, Alfred prepared to marry a young woman, then had his heart broken when he learned she had not been faithful to him. Soon Alfred's father passed away, and Alfred chose to abandon the stage to fulfill his father's obligation to Thomas and Martha Wayne as their family butler.

Later, Thomas and Martha fell victim to a mugger. Alfred and physician Leslie Thompkins (see THOMPKINS, LESLIE M.D.) raised the Waynes' young son, Bruce, in Wayne Manor after a maze of paperwork shielded the case from the influence of Gotham Child Services. When an adult Bruce decided to become the vigilante Batman, Alfred became an aide to him and the subsequent string of Robins (see ROBIN): Dick Grayson, Jason Todd, and Tim Drake.

Alfred briefly left Batman's service but soon returned after trips to Antarctica and England. Since then he has survived the destruction of Wayne Manor during a cataclysmic earthquake that turned Gotham City into a lawless No Man's Land and his own near-fatal bout with the Clench virus. Because he knew Bruce as a boy, Alfred is perhaps the only person in the world utterly unfazed by Batman's grim façade. **DW**

PEOPLE'S HEROES, THE

FIRST APPEARANCE OUTSIDERS (1st series) #10 (August 1986)
STATUS Villain group (disbanded) **BASE** The Russian Federation
MEMBERS AND POWERS
Bolshoi A formidable martial artist and superspeedster.
Hammer Possesses superhuman strength and wields a hammer.
Molotov Has an explosive touch.
Pravda Possesses psychic powers.
Sickle A martial artist, her signature weapon is a razor-sharp sickle.

COMMUNIST AVENGERS Before disbanding, the People's Heroes were Russia's most patriotic superteam. They are 1) Bolshoi 2) Pravda 3) Molotov 4) Hammer 5) Sickle.

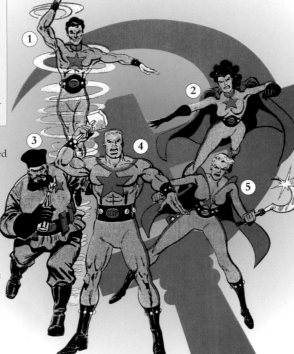

The People's Heroes were a group of superhuman agents created by Communist scientists using information learned through scientific analysis of the U.S. super-team, The Force of July. The People's Heroes were assigned to the Russian secret service and battled the U.S. OUTSIDERS twice to a standstill. The People's Heroes later came into conflict with the SUICIDE SQUAD during a kidnapping mission. The Squad squarely defeated the Heroes, leaving Pravda for dead.

After a failed attempt by HAMMER AND SICKLE to execute RED STAR, another Russian hero, on behalf of an extreme faction of the Russian government, the People's Heroes were disbanded. However, Molotov and Bolshoi were recruited by the Red Shadows, the Russian counterpart of the Suicide Squad. **PJ**

PERIL, JOHNNY

FIRST APPEARANCE COMIC CAVALCADE #22 (September 1947)
STATUS Hero **REAL NAME** Unknown
OCCUPATION Private investigator **BASE** Unnamed Midwestern city
HEIGHT 6ft 2in **WEIGHT** 195 lbs **EYES** Blue **HAIR** Blond
SPECIAL POWERS/ABILITIES Above-average hand-to-hand fighter; quick-witted and good with a gun.

Johnny Peril's past is a mystery to all who know him. His name, synonymous with adventure and intrigue, is almost certainly an alias. He has been a reporter, a soldier-of-fortune, or a troubleshooter, taking on any high-risk job where more than money is at stake. Johnny is certainly well-traveled. However, despite his apparent addiction to adventure, Johnny isn't afraid to admit a longing for a nice, normal case every once in a while. That's why he currently makes his home in a mundane, Middle American city, having set himself up as a private investigator. He is frequently aided by psychic Heather Storm, in whom Johnny has shown more than a professional interest. **SB**

PERKINS, NEPTUNE

FIRST APPEARANCE FLASH COMICS #166 (September 1945)
STATUS Hero *REAL NAME* Neptune Perkins
OCCUPATION Senator and author *BASE* Mobile
HEIGHT 6ft *WEIGHT* 187 lbs *EYES* Blue *HAIR* Black
SPECIAL POWERS/ABILITIES Amphibious and has webbed hands and feet, allowing him to swim as fast as a swordfish or dolphin; requires constant exposure to salt water for survival; fair-minded politician and accomplished author.

In 1922, Neptune Perkins was born a mutant with webbed hands and feet and a sodium salt deficiency, the result of being conceived in the light of a Vril-powered device. He grew up spending most of the time in the sea, and later became a costumed adventurer as part of the YOUNG ALL-STARS. On one such mission he fought a young Japanese girl named TSUNAMI. when she attacked a naval base. They subsequently fell in love. At one point, Perkins was being held against his will by gangsters. HAWKMAN I traveled to California and rescued him. The heroes prevented the thugs from using Perkins's houseboat as an escape craft following their crime spree, but the vessel was destroyed in the process. Eventually, Perkins retired from crimefighting and became a successful author and a senator. He and Tsunami were married and had a child, the adventurer known as Deep Blue. **RG**

PERUN

FIRST APPEARANCE FIRESTORM #72 (June 1988)
STATUS Hero *REAL NAME* Ilya Trepliov
OCCUPATION Hero *BASE* Russian Federation
HEIGHT 6ft *WEIGHT* 165 lbs *EYES* Brown *HAIR* Black
SPECIAL POWERS/ABILITIES Able to mentally control electricity within several hundred feet of himself, channeling this energy any way that he chooses.

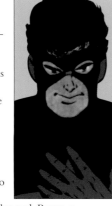

Perun is a member of SOYUZ, a group of young adventurers in Russia and one of the only super-human teams not accountable to the Russian government. Soyuz was vigorously pursued by various Russian agencies, including the K.G.B., while their activities were recorded. After Soyuz's heroic defense of Russia during an invasion by aliens, the Russian government chose to back down from their pursuit of Soyuz and allowed the youngsters freedom to act independently.

Named after the Russian thunder god, Perun, a determined young man, began his heroic career at the young age of 17, defending the rights of innocent people throughout Russia. Along with his Soyuz teammates, Perun most recently fought the terrible forces of the alien invader IMPERIEX. **PJ**

PHANTASM

FIRST APPEARANCE NEW TITANS (1st series) #73 (February 1991)
STATUS Hero (seemingly destroyed) *REAL NAME* Inapplicable
OCCUPATION Wraith *BASE* Mobile
HEIGHT None *WEIGHT* None *EYES* None *HAIR* None
SPECIAL POWERS/ABILITIES Empathic and telekinetic of staggering power; a being composed of more than a thousand souls.

During the so-called "Titans Hunt," when several TEEN TITANS were brutally murdered by the bizarre WILDEBEEST Society, young telekinetic Danny Chase faked his own demise during a Wildebeest-instigated melee at a Washington, D.C. shopping mall. From several stores, Danny then secretly assembled various items—a bolt of cloth, a hockey mask, and an electronic voice modulator—and created a costumed secret identity, the wraith-like Phantasm. Thus disguised, Danny secretly aided the Titans' leader NIGHTWING, who had infiltrated the Wildebeest Society and learned that the 'beests were possessed by disembodied Azarathian souls (*see* RAVEN). During the final conflict with the Wildebeests, Danny linked his own burgeoning powers to the Titans' Raven and her mother, Arella, to cleanse the tainted Azarathians that had taken over fellow member JERICHO and used him to control the Wildebeest Society. Danny and Arella died, but their essences merged with the freed Azarathians to create a new and more powerful Phantasm that continued to be an ally of the Titans. Phantasm was seemingly destroyed sometime later while attempting to contain the evil essence of a resurrected Raven. **SB**

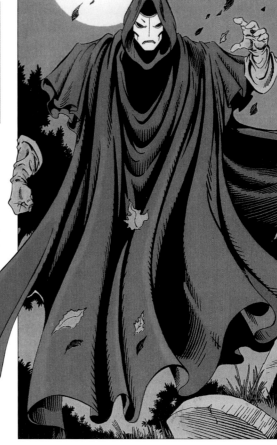

SPOOKED *Phantasm became a real wraith when Danny died and merged with the souls of Arella and her fellow Azarathians.*

PHANTASMO

FIRST APPEARANCE YOUNG ALL-STARS #22 (January 1989)
STATUS Hero *REAL NAME* Jean-Marc de Villars
OCCUPATION Adventurer *BASE* England
HEIGHT 5ft 9in *WEIGHT* 168 lbs
EYES Blue *HAIR* Black
SPECIAL POWERS/ABILITIES Could become intangible and seemed impervious to most organic objects.

Phantasmo was Jean-Marc de Villars, a Frenchman and the son of a human and an Earth elemental spirit. He had the superhuman ability to make himself intangible and an invulnerability to "Earth substances" such as common metals. Phantasmo was a member of the Young Allies, a team of international young heroes who banded together to oppose the Nazis during World War II, and once cooperated with the American Young All-Stars. Phantasmo has not been seen since 1942. but post-War activities have been hinted at. **RG**

DIVIDED SOUL *Phantasmo is actually a human and elemental spirit sharing a body, forging an uneasy alliance.*

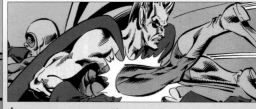

JUST PASSING THROUGH *Phantasmo was an especially effective crime fighter because adversaries' attacks failed to make contact with him.*

PHANTOM OF THE FAIR

FIRST APPEARANCE SECRET ORIGINS (2nd series) #7 (December 1986)
STATUS Hero **REAL NAME** Unknown
OCCUPATION Criminal **BASE** New York World's Fair
HEIGHT Unknown **WEIGHT** Unknown
EYES Unknown **HAIR** Unknown
SPECIAL POWERS/ABILITIES Superstrength, partial invulnerability, and enhanced agility. Apparently possesses acrobatic training and talents in the areas of stealth and camouflage.

The brief career of the Phantom of the Fair remains an enigma. On April 30, 1939, the opening day of the New York World's Fair, a masked figure swooped down on Mayor LaGuardia during the opening ceremonies. Seizing the mic, the Phantom declared: "Men and women of New York City—this World's Fair is now declared officially haunted by the Phantom of the Fair!"

LaGuardia refused to close the fair, and on June 10, New York welcomed King George VI and Queen Elizabeth of Britain. To protect them from the Phantom during their visit to the World's Fair, wealthy socialite Wesley Dodds assumed the crime-fighting identity of the SANDMAN I for the first time. The Phantom attacked the king and queen using the giant World's Fair robot Elektro, but the Sandman and the CRIMSON AVENGER I drove off the Phantom. This was arguably the first super hero conflict of the Golden Age of heroism. **DW**

PHANTOM STRANGER, THE

FIRST APPEARANCE THE PHANTOM STRANGER (1st series) #1 (September 1952) **STATUS** Hero **REAL NAME** Unknown
OCCUPATION Conscience; advocate **BASE** Mobile
HEIGHT 6ft 2in **WEIGHT** 185 lbs **EYES** White **HAIR** White
SPECIAL POWERS/ABILITIES Powers and abilities defy classification; in the past, the Phantom Stranger demonstrated teleportation, control over natural forces, and manipulation of supernatural energies.

LOST SOUL Like a Good Samaritan, the Phantom Stranger roams the world, helping those in need.

The Phantom Stranger's origin is a mystery. Some believe him to be a fallen angel forced to walk the Earth and help those in need as atonement for some great sin. The Phantom Stranger admits that he serves the cause of Order in its eternal conflict to keep Chaos in check. Whenever someone is troubled by a spiritual or moral dilemma—all too often caused by supernatural forces—the Phantom Stranger will offer counsel. Many times, the Stranger will wield his own considerable mystical powers to defend the defenseless. The Stranger is a loner, although he has counted as friends both Bruce Gordon, the scientist once possessed by the evil ECLIPSO, and Cassandra Craft, a blind woman with latent magical talent who once helped the Stranger to regain his powers and fell in love with him. Unfortunately, the Stranger could not return such feelings. The Phantom Stranger has aided the JUSTICE LEAGUE OF AMERICA and was offered membership many times, but has simply spirited away rather than refuse. However, he does belong to the Quintessence, a quintet of immortals who watch over humanity. **SB**

PHANTOM LADY I & II

FIRST APPEARANCE (I) POLICE COMICS #1 (August 1941); (II) ACTION COMICS WEEKLY #636 (Jan. 1989) **STATUS** Hero **REAL NAME** (I) Sandra Knight; (II) Delilah "Dee" Tyler **OCCUPATION** (I) Debutante; (II) TV Station employee **BASE** (I, II) Washington, D.C. **HEIGHT** (I) 5'6"; (II) 5'8" **WEIGHT** (I) 140 lbs; (II) 143 lbs **EYES** (I) Blue; (II) Brown **HAIR** (I, II) Black **SPECIAL POWERS/ABILITIES** (I) Blackout ray wrist device; (II) bracelet-mounted taser, costume circuitry defeats electronic surveillance, can project holograms of herself.

In 1939, Sandra Knight foiled the kidnap of her father, a U.S. Senator, on the steps of the Capitol Building. Scientist Abraham Davis was so impressed by her bravery he gave her a special device, a black light projector; Sandra became the crime fighter Phantom Lady.

Phantom Lady joined the ALL-STAR SQUADRON, then the FREEDOM FIGHTERS, and the government agency ARGENT I. Decades later, she opened a finishing school, the Université Notre Dame des Ombres, in Paris. Dee Tyler, daughter of the Attorney General, graduated from the Université, and returned to Washington for a political and television career. To save her father from being blackmailed by the crime cartel, Les Mille Yeux, Dee became the new Phantom Lady. Dee uses her government and media connections to fight crime in Washington. **PJ**

PHOBIA

FIRST APPEARANCE THE NEW TEEN TITANS (1st series) #14 (December 1981) **STATUS** Villain **REAL NAME** Angela Hawkins III
OCCUPATION Assassin **BASE** Mobile
HEIGHT 5ft 11in **WEIGHT** 151 lbs **EYES** Green **HAIR** Black
SPECIAL POWERS/ABILITIES Psychic ability to incapacitate her enemies by conjuring their greatest fears.

Born into the British aristocracy, blue-blooded Angela Hawkins III discovered at an early age that she possessed the psychic ability to detect the fears of others. She also found she could project those fears with nightmarish intensity. This knowledge made her cold-hearted and power-hungry. She gladly accepted an offer extended by the BRAIN and MONSIEUR MALLAH to join the New Brotherhood of Evil. Now calling herself Phobia, she helped the Brotherhood take their revenge on MADAME ROUGE, and remained with the group after its transition into the SOCIETY OF SIN. She often found herself battling the TEEN TITANS. During the Crisis (see Great Battles, pp. 320–1), Phobia nearly became the emotion-manipulating agent of the Anti-Monitor (see MONITOR), who elected to spare Phobia in favor of a different stooge. Some time later, the empath RAVEN helped excise Phobia's inner demons and childhood fears of her father, Lord Hawkins. However, she returned to her criminal ways alongside the Society of Sin, and was recently seen battling YOUNG JUSTICE on the island nation of Zandia. **DW**

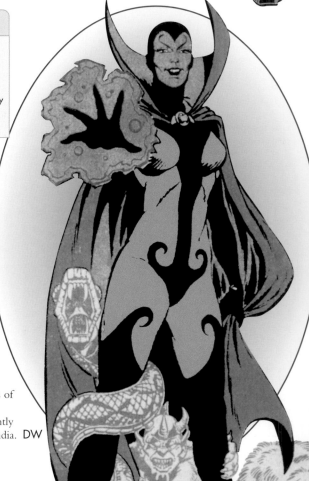

PHOBOS

FIRST APPEARANCE WONDER WOMAN (2nd series) #2 (March 1987)
STATUS Villain **REAL NAME** Phobos
OCCUPATION God of Fear **BASE** The Netherworld
HEIGHT 7ft 7in **WEIGHT** 459 lbs **EYES** Red **HAIR** Flaming red
SPECIAL POWERS/ABILITIES Invulnerability of the gods; possesses the power to physically manifest the darkest fears of his enemies; immortal; generates gouts of infernal fire from the netherworld.

Greek God of Fear, Phobos is the son of ARES and Aphrodite, and shares cruel power with his brother Deimos (God of Terror) and sister Eris (Goddess of Strife). As part of Ares's plan to dominate the Earth, Phobos pitted himself against WONDER WOMAN. He released the gorgon Decay until Wonder Woman pursued them into the Netherworld. She decapitated Deimos and Phobos fled. Deimos was resurrected by Phobos and his soul placed in the JOKER's body. Phobos, Deimos, and Eris caused havoc in Gotham City by possessing SCARECROW, the Joker, and POISON IVY until Wonder Woman and BATMAN defeated them. Phobos, deemed a failure by his angry father Ares, was chained to a giant wheel in Hades. **DW**

PLANETEERS, THE

FIRST APPEARANCE ACTION COMICS #127 (December 1948)
STATUS Hero team (disbanded) **BASE** Earth
NOTABLE MEMBERS AND POWERS
General Horatio Tomorrow Superior marksman, pilot, and tactician.
Colonel Tommy Tomorrow Ace pilot, good fighter, and crack shot.
Brent Wood Marksman, navigator, and co-pilot.

In the 22nd century, Earth and its colonies throughout the solar system and beyond were protected by the Space Planeteers. These officers of peace patrolled the spacelanes, ensuring people and supplies flowed smoothly between worlds. When Earth or its colonies were threatened, the Planeteers acted as the first line of defense. It was the Planeteers who stopped evil scientist Rotwang and his robot MEKANIQUE in addition to a race of aquatic aliens who attempted to plunder Earth's resources. Among its great leaders was General Horatio Tomorrow, who worked out of Planeteer headquarters on Earth. One day, Horatio found a young boy at Headquarters Bunker D Horatio took the boy in, named him Thomas, and raised him. In time the lad joined the Planeteers, rising to the rank of Colonel. Along with his best friend, Brent Wood, TOMMY TOMORROW protected humanity aboard his patrol craft, *The Ace of Space*. When the Planeteers ceased to exist and what replaced them has yet to be recorded. **RG**

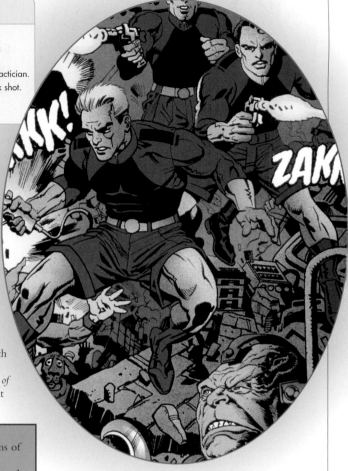

PIED PIPER

FIRST APPEARANCE THE FLASH (1st series) #106 (May 1959)
STATUS Hero (reformed villain) **REAL NAME** Hartley Rathaway
OCCUPATION Social activist **BASE** Central City
HEIGHT 5ft 10in **WEIGHT** 158 lbs **EYES** Blue **HAIR** Reddish-blond
SPECIAL POWERS/ABILITIES An expert in the science of sound who uses various pipes and technological devices to generate destructive sonic blasts or hypnotize others.

Hartley Rathaway's wealthy family spent millions of dollars on scientific experiments to restore his hearing. When Hartley's condition was finally cured, he became obsessed with sound and music. Emotionally distant and unstable, Hartley began experimenting with devices that manipulated sound, using the vast family fortune to buy the most advanced technology. Bored with his world of easy wealth, Hartley became a criminal called the Pied Piper, using his sonic pipes to commit spectacular crimes. He became a constant foe of Barry Allen, the second FLASH.

Soon after the Flash's death, however, the Pied Piper retired from crime and dedicated his life to social service. Openly gay, the Piper became an activist both for gay rights and Central City's homeless. He briefly teamed up with a group of local heroes to arrange meals for Central City's needy, and befriended Wally West, the third Flash.

The Pied Piper was framed for the murder of his parents and driven crazy in prison. The insane Piper then allied himself with the first Trickster (see TRICKSTER II). **PJ**

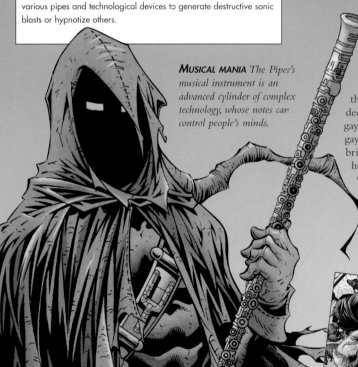

MUSICAL MANIA *The Piper's musical instrument is an advanced cylinder of complex technology, whose notes can control people's minds.*

PLASMUS

FIRST APPEARANCE THE NEW TEEN TITANS (1st series) #14 (December 1981)
STATUS Villain **REAL NAME** Otto Von Furth
OCCUPATION Criminal **BASE** Europe
HEIGHT 6ft 4in **WEIGHT** Unknown **EYES** Gray **HAIR** None
SPECIAL POWERS/ABILITIES Plasmus's touch brings fiery death and reduces living creatures to burning protoplasm.

While excavating deadly radium, miner Otto Von Furth was trapped in a cave-in for seven days. During this time he was exposed to lethal levels of radiation, which killed his co-workers and left Von Furth highly radioactive. While recovering in hospital, Von Furth was kidnapped by ex-Nazi scientist GENERAL ZAHL, whose cruel experiments mutated the mineworker into a blob-like, protoplasmic monster with a deadly, disintegrating touch.

Dubbed "Plasmus," Von Furth joined Zahl in a villainous team known as the Brotherhood of Evil, opposing the TEEN TITANS. Plasmus also belonged to the Brotherhood's successor team, the SOCIETY OF SIN. He and his terrible teammates remain an ever-present menace. **SB**

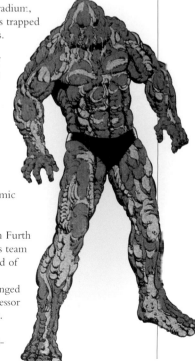

PLASTIC MAN

THE PLIABLE PRANKSTER

FIRST APPEARANCE POLICE COMICS #1 (August 1941)
STATUS Hero **REAL NAME** Eel O'Brian
OCCUPATION Adventurer **BASE** Chicago
HEIGHT 6ft 1in **WEIGHT** 178 lbs **EYES** Groovy goggles
HAIR Black **SPECIAL POWERS/ABILITIES** Capable of stretching every atom in his body into any shape he wishes. He is seemingly unbreakable and his shape-changing is limited only by his own overactive imagination; also has a mercurial sense of humor.

EEL O'BRIAN STARTED OUT on the wrong side of the law, but is working hard to make up for it. In 1941, he was just a lowlife gangster. Shot by a guard at the Crawford Chemical Works, he stumbled into a vat of acid, which seeped into his wounds. He escaped and ended up at Rest Haven, a spiritual retreat. While there, he realized that amazing changes in his human form would also allow him to change his ways. He became the hero Plastic Man.

LUCKY BREAK Eel O'Brian's life changed for the better when he ought to have died in the accident.

YOUR FLEXIBLE FRIEND

After serving in both the ALL-STAR SQUADRON and the FREEDOM FIGHTERS with distinction during World War II, Plastic Man was employed by the F.B.I. and then its sister agency, the National Bureau of Investigations. To this day, he continues to handle cases for the N.B.I., usually paired with the sloppy, lazy, and dull-witted Woozy Winks. These two improbable partners have an impressive track record. Together they have brought down numerous villains, including, the Dart, Even Steven, and the Brotherhood of the Savage Caribou.

In more recent times, Plastic Man has successfully worked alongside BATMAN on several cases, despite their strikingly different temperaments. In fact, the Dark Knight recommended Plas for membership for the JUSTICE LEAGUE OF AMERICA. Plastic Man has served the League well, despite his tendency to joke about everything.

BUGGED OUT Queen Bee manages to get the drop on Plastic Man, a rare occurrence.

Batman also learned that Plas had a son, born out of wedlock. Eel's son grew up to inherit his father's incredible "plastic man" abilities, although with greater control. Plastic Man's seeming death in the Obsidian Age, 3,000 years ago, left the JLA traumatized. Reduced to atoms, he spent the next three millennia using his conscious mind to reassemble himself. Those millennia of isolation have had a profound affect on him, and O'Brian has rededicated himself to playing a positive role in his son's life, virtually forgetting his heroic persona in favor of becoming a daily presence. When a demon from Mars's ancient past emerged on Earth, Batman forced Plastic Man to once again be a hero. Eel remains an occasional hero, a pal to Woozy Winks and a full-time father. RG

KEY STORYLINES

• **PLASTIC MAN (3RD SERIES) #1–6 (FEBRUARY–JULY 2004):** Plastic Man and Woozy Winks in one of their most madcap adventures yet.
• **JLA #65 (AUGUST 2002):** Plastic Man reconnects with his son, thanks to Batman.
• **PLASTIC MAN (3RD SERIES) #1-4 (NOVEMBER–FEBRUARY 1988-89):** Plas and Woozy face the incredibly inept Ooze Brothers.
• **POLICE COMICS #1 (AUGUST 1941):** Eel O'Brian turns from petty criminal to costumed crime fighter, thanks to a freak accident.

FIRED UP Plastic Man had to return to action in order to save the U.S. from the fiery Fernus, an ancient Martian threat.

PLASTIC SOLUTION Batman shows the still reassembling Plastic Man—after 3,000 years—to the JLA.

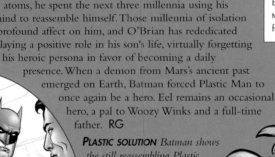

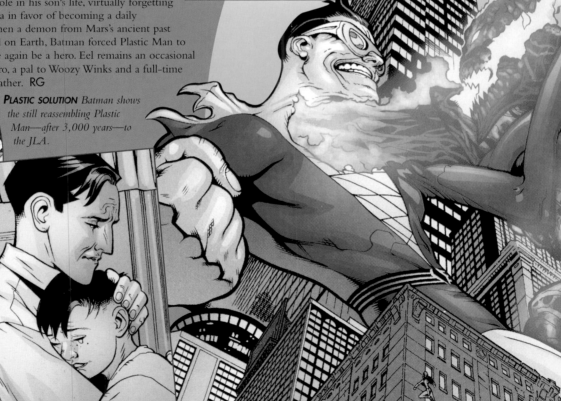

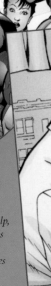

FATHER AND SON
It took Batman to help, but Eel has rebuilt his relationship with his son, who also possesses his father's incredible stretching power.

PLASTIQUE

FIRST APPEARANCE FURY OF FIRESTORM #7 (December 1982)
STATUS Reformed villain **REAL NAME** Bette Sans Souci
OCCUPATION Former terrorist **BASE** Quebec, Canada
HEIGHT 5ft 6in **WEIGHT** 141 lbs **EYES** Blue **HAIR** Red
SPECIAL POWERS/ABILITIES Is able to cause objects to explode by
touching them with her fingertips. A demolitions expert, Plastique
has received training in urban terrorism and possesses an
incendiary temper.

Plastique was a radical French-
Canadian terrorist committed to
winning Quebec's independence
by any means necessary. Originally
she possessed no superpowers, and
so she wore a suit rigged with
plastic explosives into the offices
of the *New York News Express* in an
attempt to extort the newspaper's
owners.

FIRESTORM, THE NUCLEAR MAN
foiled her incendiary plot and sent
her to prison, but behind bars
Plastique received an injection of an
experimental serum that gave her the
ability to explode objects by
touching them. A second criminal
caper teamed Plastique with KILLER FROST II in a failed
attempt to blow up the Niagara Falls power plant.

Plastique became semi-reformed when offered the
opportunity to work with the SUICIDE SQUAD in exchange
for a commuted sentence. Since then, she has changed her
criminal ways and hooked up with CAPTAIN ATOM,
eventually becoming his wife. Perhaps affected by Captain
Atom's apparent death, Plastique has largely dropped out
of sight. **DW**

PLUNDER

FIRST APPEARANCE FLASH (2nd series) #165 (October 2000)
STATUS Villain **REAL NAME** None; a mirror clone of Jared Morillo
OCCUPATION Bounty hunter **BASE** A mirror image dimension
HEIGHT 5ft 11in **WEIGHT** 190 lbs **EYES** White **HAIR** None
SPECIAL POWERS/ABILITIES Plunder is an expert hitman renowned
for his unerring aim; he also possesses numerous handguns
and other firearms in his armor; a powerful, if unsophisticated,
hand-to-hand combatant.

Plunder was a bounty hunter that
existed in a mystical "mirror
world" housed within the
diamond wedding ring of Linda
Park (*see* PARK, LINDA), the wife of
Wally West, the third FLASH.
A mercenary for the mirror
world's Thinker, Plunder
discovered that his dimension was
fading into non-existence, and hoped
to escape into our world. The
Thinker hired Plunder to
capture two of the Flash's
Rogues Gallery, MIRROR
MASTER and CAPTAIN COLD,
to lure the Flash into their
mirror dimension. The Flash
escaped the Thinker's trap and returned to our dimension.
Plunder is the mirror image of Detective Jared Morillo,
a Flash ally from the Department of Meta-human
Hostility. Plunder shot Morillo, assumed his form, and
briefly took his place. Discovered, Plunder forsook
Morillo's identity and resumed bounty hunting. **PJ**

POISON IVY

FIRST APPEARANCE BATMAN #181 (June 1966)
STATUS Villain **REAL NAME** Pamela Lillian Isley
OCCUPATION Criminal; eco-terrorist **BASE** Gotham City
HEIGHT 5ft 6in **WEIGHT** 133 lbs **EYES** Green **HAIR** Chestnut
SPECIAL POWERS/ABILITIES Poison Ivy's altered body chemistry enables
her to exude a venomous variety of floral toxins to which she alone is
immune; carries with her a plethora of pernicious plants that
germinate from fast-growing seed pods.

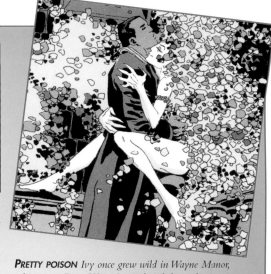

Botanist Pamela Isley was a shrinking violet when she
went to work for famed scientist (and super-villain-in-the-
making) Dr. Jason Woodrue. The future FLORONIC MAN
experimented on her, hoping to create a human/plant
hybrid like himself. Woodrue succeeded all too well,
creating the ravishing-but-deadly Poison Ivy. Where Isley
was gangly and unremarkable, Ivy was gorgeous and
unforgettable. Isley's porcelain skin soon took on a green
pigmentation as chlorophyll replaced her human blood. Ivy
even exuded man-maddening pheromones and natural
toxins. She was Poison Ivy in more than name.

Ironically, the sun-loving Ivy found herself drawn
to gloomy Gotham City, where she sowed the
seeds of a criminal career to fund her
true cause as a green guerrilla
championing the world's
diminishing fauna. Ivy also
discovered a worthy foe in
BATMAN, who has resisted
Ivy's fragrant charms
while uprooting her
terrorist schemes.
As time passes, Ivy
becomes more
plant-like and less
human, making
her increasingly
difficult to
defoliate. **SB**

GREENBACKS *Poison Ivy
loves the color of money,
especially because robbery and
extortion help to fund her exotic
environmental causes.*

PRETTY POISON *Ivy once grew wild in Wayne Manor,
taking over Bruce Wayne's mind with her seductive
pheromones. Little did Ivy know
that she had Batman
in her thrall!*

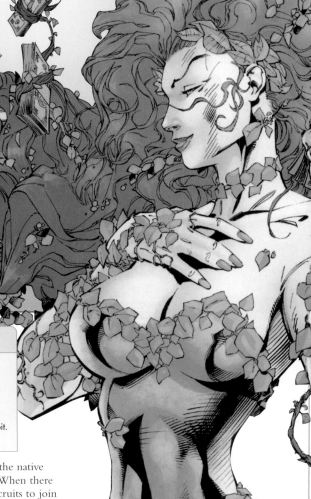

POLAR BOY

FIRST APPEARANCE LEGIONNAIRES #43 (December 1996)
STATUS Hero **REAL NAME** Brek Bannin
OCCUPATION Adventurer **BASE** Earth
HEIGHT 5ft 5in **WEIGHT** 140 lbs **EYES** Blue **HAIR** Blond
SPECIAL POWERS/ABILITIES Like all natives of Tharr, can generate
subzero temperatures as a natural defense against a near-sun orbit.

Tharr's Brek Bannin has the native
power to generate cold. When there
was an open call for recruits to join
the LEGION OF SUPER-HEROES,
Bannin was among the first to
apply. He failed the tests but
decided to team up with
other rejects as the LEGION OF SUBSTITUTE
HEROES. They were called into action when R.J.
Brande (*see* BRANDE, R.J.) summoned their help
during one of the DARK LORD Mordru's attempts to
conquer the universe. Polar Boy admitted they weren't
ready at the time, but has since acted as team leader,
hoping for the day he graduates to the real Legion. **RG**

POWER COMPANY

First appearance JLA #61 (February 2002)
Status Hero team *Base* San Francisco
Current Members and Powers
Josiah Power (managing partner) Can turn into a rock form.
Skyrocket (partner) Argo Harness lets her channel and control energy.
Manhunter (partner) Clone of Manhunter Paul Kirk; skilled combatant.
Witchfire (partner) Possesses occult conjuring abilities.
Striker Z (associate) Living battery able to power his high-tech gear.
Bork (associate) Possesses mystically-granted invulnerability.
Sapphire (associate) Alien "gem coating" can create armor, shielding, and weapons.
Jennifer Elizabeth Barbara Stuart Pilots high-tech Haunted Tank.

Billing itself as "the world's foremost supplier of professional superhuman services," The Power Company is a super-hero corporation run like a law firm and designed to make a profit. Although founder Josiah Power encourages *pro bono* work for good causes, high-paying clients often retain the Power Company for security, recovery, or investigative missions.

Josiah Power drew upon his past history as a lawyer to structure the Power Company into partners and associates. His early partners included MANHUNTER, WITCHFIRE, and SKYROCKET, the local hero of St. Louis. Associates included ex-villain Bork, the stuntman STRIKER Z, and the runaway called Sapphire.

During the time when Josiah Power lay in a coma from a gunshot wound, the other team members brought aboard FIRESTORM, THE NUCLEAR MAN as a temporary associate. Garrison Slate, the CEO of S.T.A.R. Labs, took over as interim administrator. Though Firestorm left the team, they gained new help from Jennifer Stuart and her HAUNTED TANK during the battle against the Dragoneer. Josiah Power has since returned to full health and the Power Company is actively seeking new clients. Few other super hero teams have as deep an understanding of the business market, and it appears that the Power Company is primed to make a killing. They can only hope that super-villain gangs don't follow their lead and begin marketing themselves as corporations. DW

FURY FORCE
1) Striker Z 2) Bork
3) Josiah Power 4) Witchfire
5) Manhunter 6) Sapphire
7) Skyrocket

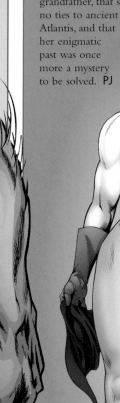

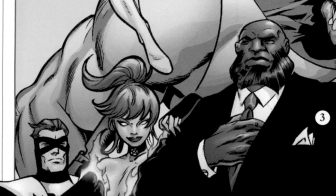

POWER GIRL

First appearance ALL-STAR COMICS #58 (February 1976)
Status Hero *Real name* Karen "Kara" Starr
Occupation Software designer; adventurer
Base Los Angeles; New York City
Height 5ft 7in *Weight* 160 lbs
Eyes Blue *Hair* Light blonde
Special powers/abilities Incredible superstrength, superspeed, near invulnerability, flight.

Almost a decade ago, Kara emerged from a mysterious ship that had crash-landed on Earth. Possessing incredible powers similar to SUPERMAN's, Kara was taken in as a kind of protégée by the Man of Steel, who then introduced her to the JUSTICE SOCIETY OF AMERICA. The headstrong young woman became Power Girl, and, after establishing a successful software development firm, briefly joined INFINITY, INC. Kara was then contacted by the spirit of ARION, LORD OF ATLANTIS, who told her that she was his granddaughter, sent thousands of years into the future to save her from her brother Garn (see DAANUTH, GARN). Upset by this news, Kara handed over control of her company to Felicity Raymond, FIRESTORM, THE NUCLEAR MAN's stepmother, and briefly joined Justice League Europe (see JUSTICE LEAGUE OF AMERICA).

Kara subsequently joined the latest incarnation of the Justice Society, where the fiercely independent Power Girl learned that Arion was not her grandfather, that she had no ties to ancient Atlantis, and that her enigmatic past was once more a mystery to be solved. PJ

BRAINS AND BRAWN *Power Girl's physical strength is matched by her aggressive personality.*

POW-WOW SMITH

FIRST APPEARANCE WESTERN COMICS #44 (April 1954)
STATUS Hero **REAL NAME** Ohiyesa
OCCUPATION Legionnaire **BASE** Elkhorn
HEIGHT 6ft 2in **WEIGHT** 190 lbs **EYES** Black **HAIR** Black
SPECIAL POWERS/ABILITIES Ohiyesa turned out to be a clever man, quickly mastering the white man's ways, becoming a crack shot and a fine detective.

Sioux brave Ohiyesa left his tribe in Red Deer Valley to learn the ways of the white man in the late 1880s. He became a small-town sheriff nicknamed Pow-Wow Smith because of his native American heritage, and clashed with various rogues, including the Fadeaway Outlaw, an escape artist turned criminal who seemed to vanish after committing his crimes. He married his fellow Sioux tribemate Fleetfoot and his peace-keeping exploits earned him honorary U.S. citizenship. Despite his sterling record in law enforcement, the prejudiced townsfolk continued to shun him socially or turn on him, given the slightest provocation. Rather than react to this, Smith let his deeds speak for him.

A descendant of Ohiyesa's adopted the name Pow-Wow Smith, settled in Red Deer Valley, and become a noted private investigator during the late 1940s and 1950s. His son, also known as Ohiyesa, followed in the family tradition. In recent times, he helped ROBIN, HUNTRESS, NIGHTHAWK, and the local county's Sheriff Shotgun Smith bring the second incarnation of the TRIGGER TWINS to justice. **RG**

POZHAR

FIRST APPEARANCE FIRESTORM #62 (August 1987)
STATUS Hero (absorbed) **REAL NAME** Mikhail Arkadin
OCCUPATION Former super hero **BASE** Moscow
HEIGHT 6ft **WEIGHT** 190 lbs **EYES** Blue **HAIR** Black
SPECIAL POWERS/ABILITIES Flight; ability to control nuclear blasts, and immunity to radiation.

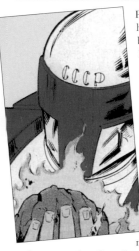

Pozhar was a Russian super hero who found a new life by becoming part of the complex history of FIRESTORM, THE NUCLEAR MAN. Exposure to a nuclear plant meltdown imbued Arkadin with atomic powers. Dubbed Pozhar by the Russian secret service, he agreed to battle Firestorm when the U.S. hero agreed to disarm the world's nuclear arsenal.

Fighting above the Nevada desert, Pozhar and Firestorm fused into a single entity when government agents fired a missile at them. This new version of Firestorm could only appear when Ron Raymond and Arkadin merged; the amnesiac mind of Martin Stein controlled this Firestorm.

Later, Raymond and Arkadin merged with the villainous Russian creation Svarozhich, then Firestorm split when Martin Stein turned Firestorm into a fire elemental. Mikhail Arkadin is now powerless. **DW**

PRANKSTER

FIRST APPEARANCE ACTION COMICS #51 (August 1942)
STATUS Villain **REAL NAME** Oswald Loomis
OCCUPATION Comedian; criminal **BASE** Metropolis
HEIGHT 5ft 9in **WEIGHT** 160 lbs **EYES** Blue **HAIR** Brown
SPECIAL POWERS/ABILITIES Weapons imbued with nanotechnology, include tear-gas squirt flowers, 3-D glasses, acid-spitting water gun.

Loomis was a successful television comedian and the host of "The Uncle Oswald Show," a children's morning show in Metropolis. When Morgan Edge, the station president, cancelled his show after 25 years, Lewis snapped and staged a number of bizarre and dangerous pranks throughout the city. Loomis kidnapped Lois Lane (see LANE, LOIS) and held her captive at his studio. When Edge tried to intervene, Loomis hurled him out of a trap door 30 stories above the streets of Metropolis.

SUPERMAN saved Edge and freed Lois before Loomis surrendered. Realizing that he could be in jail for life, the Prankster escaped his guards.

The Prankster returned several times, hoping to eliminate Edge, but each time he was captured and incarcerated by Superman. The villain later sold his soul to Lord SATANUS in exchange for an altered appearance. **PJ**

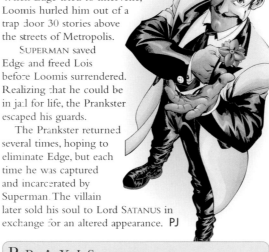

PRAXIS

FIRST APPEARANCE THE SPECTRE 2nd series #24 (February 1989)
STATUS Hero **REAL NAME** Jason Praxis
OCCUPATION Super hero; former police detective **BASE** Mobile
HEIGHT 7ft 7in **WEIGHT** 168 lbs **EYES** Blue **HAIR** Black
SPECIAL POWERS/ABILITIES Skilled, experienced detective; possesses telepathic and telekinetic control over electricity, including synaptic brain activity, allowing Praxis limited control over others' minds.

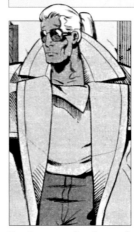

Portland police detective Jason Praxis acquired his meta-human ability to manipulate electricity after failing to prevent a serial killer from murdering his niece. Although the killer was subdued, the guilt-ridden Praxis left the police force and used his telepathy and telekinesis as a superpowered private investigator. Praxis was recruited by BOOSTER GOLD to join the short-lived corporate super-team the CONGLOMERATE. Later, Praxis returned to law enforcement, working alongside F.B.I. agent Deena Walker and preventing malevolent magician Dexter DeFarge from invoking Ghast, one of the devilish DEMONS THREE, and setting him loose on Earth. In mental combat with DeFarge, Praxis was able to transform himself into a being of pure mental energy. It is speculated that Praxis and his powers are related to the Lords of Order, ancient beings in eternal opposition to the Lords of Chaos for universal balance. Praxis continues to use his powers and skills in the cause of justice. **SB**

PREZ

FIRST APPEARANCE PREZ #1 (September 1973)
STATUS Hero **REAL NAME** Prez Rickard
OCCUPATION Ex-president of the U.S. **BASE** Steadfast
HEIGHT 5ft 7in **WEIGHT** 145 lbs **EYES** Blue **HAIR** Blond
SPECIAL POWERS/ABILITIES Possesses a sunny, enthusiastic, and optimistic outlook on life that makes people instinctively want to trust him.

A story that makes the rounds at the Inn Between Worlds concerns a teenager named Prez. When Congress changed the Constitution, lowering the minimum age of president from 35 to 18, Prez seized the opportunity to run. After Richard Nixon's time in the Oval Office, the disenchanted populace chose Prez, who served with distinction. His trusted friend, Eagle Free, became director of the F.B.I. Prez used the powers of his office to stop a new Cold War and preach a new breed of pacifism. A mentally disturbed girl shot and killed Prez's girlfriend and, feeling betrayed by the people, Prez withdrew from office and vanished from public life. A cautionary tale or fanciful yarn? Only the individual can judge. **RG**

PRIMAL FORCE

FIRST APPEARANCE PRIMAL FORCE #0 (October 1994)
STATUS Hero team **BASE** New York City
MEMBERS AND POWERS Red Tornado (controls weather); Claw (demonic claw); Golem (regenerative powers); Jack O'Lantern III (energy blasts); Meridian (teleports); Black Condor II (heightened senses); Nightmaster (Sword of Night); Willpower (living thunderbolt).

Also known as the Leymen, the short-lived supergroup Primal Force came into being following the time crisis of Zero Hour (see Great Battles, pp. 320–1). The order of the Leymen have defended Earth for over two thousand years against evil supernatural forces.

Armed with ley pendulums that augmented their natural powers in times of great stress, the new Leymen moved against villains such as Cataclysm, SATANUS, and the sinister cult called the August.

Primal Force disbanded after a confrontation with Cataclysm in New York's Central Park, though its members stand ready. JACK O'LANTERN III remembers a prophecy that foretold he would lead the team. **DW**

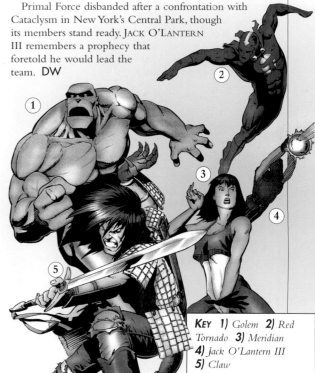

KEY 1) Golem **2)** Red Tornado **3)** Meridian **4)** Jack O'Lantern III **5)** Claw

PRINCE RA-MAN

FIRST APPEARANCE (Merlin) HOUSE OF SECRETS (1st series) #23 (August 1959); (Prince Ra-Man) HOUSE OF SECRETS #73 (August 1965)
STATUS Hero (dead) **REAL NAME** Mark Merlin **OCCUPATION** Occultist and adventurer **BASE** Mystery Hill Mansion, in the town of Cloister
HEIGHT (Merlin) 5ft 10in; (Prince Ra-Man) 6ft **WEIGHT** (Merlin) 157 lbs; (Prince Ra-Man) 178 lbs **EYES** (both) Blue **HAIR** (Merlin) Brown; (Prince Ra-Man) black
SPECIAL POWERS/ABILITIES Sorcery; illusion casting; invisibility; mental transference into his cat, Memakata; telekinetic powers projected as a beam from his forehead; matter transmutation.

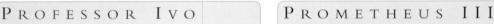

College student Mark Merlin was investigating the death of his uncle, a stage magician, who was killed for revealing the secrets of fake magicians. Exposing a group called the Council of Three as the murderers, Mark became an occult specialist and began investigating magical impostors as his uncle once had.

Mark was transported to the otherdimensional world of Ra, where several ancient Egyptians lived as immortals. There, Merlin gained various mental abilities and returned to Earth reincarnated in the body of an ancient Egyptian prince. Calling himself Prince Ra-Man, Merlin battled various mystical threats but died when the Anti-Monitor, a nihilist from the Anti-Matter Universe, invaded Earth (see Great Battles, pp. 320–1). He left behind his shattered fiancée, Elsa. **PJ**

PROFESSOR IVO

FIRST APPEARANCE THE BRAVE AND THE BOLD #30 (July 1960)
STATUS Villain **REAL NAME** Anthony Ivo (alias Professor Ives)
OCCUPATION Occultist and adventurer **BASE** Mobile
HEIGHT 5ft 10in **WEIGHT** 165 lbs **EYES** Blue **HAIR** Black
SPECIAL POWERS/ABILITIES Scientific genius; experiments to extend his lifespan have left Ivo deformed and long-lived, but not immortal.

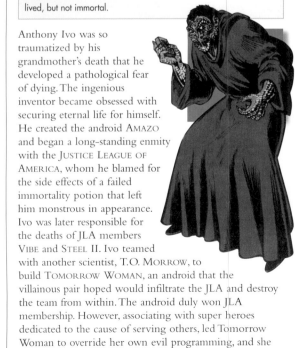

Anthony Ivo was so traumatized by his grandmother's death that he developed a pathological fear of dying. The ingenious inventor became obsessed with securing eternal life for himself. He created the android AMAZO and began a long-standing enmity with the JUSTICE LEAGUE OF AMERICA, whom he blamed for the side effects of a failed immortality potion that left him monstrous in appearance. Ivo was later responsible for the deaths of JLA members VIBE and STEEL II. Ivo teamed with another scientist, T.O. MORROW, to build TOMORROW WOMAN, an android that the villainous pair hoped would infiltrate the JLA and destroy the team from within. The android duly won JLA membership. However, associating with super heroes dedicated to the cause of serving others, led Tomorrow Woman to override her own evil programming, and she saved Earth and her teammates from IF, a time-lost weapon from the 23rd century. Nevertheless, as long as he lives, Professor Ivo poses a serious threat to the JLA. **SB**

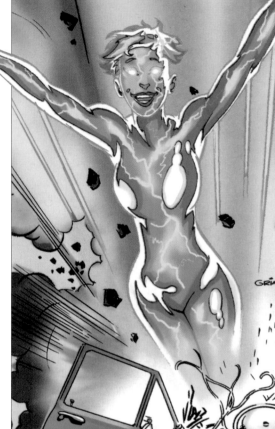

ONLY THE LONELY *"A girl without a home, a lost soul," Prysm found a friend in another alienated heroine, Supergirl.*

PROMETHEUS III

FIRST APPEARANCE PROMETHEUS #1 (December 1997)
STATUS Villain **REAL NAME** Unrevealed
OCCUPATION Hero hunter **BASE** The Ghost Zone
HEIGHT 6ft 1in **WEIGHT** 180 lbs **EYES** Brown
HAIR White **SPECIAL POWERS/ABILITIES** Brilliant designer of advanced technology and a highly skilled athlete; unique armor is laced with synaptic relays to enhance his fighting prowess; nightstick can shatter steel and override shielded electronic systems.

The first Prometheus stole fire from the OLYMPIAN GODS and brought it to Earth. The first mortal to use the name belonged to the villain team the HYBRID. The third Prometheus is by far the deadliest. His past is the mirror image of Bruce Wayne's—except that Prometheus is entirely motivated by evil. As a youngster, he saw his criminal parents gunned down by a policeman, and dedicated his life to eradicating all law officers. He traveled the world, learning ways to maim and kill.

Clad in an armored suit designed to stun opponents and augment his natural skills, he has turned himself into a master assassin, having downloaded the fighting skills of 30 martial artists into his brain. He used a device called the Cosmic Key, picked up during his studies, and found his way into the realm of nothingness he calls the Ghost Zone. There he built a Crooked House patterned after his warped soul, where he lives and schemes. He has bested the JUSTICE LEAGUE OF AMERICA on several occasions only to be defeated by CATWOMAN. He also battled GREEN ARROW II in Star City, only to have his superior technology bested by bow and arrow. He nearly died from his arrow wounds until rescued and healed by BATMAN's deadly opponent, Hush. **RG**

PRYSM

FIRST APPEARANCE TEEN TITANS #1 (October 1996)
STATUS Hero **REAL NAME** Audrey Spears
OCCUPATION Super hero **BASE** Mobile
HEIGHT 6ft 4in **WEIGHT** Indeterminate
EYES White **HAIR** Indeterminate
SPECIAL POWERS/ABILITIES Vast light controlling powers, including the ability to capture and reflect light, fire light beams, and turn invisible.

Audrey Spears was another experiment by the H'San Natall in hybrid breeding, but unlike the other Earth-based hybrids (ARGENT II, JOTO, and RISK), she grew up inside a virtual reality fantasy provided by her alien keepers. Although happy with her idyllic life based on 1950s television, she soon learned that her truth was a lie.

Returning to Earth with the other hybrid teens, Audrey adopted the codename Prysm, for her ability to manipulate light. Prysm and her fellow hybrids (along with a de-aged ATOM II) founded the post-Zero Hour TEEN TITANS. Prysm found her glassy appearance freakish and rejoiced when she lost her powers during a mission to the WARLORD's realm of Skartaris—though she voluntarily regained them in order to save her teammates.

After Joto died in battle, Prysm carried his soul inside her own body for months before finally releasing it. Prysm ultimately met her true parents—her human mother Queen Miraset and her H'San Natall father Ch'ah—and convinced the rest of the H'San Natall to leave Earth in peace. At last feeling at home, Prysm chose to remain with her parents in space. Prysm's feelings of alienation were deepened by the unrequited crush she had for her teammate RISK. **DW**

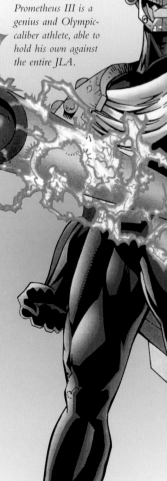

ONE-MAN ARMY *Prometheus III is a genius and Olympic-caliber athlete, able to hold his own against the entire JLA.*

PSIMON

FIRST APPEARANCE NEW TEEN TITANS (1st series) #2 (January 1981)
STATUS Villain **REAL NAME** Simon Jones
OCCUPATION Scientist; criminal **BASE** Mobile
HEIGHT 5ft 11.5in **WEIGHT** 145 lbs **EYES** White **HAIR** None
SPECIAL POWERS/ABILITIES Almost unrivaled psychic abilities, including telepathy, telekinesis, and mind control; projects mental force blasts strong enough to pulverize stone or turn a human brain to jelly.

Physicist Simon Jones was determined to breach the barriers between dimensions. During one of his experiments, a beam from another dimension struck him, endowing him with amazing psychic power. As Psimon, Jones recruited a group of villains called the FEARSOME FIVE, who came to blows with the New TEEN TITANS. One of the Teen Titans, RAVEN, discovered Psimon was an agent of her father, the demon TRIGON, who was the source of Jones's power. After failing to defeat the Titans, Trigon banished Psimon to another dimension.

The Fearsome Five freed Psimon, and fought the Titans and the OUTSIDERS, threatening New York City with nuclear annihilation. Psimon was seemingly killed during the Crisis (*see* Great Battles, pp. 320–1), but his essence survived to ravage several worlds. Psimon killed many of his former teammates before being captured by the Titans and the DARKSTARS. **PJ**

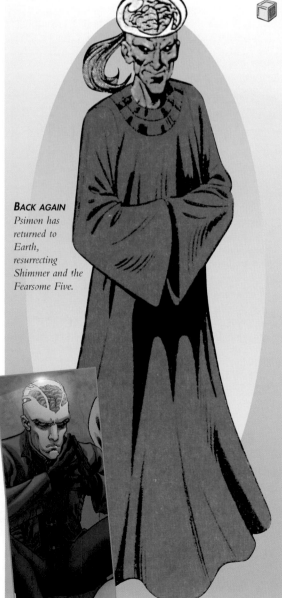

BACK AGAIN
Psimon has returned to Earth, resurrecting Shimmer and the Fearsome Five.

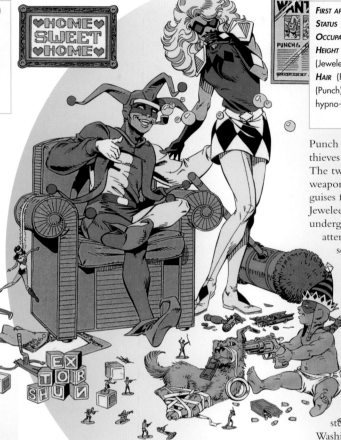

PUNCH AND JEWELEE

FIRST APPEARANCE CAPTAIN ATOM (1st series) #85 (March 1967)
STATUS Villains **REAL NAMES** Unrevealed
OCCUPATION Puppeteers; criminals **BASE** American Midwest
HEIGHT (Punch) 5ft 5in; (Jewelee) 5ft 9in **WEIGHT** (Punch) 125 lbs; (Jewelee) 139 lbs **EYES** (Punch) Brown; (Jewelee) blue
HAIR (Punch) Brown; (Jewelee) blonde **SPECIAL POWERS/ABILITIES** (Punch) Flying boot and electrically charged weapons; (Jewelee) hypno-jewels project illusions and light effects.

Punch and Jewelee were lovers, puppeteers, and part-time thieves working at Coney Island in Brooklyn, New York. The two crooks discovered a chest containing several alien weapons, and used them to craft more formidable criminal guises for themselves. As their ambitions grew, Punch and Jewelee used the alien technology to create an enormous underground headquarters in Coney Island, and even attempted to steal the minds of several prominent scientists in order to sell them to the highest bidder. The two became frequent foes of NIGHTSHADE and KING FARADAY.

The duo were renowned pranksters by now with a growing reputation for acts of mindless violence. They were thus ideal candidates for the SUICIDE SQUAD, run by Amanda Waller (*see* WALLER, AMANDA). Radically unpredictable, the duo were discharged from the Squad when Jewelee became pregnant. Punch and Jewelee moved to the U.S. heartland to raise their new baby, and briefly forsook their criminal lives. However, they later attempted to steal an experimental force-field vest on a trip to Washington, D.C., and are teaching their young scion the fine arts of thievery and mayhem. **PJ**

PSYBA-RATS

FIRST APPEARANCE ROBIN ANNUAL #2 (1993)
STATUS Undecided **BASE** Mobile
MEMBERS
Razorsharp (Raelene Sharp) Arms morph into giant blades.
Channelman (Carter Channel) Able to tap into any computer system.
Hackington (Reginald Hackman) Computer hacker.

The teenage hackers known as the Psyba-Rats, Raelene Sharp, Reginald Hackman, Carter Channel, Cullen Thane, and Michael Wasko earned their keep performing industrial espionage. When one such assignment in Gotham City went awry, their client shot and killed Mega-Biter (Wasko) and Output (Thane). On the run, the teens got caught up in an otherworldly conflict. Venev, one of several alien parasites who came to Earth as a prelude to an invasion, attacked and bit the remaining trio. The alien's venom activated their metagenes, transforming the group of cyber punks into genuine children of the digital age known as Razorsharp, Channelman (whose artificial intelligence can enter and control technology), and Hackington. A man named Branchwater hired the Psyba-Rats to retrieve the fabled formula for Zesti Cola and when problems arose, once more gunfire took a life. Channelman's human body was killed, but his essence now freely roamed all of the electromagnetic spectrum. Razorsharp briefly left the Psyba-Rats to become part of the short-lived televised darlings, the BLOOD PACK, but she soon returned to her original team. **RG**

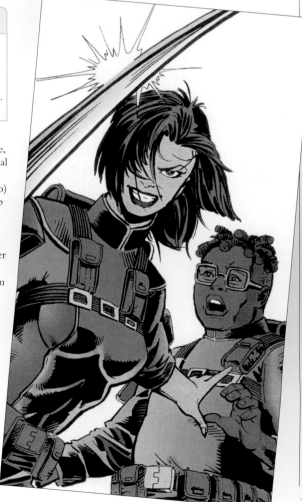

POWER SURGE *Razorsharp is not only good with a computer but, now that she has deadly arms, is a complete threat. Hackrat, though, can charm machines in more peaceful ways.*

QUANTUM MECHANICS

FIRST APPEARANCE JLA: HEAVEN'S LADDER (November 2000)
STATUS Cosmic beings **BASE** Mobile
SPECIAL POWERS/ABILITIES Possessed of virtually god-like powers and intellects, the Quantum Mechanics are capable of practically any feat that their imaginations can conceive, including teleporting entire worlds (including Earth) half-way across the universe.

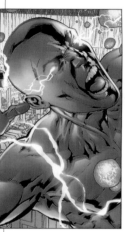

Born at the Big Bang, the Quantum Mechanics roamed the universe, seeking celestial enlightenment. Fear of their own mortality, coupled with their inability to conceive of an afterlife, prompted the Quantum Mechanics to create a vision of heaven. They created thousands of agents to study the cultures of the universe, gathering information about each version of heaven to build the perfect hereafter for themselves. The JUSTICE LEAGUE OF AMERICA first discovered the Quantum Mechanics when these ancient beings abducted planet Earth, as well as hundreds of other worlds they had been studying, to create their own "ladder" to heaven. When a rogue faction of the Quantum Mechanics threatened to destroy all these worlds, the JLA were forced to battle the cosmic creatures, eventually helping them cross over into a higher plane of existence. PJ

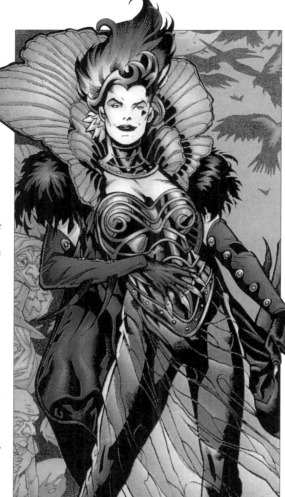

QUEEN OF FABLES

FIRST APPEARANCE JUSTICE LEAGUE OF AMERICA #47 (Nov. 2000)
STATUS Villain **REAL NAMES** Unknown
OCCUPATION Sorceress **BASE** Other-dimensional space
HEIGHT Tall and willowy **WEIGHT** Light as a feather
EYES Twin sapphires **HAIR** Sleekest ebony
SPECIAL POWERS/ABILITIES Magical ability to make the monsters and myths of storybook fables real.

Centuries ago, the Queen of Fables arrived on Earth as an exile from another dimension. Possessed of vast magical power, she carved out an empire for herself and met defeat at the hands of the virtuous princess Snow White. Imprisoned within a storybook until the dawn of the 21st century, the Queen of Fables escaped to sow chaos in New York City by conjuring various ogres, witches, and goblins.

The JUSTICE LEAGUE OF AMERICA clashed with the Queen of Fables when she attacked WONDER WOMAN, believing the Amazon to be her old nemesis Snow White. With her unique brand of sorcery, the Queen drew the Leaguers into the realm of fairy tales, where they faced the worst monstrosities of the imagination. She even transformed Manhattan island into an enchanted forest festooned with hanging moss and creeping ivy.

Eventually, Wonder Woman used her lasso to defeat the Queen of Fables, forcing the Queen to confront the truth of her own mortality. She is now imprisoned inside a new book—the *United States Tax Code*. Within its dry, literal pages, the Queen of Fables is unlikely to find any magical elements she can use to escape. DW

STORY TIME *The Queen called to life elements from fairy tales including Snow White, Sleeping Beauty, and Hansel and Gretel.*

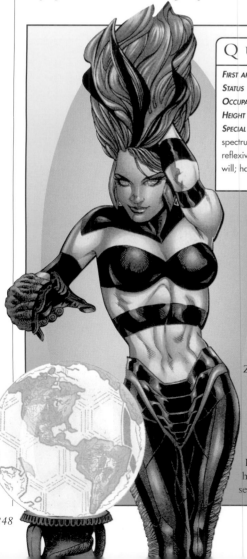

QUEEN BEE II

FIRST APPEARANCE JLA #34 (October 1999)
STATUS Villain **REAL NAME** Zazzala
OCCUPATION Royal Genetrix **BASE** The planet Korll
HEIGHT 5ft 9in **WEIGHT** 226 lbs **EYES** Blue **HAIR** Gray-black
SPECIAL POWERS/ABILITIES Multifaceted eyes see in the ultraviolet spectrum; gauntlet on right arm fires poisonous barbed stingers from reflexive venom sacs; hypno-pollen capable of bending others' to her will; has a mindless army of drones at her disposal.

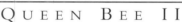

The first Queen Bee was a woman with hypnotic powers who seized control of the state of Bialya after murdering its dictator, Colonel Rumaan Harjavti (*see* HARJAVTI, RUMAAN & SUMAAN). She soon died at the hands of his brother, Sumaan.

The second Queen Bee, Zazzala, ruler of planet Korll and its ever-expanding empire, was far more dangerous. In her closest encounter with Earth, the Queen Bee and her swarms of Bee-Troopers joined Lex Luthor's INJUSTICE GANG (*see* LUTHOR, LEX) in a plot to defeat the JUSTICE LEAGUE OF AMERICA and conquer Earth. In return for the firepower of her drones, Zazzala was offered a percentage of Earth's populace as slaves. The first to suffer were the citizens of New York City, which became the site of the Queen Bee's Royal Egg-Matrix and ground zero for her planned planetary domination (after betraying Luthor). However, the Queen Bee was stung when members of the JLA—WONDER WOMAN, BIG BARDA, PLASTIC MAN, and STEEL III—attacked the Queen Bee's hive and nullified her hypno-pollen. Zazzala and her swarm were defeated and sent buzzing back to Korll via Barda's Boom Tube. SB

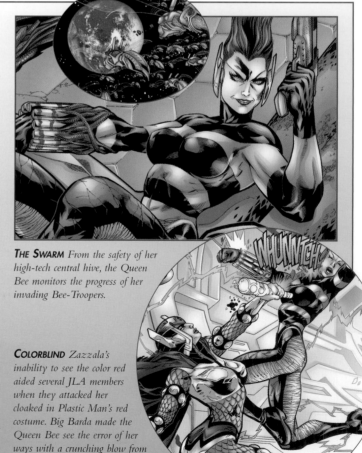

THE SWARM *From the safety of her high-tech central hive, the Queen Bee monitors the progress of her invading Bee-Troopers.*

COLORBLIND *Zazzala's inability to see the color red aided several JLA members when they attacked her cloaked in Plastic Man's red costume. Big Barda made the Queen Bee see the error of her ways with a crunching blow from her Mega-Rod!*

CRUSADER *Vic Sage became an Everyman figure, using his fists to find truth in corrupt Hub City.*

QUESTION, THE

FIRST APPEARANCE BLUE BEETLE (3rd series) #1 (June 1967)
STATUS Hero   **REAL NAME** Charles Victor Szasz
OCCUPATION Television journalist (as Vic Sage)   **BASE** Hub City
HEIGHT 6ft 2in   **WEIGHT** 185 lbs   **EYES** Blue   **HAIR** Reddish blond
SPECIAL POWERS/ABILITIES Trained by Richard Dragon, Vic is a formidable fighter and martial artist.

Victor Szasz was an angry orphan who could not understand why people did the things they did. As Vic Sage, television reporter for K.B.E.L., he took on political corruption in Hub City. Those hypocrites he couldn't expose on television he went after as the Question, his features masked by a compound called Pseudoderm devised by his friend Tot (Dr. Aristotle Rodor). Sage was also aided by Mayor Myra Connelly, (widow of the former Mayor) and Izzy O'Toole, perhaps the only honest cop on the force.

After many adventures, Sage became disillusioned with his crusading role and, entrusted with Myra's daughter Jackie, journeyed to the Amazon rain forest to find himself.

He returned to Hub City a changed man after LADY SHIVA saved his life and Richard Dragon (*see* DRAGON, RICHARD) instructed him in martial arts. Later, when the HUNTRESS was accused of murder, the Question befriended her and introduced her to Dragon, who helped the heroine learn how to channel her anger. RG

HEART TO HEART *Vic and Mayor Myra Connelly have a complex, but loving relationship.*

QWSP

FIRST APPEARANCE AQUAMAN #1 (February 1962)
STATUS Undecided   **REAL NAME** Qwsp
OCCUPATION Mischief-making imp   **BASE** The fifth dimension
HEIGHT/WEIGHT/EYES/HAIR Variable
SPECIAL POWERS/ABILITIES Fifth-dimensional being who appears to have an almost magical ability to transform people and objects as his unpredictable fancy takes.

Qwsp may have heard about a dimension full of heroes from MR. MXYZPTLK, then again he may not. This imp from another realm arrived some time back to help AQUAMAN and Aqualad (*see* TEMPEST) fend off some Fire Trolls. Fascinated by these watery types, Qwsp visited in a helpful manner, unlike Mxyzptlk or BAT-MITE.

He returned to his home dimension for a long while; but when he next arrived to visit the Sea King, he noticed the hero had changed, and was now darker in his demeanor. Qwsp followed suit and launched a war involving several of his homeworld's genies, starting with Johnny Thunder's Thunderbolt (*see* THUNDER, JOHNNY), Yz, and Lkz. Lkz corrupted TRIUMPH and set him against members of the JUSTICE LEAGUE OF AMERICA and the JUSTICE SOCIETY OF AMERICA. Qwsp, feeling only mildly ashamed, returned to the fifth dimension. RG

QUICK, JESSE

FIRST APPEARANCE JUSTICE SOCIETY OF AMERICA (2nd series) #1 (August 1992)   **STATUS** Hero (retired)   **REAL NAME** Jesse Chambers
OCCUPATION C.E.O. of Quickstart Enterprises   **BASE** Keystone City
HEIGHT 5ft 9in   **WEIGHT** 142 lbs   **EYES** Blue   **HAIR** Blonde
SPECIAL POWERS/ABILITIES Superspeed, superstrength, flight, martial arts.

Jesse Chambers is the daughter of Johnny Quick (*see* QUICK, JOHNNY) and LIBERTY BELLE, two heroes of World War II. Jesse inherited her parents' powers and gained superspeed by reciting her father's formula ("3X2(9YZ)4A"), which allowed her to tap into the Speed Force.

An ally of the FLASH III, MAX MERCURY, and Impulse (*see* KID FLASH II), Jesse Quick, as Chambers called herself, became a prominent speedster in Keystone City. She was also a member of the JUSTICE SOCIETY OF AMERICA and the TEEN TITANS. After her father's death at the hands of SAVITAR, Jesse inherited his role as C.E.O. of Quickstart Enterprises.

After lending a portion of her power to the Flash, Jesse lost her ability to recall the Quick mantra as well as her superspeed, and retired. PJ

QUICK, JOHNNY

FIRST APPEARANCE MORE FUN COMICS #71 (September 1941)
STATUS Hero   **REAL NAME** Johnny Chambers
OCCUPATION Super hero   **BASE** New York City
HEIGHT 5ft 11in   **WEIGHT** 170 lbs   **EYES** Blue   **HAIR** Blond
SPECIAL POWERS/ABILITIES Superspeed; can pass through objects by vibrating his molecules and briefly "fly".

At the dawn of the 1940s, Johnny Chambers's guardian, the celebrated Professor Gill, discovered a miraculous formula written on a piece of papyrus in the temple of Egyptian king Amen. When young Johnny said "3X2(9YZ)4A" he received the gift of superspeed, and he could close off this link by saying "Z25Y(2AB)6." So began a new life as the costumed Johnny Quick.

The outbreak of World War II caused all of America's mystery men to unite under the banner of the ALL-STAR SQUADRON. Johnny Quick worked with Jay Garrick (the original FLASH), and dated and later married LIBERTY BELLE.

Unlike others, Johnny Quick did not enter forced retirement when the House of Un-American Activities Committee ordered all mystery men to unmask themselves in the 1950s. Nevertheless, Johnny spent gradually less time in the hero game in order to build up his communications business and to spend time with his daughter, Jesse.

Though Johnny Quick claimed he didn't believe in the Speed Force, his magic formulas acted as mental mantras that channeled the extra-dimensional speed energy into his body. He became one with the Speed Force when he sacrificed himself in battle against the foul SAVITAR. He is survived by Jesse, who works with the JUSTICE SOCIETY OF AMERICA as Jesse Quick (*see* QUICK, JESSE). DW

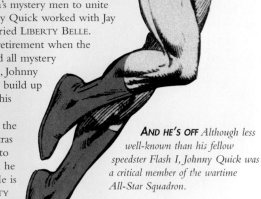

AND HE'S OFF *Although less well-known than his fellow speedster Flash I, Johnny Quick was a critical member of the wartime All-Star Squadron.*

ROMANTIC MOMENTS

SUPER HEROES ARE ESSENTIALLY SOLDIERS, ready to go into battle at a moment's notice and regularly brushing up against death. With this as a backdrop, it's understandable that these amazing superbeings form desperate, passionate, often short-lived liaisons. Although a few relationships belie that stereotype, having lasted for years, tellingly, few steady romances exist where *both* partners are costumed heroes.

CLARK KENT AND LOIS LANE

Perhaps no pair is more different, yet more perfect for one another, than the ace reporter from Metropolis and the farmboy from Smallville, Kansas. As co-workers at the *Daily Planet*, they gradually put aside their professional rivalry (as well as Lois' infatuation with SUPERMAN) and learned to embrace all that they had in common. Eventually Clark revealed his secret identity to Lois Lane (*see* LANE, LOIS) and the two were married. Fortunately—because so few know of Clark Kent's famous alter ego—the happy ceremony remained unmarred by super-villains or other occupational hazards.

To date, Lois has not expressed any jealousy over the fact that, by necessity, she has to share Superman with the world. Recently, however, Clark and Lois' relationship has come under new strain as Clark deals with work-related stress at the *Daily Planet*. Lois still provides the human grounding the Man of Steel desperately needs.

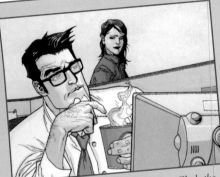

OFFICE ROMANCE *When Lois first met Clark the air crackled with tension; but eventually mutual competitiveness turned to lasting love.*

GREEN LANTERN AND CAROL FERRIS

The head of Ferris Aircraft, Carol Ferris was first and foremost Hal Jordan's boss, but the cocky test pilot did not let their professional relationship prevent him from striking up a steamy romance. Their connection became increasingly complicated when the Zamarons made Carol their unwitting queen (STAR SAPPHIRE) and pitted her against GREEN LANTERN. Immediately after Hal became the supremely powerful PARALLAX, he shared a final kiss with Carol before sacrificing his life to reignite Earth's sun.

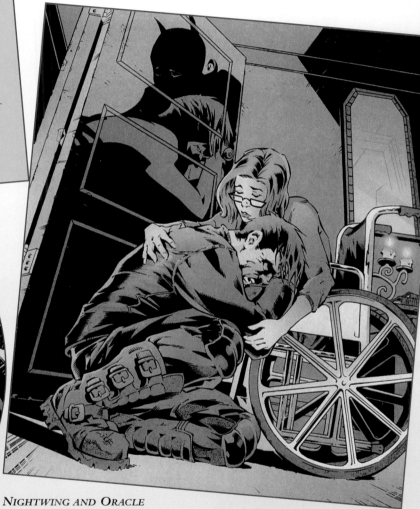

NIGHTWING AND ORACLE

Dick Grayson, as ROBIN, fell for Barbara Gordon early in her career as BATGIRL, calling her the "first person to make my heart sing." Mutual affection soon led to passion, though the only thing that remained consistent in their relationship was the inconsistency of their on-again, off-again romance. Their love survived Barbara's paralyzing injury by the JOKER and her subsequent role as ORACLE, but they eventually split up, with Barbara citing Dick's reckless disregard for his own safety as NIGHTWING as the cause. Yet how long can Nightwing and Oracle ignore their destiny?

BLACK CANARY AND GREEN ARROW

Dinah Lance and Oliver Queen are two of the world's most outspoken heroes. She is a brash self-promoter. He is a blunt liberal activist. Their strong personalities seem to draw them irresistibly together—for passionate arguments or for passionate kisses. They toured the U.S. on a cross-country road trip and still team up on the occasional mission, riding tandem on a motorcycle. It's amazing they can ever agree on a route!

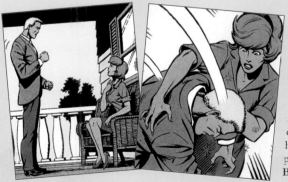

ANIMAL MAN

Suburban super hero Buddy Baker led the perfect family life with his wife, Ellen. High-school sweethearts, Buddy and Ellen raised two children, Cliff and Maxine, in between Buddy's adventuring stints as ANIMAL MAN. Eventually his powers overtook his life, causing him to start his own religion based on animal-power. This placed severe strain on Buddy's relationship with Ellen.

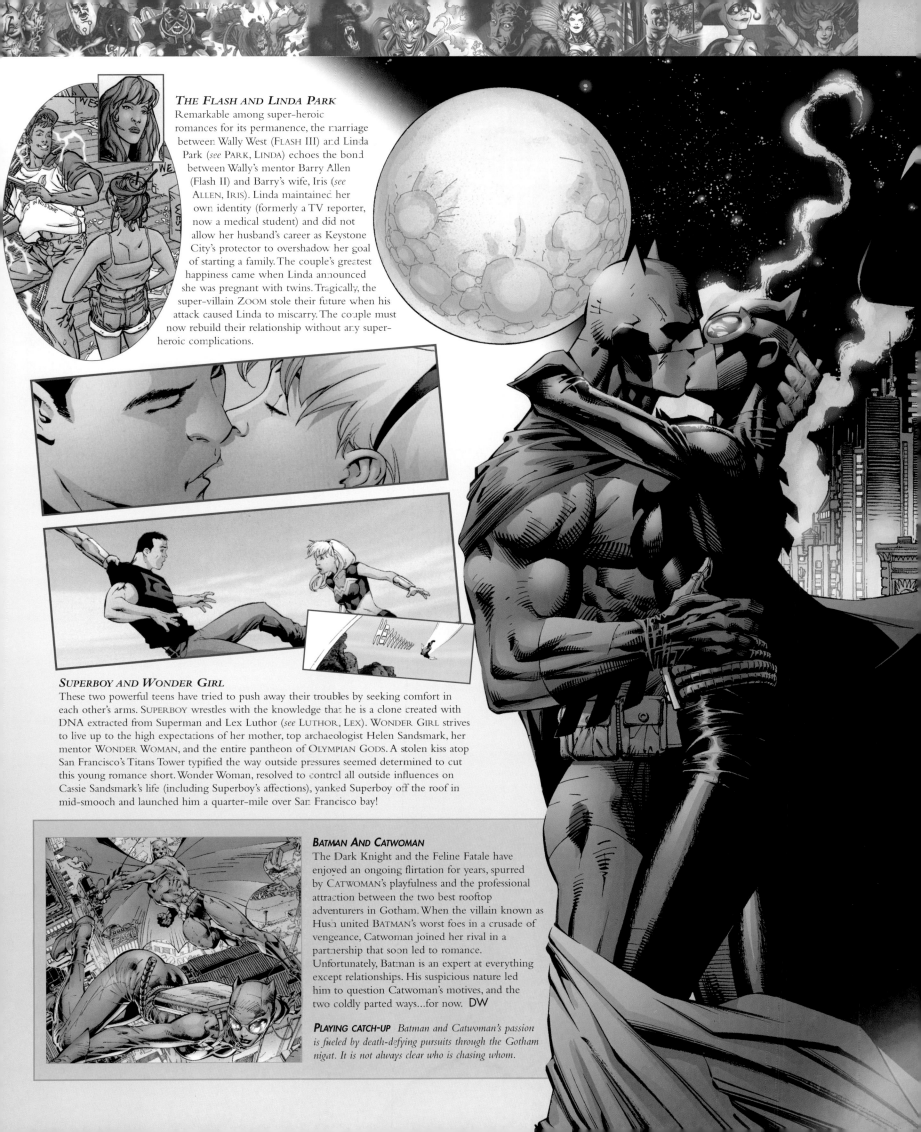

THE FLASH AND LINDA PARK

Remarkable among super-heroic romances for its permanence, the marriage between Wally West (FLASH III) and Linda Park (see PARK, LINDA) echoes the bond between Wally's mentor Barry Allen (Flash II) and Barry's wife, Iris (see ALLEN, IRIS). Linda maintained her own identity (formerly a TV reporter, now a medical student) and did not allow her husband's career as Keystone City's protector to overshadow her goal of starting a family. The couple's greatest happiness came when Linda announced she was pregnant with twins. Tragically, the super-villain ZOOM stole their future when his attack caused Linda to miscarry. The couple must now rebuild their relationship without any super-heroic complications.

SUPERBOY AND WONDER GIRL

These two powerful teens have tried to push away their troubles by seeking comfort in each other's arms. SUPERBOY wrestles with the knowledge that he is a clone created with DNA extracted from Superman and Lex Luthor (see LUTHOR, LEX). WONDER GIRL strives to live up to the high expectations of her mother, top archaeologist Helen Sandsmark, her mentor WONDER WOMAN, and the entire pantheon of OLYMPIAN GODS. A stolen kiss atop San Francisco's Titans Tower typified the way outside pressures seemed determined to cut this young romance short. Wonder Woman, resolved to control all outside influences on Cassie Sandsmark's life (including Superboy's affections), yanked Superboy off the roof in mid-smooch and launched him a quarter-mile over San Francisco bay!

BATMAN AND CATWOMAN

The Dark Knight and the Feline Fatale have enjoyed an ongoing flirtation for years, spurred by CATWOMAN's playfulness and the professional attraction between the two best rooftop adventurers in Gotham. When the villain known as Hush united BATMAN's worst foes in a crusade of vengeance, Catwoman joined her rival in a partnership that soon led to romance. Unfortunately, Batman is an expert at everything except relationships. His suspicious nature led him to question Catwoman's motives, and the two coldly parted ways...for now. DW

PLAYING CATCH-UP *Batman and Catwoman's passion is fueled by death-defying pursuits through the Gotham night. It is not always clear who is chasing whom.*

R.E.B.E.L.S WITHOUT A CAUSE *Resolved to save the universe from the demented rule of the super-intelligent grandchild of Brainiac, the R.E.B.E.L.S. were freedom fighters and former members of L.E.G.I.O.N., including* **1)** *Strata* **2)** *Lobo* **3)** *Vril Dox II* **4)** *Phase* **5)** *Stealth.*

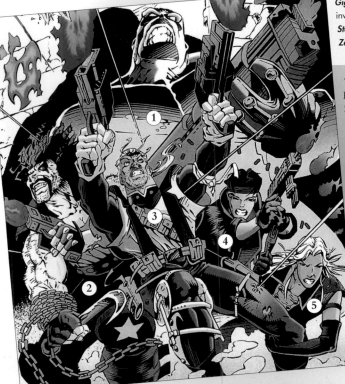

R.E.B.E.L.S.

FIRST APPEARANCE R.E.B.E.L.S. #1 (November 1994)
STATUS Hero team (disbanded) **BASE** Interstellar space
MEMBERS/POWERS *Captain Comet* various superpowers; *Amon Hakk, Garv, Strata* superstrength, invulnerability; *Darkstar* projects darkness; *Garryn Bek, Mari'jn Bek* no powers; *Gigantus, Layla* martial artists; *Lobo* superstrength, invulnerability, tracking; *Phase* becomes intangible; *Stealth* creates silence; *Telepath* psychic abilities; *Zena Moonstruk* absorbs light.

The R.E.B.E.L.S. (Revolutionary Elite Brigade to Eliminate L.E.G.I.O.N. Supremacy) was a rag-tag team of guerrilla fighters and former L.E.G.I.O.N. officers formed when Lyrl Dox, the son of Vril Dox II, used his twelfth-level intelligence and subliminal charisma program to take over the interstellar police organization. As Lyrl's L.E.G.I.O.N. began a strategic takeover of the various worlds that L.E.G.I.O.N. had once protected, the R.E.B.E.L.S. exploited their inside knowledge in a series of hit and run raids designed to disable the fascist police force.

Vril Dox finally defeated his son by infecting him with a drug that greatly diminished Lyrl's intelligence, ending his control of L.E.G.I.O.N. The R.E.B.E.L.S. then disbanded. Captain Comet subsequently reformed L.E.G.I.O.N. with a new charter and Vril Dox retired to watch over his infant son. **PJ**

RAJAK, COLONEL

FIRST APPEARANCE ADVENTURES OF SUPERMAN #590 (May 2001)
STATUS Villain **REAL NAME** Ehad Rajak
OCCUPATION Dictator **BASE** Bialya
HEIGHT 5ft 6in **WEIGHT** 155 lbs **EYES** Blue **HAIR** Black
SPECIAL POWERS/ABILITIES No superpowers, but a charismatic and willful commander who leads an army of fanatical followers.

The African country of Bialya has seen its share of iron-fisted leaders come and go. After Rajak evicted Sumaan Harjavti (see HARJAVTI, RUMAAN AND SUMAAN) from power, the Colonel took control of Bialya and perpetuated the anti-American stance for which the country had become well known. Bialy remains under economic sanctions from the U.S., which does not help the political situation. President Luthor (see LUTHOR, LEX) asked SUPERMAN to help rescue *Newstime* journalist Andrew Finch, hoping to avoid direct military intervention. Finch, however, was a C.I.A. assassin working under Luthor's orders. Superman rescued Finch but stopped him eliminating Rajak. The strongman remains a threat to the Middle East peace process and has a personal score to settle with Luthor. **RG**

RAGMAN

FIRST APPEARANCE RAGMAN 1st series #1 (September 1976)
STATUS Hero **REAL NAME** Rory Regan
OCCUPATION Defender of the weak **BASE** Gotham City
HEIGHT 5ft 11in **WEIGHT** 165 lbs **EYES** Blue **HAIR** Brown
SPECIAL POWERS/ABILITIES Costume grants superhuman strength, speed, agility, and the ability to float on air. It claims the souls of the wicked by engulfing them within the Ragman's tatters.

To protect themselves from persecution, the Jews of 16th century Prague animated a soulless Golem from river clay. Wary of the monster they created, the Council of Rabbis decreed that the Golem should be replaced with a human defender. The Rabbis chose rags to clothe their new champion who, like the Golem, was empowered by a verse in the Kaballah. Thus, the "Ragman" was first woven to guard over the Warsaw Ghetto. During World War II, Jerzy Reganiewicz took up the patchwork mantle of Ragman to protect Warsaw's Jews from the Nazis. Tragically, Jerzy failed to spare his people from the horrors of the Holocaust. Years later, Jerzy (renamed Gerry Regan after emigrating to the U.S.) passed down the Ragman's suit to his son, Rory, who first wore it to defend the oppressed denizens of Gotham City's slums. From his "Rags 'n' Tatters" junk shop, Rory continues to add new rags to the garish garment of the "Tattered Tatterdemalion," Ragman. Though working alone more often than not, Ragman has teamed with fellow Gotham avenger BATMAN on occasion and also belongs to a loose confederation of mystical heroes once dubbed the Sentinels of Magic. **SB**

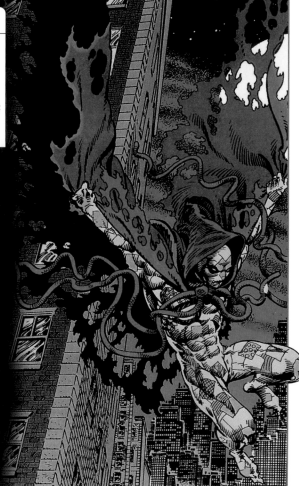

RAMULUS

FIRST APPEARANCE WORLD'S FINEST #6 (Summer, 1942)
STATUS Villain **REAL NAME** Unknown
OCCUPATION Scientist **BASE** The Magic Forest, upstate New York
HEIGHT 6ft 3in **WEIGHT** 185 lbs **EYES** White **HAIR** Green
SPECIAL POWERS/ABILITIES Can control vegetation with his mind, specifically giant vines, his so-called Tendrils of Terror.

Originally committing crimes under the name Nightshade, the green-skinned Ramulus created mechanized, murdering plants to terrorize his victims in a "magic forest" in upstate New York. In 1942, Wesley Dodds, the SANDMAN I, and his protégé, Sandy the Golden Boy, ran afoul of Nightshade when the villain kidnapped the parents of one of Sandy's friends. While Sandman and Sandy rescued the kidnapped couple, Nightshade lost control over his electronic plants and was seemingly murdered by them, while his "magic forest" burned to the ground.

Miraculously surviving, Nightshade was discovered by the Aztec priestess NYOLA. Given greater control over his technological flora, and the ability to mentally manipulate living vegetation, Nightshade changed his name to Ramulus and joined Nyola's MONSTER SOCIETY OF EVIL. **PJ**

RĀ'S AL GHŪL

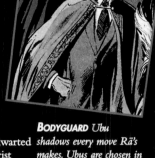

FIRST APPEARANCE BATMAN #232 (June 1971)
STATUS Villain (deceased) **REAL NAME** Unknown
OCCUPATION International terrorist **BASE** Mobile **HEIGHT** 6ft 5in
WEIGHT 215 lbs **EYES** Blue **HAIR** Gray with white streaks
SPECIAL POWERS/ABILITIES A master swordsman and ruthless hand-to-hand combatant, Rā's al Ghūl lived for many centuries, amassing great wealth and power, as well as a treasure trove of knowledge, during his near-eternal existence.

ALTHOUGH NOT TRULY IMMORTAL, the international terrorist Rā's al Ghūl was one of the most long-lived men on the planet. In Arabic, his name translates as "The Demon's Head," a fitting sobriquet for someone so sinister. Rā's al Ghūl's primary purpose during his extended life was to restore the Earth's ecological balance. Unfortunately, this seemingly altruistic goal led to him committing global genocide to reduce mankind's polluting numbers.

KYLE RAYNER

For centuries, Rā's al Ghūl maintained his existence by periodically immersing himself in "Lazarus Pits," pools filled with an alchemical mix of acids and poisons excavated above the electromagnetic ley lines crisscrossing the Earth. Following his emergence from the liquid in the the Lazarus Pits Rā's al Ghūl would, for a short time, be consumed with insane fury. For this reason, Rā's demanded solitude when rejuvenating himself.

LAZARUS PITS Like a macabre fountain of youth, these fiery pits sustained Rā's al Ghūl's incredible vim and vigor.

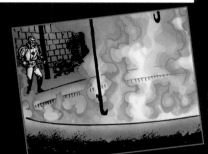

Rā's al Ghūl's schemes to restore Earth to an Eden-like splendor have been thwarted time and again by BATMAN. The Dark Knight first met the enigmatic eco-terrorist when Rā's al Ghūl, desiring an heir for his crime empire, kidnapped ROBIN in an attempt to coerce the Dark Knight into marrying his daughter, TALIA. Naturally, Batman refused, and although he had deep feelings for the beautiful Talia, he continued to oppose Rā's al Ghūl schemes.

BODYGUARD Ubu shadows every move Rā's makes. Ubus are chosen in mortal combat matches and will give their lives to protect the Demon's Head.

MASTER SCHEMER Not content with making Batman's life miserable, the Demon's Head has involved other super heroes, including the Man of Steel, in his "world-saving" plots.

Rā's al Ghūl's most ambitious attacks upon humanity occurred with his creation of the Ebola Gulf-A plague that decimated the population of Gotham City. This plague, dubbed the "Clench" due to its victims' writhing ends, was halted by the Dark Knight and his squires, who later learned that Rā's al Ghūl had deciphered the virus's genetic code from an ancient "Wheel of Plagues." With it, Rā's al Ghūl would have unleashed even more virulent contagions if not for the intervention of the Bat-Family.

Rā's al Ghūl continued to seek a suitable heir, even considering the musclebound terrorist BANE, before Talia spurned this potential suitor. The dejected Bane then set about sabotaging Rā's al Ghūl's Lazarus Pits to get revenge.

SWORDPLAY A renowned swordsman with centuries of fighting experience, Rā's has challenged Batman to duels on many occasions in order to put the Dark Knight's mettle to the test.

DAUGHTER DEAREST Nyssa succeeded where others could not, ending the long life of the Demon's Head!

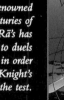

Meanwhile, Rā's al Ghūl created worldwide anarchy with his electronic "Tower of Babel," which rendered all languages unintelligible until the JUSTICE LEAGUE OF AMERICA destroyed it. Talia left her father's side soon after, hired by Lex Luthor (see LUTHOR, LEX) to run his company, LexCorp. It then transpired that Rā's had fathered another daughter, Nyssa. Unlike her sister Talia, Nyssa hated her father, and tried to brainwash Talia into killing him. What no one realized was that Rā's was grooming Nyssa to inherit his empire and had engineered events to force Nyssa to kill him! With Rā's now dead, his daughters departed to make mayhem and shake the world from its apathy, their way of furthering their father's legacy. Nyssa retains control over one final life-renewing Lazarus Pit, located somewhere in the Balkans. **SB**

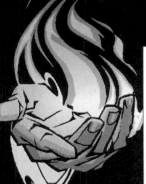

KEY STORYLINES

• *BATMAN #232 (JUNE 1971):* Rā's al Ghūl makes his first appearance, kidnapping the Boy Wonder to force Batman to do his bidding!
• *DETECTIVE COMICS #700 (AUGUST 1996):* As the multipart "Legacy" storyline begins, Rā's al Ghūl uses the ancient Wheel of Plagues, responsible for Gotham City's Clench outbreak, to unleash an even worse contagion!
• *BATMAN: DEATH AND THE MAIDENS #1-9 (OCTOBER 2003–JUNE 2004):* Nyssa, daughter of Rā's al Ghūl, plots her father's demise in order to take over his worldwide criminal empire! Is this the end for the Demon's Head, or the beginning of another villainous dynasty?

RAVEN

FIRST APPEARANCE DC COMICS PRESENTS #26 (October 1980)
STATUS Heroic victim of evil **REAL NAME** Raven
OCCUPATION Adventurer **BASE** Mobile
HEIGHT 5ft 11in **WEIGHT** 139 lbs **EYES** Blue **HAIR** Black
SPECIAL POWERS/ABILITIES Has empathic and limited healing abilities in addition to a psychic connection with all things mystical; in many ways, still an innocent and susceptible to overwhelming mystic forces.

Some time ago, a member of a cult trying to bring the devil to Earth was raped and made pregnant by the demon TRIGON. The woman, Arella, joined a group of pacifists in the sanctuary of Azarath. Nine months later, she gave birth to a girl she named Raven. As an adult, Raven approached the JUSTICE LEAGUE OF AMERICA about the imminent threat of Trigon but ZATANNA, sensing the Raven's genetic connection to the demon, urged the JLA to ignore her warnings. Instead, Raven turned to the TEEN TITANS. Trigon duly arrived, took control of Raven, and then of Earth. The Titans destroyed him… or so they thought.

For several years, Raven had countless battles with her demon father. Even after he was killed she was still subject to his cruel influence. In order to save Raven, her body was destroyed, leaving her soul-self intact. Without a body to inhabit, Raven's soul-self wandered the world until another evil claimed her: the new BROTHER BLOOD. **RG**

DEMON PARENT *Raven, daughter of Trigon the Terrible, has sought to escape his evil influence.*

RAVERS, THE

FIRST APPEARANCE SUPERBOY AND THE RAVERS #1 (Sept. 1996)
STATUS Hero team **BASE** The traveling rave Event Horizon
CURRENT MEMBERS AND POWERS
Superboy (leader) Flight, superstrength, and invulnerability.
Kaliber Qwardian with shrinking and growing powers.
Aura Possesses powerful magnetic abilities.
Hero Cruz Force field generated from Achilles Vest.
Hero H-Dial allows transformation into a super-hero identity.
Rex the Wonder Dog Enhanced intelligence.
Sparx Can wield electricity; flight.

The Event Horizon was a mobile, intergalactic party frequented by cliques of teens invited by club owner Kindred Marx—the catch was that only those with superpowers could get in. The Ravers, led by SUPERBOY, were the most outrageous of the club's regulars. By touching their hand-stamps, the Ravers could teleport to the Event Horizon from anywhere in the universe.

The Ravers came into conflict with rival clique Red Shift and the interdimensional police force InterC.E.P.T. They also helped HIGHFATHER of New Genesis foil DARKSEID's attempts to tap into the power of the Source. After Raver Half-Life perished in a battle against the Qwardians of the Anti-Matter universe (*see* WEAPONERS OF QWARD), Kindred Marx chose to end the Event Horizon, and most of the Ravers went their separate ways. **DW**

THE RAVERS 1) *Hardrock*
2) *Associate member* 3) *Half-Life*
4) *Hero Cruz*
5) *Kaliber*
6) *Aura*

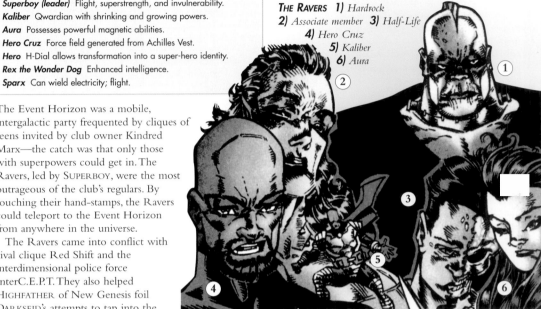

RAY I & II

FIRST APPEARANCE (I) SMASH COMICS #14 (September 1940); (II) THE RAY #1 (February 1992) **STATUS** Heroes **REAL NAMES** (I) "Happy" Terrill; (II) Raymond C. Terrill **OCCUPATIONS** (I) Reporter; (II) computer programmer **BASES** (I) New York City; (II) Philadelphia **HEIGHTS** (I) 5ft 10.5in; (II) 5ft 10in **WEIGHTS** (I) 165 lbs; (II) 155 lbs **EYES** (I) Blue; (II) green **HAIR** (I) Blonde; (II) red **SPECIAL POWERS/ABILITIES** (I) Absorbs heat, light, electricity, projects light and electrical blasts, superspeed flight; (II) absorbs sunlight for power, projects energy blasts, superspeed flight, rearranges molecular matter.

"Happy" Terrill, a reporter for the *New York Star*, was caught in an electrical storm while on a story and pummeled with thousands of volts of electricity. Instead of killing him, the energy gave the reporter strange powers. Decades later, Terrill learned that he'd been deliberately exposed to a genetic "light bomb" created by research scientist Dr. Dayzl. Terrill became the Ray, and joined the JUSTICE SOCIETY OF AMERICA as well as UNCLE SAM's FREEDOM FIGHTERS. Terrill's son Joshua inherited his father's powers and became his sidekick, Spitfire. After Joshua accidentally killed his mother, Gayle, Terrill placed him in suspended animation and retired his Ray identity.

Terrill remarried and his second son Raymond was also born with his father's potentially deadly powers. Raymond was a teenager before he was first exposed to light, which activated his powers. Ray II fought alongside BLACK CANARY and was a member of the JUSTICE LEAGUE OF AMERICA's Task Force, the Forgotten Heroes, and YOUNG JUSTICE. Ray II almost died during the Imperiex War (*see* Great Battles, pp. 320–1). **PJ**

WAR WOUND *While defending the planet Daxam, the Ray was nearly sliced in two by a warrior drone!*

SON OF THE FATHER *The second Ray is easily as powerful as the first. Despite his youth, the Ray has used his powers as a member of the JLA, Earth's greatest defenders.*

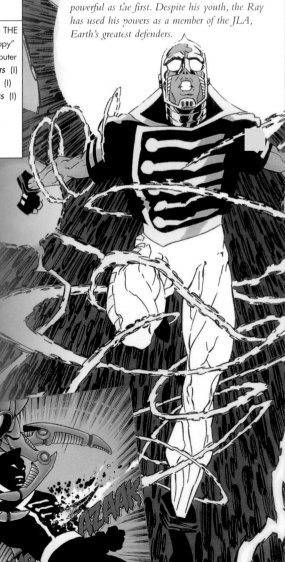

RAYMOND, ROY- TV DETECTIVE

FIRST APPEARANCE DETECTIVE COMICS #153 (November 1949)
STATUS Hero REAL NAME Roy Raymond
OCCUPATION Television host (retired) BASE Metropolis
HEIGHT 5ft 10.5in WEIGHT 175 lbs EYES Blue HAIR Brown
SPECIAL POWERS/ABILITIES Though marked by age, Raymond once possessed a brilliant analytical mind; was an average hand-to-hand combatant when push came to shove.

Roy Raymond found fame as host of the *Impossible—But True!* television series, a forum for revealing the strange and weird from all over the world. Debunking hoaxes on the show earned Raymond the title "TV Detective." Raymond's deductive skill was put to the test in many adventures; he often aided the police, and was usually accompanied by his fetching assistant, Karen Colby. Raymond eventually retired after a horrifying encounter with the "Wild Thing," a crazed creature grown by the SWAMP THING to become Earth's next plant elemental. Raymond's son, Roy Raymond, Jr. (or a young man claiming to be so), continues the family legacy with his own "true crime" reality series. However, the youthful Raymond lacks his father's good looks and keen intellect. SB

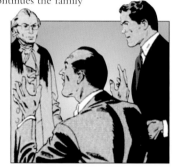

GHOSTBUSTER Roy Raymond (right) rumbles yet another phoney phantom.

RED BEE

FIRST APPEARANCE HIT COMICS #1 (July 1940)
STATUS Hero (deceased) REAL NAME Richard Raleigh
OCCUPATION Assistant District Attorney BASE Superior City
HEIGHT 5ft 9.5in WEIGHT 147 lbs EYES Blue HAIR Reddish-blond
SPECIAL POWERS/ABILITIES An amazing beekeeper, training bees to aid him in his fight against crime; also developed a special stinger gun that stunned criminals.

Assistant District Attorney Richard Raleigh became the costumed crime fighter Red Bee in Superior City, Oregon, in the 1940s. He believed that taking direct action was the only way to ensure that justice was done during this dark time in American history. In his first case as the Red Bee, he took on the city's political machine, and brought down its corrupt leader, "Boss" Storm. Raleigh's main crime-fighting asset was his trained swarm of bees; his favorite was named Michael and kept in his belt buckle for special needs. Red Bee was later recruited to join the ALL-STAR SQUADRON as the U.S. was plunged into World War II. The Apis Avenger, as he was nicknamed, appreciated being surrounded by his costumed colleagues although he recognized he was outpowered by most of them. Still, he fought with bravery, something recalled by surviving teammates years later. He survived at least into 1944 as a member of the FREEDOM FIGHTERS. He is known to have eventually perished, but the circumstances surrounding his death are unknown. RG

RED PANZER

FIRST APPEARANCE WONDER WOMAN (1st series) #228 (February 1977)
STATUS Villain REAL NAME Helmut Streicher
OCCUPATION Super-villain BASE Mobile
HEIGHT 6ft WEIGHT 190 lbs EYES Blue HAIR Brown
SPECIAL POWERS/ABILITIES Powered warsuit can withstand most damage and fire energy blasts; also provides limited resistance to damage.

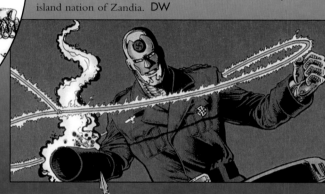

AMAZON ADVERSARY In all his incarnations, the Nazi-obsessed Red Panzer has been a foe of Wonder Woman.

Helmut Streicher, a general in the German army during World War II, developed an armored warsuit in order to prevent a vision of the Third Reich's defeat that he had witnessed through a time scanner coming true. Battling the JUSTICE SOCIETY OF AMERICA under the name Red Panzer, Streicher found his most vexing opponent to be HIPPOLYTA, who served as WONDER WOMAN throughout the war.

Streicher died after Adolf Hitler's defeat, but the Red Panzer cast such a long shadow that no less than three successors have since worn his armor. Red Panzer II was a neo-Nazi who perished in battle with the current Wonder Woman and TROIA.

The third Red Panzer got his start while still a teenager, after his father murdered his mother for perceived imperfections in her genetic history. Raised in foster homes with his father behind bars, the young man assumed a new identity as Red Panzer III, though he constantly battled with self-loathing, knowing that his blood was not 100% Aryan. Red Panzer III joined VANDAL SAVAGE's villainous team TARTARUS, but he died at the hands of the leader of the H.I.V.E. syndicate (see H.I.V.E. and DARHK, DAMIEN).

Vandal Savage hired a new Tartarus member to wear the crimson armor, and Red Panzer IV is still active today on the island nation of Zandia. DW

RED STAR

FIRST APPEARANCE TEEN TITANS (1st series) #18 (December 1968)
STATUS Hero REAL NAME Leonid Kovar
OCCUPATION Scientist; adventurer BASE Russian Federation
HEIGHT 5ft 10in WEIGHT 180 lbs EYES Green HAIR Blond
SPECIAL POWERS/ABILITIES Possesses superhuman strength and endurance; his body can turn into white hot flame.

Leonid Kovar and his father discovered a derelict spacecraft in the Yenesi River. The teenaged Leonid was bathed in alien energies emanating from the craft, giving him superpowers. Leonid became the first Russian super hero, Starfire. He met the TEEN TITANS on more than one occasion, clashing with their most conservative member, Wally West (see FLASH III). Even after Starfire's fiancée was infected with a deadly virus by an insane Russian official, Leonid remained committed to his country's communist ideals and became Red Star.

Red Star was part of an information exchange on meta-human development between the U.S. and Russian governments. The exchange was sabotaged by HAMMER AND SICKLE, and Red Star's communist beliefs were sorely tested. When JERICHO took control of the WILDEBEEST Society and attacked the Titans, Red Star joined forces with his former adversaries. After helping rebuild CYBORG, who was severely injured in the Wildebeest attack, and gaining new powers, which allowed him to generate intense heat and light, Red Star "adopted" fellow Titans PANTHA and Wildebeest as a surrogate family. The trio settled in Science City, Russia. PJ

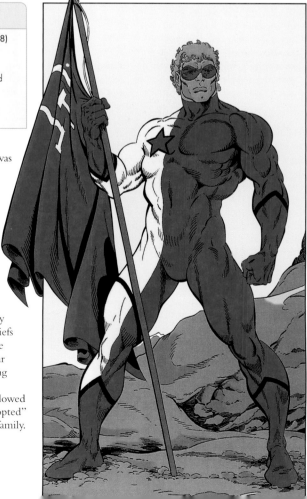

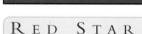

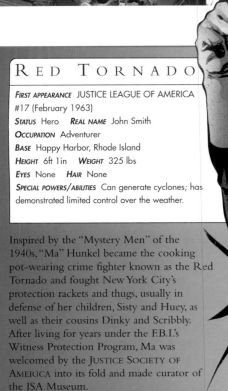

RED TORNADO

FIRST APPEARANCE JUSTICE LEAGUE OF AMERICA #17 (February 1963)
STATUS Hero **REAL NAME** John Smith
OCCUPATION Adventurer
BASE Happy Harbor, Rhode Island
HEIGHT 6ft 1in **WEIGHT** 325 lbs
EYES None **HAIR** None
SPECIAL POWERS/ABILITIES Can generate cyclones; has demonstrated limited control over the weather.

WHIRLING DERVISH *Like a crimson cyclone, the second Red Tornado uses his elemental powers to defend humanity.*

Inspired by the "Mystery Men" of the 1940s, "Ma" Hunkel became the cooking pot-wearing crime fighter known as the Red Tornado and fought New York City's protection rackets and thugs, usually in defense of her children, Sisty and Huey, as well as their cousins Dinky and Scribbly. After living for years under the F.B.I.'s Witness Protection Program, Ma was welcomed by the JUSTICE SOCIETY OF AMERICA into its fold and made curator of the JSA Museum.

The second Red Tornado was originally the Tornado Tyrant from the planet Rann, a living cyclone that journeyed to Earth and found its sentience infused within an android body created by the renegade scientist T.O. MORROW to destroy the JUSTICE LEAGUE OF AMERICA. Fortunately, Red Tornado turned on his creator and joined the JLA. The heroic android called himself John Smith, married Kathy Sutton, and adopted the orphan girl Traya. Red Tornado sacrificed his android body in the line of duty, reconstituting himself as Earth's Air Elemental. After briefly serving as mentor to YOUNG JUSTICE, the Red Tornado returned to active super-heroics and is attempting to mend fences with his estranged human family. **SB**

RED TORPEDO

FIRST APPEARANCE CRACK COMICS #1 (May 1940)
STATUS Hero **REAL NAME** James Lockhart
OCCUPATION Adventurer **BASE** Mobile
HEIGHT 5ft 8in **WEIGHT** 170 lbs **EYES** Blue **HAIR** Black
SPECIAL POWERS/ABILITIES Lockhart's Red Torpedo could not only move below the sea's surface, but also float on it and fly in the sky.

Based on an island in the South Seas, former Navy captain James Lockhart created a navigable torpedo capable of flight and became the Red Torpedo, scourge of saboteurs and Nazis. The Red Torpedo's worst foe was the Black Shark. On December 6, 1941, UNCLE SAM organized the FREEDOM FIGHTERS in a doomed attempt to turn back the Japanese attack on Pearl Harbor. Red Torpedo was one of several heroes captured by the Japanese. He was ultimately freed and returned stateside, hanging up his mask. Years later, Lockhart was asked by DOCTOR MID-NITE I to help build a star-shaped hovercraft to serve as his transportation when he temporarily protected Opal City as STARMAN II. **RG**

SUPER SUB
James Lockhart and his creation, the armored, powerful Red Torpedo.

RELATIVE HEROES

FIRST APPEARANCE RELATIVE HEROES #1 (March 2000)
STATUS Hero team **BASE** Mobile
CURRENT MEMBERS AND POWERS
Houston (leader) No superhuman abilities.
Temper Can control electricity.
Allure Possesses magically-based persuasive abilities.
Blindside Has the power of invisibility.
Omni Can imitate the superpowers of those around him.

Orphaned by a car crash, the superpowered Weinberg children embarked on a road trip in search of SUPERMAN—an odyssey that became the inaugural adventure of the Relative Heroes.

Police, child welfare officers, and DEO agents pursued the Relative Heroes team, which consisted of oldest brother Joel (Houston), younger sister Aviva (Temper), her babysitter Damara Sinclaire (Allure), and the Weinberg's adopted brothers Tyson Gilford (Blindside) and Cameron Begay (Omni). When the troupe reached Metropolis, the scientists of S.T.A.R. Labs revealed that Omni came from alien stock. The Relative Heroes convinced Omni's people to let him stay on Earth.

The Relative Heroes chose not to become full-time super heroes, but they remain potential players for the future. **DW**

RELATIVE HEROES
1) Blindside 2) Houston 3) Allure 4) Temper 5) Omni

REPLICANT

FIRST APPEARANCE THE FLASH SECRET FILES #2 (November 1999)
STATUS Villain **REAL NAME** Anthony Gambi
OCCUPATION Criminal **BASE** Central City
HEIGHT 7ft 5in **WEIGHT** 325 lbs **EYES** Mirrored **HAIR** None
SPECIAL POWERS/ABILITIES Can imitate other superpowers; projection of ice, flame; weather control.

Anthony Gambi, an orphan raised by his uncle Paul in Central City, befriended several members of the FLASH's Rogues Gallery when the villains came to the Gambi tailor shop for costumes and supplies. The Rogues took the young Anthony as a sort of ward, teaching him various tricks and becoming his surrogate family.

After CAPTAIN BOOMERANG was nearly killed during a battle with a new Flash, the Australian villain gathered the Rogues together in order to create a new super-villain capable of stopping this ruthless incarnation of the Fastest Man Alive. Volunteering for the job, Anthony was quickly transformed with various technologies into the Replicant, a villain who could manifest any of the Rogues' superpowers. The Replicant soon became the new Flash, who was in fact a version of Wally West from an alternate timeline. **PJ**

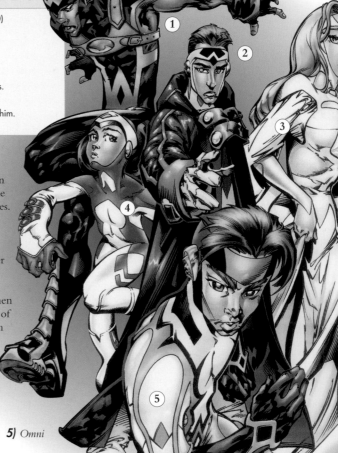

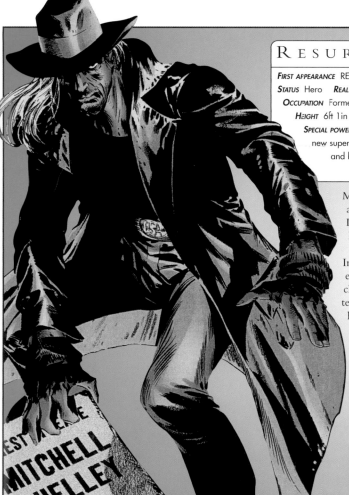

RESURRECTION MAN

FIRST APPEARANCE RESURRECTION MAN #1 (March 1997)
STATUS Hero **REAL NAME** Mitchell "Mitch" Shelley
OCCUPATION Former lawyer; adventurer **BASE** Mobile
HEIGHT 6ft 1in **WEIGHT** 190 lbs **EYES** Brown **HAIR** White
SPECIAL POWERS/ABILITIES An immortal champion imbued with
new superpowers each time he is reborn; his distinctive coat
and hat are remade by the tektites when damaged.

Mitch Shelley is an immortal man, and for
a brief time believed he was *the*
IMMORTAL MAN, imbued with eternal
life after exposure to the same meteor
that created the villain VANDAL SAVAGE.
In truth, Shelley was a lawyer,
experimented upon by the Lab, a
clandestine organization that injected
tektites—microscopic nanobots—into his bloodstream. With the tektites rebuilding his body each time
he died, Shelley possessed the closest thing to immortality. Moreover, the tektites also imbued him with
a different superpower each time he was resurrected. At first, Shelley suffered from amnesia and
traveled the U.S. in search of his lost memory while helping those in need. In the course of his
adventures, he fought AMAZO, the BODY DOUBLES, and other threats while making the acquaintances
of the JUSTICE LEAGUE OF AMERICA, SUPERGIRL, and other costumed heroes. Shelley ultimately

HEROIC PATHS
*Despite not considering himself a costumed
champion, Mitch Shelley has sided with Supergirl and other
heroes while attempting to recover his lost memories.*

discovered that he was not the Immortal Man,
although he did come into conflict with Vandal
Savage and, as has been revealed, will continue to
battle Savage through many lives and deaths well
into the 853rd century. In the present, however,
Shelley joined forces with the true Immortal Man
to stop Savage from obtaining the Temporal Meteor.
Mitch Shelley made a temporary home for himself
in Viceroy, South Carolina, with the love of this life,
private eye Kim Rebecki. **SB**

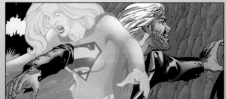

GHOST OF A CHANCE *Resurrection Man tries to give
a suddenly intangible Supergirl a helping hand.*

REVERSE-FLASH

FIRST APPEARANCE FLASH (1st series) #139 (September 1963)
STATUS Villain (deceased) **REAL NAME** Eobard Thawne
OCCUPATION Super-villain **BASE** 25th century Central City
HEIGHT 5ft 11in **WEIGHT** 179 lbs **EYES** Blue **HAIR** Reddish-blond
SPECIAL POWERS/ABILITIES Could run at near-light speeds, vibrating
through solid objects or temporal dimensions; though not a skilled
combatant, his brilliant mind led him to use his speed dangerously.

The evil Reverse-Flash, also known as Professor Zoom,
hailed from the far future of the 25th century. Eobard
Thawne became obsessed with the 20th century's second
and most prominent FLASH, Barry Allen, even going so far
as to try to duplicate his incredible powers. He found one
of the Flash's old costumes in a time capsule and the suit's
residual Speed Force energy provided the boost he needed.
Now possessed of superspeed, Thawne traveled back five centuries to meet
his idol but arrived several years after Allen's death during the Crisis (*see*
Great Battles, pp. 320–1). Conclusive evidence Thwane discovered in a
museum stating that he would one day become the evil Reverse-Flash
sent Thawne into psychological shock, and he briefly posed as a
resurrected Barry Allen before returning to his own time.

Thawne now harbored a hatred of Barry Allen. He dyed his costume
in opposite-spectrum colors and returned to the 20th century as
Professor Zoom, the Reverse-Flash. His attempts to win the heart of
Barry Allen's wife, Iris (*see* ALLEN, IRIS), failed dismally, so a bitter
Thawne apparently murdered her. Barry Allen sent his nemesis into
another dimension, but Thawne returned to menace Allen's new
fiancée, Fiona Webb. This time, Allen accidentally killed the Reverse-
Flash by snapping his neck. In the aftermath, Barry Allen was
acquitted of manslaughter, and Iris Allen revealed that she had
survived as a citizen of the 30th century. **DW**

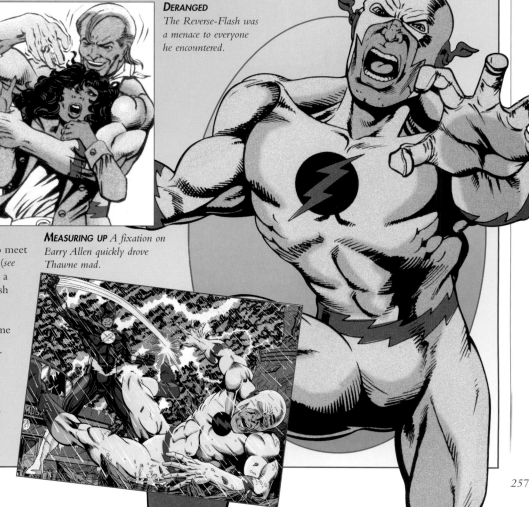

DERANGED
*The Reverse-Flash was
a menace to everyone
he encountered.*

MEASURING UP *A fixation on
Barry Allen quickly drove
Thawne mad.*

RIDDLER, THE

PRINCE OF PUZZLERS

FIRST APPEARANCE DETECTIVE COMICS #140 (October 1948)
STATUS Villain **REAL NAME** Edward Nigma (née Nashton)
OCCUPATION Professional criminal **BASE** Gotham City
HEIGHT 6ft 1in **WEIGHT** 183 lbs **EYES** Blue **HAIR** Black
SPECIAL POWERS/ABILITIES Brilliant in his own twisted way, but a poor hand-to-hand fighter; his addiction to leaving "enigmatic"clues to his crimes for Batman always proves his undoing.

EDWARD NIGMA'S SCHOOLTEACHER once held a contest to see which one of her pupils could assemble a puzzle the fastest. Little Edward secretly photographed the assembled puzzle, which he had found in the teacher's desk, and studied its formation so he could easily win. After this event, puzzles became his life. Failing in school, he took a job as a carnival barker, running a rigged puzzle booth. From there, it was only a matter of time before he turned to crime full-time as one of Gotham City's most famous rogues, the Riddler.

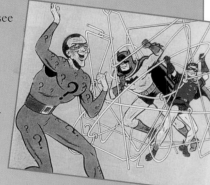

TRICKS FOR KICKS *The Prince of Puzzlers loved matching wits with the Dynamic Duo.*

ASKING THE QUESTIONS

The Riddler seemed psychologically incapable of committing a crime without first posing a riddle to BATMAN or the G.C.P.D. An admirer of the late, great escape artist Harry Houdini, the Riddler's tangled traps display a similar flair for showmanship. For years, he was considered a second-rate criminal, meeting defeat not only at the Dark Knight's hands, but also in matches against the ELONGATED MAN, FLASH I, GREEN ARROW I, BLACK CANARY, and the QUESTION. Recently, however, he has shown a more dangerous side, which seems to have attracted a score of followers. He is usually accompanied by Deidre Vance and Nina Damfino, known as Query and Echo II, who handle the rough stuff.

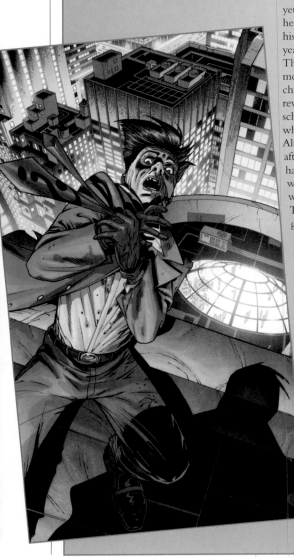

RIDDLER'S GANG *Over the years, the Riddler has used many costumed henchman, mere pawns in his master game.*

The Riddler was eventually diagnosed with terminal cancer, setting him on his most deadly path yet. He found one of RĀ'S AL GHŪL'S Lazarus Pits and healed himself. Hoping to profit from this, he turned to his doctor, Philadelphia physician Thomas Elliot. Many years before, Elliot had tried to kill his parents but Thomas Wayne (Bruce Wayne's father) had saved Elliot's mother's life. Elliott hated the Waynes for spoiling his childhood plot and conspired with the Riddler to gain revenge on Batman. Thus began an involved scheme organized and planned by the Riddler, who learned Batman's identity in the process. Although he was returned to Arkham Asylum after the plan failed, the Riddler is satisfied to have cracked the riddle of Batman's identity, while continuing to taunt the Dark Knight with the mystery of where the body of Jason Todd (ROBIN II)—a pawn in the Riddler's grand scheme—currently resides. **RG**

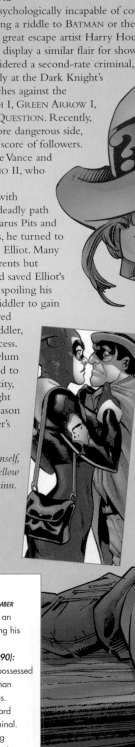

NO JOKING MATTER *Out for only himself, the Riddler has crossed many fellow rogues, including Harley Quinn.*

RETURN OF HUSH *When the Riddler's usefulness seemed at an end, he had good reason to fear the wrath of his former partner, Hush.*

KEY STORYLINES

• *BATMAN #608–619 (DECEMBER 2003–NOVEMBER 2004):* Paired with Hush, the Riddler set out an elaborate scheme to kill Batman after learning his secret identity.
• *Batman #452–454 (AUGUST–SEPTEMBER 1990):* In "Dark Knight, Dark City," the Riddler is possessed by the spirits of Gotham's founders as Batman learns about the city's gruesome beginnings.
• *SECRET ORIGINS SPECIAL (1989):* How Edward Nigma turned from cheater to master criminal.
• *THE QUESTION #26 (MARCH 1989):* Fleeing Gotham for Hub City, the Riddler wants to make a clean start, but fails once again.

REX, THE WONDER DOG

FIRST APPEARANCE THE ADVENTURES OF REX, THE WONDER DOG #1 (February 1952) **STATUS** Hero **REAL NAME** Rex
OCCUPATION Soldier; intergalactic Raver **BASE** Mobile
HEIGHT 2ft 8in **WEIGHT** 80 lbs **EYES** Blue **HAIR** White
SPECIAL POWERS/ABILITIES Incredibly intelligent, he can communicate with animals and humans alike.

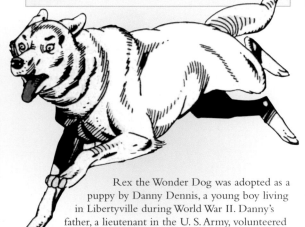

Rex the Wonder Dog was adopted as a puppy by Danny Dennis, a young boy living in Libertyville during World War II. Danny's father, a lieutenant in the U. S. Army, volunteered Rex for a series of experiments being conducted by Doctor Anabolus. These experiments transformed Rex, altering the little pup into a full-sized, superintelligent dog. Doctor Anabolus was killed soon after by Nazi agents, but Rex escaped and became a distinguished soldier during both World War II and the Korean War.

Danny grew up and joined the military himself, following in his father's footsteps. Together, the boy and his dog traveled the world, helping to defend the innocent. After drinking from the Fountain of Youth along with Bobo the DETECTIVE CHIMP, Rex became eternally spry, and eventually joined the intergalactic rave party known as the Event Horizon (see RAVERS). When the cosmic rave ended, Rex returned to Earth and, along with his friend Detective Chimp, still takes missions for the U.S. government's Bureau of Amplified Animals from time to time. **PJ**

FISTS OF FURY *Four massive arms double the danger posed by the Apokoliptian menace known as Rip Roar!*

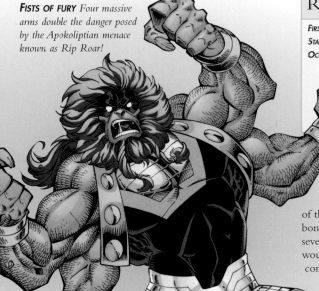

RIDDLER, THE SEE OPPOSITE PAGE

RIOT

FIRST APPEARANCE SUPERMAN: THE MAN OF STEEL #61 (Oct. 1996)
STATUS Villain **REAL NAME** Frederick Legion
OCCUPATION Super-criminal **BASE** Metropolis
HEIGHT 5ft 10in **WEIGHT** 145 lbs **EYES** Black **HAIR** Black
SPECIAL POWERS/ABILITIES Can create multiple duplicates of himself and reintegrate the copies at will.

Overworked at a high-tech laboratory, Frederick Legion decided that the only way he could complete all his experiments would be if there were somehow two Fredericks. Inspired, he stole a temporal phase shifter and plucked copies of himself from alternate microseconds in the timestream. He soon learned to duplicate without the aid of machinery, but the physical stress drove him mad and altered his appearance to that of a ghastly skeleton.

Now known as Riot, the multiplying menace clashed repeatedly with SUPERMAN but the Man of Steel's punches only created more Riots. Media mogul Morgan Edge recruited Riot into the Superman Revenge Squad (alongside Anomaly, Barrage, MAXIMA, and Misa), but the team never took off. When not terrorizing Metropolis, Riot is usually behind bars on Stryker's Island. **DW**

MULTIPLICATION *Replicating allows Riot to stand up to the mighty Man of Steel.*

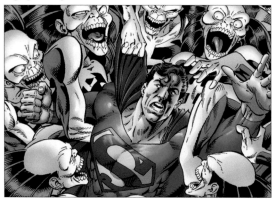

RIP ROAR

FIRST APPEARANCE YOUNG JUSTICE #2 (September 1998)
STATUS Villain **REAL NAME** None
OCCUPATION Warrior **BASE** Formerly Apokolips
HEIGHT 7ft 6in **WEIGHT** 180 lbs
EYES Red **HAIR** Strawberry blond
SPECIAL POWERS/ABILITIES Massively strong; able to project both fire and ice.

Long ago, the four-armed juggernaut Rip Roar was dispatched with his hated rival, KALIBAK the Cruel, to plunder tribute for their master DARKSEID. Rip Roar stole a Super-Cycle (see Amazing Vehicles, pp. 32–3) from New Genesis, home of the NEW GODS who opposed Darkseid. Rip Roar bonded with this sentient vehicle and rode roughshod over several worlds in Darkseid's name. Knowing that his father would look kindly on Rip Roar's destructiveness, Kalibak convinced Darkseid's majordomo DESAAD to sabotage Rip Roar's teleporting Boom Tube. Roar wound up entombed inside a mountain on Earth, until he was accidentally freed by YOUNG JUSTICE. After a battle, the teen heroes buried Rip Roar in lava. The Department of Extranormal Operations (D.E.O.) recovered the warrior, who remains in its custody for now. **SB**

RISING SUN

FIRST APPEARANCE SUPER FRIENDS #8 (November 1977)
STATUS Hero **REAL NAME** Isumi Yasunari
OCCUPATION Doctor; adventurer **BASE** Tokyo, Japan
HEIGHT 5ft 9in **WEIGHT** 165 lbs **EYES** Brown **HAIR** Black
SPECIAL POWERS/ABILITIES Absorbs solar energy and can project intense heat, light, and flame from his body; he can also generate superheated solar winds and use them to fly at great speeds.

Isumi Yasunari's grandparents were both survivors of the atom bomb dropped on Nagasaki, Japan, by the U.S. in 1945, which brought World War II to an end. Both of Isumi's grandparents later developed cancer and died. Isumi's mother also developed cancer but recovered with chemotherapy. Horrified by the genetic disposition of his family for degenerative disease, Isumi and his brother, Wataru, became doctors specializing in cancer research, while their troubled sister, Kaori, joined a religious cult.

Isumi used his abilities to absorb solar radiation and became Rising Sun, a staunch defender of Japan, who believes his country should take a less pacifistic approach in world affairs. Rising Sun joined the GLOBAL GUARDIANS, serving with them unwaveringly for years. Rising Sun is a notorious flirt and has vigorously pursued a romance with DOCTOR LIGHT II for some time. **PJ**

RISK

FIRST APPEARANCE TEEN TITANS (2nd series) #1 (October 1996)
STATUS Hero **REAL NAME** Cody Driscoll
OCCUPATION Student **BASE** Mobile
HEIGHT 5ft 10in **WEIGHT** 180 lbs **EYES** Blue **HAIR** Blond
SPECIAL POWERS/ABILITIES The result of an alien experiment, Cody is a mutant with superhuman strength, speed, and stamina.

Aliens called the H'san Natall came to Earth and conducted breeding experiments on humans. This resulted in the birth of four children who grew up to develop amazing powers. Their names were ARGENT II (Toni Monetti), JOTO (Isiah Crockett), PRYSM, and Risk (Cody Driscoll), and they were eventually gathered together by Mr. Jupiter and Omen to form a new incarnation of the TEEN TITANS. The ATOM II joined them at the point in his career when he was returned to his teenage physique. During a series of adventures, they learned of their true natures and tracked down the H'san Natall, which resulted in Prysm and FRINGE remaining in space with them. Risk and Joto chose to remain on Earth, largely forgoing their costumed identities. Risk was last seen aiding YOUNG JUSTICE in their all-out assault on LADY ZAND and the villains of Zandia. **RG**

RISKY BUSINESS *Cody lives life to the fullest, more than living up to his name.*

ROBIN

THE BOY WONDER

DICK GRAYSON (ROBIN I)
FIRST APPEARANCE DETECTIVE COMICS #38 (April 1940)
STATUS Hero   **REAL NAME** Richard "Dick" Grayson
OCCUPATION Crime fighter; police officer   **BASE** Gotham City
HEIGHT 5ft 10in   **WEIGHT** 175 lbs   **EYES** Blue   **HAIR** Black

JASON TODD (ROBIN II)
FIRST APPEARANCE DETECTIVE COMICS #526 (September 1983)
STATUS Hero (deceased)   **REAL NAME** Jason Todd
OCCUPATION Crime fighter; student   **BASE** Gotham City
HEIGHT 5ft 2in   **WEIGHT** 105 lbs   **EYES** Blue   **HAIR** Black

TIM DRAKE (ROBIN III)
FIRST APPEARANCE (as Tim Drake) BATMAN #436 (August 1989);
(as Robin) BATMAN #457 (December 1990)
STATUS Hero   **REAL NAME** Timothy Drake
OCCUPATION Student; crime fighter   **BASE** Gotham City
HEIGHT 5ft 5in   **WEIGHT** 125 lbs   **EYES** Blue   **HAIR** Black
SPECIAL POWERS/ABILITIES
Like the previous Robins, Tim Drake was trained by Batman in martial arts, as well as sleuthing skills. He is adept in the use of electronic devices, especially computers. Tim's utility belt carries the standard complement of Batarangs, gas capsules, de-cel jumplines, and other tools. His R-insignia doubles as a razor-sharp shuriken. Robin's costume is lined with Kevlar and Nomex fabrics, making it bulletproof and fire-resistant. His mask is fitted with Starlite night-vision lenses. Typically, Robins have ridden customized Batcycles in their own colors, but Tim prefers his Redbird, a crime-fighting car second only to the Batmobile.

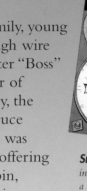

SENSATIONAL DEBUT *The introduction of Robin brought a ray of hope to the Dark Knight's nocturnal vigil.*

As a member of the Flying Graysons acrobatic family, young Dick Grayson thrilled audiences nightly on the high wire beside his circus aerialist parents. But when gangster "Boss" Zucco sabotaged the high wire because the owner of Haly's Circus refused to offer up protection money, the elder Graysons paid with their lives. Billionaire Bruce Wayne was in the audience that night; however, it was BATMAN who visited the grieving Dick Grayson, offering the boy a chance at retribution by becoming Robin, the Dark Knight's squire in his personal war on crime.

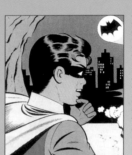

DICK GRAYSON
The first Robin was carefully schooled by Batman, learning all the skills he would need to bring "Boss" Zucco to justice. Before long, Dick was ready for action. Swearing a solemn oath, he joined the Dark Knight's crusade as his most trusted partner, Robin the Boy Wonder.

After several years in service to the Dark Knight, Grayson—then leader of the TEEN TITANS—relinquished the mantle of Robin when Batman forced him to choose between his duties with the Titans and his promise to aid the Dark Knight. Adopting the identity of NIGHTWING, Dick continued to battle crime while remaining Batman's close ally.

BRUCE WAYNE'S WARD
To give the orphaned Dick Grayson a home, billionaire Bruce Wayne became the boy's legal guardian. Wayne's trusted valet, Alfred (*see* PENNYWORTH, ALFRED) was just as much a surrogate father to Dick as Bruce was. While the Dark Knight's alter ego trained Dick in fighting and detective skills to become his second in the war on crime, Alfred made sure that Dick kept up with a more "classical" education. Bruce avoided adopting Dick because he didn't want to replace Dick's real father. However, he made Dick his legal heir in adulthood, and the two are as close as any father and son could be.

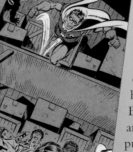

JASON TODD
Batman met juvenile delinquent and presumed orphan, Jason Todd, when the boy literally tried to steal the tires right off the Batmobile. With original partner Dick Grayson having given up the role of Robin, Batman decided to take Jason in and offer him both a home and a purpose. Jason began the same training regimen Grayson once undertook to become the Dark Knight's partner. However, Jason was a troubled soul who lacked maturity and was quick to anger.

A DEATH IN THE FAMILY
When Jason discovered clues that his long-lost mother was alive, he secretly traveled to Africa to find her. Tragically, the trail also led him straight into the clutches of the JOKER, who savagely beat the second Boy Wonder within an inch of his life. The Clown Prince of Crime left Jason and his mother to die in a booby-trapped warehouse wired from floor to ceiling with high-explosive charges. Jason courageously tried to shield his mother from the brunt of the devastating blast. She survived the explosion just long enough to tell a grief-stricken Batman that his reckless young partner had died a hero.

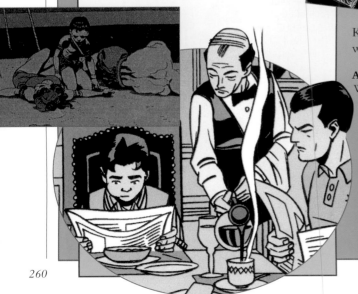

THE DEATH OF ROBIN *Batman cradled Jason in his arms, blaming himself for not rescuing him in time, consumed with rage at the Joker's latest, cruelest crime.*

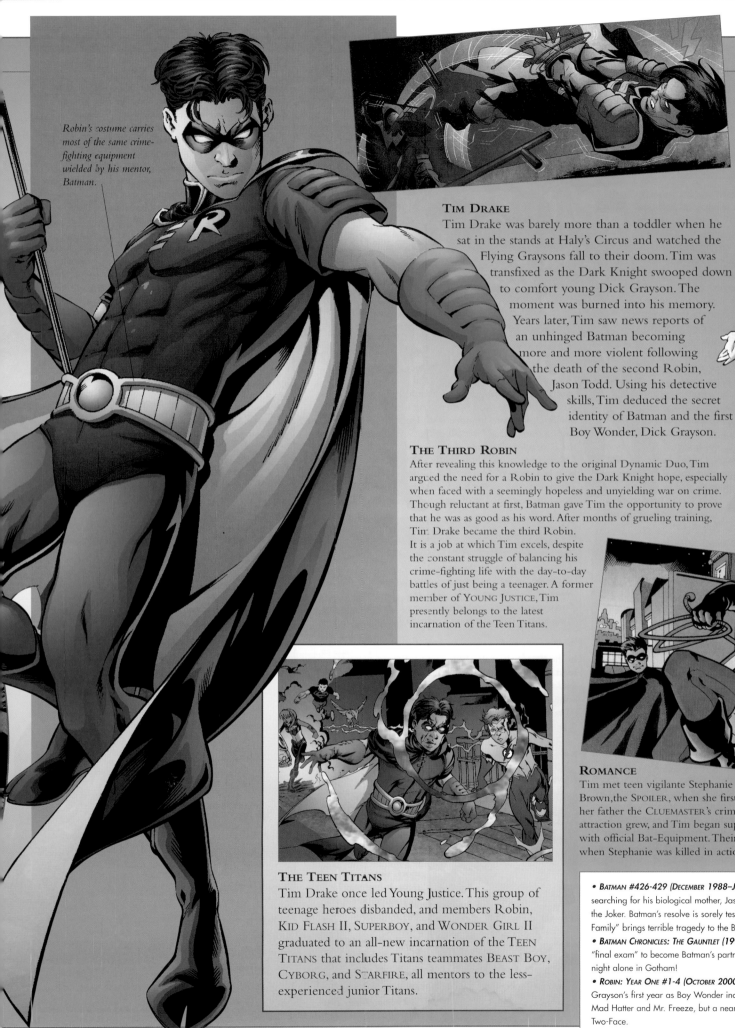

Robin's costume carries most of the same crime-fighting equipment wielded by his mentor, Batman.

TRAINING With Batman, Nightwing, Batgirl, and Azrael as sparring partners, Robin is prepared for combat with any opponent.

TIM DRAKE

Tim Drake was barely more than a toddler when he sat in the stands at Haly's Circus and watched the Flying Graysons fall to their doom. Tim was transfixed as the Dark Knight swooped down to comfort young Dick Grayson. The moment was burned into his memory. Years later, Tim saw news reports of an unhinged Batman becoming more and more violent following the death of the second Robin, Jason Todd. Using his detective skills, Tim deduced the secret identity of Batman and the first Boy Wonder, Dick Grayson.

MODEL STUDENT
Tim went to Brentwood Academy until his father had money trouble. Public education made it easier for Tim to operate as Robin.

THE THIRD ROBIN

After revealing this knowledge to the original Dynamic Duo, Tim argued the need for a Robin to give the Dark Knight hope, especially when faced with a seemingly hopeless and unyielding war on crime. Though reluctant at first, Batman gave Tim the opportunity to prove that he was as good as his word. After months of grueling training, Tim Drake became the third Robin. It is a job at which Tim excels, despite the constant struggle of balancing his crime-fighting life with the day-to-day battles of just being a teenager. A former member of YOUNG JUSTICE, Tim presently belongs to the latest incarnation of the Teen Titans.

ROMANCE

Tim met teen vigilante Stephanie Brown, the SPOILER, when she first attempted to thwart her father the CLUEMASTER's criminal schemes. Mutual attraction grew, and Tim began supplying Stephanie with official Bat-Equipment. Their love ended tragically, when Stephanie was killed in action. **SB**

THE TEEN TITANS

Tim Drake once led Young Justice. This group of teenage heroes disbanded, and members Robin, KID FLASH II, SUPERBOY, and WONDER GIRL II graduated to an all-new incarnation of the TEEN TITANS that includes Titans teammates BEAST BOY, CYBORG, and STARFIRE, all mentors to the less-experienced junior Titans.

- *BATMAN #426-429 (DECEMBER 1988–JANUARY 1989):* While searching for his biological mother, Jason Todd is murdered by the Joker. Batman's resolve is sorely tested as "A Death in the Family" brings terrible tragedy to the Batcave.
- *BATMAN CHRONICLES: THE GAUNTLET (1997):* Dick Grayson's "final exam" to become Batman's partner involves surviving a night alone in Gotham!
- *ROBIN: YEAR ONE #1-4 (OCTOBER 2000–JANUARY 2001):* Dick Grayson's first year as Boy Wonder includes victories against Mad Hatter and Mr. Freeze, but a near-fatal encounter with Two-Face.

SABBAC

FIRST APPEARANCE CAPTAIN MARVEL JR. #4 (February 1943)
STATUS Villain REAL NAME Timothy Karnes
OCCUPATION Would-be world conqueror BASE Mobile
HEIGHT 6ft 2in WEIGHT 240 lbs EYES Blue HAIR None
SPECIAL POWERS/ABILITIES Saying the word "Sabbac" gives Karnes
a range of demonic powers.

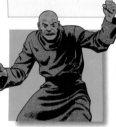

Timothy Karnes, foster brother of Freedy Freeman (see CAPTAIN MARVEL JR.), studied black magic to gain power. He succeeded beyond his wildest dreams when he conjured the spirits of six demonic entities. In a blasphemous parody of CAPTAIN MARVEL's own powers, the devils gave him unique abilities that he could wield by saying the word "sabbac."

Immediately upon uttering the magic word, Karnes felt the zap of a bolt of black lightning. He now had the powers of his benefactors: Satan's strength, Any's invulnerability, Belial's wisdom, Beelzebub's flames, Asmodeus's courage, and Craeteis's power of flight. He soon discovered that saying "Sabbac" once again turned him back into Karnes.

Sabbac battled the Marvel family and wound up behind bars. Recently, a Russian mafia boss named Ishmael Gregor sprung Karnes from prison and seemingly murdered him, taking the powers of Sabbac for himself. This new Sabbac has since gone on to menace the OUTSIDERS. **DW**

ST. CLOUD, SILVER

FIRST APPEARANCE DETECTIVE COMICS #469 (May 1977)
STATUS Hero's friend REAL NAME Silver St. Cloud
OCCUPATION Convention organizer BASE Gotham City
HEIGHT 5ft 5in WEIGHT 131 lbs EYES Blue HAIR Silver
SPECIAL POWERS/ABILITIES No superpowers, but beautiful, intelligent, and charismatic; a woman who knows her own mind.

Silver St. Cloud is a convention organizer who first met the billionaire playboy Bruce Wayne at a charity event held on Councilman Rupert Thorne's yacht. When BATMAN saved her from an assassin's bullet, Silver realized in a flash what few before her had even suspected: the Dark Knight, Gotham's grim defender, and the apparently feckless Bruce Wayne were one and the same person!

Silver and Bruce embarked on a romance, during which she told him of her suspicions about his dual identity. Rather than suffer in fear, waiting by the telephone as night after night Batman risked life and limb on Gotham City's crime-ridden streets, Silver decided she had better end her affair with Bruce Wayne before their romance became too serious. So she bid the Dark Knight a tearful farewell. **PJ**

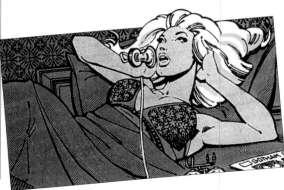

SALA

FIRST APPEARANCE GREEN LANTERN ANNUAL (2nd series) #9 (September 2000)
STATUS Hero REAL NAME Sala Nisaba
OCCUPATION Archaeologist BASE Nabeul, Tunisia
HEIGHT 5ft 7in WEIGHT 138 lbs EYES Green HAIR Brown
SPECIAL POWERS/ABILITIES Empowered by the Ringstaff of Istar, Sala possesses incredible strength, agility, and fighting skills as a modern-day Lady of Battle.

While excavating in the Syrian Desert, archaeologist Sala Nisaba discovered a gateway to the Babylonian underworld known as Kurnugi. Unfortunately, at the same time she inadvertently freed the demon lord Pazuzu and other vengeful gods. Kurnugi's ruler, NERGAL the Lord of Terror, informed Sala that she was descended from Istar, Lady of Battle, and by Nergal's mystical touch Sala was transformed into a new Istar. Teamed with Kyle Rayner (GREEN LANTERN V), a friend since attending art school together, Sala battled Pazuzu, Nergal and his wife, Ereskigal, and the monstrous Tiamat. Later, with the aid of the JUSTICE LEAGUE OF AMERICA, the Babylonian deities were returned to Kurnugi. Sala continues to use her powers as avatar of Istar to combat evils ancient and modern. **SB**

SALAKK

FIRST APPEARANCE GREEN LANTERN (2nd series) #149 (February 1982)
STATUS Hero (deceased) REAL NAME Salaak
OCCUPATION Green Lantern BASE Slyggia and Earth
HEIGHT 6ft 11in WEIGHT 207 lbs EYES White HAIR None
SPECIAL POWERS/ABILITIES With his power ring, this fearless loner could fight as well as any of his brethren.

Born on the planet Slyggia, Salakk inherited the mantle of GREEN LANTERN for sector 1418. He performed his job well but was considered a loner by his fellow GREEN LANTERN CORPS members. That did not stop him from agreeing to cover sector 1417 when its Lantern, KATMA TUI, was assigned to train John Stewart (Green Lantern IV), who was substituting for sector 2814's Hal Jordan. When the cosmic event called the Crisis caused a reduction in the number of Green Lanterns as well as the abandonment of the sector system, Salakk agreed to join several other Corpsmen based on Earth. There he developed his first true friendship with fellow Lantern CH'P. Salakk was accidentally brought to the year 5711 to portray Solar Director Pol Manning, a role Jordan had previously played several times, and he agreed to remain even after recovering his memories. Salakk later returned to the present in a futile attempt to prevent the destruction of the central power battery on Oa. In a state of deep depression, Salakk spent time with Ch'p and later joined John Stewart on Oa. Sometime after the decimation of the Corps, Salakk was captured and imprisoned by an evil clone of Guy Gardner, along with several other former Green Lanterns and was subsequently killed by parasitic aliens. **RG**

SALAMANCA

FIRST APPEARANCE FLASH (2nd series) ANNUAL #3 (2000)
STATUS Hero REAL NAME Unknown
OCCUPATION Hero BASE Buenos Aires, Argentina
HEIGHT 5ft 8in WEIGHT 142 lbs EYES Brown HAIR Black
SPECIAL POWERS/ABILITIES Sorcerous control over the elements; can leave her body as an astral form for three hours.

Salamanca, named after a supernatural location in Argentinean folklore, is the leader of the Argentinean super-hero group SUPER-MALON. Together with fellow heroes Pampero, CACHIRU, El Lobizon, Vizacacha, El Bagual, El Yaguarete, and Cimarron, she uses her incredible mastery over the weather to combat threats to her home country.

Not long ago, Salamanca's arch-enemy, the sorcerer Gualicho, imprisoned her and her former lover Cachiru in an alternate dimension. Jay Garrick, the original FLASH, could not free them, and only the current, third Flash, Wally West, succeeded in breaking Gualicho's control and liberating Salamanca and the others.

More recently, Salamanca and the Super-Malon were involved in a violent confrontation with CHEETAH III (Sebastian Ballésteros) and WONDER WOMAN in Buenos Aires. During the fight, the two rivals—Barbara Minerva and Sebastian Ballésteros—scuffled over the right to wield the Cheetah's powers, and Salamanca's team provided invaluable backup to Wonder Woman in her efforts to trap the villains and contain the damage. Salamanca is a romantic at heart, and holds out hope that one day she and Cachiru will be able to rekindle their love. **DW**

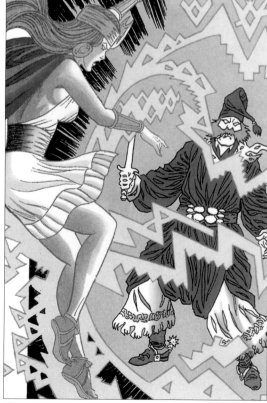

WITCHY WOMAN Salamanca is a potent magician. While in her astral form, she can sense the spirit-trails of ghosts.

SAND

FIRST APPEARANCE ADVENTURE COMICS #69 (December 1941)
STATUS Hero **REAL NAME** Sanderson Hawkins **OCCUPATION** Former chairman of JSA **BASE** New York City **HEIGHT** 5ft 11in **WEIGHT** 162 lbs **EYES** Blue **HAIR** Blond **SPECIAL POWERS/ABILITIES** Can manipulate silicon-based materials, causing earthquakes; can phase through earth, glass, or bricks; limited precognition.

Sanderson "Sandy" Hawkins is the nephew of Dian Belmont, the girlfriend of Wesley Dodds, SANDMAN I. Sandy idolized the legendary crime fighter and, unaware that Dodds was the "mystery man" in disguise, began a rigorous training program in the hope of becoming his sidekick. Dodds eventually revealed his identity to Sandy, who became the Sandman's protégé, Sandy the Golden Boy. The two heroes joined the ALL-STAR SQUADRON and fought Axis tyranny during World War II.

When a scientific experiment went awry, Sandy was transformed into a crazed silicon monster. The Sandman imprisoned the transformed Sandy in a special chamber, where his sidekick remained for decades. When a villain called the Shatterer attempted to exploit Sandy's silicon-based power, the Sandman triggered an explosion that freed his ward from his monstrous state. Sandy joined the Sandman and other members of the JUSTICE SOCIETY OF AMERICA to defend Earth against the coming of Raganarok, the end of the world.

When Dodds was killed by the DARK LORD, Sandy, now calling himself "Sand", rejoined the JSA to avenge Dodds and became the group's chairman and financier. He remains a member of the JSA, but has deferred leadership to MISTER TERRIFIC II. **PJ**

SILICON SUPER HERO
His body no longer human, Sand Hawkins is now a silicon-based life form. He can turn himself into stone or sand, and control those same elements with his mind. Sand now controls these transformations with technologies provided by Hourman II.

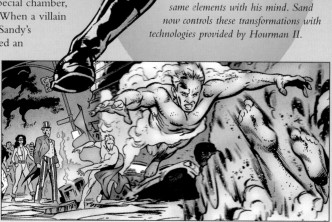

SANDMAN (MORPHEUS)

FIRST APPEARANCE SANDMAN (2nd series) #1 (March 1989)
STATUS Hero **REAL NAME** Morpheus, Dream, Oneiros, Kai'ckul and L'zoril **OCCUPATION** Guardian **BASE** The Dreaming **HEIGHT/WEIGHT** Variable **EYES** White **HAIR** Black **SPECIAL POWERS/ABILITIES** An immortal being of vast power; able to summon sleep and conjure dreams, from wistful fantasies to fevered nightmares, any of which were used to cure maladies or punish those who offended the Lord of Dreams.

Morpheus (or Dream) belonged to an eternal race of beings known as the ENDLESS. Since life began, Morpheus has watched over Earth and all mankind. More than 70 years ago, Morpheus was imprisoned by warlock Roderick Burgess, who had instead hoped to snare Dream's sister, DEATH. When he finally escaped decades later, Morpheus set about reclaiming his talismans—his sacred helm, his pouch filled with sleeping sand, and his mystic ruby—as well as restoring his realm, the Dreaming, which had fallen into disrepair during his absence. While Morpheus was imprisoned, two of his minions, Brute and Glob, enabled the human Dr. Garrett Sandford to operate from the Dreaming as a costumed hero known as the Sandman (no relation to Wesley Dodds, SANDMAN I). Upon Sandford's demise, Brute and Glob replaced him with Hector Hall (DOCTOR FATE), whose son Daniel was born in the Dreaming. Hector Hall later died and was reincarnated like his parents, HAWKMAN and HAWKGIRL, while baby Daniel and his mother, Lyta, were returned to Earth. The boy's destiny would be inextricably tied to the Dreamland.

Eventually, Morpheus was killed by the Furies, the beings known as the Eumenides or "The Kindly Ones" (*see* FURY I). However, before his death, Morpheus chose Daniel as his successor. Within the Dreaming, Daniel was aged to adulthood and has now taken Morpheus's place as Lord of Dreams and one of the Endless. **SB**

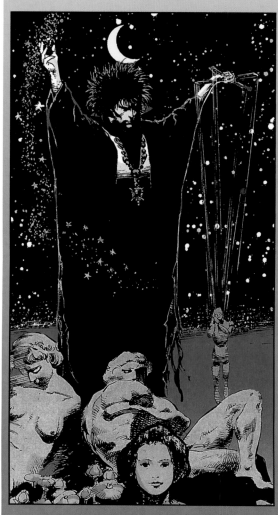

SANDMAN I

FIRST APPEARANCE ADVENTURE COMICS #40 (July 1939)
STATUS Hero (deceased) **REAL NAME** Wesley Dodds **OCCUPATION** Socialite; crime fighter **BASE** New York City **HEIGHT** 5ft 11in **WEIGHT** 210 lbs **EYES** Blue **HAIR** Black **SPECIAL POWERS/ABILITIES** Arsenal of gas weapons, including gas gun; later wielded "wirepoon" gun for climbing or snaring foes.

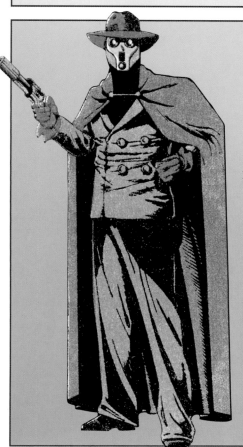

Prophetic, nightmarish dreams induced Wesley Dodds to take up the cloak, gas mask, and tranquilizing gas gun of the Sandman to thwart the evils of the waking world. The Sandman's first quarry was the PHANTOM OF THE FAIR, a villain stalking the 1939 New York World's Fair. Through his role as the Sandman, Dodds met and fell in love with Dian Belmont, who would eventually share his secret and his life. The Sandman joined the JUSTICE SOCIETY OF AMERICA as a founding member, and served the wartime ALL-STAR SQUADRON alongside his youthful partner Sandy Hawkins, Belmont's nephew (*see* SAND), trading cloak and fedora for a more colorful costume befitting the "Mystery Men" of the time. Dodds kept up the good fight for decades thereafter, until he committed suicide to prevent the sorcerer Mordru, the DARK LORD, from mining his mind to learn the location of the reincarnated DOCTOR FATE. **SB**

LIGHTS OUT *Sandman Wesley Dodds puts another villain to sleep.*

SARGE STEEL

FIRST APPEARANCE SARGE STEEL #1 (December 1964)
STATUS Hero **REAL NAME** Unknown
OCCUPATION Operative, D.E.O. **BASE** Washington, D.C.
HEIGHT 6ft 1in **WEIGHT** 198 lbs **EYES** Blue **HAIR** Black
SPECIAL POWERS/ABILITIES Expert martial artist who packs a powerful punch with his solid steel fist.

The "iron man with the fist of steel" received his trademark appendage during a stint with U.S. Special Forces, when communist agent Ivan Chong arranged for Steel to receive a booby-trapped hand grenade that exploded prematurely. Discharged from the military due to the accident, he received a solid steel prosthetic on his left stump and became a private investigator.

Steel became head of the Central Bureau of Intelligence (CBI), a spy organization whose field agents included ARSENAL and KING FARADAY. Steel also worked with CHECKMATE, a government strike team designed for high-powered combat response.

Once the CBI was absorbed into the Department of Extranormal Operations, Sarge Steel earned a place in the President's cabinet as Director of Meta-human Affairs (and briefly became a pawn of MISTER MIND). With the election of Lex Luthor (*see* LUTHOR, LEX), Amanda Waller (*see* WALLER, AMANDA) succeeded Steel in that post. Steel still works with the D.E.O, now under his former subordinates Waller and Faraday. **DW**

SARGON THE SORCERER

FIRST APPEARANCE ALL-AMERICAN COMICS #26 (May 1941)
STATUS Hero (deceased) **REAL NAME** John Sargent
OCCUPATION Stage magician **BASE** Legion World, U.P. Space
HEIGHT 5ft 11in **WEIGHT** 176 lbs **EYES** Brown **HAIR** Brown
SPECIAL POWERS/ABILITIES Possessed the magical Ruby of Life, which gave him mystical control over whatever object he touched.

In 1917, archaeologist Richard Sargent discovered the Ruby of Life, an object carved from the Ring of Life, a powerful totem once used by the SPECTRE. Unaware of its mystic origins, Sargent gave the Ruby to his wife. The jewel was the first thing their infant son John saw and touched. On an expedition with his father years later, John learned the true nature of the Ruby and discovered he could control its power. Deciding to use his abilities for good, but hiding their mystic nature behind the persona of a stage magician, John became Sargon the Sorcerer. Sargon joined the ALL-STAR SQUADRON during World War II. Decades later, he and a host of other mystics gathered together to prevent a great Shadow Creature from threatening Heaven with destruction. Sargon died when the Shadow Creature incinerated his body. **PJ**

SATANUS

FIRST APPEARANCE SUPERMAN (2nd series) #38 (December 1989)
STATUS Villain **REAL NAME** Satanus (alias Colin Thornton) **OCCUPATION** Demon lord
BASE The Netherworld **HEIGHT/WEIGHT/EYES/HAIR** Variable
SPECIAL POWERS/ABILITIES Alters size and appearance; can teleport himself and other beings; staff projects blasts of hellfire.

In the infernal netherworld, he is Lord Satanus, a demon in conflict with his demoness sister Blaze for control of an extra-dimensional purgatory, where human souls suffer endless torments. Deposed by Blaze, Satanus made his way to Earth and assumed the guise of mortal Colin Thornton, publisher of the Metropolis-based *Newstime* magazine. Satanus began a campaign to corrupt the much-coveted soul of the SUPERMAN. However, Satanus has been thwarted at every turn, either defeated by the Man of Steel, or vexed by Blaze, who desires Superman's indomitable spirit for herself. With the aid of the lesser demon Mudge, Satanus vainly attempted to take over the post-Y2K Metropolis, which was still reeling from the machine ills wrought by BRAINIAC 13. Satanus later abducted Cary Richards, a crippled boy whose psychic powers created the superpowered Adversary to punch out Superman. The Man of Steel freed Cary from Satanus's thrall, but the demon lord remains determined to drag the hero down to his level of hell. **SB**

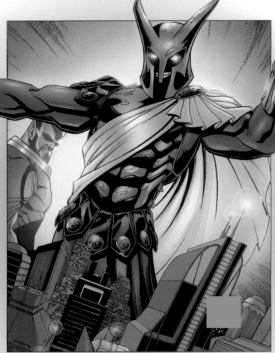

DEMON SPAWN *Satanus and his sister Blaze are the devilish children of the wizard known as Shazam!*

SATURN GIRL

FIRST APPEARANCE ADVENTURE COMICS #247 (April 1958); LEGION OF SUPER-HEROES (4th series) #0 (October 1994)
STATUS Hero **REAL NAME** Imra Ardeen
OCCUPATION Legionnaire **BASE** Legion World, U.P. Space
HEIGHT 5ft 7in **WEIGHT** 120 lbs **EYES** Blue **HAIR** Blonde
SPECIAL POWERS/ABILITIES Among the universe's top telepaths; Imra has experienced enough minds to have a unique perspective on things, making her a gifted leader.

Imra Ardeen from Titan, a moon of Saturn, was en route to Earth to join the Science Police when her telepathic powers detected an assassination plot against wealthy stargate inventor R.J. Brande (*see* BRANDE, R.J.). Working with Braal's Rokk Krinn and Winath's Garth Ranzz, the heroes foiled the plot. Impressed by their teamwork, Brande founded the LEGION OF SUPER-HEROES. Imra, dubbed Saturn Girl, discovered she hadn't fully developed the mental shielding necessary to keep from reading other minds or being influenced by evil telepaths. On one mission, she shut down the Composite Man's mind, losing her sanity in the process. The love of Garth Ranzz helped to heal her, and she subsequently accepted Garth's marriage proposal. The Legion was then split in two by the BLIGHT's attack and Saturn Girl commanded the team lost in another galaxy, using her mental skills to keep her teammates calm.

Later, they encountered a time-lost ELEMENT LAD, who had been driven mad by billions of years of isolation. Saturn Girl tried to shut his mind down, but she failed and Garth lost his life. Garth's spirit found its way back into Element Lad's crystallized body; however, this was too much for Saturn Girl, who shunned him. **RG**

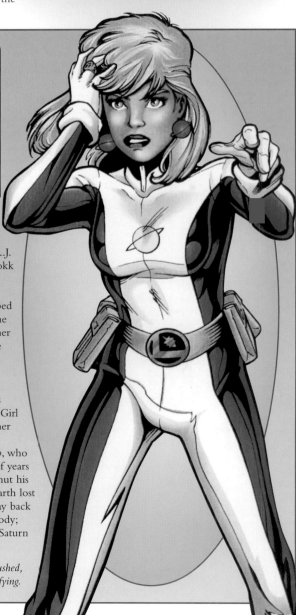

MENTAL STRENGTH *When she is pushed, Saturn Girl's thoughts can be terrifying.*

SAVAGE, MATT: TRAIL BOSS

FIRST APPEARANCE WESTERN COMICS #77 (October 1959)
STATUS Hero **REAL NAME** Matt Savage
OCCUPATION Cattle driver and trail boss
BASE The Texas Trail, 1860s–1870s
HEIGHT 5ft 10in **WEIGHT** 165 lbs **EYES** Blue **HAIR** Red-brown
SPECIAL POWERS/ABILITIES Expert tracker, horseman, and sharpshooter.

A special breed of men helped tame the post-Civil War American West. Unlike the wandering gunslingers such as BAT LASH, Trail Boss Matt Savage did an honest day's work by running a cattle drive, transporting cattle from Texas to Kansas.

Savage worked as a Union army scout and a miner before joining up with a cattle drive as a flank man. When he decided to become a trail boss and start up the Dogiron Crew, he brought aboard Union veteran Clay Dixon and Confederate veteran Jim Grant. To overshadow the Civil War of those two, Savage recruited Luther Jones, Manuel Ortega, and the mysterious Red. "Biscuits" Baker became the team's cook once Savage cleared him of a horse-thievery charge. Jebediah Kent, ancestor of Jonathan "Pa" Kent (see KENTS), briefly ran with Savage's team.

The Dogiron Crew drove their cattle between Texas and Kansas, encountering adventure along the way. Matt Savage is believed to be a relative of Brian Savage, the SCALPHUNTER. **DW**

SAVANT

FIRST APPEARANCE BIRDS OF PREY #56 (August 2003)
STATUS Villain **REAL NAME** Brian K. Durlin
OCCUPATION Extortionist; information broker **BASE** Gotham City
HEIGHT 6ft 3in **WEIGHT** 217 lbs **EYES** Blue-gray **HAIR** Blond
SPECIAL POWERS/ABILITIES Computer genius and extraordinary martial artist; Savant's brain imbalance makes him a particularly dangerous and unpredictable foe.

Wealthy Brian Durlin rarely finishes anything he starts, owing to a chemical imbalance in his brain that affects his memory. Although highly intelligent, Durlin's inability to properly distinguish the passage of time resulted in poor grades and he dropped out of school and university. Durlin's father disinherited him, leaving the young man penniless and living in Greece, where he began using blackmail to support his expensive tastes.

Durlin decided to turn his talents to heroics as the masked Savant, but was barred from Gotham City by BATMAN after Savant prioritized pursuing arsonists over saving the occupants of a burning building. Savant returned to blackmail, using his computer savvy to extort money from the wealthy. With his loyal assistant Creote, a former K.G.B. agent, Savant abducted the BLACK CANARY and held her hostage, hoping to coerce Barbara Gordon (ORACLE) to divulge Batman's civilian identity. With the Huntress's help, the Canary was freed and Savant was jailed. Oracle later opted to employ him as her assistant in the business of information brokering. **SB**

SAVITAR

FIRST APPEARANCE THE FLASH (2nd series) #108 (December 1995)
STATUS Villain (missing) **REAL NAME** Unrevealed
OCCUPATION Criminal **BASE** Tibet
HEIGHT 6ft 4in **WEIGHT** 220 lbs **EYES** Light blue **HAIR** Black
SPECIAL POWERS/ABILITIES By tapping into the Speed Force, Savitar can move his body at near light speed; can absorb motion from other objects and people, thereby slowing their movement.

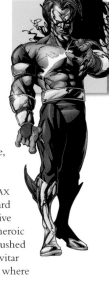

The man now known as Savitar was once an Eastern bloc military pilot. While flying an experimental supersonic plane, he was infused with Speed Force energy that gave him incredible superspeed, making him the fastest man alive. The pilot believed his superspeed was a divine gift, and named himself Savitar, after the Hindu god of motion. Curious about the true nature of this so-called Speed Force, Savitar began a cruel campaign of extortion against various other speedsters. During a battle with MAX MERCURY, Savitar was thrust forward in time to the present. After a massive battle between Savitar and Earth's heroic speedsters, Wally West (FLASH III) pushed the villain into the Speed Force. Savitar was absorbed into the energy field, where he remains trapped to this day. **PJ**

SCALPHUNTER

FIRST APPEARANCE WEIRD WESTERN TALES #39 (March 1977)
STATUS Hero (reincarnated) **REAL NAME** Brian Savage
OCCUPATION Police detective **BASE** Opal City **HEIGHT** 6ft 1in
WEIGHT 190 lbs **EYES** Blue; (as Matt O'Dare) blue **HAIR** (as Matt O'Dare) Red **SPECIAL POWERS/ABILITIES** Expert horseman; unerring aim with bow and arrow, tomahawk, rifle, or handgun.

Brian Savage was abducted from his parents by Kiowa Indians during the 1840s and renamed Ke-Woh-No-Tay, which roughly translates as "He Who Is Less Than Human." Raised in the Kiowa traditions, Savage was later known as Scalphunter to the white men he encountered on his many adventures across the Wild West. After learning the truth about his roots, Scalphunter became a gunfighter, eventually settling down in Opal City during its frontier days. As Opal's sheriff, Savage maintained law and order for more than a decade.

He eventually married and retired to a farm in Turk County. His son, Steve Savage, became famous many years later as the World War I aerial ace known as BALLOON BUSTER. Brian Savage died in 1899, shot in the back after returning to Opal City during tumultuous times. Perhaps owing in some way to his Kiowa background, Savage was reincarnated as Opal City police detective Matt O'Dare, friend and ally of STARMAN. Matt has assumed the mannerisms of the late, great Scalphunter. **SB**

SCARAB

FIRST APPEARANCE SCARAB #1 (November 1993)
STATUS Hero **REAL NAME** Louis Sendak
OCCUPATION Adventurer **BASE** New York City
HEIGHT 5ft 10in **WEIGHT** 170 lbs **EYES** Brown **HAIR** Brown
SPECIAL POWERS/ABILITIES The Scarabaeus allowed him to command mystic energies, either as raw power or in subtle manifestations.

Louis Sendak was born in Staten Island, N.Y. during the 1920s. In 1924, Louis's father brought home various mystic artifacts including the Door and the Scarabaeus. Louis later used this talisman to become the occult adventurer Scarab.

He was a successful hero, teaming with other mystics to form the Seven Shadows. When Johnny Sorrow (see SORROW, JOHNNY) murdered six of the Seven Shadows, their deaths caused Scarab to suffer a mental breakdown. During his convalescence, Louis's wife, Eleanor, was drawn into the Door and vanished. Decades later, Sendak teamed up with the JUSTICE SOCIETY OF AMERICA on their quest for the Fate child, only to be attacked by the DARK LORD. Stripped of his magic powers, he became the unwitting vessel chosen by Johnny Sorrow to enable his master, the King of Tears, to return to the known world from the plane of non-reality he was trapped in. **RG**

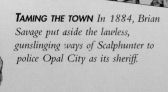
TAMING THE TOWN In 1884, Brian Savage put aside the lawless, gunslinging ways of Scalphunter to police Opal City as its sheriff.

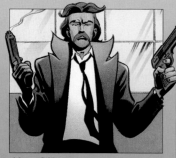
MATT O'DARE Once a corrupt cop in a family of devoted lawmen, Matt O'Dare renounced his wicked ways after discovering that he was the reincarnation of the western hero Scalphunter.

SCARECROW

FIRST APPEARANCE WORLD'S FINEST COMICS #3 (Fall 1941)
STATUS Villain **OCCUPATION** Professor and professional criminal
REAL NAME Jonathan Crane **BASE** Gotham City
HEIGHT 6ft **WEIGHT** 150 lbs **EYES** Blue **HAIR** Brown
SPECIAL POWERS/ABILITIES A psychologist and biochemist, Crane used his knowledge to create a fear-inducing gas that causes nightmarish hallucinations in the mind of anyone who inhales it; costume also designed to strike terror; a manic hand-to-hand combatant.

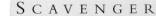

Harmless tease?
Jonathan was a spindly nerd, easily fooled by a sexy girl like Sherry.

TORMENTING TEENS
More cruel pranks fractured his already fragile psyche.

Gawky and uncoordinated as a child, Jonathan Crane was often the physical and emotional target of neighborhood bullies. Initially frightened by their horrible taunts, Crane eventually decided he would turn the tables on his attackers, and began voraciously studying phobias and the nature of fear. As an adult, Crane became an expert psychologist, specializing in fear. He also acquired some knowledge of chemistry, studying how certain combinations of chemicals could affect the human psyche. Crane became a professor at Gotham City University, but was summarily dismissed for his unorthodox teaching methods and his refusal to follow the school's safety codes.

Crane's fragile mind snapped after his dismissal and he adopted the guise of the Scarecrow, vowing to use his knowledge of fear and his own specially designed "fear gas" to gain revenge. Using this chemical, the Scarecrow killed several of Gotham University's regents by literally scaring them to death. The Scarecrow was then confronted by the BATMAN, who ended the villain's reign of terror and incarcerated him in Arkham Asylum for the Criminally Insane.

Escaping from custody over and over again, the Scarecrow used stolen funds to constantly upgrade the potency of his fear gas, mixing powerful synthetic adreno-cortical secretions with potent hallucinogens to create a pathogen strong enough to prompt almost instantaneous, terror-induced heart attacks in his victims.

A constant foe of Batman and his allies, and a spooky threat to the citizens of Gotham City, the Scarecrow is obsessed with fear in all its manifestations and relishes inflicting it. Perhaps fortunately, Crane is prey to a phobia of his own: *Chiropteraphobia*, a chronic fear of bats or, more specifically, of Batman! **PJ**

TERROR MASTER
A psychiatrist turned psychopath, the Scarecrow uses his fear gas to terrorize his victims, often leaving their minds permanently crippled.

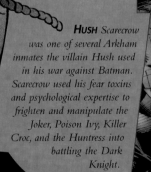

HUSH *Scarecrow was one of several Arkham inmates the villain Hush used in his war against Batman. Scarecrow used his fear toxins and psychological expertise to frighten and manipulate the Joker, Poison Ivy, Killer Croc, and the Huntress into battling the Dark Knight.*

SCAVENGER

FIRST APPEARANCE SUPERBOY (2nd series) #4 (March 1994)
STATUS Villain **REAL NAME** Unknown **OCCUPATION** Plunderer
BASE Mobile **HEIGHT** 5ft 10in **WEIGHT** 160 lbs
EYES One white; one cybernetic **HAIR** White
SPECIAL POWERS/ABILITIES Long-lived; possesses several cybernetic implants; wields weapons pillaged from various heroes and villains.

His origins a closely guarded secret, the Scavenger travels the world using stolen teleportation technology, searching for mystic talismans and items of power. He claims he was once wronged by a godlike hero and is gathering weapons for a coming battle with this mystery foe. The Scavenger also believes that all heroes are conspiring against humanity and cannot be trusted.

The Scavenger has battled SUPERBOY on several occasions, and he also engaged in a cyberspace auction hoping to outbid GREEN ARROW I for a vintage Arrow Car. The Scavenger continues to prepare for conflict with his unnamed nemesis. **SB**

SCORCH

FIRST APPEARANCE JLA #61 (February 2002)
STATUS Villain (reformed and deceased) **REAL NAME** Aubrey (second name unknown)
OCCUPATION Unrevealed **BASE** Pisboe, VA
HEIGHT 5ft 9in **WEIGHT** 140 lbs **EYES** Red **HAIR** Black
SPECIAL POWERS/ABILITIES Does not sleep and seems to have complete mastery over fire, from generating it to controlling its intensity.

The sultry young woman Aubrey, known as Scorch, escaped from a variation of reality when the JOKER briefly gained MISTER MXYZPTLK's fifth-dimensional, cosmic powers. She battled both SUPERMAN and the MARTIAN MANHUNTER as she tried to make a name for herself in the world of crime. Although offered a chance to reform and become a force for good by Superman, she refused. Later, the Manhunter asked Scorch to help him overcome his psychological fear of fire in exchange for helping her calm her tortured mind. During the resulting sessions they became lovers, although Superman remained suspicious of her motives. His doubts seemed justified when she unwittingly unleashed an ancient Martian horror; however, Scorch sacrificed herself to save not only her beloved but the entire JLA. **RG**

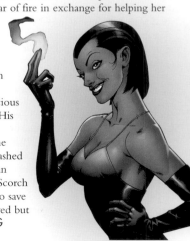

SEA DEVILS

First appearance SHOWCASE #27 (August 1960)
Status Hero team **Base** Earth's oceans and waterways
Members and Powers
Dane Dorrance (leader) Expert diver and natural leader.
Biff Bailey Powerful combatant.
Judy Walton Charismatic and athletic.
Nicky Walton Quick-witted and eager.

The Sea Devils, like the CHALLENGERS OF THE UNKNOWN, predated the modern heroic age and excelled in an era when non-superpowered teams could still capture the public's imagination. In their career they battled sea monsters, vanquished aquatic super-villains, and discovered undersea kingdoms. Dane worked for a time with the Forgotten Heroes, and eventually he and Judy married. Ardent environmentalists, the Sea Devils still aid the super-hero community, most notably during the allied alien invasion of Earth (see Great Battles, pp. 320–1). DW

THE SEA DEVILS
1) Judy Walton
2) Dane Dorrance
3) Nicky Walton
4) Biff Bailey

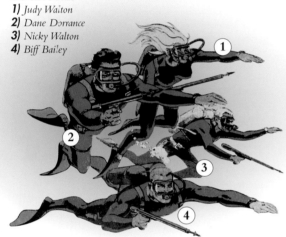

SECRET

First appearance YOUNG JUSTICE: THE SECRET #1 (June 1998)
Status Hero **Real name** Greta Hayes
Occupation Warder **Base** Mobile
Height 4ft 8in **Weight** Unknown **Eyes** Blue **Hair** Light brown
Special powers/abilities Secret is a wraithlike form which allows her to pass through solid objects and create psychic manifestations.

SUPERBOY, ROBIN III (Tim Drake) and IMPULSE helped rescue a mysterious phantom girl called the Secret from D.E.O. custody. Soon after, the trio formed YOUNG JUSTICE and Secret, nicknamed "Suzie," was welcomed as a member. During her time with the group, she developed a crush on Robin. The SPECTRE counseled Secret, revealing her origin—the demon Buzz and Greta's brother made a pact, which resulted in her becoming a warder, a spirit on the fringes of Death's domain but incapable of going to the other side herself. Worried about turning evil like her brother, now known as Harm, she kept her distance from most of the team. Soon after she was corrupted by DARKSEID, and went on a rampage until Robin managed to break through to her. Darkseid "punished" the young warder by restoring her humanity. RG

SECRET SIX

First appearance ACTION COMICS WEEKLY #601 (May 1988) **Status** Hero team **Base** Top secret
Current Members and Powers
Mitch Hoberman Arthritic special effects artist.
LaDonna Jameal Mute and disfigured actress.
Tony Mantegna Deaf reporter.
Luke McKendrick Crippled Olympic athlete.
Vic Sommers Blind combat veteran.
Dr. Maria Verdugo Epileptic mathematician.

Formed decades ago by the enigmatic MOCKINGBIRD, the original Secret Six were a team of undercover operatives fighting crime and defending democracy, though ultimately serving the goals of a covert U.S. government group, the Agency. After many successful missions, the Secret Six retired. Reunited years later, the team was flying to train a new generation of operatives when their sabotaged plane crashed into a mountain. Five of the Six—save for Carlo di Rienzi, a master escape artist—were killed instantly. Di Rienzi established another sextet of stealthy adventurers and assumed the role of a new Mockingbird. The new Secret Six comprised individuals with disabilities helped or negated by high-tech devices given them by Mockingbird. Once more, the Secret Six fought to uphold democracy. They also tracked down Agency operative Walter Fenady who had killed the first Secret Six. The Six remain active, and free from the Agency's treacherous agenda. SB

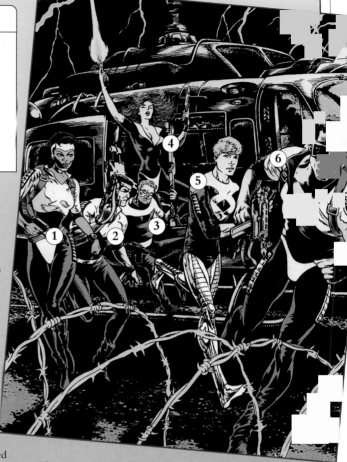

1) LaDonna Jameal **2)** Tony Mantegna **3)** Mitch Hoberman
4) Dr. Maria Verdugo **5)** Luke McKendrick **6)** Vic Sommers

SECRET SOCIETY OF SUPER-VILLAINS

First appearance SECRET SOC. OF SUPER-VILLAINS #1 (June 1976)
Notable Members (see individual entries for powers)
Darkseid, Captain Boomerang, Captain Cold, Copperhead, Gorilla Grodd, Manhunter IV, Trickster I, Mirror Master I, Sinestro, Poison Ivy, Floronic Man, Blockbuster I and II, Reverse-Flash, Chronos I, Charaxes, Killer Frost I, Rag Doll, Ultra-Humanite, Cheshire, Deadshot, Per Degaton, Scarecrow, Felix Faust, Wizard, Riddler, Scarecrow, Deadshot, Hector Hammond, Sivana, Solomon Grundy, Royal Flush Gang, Mist I, Star Sapphire III, Psycho-Pirate (manipulates emotions), **Shadow Thief** (becomes a living shadow), **Funky Flashman** (master conman), **Matter Master** (transmutes elements), **Monocle** (energy blasts), **Brainwave I** (psychic powers), **Silver Ghost** (intangibility), **Signalman** (gimmick weapons), **Quakemaster** (creates earthquakes), **Captain Stingaree** (swordsman).

One of the largest and most significant convocations of criminals ever assembled, the Secret Society of Super-Villains was created by DARKSEID as an underground organization that would rid Earth of its super heroes. After Funky Flashman and GORILLA GRODD each briefly took control of the Society, the villains, the premier enemies of the JUSTICE LEAGUE OF AMERICA and the JUSTICE SOCIETY OF AMERICA, made several attempts to destroy them both. Under the auspices of the ULTRA-HUMANITE, a new version of the Secret Society fought the JLA and the JSA before the heroes banished them to limbo.

Later, during the Crisis (see Great Battles, pp. 320–1), the Anti-Monitor used the emotion-manipulating powers of the Psycho-Pirate to mentally dominate the second FLASH. Soon after, the Pirate, one of the few beings to remember the Crisis, went mad. When the most recent incarnation of the Society was formed, the MARTIAN MANHUNTER infiltrated the Secret Society's headquarters and the JLA incarcerated those present. PJ

VILLAINS EVERYWHERE *After the first Society dissolved, Funky Flashman recruited a second, convincing its members that all they needed was strong publicity to accomplish their goals. The members included* **1)** *Star Sapphire* **2)** *Captain Boomerang* **3)** *Wizard* **4)** *Mirror Master I* **5)** *Captain Cold* **6)** *Gorilla Grodd* **7)** *Funky Flashman* **8)** *Shadow Thief* **9)** *Copperhead.*

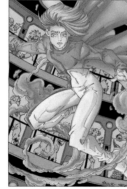

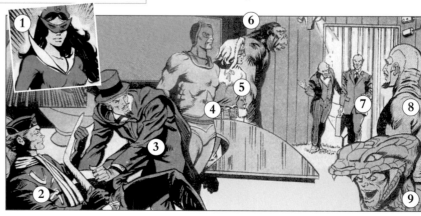

SENSOR

FIRST APPEARANCE LEGIONNAIRES #43 (December 1996)
STATUS Hero **REAL NAME** Jeka Wynzorr
OCCUPATION Legionnaire **BASE** Legion World, U.P. Space
HEIGHT 12ft **WEIGHT** 250 lbs **EYES** Green **HAIR** Purple
SPECIAL POWERS/ABILITIES Can sense the perceptions of others and create realistic illusions through hypnosis; of royal blood, she is accustomed to giving orders.

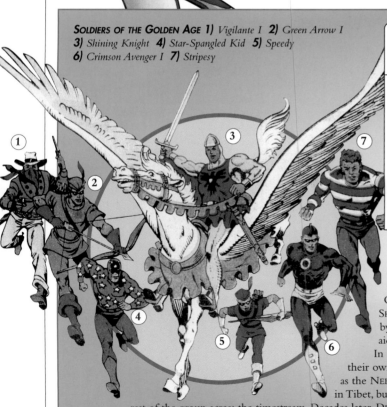

Jeka Wynzorr is a member of the royal family of Orando, a planet inhabited by gigantic serpents with the ability to cast illusions. Despite family opposition, Jeka joined the LEGION OF SUPER-HEROES as Sensor. She abandoned her claim to the Orandan throne to devote her time to the Legion, and also developed a close friendship with her shape-changing teammate CHAMELEON. Because the Legion's facilities were designed for humanoids, Sensor often wore a harness fitted with cybernetic arms. Sensor suffered a grievous injury that caused her to form a healing cocoon. When she emerged from the chrysalis she had mutated into a new form—serpentine below the waist, but humanoid above. Since then she has rescued Legionnaires KARATE KID and FERRO and has helped defeat the villain Universo. DW

SERAPH

FIRST APPEARANCE DC COMICS PRESENTS #46 (June 1982)
STATUS Hero **REAL NAME** Chaim Lavon
OCCUPATION Teacher; activist **BASE** Jerusalem, Israel
HEIGHT 5ft 10in **WEIGHT** 165 lbs **EYES** Brown **HAIR** Black
SPECIAL POWERS/ABILITIES Superstrength; Ring of Solomon enables teleportation; Staff of Moses can transform into a snake, generate forcefields, and null gravity; wears the symbolic Mantle of Elijah.

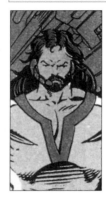

Chaim Lavon was born in Netanya, a city on the west coast of Israel. The youngest of four siblings, Chaim was horrified by the continued animosity between the Israelis and the Arab world and became a pacifist and a teacher, working at an Arab school to teach culture and language to Jews and Muslims alike. On a pilgrimage to a small synagogue outside Bethlehem, Chaim stopped on a dirt road and cried out in frustration to God for an end to the suffering in the Middle East. Chaim was answered by a brilliant light and a voice that declared that Chaim would lead the Middle East out of its destructive cycle of conflict. Chaim was given several mystic objects and became the hero Seraph.

Seraph was invited to join DOCTOR MIST's GLOBAL GUARDIANS, becoming one of its most visible members, although he resided in Israel. When the first Queen Bee (see QUEEN BEE II) hypnotized a number of the Guardians into working for her, Seraph, unaware of the Queen's cunning, distanced himself from the team. After the Queen was defeated and the Guardians were attacked by the villain Fain Y'Onia, Seraph returned, tending to injured teammate Tuatara. PJ

SERIFAN

FIRST APPEARANCE FOREVER PEOPLE 1st series #1 (March 1971)
STATUS Hero **REAL NAME** None
OCCUPATION Adventurer **BASE** New Genesis
HEIGHT 5ft 7.5in **WEIGHT** 143 lbs **EYES** Blue **HAIR** Blond
SPECIAL POWERS/ABILITIES Cosmic Cartridges create "shock-repelli-field" gravity effects, vehicle-fueling power, intense heat, or stun blasts.

A member of the FOREVER PEOPLE, Serifan was one of five children from New Genesis trained by HIGHFATHER of the NEW GODS to use their miraculous powers in the defense of their native Genesis. In one adventure, Serifan and the Forever People thwarted DARKSEID's agent, DEVILANCE, but were trapped on the distant world of Adon. VYKIN used the team's Mother Box, to evolve Adon's natives. Vykin died, but the Adonians became civilized and the Forever People built them Forevertown, their first city. Unfortunately, Serifan's sensitivity to telepathy allowed an evil entity, the Dark, to possess him. The Dark turned back time on Adon, reversing the Forever People's gifts, but inadvertently resurrecting Vykin. The INFINITY MAN ultimately drove the Dark away for good. Serifan and his friends returned to New Genesis, where they continue to help the New Gods protect their planet from warmongering Apokolips. SB

SOLDIERS OF THE GOLDEN AGE 1) *Vigilante I* 2) *Green Arrow I* 3) *Shining Knight* 4) *Star-Spangled Kid* 5) *Speedy* 6) *Crimson Avenger I* 7) *Stripesy*

SEVEN SOLDIERS OF VICTORY

FIRST APPEARANCE LEADING COMICS #1 (Winter 1941–1942)
STATUS Hero team **BASE** Mobile
MEMBERS AND POWERS
Crimson Avenger I Two-fisted crusader for justice.
Spider Expert with bow and arrow.
Shining Knight Time-tossed paladin astride winged steed.
Vigilante I Expert fighter, horseman, marksman, and singer.
Billy Gunn All guts, fists, and attitude.
Star-Spangled Kid Wealthy teen turned combatant.
Stripesy Skilled fighter, even more skilled engineer.

SOLDIERS OF THE SILVER AGE 1) *Batgirl I* 2) *Deadman* 3) *Adam Strange* 4) *Mento* 5) *Blackhawk* 6) *Metamorpho* 7) *Atomic Knight*

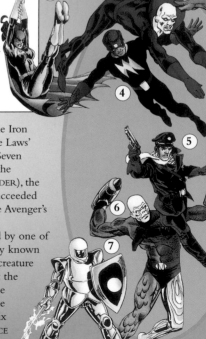

Independently stopping the villainous agents of the Iron Hand, seven heroes joined together to become the Laws' Legionnaires, more commonly referred to as the Seven Soldiers of Victory. Founding members included the CRIMSON AVENGER I, the Spider (see ALIAS THE SPIDER), the SHINING KNIGHT, VIGILANTE I, Billy Gunn (later succeeded by Stuff), the Star-Spangled Kid, and STRIPESY. The Avenger's aide, WING, was the unofficial eighth member.

In 1948, the Seven Soldiers of Victory were betrayed by one of their own, the Spider, and engaged in battle with the entity known as the NEBULA MAN. Wing sacrificed his life to destroy the creature in Tibet, but the resulting explosion of temporal energies cast the rest of the group across the timestream. Decades later, DEADMAN organized a short-lived new edition of the SSV including Adam Strange (see STRANGE, ADAM), Batgirl, Blackhawk, Mento, Metamorpho, and the second SHINING KNIGHT to defend the planet Rann from attack by the Injustice League. Soon after that, six of the time-displaced original Soldiers were rescued by the united JUSTICE SOCIETY OF AMERICA and JUSTICE LEAGUE OF AMERICA before RED TORNADO II sacrificed his life to save Earth from the Iron Hand. RG

SERGEANT ROCK
THE COMBAT-HAPPY JOE

FIRST APPEARANCE OUR ARMY AT WAR #81 (April 1959)
STATUS Hero REAL NAME Frank Rock
OCCUPATION Former leader of Easy Company BASE Mobile
HEIGHT 6ft WEIGHT 183 lbs EYES Blue HAIR White (formerly red)
SPECIAL POWERS/ABILITIES Expert combatant, marksman, and battlefield
leader; is skilled with almost every known firearm and can operate
most varieties of tanks and other heavy equipment.

THE ALL-STAR SQUADRON earned much of the U.S.'s attention during World War II with their brightly-colored costumes and their superhuman powers. Yet no one is considered a greater wartime hero than a simple, G.I.-uniformed Army sergeant named Frank Rock. Rock suffered unfathomable tragedies before he ever saw combat. His father died in World War I. His stepfather suffocated during a mine collapse. A father figure Rock looked up to while working at a Pittsburgh steel mill also lost his life. Many of his siblings similarly perished, but patriotic Rock enlisted in the army the day after the Japanese attacked Pearl Harbor in 1941 and received an immediate assignment to the European theater of war.

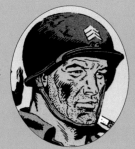

IN PRINT Sergeant Rock was immortalized by writer Kanigher and artist Kubert.

THE GOOD SOLDIER

Private Rock didn't truly distinguish himself until the D-Day invasion in 1944. Soon after, at the Battle of Three Stripes Hill, he received a battlefield promotion to sergeant. Sergeant Rock's unit, Easy Company, quickly became one of the most distinguished fighting forces in Europe. Moving from North Africa to Italy to France to Germany, the "combat-happy Joes" included such stalwarts as Wildman, Little Sure Shot, Bulldozer, Farmer Boy, and the Ice Cream Soldier. Pulling off impossible missions, the company lived up to their motto, "Nothin's ever easy in Easy."

Sergeant Rock struck up a battlefield romance with French resistance fighter MADEMOISELLE MARIE and served a brief tour in the Pacific theater. He refused promotions so often he received the nickname "the general of sergeants." According to legend, he died when struck by the last enemy bullet fired on the last day of the war.

Rock, however, survived. Performing postwar covert missions for the U.S. government, he battled his old foe the Iron Major and teamed up with Easy Company veteran Bulldozer on an assignment to Dinosaur Island. Recently, U.S. President Lex Luthor (see LUTHOR, LEX) named General Frank Rock—by then in his eighties—Chairman of the Joint Chiefs of Staff. Rock died during the Imperiex War (see Great Battles, pp. 320–1) and was buried with full honors at Arlington National Cemetery. A short time later a similar Frank Rock appeared at the head of a reconstituted SUICIDE SQUAD. It is debatable whether this Rock was the original or merely an imposter. DW

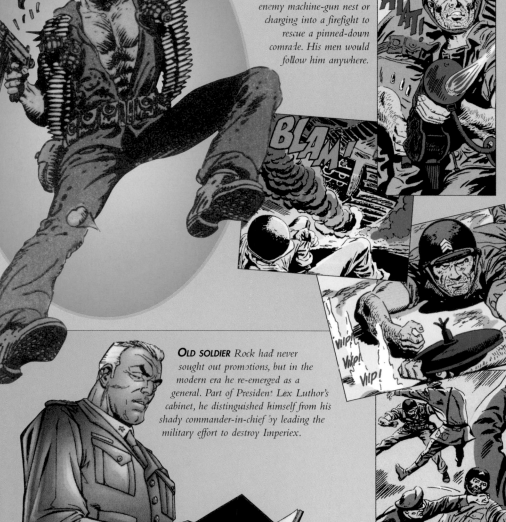

QUIET HERO Rock never thought twice about advancing on an enemy machine-gun nest or charging into a firefight to rescue a pinned-down comrade. His men would follow him anywhere.

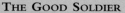

OLD SOLDIER Rock had never sought out promotions, but in the modern era he re-emerged as a general. Part of President Lex Luthor's cabinet, he distinguished himself from his shady commander-in-chief by leading the military effort to destroy Imperiex.

DEFENSIVE General Rock prevents Imperiex from invading Washington.

SHADE, THE

FIRST APPEARANCE FLASH COMICS #35 (September 1942)
STATUS Supernatural villain **REAL NAME** Richard Swift
OCCUPATION Criminal (retired) **BASE** Opal City
HEIGHT 6ft 2in **WEIGHT** 170 lbs **EYES** Gray **HAIR** Black
SPECIAL POWERS/ABILITIES Immortality; can summon
"shadowmatter"—matter of all kinds, shapes, and sizes, including
living beings—from a dimension called the Dark Zone.

Soon after acquiring the ability to manipulate
shadowmatter, Richard Swift met Simon Culp, who
possessed similar powers. When the two shadowcasters
were caught in an explosion, their souls fused together,
although Swift's essence controlled their physical body.
Swift, now an immortal who called himself the Shade,
traveled the world, amassing a fortune. No longer
believing that the moral laws of mere mortals applied
to him, the Shade settled in Opal City. During and
after World War II, the Shade joined the INJUSTICE
SOCIETY, exhilarated by the challenge of besting heroes
like FLASH I and the JUSTICE SOCIETY OF AMERICA. He
eventually gave up crime to defend his adopted home,
Opal City and befriended STARMAN
Jack Knight. Centuries into the future,
a cursed Shade transformed into the
mysterious Dark Colossus
and battled the LEGION OF
SUPER-HEROES. PJ

ROGUE AND HERO The Shade shares a
joke with his former foe, the first Starman.

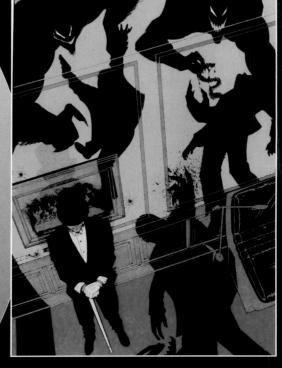

SHADOWY POWERS Motivated by the tedium of his life more
than by malice or greed, the Shade remained a criminal for years,
plunging Keystone City in darkness to loot its banks, or using his
Dark Zone creatures to rumble with the Fastest Man Alive.

SHADE, THE CHANGING MAN

FIRST APPEARANCE SHADE, THE CHANGING MAN (1st series) #1
(July 1977) **STATUS** Hero **REAL NAME** Rac Shade
OCCUPATION Adventurer **BASE** Mobile **HEIGHT** 5ft 6in
WEIGHT 108 lbs **EYES** Blue **HAIR** Red **SPECIAL POWERS/ABILITIES**
Formidable combatant; M-vest emits energy that distorts people's
perceptions of its wearer according to their emotional state, also
projects force-field, and enables flight, or travel between dimensions.

On the other-dimensional
world of Meta, security
service agent Rac Shade was
framed for causing an explosion
that crippled the parents of his
true love, Mellu Loren. Little
did Shade realize that Mellu's
mother was Sude, the Supreme
Decider, head of a conspiracy to
take over Meta's dimension, the
Meta-Zone, and the neighboring
dimension containing Earth.
Donning the M-vest, created by
the genius Dr. Miraco, Shade
embarked on a struggle to clear his
name. At one point, Shade became
trapped in the Zero-Zone between
Earth and Meta, his M-vest damaged
and unable to transport him to either
world. He was saved by the SUICIDE
SQUAD and joined the Squad in
exchange for passage to Meta.
Presumably, not much had changed for
Shade on Meta. When last seen, he was
back on Earth, perhaps for good. SB

SHADO

FIRST APPEARANCE GREEN ARROW:
THE LONGBOW HUNTERS #1 (1987)
STATUS Hero **REAL NAME** Shado
OCCUPATION Kyudo Master **BASE** Japan
HEIGHT 5ft **WEIGHT** 109 lbs **EYES** Brown **HAIR** Black
SPECIAL POWERS/ABILITIES One of the world's greatest archers, using
Japanese bamboo arrows 97.5 centimeters long, and a bow
weighing 30 kilograms; is also well trained in the martial arts.

Tomonaga worked for the Yakuza, the Japanese criminal
organization, and was sent with two million dollars in gold
bullion to the U.S. to help set up American operations.
Before he could use the money, he was placed in an
internment camp after the Japanese attack on Pearl
Harbor. Soldiers tried to learn the money's whereabouts
but failed. Once released, Tomonaga married and had a
daughter, but was tracked by soldiers who wanted the
bullion for themselves. When they tortured his wife, he
had little choice but to comply. Returning to Japan, he
committed *seppuku* for failing in his mission, and the
Yakuza raised the girl, named Shado, as one of their
own. She was trained to be their agent, and was given a
tattoo on her left arm, shoulder, breast, and shoulder
blade that formed the image of a large red dragon. Her
first assignment was to kill the men who brought
about her father's downfall. One of the men was
killed instead by Oliver Queen (GREEN ARROW)
because he had also tortured Queen's lover, BLACK
CANARY II. Later, Shado was asked to commit acts she
felt were too heinous and refused, which pitted her against
the Yakuza, who now wanted her dead. She has crossed
paths with Green Arrow on numerous occasions, which
resulted in her giving birth to their son, Robert. She has
chosen a life of seclusion to raise the boy and avoids
contact with both the Yakuza and Oliver Queen. RG

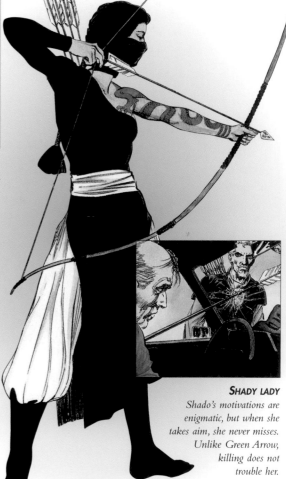

SHADY LADY
Shado's motivations are
enigmatic, but when she
takes aim, she never misses.
Unlike Green Arrow,
killing does not
trouble her.

SHADOWDRAGON

FIRST APPEARANCE SUPERMAN #97 (February 1995)
STATUS Undecided **REAL NAME** Prince Savitar Bandu
OCCUPATION Prince of Bhutan, adventurer **BASE** Metropolis
HEIGHT 5ft 9in **WEIGHT** 147 lbs
EYES Brown **HAIR** Black
SPECIAL POWERS/ABILITIES Skilled martial artist and computer hacker;
wears weapon-studded armored suit that also confers invisibility.

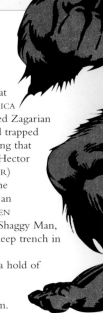

Shadowdragon is the alternate persona of Prince Savitar Bandu of Bhutan, who uses his ninja-like stealth and lightning-fast combat skills to steal technology that will benefit his developing nation. He wears an advanced X-10 battlesuit—stolen from the rival nation of Chi-Lann—that allows him to turn invisible or to fire poison darts. Shadowdragon has trained most of his life to become a master of the martial arts and is also one of the world's top computer hackers.

Despite his ongoing thefts, Shadowdragon is an honorable man who only acts in the best interests of his people. Upon first arriving in Metropolis, he uncovered reams of computer data on SUPERMAN for use by the villain Conduit; however, when Shadowdragon learned of Conduit's malevolent motives toward the Man of Steel, he erased the data. He continues to operate in both Metropolis and Bhutan, and to do everything in his power to ensure a prosperous future for the citizens he will one day rule as king. **DW**

SHAGGY MAN

FIRST APPEARANCE JUSTICE LEAGUE OF AMERICA #45
(June 1966) **STATUS** Robotic villain (destroyed)
REAL NAME/OCCUPATION Inapplicable **BASE** Mobile
HEIGHT 5ft 5in **WEIGHT** 437 lbs
EYES Red **HAIR** Brown
SPECIAL POWERS/ABILITIES Superhuman strength; near
invulnerability; body part regeneration.

The Shaggy Man was a robotic creature created by Professor Andrew Zagarian with "plastalloy," a synthetic substance resembling human tissue. The robot came to life and went on a rampage, one that even the JUSTICE LEAGUE OF AMERICA could not stop. The FLASH persuaded Zagarian to create a second Shaggy Man and trapped the two robots on an asteroid, hoping that each would destroy the other. But Hector Hammond (see HAMMOND, HECTOR) intervened and teleported one of the Shaggy Men to the JLA satellite in an attempt to destroy the heroes. GREEN LANTERN was able to capture that Shaggy Man, and AQUAMAN imprisoned it in a deep trench in the Pacific Ocean.

Later, General Wade Eiling got a hold of the Shaggy Man body hidden by Aquaman, and transferred his consciousness into its synthetic form. The now nearly indestructible GENERAL became a part of Lex Luthor's second INJUSTICE GANG (see LUTHOR, LEX). **PJ**

SHARK

FIRST APPEARANCE GREEN LANTERN (2nd series) #24 (October 1963)
STATUS Villain **REAL NAME** Has used aliases T.S. Smith and Karshon
OCCUPATION Predator **BASE** Mobile
HEIGHT 6ft 2in **WEIGHT** 243 lbs **EYES** Black **HAIR** None
SPECIAL POWERS/ABILITIES A powerful psionic able to manipulate
matter, project energy bolts, and communicate telepathically;
also able to fly and grow to gigantic size.

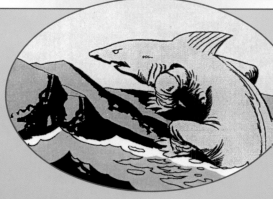

Radiation leaking from an oceanside nuclear power station transformed a tiger shark into a mutant humanoid monster. Imbued with increased intelligence and psionic powers, the Shark was still driven by his species' primal predatory urges, but now fed on the psyches of his victims rather than their flesh. The Shark attacked Hal Jordan (GREEN LANTERN II) hoping to make the fearless Green Lantern experience terror before he consumed his mind. However, Jordan defeated the Shark and devolved him to his original state. The Shark regained his humanoid form on several occasions, battling both Green Lantern and AQUAMAN, briefly deposing the latter from his throne by disguising himself as an Atlantean named Karshon and using his mental might to rule Atlantis. Later, the Shark was recruited by Green Lantern III Guy Gardner to join a squad of super-villains opposing the Qwardians during the Crisis conflict (see Great Battles, pp. 320–1).

When last seen, the Shark had returned to the Atlantean capital Poseidonis with an army of evolved sharks seeking to retake Aquaman's throne. The King of the Seas proved his worth once more, defeating the mutant with his superior telepathy. **SB**

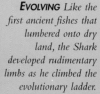

EVOLVING Like the first ancient fishes that lumbered onto dry land, the Shark developed rudimentary limbs as he climbed the evolutionary ladder.

POWER TO DESTROY With just a thought, the Shark could wreak havoc with his psionic powers or devastating energy bolts.

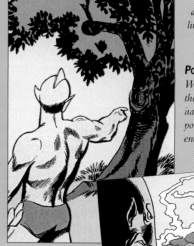

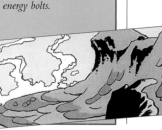

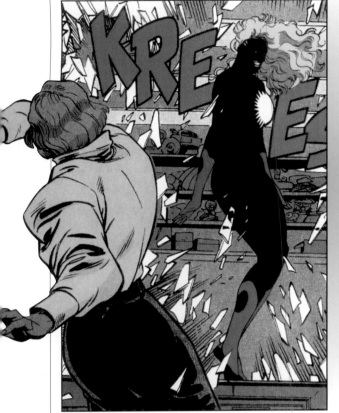

SHELLSHOCK II

FIRST APPEARANCE STEEL #6 (July 1994)
STATUS Villain   **REAL NAME** Ruth Spencer
OCCUPATION Assassin   **BASE** New Jersey
HEIGHT 5ft 4in   **WEIGHT** 120 lbs   **EYES** Brown   **HAIR** Black
SPECIAL POWERS/ABILITIES Has the ability to cause objects to explode with a single punch, but she must name the item or her power fails.

The first villain to go by the name Shellshock was a woman with the ability to generate explosive force from her body. She battled the second HAWK AND DOVE team before being defeated by SUPERMAN, and has seemingly retired from a life of crime. The current villain operating as Shellshock is a member of Black Ops, an organization of techno-pirates run by Manual Cabral, known as Hazard II (see HAZARD I). Nothing is known about how Ruth Spencer gained her energy-punch powers or came in contact with Hazard. She is fiercely loyal to Black Ops's charismatic leader, acting as his lieutenant. It is unclear if she harbors romantic feelings for Hazard II or is simply an idealistic zealot. Under Hazard's command, the Black Ops attempted to take over the entire nuclear arsenal of the U.S., only to be opposed and ultimately stopped by John Henry Irons, STEEL III. After their final defeat, Hazard turned his attention to other nefarious schemes for acquiring the latest high-tech weaponry and selling it to the highest bidder. The members of his ruthless team, including second-in-command Shellshock, await his orders. **RG**

SHINING KNIGHT

FIRST APPEARANCE ADVENTURE COMICS #66 (September 1941)
STATUS Hero   **REAL NAME** Sir Justin, a.k.a. Justin Arthur
OCCUPATION Knight   **BASE** Camelot; New York City
HEIGHT 6ft 1in   **WEIGHT** 185 lbs   **EYES** Blue   **HAIR** Blond
SPECIAL POWERS/ABILITIES Master of knightly combat; wears enchanted, bulletproof armor and wields enchanted sword; rides a flying horse.

While riding to battle the ogre Blunderbore, Sir Justin—a knight of King Arthur's Round Table—was accosted by outlaws. While driving them off, Sir Justin grazed a tree with his lance and released the wizard Merlin from mystical imprisonment. The grateful Merlin enchanted Sir Justin's sword and armor, and gave his noble steed wings. Merlin's gifts helped Sir Justin to slay Blunderbore, but not before the dying ogre buried Sir Justin and his horse, Winged Victory, beneath a mountain of ice.

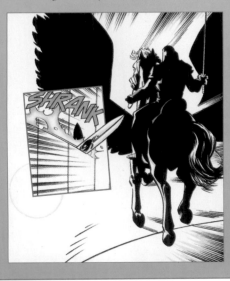

WINGED VICTORY
Sir Justin's brave horse still carries him into battle.

For centuries, Sir Justin and Winged Victory lay in suspended animation. But in 1941, the knight was freed by Dr. Moresby, who helped Sir Justin to establish the identity of Justin Arthur and make a new home in New York City. As the Shining Knight, Sir Justin joined the ALL-STAR SQUADRON, and then the SEVEN SOLDIERS OF VICTORY. He also fell in love with Danette Reilly (FIREBRAND II), and was griefstricken to learn of her death at the hands of the DRAGON KING. The Shining Knight slew the Dragon King in aerial combat, and continues to cross swords with evil wherever he finds it. **SB**

SHIMMER

FIRST APPEARANCE THE NEW TEEN TITANS (1st series) #3 (Jan. 1981)
STATUS Villain   **REAL NAME** Selinda Flinders
OCCUPATION Professional criminal   **BASE** Mobile
HEIGHT 5ft 7in   **WEIGHT** 125 lbs   **EYES** Blue   **HAIR** Red
SPECIAL POWERS/ABILITIES Could temporarily transform one element or compound into another.

Selinda Flinders and her brother Baran were born in Australia and shunned because of their superhuman abilities. Their father brought them to Doctor Helga Jace, a renowned Markovian scientist, to help them master their powers and develop a sense of right and wrong. Selinda and Baran, however, rejected their education and became professional criminals, eventually joining DOCTOR LIGHT I in his villainous organization, the FEARSOME FIVE.

Shimmer, as Selinda came to be called, and her brother, now named MAMMOTH, fought the New TEEN TITANS several times over the years, and were imprisoned more than once.

The two siblings renounced crime and found peace in a Tibetan monastery. However their former teammate PSIMON came seeking revenge for their betrayal of the Fearsome Five. Psimon turned Shimmer into glass and shattered her body, killing her instantly. Mammoth only barely survived. However, Shimmer was resurrected by DOCTOR SIVANA. She and Mammoth returned to a life of crime with a new Fearsome Five. **PJ**

SHOCK TRAUMA

FIRST APPEARANCE THE TITANS #21 (November 2000)
STATUS Villain   **REAL NAME** Unrevealed
OCCUPATION Assassin   **BASE** Japan
HEIGHT 5ft 6in   **WEIGHT** 146 lbs
EYES Unrevealed   **HAIR** Unrevealed
SPECIAL POWERS/ABILITIES Can generate and emit electricity over short distances but at lethal levels.

Shock Trauma was born and raised in Japan. He is the youngest member of the HANGMEN. This group is typical of the new generation of assassins, in it purely for the money. They are all power, no subtlety. The team, which also includes Breathtaker, Provoke, Stranglehold, and KILLSHOT, made its mark in Europe before taking assignments in America. Its first visit to the U.S. was unusual, a kidnapping, not killing assignment, at the behest of rebels from the Middle-Eastern country of Qurac. The Hangman were sent to collect Lian Harper, the daughter of Teen Titan ARSENAL and the international terrorist CHESHIRE, who set off a nuclear device in Qurac. The TEEN TITANS defeated the Hangmen, and rescued Lian. Following this encounter, Shock Trauma went into hiding, presumably readying himself for another Hangman mission. **RG**

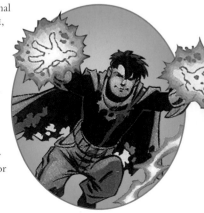

SHRECK

FIRST APPEARANCE SUICIDE SQUAD (1st series) #37 (January 1990)
STATUS Villain REAL NAME Unknown
OCCUPATION Vampire BASE Mobile
HEIGHT 6ft 3in WEIGHT 188 lbs EYES Black HAIR Black
SPECIAL POWERS/ABILITIES Superstrength; partial invulnerability; ability
to hypnotize.

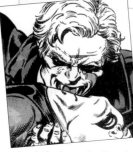

Shreck is a vampire who feeds on blood and possesses many of the powers associated with the lords of the undead. He is also an agent for the Russian government, having logged time with all the major Russian meta-human programs. Most recently he served as a member of the Red Shadows, the Russian covert strike agency that acted as the Eastern equivalent to America's SUICIDE SQUAD.

Shreck and the Red Shadows tussled with the Suicide Squad in a mission that took them to Cambodia in search of the Temple of the Dragon's Hoard. Shreck's vampiric gift for mesmerism came in handy when he took control of Suicide Squad member NIGHTSHADE, though the Red Shadows came away from the battle empty-handed. **DW**

SHRINKING VIOLET

FIRST APPEARANCE LEGION OF SUPER-HEROES (4th series) #66
(March 1995) STATUS Hero REAL NAME Salu "Violet" Digby
OCCUPATION Legionnaire BASE 30th-century Earth
HEIGHT 5ft 2in WEIGHT 105 lbs EYES Violet HAIR Black
SPECIAL POWERS/ABILITIES Can shrink to subatomic size or grow 30 feet
tall, with a proportionate increase in mass and strength.

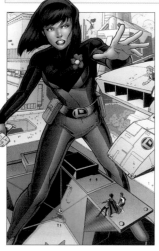

A native of the planet Imsk, whose inhabitants can all shrink to tiny size, the socially awkward Salu Digby was chosen to become a member of the LEGION OF SUPER-HEROES because of her power, her deductive skills, and her combat prowess. Using the name Shrinking Violet, Salu was quickly admitted to the Legion's Espionage Squad.

The overly shy Violet was contacted by the Emerald Eye of Ekron, a sentient talisman, who wanted to make use of her body as a host for its energies. Violet agreed to allow the mystical force to merge with her body, and the Emerald Eye possessed her. Violet took control of the Legion and hurled some of the members back in time. Eventually she was freed from the Eye's tyrannical thrall during a battle between the Legion and Mordru the DARK LORD, who desired the Eye's power for himself.

During her possession by the Eye, Violet's fellow Legionnaire LEVIATHAN perished at her hands. She failed to use the power of the Eye to revive him, but absorbed Leviathan's power to grow to great heights and took the name Le Viathan. She later changed her name to Violet and worked to rebuild her reputation as a Legionnaire, which had been severely damaged during her possession by the Emerald Eye. **PJ**

SILVER BANSHEE

FIRST APPEARANCE ACTION COMICS #495 (December 1987)
STATUS Hero REAL NAME Siobhan McDougal/Lacy MacElwain
OCCUPATION Adventurer BASE The Netherverse
HEIGHT 6ft 11in WEIGHT 180 lbs EYES White HAIR Silver
SPECIAL POWERS/ABILITIES Impervious to gunfire; possesses superhuman
speed and the strength of ten men; her siren wail is a deadly song,
killing anyone within earshot.

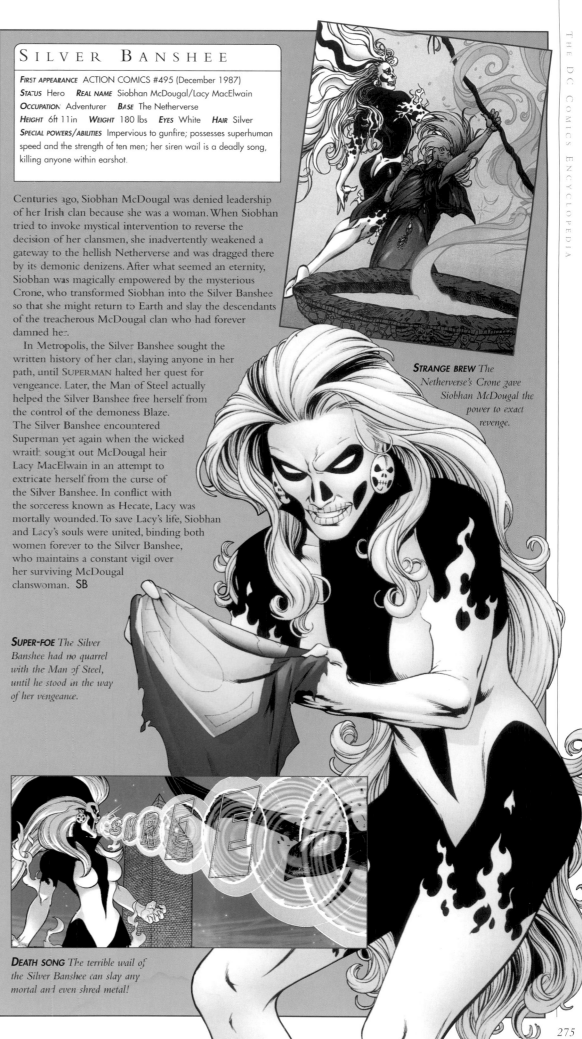

Centuries ago, Siobhan McDougal was denied leadership of her Irish clan because she was a woman. When Siobhan tried to invoke mystical intervention to reverse the decision of her clansmen, she inadvertently weakened a gateway to the hellish Netherverse and was dragged there by its demonic denizens. After what seemed an eternity, Siobhan was magically empowered by the mysterious Crone, who transformed Siobhan into the Silver Banshee so that she might return to Earth and slay the descendants of the treacherous McDougal clan who had forever damned her.

In Metropolis, the Silver Banshee sought the written history of her clan, slaying anyone in her path, until SUPERMAN halted her quest for vengeance. Later, the Man of Steel actually helped the Silver Banshee free herself from the control of the demoness Blaze. The Silver Banshee encountered Superman yet again when the wicked wraith sought out McDougal heir Lacy MacElwain in an attempt to extricate herself from the curse of the Silver Banshee. In conflict with the sorceress known as Hecate, Lacy was mortally wounded. To save Lacy's life, Siobhan and Lacy's souls were united, binding both women forever to the Silver Banshee, who maintains a constant vigil over her surviving McDougal clanswoman. **SB**

STRANGE BREW The Netherverse's Crone gave Siobhan McDougal the power to exact revenge.

SUPER-FOE The Silver Banshee had no quarrel with the Man of Steel, until he stood in the way of her vengeance.

DEATH SONG The terrible wail of the Silver Banshee can slay any mortal and even shred metal!

SILVER MONKEY

FIRST APPEARANCE DETECTIVE COMICS #685 (March 1995)
STATUS Villain (deceased) **REAL NAME** Unrevealed
OCCUPATION Assassin **BASE** Asia
HEIGHT 5ft 6in **WEIGHT** 130 lbs **EYES** Blue **HAIR** Brown
SPECIAL POWERS/ABILITIES One of the deadliest martial artists on the planet; a merciless killer.

When General Tsu and the Shan Triad attempted to corner the heroin market in Asia's Golden Triangle, they were opposed by KING SNAKE. This resulted in a gang war played out on the streets of Gotham City. Tsu, unwilling to lose the battle or face the Taiwanese Triad, hired the mercenary Silver Monkey to kill King Snake. The battle was bloody, and caught the attention of Gotham's guardian, BATMAN. He intervened, along with NIGHTWING and ROBIN III. In the climactic battle, Robin saved King Snake from Silver Monkey, and the Monkey tumbled into Gotham Harbor. Silver Monkey survived, only to be slain during a brutal gang war. **RG**

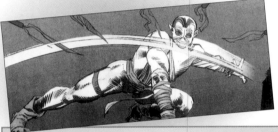

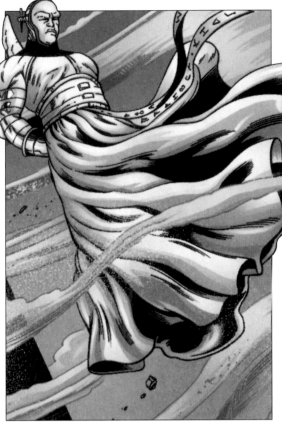

SIN-EATER

FIRST APPEARANCE JSA #23 (June 2001)
STATUS Villain (destroyed) **REAL NAME** Onimar Synn
OCCUPATION Consumer of souls **BASE** The planet Thanagar
HEIGHT 7ft 5in **WEIGHT** 480 lbs **EYES** Yellow **HAIR** None
SPECIAL POWERS/ABILITIES Absorbed power from the suffering and fear of others; could absorb the souls of innocent people and transform them into zombie warriors.

Rumored to be one of the legendary Seven Devils of Thanagar, a race of demons that has plagued the planet since birth, Onimar Synn attempted to take over the planet Thanagar and feed on the souls of its populace. Onimar enslaved the population with Nth metal, an element found only on Thanagar. He killed thousands of them, feasting on their souls and transforming them into an undead army. The Nth metal gave Onimar complete mastery over the four fundamental forces of the universe—strong, weak, gravitational, and electromagnetic.

In a desperate attempt to save the rest of their people, the high priests of Thanagar kidnapped Kendra Saunders, the hero known as HAWKGIRL, who could summon Carter Hall (HAWKMAN) back from the dead through their divine connection. Kendra succeeded, but it took the combined might of Hawkman, Hawkgirl, and the JUSTICE SOCIETY OF AMERICA to stop Synn's rampaging, undead warriors. Onimar Synn was apparently destroyed by the power of Hawkman and Hawkgirl's ancient love. **PJ**

SILVER SWAN I & II

FIRST APPEARANCE ((I) WONDER WOMAN (2nd ser.) #15 (April 1988); (II) WONDER WOMAN (2nd ser.) #171 (August 2001) **STATUS** Villains
REAL NAME (I) Valerie Beaudry; (II) Vanessa "Nessie" Kapatelis
OCCUPATION (I) Reformed villain; (II) enforcer **BASE** (I) Mobile; (II) Boston **HEIGHT** (I) 5ft 7in; (II) 5ft 6in **WEIGHT** (I) 136 lbs; (II) 130 lbs **EYES** (I) Blue; (II) blue **HAIR** (I) Blonde; (II) brown
SPECIAL POWERS/ABILITIES Flight; emit "swan song" that can flatten buildings or generate a sonic shield; II can mentally control birds.

FRAGILE PSYCHE Although graceful in flight and beautiful in appearance, both Silver Swans suffer from self-loathing.

The first Silver Swan was a true manifestation of the Ugly Duckling fable. Born with severe physical deformities, Valerie Beaudry came under the tender mercies of billionaire industrialist Henry Armbruster, who subjected her to chemical treatments that eventually made her beautiful. A side-effect of these experiments provided her with a steel-shattering sonic scream and the power of flight. Armbruster exploited Valerie's insecurities, physically and mentally abusing her to ensure her loyalty as the Silver Swan, his private enforcer. Wearing a suit with artificial wings for steering, the Silver Swan attacked WONDER WOMAN until the Amazon princess revealed the truth—Valerie's benefactor was a monster. The Silver Swan turned on Armbruster and became a free agent, later turning up alongside the Captains of Industry, a superhuman task force.

Silver Swan II once considered herself to be Wonder Woman's closest friend. Vanessa "Nessie" Kapatelis, daughter of archaeologist Julia Kapatelis, viewed Diana as a beloved older sister but eventually began to resent her Amazonian perfection. Angry and hurt when Diana chose Cassie Sandsmark to be the new WONDER GIRL, Nessie became an easy target for the evil sorceress CIRCE, who magically transformed the girl into a new Silver Swan. Bearing heavy psychological baggage made more severe by the brainwashing and mind-bending techniques of Circe's

temporary ally DOCTOR PSYCHO, Silver Swan II set herself against Wonder Woman. She launched a wall-splitting sonic attack on Wonder Girl's high school, accidentally exposing Cassie Sandsmark's Wonder Girl identity when she was forced to use superpowers to rescue her classmates. Recently, Silver Swan II became an agent of Wonder Woman's enemy, Veronica Cale, and attacked the Amazon princess in a fury. Diana defeated her former friend and brought her to Themyscira for treatment. **DW**

SINESTRO

First appearance GREEN LANTERN (2nd series) #7 (August 1961)
Status Villain   **Real name** Sinestro
Occupation Intergalactic criminal   **Base** The anti-matter universe of Qward
Height 6ft 7in   **Weight** 205 lbs   **Eyes** Black   **Hair** Black
Special powers/abilities Master tactician and military commander; his yellow power ring could create anything his fertile, fiendish imagination could conceive.

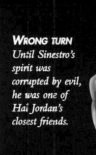

WRONG TURN
Until Sinestro's spirit was corrupted by evil, he was one of Hal Jordan's closest friends.

Sinestro became the greatest enemy of GREEN LANTERN and the GREEN LANTERN CORPS. He was, for a time, a Corps member himself—the Green Lantern of space sector 1417. Born on the planet Korugar, Sinestro was a fearless warrior. Given a power ring by the GUARDIANS OF THE UNIVERSE, Sinestro became an adept Green Lantern. He returned to Korugar and, corrupted by power, proclaimed himself ruler. Sinestro was forced to leave his homeworld to train Green Lantern Hal Jordan on Earth, and they became good friends. Sinestro then returned to Korugar, where the people were rioting against his rule. Disgusted by Sinestro's abuse of power, the Guardians stripped him of his power ring and banished him to the anti-matter universe of Qward.

Trapped in the anti-matter universe, Sinestro impressed the hardened leadership of Qward with his warrior's skills and told them of the Green Lanterns and their rings. The Qwardians created their own power ring, imbued with yellow energy, the only weakness of the Green Lanterns' rings. Using the ring, Sinestro returned to the positive-matter universe and became a constant foe of the Green Lanterns, notably his old pupil, Hal Jordan. After years of intergalactic sparring, Sinestro was imprisoned on Oa, the Guardians' homeworld. But Sinestro escaped and, enraged by his humiliation, destroyed an entire solar system. The massive genocide brought to bear the combined power of the entire Green Lantern Corps, who condemned Sinestro to death. Sinestro's body was destroyed, and his soul was trapped in the Guardians' Great Central Power Battery, which crumbled soon after. Trapped in the Battery's remains, Sinestro existed in a ghost-like state until the Guardians resurrected him. The villain was to defend Oa from an insane Hal Jordan, but in combat with Jordan, Sinestro's neck was snapped by his former friend, ending his threat forever. **PJ**

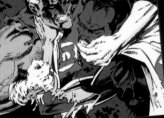

FRIENDS AND FOES *It was in final battle with Hal Jordan that the sinister Sinestro met his grisly fate.*

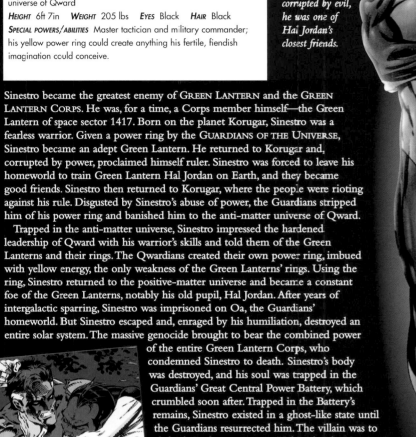

SIRIUS

First appearance ORION #10 (March 2001)
Status Wolf-demon (deceased)   **Real name** None
Occupation Guardian of the Dreggs   **Base** Apokolips
Height 20ft   **Weight** 5,618 lbs   **Eyes** Green   **Hair** Golden
Special powers/abilities A demon of gargantuan size and unbridled ferocity, but with a definite sense of good and evil.

Beneath the slums of Armagetto on Apokolips lie the labyrinthine Black Ways of the Dreggs which were guarded by Sirius, a wolf-demon imprisoned there for millennia. ORION, Dog of War, tracked his enemy DESAAD into the Dreggs and met Sirius instead. A Desaadite—an artificial life-form in Desaad's form—attacked and Sirius defended the Dog of War. Sirius took up Orion in his gaping jaws and hurled him into a Boom Tube leading to the surface of Apokolips, thus saving his life. The wolf-demon died in battle with the Desaadite, and Orion has never forgotten the noble demon beast. **SB**

SKORPIO

First appearance STEEL (2nd series) #37 (April 1997)
Status Villain   **Real name** Dennis Samuel Ellis
Occupation Medical intern; mercenary   **Base** Jersey City, NY
Height 5ft 9in   **Weight** 162 lbs   **Eyes** Brown   **Hair** Black
Special powers/abilities Costume contains hidden weaponry, such as toxin-coated blades; an above-average athlete.

Sam Ellis was a resident at Garden State Medical Center when the head of the hospital, gang boss Dr. Arthur Villain, recruited him for a special mission. Anticipating STEEL's arrival, Villain created the super-powered persona of Skorpio. Ellis was only too happy to adopt this character. He took the costume and Villain's money in the hope that he would get some kicks and earn some extra money to pay back his student loans. Skorpio became Villain's mob enforcer, until he found himself in direct competition with Steel for the affections of Dr. Amanda Quick, a doctor at Garden State Medical Center. **RG**

SKYROCKET

First appearance JLA #61 (February 2002)
Status Hero   **Real name** Celia Forrestal
Occupation Adventurer   **Base** San Francisco
Height 5ft 9in   **Weight** 137 lbs
Eyes Brown   **Hair** Black
Special powers/abilities Argo Harness allows flight and the ability to absorb, convert, or redirect energy.

As a fighter pilot in the U.S. Navy, Lt. Celia Forrestal could fly rings around her squadron mates, yet she still encountered prejudice due to her gender. Frustrated, she embarked on a new career after the terrorist group Scorpio murdered her parents over their latest technological discovery. Celia donned her parents' invention—the Argo Harness—and defeated the terrorists with help from GREEN LANTERN Hal Jordan. At Green Lantern's suggestion, she took the codename Skyrocket and became a full-time super hero.

Skyrocket worked as the protector of St. Louis for years before joining the POWER COMPANY and becoming the team's field leader. She believes that heroism is its own reward and has frequently clashed with the firm's other partners over their policy of charging for their services. **DW**

SLEEZ

First appearance ACTION COMICS #592 (September 1987)
Status Villain (deceased)   **Real name** None
Occupation Corruptor   **Base** Formerly Apokolips; later Metropolis
Height 4ft 3in   **Weight** 181 lbs   **Eyes** Black   **Hair** Black (sparse)
Special powers/abilities Psionic powers enabled Sleez to dominate others' minds and force them to surrender to their baser desires.

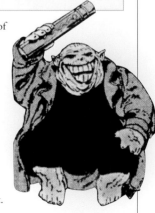

Spewed forth from the sewers of Armagetto on distant Apokolips, the dwarfish Sleez was notorious for his vileness. DARKSEID made Sleez his aide, but even Darkseid tired of Sleez's depravity. He was transported to Earth, where he captured SUPERMAN and BIG BARDA—formerly one of Darkseid's FEMALE FURIES— and mentally manipulated them into fighting for his own twisted amusement. Fortunately, Barda's husband, MISTER MIRACLE, intervened. Later, Sleez mentally enslaved the directors of Project Cadmus and forced them to create clones of themselves, thereby giving birth to a second NEWSBOY LEGION. Following a renewed conflict with Superman involving the Project's Newsboys, Sleez was apparently killed when the torture device he used to enthrall the Cadmus creations backfired. However, Sleez has been thought dead before and has always slunk back to perpetrate more amoral acts. **SB**

SOCIETY OF SIN

FIRST APPEARANCES (Brotherhood of Evil) DOOM PATROL (1st series) #86 (March 1964); (Society of Sin) NEW TITANS ANNUAL #6 (1990) **STATUS** Villain team **BASE** Mobile
MEMBERS AND POWERS
Brain Vast cyborg intellect.
Monsieur Mallah Super-evolved intelligent gorilla.
Madame Rouge (deceased) Elastic powers.
General Immortus Immortality.
Garguax Alien control of an army of android "plastic men."
General Zahl (deceased) Nazi U-boat commander.
Houngan Voodoo techno-fetishes can inflict pain or death.
Phobia Can project illusions of a subject's greatest fear.
Plasmus Protoplasmic touch can burn through most substances.
Warp Teleportation.
Trinity (destroyed) Energy blasts, illusions, and time control.

The Society of Sin was formed years ago by the BRAIN and his ape companion, MONSIEUR MALLAH. Along with MADAME ROUGE, GENERAL IMMORTUS, and Garguax, this "Brotherhood of Evil" targeted the DOOM PATROL. But the mentally unstable Madame Rouge murdered her former partners in the Brotherhood and together with GENERAL ZAHL seemingly destroyed the Doom Patrol. Years later, the Brain and Mallah, who survived Rouge's attack, returned with a new Brotherhood. This new team, which included PHOBIA, HOUNGAN, WARP, and PLASMUS, clashed with the TEEN TITANS. The Brain and Mallah left the Brotherhood and recruited Trinity, renaming themselves the Society of Sin. **PJ**

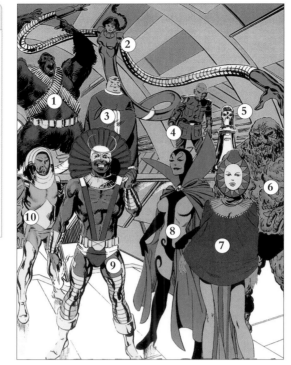

A BROTHERHOOD OF EVIL *Sinister enemies of both the Titans and the Doom Patrol, they are* **1)** *Monsieur Mallah* **2)** *Madame Rouge* **3)** *Garguax* **4)** *General Immortus* **5)** *Brain* **6)** *Plasmus* **7)** *Trinity* **8)** *Phobia* **9)** *Houngan* **10)** *Warp.*

SOLARIS I & II

FIRST APPEARANCE KOBRA #2 (May 1976)
STATUS Villain (deceased) **REAL NAME** Clifton Lacey
OCCUPATION Assassin **BASE** Houston
HEIGHT 5ft 7in **WEIGHT** 140 lbs **EYES** Blue **HAIR** Black
SPECIAL POWERS/ABILITIES Had access to high-tech equipment and scientific knowledge and skills, but was a poor fighter.

A rogue NASA engineer calling himself Solaris created the deadly Heliotron, with which he hoped to gain world domination. He was killed in battle with KOBRA and Jason Burr.

Solaris is also the name of a tyrant sun (right) who sought to conquer two eras—the 20th and the 853rd centuries. By encoding its evil in a techno-virus, Solaris literally created itself. The JUSTICE LEAGUE OF AMERICA and its future counterparts Justice Legion-A joined forces to defeat the sentient star. **RG**

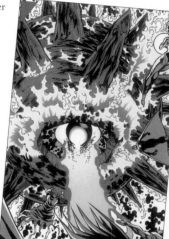

SOLOMON GRUNDY

FIRST APPEARANCE ALL-AMERICAN COMICS #61 (November 1944)
STATUS Villain **REAL NAME** None
HEIGHT 7ft 5in **WEIGHT** 517 lbs **EYES** White **HAIR** White
OCCUPATION Criminal **BASE** Mobile
SPECIAL POWERS/ABILITIES Superstrength and invulnerability; is able to lift many tons and is capable of shrugging off blows from Superman; his undead nature means that it is nearly impossible for anyone to kill him.

HOLDS A GRUDGE *Grundy still hates the Justice Society of America in a grudge that goes back to the 1940s.*

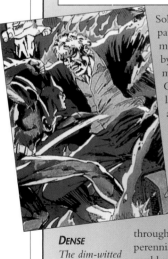

DENSE
The dim-witted Grundy is defeated by superior tactics.

Solomon Grundy is part-zombie and part-plant elemental. In 1894, a rich man named Cyrus Gold was killed by robbers. His corpse sank into the muck of Slaughter Swamp outside Gotham City. Over forty years later a pasty-white behemoth arose from Slaughter Swamp. The fiend got its name from an old nursery rhyme ("Solomon Grundy, born on Monday").

Grundy was employed as a criminal muscle-man, running up against the original GREEN LANTERN Alan Scott and the JUSTICE SOCIETY OF AMERICA throughout the 1940s. Grundy became Scott's perennial nemesis, since Scott's power ring could not affect the wood in Grundy's body. Grundy joined the INJUSTICE SOCIETY, serving with them when they crashed the press conference at which the JUSTICE LEAGUE OF AMERICA announced its formation. A gentler incarnation of Grundy became a friend to Scott's daughter JADE during her time with INFINITY, INC.

Reborn in the mud of a new swamp, the current Solomon Grundy (under the mental control of GORILLA GRODD) nearly drowned BATMAN in the Lincoln Memorial's reflecting pool. **DW**

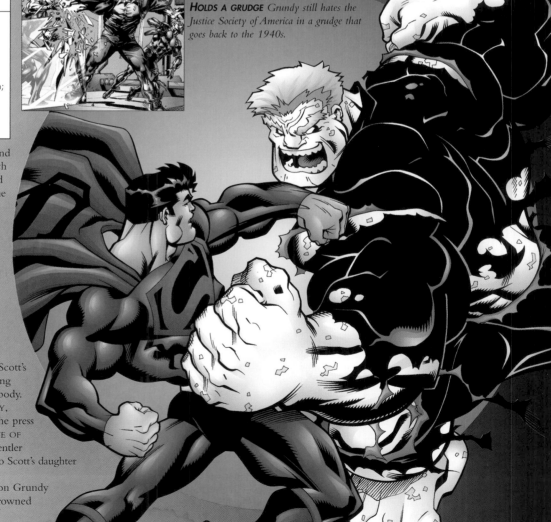

SON OF VULCAN

FIRST APPEARANCE MYSTERIES OF UNEXPLORED WORLDS #46 (May 1965) *STATUS* Hero (deceased) *REAL NAME* John Mann
OCCUPATION Reporter *BASE* Mobile *HEIGHT* 6ft 1in *WEIGHT* 210 lbs
EYES Blue *HAIR* Brown *SPECIAL POWERS/ABILITIES* Invoking the name "Vulcan" transformed his body; super-strong; invulnerable to fire; able to conjure any weapon from Vulcan's forge.

John Mann was a war correspondent working in the Mediterranean who had lost his leg covering the conflict in the region. While resting in the Temple of Jupiter, Mann demanded to know how the gods could allow such carnage. He was struck by lightning and transported to the Mount Olympus of the Roman gods. Vulcan, god of the forge, took a liking to Mann. Despite opposition from Mars, the war god, Vulcan restored Mann's leg and gave him powers and weapons to fight the forces of evil and war on Earth. As the Son of Vulcan, John returned to the Mediterranean island of Cyprete and ended a civil war there. He was killed by the evil sorceress CIRCE during the War of the Gods, a conflict she had concocted that pitted the deities of various pantheons against each other. When the war ended, Vulcan escorted Mann's soul to the eternal heroic happiness of the Elysian Fields. PJ

SONAR

FIRST APPEARANCE GREEN LANTERN (3rd series) #66 (Sept. 1995)
STATUS Villain *REAL NAME* Unknown
OCCUPATION Professional criminal *BASE* Mobile
HEIGHT 6ft 1in *WEIGHT* 215 lbs *EYES* Blue *HAIR* Red
SPECIAL POWERS/ABILITIES Subcutaneous micro-circuitry gives him the ability to absorb and amplify sound waves to destructive levels.

Through circumstances unrevealed, the criminal currently calling himself Sonar came into possession of the sonic weapons belonging to Bito Wladon, the Modoran monarch who battled GREEN LANTERN Hal Jordan as the villain of the same name. The present Sonar used Wladon's technology to surgically augment his own body with electronic implants to enable him to manipulate sound waves. Sonar battled the Green Lantern Kyle Rayner and FLASH III (Wally West) when he rocked Manhattan in an attempt to make the island his own personal kingdom. Looking increasingly horrific as he amps up his implants, Sonar is frequently incarcerated at the Slab, a meta-human prison with facilities to neutralize his sonic powers. However, he is determined to escape for an encore performance against the Emerald Gladiator and Scarlet Speedster. SB

SORROW, JOHNNY

FIRST APPEARANCE SECRET ORIGINS OF SUPER-VILLAINS 80-PAGE GIANT #1 (December 1999)
STATUS Villain *REAL NAME* Jonathan "Johnny" Sorrow
OCCUPATION Criminal leader *BASE* Mobile
HEIGHT 6ft 1in *WEIGHT* 192 lbs *EYES* Unknown *HAIR* None
SPECIAL POWERS/ABILITIES His naked face horrifies and kills any who look directly at it; teleportation; intangibility.

A petty criminal during World War II, Johnny Sorrow created a device that allowed him to phase in and out of reality. Damage to the device caused Sorrow to be transported to another dimension, the Subtle Realms. The creatures who lived there hoped to use Johnny as a conduit to our world, and they made his visage so horrifying that anyone who looked upon it died from shock. Sorrow was returned to Earth to prepare the passage for the King of Tears, a god of the Subtle Realms. But the Justice Society of America and the SPECTRE stopped the King of Tears and imprisoned him.

Decades later, Sorrow returned and assembled a new INJUSTICE SOCIETY to free the King of Tears. But the Injustice Society was defeated by the JSA, and Sorrow was transported back to the Subtle Realms by the FLASH III.

Johnny returned, however, teaming with the alien Despero against the combined might of the Justice League of America and the JSA, but was again defeated. PJ

DEADLY VISAGE *No one can look upon the face of Johnny Sorrow, demonically transformed by his stay in the Subtle Realms, and live to tell the tale.*

SOYUZ

FIRST APPEARANCE FIRESTORM, THE NUCLEAR MAN #70 (April 1988)
STATUS Hero team *BASE* Russia
CURRENT MEMBERS AND POWERS
Firebird (Serafina Arkadin, leader) Telepath with telekinetic ability.
Perun (Ilya Trepilov) Can mentally control electricity.
Ruselka (Mashenka Medvienko) Controls water or water vapor.
Igor (Moizoko Medevienko) Can create arctic cold.
Vikhor (Feodor Sorin) Expert skater who can whip up a whirlwind.

Soyuz (Russian for "alliance") is a team of adolescent Russian mutants with superhuman powers who operate under secret identities in their homeland. Their codenames are taken from Russian mythology. The team first operated together to rescue their future member Perun. They adopted their distinctive costumes and codenames after they rescued the wife and children of Mikhail Arkadin, who was part of the Firestorm persona for a time. The team had several adventures as Russian set about regaining its national identity. They were last seen helping Young Justice during their assault on Zandia. Presumably, the team remains active in Eastern Europe. RG

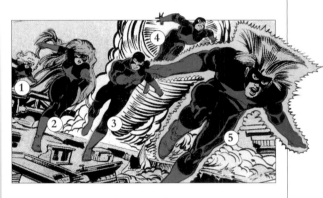

THE HEROES OF SOYUZ 1) *Firebird* 2) *Ruselka* 3) *Igor* 4) *Vikhor* 5) *Perun*

SPACE CABBY

FIRST APPEARANCE MYSTERY IN SPACE #21 (September 1954)
STATUS Hero *REAL NAME* Unknown
OCCUPATION Interstellar Multi-Species Transportation Expert
BASE Corner of Earth and Lunar
HEIGHT 5ft 10in *WEIGHT* 157 lbs *EYES* Brown *HAIR* Brown
SPECIAL POWERS/ABILITIES Skilled pilot and navigator.

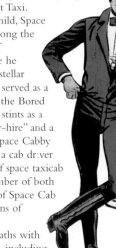

In the middle of the 22nd century, the man known only as Space Cabby began driving for 9-Planet Taxi.

Orphaned as a child, Space Cabby grew up among the military dictators of Ghengkis VII, where he showed a talent for stellar navigation. He later served as a fighter pilot during the Bored Wars of 2146. After stints as a mercenary "flier-for-hire" and a spaceport laborer, Space Cabby found his calling as a cab driver behind the wheel of space taxicab #7433. He is a member of both the Cosmic Order of Space Cab Pilots and the Veterans of Alien Wars.

He has even crossed paths with a few 20th century heroes, including LOBO and STARMAN. DW

SPACE RANGER

FIRST APPEARANCE SHOWCASE #15 (August 1958)
STATUS Hero **REAL NAME** Rick Starr **OCCUPATION** Businessman
BASE New York City; an asteroid in the 22nd century
HEIGHT 6ft 2in **WEIGHT** 194 lbs **EYES** Blue **HAIR** Black
SPECIAL POWERS/ABILITIES Weapons include thermoblaze gun (melts objects), explosidiscs, dissolverizer, anti-gravity gun, numbing gun.

Rick Star is the son of multimillionaire Thaddeus Star, owner of Allied Solar Enterprises in the New York of the 22nd century. Rick Star became the Space Ranger to patrol Earth's solar system and protect it from criminals and alien invaders. Using his millions, Rick created a base on an asteroid between Mars and Jupiter. He was often accompanied aboard his starship, the *Solar King*, by his girlfriend, Myra Mason. The Space Ranger nearly died when he was stranded on Pluto without a life support system. There, a shape-changing alien named Cyrll saved his life, and the two became lifelong friends and allies.

The Space Ranger's greatest battle came during the war against the alien Gordanians when they attempted to capture Earth. With the help of GREEN LANTERN Hal Jordan, the Space Ranger thwarted the Gordanian raid and saved the planet. PJ

SPARK

FIRST APPEARANCE LEGION OF SUPER-HEROES (4th series) #0 (October 1994) **STATUS** Hero **REAL NAME** Ayla Ranzz
OCCUPATION Legionnaire **BASE** Legion World, U.P. Space
HEIGHT 5ft 5in **WEIGHT** 120 lbs **EYES** Light blue **HAIR** Red
SPECIAL POWERS/ABILITIES Able to generate, project, and absorb highly energized blasts of lightning.

Like her twin, Garth, and older brother, Mekt (*see* LIVE WIRE *and* LIGHTNING LORD), Ayla Ranzz acquired her ability to cast lightning after the siblings from the planet Winath crashed on the remote planet Korbal. When Korbal's lightning beasts attacked the Ranzz family, the siblings gained similar electrifying powers. Garth co-founded the LEGION OF SUPER-HEROES. Ayla soon earned Legion membership as Spark, Winath's official representative on the team. Spark was among a contingent of Legionnaires briefly stranded in the 20th century. Before their return, Spark's powers were altered by the Source, allowing her to create low- or null-gravity fields as a veritable "Light Lass." Ayla later regained her lightning-casting powers, and she remains a Legionnaire in good standing. SB

SPARX

FIRST APPEARANCE ADVENTURES OF SUPERMAN ANNUAL #5 (1993)
STATUS Hero **REAL NAME** Donna Carol "D.C." Force
OCCUPATION Adventurer **BASE** New York City **HEIGHT** 5ft 5in
WEIGHT 130 lbs **EYES** Blue; white (as Sparx) **HAIR** Brown; white (as Sparx) **SPECIAL POWERS/ABILITIES** Can move faster than light, emit lightning blasts from her body, and fly; an unskilled combatant.

When alien parasites invaded Earth they infected humans with their bites, triggering dormant metagenes. Donna Force saw this as her opportunity to shine. The youngest member of the famous Canadian Force family, Donna, or "D.C.," lacked powers compared with her family. In Metropolis, she encountered the alien Gemir, who sucked out her spinal fluid, seemingly killing her. When paramedics attempted to revive her, she displayed newfound electrical powers, becoming a living thunderbolt. Working alongside SUPERBOY, D.C., now known as Sparx, helped the new bloods and the veteran heroes combat the alien horde.

Searching for her place in the world, D.C. discovered the Event Horizon, a never-ending rave that floated from reality to reality, world to world. Soon after, Superboy was invited to the rave, and with Sparx created a team known as the RAVERS. RG

SPAWN OF FRANKENSTEIN

FIRST APPEARANCE PHANTOM STRANGER (2nd series) #23 (Jan. 1973)
STATUS Villain **REAL NAME** None
OCCUPATION Wanderer **BASE** Mobile
HEIGHT 7ft **WEIGHT** 300 lbs **EYES** Green **HAIR** Brown
SPECIAL POWERS/ABILITIES Superstrength; difficult to kill due to undead nature.

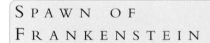

The Spawn of Frankenstein is the undead monster created by Dr. Victor Frankenstein in the late 18th century, a creature often mistakenly referred to only as Frankenstein. Composed of stitched-together corpses, the Spawn of Frankenstein moved against its creator, but Dr. Frankenstein hunted it into the Arctic, where it seemingly perished.

In the 1940s, the YOUNG ALL-STARS crossed paths with Dr. Frankenstein in the Arctic. Resurrected by scientist Victor Adams, the Spawn of Frankenstein killed Adams and knocked Marie Thirteen into a coma. Marie's husband, DOCTOR THIRTEEN, joined with the PHANTOM STRANGER to battle the monster. It is probably at large. DW

SPEED SAUNDERS

FIRST APPEARANCE DETECTIVE COMICS #1 (March 1937)
STATUS Hero **REAL NAME** Cyril Saunders
OCCUPATION Retired adventurer **BASE** Mobile
HEIGHT 5ft 11in **WEIGHT** 160 lbs **EYES** Hazel **HAIR** Gray
SPECIAL POWERS/ABILITIES World-class explorer and adventurer; expert tracker, climber, and survivalist.

Cyril "Speed" Saunders was born in Columbus, Ohio, and raised in Europe. While little has been revealed about Cyril's adolescent years, it has been said that he traveled the world in search of adventure. Speed may well have been a founder of the Office of Strategic Services, the World War II spy agency known as the O.S.S. Speed Saunders met the JUSTICE SOCIETY OF AMERICA on several occasions during the 1940s, also meeting Wesley Dodds, the first SANDMAN. The two remained close friends until Dodds committed suicide to prevent Mordru the DARK LORD from ravaging his mind.

Speed became the guardian of Shiera Saunders, his granddaughter, after the deaths of her parents. Speed trained Shiera, the reincarnation of an Egyptian princess, to become the new HAWGIRL. An elderly daredevil blessed with the vigor of a man half his age, Speed continues to travel the world, seeking adventure. PJ

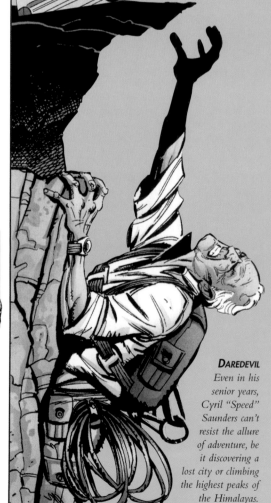

DAREDEVIL
Even in his senior years, Cyril "Speed" Saunders can't resist the allure of adventure, be it discovering a lost city or climbing the highest peaks of the Himalayas.

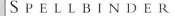

SPELLBINDER

FIRST APPEARANCE DETECTIVE COMICS #358 (December 1966)
STATUS Villain (deceased) **REAL NAME** Delbert Billings
OCCUPATION Adventurer **BASE** Gotham City
HEIGHT 5ft 11in **WEIGHT** 155 lbs **EYES** Blue **HAIR** Brown
SPECIAL POWERS/ABILITIES Utilized optical devices to hypnotize victims; minimally skilled at hand-to-hand fighting.

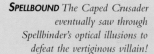

SPELLBOUND The Caped Crusader eventually saw through Spellbinder's optical illusions to defeat the vertiginous villain!

Art forger Delbert Billings decided to embellish his criminal career by developing optical devices that would enable him to hypnotize others. As the Spellbinder, Billings committed a rash of robberies but was ultimately routed by the Dynamic Duo, BATMAN and ROBIN. A second Spellbinder—mystically powered and unrelated to Delbert Billings—was briefly active during Billings' incarceration and battled the JUSTICE LEAGUE OF AMERICA as a member of the government sanctioned "Leaguebusters." Billings attempted a criminal comeback upon his release from prison, but made the mistake of his life when he turned down the demonic NERON's offer for enhanced powers in exchange for his soul. **SB**

SPELLBINDER III

FIRST APPEARANCE DETECTIVE COMICS #691 (November 1995)
STATUS Villain **REAL NAME** Fay Moffit
OCCUPATION Professional criminal **BASE** Gotham City
HEIGHT 5ft 6in **WEIGHT** 137 lbs **EYES** Blue **HAIR** Pink (dyed)
SPECIAL POWERS/ABILITIES Generates lifelike illusions, throwing victims off-kilter and making them experience whatever she desires.

Although Delbert Billings (SPELLBINDER) was unwilling to trade his soul to the Demon NERON in exchange for enhanced powers, his moll, Fay Moffit, eagerly accepted the deal and promptly shot Delbert in the head. Neron gave Moffit the ability to cast psychedelic illusions, and she became the third and most sinister Spellbinder. Her amazing power to alter others' perceptions of reality is directly tied to her own sense of vision. Cover her eyes and she is rendered powerless. While incarcerated at the the Slab prison, she was among a throng of villains "Jokerized" by the JOKER and made into capering carbon-copies of the Clown Prince of Crime. During the jailbreak that followed, Spellbinder almost killed NIGHTWING with an illusion of the inter-dimensional imp BAT-MITE. Spellbinder was later restored to normal, and any lingering effects of her "Jokerizing" remain to be seen. **SB**

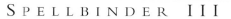

SPINNER, DOROTHY

FIRST APPEARANCE DOOM PATROL (2nd series) #14 (November 1988)
STATUS Hero **REAL NAME** Dorothy Spinner
OCCUPATION Adventurer **BASE** Kansas
HEIGHT 5ft 3in **WEIGHT** 118 lbs **EYES** Brown **HAIR** Brown
SPECIAL POWERS/ABILITIES Born with the mutant ability to bring her imaginary friends to life for short periods; one such imaginary friend even taught her to read.

Born with a deformed, simian-like face, Dorothy retreated from the world until she encountered the DOOM PATROL. While working with the team, she brought the Candlemaker to life, who, unfortunately, later wound up decapitating the CHIEF. She was one of the young adults lured by inhabitants into the other dimensional Dream Country where it was hoped that the powerful children could be convinced to maintain and expand its power. She managed to escape and then is on her own for some time. When heroes ROBOTMAN II and Coagula attempted to reunite Dorothy Spinner with her mother, the girl went berserk, wiping them both out of existence. Dorothy created a new Robotman, one "more in control, maybe more pure and certainly stronger." A group of heroes, including BEAST BOY and FEVER, eventually restored the real Robotman to life and discovered that the incarnation they knew was actually a construct of Dorothy Spinner. She is now receiving psychiatric treatment for her condition. **RG**

SPLIT

FIRST APPEARANCE STEEL #6 (July 1994)
STATUS Villain **REAL NAME** Unknown
OCCUPATION Member of Team Hazard's Black Ops **BASE** Mobile
HEIGHT 5ft 10in **WEIGHT** 145 lbs **EYES** White **HAIR** Red with blond streaks
SPECIAL POWERS/ABILITIES Able to teleport himself and others.

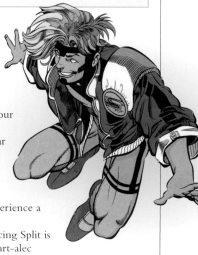

The criminal genius Hazard II (see HAZARD I) has called Split one of his most valuable assets, telling the young meta-human, "I have yet to discover another teleporter with your range and power." Split's teleportational skills appear to be almost unlimited, a fact that is even more impressive considering that Split is barely out of his teens and may yet experience a deepening of his talents.

The biggest problem facing Split is his big mouth and his smart-alec attitude, qualities that Hazard barely tolerates. Split first crossed paths with the super hero STEEL III when Split teleported several Hazard assassins away from a crime scene. Later, Steel forced Split to teleport him out of Hazard's hidden bunker. Split then teleported back to headquarters with a shrug and an unapologetic, "Sorry boss, it was him or me."

Despite his formidable teleporting powers, Split is a poor combatant. In yet another Black Ops battle with Steel, Split crumpled when hit by a glancing blow from John Henry Irons's trusty hammer. **DW**

SPECTRE

THE SPIRIT OF VENGEANCE

JIM CORRIGAN (SPECTRE I)
FIRST APPEARANCE MORE FUN COMICS #52 (February 1940)
STATUS Hero **REAL NAME** James Brendan Corrigan
OCCUPATION Police detective; spirit of vengeance
BASE New York City
HEIGHT (as Corrigan) 6ft 1in **WEIGHT** (as Corrigan) 184 lbs
EYES (as Corrigan) Blue **HAIR** (as Corrigan) Red, with white streak

HAL JORDAN (SPECTRE II)
FIRST APPEARANCE (as the Spectre) DAY OF JUDGEMENT #5
(November 1999) **STATUS** Hero **REAL NAME** Harold "Hal" Jordan
OCCUPATION Former test pilot and Green Lantern; the Spirit of Wrath
BASE Mobile
HEIGHT (as Jordan) 6ft **WEIGHT** (as Jordan) 186 lbs
EYES (as Jordan) Brown **HAIR** (as Jordan) Brown

SPECIAL POWERS/ABILITIES The Spectre is among the most powerful
beings in the universe. Limited only by its need to bond with another
host, the Spectre possesses the ability to fly at nearly any speed,
become intangible, inhabit and animate objects, read minds,
teleport, and psychically project hideous fears into the hearts and
souls of his victims. He can turn invisible, cast illusions, create
impenetrable mists, travel across the astral planes, grow to
incomprehensible size, and manipulate magic to nearly any end his
spiritual mind can conceive!

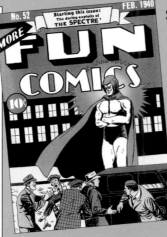

GHOSTLY *The Spectre arrived in a swirl of mist to pass sentence on criminals.*

SET LOOSE ON EARTH by the almighty Presence in 776
BC, the Spectre is the mystical embodiment of God's
wrath. When the angel Raphael, who rebelled against
Heaven with Lucifer, repented his sins, God transformed
him into an avenger that would inflict His wrath on sinful
souls. The Spectre destroyed Sodom and Gommorah,
spread the ten plagues across Egypt, and brought down the
walls of Jericho. After the birth of Jesus, whose mission
was to teach people compassion, the Presence decreed
that the spirits of vengeance and forgiveness should not
exist on Earth at the same time. The Spectre bode his
time in Limbo until Christ's death. Then, forced to bond
with mortal souls to manifest his power, the Spectre
leaped forth, meting out vengeance down the centuries.

JIM CORRIGAN

James Corrigan was the only child of the
Reverend Jedediah Corrigan, a
fundamentalist preacher who physically and
emotionally abused his son to discourage
him from the temptations of sin. As a
teenager, Corrigan ran away to New York
City and enrolled in the police academy,
excelling at detective work. Self-righteous
and arrogant, Corrigan became a pitiless cop.
Corrigan's brutality caught up with him,
when he was killed by mobster Gat Benson
in 1940. Corrigan's soul cried out for
vengeance and was answered by
the Spectre. Infused with the Spectre's power,
Corrigan's spirit returned to his body and took
revenge on Benson. The Spectre was subsequently
encouraged to use his power for good by Percival
Poplanski, a patrolmen who witnessed Benson's demise. Manifesting itself as a
ghostly spirit, the Spectre joined the JUSTICE SOCIETY OF AMERICA as one of
its most powerful members.
After World War II, the Spectre fought the demon Azmodus, who trapped
the Spirit of Vengeance in Corrigan's undead frame for nearly two decades.
The Ghostly Guardian often quarreled with his earthly host over
methodology and the nature of humanity itself.

AVENGING ANGEL *The Spectre uses his powers to horrify criminals, visiting retribution upon them in macabre ways.*

MURDER! *Gat Benson stuffed Jim Corrigan's body in a cement-filled barrel and drowned him.*

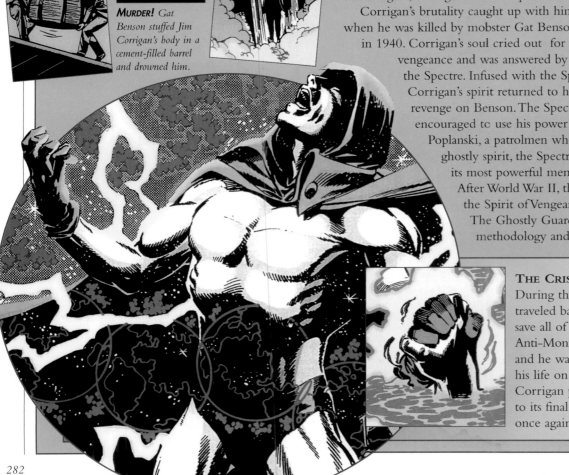

THE CRISIS

During the Crisis (*see* Great Battles, pp. 320-1), the Spectre
traveled back to the dawn of time and used his vast power to
save all of Creation as its heroes battled the universe-consuming
Anti-Monitor. The Spectre's powers were greatly diminished,
and he was once again separated from Corrigan. Exhausted by
his life on Earth, and forgiving his father for his abuses,
Corrigan pleaded with the Presence to allow his soul to travel
to its final resting place. The Spectre, nearly omnipotent, was
once again left without a human focus.

HAL JORDAN

Hal Jordan was one of the most powerful officers in the legendary GREEN LANTERN CORPS and a founding member of the JUSTICE LEAGUE OF AMERICA. When MONGUL and the CYBORG SUPERMAN destroyed Jordan's hometown, Coast City, slaughtering its seven million inhabitants, Jordan went insane, usurping the power of the Corps and transforming into the universe-threatening PARALLAX.

Parallax first tried to recreate Coast City by tampering with time during the Zero Hour crisis (see Great Battles, pp. 320–1). Failing time and time again, Parallax nonetheless helped reignite the Earth's sun, which had been extinguished by an alien creature, at the cost of his own life. His spirit consigned to Purgatory for his sins, Jordan bonded with the Spectre's energies after they briefly inhabited ASMODEL.

Returned to Earth in this new, ghostly form, the spirit of Hal Jordan and the essence of the Spectre wander the globe, seeking redemption while inflicting punishment on the guilty. **PJ**

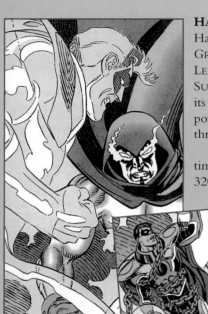

HELPING YOUNG JUSTICE

As the Spectre, Hal Jordan used his omnipotent power to help SECRET learn the truth about her past. The elder ghost helped the younger discover that her death was a sacrifice to a demon, and that she had been transformed by the Lords of Light into a spirit guide. The Spectre used his power to help Secret accept her dismal past and hopeful future.

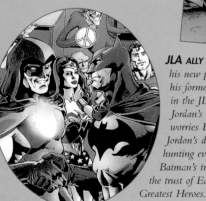

JLA ALLY Hal Jordan uses his new power to aid his former teammates in the JLA. While Jordan's vast power worries BATMAN, Jordan's diligence in hunting evil earns Batman's trust, and the trust of Earth's Greatest Heroes.

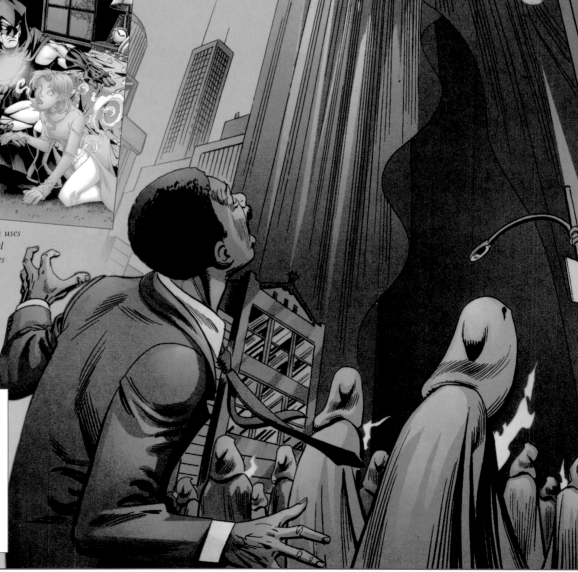

KEY STORYLINES

• *MORE FUN COMICS #52 (FEBRUARY 1940):* The first appearance of the ghostly avenger.

• *DC SPECIAL #29 (SEPTEMBER 1977):* The Spectre becomes a founding member of the Justice Society of America.

• *CRISIS ON INFINITE EARTHS (TPB, 2000)* The Spectre stops the Anti-Monitor from destroying all creation, and reignites the universe.

• *DAY OF JUDGEMENT #1–4 (NOVEMBER 1999–FEBRUARY 2000):* Hal Jordan rescues the spirit of God's wrath from Asmodel and becomes the new Spectre.

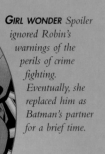

S

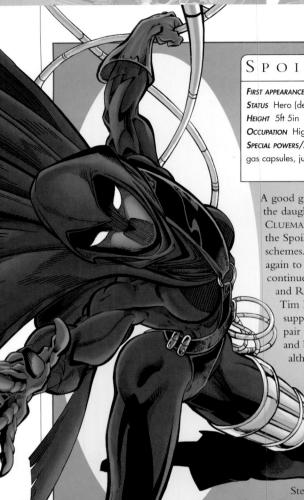

SPOILER

FIRST APPEARANCE DETECTIVE COMICS #647 (August 1992)
STATUS Hero (deceased) **REAL NAME** Stephanie Brown
HEIGHT 5ft 5in **WEIGHT** 129 lbs **EYES** Blue **HAIR** Blonde
OCCUPATION High-school student; adventurer **BASE** Gotham City
SPECIAL POWERS/ABILITIES Above-average combatant; utility bandoleer contains gas capsules, jumplines, and other equipment supplied by Robin III.

A good girl with a bad father, teenager Stephanie Brown is the daughter of Arthur Brown, better known as the criminal CLUEMASTER. Stephanie created her own costumed alter ego, the Spoiler, in an attempt to "spoil" her father's lawbreaking schemes. But even after the Cluemaster was remanded again and again to Blackgate Penitentiary for rehabilitation, the Spoiler continued to patrol Gotham City, despite the admonitions of BATMAN and ROBIN III (Tim Drake). Against the Dark Knight's wishes, Tim Drake enabled Stephanie to operate as the Spoiler, often supplying her with necessary equipment. Friends at first, the pair soon became romantically linked. Later, Batman relented and began schooling Stephanie in crime-fighting skills, although her training was cut short when the Dark Knight's alter ego, Bruce Wayne, was accused of murdering journalist Vesper Fairchild (see FAIRCHILD, VESPER). The Spoiler then apprenticed with the BLACK CANARY II for a while. She remained an active heroine, usually in the company of her boyfriend, Robin. When Tim's father, Jack Drake, learned of his son's vigilante activities, Tim was forced to give up the mantle of Robin for a brief time. With Batman's sanction, Stephanie became the first female Robin during Tim's absence. Tragically, she was killed in action not long after returning to her role as the Spoiler. **SB**

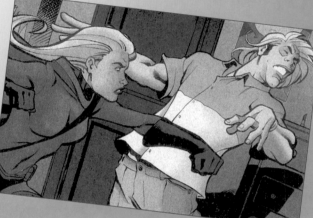

GIRL WONDER Spoiler ignored Robin's warnings of the perils of crime fighting. Eventually, she replaced him as Batman's partner for a brief time.

ABSENT FATHER
When not spoiling his Cluemaster crime sprees, Stephanie showed Arthur Brown what she thought of his parenting skills!

SPY SMASHER

FIRST APPEARANCE WHIZ COMICS #1 (February 1940)
STATUS Hero (retired) **REAL NAME** Alan Armstrong
OCCUPATION Former adventurer, former sportsman **BASE** The U.S.
HEIGHT 5ft 11in **WEIGHT** 175 lbs **EYES** Blue **HAIR** Black
SPECIAL POWERS/ABILITIES A skilled hand-to-hand combatant; for a time, he flew the technologically advanced Gyrosub.

Why Alan Armstrong thought he could help the U.S. by protecting its shores as the Spy Smasher is unknown. However, he achieved great renown for his exploits during World War II. Spy Smasher often faced his Nazi counterpart, America Smasher. His greatest foe, though, was the Mask, who went so far as to hypnotize him into becoming his lieutenant. It took the efforts of BULLETMAN to restore Spy Smasher's mind. The two heroes became good friends as a result. Bulletman, Minute-Man and Spy Smasher interfered with CAPTAIN NAZI's search for the freighter *La Poloma*, but failed to prevent the villain retrieving a mysterious tank from the vessel and disappearing. The device proved to be a cryogenic unit that the Captain believed contained Adolf Hitler's body. At the end of this incident Captain Nazi was placed in another unit, destined to be revived more than five decades into the future. Immediately following the war, Spy Smasher briefly changed his name to Crime Smasher. In the 1950s, Spy Smasher and C.C. Batson (CAPTAIN MARVEL's father) battled BARON BLITZKRIEG, now working as a Communist agent. At some point, Spy Smasher finally retired. **RG**

SQUIRE III

FIRST APPEARANCE JLA #26 (February 1999)
STATUS Hero **REAL NAME** Unknown
OCCUPATION Ultramarine **BASE** Ultramarines base, Superbia
HEIGHT 5ft 6in **WEIGHT** 131 lbs **EYES** Blue **HAIR** Black
SPECIAL POWERS/ABILITIES Scrappy fighter, who learned to stand up for herself on the backstreets of London.

The current Squire is heir to a tradition that began with Percy Sheldrake, the first Squire (see KNIGHT I and SQUIRE I) who served as the wartime aide to the SHINING KNIGHT. After World War II, Percy became the Knight and trained his son Cyril as the Squire II. Cyril, in turn, became the second Knight.

Facing up to the reality of his advancing years, Cyril has recently trained a new female apprentice as the third Squire. Cyril found the young girl brimming with punk attitude on the streets of London. He adopted her and channeled her aggression into combat expertise. His efforts paid off when the INTERNATIONAL ULTRAMARINE CORPS, an independent global peacekeeping force, asked the Knight and Squire to join their team as England's representatives.

Squire III is currently stationed in the Ultramarine floating city of Superbia, above the ruins of Montevideo, Uruguay. She and the Knight stand ready to aid the persecuted citizens of the world. **DW**

STALKER

FIRST APPEARANCE STALKER #1 (July 1975)
STATUS Villain (deceased) **REAL NAME** Unknown
OCCUPATION Warrior **BASE** Mobile
HEIGHT 8ft 2in **WEIGHT** 520 lbs **EYES** Red **HAIR** Black
SPECIAL POWERS/ABILITIES Master of armed and unarmed combat; superstrength; supersenses; enhanced reflexes; near invulnerability; unrivaled tracking ability; power blast projection from hands.

Born thousands of years ago in the city of Geranth on an unnamed world, an orphan boy offered his soul to Dgrth, god of warriors. Dgrth stripped the youth of his soul in exchange for vast power. The boy became Stalker. Eventually Stalker realized the terrible price he had paid for his vast power and pursued Dgrth, hoping to reclaim his soul and undo the bargain. However, Dgrth took his power from the warriors who worshipped him and would never relinquish Stalker's soul while his sycophants could wage battle for him. Thus, Stalker dedicated his life to ending all strife across the universe.

Stalker reasoned that if he ended all life, he would end all war, and so reclaim his soul. He traveled to Earth aiming to end all life there and created seven disciples. The disciples were destroyed, along with Stalker himself, by the JUSTICE SOCIETY OF AMERICA. **PJ**

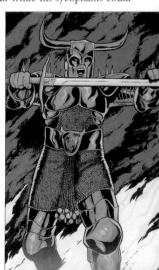

STALNOIVOLK

FIRST APPEARANCE FIRESTORM 2nd series #67 (January 1988)
STATUS Villain *REAL NAME* Ivan Illyich Gort
OCCUPATION Special agent for K.G.B. *BASE* Moscow, Russia
HEIGHT 6ft 2in *WEIGHT* 275 lbs *EYES* Blue *HAIR* Black
SPECIAL POWERS/ABILITIES Superhuman strength, speed, and agility; retarded aging; considerable resistance to pain and injury.

Peasant Ivan Illyich Gort was selected by the Soviet government to be transformed into a Russian superman and symbol of resistance to Nazi Germany during World War II. Called Stalnoivolk, a name that translates as "Steel Wolf" in English, Gort was a model Communist, utterly loyal to Josef Stalin after the war and an active participant in the dictator's bloody purges. Stalnoivolk was exiled to Siberia following his leader's death and the Soviet rejection of Stalinist politics.

Decades later, Stalnoivolk—still strong and vital as a result of the experiments that empowered him—became a K.G.B. agent and was sent to the U.S. to oppose FIRESTORM after the nuclear hero sought to eliminate the world's atomic weapons and end the arms race. While in the U.S., Stalnoivolk killed Richard Dare (CAPTAIN X), the grandfather of Ronnie Raymond, one of Firestorm's alter egos. While in federal custody, Stalnoivolk joined the SUICIDE SQUAD. He remains a Stalinist hard-liner, despite the dissolution of the U.S.S.R. into independent states. SB

STANLEY & HIS MONSTER

FIRST APPEARANCE GREEN ARROW (2nd series) #1 (April 2001)
STATUS Hero *REAL NAME* Stanley Dover
OCCUPATION None *BASE* Star City
HEIGHT 3ft 2in *WEIGHT* 65 lbs *EYES* Blue *HAIR* Blond
SPECIAL POWERS/ABILITIES No powers, but a kind heart; an innocent pawn in his Grandpa's dastardly schemes. The Monster was huge and powerful, but rather slow-moving.

Satanic worshipper Stanley Dover sought to transfer his soul into a demon. Instead, the infant grandson, who shared his name, became the recipient of a binding to the beast. Eventually the mage discovered that the monster, named Spot, had been hiding in his grandson's closet. To draw it out, the warlock imprisoned his grandson and defiled him with the blood of victims he had killed as the Star City Slayer. GREEN ARROW I entered the picture after rescuing the Stanley Sr. from a mugging. The warlock realized that the archer was a body without a soul and tried to transfer his soul into Queen's body to help him capture Stanley's monster. Before the transfer was complete, Queen's soul reentered his resurrected body, thwarting the mage. Stanley's monster then devoured the satanist. RG

STAR BOY

FIRST APPEARANCE LEGIONNAIRES #0
STATUS Hero *REAL NAME* Thom Kallor
OCCUPATION Assassin *BASE* Legion World
HEIGHT 5ft 8in *WEIGHT* 160 lbs *EYES* Blue *HAIR* Brown
SPECIAL POWERS/ABILITIES Has the ability to alter the mass of any object or person; possesses an array of superstrength, flight, and limited invulnerability.

In the 31st Century, Xanthuan hero Star Boy of a team of super-powered teens called the Uncanny Amazers used his mass-inducing powers to defeat High-Brow, Klamorr, Slopp and Violence Queen. He was nearly killed when his space cruiser was destroyed. While recovering, he gained further powers due to ingesting meat from the same space-whale that ULTRA BOY once encountered. Star Boy then left the Amazers to join the LEGION OF SUPER-HEROES. A time traveling Mikaal Tomas and Jack Knight (see STAR MAN) helped Star Boy, UMBRA and the Uncanny Amazers free the planet Xanthu from the mysterious Dark Colossus, ultimately revealed to be a transformed SHADE. Star Boy was stunned when the Shade told him that he would eventually travel to the 21st Century, assume the name of Danny Blaine, become Starman VIII and ultimately die. It's suspected he was a reincarnation of Earth's SCALPHUNTER and Matt O'Dare. His heart remained with his homeworld, however, and when it was invaded by Robotica (see C.O.M.P.U.T.O.), a race of sentient mechanical beings, he and fellow Legionnaires remained to protect Xanthu and help rebuild it. RG

STAR CONQUEROR

FIRST APPEARANCE BRAVE AND THE BOLD #28 (March 1960)
STATUS Villain *REAL NAME* Inapplicable; also known as Starro
HEIGHT Variable *WEIGHT* Variable
EYE Red sclera with yellow pupil *HAIR* None
OCCUPATION Alien invader *BASE* Mobile throughout universe
SPECIAL POWERS/ABILITIES Can exert mental control over others, fire force bolts, and release thousands of small probes that attach to their victims' faces and turn them into slaves.

A titanic intergalactic starfish, the Star Conqueror (Starro for short) may be the strangest villain the JUSTICE LEAGUE OF AMERICA has ever faced. The original team of five—FLASH II, GREEN LANTERN, AQUAMAN, MARTIAN MANHUNTER, and BLACK CANARY—tangled with Starro on their first mission, preventing the alien invertebrate from turning the residents of Happy Harbor, Rhode Island, into zombies. The JLA's mascot, Snapper Carr (see CARR, SNAPPER), luckily discovered the Starro was vulnerable to quicklime.

Starro battled the JLA many more times, but eventually a similar Star Conqueror (believed to be a probe of Starro, or vice versa) appeared in Blue Valley, Nebraska. This ushered in a new incarnation of the League, this time uniting BATMAN, SUPERMAN, Flash, Green Lantern, Aquaman, Martian Manhunter, and WONDER WOMAN against the vile face-clinging parasites that would have turned the universe's inhabitants into the Star

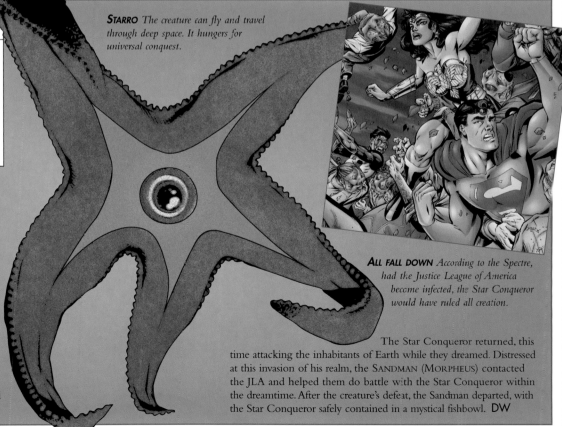

STARRO *The creature can fly and travel through deep space. It hungers for universal conquest.*

ALL FALL DOWN *According to the Spectre, had the Justice League of America become infected, the Star Conqueror would have ruled all creation.*

The Star Conqueror returned, this time attacking the inhabitants of Earth while they dreamed. Distressed at this invasion of his realm, the SANDMAN (MORPHEUS) contacted the JLA and helped them do battle with the Star Conqueror within the dreamtime. After the creature's defeat, the Sandman departed, with the Star Conqueror safely contained in a mystical fishbowl. DW

STAR HAWKINS

FIRST APPEARANCE STRANGE ADVENTURES #114 (March 1960)
STATUS Hero **REAL NAME** Star Hawkins
OCCUPATION Private detective **BASE** New City, Earth, in 2070
HEIGHT 5ft 10in **WEIGHT** 176 lbs **EYES** Blue **HAIR** Brown
SPECIAL POWERS/ABILITIES A renowned detective with amazing mystery solving skills; an excellent martial artist; carries a special laser gun.

Private detective Star Hawkins was renowned for spending his money faster than he could earn it. His ally was a robot named Ilda, a secretary and housecleaner whom he often had to pawn when he needed money. However, he always bought her right back after getting paid for his latest case. Star was eventually assigned to the U.S. government's National Science Center, Earth's premier law enforcement agency. In the year 2092, on his last case, Hawkins saved Automan, a 130-year-old robot, from destruction. Together with Stella Sterling, Star Hawkins founded the Academy of Robot Detection, a training camp for robot detectives. Ilda and Automan, were "lifepaired," the first mechanicals in history to be betrothed to each other. **PJ**

STAR ROVERS, THE

FIRST APPEARANCE MYSTERY IN SPACE #66 (March 1961)
STATUS Hero team **BASE** Mobile
MEMBERS AND POWERS
Homer Gint Novelist and sportsman.
Karel Sorensen Glamorous markswoman.
Rick Purvis Playboy athlete.

Spacefaring adventurers of the 22nd century, Homer Gint, Karel Sorensen, and Rick Purvis often find themselves rocketing to save Earth from various extraterrestrial threats. More often than not, each experiences the danger at hand through separate encounters. After comparing notes, the friendly rivals invariably discover that three heads are better than one. These Star Rovers are independent of any Earth organization, so their exploits are mostly unheralded, which suits these stellar thrill seekers just fine. **SB**

THE STAR ROVERS 1) Homer Gint **2)** Karel Sorensen **3)** Rick Purvis.

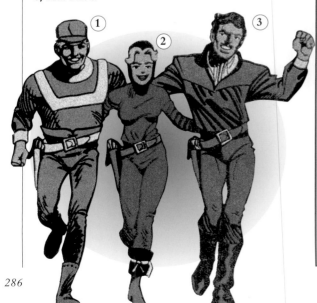

STARFIRE

FIRST APPEARANCE DC COMICS PRESENTS #26 (October 1980)
STATUS Hero **REAL NAME** Koriand'r
OCCUPATION Exiled queen; Teen Titan **BASE** Themyscira
HEIGHT 6ft 4in **WEIGHT** 158 lbs **EYES** Green **HAIR** Auburn
SPECIAL POWERS/ABILITIES Natural ability to fly, absorb solar energy, and emit light has been augmented to let her turn that light into destructive force beams; trained to be a warrior.

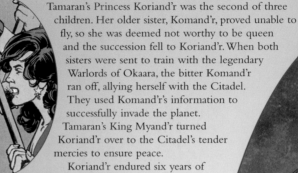

FIGHT CLUB
Sparring with Wonder Girl I was one of Koriand'r's favorite pastimes.

Tamaran's Princess Koriand'r was the second of three children. Her older sister, Komand'r, proved unable to fly, so she was deemed not worthy to be queen and the succession fell to Koriand'r. When both sisters were sent to train with the legendary Warlords of Okaara, the bitter Komand'r ran off, allying herself with the Citadel. They used Komand'r's information to successfully invade the planet. Tamaran's King Myand'r turned Koriand'r over to the Citadel's tender mercies to ensure peace.

Koriand'r endured six years of torture until she and Komand'r were both released for experimentation by the ruthless Psions (*see* Alien Races, pp. 150–1). Both sisters escaped, however, Koriand'r finding her way to Earth with the help of the TEEN TITANS. She chose to remain with the team, taking the name Starfire. She gave team member ROBIN I a passionate kiss in order to learn the English language, igniting a romance that lasted for quite some time. She also endured many missions with the Titans and many heartbreaks involving her family.

After her planet Tamaran, along with her parents and most of her people, was destroyed by the Sun-Eater; Starfire recognized Earth as her true home. She made her residence on the Amazonian island of Themyscira (*see* Amazing Bases, pp. 120–1), traveling to Titans Tower in San Francisco whenever needed. **RG**

FIRST KISS Robin was attracted to the alien Princess, who kissed him to absorb the English language and communicate.

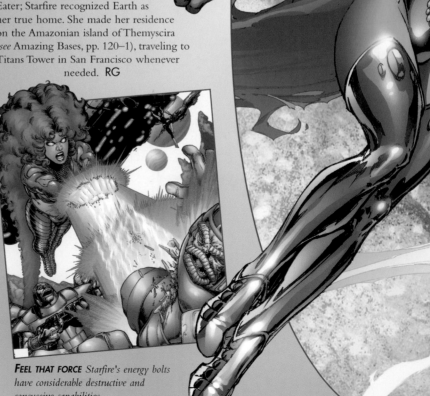

FEEL THAT FORCE *Starfire's energy bolts have considerable destructive and concussive capabilities.*

STAR SAPPHIRE

FIRST APPEARANCE GREEN LANTERN (2nd series.) #16
(October 1962) **STATUS** Villain **REAL NAME** Carol Ferris
OCCUPATION Estranged queen **BASE** Mobile
HEIGHT 5ft 7in **WEIGHT** 126 lbs **EYES** Blue **HAIR** Black
SPECIAL POWERS/ABILITIES Sapphire gem permits flight and
space travel; fires energy blasts; protects against damage.

The Zamarons, immortal female counterparts to
the GUARDIANS OF THE UNIVERSE, developed their
own warrior culture on their planet. Appointing a
queen from the ranks of the galaxy's mortals
became a tradition, and each woman selected
became known as Star Sapphire.

In the late 20th century, the Zamarons chose
Ferris Aircraft president Carol Ferris as their
queen. When she refused, they hypnotized her,
using the power of the sapphire gem to give her
superpowers and a separate Star Sapphire identity,
which she forgot every
time she awoke from the
sapphire's spell. In her first
mission she obeyed the
Zamarons' hypnotic
suggestion to attack
GREEN LANTERN Hal
Jordan, despite the love
she felt for him in her
civilian identity.

Eventually the
militaristic aggression of
the Zamarons took physical
life in Star Sapphire, creating a
separate male being known as
the Predator.

Carol Ferris's predecessor in
the role of Star Sapphire still
lives inside the "7th
Dimension," though she has
grown old and decrepit. This
Golden Age Star Sapphire was
known for tormenting Jay
Garrick (the original FLASH)
during the 1940s. **DW**

> **BEJEWELED** *A part of Carol
> Ferris relishes the role of royal
> villainess.*

> **GOLDEN AGE** *Earth's
> previous Star Sapphire has
> been all but forgotten.*

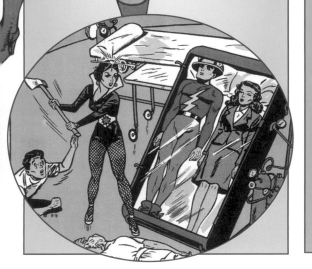

STARGIRL & S.T.R.I.P.E.

FIRST APPEARANCE (Stargirl) STARS AND S.T.R.I.P.E. #0 (July 1999);
(S.T.R.I.P.E.) STARS AND S.T.R.I.P.E. #0 (July 1999)
STATUS Heroes **REAL NAMES** (Stargirl) Courtney Elizabeth
Whitmore; (S.T.R.I.P.E.) Pat Dugan **OCCUPATION** (Stargirl) High
school student, adventurer; (S.T.R.I.P.E.) mechanic, inventor
BASE Blue Valley, Nebraska **HEIGHT** (Stargirl) 5ft 5in; (S.T.R.I.P.E.
in armor) 7ft **WEIGHT** (Stargirl) 127 lbs. (S.T.R.I.P.E. in armor)
425 lbs. **EYES** (Stargirl) Blue; (S.T.R.I.P.E.) red **HAIR** (Stargirl)
Blonde; (S.T.R.I.P.E.) None
SPECIAL POWERS/ABILITIES (Stargirl) Cosmic converter belt gives her
superstrength and reflexes and the ability to project light forms that
affect the human nervous system; also uses the cosmic rod, which
allows her to fly and project blasts of solar energy. (S.T.R.I.P.E.)
Robot with flight capabilities and damage-resistant exoskeleton,
telescopic vision, fist rocket launcher, grappling hook, net launcher,
fire-retardant spray, headlights in chest cavity, taser darts, electric
shock cables, fan, tracking device for Stargirl, satellite feeds, virtual
reality control system.

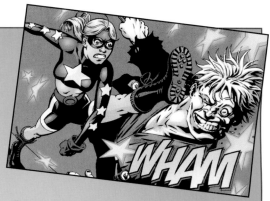

> **FULL FORCE GIRL** *Using a special belt, Stargirl gains
> strength, speed, and the power to kick butt!
> Solomon Grundy sees stars!*

> **THE INNER MAN** *The man inside the S.T.R.I.P.E. armor,
> Pat Dugan has been a hero since World War II.*

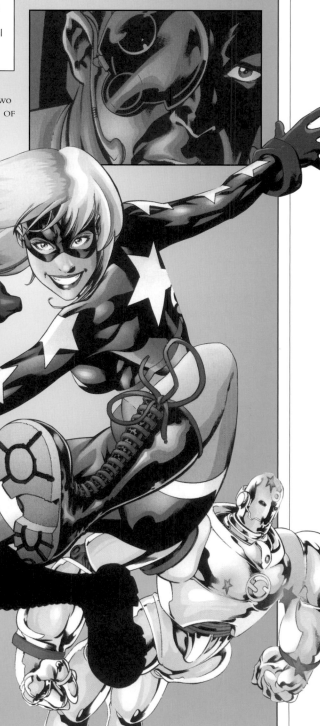

Pat Dugan, a car mechanic during World War II, was
STRIPESY, the sidekick of the Star-Spangled Kid. The two
men fought the Axis powers with the SEVEN SOLDIERS OF
VICTORY until a battle with the NEBULA MAN, a
powerful villain composed of temporal energy,
trapped the duo centuries in the past.

Dugan was rescued by the JUSTICE
SOCIETY OF AMERICA and emerged
in the present, a man out of time.
Pat married, had a son, and
settled down, but his cousin
stole the patents of his
inventions and left him penniless.
Overwhelmed by their financial
problems, Dugan's wife left them.
Dugan worked briefly with
INFINITY, INC. until the Kid's murder by
Mister Bones (*see* DIRECTOR BONES).
Distraught, he moved his new family,
including his stepdaughter, Courtney, to
Blue Valley, Nebraska.

Courtney, who disdained her stepfather
for moving her from her friends and life
in Los Angeles, learned of Dugan's past
and stumbled upon the cosmic converter
belt designed for the original Star-
Spangled Kid. Courtney used the belt and
became the second Star-Spangled Kid just to
make Dugan angry. Dugan created the
S.T.R.I.P.E. battlesuit to assist his
stepdaughter, who got herself into trouble
almost immediately.

Since then, Courtney has curbed her
recklessness and become a
professional hero. After proving
herself in battle against Mordru
(*see* DARK LORD), she was asked to
join the JSA. She inherited the
cosmic rod from STARMAN Jack
Knight and defeated her biological
father, a member of the ROYAL FLUSH
GANG. Courtney then changed her
name to Stargirl. S.T.R.I.P.E. remains a
reserve member of the JSA, dutifully watching over
Courtney as she becomes a legend herself. **PJ**

> **STATE OF INDEPENDENCE** *Stargirl has become one of the
> strongest—and strongest willed—members of the JSA!*

STARMAN

THE STARRY KNIGHT

STARMAN I
FIRST APPEARANCE ADVENTURE COMICS #61 (April 1941)
STATUS Hero (deceased) *REAL NAME* Theodore Henry Knight
OCCUPATION Astronomer, adventurer *BASE* Opal City
HEIGHT 6ft *WEIGHT* 165 lbs *EYES* Blue *HAIR* Gray
SPECIAL POWERS/ABILITIES A wealthy amateur scientific genius who helped develop the atomic bomb; also invented a method for collecting energy radiated by stars and the Gravity Rod, which allowed him to fly; an average hand-to-combatant.

STARMAN II
See DR. MID-NITE I
SPECIAL POWERS/ABILITIES Paul "Robotman" Dennis and Jim "Red Torpedo" Lockhart designed and constructed a sophisticated star-shaped hovercraft that served as Starman II's transportation.

STARMAN III
FIRST APPEARANCE FIRST ISSUE SPECIAL #12 (March 1976)
STATUS Hero *REAL NAME* Mikaal Tomas
OCCUPATION Adventurer *BASE* Opal City
HEIGHT 6ft 3in *WEIGHT* 160 lbs *EYES* Pale blue *HAIR* Purple
SPECIAL POWERS/ABILITIES The sonic crystal that was seared into his flesh allows Mikaal to fire sonic blasts and grants him invulnerability and limited flight.

STARMAN IV
FIRST APPEARANCE ADVENTURE COMICS #467 (January 1980)
STATUS Hero (deceased) *REAL NAME* Prince Gavyn
OCCUPATION Adventurer *BASE* Throneworld
HEIGHT 6ft 2in *WEIGHT* 180 lbs *EYES* Blue *HAIR* Blond
SPECIAL POWERS/ABILITIES Could absorb energy and redirect it as heat or energy bolts.

STARMAN V
FIRST APPEARANCE STARMAN (1st series) #1 (October 1980)
STATUS Hero (deceased) *REAL NAME* William Payton
OCCUPATION Adventurer *BASE* Tucson, Arizona
HEIGHT 6ft 1in *WEIGHT* 180 lbs *EYES* Brown *HAIR* Brown
SPECIAL POWERS/ABILITIES Could emit heat and light; had the power of flight, and could alter his physical form.

STARMAN VI
FIRST APPEARANCE STARMAN (1st series) #26 (September 1990)
STATUS Hero (deceased) *REAL NAME* David Knight
OCCUPATION Adventurer *BASE* Opal City
HEIGHT 5ft 11in *WEIGHT* 170 lbs *EYES* Brown *HAIR* Brown
SPECIAL POWERS/ABILITIES While possessing the cosmic rod, David could fly and direct energy bolts, although he was never especially adept at it.

THE LEGEND OF THE STARMAN, harnessing the stars for the greater good of humanity, stretches from the dawn of the atomic age through the millennia. It begins with wealthy amateur astronomer Ted Knight, who in 1939, created the Gravity Rod, which enabled him to augment or negate gravity. Crafting a super-hero costume, he took flight as Starman.

STARMAN I
Knight's heroic career led to his protecting not only his beloved Opal City, but all of the U.S. through his work with the JUSTICE SOCIETY OF AMERICA and the ALL-STAR SQUADRON. He battled the MIST I again and again, creating an enmity that would last for decades. Knight, who was haunted by his role in the creation of the atomic bomb, resigned from the JSA after helping them beat the dimensional conqueror known as STALKER. Soon after this, he suffered the first of a series of nervous breakdowns and bouts of depression, which led him to temporarily give up his heroic career.

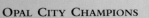

OPAL CITY CHAMPIONS
Dr. Mid-Nite took over Knight's role, becoming Starman II, and watching over Opal City. Then a time-lost David Knight (who would be Starman VI) arrived in town and was groomed by Dr. Mid-Nite to become his "secret weapon." Eventually David returned to his own time in the future and Ted Knight resumed his Starman mantle.

Ted met Adele Doris Drew at a fundraiser, and the two fell in love, married, and had two sons, David and Jack. During those years, Ted, sporting an upgraded device called the Cosmic Rod, often came out of retirement, fighting villains with such heroes as BLACK CANARY I and WILDCAT I.

CANARY KISS
When Starman took to the skies, he began an affair with the first Black Canary.

STARMAN II *Opal City guardian.*

STARMAN IV AND V
Out in the distant universe, Prince Gavyn became known as Starman IV, protector of his empire. He served his people well, sacrificing his life during the Crisis (*see Great Battles, pp. 320–1*). Reduced to pure energy, Gavyn was directed toward Earth. Teenage hitchhiker Will Payton was struck by Gavyn's lifeforce, gaining extraordinary powers. At this time, Starman I was away in Limbo with the JSA, battling demons to protect the Earth. So, to his sister Jayne's delight, Payton became Starman V. Will struggled with being both a hero and a teenager, and learned the ropes from established heroes such as BATMAN and the ATOM. Eventually he lost his life battling the villain ECLIPSO.

WILL PAYTON
Teenager who died a hero's death as Starman V.

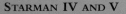

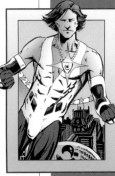

STARMAN III
Unknown to Ted Knight, the blue-skinned Mikaal Tomas escaped from his fellow race of invading aliens from Talok III. Tomas began adventuring as Starman III while Ted raised his children. Within a year, Mikaal Tomas killed the other surviving member of his race in ritual combat, then disappeared from sight for years. After his rescue from virtual imprisonment, Mikaal joined Starman VI for several adventures before going his own way once more.

STARMAN VII

FIRST APPEARANCE ZERO HOUR #1 (September 1994)
STATUS Hero **REAL NAME** Jack Knight
OCCUPATION Antique dealer; adventurer **BASE** Opal City
HEIGHT 6 ft 1in **WEIGHT** 165 lbs **EYES** Blue **HAIR** Black
SPECIAL POWERS/ABILITIES Trained in jujitsu, and uses the Cosmic Rod to fly or to project energy bolts, levitate objects or create force fields.

STARMAN VIII

FIRST APPEARANCE STARMAN (2nd series) #79 (July 2001)
See STAR BOY
SPECIAL POWERS/ABILITIES This native of Xanthu can control mass and fly.

STARMAN 1,000,000

FIRST APPEARANCE JLA #23 (November 1998)
STATUS Hero **REAL NAME** Farris Knight
OCCUPATION Adventurer **BASE** Uranus
HEIGHT 6ft 4in **WEIGHT** 265 lbs **EYES** Blue **HAIR** Brown
SPECIAL POWERS/ABILITIES Uses a revamped version of the gravity rod, enabling him to fly, alter gravimetric forces and fight with fierce determination.

STARMAN VII

Starman I, now retired, declared his son David his successor. David's run as Starman VI was cut short when he was gunned down by the Mist. David's brother, Jack Knight, then found the family legacy thrust upon him and reluctantly became Starman VII. While visiting a circus, Jack discovered and rescued Mikaal Tomas, Starman III, from captivity as a sideshow attraction. Meanwhile, Nash, the Mist's unstable daughter, vowed revenge after Jack killed her brother. As MIST II, she captured Jack and seduced him while he was only partially conscious. A year later, Jack was stunned to learn that Nash had given birth to his son, Kyle Theo Knight.

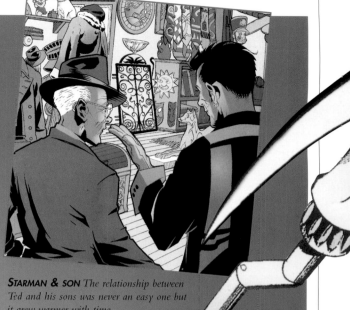

STARMAN & SON *The relationship between Ted and his sons was never an easy one but it grew warmer with time.*

TO THE STARS AND BACK

Accompanied by Mikaal, Jack voyaged into space to determine the fate of Starman V, the brother of his girlfriend Sadie Falk (who was actually Jayne Marie Payton). Jack journeyed to Throneworld, which was now ruled by a cruel, despotic regime. Jack found Will and learned of his amazing connection with Throneworld's Prince Gavyn. The three Starmen, along with political prisoners such as FASTBAK and the OMEGA MEN's Tigorr, then freed Throneworld from tyranny. Will Payton/Gavyn declined an invitation to

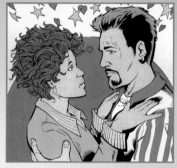

SADIE *When Jayne Payton's brother, Starman V, died, she turned to the latest Starman for help but fell in love instead.*

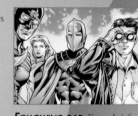

FOLLOWING DAD *For a brief time, Jack served with the JSA, his father's old team.*

return to Earth and Jack and Mikaal set off homeward. After various adventures, they returned to Opal City, which was soon threatened with nuclear holocaust by the Mist.

While they had been away, Ted Knight, Starman I, had been diagnosed with terminal cancer, contracted while battling Doctor Phosphorus. Despite the disease, Ted used an advanced cosmic rod to transport the Mist I's bomb safely into space. Ted and the Mist died in the explosion, and the super-hero community mourned his passing. Jack Knight, briefly served with the JSA before opting to retire to raise his son. He gave his cosmic rod to Star-Spangled Kid, who renamed herself STARGIRL in honor of the legacy. RG

STARMAN VIII

Jack Knight's grandson is said to have been the first villainous Starman. In the 23rd century, Tommy Tomorrow II became the latest incarnation of Starman. By the 822nd century, the heritage of Starman had been abandoned for at least three millennia until revived by Farris Knight's great-grandfather, who discovered his lineage and resurrected the heroic mantle of Starman. Farris Knight was a member of Justice Legion A and wielder of the gravity rod, who resided in his citadel in Uranus's orbit. He betrayed his team until a meeting with the Starman line's progenitor, Ted Knight, led him to mend his ways. He gave his life in the battle against the Sun-eater, Solaris.

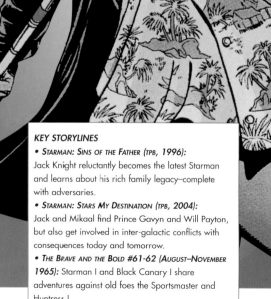

KEY STORYLINES

• *STARMAN: SINS OF THE FATHER (TPB, 1996):* Jack Knight reluctantly becomes the latest Starman and learns about his rich family legacy—complete with adversaries.
• *STARMAN: STARS MY DESTINATION (TPB, 2004):* Jack and Mikaal find Prince Gavyn and Will Payton, but also get involved in inter-galactic conflicts with consequences today and tomorrow.
• *THE BRAVE AND THE BOLD #61-62 (AUGUST–NOVEMBER 1965):* Starman I and Black Canary I share adventures against old foes the Sportsmaster and Huntress I.

STEAMROLLER

FIRST APPEARANCE GREEN LANTERN (2nd series) #176 (May 1984)
STATUS Villain **REAL NAME** Unknown
OCCUPATION Member of Demolition Team **BASE** Mobile
HEIGHT 5ft 11in **WEIGHT** 205 lbs
EYES Blue **HAIR** Black
SPECIAL POWERS/ABILITIES Drives a steamroller capable of leveling buildings.

Though his real name is unknown, the code name Steamroller is all one needs to know about this member of the DEMOLITION TEAM. Formerly a stunt-motorcyclist operating out of Chicago, Steamroller now drives a miniature, high-powered steamroller with enough muscle to knock down any structure and flatten the pieces.

Steamroller joined the Demolition Team in hopes of becoming a high-priced mercenary, and with his new comrades—Rosie, Hardhat, Jackhammer, and Scoopshovel—tore up the Los Angeles branch of Ferris Aircraft on behalf of a congressmen nursing a grudge. Steamroller's gleeful rampage came to an end courtesy of the Predator, who later turned out to be an alternate personality belonging to STAR SAPPHIRE Carol Ferris.

After the CYBORG SUPERMAN, aided by MONGUL destroyed Coast City, the Demolition Team decided to stamp out threats to the Earth and targeted a German nuclear plant. This time, the inexperienced BLOOD PACK super heroes flattened Steamroller and sent him and his teammates to prison. DW

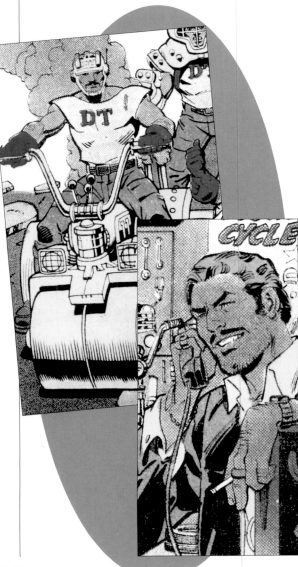

STEEL I

FIRST APPEARANCE STEEL (1st series) #1 (March 1978)
STATUS Hero (deceased) **REAL NAME** Henry (Hank) Heywood I
OCCUPATION Crime fighter **BASE** Mobile
HEIGHT 6ft **WEIGHT** 378 lbs **EYES** Blue **HAIR** Blond
SPECIAL POWERS/ABILITIES Nearly indestructible due to steel construction and bioretardant skin; possesses enhanced strength and speed.

Hank Heywood nearly died when an explosion shredded his body. Rebuilt from the skeleton up, Heywood received artificial lungs, steel tubing instead of bones, metal plating on his skull, micro-motors to power his joints, and tough, bioretardant skin. As "Steel the Indestructible Man," he battled the Nazis during World War II, received the name Commander Steel from President Roosevelt, and joined the ALL-STAR SQUADRON.

After the war, Steel retired from heroics and earned a fortune as a Detroit-based industrialist. His son died in Vietnam, but Commander Steel gave his grandson the same treatments he had received and turned Hank Heywood III into a new Steel. After AQUAMAN reformed the JUSTICE LEAGUE OF AMERICA, Commander Steel offered his Detroit bunker as an HQ if Aquaman accepted his grandson as a member. Years later, Steel died battling the villain ECLIPSO. DW

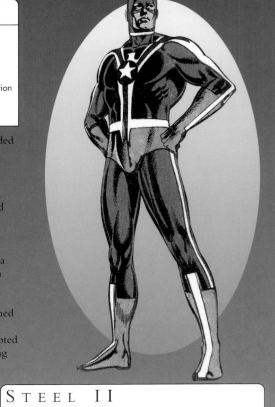

STEEL II

FIRST APPEARANCE JUSTICE LEAGUE OF AMERICA (1st series) ANNUAL #2 **STATUS** Hero **REAL NAME** Henry "Hank" Heywood III
OCCUPATION Troubleshooter **BASE** Detroit
HEIGHT 5ft 11in **WEIGHT** 379 lbs **EYES** Blue **HAIR** Red
SPECIAL POWERS/ABILITIES Superhuman strength, speed, and agility; enhanced hearing; infrared vision.

Grandson of Henry Heywood, the 1940s champion Commander Steel (see STEEL I), Hank Heywood III endured a series of painful operations to become a modern-day Steel. His bones were replaced with titanium. Micro-motors and servomechanisms enhanced his musculature. Subdermal plastisteel mesh lining a fibroplast skin made him nearly invulnerable, and cybernetic implants augmented his visual and auditory senses. After a long recovery, as his body adjusted to bio-chemical treatments and implants, the new Steel joined the JUSTICE LEAGUE OF AMERICA. He was granted membership in exchange for the League's use of a Detroit-based headquarters, the Bunker, donated by the elder Heywood, a wealthy industrialist. Steel II was mortally wounded by an android creation of the League's foe PROFESSOR IVO. Heywood died months later when DESPERO destroyed his life-support systems. SB

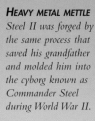

HEAVY METAL METTLE
Steel II was forged by the same process that saved his grandfather and molded him into the cyborg known as Commander Steel during World War II.

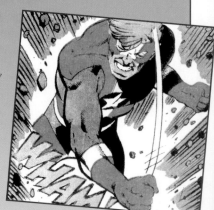

STEEL III

THE MAN OF IRON

FIRST APPEARANCE ADVENTURES OF SUPERMAN #500 (June 1993)
STATUS Hero **REAL NAME** John Henry Irons
OCCUPATION Inventor, adventurer **BASE** Metropolis
HEIGHT 6ft 7in **WEIGHT** 210 lbs **EYES** Brown **HAIR** None
SPECIAL POWERS/ABILITIES A scientific genius with amazing
manufacturing skills and a brave fighter with little formal training.
Specially designed armor confers protection in battle and enables
him to fly. His main weapon is a remote controlled hammer.

JOHN HENRY IRONS is a fighter forged from the same
mold as Superman. When the Man of Tomorrow saved
Irons from a fatal fall off a Metropolis skyscraper, he
challenged the construction worker to make his life
count for something. A former weapons engineer for
the ruthless AmerTek company, Irons longed to atone
for the deaths his designs caused. He chose the way of
the hero as the armored champion Steel.

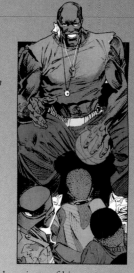

IN THE 'HOOD
John Henry Irons
loved to work with
the kids in his
Washington D.C.
neighborhood.

GREAT DEFENDER Steel and
his mighty hammer protected
Washington, New Jersey
and New York during his
brief career.

FINAL FIRES
Irons forges his
last suit of
battle armor.

THE IRON MAN

John Irons grew up, surrounded by a loving family,
in a poor section of Washington D.C. He entered
college as a physics major and quickly rose to the
top of his class. Realizing his potential as an
engineer, AmerTek hired Irons and he designed the
BG-80 assault rifle, also known as the "Toastmaster,"
as well as a flying armor prototype. Disillusioned by the misuse of his
inventions, Irons faked his death and moved to Metropolis. After SUPERMAN
died at DOOMSDAY's hands, he was one of four men to briefly claim the Man of
Steel's mantle. Irons and the resurrected Superman become close friends. John
continued to adventure as Steel, aided by his plucky niece Natasha (see IRONS,
NATASHA). Eventually, John opened Steelworks, an industrial design concern.
He also worked with the JUSTICE LEAGUE OF AMERICA.

During the Imperiex War (see Great Battles, pp. 320–1), Steel suffered
mortal wounds while releasing Doomsday from the JLA Watchtower to battle
the cosmic conqueror. At the same time, Superman was unable to turn away
the New Gods' BLACK RACER, who ushered dead souls
into the afterlife. This time, however, the Racer delivered
Irons to Apokolips, where the crafty Darkseid restored his
life. Darkseid placed Irons in the Entropy Aegis, an
Imperiex probe converted into a battle suit. Steel used it to
help during the war's final hours.

Having experienced death and resurrection, Irons now
prefers to stay working away in his lab work. However, his niece
Natasha wears a new suit of Steel armor, thereby carrying on the
proud family tradition. RG

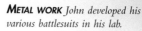

METAL WORK John developed his
various battlesuits in his lab.

LIFE-SAVER The Aegis, a piece of an Imperiex
Probe, sustained John's life in the latter days
of the Imperiex War.

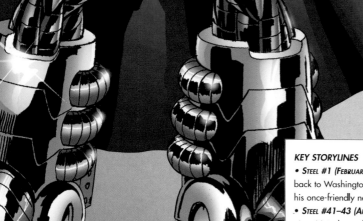

KEY STORYLINES

• **STEEL #1 (FEBRUARY 1994):** John Henry Irons moves
back to Washington, D.C. and discovers that crime has ruined
his once-friendly neighborhood.

• **STEEL #41–43 (AUGUST–OCTOBER 1997):** Steel has to handle his
niece Natasha. political intrigue at his hospital, Skorpio, and
romance all at the same time.

• **SUPERMAN VS. DARKSEID: APOKOLIPS NOW! (TPB, 2003):**
Superman braves Apokolips's worst forces to retrieve Steel's
soul and return him to life.

MELTING POINT FOR STEEL? Natasha, John Henry's
niece, shields her eyes from the terrible explosion
that claimed John's life.

STRANGE, ADAM
CHAMPION OF RANN

FIRST APPEARANCE SHOWCASE #17 (December 1958)
STATUS Hero **REAL NAME** Jean Paul Valley
OCCUPATION Adventurer **BASE** The planet Rann
HEIGHT 6ft **WEIGHT** 175 lbs **EYES** Blue **HAIR** Blond
SPECIAL POWERS/ABILITIES Adam is a brilliant strategist and expert flyer. He can teleport across space using a Rannian machine; also travels using a jet pack; wears a special suit fitted with oxygen tanks to survive in the airless vacuum of space; main weapon is a ray gun.

ARCHAEOLOGIST ADAM STRANGE was unexpectedly transported 25 trillion miles across space to the planet Rann. There, he met the scientist Sardath, who explained that his Zeta beam had been intended purely as a communications tool but had turned out to be a teleportation device instead. Over time, Adam adapted so well to this new world that he became the planet's protector, using his wits and the native technology to overcome alien invasions, rogue monsters and the occasional Tornado Tyrant.

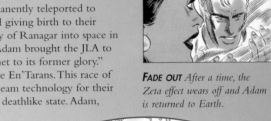

BEAMED UP The Zeta Beam conveys Adam from Earth to Alanna.

ZETA BEAM LOVE
Adam fell in love with Sardath's beautiful daughter Alanna, but their romance was regularly interrupted, for whenever the Zeta beam radiation wore off, Adam was yanked back to Earth. To return to Rann, Adam had to calculate the next time and location the Zeta Beam would strike. It was some time before Adam learned Rann's secret: Rannian men were all sterile and Adam had been brought to Rann to father a child with Alanna and perpetuate the race!

During his exploits on Rann, Adam was aided by the JUSTICE LEAGUE OF AMERICA. and many other heroes. Adam was finally drained of the toxic radiation that prevented him from making long-term stays on Rann. His romance with Alanna continued, and the JLA attended their wedding. Finally drained of the energy that kept him on Rann, Adam returned to Earth.

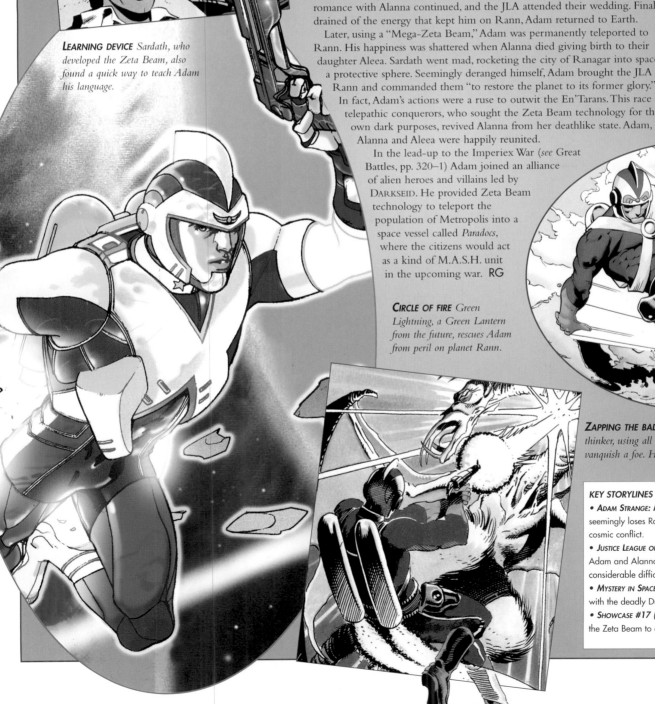

LEARNING DEVICE Sardath, who developed the Zeta Beam, also found a quick way to teach Adam his language.

Later, using a "Mega-Zeta Beam," Adam was permanently teleported to Rann. His happiness was shattered when Alanna died giving birth to their daughter Aleea. Sardath went mad, rocketing the city of Ranagar into space in a protective sphere. Seemingly deranged himself, Adam brought the JLA to Rann and commanded them "to restore the planet to its former glory."

In fact, Adam's actions were a ruse to outwit the En'Tarans. This race of telepathic conquerors, who sought the Zeta Beam technology for their own dark purposes, revived Alanna from her deathlike state. Adam, Alanna and Aleea were happily reunited.

In the lead-up to the Imperiex War (*see* Great Battles, pp. 320–1) Adam joined an alliance of alien heroes and villains led by DARKSEID. He provided Zeta Beam technology to teleport the population of Metropolis into a space vessel called *Paradocs*, where the citizens would act as a kind of M.A.S.H. unit in the upcoming war. **RG**

FADE OUT After a time, the Zeta effect wears off and Adam is returned to Earth.

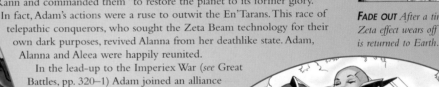

CIRCLE OF FIRE Green Lightning, a Green Lantern from the future, rescues Adam from peril on planet Rann.

ZAPPING THE BAD GUY Adam Strange is a fast thinker, using all his experience to find a way to vanquish a foe. He's also a dead shot with his ray gun.

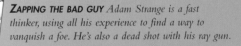

KEY STORYLINES

• *ADAM STRANGE: MAN OF TWO WORLDS* (TPB, 1990): Adam seemingly loses Rann, Alanna and his daughter in a cosmic conflict.

• *JUSTICE LEAGUE OF AMERICA #120–121 (JULY–AUGUST 1975)*: Adam and Alanna finally get married, but not without considerable difficulty.

• *MYSTERY IN SPACE #68 (JUNE 1961)*: Adam's first encounter with the deadly Dust Devils.

• *SHOWCASE #17 (NOVEMBER–DECEMBER 1958)*: Adam first rides the Zeta Beam to discover Rann.

STEPPENWOLF

FIRST APPEARANCE NEW GODS (1st series) #7
STATUS Villain **REAL NAME** Steppenwolf
OCCUPATION Military commander **BASE** Apokolips
HEIGHT 6ft **WEIGHT** 203 lbs **EYES** Red **HAIR** Black
SPECIAL POWERS/ABILITIES Dog cavalry commander; "cable snare" device fires lethal energy beams and entraps opponents; wields an electro-axe and is an expert swordsman.

The uncle of DARKSEID, ruler of Apokolips, Steppenwolf was the commander of Apokolips's military during the reign of Heggra, Darkseid's mother. Hoping to incite a war between Apokolips and its sister world, New Genesis, Darkseid suggested that Steppenwolf go and hunt the inhabitants there for "sport."

When Steppenwolf murdered the wife of Izaya the Inheritor, the New Genesis leader (see HIGHFATHER), and Darkseid pretended to kill Highfather himself, a bloody war between the two worlds began.

During a pitched battle on the plains of New Genesis, Steppenwolf was caught off guard and killed by the vengeful Izaya, whom he believed dead. Steppenwolf was later resurrected by the advanced technology of Apokolips. Mindful of his uncle's past military prowess, Darkseid once again placed Steppenwolf in command of his vast armies. **PJ**

STOMPA

FIRST APPEARANCE MISTER MIRACLE 1st series #6 (February 1972)
STATUS Villain **REAL NAME** Unknown
OCCUPATION Female Fury **BASE** Apokolips
HEIGHT 5ft 8in **WEIGHT** 330 lbs **EYES** Unknown **HAIR** Unknown
SPECIAL POWERS/ABILITIES Ruthless enforcer; heavy matter boots can pulverize even the densest material.

Reared on distant Apokolips and personally trained for terror by the vile GRANNY GOODNESS, Stompa is a member of the much-feared FEMALE FURIES, an elite squad of women warriors belonging to Darkseid's Special Powers Force. As her name implies, Stompa uses her considerable bulk to great advantage when crushing the enemies of Darkseid beneath her boot heels. Possessing considerable muscle mass, she is stronger than a Parademon and just as mean.

Recently, Stompa adopted a new costume that accentuates her feminine qualities slightly more than her previous unisex uniform. She was among the Furies dispatched to Earth by Darkseid to capture Kara Zor-El, Superman's Kryptonian cousin, so that the dreaded lord of Apokolips could mold the young SUPERGIRL to do his bidding. As expected, this mission brought Stompa and the Female Furies into direct conflict with the the Earth's finest heroes, particularly Superman and Batman, as two worlds struggled for the soul of the young Kryptonian girl. **SB**

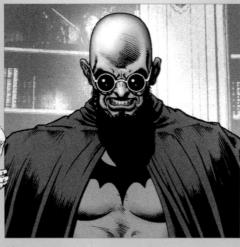

STRANGE, ADAM SEE OPPOSITE PAGE

STRANGE, PROFESSOR HUGO

FIRST APPEARANCE DETECTIVE COMICS #36 (February 1940)
STATUS Villain **REAL NAME** Hugo Strange
OCCUPATION Psychiatrist; criminal **BASE** Gotham City
HEIGHT 5ft 10in **WEIGHT** 170 lbs
EYES Gray **HAIR** None (black beard)
SPECIAL POWERS/ABILITIES Brilliant deductive mind and extensive knowledge of psychology.

Professor Hugo Strange is one of the only people to have deduced BATMAN's secret identity. Early in the caped crusader's career, Professor Strange became a media celebrity by appearing on talk shows and providing his "expert opinion" regarding the costumed vigilante's psychological makeup. Soon appointed a special consultant to Gotham City's Vigilante Task Force, Strange's obsession with the Batman gradually unhinged his mind even as it allowed him to piece together disparate clues linking Batman to Bruce Wayne.

Strange has used his knowledge of Batman's greatest secret to torment the Dark Knight, though Strange's waxing and waning levels of insanity sometimes make him unaware of his proprietary knowledge. Bruce Wayne recently underwent self-hypnosis to temporarily forget that he was the Batman, confounding Strange and allowing NIGHTWING and ROBIN to defeat the professor. Hugo Strange has also brewed mind-altering drugs that have turned Gotham's thugs into vicious killers. Although his sporadic knowledge of Bruce Wayne's costumed identity would prove invaluable to Batman's enemies, Hugo Strange has remained at arm's length from the Dark Knight's Rogues Gallery. Strange prefers to work alone. He remains a dangerous foe, and the day when his mind finally snaps will be a grim day for the citizens of Gotham. **DW**

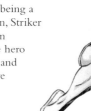

MASKED MANIA Hugo Strange has allowed his entire reality to revolve around Batman. His brain is still his greatest asset, despite his bouts of psychosis.

STRATA

FIRST APPEARANCE INVASION #2 (Summer 1989)
STATUS Hero **REAL NAME** Strata
OCCUPATION Interstellar operative **BASE** The planet Cairn
HEIGHT 7ft 2in **WEIGHT** 803 lbs **EYES** White **HAIR** None
SPECIAL POWERS/ABILITIES Superstrength; invulnerability; extremely long-lived.

Strata is from the planet Dryad, whose inhabitants are sentient, rock-like humanoids made of silicon. As a youngster, Strata was captured by aliens seeing to conquer the universe. With several other prisoners, Strata escaped with the help of Vril Dox. Strata and the others then helped Dox form an interstellar police force, L.E.G.I.O.N.

The L.E.G.I.O.N. was attacked by alien psychopath LOBO, who shredded Strata's rock-like epidermis, revealing crystalline skin beneath. It was only then that Strata realized she was female! Strata served as chief training officer of L.E.G.I.O.N and married fellow member Garv.

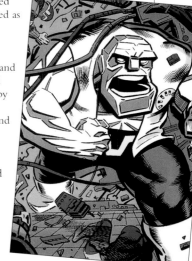

When the L.E.G.I.O.N. and its forces were transformed into a fascist organization by Vril Dox's son, Lyrl, Strata was separated from Garv and worked with the R.E.B.E.L.S. to end Lyrl's threat. Captain Comet reformed L.E.G.I.O.N. and Strata and Garv returned to its ranks. Strata later joined InterC.E.P.T., an organization specializing in interdimensional border control. **PJ**

STRIKER Z

FIRST APPEARANCE JLA #61 (February 2002)
STATUS Hero **REAL NAME** Danny Tsang **OCCUPATION** Super hero
BASE San Francisco **HEIGHT** 5ft 10in **WEIGHT** 175 lbs
EYES Black **HAIR** Black **SPECIAL POWERS/ABILITIES** Biologically-created energy powers his "flight jacket", a visor with built-in sensor arrays, sonic generators, shock cannons and other useful devices.

While working as a stuntman in the Hong Kong movie industry, Danny Tsang developed superpowers after an on-set accident when he fell into an experimental fuel-cell medium. Danny's body became a living battery capable of fueling various high-tech devices designed by Danny's pal, Charlie Lau, a former S.T.A.R. Labs engineer and special-effects expert. Danny traveled to the U.S hoping that his flashy powers would make him a Hollywood star. Dubbed Striker Z by his talent agent, Danny instead found work with the POWER COMPANY, a superpowered law firm. After he joined the Power Company, Striker Z received several offers to star in television commercials.

While he enjoys being a costumed champion, Striker Z remains uncertain whether he's in the hero game for the fame and fortune, or for more altruistic motives. **SB**

STRIPESY

FIRST APPEARANCE STAR SPANGLED COMICS #1 (October 1941)
STATUS Hero **REAL NAME** Patrick Dugan
OCCUPATION Inventor **BASE** Blue Valley, Nebraska
HEIGHT 6ft 1in **WEIGHT** 210 lbs **EYES** Blue **HAIR** Red
SPECIAL POWERS/ABILITIES Pat has an extraordinary intellect and skill as a mechanic, first inventing a flying car in the 1940s and, more recently, the S.T.R.I.P.E. armor.

Sylvester Pemberton III and his chauffeur, Pat Dugan, were independently inspired to become the Star-Spangled Kid and Stripesy. Their exploits during World War II included pursuing the hulking mad scientist Doctor Weerd and matching wits with the dart-wielding villain the Needle. The duo then joined with other heroes to form the SEVEN SOLDIERS OF VICTORY, and had several adventures before becoming lost in time.

After returning to the present, Pat hung up his costume and married a woman named Maggie. They become the parents of a son, Michael. A side effect of Pat's past exposure to the time-stream caused his son's body and intellect to age unnaturally fast. The child resembled a six-year-old before the magic-based members of the JUSTICE SOCIETY OF AMERICA could arrest this unnatural development. Pat subsequently divorced Maggie and married Barbara Whitmore. When Pat's stepdaughter, Courtney Whitmore, laid claim to Sylvester Pemberton's cosmic belt and became an adventurer, Pat returned to action in a robot battlesuit and the duo became STARGIRL AND S.T.R.I.P.E. He briefly relocated the family to Metropolis to work with John Henry Irons' Steelworks (see STEEL III). He has since moved everyone back to Blue Valley. Pat and Barbara now have a daughter, Patricia Lynn (who may grow up to be Starwoman). **RG**

CHANGING WITH THE TIMES *Pat Dugan in his first costume and in his current armored persona.*

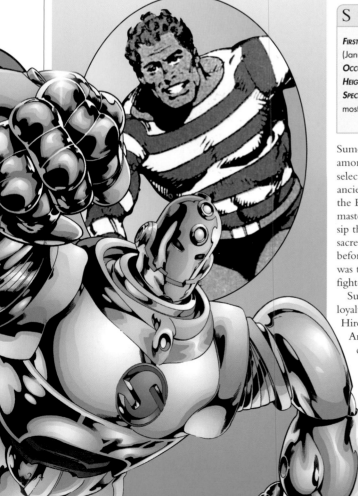

STRONG BOW

FIRST APPEARANCE ALL-STAR WESTERN #58 (May 1951)
STATUS Hero **REAL NAME** Strong Bow
OCCUPATION Peacemaker **BASE** North America
HEIGHT 6ft **WEIGHT** 165 lbs **EYES** Brown **HAIR** Black
SPECIAL POWERS/ABILITIES A wise mind and a gentle spirit; is an expert shot with a bow and arrow.

Before Columbus discovered America, Strong Bow crisscrossed North America on a mission of peace. His tribe had been massacred and Strong Bow had no home. Striking out to unite the continent's tribes and prevent further atrocities, Strong Bow became a legendary mediator who revealed only that he hailed from "beyond the misty mountains." Strong Bow's travels all took place on foot, since horses had not yet been introduced to North America.

On at least two occasions, Strong Bow had time-skipping brushes with the 20th century. During the Crisis (*see* Great Battles, pp. 320–1), he hopped through history with other Native American heroes to join a fight at Florida's Cape Canaveral. On another occasion several modern heroes encountered Strong Bow as part of the "Rough Bunch," a group recruited to battle the time-traveling villain EXTANT in the Old West. **DW**

SUICIDE SQUAD *SEE OPPOSITE PAGE*

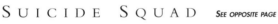

SUMO, THE SAMURAI

FIRST APPEARANCE SUPERMAN VS. WONDER WOMAN (January 1978) **STATUS** Hero **REAL NAME** Sumo
OCCUPATION Villain **BASE** Asahikawa, Japan
HEIGHT 6ft 7in **WEIGHT** 300 lbs **EYES** Brown **HAIR** Black
SPECIAL POWERS/ABILITIES Deadly warrior despite size, more agile than most men; exerts unusual control over his five senses.

Sumo was uniquely honored among the relatively few pupils selected to train under the ancient samurai known as the Enlightened One. His master permitted him to sip the Enlightened One's sacred "potion of power," and, before a year had passed, Sumo was transformed into a giant fighter and master swordsman.

Sumo the Samurai pledged loyalty to Japan's Emperor Hirohito and battled the American ALL-STAR SQUADRON during World War II as Hirohito's personal agent. Along with the shape-changer Kung and TSUNAMI, Sumo was a member of the Samurai Squad. Sumo remains a legendary figure throughout the Land of the Rising Sun. His present whereabouts are unknown. **SB**

SUNBURST

FIRST APPEARANCE NEW ADVENTURES OF SUPERBOY #45 (September 1983)
STATUS Hero (deceased) **REAL NAME** Takeo Sato
OCCUPATION Hero **BASE** Ibusuki, Japan
HEIGHT 5ft 11in **WEIGHT** 182 lbs **EYES** Brown **HAIR** Black
SPECIAL POWERS/ABILITIES Able to project solar energy as light, heat or force, allowing limited flight.

Takeo Sato was born breathing in the charged air near an active volcano in his native Japan. The fumes altered his body chemistry and, as Takeo grew up, he learned he could absorb and project solar energy. He always wanted to be an actor, and as an adult found the perfect part—Sunburst. Little did his director know that Takeo actually had powers, but once it became apparent, Takeo became an instant celebrity. Fame came at a price, however; his parents were kidnapped and Sunburst was forced to commit crimes in order to rescue them. He ultimately crossed paths with RISING SUN, who uncovered the sinister kidnap plot and helped the actor. Takeo wasn't entirely comfortable with superheroics and stayed out of the action until the cosmic event known as the Crisis (*see* Great Battles, pp. 320–1). He flew into battle one final time, losing his life to the antimatter shadow demons. **RG**

SUPER-CHIEF

FIRST APPEARANCE ALL-STAR WESTERN #117 (March 1961)
STATUS Hero **REAL NAME** Flying Stag
OCCUPATION Superpowered warrior **BASE** North America
HEIGHT 5ft 10in **WEIGHT** 170 lbs **EYES** Gray **HAIR** Black
SPECIAL POWERS/ABILITIES Meteorite fragment gives him superstrength, superspeed, flight, and an extended lifespan.

As the greatest warrior of the Wolf Clan in the late 1400s, Flying Stag knew he would win the contest to become Royaneh (Supreme Chief) of the Iroquois Nations. His rivals, however, trapped him in a pit, and when Flying Stag prayed to the Great Spirit Manitou, a radioactive meteorite fell from the sky. Wearing a shard of the meteorite around his neck, Flying Stag could access miraculous powers for one hour each day. To honor the Great Spirit he became Saganowahna, or Super-Chief.

Super-Chief led a heroic life and took a lover, White Fawn. But the energies of the meteorite caused him to outlive everyone he knew. He survived into the late 1800s. After a few time-tripping hops into the 20th century during the Crisis, a senile Super-Chief joined BAT LASH. Super-Chief's fate is unrecorded.

Recently, a new Super-Chief surfaced in the U.S. town of Dry Gulch and caused trouble until he was stopped by SUPERMAN. **DW**

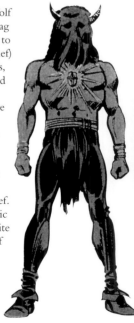

SUICIDE SQUAD

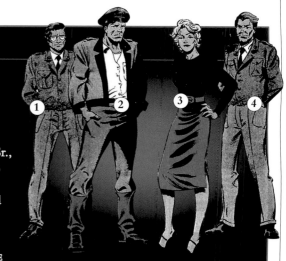

FIRST APPEARANCE THE BRAVE AND THE BOLD (1st series) #25 (Sept. 1959) **STATUS** Covert agents **BASE** Mobile; formerly Belle Reve prison, La. **NOTABLE MEMBERS** Air Wave II (as Maser); Amanda Waller; Arsenal (as Speedy); Atom II; Atom III; Batman; Big Barda; Big Sir; Black Adam; Black Orchid II; Blackstarr; Blockbuster I; Bronze Tiger; Cameron Chase; Captain Boomerang; Captain Cold; Catalyst; Chronos I; Clock King, Doctor Light I, Enchantress, Killer Frost; King Shark; Major Disaster; Manhunter III; Nemesis, Parasite, Penguin, Plastique; Punch and Jewelee; Vixen, Shade.

WORKING UNDER THE AUSPICES of Task Force X, a secret U.S. government agency, the Suicide Squad is a unit of paramilitary and meta-human operatives first assembled during World War II. Under the command of Captain Richard Flag, Sr., this "Suicide Squadron," comprised soldiers who chose service with the Squad in lieu of a court martial. The squad's assignments were considered suicide missions—hence its name!

ELITE FORCE

During the 1950s, the Suicide Squad, became an elite force assigned to covert missions abroad. After Rick Flag's wife died in a car accident, Flag himself perished in a suicide mission against the German War Wheel. Their son, Richard Flag Jr., under the eye of General J.E.B. Stuart (see HAUNTED TANK), grew up to became an Air Force colonel and the leader of a revamped Suicide Squad. Along with Karin Grace, Jess Bright, and Hugh Evans, Flag's Squad handled numerous threats to national security. After the tragic deaths of Bright and Evans on a mission in Cambodia, Karin Grace had a mental breakdown, and the Squad was disbanded.

Decades later congressional aide Amanda Waller (see WALLER, AMANDA) created a new Suicide Squad, many of whom were superhuman criminals. In exchange for a pardon and a fee, the criminals agreed to undertake one mission. Rick Flag, Jr. was recruited to be the Squad's field commander.

By maintaining a core group, the Suicide Squad undertook a number of missions, but several operatives died along the way, including Grace and Flag himself. After the terrorist KOBRA unhinged the U.S. intelligence community in one of his attempts at world domination, and Waller was sent to prison for contempt of Congress, the Squad was disbanded.

The Squad was revived as in independent organization, paying operatives one million dollars a mission, but Waller disbanded that Squad soon after. President Lex Luthor (see LUTHOR, LEX) reinstated the Squad to free DOOMSDAY during the Imperiex War (see Great Battles, pp. 320–1), and a second Squad, commanded by SERGEANT ROCK, battled the ONSLAUGHT, the Squad's most persistent foes. **PJ**

THE FIRST SQUAD
1) Jess Bright
2) Rick Flag, Sr.
3) Karin Grace
4) Dr. Hugh Evans

THE LAST SQUAD
1) Sergeant Rock
2) Modem
3) Deadshot
4) Blackstarr
5) Bulldozer

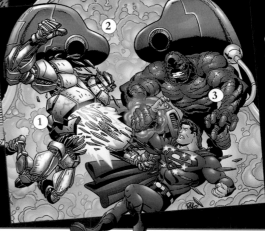

OUR WORLDS AT WAR TEAM
Recruited by Lex Luthor to destroy Imperiex, this monstrous version of the Suicide Squad was nearly impossible to control, even by Superman.
1) Shrapnel
2) Chemo
3) Plasmus

KEY STORYLINES
• BRAVE AND THE BOLD #25 (SEPTEMBER 1959): Rick Flog gathers together his covert team for the U.S. government, forming the first ever Suicide Squad.
• LEGENDS #1 (NOVEMBER 1986): A new Suicide Squad, comprised of supervillains, takes down the titanic Brimstone as Darkseid destroys Earth's legends!
• SUICIDE SQUAD (1ST SERIES) #17–18 (SEPTEMBER–OCTOBER 1988): The Suicide Squad prevents the Jihad terrorist group from destroying New York City!

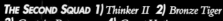

THE SECOND SQUAD 1) Thinker II **2)** Bronze Tiger **3)** Captain Boomerang **4)** Count Vertigo **5)** Deadshot **6)** Poison Ivy **7)** Atom II **8)** Amanda Waller **9)** Oracle **10)** Nightshade.

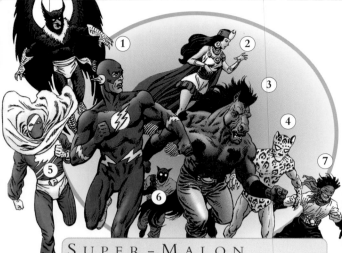

SUPER MALON:
1) *Cachiru* 2) *Salamanca* 3) *El Lobizon* 4) *El Yagaurite*
5) *Pampero* 6) *Vizacacha* 7) *Cimarrón*.

SWAMP THING *SEE OPPOSITE PAGE*

SYLPH

FIRST APPEARANCE NIGHTWING #48 (October 2000)
STATUS Villain **REAL NAME** Sylvan Scofield
OCCUPATION Criminal **BASE** Blüdhaven
HEIGHT 5ft 6in **WEIGHT** 120 lbs **EYES** Brown **HAIR** Brown
SPECIAL POWERS/ABILITIES Special textile wrap is charged with static electricity and can entangle enemies.

SYONIDE II

FIRST APPEARANCE BATMAN AND THE OUTSIDERS #20 (April 1985)
STATUS Villain (deceased) **REAL NAME** Unknown
OCCUPATION Assassin **BASE** Mobile
HEIGHT 5ft 9in **WEIGHT** 140 lbs **EYES** Blue **HAIR** Orange
SPECIAL POWERS/ABILITIES Wields electrically-charged whip and carries a gun loaded with paralysis and poison capsules.

SUPER-MALON

FIRST APPEARANCE THE FLASH (2nd ser.) ANNUAL #13 (Summer 2000)
STATUS Hero team **BASE** Buenos Aires, Argentina
MEMBERS AND POWERS
El Bagual Horseheaded humanoid with superstrength, superspeed;
Cachirú Flight with wings, razorsharp talons; *Cimarrón* A wild,
swashbuckling hero; *El Lobizon* A wolf-headed lycanthrope;
Pampero Can control wind currents; *Salamanca* Sorceress who can
project astral self and manipulate the weather; *Vizacacha* Master
thief; *El Yaguarete* Superspeedster.

Carrying on in the patriotic tradition of their heroic
predecessor from the 1950s, the Gaucho, the Super-Malon,
a team of meta-humans, are Argentina's modern defenders.
These heroes have taken the names of characters from
Argentine folklore, and many of their personal origins
remain mysterious. Their leader is the sorceress
SALAMANCA, a witch who can control the elements and
project her astral self from her body, allowing her to roam
the world as a phantom. When Barbara Minerva and
Sébastian Ballesteros vied in Buenos Aires for the powers
of the CHEETAH, the Super-Malon took to the streets to
protect bystanders and help WONDER WOMAN trap the
two villains; El Yaguarete was wounded in the process. **PJ**

Motivated by revenge, Scofield
systematically executed the
owners of the patent on the
synthetic Achilloron fabric. Her
father, a chemist, had invented
the miracle textile, but
committed suicide when others
stole his design. Sylph wrapped
herself in a bolt of Achilloron and
slew some of the most
prominent business leaders of Blüdhaven.

After Sylph's first two murders,
NIGHTWING crossed paths with
the murderess. He nearly died
when she wrapped him in a
sample of Achilloron and
dumped him on a highway.
Nightwing intercepted Sylph as
she tried to kill the final
patent-holder. In the struggle,
Sylph became entangled in her
own fabric and apparently
broke her neck. It is likely that
her death was a ruse and that
Sylph will soon return. **DW**

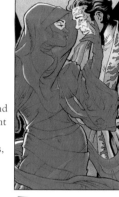

The original Syonide carved out a name
for himself as a hot-tempered and arrogant
bounty hunter who often worked for
mob kingpin Tobias Whale and the
criminal syndicate the 100. Syonide
insisted he wasn't a killer, yet he
delivered victims into the hands of
killers, making him a hypocrite at best.
Troubled by this, Syonide committed
suicide while pursuing BLACK LIGHTNING.

Tobias Whale recruited a second
Syonide, this one a cold-hearted and
lethal hitwoman. She battled the
OUTSIDERS during a mission to
track down Outsider teammate
HALO and seemingly was killed
by Sam Harper, Halo's father.
Syonide survived and joined
Strike Force Kobra, where she worked alongside the
villainess Fauna, who was also her lover. She died while
fighting a reformed version of the Outsiders. **DW**

SUPERMEN OF AMERICA

FIRST APPEARANCE SUPERMEN OF AMERICA #1 (March 1999)
STATUS Hero team **BASE** Metropolis
CURRENT MEMBERS AND POWERS
Brahma (Cal Usjak) Superstrong and invulnerable.
Loser (Theo Storm) Possesses powerful dermal force field.
Maximum (Max Williams) Channels bursts of superhuman energy.
Outburst (Mitch Anderson) Manipulates magnetic fields.
Pyrogen (Claudio Tielli) Flame-controlling pyrokinetic.
White Lotus (Nona Lin) Martial artist empowered by mystic aura.

A heroic power vacuum left
by SUPERMAN's brief
departure from Metropolis
to defend the whole of
Earth gave rise to the
Supermen of America, a
team of teen heroes once
sponsored by Metropolis
mogul Lex Luthor (see
LUTHOR, LEX).

When Junior K-D, lead
singer of the band
Crossfire, was gunned
down during the "Cause
for Pause" benefit
concert in Metropolis, the ensuing chaos between rival street gangs forced teen
hero Outburst into action. Years before he developed superpowers, Outburst and his
family had been saved from the monstrous DOOMSDAY by the Man of Steel. With
Superman as his inspiration, Outburst eagerly accepted Lex Luthor's offer to
recruit a force of young meta-humans to patrol the city in Superman's stead.

Soon enough, Outburst had gathered Brahma, Loser, Psilencer, Pyrogen, and
White Lotus to serve as Supermen of America, an ironic appellation given
Luthor's not-so-secret hatred for the Last Son of Krypton. As salaried super
heroes, the Supermen helped to quell gang violence on Metropolis's streets and
even tackle super-villains emboldened by Superman's absence. Unfortunately,
the prescient and telepathic Psilencer was killed in action, struck down by a
gang member's bullet. He was replaced by the super-athletic Maximum. The
Supermen of America eventually left Luthor's employ; however they continue
to protect and serve the citizens of Metropolis and to help the Man of Steel in
times of need. **SB**

SUPERMEN OF AMERICA
1) *Brahma*
2) *Loser*
3) *White Lotus*
4) *Outburst*
5) *Psilencer (deceased)*
6) *Pyrogen*

THE DC COMICS ENCYCLOPEDIA

SWAMP THING

THE TOXIC AVENGER

FIRST APPEARANCE HOUSE OF SECRETS #92 (July 1971)
STATUS Hero **REAL NAME** Alec Holland
OCCUPATION Plant elemental **BASE** Houma, Louisiana
HEIGHT Variable **WEIGHT** Variable **EYES** Red **HAIR** None
SPECIAL POWERS/ABILITIES Earth's plant elemental can manifest itself wherever there is organic life and can sense anything that affects said life; superstrong, with amazing regenerative powers; can change size and shape; can travel back through time.

GAEA, THE EARTH SPIRIT, has always had Elemental avatars to look after the planet and its living inhabitants. The greatest among them is the plant elemental known as Swamp Thing, who protects the planet at the risk of eliminating all human life. Several individuals have been given the role of plant elemental. The most recent is Alec Holland, who fell into a Louisiana swamp polluted with chemicals, which turned him into Swamp Thing.

UNDER GLASS *General Sunderland studies Swamp Thing's body, trying to establish dominance.*

AVATARS OF THE GREEN
The Green was established as the Earth cooled and Yggdrasil was created. Yggdrasil gained sentience, and the Parliament of Trees grew in a sacred South American grove. Other elemental forces created their own parliaments soon after, including Water, Air, Fire, and Stone. Over time, each elemental caused a human to become its avatar. Each avatar lives until circumstances demand a changing of the guard. In the 20th Century this occurred with great rapidity, from Alex Olsen in 1905 to German pilot Albert Hollerer in 1942, to 1953's Aaron Hayley, to Alan Hallman, to the current Alec Holland.

Holland's spirit was enveloped in a plant body that thought it was still human, until he learned the truth after being captured by the vile Sunderland Corporation. Though shaken by the revelation, Swamp Thing eventually came to terms with this life. Swamp Thing endured much, environmental pollution as well as mystic threats. He also fell in love with Abigail Cable, daughter of Anton Arcane (see ARCANE, ANTON), one of the recurring threats to the creature. At one point, Swamp Thing took an unwanted sojourn into outer space. To fill the void, the Parliament of Trees sought to replace him with his child, dubbed Sprout and ultimately named Tefe (a child conceived with more than a little help from John Constantine).

Upon his return, Swamp Thing endured a series of trials that had him master each neighboring Parliament until he gained total control over the world's elements. The WORD I intervened and stopped Swamp Thing from being corrupted by his own absolute power. Now representing the Earth as a whole, Swamp Thing took his place in the Parliament of Worlds.

Tefe grew to adulthood, trying to find her way, rebelling against Abby's love. Swamp Thing, stripped of Holland's human consciousness, sought to destroy all life, starting with Tefe. Constantine restored Holland to the elemental and the new unified being is establishing his place in the world anew. **RG**

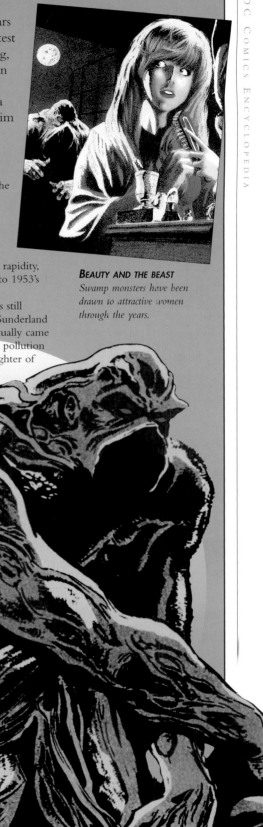

BEAUTY AND THE BEAST *Swamp monsters have been drawn to attractive women through the years.*

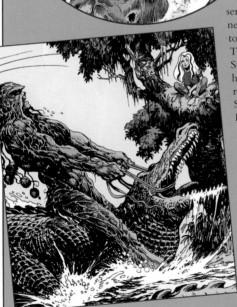

GATOR TAMER *Swamp Thing loved Abby and protected her from every conceivable danger.*

KEY STORYLINES
• *SWAMP THING: DARK GENESIS (TPB, 1991):* The original storyline of the Swamp Thing and Abby.
• *SWAMP THING (2ND SERIES) #61 (JUNE 1987):* In "All Flesh is Grass," while exiled in space, he encounters Green Lantern Medphyl's homeworld.
• *SAGA OF THE SWAMP THING #34 (MARCH 1985):* Abby eats a tuber and experiences life from Swamp Thing's perspective.
• *SWAMP THING #21 (FEBRUARY 1984):* Swamp Thing learns he is not Alec Holland but a plant elemental.
• *HOUSE OF SECRETS #92 (JULY 1971):* The first ever Swamp Thing story.

THE DC COMICS ENCYCLOPEDIA

SUPERBOY

THE TEEN OF STEEL

FIRST APPEARANCE ADVENTURES OF SUPERMAN #500 (June 1993)
STATUS Hero **REAL NAMES** Kon-El; Conner Kent
OCCUPATION Student, adventurer **BASE** Smallville; San Francisco
HEIGHT 5ft 7in **WEIGHT** 150 lbs **EYES** Blue **HAIR** Black
SPECIAL POWERS/ABILITIES Superboy has "tactile telekinesis" which mimics superstrength and flight and other Kryptonian abilities; can disassemble objects by touching them.

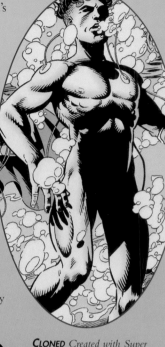

A CLONE OF SUPERMAN created by the Cadmus Project, the world's most advanced genetic research facility, Superboy is a custom-made copy of the Man of Steel. In fact, Superboy was one of many such clones engineered by Cadmus for the purpose of replacing Superman, using DNA samples taken from the Kryptonian champion after his battle with DOOMSDAY. Superboy, however, was the only clone to survive.

CREATING A SUPER HERO

The Cadmus scientists stabilized Superboy's gene code by grafting Superman's alien DNA on to a human DNA strand. The clone was then transformed through a rapid-aging process, becoming a 16-year-old boy in weeks.

The teenage duplicate was rescued from his confines at Cadmus by the NEWSBOY LEGION, who had learned that Superboy's "creator," the unscrupulous Doctor Paul Westfield, had planned to use the young clone's power for his own ends. Altering his costume, the headstrong Superboy then revealed himself to the world. Superboy soon became a close ally of Superman, but moved to Hawaii, hoping the distance from Metropolis might better help him attain an identity separate from his genetic "father." There he began dating Tana Moon, a journalist who moved to Hawaii after helping Superboy make a splash at television station W.G.B.S. as the "Metropolis Kid." After his body started to deteriorate from a clone plague, Superboy's DNA became "frozen" at his 16-year old age. Superman gave the young clone the Kryptonian name "Kon-El". Soon after, Superboy had a brief affair with KNOCKOUT; Tana Moon broke up with him and moved away.

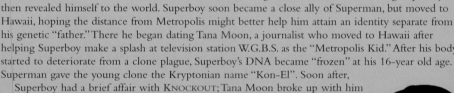

Superboy returned to Metropolis as Project Cadmus' special agent and also helped found YOUNG JUSTICE. Superboy was then kidnapped by the Agenda, a clandestine organization of cloners, and was replaced for months by an evil duplicate named Match. Superboy eventually escaped the Agenda, but not before, Tana Moon was killed by the Agenda's leader Amanda Spence, Paul Westfield's cyborg daughter.

Superboy was then adopted by Superman's parents, Jonathan and Martha Kent (see KENTS, THE), and enrolled in Smallville High School as Conner Kent, Clark Kent's young cousin. After Young Justice's dissolution, Superboy joined the TEEN TITANS. He then learned that his human strand of DNA is Lex Luthor's, a horrifying secret he has only shared with Titans teammate ROBIN. **PJ**

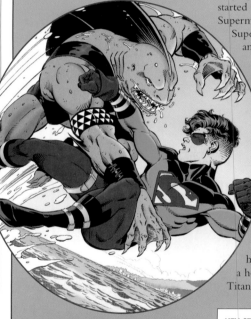

TEST-TUBE HERO Superboy emerges from his cloning tube at Project Cadmus, the spitting image of Superman at 16!

BOY OF STEEL Superboy lived in Honolulu for some time, finding enemies in the Scavenger, King Shark (above), and Black Zero, and both friend and foe in Knockout, one of the Female Furies.

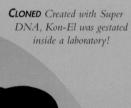

CLONED Created with Super DNA, Kon-El was gestated inside a laboratory!

KEY STORYLINES

• ADVENTURES OF SUPERMAN #500 (JUNE 1993): Superboy and three others begin the Reign of the Supermen after Doomsday nearly killed the Man of Steel!

• SUPERBOY (3RD SERIES) #74 (MARCH 2000): Tana Moon, Superboy's girlfriend, dies at the hands of the villainous Agenda!

• TEEN TITANS (3RD SERIES) #1 (AUGUST 2003): After joining the latest incarnation of the Teen Titans, Superboy discovers that he shares Lex Luthor's DNA!

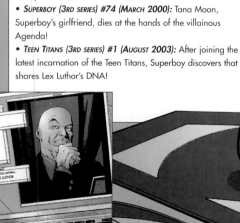

SUPER SECRET Robin helped Superboy deduce the secret from the young clone's past—the source of his human DNA—a secret the Boy Wonder is sworn to conceal.

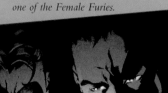

SUPERGIRL

THE MAID OF MIGHT

FIRST APPEARANCE ACTION COMICS #252 (May 1959)
STATUS Hero **REAL NAME** Kara Zor-El
OCCUPATION Adventurer **BASE** Metropolis
HEIGHT 5ft 5in **WEIGHT** 135 lbs **EYES** Blue **HAIR** Blonde
SPECIAL POWERS/ABILITIES Under the Sun's solar radiation, Supergirl's kryptonian physique absorbs energy and can fly, has superstrength, superspeed, invulnerability, acute hearing, and a range of vision, including emitting X-rays and heat.

THERE EXIST COUNTLESS parallel universes, some with super heroes, some without. In one such pocket universe, Superman was not the sole survivor of Krypton. That world's Superboy, however, died in the 30th century while saving that universe's LEGION OF SUPER-HEROES. Three Kryptonian criminals managed to survive as well, and found their way to Earth. No one powerful enough was left to stop them. That world's Lex Luthor (see LUTHOR, LEX), a noble scientist, created a lifeform from protomatter, using genetic material supplied by Lana Lang (see LANG, LANA), hoping it could help defeat the deadly trio.

THE MATRIX

This shape-changing being was dispatched to a parallel world, hoping SUPERMAN could help. The Man of Steel answered the call to arms and was forced to kill the three Kryptonians to save the world, but not before the lifeform, known as Matrix, was reduced to an amorphous mass. Superman brought Matrix to his world and there it recuperated on the Kent family farm. Out of respect for its savior, Matrix took on a feminine form and used her more limited superpowers to become Supergirl. When Superman exiled himself to space to atone for having killed for the first time, Supergirl took on his peace-keeping role.

She naïvely fell under Lex Luthor's thrall for a while, until she saw him for the manipulative despot that he was. She then saved the life of Linda Danvers in the town of Leesburg, VA., by merging her life essence with Linda's. This created an entirely new being with different abilities, such as more limited shape-changing, psychokinetic skills, and increased strength and endurance.

In time, Linda/Supergirl/Matrix discovered the violent and haunted life Linda had led and sought to redeem her existence. During her encounters with the demon Buzz and other supernatural entities, she discovered she was a reborn being known as an Earth-Angel, one of three on Earth. After several weird adventures, Linda met up with a Supergirl from yet another parallel timeline. This Supergirl was Superman's cousin from Krypton, a more innocent heroine who needed to die in order to keep the fabric of time from fraying. Linda also gave up her angelic abilities and left Leesburg hoping to lead a "normal" life.

Some time thereafter, the enigmatic Futuresmiths altered time. As a result, a young teen named Cir-El arrived in Metropolis, claiming to be the daughter of Clark Kent and Lois Lane (see LANE, LOIS). She was gradually accepted by Superman until the Futuresmith's plans were undone to preserve the timeline and Cir-El vanished. The repercussions of the constant changes to the timestream had unexpected results. One was the imminent arrival of an asteroid that scientists traced back to Krypton. The asteroid broke apart as it entered Earth's atmosphere but a spacecraft managed to splash down in the ocean. Within the damaged craft was a young teenager, from Superman's homeworld. News of the arrival of a *second* survivor from Krypton spread and a scramble began to gain influence over the girl, Kara Zor-El. Finally, it was agreed that Kara would stay in America, under Superman's watchful gaze. When she is deemed ready, Superman has a costume, complete with S-shield, waiting for his cousin. **RG**

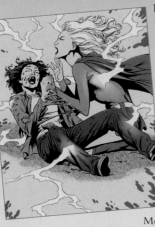

WITHOUT SUPERMAN *Supergirl selflessly used her powers to protect one and all.*

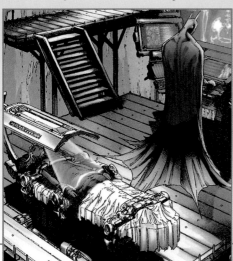

TWO BECOME ONE *Supergirl and Linda Danvers confront cosmic forces to restore balance to reality.*

NEW ARRIVAL *A rocket arrives on Earth and a suspicious Batman doubts its occupant's claims of Kryptonian birth.*

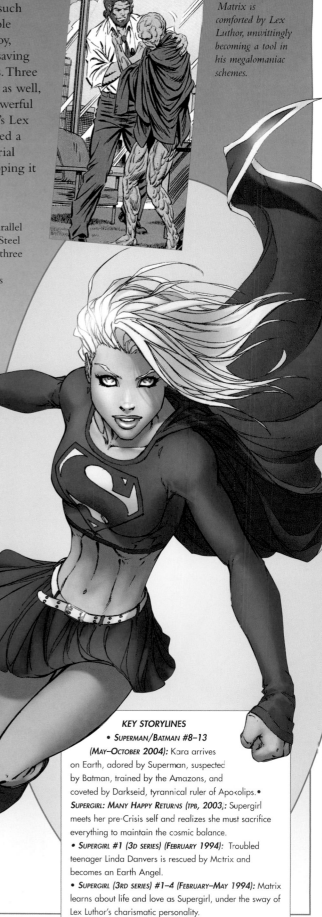

LUTHOR'S TOY *Matrix is comforted by Lex Luthor, unwittingly becoming a tool in his megalomaniac schemes.*

KEY STORYLINES

- **SUPERMAN/BATMAN #8–13 (MAY–OCTOBER 2004):** Kara arrives on Earth, adored by Superman, suspected by Batman, trained by the Amazons, and coveted by Darkseid, tyrannical ruler of Apokolips.•
- **SUPERGIRL: MANY HAPPY RETURNS (TPB, 2003,):** Supergirl meets her pre-Crisis self and realizes she must sacrifice everything to maintain the cosmic balance.
- **SUPERGIRL #1 (3D SERIES) (FEBRUARY 1994):** Troubled teenager Linda Danvers is rescued by Matrix and becomes an Earth Angel.
- **SUPERGIRL (3RD SERIES) #1–4 (FEBRUARY–MAY 1994):** Matrix learns about life and love as Supergirl, under the sway of Lex Luthor's charismatic personality.

SUPERMAN

THE MAN OF STEEL

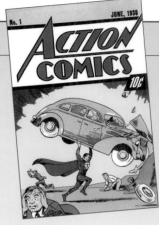

FIRST APPEARANCE ACTION COMICS #1 (June 1938)
STATUS Hero   REAL NAME Kal-El; Clark Joseph Kent (adoptive name)
OCCUPATION Super hero; (as Clark Kent) journalist   BASE Metropolis
HEIGHT 6ft 3in   WEIGHT 235 lbs   EYES Blue   HAIR Black
SPECIAL POWERS/ABILITIES Kal-El's powers were latent until his teenage years. His kryptonian physiology absorbs immense energy from Earth's yellow sun, enabling him to fly at incredible speeds, and endowing him with superstrength, invulnerability (his only weaknesses are green kryptonite radiation and magic), ultra-acute hearing, freezing breath, immense lung capacity and a range of vision including X-ray vision (he can see through anything except lead) and heat vision.

SUPERMAN, THE LAST SON OF KRYPTON, represents the very best in humanity. His native world of Krypton, a giant planet orbiting a dying red sun, was doomed by the radioactive elements at its core and exploded many years ago, but not before scientist Jor-El and his wife Lara rocketed their son to safety, hoping against hope that his spacecraft would find him a new home in the vast reaches of the universe. Their gamble paid off in ways that have enormously benefited humanity.

FIRST ISSUE *The Man of Steel first flexed his muscles on the cover of Action Comics #1.*

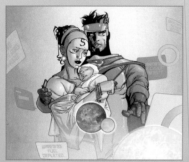

THE SOLE SURVIVOR
Jor-El had warned Krypton's Council that the planet was doomed, but his fears had been dismissed. Now there was no fleet of starcraft to carry the people to safety. There was only Jor-El's own tiny prototype, a craft just large enough to contain their own son, Kal-El. All Jor-El could do was program the capsule's navigational intelligence to search for a world where life could thrive. Then, at the last moment, he located a blue planet lit by a yellow star. If Kal-El could survive the long journey, his Kryptonian metabolism could absorb so much energy from that yellow star he would become a superman! Lara placed a holographic chronicle of Krypton's history so that one day Kal-El would understand his true origins. The capsule took off, just as Krypton exploded!

SMALLVILLE DAYS
Kal-El's ship traveled countless light-years until it crashed in a remote field near Smallville, Kansas, where it and its infant cargo were found by farmers Jonathan and Martha Kent. Raising him as their own, the kind-hearted Kents named the boy Clark Joseph and watched in amazement as, little by little, his unique abilities began to manifest themselves. Clark's body proved to be a veritable solar battery. He absorbed the sun's energy, which gave him incredible strength, invulnerability, heightened senses, and the ability to fly. Fearing that various governments or factions would claim Clark as their own, the Kents encouraged the boy to act as "normal" as possible and to keep his powers a secret. After graduating from high school, Clark left the little town of Smallville to begin a seven- year exploration of the globe, eager to find some purpose for his amazing abilities as he searched for a suitably heroic role in life.

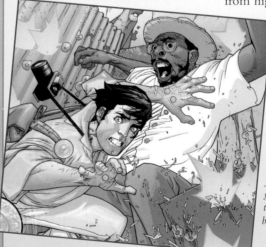

AFRICAN ADVENTURE *Before Clark Kent made his name in Metropolis, he traveled the world on an eight-year personal journey of discovery. Eager to try out his growing superpowers, he headed for some of the worlds trouble spots, helping to resolve a bloody intertribal conflict in Africa.*

SUPERMAN'S COSTUME
In time, however, Clark realized that he'd made a mistake by ignoring his alien heritage in favor of his human upbringing. Once he acknowledged that there was a place in this world not only for Clark Kent but for Kal-El, Clark used materials from his spacecraft to create a costume signifying and reflecting his Kryptonian roots—one he could wear openly whenever he wasn't disguising himself as a mild-mannered journalist.

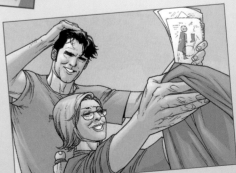

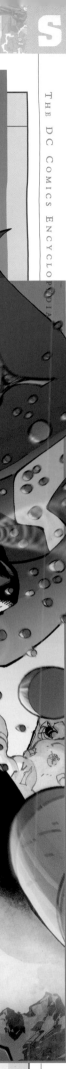

LIFESAVER!
Superman's first costumed adventure saw him saving Jimmy Olsen and Lois Lane from certain death.

LOIS LANE *As time went by, Clark Kent became a celebrated reporter and fell in love with Lois. She got over her crush on the Man of Steel, realizing what a good catch Clark was. Marriage soon beckoned.*

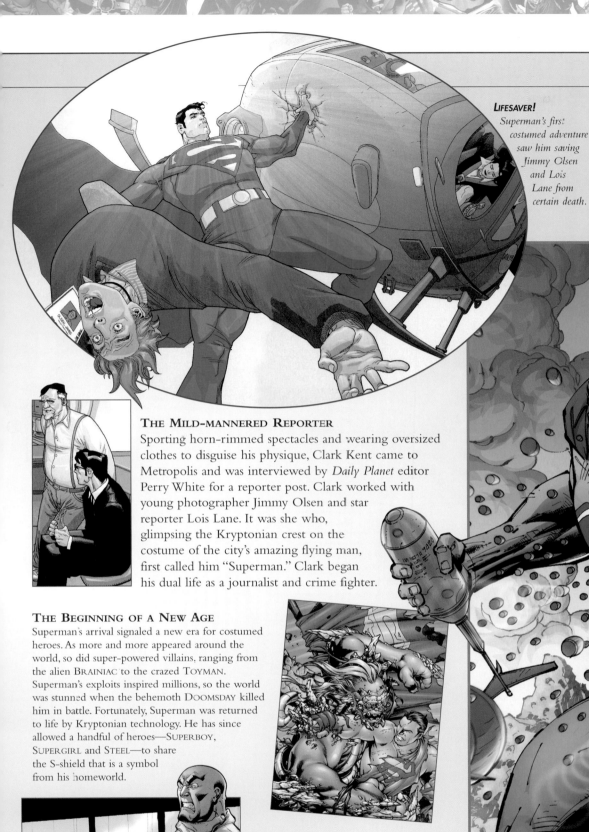

THE MILD-MANNERED REPORTER

Sporting horn-rimmed spectacles and wearing oversized clothes to disguise his physique, Clark Kent came to Metropolis and was interviewed by *Daily Planet* editor Perry White for a reporter post. Clark worked with young photographer Jimmy Olsen and star reporter Lois Lane. It was she who, glimpsing the Kryptonian crest on the costume of the city's amazing flying man, first called him "Superman." Clark began his dual life as a journalist and crime fighter.

THE BEGINNING OF A NEW AGE

Superman's arrival signaled a new era for costumed heroes. As more and more appeared around the world, so did super-powered villains, ranging from the alien BRAINIAC to the crazed TOYMAN. Superman's exploits inspired millions, so the world was stunned when the behemoth DOOMSDAY killed him in battle. Fortunately, Superman was returned to life by Kryptonian technology. He has since allowed a handful of heroes—SUPERBOY, SUPERGIRL and STEEL—to share the S-shield that is a symbol from his homeworld.

AN EVERLASTING INSPIRATION

Superman has had to contend with scheme after malicious scheme to discredit or destroy him. Virtually all of them have been engineered by Lex Luthor, first through his LexCorp business and then as U.S. President.

Alone and with the JUSTICE LEAGUE OF AMERICA, Superman has become a symbol for truth and justice across the world. In the 31st century, the legacy of Superman led many people to become adherents of a secular belief called "The Spirit of the Last Son," which sees the Man of Steel as a model for mature, altruistic living. **RG**

KEY STORYLINES
• *SUPERMAN #75 (JANUARY 1993):* Superman dies defeating Doomsday, an alien genetic experiment designed to be the ultimate killing machine in the "The Death of Superman!"
• *ACTION COMICS #689 (SEPTEMBER 1993):* The Man of Steel returns from the dead.
• *SUPERMAN #171 (AUGUST 2001):* Superman begins a tumultuous defence of Earth and the Universe against the might of Imperiex as the Our Worlds at War storyline commences.
• *SUPERMAN BIRTHRIGHT #1 (SEPTEMBER 2003):* Superman's origins from his escape from Krypton to him becoming the world-renowned Man of Steel is thoroughly redefined and expanded.

T.O. MORROW

FIRST APPEARANCE FLASH (1st series) #143 (March 1964)
STATUS Villain **REAL NAME** Thomas Oscar Morrow
OCCUPATION Criminal scientist **BASE** Mobile
HEIGHT 5ft 10in **WEIGHT** 191 lbs **EYES** Blue **HAIR** Gray
SPECIAL POWERS/ABILITIES Brilliant intellect; possesses technology that can see into or retrieve objects from the future.

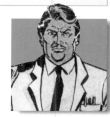

Thomas Oscar Morrow studied cybernetics and computers at Harvard, where, as one might expect from a man named T.O. Morrow, he became obsessed with the future. Inventing a viewscreen that allowed him to witness events that would occur in 100 years' time, Morrow copied the designs he saw and became known as a brilliant roboticist. He also developed a "fourth dimensional grappler" that could pluck actual objects from the future. Undoubtedly, Morrow's greatest creation is the android RED TORNADO, who rebelled against his creator and joined the JUSTICE SOCIETY OF AMERICA.

At one point, T.O. Morrow briefly split into two beings, including the big-headed Future Man. Later, he witnessed distressing future events and sank into a deep depression, though he has since shaken off his melancholy.

In a team-up with PROFESSOR IVO, Morrow developed the android TOMORROW WOMAN as a sleeper agent whose only purpose was to infiltrate the JUSTICE LEAGUE OF AMERICA. When Tomorrow Woman developed a conscience and sacrificed her life to save her teammates, Morrow was delighted—in his eyes, such humanlike behavior was evidence of his programming genius. **DW**

TAKION

FIRST APPEARANCE TAKION #1 (June 1996)
STATUS Hero **REAL NAME** Joshua Sanders
OCCUPATION Leader of the New Gods **BASE** New Genesis
HEIGHT 6ft 2in **WEIGHT** Variable **EYES** Red **HAIR** None
SPECIAL POWERS/ABILITIES A being of limitless power who can manipulate matter and energy in all its forms.

Blind since birth, Joshua Sanders had the most profound epiphany when HIGHFATHER of New Genesis stripped him of his corporeal shell. Transformed into the living embodiment of the Source, Sanders merged with the light of the universe and became a conduit between the life-stuff of creation and the NEW GODS empowered by it. Sanders became Takion, omniscient and omnipotent avatar of the Source. Since Highfather's death, Takion leads the New Gods and helps them protect the peaceful planet of New Genesis from the unending threat of its neighbor Apokolips. As Takion, the formerly sightless Sanders briefly enjoyed seeing the FOREVER PEOPLE's BEAUTIFUL DREAMER in both a literal and romantic sense. **SB**

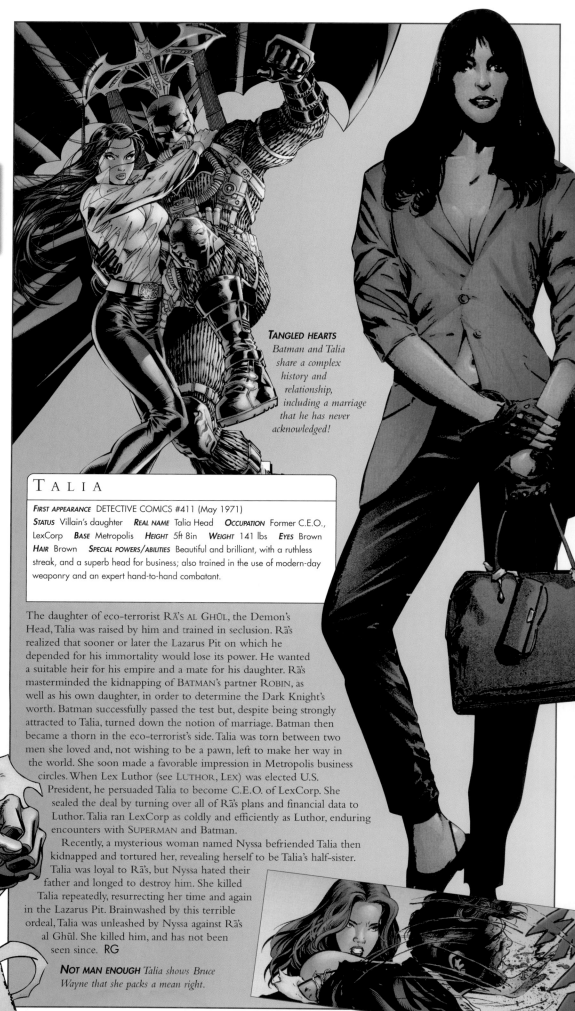

TANGLED HEARTS
Batman and Talia share a complex history and relationship, including a marriage that he has never acknowledged!

TALIA

FIRST APPEARANCE DETECTIVE COMICS #411 (May 1971)
STATUS Villain's daughter **REAL NAME** Talia Head **OCCUPATION** Former C.E.O., LexCorp **BASE** Metropolis **HEIGHT** 5ft 8in **WEIGHT** 141 lbs **EYES** Brown **HAIR** Brown **SPECIAL POWERS/ABILITIES** Beautiful and brilliant, with a ruthless streak, and a superb head for business; also trained in the use of modern-day weaponry and an expert hand-to-hand combatant.

The daughter of eco-terrorist RĀ'S AL GHŪL, the Demon's Head, Talia was raised by him and trained in seclusion. Rā's realized that sooner or later the Lazarus Pit on which he depended for his immortality would lose its power. He wanted a suitable heir for his empire and a mate for his daughter. Rā's masterminded the kidnapping of BATMAN's partner ROBIN, as well as his own daughter, in order to determine the Dark Knight's worth. Batman successfully passed the test but, despite being strongly attracted to Talia, turned down the notion of marriage. Batman then became a thorn in the eco-terrorist's side. Talia was torn between two men she loved and, not wishing to be a pawn, left to make her way in the world. She soon made a favorable impression in Metropolis business circles. When Lex Luthor (see LUTHOR, LEX) was elected U.S. President, he persuaded Talia to become C.E.O. of LexCorp. She sealed the deal by turning over all of Rā's plans and financial data to Luthor. Talia ran LexCorp as coldly and efficiently as Luthor, enduring encounters with SUPERMAN and Batman.

Recently, a mysterious woman named Nyssa befriended Talia then kidnapped and tortured her, revealing herself to be Talia's half-sister. Talia was loyal to Rā's, but Nyssa hated their father and longed to destroy him. She killed Talia repeatedly, resurrecting her time and again in the Lazarus Pit. Brainwashed by this terrible ordeal, Talia was unleashed by Nyssa against Rā's al Ghūl. She killed him, and has not been seen since. **RG**

NOT MAN ENOUGH *Talia shows Bruce Wayne that she packs a mean right.*

302

T

TANNARAK

FIRST APPEARANCE PHANTOM STRANGER (2nd series) #10 (December 1970) **STATUS** Villain **REAL NAME** Unknown **OCCUPATION** Sorcerer; nightclub owner **BASE** The Bewitched nightclub **HEIGHT** 6ft **WEIGHT** 187 lbs **EYES** Blue **HAIR** Black **SPECIAL POWERS/ABILITIES** Immortal and a powerful sorcerer; can project magical force blasts from his hands; master alchemist.

Tannarak is the owner of Bewitched, an interdimensional nightclub in San Francisco catering to Earth's mystic community. The magician, born over one hundred years ago, became obsessed with his own mortality and vowed to live forever. He concocted an elixir that stopped his body aging; however he had to steal souls to maintain his youth. The PHANTOM STRANGER became Tannarak's enemy, trying to thwart the alchemist's sinister drive for immortality. Tannarak became a member of the Dark Circle, an organization of mystics run by the evil sorceress Tala. When Tala summoned the Four Horsemen of the Apocalypse to destroy the world, Tannarak summoned the Phantom Stranger to help end her rampage. Tannarak seemed to have perished in the battle, but he somehow survived and remains a dark force in Earth's mystical community. **PJ**

TAR PIT

FIRST APPEARANCE FLASH (2nd series) #174 (July 2001) **STATUS** Villain **REAL NAME** Joey Monteleone **OCCUPATION** Criminal **BASE** Keystone City **HEIGHT** Variable **WEIGHT** Variable **EYES** Yellow **HAIR** None **SPECIAL POWERS/ABILITIES** Body made of molten asphalt is nearly invulnerable; can hurl flaming chunks of tar at enemies. Can maintain a remote consciousness in inanimate objects.

Joey Monteleone had no interest in his family's business, namely the drug trade in Keystone City. Arrested instead on a theft charge, he landed in the Iron Heights penitentiary to serve his sentence. There he learned that he could transfer his consciousness into inanimate objects, and mischievously "became" a vat of hot tar one evening to cause a ruckus at a local hockey game.

The FLASH III fought the sticky lump called Tar Pit, but found he could not defeat an enemy with no real body, and therefore no weaknesses. He finally located an acid that dissolved the tar, reducing Tar Pit to puddles. Joey Monteleone, however, could not unstick his mind from the form of Tar Pit, and his body lay comatose in Iron Heights prison. Recently, a jailbreak orchestrated by GORILLA GRODD let Tar Pit's molten form escape into Keystone once more. **DW**

TARANTULA I

FIRST APPEARANCE STAR-SPANGLED COMICS #1 (October 1941) **STATUS** Hero (deceased) **REAL NAME** Jonathan Law **OCCUPATION** Crime novelist **BASE** Blüdhaven **HEIGHT** 5ft 10in **WEIGHT** 180 lbs **EYES** Blue **HAIR** Blond **SPECIAL POWERS/ABILITIES** A skilled acrobat and combatant; uses a web-gun that shoots strands of sticky webbing that entraps foes.

A crime novelist in the late 1930s who became intrigued by the rising crop of "mystery men" fighting crime, Jon Law interviewed Dian Belmont, longtime companion of the first SANDMAN, about her association with the hero. After Belmont gave a sketch of a costume she had designed for the Sandman to Law, the novelist secretly created a copy of the costume for himself and began fighting crime as the Tarantula, taking his name and weapons from his pet spider.

The Tarantula's first case was in 1941, when the new crime fighter stopped a Nazi saboteur. He later became a more public figure after stopping a crime at a Broadway theater. The Tarantula joined the wartime heroes known as the ALL-STAR SQUADRON until they disbanded in 1945.

In the 1960s, Law wrote a book called *Altered Egos*, about the mystery men of the 1940s. Decades later, the novelist moved from New York City to Blüdhaven, where he was murdered by BLOCKBUSTER II. **PJ**

TARANTULA II

FIRST APPEARANCE NIGHTWING #71 (September 2002) **STATUS** Anti-hero **REAL NAME** Catalina Marie Flores **OCCUPATION** Social worker; vigilante **BASE** Blüdhaven **HEIGHT** 5ft 7in **WEIGHT** 135 lbs **EYES** Brown **HAIR** Black **SPECIAL POWERS/ABILITIES** Athlete trained in F.B.I. techniques; arsenal includes web-gun firing grapnel lines or adhesives to ensnare foes.

Strong and streetwise, Catalina Flores studied at the F.B.I. Academy in Quantico, Virginia. However, for reasons unrevealed, she left the program and returned to her native Blüdhaven. She became a social worker and befriended Jonathan Law, retired mystery novelist and the former masked "Mystery Man" Tarantula (*see* TARANTULA I). Catalina stole Law's vigilante gear and became a second Tarantula, a cold-blooded vigilante. Catalina sharpened her fighting skills under the tutelage of crime boss Roland Desmond (BLOCKBUSTER II). This association made Tarantula and Blüdhaven's guardian NIGHTWING adversaries, especially after the Tarantula murdered corrupt Blüdhaven Police Chief Frances Redhorn.

When Blockbuster played a part in John Law's death Tarantula shot him dead. Meanwhile, she and Nightwing began a tempestuous affair. She followed Nightwing to Gotham City, helping Batman end a bloody gang war The Dark Knight's influence has encouraged Catalina to rethink her murderous methods and to realign her ambiguous moral compass. **SB**

TARTARUS

FIRST APPEARANCE THE TITANS #6 (August 1999) **STATUS** Villain team **BASE** Mobile **MEMBERS AND POWERS** **Vandal Savage** Immortal conqueror. **Gorilla Grodd** Telepathic psychopath. **Lady Vic** International assassin. **Cheshire** International terrorist. **Siren** Mesmerizing criminal. **Red Panzer III** Deadly Nazi sympathizer.

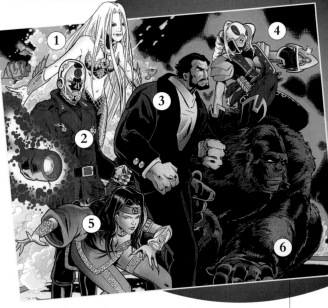

TARTARUS 1) Siren 2) Red Panzer III 3) Vandal Savage 4) Lady Vic 5) Cheshire 6) Gorilla Grodd

VANDAL SAVAGE kidnapped former TEEN TITAN Omen (Lilith Clay) and forced her to use her telepathic skills to form the perfect team of adversaries to defeat the Titans. She subverted his plans, however, by selecting villains who would never gel long enough to become a true threat. Omen recruited GORILLA GRODD, LADY VIC, CHESHIRE, the mesmerizing Siren and RED PANZER III. Savage named the group Tartarus, after the prison that housed the TITANS OF MYTH. He planned to use Tartarus to gain access to the H.I.V.E. Queen. DEATHSTROKE's ex-wife Adeline Kane, in the country of Zandia. He hoped to secure a sample of Kane's blood, which contained special regenerative properties. The Titans teamed with Deathstroke and went to Zandia. There, they had to fight not only Tartarus, but the H.I.V.E., which tried to protect their Queen. During the conflict, Savage mortally wounded Kane and Red Panzer III died. Savage allowed Justin from the H.I.V.E. to become the fourth Panzer. After the battle, TEMPEST learned of Omen's capture and led the Titans to Tartarus's base in Scotland. The villains scattered, with Siren aiding Tempest. **RG**

303

TATTOOED MAN

FIRST APPEARANCE GREEN LANTERN (2nd series) #23 (Sept. 1963)
STATUS Occasional villain **REAL NAME** Abel Tarrant
OCCUPATION Reformed criminal **BASE** New York City
HEIGHT 6ft **WEIGHT** 195 lbs **EYES** Blue **HAIR** Brown
SPECIAL POWERS/ABILITIES Can manifest his tattoos as physical objects
by concentrating on one tattoo at a time.

Abel Tarrant, was a sailor based in Coast City who
turned to burglary. During one heist, exposure to a spill
of mystery chemicals left him with the mental ability to
conjure actual objects from the chemicals. He promptly
created a bomb, blasted a hole in the wall to escape from
a police shoot-out, and returned home to tattoo his
body with various shapes (including an axe, a shield, a
cannon, and a dragon), using the chemical as body ink.

The Tattooed Man began stealing from local billionaire
Baron Cranfield until opposed by GREEN LANTERN Hal
Jordan. The Tattooed Man sent his shapes into battle
against the Emerald Crusader, discovering that the yellow
base used in the ink made the tattoos impervious to his
enemy's power ring. Green Lantern eventually triumphed
by forcing the Tattooed Man to concentrate on more than
one tattoo at a time in order to shake his mental focus.

Joining the INJUSTICE GANG, the Tattooed Man made
a near-fatal mistake when he stole money from
GOLDFACE. Shot and left for dead by Goldface's agents,
the Tattooed Man started a new life as a tattoo artist in
New York City. Recently, the Tattooed Man used the
time-travel equipment of his dead teammate CHRONOS I
to go back 20 years and warn his younger self away from
a life of crime, an experiment that failed. **DW**

INTERROGATION
The Outsiders leaned
on the Tattooed Man
in order to learn the
whereabouts of the
villain Sabbac.

A STORY IN INK
Every one of the
Tattooed Man's
tattoos can come to
life, spelling trouble
for his enemies.

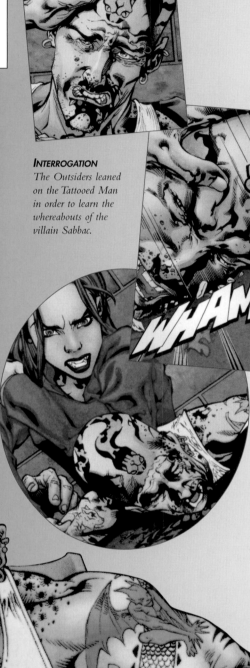

TASMANIAN DEVIL

FIRST APPEARANCE SUPER FRIENDS #7 (October 1977)
STATUS Hero **REAL NAME** Hugh Dawkins
OCCUPATION Ex-engineer; drama coach **BASE** Sydney, Australia
HEIGHT 6ft **WEIGHT** 176 lbs **EYES** White **HAIR** Red
SPECIAL POWERS/ABILITIES Transforms into a 9ft-4in, 535-pound,
werewolf-like creature with superstrength, and razor-sharp claws.

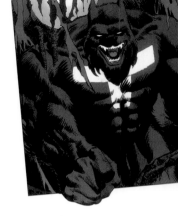

Hugh Dawkins was
born in Launceton,
Tasmania. His mother
was a werewoman and
his father was the
leader of a Tasmanian
Devil cult that
worshipped her. The
couple eventually
decamped to Perth,
Australia, with Hugh,
and tried to lead
ordinary lives.

As a teenager, Hugh
told his parents that he
was gay, and his stern
father rejected him. Hugh also acquired his mother's
powers and found that he could turn into a giant
werecreature. He took the name Tasmanian Devil and
became a crime fighter in Sydney, and later joined the
GLOBAL GUARDIANS. Tasmanian Devil then joined the
international branch of the JUSTICE LEAGUE OF AMERICA
and met and fell in love with JLA liaison Joshua Barbazon.
Tasmanian Devil returned to the Global Guardians before
settling in Sydney, where he lives with Joshua and teaches
drama at a local university. He continues to build a new,
more loving relationship with his father. **PJ**

TECHNOCRAT

FIRST APPEARANCE OUTSIDERS (2nd series) #1 (Alpha) (November
1993) **STATUS** Hero **REAL NAME** Geoffrey Barron
OCCUPATION Inventor **BASE** Mobile **HEIGHT** 6ft
WEIGHT 188 lbs **EYES** Brown **HAIR** Black, streaked with white
SPECIAL POWERS/ABILITIES Armored techno-suit enables flight,
superstrength, and is outfitted with an arsenal of weapons.

While visiting the European principality of Markovia to
promote his Technocrat 2000 prototype battle armor,
businessman Geoffrey Baron had no choice but to don the
techno-suit himself after his assistant, Charlie Wylde, was
mortally injured by a maddened bear. Barron protected
Wylde as the sorcerer FAUST magically merged the injured
Wylde with his beastly attacker. Later, with the man-beast
Wylde still by his side, Barron became Technocrat. Both
men joined a second incarnation of the OUTSIDERS
led by the Markovian meta-human Prince Brion
Markov (see GEO-FORCE), who had been
deposed by Queen Ilona and her
vampire consort, Roderick. As an
Outsider, Barron helped the team to
liberate planet Nekrome from the evil
influence of ECLIPSO, a conflict
that saw the Technocrat's
armor fused with an alien
weapon. Since the
Outsiders disbanded,
Technocrat has been
working at
mastering the
alien-altered
Technocrat
technology. **SB**

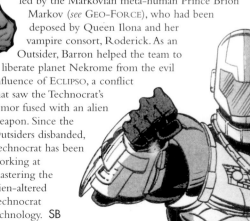

TEMPEST

ATLANTEAN MAGE

FIRST APPEARANCE ADVENTURE COMICS #269 (February 1960)
STATUS Hero REAL NAME Garth OCCUPATION Ambassador; sorcerer
BASE Poseidonis, Atlantis HEIGHT 5ft 10in WEIGHT 235 lbs
EYES Purple HAIR Black SPECIAL POWERS/ABILITIES Amphibious;
swims at speeds of 97.76 knots (85 mph); superstrength; high
resistance to deep-sea pressures; projection of powerful optic force
blasts; manipulation of water currents; creation of whirlpools; can
boil or freeze water; mystic powers include postcognition, telepathy,
dimensional travel, and astral projection; partially colorblind.

ABANDONED AT BIRTH by the superstitious Atlanteans, Garth survived alone in the ocean depths for years until he was discovered by AQUAMAN. Adopted by the Sea King and called Aqualad, Garth was the least powerful member of the TEEN TITANS, until he realized his potential for wizardry and became the powerful mage Tempest!

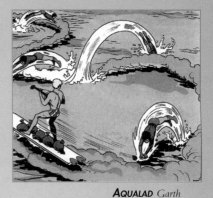

AQUALAD Garth earned his stripes against enemies that were vexing, but rarely lethal.

UNLUCKY EYES

Garth's heritage is of the Idylists, a group of Atlantean pacifists who established the colony of Shayeris in the Hidden Valley. When Garth's father, King Thar, assembled weapons to destroy his brother Zath's invading armies, his palace guards mistakenly believed he was going insane, and murdered him. Thar's pregnant wife Berra was exiled to Atlantis, where she gave birth to Garth. Believing his purple eyes to be a bad omen, the Atlanteans seized the infant and left him to die, abandoned to the sea. Thanks to the sorcerer ATLAN, Garth survived and grew up to cross paths with Aquaman, who adopted him as his ward. After Aquaman joined the JLA, and following formal schooling in Scotland, Aqualad became a founding member of the Teen Titans. He fell in love with AQUAGIRL, who tragically died during the Crisis (see Great Battles, pp. 320–1).

Sometime later, Garth's uncle Zath, now the necromancer Slizzath, returned to conquer Atlantis. Under the tutelage of Atlan, the father of Aquaman, Aqualad acquired a host of magical abilities, refined his own powers, and became the mage Tempest. Garbed in the flag of his people, Tempest defeated his uncle and saved the undersea realms. Soon after, he became an Atlantean ambassador. Tempest soon found new love with DOLPHIN—who, awkwardly, was seeing Aquaman at the time—and the two were married. In time they bore a son, whom they named Cerdian. During the Imperiex War, Tempest used his powers as a wizard to protect Atlantis, but accidentally sent the city thousands of years back in time to the Obsidian Age. Later he served as a living conduit for the Apokoliptian power used to send IMPERIEX back to the birth of the universe. Since Atlantis' return from the ancient past, Tempest has helped protect Aquaman from persecution by vengeful Atlanteans. DW

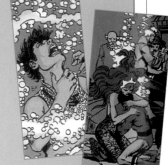

TULA The love of Garth's life succumbed to the monster Chemo during the great Crisis.

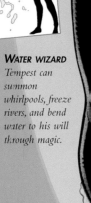

WATER WIZARD
Tempest can summon whirlpools, freeze rivers, and bend water to his will through magic.

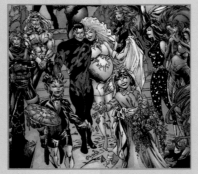

WEDDING Surrounded by the Titans and other super heroes, Tempest married Dolphin.

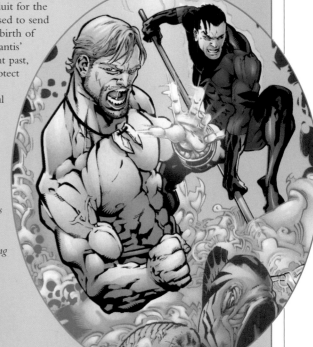

PEERS Like Nightwing and Arsenal, Tempest has shed the label of "super-hero sidekick" and now stands on an equal footing with Aquaman.

KEY STORYLINES

• *TEMPEST #1–4 (NOVEMBER 1997–FEBRUARY 1997)*: Aqualad no more! Garth assumes his new name and new identity as Tempest while fighting his villainous uncle with the power of Atlantean sorcery.

• *WONDER WOMAN #178 (OCTOBER 2001)*: Tempest joins with Darkseid and Wonder Woman to help save the universe from Imperiex, Destroyer of Worlds, accidentally sending Atlantis back in time.

• *AQUAMAN #63 (JANUARY 2000)*: Dolphin gives birth to Tempest's son Cerdian, a child who may become an Aquaman for a future generation.

TEEN TITANS

ADOLESCENT AVENGERS

FIRST APPEARANCE (Teen Titans I) BRAVE AND THE BOLD #54 (July 1964); (New Teen Titans) DC COMICS PRESENTS #26 (December 1980); (Teen Titans II) TEEN TITANS (2nd series) #1 (October 1996); (current team) TEEN TITANS (3rd series) #1 (July 2003)
STATUS Hero team **BASE** Titans Tower, San Francisco Bay
CURRENT MEMBERS AND POWERS
Robin III Team leader; skilled martial artist and tactician.
Kid Flash II Superspeed.
Wonder Girl II Superstrength, flight.
Beast Boy Shape-changing into animal forms.
Starfire Flight, star bolts, solar absorption.
Cyborg Superstrength, white sound blaster, computer skills.
Raven Teleportation, empathic powers, sorcery.

ALMOST A DECADE AGO, teen heroes Robin I (NIGHTWING), Kid Flash I (FLASH III) and Aqualad (TEMPEST) brought an end to the reign of Mister Twister, a deranged weather-controlling villain. Soon after, Wonder Girl I (*see* TROIA) and Speedy (*see* ARSENAL) joined the three teenagers and the quintet stopped a mind-controlled JUSTICE LEAGUE OF AMERICA from committing a crime spree. Calling themselves the Teen Titans, the young sidekicks fought criminals like DOCTOR LIGHT I and the ANTITHESIS before parting ways for college and to further their budding careers.

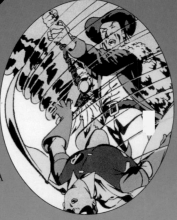

IT'S A TWISTER! *The weather-controlling Mister Twister attacks the first Teen Titans team.*

THE NEW TEEN TITANS
Years later, Robin, KID FLASH II, Wonder Girl and Changeling (*see* BEAST BOY) and new heroes STARFIRE and CYBORG were united by RAVEN as the New Teen Titans to thwart the demon TRIGON, Raven's father, from invading the Earth. After defeating Trigon, the Titans quickly ran afoul of the villainous forces of DEATHSTROKE the Terminator, the FEARSOME FIVE, the SOCIETY OF SIN, and BROTHER BLOOD.

Meanwhile, the Titans accepted an enigmatic young girl named TERRA into their ranks. Unbeknownst to the Titans, however, Terra was a spy for Deathstroke, sent to infiltrate their ranks and learn their secrets. The insane Terra then helped Deathstroke capture the Titans and turn them over to the H.I.V.E. terrorist group before killing herself. During this time, Kid Flash retired, Robin became Nightwing, and Deathstroke's son JERICHO joined the team.

DEMON SEED *Trigon has frequently tried to conquer Earth, using Raven as a pawn.*

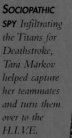

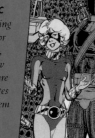

SOCIOPATHIC SPY *Infiltrating the Titans for Deathstroke, Tara Markov helped capture her teammates and turn them over to the H.I.V.E.*

COMINGS AND GOINGS
When the Anti-Monitor invaded Earth, Dove (HAWK AND DOVE), AQUAGIRL, and new Titan KOLE died during the ensuing Crisis (*see* Great Battles, pp. 320–1). Starfire left the planet for an arranged marriage and the original Titans reformed under Wonder Girl's unsteady leadership. After an epic battle with Brother Blood, the return of Starfire and Raven, newly purged of her father Trigon's evil, and Wonder Girl's transformation into TROIA, the Teen Titans took the more adult name the New Titans.

THE TEEN TITANS II
A second group of Teen Titans were genetic experiments created by the evil alien H'San Nattall empire. Managed by billionaire Mister Jupiter, and led by the ATOM II, who had been reduced in age by EXTANT, these half-human/half-alien Titans faced villains like DARK NEMESIS and Haze before splitting up.

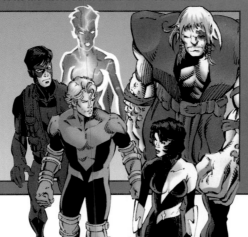

THE TITANS HUNT
Jericho, whose body been contaminated by souls corrupted by the evil of Trigon, ordered the villainous WILDEBEEST Society to hunt the Titans one by one. After killing Golden Eagle, severely injuring Aqualad and Cyborg, and destroying Titans Tower, Jericho was finally stopped when his father Deathstroke killed him. Programmed assassins for EXTANT, the Team Titans arrived from an alternate timeline, and Cyborg became the alien robot Cyberion. After several membership changes, the Titans teamed to stop an alien invasion and the spread of Trigon's progeny. The New Titans then disbanded.

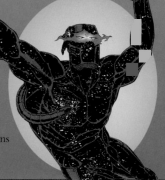

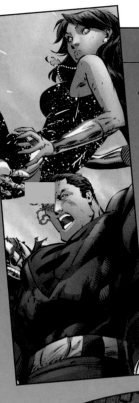

TITANS REBORN

When Cyberion returned to Earth and threatened the planet, the Titans reunited and saved their former friend. The original Titans, all adults, decided to reform the Titans to train younger heroes. The team stayed together for some time, fighting criminals like CHESHIRE, Deathstroke, and the HANGMEN.

The Titans briefly recruited a group of youngsters from an orphanage in the D.E.O., until one of them died. Later, after a rogue SUPERMAN Robot murdered Troia and Lilith, the daughter of Mister Jupiter, this incarnation of the team disbanded.

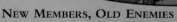

NEW MEMBERS, OLD ENEMIES

But the members of Young Justice, honoring the legacy of the Titans, reestablished the team, based in San Francisco. The latest wave of Teen Titans includes SUPERBOY, ROBIN II, Beast Boy, Cyborg, and Starfire, and WONDER GIRL II. Raven, her soul housed in a new body, joined the teen heroes, and Deathstroke, possessed by the spirit of his son Jericho, returned to attack them, as did Brother Blood. **PJ**

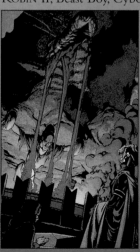

RAVEN'S BLOOD *Brother Blood has long craved Raven's magic powers, and was responsible for restoring the half-breed demon's human body, lost in battle with Trigon.*

SPARE-TIME HEROES

The Teen Titans are weekend warriors —they are only available to fight crime when they're not busy doing their high-school homework during the week. They remain powerful crusaders for justice and powerful inspirations to teens, and adults, all over the world.

THE CURRENT LINEUP 1) *Raven* **2)** *Cyborg* **3)** *Starfire* **4)** *Robin III* **5)** *Superboy* **6)** *Kid Flash II* **7)** *Beast Boy* **8)** *Wonder Girl II*

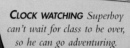

CLOCK WATCHING *Superboy can't wait for class to be over, so he can go adventuring.*

TERRA

FIRST APPEARANCE NEW TEEN TITANS (1st series) #26 (December 1982) **STATUS** Hero **REAL NAME** Tara Markov **OCCUPATION** Adventurer **BASE** San Francisco **HEIGHT** 5ft 1in **WEIGHT** 112 lbs **EYES** Blue **HAIR** Blonde **SPECIAL POWERS/ABILITIES** A powerful geomorph, Terra has complete control over the earth, creating flying islands or moving creatures of soil or stone, generating earthquakes, or calling forth molten lava or mudslides with just a thought.

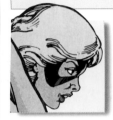

Like her brother Brian, GEO-FORCE of the OUTSIDERS, Tara Markov was given powers over the earth by Markovian scientist Dr. Helga Jace. But where Brion was a prince-in-waiting of their tiny European kingdom, Tara was the monarch's illegitimate daughter and grew up isolated and resentful in the United States. In her teens, Tara molded a pact with DEATHSTROKE the Terminator to destroy the TEEN TITANS by securing membership as the earth-shaking Terra and spying on the group from within. When her betrayal was revealed, Terra died battling the Titans. Sometime later, a new Terra emerged from an alternate future as one of the time-lost Team Titans. In stark contrast to the sociopath Tara Markov, the second Terra wants nothing more than to use her powers for good. Following a genetics test, Brion Markov learned that this second geomorph is genetically identical to her predecessor, information he has kept from Terra for her own peace of mind. Whether or not she is a clone or twin of Tara Markov remains to be seen. **SB**

TEZUMAK

FIRST APPEARANCE JLA # 66 (July 2002) **STATUS** Hero (deceased) **REAL NAME** Tezumak **OCCUPATION** Warrior **BASE** South America **HEIGHT** 6ft **WEIGHT** 340 lbs **EYES** White **HAIR** Bronze **SPECIAL POWERS/ABILITIES** Wearing bronze armor that had once been oiled with the blood of sacrificial victims gave Tezumak enhanced strength and endurance.

3,000 years ago, a group of people were gathered by the sorceress GAMEMNAE to help her achieve great power. Tezumak, a South American monk from a pre-Aztec, Mesoamerican civilization in Mexico, joined her band of followers and did Gamemnae's bidding. He wore bronze armor, honoring the gods who first brought science to the people. Working with Gamemnae pitted him against the JUSTICE LEAGUE OF AMERICA, who had been lured back in time to search for the missing AQUAMAN. When Tezumak learned the full extent of Gamemnae's plans, which involved exterminating the JLA, he revolted, ultimately sacrificing his life to help bring about her defeat. **RG**

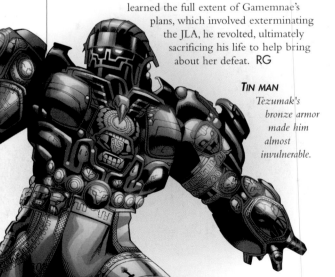

TIN MAN
Tezumak's bronze armor made him almost invulnerable.

THAROK

FIRST APPEARANCE ADVENTURE COMICS #352 (January 1967); LEGION OF SUPER-HEROES (4th series) #79 (April 1996). **STATUS** Villain **REAL NAME** Tharok **OCCUPATION** Criminal **BASE** Mobile **HEIGHT** 6ft 4in **WEIGHT** 225 lbs **EYES** Black **HAIR** None **SPECIAL POWERS/ABILITIES** Brilliant cyborg intelligence; enhanced strength in mechanical limbs; a genius at manipulating others, he always rises to a leadership position.

Once a petty crook on his home planet of Zadron, Tharok made one heist too many and wound up with much of his body vaporized after a run-in with law officers. In the late 30th century, he was saved from death through extensive cyborg reconstruction. Tharok became half-man, half-metal with a computerized intelligence that transformed him into a criminal mastermind.

When the star-devouring Sun-Eater menaced the United Planets, the LEGION OF SUPER-HEROES assembled five criminals to battle the entity in exchange for amnesty. Tharok became a member of this "FATAL FIVE" (alongside Validus, the Persuader, Empress, and Mano) which proceeded to set itself against the Legion after the Sun-Eater's defeat. Tharok and his comrades have failed to defeat the Legion several times, but always escape from prison. On his most recent rampage, Tharok and the rest of the Fatal Five lost to Legionnaire TIMBER WOLF, who was embarking on his first official mission. **DW**

THIRST, THE

FIRST APPEARANCE AQUAMAN (4th series) #5 (June 2003) **STATUS** Villain (destroyed) **REAL NAME** None **OCCUPATION** Supernatural destroyer **BASE** The Secret Sea **HEIGHT** Variable **WEIGHT** Variable **EYES** Red **HAIR** None **SPECIAL POWERS/ABILITIES** Absorbs life energy, leaving his victims withered husks; possesses mental control over his zombie-like armies; absorbs moisture from all water sources, which gives him power and also affects his physical size.

The Thirst is a golem composed of dry river mud, the mystical "brother" of a being called the Waterbearer, an ancient goddess. The Thirst has preyed on the deities who have watched over the Secret Sea, a metaphysical realm composed of the shared imagination of humanity, for millennia, absorbing their power. When AQUAMAN became guardian of the Secret Sea, the Thirst set its sights on the hero.

The evil, magical parasite battled Aquaman several times, attempting to drain not only the rivers of Earth and the magical waters of the Secret Sea of all life, but the Sea King's very essence as well. In their final battle, Aquaman and the Thirst merged into a single, monstrous being. When Aquaman stopped fighting the Thirst and surrendered his control to the light of the universe, the evil parasite was consumed by the holy power and destroyed, seemingly forever. **PJ**

THOMPKINS, LESLIE M.D.

FIRST APPEARANCE DETECTIVE COMICS #457 (March 1976) **STATUS** Hero **REAL NAME** Dr. Leslie Thompkins **OCCUPATION** Physician **BASE** Gotham City **HEIGHT** 5ft 7in **WEIGHT** 130 lbs **EYES** Blue **HAIR** Gray **SPECIAL POWERS/ABILITIES** Gifted and compassionate physician; considers herself a general practitioner, but is also a surgeon of great skill and follows advances in medical science with great interest.

Born to affluence in Gotham City, Leslie Thompkins graduated with honors from Gotham State Medical School. She decided to devote herself to helping the less fortunate and opened a free clinic to benefit Gotham's poorest citizens. Returning from a house call late one night, Leslie found young Bruce Wayne kneeling by the bodies of his murdered parents in the city's notorious "Crime Alley." Along with the Wayne family butler Alfred (*see* PENNYWORTH, ALFRED), Leslie befriended Bruce, helping the orphan remain free from the dubious clutches of Gotham's Social Services. She later encouraged him to undertake the global sojourn that would lead him to becoming BATMAN. Leslie is one of the select few privy to the Dark Knight's secrets. She remains a close ally to the Bat-Family, providing emergency medical attention when called upon. Leslie is particularly close to Bruce Wayne's valet Alfred; however their romance has always taken second place to their unstinting support for Batman's war on crime. **SB**

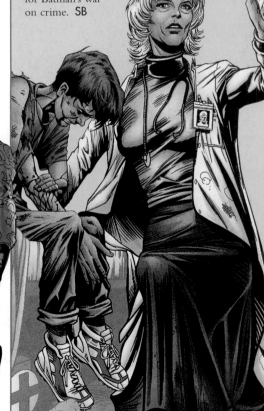

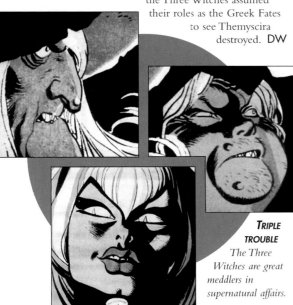

ALIEN PROGENY *The twin sons of a human and an alien, the brothers Thunder and Lightning are the living embodiment of their names, able to manipulate the elements to destructive effect!*

THREE WITCHES, THE

FIRST APPEARANCE THE WITCHING HOUR #1 (December 1970)
STATUS Villains **REAL NAMES** Mildred, Mordred, and Cynthia
OCCUPATION Oracles **BASE** Mobile **HEIGHT** The Witches refuse to be measured **WEIGHT** The Witches refuse to divulge **EYES** Variable
HAIR Variable **SPECIAL POWERS/ABILITIES** Supernatural talents from their role as deities; aware of every event on the physical and metaphysical planes.

The Three Witches are goddesses who belong to no particular pantheon. They have appeared in various guises, known to the Egyptians, Romans, and Vikings alike. In ancient Greece they were called the Fates and went by the names Clotho, Lachesis, and Atropos. The Three Witches disappeared during the witch-hunts of the Middle Ages, but have recently returned in new forms.

In the modern era, The Three Witches most commonly go by the names Mildred, Mordred, and Cynthia. Their different personalities embody the three aspects of the Triple Goddess: the mother (Mildred), the crone (Mordred), and the maiden (Cynthia). They claim their magic powers are strongest at midnight, and will answer any three questions if asked with the proper ritual.

During the Imperiex War (*see* Great Battles, pp. 320–1), the Three Witches assumed their roles as the Greek Fates to see Themyscira destroyed. **DW**

TRIPLE TROUBLE *The Three Witches are great meddlers in supernatural affairs.*

THUNDER AND LIGHTNING

FIRST APPEARANCE THE NEW TEEN TITANS (1st series) #32
STATUS Undecided **REAL NAMES** Gan Williams; Tavis Williams
OCCUPATION Adventurers **BASE** San Francisco
HEIGHT 6ft 5in; 6ft 4in **WEIGHT** 230 lbs; 215 lbs
EYES (both) Brown **HAIR** (both) Black
SPECIAL POWERS/ABILITIES Both share a psychic link; (Thunder) explosive force from hands; (Lightning) electricity bolts from hands; projects energy "surfboards".

Several hundred years ago, an alien crashlanded in Cambodia, traveling the world until it finally disguised itself as Walter Williams and joined the U.S. Army. Williams returned to Asia, hoping to find his buried spacecraft. During his search, he fell in love with a Vietnamese woman, who gave birth to cojoined twins. The twins were separated by a magician, who discovered that they possessed destructive powers. As adults, the twins, now called Thunder and Lightning, sought out their father for a cure, only to discover he was under the control of the criminal organization H.I.V.E. After a brief conflict with the TEEN TITANS, Thunder and Lightning were forced to kill their father. A blood transfusion gave them full control of their powers, and they settled in San Francisco to work with S.T.A.R. Labs to hone their powers. After being possessed by the souls of the demon TRIGON's unborn children, Thunder and Lightning returned to Vietnam and became two of Southeast Asia's most prominent defenders. **PJ**

THUNDER II

FIRST APPEARANCE POWER OF SHAZAM ANNUAL #1 (1996)
STATUS Undecided **REAL NAME** CeCe Beck
OCCUPATION Assassin **BASE** United Planets
HEIGHT 5ft 6in **WEIGHT** 130 lbs **EYES** Blue **HAIR** Blonde
SPECIAL POWERS/ABILITIES Strength, stamina, flight, wisdom, and invulnerability derived from gods that lent their powers to Shazam.

Hailing from 6,000 years after the 30th century, when the Earth is long dead, CeCe Beck (or just Beck) was granted powers by a wizard (formerly CAPTAIN MARVEL of the 20th century) following a terrorist attack that transported her to the Rock of Eternity at the edge of space and time. Whenever Beck invokes the name "Captain Marvel," lightning strikes, transforming her into Thunder, a slightly older woman with the godly powers of the wizard Shazam. While returning from a mission in the 20th century, Thunder was shunted to the 30th century when pro-science terrorists blew up the Rock of Eternity. After stopping the terrorists, she was offered membership in the LEGION OF SUPER-HEROES. Lord Pernisus gathered the scattered fragments of the Rock of Eternity in a bid for power, but was defeated by Thunder and the Legion. The Rock of Eternity was restored, but since it was still in its radioactive state, Thunder couldn't immediately use it to return home. She took some satisfaction in the fact that she can now return to the 90th Century as CeCe Beck by saying "Captain Marvel." **RG**

THUNDER III

FIRST APPEARANCE OUTSIDERS 3rd series #1 (August 2003)
STATUS Hero **REAL NAME** Anissa Pierce **OCCUPATION** Adventurer
BASE Metropolis **HEIGHT** 5ft 7in **WEIGHT** 119 lbs **EYES** Brown
HAIR Black (blonde wig as Thunder III)
SPECIAL POWERS/ABILITIES Can control her body's density, making Thunder II invulnerable and heavy enough to make a thunderous and destructive shock wave whenever she stomps her feet.

Growing up, Anissa Pierce wanted to be just like her crime-fighting father, Jefferson Pierce, alias BLACK LIGHTNING. Anissa developed her own meta-human traits when she was just 11 years old, manifesting the ability to manipulate her own density. However, her parents divorced and Anissa went to live with her mother, affording Anissa little opportunity to master her powers under her father's tutelage—even if he had been willing to help. For Jefferson Pierce wanted his daughter to forget about superheroics and lead a normal life. He made Anissa promise to wait until after she graduated from the pre-med program at Tulane University before considering a career in costumed crime fighting. Anissa kept her promise, assuming the identity of Thunder II just hours after accepting her degree. Thunder has since joined the OUTSIDERS, a new incarnation of the team to which Black Lightning once belonged. With time and hard work, Anissa hopes to earn her father's approval by showing him that Thunder inevitably follows lightning! **SB**

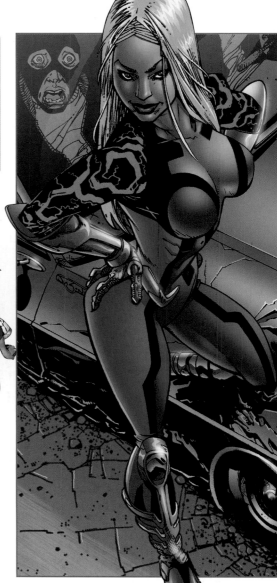

THUNDER, JAKEEM & THUNDERBOLT

FIRST APPEARANCE THE FLASH (2nd series) #134 (February 1998) **STATUS** Hero **REAL NAME** Jakeem John Williams
OCCUPATION High-school student **BASE** Keystone City
HEIGHT 5ft 4in **WEIGHT** 140 lbs
EYES Brown **HAIR** Black
SPECIAL POWERS/ABILITIES Born in the 7th hour on July 7th, Jakeem controls the 5th-dimensional genie Thunderbolt, who is capable of flight and vast feats of magic; Jakeem controls the Thunderbolt with the magic words "So cool."

Jakeem Williams, also known as J.J. Thunder, was born in Keystone City. His parents left him to be raised by his aunt Lashawn, and J.J. grew up with a rebellious streak, alienating his friends and family and getting into trouble at school.

One day, Jakeem asked Jay Garrick, the original FLASH, for his autograph and inadvertently grabbed a pen that housed a genie. The genie, a Fifth-Dimensional imp named Yz, had at one time been the sidekick of Johnny Thunder (see THUNDER, JOHNNY), a member of the JUSTICE SOCIETY OF AMERICA. The genie was trapped in the pen and looking for a new companion.

When another Fifth-Dimensional imp attacked the Earth, Jakeem was able to summon Yz from his pen and save the planet. Later, when Johnny Thunder was killed by the ULTRA-HUMANITE, Yz was able to merge with his former mentor's body, creating a new Thunderbolt that Jakeem controlled with the words "so cool." Soon after, Jakeem became a part-time member of the JSA. Jakeem briefly met his father, Phil, in Michigan, but did not reveal his true identity to him. **PJ**

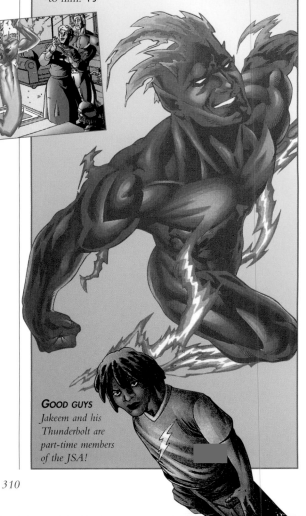

GOOD GUYS
Jakeem and his Thunderbolt are part-time members of the JSA!

THUNDER, JONNI

FIRST APPEARANCE JONNI THUNDER #1 (February 1985)
STATUS Hero **REAL NAME** Jonni Thunder
OCCUPATION Private investigator **BASE** Los Angeles
HEIGHT 5ft 6in **WEIGHT** 130 lbs **EYES** Green **HAIR** Blonde
SPECIAL POWERS/ABILITIES Skilled fighter; once possessed the power to act as a living thunderbolt with flight and energy-casting abilities.

The best private detective in Los Angeles learned her craft from her father Jim, a veteran of the LAPD. Jonni would have been content to ply her trade the old-fashioned way— but a bizarre accident gave her powers that coincidentally mirrored those of Johnny Thunder (see THUNDER, JOHNNY) of the JUSTICE SOCIETY OF AMERICA.

When crooks tried to steal a statue of Apu Illapu, the Incan god of lightning, Jonni found herself filled with energy. She was now able to become a living thunderbolt through an "out of body" experience—while her true form lay unconscious, Jonni could fly and control electrical discharges. Her thunderbolt self was often more ruthless than her waking self.

Jonni soon learned that the thunderbolt was an energy-based alien. Freed from the statue, it now wanted to free all its imprisoned brethren, but Jonni and INFINITY INC. stopped the aliens before they could take over the world. She is now cut off from her thunderbolt powers. **DW**

THUNDER I, JOHNNY

FIRST APPEARANCE ALL-AMERICAN COMICS #100 (August 1948)
STATUS Hero **REAL NAME** John Stuart Mill Tane
OCCUPATION Gunslinger **BASE** Mesa City
HEIGHT 6ft 2in **WEIGHT** 210 lbs **EYES** Blue **HAIR** Blond
SPECIAL POWERS/ABILITIES An expert marksman, fine horseman, and an above-average hand-to-hand combatant.

When a gang of thugs publicly humiliated his father, Sheriff William Tane, schoolmaster John Tane donned a colorful costume, dyed his hair black, and armed himself with a six-shooter. Teaching by day and fighting crime in the Old West by night, John Tane became the first Johnny Thunder. Soon after, he acquired a valiant horse named Black Lightning. Over the next few years, Johnny Thunder clashed with foes such as Silk Black and befriended a Cheyenne youth named Swift Deer.

In 1872, Jeanne Walker's father was cheated out of a rich strike at a gold mine by swindlers. Jeanne assumed the secret identity of MADAME .44 and became a thief, robbing from unscrupulous men. At first, this put her at odds with Johnny. However, Johnny Thunder and Madame .44 eventually became allies during a battle with the outlaw Silk Black. When it was over, they fell in love and married. **RG**

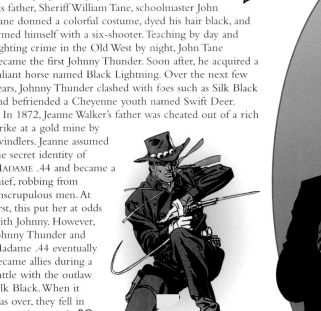

THUNDER II, JOHNNY

FIRST APPEARANCE FLASH COMICS #1 (January 1940)
STATUS Hero (deceased) **REAL NAME** Johnny Thunder
OCCUPATION Adventurer **BASE** New York City
HEIGHT 5ft 11in **WEIGHT** 225 lbs **EYES** Blue **HAIR** Blond
SPECIAL POWERS/ABILITIES No superpowers and an average combatant, usually relying on his Thunderbolt to fight for him. Since merging with the Thunderbolt, Johnny possesses unlimited magical power.

Johnny Thunder was born on the seventh day of the seventh month in a year that ended in seven. Realizing that a child born under this numerological sign would wield great power, the Badhnisian High Priest of Aissor kidnapped Johnny and placed the mystical Zodiac Belt on him. The High Priest cast a magic spell that granted Johnny magical powers on his seventh birthday. By uttering "Cei-U" (or "Say, You!"), Johnny commanded a magical pink Thunderbolt. Though smarter than Johnny, the Thunderbolt—a mystical Fifth-Dimensional sprite—had to obey his master for one hour. Together, Johnny and the Thunderbolt served as "mascot" to the JUSTICE SOCIETY OF AMERICA and Johnny served in the U.S. Navy in World War II.

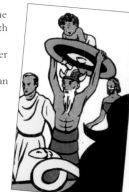

STOLEN *Johnny's upbringing was distinctly unusual.*

Johnny was a member of the JSA in the decades that followed, until, suffering from Alzheimer's disease, Johnny passed control of the Thunderbolt to young Jakeem J. Williams (see THUNDER, JAKEEM). However, Johnny took back the Thunderbolt while mind-controlled by the evil ULTRA-HUMANITE, who tried to use him to take over the world. The JSA fought back and Johnny's body was killed; however the Thunderbolt saved Johnny's soul and merged with it, creating Johnny Thunderbolt, a mix of both old friends and now a mentor and partner to Jakeem. **SB**

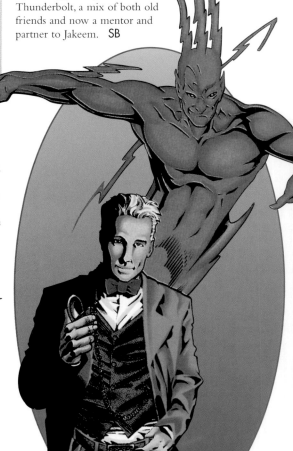

TIGGRA

FIRST APPEARANCE NEW GODS (1st series) #7 (March 1972)
STATUS Undecided (deceased) **REAL NAME** None
OCCUPATION Former concubine **BASE** Apokolips
HEIGHT 5ft 9in **WEIGHT** 130 lbs **EYES** Red **HAIR** Reddish-blonde
SPECIAL POWERS/ABILITIES A fierce fighter possessing energy-blasting powers; traversed space via Boom Tube.

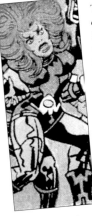

Tiggra was the second spouse of the dreaded DARKSEID, and the mother of his son, ORION. Moments after Orion's birth, Darkseid seized the infant from Tiggra's arms and presented him to HIGHFATHER of New Genesis to seal a peace between their warring worlds. Tiggra was imprisoned cryogenically for years until the adult Orion returned to Apokolips aiming to destroy Darkseid. With the help of the rebel scientist Himon, Orion freed Tiggra and sheltered her on New Genesis. Tiggra convinced Orion that Darkseid was not his father, as part of her plan to see Orion slay Darkseid and rule Apokolips. However, Tiggra was attacked by Apokoliptian Suicide Jockeys and died in Orion's arms before she could confess the truth. Tiggra later appeared to Orion when he was lost in the Abysmal Plane, but she was merely an animated construct created by the evil Ecruos, a monstrous creature of that realm, to torment the Dog of War. **SB**

TIMBER WOLF

FIRST APPEARANCE LEGION WORLDS #6 (November 2001)
STATUS Hero **REAL NAME** Brin Londo
OCCUPATION Hero **BASE** Rimbor and Earth
HEIGHT 6ft **WEIGHT** 190 lbs **EYES** Brown **HAIR** Brown
SPECIAL POWERS/ABILITIES Has above-average strength, speed and agility. The origin of these abilities is unknown.

Brin Londo ran with Crody, Hubble, Rn'dbrr, Mash, and Rac, a street gang on the planet Rimbor in the 31st century. Brin's gang was a rival of a gang including Jo Nah (see ULTRA BOY). Some time after Jo gained powers and joined the LEGION OF SUPER-HEROES as ULTRA BOY, Brin's life was endangered during a brawl. The Legion's APPARITION, looking to find Jo Nah and tell him of her pregnancy, intervened, saving his life. Brin repaid her kindness by becoming her protector, starting with preventing bounty hunters from kidnapping her. When half the Legion— including Jo Nah— was seemingly lost in the Second Galaxy, Brin provided friendship to Apparition during her pregnancy. After the team was reunited, Brin accompanied Apparition and her child, Cub, to Earth. Brin was invited to join the Legion as Timber Wolf. His loyalty extends to the entire team. **RG**

TIME COMMANDER

FIRST APPEARANCE THE BRAVE AND THE BOLD #59 (May 1965)
STATUS Villain **REAL NAME** John Starr
OCCUPATION Criminal **BASE** Mobile
HEIGHT 6ft 2in **WEIGHT** 210 lbs **EYES** Blue **HAIR** Brown
SPECIAL POWERS/ABILITIES Is able to travel through time using a special hourglass.

The Time Commander started out as a scientist before turning to crime, developing a time-shifting hourglass while serving time behind bars. He escaped prison by traveling back to a point before the prison had been made, then simply walking away. Using his hourglass to uncover the secret identities of BATMAN and GREEN LANTERN, the Time Commander tried to defeat both foes but wound up back in prison. He returned, this time apparently mad, and jumbled up time to reunite Parisians with their lost loves, until he was stopped by ANIMAL MAN. The Time Commander joined with time-themed villains CHRONOS I, CLOCK KING, and Calendar Man to form the Time Foes. Assembled by the 2000 Committee, the Time Foes met their end at the hands of several Team Titans, a teen team of heroes from a potential future. **DW**

TIME MASTERS

FIRST APPEARANCE SHOWCASE #20 (June 1959)
STATUS Hero team (disbanded) **BASE** Upstate New York
MEMBERS AND POWERS
Rip Hunter Time travel expert.
Jeffrey Smith Hunter's research partner and MIT graduate.
Bonnie Baxter Researcher and onetime lover of Rip Hunter.
Corky Baxter (deceased) Teenage rock'n'roll brother of Bonnie.
Dan Hunter Rip Hunter's cousin and team financier.
Antonia ("Tony") A car thief and computer expert.

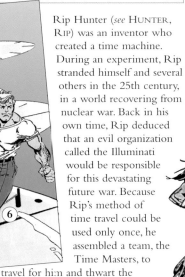

Rip Hunter (see HUNTER, RIP) was an inventor who created a time machine. During an experiment, Rip stranded himself and several others in the 25th century, in a world recovering from nuclear war. Back in his own time, Rip deduced that an evil organization called the Illuminati would be responsible for this devastating future war. Because Rip's method of time travel could be used only once, he assembled a team, the Time Masters, to travel for him and thwart the Illuminati. He enlisted the aid of Bonnie and Corky Baxter, his cousin Dan, and Tony, a computer expert. When Rip's lab was destroyed by the Illuminati, the team relocated to an underground base belonging to Cave Carson (see CARSON, CAVE), Bonnie's lover.

One of the LINEAR MEN, Matthew Ryder, later brought the Time Masters to the Vanishing Point, a platform from which they could study disruptions in the space/time continuum. After helping the JUSTICE LEAGUE OF AMERICA defeat Gog, the Time Masters were erased from existence. **PJ**

TITANS OF MYTH

FIRST APPEARANCE THE NEW TEEN TITANS (1st series) #11 (June 1981) **STATUS** Godlike beings **BASE** New Cronus
SPECIAL POWERS/ABILITIES
Cronus & Rhea (Titans of the Earth, both deceased) Controlled earth and vegetation. Parents of Olympian gods.
Hyperion & Thia (Titans of the Sun) Can control and project sunfire, enough to incinerate entire city blocks.
Iapetus & Themis (Titans of Justice) Arbiters of law.
Coeus & Phoebe (Titans of the Moon, Phoebe deceased) Can project nighttime darkness, absorbing all light and heat.
Oceanus & Tethys (Titans of the Seas) Able to control the oceans and all the creatures that live within the seas.
Crius & Mnemosyne (Titans of Memory) Pre- and post-cognitive, as well as possessing the memories of the universe; able to psychically manifest the memories of others.

Spawn of Uranus and Gaea, the twelve Titans of Myth were granted dominion over Earth in the very earliest days of mankind. The paired siblings eventually sired their own children, the OLYMPIAN GODS and goddesses who would eventually inherit the Earth after defeating the Titans. CRONUS was transformed into a gnarled tree, his prison until modern times. The remaining Titans were banished to the furthest reaches of outer space. They settled upon a distant planet, which the Titans named New Cronus in honor of their lost brother.

Many centuries later, the Titans adopted twelve children, each from a different world and intended to be an individual "seed" from which a new order of gods would spring. One such child was Donna Troy, (see TROIA), whose memory of her time on New Cronus remained lost until she accompanied her fellow TEEN TITANS to the ancient Titans' home.

Despite their brother Cronus's latter-day conflicts with WONDER WOMAN and the Olympian gods, the Titans of Myth are content to remain on New Cronus, far-removed from the affairs of humans and their Olympian children. **SB**

THE TITANS OF MYTH 1) *Oceanus* 2) *Cronus* 3) *Thia* 4) *Hyperion* 5) *Coeus* 6) *Phoebe* 7) *Rhea* 8) *Crius* 9) *Mnemosyne* 10) *Themis* 11) *Iapetus* 12) *Tethys*.

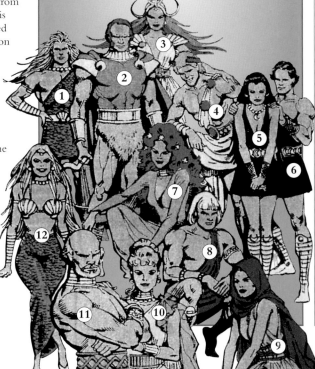

TNT & DAN THE DYNA-MITE

FIRST APPEARANCE WORLD'S FINEST COMICS #5 (Spring 1942)
STATUS Heroes (TNT is deceased) **REAL NAMES** (TNT) Thomas N. Thomas; (Dyna-Mite) Daniel Dunbar
OCCUPATION (TNT) High School teacher; (Dyna-Mite) High-school student **BASE** New York City
HEIGHT (TNT) 5ft 11in; (Dyna-Mite) 5ft 6.5in **WEIGHT** (TNT) 175 lbs; (Dyna-Mite) 140 lbs **EYES** (TNT) Brown; (Dyna-Mite) Blue
HAIR (TNT) Brown; (Dyna-Mite) Red
SPECIAL POWERS/ABILITIES When imbued with atomic energy, both heroes gained immense strength and the ability to hurl energy from their hands.

Schoolteacher Thomas N. "Tex" Thomas and his student, Daniel Dunbar accidentally discovered a derivative of 27-QRX and assumed the costumed identities of TNT and Dyna-Mite. Both served in the ALL-STAR SQUADRON with distinction for several months. In April 1942, TNT was killed in Colorado by Gudra the Valkyrie, who was part of AXIS AMERIKA. The traumatized Dyna-Mite was rescued by Iron Munro and they in part formed a subgroup of the All-Star Squadron, the YOUNG ALL-STARS. In Rioguay in South America, the paths of Iron Munro and Dyna-Mite crossed again as Hugo Danner and the Sons of Dawn attacked. Dunbar's life remained unknown until he next turned up as a member of Old Justice, costumed survivors of the early heroic era who feel today's youth should not be exposed to such dangers. They took on YOUNG JUSTICE but learned there remains a need to train those with special abilities. **RG**

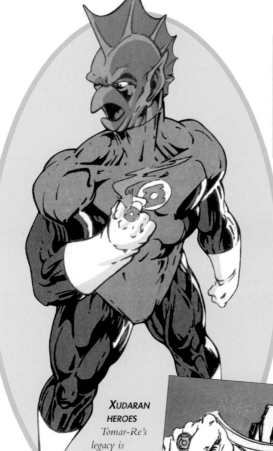

XUDARAN HEROES
Tomar-Re's legacy is carried on by his son, Tomar-Tu!

TOMAR-RE

FIRST APPEARANCE GREEN LANTERN (1st series) #6 (June 1961)
STATUS Hero (deceased) **REAL NAME** Tomar-Re
OCCUPATION Former scientist; Green Lantern **BASE** Mobile
HEIGHT 6ft 2in **WEIGHT** 210 lbs **EYES** Black **HAIR** Fused feathers
SPECIAL POWERS/ABILITIES Flight; Green Lantern ring granted him incredible powers based on his imagination and willpower.

Tomar-Re was a scientist on planet Xudar chosen by the GUARDIANS OF THE UNIVERSE to become a GREEN LANTERN. One of Tomar-Re's first assignments was to rescue the inhabitants of the doomed planet Krypton, located in space sector 2813. Tragically, Tomar-Re was unable to prevent Krypton's destruction and was forced to watch the planet explode. Tomar-Re later became fast friends with Green Lantern Hal Jordan. The two became the premier members of the GREEN LANTERN CORPS and legends throughout the universe. Tomar-Re retired from the GLC, although he was appointed to their Honor Guard after years of distinguished service. Tomar-Re was killed during a Qwardian invasion while trying to save the universe from the Anti-Monitor (*see* MONITOR). Before he died, Tomar-Re passed his ring on to John Stewart. **PJ**

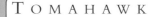

THE PATRIOT *Tomahawk helped change the course of the Revolutionary War, earning a place alongside the Founding Fathers of the United States.*

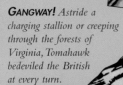

GANGWAY! *Astride a charging stallion or creeping through the forests of Virginia, Tomahawk bedeviled the British at every turn.*

TOMAHAWK

FIRST APPEARANCE STAR SPANGLED COMICS #69 (July 1949)
STATUS Hero (deceased) **REAL NAME** Thomas Hawkins (alias Tom Hawk)
OCCUPATION Frontiersman; freedom fighter **BASE** U.S. circa 1750–1820
HEIGHT 6ft 1in **WEIGHT** 184 lbs **EYES** Blue **HAIR** Blonde
SPECIAL POWERS/ABILITIES Hunter, tracker, marksman, and combatant.

The U.S. might never have gained its independence from Britain had it not been for Tomahawk, the greatest hero of the Revolutionary War. As a young man, Thomas Hawkins spent a year living with an Indian tribe where he learned the ways of the frontier and how to handle the short throwing-axe, whose name he adopted as his own. Tomahawk and his sidekick, Dan Hunter, had already made a name for themselves as heroes of the American colonies by the time armed conflict broke out in 1776.
In war, Tomahawk truly came into his own. General George Washington agreed to create a stand-alone military unit called Tomahawk's Rangers to undertake special missions. Tomahawk led the team, whose members included Big Anvil, Kaintuck Jones, Stovepipe, and Cannonball. British intelligence agent Lord Shilling became Tomahawk's cruelest foe, aided at times by Lady Shilling, who also went by the alias the Hood.
After the war's end, Tomahawk wound up in an eastern city working as a tax collector. However, in 1800 a romantic encounter with an Indian woman named Moon Fawn—and a final clash with Lord Shilling—brought about a completely new direction in his life. Retiring to Echo Valley in what is now the American Midwest, he had two children with Moon Fawn—Hawk (*see* HAWK, SON OF TOMAHAWK) and Young Eagle—and ran a farm on the wild frontier. Tomahawk's final fate is unrecorded, but he is known to have survived into the 1820s. Despite his advancing age, Tomahawk remained a vital force, famous for his proficiency with a musket and his flinty temper. **DW**

TOMMY TOMORROW

FIRST APPEARANCE REAL FACT COMICS #6 (January 1947)
STATUS Hero **REAL NAME** Kamandi Blank
OCCUPATION Space Planeteer **BASE** Planeteer HQ,
Gotham City
HEIGHT 5ft 11in **WEIGHT** 179 lbs
EYES Blue **HAIR** Blond
SPECIAL POWERS/ABILITIES Owing to Planeteer
training, in peak physical shape; highly
intelligent; carries a personalized ray gun and
travels by Planeteer spacecraft.

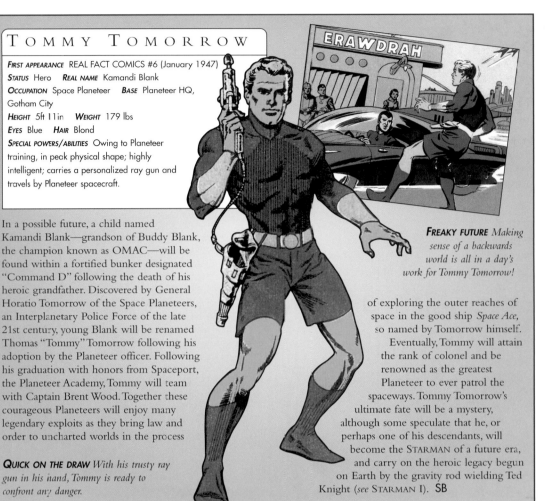

In a possible future, a child named
Kamandi Blank—grandson of Buddy Blank,
the champion known as OMAC—will be
found within a fortified bunker designated
"Command D" following the death of his
heroic grandfather. Discovered by General
Horatio Tomorrow of the Space Planeteers,
an Interplanetary Police Force of the late
21st century, young Blank will be renamed
Thomas "Tommy" Tomorrow following his
adoption by the Planeteer officer. Following
his graduation with honors from Spaceport,
the Planeteer Academy, Tommy will team
with Captain Brent Wood. Together these
courageous Planeteers will enjoy many
legendary exploits as they bring law and
order to uncharted worlds in the process

QUICK ON THE DRAW With his trusty ray
gun in his hand, Tommy is ready to
confront any danger.

FREAKY FUTURE Making
sense of a backwards
world is all in a day's
work for Tommy Tomorrow!

of exploring the outer reaches of
space in the good ship *Space Ace*,
so named by Tomorrow himself.
Eventually, Tommy will attain
the rank of colonel and be
renowned as the greatest
Planeteer to ever patrol the
spaceways. Tommy Tomorrow's
ultimate fate will be a mystery,
although some speculate that he, or
perhaps one of his descendants, will
become the STARMAN of a future era,
and carry on the heroic legacy begun
on Earth by the gravity rod wielding Ted
Knight (*see* STARMAN I). **SB**

TOR, MAGIC MASTER

FIRST APPEARANCE CRACK COMICS #10 (October 1940)
STATUS Hero (deceased) **REAL NAME** Jimmy Slade
OCCUPATION Press photographer **BASE** Mobile
HEIGHT 5ft 10in **WEIGHT** 165 lbs **EYES** Brown **HAIR** Black
SPECIAL POWERS/ABILITIES Minor magician capable of creating spells of
limited intensity, including levitation; usually spoke his spells
backwards to focus his power.

Jimmy Slade was a photographer
working for a major newspaper in
1941 who, inspired by the heroes
of the Golden Age JUSTICE
SOCIETY OF AMERICA, chose to
create a costumed identity for
himself to fight crime. Able to
cast low level spells, Slade wore
makeup and a fake mustache and
created the identity of Tor, the
Magic Master. Like ZATARA
the Magician and his daughter
ZATANNA, Tor spoke his spells
backwards.

Tor the Magic Master
fought criminals and Axis
spies throughout World War II. As Jimmy Slade, Tor also
became a successful photojournalist, taking award-winning
photographs of the war. In 1945, Tor was one of several
heroes with magical powers, including Zatara, DOCTOR
OCCULT, SARGON THE SORCERER and Merlin. who joined
forces to fight the threat of the STALKER, an evil entity that
threatened the Earth. Despite the JSA's intervention, Tor
and Merlin were killed by the Stalker. **PJ**

TOMORROW WOMAN

FIRST APPEARANCE JLA #5 (May 1997)
STATUS Villain (destroyed) **REAL NAME** None
OCCUPATION Would-be assassin **BASE** JLA Watchtower
HEIGHT 5ft 11in **WEIGHT** 320 lbs **EYES** Blue **HAIR** Black
SPECIAL POWERS/ABILITIES Tomorrow Woman's robotic powers were
telekinetic and telepathic in nature.

The scientists T.O. MORROW
and PROFESSOR IVO,
longtime opponents of the
JUSTICE LEAGUE
OF AMERICA,
pooled their
resources to build the
perfect simulacrum, and
named her
Tomorrow Woman.
As per her
programming, she
played the heroine to
perfection. Invited to
join the JLA, she was
soon ensconced in the
JLA's Watchtower.
Morrow and Ivo hoped
their "Trojan horse" would
wreak havoc among the
unsuspecting heroes. However,
the two villains had built too good a
machine: Tomorrow Woman developed her own
personality and feelings. She disobeyed their orders,
sacrificing herself rather than murder the JLA. A statue in
her memory was erected in the Garden of Heroes. **RG**

TOP

FIRST APPEARANCE FLASH (1st series) #122 (August 1961)
STATUS Villain **REAL NAME** Roscoe Dillon
OCCUPATION Criminal **BASE** Central City/Keystone City
HEIGHT 6ft **WEIGHT** 179 lbs **EYES** Blue **HAIR** Brown
SPECIAL POWERS/ABILITIES Can spin himself at incredible
speeds and induce vertigo in his victims.

Fascinated by tops, gyroscopes, and
all spinning things, crook
Roscoe Dillon became the
costumed criminal the Top in
order to dominate crime in
Central City. His ability to
spin at great speeds made him
a recurring foe of the second
FLASH, Barry Allen, and a
member of the Flash's
Rogues Gallery. He struck up a
romance with CAPTAIN COLD's
sister Lisa Snart (the GOLDEN
GLIDER), but eventually
learned that the Flash's
superspeed vibrations had
overheated the cells in his brain.

The Top died, but his spirit lived on. He possessed Barry
Allen's father, and years later he took over the body of
slain senator Thomas O'Neill. The third Flash, Wally West,
uncovered the Top's deception before O'Neill could be
elected vice president. Imprisoned in Iron Heights, the Top
recently escaped and tried to murder the Keystone City
mayor. Now exhibiting the power to scramble the way his
opponents' eyes interpret images (triggering crippling
nausea), the Top was defeated by Wally West. **DW**

TORQUE

FIRST APPEARANCE NIGHTWING #1 (October 1996)
STATUS Villain (deceased) **REAL NAME** Dudley Soames
OCCUPATION Former police inspector; criminal **BASE** Blüdhaven
HEIGHT 6ft 1in **WEIGHT** 186 lbs **EYES** Hazel **HAIR** Brown (graying)
SPECIAL POWERS/ABILITIES Favored a vintage Thompson .45 caliber
machine gun (the "Tommy Gun"). Mirrored glasses helped his aim.

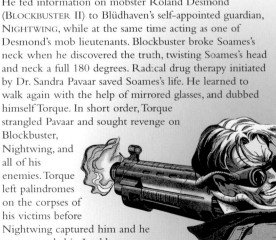

Inspector Dudley Soames was Blüdhaven's crookedest cop.
He fed information on mobster Roland Desmond
(BLOCKBUSTER II) to Blüdhaven's self-appointed guardian,
NIGHTWING, while at the same time acting as one of
Desmond's mob lieutenants. Blockbuster broke Soames's
neck when he discovered the truth, twisting Soames's head
and neck a full 180 degrees. Radical drug therapy initiated
by Dr. Sandra Pavaar saved Soames's life. He learned to
walk again with the help of mirrored glasses, and dubbed
himself Torque. In short order, Torque
strangled Pavaar and sought revenge on
Blockbuster,
Nightwing, and
all of his
enemies. Torque
left palindromes
on the corpses of
his victims before
Nightwing captured him and he
was remanded in Lockhaven
Penitentiary. After months in jail, Torque
enlisted Tad Ryerstad, the rogue Nite-
Wing, to help him escape. Soames
planned to kill Ryerstad as soon as they
were free, but was double-crossed and
murdered by Ryerstad instead. **SB**

THE DC COMICS ENCYCLOPEDIA

TOYMAN

FIRST APPEARANCE ACTION COMICS #64 (September 1943)
STATUS Villain **REAL NAME** Winslow P. Schott
OCCUPATION Professional criminal **BASE** Metropolis
HEIGHT 5ft 4in **WEIGHT** 155 lbs **EYES** Blue **HAIR** Brown
SPECIAL POWERS/ABILITIES Although psychotic, Schott is a skilled inventor and mechanical engineer.

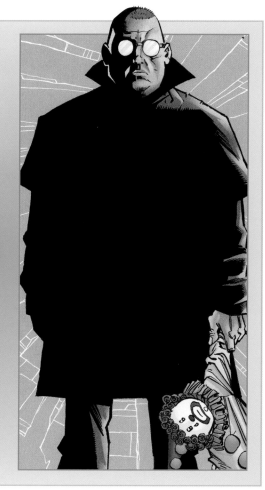

Winslow P. Schott was only a small boy when he made his first toy, a balsa-wood airplane painted blue and red. Another boy stole the plane, an act that had a profound effect on Winslow and may have ultimately driven him to use toys to rob others. When he grew up, Schott created some of the most amazing toys ever conceived, for which he received widespread acclaim. However, LexCorp's acquisition of Schott's toy company left him jobless and burning for revenge against LexCorp's owner, Lex Luthor (see LUTHOR, LEX). Schott's failed attempts to kill Luthor with various lethal toys eventually led to an association with INTERGANG and a criminal career as the Toyman. His worst act was to murder Adam Grant, the son of television chat-show host and Metropolis celebrity Cat Grant. However, in the main, Schott has a soft spot for children, especially those in need. Clearly insane, the Toyman is one of SUPERMAN's most unpredictable, and therefore deadliest, opponents. The Toyman name has also been applied to Hiro Okamura, 13-year-old mechanical genius, whose family developed the alloy "metallo," which helped save the planet from the Kryptonian asteroid that brought SUPERGIRL to Earth. Schott is now on retainer to built equipment as BATMAN needs. **RG**

TRACI 13

FIRST APPEARANCE SUPERMAN (2nd series) #189 (December 2002)
STATUS Hero **REAL NAME** Traci (last name unrevealed)
OCCUPATION Adventurer **BASE** Metropolis **HEIGHT** 5ft 5in
WEIGHT 127 lbs **EYES** Sometimes black, sometimes purple
HAIR Black and purple **SPECIAL POWERS/ABILITIES** Urban sorceress with magical powers linked to her proximity to cities; her magic is manifested as purple panes of stained glass.

Traci 13 is a young witch with the power to tap into the magical energies found in all urban environments and draw on those living energies for power. Born a natural sorceress, one of the rare *Homo magi*, Traci was nonetheless orphaned at an early age when her mother, also a sorceress, perished trying to harness her power. Traci's father, reputed to be DOCTOR THIRTEEN, the ghost-breaker, chose to completely reject magic in his life after Traci's mother died, and that denial has caused a great rift to form between him and his daughter.

Along with her magical familiar, an iguana named Leroy, Traci moved to Metropolis and allied herself with Natasha Irons (see IRONS, NATASHA), the niece of John Henry Irons, alias STEEL III. **PJ**

TREVOR, STEVE

FIRST APPEARANCE ALL-STAR COMICS #8 (Winter 1941)
STATUS Hero **REAL NAME** Steven Rockwell Trevor
OCCUPATION Retired U.S. Air Force colonel **BASE** Mobile
HEIGHT 6ft 1in **WEIGHT** 195 lbs
EYES Blue **HAIR** Blonde with white [only looks blonde in pic?]
SPECIAL POWERS/ABILITIES Expert pilot and military commander.

One of WONDER WOMAN's oldest friends, Steve Trevor inherited his military background from his father, Ulysses Steven Trevor, and his connection with the AMAZONS from his mother, Diana Trevor, who sacrificed her life to save the women of Paradise Island from the demon Cottus. As a pilot in the U.S. Air Force, Steve Trevor flew a bomber to Themyscira (see Amazing Bases, pp. 120–1) as part of a plot orchestrated by the war god ARES to destroy the island. Ares's scheme failed, but Trevor became a wanted man among some Air Force leaders.

Trevor fled with his aide, Etta Candy, and helped Wonder Woman end the threat of the war god. Although eventually cleared of all charges related to the Paradise Island incident, Trevor resigned his Air Force commission and started work as a freelance aircraft design engineer. He soon married Etta Candy; his relationship with Wonder Woman remains one of a deep mutual respect, and Steve regards Diana as a sort of younger sister. Trevor still plays an important role in Wonder Woman's affairs, recently helping the Amazons battle the galaxy-conquering IMPERIEX. **DW**

TRIAD

FIRST APPEARANCE LEGION OF SUPER-HEROES (4th series) #0
STATUS Hero **REAL NAME** Luornu Durgo
OCCUPATION Legionnaire **BASE** Legion World, U.P. Space
HEIGHT 5ft 7in **WEIGHT** 136 lbs **EYES** (right) orange; (left) violet **HAIR** Auburn **SPECIAL POWERS/ABILITIES** Triad can split into three different bodies, each with three different personalities—flirtatious, shy, and intellectual.

Born on the planet Cargg in the latter half of the 30th century, Luornu Durgo inherited her species' ability to split into identical duplicates. Unlike other Carggites, however, Luornu's three duplicates manifested their own individual personalities, and she was forced to spend time in a mental institution for this unusual aberration.

Luornu escaped from the hospital and made her way to Earth. There, she met industrialist R.J. Brande (see BRANDE, R.J.) who became her legal guardian. Luornu also became his assistant. After saving his life during a terrorist attack by the villainous White Triangle gang, she was inducted into the hero team Brande had founded, the LEGION OF SUPER-HEROES, as Triad.

Triad soon became a member of the Legion Espionage Squad, a covert action team. Over the years, Triad's bodies and their personalities became more and more distinct and more and more independent of each other, sharing less time in the same body. While one of those bodies is infatuated with M'ONEL, another romantically pursued Legion mechanic Chuck Taine until their affair ended tragically when the Earth was overrun by the insidious alien BLIGHT. **PJ**

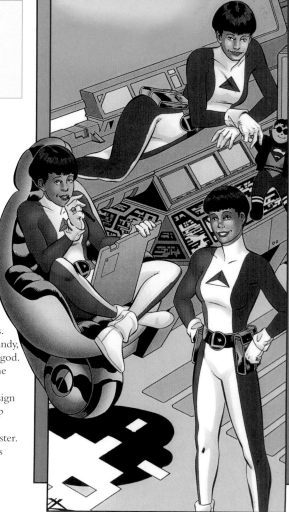

TRIGGER TWINS

FIRST APPEARANCE ALL-STAR WESTERN #58 (May 1951)
STATUS Heroes (deceased)   **REAL NAMES** Walter and Wayne Trigger
OCCUPATION Sheriff   **BASE** Rocky City
HEIGHT (both) 6 ft   **WEIGHT** (both) 160 lbs
EYES (both) Blue   **HAIR** (both) Reddish blond
SPECIAL POWERS/ABILITIES Skilled marksmen and horsemen, more than capable hand-to-hand combatants.

The original Trigger Twins, Walt and Wayne Trigger, kept law and order in Rocky City during the 1870s. Walt's (greatly exaggerated) Civil War exploits earned him the position of Rocky City's sheriff. Wayne, who had been the true hero in most of Walt's tales, agreed to assume the identity of sheriff whenever danger threatened the town. The Trigger Twins became a legend of the Old West.

The modern-day Trigger Twins, Tom and Tad Trigger, are believed to be descendants of the original western heroes. They wear cowboy clothing, but unlike Walt and Wayne, the current Trigger Twins are criminals. They have battled most of Gotham's defenders, including ROBIN, and are now in Blackgate prison. During Gotham's year as a No Man's Land, the Trigger Twins worked with fellow inmates Lock-Up and the KGBeast to keep order at Blackgate, after the guards abandoned the facility. **DW**

TRICKSTER II

FIRST APPEARANCE THE FLASH (2nd series) #183 (April 2002)
STATUS Villain   **REAL NAME** Axel Walker
OCCUPATION Professional criminal   **BASE** Keystone City
HEIGHT 5ft 7in   **WEIGHT** 150 lbs   **EYES** Blue   **HAIR** Brown
SPECIAL POWERS/ABILITIES A variety of technological gadgets allows him to cause mayhem; he is still mastering their use and has no great athletic skill.

The first villain to be known as the Trickster was James Jesse, the stage name of Giovanni Giuseppe, a trapeze artist with a fear of heights who invented a pair of "air walker shoes" that allowed him to perform stunts safely. Eventually he turned to crime, employing numerous ridiculous gadgets, before turning F.B.I. informant and retiring.

The villain Blacksmith wanted someone with similar skills in her new gang. She selected wayward teenager Axel Walker, giving him a complete set of equipment, upgraded and more technologically sophisticated versions of the Trickster's tools. Axel was sent to attack Wally West, the FLASH III, as a test. He acquitted himself well. Being a modern day teen, Axel lives for the rush and thrill of danger, apparently not entirely clear on the distinction between real life and the fantasy realms depicted in his beloved video games. **RG**

NEW KID ON THE BLOCK *Young Axel Walker loves being part of the Flash's Rogues Gallery, even though he has nothing in common with his villainous peers.*

TRIGON

FIRST APPEARANCE NEW TEEN TITANS (1st series) #4 (February 1981)
STATUS Villain   **REAL NAME** Trigon; also known in other dimensions as Skath and Ddrez
OCCUPATION Demon lord; conqueror   **BASE** Another dimensional plane
HEIGHT Variable   **WEIGHT** Variable   **EYES** Red   **HAIR** Red
SPECIAL POWERS/ABILITIES Nearly immeasurable demonic powers; has drained the souls of millions of worlds and reshaped planets; can change size, fire destructive energy blasts, teleport, control demons, and transmute elements, such as stone into water.

The personification of evil, Trigon was a demon lord who destroyed his homeworld by the age of six. Slaying billions of souls in his own dimension, Trigon eventually sired a child by the woman Arella. Their child was RAVEN, a powerful mystic, who rejected her father's evil and was raised in Azarath, a pacifist community nestled in another dimension. Trigon tried to breach the barriers between his dimension and Earth's but was stopped by sorcerers from Azarath. Finally tearing through the interdimensional wall, Trigon attacked Earth. Horrified, his daughter Raven, now a teenager, agreed to rule by his side if he spared the planet. But Raven realized her father would not honor the bargain and hurried to Earth, gathering a group of teenage heroes to stop Trigon's invasion. These heroes were the NEW TEEN TITANS, and together they drove Trigon into a distant nether universe that Arella agreed to guard for eternity. As time passed, Raven began to succumb to her father's evil. Trigon murdered a billion beings in his dimension and stole their energy. He once again invaded Earth's dimension, turning Earth into a wasteland. But the Titans were able to help the souls of Azarath channel all their power into Trigon, seemingly destroying the demon.

Purged of her father's evil, Raven's body was nonetheless taken over by the soul of one of her slain siblings. However, her soul was placed in STARFIRE's body, and the Titans were able to destroy the rest of Trigon's progeny, ending his threat, they believed, forever. **PJ**

BACK FROM THE DEAD *The demon Trigon has taken over the Earth twice, but each time he has been defeated by the Teen Titans. Brother Blood recently took Raven as his bride, resurrecting Trigon once again, who attacked the Titans from his watery grave.*

315

TRIUMPH

FIRST APPEARANCE JUSTICE LEAGUE EUROPE #67 (August 1994)
STATUS Villain (deceased)   **REAL NAME** William MacIntyre
OCCUPATION Adventurer   **BASE** JLA Watchtower, the Moon
HEIGHT 6ft 1in   **WEIGHT** 200 lbs   **EYES** Blue   **HAIR** Blond
SPECIAL POWERS/ABILITIES Possessed enhanced strength, speed, endurance and the ability to fly.

Eight-year-old William MacIntyre discovered that his father was a thug working for an evil scientist, Dr. Cobalt. When HOURMAN I battled Dr. Cobalt, Jimmy saved the hero from a magnetic blast. Hourman I cautioned young Will to "learn from your father's mistakes."

When plasma aliens invaded Earth, MacIntyre—now the hero Triumph—gathered a team to defeat them. During the fight, Triumph disappeared from the time-stream, and was actually forgotten. A decade later, he emerged to beat the Plasma-Men. He then joined the JUSTICE LEAGUE OF AMERICA. Triumph sold his soul to the demon NERON to regain the decade he had lost, but in so doing, the world forgot about him again! Embittered, he sold items stolen from the JLA Watchtower, including a pen containing the genie LKZ. LKZ corrupted Triumph further and led the JLA and the JUSTICE SOCIETY OF AMERICA into a war between itself and QWSP. SPECTRE turned Triumph into ice, and he is now stored in the Watchtower Trophy Room. RG

TSUNAMI

FIRST APPEARANCE ALL-STAR SQUADRON #33 (May 1984)
STATUS Hero   **REAL NAME** Miya Shimada
OCCUPATION Warrior   **BASE** San Francisco
HEIGHT 5ft 6in   **WEIGHT** 131 lbs   **EYES** Brown   **HAIR** Black
SPECIAL POWERS/ABILITIES Psionically creates sea-waves; able to swim at superspeed and breathe underwater.

Racial prejudice during World War II forced Miya Shimada's family to return to their native Japan, despite their status as U.S. citizens. A *nisei*, or first-generation American, Miya nevertheless offered to use her amazing water-manipulating powers as the Imperial Japanese operative code-named Tsunami. Riding atop her giant sea-waves, Tsunami battled the ALL-STAR SQUADRON on several occasions before switching sides and joining the YOUNG ALL-STARS to fight against the very Axis powers she had once served.

Following the end of World War II, Tsunami's aging was slowed as a result of a mystic pact with the Atlantean sorcerer ATLAN. Tsunami's romantic dalliance with her fellow All-Star Neptune Perkins (see PERKINS, NEPTUNE) resulted in a daughter, Deborah, who is now known as the aquatic heroine Deep Blue. Tsunami continues to train Deep Blue in the use of her superpowers, occasionally making waves herself as a reluctant super heroine. She has been known to ally herself with AQUAMAN if called upon to lend her wonderful water-based abilities for the good of the Seven Seas. SB

TWILIGHT

FIRST APPEARANCE SUPERGIRL (3rd series) #15 (November 1997)
STATUS Undecided   **REAL NAME** Molly (last name unrevealed)
OCCUPATION Angel; former destroyer   **BASE** Mobile
HEIGHT 5ft 7in   **WEIGHT** 135 lbs   **EYES** Blue   **HAIR** White
SPECIAL POWERS/ABILITIES Can resurrect the dead; possesses wings of fire and devastating flame vision.

During the Black Death that ravaged 14th-century Europe, a girl named Molly discovered she had the God-given power to bring the dead back to life. After exhausting herself and her power, Molly discovered the body of her sister Jane but was unable to resurrect her.

Outraged, Molly declared war on God.

Centuries later, Molly, as Twilight, became the enemy of God's agents on Earth, including the angel SUPERGIRL. After several devilish intrigues, Twilight confronted Supergirl and her ally, MARY MARVEL in Eden. Linda Danvers, a part of Supergirl's alter ego, died in the skirmish. The Matrix aspect of Supergirl merged with Twilight and resurrected Linda as the true Supergirl. Twilight then became the Angel of Fire, seeking redemption for her sins. PJ

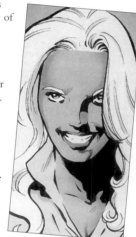

TROIA

FIRST APPEARANCE THE BRAVE AND THE BOLD #60 (July 1965)
STATUS Hero (presumed deceased)   **REAL NAME** Donna Hinkley Stacey Troy   **HEIGHT** 5ft 9in   **WEIGHT** 143 lbs   **EYES** Blue
HAIR Black   **OCCUPATION** Photographer   **BASE** New York City
SPECIAL POWERS/ABILITIES Superstrength, superspeed, flight; truth-coaxing abilities; psychic link to Wonder Woman; trained warrior respected and admired by everyone she worked with.

Donna Troy was originally a magically-created playmate and "sister" for the young Princess Diana, later the champion of the AMAZONS of Themyscira known as WONDER WOMAN. An identical twin created with a fraction of Diana's own soul, Donna was kidnapped by the villainous Dark Angel (see VON GUNTHER, BARONESS PAULA), who believed she had captured Diana instead, and forced to live a string of alternate lives, each ending in tragedy and pain.

Her most recent life began in the body of an orphaned baby put up for adoption. Saved from a burning building by Rhea, one of the TITANS OF MYTH, the infant Donna grew up on New Cronus, where the Titans gave her powers, taught her the mysteries of the universe, and named her Troy. Returning to Earth, Donna took the name Wonder Girl, inspired by HIPPOLYTA, the Wonder Woman of World War II, and founded the original Teen Titans with Robin (see NIGHTWING), Kid Flash (see Wally West, FLASH III), Aqualad (see TEMPEST) and Speedy (see ARSENAL).

Later, Donna assumed the codename Troia to reflect her upbringing with the Titans of Myth. She married history professor Terry Long, had a son, Robert, and became a member of the DARKSTARS. Tragically, Terry and Robert were killed in a car accident. Dark Angel arrived to cast Troia into another tragic life. But Wonder Woman and the Flash III defeated Dark Angel. Donna later seemed to perish battling a malfunctioning Superman robot, but her fate remains a mystery. DW

MAGALA The Amazon sorceress Magala brings Princess Diana's reflection to life, creating Donna Troy!

SOUL SISTER Troia, Wonder Woman's "sister," was created from a fragment of Wonder Woman's own soul.

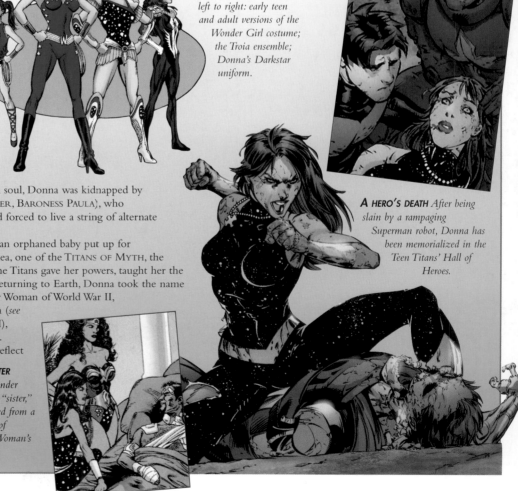

CHANGING STYLES From left to right: early teen and adult versions of the Wonder Girl costume; the Troia ensemble; Donna's Darkstar uniform.

A HERO'S DEATH After being slain by a rampaging Superman robot, Donna has been memorialized in the Teen Titans' Hall of Heroes.

TWO-FACE

SCHIZOID CRIMINAL MASTERMIND

FIRST APPEARANCE DETECTIVE COMICS #66 (August 1942)
STATUS Villain **REAL NAME** Harvey Dent
OCCUPATION Former D.A.; professional criminal **BASE** Gotham City
HEIGHT 6ft **WEIGHT** 182 lbs **EYES** Blue **HAIR** Brown
SPECIAL POWERS/ABILITIES A criminal genius, whose crimes reveal an obsession with duality and the number two. An average combatant, but capable of savage violence.

HARVEY DENT IS A MAN DIVIDED. Childhood abuse fractured Dent's psyche right down the middle, leaving the respected Gotham City District Attorney subconsciously sublimating a darker and more violent persona as an adult. This duality was mirrored by Dent's good luck charm, a "two-headed" silver dollar. Once Batman's ally in justice, Dent's evil side reared its ugly head when, amid a packed courtroom, gangster Vincent Maroni hurled acid in the D.A.'s handsome face!

THE DARK SIDE

As the left side of Dent's face dissolved, so did the psychic wall keeping his dark persona in check. With good and evil wrestling for control, Dent scarred one side of his lucky coin. It became the final arbiter for his new persona, Two-Face, whose every act would be decided by the flip of a coin. If the unmarked side came up, he would show mercy; if the scarred side came up he would do evil. Dent abandoned his wife Gilda Grace, who had hoped plastic surgery would restore her husband's face and help his mind heal. Gilda married Doctor Paul Janus and they became the parents of twins, children conceived utilizing Harvey Dent's frozen sperm.

THE DARK SIDE *Although a crusading D.A, Harvey Dent was prey to strange, inner fears.*

DEFINING MOMENT *Gangster Boss Moroni hurls acid in Harvey Dent's face, scarring him both physically and psychologically.*

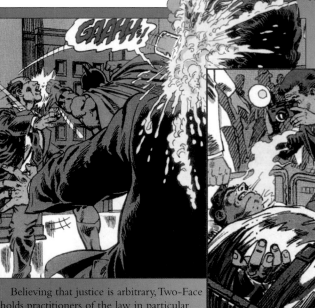

Believing that justice is arbitrary, Two-Face holds practitioners of the law in particular contempt. As judge, jury and executioner, he has murdered his own court-appointed attorneys and carried out lethal litigation against scores of Gotham's legal eagles.

During Gotham's year-long experience as a lawless No Man's Land, Dent turned prosecutor once more, "indicting" Commissioner Gordon (*see* GORDON, JAMES W.) for his law-breaking alliance—with Two-Face! Dent's cross-examination of his own alter ego led to a temporary mental brainstorm and an acquittal for Gordon. During that time, detective Renee Montoya (*see* MONTOYA, RENEE) was Two-Face's prisoner for five months, and she glimpsed a kinder, gentler Dent. He professed love for her, but felt betrayed when he learned she was a lesbian.

Two-Face remains Batman's most unpredictable foe, even more so since surgeon Tommy Elliot successfully repaired Dent's face. He helped Gordon when the RIDDLER and Elliot tried to destroy Batman. How this has affected Two-Face's conflicted personality remains to be seen. **RG**

FICKLE FATE *Every key decision Two-Face makes is decided by his two-sided coin, one side of which is scarred, and one side of which is unblemished.*

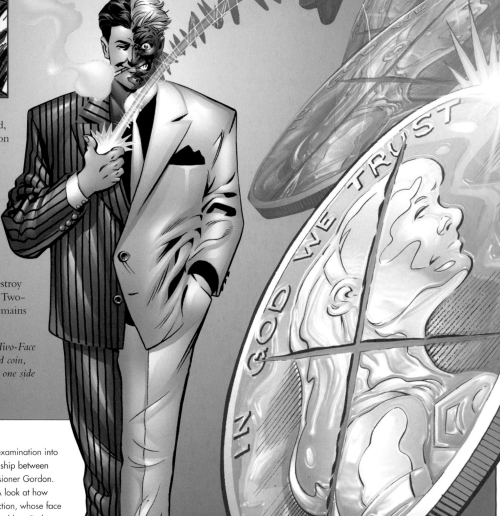

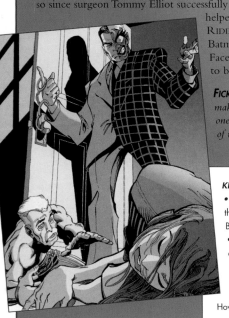

KEY STORYLINES

• **BATMAN: FACES (TPB, 1995):** An examination into the tortured, often violent relationship between Batman, Two-Face, and Commissioner Gordon.
• **BATMAN ANNUAL #14 (1990):** A look at how difficult it is for Two-Face to function, whose face never fits in either the normal world or Gotham City's underworld.
• **SECRET ORIGINS SPECIAL (TPB, 1989):** How Harvey Dent changed from successful District Attorney to psychopathic madman.

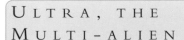

UBERMENSCH

FIRST APPEARANCE YOUNG ALL-STARS #1 (June 1987)
STATUS Villain (deceased)   **REAL NAME** Unknown
OCCUPATION Nazi hero   **BASE** Mobile
HEIGHT 6ft 3in   **WEIGHT** 225 lbs   **EYES** Blue   **HAIR** None
SPECIAL POWERS/ABILITIES Ubermensch was capable of leaping tall buildings in a single bound, but squandered his enhanced gifts in the service of evil; possessed superstrength and superspeed; his skin was invulnerable to bullets.

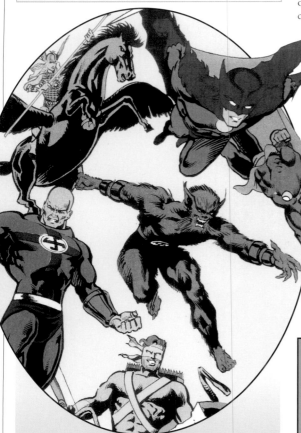

UBERMENSCH ÜBER ALLES! Hitler's follicly-challenged muscleman leads out Axis Amerika, the Third Reich's favorite team of super-villainous bullies.

Ubermensch was the epitome of Adolf Hitler's ideal of racial purity, selected by Nazi scientists to undergo painful treatments that transformed him into the ultimate Aryan super hero. He possessed remarkable strength, speed, and agility, while his skin was so tough he could shrug off the bullets of small-arms fire!

As World War II unfolded, Ubermensch became the head of AXIS AMERIKA, leading Gudra, SEA WOLF, Usil, Die Grosshorn Eule, Die Fledermaus, and Kamikaze against the American heroes of the ALL-STAR SQUADRON and its youthful spinoff, the YOUNG ALL-STARS. Ubermensch's fate at the end of the war is still unrecorded.

Recently, an American claimed the notorious name of Ubermensch as a member of a revived incarnation of Axis America. The man called Shepherd was the leader of the religious commune Safe Haven and persuaded the world that the JUSTICE LEAGUE OF AMERICA had destroyed the commune and killed 1,000 innocent people! This accusation was soon exposed as a blatant lie, and Shepherd, revealed as the ideologue Ubermensch II, met defeat at the hands of the JLA. **DW**

ULTRA BOY

FIRST APPEARANCE LEGION OF SUPER-HEROES (4th series) #64 (January 1995)   **STATUS** Hero   **REAL NAME** Jo Nah
OCCUPATION Legionnaire   **BASE** 30th-century Earth
HEIGHT 5ft 8in   **WEIGHT** 155 lbs   **EYES** Brown   **HAIR** Brown
SPECIAL POWERS/ABILITIES Vast superstrength, speed, invulnerability, flight and vision powers, but can only use one power at a time.

Jo Nah grew up in the latter half of the 30th century on Rimbor, a planet known for neglecting its children. Jo was on a scavenging mission in outer space when a giant space creature swallowed his ship. By eating some of the creature's flesh, Jo gained various superpowers. He used them to escape Rimbor and joined Leland McCauley's Workforce as Ultra Boy. Ultra Boy later joined the LEGION OF SUPER-HEROES, the 31st century's premier superteam, and fell in love with teammate APPARITION. He eventually married her when the two were trapped in the past.

After the BLIGHT attacked the Earth, Ultra Boy was hurled into another dimension. Although he managed to return to his wife, their marriage remains on shaky ground. Their son, Cub Wazzo-Nah, appears to have inherited meta-human powers from both his parents, although the extent of his abilites has yet to be revealed. **PJ**

ULTRA, THE MULTI-ALIEN

FIRST APPEARANCE MYSTERY IN SPACE #103 (November 1965)
STATUS Hero   **REAL NAME** Ace Arn
OCCUPATION Adventurer   **BASE** Mobile
HEIGHT 5ft 10in (as Arn); 6ft 2in (as Ultra)   **WEIGHT** 157 lbs (as Arn); 163 lbs (as Ultra)   **EYES** Blue (as Arn); Black (as Ultra); **HAIR** Brown (as Arn); Half bald, half green, later half bald, half white (as Ultra)
SPECIAL POWERS/ABILITIES Each quarter of Arn's body possesses a unique property such as magnetism, increased strength, cohesive energy and the power of flight.

In the late 21st century, Captain Ace Arn's spacecraft accidentally crashed into an asteroid in another solar system. The rock turned out to be the secret hideout for interstellar criminal Zobra. Arn learned the four planet solar system was artificially created with one member from each race— Ulla, Laroo, Trago, and Raaga— serving Zobra. Zobra accidentally killed himself with a poisonous gas and a free-for-all began among his underlings. When they arrived at the asteroid and found Arn there, they all fired their unique duplication weapons simultaneously. As a result, Arn was transformed into a four-segmented composite alien, representing each alien race. Granted phenomenal new powers, Arn subdued the aliens, repaired his craft and returned to Earth. He gave up piloting to fight crime as Ultra, but is haunted by regret for the loss of his humanity and his girlfriend from his previous life, Bonnie. **RG**

ULTRA-HUMANITE

FIRST APPEARANCE ACTION COMICS #13 (June 1939)
STATUS Villain (deceased)   **REAL NAME** Unknown
OCCUPATION Criminal scientist   **BASE** Mobile
HEIGHT Varied   **WEIGHT** Varied   **EYES** Varied   **HAIR** Varied
SPECIAL POWERS/ABILITIES A brilliant inventor, the Ultra-Humanite's greatest achievement was the process he devised to transplant his brain into different bodies, human or otherwise.

The Ultra-Humanite was one of the JUSTICE SOCIETY OF AMERICA's most terrible foes, responsible for the deaths of the CRIMSON AVENGER I and Johnny Thunder (see THUNDER I, JOHNNY) among many atrocities. Originally a criminal scientist active during the 1940s, the Ultra-Humanite escaped death by transplanting his brain into other bodies, including film star Dolores Winters, a giant ant, and finally a genetically mutated albino ape. He continued his assaults upon the JSA, as well as the team's superpowered progeny in INFINITY INC., and also led the SECRET SOCIETY OF SUPER-VILLAINS. Shaving his gorilla body, an even more terrifying Ultra-Humanite utilized resources usurped from the Council (see MANHUNTER II). Recently, the villain gave up his primate shell and hid his brain while taking mental control of the aged Johnny Thunder. The Ultra-Humanite then stole the power of Johnny's Thunderbolt to dominate the world. Once more, the JSA rallied and CRIMSON AVENGER II shot a bullet through his corrupt brain. **SB**

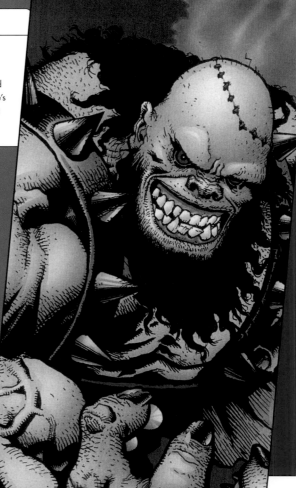

UMBRA

FIRST APPEARANCE (as Shadow Lass) ADVENTURE COMICS #365
(February 1968); (as Umbra) LEGIONNAIRES #43 (December 1996)
STATUS Hero **REAL NAME** Tasmia Mallor **OCCUPATION** Legionnaire
BASE Legion World **HEIGHT** 5ft 7in **WEIGHT** 130 lbs
EYES Dark blue **HAIR** Black **SPECIAL POWERS/ABILITIES** Can
manipulate "shadow energy" to attack or create a field of darkness.

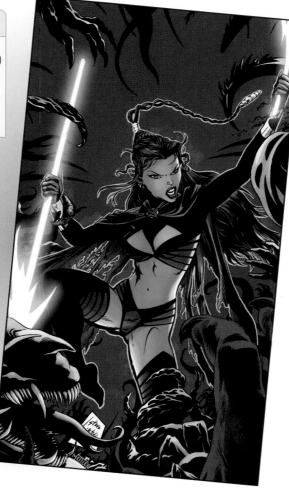

A descendant of L.E.G.I.O.N.'s Lydea Mallor, Tasmia
Mallor always knew that one day she would become
the Shadow Champion of her native planet Talok
VIII. Last in the ancestral line of Talokian champions,
she trained under the Shadow Maven to wield the
light-absorbing energies that were her ritual
inheritance. But the people of Talok VIII cast Tasmia
out from their company, viewing her politics as too
insular. To gain the benefits of a pan-species
education, Tasmia joined the LEGION OF SUPER-
HEROES under the codename Umbra.

Cold and aloof, Umbra made few friends among
the Legionnaires but impressed them with her raw
skill. When Umbra lost her shadow-casting powers she
returned to Talok VIII, where she discovered that the
fearful Talokians had withdrawn from the United
Planets and encased the entire planet in shadowforce.
A new Shadow Champion—Umbra's insane cousin
Grev—now controlled the shadows through a
technological rig. Umbra defeated Grev and learned
that the shadowforce had been animating his dead
body for months. Restoring her connection with the
darkness, Umbra re-established Talok VIII's place in
the U.P. and returned to the Legion. DW

UNKNOWN SOLDIER

FIRST APPEARANCE STAR-SPANGLED WAR STORIES #151
(July 1970) **STATUS** Hero **REAL NAME** Unrevealed
OCCUPATION Secret agent **BASE** Washington, D.C.
HEIGHT 5ft 9in **WEIGHT** 155 lbs **EYES** Blue **HAIR** Blond
SPECIAL POWERS/ABILITIES Weapons and explosives expert;
expert combatant; master of disguise and impersonation.

The man who became known in U.S. intelligence
as the Unknown Soldier enlisted with his older
brother Harry in World War II. Harry died saving
his sibling from a Japanese grenade, which left the
young soldier's face horribly disfigured. He
continued as an undercover agent, disguising his
ruined face to resemble anyone he wished and
then infiltrating enemy lines. The Unknown
Soldier's daring exploits earned him the enmity of
Adolf Hitler, who frequently pitted a Nazi
operative known as the Black Knight against him.

Later, as the war was ending, the Unknown
Soldier infiltrated Hitler's Berlin bunker, where he
facilitated the Führer's suicide. Many believed the
Soldier had died saving a child from an explosion
on the streets of war-torn Berlin. In reality, he
continued to serve U.S. interests throughout other
wars and various clandestine conflicts in the
decades to follow as the U.S.
military's favorite cleanup agent,
a man with neither a face nor a
name. SB

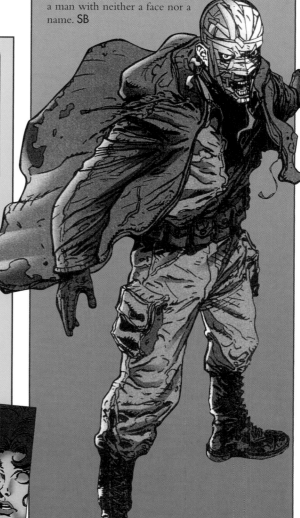

UNCLE SAM

FIRST APPEARANCE NATIONAL COMICS #1 (July 1940)
STATUS Hero **REAL NAME** Unknown **OCCUPATION** Patriotic spirit
BASE The United States **HEIGHT** 6ft 3in **WEIGHT** 210 lbs
EYES Blue **HAIR** White **SPECIAL POWERS/ABILITIES** Superstrength,
invulnerability; can change size; powers are proportionate to the the
country's faith in the ideals of freedom and liberty.

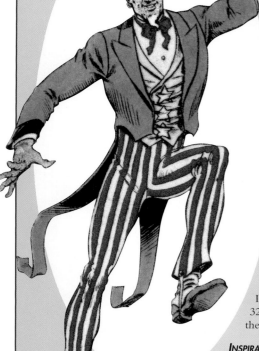

Several hundred years ago, soon after the formation of the
United States, Benjamin Franklin and other Founding
Fathers used a mystic ritual to create the American
Talisman. The Talisman would embody the very spirit
of the U.S., and materialize by magically binding
itself to a nationalistic citizen. During World War II,
the spirit linked itself to a man named Samuel and
became the star-spangled superpatriot Uncle Sam.

Uncle Sam joined the ALL-STAR SQUADRON and
later formed an auxiliary unit called the FREEDOM
FIGHTERS. After World War II, the American talisman was
destroyed and Uncle Sam's energies waned. An evil group
called the National Interest tried to recreate the shattered
Talisman, but the SPECTRE defeated the Interest as well as
the American Scream, the insane personification of
American culture. The Talisman
was reassembled and Uncle Sam
became the Patriot, defending the
U.S., most notably during the
Imperiex War (see Great Battles, pp.
320–1). The spirit then reclaimed
the title Uncle Sam. PJ

INSPIRATION During the great Crisis,
Uncle Sam led members of the JLA and the
Titans into battle against the Anti-Monitor.

GREAT BATTLES

Why are there super heroes? Perhaps the cosmic presence that governs the universe created so many meta-humans in the 20th century in preparation for the creation-shaking threats soon to follow. Without the JLA, the JSA, and other champions of freedom, the Earth and all of reality would long since have ceased to exist!

THE APPELLAXIAN CONTEST

Seven champions came from a distant star to slug it out on an Earth battlefield and determine which of the seven was fit to rule the Appellaxian empire. Assuming "battle forms" of glass, fire, rock, mercury, wood, ice, and a giant golden bird, the seven met swift defeat thanks to the embryonic JUSTICE LEAGUE OF AMERICA—AQUAMAN, GREEN LANTERN, the FLASH, MARTIAN MANHUNTER, and BLACK CANARY. An eighth Appellaxian went unnoticed. He called seven thousand of his planet's top shock troops for a full-scale alien invasion.

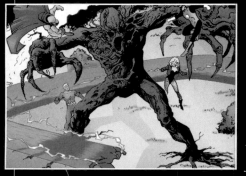

GIANT STEPS
All of Earth's heroes united to defeat the Appellaxian horde, ultimately sending them back to their own planet through a mystical wormhole. The conflict is still remembered as the JLA's baptism of fire

The cosmic tyrant IMPERIEX hungered to reignite the universe in a new Big Bang, wiping out all that had gone before. SUPERMAN led a galaxy-wide coalition of champions to oppose his cataclysmic scheming. The Imperiex War—a period sometimes referred to as "Our Worlds at War"—was inevitable if the universe was to be saved. Earth's defenders included an unlikely alliance of DARKSEID and U.S. President Lex Luthor (*see* LUTHOR, LEX), whose combined forces provided the necessary edge when the computerized monster BRAINIAC 13 entered the fight on the side of evil. Among the war's many casualties were most of the population of Topeka, Kansas as well as HIPPOLYTA—Princess Diana's mother, and the Golden Age WONDER WOMAN.

DESTROYED BY FIRE
Topeka is set ablaze during the Imperiex War.

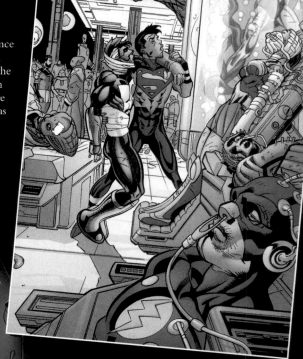

HAVEN *Orbiting 'Paradocs' sheltered those wounded in the shocking conflict, including some of the greatest heroes the Earth has ever seen.*

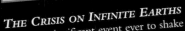

THE MAGEDDON WAR

Those who lived through it called it World War III. When the ancient doomsday device Mageddon slipped its moorings outside space-time and approached Earth, its aggressive energies caused the planet to erupt in a fury of violence. Angels from Heaven helped calm the leaders of nations, while Wonder Woman spearheaded an effort to turn ordinary citizens into temporary super heroes. In the end Superman switched off the Mageddon warhead, ensuring Earth's survival—until the next extraterrestrial threat.

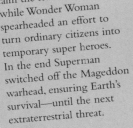

LOSS *Though Superman secured a victory, the young hero Aztek perished in his efforts to halt the advance of the warbringer.*

THE CRISIS ON INFINITE EARTHS

The most significant event ever to shake the universe is the one that almost no one can remember. In an earlier reality, creation was ordered into a "multiverse" with multiple parallel Earths—an Earth-2 for the Justice Society and an Earth-S for the CAPTAIN MARVEL family, alongside an infinite number of others. The omnipotent Anti-Monitor began destroying all parallel universes, and his heroic mirror-image the MONITOR gathered heroes from all realities and timeframes to fight him.

In order to save what was left, the Monitor merged five Earth-histories into one and the universe was reborn as if it had always been that way. Thus, while modern heroes remember a battle called the Crisis, they have no memory of a multiverse. Some heroes who died in the Crisis (such as the Barry Allen Flash) still perished in the rebooted version of the event, while others (such as the pre-Crisis version of SUPERGIRL) had their deaths—and entire histories—retroactively wiped from existence. Among the characters who can remember bits of pre-Crisis reality are the Psycho Pirate, the LINEAR MEN, and presumably some of God's agents, such as the PHANTOM STRANGER and the SPECTRE.

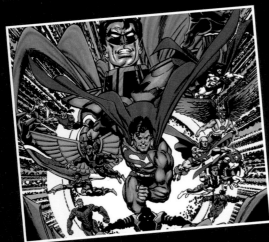

ZERO HOUR

Essentially a Crisis aftershock, the history-altering Zero Hour united the villainous EXTANT with the delusional hero PARALLAX, who wanted to remake the universe and remove all pain and loss. A team of super heroes followed Parallax back to the dawn of time and prevented his larger plan, though reality was still reborn in a slightly modified form. Zero Hour's biggest effects were felt in the 30th century, where the history of the LEGION OF SUPER-HEROES experienced a complete restart. **DW**

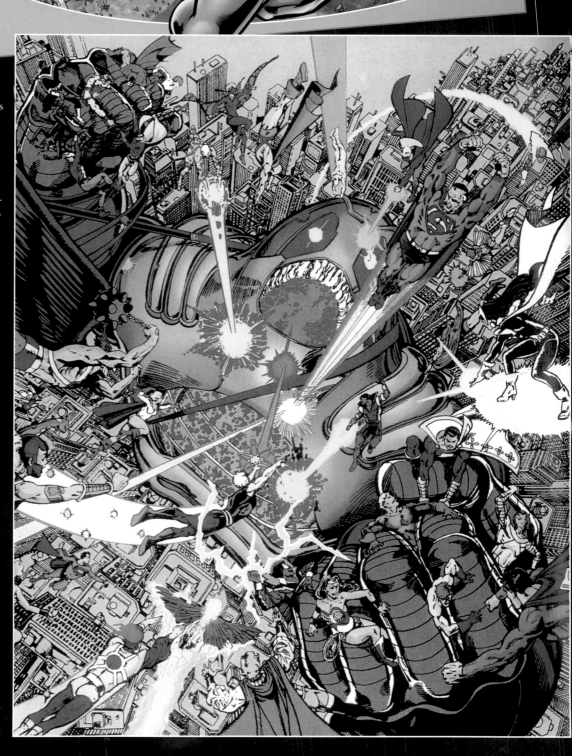

VALDA

FIRST APPEARANCE ARAK, SON OF THUNDER #3 (November 1981)
STATUS Hero **REAL NAME** Valda
OCCUPATION Knight **BASE** Aix-le-Chapelle, Frankland
HEIGHT 5ft 6in **WEIGHT** 130 lbs **EYES** Blue **HAIR** Brown
SPECIAL POWERS/ABILITIES Valda was quick-witted and courageous, and an expert hand-to-hand combatant and swordsman.

Nicknamed the Iron Maiden of Europe, Valda was the daughter of Bradamante, the legendary female knight. When her mother did not return alive from the ambush at the pass of Roncesvalles in the Pyrenees mountains in 778, when part of King Charlemagne's army was destroyed by the Basques, Valda was raised by Charlemagne and his court sorcerer, Malagigi.

The young woman used a spell she learned from Malagigi to summon the spirit of Amadis of Gaul, a valiant warrior, and the ghost tutored her as a warrior into Valda's adulthood.

Charlemagne was so impressed with Valda's talents and bravery that he eventually made her a knight. Soon after, Valda came under the control of the sorcerer Baledor and was freed by ARAK, SON OF THUNDER. Arak and Valda became lovers, adventuring throughout Europe until the end of their lives, which remain unchronicled. **PJ**

VALE, VICKI

FIRST APPEARANCE BATMAN #49 (October 1950)
STATUS Hero **REAL NAME** Victoria "Vicki" Vale
OCCUPATION Talk-show host **BASE** Gotham City
HEIGHT 5ft 6in **WEIGHT** 121 lbs **EYES** Blue **HAIR** Red
SPECIAL POWERS/ABILITIES No superpowers, but few journos have a better nose for a good story or are more persistent when on the trail of a possible scoop.

Among the so-called "Fourth Estate" of professional newspaper reporting, Vicki Vale was highly respected and acclaimed for her determination in rooting out the truth with her writing. In Gotham City social circles, Vicki was also known for her on-again/off-again romance with billionaire Bruce Wayne, who—despite caring deeply for Vicki—was ultimately unable to reveal to her the fact that he was BATMAN. In the past her relationship with

Bruce drove Selina Kyle, CATWOMAN, into fits of murderous jealousy. On one occasion Selina caused the car Vicki and Bruce were traveling in to plunge into a lake. Vicki would have drowned if Bruce had not rescued her.

Vicki has since left both Bruce Wayne and print journalism behind and now hosts *The Scene* TV show. **SB**

VANDAL SAVAGE

FIRST APPEARANCE GREEN LANTERN (1st series) #10 (Winter 1943)
STATUS Villain **REAL NAME** Vandar Adg
OCCUPATION Would-be conqueror **BASE** Mobile
HEIGHT 5ft 10in **WEIGHT** 170 lbs **EYES** Brown **HAIR** Black
SPECIAL POWERS/ABILITIES Savage is immortal. He is a brilliant strategist and scientist with 50,000 years of experience to draw upon.

Fifty thousand years ago, Vandar Adg was a chieftain of the Blood tribe of Cro-Magnons in Europe. Adg was exposed to the radiation from a meteor that advanced his intellect and gave him immortality. The ruthless Adg spent millennia acquiring wealth and power, and became a leader of the Illuminati, a secret society out to control the world. Over the centuries, Savage was a pharaoh in Egypt; a Caesar in Rome; led the Mongol hordes as Genghis Khan; led the Spanish Armada; advised Napoleon; and committed serial murders as Jack the Ripper.

During World War II, Vandal Savage fought the JUSTICE SOCIETY OF AMERICA in the INJUSTICE SOCIETY. He collected DNA samples of the team and used them to create DAMAGE. Savage engineered the congressional hearings that forced the JSA to disband in 1951. In recent years, Savage created the super-drug Velocity 9, joined several villains in TARTARUS while fighting the TEEN TITANS, plotted nuclear extortion, and destroyed Montevideo, Uruguay. A sworn enemy of Rip Hunter (*see* HUNTER, RIP), RESURRECTION MAN, and the JSA, Savage uses transplanted organs from his descendants to ensure his survival, which extends well into the 853rd century. There, he unleashed the HOURMAN virus before traveling back to the present, where his current self watched his future incarnation immolated in the Montevideo attack. The present-day Savage escaped, however, knowing that he has millennia to plot his revenge. **PJ**

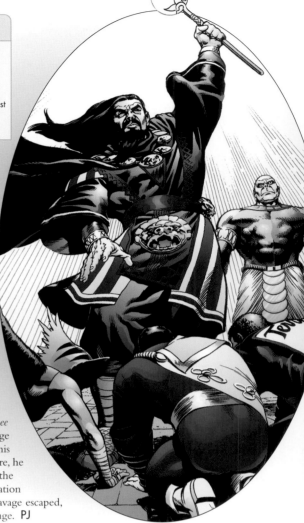

MEETING OF HEROES The Teen Titans join forces with the members of Vanguard: **1)** Scanner **2)** Solaar **3)** White Dwarf **4)** Anti-Matterman.

VANGUARD

FIRST APPEARANCE NEW TEEN TITANS (1st series) ANNUAL #1 (1985)
STATUS Hero team **BASE** Mobile
MEMBERS AND POWERS **Anti-Matterman** Draws power from anti-matter universe; **Scanner** Powerful mental abilities; **White Dwarf** Controls gravity and density of objects; **Solaar** Controls heat and energy of solar winds; **Black Nebula (deceased)** Could generate a field of darkness; **Drone** Entity of living metal; Vanguard space transport.

The Vanguard are a mobile team of superpowered entities whose territory is the entire cosmos. Roaming the stars in their sentient starship Drone, they visit planets, doing what good they can before departing to the next star system. Their membership is composed primarily of individuals who command some fundamental cosmic power, such as White Dwarf, Solaar, and Anti-Matterman.

The Vanguard's first and only visit to Earth to date was largely a case of mistaken identity. The core Vanguard team attempted to capture SUPERMAN but only succeeded in netting a Superman robotic duplicate. The New TEEN TITANS arrived to help. Both teams soon discovered that BRANIAC had murdered Vanguard member Black Nebula and abducted Superman to serve as an organic power source for his interstellar war machines.

Only the united strength of the Vanguard team and the Teen Titans could defeat Braniac and return Superman to Earth. Although grateful to the Titans for the assistance, the Vanguard chose to resume wandering across the light-years of space rather than remain tied to a single planet. **DW**

VAPOR

FIRST APPEARANCE JUSTICE LEAGUE QUARTERLY #1 (Winter 1990)
STATUS Hero *REAL NAME* Carrie Donahue
OCCUPATION Activist *BASE* Formerly New York City
HEIGHT 5ft 5in *WEIGHT* 124 lbs *EYES* Hazel *HAIR* Brown
SPECIAL POWERS/ABILITIES Able to transform into a living vaporous mist with acidic, anesthetic, or transparent properties.

Although Carrie Donahue was less than overjoyed upon acquiring superpowers, the admitted liberal decided to use her ability as the adventuring activist known as Vapor. The origins of Carrie's gifts are unknown, although they may be the result of a latent metagene, as is often the case with spontaneous superpowers. Ironically, this intelligent and haughty young woman accepted businesswoman Claire Montgomery's offer to join The Conglomerate (*see* CONGLOMERATE, THE), a team supplying its super heroic services to several corporate sponsors. Based on Wall Street, The Conglomerate soon battled the JUSTICE LEAGUE OF AMERICA—whom Vapor regarded as a "pathetic joke"—after violating U.N. protocols by ousting the tyrannical leader of the nation of San Sebor. The Conglomerate broke apart shortly after, and Vapor became a spokesperson for an environmental group. Her present location and activities are unknown. **SB**

VEXT

FIRST APPEARANCE DCU HEROES SECRET FILES AND ORIGINS #1 (February 1999) *STATUS* Undecided *REAL NAME* Vext
OCCUPATION Patron deity of misfortune *BASE* Delta City
HEIGHT 6ft 2in *WEIGHT* 210 lbs *EYES* Blue *HAIR* Brown
SPECIAL POWERS/ABILITIES Immortality; teleportation; can manipulate all manner of unfortunate occurrences; suffers constant bad luck.

Vext is a god of mishap and misfortune, the personification of the so-called "Murphy's Law," where anything that can go wrong will, and at the worst possible moment! Vext once resided in the Jejune Realm, also known as the Borough of Mawkish Indifference, a land of minor gods and goddesses who oversee the mundane aspects of people's everyday life.

The Jejune Realm was erased from existence when mortals no longer chose to actively worship its gods and Vext was sent to Earth. He arrived in Delta City, under strict orders from the cosmic powers not to interfere in human affairs. Struggling to fit into the world as a normal person, Vext was often joined by Paramour, the beautiful but unlucky Goddess of Relationships Gone Horribly Wrong. After being pursued by Aaron Caldwell, an archaeologist devoted to the study of minor gods such as the Jejune pantheon, Vext settled down with Colleen McBride, an aspiring writer and Vext's next-door neighbor. **PJ**

VIBE

FIRST APPEARANCE JUSTICE LEAGUE OF AMERICA (1st series) ANNUAL #2 (November 1984)
STATUS Hero (deceased) *REAL NAME* Paco Ramone
OCCUPATION Super hero *BASE* Detroit
HEIGHT 5ft 10in *WEIGHT* 157 lbs *EYES* Brown *HAIR* Brown
SPECIAL POWERS/ABILITIES Could emit shockwaves to trigger earthquakes.

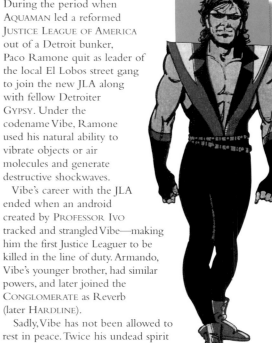

During the period when AQUAMAN led a reformed JUSTICE LEAGUE OF AMERICA out of a Detroit bunker, Paco Ramone quit as leader of the local El Lobos street gang to join the new JLA along with fellow Detroiter GYPSY. Under the codename Vibe, Ramone used his natural ability to vibrate objects or air molecules and generate destructive shockwaves.

Vibe's career with the JLA ended when an android created by PROFESSOR IVO tracked and strangled Vibe—making him the first Justice Leaguer to be killed in the line of duty. Armando, Vibe's younger brother, had similar powers, and later joined the CONGLOMERATE as Reverb (later HARDLINE).

Sadly, Vibe has not been allowed to rest in peace. Twice his undead spirit has been reanimated to vex his former teammates in the JLA. **DW**

VENTRILOQUIST & SCARFACE

FIRST APPEARANCE DETECTIVE COMICS #583 (February 1988)
STATUS Villainous pair *REAL NAME* Arnold Wesker
OCCUPATION Gang boss; assassin *BASE* Gotham City
HEIGHT 5ft 7in *WEIGHT* 142 lbs *EYES* Blue *HAIR* Gray
SPECIAL POWERS/ABILITIES Out of shape and a poor ventriloquist (he speaks "b"s as "g"s); however his shattered psyche harbors dark passions, which find murderous outlet through his dummy, Scarface.

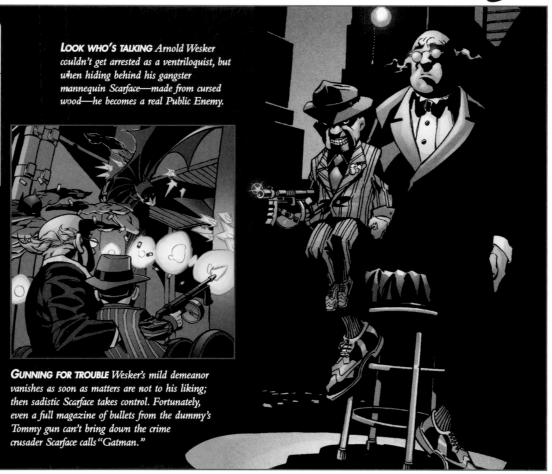

LOOK WHO'S TALKING *Arnold Wesker couldn't get arrested as a ventriloquist, but when hiding behind his gangster mannequin Scarface—made from cursed wood—he becomes a real Public Enemy.*

GUNNING FOR TROUBLE *Wesker's mild demeanor vanishes as soon as matters are not to his liking; then sadistic Scarface takes control. Fortunately, even a full magazine of bullets from the dummy's Tommy gun can't bring down the crime crusader Scarface calls "Gatman."*

Arnold Wesker was orphaned as a child and repressed his feelings so deeply that he developed a multiple personality disorder. As an adult, he let those angry feelings out and killed a man, landing him in Gotham's Blackgate Penitentiary. His cellmate, Donnegan, showed him a ventriloquist's dummy he had carved from the wood of Blackgate's Gallows Tree. Perhaps the wood was cursed, for Wesker was irresistibly drawn to the doll, and killed Donnegan for it. The psychopathic personality of Scarface emerged, speaking through the dummy.

Wesker and Scarface became major players in Gotham's underworld. When stopped by BATMAN, Wesker's defense was that he was an innocent dupe of the Scarface persona. When Gotham was devastated by an earthquake, Wesker created a new puppet, the Quakemaster, and tried to extort $100,000,000 from the city. Wesker committed more mundane crimes until Lt. Mackenzie Bock shot the dummy, shattering its wooden head. Since then Wesker has been in therapy, but late at night, he continues to hear the snarling voice of a very angry ghost. **RG**

VIGILANTE I

FIRST APPEARANCE ACTION COMICS #42 (November 1941)
STATUS Hero **REAL NAME** Gregory Sanders
HEIGHT 6ft **WEIGHT** 188 lbs **EYES** Blue **HAIR** Black
OCCUPATION Adventurer **BASE** Mobile
SPECIAL POWERS/ABILITIES A trained fighter, an expert motorcycle rider, is skilled with a pistol and lariat, and can sing a pretty mean tune.

Nathaniel Sanders and his wife had three children, Rebecca, Gregory and Jeffrey. Jeff Sanders died of "the fever" in 1936 and Nathaniel was killed by stagecoach bandits. Greg grew up to become the famous radio star known as the "Prairie Troubadour." However, to avenge his father, he donned the costumed identity of the Vigilante. He had numerous exploits on his own, and with the SEVEN SOLDIERS OF VICTORY. Billy "Pop" Gunn, an old man from New Jersey who loved the Old West, hooked up with the Vigilante for several adventures.

While trying to prevent the Head from instigating a tong war in Chinatown, the Vigilante met the youthful Daniel Leong, who soon becomes his partner, Stuff. Gangster Benjamin "Bugsy" Siegel killed Stuff, sending Vigilante on a new mission of vengeance. At some point thereafter, Leong's brother Victor took over his brother's role as Stuff, the Chinatown Kid. On June 20 1947, Vigilante finally gained revenge in a one-on-one confrontation with Bugsy Siegel. Shortly thereafter, the SSOV were tossed back in time and Sanders spent 1875-1895 roaming the Old West. He was rescued by the JUSTICE LEAGUE OF AMERICA and the JUSTICE SOCIETY OF AMERICA. Now better known for his Greg Sanders's Round-Up fast-food franchise, he enjoys a well-deserved retirement with his wife, Sally. **RG**

VIGILANTE II

FIRST APPEARANCE THE NEW TEEN TITANS ANNUAL (1st series) #2 (Summer 1983)
STATUS Hero (deceased) **REAL NAME** Adrian Chase
OCCUPATION Criminal hunter **BASE** Mobile
HEIGHT 6ft 2in **WEIGHT** 197 lbs **EYES** Blue **HAIR** Blond
SPECIAL POWERS/ABILITIES Master of unarmed combat and skilled in the use of firearms and other weapons; practiced meditative processes to overcome pain and heal injuries; rode a heavily armed motorcycle.

As an indefatigable Manhattan District Attorney, Adrian Chase worked doggedly within the system to dismantle the city's Mafia infrastructure. But when Chase's wife Doris, son Adam, and daughter Drew were killed by a bomb planted by the Scarapelli mob family, Chase sought his own justice as Vigilante. Guilt-ridden over his abandonment of the rule of law, Chase attempted to cease his Vigilante activities on several occasions and ultimately committed suicide. **SB**

VIGILANTE III

FIRST APPEARANCE DEATHSTROKE THE TERMINATOR #6 (January 1992) **STATUS** Hero **REAL NAME** Patricia "Pat" Trayce
OCCUPATION Retired police detective; crime fighter **BASE** Mobile
HEIGHT 5ft 9in **WEIGHT** 144 lbs **EYES** Blue **HAIR** Blond
SPECIAL POWERS/ABILITIES Markswoman and martial artist; costume has night-vision goggles and flak jacket; weapons and equipment include pistol, ropes, grenades, and a molybdenum-alloy fighting baton.

After her partner was killed by mob hitman Barker, G.C.P.D. detective Pat Trayce was suspected of jeopardizing Barker's safety in the witness protection program. When DEATHSTROKE kidnapped Barker to smoke out the true traitor within the justice department, Trayce was blamed and suspended from duty. Determined to prove her innocence, Trayce began her own investigation, during which time she met the informant Scoops, who had once assisted the late Adrian Chase, (VIGILANTE II). Scoops gave Trayce the costume and weapons of the Vigilante. Trayce then helped Deathstroke flush out the justice department mole. Realizing the benefits of working outside the law, Trayce turned in her badge and became the Vigilante full-time. She has been a CHECKMATE agent, set up a detective agency, Vigilance, and worked with the FORGOTTEN HEROES and the JSA All-Stars. **SB**

VIKING PRINCE

FIRST APPEARANCE THE BRAVE AND THE BOLD #1 (August 1955)
STATUS Hero (deceased) **REAL NAME** Jon Haraldson
OCCUPATION Adventurer **BASE** Formerly 10th-century Scandinavia, now Valhalla, home for Norse warriors who have died in battle.
HEIGHT 5ft 11in **WEIGHT** 171 lbs **EYES** Blue **HAIR** Blond
SPECIAL POWERS/ABILITIES A powerful hand-to-hand combatant and swordsman; some legends claim that he was invulnerable to harm from metal, wood, fire, and water.

The origins of Jon the Viking Prince remain a mystery. One legend asserts that Jon was brought to Valhalla after a great battle, granted superpowers by Odin, the Asgardian god, and sent back to Earth to battle evil for eternity.

Jon's mysterious past became linked to the present when CHESHIRE and her band of female assassins, the Ravens, traveled back in time to the 10th century. BLACK CANARY pursued them and the Viking Prince fell in love with her. But Cheshire shot the Prince, and the Ravens and Canary returned to the present.

Suspended in ice by a Valkyrie who had fallen in love with him, the Viking Prince was freed from his frozen state centuries later during World War II. After dying fighting the Nazis, Jon was finally taken to Valhalla.

Black Canary later learned that the Viking Prince had survived Cheshire's bullet when she found an artifact that referred to their affair. Upon it was carved the inscription: "His heart mourned for a love lost to time." **PJ**

VILLAINY INC.

FIRST APPEARANCE WONDER WOMAN: OUR WORLDS AT WAR #1 (August 2001) **STATUS** Villain team **BASE** Mobile
CURRENT MEMBERS AND POWERS Queen Clea (leader, deceased) Atlantean monarch who carried the Trident of Poseidon.
Cyborgirl Cyborg who can interface with machinery.
Doctor Poison II Expert in toxins and plagues. Giganta Can grow to towering heights. Jinx Vast mystical abilities.
Trinity (destroyed) Her three faces, Time, War, and Chaos, possessed specialized powers; revealed as a computer virus.

This all-female super-villain team has made life awful for WONDER WOMAN, starting in the 1940s. Led by the Atlantean Queen Clea (whose roster included CHEETAH I, Doctor Poison, Hypnotic Woman, and Zara) the wartime team failed to score lasting victories. Clea resurrected Villainy, Inc. and recruited a new roster: Cyborgirl, outfitted with CYBORG's machinery and weapons, GIGANTA, JINX, the enigmatic TRINITY, and the second DOCTOR POISON, the granddaughter of the original.

Clea led the new team to Skartaris, home of the WARLORD, hoping to capture the Golden City of Shamballah and its computer core. Wonder Woman united the peoples of Skartaris in a counter attack, but Trinity revealed herself to be a living computer virus created by ancient Skartaran scientists to infect Shamballah's computer core and "reboot" the land to its previous, more harmonious state. Wonder Woman stopped Trinity and Clea was de-aged into nothingness. The surviving members joined Wonder Woman on a time-hop to 1943, where a younger Clea and Hippolyta were joined in battle. After helping defeat Clea, Wonder Woman escorted Villainy Inc. back to the modern era. **DW**

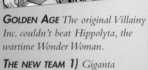

GOLDEN AGE The original Villainy Inc. couldn't beat Hippolyta, the wartime Wonder Woman.

THE NEW TEAM 1) Giganta
2) Doctor Poison II
3) Trinity **4)** Queen Clea
5) Cyborgirl **6)** Jinx.

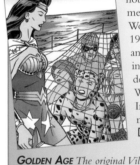

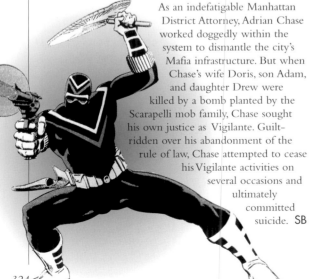

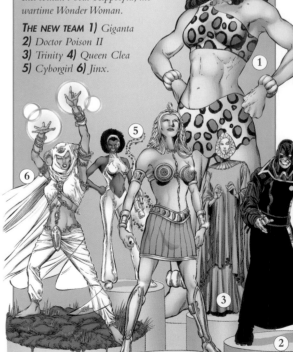

VIXEN

FIRST APPEARANCE ACTION COMICS #521 (July 1981)
STATUS Hero **REAL NAME** Mari Jiwe McCabe
OCCUPATION Adventurer **BASE** Ultramarines base, Superbia
HEIGHT 5ft 7in **WEIGHT** 140 lbs **EYES** Brown **HAIR** Brown
SPECIAL POWERS/ABILITIES Mystical Tantu totem gives her the abilities of one animal at a time.

Mari McCabe grew up in Africa, the daughter of the Reverend Richard Jiwe. Her father had inherited a magical totem that had supposedly been given to the ancient hero Tantu by the trickster Anansi the Spider of African folklore and myth. The reverend's envious and corrupt half-brother, General Maksai, killed Richard for the totem, and Mari fled to the U.S., where she found remarkable success as a fashion model.

Soon, Mari recovered the Tantu totem and, under the codename Vixen, used its amazing animal powers to become a member of the Detroit-based JUSTICE LEAGUE OF AMERICA. General Maksai tried to force her to turn the totem over to him, but received his comeuppance when he used the totem in selfishness, and was transformed into an ox! Vixen joined the SUICIDE SQUAD after leaving the JLA, striking up a failed romance with teammate BRONZE TIGER. She later worked with the Justice League Task Force and is now a member of the INTERNATIONAL ULTRAMARINES CORPS. Alongside her fellow heroes in the Ultramarines, Vixen now operates from the floating city of Superbia and keeps a lookout for global crises. **DW**

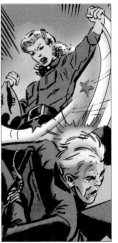

SHARED LINK Like Animal Man, Vixen shares a connection to the "morphogenic field" that bestows animal powers.

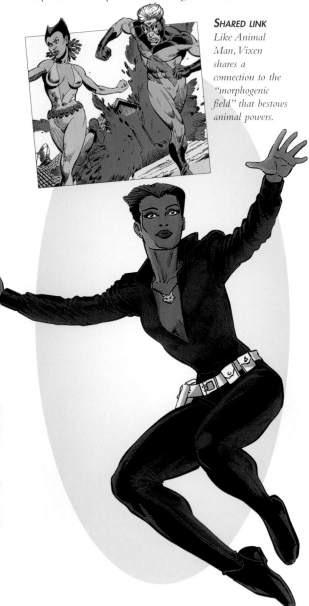

VUNDERBARR, VIRMIN

FIRST APPEARANCE MISTER MIRACLE (1st series) #5 (DECEMBER 1971)
STATUS Villain **REAL NAME** Virmin Vunderbarr
OCCUPATION Assassin **BASE** Apokolips
HEIGHT 5ft 2in **WEIGHT** 130 lbs **EYES** Blue **HAIR** Black
SPECIAL POWERS/ABILITIES A highly skilled, if inflexible, tactician; good hand-to-hand combatant, but handicapped by small size. He relies on his troops to fight his battles for him; has delusions of grandeur and believes he deserves more power than he has.

Virmin Vunderbarr was one of DARKSEID's best skilled soldiers, quickly rising to become a military leader. He has ensconced himself as one of Darkseid's trusted aides even though he schemes with the other acolytes to amass his own power. After a campaign on Earth, Vunderbarr styled himself after 19th-century Prussian soldiers. On occasion, he has angered Darkseid and been destroyed by the Omega Force, only to be resurrected when needed by the tyrant. Virmin spends more time currying his master Darkseid's favor than being an effective leader. Despite his keen intellect and tactical acumen he has failed time and again, usually because of the intervention of Scott Free, MR. MIRACLE.

Virmin's niece Malice is the youngest, but by no means the least dangerous, of Granny Goodness' Female Furies. She controls the terrifying shadow monster Chessure. **RG**

JACKBOOT JERK Virmin Vunderbarr styles himself after the rigid and domineering Prussian military of days gone by.

MALICE IN MIND Despite her innocent appearance, Virmin's niece Malice has the makings of being far deadlier and more effective than he ever was.

VON GUNTHER, BARONESS PAULA

FIRST APPEARANCE WONDER WOMAN (2nd series) #131 (March 1998) **STATUS** Reformed villain **REAL NAME** Paula Von Gunther
OCCUPATION Scientist **BASE** Themyscira
HEIGHT 5ft 10in **WEIGHT** 155 lbs **EYES** Blue **HAIR** Blonde
SPECIAL POWERS/ABILITIES Expert occultist; (as Dark Angel) teleportation; can change size and shape; mind control; manipulation of time.

Baroness Paula Von Gunther was a ruthless Nazi occultist and a personal assistant to Adolf Hitler during World War II. Hoping to harness the power of Johnny Thunder's mystic Thunderbolt (see THUNDER II, JOHNNY) for her own evil ends, the Baroness summoned the ancient spirit Dark Angel, who took over her body. Channeling Dark Angel's mystic powers, Von Gunther attacked the JUSTICE SOCIETY OF AMERICA and trapped them in a magical cage. HIPPOLYTA, the Golden Age WONDER WOMAN, freed her heroic teammates, and Von Gunther was separated from the Dark Angel spirit. Dark Angel became a constant foe of Hippolyta and her daughter, TROIA, while Von Gunther renounced her ties to the Nazi party and relocated to Themyscira (see Amazing Bases, pp. 120–1). There, the Baroness became a prominent scientist, the inventor of the Purple Healing Ray. **PJ**

VYKIN

FIRST APPEARANCE FOREVER PEOPLE 1st series #1 (March 1971)
STATUS Hero **REAL NAME** None **OCCUPATION** Adventurer
BASE Earth **HEIGHT** 6ft 1in **WEIGHT** 201 lbs **EYES** Brown
HAIR Black **SPECIAL POWERS/ABILITIES** "Magno-Power" enables him to project magnetic energy; a natural tracker able to mentally trace atomic patterns; carries the Forever People's Mother Box computer.

Like his five human friends in the FOREVER PEOPLE, Vykin was plucked from Earth and transported through time and space to New Genesis. There the enigmatic Highfather imbued him with incredible powers. When BEAUTIFUL DREAMER of the Forever People was abducted by DARKSEID, sworn enemy of New Genesis, and taken to Earth, Vykin and the others returned to the planet of their birth to rescue her. Later, after battling Darkseid's agent, DEVILANCE the Pursuer, Vykin and the Forever People were marooned on the planet Adon. Vykin died using the Forever People's Mother Box, a living computer, to increase the intelligence of Adon's native populace. The remaining Forever People taught the Adonians culture and established the city of Forevertown. However, when SERIFAN was possessed by an evil entity called the Dark, Adon was regressed to its original primitive state. The Dark's reversal of time fortunately raised Vykin from the dead. Vykin and the team have since returned to New Genesis. **SB**

WALLER, AMANDA

FIRST APPEARANCE LEGENDS #1 (November 1986)
STATUS Villain **REAL NAME** Amanda Blake Waller
OCCUPATION Leader of the Suicide Squad **BASE** Washington, D.C.
HEIGHT 5ft 1in **WEIGHT** 200 lbs **EYES** Brown **HAIR** Brown
SPECIAL POWERS/ABILITIES No combat training, but her steel will allows
her to see straight through to the heart of a problem.

Amanda Waller grew up in the Cabrini-Green section of
Chicago and married her sweetheart, Joseph Waller, at
the age of 18. They made a good life for themselves
and their five children. Then tragedy struck: their
son, Joe Jr., was gunned down by local thugs and,
six months later, their daughter Damita was
raped and killed by a drug-dealer known as
Candyman. Joe went seeking revenge, only to
die in a hail of bullets. Amanda fiercely
protected her remaining three children,
pushing them to finish their education. She
also went to college herself, majoring in
psychology and political science. When all
three children finished high school, she told
them they had to fend for themselves.

While working for Illinois Congressman
Marvin Collins, she found some old,
dusty files about Task Force X and
its two divisions, Argent and
the Suicide Squad.

TOUGH NUT *Waller has been through
much, helping her to endure any threat.*

Managing with an iron hand, Waller
saw to it that the Squad took on the
nastiest operations around the world.
Concealed in Louisiana's Belle Reve
prison, the Squad was a political hot
potato and Waller expertly played the
political game, determined to preserve the
team. She remains an active force in
Washington, having survived under several
administrations. **RG**

Waller conceived the idea of a
revived Force, using meta-humans
and costumed criminals alike, if
necessary granting them pardons
to persuade them to go on suicide
missions. She managed to wrangle
government approval and funding,
and Task Force X was reborn.

BACK OFF! *"The Wall"
is not intimidated—not
even by the most feared
"cape" of them all!*

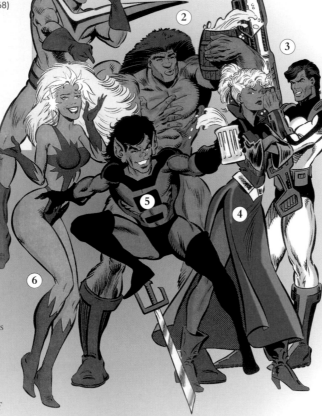

WANDERERS, THE

FIRST APPEARANCE ADVENTURE COMICS #375 (December 1968)
STATUS Hero team **BASE** Mobile
MEMBERS AND POWERS
Re-Animage (leader) Immortal.
Dartalon Carries a blowgun that fires special darts.
Elvar Master swordsman with an energy-charged blade.
Aviax Shapeshifter; can turn into any type of bird.
Psyche Empath capable of manipulating others' moods.
Quantum Queen Can change her body into light radiation.
Celebrand (not active) Skilled marksman; natural leader.

The Wanderers are considered by many to be a
smaller, more mobile version of the LEGION OF
SUPER-HEROES. They earned their stripes as
adventurers but first saw widespread fame as
villains, when the corrupt influence of the
Nefar Nebula caused them to turn to crime
and steal the Seven Stones of Alactos.

Though their time on the dark side proved
short-lived, the Wanderers appeared to have
met their ultimate end when the mad wife of
the Controller called Clonus murdered them.
Clonus, however, grew clones of every Wanderer
(except Celebrand) with memories of their past lives
intact. A few of the clone Wanderers adopted new
names: Immorto became Re-Animage, Dartalg
became Dartalon, Elvo became Elvar, and Ornitho
became Aviax.

Once the clone Wanderers solved the mystery of
their own murders they became deputized agents of
the United Planets. They even created a clone of
Celebrand, but vanished into deep space before the clone
could mature. Although the Wanderers have not been seen
for some time, they are presumably still active somewhere
in the greater galaxy. **DW**

THE WANDERERS 1) *Aviax* **2)** *Dartalon* **3)** *Re-Animage*
4) *Psyche* **5)** *Elvar* **6)** *Quantum Queen.*

WARRIOR

FIRST APPEARANCE GREEN LANTERN (2nd series) #59 (March 1968)
STATUS Hero **REAL NAME** Guy Gardner
OCCUPATION Adventurer; bar owner
BASE Warriors Bar, New York City
HEIGHT (Guy) 6ft 2in; (Warrior) up to 9ft **WEIGHT** (Guy) 240 lbs;
(Warrior) up to 750 lbs **EYES** Blue **HAIR** Red
SPECIAL POWERS/ABILITIES Vast superstrength; near invulnerability;
transformation of appendages into weapons; absorption of
energy; alien martial arts skills.

Born with the DNA of the alien Vuldarians spliced into his
own, Guy Gardner was a college football star who had been
selected to become a GREEN LANTERN. Guy ultimately
acquired his own ring after Hal Jordan became Earth's
premier Green Lantern. Guy suffered brain damage while
trapped in the Phantom Zone, another dimension where
beings exist in ghostlike states. After briefly betraying the
Green Lantern Corps, Guy returned to Earth and joined
the JUSTICE LEAGUE, falling
for fellow Leaguer ICE.

After a conflict with Hal
Jordan, Guy was forced to
resign from the Corps, but
he tricked LOBO into
finding SINESTRO's yellow
power ring and made it
his own. An attack by
Jordan left Guy powerless,
but his Vuldarian DNA
became active and Guy's
new powers transformed
him into Warrior.

Tragically, Ice died, but Guy's brain damage was finally
healed. Soon after, Guy opened Warriors, a super-hero-
themed bar in New York City. **PJ**

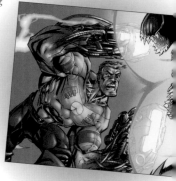

WARLORD

FIRST APPEARANCE FIRST ISSUE SPECIAL #8 (November 1975)
STATUS Hero **REAL NAME** Travis Morgan
OCCUPATION Warlord **BASE** Skartaris
HEIGHT 6ft **WEIGHT** 188 lbs **EYES** Blue **HAIR** White
SPECIAL POWERS/ABILITIES An exceptional athlete and tactical thinker, a proven swordsman, horseback rider, and brawler.

OUT OF TIME
Travis found his place in the world…the lost world of Skartaris.

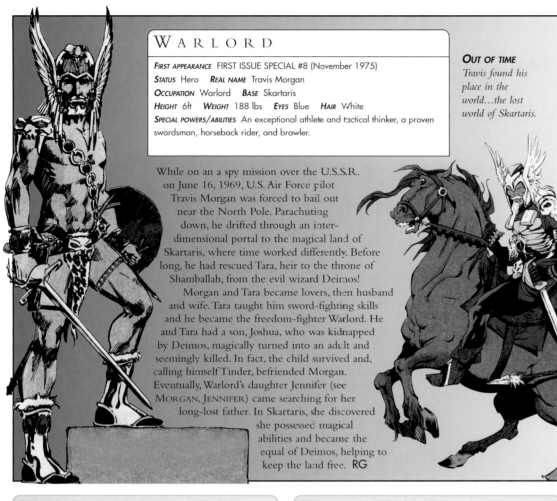

While on a spy mission over the U.S.S.R. on June 16, 1969, U.S. Air Force pilot Travis Morgan was forced to bail out near the North Pole. Parachuting down, he drifted through an inter-dimensional portal to the magical land of Skartaris, where time worked differently. Before long, he had rescued Tara, heir to the throne of Shamballah, from the evil wizard Deimos! Morgan and Tara became lovers, then husband and wife. Tara taught him sword-fighting skills and he became the freedom-fighter Warlord. He and Tara had a son, Joshua, who was kidnapped by Deimos, magically turned into an adult and seemingly killed. In fact, the child survived and, calling himself Tinder, befriended Morgan. Eventually, Warlord's daughter Jennifer (see MORGAN, JENNIFER) came searching for her long-lost father. In Skartaris, she discovered she possessed magical abilities and became the equal of Deimos, helping to keep the land free. **RG**

WARP

FIRST APPEARANCE THE NEW TEEN TITANS (1st series) #14 (December 1981) **STATUS** Villain **REAL NAME** Emil LaSalle
OCCUPATION Mercenary **BASE** Saint-Tropez, France
HEIGHT 5ft 8in **WEIGHT** 148 lbs **EYES** Brown **HAIR** Brown
SPECIAL POWERS/ABILITIES Ability to fly; can open warps, and teleport between two locations.

Driven by hatred, Frenchman Emil LaSalle is a dangerous enemy with the extraordinary ability to teleport himself anywhere in the world. For unknown reasons, he nursed a grudge against MADAME ROUGE, even joining the New Brotherhood of Evil to help them track down Rouge after she betrayed their organization. Following Rouge's death, Warp remained with his new comrades during the Brotherhood's reorganization into the SOCIETY OF SIN.

Warp possesses the power to create wormholes between two points in space, through which he can transport himself or others. It is believed that he needs specific coordinates for both locations in order to open a wormhole, but Warp's powers are still undefined.

Warp participated in the Crisis (*see* Great Battles, pp. 320–1) and has battled the TEEN TITANS and ELONGATED MAN. More recently he participated in The JOKER's "Last Laugh" rampage. Warp bears a grudge toward CAT-MAN, a fellow villain who once confessed secrets to court prosecutors. **DW**

WAVERIDER

FIRST APPEARANCE ARMAGEDDON 2001 #1 (May 1991)
STATUS Hero **REAL NAME** Matthew Ryder
OCCUPATION Scientist **BASE** Mobile
HEIGHT 6ft **WEIGHT** 185 lbs **EYES** Blue **HAIR** Blond
SPECIAL POWERS/ABILITIES Time travel; flight; project of quantum-powered force blasts; can access a person's aura and predict their most probable future.

Matthew Ryder was a scientist from a future Earth ruled by MONARCH, an armored despot who had eliminated all heroes. Ryder believed that one of Earth's erstwhile heroes had evolved into Monarch, and, using his scientific skills, Ryder created a time machine to journey into the past and change history. Ryder convinced Monarch to let him be a guinea pig in his own device, and Monarch agreed, believing Ryder, like several initial test subjects, would die in the process. Ryder survived, however, merging with the timestream and transforming into Waverider.

Traveling back to the past, he joined forces with Earth's heroes, including the JUSTICE LEAGUE OF AMERICA, the TEEN TITANS, and CAPTAIN ATOM, to defeat Monarch, who was revealed to be Hank Hall, formerly the hero Hawk (see HAWK & DOVE). Waverider then joined the LINEAR MEN, a group devoted to maintaining the timestream. **PJ**

WEAPONERS OF QWARD

FIRST APPEARANCE GREEN LANTERN (2nd series) #2 (October 1960)
STATUS Villains **BASE** Qward, the Anti-Matter Universe
NOTABLE AGENTS AND WEAPONERS
Borbrydi, Chomin, Drik, Gnaxos (a robot), Gyn-Gryngg, Gypo-Bax, Karo-Thynn, Kiman the Chief Weaponer, Kramen, Magot, Rengan the Abominable, Sinestro, Telle-Teg, Vestry the Thinker, Yokal the Atrocious.
SPECIAL POWERS/ABILITIES Armed with "qwa-bolts"; yellow shields, render the power rings of the Green Lantern Corps ineffective.

In the anti-matter universe of Qward, wrong is quite literally right. The Qwardians worship evil and hate beings in the positive matter universe who believe in the ideal of goodness. Ten billion years ago, the Anti-Monitor was born on a lifeless moon of Qward. This creature—absolute evil incarnate—seized control of the anti-matter universe and created an army of Thunderers to battle his munificent reflection in the positive-matter universe, the MONITOR.

When a backlash of their equal-but-opposite assaults sent the Anti-Monitor and the Monitor into slumbering stasis for billions of years, a Qwardian named Yokal the Atrocious seized the opportunity to unite his people as the Weaponers of Qward. Declaring himself Chief Weaponer, Yokal initiated the ongoing Qwardian offensive to undermine the GUARDIANS OF THE UNIVERSE in the positive-matter universe and wage war with the Guardians' peacekeeping agents, the heroic GREEN LANTERN CORPS. Over the years, the Weaponers have launched even more ambitious campaigns to overrun the positive matter universe, but none more successful than the return of the Anti-Monitor, who transformed his Thunderers into shadow demons that killed trillions during the Crisis (*see* Great Battles, pp. 320–1). **SB**

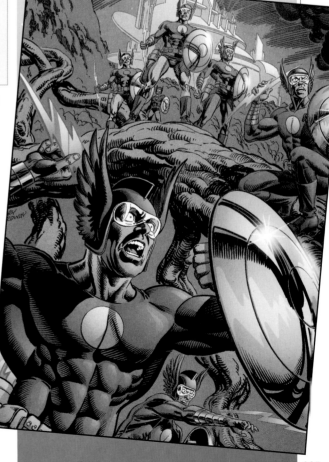

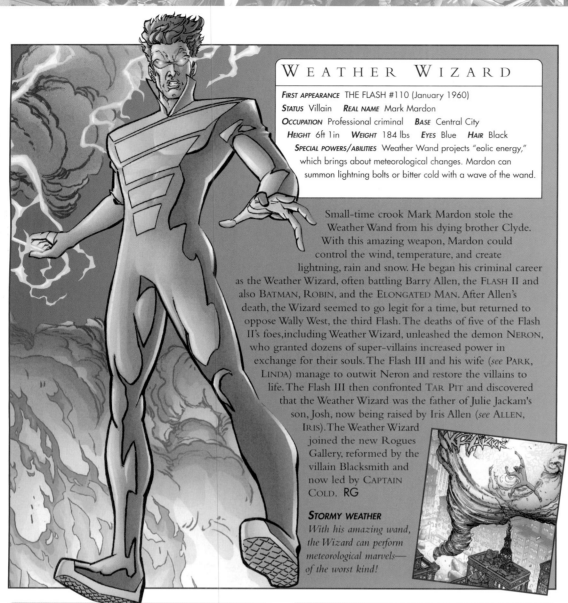

WEATHER WIZARD

FIRST APPEARANCE THE FLASH #110 (January 1960)
STATUS Villain **REAL NAME** Mark Mardon
OCCUPATION Professional criminal **BASE** Central City
HEIGHT 6ft 1in **WEIGHT** 184 lbs **EYES** Blue **HAIR** Black
SPECIAL POWERS/ABILITIES Weather Wand projects "eolic energy,"
which brings about meteorological changes. Mardon can
summon lightning bolts or bitter cold with a wave of the wand.

Small-time crook Mark Mardon stole the Weather Wand from his dying brother Clyde. With this amazing weapon, Mardon could control the wind, temperature, and create lightning, rain and snow. He began his criminal career as the Weather Wizard, often battling Barry Allen, the FLASH II and also BATMAN, ROBIN, and the ELONGATED MAN. After Allen's death, the Wizard seemed to go legit for a time, but returned to oppose Wally West, the third Flash. The deaths of five of the Flash II's foes, including Weather Wizard, unleashed the demon NERON, who granted dozens of super-villains increased power in exchange for their souls. The Flash III and his wife (see PARK, LINDA) manage to outwit Neron and restore the villains to life. The Flash III then confronted TAR PIT and discovered that the Weather Wizard was the father of Julie Jackam's son, Josh, now being raised by Iris Allen (see ALLEN, IRIS). The Weather Wizard joined the new Rogues Gallery, reformed by the villain Blacksmith and now led by CAPTAIN COLD. **RG**

STORMY WEATHER
With his amazing wand, the Wizard can perform meteorological marvels— of the worst kind!

WEIRD, THE

FIRST APPEARANCE THE WEIRD #1 (April 1988)
STATUS Hero (deceased) **REAL NAME** None
OCCUPATION Dimensional guardian **BASE** Mobile
HEIGHT 6ft 5in **WEIGHT** 185 lbs **EYES** Brown **HAIR** Brown
SPECIAL POWERS/ABILITIES Could change molecular density of his body
or anything he was in contact with; flew by riding magnetic currents.

The Weird came from an alternate dimension inhabited by the energy-seething Zarolatts and the brutish Macrolatts, who exploited the Zarolatts as power sources. When several Macrolatts decided to attack Earth, the Weird rushed to Earth to prevent it.

To contain his energy form in this new world, the Weird possessed the body of a dead man named Walter Langley. Unfortunately, the Weird was approaching critical mass—when he exploded, he would take out half the Earth. The Weird stopped the Macrolatt invasion and was then taken into space by SUPERMAN and GREEN LANTERN Guy Gardner. There, the Weird perished in a colossal blast. **DW**

WHIP, THE

FIRST APPEARANCE FLASH COMICS #1 (January 1940)
STATUS Hero **REAL NAME** Rodney Elwood Gaynor
OCCUPATION Playboy **BASE** Seguro, New Mexico; New York City
HEIGHT 6ft 2in **WEIGHT** 210 lbs **EYES** Blue **HAIR** Blond
SPECIAL POWERS/ABILITIES Expert with a bullwhip, and a superb
horseback rider; well-developed social conscience, despite wealth.

In 1939, millionaire socialite Rod Gayner was traveling through Seguro, New Mexico, when he learned of the legendary Don Fernando Suarez, a 19th-century hero known as El Castigo, "the Whip." Gayner discovered many of Suarez's belongings and decided to perpetuate the hero's legend. He became an expert with a bullwhip and an expert equestrian, riding his stallion Diablo as the new Whip.

As the Whip, Gayner fought crime in New Mexico, preventing the exploitation of the poor Mexican immigrants who lived there. When the United States entered World War II, however, Gayner moved to New York City and joined the ALL-STAR SQUADRON.

Nothing is known about the Whip's activities after 1944, and his final fate has yet to be revealed. **PJ**

WHITE MARTIANS

FIRST APPEARANCE JLA #1 (January 1997)
STATUS Villains **BASE** Z'onn Z'orr
MAIN MEMBERS AND POWERS (HYPERCLAN)
PROTEX A Martian superman.
PRIMAID Warrior woman.
ZÜM Superspeedster.
ZENTURION Shield-carrying soldier.
FLEXUS Rocky powerhouse.
ARMEK Armored juggernaut.
TRONIX Possessor of devastating gaze.
A-MORTAL Fearsome wraith.

Possessing superstrength, telepathy, the power of flight, and force-blasting "Martian Vision" like their Green Martian kin, the White Martians are a thousands-strong race of shape-shifters. They share the Green Martians' weakness to fire, which renders them virtually powerless. Eons ago, the bloodthirsty White Martians had dominated Earth. However the more peaceful Green Martians (of whom the JLA's MARTIAN MANHUNTER J'onn J'onzz is the sole survivor) banished them to the inter-dimensional Still Zone for an environmental catastrophe the White Martians had wrought on Earth. Eons later, the White Martians escaped from exile. Eight of their leaders arrived on Earth, calling themselves the Hyperclan. These handsome-seeming superbeings proclaimed they had come to save the world and quickly gained mankind's trust with a few good deeds. Fortunately, the JLA saw through the Hyperclan's deception and thwarted the White Martians' plans for global invasion.

Despite having their memories wiped, and being shape-shifted into harmless human forms, the Hyperclan again attempted to wreak havoc on Earth. The JLA defeated the White Martians once more and returned them to the Still Zone, where J'onn J'onzz monitors their imprisonment as his ancestors once did. **SB**

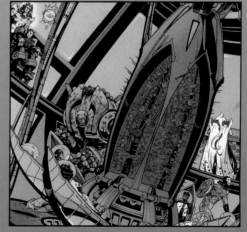

FLOWER OF WRATH *The Hyperclan subject the JLA heroes to a ghastly White Martian torture device!*

WHITE WITCH

FIRST APPEARANCE ADVENTURE COMICS #350 (November 1996)
STATUS Hero REAL NAME Mysa
OCCUPATION Adventurer BASE Earth
HEIGHT 5ft 8in WEIGHT 118 lbs EYES Red HAIR White
SPECIAL POWERS/ABILITIES Can perform magic spells of defense or offense. Still learning, but has the potential to become one of the most powerful mages of her millennium.

A group of 30th century mages, including Mysa, the White Witch, mobilized to defeat the all-powerful DARK LORD Mordru, stripping him of his objects of power (most notably the Emerald Eye) and entombing him. Few

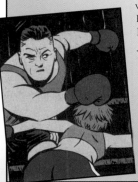

knew, until much later, that Mysa was Mordru's firstborn child. Transformed into a withered old crone by Mordru, Mysa is the lone survivor of the mystic heroes. On planet Tharn, Mysa used the Scepter of Sybolla to save the life of the pregnant Azra Saugin, unintentionally gifting the baby Zoe with telekinesis. Later, KINETIX of the LEGION OF SUPER-HEROES lost her powers, unaware that Mysa (using the Star of Akkos) was to blame for this. Mysa revealed her role and restored Kinetix's abilities just before Mordru escaped from his prison. In the ensuing battle, Mysa, the White Witch was returned to her youthful form by magic. She continues to perfect her abilities and works with Legionnaires on occasion. RG

WHITE, PERRY

FIRST APPEARANCE SUPERMAN (1st series) #7 (November 1940)
STATUS Hero REAL NAME Perry Jerome White
OCCUPATION Managing editor of The Daily Planet BASE Metropolis
HEIGHT 5ft 10in WEIGHT 200 lbs
EYES Blue HAIR Brown with white at temples
SPECIAL POWERS/ABILITIES Indomitable will and relentless thirst for truth.

In a city dominated by the Man of Steel, The Daily Planet's Perry White has become one of the most influential figures in Metropolis, due to the power of the press. His life is inseparable from the modern history of the Planet, having started there as a copy boy at the age of ten. White's rough childhood in Suicide Slum was brightened somewhat by his friendship with a boy named Lex Luthor (see LUTHOR, LEX).

Luthor made a fortune in his early twenties and purchased the Planet; Perry left the country on assignment as an overseas reporter. In that time, Luthor seduced White's girlfriend, Alice Spencer, who conceived a child. White married Spencer upon his return and she gave birth to his son (really Luthor's natural son), Jerry White. Meanwhile, financiers bought the newspaper back from Luthor on the condition that Perry White become managing editor.

White hired both Lois Lane (see LANE, LOIS) and Clark Kent (see SUPERMAN), and has weathered a number of tragedies that would have broken lesser men, including the death of his son and a bout with lung cancer. After a recent stint as a professor at Metropolis University, White returned to his first love, The Daily Planet. One of his toughest recent decisions was to demote Clark Kent to a lesser reporting job and hire Jack Ryder (see CREEPER, THE) as his replacement. DW

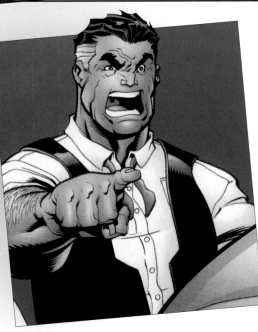

STOP THE PRESSES! Perry White is a newspaperman through and through, who remains a tireless advocate for the Daily Planet. It's often said that if you cut him open, you'd find printer's ink running through his veins!

WILDCAT I

FIRST APPEARANCE SENSATION COMICS #1 (January 1942)
STATUS Hero REAL NAME Ted Grant
OCCUPATION Boxer BASE New York City
HEIGHT 6ft 5in WEIGHT 250 lbs EYES Blue HAIR Gray
SPECIAL POWERS/ABILITIES Master of hand-to-hand combat, especially boxing; slowed aging (like other JSA members).

Raised by a timid father, Ted Grant grew up to become a heavyweight boxing champion in the 1930s. Framed for murder in the boxing ring by mafioso Victor Moretti, Ted became a fugitive from justice. Inspired by Alan Scott, the first GREEN LANTERN, Ted donned a black costume and became Wildcat. He used his new uniform and fighting skills to pound out a confession from Moretti and clear his name. As Wildcat, Grant began patrolling the streets of New York City and ridding them of mob-related crime. He joined the JUSTICE SOCIETY OF AMERICA during World War II and had a love affair with HIPPOLYTA, the Golden Age Wonder Woman. In 1947, Grant's son Jake was kidnapped by the Golden Wasp and Wildcat temporarily retired from crime fighting. He opened his own gym, and trained some of the world's greatest fighters, including BATMAN, BLACK CANARY II, and CATWOMAN. Claiming to possess nine lives, Wildcat now serves with the JSA. Tragically, while fighting the INJUSTICE SOCIETY, he learned that his son Jake had been murdered by the Golden Wasp's son, Killer Wasp. PJ

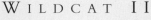

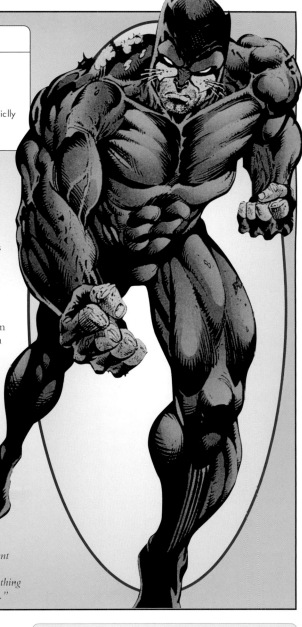

SPARRING PARTNER Ted Grant teaches Holly Robinson, Catwoman's close friend, a thing or two about the "noble art."

WILDCAT II

FIRST APPEARANCE (Yolanda Montez) INFINITY INC. #12 (Mar. 1985); (Wildcat II) CRISIS ON INFINITE EARTHS #6 (Sept. 1985)
STATUS Hero (deceased) REAL NAME Yolanda Montez
OCCUPATION Journalist for Rock Stars magazine BASE Los Angeles
HEIGHT 5ft 8in WEIGHT 143 lbs EYES Brown HAIR Reddish brown
SPECIAL POWERS/ABILITIES A ferocious fighter with cat-like reflexes and retractable claws, enhanced speed, and superhuman agility.

The original Wildcat (see WILDCAT I), Yolanda Montez's godfather, suffered crippling injuries during the Crisis. Yolanda decided to honor her godfather by using her cat-like abilities to carry on in the battling boxer's stead. As Wildcat II, Yolanda joined INFINITY INC. and learned that her powers resulted from experiments conducted by Dr. Benjamin Love upon pregnant mothers, including Yolanda's own (see HELIX). Wildcat II remained semi-active after the Infinitors disbanded, and later joined a squad of super heroes fighting to liberate Parador, from ECLIPSO. Sadly, she was killed by the villain. SB

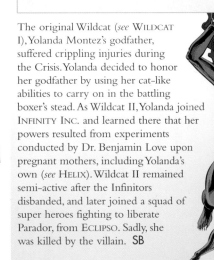

WILD DOG

FIRST APPEARANCE WILD DOG #1 (September 1987)
STATUS Hero **REAL NAME** Jack Wheeler
OCCUPATION Ex-soldier; mechanic; vigilante **BASE** Quad Cities, Iowa
HEIGHT 6ft **WEIGHT** 175 lbs **EYES** Blue **HAIR** Blond
SPECIAL POWERS/ABILITIES An exceptional soldier, excellent with firearms. As Wild Dog, his gloves emit an electric shock, similar to a taser.

Star athlete Jack Wheeler went to college on a football scholarship. After an injury forced him off the team, he dropped out, unable to afford tuition. He opted instead for a tour of duty with the U.S. Marines, which ended in tragedy when most of his comrades were killed by a terrorist bomb. Disheartened, Wheeler left the army and returned to Quad Cities, Iowa taking night classes at State University. He also fell in love with Claire Smith—only to see her struck down by a gunman. The police investigation revealed that her last name was really Carmonti and that she was the daughter of a recently killed Chicago mob boss. She was not a random victim, but a target. Something inside Wheeler snapped. Donning a hockey mask, khakis, and a State U. T-shirt, he became the crime fighter Wild Dog. He was soon a local hero, even though wanted by the police for his ruthless vigilantism. Wheeler spends his days as an auto mechanic and his nights as a protector of the innocent. **RG**

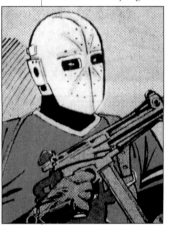

WILDEBEEST

FIRST APPEARANCE (Wildebeest Society) THE NEW TEEN TITANS (2nd series) #36 (October 1987); (Baby Wildebeest) NEW TITANS #84 (February 1982) **STATUS** Hero **REAL NAME** None **OCCUPATION** Hero **BASE** Science City, Russia **HEIGHT** Up to 12ft **WEIGHT** Up to 635 lbs **EYES** Yellow **HAIR** Auburn **SPECIAL POWERS/ABILITIES** Can transform into a giant, superstrong powerhouse; has the mind of an infant and the temper to match.

The Wildebeest Society started as a criminal organization designed to make obscene amounts of money by posing as a single super-criminal called "Wildebeest," whose random appearances and varying styles of operation baffled investigators.
JERICHO, mute member of the TEEN TITANS, became the leader of the Wildebeest Society when a demonic force held him in its thrall. He turned the society's resources toward the creation of human/animal hybrid bodies to serve as new hosts for the evil energy. When the new Wildebeest kidnapped the Titans, DEATHSTROKE the Terminator had no choice but to kill Jericho, his own son.
One Wildebeest survived the destruction of the Society. Nicknamed Baby Wildebeest, this genetically engineered behemoth lives with RED STAR and PANTHA, its surrogate parents, in Russia. **DW**

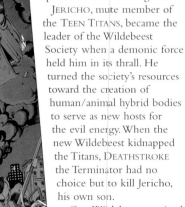

WILDFIRE

FIRST APPEARANCE LEGIONNAIRES #76 (October 1999)
STATUS Hero **REAL NAME** (Atom'x) Leroy Drake; (Blast-Off) Randall Burroughs; (Wildfire amalgam) Drake Burroughs **OCCUPATION** Legionnaire **BASE** Legion World, U.P. Space **HEIGHT** 6ft 2in
WEIGHT Variable **EYES** None **HAIR** None **SPECIAL POWERS/ABILITIES** Projects blasts of energy and absorbs energy; can fly at superspeed.

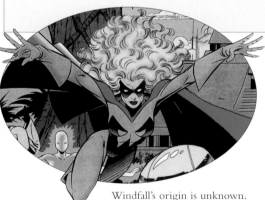

After the evil Mordru, the DARK LORD destroyed the bodies of the energy-powered heroes Atom'x and Blast-Off, the souls of the young heroes were contained in a special containment suit created by Professor Vultan. Dubbed "Drake Burroughs," the energy creature quickly became an ally of the LEGION OF SUPER-HEROES under the codename Erg-1. As Erg-1, Burroughs helped the Legionnaires battle the parasitic BLIGHT as they took over the universe of the 31st century. Soon after, Erg–1 was transported across the galaxy through a tear in the fabric of space and his containment suit was destroyed. Erg-1 then found the Kwai, a nomadic race of space trackers, who led his disembodied energies back to the Legion. Reincorporated in one of Professor Vultan's special suits, Burroughs took the name Wildfire and rejoined the Legion as one of its most powerful members. **PJ**

WINDFALL

FIRST APPEARANCE BATMAN AND THE OUTSIDERS #9 (April 1985)
STATUS Hero **REAL NAME** Wendy Jones
OCCUPATION Adventurer **BASE** Los Angeles
HEIGHT 5ft **WEIGHT** 105 lbs **EYES** Blue **HAIR** Blonde
SPECIAL POWERS/ABILITIES Can generate and control winds, from gentle breezes to gale force, tornado-level windstorms.

Windfall's origin is unknown. Sister to water-wielding villainess Becky Jones, (New-Wave), Wendy Jones fought for justice with the OUTSIDERS, befriending HALO. Windfall was captured and cloned by New-Wave, her diabolical double infiltrating the Outsiders. The Windfall clone was discovered by BATMAN and died in battle. The real Windfall went back to the Outsiders, but left when Violet, Halo's evil double, convinced her to join Strikeforce KOBRA. Realizing her mistake, Windfall rejoined the Outsiders until it disbanded. She was romantically linked to teammate Gardner Grayle, (the Atomic Knight). Windfall was last seen defending the rogue nation of Zandia from YOUNG JUSTICE, perhaps duped into siding with the wrong team yet again. **SB**

WING

FIRST APPEARANCE DETECTIVE COMICS #20 (November 1938)
STATUS Hero (deceased) **REAL NAME** Wing How
OCCUPATION Adventurer **BASE** England
HEIGHT 5ft 6in **WEIGHT** 140 lbs **EYES** Brown **HAIR** Black
SPECIAL POWERS/ABILITIES Possesses a bright mind and a deep knowledge of Chinese martial arts.

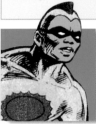

A Chinese immigrant named Wing How, came to the U.S. and learned to drive, ultimately becoming the trusted chauffeur of newspaper publisher Lee Travis. In 1938, when Travis chose the crime-fighting costume of the CRIMSON AVENGER I, Wing stayed in his driver's uniform, but came to his employer's aide when needed. A deep friendship formed between the two men, as they shared a common sense of justice. Wing subsequently adopted a distinctive costume to disguise his identity. When World War II broke out, they joined the ALL-STAR SQUADRON. Wing also became the unofficial eighth member of the SEVEN SOLDIERS OF VICTORY. When the SSV was betrayed by one of their own members, the Spider, and attacked by the NEBULA MAN, Wing sacrificed his life to destroy the entity. His sacrifice has been remembered by heroes from the Golden Age and Modern Age, inspiring all who followed in his path. **RG**

WITCHFIRE

FIRST APPEARANCE JLA #61 (February 2002)
STATUS Hero **REAL NAME** Rebecca Carstairs
OCCUPATION Super hero **BASE** San Francisco
HEIGHT 5ft 8in **WEIGHT** 128 lbs **EYES** White **HAIR** Red
SPECIAL POWERS/ABILITIES Skilled daredevil who possesses spell-based occult powers.

Witchfire remembers a childhood spent in an orphanage, where a book of spells exposed young Rebecca Carstairs to the wickedly fun world of magic. As an adult she assumed the stage name Witchfire and set out to conquer the entertainment world, winning fame as a singer, actress, model, and motorcycle daredevil.
At a concert in Boston, Witchfire cast a careless spell and unwittingly released a demon. WONDER WOMAN helped her capture the beast, and Witchfire committed herself to refining her supernatural abilities. She eventually joined the San Francisco-based super-hero firm The POWER COMPANY as a partner, though some members (notably SKYROCKET) considered her little more than a publicity seeker.
After her first year with the Power Company, Witchfire discovered a disturbing truth—she was a homunculus, a magically-created artificial being and not the true Rebecca Carstairs. How she will deal with this revelation remains to be seen. She hopes to win new clients for the Power Company. **DW**

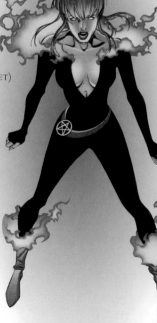

WIZARD

FIRST APPEARANCE ALL-STAR COMICS #34 (April 1947)
STATUS Villain **REAL NAME** William Asmodeus Zard
OCCUPATION Professional criminal **BASE** Mobile
HEIGHT 6ft **WEIGHT** 182 lbs **EYES** Blue **HAIR** Black
SPECIAL POWERS/ABILITIES A sorcerer who can cast illusions, hypnotize others, and project his psyche on the astral plane.

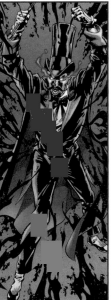

A career criminal from a young age, William Zard was in and out of prison during the 1930s. Deciding to refashion his criminal career, he left the U. S. and traveled to a Tibetan monastery. There he studied with a Master Lama and learned hypnotism and astral projection. He then used his newfound skills to kill the monk who had been training him!

Zard then became the Wizard, returning to the U.S. at the end of World War II. He assembled the INJUSTICE SOCIETY, a villainous counterpart to the JUSTICE SOCIETY OF AMERICA, whose heroes he was determined to defeat and discredit.

The Wizard has continued to clash with the JSA. He gained greater powers recuperating in a magical fairyland, but was then absorbed into RAGMAN's cloak. However he freed himself to attack the JSA again. **PJ**

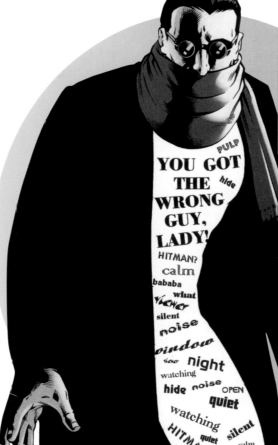

WORD II, THE

FIRST APPEARANCE DCU VILLAINS SECRET FILES #1 (April 1999)
STATUS Villain **REAL NAME** Unknown
OCCUPATION Assassin **BASE** Mobile
HEIGHT 5ft 9in **WEIGHT** 175 lbs **EYES** Unknown **HAIR** Black
SPECIAL POWERS/ABILITIES The Word II may be a mutant with the ability to assimilate any written word onto his body.

The first Word is a cosmic entity created at the dawn of the universe by the Voice. In recent times, the Word destroyed the Parliament of Trees and Lady Jane, an elemental, as well as the Parliaments of Stones, Waves and Vapors—elemental nature spirits—in an attempt to stop SWAMP THING from becoming all-powerful. The Word was eventually defeated by Swamp Thing and his daughter, Tefe.

The Word II (pictured left) is a mortal costumed criminal. What this man truly is or does, however, remains a mystery. He seems to have no mouth and uses the written word to communicate. A mercenary for hire, his specialty is gathering intelligence, and he has been employed by the likes of VANDAL SAVAGE. **RG**

WONDER GIRL

FIRST APPEARANCE WONDER WOMAN (2nd series) #105 (February 1996)
STATUS Hero **REAL NAME** Cassandra "Cassie" Sandsmark
OCCUPATION Member of Teen Titans **BASE** San Francisco
HEIGHT 5 ft 3in **WEIGHT** 124 lbs **EYES** Blue **HAIR** Blonde
SPECIAL POWERS/ABILITIES Flight, superstrength, and enhanced speed bestowed upon her by Zeus; carries magical lasso; some invulnerability; trained in combat by the Amazons. Wonder Girl is still young and her powers may deepen with time.

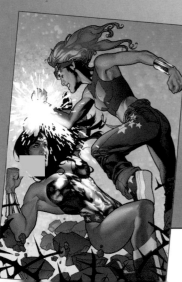

YOUNG JUSTICE *Cassie is happiest around heroes her own age, and currently serves with the Teen Titans.*

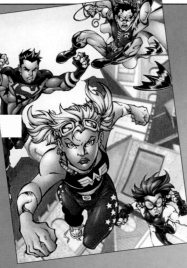

Prominent archaeologist Helena Sandsmark always reprimanded her daughter for her lack of responsibility, but Cassie seized the mantle of a hero when WONDER WOMAN came to her hometown of Gateway City. Temporarily "borrowing" Wonder Woman's Sandals of Hermes and Gauntlet of Atlas, Cassie received prodigious strength and the ability to fly—superpowers she used to help smash a clone of DOOMSDAY. She later helped Wonder Woman defeat a manifestation of entropy called Decay, donning goggles and a black wig to disguise herself in her new role as the second Wonder Girl, bearing a name once used by Donna Troy (see TROIA).

Summoned to Olympus, Cassie brashly asked Zeus for her own powers. He granted her wish and Wonder Girl became Gateway City's teen hero. She honed her fighting skills through training sessions with ARTEMIS. Cassie joined the heroes of YOUNG JUSTICE alongside ROBIN, SUPERBOY, EMPRESS, ARROWETTE, Impulse (see KID FLASH), the SECRET, and LOBO, and served as team spokesperson.

Wonder Girl struggled to maintain her secret identity. Her charade came to an end when SILVER SWAN II attacked Gateway City High School, exposing Cassie's secret.

Since then Wonder Girl has joined the newest team of TEEN TITANS, and hinted at a romance with SUPERBOY. She wields a golden lasso given to her by ARES, though the motives behind the war god's gift remain a mystery. **DW**

GIRL POWER *Cassie has a warrior's spirit and can even stand up to Wonder Woman in battle.*

WONDER WOMAN

THE AMAZING AMAZON

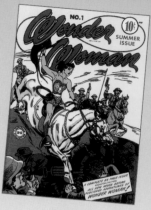

FIRST APPEARANCE ALL-STAR COMICS #8 (Winter 1941)
STATUS Hero **REAL NAME** Diana
OCCUPATION Ambassador of peace; adventurer
BASE New York City; Themyscira
HEIGHT 6ft **WEIGHT** 165 lbs **EYES** Blue **HAIR** Black
SPECIAL POWERS/ABILITIES Blessed with the gifts of the Olympian Gods, Wonder Woman is one of the strongest beings on the planet; she can fly at sublight speed; while not invulnerable, she is highly resistant to bodily harm; she can psychically communicate with animals; she is an expert at all forms of classical armed and unarmed combat; a master of the sword, ax, and bow and arrow; a skilled tactician and diplomat; her arsenal includes a magic lasso that forces anyone within its confines to tell the absolute truth; her bracelets can deflect bullets.

WISE AS ATHENA, stronger than Heracles, swift as Hermes and beautiful as Aphrodite, Wonder Woman is Princess Diana, champion of Themyscira, the home of the immortal AMAZONS. Sculpted from clay by her mother, Queen HIPPOLYTA, and brought to life by the OLYMPIAN GODS, Diana secretly entered a contest to find the worthiest Amazon and emerged as the victor. Given the task of ending the war god Ares's scheme to destroy the planet, Diana stepped forth from her idyllic existence into the chaotic world of Man as one of Earth's greatest defenders, Wonder Woman, the Amazing Amazon!

REBIRTH The Amazon warrior emerges from seclusion on Paradise Island to thwart Nazi tyranny.

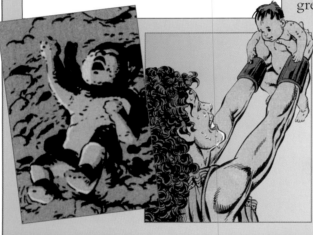

SCULPTED FROM CLAY

The reincarnated soul of a woman who had died 30,000 years ago, Hippolyta longed for the child she had carried centuries before. An oracle told her to sculpt a baby from clay; the gods themselves then gave the child life. The only child ever born on Themyscira, the infant was named Diana, after aviator Diana Trevor, who once crashed on Themyscira and died a hero defending the island. Princess Diana was raised by a nation of 3,000 teachers and sisters, always under the watchful eye of her overprotective mother.

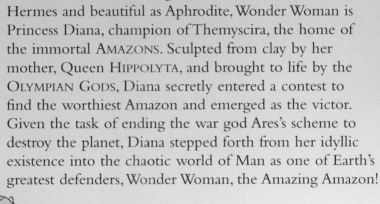

THE AMAZONS AND THEIR ISLAND

Created 3,000 years ago by five goddesses of Olympus, the Amazons are a race of warrior women charged with the responsibility of promoting the peaceful ways of Gaea, the earth spirit. After Heracles and his men ransacked the Amazons' home of Themyscira, the Amazons, by decree of the goddesses, were led to a remote island paradise, where they were granted immortality and the task of guarding Doom's Doorway, the portal to Pandora's Box, behind which a host of monsters were imprisoned.

Rebuilding their great city-state of Themyscira, the Amazons lived in idyllic solitude for millennia, until a pilot from beyond their shores named Diana Trevor arrived on Paradise Island, changing their fate forever.

DIANA TREVOR A pilot for the Women's Auxiliary Ferrying Squadron, Diana Rockwell Trevor pierced the mystic barrier between our world and Themyscira. Crash-landing on the island, the startled pilot used her weapons to force Cottus, a creature that had escaped from Doom's Doorway, back to the underworld. Diana gave her life to save the Amazon nation.

THE CONTEST

The goddesses ordered the Amazons to send for their greatest warrior to thwart ARES's mad schemes. Forbidden by Hippolyta to enter the Contest, Diana disguised herself and became Themyscira's champion. Garbed in a uniform decorated with symbols honoring Diana Trevor, Diana was rewarded with a magic lasso and silver bracelets. Soon after, Steve Trevor, Diana Trevor's son and an unwitting pawn of Ares, crash-landed on Themyscira. Diana was charged with taking him back to Patriarch's World, the mortal world of humankind, as part of her sacred mission.

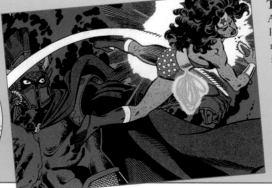

THE MADNESS OF ARES

After battling Ares' monstrous sons upon her arrival in Patriarch's World, Diana, Steve, and several allies were mystically transported to a commandeered military base in Colorado where Wonder Woman stopped Ares from launching his nuclear arsenal and ended his insane threat. Diana then embarked on a worldwide tour promoting peace and Amazon ideals. Living with Julia and Vanessa Kapatelis in their Boston brownstone, Wonder Woman garnered a formidable Rogues Gallery which included the CHEETAH II, SILVER SWAN, DOCTOR PSYCHO, and the sorceress CIRCE, who most resented Diana's pleas for peace and harmony.

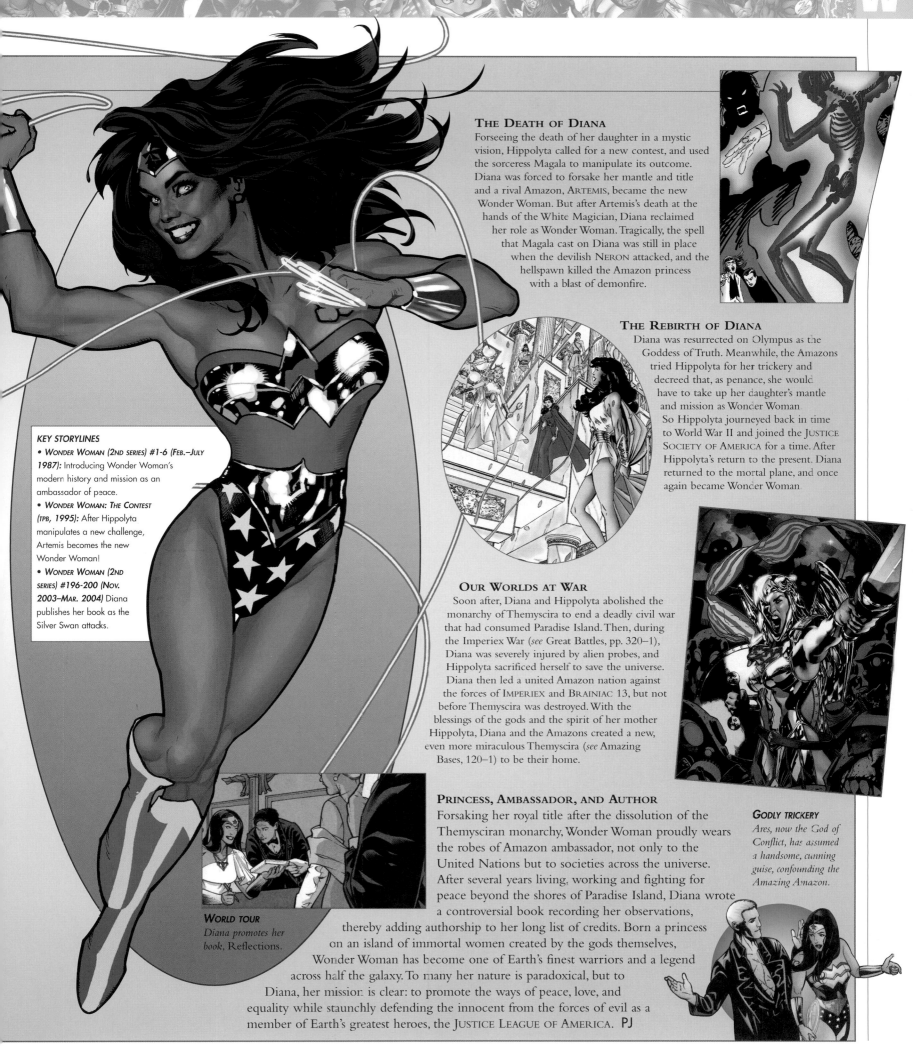

THE DEATH OF DIANA

Forseeing the death of her daughter in a mystic vision, Hippolyta called for a new contest, and used the sorceress Magala to manipulate its outcome. Diana was forced to forsake her mantle and title and a rival Amazon, ARTEMIS, became the new Wonder Woman. But after Artemis's death at the hands of the White Magician, Diana reclaimed her role as Wonder Woman. Tragically, the spell that Magala cast on Diana was still in place when the devilish NERON attacked, and the hellspawn killed the Amazon princess with a blast of demonfire.

THE REBIRTH OF DIANA

Diana was resurrected on Olympus as the Goddess of Truth. Meanwhile, the Amazons tried Hippolyta for her trickery and decreed that, as penance, she would have to take up her daughter's mantle and mission as Wonder Woman. So Hippolyta journeyed back in time to World War II and joined the JUSTICE SOCIETY OF AMERICA for a time. After Hippolyta's return to the present, Diana returned to the mortal plane, and once again became Wonder Woman.

KEY STORYLINES

- *WONDER WOMAN (2ND SERIES) #1-6 (FEB.–JULY 1987):* Introducing Wonder Woman's modern history and mission as an ambassador of peace.
- *WONDER WOMAN: THE CONTEST (TPB, 1995):* After Hippolyta manipulates a new challenge, Artemis becomes the new Wonder Woman!
- *WONDER WOMAN (2ND SERIES) #196-200 (NOV. 2003–MAR. 2004)* Diana publishes her book as the Silver Swan attacks.

OUR WORLDS AT WAR

Soon after, Diana and Hippolyta abolished the monarchy of Themyscira to end a deadly civil war that had consumed Paradise Island. Then, during the Imperiex War (*see* Great Battles, pp. 320–1), Diana was severely injured by alien probes, and Hippolyta sacrificed herself to save the universe. Diana then led a united Amazon nation against the forces of IMPERIEX and BRAINIAC 13, but not before Themyscira was destroyed. With the blessings of the gods and the spirit of her mother Hippolyta, Diana and the Amazons created a new, even more miraculous Themyscira (*see* Amazing Bases, 120–1) to be their home.

PRINCESS, AMBASSADOR, AND AUTHOR

Forsaking her royal title after the dissolution of the Themysciran monarchy, Wonder Woman proudly wears the robes of Amazon ambassador, not only to the United Nations but to societies across the universe. After several years living, working and fighting for peace beyond the shores of Paradise Island, Diana wrote a controversial book recording her observations, thereby adding authorship to her long list of credits. Born a princess on an island of immortal women created by the gods themselves, Wonder Woman has become one of Earth's finest warriors and a legend across half the galaxy. To many her nature is paradoxical, but to Diana, her mission is clear: to promote the ways of peace, love, and equality while staunchly defending the innocent from the forces of evil as a member of Earth's greatest heroes, the JUSTICE LEAGUE OF AMERICA. PJ

WORLD TOUR
Diana promotes her book, Reflections.

GODLY TRICKERY
Ares, now the God of Conflict, has assumed a handsome, cunning guise, confounding the Amazing Amazon.

XER0

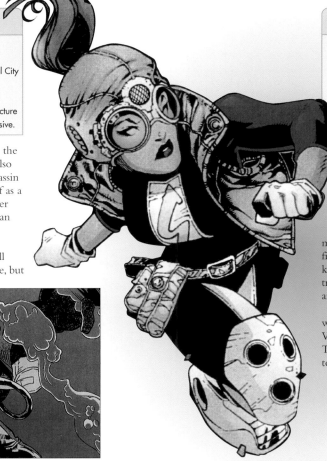

FIRST APPEARANCE XER0 #1 (May 1997)
STATUS Hero **REAL NAME** Coltrane "Trane" Walker
OCCUPATION Closer; professional basketball player **BASE** National City
HEIGHT 6ft 7in **WEIGHT** 218 lbs **EYES** Brown (blue as Xer0)
HAIR Black (blonde as Xer0)
SPECIAL POWERS/ABILITIES Can speed up any object's molecular structure
to walk on water or through walls; Deadeye laser; Deadlok adhesive.

African-American athlete Trane Walker was famous as the
power forward for the National City Vipers. He was also
Coltrane Walker, a clandestine government agency assassin
who preserved his secret identity by disguising himself as a
blond and blue-eyed Caucasian covert operative. Walker
died on his very first mission, but was resurrected via an
experimental X-enzyme that restored him to physical
health, but also left him emotionally empty. Thus, he
became both the perfect killer and the perfect basketball
player, blunt and remorseless in getting either job done, but
especially as the "closer"
Xer0. Unfortunately, Walker
perished again during a test
set up by his superior,
Frank Decker, to measure
Xer0's abilities. Walker's
second resurrection left
him brain damaged.
Whether or not Walker was
left to die in peace, or if his
agency will seek some way
to return him to his role
as Xer0, remains to
be seen. SB

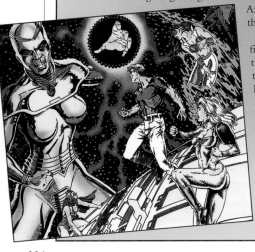

XS

FIRST APPEARANCE LEGIONNAIRES #0 (October 1994)
STATUS Hero **REAL NAME** Jenni Ognats
OCCUPATION Legionnaire **BASE** Earth
HEIGHT 5ft 6in **WEIGHT** 135 lbs **EYES** Amber **HAIR** Brown
SPECIAL POWERS/ABILITIES Can run at supersonic speed while
projecting a protective aura around her body.

Dawn Allen, daughter of the FLASH II (Barry
Allen), and Jeven Ognats married and had a child,
Jenni, on the planet Aarok. As a teenager, Jenni
found that she could tap into the Speed Force (see
FLASH). When she had fully mastered her hereditary
speed powers, Jenni was invited to join the LEGION OF
SUPER-HEROES at the dawn of the 31st century. On a
mission back in time, at the end of the 20th century, Jenni
first encountered SUPERBOY and her cousin Bart, then
known as Impulse (see KID FLASH). For a time, she was
trapped in the 20th century and worked alongside her
ancestors as they battled the villainous SAVITAR.

Jenni was then thrust into the 100th Century for a
while, before being shunted to the *end* of time known as
Vanishing Point. Thanks to the intervention of the Time
Trapper, who lives there, Jenni finally managed to return
to her proper time period. RG

EMPOWERED *Like all Legionnaires, Xs
is able to fly at great speed, thanks to
her Legion Flight Ring.*

YOUNG ALL-STARS

FIRST APPEARANCE YOUNG ALL-STARS #1 (June 1987)
STATUS Hero team (disbanded) **BASE** The Perisphere, New York City
MEMBERS AND POWERS
Dyna-Mite Can generate explosive blasts.
Flying Fox Shaman that can generate forcebolts, and cast spells;
flight with fur cape and cowl.
Fury Superstrength; can summon the spirit of the Fury Tisiphone.
Iron Munro Superstrength, invulnerability.
Neptune Perkins Amphibious; can swim at superspeed.
Tsunami Can generate tidal waves.

The Young-All Stars were a short-lived teenage division
of the ALL-STAR SQUADRON, the U.S.'s greatest
assemblage of World War II heroes. The Young All-Stars
were created by President F. D. Roosevelt in April,
1942, after the young heroes helped the All-Star
Squadron defeat the Nazi superteam AXIS AMERIKA.

Initially assigned to fund-raising events and
morale boosters like celebrity baseball
games, the Young All-Stars began their
crime-fighting careers battling
villains such as the despotic
Per Degaton, Deathbolt, and
the ULTRA-HUMANITE when
the villains infiltrated the
government's mysterious
Project M organization. The
Young All-Stars also thwarted a gang of Nazi occultists, who had invaded an alien colony
in Antarctica hoping to steal its secrets, and stopped the robotic MEKANIQUE's plot to take
over the future. The team's most frequent enemies, however were the wartime version of
Axis Amerika. Fighting alongside the Allies or by themselves, the Young All-Stars battled
Axis Amerika, led by UBERMENSCH, no less than
three times within weeks of their inception.

When team member Iron Munro set out to
find his missing father, Hugo Danner, he learned
that Danner had used a special serum to create
the Sons of the Dawn, a group of mutated
human experiments. After Munro defeated Danner
and the Sons in June of 1942, LIBERTY BELLE put
an end to the probationary mascot status of the
Young All-Stars and made them full-fledged
members of the All-Star Squadron. PJ

WAR-TIME TEENS *The Young All-Stars did more
than sell war bonds; they fought Nazi
supercriminals and stopped the robot
Mekanique from destroying the future by
changing the past!*

TREND SETTERS *The first superpowered teen team, the
Young All-Stars eventually became fully Squadron
members. They were:* **1)** *Dan the Dyna-Mite* **2)** *Fury I*
3) *Iron Munro* **4)** *Tsunami* **5)** *Neptune Perkins*
6) *Flying Fox* **7)** *Tigress.*

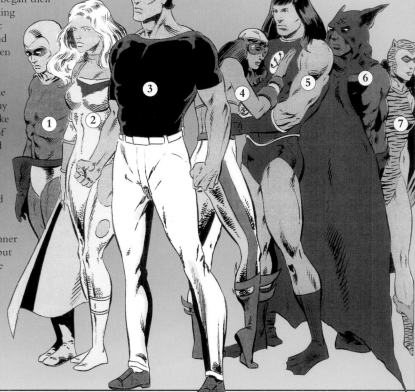
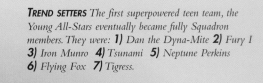

YOUNG HEROES IN LOVE

FIRST APPEARANCE YOUNG HEROES IN LOVE #1 (June 1997)
STATUS Heroes (sexually active)   BASE A very cool warehouse loft
MEMBERS AND POWERS
Bonfire (Annie Fletcher) Pyrokinetic with control over fire; Frostbite
(real name unrevealed) Generates extreme cold; Hard Drive
(Jeremy Horton) Possesses telepathy and telekinesis; Junior
(Benjamin Newton) Brilliant scientist only four inches tall;
Monstergirl (Rita Lopez) Transforms into a monster; Off-Ramp
(George Sloan) Teleporter Thunderhead (Scott Tucker)
Superstrength; limited invulnerability; Zip Kid (Stacey Taglia) Flies;
shrinks; fires pink energy bolts.

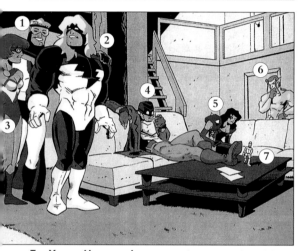

THE YOUNG HEROES IN LOVE Raging hormones and wistful
longings are just par for the course for this super-team:
1) Hard Drive 2) Thunderhead 3) Zip Kid 4) Off-Ramp
5) Monstergirl 6) Frostbite 7) Junior.

The Young Heroes are just that, young and relatively
inexperienced super heroes brought together by the
telepathic Jeremy Horton (Hard-Drive) and his lover Rita
Lopez (Monstergirl) to form their own titanic team.
However, most of the Young Heroes did not know until
much later that Hard Drive had secretly used his powers
to coerce each member into joining to achieve his own
self-aggrandizing ends. He was summarily booted out by
his teammates when they learned the truth.

When not struggling with internal strife from several
intersecting love triangles, the Young Heroes distinguished
themselves in battle with such monsters as Totenjager the
Relentless, the Beast Grundomu, and KALIBAK the Cruel.
When last seen, the Young Heroes were attending the
inaugural ball of Jeremy Horton, who had used his powers
to influence and win the Connecticut gubernatorial
election. The Young Heroes are presumably still active,
though it is just as likely that those thorny romantic
entanglements may have finally torn the team asunder. SB

YOUNG JUSTICE

FIRST APPEARANCE YOUNG JUSTICE: THE SECRET (April 1998)
STATUS Hero team   BASE The Secret Sanctuary
ORIGINAL MEMBERS AND POWERS
Superboy Superstrength, flight, tactile telekinesis
Robin III (Tim Drake) Athlete, Boy Wonder
Impulse Superspeedster.
Empress Amazing athlete.
Wonder Girl Flight, superstrength, bravado
The Secret Ephemeral wraith.

SUPERBOY, ROBIN III and IMPULSE helped rescue a
mysterious girl called the SECRET from custody by
the U.S. government-backed D.E.O. The teens
united as Young Justice and begin operating
out of the JUSTICE LEAGUE OF AMERICA's
abandoned Secret Sanctuary. The boys
were soon joined by ARROWETTE,
WONDER GIRL and the Secret. The
team was given the stamp of approval by
the JLA, and RED TORNADO became Young
Justice's mentor.

KLARION THE WITCH BOY cast a spell that
transformed the adult heroes into children while
having the reverse effect on the members of
Young Justice. The process was ultimately
reversed for all but LOBO, who took on the
name Slobo. Young Justice journeyed to
Australia where they fought a team of villains
representing the rogue state
Zandia. The mysterious EMPRESS
joined the team after Young
Justice learned that she was
Anita, daughter of government
ally Donald Fite. After a devastating
mission to Apokolips, Snapper Carr (see
CARR, SNAPPER) came aboard as a senior
member, succeeding Red Tornado as team mentor.
The RAY II also joined Young Justice at that time.

After Baron Agua Sin Gaaz murdered Empress'
father, Young Justice led a squad of heroes in an
attack on his Zandian fortress. Corrupted by
DARKSEID, the Secret then went on a rampage
until Robin managed to break through to her.
Darkseid punished the young warder by
restoring her humanity. He also banished
Slobo to the 853rd Century, condemning him
to an eternity as a statue. A mysterious blue
cyborg-girl named INDIGO did serious damage to
the Titans and Young Justice and unleashed a
defective Superman Robot which killed Teen
Titan Lilith and TROIA. In a state of shock,
both teams disbanded. RG

TRAGIC CONCLUSION In their final
mission, the team was devastated
when they were manhandled by
Indigo and a Superman robot and
were unable to save Troia's life.

YOUNG
WARRIORS
Regardless of
threat, Young
Justice enters
every fray with
gusto and more
than a little
recklessness.

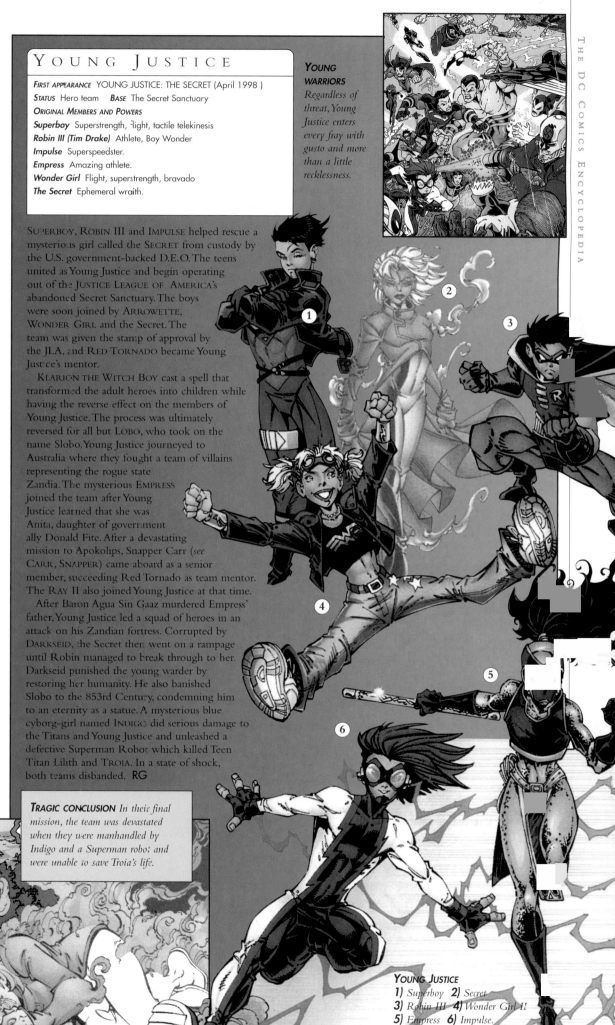

YOUNG JUSTICE
1) Superboy 2) Secret
3) Robin III 4) Wonder Girl II
5) Empress 6) Impulse.

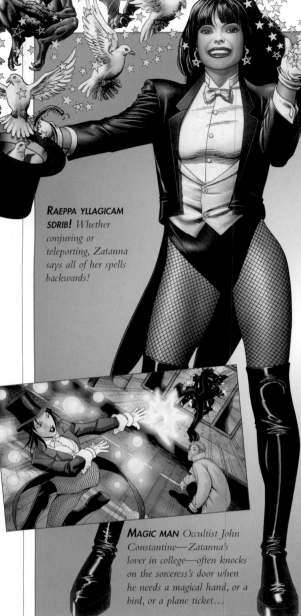

RAEPPA YLLAGICAM SDRIB! Whether conjuring or teleporting, Zatanna says all of her spells backwards!

MAGIC MAN Occultist John Constantine—Zatanna's lover in college—often knocks on the sorceress's door when he needs a magical hand, or a bird, or a plane ticket…

ZATANNA

FIRST APPEARANCE HAWKMAN (1st series) #4 (November 1964)
STATUS Hero **REAL NAME** Zatanna Zatara
OCCUPATION Stage magician; adventurer
BASE San Francisco
HEIGHT 5ft 7in **WEIGHT** 137 lbs **EYES** Blue **HAIR** Black
SPECIAL POWERS/ABILITIES Genetically imbued with the ability to manipulate magic; sorcery includes elemental manipulation, transmutation, and teleportation; she says her spells backwards as an aid to concentration.

Zatanna is the daughter of Golden Age adventurer John ZATARA and his wife Sindella, a member of the mystic tribe of sorcerers called the Hidden Ones, or *Homo magi*. Zatanna inherited her mother's ability to manipulate magic and her father's penchant for heroism. When Sindella faked her own death and returned to the Hidden Ones' sanctum in Turkey, she left her daughter to John Zatara's care.

Zatara traveled the world with his daughter and taught her how to harness her magical abilities. Zatanna was later raised by strangers, however, when a curse by the evil witch Allura prevented Zatanna from seeing her father, leaving the young girl in a constant, fruitless search for her natural parents.

Zatanna discovered her father's diary and created a stage persona for herself. The young magician's quest to find her father led her into a brief affair with the occultist John Constantine (see Great Team-Ups, pp. 232–233). Later, with the help of the JUSTICE LEAGUE OF AMERICA, Zatanna was able to lift Allura's curse and reunite with her father and, soon after, her mother. Tragically, Sindella died rescuing her daughter from the city of Homo Magi.

As a long-standing member of the JLA, Zatanna fought countless super-villains and mystical threats. However, after the death of her father, Zatanna retired from active adventuring. She now lives in San Francisco, seeking some semblance of a normal life, while acting as a constant peacemaker between the light and dark forces of Earth's mystic community. **PJ**

ZATARA

FIRST APPEARANCE ACTION COMICS #1 (June 1938)
STATUS Hero **REAL NAME** Giovanni "John" Zatara
OCCUPATION Stage magician; adventurer **BASE** Washington, D.C.
HEIGHT 5ft 11in **WEIGHT** 170 lbs **EYES** Blue **HAIR** Gray
SPECIAL POWERS/ABILITIES Limitless magic enabled by speaking his spells backward; merely an average fighter, who preferred sleight-of-hand over hand-to-hand combat.

John Zatara was a stage magician at age nineteen. However, when he read the lost journals of Leonardo Da Vinci, his reputed ancestor, he discovered the true secrets of sorcery. By uttering his spells backwards, he could perform *real* magic! As his fame grew, Zatara also became a crime fighter, serving with the ALL-STAR SQUADRON during World War II.

While traveling in Turkey, Zatara met and married the enigmatic Sindella. Sindella gave birth to Zatara's daughter, Zatanna, and seemingly died not long after. While raising Zatanna alone, Zatara battled Allura, an evil elemental who cursed father and daughter with a spell prohibiting either from seeing the other lest both be struck dead. It took Zatara years to lift the curse and be reunited with his daughter.

Zatara retired from the stage and super heroics, but answered the call to action when a primordial shadow creature from Earth's prehistory threatened to tear both

Heaven and Earth asunder. Alongside warlock John Constantine, Zatanna, and a circle of several other sorcerers, Zatara engaged in a séance to help the SWAMP THING battle the creature. When the creature attempted to destroy Zatanna, Zatara cast a spell to save her from its staggering power. He died in Zatanna's place, the ancient darkness causing the master magician to spontaneously combust, incinerating him before the eyes of all in attendance. **SB**

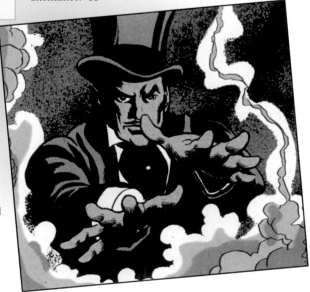

ZAURIEL

FIRST APPEARANCE JLA #6 (June 1997)
STATUS Hero **REAL NAME** Zauriel
OCCUPATION Adventurer **BASE** The Aerie, high above Los Angeles
HEIGHT 6ft 1in **WEIGHT** 180 lbs **EYES** Purple and red **HAIR** Silver
SPECIAL POWERS/ABILITIES Now a mortal, Zauriel retains his wings, granting him flight, but his angelic abilities, such as a sonic cry, have been reduced or removed. He can still speak to animals.

A Guardian-Angel of Heaven's Eagle-Host, Zauriel left heaven pursued by forces loyal to renegade King-Angel ASMODEL. Falling to Earth, Zauriel found kindred spirits in the JUSTICE LEAGUE OF AMERICA and Asmodel was routed. Zauriel kept his wings and remained on Earth. When MAGEDDON threatened all life, Zauriel sacrificed himself so others might live. His spirit pleaded humanity's cause in Heaven. As Mageddon neared Earth, Zauriel convinced the angels of the Pax Dei to fight for Heaven and Earth. Zauriel has renounced his immortality and lives among men. He has left the JLA, and protects others on his own, hoping to convince people of God's love for life. **RG**

ZUGGERNAUT

FIRST APPEARANCE FIRESTORM, THE NUCLEAR MAN #69 (March 1988)
STATUS Hero **REAL NAME** Matvei Rodor
OCCUPATION (Rodor) black marketeer; (Zuggernaut) inapplicable
BASE Moscow, Russian Federation
HEIGHT (Rodor) 5ft 9in; (Zuggernaut) 7ft **WEIGHT** (Rodor) 170 lbs; (Zuggernaut) 250 lbs **EYES** (Rodor) Blue; (Zuggernaut) Red
HAIR (Rodor) Brown; (Zuggernaut) None
SPECIAL POWERS/ABILITIES Superhuman strength; leaping ability; resistance to physical injury; generation of explosive energy from its mouth and a jewel in its forehead.

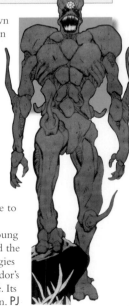

The extraterrestrial creature known as the Zuggernaut crash-landed on Earth in Russia, near the dacha of black marketer Matvei Rodor. Merging its monstrous alien body with Rodor's human desires, the Zuggernaut found its way to Moscow and tried to kill one of Rodor's enemies, a prosecutor named Soliony. The Zuggernaut was driven off by the American hero FIRESTORM and resumed its human shape as Rodor.

Later, after returning once more to kill Soliony, the Zuggernaut was thwarted by Firestorm and the young superteam, SOYUZ. Firestorm used the Zuggernaut's own explosive energies against it, mortally wounding Rodor's body and causing the alien to flee. Its current whereabouts are unknown. **PJ**

THE DC COMICS ENCYCLOPEDIA

ZOOM

PSYCHOTIC SPEEDSTER

FIRST APPEARANCE FLASH SECRET FILES #3 (November 2001)
STATUS Hero **REAL NAME** Hunter Zolomon
OCCUPATION Super-villain **BASE** Keystone City
HEIGHT 6ft 1in **WEIGHT** 181 lbs **EYES** Brown **HAIR** Brown
SPECIAL POWERS/ABILITIES Ability to travel at superspeed due a limited control of time. Zoom has essentially shifted himself to a "faster" timeline, allowing him to surpass even the feats of speed evidenced by the current Flash, Wally West.

HEIR TO THE SINISTER LEGACY of Professor Zoom the Reverse-Flash, Hunter Zolomon was one of FLASH III's closest friends before a series of tragedies ruined his life. Hunter came from a nightmarish family. His father was a serial killer, a fact that Hunter only learned when police gunned down his father for the murder of his mother. Zolomon joined the F.B.I. and found love with a fellow agent named Ashley, whom he later married. Once again, his world imploded when a shootout with a criminal called the Clown left him with a shattered kneecap and brought about the death of Ashley's father. She divorced him soon after and the F.B.I. eventually fired him.

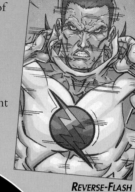

REVERSE-FLASH
Zolomon follows the bad example of Eobard Thawne, the original Prof. Zoom.

STRANGLEHOLD *In his psychosis, Zoom believes that he can make the Flash a better hero by forcing him to deal with tragedy.*

BAD LUCK AND TROUBLE

Desperate for even the pretense of stability, Zolomon wound up in Keystone City where he became a profiler of meta-human activities for the police department. He befriended the current Flash, Wally West, but his position with the K.C.P.D. made him a target for super-villains. An assault on Keystone by GORILLA GRODD left Zolomon with a broken back.

Now a paraplegic, Zolomon felt his only recourse was to beg the Flash to use the Cosmic Treadmill from the Flash Museum to travel back in time and prevent the calamities that had led to this point. Although sympathetic to his friend's plight, the Flash refused to alter time. Zolomon decided to do it himself. The resulting explosion of the Cosmic Treadmill shifted him onto a different frame of relative time, allowing him to move at superspeed by controlling time's passage. With new powers and threadbare sanity, Zolomon decided to teach the Flash a lesson about tragedy. He donned a costume similar to the one worn by the deceased REVERSE-FLASH and christened himself Zoom. Zoom attacked Wally West's family, causing Wally's wife Linda (see PARK, LINDA) to miscarry twins. Wally battled the mad monster at superspeed, ringing the globe before trapping Zoom in a repeating window of time, where he was forced to witness his disastrous shootout with the Clown again and again. In the aftermath, Wally wished that he could protect his family by having everyone forget his secret identity—a request granted by the SPECTRE. **DW**

TRAGIC EFFECTS *Zoom's vicious attack on Linda Park caused her to miscarry twin babies.*

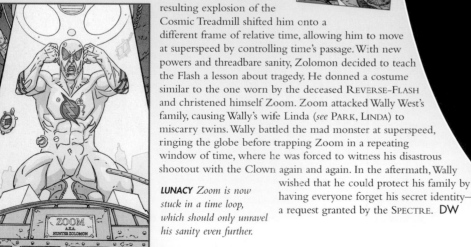

LUNACY *Zoom is now stuck in a time loop, which should only unravel his sanity even further.*

KEY STORYLINES

• *FLASH SECRET FILES #3 (NOVEMBER 2001):* Hunter Zolomon makes his first appearance in these pages, which barely hint at his villainous future.

• *THE FLASH: BLITZ (TPB, 2004):* This trade paperback, reprinting FLASH issues #192–200, is the definitive collection of the Zoom saga. By the time this series had finished its run, the status quo had been upended and Wally West had embarked on a new, controversial direction.

STRANGE TIMES AND PLACES

IN ELSEWORLDS, heroes and villains are taken from their usual, familiar settings and thrust into alternate worlds, divergent timelines, or parallel realities. Some are strange forgotten times that have existed or histories that might have been. Others are places that can't, couldn't, or *shouldn't* exist. Origins begin at divergent points and the outcomes of major crises may vary dramatically. And in all these imaginary stories made real, it all begins with the question, "What if…?"

WONDER WOMAN: AMAZONIA

In another reality, Diana is stolen away from paradise by Steve Trevor and the Royal Air Marines of the 19th-century British Empire. Forced to marry the vile Trevor, Diana becomes the star of a London show, reenacting tales of heroic women immortalized in the Bible. She shows herself to be a true heroine, freeing oppressed women all over the Empire, from the terrible reign of King Jack Planters, alias Jack the Ripper!

KINGDOM COME

This futuristic, apocalyptic tale begins in the Kansas wheat fields. A battle between the Justice Battalion and the villain PARASITE results in CAPTAIN ATOM's death and his nuclear energies lay waste to America's heartland. As a disillusioned SUPERMAN retreats into seclusion, a new generation of meta-humans—the uncontrollable sons and daughters of the world's greatest super heroes—inherits the Earth. Unfortunately, without Superman and his contemporaries to guide them, these super-menaces might well herald Armageddon. As witnessed by a holy man and his spiritual guide, the SPECTRE, Superman must embrace his role as leader and unite the divided super-heroes lest his adopted world be torn asunder. The fate of all mankind is in the balance.

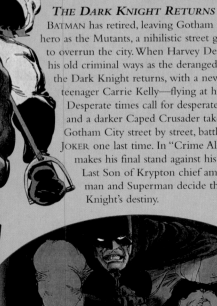

THE DARK KNIGHT RETURNS

BATMAN has retired, leaving Gotham in need of a hero as the Mutants, a nihilistic street gang, threaten to overrun the city. When Harvey Dent returns to his old criminal ways as the deranged TWO-FACE, the Dark Knight returns, with a new ROBIN—teenager Carrie Kelly—flying at his side. Desperate times call for desperate measures, and a darker Caped Crusader takes back Gotham City street by street, battling the JOKER one last time. In "Crime Alley," Batman makes his final stand against his enemies, the Last Son of Krypton chief among them, as man and Superman decide the Dark Knight's destiny.

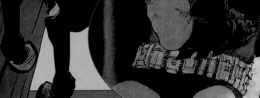

GRIEF-STRICKEN

On the devastated Kansas plains, Superman tends the graves of the victims of an accidental atomic holocaust.

LAST SON OF EARTH

Rocketed to distant Krypton from the dying planet Earth, baby Clark Kent is adopted by the scientist Jor-El and renamed Kal-El. Clad in a cumbersome exoskeleton to counter Krypton's oppressive gravity, Kal-El's discovery of a dead Green Lantern's power ring frees him to walk unfettered upon Kryptonian soil before journeying to the planet of his birth in search of his origins. There, amid the ragtag survivors of the blasted world, Clark meets the love of his life, Lois Lane (right, *see* LANE, LOIS), and his greatest foe, Lex Luthor (*see* LUTHOR, LEX)!

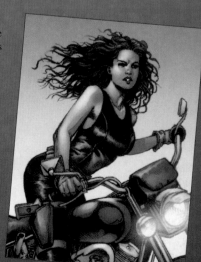

BLOODSTORM

In a Gotham City where vampires rule the underworld, Batman is a bloodsucking monster who hunts those like him! Sating his own bloodlust to cleanse Gotham, Batman finds his undead foes united by the Clown Prince of Crime. Batman's only ally is doomed were-CATWOMAN Selina Kyle. One-by-one, Batman slays his immortal foes and bathes Gotham in red rain until only one is left. In the end, the Dark Knight knows that the killing might begin anew if a single vampire remains. Commissioner Gordon (see GORDON, JAMES W.) and Alfred (see PENNYWORTH, ALFRED) have little choice but to drive a stake through the heart of Batman, bringing him the peace he has long sought.

SUPERMAN: RED SON

What if Kal-El of Krypton had landed on an agricultural collective in the Soviet Union rather than a farm in Kansas? Earth's greatest hero would fight for truth, justice, and the *Russian* way of a life as the Soviets' most powerful secret weapon! What follows is an arms race of unparalleled intensity as the U.S. commissions its greatest scientist, the brilliant Lex Luthor (see LUTHOR, LEX), to tilt the balance of power in America's favor. The world stands on the brink of annihilation as Superman assumes leadership of the Soviet Union, bidding to unite the planet under Communism.

THE BIG RED With a hammer and sickle emblazoned on his chest, Superman is a propaganda tool of the Stalinist regime. But the Man of Steel cares only for helping his fellow man, regardless of politics or nationality.

SECRET WEAPONS The U.S.'s elite troops are the Green Lantern Marine Corps, led by Hal Jordan.

JLA: THE NAIL

Imagine a world without the Man of Steel. On an Earth resembling the DC Universe in every way—with all its requisite heroes and villains save one—for want of a nail Superman was lost. When infant Kal-El's rocket plummeted to Earth, Jonathan and Martha Kent (see KENTS, THE) missed their fateful rendezvous with the Last Son of Krypton because of a flat tire… all for want of a nail. Instead, Kal-El was adopted by an Amish family and never ventured forth from his rural backwater to become a hero. That is, until an evil regime outlawed all meta-humans and tried to drive the planet's heroes into imprisonment or extinction. The plains of Kansas become the scene of the final battle between a power-mad Jimmy Olsen (see OLSEN, JIMMY) and what remains of the world's greatest super heroes.

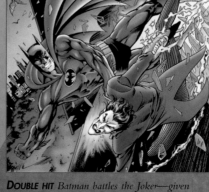

DOUBLE HIT Batman battles the Joker—given staggering power by Jimmy Olsen—and Olsen finally meets his match when Kal-El of Krypton saves humanity (right)!

AT EARTH'S END

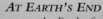

Welcome to the Earth after disaster! It is one year since a bearded and remarkably long-lived Superman helped the young humans Kamandi, Saphira, Sleeper Zom, and the cyborg Ben Boxer to defeat the maniacal Mother Machine, cause of Earth's second apocalypse. When Boxer targets Gotham City for destruction, Superman flies to Batman's old stomping ground armed to the teeth to aid a band of youths and free the remains of Bruce Wayne, alias Batman, from the DNA Dictators!

INDEX

Entries in **bold** type signify that a character has his or her own entry.

Acknowledgments

SCOTT BEATTY would like to thank his editors Chris Cerasi, Alastair Dougall, Laura Gilbert, and Robert Perry for their enduring patience. Thanks also to fellow writers Bob Greenberger, Phil Jimenez, and Dan Wallace for always watching my back. Additional gratitude goes to Ed Brubaker, Joey Cavalieri, Chuck Dixon, Devin Grayson, Scott McCullar, Jerry Ordway, Greg Rucka, Gail Simone, and Michael Wright for helping to ply the choppy waters of comic book continuity. Finally, special thanks to Jennifer Myskowski, my first and best reader, and Wilbur, a dog's dog and source of endless distraction.

BOB GREENBERGER would like to thank John Wells (first and foremost, much of this book wouldn't be this good without him).

PHIL JIMINEZ would like to thank the writers and artists who created the DC Universe with their talent and imagination; few places feel so much like home. I'd also like to thank Chris Cerasi for the hot fruit, the Diablo Dogs, and the grape sodie; Alastair Dougall for actually reading my hundreds of e-mails, even the ones about Tempest; and as ever, George Pérez, for without his influence on my work I'd never have had a career. And finally, a nod to Neal Pozner, a decade after his death, for so much, to Jack Mahan, for taking care of me for so long, and to Joe Hosking, for just about everything.

DAN WALLACE would like to thank DC Comics' Chris Cerasi for his unceasing cheer and for bringing him on board to play in the biff-bam-sockiest fictional universe ever created; his co-writers Phil Jimenez, Scott Beatty, and Bob Greenberger for producing such great work and for supplying arcane bits of DC lore; DK's Alastair Dougall and Laura Gilbert for always coming through at the eleventh hour; Kelly, Andrew, Grant, and Emma for their love and support; Detroit's own Time Travelers Comics and Books for their back-issue bins, and Jerry Siegel and Joe Shuster for birthing a genre.

DORLING KINDERSLEY WOULD LIKE TO THANK THE FOLLOWING AT DC COMICS:
Chris Cerasi, Steve Korté, Paul Levitz, Georg Brewer, Allan Asherman, Triss Stein, Roger Bonas, Anton Kawasaki, Ivan Cohen, Kilian Plunkett, Patrick Gleason, Christian Alamy, Carla Johnson Demetri Detsaridis, and Richard Callender.
And of course Scott Beatty, Bob Greenberger, Phil Jimenez, and Dan Wallace.

DORLING KINDERSLEY WOULD ALSO LIKE TO THANK THE FOLLOWING:
Nick Avery, Dan Bunyan, Lisa Crowe, and Sandra Perry for additional design assistance, Julia March and Kate Simkins for editorial assistance, and Ann Barrett for the index.

ARTIST ACKNOWLEDGMENTS

Dusty Abell, Jerry Acerno, Arthur Adams, Neal Adams, Dan Adkins, Charlie Adlard, Ian Akin, Christian Alamy, Gerry Alanguilan, Jeff Albrecht, Alfredo Alcala, Alcatena, Michael Allred, Bob Almond, Marlo Alquiza, Sal Amandola, Brent Anderson, Murphy Anderson, Ross Andru, Jim Aparo, Jason Armstrong, Tom Artis, Stan Asch, Derec Aucoin, Terry Austin, Brandon Badeaux, Mark Badger, Bernard Baily, Michael Bair, Kyle Baker, Jim Balent, Darryl Banks, Carlo Barberi, Dell Barras, Mike Barreiro, Eduardo Barreto, Al Barrionuevo, David Baron, Sy Barry, Hilary Barta, Chris Batista, Eric Battle, John Beatty, Terry Beatty, C.C. Beck, Howard Bender, Scott Benefiel, Ed Benes, Ramon Bernado, D. Bruce Berry, Jack Binder, J.J. Birch, Simon Bisley, Stephen Bissette, Fernando Blanco, Greg Blocks, Bret Blevins, Will Blyberg, Jon Bogdanove, Brian Bolland, Philip Bond, Richard Bonk, Wayne Boring, John Bolton, Ron Boyd, Craig Brasfield, Ken Branch, Brett Breeding, Ryan Breeding, Jeff Brennan, Norm Breyfogle, Mark Bright, June Brightman, Pat Broderick, Greg Brooks, Joe Brozowski, Mark Buckingham, Rich Buckler, Danny Bulanadi, Rick Burchett, Ray Burnley, Sal Buscema, Buzz, Mitch Byrd, John Byrne, Ralph Cabrera, Jim Calafiore, Talent Caldwell, Robert Campanella, Marc Campos, W.C. Carani, Nick Cardy, Sergio Cariello, Richard Case, John Cassaday, Anthony Castrillo, John Cebollero, Joe Certa, Gary Chaloner, Keith Champagne, Travis Charest, Howard Chaykin, Michael Chen, Jim Cheung, Cliff Chiang, Tom Chiu, Ian Churchill, Matthew Clark, Mike Clark, Dave Cockrum, Olivier Coipel, Gene Colan, Jack Cole, Simon Coleby, Hector Collazo, Vince Colletta, Bill Collins, Mike Collins, Ernie Colon, Kevin Conrad, Darwyn Cooke, Pete Costanza, Denys Cowan, Dennis Cramer, Reed Crandall, Saleen Crawford, Steve Crespo, Jake Crippen, Chris Cross, Charles Cuidera, Paris Cullins, Rodolfo Damaggio, Antonio Daniel, Alan Davis, Dan Davis, Ed Davis, Shane Davis, Francisco Rodriguez De La Fuente, Sam De La Rosa, Mike DeCarlo, Nelson DeCastro, Randy DeBurke, Adam Dekraker, Jose Delbo, John Dell, Jesse Delperdang, J. M. DeMatteis, Mike Deodato, Jr., Tom Derenick, Stephen DeStefano, Tony Dezuniga, Dick Dillin, Steve Dillon, Steve Ditko, Rachel Dodson, Terry Dodson, Colleen Doran, Evan Dorkin, Alberto Dose, Bob Downs, Mike Dringenberg, Armando Durruthy, Jan Duursema, Bob Dvorak, Kieron Dwyer, Joshua Dysart, Dale Eaglesham, Scot Eaton, Marty Egeland, Lee Elias, Chris Eliopulos, Randy Emberlin, Steve Epting, Steve Erwin, Mike Esposito, Ric Estrada, George Evans, Rich Faber, Mark Farmer, Wayne Faucher, Duncan Fegredo, Tom Feister, Jim Fern, Pascual Ferry, John Fischetti, Creig Flessel, John Floyd, John Ford, John Forte, Ramona Fradon, Gary Frank, Frank Frazetta, Fred Fredericks, George Freeman, Ron Frenz, Richard Friend, James Fry, Kerry Gammill, German Garcia, José Luis García-López, Ron Garney, Brian Garvey, Ale Garza, Carlos Garzon, Stefano Gaudiano, Drew Geraci, Frank Giacoia, Vince Giarrano, Dave Gibbons, Joe Giella, Keith Giffen, Michael T. Gilbert, Craig Gilmore, Dick Giordano, Sam Glanzman, Patrick Gleason, Frank Gomez, Fernando Gonzales, Jason Gorder, Al Gordon, Chris Gordon, Sam Grainger, Jerry Grandinetti, Mick Gray, Dan Green, Sid Greene, Mike Grell, Tom Grindberg, Peter Gross, Tom Grummett, Fred Guardineer, Butch Guice, Yvel Guichet, Paul Guinan, Mike Gustovich, Matt Haley, Craig Hamilton, Cully Hamner, Scott Hanna, Ed Hannigan, Norwood Steven Harris, Ron Harris, Tony Harris, Irwin Hasen, Fred Haynes, Doug Hazlewood, Russ Heath, Don Heck, Marc Hempel, Andrew Hennessy, Phil Hester, Everett E. Hibbard, Bryan Hitch, Rick Hoberg, James Hodgkins, Josh Hood, Ken Hooper, Dave Hoover, Alex Horley, Richard Howell, Tan Eng Huat, Mike Huddleston, Adam Hughes, Dave Hunt, Jamal Igle, Stuart Immonen, Carmine Infantino, Geof Isherwood, Chris Ivy, Dennis Janke, Klaus Janson, Dennis Jensen, Oscar Jimenez, Phil Jimenez, Geoff Johns, Dave Johnson, Drew Johnson, Staz Johnson, Arvell Jones, Casey Jones, Kelley Jones, Malcolm Jones III, Arnie Jorgensen, Dan Jurgens, Justiniano, Barbara Kaalberg, John Kalisz, Michael Kaluta, Bob Kane, Gil Kane, Kano, Rafael Kayanan, Stan Kaye, Joe Kelly, Dale Keown, Karl Kerschl, Karl Kesel, Jack Kirby, Leonard Kirk, Barry Kitson, Scott Kolins, Don Kramer, Peter Krause, Ray Kryssing, Andy Kubert, Joe Kubert, Andy Kuhn, Alan Kupperberg, Harry Lampert, Greg Land, Justin Land, Andy Lanning, Michael Lark, Greg Larocque, Bud Larosa, Salvador Larroca, Erik Larsen, Bob Layton, Jim Lee, Norman Lee, Alex Lei, Steve Leialoha, Rob Leigh, Jay Leisten, Rick Leonardi, Bob Lewis, Mark Lewis, Steve Lieber, Rob Liefeld, Steve Lightle, Mark Lipka, Don Lomax, Alvaro Lopez, David Lopez, Aaron Lopresti, John Lowe, Greg Luzniak, Tom Lyle, Mike Machlan, Dev Madan, Kevin Maguire, Rick Magyar, Larry Mahlstedt, Doug Mahnke, Alex Maleev, Tom Mandrake, Mike Manley, Lou Manna, Pablo Marcos, Bill Marimon, Cindy Martin, Gary Martin, Marcos Martin, Shawn Martinbrough, Kenny Martinez, Roy Allan Martinez, José Marzan, Jr., William Messner-Loebs, Rick Mays, Trevor McCarthy, Tom McCraw, John McCrea, Scott McDaniel, Luke McDonnell, Todd McFarlane, Ed McGuinness, Dave McKean, Mark McKenna, Mike McKone, Frank McLaughlin, Bob McLeod, Shawn McManus, Lan Medina, Paco Medina, Linda Medley, Carlos Meglia, David Meikis, Adriana Melo, Jaime Mendoza, Jesus Merino, J.D. Mettler, Pop Mhan, Grant Miehm, Mike Mignola, Danny Miki, Al Milgrom, Frank Miller, Mike S. Miller, Steve Mitchell, Lee Moder, Sheldon Moldoff, Steve Montano, Jim Mooney, Jerome Moore, Marcio Morais, Mark Morales, Rags Morales, Ruben Moreira, Gray Morrow, Win Mortimer, Jeffrey Moy, Philip Moy, Brian Murray, Todd Nauck, Paul Neary, Rudy Nebres, Mark Nelson, Denis Neville, Dustin Nguyen, Tom Nguyen, Art Nichols, Troy Nixey, Cary Nord, Graham Nolan, Irv Novick, Kevin Nowlan, John Nyberg, Bob Oksner, Ariel Olivetti, Jerry Ordway, Joe Orlando, Richard Pace, Carlos Pacheco, Mark Pajarillo, Tom Palmer, Jimmy Palmiotti, Peter Palmiotti, Dan Panosian, George Papp, Yanick Paquette, Francisco Paronzini, Ande Parks, Mike Parobeck, Sean Parsons, James Pascoe, Bruce Patterson, Chuck Patten, Jason Pearson, Paul Pelletier, Mark Pennington, Andrew Pepoy, George Pérez, Mike Perkins, Frank Perry, Harry G. Peter, Bob Petrecca, Joe Phillips, Wendy Pini, Al Plastino, Kilian Plunkett, Keith Pollard, Adam Pollina, Francis Portela, Howard Porter, Howie Post, Joe Prado, Miguelanxo Prado, Mark Propst, Javier Pulido, Joe Quesada, Frank Quitely, Mac Raboy, Pablo Raimondi, Humberto Ramos, Rodney Ramos, Ron Randall, Tom Raney, Rich Rankin, Norm Rapmund, Ivan Reis, Roy Richardson, Robin Riggs, Eduardo Risso, Paul Rivoche, Trina Robbins, Clem Robins, Andrew Robinson, Jerry Robinson, Roger Robinson, Denis Rodier, Anibal Rodriguez, Danny Rodriguez, Jasen Rodriguez, Rodin Rodriguez, Marshall Rogers, Prentis Rollins, T.G. Rollins, William Rosado, Alex Ross, Dave Ross, Duncan Rouleau, Craig Rousseau, George Roussos, Jim Royal, Mike Royer, Josef Rubinstein, Steve Rude, P. Craig Russell, Vince Russell, Paul Ryan, Bernard Sachs, Stephen Sadowski, Tim Sale, Javier Saltares, Jose Sanchez, Medina Sanchez, Clement Sauve, Jr, Alex Saviuk, Kurt Schaffenberger, Mitch Schauer, Christie Scheele, Damion Scott, Trevor Scott, Bart Sears, Mike Sekowsky, Mike Sellers, Val Semeiks, Eric Shanower, Hal Sharp, Howard Sherman, Howard M. Shum, Joe Shuster, Bill Sienkiewicz, Dave Simons, Tom Simmons, Walter Simonson, Howard Simpson, Alex Sinclair, Louis Small, Jr., Andy Smith, Bob Smith, Cam Smith, Dietrich Smith, Todd Smith, Peter Snejbjerg, Ray Snyder, Aaron Sowd, Dan Spiegle, Chris Sprouse, Claude St. Aubin, John Stanisci, Joe Staton, Jim Starlin, Arne Starr, Rick Stasi, John Statema, Joe Staton, Ken Steacy, Brian Stelfreeze, Dave Stevens, Cameron Stewart, Dave Stewart, Roger Stewart, John Stokes, Karl Story, Larry Stroman, Lary Stucker, Rob Stull, Tom Sutton, Curt Swan, Bryan Talbot, Romeo Tanghal, Christopher Taylor, Ty Templeton, Greg Theakston, Art Thibert, Frank Thorne, Alex Toth, John Totleben, Tim Truman, Chaz Truog, Dwayne Turner, Michael Turner, George Tuska, Angel Unzueta, Juan Valasco, Ethan Van Sciver, Rick Veitch, Sal Velluto, Charles Vess, Al Vey, Carlos Villagran, Ricardo Villagran, Dexter Vines, Juan Vlasco, Trevor Von Eeden, Wade Von Grawbadger, Matt Wagner, Kev Walker, Chip Wallace, Bill Wray, Lee Weeks, Alan Weiss, Kevin J. West, Chris Weston, Doug Wheatley, Mark Wheatley, Glenn Whitmore, Bob Wiacek, Mike Wieringo, Anthony Williams, J. H. Williams III, Scott Williams, Bill Willingham, Phil Winslade, Chuck Wojtkiewicz, Walden Wong, Pete Woods, John Workman, Moe Worthman, Chris Wozniak, Bill Wray, Jason Wright, Berni Wrightson, Tom Yeates, Steve Yeowell, Leinil Francis Yu.

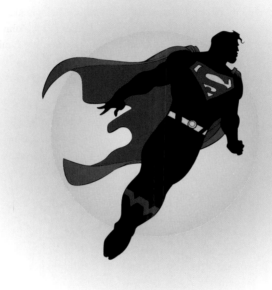